# Bannerman Catalogue

## of

## Military Goods

## 1927

DBI BOOKS, INC., NORTHFIELD, ILL.

ISBN 0-910676-20-8

# INTRODUCTION

Francis Bannerman Sons, Inc., was a unique organization. It was begun during the Civil War as a part-time business, when young Frank Bannerman supplemented the family income by dragging river bottoms for scrap to be sold to junk dealers, but eventually the company grew to become what was probably at its height the largest dealer in military surplus in the world. Bannerman claimed to have purchased 90 percent of the surplus from the Spanish American War, a claim that was never challenged. Though many large firms have developed from the military residue of World War II and subsequent conflicts around the world, Bannerman is still unique in having managed to corner 90 percent of the spoils and leftovers of a major war's victor.

Francis Bannerman VI was a Scotsman, born in Dundee March 24, 1851. He emigrated to the United with his family in 1854. When his father joined the Union army early in the Civil War, young Frank went to work to help support the family. He developed a part-time business selling the rope, chain and other scrap he could dredge out of waters near the Brooklyn Navy Yard, and when his father returned from service partially disabled, father and son joined forces in an expanded scrap business.

Their business prospered, bolstered with purchases of Navy surplus, necessitating a move to a combination store and warehouse in Brooklyn in 1867. On a buying trip to Europe in 1872 he met Helen Boyce in Ulster, Ireland, and when he returned to Brooklyn later that year he brought a bride with him.

Upon his return Frank, with the encouragement of his father, expanded the business to deal in Army as well as Navy surplus. Noting that the historical value of some of the war materials he was buying far exceeded their scrap value, Bannerman put together a catalogue describing the various guns, swords and related militaria he'd purchased. Bannerman's catalogue served to whet interest in historical militaria, and—in the view of some historians—provided a major stimulus toward establishing a serious interest in arms collecting in the United States.

But, arms collectors comprised only one segment of Bannerman's market. Because of the quantity and variety of military equipment Bannerman had purchased, he could truly provide for the needs of a major museum or outfit an army . . . and undoubtedly did both. As the company and its inventory grew, it went through a series of moves. In the 1890s he moved it to New York City, seeking out progressively larger quarters until he purchased the famous 501 Broadway building from the Metropolitan Museum. According to the company's archives, the Metropolitan's trustees made a considerable reduction in the price of the building for Bannerman, "in recognition of his public spirit in maintaining a free public war museum at his own expense in New York City."

When Bannerman scored his coup of buying out essentially all of the United States Government's captured booty from the 1898 war with Spain, his downtown New York store and Brooklyn warehouse could simply not accommodate the volume of new material. In small arms alone he had acquired 20 million rounds of Mauser ammunition, and tens of thousands of rifles to shoot it. In addition, the New York City authorities were taking a very dim view of Bannerman's burgeoning stock of explosives and pyrotechnics being stored in their city. Thus it was in 1900 Bannerman bought Pollepel Island, a rocky 6¾-acre chunk of land sticking out of the Hudson River about 50 miles upstream from New York and only 4 miles from West Point.

Pollepel Island has a long and interesting history. Henry Hudson's journal mentions anchoring the *Half Moon* in the lee of a small island that can only be Pollepel, as he traveled up the Hudson looking for the northwest passage. It is mentioned in pre-Revolutionary Dutch journals (spelled "Pollaples") and was the site of a *chevaux de frise*—an underwater fence of iron-tipped poles anchored in the river bottom to prevent the passage of British war ships—during the Revolution. It later became the property of a Henry Taft, from whom Bannerman bought it in 1900.

Bannerman's Island, as it is now popularly known, was an excellent choice for a munitions storage facility. Even the

largest cannon could be delivered by barge up the Hudson to its dock, and the surrounding water provided at least moderate protection from casual visitors. The first warehouses and a caretaker's quarters were constructed in 1900, but Bannerman quickly took advantage of the opportunity provided by the beautiful setting to begin building himself a castle. Patterning it after the historical castles of his native Scotland,. Bannerman began his castle in the early 1900s and continued construction until his death in November 1918. Though much of the castle provided a warehouse for his growing inventory of arms, munitions and equipment, it was also summer living quarters for the Bannerman family.

Though today Bannerman's picturesque island arsenal looks as impressive from a distance as it did when it was still new, a close-up view reveals crumbling parapets and cracked walls throughout much of the intricate structure. There's a typical Bannerman reason for this, according to one story. At the turn of the century Bannerman refused to sell a large amount of military ammunition to a buyer who wanted it concealed in barrels of dry cement before shipping. The buyer made his purchase anyway, from another source, but Bannerman ended up with both ammunition and cement by buying it at Government auction after U.S. Customs had seized it. Ever the thrifty Scot, Bannerman used the cement to build his castle while eventually selling the would-be smuggler's ammunition to the government of Santo Domingo. Unfortunately, the smuggler had apparently used the cheapest cement he could find for his abortive smuggling attempt, and Bannerman's castle was the eventual loser!

As if crumbling cement wasn't enough of a problem for Bannerman's castle, a portion of the warehouse was destroyed when 200 pounds of gunpowder blew up on August 15, 1920. Three people on the island were slightly injured in the blast, which blew a 25-foot section of the concrete wall a quarter-mile across the river and onto the New York Central Railroad tracks, where they ran along the river bank. Contemporary newspaper reports state that rescue boats were kept from approaching the island for some time by a barrage of shot and bullets from exploding ammunition. In addition to extensive damage to the island, the blast blew out hundreds of windows in nearby communities up and down the river.

By the 1950s Bannermans had slipped badly from its former preeminence as a merchandiser of second hand military wares. The store, often described as New York City's "military museum," was a dusty, dirty, disorganized junk shop—though it was still capable of coming up with some real treasures for the knowledgeable and enterprising collector willing to get his hands and clothes dirty. Conditions on the island were even worse. The deteriorating buildings and just plain neglect had destroyed much of the material in the island's warehouses, and the condition of the live ammunition, much of it corroded beyond use, was cause for alarm.

Thus it was that Val Forgett, founder of Service Armament and Navy Arms, and Bill Edwards, then editor of *Guns* Magazine and well-known gun book author, visited Pollepel Island in 1958. Val had been hired by Bannermans to deactivate the live artillery ammunition, some of it dating from the Civil War, while Bill had come along for the ride. Val's efforts were apparently successful, as he—and the island—both survived. He recently told me of his final acts before leaving the island.

Noting there'd been no check of two giant 16-inch shells flanking the entrance to the harbor, Val grabbed a wrench and had an assistant boost him up to the nose so he could unscrew the fuse. Needless to say, the fuses were live and the projectiles full of high explosive—enough in either to change a good chunk of island into a hole in the river bottom!

That exploratory visit was described at length in a fascinating article Bill wrote in the January, 1959, issue of *Guns*. In it he reports finding 1-inch Gatling cartridges in their original box, so corroded they disintegrated as he picked them up. The wreckage of a dozen Gatling guns, smashed beyond repair for the brass their actions would yield, was also found. Rusting artillery, rotting knapsacks, incomplete rifle actions and uncountable rounds of small arms and artillery ammunition littered the floors and grounds. Surely a collector's Mecca, but one to make him break down and cry.

Fortunately the catalogue whose pages follow hails from Bannerman's happier days. It's filled with firearms and militaria, and when it came out in 1927 such things as Gatling guns in rusty condition were still available "for lawn decoration, at bargain prices." An extremely rare Civil War Billinghurst and Requa Mitraleuse was offered for $500 (single cartridges were only 20¢), and a Spanish Nordenfelt "machine gun" was $285 (I saw one, incomplete, sold in Europe 2 years ago for over $10,000!).

This listing of exotica could go on indefinitely, of course, but why should it when the actual pages are here to be studied and enjoyed? One word of warning, however. This is not a well organized book, though the sketchy General Index on page 371 will often but not always lead you to what you're looking for. I say usually, because over the years of its evolution Bannerman's catalogue often expanded by adding new pages where it was convenient, even if not necessarily appropriate. That's why you'll find a special section of one-of-a-kind collectors items beginning on page 16a, for example, or a page of swords, daggers and battle axes on page 147, in the midst of "Cannon, Projectiles." However, such minor inconveniences should be considered part of the book's great charm.

Dig in, then, and we're sure you'll find Bannerman's 1927 "Military Goods Catalogue" not only entertaining but instructive, a classic bit of American arms literature.

*Joseph Schroeder*

**FOUNDED 1865**

ILLUSTRATED DESCRIPTIVE HISTORICAL

# MILITARY GOODS

**FRANCIS BANNERMAN SONS**

| | |
|---|---|
| Cable Address: | **BANNERMAN** |
| Cable Codes: | Liebers<br>A B C 4th Edition<br>Western Union |

*Bannerman*

**JANUARY, 1927**

WHOLESALE AND RETAIL PRICE LIST

# CATALOGUE

**501 BROADWAY, NEW YORK**

Few are the sights that Gotham has to offer
Of greater interest and instructive aid,
Than the rare contents of this famous coffer
From all earth's ransacked corners here displayed.

### 1865    1927

# War Weapons, Antique and Modern---Cannon, Pistols, Muskets, Rifles, Saddles, Uniforms, Cartridges

*View of Lighter Shipping Six Inch Navy Cannon from Our Island Arsenal*

## THIS CATALOGUE IS OFFERED AT 50 CENTS PER COPY, MAILED
### The DeLuxe Edition on Heavy Glazed Paper Is $2.50 per Copy

BANNERMAN, Francis, merchant and antiquarian, born in Dundee, Scotland, 24 March, 1851, coming with his parents to the United States in 1854, residing in Brooklyn since 1858. He is the sixth of the name of Frank from the first Frank Bannerman, standard-bearer of Clan Macdonald, who escaped the massacre at Glencoe in 1692, by sailing to the Irish coast, and landed in County Antrim, where his descendants resided for many years. It has been a rule in the family that the eldest son shall be named Frank. Tradition states that the name originated at Bannockburn, when during the battle a member of the Macdonald clan rescued a clan pennant, whereupon King Robert Bruce cut off the streamer part of the flag from the national St. Andrew's Cross, and pronounced him a "Bannerman." The family came to America in 1854, locating in Brooklyn, where Frank (6th) attended public schools until the age of ten. It was then that his father, Frank Bannerman (5th), joined the colors for the defense of the Union, and it became necessary for the boy to leave school, and secure some paying occupation, to help provide for the younger members of the family. He obtained a position as errand boy at $2.00 a week in a lawyer's office at 37-39 Jauncey Court (an old court off Wall Street). Since the family resided alongside the Brooklyn Navy Yard near the river, Frank obtained the use of a captured southern dugout canoe, and every morning before going to the lawyer's office at 9 A. M., he supplied the officers and crews of the warships anchored in the Navy Yard Bay with the morning papers, usually the New York "Herald," which contained the shipping news. He never missed a morning, although often suffering considerable hardships. About 1863 a naval officer gave him a bag of rope lines, collected while cleaning ships, which contained also a small four-pronged boat anchor. This anchor the boy used as a grapple to drag the

river bottom in the summer evenings, picking up odd bits of rope, chain, etc., which he sold to a local junkman. On his father's return from the war, disabled and of "no further service to the United States"—so states his honorable discharge—he attended to the selling of the junk, and as his strength returned, he branched out into buying from others. He was thus able to earn enough to send Frank back to Public School No. 7, where he soon got into a misunderstanding with the principal and was expelled, only to be sent for a few days later, and reinstated with high honors by the superintendent, who had learned that Frank was blameless and had acted on high moral principles. The superintendent became much attached to him and later awarded him one of the Cornell University scholarships allowed for prize scholars. But his father was still suffering from his war disability, which at times wholly incapacitated him for business, and so Frank had to decline with great regret (for he had always earnestly desired a university education), feeling that his duty was then to stay with his father and help carry on the business for the welfare of the family. Even these short-time schooldays were broken into by the many days in which he was absent with his father attending navy auctions, and these frequent sales, soon necessitating his whole time, ended school for him. The business soon outgrew the little storehouse near the navy yard, and the large store and warehouse at 14 Atlantic Avenue was opened in the fall of 1867, for the sale of ship chandlery in connection with navy auction goods, including the original business of supplying paper makers with old rope. In 1872 when old rope became very scarce in the United States, Frank made a business trip to Europe, and made large purchases of rope for export to New York. For a while he made his home with his grandmother in Ulster, and there met Helen Boyce, daughter of a well-to-do farmer of Huguenot Scotch-Irish descent, to whom he was married 8 June, 1872, in Ballymena, Ireland, by the Rev. Frederick Buick, who had also officiated at the marriage of his father. Three sons, Frank (7th), David Boyce, and Walter Bruce, also a daughter who died in infancy, are the result of the union. The two eldest sons assist the father in business, while Walter Bruce is a practicing physician at Bridgewater, Mass. On his return with his bride to Brooklyn, Frank Bannerman desired to start in business for himself, his younger brother then being able to take his place. His father favored his ambition, and helped him locate near by in a nearly similar business, claiming that competition would help both. He then began attending army auctions, and noted the destruction of old muskets and swords for scrap metal, for which there was often a demand from small states, unable to afford the expensive modern weapons of first-class nations; also that many weapons broken up for junk had been used on historical battlefields and were

worthy of preservation. He began, accordingly, the publication of a catalogue illustrating, describing, and giving the history of the weapons he had for sale. As the New York "Sun" reporter said, "Bannerman could tell an interesting story about everything he had for sale." His catalogue induced many to start collecting war weapons. To emigrants coming from Europe, where the use of firearms was prohibited, he sold the old army musket altered over into a five-pound Quaker gun made out of the old ten-pound army rifle by replacing the heavy steel barrel with one of wood and reducing the length and grasp of the stock. The store at 43 Atlantic Avenue soon became too small, and since the Brooklyn express and freight facilities at that time were too slow for handling the rapidly increasing mail order business, it became necessary to open store in New York City. The first was at 118 Broad Street, a later one at 27 Front Street (where thirty years before he had, while in the lawyer's office, delivered his first message). In 1897 he leased the store, 579 Broadway, from which place he fitted out many regiments of volunteers in the Spanish War. The assistant chief of ordnance claimed that Bannerman had done so much good toward training the youth of America with his Quaker gun that the U. S. government should pay him a royalty on each gun made. At the close of the war with Spain, he purchased over 90 per cent. of the captured guns, ammunition, and equipment, making it necessary to obtain a place outside any corporate limits for the storage of millions of cartridges. Polopels Island in the Hudson, at the northern entrance to the Highlands, was purchased for this purpose, and there he constructed harbors and built storehouses patterned after the baronial castles of his native Scotland; he also makes the island his summer home. In 1905 he secured 499 and 501 Broadway, extending through the block 200 feet to Mercer Street. The trustees of the Metropolitan Museum, who had the 501 property for sale, made a reduction of many thousands of dollars in the price "in recognition of his public spirit in maintaining a free public war museum at his own expense in New York City." Government officials say that Bannerman is the father of the sealed bid plan of selling obsolete stores. All acknowledge him to be the founder of the military goods business. All his goods are sold on government auction sale, terms cash with order. At the outbreak of the great European war in 1914 he was able in seven weeks from his island arsenal to supply saddles (a year's output for a large factory). He showed his love for the land of his birth by donating thousands of rifles, cartridges, equipment, and money to help the British in their great fight. Collectors claim that Bannerman's large illustrated book catalogue is the best book published on weapons of war. A great lover of boys, he has been connected with boys' club church work for many years, devoting one night each week to them for the study of the Sabbath school lesson. He was among the first trustees of the Caledonian Hospital, and a member of the St. Andrew's and many other societies.— From *Appleton's Cyclopaedia of American Biography.*

# Blowing Our Own Horn

Quite a number have undertaken at different times to tell about our business. We prefer, however, to tell the public here in this catalogue, our own story, in order to answer the many inquiries made by interested customers and others, such as "How did you come to start this business? How long have you been at it? Who buys your goods? Do you occupy all of this large building?" etc., etc.

This business was commenced in 1865, by attending auction sales, where large quantities of military goods were offered for sale by the U. S. Government, at the close of the civil war. In those days it was customary with buyers, ourselves along with others, to purchase old swords and guns for their value in old metal. Sword handles, usually of brass, weighed about ¾ of a pound. The steel blade and scabbard about 3 pounds. Old muskets would net about 7 pounds of iron. Buyers could always find a market for old metal from broken up swords and guns. This breaking up of large numbers of old guns accounts for the present scarcity of some of the old types of army weapons. This destructive practice not only prevailed in America, but also in Europe.

The U. S. Government also adopted this method in disposing of many of the old captured guns. We remember, at the close of the civil war, making the highest bid at a Government sale, on a lot of 11,000 old guns, "veterans of many wars," part of the lot surrendered by General Lee, classified as "Rebel." The U. S. A. Ordnance Officer refused to accept our bid for the guns, alleging "that Bannerman would repair the guns and put them in serviceable order, and that they would then enter into competition with the now obsolete guns that the Government had for sale," so this lot of "Rebel" guns, which contained many heirlooms of patriots who had fought with WASHINGTON and JACKSON, were consigned to the fire, and the old burnt locks and barrels sold to us later as scrap iron.

IN UTILIZING THE WASTE MILITARY PRODUCTS that came to us in the course of our business, we endeavored to stop this destruction and to educate the people to use the old swords and guns in making beautiful decorations for library or den.

By removing the heavy steel barrel, and replacing with a light wooden barrel, and reducing the thickness of the gun stock, we have altered 10 pound muskets into 5 pound Quaker drill guns, suitable for Boys Brigade Companies attached to the churches. Again by boring out the rifling in the gun barrel, and reducing the length and weight of the stock, we convert the army rifle into a smooth bore fowling gun, of which many thousands have been supplied to immigrants settling in our Northwest, who come from countries where the use of fire arms is prohibited, and who find that in their new home a gun is almost as much of a necessity as a plow in protecting stock, providing game for food, etc.

During the sixty years in which we have been engaged in this work, our business has grown so that the U. S. Government now depends upon us to purchase at their sales, the large quantities of obsolete and discarded goods.

**We purchased 90 per cent. of the guns, ammunition and other military goods captured in the Spanish War.**

We also have agents in foreign countries who buy and sell military goods for us. Our London agent personally delivered goods for trading purposes, that his father had sold to Dr. David Livingston, the famous African missionary explorer, and the books of our agent's forbears showed sales of trading goods, made to Captain Cook, the British naval explorer, in 1770.

Our reputation is known to all as the **Largest Dealers in the World in Military Goods.** Round the world travelers tell us that there is no other establishment in the world, where is carried such a large and assorted stock as ours. Even in great London, buyers would have to visit at least six different places, in order to purchase the variety of goods that could be obtained in greater assortment, and in larger quantities, in our store.

In our salesroom, we have on view upwards of **1,000 Different Kinds of Guns**, from the early matchlock, up to the present day automatic. What a story some of these old arms could tell, of victories and reverses, of heroism and valor, but they lie silent now, and one would never think that the fate of armies has more than once depended upon them and the men who carried them.

We have on exhibition over a **Thousand Different Kinds of Pistols**, from the earliest hand cannon, fired with fuse, up to the latest self-loading automatic. **A Thousand Different Kinds of Swords**, from the bronze blade, carried by the ancient Romans, up to the present day regulation. **No Museum in the World Exceeds Ours in the Number of Weapons.** In our uniform department, we have had for sale at one time, over 170,000 military uniforms of one particular kind. In cannon we have a large and complete stock, from the ancient iron barrel, encased in a wood log, up to the present day semi-automatic rifled cannon for battle ships. On short notice we can deliver promptly from our stock 100 high power rapid fire guns at bargain price.

Recently, a shipping firm in Europe, gave us an order to convert a large ocean passenger steamship into a warship they had sold to a South American Government. In one week the peaceful passenger ship sailed, altered by us into a man-of-war, fully armed and equipped; a record for quickness that could scarcely be beaten to-day in any up-to-date government establishment.

During the Russian-Japanese war, we personally submitted samples to the Japanese War Department, in Tokyo, of 10,000 McClellan army saddles, 100,000 army rifles, 100,000 knapsacks, 100,000 haversacks, 100,000 sets of equipments, 150,000 gun slings, 100,000 new khaki uniforms, 150,000 white summer uniforms, 20,000,000 cartridges, together with a shipload of assorted military goods.

For twenty-four years we were located on Atlantic avenue, Brooklyn; next at 118 Broad street, New York City. Our stock increasing, and needing more room, we located at 27 Front street. In 1897 we moved to 579 Broadway, where we had about 15,000 feet for salesroom and storage. At the close of the Spanish war, we made such large purchases from the U. S. Government, of captured arms and war supplies, and also personally from the Spanish Government, before the evacuation of Cuba, that it became necessary for us to lease three large warehouses on the Brooklyn water front; and for the storage of over thirty millions of cartridges, we purchased the island in the Hudson River opposite Cornwall, New York, whereon we have erected store houses built after the style of old Scotch castles.

In 1905, the Directors of the Metropolitan Museum of Art, J. P. Morgan, D. O. Mills and others, offered for sale the building 501 Broadway, which had been bequeathed to the Museum by the late Jacob Rogers, the locomotive builder. We offered to purchase the property and asked the Directors to make a reduction in price, in consideration of the fact that we were, at our own personal expense, exhibiting free to the public, our museum collection of war relics and trophies, on similar lines to what they were doing at the public cost. The Directors answered our request by letter, saying, "That in recognition of the public spirit shown by us, they would sell to us at a lower price." We accepted their offer, and after six months fitting up the place, making the building ready for our business, we were able in November, 1905, to move our immense stock and open up at 501 Broadway. This fine property occupies a space of 30 feet on Broadway, extending 200 feet through to Mercer street in the rear. The building contains seven floors, which gives us over 40,000 feet for sales room and the exhibition of our museum collection. We have lately secured the adjoining premises, 499 Broadway, which now gives us a property of 10,000 feet ground measurement—50 feet on Broadway, through the block 200 feet with a frontage of 50 feet on Mercer street. We mention these facts to show our responsibility and the growth and extent of our business, which now, with our salesroom, store, armory, warehouse and island, gives us a storage space of about 15 acres.

When we first came to Broadway in 1897, our neighbors thought that in about one month we would have to move for lack of business. It does seem in these days, when so many are advertising free samples of goods, offering to send them with the privilege of using before payment, that the **"Government Auction Sale Terms,"** which we adopted sixty years ago, would prevent us from doing a successful business. We can only account for our success, in that those who order our goods, and send us the money in advance with the order, in compliance with our terms, find that we fulfill our offers to the letter, without any substitution; that we give good value, as per our catalogue advertisement; that our motto is the **"Golden Rule, in Action."** We receive large numbers of letters from customers, who write us that the goods sent them are better than we advertised. Satisfied customers are our best advertisement—**We try to be fair and just with all.**

Our customers include many of the South and Central American Governments. Some of the Mauser rifles purchased after the war of 1898, were delivered to European and Asiatic Governments. For years we have supplied the Dominican and Haytian Governments. Our largest customers are governments who, having limited financial resources, must necessarily purchase army guns and supplies at low prices, and who are not averse to adopting a good serviceable gun which has been cast aside by a richer and stronger government. We purchase large quantities of arms, which we hold in our island store house, for times of emergency, when arms are in demand, when even obsolete serviceable guns are purchased by first-class governments, as in 1861, when President Lincoln sent agents to Europe to buy up all the guns available, to arm the volunteers, and also to keep them from the Southern Confederacy. At the first defeat of the French in the Franco-German war, agents were sent to the United States by the French Government to purchase arms left over from our civil war. Cuba depended upon us to furnish, on short notice, millions of cartridges and other military supplies.

**No Fire Arms are Ever Sold in Our Store to Any Minor.** We will not sell weapons to any one whom we think would endanger the public safety. Only museums and licensed persons can purchase cane swords. The peace of the world is preserved to-day by the use of weapons. "Oh, dear," said a reverend friend whom we met in boys' Church Club work, "What a horrid business you are in; dealing in weapons of war." We answered his remark by asking him if he could tell us how many swords were reported in the company of the twelve Apostles, who accompanied the Lord Jesus Christ on his three years' preaching journeys. He saw the point and answered, "Two, and Peter used one of them with good effect." Two swords in a company of twelve make rather a good percentage in favor of weapons being carried by travelers, made necessary by the conditions of those times, for did not the Master, in answer to the lawyer's question of "Who is my neighbor," illustrate by telling the story of the Jew who was robbed and beaten on his journey between Jerusalem and Jericho, and who was rescued by the kind-hearted Samaritan business man. If the carrying of weapons met the approval of the Prince of Peace, then, we think that weapons are necessary to the peace of the world as it is to-day. Who would advise disarming the police or soldier, our peace protectors.

St. John's vision of Satan bound and the one thousand years of peace is not yet in sight. We believe the millennium will come, and have for years been preparing by collecting rare weapons now known as Bannerman's Military Museum, but which we hope some day will be known as **"The Museum of Lost Arts,"** when law and order will be preserved without the aid of weapons. As a sincere Christian life is the surest individual safeguard against wrongdoing, so we believe that when the nations and their rulers, who now profess to be Christians, shall live up to their prayer of "Our Father," there will be no more violations of His commandment "Love thy neighbor," then war shall be done away, and **Peace Shall Reign On Earth.**

# ARMY AUCTION BARGAINS
## Office & Museum Salesroom, 501 Broadway, N. Y. City
### Containing the Most Wonderful Collection of Ancient and Modern Military Goods Ever shown.

ESTABLISHED
1865.

NOTHING TO EQUAL IT IN THE WORLD.
OUR GOODS ARE FOUND ON EVERY SEA.
IN EVERY LAND ROUND THE WORLD.
EVEN WITH PEARY AND COOK (?) TO THE NORTH POLE.

JANUARY,
1927

In these pages will be found illustrations and descriptions of GOODS PURCHASED AT ARMY AND NAVY AUCTION SALES. OUR COMPLETE ILLUSTRATED CATALOGUE CONTAINS 372 PAGES, size 9 by 11½ inches, with 5,000 illustrations and descriptions of military goods, and numerous interesting military stories. Complete catalogue sold at 50 cents; mailed to foreign countries, 75 cents; copies bound, for library use (edition De Luxe) $2.50.

Prices in catalogue are both wholesale and retail, in that as far as possible we offer case lots at a lower rate than single pieces.

## IMPORTANT NOTICES WHICH GOVERN THE SALES IN THIS CATALOGUE.

We do not guarantee firearm mechanisms or ammunition; we describe faithfully the goods offered as far as it is possible to describe job lots, second-hand, assorted goods, and so guarantee goods as per our description and sell firearms and ammunition "AS ARE." Many old guns are valuable only to collectors as showing the evolution of firearms; some are inventors' models and would never have stood a proof test. The larger part of our stock we purchased from the United States Government and which bears Government proofs—"Hall-marks of the best in the world" quality, but even these guns, originally intended for black powder, could be made dangerous by using dense smokeless powders. So, caveat emptor, the buyer takes the risk; we will not be responsible for any use made of goods sold by us.

Our terms are the same as at Government auction.

FIRST YOU PAY YOUR MONEY THEN YOU GET THE GOODS. Commercial rating is of no interest to Government paymasters, or to us. THE STANDARD OIL CO. WHEN ORDERING GOODS FROM us sent us New York City check WITH THEIR ORDER. Send express or post office money order, or New York draft with your order. U. S. postage stamps taken from out-of-town customers in payment for orders under $1.00. Foreign stamps not received. Out-of-town bank checks not received as cash, as there is a charge for collecting and delay in shipment of one week or more while waiting for collection. Goods ordered sent by mail, the necessary postage must accompany the order.

We box and deliver goods to the express company in New York City, or case lots to freight depot free of charge. Single guns, price of which is under $2.00, charge of 30 cents will be made for packing box.

Single saddles are packed in bagging. If ordered "ship by freight" add 25 cents extra for New York cartage. Our responsibility ceases when we make delivery in New York City.

C. O. D. shipments are not made, unless we first receive remittance enough to cover express charges both ways. All goods are offered "as

are" (Caveat Emptor); the buyer takes the risk. We guarantee goods to be as described. NOT RESPONSIBLE FOR ANY USE MADE OF OUR GOODS, OR FOR TRANSPORTATION COMPANIES OR U. S. MAIL DELIVERIES.

Most of the goods offered in our catalogue bear the U. S. Government marks as having been made at Government arsenals—quality passed upon and accepted by U. S. Government inspectors.

All prices quoted are NET PRICES WITHOUT OPTION. On receipt of money order we will ship goods ordered as buyer may direct. If you do not care to send the full amount, we accept remittance of enough to cover the expenses both ways and ship C. O. D. for the balance and collection charges, the buyer having the privilege of examining the goods at his own express office. On C. O. D. orders for case lots we will accept 25 per cent. of the amount with the order, and will ship by freight consigned to our order, and send draft with bill of lading endorsed to your bank for the balance, with instructions for freight agent to allow you to examine on arrival at your railroad station.

Any Government officer will tell you we are the largest buyers at the Government auctions, taking upwards of 90 per cent. of all the goods offered. By our catalogue you will see the immense stock we have for sale, which takes upwards of fifteen acres for storage—the largest stock in the world of new and second-hand military goods from Government auction.

Catalogues will be sent out wrapped in heavy paper, stamped with necessary postage.

We have frequently supplied Government museums with rare weapons. Every collector in America—many in Europe, and, in fact, all over the world—send for our catalogue for record and preservation.

The office of war chiefs in nearly every nation, of every commandant of U. S. arsenals and navy yards, as well as chiefs of departments at Washington, have on file "Bannerman's Office Copy Catalogue," finding therein information obtained in no other book.

All the great sculptors and artists are our customers and nearly all the great statues, paintings and plays in America of military subjects since 1865, appear equipped with guns and equipment that we have furnished. Illustrators of military art in America, either in marble, canvas or on the stage—rely upon us for correctness as to detail of equipment.

Our catalogue has now gotten so large that it is impossible to continue mailing it for fifteen cents. At the price of 50 cents we do not near get back the money it costs us for paper, printing and postage—not to speak of the costly work of illustrating and compiling. Many authors in America and Europe are writing about old military weapons with knowledge gained from our catalogue. Bookseller in Germany recently wrote us for discounts on catalogue in lots of 100. No wonder an Ohio man writes us: "YOUR CATALOGUE IS WORTH ITS WEIGHT IN GOLD. MY WIFE CALLS IT MY BIBLE."

Do not write us to "Ship goods and we will remit." You may be rated a millionaire, but if you attended a Government auction sale your bid would not be entertained unless you complied with the terms, which are cash down. Therefore, in order for us to buy Government goods it is necessary to sell for spot cash. This rule is strictly adhered to. Do not write on receipt of catalogue for our discount sheet, that you are a dealer, perhaps proprietor of a large department store. Whoever you are the prices in this catalogue are intended to govern all cases; as will be seen within, that we quote prices on a single gun, lower prices per case lot and still lower prices for larger quantities. In this way the catalogue is both for wholesale and retail and prices are exactly as stated and strictly adhered to, either for one gun or for 25,000 guns.

Case lot goods delivered free of charge for cartage to railroad, steamship or express company's depot in New York City south of Fourteenth street.

All goods are quoted IF ON HAND WHEN THE ORDER IS RECEIVED. On some of the articles quoted as refinished it may be necessary to allow time to send them to the armory for the work to be performed. Prices subject to change without notice.

Our liability ceases when we receive transportation company's receipt. Will accept no responsibility for packages and catalogues mailed unless insured. All claims must be made within three days after receipt of goods. We do not guarantee delivery within certain time.

MUSKET CAPS, CARTRIDGES AND EXPLOSIVES CANNOT BE SENT BY MAIL. Packages can be insured at cost of 10 cents extra, insuring safer delivery. Do not forget to send postage for goods ordered sent by mail. We advise all mail orders to be insured. When answering letters please give us the date of our letters to you. When enclosing stamps for catalogue do not wet the edge—moisten a small part in the CENTER of the stamp. Where no shipping directions are given we use our best judgment in forwarding. Buyer pays freight or express charges; also, the express company's charge for returning the amount collected to us; you can avoid this needless expense by sending us the full amount. FREIGHT: All shipments under 100 pounds are charged for by the transportation companies as 100 pounds, as this is their MINIMUM charge; over 100 pounds is charged for at pound-rate basis. EXPRESS: Nearly all the express companies will accept all packages. DO NOT SEND US LOCAL BANK CHECKS, AS THEY ARE SUBJECT TO COLLECTION CHARGES. All orders are filled in turn. No goods held in reserve unless deposit has been made.

We receive many letters written in German, evidently from Germans who believe from our name that we are Germans. This is an error—the name Bannerman is an old Scotch name given to our forebear, who rescued his chieftain's (Macdonald's) pennant at the battle of Bannockburn, for which act King Robert Bruce, with his sword, cut off the clan pennant part attached to the National Saint Andrew's Cross banner and pronounced him a Bannerman.

REFERENCES—Any of the Commercial Agencies will tell you all about us, although we are not subscribers to their books of reference, having no need for their valuable services on account of our purchases being made direct with the Government, who by law are bound to sell only for cash, without regard to credit. We can also refer to the bank where we transact our business, viz.: Corn Exchange Bank (Broadway branch), Broadway, corner of Spring street.

Note that we have for the benefit of our out-of-town customers shown illustrations and given descriptions of many rare guns of which we have only the one piece. Should you order and the piece wanted is sold we cheerfully return your money.

NO GOODS WILL BE TAKEN BACK OR EXCHANGED, EXCEPT BY SPECIAL AGREEMENT IN WRITING MADE AT TIME OF PURCHASE. (We have known of parties purchasing uniforms, then having their photographs taken in military costumes and afterwards returning the uniforms and receiving back their money. This is one of the reasons for this clause.)

Note that we are giving up making Spencer guns since we were defeated in the courts (by a mere technicality) from stopping the Winchester, Colt and Marlin Arms Companies from what we claimed was an infringement of our Spencer gun patents.

Please send us with your letter:

Name—Please write plainly; often we have to hold back orders, or goods go to wrong place, because the writer did not write his signature plainly.

Street and Number, Town or City, County, State, Number of Post Office Box.

When ordering, send us page number and item, also date of any previous correspondence.

When ordering uniforms, please send us:

Size of cap or hat worn, chest measure for coat or blouse, waist and inside of leg seam for trousers; boots—number of size. Please note that Cadet means young men's size, that our uniforms in ready-made goods are from 33 to 38 chest.

It is unnecessary to say anything regarding the location of Broadway, New York. It is known and acknowledged in all civilized lands as THE GREATEST BUSINESS THOROUGHFARE ON EARTH. Our number is 501, on the west side (best side), three doors north of Broome street.

**11055**

**11056**

**11055.** Hand Hammer or Crusher Stones, chipped round and flat, disc shaped like a small cheese, then rubbed smooth for use in grinding grain and for use as a hand hammer. Price $1.50

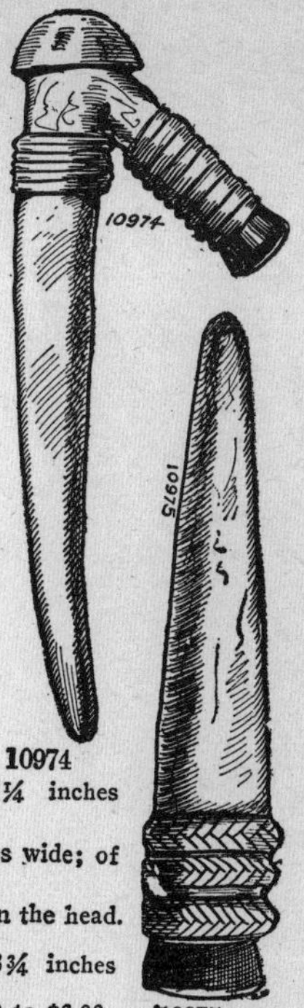

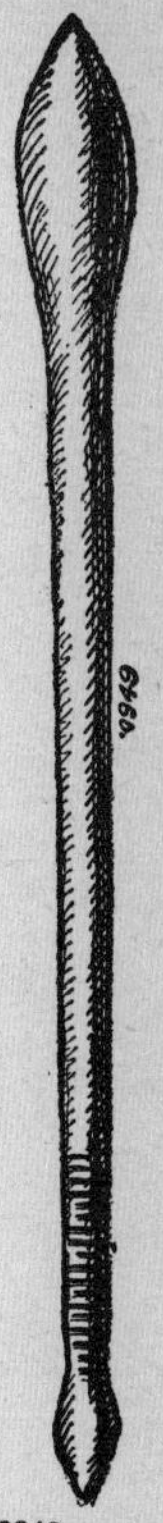

**11055 A.** Hammer-Crusher Stone Disks; average diameter 2¾ inches, 1¼ inch thick. Price $1.00.

**11056.** Hammer-Crusher Stone Disks; average diameter 3 inches, 1¾ inch thick; polished smooth; fine specimen. Price $1.50.

Portable Mortar or Mealing Stone; large heavy stone slightly hollowed on the flat surface wherein grain was reduced by rubbing with a crusher stone; length is 11 inches, 8 inches at the widest part, 3¾ inches high; has hollow in the center on both top and bottom sides. Price, with crusher $10.00.

**11056 A** Portable Mortar or Mealing Stone; is 10 inches length, 7 inches width and 4½ inches high; it is hollowed on both sides. Price with the crusher stone is $10.00.

Adam Oliver, who collected Georgia and South Carolina stone weapons, was Master Armorer and Ordnance Storekeeper at the U. S. Augusta Arsenal, Ga., from the period of the Mexican War until his death 30 years after the close of the Civil War, serving both the United States and the Southern Confederacy as Ordnance Storekeeper. The following description is taken from letter describing a collection of stone weapons Mr. Oliver presented to the Public Museum in his native town, Jedburg, Scotland.

"Polished Stone Axes or Celts; wedge shaped tough stone with groove for handle in the center. Some with groove on the sides for tightening handle with wedge. Peculiar to the United States. Found in sites of ancient villages along the banks of the Savannah River, where it washes the counties of Richmond and Columbia in Georgia, and Edgefield and Barnewell counties in South Carolina. Probably the handiwork of the Uchees and the Kiokees, component tribes of the Creek Confederacy, natives here when the region was first peopled by Europeans. The grooved axes were made chiefly of dionite and were hafted by means of a stout withe fastening around the groove, the ends being brought together below and were lashed with thongs of deer skin thus forming a handle. Some of the axes in the lot have grooves at the side in order to hold wedge for tightening the handle. These weapons were frequently used by these primitive peoples in girdling trees, in removing the charred portions from log tree canoes while they were being hollowed out by firing, and as offensive weapons of war."

**11058**

**11058.** Polished Stone Axe, with groove for handle. One side almost straight for handle wedge. Size about 5 inches long. Price, $10.00.

**11059.** Polished Stone Battle Axe, about 7 inches long, with grooves for handle. Slightly chipped. This size rare. Price, $12.00.

**11061A.** Polished Stone Battle Axe; 4¼ inches long, 3¼ inches wide; perfect condition. Price $3.75.

**11062.** Unpolished Groove Battle Axe; 7 inches long, 4½ inches wide; of a much earlier period than the polished axe. Price $5.00.

**11063.** Battle Axe; 3 inches long, 3 inches wide; very slight chip on the head. Price $2.85.

**11064.** Battle Axe with rounded head; 4½ inches long, 3¾ inches wide; broken condition. Price $4.00.

Assorted Battle Axes, polished, in broken condition. From $1.00 to $3.00.

Plain Polished Celts, 3½ inches long, 2¼ inches wide. Price $1.50.

Polished Celts, with round heads with cutting edge; 2 inches by 5½ inches. Price $2.00.

Ceremonial Stones or Sinkers, 5x3½x⅝ inches. Price $1.50.

**10854.** Ivory Tusk used by African natives for pounding sago; diameter 1¾ inches, length 13 inches, weight 24½ ounces. Price $6.50.

**10887.** Native Harpoon from Terre del Fuego; bone; 11½ inches long. Price $3.85.

**10962.** Six Solomon Island Native's Hand Carved Fish Spear Arrows; sharp pointed hardwood, carved in relief and colored; attached to bamboo shaft, with notch for bow string; 4 feet long. From Arnold's Museum. Price $10.00.

**10963.** Solomon Island Native's South Sea Arrow Fish Spear; 4½ feet long; hardwood pointed, fitted into bamboo shaft, with notch for bow string; 45 in the lot. Price singly $1.00 each; 90 cents each the lot.

**10964.** Three Bows, from Solomon Island in the South Sea; 6 and 7 feet long; 2 with string. From Arnold's Museum collection. Price $20.00.

**10965.** Curious African Native Bow, made of elephant hide; 5¼ feet long, ½ inch thick, 1¼ inch wide; complete with bow string. Price $15.00.

**10966.** Six Assorted Bows, from 3½ to 5 feet long. From Lady Stewart's collection. Price $40.00.

**10974**

**10875**

**10949**

**10974.** Ancient Stone Axe from New Guinea. Purchased at sale of George Arnold Museum, Milton Hall, Gravesend, England. The adze stone is jade or green stone; round shaped edge 2¼ inches in width fitted into the cleft of bow or tree and bound around with bamboo cane; length of handle 22 inches, cleft shaft and stone adze 7 inches; rare relic. $15.00.

**10975.** Ancient Stone Head Chisel from New Guinea; with round shaped edge stone, fastened between the cleft of branch of tree and bound around with cane fibre; full length 13 inches, diameter 2½ inches. Price $9.85.

**10949.** Australian Aboriginal Native's Weapon, called Waddia; hard dark colored wood, crudely ornamented; from Arnold's Museum; 25 inches long. Price $4.50. 29 inches long, $5.50. 32 inches long, $6.50.

**10951.** African Native's Spoon; made of cocoanut shell, crudely fitted into wood handle fastened by fibres. Price $3.50.

**10950.** Australian Aboriginal Throwing Spear; polished, dark colored hardwood; flat with sharp edges; 29 inches long by 2⅜ inches wide, ¼ inch thick. Price $6.00.

**10952.** African Native's Quiver; made of the hide of some wild animal; contains 24 fine steel metal tipped barbed arrows; bamboo shaft; wood hand grip. Price $24.00 the outfit.

**10953.** African Native Hide Quiver, with 13 metal tipped needle pointed double barbed arrow spears. From Lady Stewart's collection. Price $13.00.

**10954.** African Native's Decorated Hide Quiver, containing 14 barbed pointed double and triple barbed arrow spears. From sale of Lady Stewart's collection. Price $15.00.

**10955.** Eleven Native Made Arrow Spears, with 5 inch iron shank attached to bamboo shafts with gum and fibre. Each spear of curious shaped double barbed and fluted with sharpened edged blades, to rotate the arrows the same as a rifle bullet. From Lady Stewart's collection, England. All contained in quiver with shoulder belt and small brass tube with leather bottom attached, which we think contained the poison in which the native dipped his arrow before shooting. Price the outfit, $20.00.

**10955A.** African Native Bow with String; made of bamboo; shows much service. From Lady Stewart's collection. Price $5.00.

**10956.** Thirteen Curious Native Made Arrow Spears in Quiver, attached to bamboo shaft. Also five spears without shafts; same description as No. 10955 only that there is a slight difference; the spears are a trifle longer in depth and fluted. Quiver is dark tan leather, embossed, and is heavier in the bottom to keep it upright. From Lady Stewart's collection. Price $20.00.

## ANCIENT BRITONS STONE AGE WEAPONS

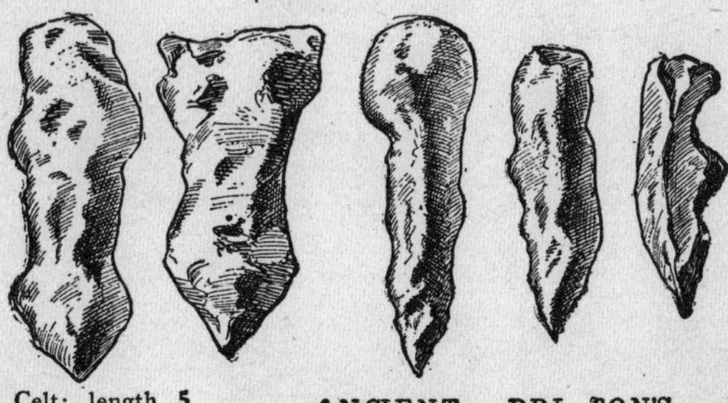

**10968.** Ancient Briton Flake Celt; length 5 inches, width 2¾ inches. Price $2.50.

**10968A.** 5x2 inches. Price $1.50.

4½x3 inches; marked Neolithic. Price $2.50.

**10968B.** 4x3 inches, with groove clearly produced by some sharp edged instrument; portion filled in with cement and afterwards petrified. From Gravesend, England, 1901. Price $3.85.

Large size double edge flake flint scraper; size 7x3 inches, weight 15 ounces. Price $3.50.

Briton's Flaked Spear War Head; heart shaped indented base; size about 2 inches; very old; partly petrified. Price $1.85.

**11058A.** Round Hammer Head, which shows numerous pitted marks of service; found in England; average length 3 inches, 2 inches wide. Price $1.00.

Heart Shaped Hammer Head and Drill, all pitted with hammer marks; one surface worn concave; size 3¼ inches; marked as having been found at West Cliff, South End, England, 1899; a rare specimen. Price $3.00.

### ANCIENT BRITON'S HAND BATTLE AXES AND CLUBS found

in the Southern counties of England. Some are coated smooth from deposit of mineral substance which must have been the work of ages. Interesting and curious specimens that show very plainly the hand hold, hammer and pick formation. The average weight of the largest is 3 pounds, and some measure 7 inches in length. Price for choice of the three largest, $4.85 each; price for choice of two smaller sizes, $3.50 each.

Hand Hammer; pike shaped; size 5x1¼ inches. Price $1.50.

I flaked a flint to a cutting edge,
  And shaped it with brutish craft;
I broke a shank from the woodland dank
  And fitted it head and haft.
Then I hid me close to the reedy tarn,
  Where the mammoth came to drink.
Through the brawn and bone I drove the stone,
  And slew him on the brink.

STONE AGE. FROM AN OLD GERMAN ILLUSTRATION SHOWING ANCIENTS DRESSED IN SKIN OF WILD ANIMALS. THEIR STONE WEAPONS, AXE, KNIFE, SPEAR, BOW, ARROWS, AND QUIVER.

Congo Natives' Neck Breaker. Heavy sharpened edged wood club. Length 25 inches; pounds. Price, $7.00.

Collection Stone Age Weapons, showing the early weapons made by man for his defense and needs of every-day life. These crude weapons acquired a sanctity in olden times which caused them to be retained for ceremonial use long after the introduction of metal. The Egyptians used stone or flint knives in embalming their dead. The ancient priests of Mexico cut out the hearts of their victims with blades of stone. To-day there are in many countries those who make use of these ancient flint weapons mounted as

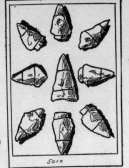

5010.

5009.

**5009. SET OF NINE ASSORTED ARROW HEADS** from various parts of the United States. Not all perfect, but valuable for collections. NOT MOUNTED ON CARD. Price, $1.00 per set of 9.

**5010. SET OF SMALL ARROW HEADS,** of different sizes, from many parts of the United States. Assorted colors and shapes. Price, $3.00 for set of 10. NOT ON CARD.

We take in trade for other goods from our catalog—stone axes, arrow heads and similar goods—and if you have any to dispose of, we shall be glad to have list with YOUR price for lot.

amulets to protect the wearer from disease and the evil eye. Only a few years ago application was made to the director of the Liverpool museum for permission to apply an old flint stone axe to the body of a sick child. This set of specimens are exact *reproductions*, made at the same flint beds in England that the ancient Britain obtained his flint weapons. This set is as fine as any exhibited in the best museums of Europe. Price, for the six pieces, $35.00.

**712-713-714.** South Sea Islanders' War Clubs or Battle Axe. Made of stone. They have made some round and some shield-shaped, with hole formed in centre for pole, used as battle axe. Purchased from London collector. Choice of three patterns—circular, shield or egg-shaped. Price, $9.50 each.

Triangular-shaped Flint Axe, Pick or Lance Head. Length, 3 inches; width, 2½ inches; ⅞-inch thick sharpened blades and point. Grey-colored flint.
Flint Scraper, sharpened points and edges. Length, 2½ inches; width, 2 inches; ⅜-inch thick. Dark-colored flint.
Flint Pick or Lance Head, sharpened edges and point. Length, 3¾ inches; width, ¾-inch. Dark-colored flint.
Flint Axe Head. Length, 5⅝ inches; width, 2½ inches; thickness, 1 inch. Sharpened edges. 4-inch blade.

Flint Knife or Sickle, with head for attaching to handle. Sharpened double edge.

Flint Saw. 2½ inches long, 1 1-16-inch wide, sharpened edge, ⅝-inch thick; dark colored.

Flint Disc Axe or Knife, 2½ inches in diameter, 3-16-inch thick; sharpened blade; dark colored.

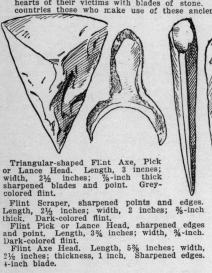

ILLUSTRATION SHOWING METHOD OF HOLDING ANCIENT STONE HAMMER.

2415. African Natives' War Spear. Barbed metal head shows artistic skill workmanship. Offered complete with shaft; length, 3 feet. Price, $4.85.
2415a. Congo Native-made Spear, with double edge sharpened blade, mounted on wood shaft. Price, $3.85.

**0-863. ANCIENT STONE AXE FROM NEW GUINEA.** Extra large jade or green stone, sharpened blade 8¾ inches long, 4 inches wide. Polished and sharpened cutting edges, inserted in the cleft of forked branch of a tree, fastened with woven fibre cane. Handle 19½ inches, axe and cleft part 17 inches, weight 2¾ pounds. A rare specimen. Price, $18.85.

N, DUPRE'S PAINTING— BATTLE OF AGINCOURT, 1415" SHOWING USE OF BOW, SPEAR, MACE SWORD WITH CHAIN MAIL AND OTHER ARMOR

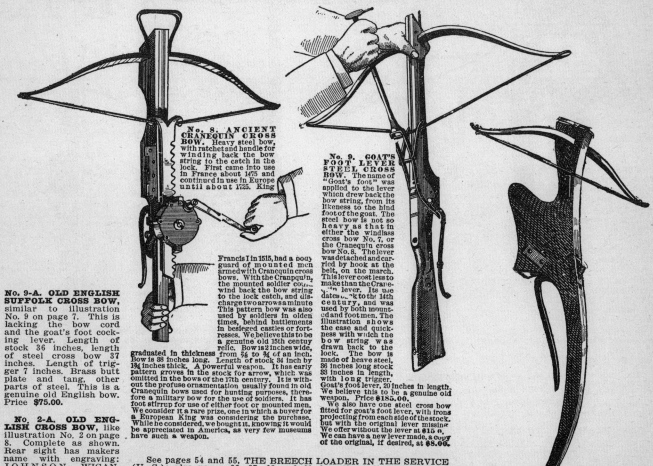

**No. 8. ANCIENT CRANEQUIN CROSS BOW.** Heavy steel bow, with ratchet and handle for winding back the bow string to the catch in the lock. First came into use in France about 1475 and continued in use in Europe until about 1725. King Francis I in 1515, had a body guard of mounted men armed with Cranequin cross bows. With the Cranequin, the mounted soldier could wind back the bow string to the lock catch, and discharge two arrows a minute. This pattern bow was also used by soldiers in olden times, behind battlements in besieged castles or fortresses. We believe this to be a genuine old 15th century relic. Bow is 2 inches wide, graduated in thickness from 5⁄8 to 3⁄4 of an inch. Bow is 38 inches long. Length of stock 34 inch by 1¾ inches thick. A powerful weapon. It has early pattern groves in the stock for arrow, which was omitted in the bows of the 17th century. It is without the profuse ornamentation usually found in old Cranequin bows used for hunting purposes, therefore a military bow for the use of soldiers. It has foot stirrup for use of either foot or mounted men. We consider it a rare prize, one in which a buyer for a European King was considering the purchase. While he considered, we bought it, knowing it would be appreciated in America, as very few museums have such a weapon.

**No. 9. GOAT'S FOOT LEVER STEEL CROSS BOW.** The name of "Goat's foot" was applied to the lever which drew back the bow string, from its likeness to the hind foot of the goat. The steel bow is not so heavy as that in either the windlass cross bow No. 7, or the Cranequin cross bow No. 8. The lever was detached and carried by hook at the belt, on the march. This lever cost less to make than the Cranequin lever. Its use dates back to the 14th century, and was used by both mounted and foot men. The illustration shows the ease and quickness with which the bow string was drawn back to the lock. The bow is made of heave steel, 36 inches long stock 33 inches in length, with long trigger. Goat's foot lever, 20 inches in length. We believe this to be a genuine old weapon. Price $185.00. We also have one steel cross bow fitted for goat's foot lever, with irons projecting from each side of the stock, but with the original lever missing. We offer without the lever at $15 0. We can have a new lever made, a copy of the original, if desired, at $8.00.

**No. 9-A. OLD ENGLISH SUFFOLK CROSS BOW,** similar to illustration No. 9 on page 7. This is lacking the bow cord and the goat's foot cocking lever. Length of stock 36 inches, length of steel cross bow 37 inches. Length of trigger 7 inches. Brass butt plate and tang, other parts of steel. This is a genuine old English bow. Price $75.00.

**No. 2-A. OLD ENGLISH CROSS BOW,** like illustration No. 2 on page 8. Complete as shown. Rear sight has makers name with engraving: JOHNSON, WIGAN. Length of stock 26 inches, with stud end. Length of bow 26 inches. Heavy brass butt plate marked: 14. Price $60.00.

See pages 54 and 55, THE BREECH LOADER IN THE SERVICE (U. S.); also pages 66, 67, 68 and 69 for all small arms used in World War. See pages 90, 94, 101 and 103 for ILLUSTRATED HISTORY OF U. S. MILITARY SMALL ARMS. Any of these features alone worth many times the price we ask for catalog, and do not appear in any other printed form. Note that this entire catalog and contents is copyrighted and cannot be used.

**No. 11. OLD CROSS BOW,** complete with bow string and stirrup, without windlass. Steel bow is 36 inches long stock 27 inches. Has been repaired. In poor order price $40.00

**NO. 4-A. ANTIQUE EUROPEAN CROSS BOW,** similar to illustration No. 4 on page 8, except that the butt plate or rest is pine apple shape of heavy brass. Fitted with grooved rear sight, adjustable for height, and front sight movable from side to side. Rest is ornamented with two white ivory discs. Full length of stock 55 inches, length of bow 30½ inches. Offered without cocking device. Price $65.00.

**NO. 00. ANTIQUE CHINESE IMPERIAL BOW,** whale bone reinforced. Length 3 ft. 5 inches; 20 inches deep; second-hand; serviceable order. Price $20.00.

**NO. 1803. STEEL BOW,** 1⅝ inches wide, 2¾ ft. long, 7 inches deep. Good serviceable order. Price $8.00.

**NO. 000. SMALL BOW,** shaped similar to No. 0. Length 25 inches; 12 inches deep, with bow string. Price $7.50.

**NO. 1802. 4 ORIENTAL HORN BOWS,** 3 feet 4 inches long, 6½ inches deep, made of horn, painted and decorated. From London collection. Price $7.50 each.

**NO. 2. BULLET SHOOTING CROSS BOW,** very finely made by gun makers about the year 1800. The lever is in the butt stock for drawing back the bow string. Bow is complete with peep and wind gauge sights. Inlaid steel ornamentation. In working order, complete, with bow strings. With leather pocket attached for holding bullet. These bows were reproductions of the 16th century stone shooting bows, being sold by the English gun makers at from $50 to $100 for hunting crows and rabbits. A favorite weapon of poachers. We believe these are genuine old English made bows. We offer:

2 with 28 inch bows, 30 inch stock, price $35.00
1 with 27 inch bows, 28 inch stock, price $32.00
1 with 24 inch bows, 26 inch stock, price $30.00

Handsome Old Bullet Cross Bow, in fine case, with extra steel bow and parts well preserved. Practically good as new. Will sell case with box and extras for $45.00.

**NO. 5. 2 STONE CROSS BOWS,** shooting small stones in hunting game. In use about the 16th century. Bow is 29 inches; stock 30 inches in length. Offered complete, with new bow strings and leather pouch to hold stone bullet. Price $32.00.

Ancient method of carrying bow.

**NO. 1855. FINE NEW BOW, MODEL FOR EUROPEAN BOW CLUB,** 4 ft. 8½ inches long. Swiss butt; 22½-inch bow; handsome curly walnut stock; checkered grip; ornamented mountings; cheek piece on stock, with new Goat's Foot Lever. Blued strap. All in fine serviceable order. steel guide for arrow, with sling. With two arrows, Price $45.00.

**NO. 4. 17TH CENTURY CONTINENTAL GOAT'S FOOT LEVER CROSS BOW.** The Knights of St. George used similar bows in olden times, at their tournaments. The bow is 30 inches long, stock 4½ ft., complete, with Goat's Foot Lever. Lock has revolving ivory nut catch for the bow string. Stock has polished brass ball ornament. Also ornamental metal tip. Double or set triggers with sight. Stock shows repairing. Has all the marks and tokens of being a genuine old time bow. The Curator of the Antwerp Museum went on a 200 mile journey to examine bows No. 4 and No. 6, and we understand made a favorable report to the Directors regarding their purchase, but before action could be taken, we purchased these two fine bows. Price for No. 4 $125.00.

**NO. 6. OLD CONTINENTAL CROSS BOW.** Kind used for deer hunting in Europe, about period of 1750. Ordinary range about 100 yards. Extreme range 250 yards. Fitted with bow string. Rare old weapon, with Goat's Foot Lever. Lock has set or hair trigger. Length 2½ ft. long, bow 22 inches. Bargain price $95.00.

**NO. 1355. A GOAT'S FOOT LEVER** for drawing back bow string, with bow. No. 1855.

**NO. 7. CROSS BOW WITH WINDLASS** for winding back the bow string. Steel bow was made so heavy it was beyond the power of man to stretch it, so it was necessary to use a windlass or lever. On the march the windlass was detached and carried at the belt. This old bow is a good specimen. Complete, with foot stirrup, with old windlass and ropes. We do not think, however, that it is a genuine early 16th century period made bow. Bow is 22 inches long, 2 inches wide, ¼ inch thick; stock 2 inches thick, 36 inches long; handles 9 inches long. From an old English collection.

**NO. 11. OLD CROSS BOW,** complete, with bow string and stirrup, without windlass steel bow; is 36 inches long, stock 37 inches. Has been repaired. In fair order. Price $40.00.

**Chevy-Chase**

With fifteen hundred bowmen bold,
All chosen men of might,
Who knew full well in time of need
To aim their shafts aright.

*       *       *       *       *

He had a bow bent in his hand,
Made of a trusty tree;
An arrow of a cloth—yard long
To the hard head hailed he.

*Anon.*

Ancient winding up windlass bow.

# Bows and Hand Cannon Guns.

**2306. OLD TIME RELIC HUNTING BOW.** Iron frame, filled in at center with wood. Has been fitted with carbine butt stock. Eight-inch cocking lever on under side. Long spike at forward end, which was used as bayonet, also to hold cross bow in place. Cross bow missing, and NOT complete in parts or in working order. Total length, 33 inches. Price, $12.00.

**0-A. ANCIENT BOW, SHAPED LIKE No. 0.** SO VERY OLD that the wood has lost its strength; a small part broken off. Length is 44 inches. Price, $7.85.

**0-934. ANCIENT ORIENTAL HAND CANNON, FIRED BY MATCHLOCK;** 24-inch barrel, with flatted rib for sighting, fastened to hardwood stock. Outside diameter at the breech 4 inches, at the muzzle 3 inches. Ancient bronze lock. Three sight-studs. Full length 3 feet 2 inches, 1¼-inch smooth bore. Oriental cannons are rarely met with for sale. Fired with matchlock, are extremely rare. A museum exhibit. Price, $100.00.

**2309. ANTIQUE CROSS BOW, with iron barrel** for guiding the arrow. Found in old-time gun-maker's collection. Rusted from age; slit in barrel for rear sight; with modern front sight; with trigger guard. The old bow shows about the last advance from the bow to the gun. Rare weapon for museum. Price, $175.00.

**2408. ANCIENT WHEEL LOCK,** taken from old gun. Lock is 7 inches in length, and is handsomely ornamented. Price, $18.50.

**0-62. ANCIENT STEEL BOW.** Size, 21½ inches. Blued steel, wood-covered center; 4½-inch groove. Price, $6.85.

**MODEL OF ANCIENT HAND CANNON.** The first powder gun. This specimen was obtained from Professor of Gunnery in famous European College. It is considered a perfect reproduction, and was on exhibition in museum, showing the evolution in weapons of war. Full length 29 inches; 1¼-inch bow; the iron barrel is 7 inches long, attached to wood stock. Interesting exhibit that daily attracts thousands of sightseers to our windows. Price, $45.00.

**0-866A. ORIENTAL NATIVE'S BOW,** with arrow. Price, $8.85.

**No. O-866-B. AFRICAN NATIVE BOWS,** average length 56 inches. Some with rawhide cords. All serviceable. $8.50 each. African native arrows for use with these bows, from $1.00 up.

**2416. ANCIENT OAK BOX,** containing ivory lock parts for antique bows. Size 22 by 9½ by 8½ inches. Price, $25.00.

**2304. ANCIENT CROSS BOW,** walnut stock, steel bow; rusty with age; poor order. Price, $18.00.

**2308. ANCIENT HUNTING BOW,** single trigger; 30-inch steel bow; gun-shaped stock; ornamental rest; brass grooves for arrow; hand grip guard. In fair order. Price, $65.00.

**2234. ANTIQUE CROSS BOW** with metal bar; ½-inch bore; length 33 inches; steel bow, 33 inches; full length 4 feet; double trigger. Rare old weapon. Price, $65.00.

**0-997. ANTIQUE STONE-SHOOTING CROSS BOW,** with rare pattern rear sight, with peep-holes. Original butt stock attached to modern shotgun pattern stock. In working order. 35-inch steel bow, similar to illustration bow No. 2. Price, $37.50.

**0-998. SEVENTEENTH CENTURY BOLT-SHOOTING CROSS BOW;** 31-inch steel bow; 27½-inch square-shaped stock, of dark-colored hardwood, with cheek-piece. Brass butt. Double, or hair trigger. Ivory front sight and arrow groove. Rare old weapon. Price, $50.00.

**0-949. ANCIENT HINDOO-CHINESE LONG BOW;** 6 feet 9 inches, with the orignal bowstring. Bow is of hard, tough, black-colored wood, ⅝ inch thick, 1 inch wide, with red enameled fibre strengthening bands. Leather-covered arrow guide. Such a *long* bow, in fine condition, is rarely met with. Bargain price, $15.00.

**10523. ANCIENT CHINESE HAND CANNON,** believed to be one of the OLDEST WEAPONS IN EXISTENCE, showing the cannon complete, with projection at the breech forming a handle. This specimen has the SWIVEL for supporting the gun on the wall or for firing from a boat. Barrel and handle stock has, for additional strength, a piece of wood fastened with bamboo around the barrel. The cannon shows the usual Chinese faulty casting at the mouth, by not allowing, when casting, sufficient metal to carry off the sprue. Length of barrel 12 inches; full length, with handle, 22 inches; diameter at the breech, 1¾ inches; smallest diameter of the barrel, 1 inch. In no museum or collection have we seen a finer specimen of the earliest shooting cannon of pistol size. Price, $350.00.

**2307. ANTIQUE EUROPEAN CROSS BOW,** with rear peep sight, front sight; ancient walnut stock; gun-shaped butt stock; brass groove for guiding arrow; 3-foot steel bow, ⅝ inch thick, ⅞ inch wide; with foot stirrup; double trigger; guard, with side plate for attaching "goat's-foot lever." (No lever.) In well preserved order. Price, $75.00.

**No. O-1185-A. EUROPEAN CROSS BOW,** similar to illustration No. O-1185 on page 10. Heavy brass ball rest on end of butt stock, brass mounted throughout, with front sight adjustable for height, rear sight missing. Butt inlaid with wooden stars and small circles of wood. Price $50.00.

**No. O-1270-A. SHORT EUROPEAN CROSS BOW,** like illustration No. O-1270 on page 10. Heavy white metal butt plate and trigger guard, checkered pistol grip, fixed front sight, rear sight adjustable for height and windage. Large ring in tip for use in hanging or storing away. Length of stock 29 inches, length of bow 23½ inches. Complete with GOAT'S FOOT COCKING LEVER. Bow is made like a wagon spring, with full width bow built up and re-inforced with three shorter pieces. Price $60.00.

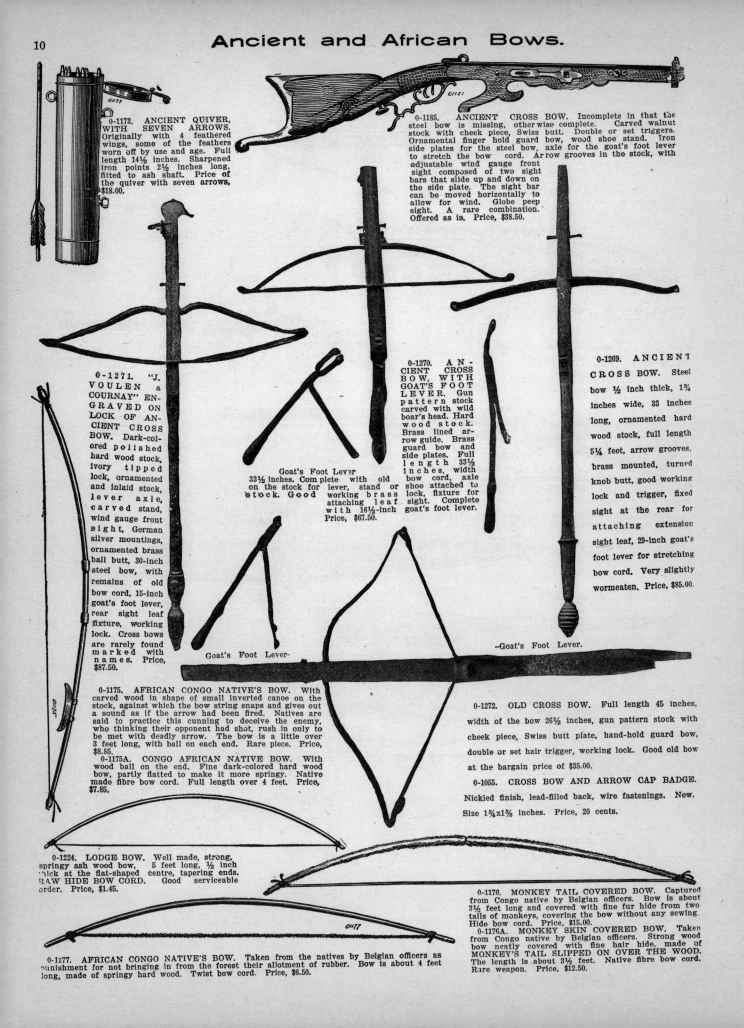

**0-1173. ANCIENT QUIVER, WITH SEVEN ARROWS.** Originally with 4 feathered wings, some of the feathers worn off by use and age. Full length 14½ inches. Sharpened iron points 2½ inches long, fitted to ash shaft. Price of the quiver with seven arrows, $18.00.

**0-1185. ANCIENT CROSS BOW.** Incomplete in that the steel bow is missing, otherwise complete. Carved walnut stock with cheek piece, Swiss butt. Double or set triggers. Ornamental finger hold guard bow, wood shoe stand. Iron side plates for the steel bow, axle for the goat's foot lever to stretch the bow cord. Arrow grooves in the stock, with adjustable wind gauge front sight composed of two sight bars that slide up and down on the side plate. The sight bar can be moved horizontally to allow for wind. Globe peep sight. A rare combination. Offered as is. Price, $38.50.

**0-1271. "J. VOULEN a COURNAY" ENGRAVED ON LOCK OF ANCIENT CROSS BOW.** Dark-colored polished hard wood stock, ivory tipped lock, ornamented and inlaid stock, lever axle, carved stand, wind gauge front sight, German silver mountings, ornamented brass ball butt, 30-inch steel bow, with remains of old bow cord, 15-inch goat's foot lever, rear sight leaf fixture, working lock. Cross bows are rarely found marked with names. Price, $87.50.

Goat's Foot Lever 33½ inches. Complete with old on the stock for lever, stand or stock. Good working brass attaching leaf with 16½-inch Price, $67.50.

**0-1270. ANCIENT CROSS BOW, WITH GOAT'S FOOT LEVER.** Gun pattern stock carved with wild boar's head. Hard wood stock. Brass lined arrow guide. Brass guard bow and side plates. Full length 33½ inches, width bow cord, axle shoe attached to lock, fixture for sight. Complete goat's foot lever.

**0-1269. ANCIENT CROSS BOW.** Steel bow ½ inch thick, 1¾ inches wide, 33 inches long, ornamented hard wood stock, full length 5¼ feet, arrow grooves, brass mounted, turned knob butt, good working lock and trigger, fixed sight at the rear for attaching extension sight leaf, 29-inch goat's foot lever for stretching bow cord. Very slightly wormeaten. Price, $85.00.

Goat's Foot Lever-

—Goat's Foot Lever.

**0-1175. AFRICAN CONGO NATIVE'S BOW.** With carved wood in shape of small inverted canoe on the stock, against which the bow string snaps and gives out a sound as if the arrow had been fired. Natives are said to practice this cunning to deceive the enemy, who thinking their opponent had shot, rush in only to be met with deadly arrow. The bow is a little over 3 feet long, with ball on each end. Rare piece. Price, $8.85.

**0-1175A. CONGO AFRICAN NATIVE BOW.** With wood ball on the end. Fine dark-colored hard wood bow, partly flatted to make it more springy. Native made fibre bow cord. Full length over 4 feet. Price, $7.85.

**0-1272. OLD CROSS BOW.** Full length 45 inches, width of the bow 26½ inches, gun pattern stock with cheek piece, Swiss butt plate, hand-hold guard bow, double or set hair trigger, working lock. Good old bow at the bargain price of $35.00.

**0-1055. CROSS BOW AND ARROW CAP BADGE.** Nickled finish, lead-filled back, wire fastenings. New. Size 1¾x1⅜ inches. Price, 20 cents.

**0-1224. LODGE BOW.** Well made, strong, springy ash wood bow, 5 feet long, ½ inch thick at the flat-shaped centre, tapering ends. RAW HIDE BOW CORD. Good serviceable order. Price, $1.45.

**0-1176. MONKEY TAIL COVERED BOW.** Captured from Congo native by Belgian officers. Bow is about 3½ feet long and covered with fine fur hide from two tails of monkeys, covering the bow without any sewing. Hide bow cord. Price, $15.00.

**0-1176A. MONKEY SKIN COVERED BOW.** Taken from Congo native by Belgian officers. Strong wood bow neatly covered with fine hair hide, made of MONKEY'S TAIL SLIPPED ON OVER THE WOOD. The length is about 3½ feet. Native fibre bow cord. Rare weapon. Price, $12.50.

**0-1177. AFRICAN CONGO NATIVE'S BOW.** Taken from the natives by Belgian officers as punishment for not bringing in from the forest their allotment of rubber. Bow is about 4 feet long, made of springy hard wood. Twist bow cord. Price, $6.50.

**1819. 48 AFRICAN NATIVE SPEAR HEAD ARROWS,** average length of shaft, 2½ ft. With native-made double edge metal points. Price $1.00 each.

**1820. 10 AFRICAN NATIVE BARBED ARROWS,** with detachable metal lance head for large game. Length 3 ft. Feathered shaft. The barbed lance is attached to the shaft by cords, which detach from the shaft on striking. Price $3.50 each.

---

**When ordering special guns allow a second choice.**

---

**1858. 30 AFRICAN NATIVE ARROWS.** Bamboo shafts. With long double barbed spear points. With sharpened edges, with blood grooves, attached to shaft by metal rod. The spear head is over 4 inches long with 2 large barbs. Price $2.00 each.

**1859. 50 AFRICAN NATIVE ARROWS,** with double barbed spear heads attached to shaft by metal shank. Average length 2 ft. Price $1.50 each.

**1862. NATIVE QUIVER** made of light wood and covered with hide and ornamented with designs in leather, with 24 inch streamers at top and 6 inch streamers at bottom. 4 inch cap covers the quiver to keep arrows from falling out. Set includes 11 arrows with bamboo shafts with sharp iron tips, average length 24 inches. Price $18.50.

**1861. QUIVER WITH 10** barbed African native arrows. All from the same tribe. Bamboo shaft, with metal barbed heads, attached to shaft by metal socket. Length is over 2 ft. Quiver is made of wood, crudely covered with leather. Length 19 inches. Price of this collection, 10 arrows with quiver, $20.00.

This Catalog besides being a list of what we have for sale, is offered as a reference book for collectors and museums and for that reason many special articles that have been sold are still shown. Some of the articles marked off may be in stock later.

**1863. 30 AFRICAN NATIVE, DOUBLE BARBED,** fluted grooves, revolving spear head arrows, attached to metal shaft by long metal shank. Spear heads 2 inches long, and is made so that the blood gutter grooved flanges will cause a slight revolving motion. Rare pattern arrows. Price $1.50 each.

**1864. 20 ARROWS WITH METAL BARBED POINTS,** with feathered wood shaft 2¾ ft. long. Price 75 cts. each.

**1862-A. NATIVE QUIVER WITH 13** arrows. Quiver is 24 inches long, made of bamboo, covered with leather and ornamented with leather strips, has leather carrying cord. Arrows have bamboo shafts with long metal tips in assorted shapes. Length of arrows 23 inches. Price $15.00.

**1866. 25 ARROWS,** assorted patterns (as illustrated); 3 and 4 sided and round spear heads. Length over 2 ft. Price 75 cts. each.

**1866-A. 8 AFRICAN NATIVE, DOUBLE BARBED ARROWS,** spear head on metal shank, attached to shaft. Length 2½ ft. Price $1.50 each.

**10950.** Australian Aboriginal Throwing Spear; polished, dark-colored hardwood; flat with sharp edges; 29 inches long by 2⅜ inches wide, ¼ inch thick. Price, $6.00.

**10952.** African Native's Quiver; made of the hide of some wild animal; contains 24 fine steel metal-tipped barbed arrows; bamboo shaft; wood hand grip. Price, $24.00 the outfit.

**10953.** African Native Hide Quiver, with 13 metal-tipped, needle-pointed, double-barbed arrow spears. From Lady Stewart's collection. Price, $13.00.

**10954.** African Native's Decorated Hide Quiver, containing 14 barbed-pointed, double- and triple-barbed arrow spears. From sale of Lady Stewart's collection. Price, $15.00.

**10955.** Eleven Native-Made Arrow Spears, with 5-inch iron shank, attached to bamboo shafts with gum and fibre. Each spear of curious shape, double-barbed and fluted with sharp-edged blades, to rotate the arrows, the same as a rifle bullet. From Lady Stewart's collection, England. All contained in quiver with shoulder belt and small brass tube with leather bottom attached, which we think contained the poison in which the native dipped his arrow before shooting. Price, the outfit, $20.00.

**10956.** Thirteen Curious Native-Made Arrow Spears in Quiver, attached to bamboo shaft. Also five spears without shafts; same description as No. 10955 only that there is a slight difference; the spears are a trifle longer in depth and fluted. Quiver is dark tan leather, embossed, and is heavier in the bottom to keep it upright. From Lady Stewart's collection. Price, $20.00.

**1804. 14 AFRICAN NATIVE BOWS.** 5 feet long, 6 inches deep, with rawhide bow-string. These are similar in shape to that in illustration, showing Congo native in act of shooting. Price for bow, with 2 barbed arrows, $10.00.

**1810. 4 NATIVE-MADE BOWS.** 6½ feet long. Broad, flat, springy-shaped whalebone-colored wood. Fitted with bow-string and 2 barbed arrows. Price, $10.00 each.

**1814. CONGO NATIVE BOW.** Partly covered with snakeskin. Price, $12.50.

**1815. 55 CONGO NATIVE ARROWS,** with double-barbed, pointed arrows. Length of feathered shaft, 2½ feet. Barbed point. Average length, 2½ inches. Price, $1.35 each.

**1816. 60 SINGLE-BARBED CONGO NATIVE ARROWS,** similar in length and size to No. 1815. Price, $1.15 each.

**10951.** African Native's Spoon; made of cocoanut shell, crudely fitted into wood handle, fastened by fibres. Price, $3.50.

**2216. 70 CONGO NATIVE'S ARROWS,** used in hunting game. Note the upper end in illustration, showing the fibre leaf wrapping, wherein we presume the native places the poison. We offer these weapons with the **cautionary notice regarding the Poison. AS ARE,** at price of 70 cts. each.

**1811. NATIVE MADE BOWS.** Assorted patterns. 4½ ft. long without bow strings. $5.85 each.

**1817. 15 CONGO NATIVE BARBED ARROWS,** with two barbs. Price $1.85 each; with 3 barbs, $2.50 each.

**1818. CONGO NATIVE ARROW** with sharpened metal point; with feathered guide. Price 75 cts.

2:27

1862

1819

1820

1869    1816    1815    1857    1866

1858    1863

1859

2216

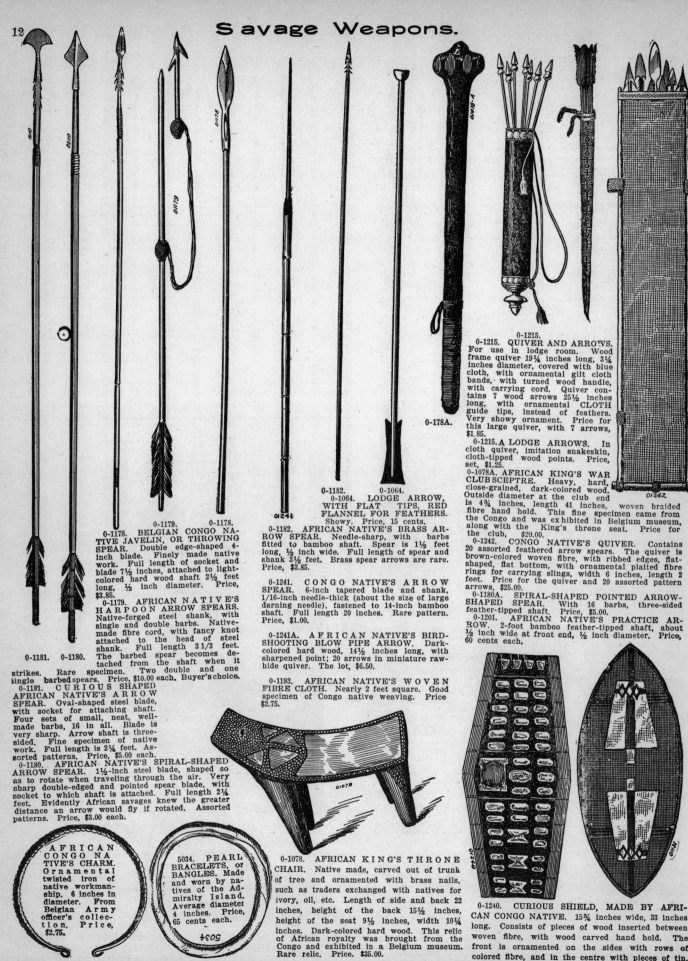

# Savage Weapons.

**0-1178.** BELGIAN CONGO NATIVE JAVELIN, OR THROWING SPEAR. Double edge-shaped 4-inch blade. Finely made native work. Full length of socket and blade 7½ inches, attached to light-colored hard wood shaft 2½ feet long, ½ inch diameter. Price, $3.85.

**0-1179.** AFRICAN NATIVE'S HARPOON ARROW SPEARS. Native-forged steel shank, with single and double barbs. Native-made fibre cord, with fancy knot attached to the head of steel shank. Full length 3 1/3 feet. The barbed spear becomes detached from the shaft when it strikes. Rare specimen. Two double and one single barbed spears. Price, $10.00 each. Buyer's choice.

**0-1181.** CURIOUS SHAPED AFRICAN NATIVE'S ARROW SPEAR. Oval-shaped steel blade, with socket for attaching shaft. Four sets of small, neat, well-made barbs, 16 in all. Blade is very sharp. Arrow shaft is three-sided. Fine specimen of native work. Full length is 2¼ feet. Assorted patterns. Price, $5.00 each.

**0-1180.** AFRICAN NATIVE'S SPIRAL-SHAPED ARROW SPEAR. 1½-inch steel blade, shaped so as to rotate when traveling through the air. Very sharp double-edged and pointed spear blade, with socket to which shaft is attached. Full length 2¼ feet. Evidently African savages knew the greater distance an arrow would fly if rotated. Assorted patterns. Price, $3.00 each.

AFRICAN CONGO NATIVE'S CHARM. Ornamental twisted iron of native workmanship. 6 inches in diameter. From Belgian Army officer's collection. Price, $2.75.

**5034.** PEARL BRACELETS, or BANGLES. Made and worn by natives of the Admiralty Island. Average diameter 4 inches. Price, 65 cents each.

**0-1064.** LODGE ARROW, WITH FLAT TIPS, RED FLANNEL FOR FEATHERS. Showy. Price, 15 cents.

**0-1182.** AFRICAN NATIVE'S BRASS ARROW SPEAR. Needle-sharp, with barbs fitted to bamboo shaft. Spear is 1½ feet long, ½ inch wide. Full length of spear and shank 3½ feet. Brass spear arrows are rare. Price, $3.85.

**0-1241.** CONGO NATIVE'S ARROW SPEAR. 6-inch tapered blade and shank, 1/16-inch needle-thick (about the size of large darning needle), fastened to 14-inch bamboo shaft. Full length 20 inches. Rare pattern. Price, $1.00.

**0-1241A.** AFRICAN NATIVE'S BIRD-SHOOTING BLOW PIPE ARROW. Dark-colored hard wood, 14½ inches long, with sharpened point; 20 arrows in miniature rawhide quiver. The lot, $6.50.

**0-1193.** AFRICAN NATIVE'S WOVEN FIBRE CLOTH. Nearly 2 feet square. Good specimen of Congo native weaving. Price $2.75.

**0-1215.** QUIVER AND ARROWS. For use in lodge room. Wood frame quiver 19¼ inches long, 3¼ inches diameter, covered with blue cloth, with ornamental gilt cloth bands, with turned wood handle, with carrying cord. Quiver contains 7 wood arrows 25½ inches long, with ornamental CLOTH guide tips, instead of feathers. Very showy ornament. Price for this large quiver, with 7 arrows, $1.85.

**0-1215.** A LODGE ARROWS. In cloth quiver, imitation snakeskin, cloth-tipped wood points. Price, set, $1.25.

**0-1078A.** AFRICAN KING'S WAR CLUB SCEPTRE. Heavy, hard, close-grained, dark-colored wood. Outside diameter at the club end is 4¾ inches, length 41 inches, woven braided fibre hand hold. This fine specimen came from the Congo and was exhibited in Belgium museum, along with the King's throne seat. Price for the club, $20.00.

**0-1242.** CONGO NATIVE'S QUIVER. Contains 20 assorted feathered arrow spears. The quiver is brown-colored woven fibre, with ribbed edges, flat-shaped, flat bottom, with ornamental plaited fibre rings for carrying slings, width 6 inches, length 2 feet. Price for the quiver and 20 assorted pattern arrows, $25.00.

**0-1180A.** SPIRAL-SHAPED POINTED ARROW-SHAPED SPEAR. With 16 barbs, three-sided feather-tipped shaft. Price, $5.00.

**0-1201.** AFRICAN NATIVE'S PRACTICE ARROW. 2-foot bamboo feather-tipped shaft, about ½ inch wide at front end, ½ inch diameter. Price, 60 cents each.

**0-1078.** AFRICAN KING'S THRONE CHAIR. Native made, carved out of trunk of tree and ornamented with brass nails, such as traders exchanged with natives for ivory, oil, etc. Length of side and back 22 inches, height of the back 15½ inches, height of the seat 9½ inches, width 10¼ inches. Dark-colored hard wood. This relic of African royalty was brought from the Congo and exhibited in a Belgium museum. Rare relic. Price. $35.00.

**0-1131.** CONGO NATIVE'S WAR SHIELD. Made of heavy woven fibre, oval shape, 14½ inches wide, nearly 3 feet long, colored in black and white, projecting rim around the edges, on the reverse side wood centre with carved hand hold. Brought from the Congo by Belgian officer. Price, $12.85.

**0-1240.** CURIOUS SHIELD, MADE BY AFRICAN CONGO NATIVE. 15¾ inches wide, 33 inches long. Consists of pieces of wood inserted between woven fibre, with wood carved hand hold. The front is ornamented on the sides with rows of colored fibre, and in the centre with pieces of tin, oval-shaped, supposed to make arrow proof. Perhaps the only one of its kind ever made. Curiosity. Price, $14.85.

# Matchlock Guns.

**2222.** Asiatic Matchlock Gun with silvered Damascus barrel; 46 inches long; fine pin-point damaskeen figures; ornamented muzzle; working order. Price, $38.00.

**2222b.** Asiatic Matchlock, steel barrel; length 49 inches; serviceable order. Price, $20.00.

**2222c.** Two Antique Long-Barrel Matchlock Guns, in fair order. Price, $18.00 each.

**2222a.** Asiatic Matchlock Gun, with steel barrel; 53 inches long. Price, $20.00.

**7135.** African Trader's MATCHLOCK GUN, with red stock, with brass bands, slightly blunderbuss shaped; 32-inch barrel; full length 44 inches; leg handle butt stock, complete. Price, $18.00.

Illustration from our book on War Weapons, showing soldier in dress of the 16th Century, with Bandolier, matchlock gun and gun rest.

**No. 1064. ANCIENT EUROPEAN MATCHLOCK RAMPART GUN.** Five feet long, octagonal barrel, ⅝-inch bore, 7 rifle grooves. Hand grip trigger guard, slightly carved and ornamented; cheek piece on butt stock; front sight; also rear sight. Width of barrel at muzzle, 1¾ inches. Double or set triggers. European matchlocks are very rare. The National Museum representative called and examined this fine old relic, with view of exhibiting same at the Jamestown Exposition. Rampart guns, however, were not used at the founding of the Jamestown Colony. Catalogue price **$200.00.**

**No. 1063. EUROPEAN MATCHLOCK,** about ¾-inch bore. F. R. engraved on lock plate; in serviceable working order. Evidently not a 16th century period gun. Bargain price **$65.00.**

**No. 1021-B. JAPANESE MATCHLOCK,** similar to No. 1021-A, with 39½ inch barrel, inlaid in silver with trees and other designs. Price $28.00.

**INDIA MATCH LOCKS.** Extra long twisted iron barrel. Rare specimen, seldom met with outside of best museums. Price **$40.00.**

**No. 1021-1030. 10 CHINESE MATCHLOCK GUNS,** fired with fuse; plain barrels, with reinforced muzzle; in working order. Price, $15.00 each. Three with ornamented barrels, $17.50 ea. Three with ornamented barrels and stock, with hole in stock for carrying slings, $20.00 ea.

**No. 215.** Antique Matchlock Gun, fired with fuse; first type of powder gun, with the old bow-shaped stock barrel; is finely inlaid with ornamental scroll work, flowers, birds, etc., in silver designs; cannon-shaped barrel muzzle, outside hammer and springs; knob-shaped trigger; length, 3 feet. Price $20.00.

**No. 1021-A. JAPANESE MATCHLOCK,** with heavy octagon barrel, slightly belled at muzzle. Full length 50 inches, barrel 38 inches. Two brass bands, brass outside hammer spring, brass escutcheons, flower ornament in brass at tang, Imperial seal inlaid in silver on barrel. This is a very old piece. Price $35.00.

**When ordering special guns allow a second choice.**

Heavy Matchlock or Hackbuss Hand Gun; fired with fuse of lighted rope, fixed in the forked hammer, which, when released by pulling the little knob which served for a trigger, moved forward and ignited the powder in the pan, which in turn set off the charge in the barrel; the oldest type of powder gun made. This gun is in perfect order; polished hard wood stock; silver inlaid barrel; full length, 38½ inches; barrel, 29½ inches; weight, 13 pounds. Price **$28.00.**

Antique Matchlock Gun from China after the Boxer War, when many valuable old antiques were received from China. This pattern gun is the first powder gun made; originally fired with match or coil of thin rope held in the hand. Sometimes these guns are called Hand Guns, and were used in Europe prior to the Wheelock, 1510. dark colored hard wood polished stock; full length, 36 ins.; weight, 6 lbs. Price, **$25.00.**

**No. 118. CHINESE MATCHLOCK,** 24-inch barrel; poor order; with sighting rib. With reinforced muzzle. Price **$25.00.**

**No. 1117. CHINESE MATCHLOCK,** with sighting rib, 24-inch barrel, ¾-inch bore; weight 9 pounds. Price **$25.00.**

**No. 1118. CHINESE MATCHLOCK,** 24½ inch barrel; poor order. **$15.50.**

**No. 1698. INDIA RAJAH'S GOLD AND SILVER ORNAMENTED HIGH CLASS MATCHLOCK;** 52-inch octagonal barrel, ⅝ smooth bore. Full length, 77½ inches. Ornamented open steel decorative work, with cover to flash pan. Handsome open work steel pick for cleaning vent, attached by small chain. Price **$100.00.**

**No. 1696. HANDSOME SILVER MOUNTED MATCHLOCK.** Highly ornamented; full length, 63½ inches, 11-16 smooth bore, 44½-inch barrel. High class chieftain's gun. Price **$65.00.**

Old Arabian Matchlock, with twist steel barrel; the rings of the steel can be seen and felt; about 5 feet long; in fair order. Price **$45.00.**

India Matchlock Long Gun (6 feet); in fair order. Price **$35.00.**

Persian Matchlock Gun, over 6 feet long; fine order; rare old relic. Price **$38.00.**

**No. 1062. KURDISTAN MATCHLOCK MUSKET,** altered to percussion lock. Rare pattern; ornamented stock, with brass work. Native sling strap. Working order. Price, $18.00.

**No. 1070. OLD INDIA MATCHLOCK.** Full length, 62 inches. Barrel tied to stock with hide thongs. In poor order. Price, $10.00.

**AN ENTHUSIASTIC JACOBITE.**—The Episcopalian clergyman of Stonehaven, at the time of the "Forty-five," an old man by the name of Troup was so enthusiastic a Jacobite that when a party by the name of Bannerman came marching through the town to join the chevalier, he, though it was Sunday, took a set of bagpipes and escorted them for some distance, playing "O'er the Water to Charlie." For this act of rebellion he was deprived by Government and obliged to perform all the functions of his sacred office in the strictest secrecy. The Scottish Episcopal Church long adhered to the cause of the Jacobites, and omitted the prayer for the king and the royal family from their service. It was not until the death of the unfortunate Charles Edward, in January, 1788, that they at length (not without some difficulty) agreed to pray for King George.—*Scottish American*, May, 1905.

(Bannerman was the standard bearer, Clan Macdonald, of Glencoe, the last of the Scottish clans to give in their allegiance to the English.

Soldier of the 16th Century, showing powder flask, shot bag, Bandolier and matchlock gun in rest, in firing position.

13

# MATCH AND WHEEL-LOCK GUNS

WHEEL-LOCK. An improvement on the matchlock. It was invented in Nuremberg about 1517, was used at the siege of Parma in 1521, and was carried to England in 1530. It consisted of a steel wheel rasped at the edge, which protruded into a priming pan; a strong spring; and a cock into which was fixed a piece of pyrites (sulphuret of iron). The wheel fitted on the square end of an axle or a spindle, to which the spring was connected by a chain swivel, and the cock was so fitted that it could be moved backwards or forwards at pleasure, a strong spring being connected with it to keep it firm in its position. When it was required to discharge the gun, the lock was wound up by means of a key or spanner which fitted on the axle or spindle, and the cock was let down to the priming pan, the pyrites resting on the wheel. On pressing the trigger, the wheel was released and put in motion, when sparks were emitted which set fire to the powder in the pan. The wheel-lock frequently missed fire, as the pyrites, which is of a friable nature, broke in the pan, and impeded the free action of the wheel, hence the match was usually retained to be ready for use when required.

FL-38. SNAUHAUNCE PISTOL, forerunner of flint lock. 5 inch lock engraved. 12½ inch octagonal barrel inlaid full length with silver. Entire wood stock ornamented in inlaid silver with designs of flowers, moon, etc. Silver trigger guard. Flat butt with round silver butt plate ornament. Tip of stock slightly chipped. Price, $50.00.

R44-A. OLD ENGLISH FLINT LOCK PISTOLS, with double barrels, superposed. The lever on side turns one vent in the pan, together with priming pan for shooting second barrel. All with British marks. See illustration No. R44 on page 93 in big catalog. Price, $25.00.

MATCHLOCK. The name formerly given to a small arm or musket. The earliest muskets were fired by means of a piece of slow-match applied by the hand to the touch hole. Towards the end of the 14th century, the first improvement appeared in the MATCHLOCK. This consisted of a crooked iron lever, in the end of which the match was fixed. By a pin gear of a very simple nature, pressure on the trigger brought the match accurately down on the powder pan, on which the lid or cover to hold in the priming powder, had been pushed forward by hand. This mode of firing involved the carrying of several yards of slow-match, usually wound around the body and the piece; rain extinguished the match, and the wind dispersed the powder in the pan so that the matchlock, clumsy withall, was but an uncertain apparatus. (From Farrow's Military Encyclopedia.)

---

**See page 16a for two views of fine old Wheellock Gun. Also page 16b for Wheellock Pistols, No. C-I W, C-W L, and C-I W-1, and Matchlock Pistol No. C-M L.**

---

10588. DANISH 1695 FLINTLOCK WALL GUN. The lock has seal with letters H. Z.; the barrel is engraved "Hans Zimmerman A. Kopenhagen 1695;" barrel is about 4 feet long; ¾ inch rifle bore; 2 leaf folding rear sight; large hand grip guard bow; cheek piece; comb shaped butt plate; heavy walnut stock; in fine serviceable order. Price $250.00.

10585. FRENCH FLINTLOCK RIFLED WALL GUN; 5 feet 3 inches long; ¾ inch rifle bore; octagonal barrel; front, middle and rear sight; Swiss butt stock; originally socket swivel removed and plate has been substituted for resting on the wall; walnut stock, checkered grip; finger grip guard bow check piece on each side of the butt stock; gun is in poor order from extensive service; lock is engraved Charleville. Price $50.00.

0-936. ANCIENT HEAVY FLINTLOCK WALL GUN. Full length 69 inches; octagonal 50-inch barrel; 1-inch bore. Bell-shaped at the muzzle. Front and rear sights; large lock; heavy black oak stock; armorer's seal on the barrel, and the letters S. N. From the Lawson-Johnston sale. Weight 37 pounds. Price, $45.00.

**When ordering special articles allow a second choice when possible.**

10590. ANCIENT EUROPEAN MATCHLOCK WALL GUN, nearly six feet long, with artistic CARVED WALNUT GUN REST, which measures 6x5¼ inches, 1⅝ inches thick; carved with FIGURE OF WOMAN WITH BOOK, WITH SWORD AND CASTLE; on the reverse side a MAN WITH BOOK, WITH CROSS; fluted barrel 44½ inches, ⅝ inch smooth bore; brass tube projecting on side for peep sight; lead capped butt plate with metal eye bolt; gun shows much use; is in fair order.

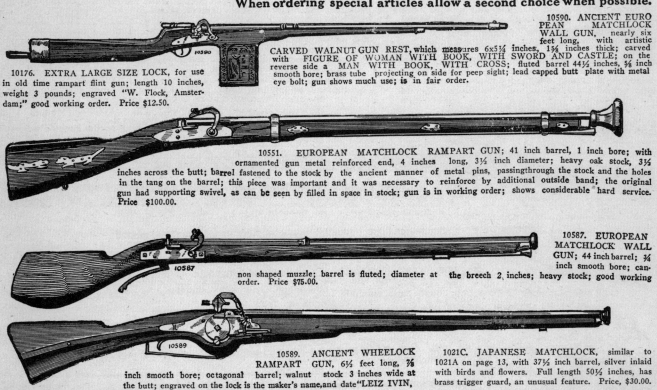

10176. EXTRA LARGE SIZE LOCK, for use in old time rampart flint gun; length 10 inches, weight 3 pounds; engraved "W. Flock, Amsterdam;" good working order. Price $12.50.

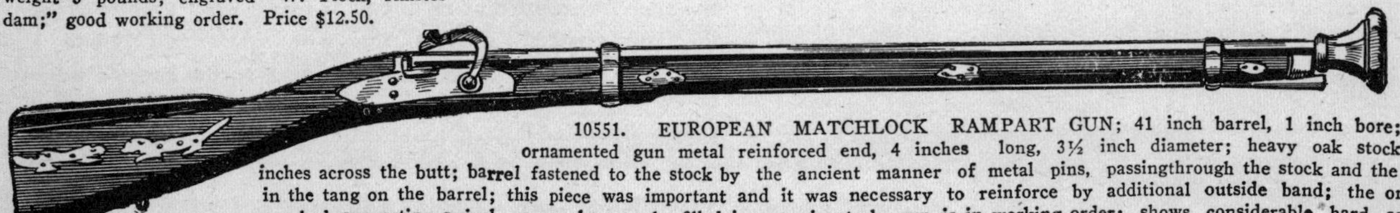

10551. EUROPEAN MATCHLOCK RAMPART GUN; 41 inch barrel, 1 inch bore; with ornamented gun metal reinforced end, 4 inches long, 3½ inch diameter; heavy oak stock, 3½ inches across the butt; barrel fastened to the stock by the ancient manner of metal pins, passingthrough the stock and the holes in the tang on the barrel; this piece was important and it was necessary to reinforce by additional outside band; the original gun had supporting swivel, as can be seen by filled in space in stock; gun is in working order; shows considerable hard service. Price $100.00.

10587. EUROPEAN MATCHLOCK WALL GUN; 44 inch barrel; ¾ inch smooth bore; cannon shaped muzzle; barrel is fluted; diameter at the breech 2 inches; heavy stock; good working order. Price $75.00.

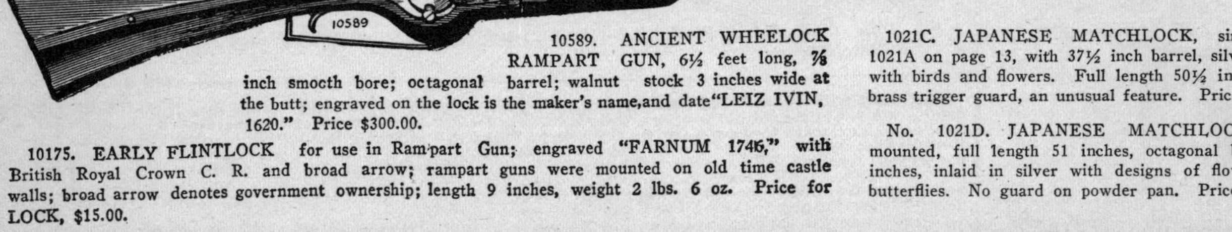

10589. ANCIENT WHEELOCK RAMPART GUN, 6½ feet long, ⅞ inch smooth bore; octagonal barrel; walnut stock 3 inches wide at the butt; engraved on the lock is the maker's name,and date "LEIZ IVIN, 1620." Price $300.00.

10175. EARLY FLINTLOCK for use in Rampart Gun; engraved "FARNUM 1746," with British Royal Crown C. R. and broad arrow; rampart guns were mounted on old time castle walls; broad arrow denotes government ownership; length 9 inches, weight 2 lbs. 6 oz. Price for LOCK, $15.00.

1021C. JAPANESE MATCHLOCK, similar to 1021A on page 13, with 37½ inch barrel, silver inlaid with birds and flowers. Full length 50½ inches, has brass trigger guard, an unusual feature. Price, $30.00.

No. 1021D. JAPANESE MATCHLOCK, iron mounted, full length 51 inches, octagonal barrel 38 inches, inlaid in silver with designs of flowers and butterflies. No guard on powder pan. Price, $25.00.

# Ancient Match and Wheelock Guns.

15

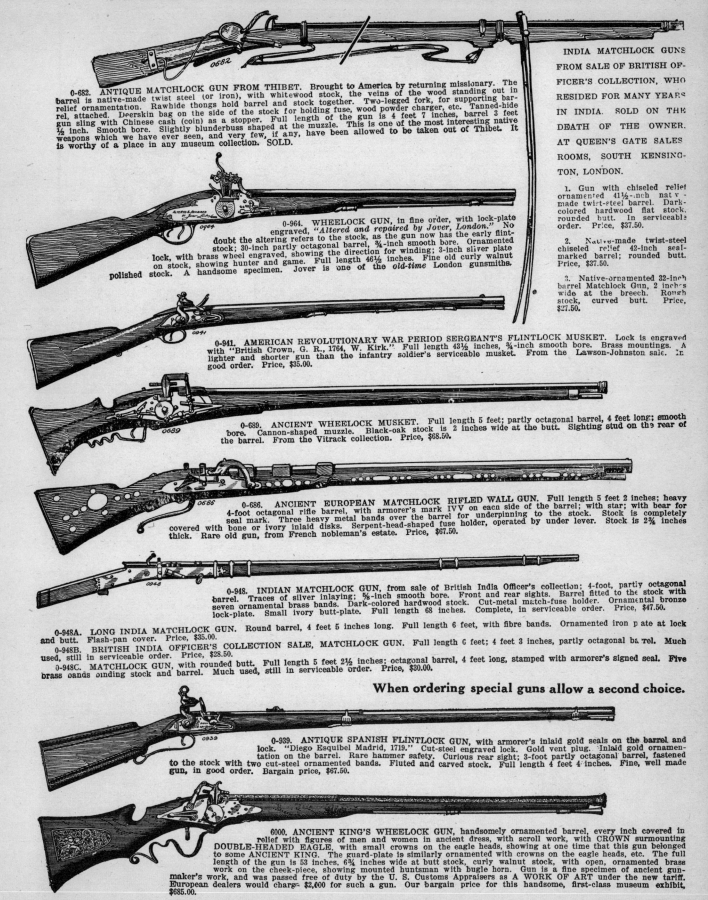

**0-682. ANTIQUE MATCHLOCK GUN FROM THIBET.** Brought to America by returning missionary. The barrel is native-made twist steel (or iron), with whitewood stock, the veins of the wood standing out in relief ornamentation. Rawhide thongs hold barrel and stock together. Two-legged fork, for supporting barrel, attached. Deerskin bag on the side of the stock for holding fuse, wood powder charger, etc. Tanned-hide gun sling with Chinese cash (coin) as a stopper. Full length of the gun is 4 feet 7 inches, barrel 3 feet ½ inch. Smooth bore. Slightly blunderbuss shaped at the muzzle. This is one of the most interesting native weapons which we have ever seen, and very few, if any, have been allowed to be taken out of Thibet. It is worthy of a place in any museum collection. SOLD.

**INDIA MATCHLOCK GUNS FROM SALE OF BRITISH OFFICER'S COLLECTION, WHO RESIDED FOR MANY YEARS IN INDIA. SOLD ON THE DEATH OF THE OWNER. AT QUEEN'S GATE SALES ROOMS, SOUTH KENSINGTON, LONDON.**

1. Gun with chiseled relief ornamented 41½-inch native-made twist-steel barrel. Dark-colored hardwood flat stock, rounded butt. In serviceable order. Price, $37.50.

2. Native-made twist-steel chiseled relief 42-inch seal-marked barrel; rounded butt. Price, $37.50.

3. Native-ornamented 32-inch barrel Matchlock Gun, 2 inches wide at the breech. Rough stock, curved butt. Price, $27.50.

**0-964. WHEELOCK GUN**, in fine order, with lock-plate engraved, *"Altered and repaired by Jover, London."* No doubt the altering refers to the stock, as the gun now has the early flint-stock; 30-inch partly octagonal barrel, ¾-inch smooth bore. Ornamented lock, with brass wheel engraved, showing the direction for winding; 3-inch silver plate on stock, showing hunter and game. Full length 46½ inches. Fine old curly walnut polished stock. A handsome specimen. Jover is one of the *old-time* London gunsmiths.

**0-941. AMERICAN REVOLUTIONARY WAR PERIOD SERGEANT'S FLINTLOCK MUSKET.** Lock is engraved with "British Crown, G. R., 1764, W. Kirk." Full length 43½ inches, ¾-inch smooth bore. Brass mountings. A lighter and shorter gun than the infantry soldier's serviceable musket. From the Lawson-Johnston sale. In good order. Price, $35.00.

**0-689. ANCIENT WHEELOCK MUSKET.** Full length 5 feet; partly octagonal barrel, 4 feet long; smooth bore. Cannon-shaped muzzle. Black-oak stock is 2 inches wide at the butt. Sighting stud on the rear of the barrel. From the Vitrack collection. Price, $68.50.

**0-686. ANCIENT EUROPEAN MATCHLOCK RIFLED WALL GUN.** Full length 5 feet 2 inches; heavy 4-foot octagonal rifle barrel, with armorer's mark IVV on each side of the barrel; with star; with bear for seal mark. Three heavy metal bands over the barrel for underpinning to the stock. Stock is completely covered with bone or ivory inlaid disks. Serpent-head-shaped fuse holder, operated by under lever. Stock is 2¾ inches thick. Rare old gun, from French nobleman's estate. Price, $67.50.

**0-948. INDIAN MATCHLOCK GUN**, from sale of British India Officer's collection; 4-foot, partly octagonal barrel. Traces of silver inlaying; ⅝-inch smooth bore. Front and rear sights. Barrel fitted to the stock with seven ornamental brass bands. Dark-colored hardwood stock. Cut-metal match-fuse holder. Ornamental bronze lock-plate. Small ivory butt-plate. Full length 68 inches. Complete, in serviceable order. Price, $47.50.

**0-948A. LONG INDIA MATCHLOCK GUN.** Round barrel, 4 feet 5 inches long. Full length 6 feet, with fibre bands. Ornamented iron plate at lock and butt. Flash-pan cover. Price, $35.00.
**0-948B. BRITISH INDIA OFFICER'S COLLECTION SALE, MATCHLOCK GUN.** Full length 6 feet; 4 feet 3 inches, partly octagonal barrel. Much used, still in serviceable order. Price, $28.50.
**0-948C. MATCHLOCK GUN**, with rounded butt. Full length 5 feet 2½ inches; octagonal barrel, 4 feet long, stamped with armorer's signed seal. Five brass bands binding stock and barrel. Much used, still in serviceable order. Price, $30.00.

### When ordering special guns allow a second choice.

**0-939. ANTIQUE SPANISH FLINTLOCK GUN**, with armorer's inlaid gold seals on the barrel and lock. "Diego Esquibel Madrid, 1719." Cut-steel engraved lock. Gold vent plug. Inlaid gold ornamentation on the barrel. Rare hammer safety. Curious rear sight; 3-foot partly octagonal barrel, fastened to the stock with two cut-steel ornamented bands. Fluted and carved stock. Full length 4 feet 4 inches. Fine, well made gun, in good order. Bargain price, $67.50.

**6000. ANCIENT KING'S WHEELOCK GUN**, handsomely ornamented barrel, every inch covered in relief with figures of men and women in ancient dress, with scroll work, with CROWN surmounting DOUBLE-HEADED EAGLE, with small crowns on the eagle heads, showing at one time that this gun belonged to some ANCIENT KING. The guard-plate is similarly ornamented with crowns on the eagle heads, etc. The full length of the gun is 53 inches, 6¾ inches wide at butt stock, curly walnut stock, with open, ornamented brass work on the cheek-piece, showing mounted huntsman with bugle horn. Gun is a fine specimen of ancient gun-maker's work, and was passed free of duty by the U. S. Customs Appraisers as A WORK OF ART under the new tariff. European dealers would charge $2,000 for such a gun. Our bargain price for this handsome, first-class museum exhibit, $685.00.

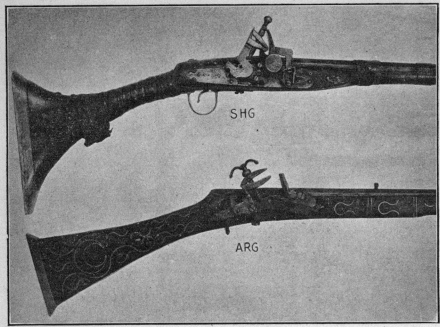

View of 16th Century Infantry Soldier, with Wheellock Gun.

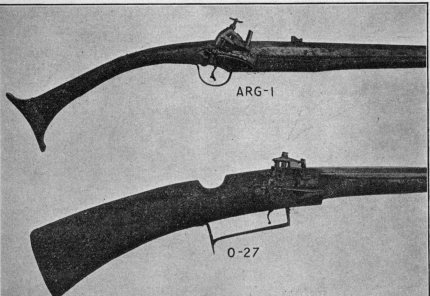

Shooting Ancient Wheellock Rifle.

**S H G. ARABIAN SNAPHAUNCE GUN** (see illustration No. 10915 on page 18 for full length). Octagon barrel 48½ inches long, bore 9/16 inch, full length 63 inches. Barrel has 13 brass bands, silver front sight, raised rear sight mounted on barrel at breech end. Three armourer's marks set in barrel, maybe in silver. Hand grip bound in leather, and ornamented with brass tacks. Foot shaped butt of white ivory, 8 inches long, 2½ inches wide, with circle ornaments. The lock is the SNAPHAUNCE, partly engraved, 7 inches long, with one maker's mark. There is a slide attachment to go over the powder pan after it has been filled, if not intended for immediate use. This is a very long specimen. Price, $75.00.

**S H G-1. ARABIAN CHIEFTAIN'S SNAPHAUNCE GUN**, full length 58 inches, octagon barrel 45 inches, bore ½ inch. Barrel inlaid full length with what appears to be silver, with 4 ornamental barrel bands, with reinforced muzzle, metal front sight, raised rear sight on breech end of barrel. One proof mark on barrel. Foot shaped butt with white ivory butt plate, 7¼ inches long, 1 inch wide. (Ivory slightly chipped off at heel.) Stock inlaid with fine silver wire in floral designs, 6 inch SNAPHAUNCE lock, with crescent moon ornament, and maker's mark. Hammer and other parts finely engraved. This is a very handsome specimen. Price, $115.00.

**S H G-2. ARABIAN SNAPHAUNCE GUN**, full length 52 inches, part octagon barrel 38½ inches, bore ½ inch. 6 ornamented brass barrel bands, 3 armourer's marks, low front sight and raised rear sight. Stock inlaid with stars and other designs in silver and shells. 8 inch white ivory butt plate, 1¾ inches wide. Tang engraved and inlaid with gold surrounded by silver wire inlay. 6½ inch engraved lock with pan cover. Price, $85.00.

**S H G-3. SNAPHAUNCE GUN FROM MOROCCO.** Full length 52 inches, part octagon barrel 38 inches, bore 9/16 inch, 5 wide brass barrel bands. Engraved barrel with armourer's marks set in gold. Butt stock inlaid with silver wire and shells in various designs. White ivory butt, foot shape, 7½ inches long by 1½ inches wide. 6 inches engraved lock, with gold inlay and one maker's mark. Trigger guard engraved with gold inlay. Price, $70.00.

**S H G-4. SNAPHAUNCE GUN FROM MOROCCO.** Part octagon barrel 31 inches long, full length 44 inches, bore 9/16 inch. 5 brass and one silver barrel bands, front and rear sights, engraved barrel with SEVEN armourer's marks. Butt stock inlaid with silver wire and shells. White ivory butt. 6¾ inches by 1½ inches. 6 inch engraved SNAPHAUNCE lock with powder pan cover. Price, $50.00.

**A R G. ARABIAN FLINTLOCK GUN**, full length 65 inches, octagon barrel 50 inches, bore ⅝ inch. Wood stock runs to within 14 inches of muzzle, and is decorated throughout with various designs of silver wire and red shell inlay. 4 ornamental silver barrel bands 2½ inches wide. Solid brass butt plate, 5 inches long, 1 inch wide. A very much decorated piece. Outside Spanish lock 6½ inch, brass, slightly curved. Stud trigger through ivory inlaid opening. Price, $40.00.

**A R G-1. ALBANIAN FLINTLOCK GUN**, with part octagon barrel 44 inches long, bore ¾ inch, full length 58 inches. Barrel has high rear sight, bell muzzle, 4 ornamented brass bands. Entire stock is metal covered and engraved. Butt stock brass trimmed, 2 rings for carrying sling, outside Spanish lock, 3½ inches long, engraved. Price, $45.00.

**O-27. MOORISH CHIEF'S FLINTLOCK GUN**, full length 63 inches, part octagon barrel 47 inches, bore 9/16 inch. Outside Spanish lock 4 inches long, square cornered trigger guard engraved with fish, butt plate of brass, embossed showing two large fish. Full length of stock covered with brass, embossed throughout, with floral designs, birds, fish and sea serpents. Note stud on trigger guard, and cut out stock for thumb hold. A very handsome piece. Price, $85.00.

The origin of the terms "bore" and "gauge," as indicating the size of the cylindrical cavity in gun barrels, arose from the fact that in olden times, the round ball was in general use, and the size of the hole in the gun barrel was known by the number of balls to the pound that the gun would shoot. That gun was called a 10 ball gun that would shoot balls 10 of which would weigh a pound. A 12 ball gun would shoot balls of a size weighing 12 to a pound. In this way the standard was fixed, and we believe it was an easy step to change the word "ball" later on to the term "bore," which gun makers used in connection with the process of making the bun barrel, by boring, to the standard fixed by the number of balls. In these later times the word "bore" is giving way to the word "gauge," retaining the old standard first fixed by the number of balls to the pound. "FROM BANNERMAN'S BOOK, 'WEAPONS OF WAR.'"

The various guns, pistols and other articles shown on this and succeeding special pages formed part of a collection shown at the BRITISH EMPIRE EXHIBITION 1924, at WEMBLEY, ENGLAND. We secured from the exhibitors the choicest pieces in the collection and now offer them for sale singly. Many of these articles have never been seen in this country and this collection contains several items not to be found in any museums or other collections in this country. We consider ourselves very fortunate to be able to offer such for the first time to collectors and museums. Please note the various four barrel flint lock pistols, the inlaid wheelock, and the two barrel FORSYTH pistol. Our suggestion to curators of museums and to collectors is to make selections as soon as possible as many of the rare pieces will be sold quickly.

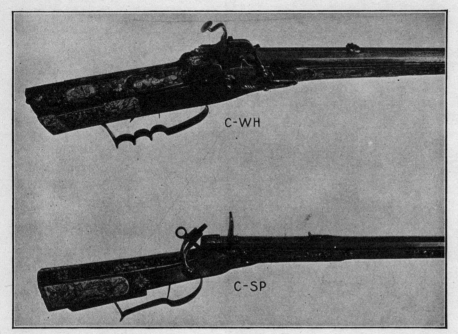

C-WH. WHEELOCK SPORTING GUN, period mid 17th century, German made. Heavy octagon barrel, 30 inches, with brass front sight, rifled barrel with 8 grooves or lands. A rear sight has been attached later. Armourer's mark a DOG is set in barrel in brass, with dates which have been almost obliterated, but one set of figures looks like 1676. Full length 40½ inches. 8-inch lock engraved with hunting scene, 5-inch patch box with spring catch, tipped with white ivory and inlaid with ivory in various designs. Full length stock inlaid throughout with ivory in different colors, with heads of men, deer, dogs, grotesque animals, such as kneeling camel with wings, wild boar with long upturned nose, fish with bull of head, and smaller designs of flowers, vines and leaves. 7½-inch trigger guard with place for three fingers. A most handsome piece. Note that illustration shows BOTH sides of gun. From MARQUIS OF RIPON COLLECTION. Price $500.00.

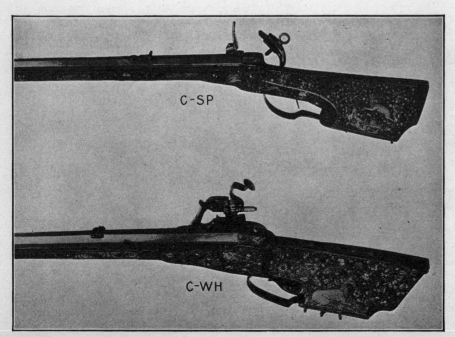

C-SP. RARE PATTERN SPORTING RIFLE fired by PYRITES, NOT FLINT. This style of firing was contemporary with the wheelock. Full length 43 inches, octagon barrel 33-inch, ⅝-inch bore, RIFLED, with brass front sight and ornamental rear sight. Armourer's or maker's mark on barrel, initials: M. K. This is thought to be the mark of KINN DE MUNLEUN, a German gun maker of the 17th century. Lock is 6 inches long, and somewhat resembles the outside Spanish locks. Has long dog's head hammer with two jaws to hold the pyrites. Full length stock ornamented throughout with ivory designs of various patterns. 5-inch patch box has spring catch, and cover of one piece of white ivory showing wild cat in foreground, and castles or forts in background. The cover of flash pan can be turned to prevent accidental firing. This rare gun was bought at the sale of the collection of the MARQUIS OF RIPON. Note illustration shows BOTH sides of gun. Price $400.00.

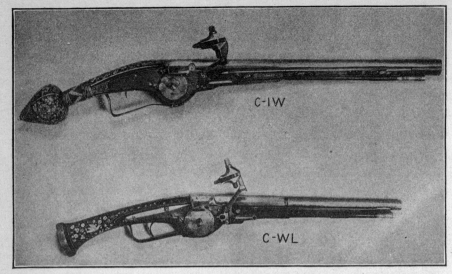

**C-I W. PAIR ITALIAN WHEELOCK PISTOLS,** full length 26½ inches, part octagon barrels 17¼ inches, round knob butt with pointed end, 6-inch locks. Entire wood stock is inlaid with ivory in many designs showing flowers, birds, rabbits, wild boar, fruit and faces. Pistols of this very early type seldom come in pair. One piece in fine complete condition, the other with imperfect stock, and part of lock missing. Price for the pair, AS IS, $150.00.

**C-W L. PAIR FINE ITALIAN WHEELOCK PISTOLS,** with 7-inch locks, full length 21½ inches, part octagon barrels, 13¼ inches. Hard wood stocks inlaid throughout with ivory and shell in various designs, showing birds, flowers, and moons. Oval butts, gold plated showing woman playing guitar. White ivory tips on ramrods. Period of 1620. From the MARQUIS OF RIPON COLLECTION. Top of barrel on one pistol marked: PIERO INZI FRANCI. Price for pair, $200.00.

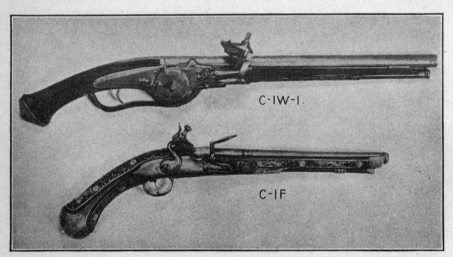

**C-I W-1. PAIR FINE ITALIAN WHEELOCK PISTOLS,** period 1640. Full length 22½ inches, round barrels 14¾ inch, bore ⅞ inches. Barrels are engraved in floral designs at muzzle and breech ends. Ebony stocks, with butt plates engraved with military designs of flags, spears, helmets, cannon, drum, etc. Wood rod with brass tip, guide of filigree work as is also the stock tip and band. The trimmings appear to be gold plated. Price for pair $160.00.

**C-IF. FINE ITALIAN FLINT LOCK PISTOL,** full length 18 inches, cannon shaped barrel, 10¾ inches, plain lock 5 inch. From the MARQUIS OF RIPON COLLECTION. Ivory tipped wood ramrod, round ball butt with heavy metal plate, short guard with plume end. Entire stock inlaid with ivory and shell in designs showing rabbits, hunting dogs, fish and human figures. Also small ivory and shell circular discs. A very handsome piece. Price $100.00.

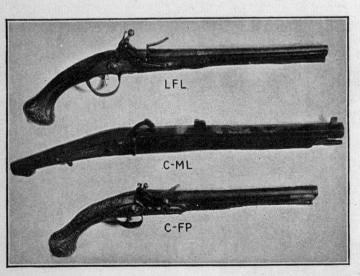

**L F L. FINE FLINT LOCK PISTOL,** full length 21½ inches, barrel, cannon shaped. 14 inches long, bore ½ inch. Full length stock, horn tipped. All mounting gold plated, plain trigger guard with embossed end, heavy fish tail butt with ornamented plate, embossed side plate showing castle with siege gun and two soldiers smoking. Maker's mark in gold on barrel. 5¼-inch brass lock with hunting scene, and marked: TO FISCHER, IN PRESBURG. This is a horseman's pistol of the period of 1740. Price $50.00.

**L F L-1. PAIR LONG FLINT LOCK PISTOLS,** with 11¼-inch ribbed barrels, raised front sights, metal tipped wood rods, fish tail butts, ornamented with satyr heads, long trigger guards with same designs, with urn tips. Monogram plates with monks heads. 5¼-inch ornamented locks, marked: adv. commvn. A very handsome pair of pistols, Period of 1750. From the collection of MARQUIS OF RIPON. Price for pair $60.00.

**C-M L. JAPANESE MATCH LOCK PISTOL,** full length 23¼ inches, octagon barrel 14¼ inches long, with front and rear sights, with heavy silver ornaments inlaid in barrel, with Japanese inscriptions. Bore ½ inch. All mountings of brass. Price $75.00.

**C-F P. FRENCH FLINT LOCK PISTOL,** made for the French Government for presentation to an ORIENTAL PRINCE. Full length 19 inches, 11¾-inch cannon shaped barrel, metal ramrod, 4½-inch lock engraved with bird and palm tree, with characters or inscription. Round butt with heavy silver plate in floral designs. Heavy silver guard and stock tip. Side plate, ramrod guides, front sight all in silver, with entire stock inlaid with fine silver wire in floral designs. A very handsome piece. Price $200.00.

# RARE COLLECTION PIECES

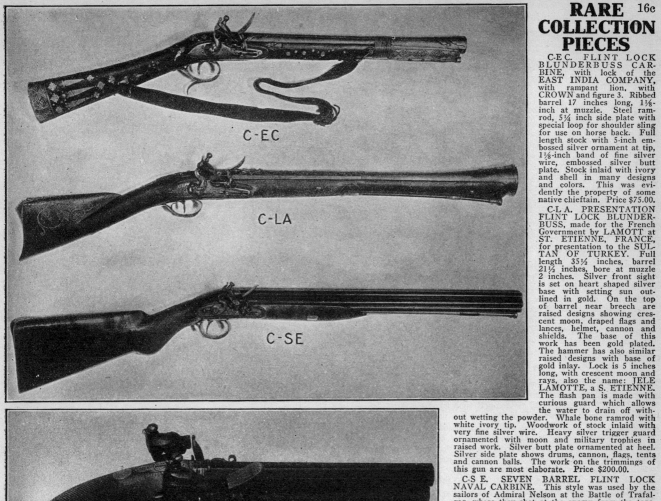

C-EC

C-LA

C-SE

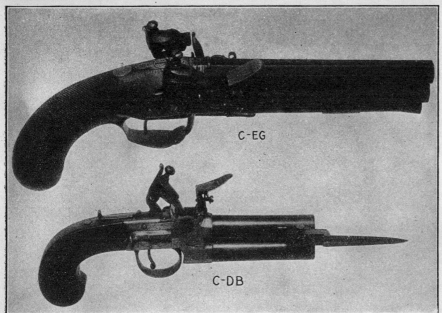

C-EG

C-DB

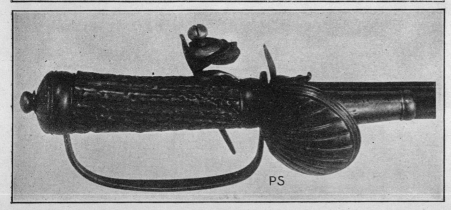

PS

**C-EC. FLINT LOCK BLUNDERBUSS CARBINE,** with lock of the EAST INDIA COMPANY, with rampant lion, with CROWN and figure 3. Ribbed barrel 17 inches long, 1⅛-inch at muzzle. Steel ramrod, 5¼ inch side plate with special loop for shoulder sling for use on horse back. Full length stock with 5-inch embossed silver ornament at tip, 1⅛-inch band of fine silver wire, embossed silver butt plate. Stock inlaid with ivory and shell in many designs and colors. This was evidently the property of some native chieftain. Price $75.00.

**C-LA. PRESENTATION FLINT LOCK BLUNDERBUSS,** made for the French Government by LAMOTT at ST. ETIENNE, FRANCE, for presentation to the SULTAN OF TURKEY. Full length 35½ inches, barrel 21½ inches, bore at muzzle 2 inches. Silver front sight is set on heart shaped silver base with setting sun outlined in gold. On the top of barrel near breech are raised designs showing crescent moon, draped flags and lances, helmet, cannon and shields. The base of this work has been gold plated. The hammer has also similar raised designs with base of gold inlay. Lock is 5 inches long, with crescent moon and rays, also the name: JELE LAMOTTE, a S. ETIENNE. The flash pan is made with curious guard which allows the water to drain off without wetting the powder. Whale bone ramrod with white ivory tip. Woodwork of stock inlaid with very fine silver wire. Heavy silver trigger guard ornamented with moon and military trophies in raised work. Silver butt plate ornamented at heel. Silver side plate shows drums, cannon, flags, tents and cannon balls. The work on the trimmings of this gun are most elaborate. Price $200.00.

**C-SE. SEVEN BARREL FLINT LOCK NAVAL CARBINE.** This style was used by the sailors of Admiral Nelson at the Battle of Trafalgar, where they shot at the enemy from the tops. Full length 36½ inches, barrels 20½ inches, bore 13/32nd inches. ALL THE BARRELS WERE FIRED AT ONE TIME, BY ONE LOCK. Each barrel is proof marked; on top rib is maker's name: E. BAKER, LONDON. He was the first gunmaker to make RIFLED ARMS as used by the BRITISH TROOPS. Highly polished walnut stock, checkered pistol grip, heavy butt plate engraved at heel. Silver monogram plate, and escutcheons. Metal ramrod, engraved tang, case hardened barrels, gold touch hole, 4½-inch lock with safety catch, with makers name in gold: BAKER under CROWN. This is only the second gun of this kind that we have been able to get in nearly 25 years. Price $500.

**C-EG. FINE FLINT LOCK PISTOL, WITH SUPERPOSED BARRELS.** Gold monogram plate with the crest of the MARQUIS OF QUEENSBURY. Full length 12½ inches, octagon barrels, one over the other, 7 inches long, fitted with GOLD front sight, and steel rear sight, bore ½ inch. Upper barrel is lined with two strips of gold at breech and marked on top in gold: D. EGG, LONDON. Round butt with engraved metal plate, checkered grip, horn tipped wood rod, 2¼-inch BELT HOOK. French type trigger guard, engraved. Note that both locks are fired by SINGLE trigger. 3½-inch engraved locks, marked: D. EGG. Gold lined touch holes, and gold lined flash pans. This is a very handsome piece of rare pattern. Price $150.00.

**C-DB. BRITISH FLINT LOCK OVER AND UNDER POCKET PISTOL,** fitted with SPRING BAYONET ON SIDE. 3-inch removable barrel, with muzzle grooves for wrench, spring bayonet fitted on upper barrel on right side. Full length 8¼ inches. Flat wood grip, one center hammer with safety catch on top of flange. Old English proof mark, and makers name on frame: BLAIR, LONDON. By using an attachment on left side the lower barrel may be kept from firing while the first or upper barrel is used. Price $38.00.

**PS. C-SW. HUNTING SWORD WITH FLINT PISTOL ATTACHED.** Old English hunting sword with 23-inch wide blade with stag horn grip, metal pommel with stud, clam shaped hand guard under which is attached the barrel of pistol. This barrel is 3 inches long, removable for quick loading. The hammer and springs are set in the horn grip, and can be fired readily. The barrel bears the old London proof mark. Combination pistol-swords of this style are rare, and this is the second one we have obtained within twenty years. Price $100.00.

FERGUSON RIFLE. A curious breech-loader used early in the Revolutionary War. Major Ferguson, a British officer, was authorized to arm and drill his troops according to his own ideas; and if tradition and circumstantial evidence are to be relied on, it was his purpose to place in their hands a breech-loading rifle with a variety of improvements, considered of recent date. Some of these rifles were used in the battle of King's Mountain, 7th October, 1780, the turning point of the war at the south, as Oriskany, another riflemen's fight, 6th August, 1777, had been at the north, a battle in which he was defeated and slain. Although a breech-loader not of American invention, it has become American from the fact that it made its first appearance as a weapon of war on the battlefields of America, and is the first instance of a breech-loading rifle ever having been used on this Continent or any other. Referring to the plate, a few details will serve to explain its peculiarities. The length of the piece itself is 50 inches, weight 7½ pounds. The bayonet is 25 inches in length and 1½ inch wide, and is what is commonly called a sword-blade bayonet; flat, lithe, yet strong, of fine temper and capable of receiving a razor edge, and, when unfixed, as serviceable as the best balanced cut-and-thrust sword. The sight at the breech is so arranged that by elevating it is equally adapted to ranges varying from one hundred to five hundred yards. Its greatest curiosity is the arrangement for the loading at the breech. The guard-plate which protects the trigger is held in its position by a spring at the end nearest the butt. Released from this spring and thrown around by the front, so as to make a complete revolution, a plug descends from the barrel, leaving a cavity in the upper side of the barrel sufficient for the insertion of a ball and cartridge or loose charge. This plug is an accelerating-screw, and is furnished with twelve threads to the inch, thereby enabling it, by the one revolution, to open or close the orifice; so that the rifle is thereby rendered capable of being discharged, it has been claimed, as rapidly as Hall's United States (flint-lock) carbine. This accelerating-screw constitutes the breech of the piece, only instead of being horizontal, as is usually the case, it is vertical. Were there not twelve independent threads to this screw, it would require two or three revolutions to close the orifice; whereas one suffices. Many of the muskets fabricated in the French arsenals during the last years of Napoleon and bayonets of the shape mentioned herein adapted to them, specimens of which were deposited among the French Trophies in the Tower of London. In case of an injury to the fire-arm, the sword blade bayonet would have been as effective a weapon as the artillery or even the infantry sword carried by foreign troops. From Farrow's Military Encyclopedia. The above description is of the regular arm as furnished to the British troops. The gun shown in photograph is a sporting gun, probably made for presentation, as it has a nobleman's crest on the silver monogram plate. Full length 47½ inches, 32-inch octagon barrel, case hardened, with two proof marks and word: NEWARK. Barrel is RIFLED, 1⅛-inch bore. Stock is sporting length, fitted with groove on under side for the brass tipped wood rod. Silver front sight and base, also rear sight with folding leaf for long ranges. Stock is of hard wood, highly polished, finely checkered pistol grip, blued steel butt plate, 5½-inch lock with safety, marked: BARBER. Pan cover fits securely over pan to keep out rain and prevent the spilling of priming powder. This is the second gun of this type that we have secured in nearly 30 years, and was bought by us in London this year. Price $800.00. (See also page 22.)

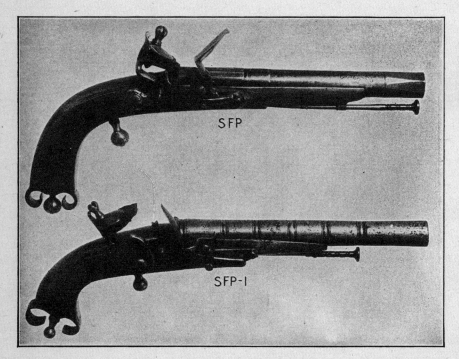

SFP

SFP-1

**MAJOR FERGUSON**
A British officer, Major Ferguson, of the 43rd Foot, tells of an incident in which General Washington had a narrow escape, just before the battle of Brandywine. Two mounted American officers approached very near the British lines, to reconnoiter. One wore a very high cocked hat, and the other a French Hussar's uniform. Major Ferguson ordered three good marksmen to creep near and fire at them, but soon countermanded the order, as the two officers rode away. One was General Washington and the other a French officer.
This incident is cited to show the presence of Major Ferguson in America with the British troops.

S F P-1-C-S C. ALL STEEL SCOTCH FLINT LOCK PISTOL, early Highland pattern, with 7½-inch cannon barrel, with 4¾-inch sash or belt hook on left side, stud trigger, short grip with ram's horn butt with stud ornament. Lock marked: I. C. for JOHN CAMPBELL. Full length 12 inches. In good condition, shows use. Price $100.00. (See page 58.)

S F P-C-S C-1. ALL STEEL SCOTCH FLINT LOCK PISTOL, in fine order, like new, Highland pattern, with 7½-inch cannon barrel, ridged at breech end, engraved at muzzle. 3¾-inch belt hook on left side. Stud trigger without guard. Long grip with ram's horn butt with stud ornament. Frame marked: I. C. for JOHN CAMPBELL. In connection with this pistol and No. C-S C, please see page 58 of this catalog for the pistols captured at LEXINGTON, MASS., from MAJOR PITCAIRN by the Minute Men. Price of this rare piece is $150.00.

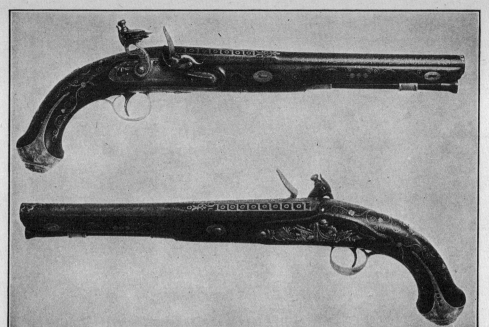

**INDIAN PRINCE'S PRESENTATION FLINT PISTOLS.** This pair made to order for the BRITISH GOVERNMENT for a gift to an Indian Prince. Full length 17½ inches, half octagon barrels 11½ inches, with silver inlaid wire scroll at muzzle, with elaborate silver designs at breech end, with gold inlaid Indian characters on tops of barrel, bore ⅝ inch, damascus steel. Wood ramrods with gun metal tips, and silver guides. All wood work inlaid with fine silver wire, silver trigger guards with acorn ends, engraved silver butt with tip in design of crossed flags and cannon. Side plates of silver in military trophy design. All silver parts have the HALL MARKS. Four-inch engraved locks, with safety catches, marked: TATHAM, LONDON. This is a very handsome pair of pistols. Price for pair $200.00.

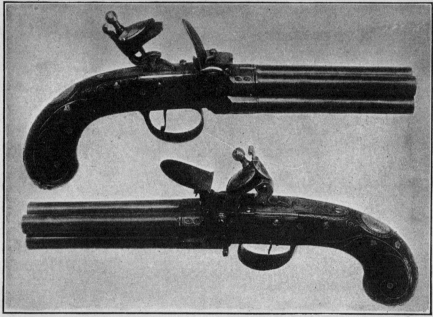

**PAIR BRASS BARREL FOUR SHOT FLINT LOCK PISTOLS,** full length 11½ inches, round brass barrels 5¼ inches, engraved brass frames, marked: BARBAR, LONDON. Round wood butts, silver wire inlaid, with silver mask butt plates with HALL MARK for 1781. These pistols have one center hammer, with side attachment by which the two lower barrels may be fired after the first two. Both top barrels are fired at the same time. Barrels are numbered from 1 to 8, and all have early British proof marks. Pistols with four barrels are scarce, and much rarer in pairs. Price for this pair $175.00.

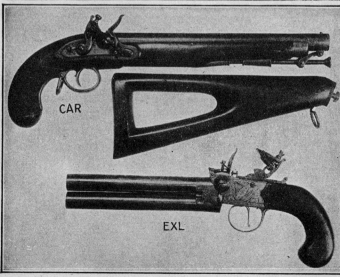

**C A R. PAIR BRITISH FLINT LOCK HOLSTER PISTOLS, FITTED WITH SKELETON BUTT STOCKS,** which are detachable. Full length with stocks 29 inches, length of pistols only, 17½ inches. Stocks and butts highly polished, with shoulder sling ring on butt stocks. Short round grips, checkered, engraved brass butt guards, brass stock tips and ramrod guides. Swivel rods. 12-inch round barrels, with flat tops, marked: BRANDER & POTTS, 70 MINORIES, LONDON. 3¾-inch locks marked: BRANDER & POTTS. Pistols and butt stocks are numbered 77 and 78. These are an unusual type and scarce in pairs. Price for pair $120.00.

**E X L. RARE TYPE FLINT LOCK PISTOL,** modeled after the small pocket pistols, and made to order for use of British officer in India. Superposed barrels, 8½ inches long, proof marked, with grooves at muzzle for use of wrench in removing. Round wood butt, polished, engraved steel frame marked: H. NOCK, LONDON. Safety catch on tang, locks hammer and striker at same time. Full length 14½ inches. Center hammer, engraved guard, side catch at left to cut off lower barrel when top one is being fired. Price $40.00.

# RARE COLLECTION PISTOLS

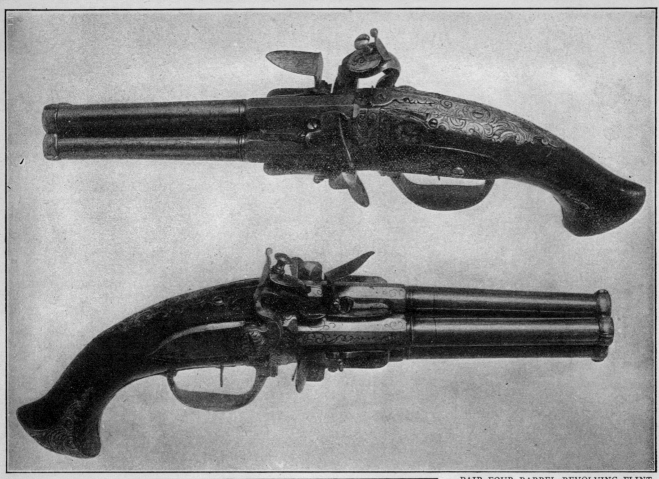

PAIR FOUR BARREL REVOLVING FLINT LOCK PISTOLS, period of 1680. Full length 13 inches, cannon shaped barrels 6⅞ inches, each barrel with its own front sight. Rear sight mounted on frame. Barrels are part octagon and inlaid at this point with gold wire. Each barrel has its own pan and striker, and is numbered. Lock 2½ inches long, engraved with figures of two men in combat with swords. Heavy brass trigger guard, which is pressed down to release the spring which holds the barrels in place. The barrels are REVOLVED by hand. Narrow fish tail butts, with ornamented gold plated butt plates, engraved tang, with gold plated scroll ornament, and gold plated side plate. This pair is rare, and as such is illustrated in Pollocks book of fire arms. Price for pair $400.00.

FOUR BARREL FLINT LOCK POCKET PISTOL, with center hammer, one trigger, with wide guard. Highly polished flat walnut butt. 3¼-inch removable barrels, with grooves for barrel wrench. Each barrel numbered. Frame marked: MULEY, DUBLIN. Catch on left side turns to bring the lower barrels ready for firing. Slide on right side comes over the two right barrels to keep them from firing when left side barrels are to be used. This arrangement is rare in pistols of this type. This piece was once the property of SIR EYRE COOTE, COMMANDER-IN-CHIEF IN INDIA IN 1783. There is a monument to him in Westminster Abbey in London. Price $75.00.

PAIR FOUR BARREL REVOLVING FLINT LOCK PISTOLS, ALL METAL. 2 inside hammers with two triggers, with safety catch on top. Full length 7½ inch, each barrel 3½ inches, cannon shaped, removable for quick loading. Each barrel is numbered by dots instead of figures. After the two upper barrels have been fired, the barrels are revolved by hand by pressing back the trigger guard to release the catch. Each barrel has its own striker. Frames are marked: LONDON. Each pistol weighs 1¾ pounds. Price for pair $500.00.

PAIR FINE ITALIAN FLINT LOCK PISTOLS, from the MARQUISE OF RIPON COLLECTION. Full length 15½ inches, cannon shaped barrels 8½ inches, with brass front sight, bore ½ inch. 4½-inch locks, ivory tipped wood rods, round butts with heavy metal plate. Ornamented guards end in open wings design. Stock inlaid over the entire surface with white ivory and shells in designs of hunting dogs, squirrels, birds, rabbits, moons and small circular discs. A very handsome pair of pistols, in good order. Price for pair $175.00.

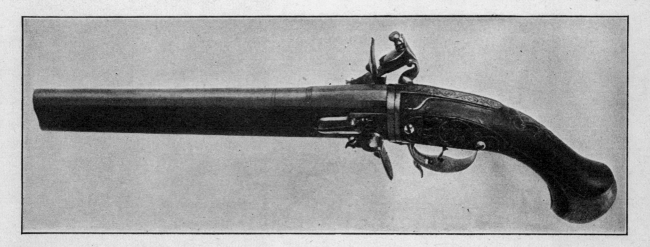

DOUBLE BARREL FLINT LOCK PISTOL, period of WILLIAM III, the Prince of Orange. This rare piece is illustrated in Meyrock's Arms & Armour. Full length 18½ inches, cannon shaped barrels, superposed (one over the other) made to REVOLVE by hand. ONLY ONE LOCK AND HAMMER, but each barrel fitted with its own PAN AND STRIKER. Barrels 11 inches long, bore ₁₆ inches, wood ramrod on side. Complete lock 5½ inches long, engraved and marked: DESELLIER. Fish tail butt with heavy metal butt plate, guard ornamented with head of man in judge's wig. Metal scroll side plate showing two wood nymphs. A catch in trigger guard releases the spring which holds barrels in position, so that they may be revolved. Price $150.00.

# RARE FORSYTH PISTOLS

**10583-A. FORSYTH MAGAZINE LOCK PISTOL** with the unusual arrangement of barrels, superposed, with TWO LOCKS, ONE ON EACH SIDE. This is one of the rarest pistols known, as most of the Forsyth's pistols were made in single barrel only. Weight 3½ pounds, full length 11¾ inches, octagon barrels 6⅛ inches with front sight. Top barrel with gold inlaid breech, lower barrel with silver inlaid breech. Barrels case hardened and marked on top: FORSYTH & CO. (PATENT), GUNMAKERS, LONDON. Round narrow wood butt, checkered grip, silver monogram plate, 4¼-inch locks engraved and marked: FORSYTH & CO. PATENT. Note ornamental magazines. Tang, locks and trigger guard finely engraved. SWIVEL RAMROD under the barrels, with swivel adjusted to use both barrels. This pistol made for use in the INDIAN SERVICE, and is the only KNOWN PISTOL OF THIS TYPE. This invention has been probably the greatest in the history of fire arms. Price $1,500.00.

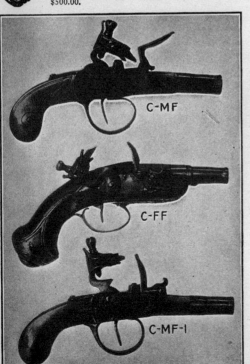

**10583. FORSYTH MAGAZINE LOCK PISTOL**, the smallest size made, and extremely rare. Full length 5¾ inches, octagon barrel 2⅛ inches, with front and rear sights, marked: FORSYTH & CO., PATENT, LONDON. Round wood butt, finely checkered grip, silver monogram plate, engraved frame, hammer and magazine. Two proof marks on barrel. SWIVEL RAMROD, under the barrel. SECRET TRIGGER. Bore ⅜ inch. Price $500.00.

**FORSYTHE MAGAZINE LOCK PISTOL.** The first percussion system. In 1805 the Rev. Alexander John Forsythe of Belhelvie, Scotland, conceived the idea of firing a charge in the old flintlock gun by percussion so as to avoid the flash giving warning to the game. In 1807, assisted by his friend, the famous James Watts, he applied for a patent, which was granted—"For exploding gun powder in firearms by placing detonating powder in small quantities in a small cylindrical touch hole, which is struck by an exploding rod, or is fed in from a SELF-ACTING MAGAZINE." The British Government assigned Dr. Forsythe a room in the Tower of London for perfecting his invention for military use. Later officials opposed to the invention ordered him to clear out with his rubbish, and treated him very badly. In order to introduce the invention to the public, he formed partnership with a London gunmaker, which lasted for ten years, until 1819. The shop was at 10 Piccadilly. The patent was disputed in 1819, but the Court decided that Forsythe was the legal inventor. The Brunswick rifle was the first British Army percussion rifle. In 1840 the 42d Royal Highlanders (Black Watch) had their old Brown Bess flint guns altered to percussion. In 1843, Alexander Bannerman, Parliamentary Representative for Forsythe District, succeeded in having the Government award the sum of 1,000 pounds for the patent. (It is stated that Emperor Napoleon offered Forsythe 20,000 pounds sterling for the invention.) The hammer is connected by side bar with small box which slides back and forth in connection with the working of the hammer. In this box was placed about 40 charges of detonating powder. At the cocking of the hammer the box magazine moved backwards so that the hole in the center was over the touch hole. As the hammer descended the box moved forward, clearing the way for the firing pin in the head of the hammer to strike and explode the small charge of detonating powder dropped into the touch hole while the magazine was in position. Forsythe model pistols are very scarce.

**C-MF. ALL-STEEL FLINTLOCK POCKET PISTOL,** with frame marked: LONDON, two-inch cannon barrel removable, with muzzle grooves for barrel wrench. Center hammer, with trigger guard, which slides forward to lock pan cover. Bulging shaped butt. Full length 5¾ inches. Price $45.00.

**C-FF. PAIR MINIATURE FRENCH FLINT POCKET PISTOLS,** made in the same shape as the army horseman's pistols, with fish tail butts with metal plates. Cannon barrels, 2½ inch, detachable, with muzzle grooves for barrel wrench. 2½-inch locks, one marked: ST. ETIENNE, the other marked: JODIN PERREEST FILS. Ornamental side plates, fancy trigger guards with URN ends. Full length only SIX inches. A very handsome pair. Price for pair $50.00.

**C-MF-1. PAIR ALL-STEEL FLINT POCKET PISTOLS.** Full length 5¾-inches, cannon shaped barrels, 2 inches, removable. Center hammers, trigger guards, which slide forward to lock pan cover. Bulging shaped butts. This is a rare type and especially scarce in pairs. Price for this pair $100.00.

**10568. ANTIQUE 4 BARREL REVOLVING EUROPEAN FLINTLOCK MUSKET.** Full length 55 inches 30 inch barrel, ¾-inch smooth bore with brass mask reinforced muzzle. CYLINDERS ARE 6½ INCHES LONG. FLASH PAN attached TO EACH BARREL. SIDE LOCK AND HAMMER. VERY OLD walnut stock. Checkered grip. Brass butt plate and ramrod thimbles. Barrels and cylinders were originally ornamented with silver inlaid checkered designs (partly worn off from great age). We have never seen a weapon of this kind outside of the highest class museums. Price $350.00.

**10526. HANDSOMELY DECORATED FLINTLOCK BLUNDERBUSS,** from French Nobleman's estate. The barrel still retains the ancient bluing. Gilt ornamental work in relief on barrel and muzzle. Relief ornamented lock and mountings. Wood stock and fore end is covered with gold plated ornamental brass work. Length of the barrel 21½ inches, diameter at the bell mouth 1½ inches, smallest diameter of the barrel ⅞ inch, full length of the gun 33¼ inches. Weight a trifle over 4 pounds. Fine enough to have been made for ancient French Prince. The mate of this gun was purchased in London by British Duke at 50 Guineas. Our price for this work of art, in working order, $175.00.

**10567. ANCIENT FRENCH FLINTLOCK MITRAILLEUSE 4 barrel Gun,** illustrated in February 1911 Field & Stream among rare guns in the famous Paris Musee. Length of barrel 34½ inches, about ¾ inch SMOOTH BORE. Socket swivel also gun sling swivels, 2 flint hammers, 2 triggers. Walnut stock. Brass bands and butt plate. Barrels are heavier from the front band to the breech to stand the force of the powder gases. At the front hammer and at the breech in front of the rear hammer is priming pans with holes leading into a channel connecting with vent hole of the four barrels. No doubt the inventor intended to FIRE THIS GUN MORE THAN TWO SHOTS FROM EACH BARREL. The gun is in good working order and is a rare weapon. It came from a French Nobleman's collection and is fine exhibit for any first class museum. Price $350.00.

**11049. ANCIENT SNAP HAUNCE FLINTLOCK,** with automatic flash pan cover, automatic lever that uncovers the pan as hammer descends on the striker. LENGTH 8 inches, weight 14 ounces. Price $20.00.

**8003.** Antique German Flintlock Sporting Gun, barrel partly octagonal, with sighting rib, with Wheelock pattern stock, with cheek piece, ornamented old pattern lock, relief ornamented brass mountings, stock slightly worm eaten; serviceable. Price, $18.50.

**8003a.** Similar gun to 8003, which has been altered to percussion lock, 28-inch barrel. Price, $8.50.

**10582. FLINTLOCK RAMPART GUN,** octagonal 18-inch iron barrel, ¾ inch smooth bore, with brass detachable cup shaped attachment for holding explosive shell or grenade. Outside diameter 3½ inches, length 2½ inches. Butt stock is nearly 8 inches long by 3 inches wide and has hole 3 inches long, 1⅛ wide, 2¼ deep intended to rest on socket for elevation and recoil in high angle firing. Crude ornamentation. Brass band fastening stock and barrel. Brass shield in front of trigger is inscribed R. Babarani G., evidently a gun that has been used considerably. Price $100.00.

**10479. RUSSIAN ARMY MUSKET,** relic of the Crimean War. Stamped with Greek letters, dated 1849. Russian double headed eagle on gun and on the butt plate. From Lord Wolsley's collection. Price, $20.00.

**10515A. PAIR ANTIQUE WOOD POWDER FLASKS,** bound with hand wrought metal, with metal ornamental disc, with neck charger, with 6½ inch belt hook. 17th Century relics Price for pair, **$38.00.**

**BS1. BRITISH FLINTLOCK SMOOTH BORE GUN,** with extra long barrel. Total length of gun 62½ inches, barrel 46½ inch, the first 16½ inches octagonal, the balance round. Antique browned finish. Wood ramrod with horn tip. Barrel marked BARNETT & SONS, LONDON. Plain lock plate 5¼ inch. Brass butt plate, side plate and ornamented guard bow. Four proof marks on barrel. Guns of this length are rare. Price, **$35.00.**

**01276C. KENTUCKY FLINTLOCK SHOT GUN,** with 41 inch barrel. First twelve inches octagonal, balance round. Front and rear sights. Brass butt plate, and acorn end brass trigger guard. Metal tipped wood rod. Price, **$42.00.**

**10833. "IOH, AND, KUCHENREUTER AU REGENSBURG,"** inlaid silver lettered inscription on FINE OLD FLINTLOCK GERMAN GUN. The lock is covered with hunting scenes in relief engraving. Mountings are in gilt with artistic relief engraving of hunting scenes and scroll work. Curly walnut carved stock with ancient cheek piece. Blued steel barrel 3 feet long, ⅝ inch smooth bore with silver front sight. Handsome old weapon purchased FROM A EUROPEAN MUSEUM. Price, **$100.00.**

NOTE—This fine old gun is a facsimile of gun altered to Percussion lock illustrated in Sporting Goods Dealer, December issue, 1911 as seen in the Arnsburg Museum, Brussels, Belgium, except that our gun is original Flintlock.

**01277K. KENTUCKY FLINTLOCK RIFLE,** with octagon barrel, 31½ inches, total length 47 inches. Front and rear sights, wood rod. Brass trimmings, with oval shaped brass patch box. In fair condition, in working order. Price, **$35.00.**

10515-A

**10814.** FLINTLOCK 1766 RIFLED GUN, 21 inch octagonal barrel, slightly bell mouth, engraved "FOWLER," on the barrel "1766." Carved walnut stock. Box in the stock for holding extra flints; with cheek piece, ornamented brass mountings. Price $25.00.

**10617.** SwISS CROSS BOW. From collection of H. T. Ashley, J. P., England. Made for shooting short bolts. Heavy Walnut stock. Brass Swiss butt plate. Hand hold guard. Brass frame. 3 peep rear sight. Adjustable pendulum for elevating. Heavy steel bow, 24 inches long, ½-inch thick, 1-inch wide. Swivel shackle, ½-inch groove for arrow bolts. Rare old weapon. Price $85.00.

**11031.** "POTSDAM, MONOGRAM F. R. W. (Frederick the Great), ROYAL CROWN," engraved on old time Flintlock Army Musket. Full length 56 inches; walnut stock. Serviceable order. Real old relic. Price, $22.00.

ENGLISH FLINTLOCK BLUNDERBUSS with extra long angular blade SPRING bayonet; 13½-inch steel barrel, 1¾-inch at the muzzle. Bayonet lies ON TOP of the barrel. Thumb catch safety. Walnut stock. In good order. Price, $30.00.

LOUIS XV FLINTLOCK FOWLING GUN, 35-inch barrel half octagonal, ⅝-inch bore. Carved walnut stock. Brass mountings. Has been a fine gun. Complete, but rusty. Offered as is. Price, $14.50.

Sealed bids are used in auctioning property in Japan. There is no shouting. The auctioneer announces to the audience that he has such and such a piece of property for sale and invites bids. Those who wish to bid write their bids and names on slips of paper. The paper is folded and placed in a box. When the auctioneer sees no more bids coming he opens the box and sorts out the bids. The highest bid takes the property.—Chicago News.

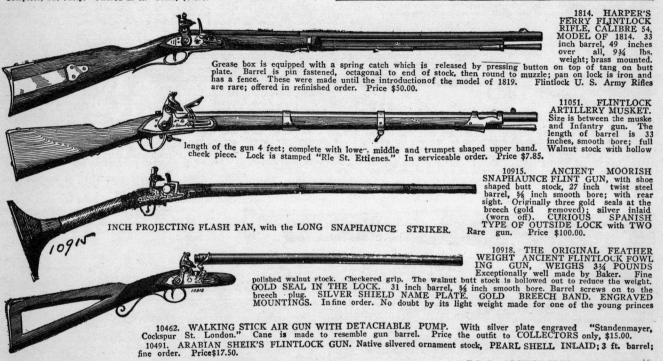

**1814.** HARPER'S FERRY FLINTLOCK RIFLE, CALIBRE 54, MODEL OF 1814. 33 inch barrel, 49 inches over all, 9¾ lbs. weight; brass mounted. Grease box is equipped with a spring catch which is released by pressing button on top of tang on butt plate. Barrel is pin fastened, octagonal to end of stock, then round to muzzle; pan on lock is iron and has a fence. These were made until the introduction of the model of 1819. Flintlock U. S. Army Rifles are rare; offered in refinished order. Price $50.00.

**11051.** FLINTLOCK ARTILLERY MUSKET. Size is between the musket and Infantry gun. The length of barrel is 33 inches, smooth bore; full Walnut stock with hollow length of the gun 4 feet; complete with lower, middle and trumpet shaped upper band. cheek piece. Lock is stamped "Rle St. Ettienes." In serviceable order. Price $7.85.

**10915.** ANCIENT MOORISH SNAPHAUNCE FLINT GUN, with shoe shaped butt stock, 27 inch twist steel barrel, ⅝ inch smooth bore; with rear sight. Originally three gold seals at the breech (gold removed); silver inlaid (worn off). CURIOUS SPANISH TYPE OF OUTSIDE LOCK with TWO INCH PROJECTING FLASH PAN, with the LONG SNAPHAUNCE STRIKER. Rare gun. Price $100.00.

*10915*

**10918.** THE ORIGINAL FEATHER WEIGHT ANCIENT FLINTLOCK FOWLING GUN, WEIGHS 3¼ POUNDS Exceptionally well made by Baker. Fine polished walnut stock. Checkered grip. The walnut butt stock is hollowed out to reduce the weight. GOLD SEAL IN THE LOCK. 31 inch barrel, ⅝ inch smooth bore. Barrel screws on to the breech plug. SILVER SHIELD NAME PLATE. GOLD BREECH BAND. ENGRAVED MOUNTINGS. In fine order. No doubt by its light weight made for one of the young princes

**10462.** WALKING STICK AIR GUN WITH DETACHABLE PUMP. With silver plate engraved "Standenmayer, Cockspur St. London." Cane is made to resemble gun barrel. Price the outfit to COLLECTORS only, $15.00.

**10491.** ARABIAN SHEIK'S FLINTLOCK GUN. Native silvered ornament stock, PEARL SHELL INLAID; 3 ft. barrel; fine order. Price $17.50.

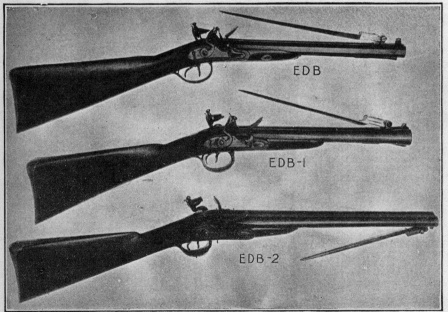

EDB

EDB-1

EDB-2

E D B. BRITISH FLINT LOCK CARBINE WITH DOUBLE BARRELS, full length 30 inches, barrels 14½ inches, with SPRING BAYONET on top side, 12½ inches long. Barrels are octagon, browned finish, marked: HENSHAW, NEW BOND STR., LONDON. The spring bayonet is released by catch on tang. Horn tipped ramrod, with silver guide. Hardwood stock, half length, with silver escutcheon at barrel pin. Heavy brass butt plate, long brass trigger guard with pineapple end. Silver monogram plate. 4¼ inch lock, with safety catches, marked: HENSHAW. Goose neck hammers, engraved. Price, $65.00.

E D B-1. BRITISH FLINTLOCK CARBINE WITH BRONZE BLUNDERBUSS BARRELS, with SPRING BAYONET on top. Full length 29 inches, double barrels, bell muzzles, 13 inches long, spring bayonet 11 inches. The barrels are part octagon, 15/16 inch at muzzle, with 2 proof marks on each and letters: T R. Catch on tang releases the spring bayonet. Whale bone ramrod, with bronze guide. Polished wood stock, with checkered grip, bronze butt plate, long bronze guard with pineapple end, French type. 4½ inch locks have safety catches, and are marked: THEOP. RICHARDS. Silver monogram plate has crest with ANIMAL'S HEAD. This is a rare piece. Price, $90.00.

E D B-2. BRITISH DOUBLE BARREL FLINT CARBINE, with Spring BAYONET attached under the barrels. Full length 32½ inches, round blued barrels, 16½ inches, spring bayonet 9½ inches. Barrels have 2 proof marks on each one, and marked: CORN HILL, LONDON. Heavy brass butt plate, with opening by spring catch for ramrod. Checkered wood grip, long French type trigger guard with pineapple end. 5 inch locks with safety catches, marked: BOND. Spring bayonet is released by catch in front of trigger guard. This style of gun carried on the inside of traveling coaches. Price, $70.00.

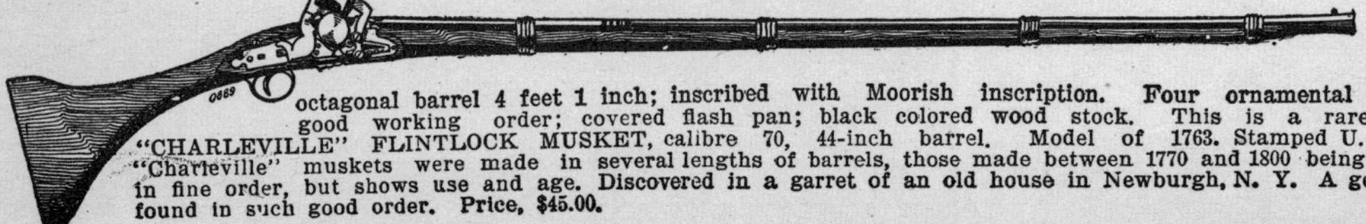

**0-899.** MOORISH SNAPHAUNCE MUSKET. Rare pattern lock. Full length 5 feet 5 inches; partly brass bands; 7-inch butt; in octagonal barrel 4 feet 1 inch; inscribed with Moorish inscription. Four ornamental good working order; covered flash pan; black colored wood stock. This is a rare pattern snaphaunce. Price, $87.50.

"CHARLEVILLE" FLINTLOCK MUSKET, calibre 70, 44-inch barrel. Model of 1763. Stamped U. S. on lock plate in rear of hammer. "Charleville" muskets were made in several lengths of barrels, those made between 1770 and 1800 being shorter than this specimen. Gun is in fine order, but shows use and age. Discovered in a garret of an old house in Newburgh, N. Y. A genuine Revolutionary relic and rarely found in such good order. Price, $45.00.

*1119-A*

**1119A. BRITISH FLINTLOCK BLUNDERBUSS WITH SPRING BAYONET** on top of barrel. Heavy brass barrel 29 inch, bell muzzle 1¼ inch, bayonet 13 inch. Made by BARNETT. In fine order. Brass barrels are rare. Price, $40.00.

**1086. FLINT LOCK BLUNDERBUSS,** with worn eaten stock. From butt to trigger guard good, balance missing. Lock 6½ inches, barrel 16½ inches, muzzle, 1¼ inches. Full length 32 inches. Offered as is. Price, $12.00.

**X27. FLINT LOCK BLUNDERBUSS** from Europe. Cleaned and in good order. Barrel 15 inches long, bore 1¾ inches, full length 30 inches. Fitted with ramrod, brass butt and trigger guard, and six inch lock. Price, $22.50.

**X. BRITISH FLINTLOCK BLUNDERBUSS,** lock marked with TOWER CROWN and G R with ARROW. Barrel 17¼ inches, muzzle 1¼ inches. Full length, 33½ inches. In good order. Price, $24.00.

**7104. PERRY FLINTLOCK BRASS BARREL BLUNDERBUSS,** with spring bayonet 4½-inch barrel, cannon-shaped at the muzzle, 1⅝-inch diameter bell mouth, 12-inch bayonet, with needle point, held in place by safety catch at the breech. British proof marks, engraved brass mountings, with military decorations; walnut stock; requires slight repairs near the muzzle; serviceable order. Price, $35.00. Like illustration No. 1119A.

**7135. AFRICAN TRADERS MATCHLOCK BLUNDERBUSS.** Full length 43 inches, barrel 32 inches, bell muzzle 1½ inch. Very heavy round barrel. Red wood stock with metal bands. Stock has 7-inch drop at butt. Fired from hip. Traders guns in this early type are rare. Price, $15.00.

**1128. OCTAGONAL BARREL, FLINTLOCK BLUNDERBUSS GUN;** 17-inch barrel that looks as if it has been in use on wheel-lock; six grooved old time rifle gun; carved walnut stock; brass mountings; guard bow extension hand grip; engraved lock; flint box on the side; cheek piece. Price, $45.00.

When ordering blunderbusses please allow a second choice when possible.

**1078. LARGE OLD FLINTLOCK BLUNDERBUSS GUN;** engraved with East India Company's Coat of Arms; made by Memory 1791; fluted at the muzzle; twist steel, partly octagonal, 30-inch barrel; 2⅝-inch bell mouth; in serviceable order; price, $100.00.

**8739. FLINTLOCK BLUNDERBUSS RIFLE.** 12 rifle grooves, with increased depth at the muzzle, the barrel is larger in diameter at both muzzle and breech ends than in the center. Twist steel octagonal barrel 29 inches long. Diameter of the rifle muzzle ¾ inch. Carved decorated walnut stock. Engraved brass mountings, evidently of ancient German make. Stock is in need of repairs. Old blunderbuss rifles are rare. Price, $85.00.

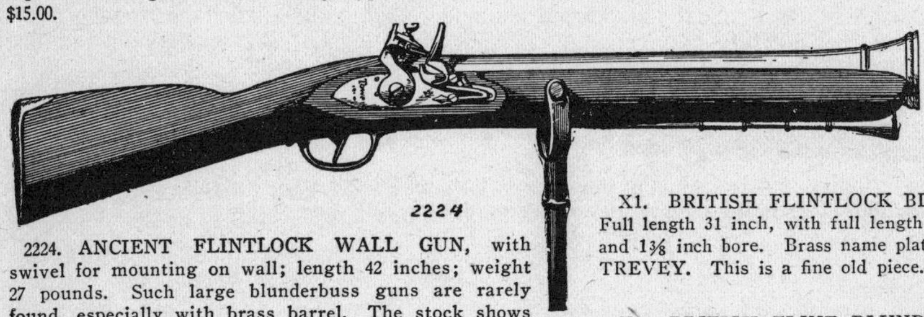

*2224*

**2224. ANCIENT FLINTLOCK WALL GUN,** with swivel for mounting on wall; length 42 inches; weight 27 pounds. Such large blunderbuss guns are rarely found, especially with brass barrel. The stock shows extensive use, evidently a blunderbus used on the old castle wall; offered in working order.

**8702. 2 THEOPS. RICHARDS BRITISH FLINTLOCK BLUNDERBUSSES,** with 13 inch TOP spring bayonets, released by finger catch on top of barrel near hammer. 14½ inch round barrel, bore 1⅛ inches, full length walnut stock, wood rod horn tipped. Brass butt plate and brass guard with acorn end. 4¾ inch barrel. Lock and barrel each marked: THEOPS. RICHARDS, with two old proof marks on barrel. Price, $35.00 each. See illustration below.

**X1. BRITISH FLINTLOCK BLUNDERBUSS, QUEEN ANNE** type, period 1710 to 1720. Full length 31 inch, with full length stock. Brass cannon barrel. 16 inches, with 3 proof marks and 1⅜ inch bore. Brass name plate, butt and guard with ball end. 6 inch lock marked: NAT TREVEY. This is a fine old piece. Price, $32.00.

**X2. BRITISH FLINT BLUNDERBUSS** with brass cannon barrel. 15¾ inches marked: LONDON, with three proof marks. 6 inch lock marked: WILSON. Full length 31 inches, bore 1¼ inches. Brass trimmed, with long guard with ball end. Price, $28.00.

**X3. BRITISH FLINTLOCK BLUNDERBUSS** with 5 inch lock marked: BOND. 11 inch steel barrel, with three proof marks, bore 1⅛ inches, brass trimmed, with guard with acorn end. Full length 26½ inches. Price, $25.00.

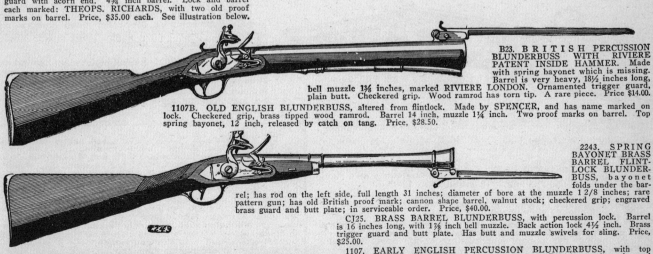

**B23. BRITISH PERCUSSION BLUNDERBUSS WITH RIVIERE PATENT INSIDE HAMMER.** Made with spring bayonet which is missing. Barrel is very heavy, 18½ inches long, bell muzzle 1⅜ inches, marked RIVIERE LONDON. Ornamented trigger guard, plain butt. Checkered grip. Wood ramrod has torn tip. A rare piece. Price, $14.00.

**1107B. OLD ENGLISH BLUNDERBUSS,** altered from flintlock. Made by SPENCER, and has name marked on lock. Checkered grip, brass tipped wood ramrod. Barrel 14 inch, muzzle 1¼ inch. Two proof marks on barrel. Top spring bayonet, 12 inch, released by catch on tang. Price, $28.50.

**2243. SPRING BAYONET BRASS BARREL FLINTLOCK BLUNDERBUSS,** bayonet folds under the barrel; has rod on the left side, full length 31 inches; diameter of bore at the muzzle 1 2/8 inches; rare pattern gun; has old British proof mark; cannon shape barrel, walnut stock; checkered grip; engraved brass guard and butt plate; in serviceable order. Price, $40.00.

**CJ25. BRASS BARREL BLUNDERBUSS,** with percussion lock. Barrel is 16 inches long, with 1⅞ inch bell muzzle. Back action lock 4½ inch. Brass trigger guard and butt plate. Has butt and muzzle swivels for sling. Price, $25.00.

**1107. EARLY ENGLISH PERCUSSION BLUNDERBUSS,** with top spring bayonet. Barrel marked on top with two British proof marks and C N 8621. Evidently a Government piece. Barrel 16½ inches wth 1 7/16 inch muzzle. Spring bayonet 15 inches. 6-inch lock marked with CROWN and TOWER PROOF. Brass trigger guard and butt plate. In fine order. Price, $27.50.

**B22. ALTERED BLUNDERBUSS, PERCUSSION,** originally flintlock. Very early type with very long spring bayonet, 15 inch, ON SIDE. Barrel is 18½ inches with 1 5/16 inch bell muzzle, with two early British proof marks. 6¼ inch lock. Side ring for shoulder sling. Brass trigger guard and butt plate both ornamented. Price, $30.00.

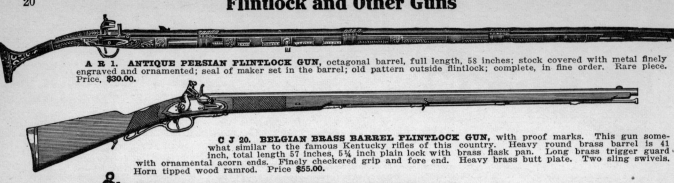

**A R 1. ANTIQUE PERSIAN FLINTLOCK GUN,** octagonal barrel, full length, 58 inches; stock covered with metal finely engraved and ornamented; seal of maker set in the barrel; old pattern outside flintlock; complete, in fine order. Rare piece. Price, **$30.00.**

**C J 20. BELGIAN BRASS BARREL FLINTLOCK GUN,** with proof marks. This gun somewhat similar to the famous Kentucky rifles of this country. Heavy round brass barrel is 41 inch, total length 57 inches, 5¼ inch plain lock with brass flask pan. Long brass trigger guard with ornamental acorn ends. Finely checkered grip and fore end. Heavy brass butt plate. Two sling swivels. Horn tipped wood ramrod. Price **$55.00.**

**ARABIAN FLINTLOCK GUNS.** Large assortment in poor order, just as they were turned in after capture. Price, **$14.00.**

**213. ARABIAN FLINTLOCK GUNS,** in various lengths, all complete but NOT offered in working order. These guns were in Belgium when the Germans invaded it, and these and all other guns were ordered dismantled. The locks and other working parts were removed. They have been reassembled and are offered "AS ARE" for collectors, or for movie or theatrical productions. We are offering these at a reduced price of **$12.00** each.

**213A. ARABIAN FLINTLOCK GUNS,** in similar condition to those in lot No. 213. The butts are not shaped like No. 213, but have a military style, but with much drop, very similar to the early American Kentucky rifles. These are all very long, and are offered at **$13.00** each.

**INVENTION OF GUNPOWDER.** In 1320, gunpowder was invented by Friar Schwartz, a German. There is reason to believe that an English monk, Roger Bacon, was acquainted with its properties in the preceding century, but Schwartz seems to have the credit of applying it to military uses. It is said that he was operating in a mortar on a mixture of nitre, charcoal and sulphur (gunpowder in fact), and accidentally firing the mixture it exploded, urging the pestle to a considerable distance; that hence originated cannon, and also the military term mortar, as applied to a particular variety of cannon.

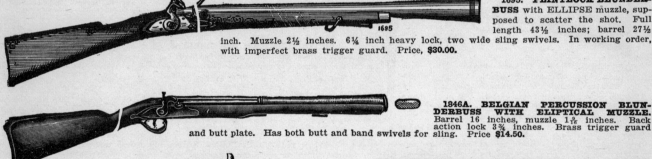

**1695. FLINTLOCK BLUNDERBUSS** with **ELLIPSE** muzzle, supposed to scatter the shot. Full length 43½ inches; barrel 27½ inch. Muzzle 2½ inches. 6¼ inch heavy lock, two wide sling swivels. In working order, with imperfect brass trigger guard. Price **$30.00.**

**1846A. BELGIAN PERCUSSION BLUNDERBUSS WITH ELIPTICAL MUZZLE.** Barrel 16 inches, muzzle 1⅞ inches. Back action lock 3¾ inches. Brass trigger guard and butt plate. Has both butt and band swivels for sling. Price **$14.50.**

**B. F. JOSLYN'S ORIGINAL MODEL OF HIS BREECH-LOADING PERCUSSION CARBINE** for which he received a patent in 1855. The arm is made with an entirely different lock and hammer, as our illustration shows, from the regular model. This historical piece is a rare prize for some collector. We price it at **$75.00.**

On page 131 gun number 6 will be found an illustration of Joslyn's first carbine. Full details of this historical piece is given in the reading matter on the same page. We have a fine specimen of this arm which is priced at $25.00. These two guns together will make an interesting exhibit.

**No. 1.** Old Flint Lock, Horseman Gun, with swivel ramrod, full length, 27 inches; fine order; metal inlaid ornaments. Price **$14.00.**

**No. 2.** Percussion Lock, Octagonal Barrel Gun, with ivory inlaid ornamental work on stock; fine order; full length, 32 inches. Price **$15.00.**

**No. 4.** Handsomely Ornamented Old Flint Lock Gun, ivory and pearl inlaid on stock, in form of spears, scimetars, battle axes, stars, etc. Outside lock; full length, 38 inches. Price **$35.00.**

**No. 3.** Antique Flint Lock Gun, with stock inlaid in pearl in form of dagger, scimetars, crescents, stars, etc.; handsome; full length, 33 inches. Price **$35.00.**

**No. 1058. 1793 SMOOTH BORE FLINT LOCK CARBINE, MADE FOR THE EAST INDIA COMPANY.** Engraved "Tower," 1793, with E I C in heart-shaped circle. 22-inch barrel, 12 gauge. Price **$12.00.**

**No. 1598. 2 FRENCH FLINT LOCK CARBINES.** Arsenal name on the lock plate indistinct from age. Guns are the same pattern as other French Flint Lock guns. Barrel 26 inches long, ⅝ cal. smooth bore. Full length, 41 inches. Brass mountings; in good clean polished order. **$10.00** each.

The rifle made at Harper's Ferry, and known officially as Model 1841, calibre 54, has often been called by the names of Mississippi rifle, Kentucky rifle, Yaeger and Windsor rifle. This rifle had a heavy barrel finely rifled, and possessed good shooting qualities. A regiment from Mississippi, during the Mexican War, under the command of Colonel Jefferson Davis (afterwards President of the Southern Confederacy) was armed with these rifles. After the war was over the soldiers were so pleased with their guns that they agreed to retain them, the War Department deducting the cost (about $14.00) from their pay. This gave rise to the name Mississippi. About this time a similar rifle was issued to sharpshooters in Germany, and called the Yaeger rifle. Kentucky troops armed with this gun called it the Kentucky rifle, and the name Windsor arose from the fact that Lamberson and Furman of Windsor, Vermont, made up, under contract, a number of this model rifle for the U. S. Government.—From Bannerman's Book, War Weapons.

**50 FLINT LOCK MUSKETOONS.** Length of barrel, 26 inches. Full length, 41 inches; in working order, only requiring cleaning. ⅝-inch smooth bore; hardwood stock, with long guard straps for strengthening the stock. A strong, well-made gun; for use of cavalry or infantry. Offered complete, with extra flints, $10.00 each.

Admiral Melville, U. S. N., in his search for De Long and his companions, tells how he was informed that a native had found a gun. Thinking this was a clue, he sent for the native, who described the action of the gun by cutting a long shaving of wood and twisting it to resemble the spiral spring such as is used in magazine guns, and said: "No good." It was one of the best Winchester rifles. No good to the native who could not obtain cartridges. As a reward the United States Government sent them flint-lock guns.

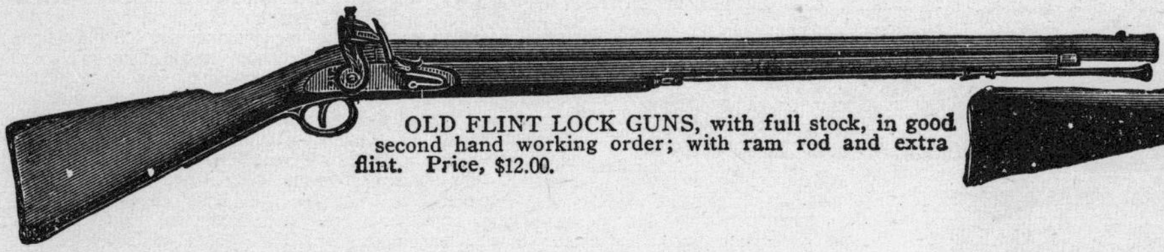

**OLD FLINT LOCK GUNS,** with full stock, in good second hand working order; with ram rod and extra flint. Price, $12.00.

**No 53A.—British Blunderbuss** in fine serviceable order. Price $20.00.

**B23. BRITISH PERCUSSION BLUNDERBUSS, WITH RIVIERE PATENT INSIDE HAMMER.** Made with spring bayonet which is missing. Barrel is very heavy, 18½ inches long, bell muzzle 1⅜ inches, marked RIVIERE, LONDON. Ornamented trigger guard, plain butt, checkered grip. Wood ramrod has horn tip. A rare piece. Price, $14.00.

**8702. THEOR, RICHARD'S FLINTLOCK BLUNDERBUSS.** With spring bayonet on top of the barrel, controlled by finger lever at the breech, 14-inch steel barrel, 1½-inch bell mouth. Brass mountings. Walnut stock; 13-inch bayonet. Price, $30.00.

**7135. AFRICAN TRADERS' MATCHLOCK BLUNDERBUSS.** Full length, 43 inches; barrel, 32 inches; bell muzzle, 11/16 inch. Very heavy round barrel. Red wood stock with metal bands. Stock has seven-inch drop at butt. Fired from hip. Traders' guns in this early type are rare. Price, $15.00.

**B22. ALTERED BLUNDERBUSS, PERCUSSION,** originally flint lock. Very early type with very long spring bayonet, 15 inch, ON SIDE. Barrel is 18½ inches, with 1⅛-inch bell muzzle, with two early British proof marks. 6¼-inch lock. Side ring for shoulder sling. Brass trigger guard and butt plate both ornamented. Price, $30.00.

**10 Antique Dragoon Flint-Lock Short-Barrel Guns,** with ramrod working on swivel, so that mounted soldiers would not lose the ramrod while loading gun. Guns are in splendid condition, cleaned and polished. Full length, 34 inches; barrel is 18 inches long; nearly 12-gauge smooth bore. Rare pattern. Price, $8.75.

**No. 1110** relates to old Tower Flint-lock Cannon Lighter, with round stock, with projecting flash pan, used to ignite the charge in old-time cannons; rare old relic. Price, $40.00. Very few in existence, even in high-class museums.

**1110. BATTLEFIELD RELIC BLUNDERBUSS.** Lock stamped Miller. Butt plate stamped B., with what looks like 1744. Original stock replaced with home-made stock, but even this rough replaced stock is all worm-eaten, cracked and in poor order. Barrel shows marks of long, hard service. Old relic. Offered as is, $19.75.

**1059. FLINT LOCK RIFLE.** Engraved on barrel, "Thomas Crodler, 1661." With gold seal; with lion rampant; with old pattern rear sight; engraved lock and mountings; fancy guard and rod holder, with butt plate, side plate, artistic cheek piece; gold lined breech; carved stock and fore-end. Rare old gun. Price, $175.

**Antique Flint-Lock Dragoon Carbine.** Used by cavalrymen in the olden time. Are in good, serviceable order. Flint in each, which, when trigger is pulled throws a shower of sparks. Handsome relics. Price, $10.00 each.

**1789** Flint-Lock Gun. Gold inlaid, ornamented, ramrod rib on barrel; ⅝inch bore; full length, 57 inches; fine order. Price, $25.00.

**100 Portuguese Flint Lock Mousquetoones,** swivel ramrods, ⅝-inch smooth bore, 20-inch barrel; sliding ring for shoulder sling. Lock is in working order; metal parts slightly rusty; walnut stock shows age. Full length, 35 inches. Brass butt plate, brass ramrod holder and guard. Price, $8.00 each.

**European Army Flint Lock Carbine.** Used by cavalry. Fine order, with flint. $6.75.

**1094.—SAMUEL EDWARDS FLINT BLUNDERBUSS;** barrel, 14½ inches long; 1½ inches across bell. Fine curly walnut stock, checkered grip, engraved mountings. Price, $20.00.

**1106.—BRASS BARREL FLINT LOCK BLUNDERBUSS.** 14 inches long, 1¾ at muzzle. Fine spring bayonet cannon-shaped ornamented barrel. Made by P. Bond, old British proof marks. Hammer broken; will replace with new one. Walnut stock. Checkered grip; ornamented brass mountings. $27.50.

**KING GEORGE THE III. FLINT LOCK BLUNDERBUSS.** 16½-inch steel barrel; 1¾ across bell mouth muzzle. Engraved lock, with British crown and Tower proof marks, 8621 N. C. stamped on butt plate, which shows having been in government service. Complete with spring bayonet; in good working order. Spring bayonet blunderbusses are seldom found with the government service marks. Price, $27.50.

**CJ25. BRASS BARREL BLUNDERBUSS,** with percussion lock. Barrel is 16 inches long, with 1⅞-inch bell muzzle. Back action lock, 4½-inch. Brass trigger guard and butt plate. Has butt and muzzle swivels for sling. Price, $25.00.

**1119B. BRITISH FLINT LOCK BLUNDERSBUSS,** with 14-inch cannon brass barrel, bore 1⅜ inches, with two old proof marks, with LONDON on top of barrel. 13-inch top spring bayonet, released by catch on tang near hammer. 5¾-inch flat lock marked: BUNNEY, with safety catch. Brass butt and plain brass guard, checkered grip. Full length 28½ inches. Price $38.00. See No. 1119 on page 19.

**1119C. BRITISH FLINT BLUNDERBUSS** with top SPRING bayonet, 13 inches long. Cannon brass barrel 14½ inches with two proof marks, and LONDON. Bore 1¼ inches. 5½-inch flat lock marked: WARRANTED. Full length 30 inches. Brass mounted throughout, with guard with urn end with three feathers, (the emblem of the Prince of Wales). Price $36.00.

**1119D. BRITISH FLINT LOCK BLUNDERBUSS WITHOUT** bayonet. 15¾-inch cannon shaped brass barrel, with bell muzzle 1¼ inches, with 3 old proof marks. 6¾-inch lock marked: FARMER 1750, G R with CROWN, also CROWN and ARROW mark. FARMER was a Government contractor. This type used by Royal Mail coaches. Wood ramrod, horn tipped. Brass mounted, with plain guard with ball end. Price $40.00.

**1119E. BRITISH FLINT BLUNDERBUSS WITHOUT** bayonet. Full length 31 inches, cannon brass barrel 15¾ inches, bore 1¼ inches. Three early proof marks on barrel. Flat lock 5¾ inches. Brass mounted with guard with ball end. Price $28.00.

**1119F. BRITISH FLINT LOCK BLUNDERBUSS,** no bayonet, full length 29¾ inches, brass cannon barrel 14¼ inches, with 2 proof marks and word: LONDON. 5½-inch plain lock, wood rod, horn tipped. Brass mounted, ornamented guard with acorn end. Initials of owner cut in stock at butt: I. D. Checkered grip with oval name plate. Price $30.00.

**1119G. BRITISH FLINT BLUNDERBUSS,** no bayonet. 5¾-inch lock marked: KETLAND & CO. Brass cannon barrel 14¼ inches with 2 proof marks. Bore 1⅜ inches. Fancy brass lock strap, brass guard with acorn end. Full length 30 inches. Price $32.00.

**1119H. BRITISH FLINT LOCK BLUNDERBUSS,** without spring bayonet, full length 30½ inches, barrel, cannon shaped, brass, 14½ inches with 2 proof marks, 7-inch plain lock, long lock strap, checkered grip, brass guard with acorn end. Price $27.00.

File of three men, 1812 period. Front rank firing, second rank faced about handing the firelock to the rare rank man, who presents his loaded firelock to centre rank man. —From Bannerman's book. "Weapons of War."

Full-length view of Ferguson Revolutionary War Pattern Breech Loading Flintlock Rifle.

See also another gun on page 16-b.

This rare old relic was the invention of Major Ferguson, attached to one of the Scotch regiments in King George III.'s army. This type of gun was used at the battle of King's Mountain during the Revolutionary War, and is mentioned in Farrow's Military Encyclopedia. The full length of gun is 60 inches. The barrel is 44 inches long and the weight about 9 pounds. The gun is in fairly good preserved order. What appears to be the British crown-mark is easily discernible on the lock plate. On top of the barrel is engraved, as near as can be made out, "S. Turner, London." The old gunmaker's proof-mark, with crown on V, is stamped on the barrel. The V stands for "viewed" while in process of manufacture by Government official. The plate opposite the lock, also the guard bar, is chased with designs of flowers and scroll work. The bore is ⅝-inch and the barrel has six rifle grooves. Stock extends the full length—no place for a bayonet—evidently a rifle intended for officer. The stock at the butt is slightly worm eaten. Original ramrod is missing; we can supply similar one. The flashpan is very shallow; fine working lock; small brass front sight, also notched rear sight. The breech-pin is engraved. We have been looking for one of these guns for over twenty years; have instructed an agent to advertise for one. This is the only one known to be in existence here in America in addition to the one owned by General De Peyster's family, which money could not buy, as it is an old heirloom, Major Ferguson being a cousin of the De Peysters. The United States Government gave a bond for $1,500 to General De Peyster for the safe return of the gun from Chicago's World's Fair. It will take $1000.00 to induce us to part with this famous old relic.

Sectional view showing lock and breech-loading mechanism in the famous old Revolutionary War Ferguson Flintlock Rifle.

**No. 1370. DOUBLE BARREL FLINT LOCK REVOLVING GUN.** In fine order; real old timer. Name engraved on the lock, but worn with age, so that only the last three letters "E R S" can be seen. Evidently of German manufacture. Curly walnut stock, with cheek piece. Carving worn smooth. Length of smooth bore barrels, 27½ inches. Lock and hammer for each barrel. Barrels revolve by hand. Price $100.00.

Early European Flint Lock Breech Loading Rifle Wall Gun. Made in Belgium in 1830. Bore ¾ of an inch. Has swivel for mounting upon wall. Fine order. Price $25.00.

**No. 260.** Revolving Double-Barrel Flintlock Gun; one hammer with two flash pans, one attached to each barrel; ramrod fits in the side between the two barrels; has fine old fashioned stock with name plate; chased mountings; all in good working order; muzzles of barrels are cannon-shaped; bore is about ⅝-inch; length of barrels, 19 inches; total length, 35 inches; spring in front of guard holds barrels in position for firing. Price $120.00.

**No. 263.** Four-Barrel Revolving Flintlock Gun with two hammers and four flash pans (one on each barrel); gun is in fine order; barrels are twist steel, 34½ inches long; total length, 51 inches; is revolved by hand; spring in front of guard bow holding barrels in place for firing. The Czar of Russia had similar gun in his private collection and loaned it to the French World's Fair in Paris, 1900.

First American Breech-Loading Flint-Lock Rifle. New guns found lying stowed away at one of the United States arsenals. "Packed away in 1843," so reads the label found inside the case. Invented by Colonel John H. Hall, of North Yarmouth, Mass., in 1811. Used in 1816 when 100 guns were made and issued to United States troops. 2,000 were made and used by United States army in the Seminole and other Indian wars in 1827. Also used in Mexican War and War of Rebellion. It was considered a wonderful gun in the olden days, when the guards at Sing Sing, armed with these guns, were able to fire eight shots before an escaping prisoner could get out of range. This particular lot of guns are stamped "Harper's Ferry, Va., 1837." United States Harper's Ferry Arsenal, where these guns were made, was the scene of John Brown's raid. Possibly some of these guns were there when Brown tried to capture the arsenal and obtain guns to arm the negroes to fight for freedom. The guns are beautiful specimens of old-time workmanship. The barrel and bayonet are browned (not blued) and are complete with flints, which, when struck, throw a lingering spark into the flash pan. We expect to get $50.00 each for some of these guns as no collection is complete without one; but for the present to start with we will pack gun in case ready for express (buyer pays expressage) for $30.00 each.

**ANCIENT MEN-OF-WAR.** The Greeks, and subsequently the Romans and other ancients, fought at sea in galleys propelled by oars, which were arranged in banks, one, two, and sometimes three deep. Their contests were principally decided by boarding, and depended much on personal prowess as well as on numbers. The galleys were constructed with heavy iron beaks, in order to destroy an opponent by piercing or crushing its sides. It was customary however to use a species of artillery.

**ANCIENT ARTILLERY.** The Greeks threw, by means of a machine, a composition known as Greek fire, which is represented to have been inextinguishable, and with which they destroyed an enemy while at a distance. It is now supposed that naphtha was the basis of Greek fire. Sometimes suffocating mixtures in earthen jars were thrown upon an enemy's deck to stifle and blind the crew, and venomous reptiles were thrown in the same way to produce terror and dismay. The catapult was the light artillery of the ancients, which was fitted for use on their light vessels.

In the middle ages, especially during the crusades, various other means of annoying a distant enemy from vessels were devised; the English galleys used windmills, which turning rapidly threw by centrifugal force heavy stones, combustible balls, and other missiles. There are enumerated no less than twelve different machines for throwing missiles which had come into use in the 11th and 12th centuries, but their forms, construction, and manner of use, are entirely lost to history.

Inventor's Model, Breech-Loading, Flint-Lock, large bore, heavy gun, with the interrupted screw breech same as used in the modern cannon on board U. S. Navy battleship. Gun must be over 100 years old. It has been altered from an old G. R. Tower Musket. Has lever on the part in front of the breech which turns the barrel and slides the whole barrel forward in order that the breech part can be opened; has buckhorn sight; smooth bore; the barrel is about 40 inches long; rare prize for collection. Price $285.00. We had to tempt the owner with a big offer to sell it to us. Rare gun that will top off a collection.

Musket, a large and heavy Arquebus Gun, first used in Italy about 1530, and in France and England about 1570. The names of animals were generally bestowed on Ordnance, as the falcon and its diminutive the falconet, etc. And as the musket was the most important small arm, the name of the smallest bird of prey might be very conveniently given to it. The musket is the male young of the Sparrow-hawk. Rifling of gun barrels was patented in England in 1635. Ancient Bowmen had the idea when they arranged the feathers on the shafts of their arrows in a spiral form in order to impart a rotary motion to the arrow in its flight.—Boutelle.

# Flint Lock Fowling Guns, Poachers' Flint Alarm Guns.

**1369. ADAM AND EVE FLINT LOCK GUN.** Barrel is old Damascus, octagonal for half its length, with figures of Adam and Eve under the apple tree, with sun, moon, and thirty-five figures of animals, beautifully engraved on the barrel with crouching lions engraved on the side plate. Name on the lock looks like "Tuklers" silver plate in the carved wood guard. "J. D." on the carved checkered stock, with antique cheek piece. Fine lock; barrel is 36 inches long. Full length, 52 inches; in serviceable order. Price $100.00.

**No. 1074. OLD FLINT LOCK SPORTING GUN.** 38-inch barrel, ⅝ bore; barrel has raised sighting rib the entire length. Gold inlaid pictures at the breech nearly worn off. Raised engraved work on the steel lock plate. Raised pictorial engravings on butt and guard plate. Silver name plate. Fine walnut stock with checkered grip and cheek piece. Handsome old gun. Price $25.00.

**No. 1069. 1780 PERIOD FLINT LOCK SPORTING GUN.** ⅝ bore, 38-inch barrel, fair order. $10.00.

**No. 1071. 17TH CENTURY FLINT LOCK SPORTING SHOT GUN.** Engraved on barrel in gold letters "J. A. Kuchenreuter," a famous German gun maker of the 17th century. Engraved with seal, mounted horsemen, and name on barrel. Carved walnut stock with cheek piece; with old fine wood guard and hand grip; in fair order. Full length 50 inches; about 9-16 bore. Rare old gun. Price $85.00.

**No. 1079. ENGLISH FLINT LOCK SPORTING GUN MADE BY "JOVER, LONDON."** 34-inch twist steel barrel, ⅝ bore, gold plated flash pan. Fine walnut stock, checkered grip, engraved lock and mountings. In working order. Original hammer has been replaced. Price $18.00.

**No. 1511. 10 FLINT LOCK SPORTING GUNS.** Average 34-inch barrel. Kind used in olden times for hunting small game. With old style pin fastening barrel to the stock; ½-inch bore; in working order; requires cleaning. Price, $12.00 each.

**No. 176A.** Damascus Barrel Flint Lock Fowling Gun, ⅝-in. smooth bore, 37-in. barrel, gilt inlaid: "Damas Anglais." In good, serviceable order. $14.00.

**No. 176B.** Extra Fine Damascus Barrel Flint Lock Gun, with chased and inlaid ornamental work on barrels and mountings; ⅝-in. smooth bore, 32½-in. barrel. Price $16.50.

**10919. ANCIENT SPANISH FLINT-LOCK MUSKET.** Lock dated "1751," with two seals "E. N. Altma" with rampant lion. Polished walnut fluted butt stock. Fine easy working outside lock engraved Mutueiza; 36 inch blued steel barrel, covered with silver inlaid ornamental work. Fine old gun. Price, $42.00.

**11028. "ROYAL FORESTERS" FLINT-LOCK CARBINE** (1774 period) from Lord Sheffield sale. Figure 13 engraved on the brass name plate; brass mounted. Walnut stock. Used by mounted foresters under Lord Sheffield to protect King George III's deer. Stock is slightly worm eaten. Valuable chiefly as relic. Price, $25.00.

**11029. FRENCH ARMY FLINTLOCK MUSKET,** brass mounted, 37 inch steel barrel and .71 smooth bore. Name on the lock worn off with age. Rusty, but in complete working order. Price, $10.00.

**8002.** Flintlock Octagonal Barrel Gun, 30-inch barrel, ⅝ bore, brass mounted with sling swivels, cleaned working order. Price, $15.00.

**No. 1047. FLINT LOCK, ALTERED FROM FRENCH MILITARY PERCUSSION LOCK GUN.** ⅝ smooth bore, about 40-inch barrel. Price $8.00.

Antique Flint Lock Trap Gun, used in olden times to set in ground with wires attached 'o give the alarm to game keepers when poachers were on the grounds. Blunderbuss-shaped barrel set in oak wood frame, as per photo illustration; full length, 19 inches; diameter of bell-mouth barrel 1½ inches; serviceable order. Price $18.50.

**No. 176.** Twist Steel Flint Lock Fowling Gun; about ⅝-inch bore, 37-inch barrel; weight about 6 pounds; part octagonal barrel, smooth bore; light-colored European hardwood stock; in fine order, like new. Price $5.50 each. Same kind of gun, with rosewood colored hardwood stocks; some with ebony colored wood stocks. $9.50 each.

**When ordering special guns allow a second choice when possible.**

**No. 105.** Fine Twist Barrel, Flint Lock Fowling Piece, made by Barnett, London; nearly ¾-inch bore; length of barrel 44½ inches; total length 60 inches, with ramrod rib, polished and checkered walnut stock. Almost new gun. Price $22.00.

**No. 1107. EARLY ENGLISH PERCUSSION BLUNDERBUSS,** with top spring bayonet. Barrel marked top with two British proof marks and C N 8621. Evidently a Government piece. Barrel, 16½ in., with 1⅞-in. muzzle. Spring bayonet, 15 in. 6-in. lock marked with CROWN AND TOWER PROOF. Brass trigger guard and butt plate. Fine order. Price, $27.50.

**No. 105B. FLINTLOCK FOWLING GUN,** with ramrod rib; about ¾-inch smooth bore; barrel measures 43 inches; total length of gun 59 inches. Guard extends for purpose of affording better hand grip. Engraved Brander & Potts, London; old English polished and checkered walnut stock; like new. Price $25.00.

**No. 105C.** Gamekeeper's Flint Lock Sporting Gun; ⅝-inch bore; 36-inch barrel; fine grooved rib octagonal barrel; curly walnut stock; fine order; good as new. $25.00.

**AUSTRIAN ARMY FLINTLOCK CARBINE,** caliber 72, with 12 deep rifled grooves. Barrel is 14½ inches long, full length 30 inches, weight 6½ pounds. On the left side is a long swivel bar with two rings, also cheek piece. These guns are all in fine cleaned condition, with sure fire flint locks with flint. Originally issued to mounted troops in the Austrian Army about the time of the accession of Emperor Ferdinand, when his empire was having trouble with Italy, 1835. Some of these guns were altered in the fifties to percussion and when our Civil War broke out, the United States Government purchased 10,000 of the altered guns at cost of $6.50 each. On account of the large caliber they were soon discarded. We offer these fine historical flint lock guns at $7.50 each.

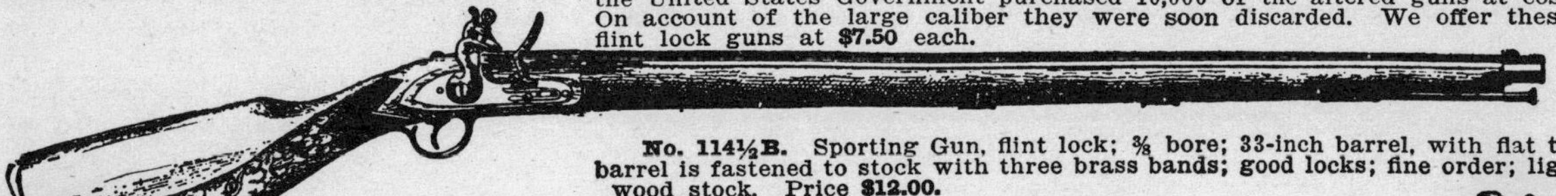

Twist Barrel Flint Lock Sporting Gun; barrel is 41 inches long, of twist steel, nicely browned, showing steel and wire figure, maple stock, sure fire, like new. Price $10.00.

20-Gauge Flint Lock Gun, with carved walnut stock and ramrod; barrel has ribs with fancy designs; like new; sure fire. Price $12.00.

2 British-make Sporting Flint Lock Shotguns; stamped "G. R.," with the Crown and Tower, also with broad arrow, showing Government ownership; fine gun, with rib on barrel for ramrod; good condition. Price $17.50.

**No. 110.** Flint Lock Twist Steel Barrel Shot Gun, ⅝-inch bore; 41½-inch barrel; total length 57 inches; old proof marks; good order. Price $15.00.

**No. 107.** Ropriedale Particular stamped on the lock of old flint lock carbine, swivel ram-rod full length, 42 inches. Price $10.00.

**No. 114½B.** Sporting Gun, flint lock; ⅝ bore; 33-inch barrel, with flat top for sighting; barrel is fastened to stock with three brass bands; good locks; fine order; light colored hardwood stock. Price $12.00.

Antique, Long, Heavy Barrel, Flint Lock Gun; 50-inch octagon barrel, with muzzle slightly bell shaped; short, old-fashioned stock; kind made in the 16th century; odd marks on the hardwood ramrod; barrel is fastened to the stock with metal pins instead of bands. Rare old relic. Price $40.00.

**No. 109.** Flint Lock Sporting Gun, ½-inch bore; octagonal barrel; total length 47 inches; brass mounted; good order. Price $12.50.

**No. 1080. DOUBLE BARREL ENGLISH SPORTING GUN LOCKS MADE BY FUNLEY.** Barrels by S. W. Olden. One hammer is missing. Fine twist steel barrels. Stock is in poor order. Offered as is, with extra hammer. Bargain for gunsmith who can repair. $18.00.

**No. 1113. FINE OLD SPORTING GUN MADE BY LANCASTER, LONDON,** with 30-inch barrel, ½-inch bore, percussion lock, plain walnut stock, easy working lock. Guard plate has hand grip extension. In working order. Price $8.50.

Ancient Cavalry Soldier with Armor and Fire-lock Carbine.

# Ancient Guns.

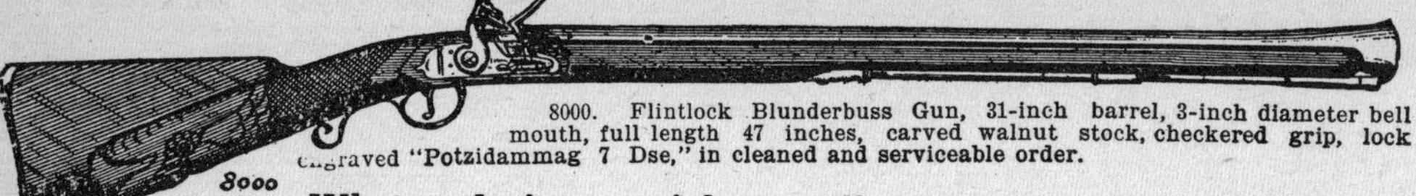

8000. Flintlock Blunderbuss Gun, 31-inch barrel, 3-inch diameter bell mouth, full length 47 inches, carved walnut stock, checkered grip, lock engraved "Potzidammag 7 Dse," in cleaned and serviceable order.

**When ordering special guns allow a second choice when possible.**

8735.—EARLY FLINTLOCK SHOT GUN. (Period about 1760.) Made by Baro. Barrel is 11/16 inch smooth bore, 23 inches long. Walnut stock has brass capped divided fore end. Serviceable order. Price, $14.50.

8736.—QUEEN ANNE ENGLISH BLUNDERBUSS FLINTLOCK. Engraved inscription as having been made by *"Oakes, London, 1718."* Heavy steel barrel 18 inches long, 1⅝ inch diameter at the bell mouth, with brass mountings, and name plate. Old British proof marks. Walnut stock. Full length 34 inches. Rare piece. Price, $50.00.

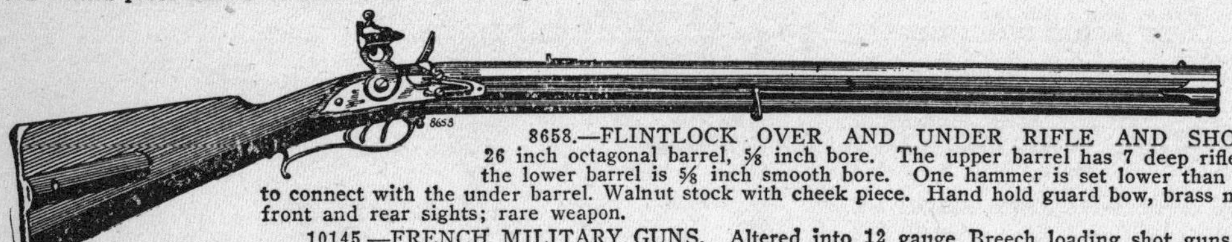

8658.—FLINTLOCK OVER AND UNDER RIFLE AND SHOT GUN. 26 inch octagonal barrel, ⅝ inch bore. The upper barrel has 7 deep rifle grooves, the lower barrel is ⅝ inch smooth bore. One hammer is set lower than the other to connect with the under barrel. Walnut stock with cheek piece. Hand hold guard bow, brass mountings, front and rear sights; rare weapon.

10145.—FRENCH MILITARY GUNS. Altered into 12 gauge Breech loading shot guns, shooting the regular 12 gauge center fire cartridge. French arsenal marks on the lock. Price, refinished like new, $4.85 each.

8737.—FLINTLOCK SPORTING GUN. With gold seal set in the barrel, lettered "H. Nock, London." With gold seal set in the lock, lettered "Lott." Gold touch hole. 31 inch barrel, ⅝ inch smooth bore. Brazed rib for the ramrod. Swan shaped hammer. Engraved mountings. Checkered grip. Walnut stock. Ebony fore end cap. Price, $22.50.

8738.—ANTIQUE FLINTLOCK SPORTING GUN. Made by Moore. Gold vent hole. Brass capped divided fore end stock. Brass mountings. Walnut stock. Old British proof marks, chased rear sight. Small muzzle end (looks as if detachable). Silver front sight. Price, $22.50.

8739.—FLINTLOCK BLUNDERBUSS RIFLE. 12 rifle grooves, with increased depth at the muzzle, the barrel is larger in diameter at both muzzle and breech ends than in the center. Twist steel octagonal barrel 29 inches long. Diameter of the rifle muzzle ¾ inch. Carved decorated walnut stock. Engraved brass mountings, evidently of ancient German make. Stock is in need of repairs. Old blunderbuss rifles are rare. Price, $85.00.

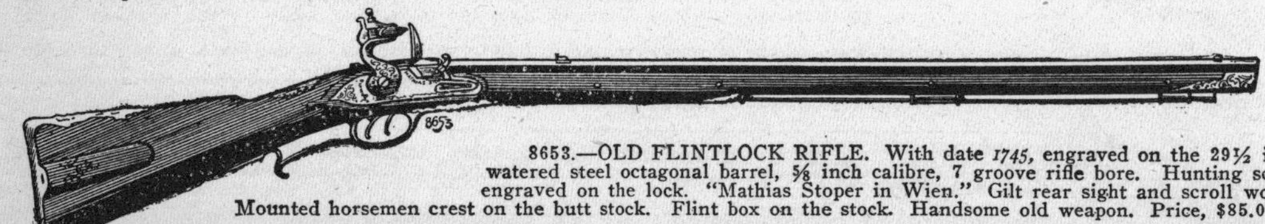

8653.—OLD FLINTLOCK RIFLE. With date *1745*, engraved on the 29½ inch watered steel octagonal barrel, ⅝ inch calibre, 7 groove rifle bore. Hunting scene engraved on the lock. "Mathias Stoper in Wien." Gilt rear sight and scroll work. Mounted horsemen crest on the butt stock. Flint box on the stock. Handsome old weapon. Price, $85.00.

8740.—PERIOD OF 1795 FLINTLOCK DOUBLE BARREL FOWLING GUN. 36 inch barrel, ⅝ inch smooth bore. Engraved brass mountings. Common gun of the period of over one hundred years ago. Small split in the stock. Bargain price, $40.00.

8653A.—FRENCH FLINTLOCK RIFLE. Time of LOUIS XV, like illustration No. 8653 on this page. Very heavy octagonal barrel, 26 inches long, slightly belled at muzzle. Inlaid with roses in silver near sight. Sight base is of silver, marked in monogram: R L. Brass upright sight fitted on this. Brass butt plate, heavy brass ramrod guides, extra long trigger guard of brass of the early French type. 5½ inch ornamented wood cheek piece. 5½ inch patch box with sliding wood cover with spring snap to keep it shut. In good order, except for small piece chipped off stock at muzzle end. Price, $38.00.

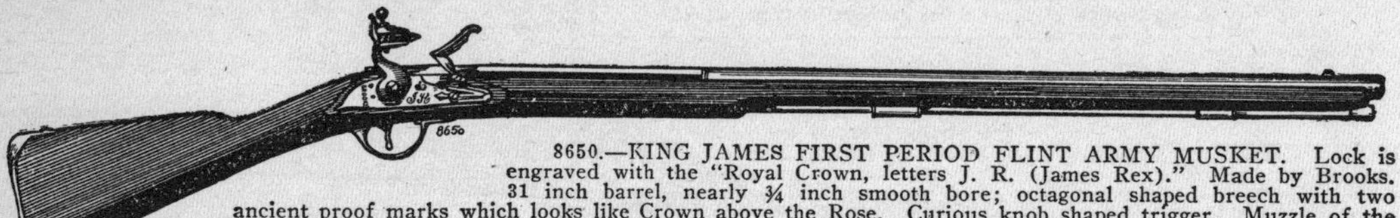

8650.—KING JAMES FIRST PERIOD FLINT ARMY MUSKET. Lock is engraved with the "Royal Crown, letters J. R. (James Rex)." Made by Brooks. 31 inch barrel, nearly ¾ inch smooth bore; octagonal shaped breech with two ancient proof marks which looks like Crown above the Rose. Curious knob shaped trigger. Muzzle of the barrel slightly blunderbuss. This is one of the earliest muskets. King James was son of Mary Queen of Scotland. Price, $100.00.

8749.—EARLY ENGLISH FLINTLOCK FOWLING PIECE. Made by Flood & Co.; 32 inch barrel, ⅝ inch smooth bore. Checkered grip. Walnut stock. Silver fore end and escutcheons; ramrod rib; engraved mountings. Price, $20.00.

8750.—FINELY MADE ANTIQUE FLINTLOCK FOWLING PIECE. Heavy silver mountings bearing London hall mark period 1759, with crest on the heel plate. Found in old mansion at Newark on Trent, England. 38 inch barrel, 11/16 inch smooth bore. Marked "Bailey, Newark" on the lock. Bronze ramrod rib. Carved walnut stock. All mountings are in heavy silver. Gold breech band. Handsome well finished gun. Old curly walnut stock. Price, $68.00.

8751.—BROMPTON, DONCASTER. Maker of English Fowling piece about the period of 1798. 33 inch twist steel barrel, ⅝ inch smooth bore. Gold band and vent hole. Brazed ramrod rib; silver name plate and escutcheons. Checkered grip. Walnut stock. Price, $25.00.

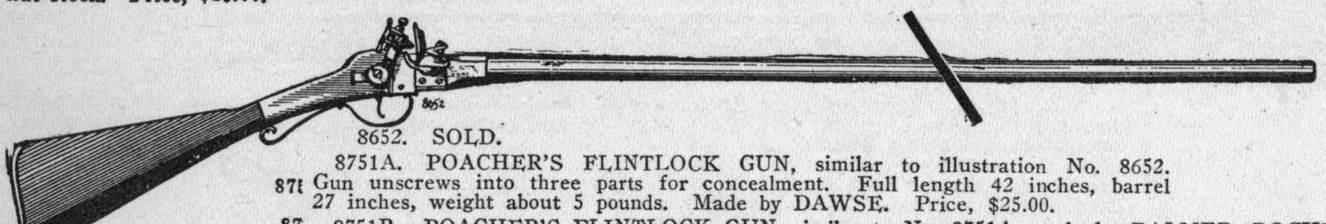

8652. SOLD.

8751A. POACHER'S FLINTLOCK GUN, similar to illustration No. 8652. 87! Gun unscrews into three parts for concealment. Full length 42 inches, barrel 27 inches, weight about 5 pounds. Made by DAWSE. Price, $25.00.

87 8751B. POACHER'S FLINTLOCK GUN, similar to No. 8751A, made by PALMER, ROCHES-Price $ TER, ENGLAND. Has cheek piece on left side of stock. Price, $25.00.

8752.—OLD BROWN BESS FLINTLOCK ARMY MUSKET. Type of the gun used in the British Army for over one hundred years. Stamped on the lock with "Two Royal Crowns, Tower, G. R." Fore stock of the barrel has been shortened for use as a shot gun. 32 inch barrel, ¾ inch smooth bore. Price, $25.00.

8753.—REVOLUTIONARY WAR PERIOD MUSKET. With brass name plate, engraving on the lock indistinct, 42 inch barrel, ¾ inch smooth bore with London proof mark, period of 1775. This type of gun sold by the British gun makers Guild to American colonists. The gun is in fine order, shows extensive use. Price, $35.00.

8755B.—REVOLUTIONARY WAR GUN. With 41½ inch barrel, made by Barber. Price, $20.00.

8753A.—REVOLUTIONARY WAR TROPHY SABRE. Marked 1 *Va. Reg't.* from its connection with old Revolutionary arms; we believe it to have been used also in the Civil War. 35 inch blade with deep and narrow grooves. Old style pierced guard. Wired wrapped hilt. Price, $25.00.

8744.—LONDON MADE FLINTLOCK MUSKET. 37 inch barrel, ⅝ inch smooth bore. Old British proof marks, period of 1775. Brass mounted, light weight gun, in serviceable order. Price, $20.00.

8745.—ENGLISH FOWLING PIECE. Made by Higgs, period of 1775. 39 inch twist steel barrel, ¾ inch smooth bore. Flatted top firing rib. Checkered grip. Walnut stock. Price, $22.00.

8746.—MIDDLEBROOK MUSEUM, (E burgh Castle) RELIC FLINTLOCK MUSK With ancient flat bladed bayonet. Label pas on the stock giving the history of the gur faded out. The proprietor of the Middlebr Museum made a specialty of securing rare m tary weapons. In 1907 his executors offe for sale the American flag from the captu frigate Chesapeake, 1813, also the bugle t sounded the charge of the Light Brigade Balaclava. This old musket is rusty, valua only as a relic. We were unable to learn history. The lot number at the sale was Length of the barrel is 39 inches, ¾ i smooth bore, full length 55 inches; the len of the bayonet is 22 inches. Price, $68.00.

8747.—OLD SINGLE BARREL FLI LOCK FOWLING GUN. Made by Sutherla London, about period of 1785. 34 inch bar ⅝ inch smooth bore. Brazed ramrod rib. Pr $16.00.

8748.—EARLY ENGLISH FLINTLO FOWLING GUN. Made by Gore. 27½ i barrel, ⅝ inch smooth bore. Gold vent, graved mountings. Silver wire inlaid or mentation on the butt stock. Carved wal stock. Price, $20.00.

10102. **Hall's Harper's Ferry 1834 Flintlo One of the first U. S. regulation breech-loa ers.** Serviceable order. U. S. Arsenal ma and dates. Price, $20.00.

2224. Ancient Brass Barrel Flintlock Blu derbuss, kind used in olden times moun on castle walls; "G. R. Crown and Towe stamped on the lock; 25-inch barrel, 3-inch muzzle; at the breech measures 2¼ inch fitted with swivel. Price, $48.00.

Antique German Flintlock Rifle, octago barrel, with blunderbuss-shaped muzzle; namented brass mountings with sporti scenes. Box for spare flints in the butt sto in working order. Price, $25.00.

8679. SPANISH EIGHTEENTH CENTU CARBINE. 14-inch Damascus barrel, w inlaid gold seal of the maker. Silver inl decorative scroll work. Crown and shi shape, silver name plate. Walnut stock w cheek piece. Engraved mountings. Fi easy-working locks. Full length 28 inch Price, $30.00.

COMMODORE OLIVER H. PERRY'S PI CASE. Came from the Brooks' collecti Made of dark-colored hard wood, polishe hollowed out for the bowl and pipe ste with metal hinge at the back of the bo Length, 7 inches; ¾-inch diameter; 1⅞ inch at the bowl. Vouched for by A. E. Brook Hartford, Conn., it having belonged to a used by Commodore Perry. Price, $15.00.

---

### TO A PAIR OF OLD PISTOLS.

How long ago since you were out one day—
With whom, and where, and why, I'd like know;
'Twas after that, they put you well away,
And now you're in a shop for "curio."

I wonder how the coffee tasted then—
I hope, indeed, they had it fresh and stror
As some one stalked the paces up to ten,
Another brought your shining case along.

It was perhaps upon a strip of beach,
Where stealthy mist crept in from off t sea;
While one, alone—most probably the leech
Skipped stones and idly pondered whi 'twould be.

I wonder if inheritance you changed,
If some old title passed beyond debate,
If you were there with erstwhile frie estranged,
Or if you settled some affair of state.

At all events, I hope the clean old code
Was well upheld and saw its justice done;
With no advantage in the flint or load,
You spoke together and the best man won.

O. C. A. CHILD.

*New York Times*, Aug. 17, 1925.

# DOUBLE BARREL FLINT LOCK GUNS, ETC.

**No. 111. FRENCH DOUBLE BARREL FLINT LOCK FOWLING PIECE,** with checkered pistol grip, two sling swivels, silver monogram plate. Knife bayonet with 4½ inch wide blade to fit over the muzzle of both barrels. When not in use it is carried in a compartment in the butt fitted with spring cover. 32 inch barrels. In fair condition. Price $35.00.

**No. 111-B. FRENCH FLINT LOCK DOUBLE BARREL FOWLING PIECE,** made with detachable butt stock, for convenience in carrying. This style also used by poachers. 34 inch round barrels with silver front sight. Right hand lock marked: A. BERNARD. Left lock marked: LIEGE. Wide trigger guard. Two sling swivels. In fine order. Price $40.00.

**No. 111A. FINE DOUBLE FLINT LOCK GUN,** similar to No. 111, without gold ornamented work on barrels, and not such a fine stock. In good order; never used. Sample old time gun. Price $37.50.

Beautiful Old Double-Barrel Flintlock Fowling Gun. This illustration is from a photograph. Note the carved and checkered polished stock, the chasing on the lock and mountings. Gun is in perfect order; good as new; in fact, never was used. It was found in a sample case of an old gunmaker in Europe who had long ago given up working. Fine old flint gun, 16 gauge. Price $45.00.

**No. 112. DOUBLE BARREL FLINT LOCK FOWLING GUN.** 16 gauge, fine working lock; engraved and decorated mounting. Carved and checkered stock; never used. Old time sample gun. One of our customers who collects old guns and sells off duplicates, informed us that he got $300 for an old flint lock gun of this pattern. Our bargain price is $30.00.

**No. 112A. FLINT LOCK DOUBLE BARREL FOWLING GUN.** 20 gauge, 34-inch barrels; finely ornamented and engraved; bronze mountings. Fine checkered Walnut stock, with cheek piece; with sling swivel; in perfect order; never used. Old time sample gun. Bargain price $30.00.

**No. 112B. FINE FLINT LOCK DOUBLE GUN,** twist steel barrels, plain finish; with sling swivel; in perfect order. Price $25.00.

**No. 1851. ANCIENT FLINT LOCK AIR GUN.** The use of guns firing shot with compressed air was prohibited in olden times. This gun looks like the regular flint lock, excepting that the stock which contains the air chambers is a trifle larger. The inside lock mechanism, when the trigger was pulled, released the charge of air and fired the shot. The hammer on the lock is only a blind.
The air chamber can be filled by an ordinary bicycle pump. Length of barrel, 37 inches; ⅜-inch smooth bore. Price $40.00.

**No. 1366. FRENCH DOUBLE BARREL LOCK FOWLING PIECE,** with checkered grip and fore end, with fancy ALL WOOD trigger guard. Gold touch holes. Two sling swivels. Five inch cheek piece with ornament. Right lock marked: P. GREVERATH. Left lock marked: a DYCK. 32 inch barrels with silver sight. In good order. Price $50.00.

**No. 1366-A.** Similar to No. 1366 with 35 inch barrels with front sight, with French locks; unmarked, with wood trigger guard. In good order. Price $38.00.

Double-Barrel Flintlock Gun, with fine walnut stock, ½-inch bore, 36-inch steel barrels, plain finished; stock has split in it, otherwise in fine order; like new. Will sell as it is for $28.75.

Handsome Flintlock Sporting Rifle; 36-inch octagonal barrel, fine English walnut stock with Swiss-shaped butt, ½-inch bore, made by Barnett of London, for English nobleman; new gun; has to be seen to be appreciated; bargain at $35.00.

FLINTLOCK DOUBLE SUPERPOSED BARREL REVOLVING GUN. 28-inch barrel; old style muzzle rifling; ½-inch bore; fancy brass mounting; carved walnut stock; full length, 44 inches; in good order; rare old gun.

Double-Barrel Flintlock Sporting Gun; about 24 gauge; barrels 36 inches long, of blued steel, with gilt decorations, engraved mountings, fine walnut stock, carved, checkered and inlaid; silvered name plate; beautiful gun, in perfect order; like new. Price $75.00.

Double-Barrel Flintlock Fowling Gun, with carved black ebonized stock; with polished silvered barrels and mountings; 36-inch barrels, ½-inch bore; in perfect order; new. Price $55.00.

**No. 1564. 17TH CENTURY FLINT LOCK GUN—2 SHOTS FROM ONE BARREL WITH ONE TRIGGER.** Inventor's model. Shows evidence of much hard service. Still in working order. Rare mechanism. Confirming the old saying, "Nothing new under the sun." The praises of the one trigger gun are still being sung, and here is a one-trigger gun anywhere from 150 to 200 years old. Two shots out of one barrel was considered new during the civil war period, and in 1862, the U. S. Government at the Springfield Armory, made up a number of percussion lock guns, under Lindsay patent, to fire two shots out of one barrel, but here is the same idea worked out in this ancient flint lock with two flint hammers. The gun also has the extended guard bow, serving as and furnishing the idea for the pistol grip hand hold. Hard wood stock with cheek piece on side. A rare prize for any high class museum. Bore ¾-inch, length of barrel, 23 inches. Price $500.00.

Double-Barrel Flintlock Gun, with polished steel engraved barrels with figures of game; with black ebonized carved stock; with old fashioned cheek piece. Decorated with ornamental scroll-work; beautiful piece of work; ½-inch bore, 36-inch barrels; in fine order; new. Price $60.00.

Double-Barrel Flintlock Shot Gun; 1 hammer is not original; in good order; about 20 gauge. Price $25.00.

Double-barrel Flint Lock Shot Gun; 16 gauge; in fine order, like new; checked grip; cheek piece on stock; polished walnut stock; rare old style gun of kind used 75 to 150 years ago. Price $28.00.

Ancient Flint-lock Rocket Gun. Only limited number made. Iron barrel that holds the colored fire is 15 inches long, 2 inches in diameter; the handle is 4 feet 5 inches long; full length, 5 feet 8 inches. Trigger is 2 feet 3 inches from the butt of handle. By pulling the trigger the flint hammer fires the spark into the flash pan that ignites the rocket fire. This is a very rare gun; we do not know of the existence of another specimen. Price $100.00.

File of three soldiers of 1812 period. Front rank man firing, center rank priming, rear rank loading.—Bannerman's History of War Weapons.

**No. 1693A. DOUBLE BARREL FLINT LOCK SPORTING GUN;** ⅝ smooth bore, 35-inch engraved barrel; lock and mountings. Carved walnut stock, with cheek piece. With name plate; with flints. Full length, 51 inches. In good working order. Barrel requires cleaning. Price $45.00.

**No. 1693B. DOUBLE BARREL FLINT LOCK WITH EBONY STOCK.** With ramrod broken. Ramrod holder missing. Requires cleaning. Offered as is, $40.00. Offered refinished; made to look like new, $45.00.

"Flintlock guns, originally called snaphaunce, were first introduced about the year 1580. It seems to have been a Dutch invention and to have by no means a dignified origin, for this lock is said to have been brought into use by certain marauding bands, who by the Dutch were called 'Snaphaans'—hen snappers, or poultry stealers. These worthies could not afford wheel-locks and the lighted matches, for the match-lock guns were liable to lead to detection, so they devised their own snaphaunce, little suspecting, doubtless, that their ingenius invention would be universally adopted and would maintain its supremacy for nearly three centuries."—Bou-

# RARE PATTERN FLINTLOCK GUNS

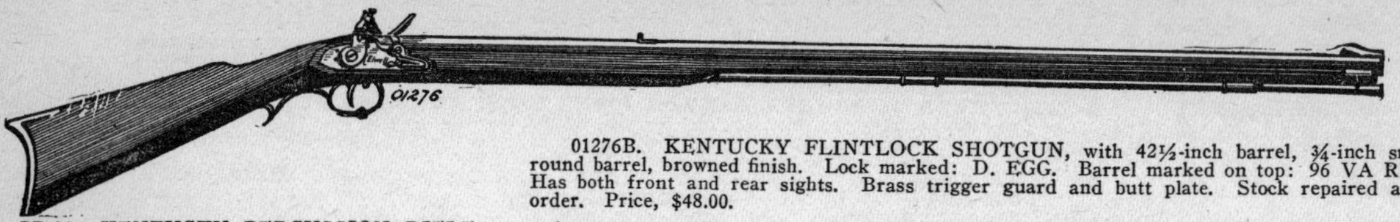


01276B. KENTUCKY FLINTLOCK SHOTGUN, with 42½-inch barrel, ¾-inch smooth bore. Plain round barrel, browned finish. Lock marked: D. EGG. Barrel marked on top: 96 VA RE ALEXANDRIA. Has both front and rear sights. Brass trigger guard and butt plate. Stock repaired at tip. In working order. Price, $48.00.

SP-30. KENTUCKY PERCUSSION RIFLE, set triggers; octagonal barrel 48 inches, full length 64 inches, bore 11/16 inch. Lock marked: R. & W. C. BIDDLE, WARRANTED. Barrel marked: E. SCHAUB, WARRANTED. Mould for round ball included. Brass front sight, butt plate and trigger guard. Price, $35.00.

SP-0. KENTUCKY PERCUSSION RIFLE, with two barrels, over and under, made to revolve by releasing catch in front of trigger guard. Barrels 35½ inches, octagonal, with rear and front sights, ONE HAMMER, two triggers, ramrod fitted at side with four brass guides. Lock marked: HENRY PARKER, WARRANTED, and gun made by D. Mosser, of Danville, Pa. French pattern long brass trigger guard, heavy brass butt plate, brass side plate, and 8-inch brass patch box. 2½-inch cheek piece inlaid with silver crescent moon. Two silver disk ornaments set in stock. Total length 51½ inches, weight 10¾ lbs. Bore of both barrels, 7/16 inch. Price, $45.00.

SP-1. KENTUCKY PERCUSSION RIFLE, with two barrels, over and under, barrels revolve, as there is only ONE hammer and two triggers. Full length 51½ inches, barrels 36½ inches, bore ½ inch, weight 9¼ lbs. Wood ramrod fitted at side, long brass trigger guard, butt plate, and 8-inch ornamented patch box. 2½-inch cheek piece with brass star set in. Brass side plate marked with maker's name, D. MOSSER, of Danville, Pa. Barrels are octagon with both rear and front sights. Price, $44.00.

SP-2. KENTUCKY PERCUSSION RIFLE, over and under, both barrels rifled, with TWO hammers and two triggers. Total length 52½ inches, barrels 36¼ inches, octagonal, with rear and front sights, fore ⅜ inch. Sporting style stock with silver ornaments set in, with silver long trigger guard and butt plate. Five-inch cheek piece ornamented with silver stag. Gun made by P. KOCKLER, LEWISBURG, and so marked on the barrel. Five inch oval silver patch box. Price, $48.00.

SP-3. KENTUCKY PERCUSSION RIFLE, with 30-inch octagonal barrel, with rear and front sights. Bore ⅜ inch. Full length wood stock with brass tip with brass holders or guides for ramrod. Long brass trigger guard, brass butt plate and side plate. Eight-inch ornamental patch box. Stock inlaid with silver pieces to represent fish, hearts, arrowheads, etc. Two-inch cheek piece, brass mounted, with a silver crescent moon. Gun made by GOLCHER. Total length 45½ inches, weight 7 lbs. Price, $45.00.

SP-4. KENTUCKY PERCUSSION RIFLE, for hunting and target use. Made by JOHN SHULER, LIVERPOOL, PA., and so marked on lock. Heavy octagonal barrel, 34 inches with front and rear sights, sporting style stock. Full length rib under the barrel fitted with ramrod guides. Stock checkered at fore end and grip, and inlaid with silver ornaments. Long brass trigger guard and butt plate. Two-inch cheek piece, and 8-inch fancy brass patch box. Total length 49½ inches, weight 9½ lbs., bore 7/16 inch. Price, $40.00.

SP-6. KENTUCKY PERCUSSION RIFLE, with 38½-inch barrel, ½-inch bore, total length 53½ inches. Weight 9¼ lbs. Made by P. Leman, Lancaster, Pa. Price, $42.00.

SP-7. KENTUCKY PERCUSSION RIFLE, similar to Nos. 5 and 6. Full length 53 inches, octagonal barrel 38 inches, bore ½ inch, weight 8½ lbs. Made by G. Avery, Hamburg, Pa., and marked G. A. on barrel. Price, $40.00.

SP-8. KENTUCKY PERCUSSION RIFLE, with 37½-inch octagonal barrel, bore 7/16 inch, full length 52 inches, weight 7¼ lbs. Made by S. Miller, Hamburg, Pa. Similar to Nos. SP-5, 6 and 7, Price, $42.00.

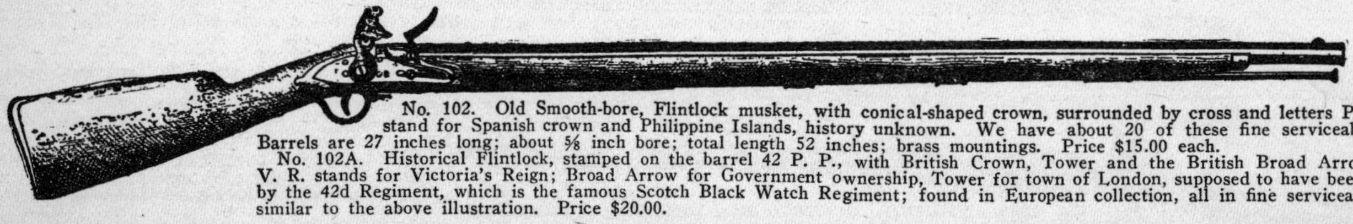

No. 102. Old Smooth-bore, Flintlock musket, with conical-shaped crown, surrounded by cross and letters P. I.; may stand for Spanish crown and Philippine Islands, history unknown. We have about 20 of these fine serviceable guns. Barrels are 27 inches long; about ⅝ inch bore; total length 52 inches; brass mountings. Price $15.00 each.

No. 102A. Historical Flintlock, stamped on the barrel 42 P. P., with British Crown, Tower and the British Broad Arrow V. R. V. R. stands for Victoria's Reign; Broad Arrow for Government ownership, Tower for town of London, supposed to have been carried by the 42d Regiment, which is the famous Scotch Black Watch Regiment; found in European collection, all in fine serviceable order similar to the above illustration. Price $20.00.

VA-1. REVOLUTIONARY WAR MUSKET, manufactured at WILLIAMSBURG, VIRGINIA in 1778, and issued to the 26th VIRGINIA LINE REGIMENT OF MUSKETEERS. This is one of 600 military muskets first manufactured for military purposes under authorization of CONTINENTAL CONGRESS. Full length 58 inches, fitted with British spade bayonet with 12-inch blade, 42-inch round barrel, browned, with British proof marks, 6-inch flintlock marked: KETLAND. 5½-inch ornamented brass side plate. Brass butt plate into which has been scratched the name: CULLEN. Long brass monogram plate also marked: CULLEN. Long brass trigger guard with urn end. Swivels in guard and barrel for gun sling. Steel ramrod with 4 long brass rod guides. This is a rare and genuine relic. Price, $250.00.

SP-9. KENTUCKY PERCUSSION RIFLE, made by P. Leman, Lancaster, Pa. Has set trigger, and stock ornamented with silver crescent and circles. Bore ⅜ inch, octagonal barrel 34 inches, total 49½ inches, weight 7¼ lbs. Price, $44.00.

SP-10. KENTUCKY PERCUSSION RIFLE, with extra heavy octagonal barrel, 35 inches, total 50 inches, bore ½ inch. Similar to Nos. SP-5, 6, 7, 8, and 9. Weight 10¼ lbs. Price, $46.00.

SP-11. KENTUCKY PERCUSSION RIFLE, with two barrels, over and under, with one hammer. Barrels revolve by releasing catch in front of trigger guard. Lock marked: G. GOULCHER. Both barrels marked: D. YOUNG. One barrel also marked: H. WORL. Both barrels octagon, 37½ inches, with brass ramrod guides, on one side. Bore ½ inch, full length 62 inches. Silver stock ornaments, and silver plated guard. 6½-inch brass patch box, 3-inch cheek piece, weight 10½ lbs. Price, $50.00.

SP-13. KENTUCKY PERCUSSION RIFLE, with two barrels, over and under, with one hammer, two triggers. Total length 51½ inches, barrels 35½ inches octagon, bore ½ inch. Barrels revolve. Fitted with front and rear sights on each barrel. Ornamented lock marked: KELKER & BROS., HARRISBURG. Each barrel marked: JOHN SHULER, LIVERPOOL, PA. Eight-inch fancy brass patch box, 2-inch cheek piece inlaid with silver disk. Price, $48.00.

No. 104A. AFRICAN CHIEFTAIN FLINTLOCK GUN, with long barrel, 51 inches; ⅝-inch bore; total length, 70 inches. New gun, stamped "Barnett, London." Bright redwood stock. Made for sale by traders to African chieftain. Price, $12.00.

No. 104B. AFRICAN CHIEFTAIN GUN, similar to No. 104A, but with ebony-colored stock and 50-inch barrel. Barnett, London. New. Price, $12.00.

No. 101C. G. R., TOWER, CROWN, BRITISH ARMY FLINTLOCK MUSKET, about ¾-inch bore, 40-inch barrel; total length, 56 inches. All in good order, except stock, which has through age become slightly worm-eaten. Barrel is fastened to stock with 3 bands. Price, $20.00.

No. 104G. LARGE BORE, FLINTLOCK GUN, ornamented trimmings, ⅞-inch bore, octagonal barrel; fine lock; good order. Price, $20.00.

No. 104I. BARNETT & SONS, LONDON, LONG BARREL, FINE FLINTLOCK FOWLING PIECE; barrel is 46½ inches long, about ¾-inch bore; total length, 62 inches; stamped with maker's name on the barrel; also Baker & Sons stamped on the lock; stock is fine old English curly walnut, polished, stock extending to muzzle. In fine order. Price, $25.00.

SP-15. KENTUCKY PERCUSSION RIFLE, with octagonal barrel, 41 inches, total 56 inches, bore 7/16 inch. Raised rear sight, with brass front sight. Brass stock tip and rod guides, and butt plate. Flat steel trigger guard. Wood cheek piece 3 inches, marked A. M. Set triggers. Barrel marked: J. DERR, weight 8 lbs. Price, $42.00.

OLD REVOLUTIONARY WAR FLINTLOCK MUSKET, with part of the barrel cut off for use as saddle gun, with letters C. S. A. and skull and crossbones, in bone, set in the stock; rare relic. Evidently some old heirloom used during the Civil War. Price, $25.00.

SP-22. KENTUCKY PERCUSSION RIFLE, with octagonal barrel, 40½ inches, total 55 inches, bore ½ inch, weight 9¼ lbs. Brass bound with 7-inch extra wide brass patch box in scroll style. Silver disk set in 2½-inch cheek piece. Lock marked: JAMES GOLCHER. Barrel marked: F. A. Price, $44.00.

SP-24. KENTUCKY PERCUSSION RIFLE, octagonal barrel marked: E. S. Lock marked: WARRANTED. Set triggers, with brass guard, butt plate and patch box. Crescent moon set in good cheek piece. Bore 7/16 inch, total length 53½ inches, barrel 38 inches, weight 8½ lbs. Price, $30.00.

SP-25. KENTUCKY PERCUSSION RIFLE, extra light weight, only 6¾ lbs. Octagonal barrel 41 inches, bore ½ inch, total length 56½ inches. Cheek piece set with silver 8-pointed star. Long wide brass patch box; other trimmings are brass. Lock marked: J. ROOP. Price, $38.00.

SP-28. KENTUCKY PERCUSSION RIFLE, extra light weight, only 7¾ lbs. Octagonal barrel 38 inches, total 54 inches, bore ½ inch. Brass trimmings, with patch box, and French type guard. Price, $38.00.

HANDSOME FLINTLOCK RIFLE, with half octagon barrel, in perfect order. Price, $25.00.

SP-16. KENTUCKY PERCUSSION RIFLE, with half octagonal, half round barrel, extra light. Total length 57½ inches, barrel 42 inches, bore ½ inch. Rear sight and brass front sight. Brass trimmed throughout, with 2-inch brass bound cheek piece, inlaid with silver crescent. Lock marked: N. ASHMORE, weight 6½ lbs. Price, $38.00.

No. 53E. FINE TWIST STEEL FLINTLOCK BLUNDERBUSS, with carved and checkered stock; engraved mountings; length of barrel, 17 inches; width at flash pan, 1 1/16 inches; width across the bell-mouth muzzle, 2¼ inches; total length of the gun, 32 inches; in fine, serviceable order. Price, $25.00.

No. 108. OCTAGONAL BARREL FLINTLOCK SHOT GUN, about ¾-inch bore; 38-inch barrel; total length, 53 inches; handsomely ornamented; old proof marks; stock slightly worm-eaten; pin fastening. Price, $17.50.

SP-17. KENTUCKY PERCUSSION RIFLE, with heavy octagonal barrel, 42 inches, total length 57½ inches, bore 9/16 inch. Brass trimmed, with 2-inch cheek piece with brass edge, and silver moon, 7-inch ornamental patch box. Barrel marked L. E., weight 7½ lbs. Price, $40.00.

0-902. LONG BARREL, BROWN BESS, FLINTLOCK MUSKET. Lock engraved with maker's name, "Cook, British Crown." Full length, 6 feet 4 inches; regulation calibre, 13-16, smooth bore; barrel 5 feet. Bronze guard and butt plate. Walnut stock. SHORT FORE-END. Price, $35.00.

0-967. ANCIENT GERMAN FLINTLOCK GUN. Stock inlaid with ivory (or bone), pearl ornaments; 33½-inch, partly octagonal, barrel, ⅝-inch smooth bore. Bronze medallion head inlaid on barrel. Brass mountings. Good order; fine-looking relic. Price, $25.00.

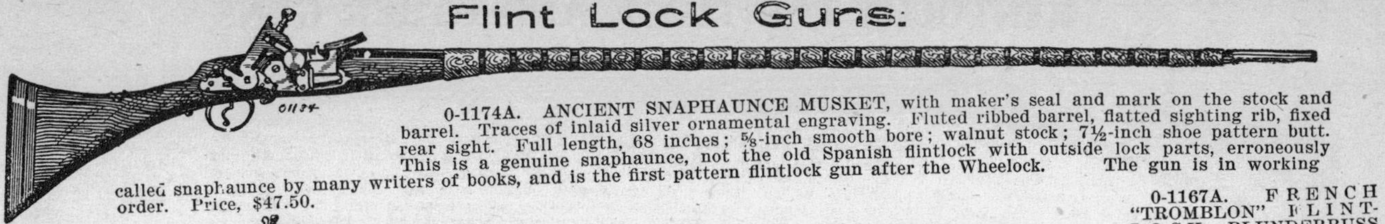

**0-1174A. ANCIENT SNAPHAUNCE MUSKET**, with maker's seal and mark on the stock and barrel. Traces of inlaid silver ornamental engraving. Fluted ribbed barrel, flatted sighting rib, fixed rear sight. Full length, 68 inches; ⅝-inch smooth bore; walnut stock; 7½-inch shoe pattern butt. This is a genuine snaphaunce, not the old Spanish flintlock with outside lock parts, erroneously called snaphaunce by many writers of books, and is the first pattern flintlock gun after the Wheelock. The gun is in working order. Price, $47.50.

**0-1155. BARNETT FLINTLOCK RED STOCK MUSKET.** The lock stamped with Royal British Crown, V. R., Tower, 1842. Barrel is 45 inches long, full length 61 inches, bore nearly ¾ inch. Heavy lower and middle bands, with antique trumpet-shaped upper band. Stock is stamped "BARNETT MINORIES, LONDON." This gun was built for trading purposes, 70 years ago. Last year we bought out the entire stock of J. Barnett & Sons, Ltd., the last one of the oldest gun firms in Europe. The first Barnett was President of the Gun Makers' Guild, chartered in 1628, by King Charles the First. The Guild proof mark was the monogram G. and P., the first British Government proof mark on record. The gun is in serviceable order. Price, $9.50. Another similar serviceable flintlock gun, in serviceable order, but without the marks on the lock, $8.50.

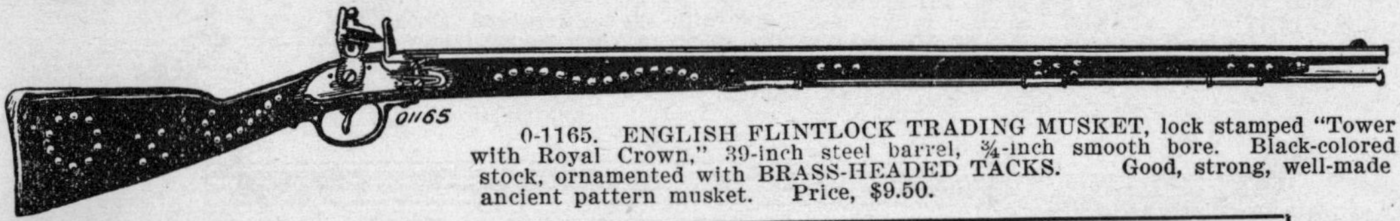

**0-1165. ENGLISH FLINTLOCK TRADING MUSKET**, lock stamped "Tower with Royal Crown," 39-inch steel barrel, ¾-inch smooth bore. Black-colored stock, ornamented with BRASS-HEADED TACKS. Good, strong, well-made ancient pattern musket. Price, $9.50.

See THE BREECH LOADER IN THE SERVICE (U. S.); also pages 66, 67, 68 and 69 for all small arms used in World War. See ILLUSTRATED HISTORY OF U. S. MILITARY SMALL ARMS. Any of these features alone worth many times the price we ask for catalog, and do not appear in any other printed form. Note that this entire catalog and contents is copyrighted and cannot be used.

**0-1169. FLINTLOCK BLUNDERBUSS**, with elliptical mouth, for scattering shot horizontally; 27½-inch barrel. The mouth is 3 inches horizontally, 1½ inches vertically. Walnut stock fastened to the barrel by stud pinning. Brass name plate. Lock engraved with monogram F. B. Cheek-piece. Brass mountings. Originally made with axle through the stock for use in swivel mount on castle walls. The gun is in good working order, with the exception that the butt stock is a trifle wormy. Price, $28.50.

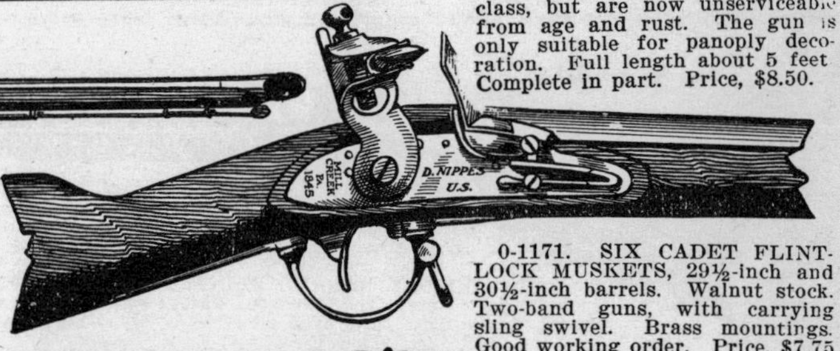

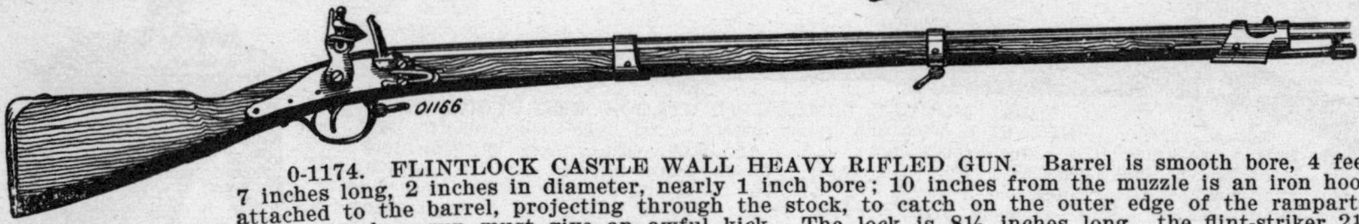

**0-1174. FLINTLOCK CASTLE WALL HEAVY RIFLED GUN.** Barrel is smooth bore, 4 feet 7 inches long, 2 inches in diameter, nearly 1 inch bore; 10 inches from the muzzle is an iron hook attached to the barrel, projecting through the stock, to catch on the outer edge of the ramparts, for taking up the recoil, for such a gun must give an awful kick. The lock is 8½ inches long, the flint-striker 2¼ inches long. Everything about the gun is large. Old walnut stock, now very slightly worm-eaten. Mark on the stock, with monogram "F. R.," and on the reverse side the figures "30." The recoil spur projection measures 2⅝ inches below the stock; full length is 6 feet. Fore stock shows repairing. Weight, 20 lbs. Bargain price, $22.50.

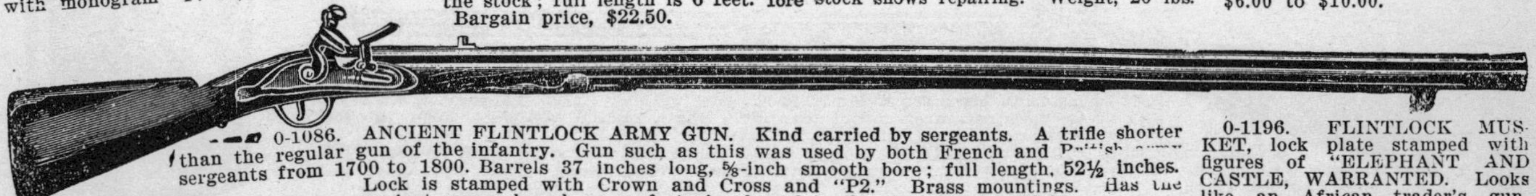

**0-1086. ANCIENT FLINTLOCK ARMY GUN.** Kind carried by sergeants. A trifle shorter than the regular gun of the infantry. Gun such as this was used by both French and British armies sergeants from 1700 to 1800. Barrels 37 inches long, ⅝-inch smooth bore; full length, 52½ inches. Lock is stamped with Crown and Cross and "P2." Brass mountings. Has the ancient square breech screw fastening barrel to the stock. Price, $9.85.

**0-2166A. CURIOUS SPANISH FLINTLOCK MUSKET, OUTSIDE PATTERN LOCK.** The battery which receives the blow of the flint hammer is 1⅝ inches wide; hammer is held cocked by outside tumbler. Curious rear sight on the barrel. Full length, 5 feet. Walnut stock. In serviceable order. Price, $17.50.

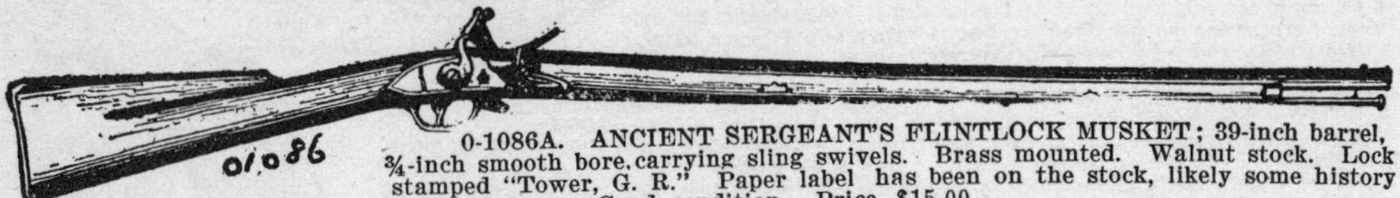

**0-1086A. ANCIENT SERGEANT'S FLINTLOCK MUSKET;** 39-inch barrel, ¾-inch smooth bore, carrying sling swivels. Brass mounted. Walnut stock. Lock stamped "Tower, G. R." Paper label has been on the stock, likely some history now unknown. Good condition. Price, $15.00.

**0-1086B. SERGEANT'S FLINTLOCK MUSKET,** similar to No. 0-1172, but without sling swivels and butt plate. Price, as is, $12.00.

**0-1167A. MAHOGANY STOCK SPANISH FLINTLOCK MUSKET.** Rare pattern outside lock. Set trigger. The hammer is held at half and full cock by projecting inside lock parts. Mahogany stock, with ivory butt plate. Full length, 61¼ inches. Octagonal barrel, gilt inlaid cross, cannons, drums, flags, etc.; 4 brass bands fastening stock and barrel. Serviceable order. Price, $28.50.

**0-1167A. FRENCH "TROMBLON" FLINTLOCK BLUNDERBUSS GUN**, issued to French Oriental Soldier. 22-inch barrel, about 2 inches across the bell-mouth muzzle. Known as the Tromblon de Mameluke, Versailles. Cost 150 francs the pair in 1813. Polished-steel barrel, brass name plate, brass wing-shaped rear sight, brass mountings. Good, strong lock. Walnut stock. Price, $27.50.

**0-1301. N. STARR & SON 1841 FLINTLOCK RIFLE**, with U. S. on lock and barrel, with inspector's mark, "J. H."; 36-inch round barrel, about 55 calibre; 7 deep rifle grooves. Steel patch box. Full length walnut stock. Three-banded gun with carrying swivels. In perfect order. Price, $25.00.

**0-1170. ANCIENT FLINTLOCK RELIC MUSKET.** Stock shows fine carved work. Lock and mountings were originally high class, but are now unserviceable from age and rust. The gun is only suitable for panoply decoration. Full length about 5 feet. Complete in part. Price, $8.50.

**0-1171. SIX CADET FLINTLOCK MUSKETS,** 29½-inch and 30½-inch barrels. Walnut stock. Two-band guns with carrying sling swivel. Brass mountings. Good working order. Price, $7.75 each.

**Lot XX. 18 OLD AMERICAN POWDER HORNS,** made by hand from cow and bull horns. The style used by American colonists with their flintlock muskets. Assorted sizes. Prices from $6.00 to $10.00.

**0-1196. FLINTLOCK MUSKET,** lock plate stamped with figures of "ELEPHANT AND CASTLE, WARRANTED." Looks like an African trader's gun. Full length, 5 feet. In good working order. Requires cleaning. Price, $8.85.

COSSACK SOLDIER, showing uniform, cartridge holder, gun and sword.

# KENTUCKY FLINTLOCK AND OTHER GUNS

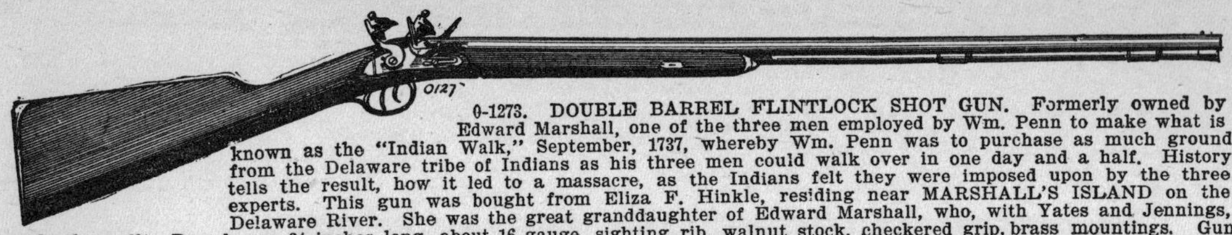


0-1273. DOUBLE BARREL FLINTLOCK SHOT GUN. Formerly owned by Edward Marshall, one of the three men employed by Wm. Penn to make what is known as the "Indian Walk," September, 1737, whereby Wm. Penn was to purchase as much ground from the Delaware tribe of Indians as his three men could walk over in one day and a half. History tells the result, how it led to a massacre, as the Indians felt they were imposed upon by the three experts. This gun was bought from Eliza F. Hinkle, residing near MARSHALL'S ISLAND on the Delaware River. She was the great granddaughter of Edward Marshall, who, with Yates and Jennings, made the walk. Barrels are 34 inches long, about 16 gauge, sighting rib, walnut stock, checkered grip, brass mountings. Gun is in complete, serviceable order. Has been well cared for. Price for this HISTORICAL RELIC, $100.00.

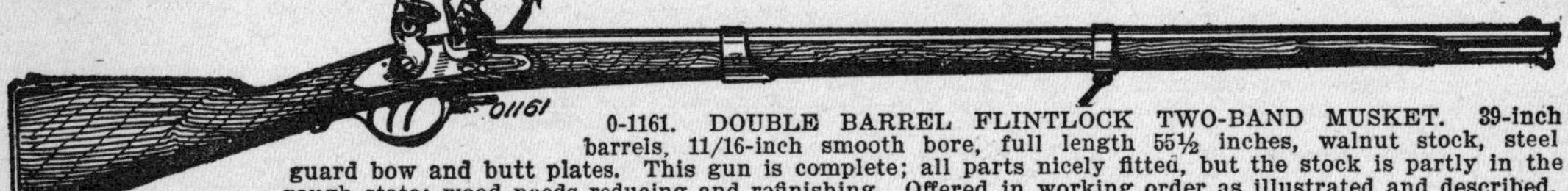


0-1161. DOUBLE BARREL FLINTLOCK TWO-BAND MUSKET. 39-inch barrels, 11/16-inch smooth bore, full length 55½ inches, walnut stock, steel guard bow and butt plates. This gun is complete; all parts nicely fitted, but the stock is partly in the rough state; wood needs reducing and refinishing. Offered in working order as illustrated and described. Double barrel flintlock muskets are rare. Price, $36.00.

0-1161A. DOUBLE BARREL FLINTLOCK MUSKET. Similar to No. 0-1161, but with shorter fore-end stock, 39½-inch barrels, 11/16-inch smooth bore. Neat fore-end. STEEL BAND fastening the stock and barrels together. Lock is in working order. Stock needs reducing and refinishing. Price, $30.00.

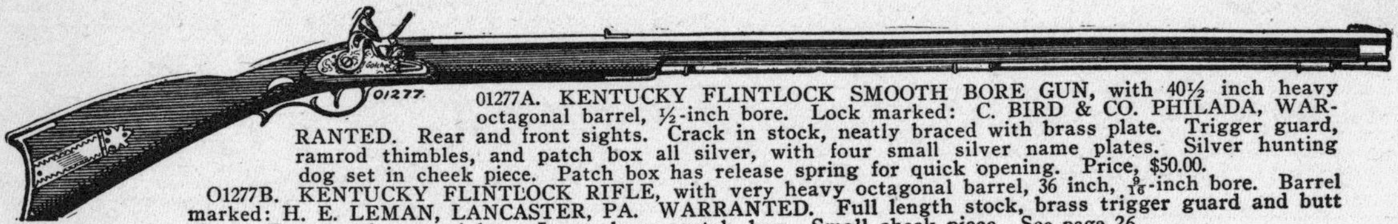


01277A. KENTUCKY FLINTLOCK SMOOTH BORE GUN, with 40½ inch heavy octagonal barrel, ½-inch bore. Lock marked: C. BIRD & CO. PHILADA, WARRANTED. Rear and front sights. Crack in stock, neatly braced with brass plate. Trigger guard, ramrod thimbles, and patch box all silver, with four small silver name plates. Silver hunting dog set in cheek piece. Patch box has release spring for quick opening. Price, $50.00.

O1277B. KENTUCKY FLINTLOCK RIFLE, with very heavy octagonal barrel, 36 inch, 7/16-inch bore. Barrel marked: H. E. LEMAN, LANCASTER, PA. WARRANTED. Full length stock, brass trigger guard and butt plate. Front and rear sights. Large brass patch box. Small cheek piece. See page 26.

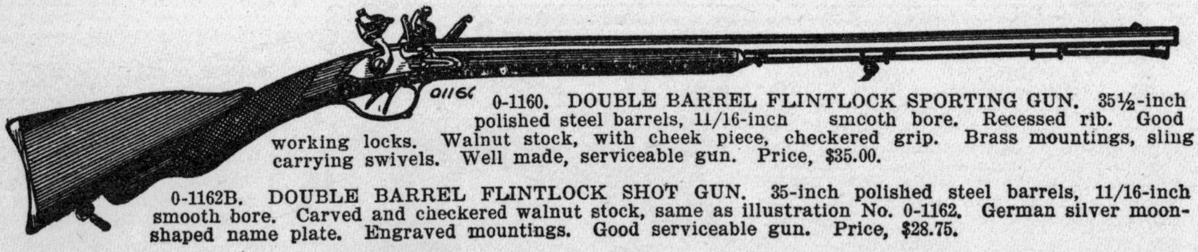


0-1160. DOUBLE BARREL FLINTLOCK SPORTING GUN. 35½-inch polished steel barrels, 11/16-inch smooth bore. Recessed rib. Good working locks. Walnut stock, with cheek piece, checkered grip. Brass mountings, sling carrying swivels. Well made, serviceable gun. Price, $35.00.

0-1162B. DOUBLE BARREL FLINTLOCK SHOT GUN. 35-inch polished steel barrels, 11/16-inch smooth bore. Carved and checkered walnut stock, same as illustration No. 0-1162. German silver moon-shaped name plate. Engraved mountings. Good serviceable gun. Price, $28.75.

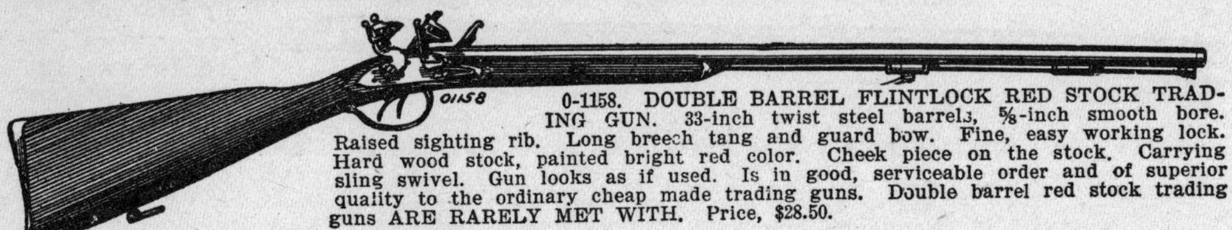


0-1158. DOUBLE BARREL FLINTLOCK RED STOCK TRADING GUN. 33-inch twist steel barrels, ⅝-inch smooth bore. Raised sighting rib. Long breech tang and guard bow. Fine, easy working lock. Hard wood stock, painted bright red color. Cheek piece on the stock. Carrying sling swivel. Gun looks as if used. Is in good, serviceable order and of superior quality to the ordinary cheap made trading guns. Double barrel red stock trading guns ARE RARELY MET WITH. Price, $28.50.

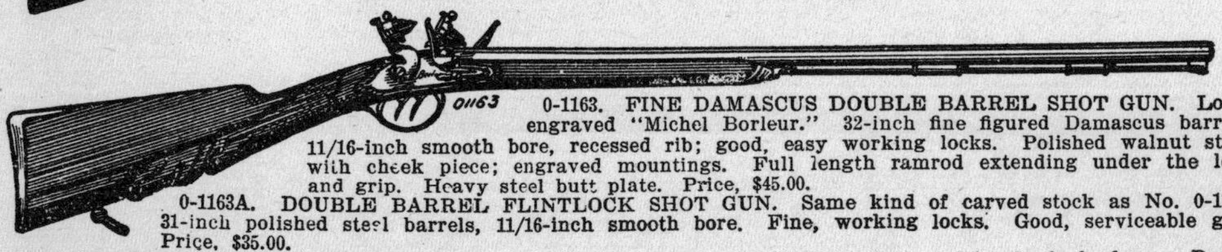


0-1163. FINE DAMASCUS DOUBLE BARREL SHOT GUN. Locks engraved "Michel Borleur." 32-inch fine figured Damascus barrels, 11/16-inch smooth bore, recessed rib; good, easy working locks. Polished walnut stock with cheek piece; engraved mountings. Full length ramrod extending under the lock and grip. Heavy steel butt plate. Price, $45.00.

0-1163A. DOUBLE BARREL FLINTLOCK SHOT GUN. Same kind of carved stock as No. 0-1163. 31-inch polished steel barrels, 11/16-inch smooth bore. Fine, working locks. Good, serviceable gun. Price, $35.00.

01277C. KENTUCKY FLINTLOCK RIFLE, with heavy octagonal barrel. 34 inch, with 7/16 inch bore. Barrel marked: HENRY FOLSOM & CO., ST. LOUIS, MO. Brass trigger guard, brass butt plate with extension tip. Front and rear sights. Small brass patch box. Price, $48.50.

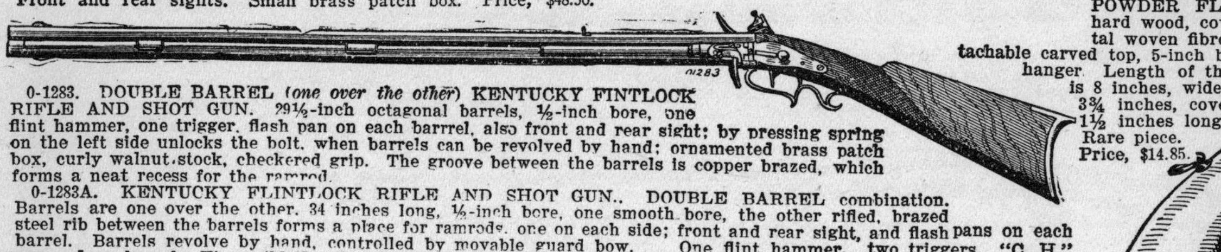


0-1283. DOUBLE BARREL (*one over the other*) KENTUCKY FINTLOCK RIFLE AND SHOT GUN. 29½-inch octagonal barrels, ½-inch bore, one flint hammer, one trigger, flash pan on each barrel, also front and rear sight; by pressing spring on the left side unlocks the bolt, when barrels can be revolved by hand; ornamented brass patch box, curly walnut stock, checkered grip. The groove between the barrels is copper brazed, which forms a neat recess for the ramrod.

0-1283A. KENTUCKY FLINTLOCK RIFLE AND SHOT GUN.. DOUBLE BARREL combination. Barrels are one over the other. 34 inches long, ½-inch bore, one smooth bore, the other rifled, brazed steel rib between the barrels forms a place for ramrods, one on each side; front and rear sight, and flash pans on each barrel. Barrels revolve by hand, controlled by movable guard bow. One flint hammer, two triggers. "C. H." engraved on barrels. Fine, ribbed, colored maple stock, with the characteristic Kentucky drop butt stock; ornamented brass patch box, half cheek. Fine old gun in good condition.

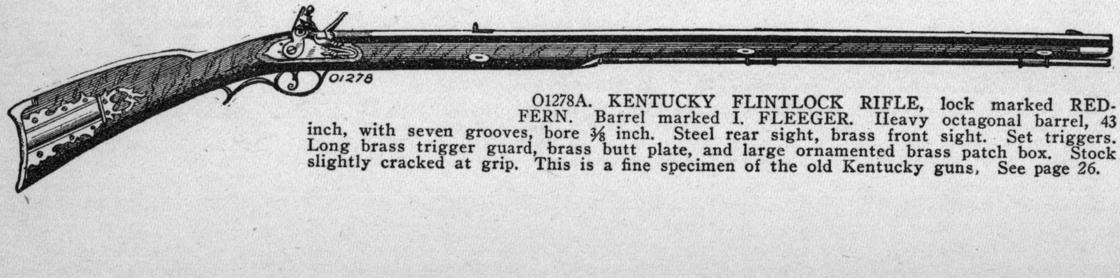


O1278A. KENTUCKY FLINTLOCK RIFLE, lock marked REDFERN. Barrel marked I. FLEEGER. Heavy octagonal barrel, 43 inch, with seven grooves, bore ⅜ inch. Steel rear sight, brass front sight. Set triggers. Long brass trigger guard, brass butt plate, and large ornamented brass patch box. Stock slightly cracked at grip. This is a fine specimen of the old Kentucky guns, See page 26.

0-1159B. DOUBLE BARREL FLINTLOCK SPORTING GUN. 39½-inch steel barrels, 11/16-inch smooth bore. Walnut stock. Good working lock. Serviceable gun. Price, $28.75.

0-1162BB. DOUBLE BARREL FLINTLOCK SPORTING GUN. Similar to No. 0-1162, with 34-inch barrels. Good serviceable order. Price, $28.75.

0-1163BB. DOUBLE BARREL FLINTLOCK SHOT GUN. 35-inch polished steel barrels, 11/16-inch smooth bore. Full length, partly concealed, ramrod. Carved walnut stock, with cheek piece. German silver crescent-shaped name plate. Engraved lock and mountings. Good, serviceable order. Good working locks. Price, $32.50.

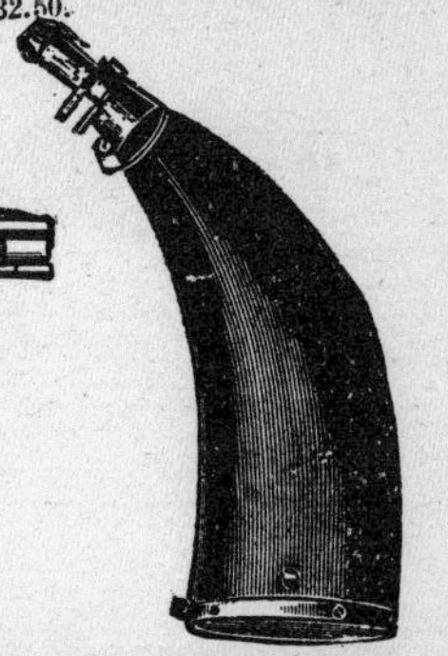

See other pages in this catalog for large assortment of powder horns and powder flasks of various periods, as used both in this country, England and Europe. We can supply the horn of the proper period to go with any of the guns listed.

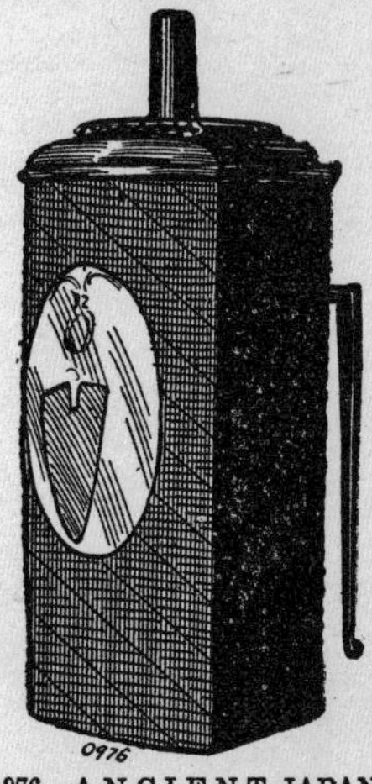


0-976. ANCIENT JAPANESE POWDER FLASK. Dark-colored hard wood, covered with ornamental woven fibre, with gilt seal, detachable carved top, 5-inch bronze engraved belt hanger. Length of the flask is 8 inches, widest width 3¾ inches, cover 1½ inches long. Rare piece. Price, $14.85.

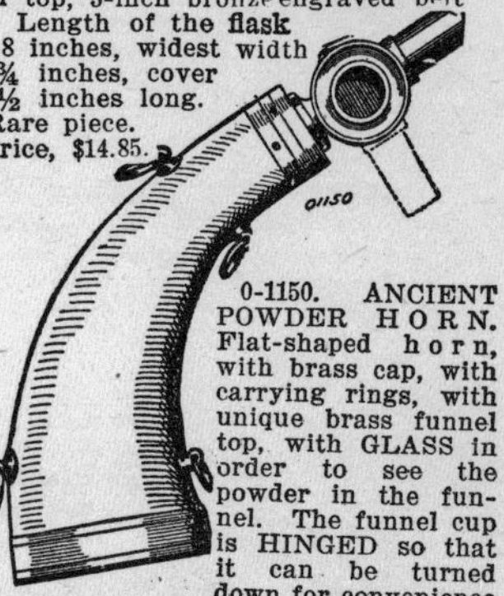


0-1150. ANCIENT POWDER HORN. Flat-shaped horn, with brass cap, with carrying rings, with unique brass funnel top, with GLASS in order to see the powder in the funnel. The funnel cup is HINGED so that it can be turned down for convenience in pouring the charge into the gun. Length is 9 inches. In good order. Price, $4.85.

**20 OLD SMOOTH-BORE FLINTLOCK MUSKETS**, ¾-inch bore; good, cleaned condition. Perhaps made about 1840. We offer them as they are for good, old-fashioned flint muskets. Price, $15.00 each. 6 Barnett's London-Make Flint-Lock Guns; good condition; assorted length of barrels and calibres. Price, $14.00 each.

**BURNSIDE'S B/L CARBINE CALIBRE 54.** The FIRST of the many models of guns used so largely in the Civil War, invented by General Burnside—stamped as having been made by the "Bristol Firearms Co." The breech block is unjointed, and the gun is without a fore stock. Made and issued to U. S. Troops before the Civil War. Rare. Price, $17.50.

**0-1300. "TRYON, PHILAD" STAMPED ON CHASED LOCK OF KENTUCKY FLINT GUN;** heavy 42½-inch octagonal barrel, ½-inch smooth bore. Dark-colored maple stock, slightly ribbed at the butt; half check-piece; neat patch box. In good condition. Weight, 10½ lbs. Price, $37.50.

**0-966. FRENCH DOUBLE BARREL FLINTLOCK SHOT GUN.** Lock is engraved "J. B. Brunon a St. Etienne;" 3-foot partly octagonal barrel, engraved "Canon-roi;" ½-inch smooth bore. Silver name plate; carrying swivels; rounded butt plate. Well preserved old gun, serviceable order. Price, $37.50.

**BALLARD B/L RIFLE,** calibre 56, rimfire, triangular bayonet. Made at "Fall River, Mass." Only a few Ballard rifles were used during the Civil War. The rifles are rare. Price, $25.00.

**NEW U. S. SPRINGFIELD FLINTLOCK MUSKET 1816.** Price, $40.00.

**ELI WHITNEY 1831 MUSKET,** originally flintlock. Altered in 1862 to percussion lock for arming the Civil War volunteers. The gun has the original lock plate stamped with the ARROW AND OLIVE BRANCH (Peace and War Emblem), "E. Whitney, U. S., New Haven, 1831." The barrel is stamped 1862; 69 calibre. Rare weapon. Price, $20.00.

**REMINGTON-MAYNARD PRIMER LOCK CIVIL WAR RIFLED MUSKET** (converted model '42 musket), altered by Remington, Ilion, N. Y., in 1857, at the contract price of $3.00 each. Issued to volunteers at the outbreak of the Civil War. Calibre 69; rifled bore; has button on the gate of primer lock; large hammer. Rare. Price, $18.00.

**J. H. MERRILL, BALTO. 1858. B/L RIFLE,** made for the U. S. Navy at cost price $60.00 each; calibre 52, complete with sword bayonet. Merrill rifles are rare. Price, $25.00.

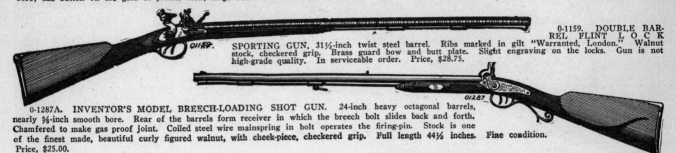

**SPORTING GUN,** 31½-inch twist steel barrel. Ribs marked in gilt "Warranted, London." Walnut stock, checkered grip. Brass guard bow and butt plate. Slight engraving on the locks. Gun is not high-grade quality. In serviceable order. Price, $28.75.

**0-1159. DOUBLE BARREL FLINT LOCK**

**0-1287A. INVENTOR'S MODEL BREECH-LOADING SHOT GUN.** 24-inch heavy octagonal barrels, nearly ⅝-inch smooth bore. Rear of the barrels form receiver in which the breech bolt slides back and forth. Chamfered to make gas proof joint. Coiled steel wire mainspring in bolt operates the firing-pin. Stock is one of the finest made, beautiful curly figured walnut, with cheek-piece, checkered grip. Full length 44½ inches. Fine condition. Price, $25.00.

**CULVERIN.** The introduction of cast-iron projectiles, which are much stronger and denser than those of stone, led to the invention of a new species of cannon called culverins, which very nearly correspond in construction and appearance to the guns of the present day. The great strength of these pieces and their projectiles permitted the use of a large charge of powder and their introduction proved an important step in the improvement of artillery. The idea was entertained by ancient artillerists founded on the relation which cannon were erroneously supposed to bear to small-arms that the range increased with the length of the piece; and in consequence many culverins were made of enormous length. A remarkable piece of this description still exists at Dover, England, familiarly known as "Queen Anne's pocket-piece." While it carries a ball weighing only 18 pounds, it is more than 25 feet long.—From *Farrow's Military Encyclopedia.*

**1 KENTUCKY GUN,** marked Ketlaand and Jacob Adam. Has patchbox. This flint-lock rifle is in good order. Price, $30.00.

**1 KENTUCKY FLINT-LOCK RIFLE,** marked Ashmore. Has heavy octagon barrel with seven grooves about calibre 40. Has set trigger. Complete with mould for $48.00.

**3054. ONION & WHEELOCK ENGLISH P/L DOUBLE GUN,** 30-inch barrels, 11-inch bore, engraved with hunting scenes. Weight, 10 pounds 8 ounces. Checkered grip, walnut stock. Serviceable order. Price, $25.00.

**3059. R. S. CLARKE P/L DOUBLE BARREL SHOT GUN,** 33 inch twist steel barrels. Weight, 8¼ pounds, not a high class gun, rusty, poor order. Price, "as is" $5.00.

**B/L LIGHT WEIGHT ENGLISH SHOT GUN.** Hammer model, with 30-inch barrels, 12 gauge. Left bbl. full choke, right bbl. cylinder bore. Weight about 6¾ pounds. Made by Wilkes of London. High grade gun in very good condition. Price, $50.00.

**3067. 14 BORE DOUBLE GUN,** 31½-inch barrels. Weight, 7 pounds 14 ounces. In poor order, rusty. Low class gun. Price, $4.85.

**3068. LIGHT WEIGHT CHEAP MADE OLD DOUBLE BARREL SHOT GUN,** 18 bore, 33-inch twist steel barrel. Weight, 6 pounds. Working order. Price, $4.85.

**3052. MORTIMER LONDON P/L DOUBLE GUN,** 38-inch smooth bore, 10 gauge, fine twist steel barrels. Weight, 13 pounds 3 ounces. Twist steel rib. Platinum side tip, silvered side, name and fore end plates. Lock engraved Mortimer, curly walnut checkered grip stock. Old pattern, pineapple engraving on guard plate. Silver cap box in the butt stock. Mortimer is considered one of the best of the last century gun makers. Gun in second hand, serviceable order. Price, $35.00.

**3062. OLD DOUBLE BARREL, PERCUSSION LOCK SHOT GUN,** 13 bore, 35 inch barrels, weight 8 pounds. Serviceable, second hand order. Eagle head engraved on the butt stock. Good old gun. Price, $8.00.

**3063. OLD DOUBLE BARREL P/L SHOT GUN,** checkered grip, cheek piece on stock. Strong, well made gun. 17 bore, 30 inch barrels. Weight 7 pounds 10 ounces. Serviceable, second hand order. Price, $8.00.

**3072. 13 BORE VERY OLD DOUBLE BARREL SHOT GUN,** percussion lock, 31½ inch barrel. Weight, 9 pounds 6 ounces. Walnut stock, broken and repaired a number of times. An old relic. Platinum breech lining. Price, $4.85.

**3074. PAIR OF LONDON FINE TWIST STEEL DOUBLE BARRELS,** 13 bore, with locks made by Brownson, Slomen & Hopkins, complete gun all but the butt stock. Price, "as is" $4.85.

**U. S. FLINT-LOCK MUSKET. MODEL OF 1822.** Calibre .69. This type of musket was made at Springfield and Harper's Ferry arsenals and also by contractors. The first of these arms appeared about 1825, in spite of the fact that lock plates are found marked "1822." They continued to be supplied to the army and militia until 1836, when the new model first appeared. Guns weigh ten pounds and are in excellent original condition in spite of their age. Price, $25.00.

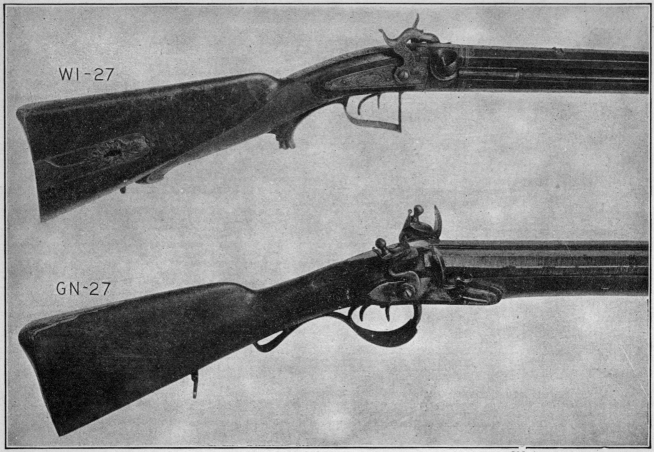

**WI-27. DOUBLE BARREL OVER & UNDER SPORTING RIFLE,** with 24-inch octagon barrel with inlaid silver breeches. Brass tipped wood rod fitted on right side. Checkered wood grip, 4½-inch patch box, 6-inch cheek piece. Ornamented 4-inch back action locks. Square front trigger guard, with wood pistol grip. Locks marked: C. PIRKO, IN WEIN. This is evidently a sporting gun made to order. Sights missing.   Price **$25.00.**

**GN-27. FRENCH FLINT LOCK DOUBLE BARREL SHOT GUN,** period LOUIS XIV, with 27-inch half octagon barrels, silver front sight, top rib or gutter for sighting. 5½-inch wood cheek piece, 5-inch locks, extra wide trigger guard with acorn end. Brass tipped wood rod, 2 sling swivels. Bore 13/16 inches. Heavy guns of this type are rare. Sold to collector.

**GN-27-1. FRENCH FLINT LOCK DOUBLE BARREL FOWLING PIECE,** light weight, with 29-inch half octagon barrels, bore 9/16th inches. Barrel muzzle worn through at tips. 5¼-inch locks, 6-inch cheek piece, checkered grip, wide trigger guard with acorn end. Spring bayonet with 6¼-inch flat blade fitted to the under side of barrels at muzzle and released by spring catch at tip of fore end. This type of gun used in hunting boars.   Price **$50.00.**

### VETERAN OF MANY WARS.

U. S. Springfield, 1812, Flint Lock stamped on the barrel U.S.—S. N. Y., with Eagle head P. V. Viewed and Proved—S. N. Y. indicates that the gun was issued to New York State Soldiers in war of 1812. This old veteran was purchased in lot from U. S. Arsenal after the Civil war. No doubt used in all the wars at and since 1812 up to close of 1865. Good working order. Price **$30.00.**

**No. 1822. FLINT LOCK MUSKETOON;** ⅝ smooth bore, 29-inch barrel. Full length, 45 inches. 2 band gun; in working order.   Price **$10.00.**

**CHARLEVILLE FLINT LOCK MUSKETOON.** 25-inch barrel, ⅝ smooth bore. Full length, 39½ inches. 2 band gun. The U. S. Government took the Charleville musket for a model when it began making guns at the National Armory in 1800. Charleville **Musketoons** are quite rare.   Price **$30.00.**

**No. 1515. FRENCH FLINT LOCK ARMY MUSKET,** engraved on the lock plate the name De Mauberg. Full length, 53½ inches. 38-inch barrel, ⅝ smooth bore. In working order.   **$10.00.**

**No. 1516. 1777 FRENCH ARMY FLINT LOCK MUSKET,** engraved on the breech 1777; on the lock "Mre. Imp. de Versailles." 41-inch barrel; full length, 56 inches. Brass guard, butt plate and side plate. Brass bands; ⅝ smooth bore. Many French lock muskets were used during the American Revolutionary War. This gun may be part of the lot brought over by Lafayette, and which the American Government took as model when the National Armory at Springfield, Mass., in 1800, commenced to manufacture flint lock muskets. This gun is in working order.   Price **$28.00.**

War of 1812. View of U. S. A. soldier file three deep. Front and center rank men firing, rear rank man priming.—From Bannerman's Book on War Weapons.

Old American Flint Lock Musket, with brass butt on which there is hammerlike head projection for using the gun as a club. Made by Eli Whitney, New Haven, Conn.; good order. Price **$15.00.**

1812 Flint Lock Musket; stamped on lock "S. N. Y."; vouched for as having been used in the Battle of Plattsburgh; small piece of the muzzle blown off, otherwise in good order. Price **$25.00.**

Old Flint Lock Musket; altered to percussion lock by closing up the vent and screwing nipple on the top of barrel. The flint lock hammer has been retained, with a piece of steel inserted in place of the flint stone; in good condition; requires cleaning; this hammer is rare. Price **$18.00.**

Old Flint Lock, from collection made of battlefield relics by Southern gentleman; stamped on lock plate "Mauberg Manf. R. Co."; barrel is 45 inches long, about ¾ bore; barrel fastened to the stock with bands, as in Revolutionary War period; flint lock made in France; rusty relic; cleaned. Price **$18.00.**

G. R. Tower and Crown Flint Lock Musket, which means George's Reign, inspected at Tower of London, with British Crown Mark; gun has 27-inch barrel; in good order. Price **$9.75.**

G. R. Tower and Crown Flint Lock Musket with ashwood stock; short barrel. Price **$8.75.**

Dublin Castle S. R. with cross over the crown engraved on the lock of an old flint lock gun. Barrel is 28 inches long. Period of manufacture, about 1750. Serviceable order. **$25.00.**

**No. 0-1112A. FRENCH FLINT LOCK BLUNDERBUSS PISTOL.** Length 13 inches, brass barrel 7¼ inches, with ellipse muzzle, 7/16th inches. Round wood butt, iron ramrod, trigger guard with acorn end. Period Louis XIV. Price **$25.00.** (See No. 0-1112, page 98.)

Holland Rampart Flint Lock Guns; full length, 6 feet 4 inches; octagonal barrel; slightly bell-mouthed at muzzle; weight, 17 pounds; stock shows signs of age, also slightly worm-eaten; complete working order; ramrod missing; rusted, requires cleaning; small projection at rear of barrel for use in sighting. Genuine old relic; ¾-inch bore; barrel is nearly 5 feet long. Price $15.00.

10159. "Wilson Flintlock, 1727 Minories, London," stamped on old flint-lock, long-barrel musket, with ancient proof marks on the 42-inch barrel. Small brush for cleaning flash-pan, attached with brass chain; stock shows repairing; in second-hand serviceable order. Price, $30.00.

**No. 000. OLD CASTLE WALL RAMPART FLINT-LOCK MUSKET**, length over six feet, weight 20 pounds; one-inch muzzle; has spike for resting on the wall; old proof marks; second hand shooting order, with large flint. Price $17.50.
Another Gun which is similar, which has been altered to percussion lock. Price $10.00.

7131. African Trader's Female Flintlock Gun, 52-inch barrel, full length 62 inches, ⅝-inch smooth bore, red stock with hook-shaped comb; called by traders the Female Gun. The regular form of stock is designated in Africa as the male. Gun is in good working order. Price, $9.85.

**No. 1368. ANTIQUE GERMAN FLINT LOCK RIFLE ENGRAVED "FRANTZ HALM."** Octagonal barrel; ½-inch bore; 7 rifle grooves with cheek piece on stock; flint box; cover finely carved; bronze mountings; engraved guard, with armored soldier; side plate engraved with dogs chasing deer. Curly walnut stock, carved black horn tip; old time weapon; serviceable order. 28 inches full length; hand grip guard; double trigger. Price $25.00.

**No. 1498. AFRICAN CHIEFS' LONG FLINT LOCK MUSKET**; stock painted bright red. Good strong serviceable gun. Full length, 67½ inches. Barrel has two proof marks. Lock stamped "warranted," with elephant bearing castle. Brass guard, butt plate and ramrod holders; also name plate. Has old style under-pin fastening barrel to stock. The German Government forbade the importation into their African Colonies of guns for natives, that have the barrel and stock fastened together with a band. We presume for the reason that the natives could use the gun as an old time war club. A very showy gun. Like new. A sample should be included in all complete collections. Price $8.50.

Flint Lock Traders' Guns; assorted lengths; with barrel fastened to stock with brass bands. Black or red painted stock. Price, $12.00 each.

Flint Lock Fowling Gun, with twist steel barrel; new; made for the African trade. Various calibres and lengths. Price, $14.00 each.
One Rampart Percussion Lock Gun; 6 feet long; serviceable, second-hand; antique. Price, $15.00.
Two Portugese Traders' Flint Lock Lazarino Guns; stock colored red; new guns; shopworn. Price, $9.00.
Flint Lock Sporting Gun, with pistol grip. Damascus 34-inch barrel; ½-inch smooth bore; checkered stock. Price, $13.00.
**No. 1066. OLD GERMAN RIFLE WITH J. J. KLINKELBERG** in gold letters on barrel. Percussion lock; fair order; with web sling. Walnut stock, checkered grip, with cheek piece. Price $8.85.
**EARLY 18TH CENTURY GERMAN FLINT LOCK SPORTING RIFLE**; 31-inch octagonal barrel; ⅝ bore; 7 rifled grooves. Fine old Wheelock style; handsomely carved stock with cheek piece; with beautiful gilt metal ornamentations. Handsome old gun. Price $60.00.
**No. 1367. FLINT LOCK SPORTING GUN.** Bright steel barrel, checkered walnut stock with grip and fore-end. Fine order. Length of barrel, 41 inches; 9-16 smooth bore with sling swivels. Original ramrod replaced. Price $15.00.

Sebago Lake, Me.
Dec. 22, 1925.

Dear Sir:
Received old Belgian Flintlock Pistol and was very much pleased with it. I immediately loaded it up with powder and shot and fired it and it worked O. K.

Yours truly,
HARRY INGALLS.

## MYSTERY OF AN ANCIENT INDUSTRY

A brief account of the revival of flint knapping in Brandon, Suffolk, England, recently reprinted on this page from the London *Daily Express*, cannot have failed to excite wonder in the minds of many who read that Brandon knappers are fashioning flints for guns. According to an official statement, improvements in machine guns will enable them to fire 600 bullets a minute. Why, then, should there be a demand for flint-lock guns; where are they used? To whom is sold a weapon which it must take minutes to load and prime in order to fire a single shot?

Knapping of flint may be the oldest living industry. It certainly must be the one industry carried on now nearly in the manner the American Indian fashioned his spear and arrow heads, as prehistoric man must have worked to produce his knives and axes. There has been some improvements in the methods of knapping, according to one authority, who writes:

"The most difficult process is the flaking, or driving off of flakes, at a single blow, of a given width and thickness, with two ribs running down them. In this, the Brandon knappers excel the prehistoric workman, but the process is so delicate that few attain to great proficiency."

Even to-day the knapper's tools consist of three simple forms of hammer and chisel.

Poets from the time of the earliest English bards down to the including so modern a singer as *Burns* have made much use of the various forms of the word knapper to describe a sound, a blow, the act of breaking. A new poet should sing of the men of Brandon knapping flints from the flint deposits of Suffolk, where, says our London contemporary, "the industry has been carried on since the neolithic age." And always with the same purpose—to make deadly weapons.

—*From N. Y. Sun, Aug. 2, 1920.*

Illustration of ancient battle scene.

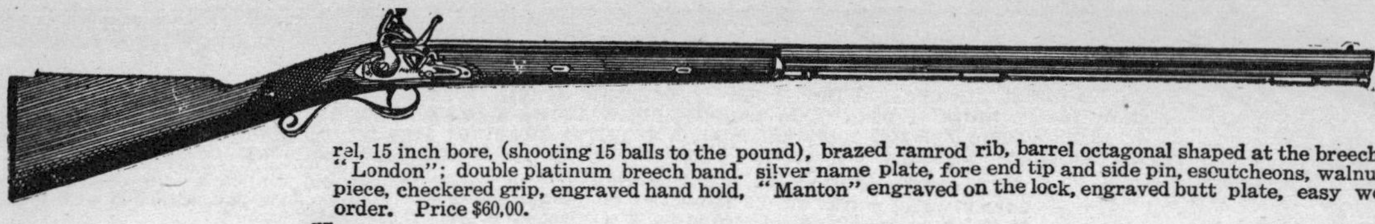

**6927. Manton.** London Flintlock Sporting Gun, 36 inch twist steel bar- rel, 15 inch bore, (shooting 15 balls to the pound), brazed ramrod rib, barrel octagonal shaped at the breech, inlaid gold letters, "London"; double platinum breech band, silver name plate, fore end tip and side pin, escutcheons, walnut stock with check piece, checkered grip, engraved hand hold, "Manton" engraved on the lock, engraved butt plate, easy working lock, in fine order. Price $60.00.

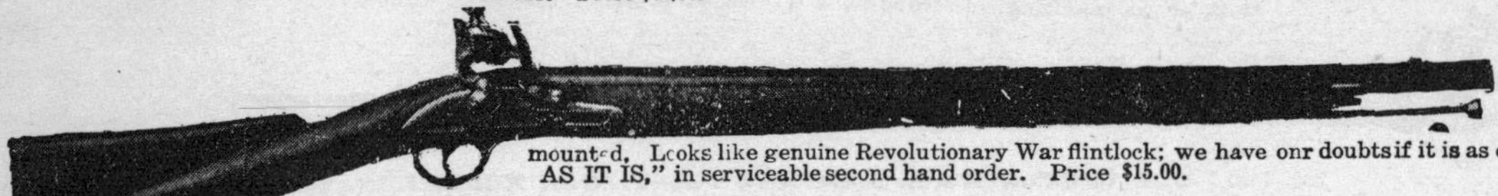

**3411. British Tower Flintlock Musket,** full length 55 ½ inche s barrel 34 ½ inches, smooth bore, under pin fastening, Tower and crown, G. R., and broad arrow marks on the lock. Brass mounted. Looks like genuine Revolutionary War flintlock; we have our doubts if it is as old a gun as it looks. We offer it AS IT IS," in serviceable second hand order. Price $15.00.

**3111. Early Pattern Percussion Lock Gun** marked "Pennsylvania Rifle Works"; 38 inch smooth bore, barrel with ramrod rib. Brass mountings, wood stock, good serviceable guns work of early American gun makers. Price $8.50.

**Military Cadet Flintlock Musket,** 37 ½ inches, barrel about calibre 70, full length 52 ½ inches. Walnut stock, polished barrel and mountings. Fine serviceable order. Price $9.85.

**3130. Early American Hunting Rifle,** heavy octagonal barrel, 40 calibre, ramrod rib, curly walnut stock, checkered grip, check piece, inlaid silver mounting with eagle and shield, double trigger, brass mountings. Price $18.00.

**Harper's Ferry 1824 Flintlock Musket,** with old Revolutionary War spade      et from collector in Maine; 42 inch barrel, in second hand working order. Small piece of this stock broken out, caused by stroke of lightning. Price $14.85.

**7121. Long Barrel Gun Made for African Traders,** captured from the natives in war with British. The gun shows where natives have repaired the broken metal bands with bands of fibre. It is the policy of Great Brit- ain to destroy all guns captured in war from their enemies. As an officer said to the writer, 'While we might get a pound ($5.00) for the gun, it would cost us 20 pounds ($100.00) to re- capture it." This captured gun no doubt was brought home to England as a souvenir by a returning soldier. Price $8.85.

**3390. EMPEROR FREDERICK, 1777 POTSDAM FLINTLOCK MUSKET,** smooth bore; serviceable relic of the great battles in which Frederick the Great's soldiers took part; 1777 stamped on the breech. Potsdam on the lock; a second date on the barrel 1810, evidently the date when the gun was sent to the Armory to be repaired. Also stamped I-C, No. 190. Perhaps used in the battle of Waterloo, June 1815. Full length 57 inches, barrel 41 inches, brass mounted; rare relic. Price $35.00.

**3390A. GERMAN ARMY FLINTLOCK MUSKET,** marked on the lock with crown, Potsdam, letters S. G., brass mounted; repair mark on the barrel 1817, ser- viceable relic. Price $18.00.

**3300B. FREDERICK WILHELM FLINTLOCK ARMY MUSKET,** marked on the lock F. W., crown and S. O. A. R. R. In appearance like No. 3390. Price $20.00.

**3390C. POTSDAM AND CROWN ON LOCK PLATE OF OLD FLINTLOCK,** smooth bore musket, Armory repair date on the barrel 1828, crown F. B., letter A, similar in appearance to gun No. 3390, BROKEN STOCK. Offered, "as is," $10.00.

**3390D. OLD GERMAN ARMY FLINTLOCK SMOOTH BORE MUSKETS,** from old German Arm- ory; similar in appearance to No. 3390. Guns are without any marks. Are in serviceable order. Price $10.00 each.

**5015. ANCIENT INDIA HIDE SHIELD,** four ornamental bosses, with arm loops on the reverse side, 21 ½ inches in diameter, same as illustration of 1790; carried by native Indian warriors. Price $12.50.

**6926.** Ancient Moorish Flintlock Gun with outside lock, pan primer (projects 1 ½ inches), barrel is almost entirely covered with ornamented brass. Full length 63 inches, shoulder piece at the butt 10 ¼ inches long, 3 ¼ inches in width. Leather grip stock orna- mented with small red stones. Gun is from the Kyble tribe, who are always fighting. Rare weapon. Price $40.00.

**Flintlock Blunderbuss,** inlaid silver engraving, in fine order like new, length 21 inches, diameter at the muzzle, 1 ¼ inches. Evidently from the engravings once belonged to some Persian officer. Octagonal bar- rel, inlaid gold seals, ornamented with sun's rays, in- scription from the Koran, etc. Price $40.00.

**First American Breech-loading Flintlock Musket,** stamped "J. H. Hall, H. Ferry, U.S., 1831." This is the earliest date B/L made at the U. S. Arsenal, Harper's Ferry, Va. The armory buildings which the Hall's rifles were made was the only one captured by John Brown. It was raided to obtain guns to arm the negroes. This particular gun came from the collection of Adam Oliver, who was master armorer for the Confederates at Augusta, Arsenal, Ga. Rare gun. Price $75.00.

**3108.** Old Flintlock Musket, lacks two inches of 6 feet, large bore, brass butt and guard plate, good working order. Price $10.00.

**3109.** War of 1812 Flintlock Army Musket, stamped on lock "E. Buell, Marlborough, Conn," pattern 1808. Evidently army contract guns. Full length 57 ½ inches, from the Stillwell collection, complete with bayonet, in working order. Price $25.00.

**3116.** "D. Egg, London," Flintlock Shot Gun, 41 ½ inches, smooth bore, barrel 20 inches, broad ivory for end tip, walnut stock, working order. Price $10.00.

**3118.** U. S. Mi  r y 1825 Percussion Lock Gun, German Eagle proof mark barrel. U. S. lock and butt plate, (rear sight missing). Price $12.00.

**3119.** U. S. A. Flintlock Musket, 1838 marked on the barrel, cap box, and butt plate, V. P  in working order. Price $12.00.

**3120.** Army Flintlock Musket, facsimile of the famous Charleville French musket, adopted by the U. S. Government in making first pattern guns. This gun is without any marks. Muzzle end of the barrel worn almost through. In working order. Price $15.00.

**AM271. FINE PAIR FRENCH FLINT LOCK PISTOLS WITH BELL MUZZLES.** Seven-inch octagonal barrel with small flare at muzzle. Total length 12½ inches. 4½-inch lock marked: LE JEUNE MOREAU. Ornamented trigger guard with urn end, flat butt with ornament. Engraved side and hammer screws. French pistols of this type are rare. Price for pair $38.00.

Illustration of India soldier, period of 1756, with matchlock and embossed hide shield and scimitar shaped sword, from Bannerman's book "Weapons of War."

**7106A. BRITISH FLINT LOCK FOWLING PIECE,** with 33-inch round bar- rel, browned finish. Barrel marked: BATH STREET BIRMINGHAM. Bore 13/16th, brass tipped wood rod, square front trigger guard, checkered grip, 5-inch cheek piece. Fore end tip, escutcheons of silver, with silver monogram oval. Breech inlaid with two gold strips. Ornamented lock marked: WILLM. HOLLIS. Price, $32.00. See No. 7106 on page 33.

**7106B. BRITISH FLINT LOCK FOWLING PIECE,** light weight, with 33- inch round barrel, bore ⅝ inch. Breech re-inforced with two strips of gold, also makers name set in gold: WAKLEY BRIDGEWATER. Silver mounted, check- ered grip, round guard with pineapple end. 4¾-inch lock marked: M. & W. WAKLEY. Price, $38.00.

**X4. FRENCH FLINTLOCK BLUNDERBUSS PISTOL,** half- length stock, round butt, brass mounted, with brass trigger guard. 5½-inch flat lock, 8½-inch barrel, part octagon, with very large muzzle, 2⅛ inches. Full length 15 inches. Price $21.00.

**685. ANCIENT FLINTLOCK RIFLE,** with hair trigger, octagonal barrel, with slight increase in diameter at the muzzle. Letters PTM set in gold oval on each side of the barrel, with lion seal in the center. Finger-guard lever. Barrel knot fore end. Has been a fine rifle. Shows much usage. Fair order. From the Vitrac collection. Price, $25.00.

# Double and Single Barrel Flint Guns

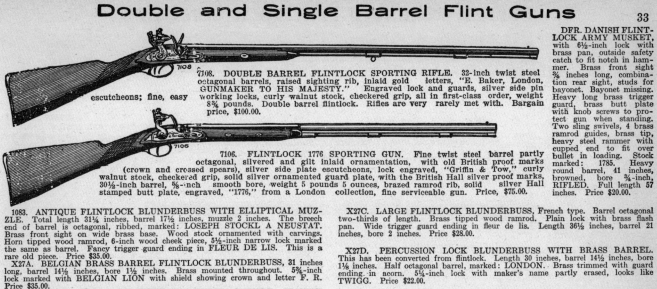

**7108. DOUBLE BARREL FLINTLOCK SPORTING RIFLE.** 32-inch twist steel octagonal barrels, raised sighting rib, inlaid gold letters, "E. Baker, London, GUNMAKER TO HIS MAJESTY." Engraved lock and guards, silver side pin working locks, curly walnut stock, checkered grip, all in first-class order, weight 8¾ pounds. Double barrel flintlock. Rifles are very rarely met with. Bargain price, $100.00.

escutcheons; fine, easy

**7106. FLINTLOCK 1776 SPORTING GUN.** Fine twist steel barrel partly octagonal, silvered and gilt inlaid ornamentation, with old British proof marks (crown and crossed spears), silver side plate escutcheons, lock engraved, "Griffin & Tow," curly walnut stock, checkered grip, solid silver ornamented guard plate, with the British Hall silver proof marks, 30½-inch barrel, ⅝-inch smooth bore, weight 5 pounds 5 ounces, brazed ramrod rib, solid silver Hall stamped butt plate, engraved, "1776," from a London collection, fine serviceable gun. Price, $75.00.

**DFR. DANISH FLINT-LOCK ARMY MUSKET,** with 6½-inch lock with brass pan, outside safety catch to fit notch in hammer. Brass front sight ¾ inches long, combination rear sight, studs for bayonet. Bayonet missing. Heavy long brass trigger guard, brass butt plate with knob screws to protect gun when standing. Two sling swivels, 4 brass ramrod guides, brass tip, heavy steel rammer with cupped end to fit over bullet in loading. Stock marked: 1785. Heavy round barrel, 41 inches, browned, bore ¾-inch, RIFLED. Full length 57 inches. Price $20.00.

**1083. ANTIQUE FLINTLOCK BLUNDERBUSS WITH ELLIPTICAL MUZZLE.** Total length 31¼ inches, barrel 17½ inches, muzzle 2 inches. The breech end of barrel is octagonal, ribbed, marked: LOSEPH STOCKL A NEUSTAT. Brass front sight on wide brass base. Wood stock ornamented with carvings. Horn tipped wood ramrod, 6-inch wood cheek piece, 5½-inch narrow lock marked the same as barrel. Fancy trigger guard ending in FLEUR DE LIS. This is a rare old piece. Price $35.00.

**X27A. BELGIAN BRASS BARREL FLINTLOCK BLUNDERBUSS,** 31 inches long, barrel 14½ inches, bore 1½ inches. Brass mounted throughout. 5¾-inch lock marked with BELGIAN LION with shield showing crown and letter F. R. Price $35.00.

**X27B. EXTRA LARGE BLUNDERBUSS WITH OUTSIDE SPANISH FLINTLOCK.** Total length 37½ inches, barrel 23½ inches, bore 2⅛ inches. Heavy wood stock, iron mounted. Blunderbusses with Spanish lock are rare. Price $32.00.

**X27C. LARGE FLINTLOCK BLUNDERBUSS,** French type. Barrel octagonal two-thirds of length. Brass tipped wood ramrod. Plain lock with brass flash pan. Wide trigger guard ending in fleur de lis. Length 36½ inches, barrel 21 inches, bore 2 inches. Price $28.00.

**X27D. PERCUSSION LOCK BLUNDERBUSS WITH BRASS BARREL.** This has been converted from flintlock. Length 30 inches, barrel 14½ inches, bore 1⅛ inches. Half octagonal brass, marked: LONDON. Brass trimmed with guard ending in acorn. 5¼-inch lock with maker's name partly erased, looks like TWIGG. Price $22.00.

**X27E. BELGIAN FLINTLOCK BLUNDERBUSS,** with heavy brass guard and butt plate. 5½-inch lock, 17½-inch barrel, part octagon, with extra large bell muzzle, 2⅛ inches. Sporting length stock, polished. Price $23.00.

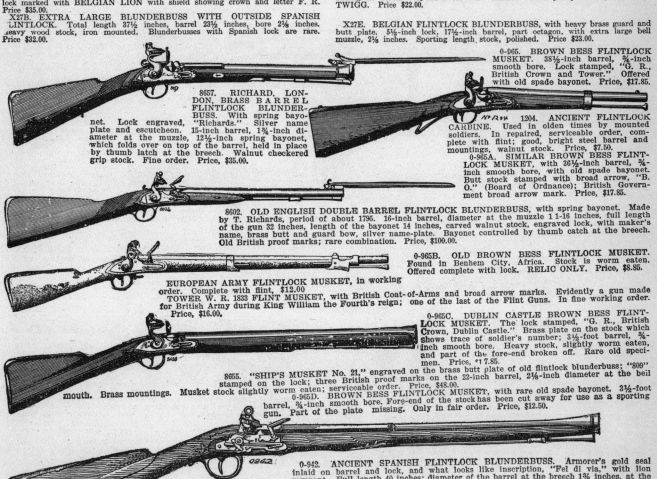

**8657. RICHARD, LONDON, BRASS BARREL FLINTLOCK BLUNDERBUSS.** With spring bayonet. Lock engraved, "Richards." Silver name plate and escutcheon. 15-inch barrel, 1¾-inch diameter at the muzzle, 12½-inch spring bayonet, which folds over on top of the barrel, held in place by thumb latch at the breech. Walnut checkered grip stock. Fine order. Price, $35.00.

**0-965. BROWN BESS FLINTLOCK MUSKET.** 38½-inch barrel, ¾-inch smooth bore. Lock stamped, "G. R., British Crown and Tower." Offered with old spade bayonet. Price, $17.85.

**1204. ANCIENT FLINTLOCK CARBINE.** Used in olden times by mounted soldiers. In repaired, serviceable order, complete with flint; good, bright steel barrel and mountings, walnut stock. Price, $7.50.

**0-965A. SIMILAR BROWN BESS FLINTLOCK MUSKET,** with 36½-inch barrel, ¾-inch smooth bore, with old spade bayonet. Butt stock stamped with broad arrow, "B. O." (Board of Ordnance); British Government broad arrow mark. Price, $17.85.

**8602. OLD ENGLISH DOUBLE BARREL FLINTLOCK BLUNDERBUSS,** with spring bayonet. Made by T. Richards, period of about 1795. 16-inch barrel, diameter at the muzzle 1 1-16 inches, full length of the gun 32 inches, length of the bayonet 14 inches, carved walnut stock, engraved lock, with maker's name, brass butt and guard bow, silver name-plate. Bayonet controlled by thumb catch at the breech. Old British proof marks; rare combination. Price, $100.00.

**0-965B. OLD BROWN BESS FLINTLOCK MUSKET.** Found in Benhem City, Africa. Stock is worm eaten. Offered complete with lock. RELIC ONLY. Price, $8.85.

**EUROPEAN ARMY FLINTLOCK MUSKET, in working order.** Complete with flint, $12.00

**TOWER W. R. 1833 FLINT MUSKET,** with British Coat-of-Arms and broad arrow marks. Evidently a gun made for British Army during King William the Fourth's reign; one of the last of the Flint Guns. In fine working order. Price, $16.00.

**0-965C. DUBLIN CASTLE BROWN BESS FLINTLOCK MUSKET.** The lock stamped, "G. R., British Crown, Dublin Castle." Brass plate on the stock which shows trace of soldier's number; 3½-foot barrel, ¾-inch smooth bore. Heavy stock, slightly worm eaten, and part of the fore-end broken off. Rare old specimen. Price, $17.85.

**8655. "SHIP'S MUSKET No. 21,"** engraved on the brass butt plate of old flintlock blunderbuss; "809" stamped on the lock; three British proof marks on the 22-inch barrel, 2⅛-inch diameter at the bell mouth. Brass mountings. Musket stock slightly worm eaten; serviceable order. Price, $48.00.

**0-965D. BROWN BESS FLINTLOCK MUSKET,** with rare old spade bayonet. 3½-foot barrel, ¾-inch smooth bore. Fore-end of the stock has been cut away for use as a sporting gun. Part of the plate missing. Only in fair order. Price, $12.50.

**0-942. ANCIENT SPANISH FLINTLOCK BLUNDERBUSS.** Armorer's gold seal inlaid on barrel and lock, and what looks like inscription, "Fel di via," with lion rampant. Full length 40 inches; diameter of the barrel at the breech 1⅜ inches, at the bell-mouth muzzle 2⅜ inches. Outside lock, erroneously called by some writers "Snaphaunce." Good working order. Price, $37.50.

**0-898. BROWN BESS FLINT MUSKET USED AT THE BATTLE OF PRESTON PANS** (near Edinburgh, Scotland), September 21, 1745. Lock is stamped, "1741, Tower, G. R." The brass plate on the stock has the soldier's number "66." Full length 5 feet 2 inches. Barrel is 13-16-inch smooth bore, 46 inches long, fastened to the stock by stud pinning. Bronze guard and butt plate. Genuine old relic gun from the Lawson Johnstone sale. Price, $50.00.

**"J. J. HENRY, PHILA., U. S." FLINTLOCK MUSKET.** Calibre 69. Barrel is 42 inches long. This musket, which is in fine, almost new, order, was found in the old New Jersey State Arsenal many years ago. The various details of its construction indicate that it was made about 1812, so that it was undoubtedly purchased by New Jersey for use in the War of 1812. Henry's factory was in Philadelphia and arms were made there by him as early as 1752. The barrel is stamped, "Salem," a county and town in southern New Jersey. Price, $20.00.

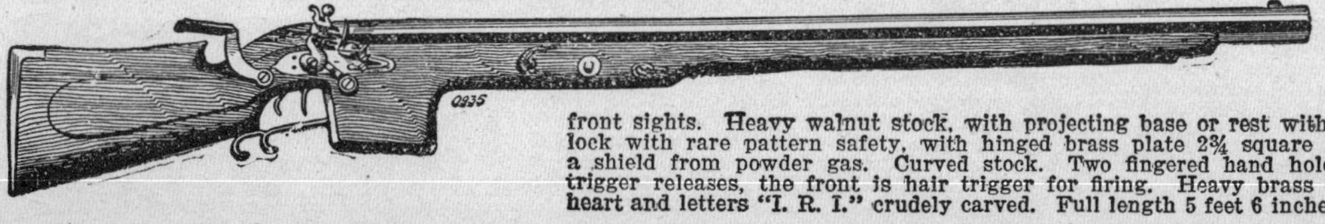

**0-935. ANCIENT HEAVY FLINTLOCK RIFLED WALL GUN.** Stamped, "Montaur A. Geneva, 1774." 50½-inch octagonal barrel, 1⅛-inch rifled bore. Diameter at breech 2⅝ inches, at the muzzle 1¾ inches. With rear and front sights. Heavy walnut stock, with projecting base or rest with axles for swivel mounting. Flintlock with rare pattern safety, with hinged brass plate 2⅜ square back of the lock, perhaps used as a shield from powder gas. Curved stock. Two fingered hand hold guard. Double trigger: the rear trigger releases, the front is hair trigger for firing. Heavy brass butt plate engraved with shape of heart and letters "I. R. I." crudely carved. Full length 5 feet 6 inches. Weight 49 pounds. Price, $67.50.

# PELLET, TUBE AND FLINTLOCK GUNS, ETC.

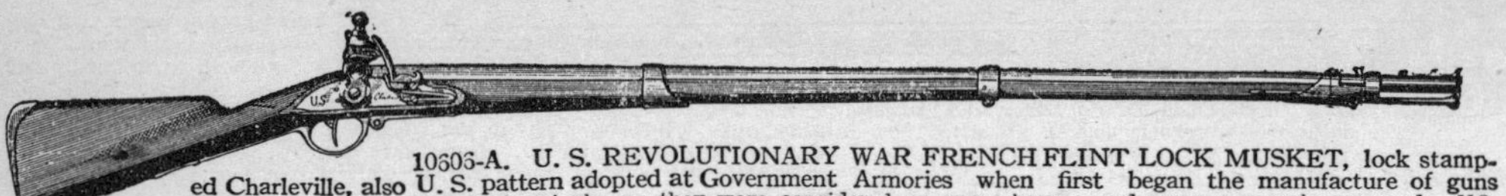

10606-A. U. S. REVOLUTIONARY WAR FRENCH FLINT LOCK MUSKET, lock stamped Charleville, also U. S. pattern adopted at Government Armories when first began the manufacture of guns Springfield, 1795. No sling swivels, as they were considered an encumbrance and were purposely removed. NO, bayonet, as less than half the soldiers in the Revolutionary War had bayonets on their guns. This is an INTERESTING GUN. IT IS IN SERVICEABLE ORDER. Price $50.00.

10606-B. FLINT LOCK MUSKET. Perfect order marked on the barrel "S. N. J." and on the lock "Essex Brigade." Found many years ago in Morristown, N. J. Gun is known as the model 1808, made by J. Henry, Phila., Pa. Price $25.00.

10606-C. "U. S. N. STARR MIDDLETOWN, CONN. 1824" stamped on old Flintlock musket complete with the original old white buff leather sling strap in perfect order like new. Price, $20.00.

10497. MUSHROOM PATTERN PERCUSSION CAP. The flanges on the cap fit over the nipple tube. The fulminate powder is contained in the cap TUBE. The copper flanges are merely to hold in place. Rare specimen for collectors. Price 50 cents each (cannot be mailed).

10498. GUN PRIMER TUBE, made for use between the period of flint and percussion cap guns. We have old flintlock guns that show alteration from the flint to this tube-lock. Primer tube is inserted in the vent and fired by the blow of the hammer descending on the metal covering over the tube. Price 50 cents each tube.

01285-A. COMBINATION KENTUCKY RIFLE AND SHOTGUN. Percussion lock. Barrels originally made to revolve, but now stationary, with the hammer for lower barrel lengthened to fire cap without turning. Like illustration except there is no tang sight, and trigger guard has no extension. Two hammers, two triggers. 34-inch octagonal barrels, with iron rod for rifle barrel, and wood rod for shot barrel. One fitted in groove on each side. Rifle barrel $\frac{7}{16}$ inch, shot barrel $\frac{9}{16}$ inch. Brass patch box as shown, checkered grip. Lock marked RIDDLE. Price, $38.00.

01277-D. KENTUCKY FLINTLOCK RIFLE, similar to 01277-C with larger brass patch box, with same name on barrel. In good order. Barrel 32½ inch, heavy octagonal. Price, $47.00.

01277-E. KENTUCKY FLINT LOCK RIFLE, with 29½ inch very heavy octagonal barrel, $\frac{7}{16}$ inch bore. Brass ornamented trigger guard and butt plate. Long brass patch box. Barrel marked: H. E. LEMAN, LANCASTER, PA. WARRANTED. Front and rear sights. Price, $55.00.

01277-F. KENTUCKY FLINTLOCK RIFLE, similar to 01277-E with same maker's name on barrel. Brass trigger guard, butt plate and patch box. Heavy octagonal barrel 24½ inch, an unusual length in this style. Bore 17/32 inch. In good order. Price, $42.00.

10604. SHIPS MUSKET FLINTLOCK, STAMPED 1787, BLUNDERBUSS pattern, kind furnished in olden times to merchant ships for repelling the attack of pirates and savages. Length of the barrel 2 feet, diameter at the bell mouth 2¾ inches, smallest diameter of the barrel near the breech 1¼ inches, full length 40 inches, with socket swivel for mounting on ships bulwarks, or on small boat.

10873A. OLD FLINTLOCK DOUBLE BARREL FOWLING GUN, rusty, stock needs repairing, ramrod missing, otherwise complete. Offered as is. $18.85.

10873B. OLD FLINTLOCK DOUBLE BARREL FOWLING GUN, fairly good order. Fine walnut stock with cheek piece. Brass mountings. Rammer missing. Price $24.00.

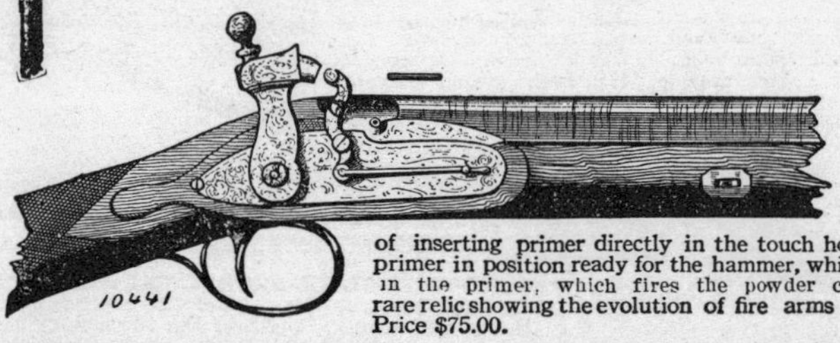

10441. TUBE-LOCK ALTERED FROM FLINT-LOCK SHOT GUN, made by Jackson, London, 8-gauge twist steel, 32-inch barrel. Fine old gun in serviceable order, complete with two of the copper priming tubes, the first improvement over the flint. The illustration shows the hammer raised, the method of inserting primer directly in the touch hole. The hinged clasp holds the primer in position ready for the hammer, which on falling explodes the charge in the primer, which fires the powder charge in the gun. This is a rare relic showing the evolution of fire arms as well as good serviceable gun. Price $75.00.

No. 0-940. H. W. MORTIMER FLINTLOCK MUSKET, cut down to carbine size. Fine easy working lock. In good order. Full length, 3 feet 4½ inches. Price, $12.50.

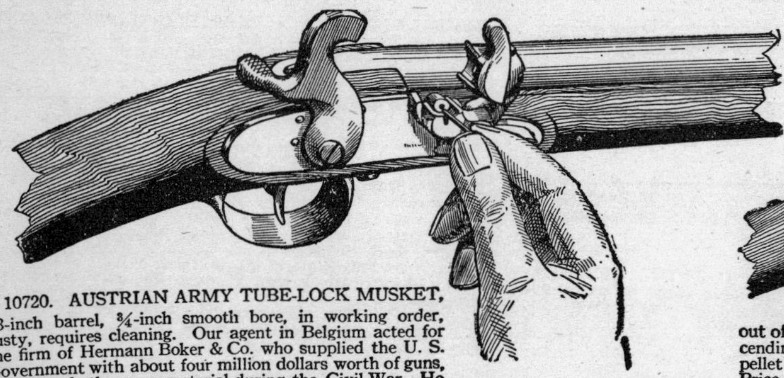

10720. AUSTRIAN ARMY TUBE-LOCK MUSKET, 33-inch barrel, ¾-inch smooth bore, in working order, rusty, requires cleaning. Our agent in Belgium acted for the firm of Hermann Boker & Co. who supplied the U. S. Government with about four million dollars worth of guns, sabers, and other war material during the Civil War. He informed me that he altered over 60,000 Austrian tube-lock guns into regular percussion cap muskets which were used to arm the Union Army Volunteers, 1861–1865. Consequently tube-lock guns are now rare, every gun collector needs one to show evolution in fire arms. Offered complete. Price $16.00.

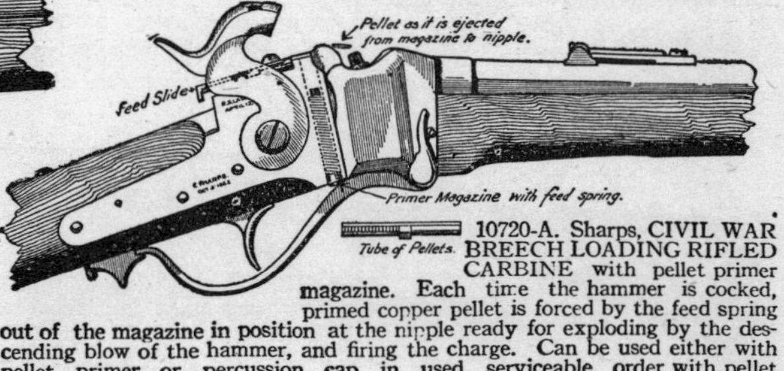


10720-A. Sharps, CIVIL WAR BREECH LOADING RIFLED CARBINE with pellet primer magazine. Each time the hammer is cocked, primed copper pellet is forced by the feed spring out of the magazine in position at the nipple ready for exploding by the descending blow of the hammer, and firing the charge. Can be used either with pellet primer or percussion cap in used serviceable order with pellet Price $7.85.

10579. ANCIENT FLINTLOCK RAMPART GUN, with socket swivel, full length 6 ft. SPANISH LOCK WITH OUTSIDE MECHANISM; ¾-inch smooth bore RIBBED shaped barrel; KNOB shaped muzzle end, silver inlaid front sights, notch in the breech protection forms rear sight. Stock is slightly worm eaten. In working order. Price $45.00.

10875. ANCIENT AUSTRIAN FLINTLOCK ARMY CARBINE, full length 30 inches, ⅝ smooth bore. In fine order refinished like new. Complete with side ring for attaching to mounted soldier's shoulder belt. Hand grip guard bow. Walnut stock with cheek piece. This type of gun was altered in large numbers during the Civil War from flintlock into cap guns for the use of the Union Cavalry. Our agent, a German residing in Belgium, was knighted by the King for the great work he gave to Belgium workmen in altering guns during the period 1861–1865. As he remarked, "I had Barbers, Tailors, Shoemakers, and all kinds of trades people employed as gun makers." Price of this ancient flintlock in fine order, $6.85.

10816. ANTIQUE FLINTLOCK AIR GUN with hollow copper cylinder for holding air, brass band engraved "T. Porter, London" period of 1790, 20½-inch barrel. Shows off well in collection of guns. Price $15.00.

10834. ELLIPTICAL MOUTHED FLINTLOCK BLUNDERBUSS, engraved on the lock "Lambert Dit Biron"; 17-inch barrel, 1⅜-inch at the breech, muzzle 2½ by 1½ inches. Walnut stock. Good working order. Price $38.00.

10835. FLINT BLUNDERBUSS, engraved on the barrel "Gio Battay Dafino," and on the LOCK 1764. Barrel is 22 inches long, 1¾-inch bell mouth. Walnut STOCK, CARVED with head of ancient warrior. Brass mountings. Good working order. Price $28.00.

10489. VICTORIAN REIGN FLINTLOCK CARBINE with British Army Royal Crown, Tower, V. R. and Broad Arrows. Serviceable order. Price $12.50.

10610. TAYLOR, LONDON, BRASS BARREL BLUNDERBUSS, in fine order. Price $25.00.

10872. ANCIENT FLINT FOWLING GUN. Early transformation into percussion. Crown and name plate in CUT STEEL. Fine easy working lock, with rare type hammer. Name on the lock worn off. Walnut stock is worm eaten. Full length 52 inches. In fair working order. Price $10.00.

10177. FLINTLOCK GUN, altered to fire tube primer, steel inserted in the place of the flint, retaining part of the flash pan, with a steel pin inserted in the striker, which, when closed, rests on the tube and explodes, when struck bye the stud in the flint hammer. Seal on the lock place B. S. 39. Rare piece, shows the evolution of the flint to percussion type. Offered with four loaded primed tubes, in fine working order. Price $25.00.

## MUSKETRY RULE

This instrument enables a rifleman to determine with reasonable accuracy the range at any long distance and to set his sight accordingly. It is an invaluable aid to a hunter who is compelled to make long shots and was successfully used by the riflemen of the American Army in France in 1917-1918. Every rifleman should have one.

**Price $1.00 Each**

Sectional view showing the lock mechanism, with pan and entrance for the capsule. Note hammer resting on the firing-pin, which explodes the pill-like fulminating charge when struck by the hammer.

**Pill-Lock Musket.** Rare type of gun, between the flint and percussion-cap periods. The charge is loaded from the muzzle and fired by a pill-shaped fulminate capsule, inserted in receptacle on the side of the gun, somewhat similar to the vent in the flint-lock. This capsule is exploded by a firing-pin, that is contained in the steel part, which caused the old flint, when struck, to give out the sparks (see sectional view illustration). Austria adopted these guns, which were afterward altered to percussion-lock guns, for use of Northern army during the Civil War. This gun is a fine, neat cadet style gun, 7-16 bore, 33-inch barrel, 47 inches full length, brass mounted, check-piece on the stock. Price, $15.00 each.

**1061.—PILL-LOCK DOUBLE BARREL SHOTGUN.** Barrels and rib have gold inlaid letters, Gregorio Lopez Arcabvcero del Rey. E. M. Madrid Ano

**1796.** Engraved lock and mounting. Gold front sight, with box of fulminate, tubes or pills.

Pill-lock guns followed after the flint-locks. They were of many different mechanisms before the advent of the percussion lock gun with nipple on the barrel, the early models retained the old flint flash pan, fulminate primers, enclosed in small tube or pill, was inserted in the vent hole, the hammer striking the tube, fired the charge. This is a real handsome old gun, with date engraved thereon. Price, $150.00.

**300** Harper's Ferry and Whitney 54-Calibre, Heavy Steel-Barrel Muzzle-Loading Rifles. Rifle has fine steel barrels; brass bands and mountings; brass butt plate; also patch box or place cut in the butt stock to hold cleaning rag or caps; has brass cover with spring. Guns were made in period from 1845 to 1855. All in serviceable order. Price $10.00 each. Many of the above rifles were made for the Government under contract. Some by Eli Whitney of New Haven, who first made guns with interchangeable parts.

**Derringer Muzzle Loading Muskets;** 58 Calibre; made by gun makers of Philadelphia, famous for fine pistols and guns 60 years ago; calibre 58; serviceable; second hand order. Price, $8.00 ea.; one stamped North Middletown, Conn., 1826. Price, $10.00. All have the old cap box on the butt stock. Derringer Rifles were used in the Mexican War, also Civil War.

**100** Smooth Bore Army Muskets, long barrel; very desirable for use as long range shotguns. These are not rifled barrels bored out, but genuine, original smooth bore; percussion lock, guns with walnut stock; in good second-hand serviceable order. Price, $10.00 each.

**ANCIENT AMSTERDAM FLINT LOCK 2-GROOVED RIFLE.** Made by J. Donahy. Octagonal barrel, with front and rear sight. ⅝-inch bore, 34-inch barrel. Fine walnut stock; handsomely carved at grip and fore-end. Ramrod, rib, old style wood guard and grip, engraved lock and mountings, hair trigger. Swiss butt. Price, $30.00.

> This Catalog besides being a list of what we have for sale is offered as a reference book for collectors and museums and for that reason many special articles interesting to them are shown though sold. Some of the articles marked off may be in stock later or we may have something similar.

See THE BREECH LOADER IN THE SERVICE (U. S.); also pages 66, 67, 68 and 69 for all small arms used in World War. See ILLUSTRATED HISTORY OF U. S. MILITARY SMALL ARMS.
Any of these features alone worth many times the price we ask for catalog, and do not appear in any other printed form. Note that this entire catalog and contents is copyrighted and cannot be used.

**1517. PILL LOCK MUSKET.** Length of barrel, 40½ inches. Full length, 56 inches; ⅝ smooth bore. This gun is of the period between the flintlock and the percussion lock, with nipple in barrel. The Austrian army at one time were armed with these guns. In 1861, at the breaking out of the Civil War, when President Lincoln sent agents abroad to purchase arms, gentleman who now acts as our agent in Europe had 60,000 of these Austrian pill lock rifles converted into percussion lock guns by removing the pill lock and replacing with percussion lock, with nipple in the barrel. Rare relic. Price, $40.00.

Illustration shows Civil War Cavalry man with full equipment consisting of Sharps carbine with wide shoulder sling, saber with belt and shoulder sling, short jacket, trousers with stripe, and large black hat with ornaments and feathers. We can supply the full outfit as shown in other pages of the catalog. We can fit out military pageants with all necessary articles. Write for prices.

**1518. FRENCH MILITARY RIFLE,** with odd-shaped long neck hammer. With patent breech barrel, percussion lock, 42½-inch barrel. Full length, 58 inches. 3-band gun. Engraved on lock, MR. le de Mauberg. Price, $8.85.

## QUESTIONS AND ANSWERS

H. A. M. Wisconsin.
Is the Russian-Springfield rifle a dependable gun?

This is a very good rifle, and while no beauty to look at nor accurate enough for fine target work, it is O. K. for hunting purposes.

*National Sportsman, Dec., 1924.*

**D25. BAMBOO CANE GUN.** Made of bamboo with brass barrel inside. Handle is made of steel, nickel plated with hole in center. By blowing, the firing pin is forced against the cartridge. The ferrule is removed when used as gun, and is fitted with prong to extract empty shells. Uses cal. 30 cartridges, center fire. Full length, 36 inches. Unscrews in center for packing, and for loading cartridges. Price, $4.50 each.

**1600. 2 FRENCH PERCUSSION LOCK MUSKETS.** Stamped, "St. Etienne." ⅝ smooth bore; 36-inch barrel; working order. Price, $6.85 each.

**1549. OBENDORF RIFLE PERCUSSION LOCK.** About 69 calibre, with double-edged blade side arm sword bayonet, fitting on at side of the barrel (early style fastening). Octagonal barrel 29½ inches in length, rifled. Rare pattern ramrod. Sling swivels. Walnut stock, slightly worm eaten; in working order. Relic. Price, $8.50.

**1848. SPANISH PERCUSSION LOCK RIFLED MUSKET.** Marked on lock date, "Fabb R. in Toreno." Patent breech. Good order. Modified Swiss-shaped butt stock. Full length, 44 inches. Price, $8.50.

**1849. SPORTING RIFLE, WITH PE)P SIGHTS.** Marked, "Lt. Colot Rit," on barrel. Full length, 5( inches. Checkered walnut stock, with extension hand-grip Swiss butt; about 40 calibre; serviceable order. Price, $8.50.

**10477. BRUNSWICK RIFLE.** The first percussion lock guns used in the British Army. Engraved as having been made at the Royal Manufactory, Enfield, 1838, with V. R. (Queen Victoria's Reign). Crown mark. Back action lock. Twist steel barrel has two rifle grooves for round belted ball. Brass mounted. Complete with side arm sword. A double-edged Roman pattern. Rare gun; choice of date, 1838-1847. With bullet mould $17.85.

**10572. ORIENTAL CHIEFTAINS PRESENTATION MUSKET.** Damascus barrel, inlaid with silver and gold ornamentation. Percussion hammer is in the shape of winged dragon. Engraved lock and mountings. Fine order. Full length 57 inches, barrel 39 inches, ½-inch smooth bore. Ebony stock. Price $50.00.

**10877. ANTIQUE MUSKETOON PERCUSSION LOCK RIFLE,** 4 grooves, 11/16 bore, full length 34 inches. In good refinished order. Price $2.85.

**10478. GERMAN ARMY POTSDAM 1855 PERCUSSION LOCK RIFLE,** with Crown, letters G. S. and W stamped on the stock. Old relic of German War. With swivel bayonet and fastening spring. Price $10.00.

**10827. INVENTOR'S MODEL BREECH LOADING RIFLE;** 30-inch twist steel barrel and breech. Top lever raises slide, breech block springs up for entrance of cartridge in the chamber; lever forward of the guard cocks the concealed hammer. Rear sight is on the breech block; 20-inch triangular bayonet folds under the gun. Rare weapons. Price $25.00.

**When ordering special guns allow a second choice.**

**10877-A. MILITARY PERCUSSION LOCK RIFLE** altered to sporting model by cutting off part of the muzzle and part of the fore end stock. Barrel is 26 inches long, 9/16 inch rifle bore. Walnut stock, with cheek piece, side bar with ring for attaching to shoulder sling. Good refinished order. Price $6.50.

**10869. BREECH LOADING CAP AND BALL SPORTING RIFLE,** engraved "Montegny, Brussels." Engraved lock and mountings. UNDER LEVER WHICH SLIDES THE BREECH FORWARD FOR LOADING. Combustible cartridge, calibre .45. Walnut stock, blued finish breech and mountings; very fine gun. Price $17.50.

**11032. RESTELS PATENT BREECH LOADING PERCUSSION LOCK RIFLE,** evidently inventor's model. British Government proof marks. Full length 55 inches. Rusty but in complete working order. Levers on the left side with projecting handle which moves back in opening first a bolt and then the breech block for the insertion of the paper cartridge. The reverse operation closes the gun for firing. Restels patent breech loading gun was before the British Government Board of Officers and was one of the eight rifles selected for trial at the time the Snider breech loading rifle was adopted. Price $20.00.

**10477. BRUNSWICK RIFLE, Belted Ball Bullet Mould** for casting balls for use in the first British Army percussion lock rifle. Offered as outfit with the rifle, period 1838 to 1847.

**1865. JEFFERSON DAVIS RIFLE;** facsimile of the rifle now on exhibition at the Springfield Armory Museum, claimed to have been taken from Jefferson Davis, President of the Southern Confederacy, while trying to escape at the close of the Civil War; gun is the regular Enfield muzzle loading rifle; with FINE WALNUT STOCK, with CHECKERED GRIP and FORE END; in good serviceable order. Price $10.00.

**10700. ANTIQUE MILITARY CARBINE,** Italian, percussion lock. 13¾-inch barrel, ¾-inch rifle bore. Walnut stock. Ring attached for shoulder strap, saddle hook on the butt stock. The metal butt plate is made to extend an inch on the lower side of the stock. Evidently for use as a *club by the mounted soldier*. The guard has finger hold projection. Rare old weapon, period 1830 to 1840.

**10702. NAPOLI 1860 PERIOD ITALIAN** ¾-inch bore. Walnut stock. Complete CARABINEERS' Musquetoon, 13-inch barrel serviceable cleaned order. Price $4.85.

**10830. CURIOS MECHANISM SHOT GUN,** Under lever acts as hammer. Fired by ring trigger; eccentric mechanism; 36 inch steel twist barrel, walnut stock. In good order. Price $20.00.

**10570. ALLEN'S PATENT 1855 SPORTING RIFLE,** made by Allen & Wheelock, Worcester. Calibre is about .36, length of barrel 26 inches. Walnut stock. Top lever forms a breech opening for the insertion of the cartridge; closed for firing. Gun is in good order. Rare piece.

**10701. ITALIAN CARBINE.** Facsimile 10700. Without the carrying rings. Price $4.85.

**10721. ALTERED FLINT MUSKET** to percussion lock, retaining the battery spring to operate a nipple lever safety, one of the very early transformations. Lock is stamped "Cesar Rd Man Breian." Brass mounted walnut stock, smooth bore. Full length 4 feet. Serviceable. Price $6.85.

**1844. JENKS U. S. N. BREECH LOADING PERCUSSION LOCK RIFLE,** side hammer and nipple is on the right side. Top lever swings back to the rear, connected at the base with plunger that pushes the cartridge into the chamber of the gun. Full length 52 inches. Practically new. Brass mountings. Jenks rifles are rare. This one formed part of the lot captured by New York City Police about the time of War Draft Riots, and was held at Police Headquarters for *forty years waiting for an owner* to turn up finally turned over to the U. S. A. Ordnance Department. No doubt the rifles were on their way to the *Southern Confederacy* when captured. Price, $25.00.

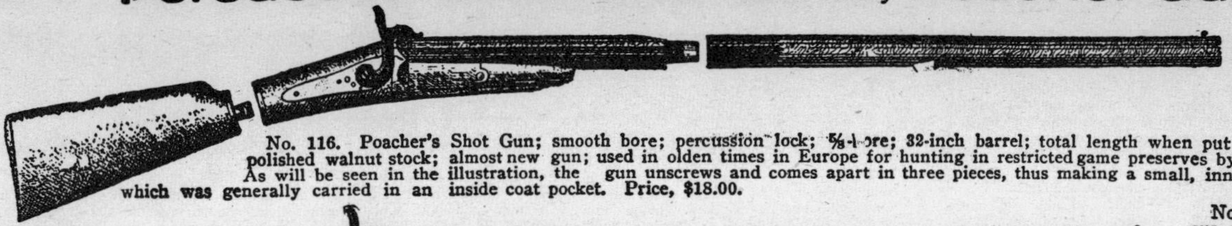

**No. 116.** Poacher's Shot Gun; smooth bore; percussion lock; ⅝-bore; 32-inch barrel; total length when put together, 48 inches; polished walnut stock; almost new gun; used in olden times in Europe for hunting in restricted game preserves by unlicensed persons. As will be seen in the illustration, the gun unscrews and comes apart in three pieces, thus making a small, innocent-looking parcel, which was generally carried in an inside coat pocket. **Price, $18.00.**

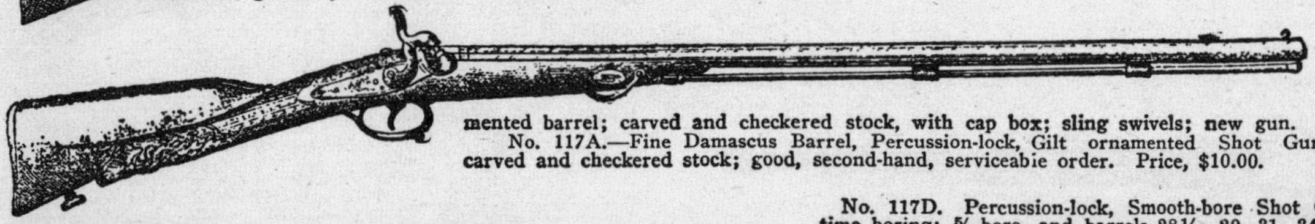

**No. 117. Fine Damas-cus Barrel, Percussion-lock Shot Gun, with ram-rod rib; ⅝-bore; 24-inch barrel; 40 inches total length; gilt inlaid orna-**mented barrel; carved and checkered stock, with cap box; sling swivels; new gun. Price, $12.00.
**No. 117A.**—Fine Damascus Barrel, Percussion-lock, Gilt ornamented Shot Gun, ⅝-bore, 33-inch barrel, carved and checkered stock; good, second-hand, serviceable order. Price, $10.00.

**No. 117B.** Fine Damascus Barrel, Percussion-lock Shot Gun, gilt inlaid letters, "Fin Damas Moire," ⅝-bore, 38-inch barrel. Price, $12.00.
**No. 117C.**—Shot Gun, same as 117B, with barrels in various lengths. Price, $12.00 each.

**No. 117D.** Percussion-lock, Smooth-bore Shot Gun, steel barrel, with old-time boring; ⅝-bore, and barrels 28½, 29, 31, 34 and 37 inches. These fine guns were made for some Spanish merchant and have Spanish names on the barrels; they are all in good, serviceable order, slightly shopworn; many are dated 1868; have carved and checkered stocks complete, with sling swivels, with cap box in butt. The ramrod passes under the lock, making a fine gun for taxidermists. Your choice, price, $8.00 each.

Light-Weight Single-Barrel Breech-Loading Shot Gun, in serviceable order; about 20-gauge, centre-fire, genuine twist steel 21-inch barrel; total length of gun, 36 inches; weight, 2 pounds 10 ounces; barrel unscrews from frame for insertion of cartridge; the lock mechanism is contained in the stock and the inside hammer is cocked by slight pull on the small folding trigger which is on the bottom of the stock; the regular trigger firing the gun is contained within the guard bow as on regular made guns. The light weight of this gun, together with its take-apart feature, the barrel part measuring 21 inches, the stock part 15 inches, makes it a very desirable gun for carrying in small space. We think this is some inventor's model. We have never seen or heard of gun like it. It is in serviceable order. Price, $15.00.

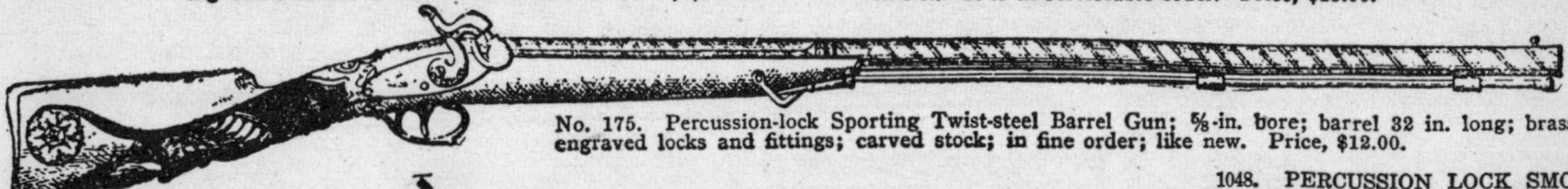

Lightest Weight Serviceable Shot Gun made; 28-inch barrel; about 24-gauge centre-fire; weight, 3¾ pounds; walnut stock, which contains the firing mechanism and inside hammer, locked by lever underneath the stock, back of the guard lever. In taking down barrel unscrews from frame. Price, $12.00.

**No. 175.** Percussion-lock Sporting Twist-steel Barrel Gun; ⅝-in. bore; barrel 32 in. long; brass mountings; engraved locks and fittings; carved stock; in fine order; like new. Price, $12.00.

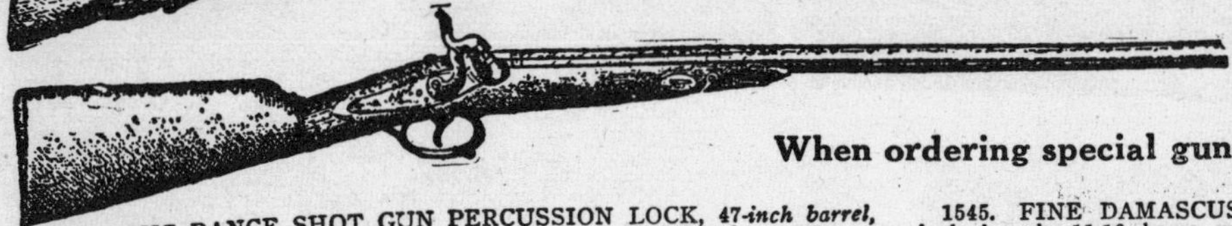

**1048.** PERCUSSION LOCK SMOOTH BORE SHOT GUN, 38-inch barrel, ⅝ bore, walnut stock, checkered grip; ramrod rib; serviceable order. $6.00.

## When ordering special guns allow a second choice.

**1050.** LONG RANGE SHOT GUN PERCUSSION LOCK, 47-inch barrel, ¾-inch bore; ramrod rib; 1⅝-inch diameter at breech. Suitable for sportsmen who need long barrel. Price, $9.00.
**1051.** LONG RANGE LARGE BORE SHOT GUN, percussion lock, fine checkered stock and grip; ramrod rib. Price, $8.75.
**1547.** TWIST STEEL BARREL SHOT GUN; length of barrel, 36 inches; 11-16 smooth bore; carved head stock; sling swivels; in working order; octagonal shaped barrel. The twist metal stands out in relief on the barrel. Price, $6.85.

**1545.** FINE DAMASCUS BARREL SHOT GUN. Percussion lock; 37-inch barrel; 11-16 bore; with sling swivels, ramrod, checkered stock. In working order. $6.50.
FRENCH SPORTING GUN; lock stamped "Verney Cabron a St. Etienne;" 30½-inch twist barrel; ⅝ smooth bore; not a high quality gun. In working order. Price, $5.00.

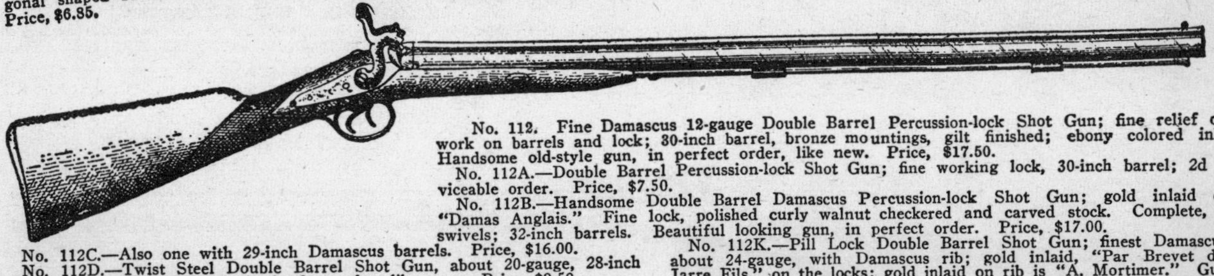

**No. 112.** Fine Damascus 12-gauge Double Barrel Percussion-lock Shot Gun; fine relief ornamented work on barrels and lock; 30-inch barrel, bronze mountings, gilt finished; ebony colored inlaid stock. Handsome old-style gun, in perfect order, like new. Price, $17.50.
**No. 112A.**—Double Barrel Percussion-lock Shot Gun; fine working lock, 30-inch barrel; 2d hand, serviceable order. Price, $7.50.
**No. 112B.**—Handsome Double Barrel Damascus Percussion-lock Shot Gun; gold inlaid on barrel, lock, polished curly walnut checkered and carved stock. Complete, with sling swivels; 32-inch barrels. Beautiful looking gun, in perfect order, like new. Price, $17.00.
**No. 112C.**—Also one with 29-inch Damascus barrels. Price, $16.00.
**No. 112D.**—Twist Steel Double Barrel Shot Gun, about 20-gauge, 28-inch barrels, checkered walnut stock; in fine order, like new. Price, $9.50.
**No. 112E.**—Rubens Fine Twist Steel Double Barrel Shot Gun, percussion lock, fine walnut checkered stock, 30-inch barrels; perfect order, like new. Price, $12.00.
**No. 112F.**—Mortimer Fine Twist Steel Double Barrel Shot Gun, about 12-bore, with 33-inch fine twist steel barrels; lock stamped Mortimer; new. Price, $12.00.
**No. 112G.**—Fine Twist Steel Double Barrel Percussion-lock Shot Gun, with engraved locks and mounting; 30-inch barrels; about 16-gauge; fine order; new. Price, $10.00.
**No. 112H.**—Pin Fire Double Barrel 12mm. Shot Gun; total length, 3½ feet; about 5½ pounds; barrels are 25 inches long. All in fine order (no cartridges). Price, $7.50.
**No. 112I.**—Inventor's Double Barrel Hammerless Damascus 12-gauge Breech-loading Centre-fire Shot Gun; has long top lever, which, when lifted up, opens the breech and cocks the hammer; also has small outside lever whereby the hammer can be cocked independent of the lever; rare mechanism; in serviceable order; barrel is engraved (with rib). Valuable gun for gun makers; as the hammers are contained inside the frames it affords fine sighting without obstruction over the barrels. No cartridges. Bargain, $18.00.
**No. 112J.**—Inventor's Model Breech-loading Double Barrel Percussion-lock Shot Gun, about 20-gauge; 27-inch barrel, with under lever action; lacks the guard lever; valuable as a type for collection, showing the progress of invention. Fair order only. Price, $8.50.
Double-barrel 10-gauge Damascus Shot Gun; under-lever action, breech-loading for any paper or brass 10-gauge, centre-fire shot or shell; in fine order. Price, $12.80.

**No. 112K.**—Pill Lock Double Barrel Shot Gun; finest Damascus barrels; about 24-gauge, with Damascus rib; gold inlaid, "Par Brevet d'Invention, Jarre Fils," on the locks; gold inlaid on rib is "A. Mortimer." Gun has two outside hammers like on the ordinary old percussion-lock guns; the face of the hammer is shaped like a nipple; the breech of the barrels, where the nipple would be in the old percussion gun, is cut out and the hammer strikes with its nipple in the hole, making neat, tight fit. We have no primers or cartridges. Gun is in fine, serviceable order, valuable to collectors, showing progress of invention. Price, $65.00.
4 Double-Barrel, Breech-Loading Shot Guns, with top snap, same appearance as illustration shown above (No. 112). Imitation twist steel barrels; 12-gauge; centre-fire; 29-inch barrel believed to be a cylinder bore barrel, fit only for field shooting; weight about 9 lbs.; shop worn new guns, serviceable order; checked pistol grip; Belgium make; not fine quality guns; sell as are. Price, $8.25 each.
1 Gun, same description as above, with 31-inch cylinder bore barrels, $8.50.
1 Gun, same description as above, with 31½-inch cylinder bore barrels, lighter weight, about 8 lbs. $9.00.
3 Double-Barrel, Breech-Loading Shot Guns, with under lever (Lefaucheaux) action; 12 gauge; 29-inch blued barrels; stamped on the barrels, "Belgium cast steel;" checked pistol grip, cylinder bore barrels; weight of guns, about 9 lbs. Offered as a new gun, shop worn, not best quality gun. Price, $6.00 each.
3 Top Snap, Double-Barrel, Breech-Loading, Centre-fire, 12-gauge Shot Guns; blued barrels, stamped "Belgium cast steel;" 29-inch barrels, cylinder bore; new, stiff-working guns, shop worn; offered as are, $7.00 each.
Fine New Double-Barreled Inventor's Model 12-gauge Shot Gun, with patent ejectors; Damascus barrels; cost over $300.00 to manufacture. Price, $100.00.
Fine Spencer Breech-loading Repeating Rifle. Inventor's model; gold-plated; only one made; cost $1,000.00. Price, $500.00.
Double-Barreled Gun, one barrel 44-rifled, one short barrel 24 gauge; barrels are superposed; has two locks and hammer with mould; good second-hand order. Price, $15.00.

After the close of the Civil War a number of army officers were disputing as to which officer displayed the best generalship. Some favored General Grant, some Sherman, others Sheridan; finally they decided to leave it to General Grant, and he rather surprised them all by saying that, in his opinion, "Old Brains," (nickname among army officers for Gen. Rufus Ingalls) was the best general of the Civil War, for no matter what situation our armies got into, Quartermaster Ingalls always had ready fresh supplies, and that, in his opinion, required greater generalship than to lead an army in battle.

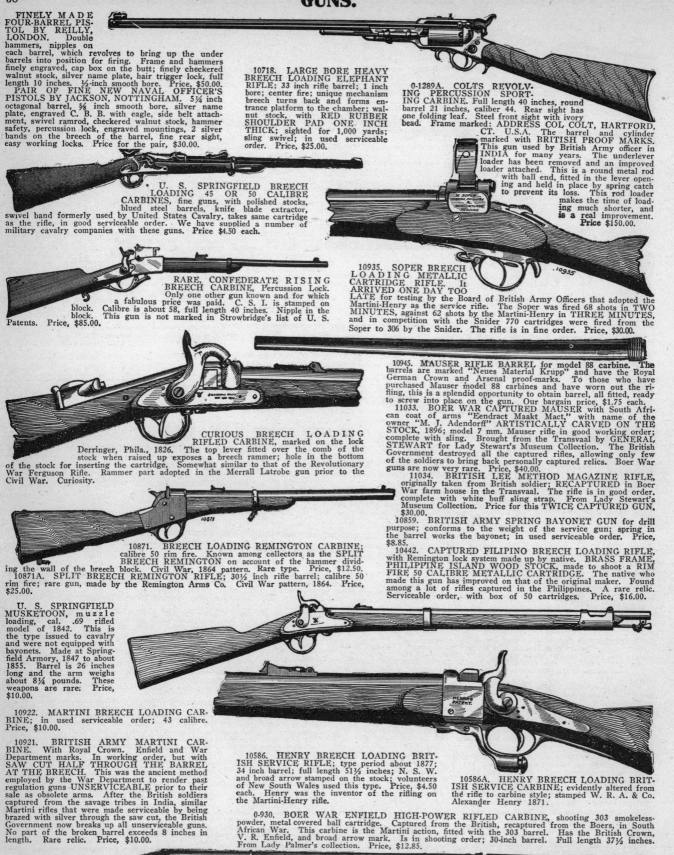

**FINELY MADE FOUR-BARREL PISTOL BY REILLY, LONDON.** Double hammers, nipples on each barrel, which revolves to bring up the under barrels into position for firing. Frame and hammers finely engraved, cap box on the butt; finely checkered walnut stock, silver name plate, hair trigger lock, full length 10 inches. ½-inch smooth bore. Price. $50.00.
**PAIR OF FINE NEW NAVAL OFFICER'S PISTOLS BY JACKSON, NOTTINGHAM.** 5¼ inch octagonal barrel, ⅝ inch smooth bore, silver name plate, engraved C. B. B. with eagle, side belt attachment, swivel ramrod, checkered walnut stock, hammer safety, percussion lock, engraved mountings, 2 silver bands on the breech of the barrel, fine rear sight, easy working locks. Price for the pair, $30.00.

**U. S. SPRINGFIELD BREECH LOADING 45 OR 50 CALIBRE CARBINES,** fine guns, with polished stocks, blued steel barrels, knife blade extractor, swivel band formerly used by United States Cavalry, takes same cartridge as the rifle, in good serviceable order. We have supplied a number of military cavalry companies with these guns. Price $4.50 each.

**RARE, CONFEDERATE RISING BREECH CARBINE,** Percussion Lock. Only one other gun known and for which a fabulous price was paid. C. S. I. is stamped on block. Calibre is about 58, full length 40 inches. Nipple in the block. This gun is not marked in Strowbridge's list of U. S. Patents. Price, $85.00.

**CURIOUS BREECH LOADING RIFLED CARBINE,** marked on the lock Derringer, Phila., 1826. The top lever fitted over the comb of the stock when raised up exposes a breech rammer; hole in the bottom of the stock for inserting the cartridge. Somewhat similar to that of the Revolutionary War Ferguson Rifle. Rammer part adopted in the Merrall Latrobe gun prior to the Civil War. Curiosity.

**10871. BREECH LOADING REMINGTON CARBINE;** calibre 50 rim fire. Known among collectors as the SPLIT BREECH REMINGTON on account of the hammer dividing the wall of the breech block. Civil War, 1864 pattern. Rare type. Price. $12.50.
**10871A. SPLIT BREECH REMINGTON RIFLE;** 30½ inch rifle barrel; calibre 50 rim fire; rare gun, made by the Remington Arms Co. Civil War pattern, 1864. Price, $25.00.

**U. S. SPRINGFIELD MUSKETOON,** muzzle loading, cal. .69 rifled model of 1842. This is the type issued to cavalry and were not equipped with bayonets. Made at Springfield Armory, 1847 to about 1855. Barrel is 26 inches long and the arm weighs about 8¼ pounds. These weapons are rare. Price, $10.00.

**10922. MARTINI BREECH LOADING CARBINE;** in used serviceable order; 43 calibre. Price, $10.00.

**10921. BRITISH ARMY MARTINI CARBINE.** With Royal Crown. Enfield and War Department marks. In working order, but with SAW CUT HALF THROUGH THE BARREL AT THE BREECH. This was the ancient method employed by the War Department to render past regulation guns UNSERVICEABLE prior to their sale as obsolete arms. After the British soldiers captured from the savage tribes in India, similar Martini rifles that were made serviceable by being brazed with silver through the saw cut, the British Government now breaks up all unserviceable guns. No part of the broken barrel exceeds 8 inches in length. Rare relic. Price, $10.00.

**10718. LARGE BORE HEAVY BREECH LOADING ELEPHANT RIFLE;** 33 inch rifle barrel; 1 inch bore; center fire; unique mechanism breech turns back and forms entrance platform to the chamber; walnut stock, with RED RUBBER SHOULDER PAD ONE INCH THICK; sighted for 1,000 yards; sling swivel; in used serviceable order. Price, $25.00.

**0-1289A. COLTS REVOLVING PERCUSSION SPORTING CARBINE.** Full length 40 inches, round barrel 21 inches, caliber 44. Rear sight has one folding leaf. Steel front sight with ivory bead. Frame marked: ADDRESS COL COLT, HARTFORD, CT. U.S.A. The barrel and cylinder marked with BRITISH PROOF MARKS. This gun used by British Army officer in INDIA for many years. The underlever loader has been removed and an improved loader attached. This is a round metal rod with ball end, fitted in the lever opening and held in place by spring catch to prevent its loss. This rod loader makes the time of loading much shorter, and is a real improvement. Price $150.00.

**10935. SOPER BREECH LOADING METALLIC CARTRIDGE RIFLE.** It ARRIVED ONE DAY TOO LATE for testing by the Board of British Army Officers that adopted the Martini-Henry as the service rifle. The Soper was fired 68 shots in TWO MINUTES, against 62 shots by the Martini-Henry in THREE MINUTES, and in competition with the Snider 770 cartridges were fired from the Soper to 306 by the Snider. The rifle is in fine order. Price, $30.00.

**10945. MAUSER RIFLE BARREL for model 88 carbine.** The barrels are marked "Neues Material Krupp" and have the Royal German Crown and Arsenal proof-marks. To those who have purchased Mauser model 88 carbines and have worn out the rifling, this is a splendid opportunity to obtain barrel, all fitted, ready to screw into place on the gun. Our bargain price, $1.75 each.
**11033. BOER WAR CAPTURED MAUSER** with South African coat of arms "Eendract Maakt Mact," with name of the owner "M. J. Adendorff" ARTISTICALLY CARVED ON THE STOCK, 1896; model 7 mm. Mauser rifle in good working order; complete with sling. Brought from the Transvaal by GENERAL STEWART for Lady Stewart's Museum Collection. The British Government destroyed all the captured rifles, allowing only few of the soldiers to bring back personally captured relics. Boer War guns are now very rare. Price, $40.00.
**11034. BRITISH LEE METHOD MAGAZINE RIFLE,** originally taken from British soldier; RECAPTURED in Boer War farm house in the Transvaal. The rifle is in good order, complete with white buff sling strap. From Lady Stewart's Museum Collection. Price for this TWICE CAPTURED GUN, $30.00.
**10859. BRITISH ARMY SPRING BAYONET GUN for drill** purpose; conforms to the weight of the service gun; spring in the barrel works the bayonet; in used serviceable order. Price, $8.85.
**10442. CAPTURED FILIPINO BREECH LOADING RIFLE,** with Remington lock system made up by native. BRASS FRAME, PHILIPPINE ISLAND WOOD STOCK, made to shoot a RIM FIRE 50 CALIBRE METALLIC CARTRIDGE. The native who made this gun has improved on that of the original maker. Found among a lot of rifles captured in the Philippines. A rare relic. Serviceable order, with box of 50 cartridges. Price, $16.00.

**10586. HENRY BREECH LOADING BRITISH SERVICE RIFLE;** type period about 1877; 34 inch barrel; full length 51½ inches; N. S. W. and broad arrow stamped on the stock; volunteers of New South Wales used this type. Price, $4.50 each. Henry was the inventor of the rifling on the Martini-Henry rifle.

**10586A. HENRY BREECH LOADING BRITISH SERVICE CARBINE;** evidently altered from the rifle to carbine style; stamped W. R. A. & Co. Alexander Henry 1871.

**0-930. BOER WAR ENFIELD HIGH-POWER RIFLED CARBINE,** shooting 303 smokeless-powder, metal covered ball cartridge. Captured from the British, recaptured from the Boers, in South African War. This carbine is the Martini action, fitted with the 303 barrel. Has the British Crown, V. R. Enfield, and broad arrow mark. Is in shooting order; 30-inch barrel. Full length 37½ inches. From Lady Palmer's collection. Price, $12.85.

25 U. S. Army Fencing Muskets and Bayonets. Regular Springfield gun stock with steel barrel fastened to the stock with two steel bands, with butt and guard plates. No lock. Full length, 51½ inches. Bayonet of the steel blade is ground flat, the point turned into a knob and covered with russet leather. All in good second hand serviceable order. Price, $3.25 each outfit.
3 Pieper Bolt-action Cadet Guns, with bronze frame, steel-barrel center-fire; for about 40-calibre cartridges; good condition. Price, $4.50 each.

# SINGLE BARREL GUNS

**ANCIENT CANNON.** The term cannon is derived from canna (a reed); the first cannon were called bombardoe, from the great noise which the firing of them occasioned.

The first cannon employed were nothing more than bars of iron arranged in such a manner that their internal aspects should form a tube; the bars were not welded, but merely confined by hoops. On some occasions, expedients much less efficient than this have been had recourse to, cannon having been made of coils of rope arranged in a tubular form, and even of leather or wood.

Earliest uses of Cannon. The earliest uses of this new description of artillery are noticed as having occured at Cressy in 1346, where they were employed on land by the Black Prince; and at sea in 1350, in an action between the Moorish king of Seville and the King of Tunis, and again by the Venetians in 1380. On this last occasion it is remarkable that nations generally exclaimed against its use as unfair in war. It was not then foreseen, as has since proved the case, that gunpowder would render war, especially in naval battles, less sanguinary. Formerly, the great object in sea engagements was to board the enemy, and in hand to hand combats destroy life; but the chief effort now in fighting ships with guns, is to cripple or destroy the ship, which being accomplished, men are compelled by necessity to surrender.

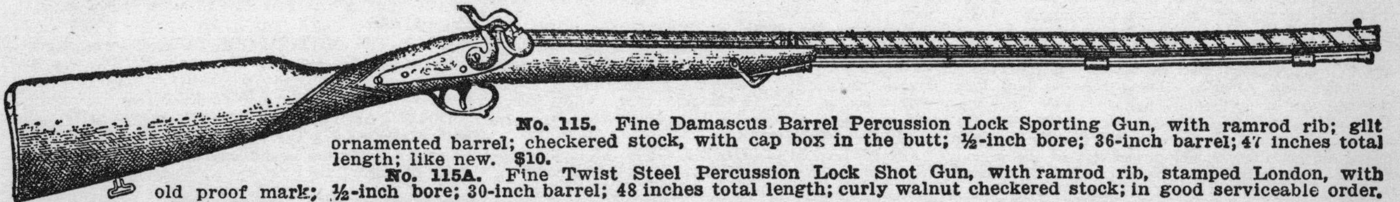

**No. 115.** Fine Damascus Barrel Percussion Lock Sporting Gun, with ramrod rib; gilt ornamented barrel; checkered stock, with cap box in the butt; ½-inch bore; 36-inch barrel; 47 inches total length; like new. $10.

**No. 115A.** Fine Twist Steel Percussion Lock Shot Gun, with ramrod rib, stamped London, with old proof mark; ½-inch bore; 30-inch barrel; 48 inches total length; curly walnut checkered stock; in good serviceable order. Price $9.00.

**No. 115B.** Parker & Fields Fine London Twist Percussion Lock Shot Gun; chased lock; dated 1837; German silver mountings; handsome miniature cap box set in the stock; checkered walnut stock; ⅝-bore; 33½-inch barrel; total length 50 inches; brass guard; has extension forming pistol grip; serviceable order. Price $10.00.

**No. 115C.** Twist Steel Barrel Fowling Piece; percussion lock; ⅝-bore; 36-inch barrel; 52 inches; total length, with ramrod rib; engraved lock and mountings, fine order, like new. Price $7.75.

**No. 115D.** 12-Gauge Damascus Barrel Percussion Lock Gun, part barrel octagonal, 33 inches long; 49 inches total length; engraved lock and mountings; almost new. Price $10.00.

**No. 115E.** 9-16-Bore Damascus Barrel Shot Gun; percussion lock; engraved lock and mountings, beautifully ornamented, partly octagonal shaped barrel; checkered grip; cap box in the butt stock; fine locks; almost new gun; 37-inch barrel; total length, 52 inches. Price $10.00.

**No. 115F.** Twist Steel Octagonal Barrel Rifle, about 44 calibre; heavy barrel; fine lock; fine curly walnut inlaid stock checkered, with cheek piece; good, second-hand, serviceable order. Price $10.00.

**No. 115G.** Spanish Shot Gun; ⅝-bore; 24-inch barrel; total length 40 inches; percussion lock with Spanish lettering on barrel; chased stock with cap box; serviceable (not new). Price, $5.50.

**No. 115H.** Maple Stock Shot Barrel Gun; gilt inlaid barrel; fine locks; checkered stock with cap box in butt; chased lock and mountings; fine order. Price $8.75.

**No. 115I.** Percussion Lock Twist Steel Barrel Shot Gun; ⅝-bore; 37-inch smooth-bore barrel; cap box in butt; almost new gun. Price $5.50.

**No. 115J.** Same as No. 115I, but 26-inch. $5.00.

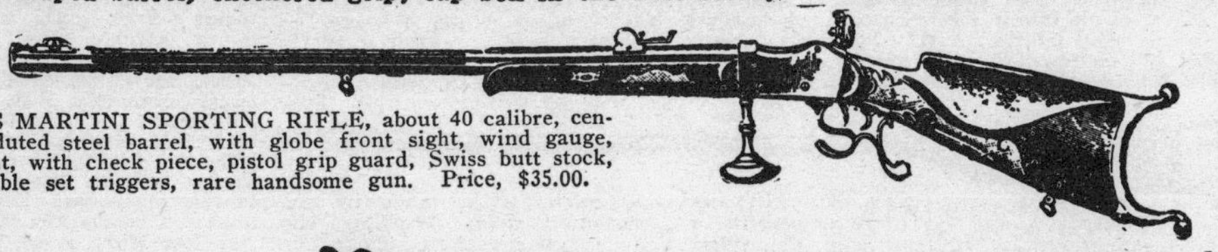

**0-759.** LARGE-BORE DUCK GUN BY PATON & WALSH, PERTH (SCOTLAND). About 1-inch smooth bore; 35½-inch barrel. Weighs 17¾ lbs. Extremely well made gun, engraved mountings, ramrod rib. Silver vent plug. Solid breech, and good thickness of metal in the barrel. Curly walnut stock. Checkered grip and fore end. Full length 52 inches. Good, serviceable order. Price, $20.00.

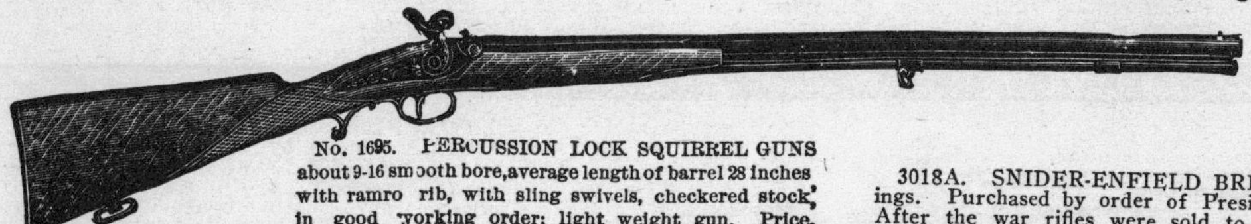

**SWISS MARTINI SPORTING RIFLE,** about 40 calibre, centre-fire, fluted steel barrel, with globe front sight, wind gauge, peep sight, with check piece, pistol grip guard, Swiss butt stock, with double set triggers, rare handsome gun. Price, $35.00.

**THE STRAIN OF MODERN WARFARE.**
She—The strain on the soldier in modern warfare must be very great.
He—It is. Sometimes the photographer isn't ready, and you have to wait hours, and then the pictures may prove failures.—Judge.

**No. 1695. PERCUSSION LOCK SQUIRREL GUNS** about 9-16 smooth bore, average length of barrel 28 inches with ramro rib, with sling swivels, checkered stock, in good working order; light weight gun. Price, $10.00.

**3018A. SNIDER-ENFIELD BREECH-LOADING RIFLES.** With iron mountings. Purchased by order of President Lincoln to arm Union Army Volunteers. After the war rifles were sold to English gunmakers, who altered the guns to breech-loaders, with the Snider system. All refinished like new. Price, $4.25. Cartridges, blank or ball, $1.75 per 100.

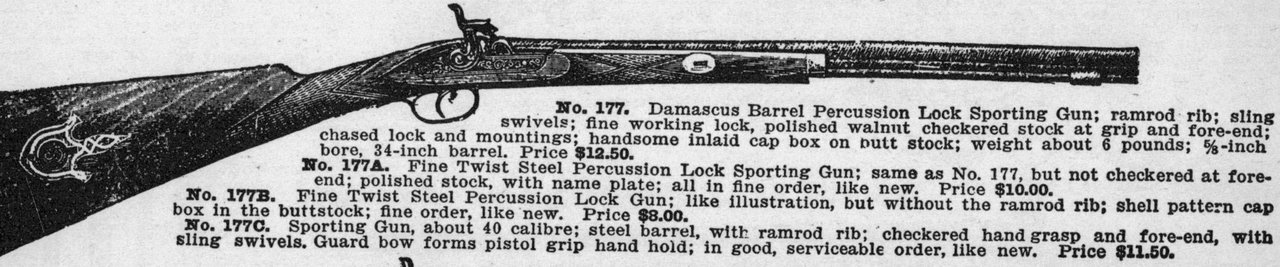

**No. 177.** Damascus Barrel Percussion Lock Sporting Gun; ramrod rib; sling swivels; fine working lock; chased lock and mountings; handsome inlaid cap box on butt stock; weight about 6 pounds; ⅝-inch bore, 34-inch barrel. Price $12.50.

**No. 177A.** Fine Twist Steel Percussion Lock Sporting Gun; same as No. 177, but not checkered at fore-end; polished stock, with name plate; all in fine order, like new. Price $10.00.

**No. 177B.** Fine Twist Steel Percussion Lock Gun; like illustration, but without the ramrod rib; shell pattern cap box in the buttstock; fine order, like new. Price $8.00.

**No. 177C.** Sporting Gun, about 40 calibre; steel barrel, with ramrod rib; checkered hand grasp and fore-end, with sling swivels. Guard bow forms pistol grip hand hold; in good, serviceable order, like new. Price $11.50.

**No. 178.** Percussion Lock Shot Gun; ⅝-inch smooth bore; 36-inch barrel, with old-style browning; with Spanish names, etc.; with sling swivels; fine lock, carved stock; good, second-hand, serviceable order. Note that ramrod looks too small for the gun; ramrod is of steel and is made to spring lightly and fit into bed under the lock. Gun is in good, second-hand, serviceable order. Price $8.50.

**No. 178A.** Fine Percussion Lock Sporting Gun, with carved and checkered stock; Spanish names, places and dates on barrel, 1869; good, second-hand, serviceable order. Price $7.50.

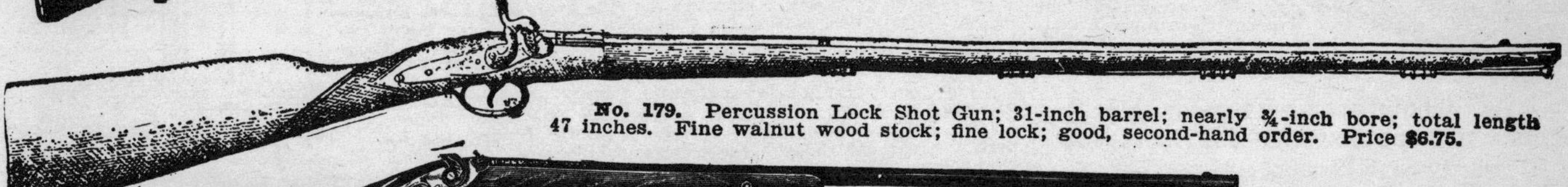

**No. 179.** Percussion Lock Shot Gun; 31-inch barrel; nearly ¾-inch bore; total length 47 inches. Fine walnut wood stock; fine lock; good, second-hand order. Price $6.75.

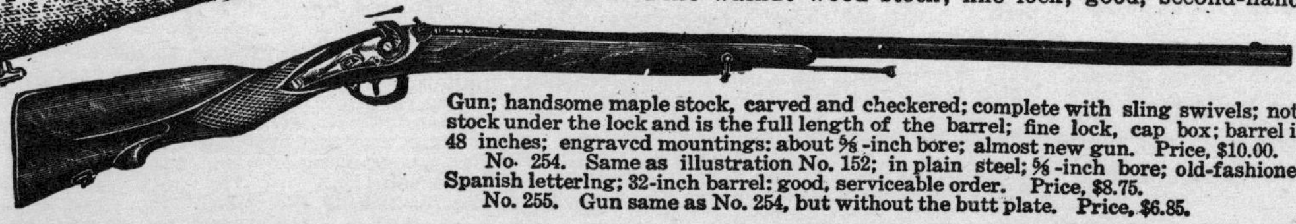

**No. 252.** Fine Damascus Barrel Percussion Lock Shot Gun; handsome maple stock, carved and checkered; complete with sling swivels; note ramrod is contained in the stock under the lock and is the full length of the barrel; fine lock, cap box; barrel is 32 inches long; total length 48 inches; engraved mountings; about ⅝-inch bore; almost new gun. Price, $10.00.

**No. 254.** Same as illustration No. 152; in plain steel; ⅝-inch bore; old-fashioned boring in the barrel; with Spanish lettering; 32-inch barrel; good, serviceable order. Price, $8.75.

**No. 255.** Gun same as No. 254, but without the butt plate. Price, $6.85.

**No. 1596. L. WURZINGER PERCUSSION LOCK MUSKET,** 29½-inch barrel, 12-gauge, smooth bore. Price $6.85.

This Catalog besides being a list of what we have for sale is offered as a reference book for collectors and museums and for that reason many special articles interesting to them are shown though sold.

**TEN FLINT LOCK MUSKETS WITH BAYONETS**, stamped on the butt plate "Lord Sydney," the leader in the British House of Commons, 1783, who was related to the Chancellor whose Stamp Act brought about the American revolution. Lord Sydney took a prominent part in drawing up the Treaty of Peace with America. These ten old flint lock muskets are from the old Sydney castle in Kent, England, rich in relics, which took three weeks in selling. The guns are genuine old flint locks made by Griffin and Tower, old gunmakers of the period of 1770, and are similar to the guns which the American and British soldiers fought with in the Revolutionary War; ¾ inch smooth bore, length 54 inches, 10 in. spade bayonet. All are in working order. Some of the stocks are a trifle worm eaten. Sydney, Australia, is named after the owner of these old muskets. Price, $15.00, each.

One gun with the *printed history* of the Sydneys, price $20.00.

**ANCIENT ENGLISH FLINT LOCK CADET GUN**; kind used by ladies or boys, length 37½ inches. Price, $7.85.

**FAMOUS MANTON FLINT LOCK SPORTING GUN**, 34 inch twist steel barrel, about ⅝ inch smooth bore. Ramrod ribbed barrel, flatted at the breech, stamped "MANTON, LONDON." Fine easy working lock. Inlaid gold vent. Silver name and side plate. Curly walnut checkered grip. In good order. Price $47.50.

**ORIENTAL MATCHLOCK GUN**, 37 inch octagonal barrel inlaid with silvered relief decoration.

Silvered band at the muzzle and on the butt stock. Hole through the stock for holding the fuse. Fine specimen. Price $25.00.

**ORIENTAL MATCH LOCK GUN.** 6 ft. long. Barrel is covered with raised ornamented decorations. Butt stock covered with camel's hide. Very old gun, in working order. Price $28.50.

**ORIENTAL MATCH LOCK GUN**, lacks 2 inches short of 6 ft. Working order. Fine nice light weight gun. Small part of the stock worm eaten. Price $17.85.

**ORIENTAL MATCHLOCK GUN**, 63 inches long. Silvered band. Long ROLL OF FUSE wound around stock ready for the match. Large curved butt. In working order. Price $21.00.

**ORIENTAL FLINT LOCK MUSKET**, 64 inches with ornamented silver band and butt plate. Inlaid silvered decorations on the barrel. In working order. Price $15.00.

**0-1081. ANCIENT PRUSSIAN MODEL, 1832, MUZZLE-LOADING SMOOTH-BORE MUSKET.** Lock stamped "Potzdam"; stamped on the gun, "1832." Barrel is 41½ inches long, ¾-inch smooth bore. Full length of the gun, 56½ inches; brass butt plate; guard bow; side plate bands and fore-end cap. Ancient pattern carrying sling swivels. Early model percussion hammer and vent. Walnut stock. Offered in working order. Price, $4.50.

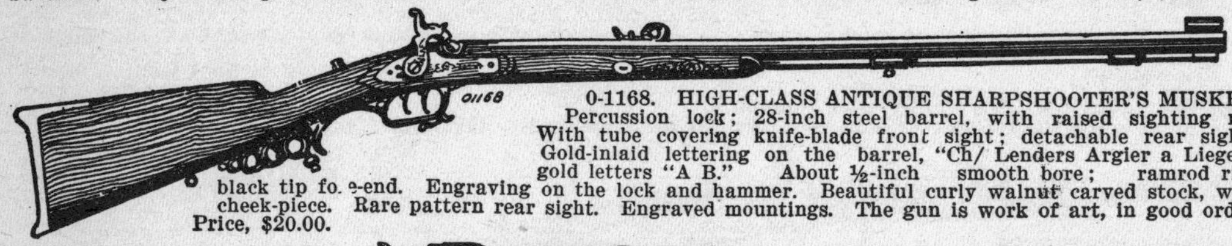

**0-1168. HIGH-CLASS ANTIQUE SHARPSHOOTER'S MUSKET.** Percussion lock; 28-inch steel barrel, with raised sighting rib. With tube covering knife-blade front sight; detachable rear sight. Gold-inlaid lettering on the barrel, "Ch/ Lenders Argier a Liege," gold letters "A B." About ½-inch smooth bore; ramrod rib; black tip fore-end. Engraving on the lock and hammer. Beautiful curly walnut carved stock, with cheek-piece. Rare pattern rear sight. Engraved mountings. The gun is work of art, in good order. Price, $20.00.

**0-1168AA. PHŒNIX BREECH-LOADING SHOTGUN**, made by the Whitney Arms Co., of Whitneyville, Ct., patented 1874. Whitney, the manufacturer, claimed that this rifle had less parts than any other breech-loading arm. 31½-inch smooth-bore barrel, about .40 calibre. In fair order only. Price, $9.85.

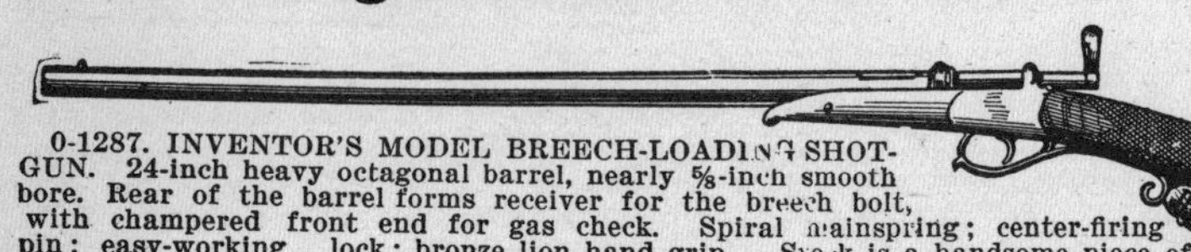

**0-1287. INVENTOR'S MODEL BREECH-LOADING SHOTGUN.** 24-inch heavy octagonal barrel, nearly ⅝-inch smooth bore. Rear of the barrel forms receiver for the breech bolt, with champered front end for gas check. Spiral mainspring; center-firing pin; easy-working lock; bronze lion hand grip. Stock is a handsome piece of figured curly walnut, with cheek-piece. Full length is 44½ inches. From the Harmer collection. Rare pattern. Good condition. Price, $20.00.

**0-1154. FRENCH CHASSEPOT MAGAZINE RIFLE**, altered from the Chassepot Rifle of the French and German wars into a magazine rifle for clip cartridges; 32-inch barrel. Magazine extends 1⅞ inches below the guard. No doubt inventor's model gun. Price, $25.00.

**0-1288. FINE TARGET RIFLE**, made by Dooley, of Scranton, Pa. Barrel was rifled by J. M. Gardner, of the same town. Both were noted craftsmen in their day. Heavy octagonal 29½-inch barrel; nearly ½-inch rifle bore. The RIFLING AT THE MUZZLE IS ALMOST SQUARE. Fine front sight is enclosed in tube; rear sight; fine peep sight on the stock. Double or set triggers. Fine, easy-working lock. German silver engraved mountings. Lock engraved "Dooley." Stock is half cheek-piece, and is a BEAUTIFUL SPECIMEN OF BIRD'S-EYE MAPLE. Full length of the gun, 45 inches. In fine order. From the Harmer collection. Price, $17.50.

**0-820. ARMY MUSKET SHOTGUN.** Old-time musket altered for use as a shotgun by cutting the long barrel down to 32 inches, boring out the rifle grooves to shoot bird-shot (about ¾-inch bore), attaching ramrod thimbles, putting on front sight, cutting off the heavy fore-end of the stock, changing the nipple from musket to shotgun size. Full length 48 inches. Finger-grip guard. Weight 7 pounds. Walnut stock. Blued steel barrel. 200 in stock. Price, $4.85 each.

**1114. WINCHESTER REPEATING ARMS CO. BREECH-LOADING SPORTING RIFLE** about .45 calibre. Found in London collection, with two British proof marks and the figure 400 on barrel. Short-leaf rear sight. Dropping breech-block action. Fine curly walnut pistol-grip stock and fore-end, with sling swivels. Barrel is 29 inches long.

**0-766. BRITISH ARMY MARTINI RIFLE**, obsolete pattern. The British Government, before offering for sale these obsolete pattern rifles, endeavored to destroy them for further use by putting a saw-cut through the receiver which contains the lock mechanism. This rifle is from the sale of Lady Palmer's collection, and shows THE CUT NEATLY BRAZED and the gun made serviceable. Evidently captured from Indian natives, which caused the British War Department to break up these old and obsolete guns into small pieces. As an officer said, "We might get a pound ($5.00) for the dead gun, but it might cost us 100 pounds to get it back." All CAPTURED GUNS are broken up, and it is only in the sale of some titled owner's collection that these relics can be obtained by collectors. An interesting,

**1850. SPORTING RIFLE.** Marked on lock "J. G. Zuzer, Arnheim." Octagonal FLUTED STEEL BARREL, with front and rear sights; about .40 calibre. Large hand-hold grip guard; Swiss butt; curly walnut stock, with checkered and engraved mountings. Price, $18.00.

**0-928. BRITISH BOER WAR LEE-ENFIELD CARBINE.** From sale of Lady Palmer's collection of rifles, which served in the war in South Africa. Gun is in good, serviceable order. Stock shows signs of hard usage. Stamped with British Crown, V. R. (Queen Victoria's Reign), England, 1885-L." Sighted for 2,000 yards. 21-inch barrel; full length 40 inches. Serviceable gun, as well as relic of the Boer War. Price, $20.00.

**CONFEDERATE ARMY WEB GUN SLINGS.** Made by the women of the South, 1861-1865. Cotton cloth, doubled to 1¼ inches in width, machine-sewed edges; iron adjusting hook; hand-sewed leather tightening strap and loops. Sold at one of the numerous AFTER-THE-WAR AUCTIONS, classified as WEB GUN SLINGS, REBEL. Offered in cleaned, serviceable order. Rare relics of the war between the States. Full length, opened out, 34 inches. Price, $1.00 each.

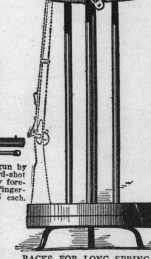

**RACKS FOR LONG SPRINGFIELD RIFLES SOLD.** U. S. ARMY RACKS for Krag rifles, similar to illustration but somewhat shorter. Will hold other late model rifles. For use in company rooms for holding rifles when not in use. Price, $5.85 each.

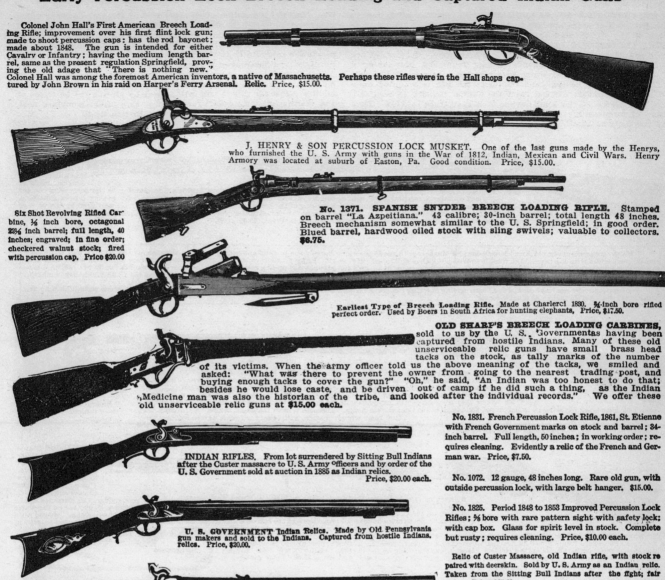

Colonel John Hall's First American Breech Loading Rifle; improvement over his first flint lock gun; made to shoot percussion caps; has the rod bayonet; made about 1848. The gun is intended for either Cavalry or Infantry; having the medium length barrel, same as the present regulation Springfield, proving the old adage that "There is nothing new." Colonel Hall was among the foremost American inventors, a native of Massachusetts. Perhaps these rifles were in the Hall shops captured by John Brown in his raid on Harper's Ferry Arsenal. Relic. Price, $15.00.

J. HENRY & SON PERCUSSION LOCK MUSKET. One of the last guns made by the Henrys, who furnished the U. S. Army with guns in the War of 1812, Indian, Mexican and Civil Wars. Henry Armory was located at suburb of Easton, Pa. Good condition. Price, $15.00.

Six Shot Revolving Rifled Carbine, ⅛ inch bore, octagonal 23½ inch barrel; full length, 40 inches; engraved; in fine order; checkered walnut stock; fired with percussion cap. Price $20.00

No. 1371. SPANISH SNYDER BREECH LOADING RIFLE. Stamped on barrel "La Azpeitiana." 43 calibre; 30-inch barrel; total length 48 inches. Breech mechanism somewhat similar to the U. S. Springfield; in good order. Blued barrel, hardwood oiled stock with sling swivels; valuable to collectors. $6.75.

Earliest Type of Breech Loading Rifle. Made at Charleroi 1830. ¾-inch bore rifled perfect order. Used by Boers in South Africa for hunting elephants, Price, $17.50.

OLD SHARP'S BREECH LOADING CARBINES, sold to us by the U. S. Governmentas having been captured from hostile Indians. Many of these old unserviceable relic guns have small brass head tacks on the stock, as tally marks of the number of its victims. When the army officer told us the above meaning of the tacks, we smiled and asked: "What was there to prevent the owner from going to the nearest trading post, and buying enough tacks to cover the gun?" "Oh," he said, "An Indian was too honest to do that; besides he would lose caste, and be driven out of camp if he did such a thing, as the Indian Medicine man was also the historian of the tribe, and looked after the individual records." We offer these old unserviceable relic guns at $15.00 each.

INDIAN RIFLES. From lot surrendered by Sitting Bull Indians after the Custer massacre to U. S. Army officers and by order of the U. S. Government sold at auction in 1885 as Indian relics. Price, $20.00 each.

No. 1831. French Percussion Lock Rifle, 1861, St. Etienne with French Government marks on stock and barrel; 34-inch barrel. Full length, 50 inches; in working order; requires cleaning. Evidently a relic of the French and German war. Price, $7.50.

No. 1072. 12 gauge, 48 inches long. Rare old gun, with outside percussion lock, with large belt hanger. $15.00.

No. 1825. Period 1848 to 1853 Improved Percussion Lock Rifles; ⅝ bore with rare pattern sight with safety lock; with cap box. Glass for spirit level in stock. Complete but rusty; requires cleaning. Price, $10.00 each.

U. S. GOVERNMENT Indian Relics. Made by Old Pennsylvania gun makers and sold to the Indians. Captured from hostile Indians. relics. Price, $20.00.

Relic of Custer Massacre, old Indian rifle, with stock repaired with deerskin. Sold by U. S. Army as an Indian relic. Taken from the Sitting Bull Indians after the fight; fair order. Price, $25.00.

No. 1882. C. Sharp, 1848 patent BREECH-LOADING RIFLE, about calibre 44, used with linen cartridge, with Maynard's patent 1845 tape primer box in the lock. With brass cap box in stock. Under lever action depresses the breech block for the removal and insertion of the cartridge in the chamber of the barrel. Heavy round barrel, 27 inch rifled. This lot was used in the Civil War by General Berdan's marksmen, which gave rise to the name "SHARP SHOOTER."

No. 1835. INVENTOR'S MODEL RIFLE WITH BREECH BOLT SERVING AS COVER, with side lever hammer; in working order. 52 inches long. Blued steel barrels and mountings; stock cracked. Price $20.00.

No. 1832. BRITISH MARTINA RIFLED CARBINE STAMPED ON LOCK WITH BRITISH CROWN V. R. (Victoria's reign). Enfield, 1879. With proof marks. In good working order. Price $15.00.

No. 1844. PERCUSSION LOCK RIFLE WITH EARLY PATTERN BAYONET which fits on the side of the gun muzzle in a triangular-shaped socket, with cheek piece on stock. Length of gun, 45 inches; ¾-inch rifle bore. Price $10.00.

No. 1829. FINE TWIST STEEL MODEL BREECH LOADING RIFLE, with top lever. Inventor's model. Checkered walnut stock. Enfield pattern lock plate. Full length, 45½ inches. Price $38.00.

## THE WORLD'S CURIOSITY SHOP.

Respectfully Dedicated to Francis Bannerman.

When Virgil sang of troops with arms disabled,
He little dreamed, in those old times gone by,
How Bannerman, to-day, if promptly cabled,
With arms the Roman legions could supply.

Yes, here could Caesar's troops become possessed of
Axe, helmet, breastplate, broadsword, shield and spear,
And all the modern arms they never guessed of,
From war's grim implements collected here.

All that is quaint and curious in history,
From cloth-yard shaft to matchlocks we behold;
And in their silent ranks how much of mystery
And deeds adventurous may rest untold.

From many a battlefield where cannon thundered,
Where charging squadrons swept the lines of steel;
From many a camp and port, dismantled plundered,
War's trophies numerous these stores reveal.

And vessels, too, their various goods and chattels,
Contribute here to swell the vast array,
With types of ordnance used in naval battles,
From ancient Actium to Manila Bay.

Old relics, too, now battered, rusted, broken,
Speak all too plainly of wild havoc wrought
By bursting shells, where men find many a token
When harvesting the fields where once they fought.

Guns whose quaint bayonets found many uses;
Long barrelled flintlock pistols of dragoons;
Carbines, and needle guns, and arquebuses,
With crossbows, blunderbusses, musketoons.

Halberds and pikes once used in border foray,
Broadswords and claymores from some Highland clan;
Javelins and shields that tell of conflict
By dusky warriors from the far Soudan;

Old guns that date from Saracen invaders,
Rare antique types collected through the years;
Weapons that once served warriors, knights, crusaders,
Italian brigands, Spanish bucaneers.

Ah, if these arms now silent could, awaking,
But find a tongue to tell of combats known,
What tales of blood, what scenes of carnage making
A hell of war's horrors would be shown.

But peaceful now, collected and united,
A grandeur mission do their ranks fulfill,
Where hundreds daily throng to gaze delighted
On their rare specimens of art and skill.

Few are the sights that Gotham has to offer
Of greater interest and instructive aid,
Than the rare contents of this famous coffer
From all earth's ransacked corners here displayed.

Greenwich, N. Y.                    D. Louis Bodge.

Published by Leslie's Weekly, July, 1906.

**INTRODUCTION OF CARRONADES.** No marked alteration in the batteries of ships appears to have occured down to the destruction of the French and Spanish maritime power at Trafalgar, in 1806. Carronades of small weight and calibre had taken the place in many cases of the 9 and 12-pounder long guns. Carronades are a short description of ordnance without trunnions, but having a loop under the reinforce which sets between lugs on a bed, a bolt passing through the lugs and the loop; the bed is mounted on a slide. The name is derived from the Carron foundry in Scotland, the first pieces of the kind having been cast there in 1779. They were of large calibre and of light proportional weight, the charge of powder was small, but at close quarters they were very effec- tive. In the composition of the batteries of the ships already cited, one great objection is the variety of calibres that were crowded together in the same ship, and sometimes on the same deck; of course each calibre had its own ammunition, which was required to be stowed separate from the ammunition of the other calibres, thus multiplying difficulties of stowage, and complicating the work of the powder division; the introduction of carronades operated to a considerable degree in bringing about an approach to uniformity of calibre. How far this is true will appear by stating the batteries of the "Santissima Trinidada," the heaviest ship of the combined fleet, and of the "Victory" and others of the British fleet.

**1,000 United States Springfield Primer-Lock, Muzzle-Loading, 58-Calibre Rifle Musket, made at** United States Springfield and United States Harper's Ferry Government Arsenals. In addition to the percussion cap the lock contains a receptacle for holding Dr. Maynard's patent primers, consisting of tape, with powder primer fulminate, about ⅜ of an inch apart, which at each cocking of the hammer one is forced out over the nipple and fired by the blow of the hammer. Percussion caps can also be used. Guns are the same as the United States troops used during the Civil War. This lot is complete with bayonets: packed 20 guns in each arm chest, all in serviceable order. Price, $5.00 each.

"Many thousands of the old Army Muzzle-loading Muskets with the 36-inch long barrels are in constant use by hunters throughout the country, and while they bear no comparison with the newest and most improved guns, they still do effective work. Many a countryman who would never dare (nor afford) to use a smokeless powder magazine gun clings to his old army musket, carries his powder in a bottle and his shot tied up in a rag, and when he goes hunting his family are seldom disappointed in their anticipation of rabbit pie for dinner. In one Maryland county within 20 miles of the Nation's capital there are no less than 1,000 single-barrel muzzle-loading guns in service."—Extract from Professor George C. Maynard, of the National Museum, in the Sporting Goods Dealer, January, 1903.
We suppose every one has heard of the Thanksgiving shooting for prize turkeys and how the up-to-date sportsmen with their fine repeaters were beaten by the countryman with his old fashioned muzzle-loader.

**No. 191.** Twice captured Confederate Muzzle-loading Rifle Musket, calibre 58. The parts for the guns were in process of manufacture at the U. S. Arsenal, Harper's Ferry, Virginia, in the early part of the Civil War, intended to be made up into the Primer-lock Musket. Just before completion the Confederates captured Harper's Ferry Armory and for safety sent the parts to Richmond, Va., where they were assembled into guns without the locks having the primer-lock attachment, the percussion lock answering for firing the musket cap, and issued to the Confederate Army. These guns show marks of usage. Eventually they were captured and sent to New York Arsenal at Governor's Island and 12 of them were laid aside, with other rare guns, as a collection. They were sold by the United States Ordnance Department July, 1902, after keeping them over 37 years. We offer these fine relics, with the marks and dates stamped on the locks, which tell their history, for $10.00 each.

Enlarged view of lock in the captured Confederate muskets.

**1,000 United States Springfield Muzzle-Loading Rifles.** Calibre 58, with bayonets. Same as used by the Union soldiers in the Civil War, when many a proud lad marched down Broadway in the early sixties with a Springfield musket on his shoulder, and it seemed light, even if its weight was over nine pounds. The barrel is 40 inches long and the bayonet measures 18 inches: on the plate is stamped the U. S. eagle, On the barrel the eagle head and the letters "V. P.," which means "viewed and proved." These rifles have small projections at the breech with vent screw whereby powder can be inserted in case a bullet has been loaded in the barrel without powder, or to remove dirt— a very useful improvement. These guns are in serviceable order. In 1861 they cost upwards of $18.00. This lot of guns was purchased from California Arsenal, where they were sent during the Civil War by convoyed steamer around Cape Horn at the time the Confederate Privateer Alabama was operating on the Pacific. To Grand Army Posts, Military organizations and the trade we offer these guns. For single gun with bayonet and gun sling, **$3.50.** Price for case of 20 guns and bayonets, packed in arm chests, **$48.00.**

**Calibre 58 Muzzle-loading Rifle Ball Cartridge.** Price, 10 cents each: $2.00 per 100. These are the kind the soldiers used to bite off the end before loading into the gun.
**8,000 Civil War Musket Blank Cartridges for Calibre 58 guns.** Price $1.25 per 100, $15 per 1,000.

**40 Enfield Muzzle-loading Civil War Rifles,** with bayonet. These guns were largely used by Confederate soldiers. Imported from England by blockade-running steamer. This particular lot came from an arsenal in Louisiana long after the war, and we have every reason to believe were carried by the famous Louisiana Tigers Confederate Regiment. In serviceable order. Price, $4.75 each.

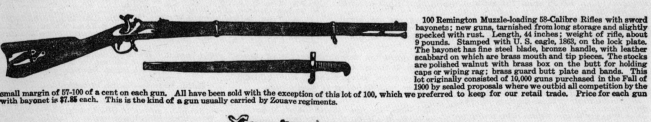

**100 Remington Muzzle-loading 58-Calibre Rifles** with sword bayonets; new guns, tarnished from long storage and slightly specked with rust. Length, 44 inches; weight of rifle, about 9 pounds. Stamped with U. S. eagle, 1863, on the lock plate. The bayonet has fine steel blade, bronze handle, with leather scabbard on which are brass mouth and tip pieces. The stocks are polished walnut with brass box on the butt for holding caps or wiping rag; brass guard butt plate and bands. This lot originally consisted of 10,000 guns purchased in the Fall of 1900 by sealed proposals where we outbid all competition by the small margin of 57-100 of a cent on each gun. All have been sold with the exception of this lot of 100, which we preferred to keep for our retail trade. Price for each gun with bayonet is **$7.85** each. This is the kind of a gun usually carried by Zouave regiments.

**500 U. S. Springfield Muzzle-loading Rifles, 58-Calibre, Model 1863,** with eagle stamped at breech; sighted for 800 yards. These rifles were used during the Civil War. Are offered in good serviceable order, with bayonets, at $4.50 each.

**Illustration of 10,000 Triangular Steel Bayonets,** for all Springfield Rifles, the only difference for various models is in the size of the socket; all have the locking clasp. Calibre 58 and all Calibre 50 Models are interchangeable; calibre 45 bayonet has smaller socket; all models of calibre 45 bayonets are interchangeable. Price of calibre 50 and 58 bayonets, 35 cents each, or $3.50 per dozen; $25.00 a hundred; in serviceable order. Calibre 45 bayonets, 90 cents each; $9.00 per dozen.

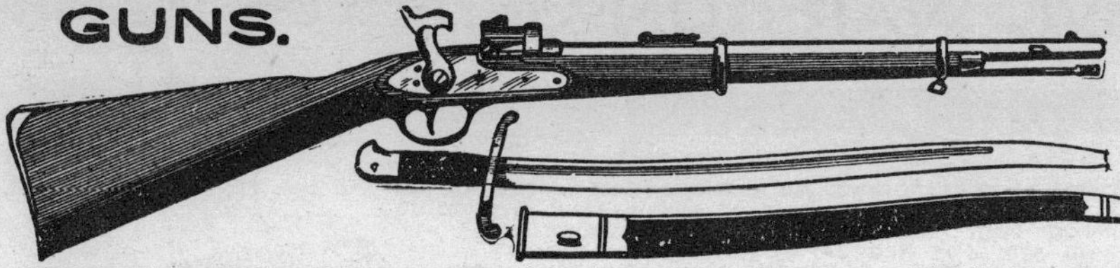

# GUNS.

**SNIDER ENFIELD BREECH-LOADING RIFLED CARBINE.** The British Government in the sixties paid a large sum of money to Snider, an American residing in Baltimore, for his invention for altering the 1,000,000 muzzle-loading Enfield Calibre 58 rifles into the breech-loader the cost of altering being about $5.00 per gun. The period of 1860 to 1870 was known as the Transition Period, regarding improvements in Government guns, nearly all the nations economized by altering the old guns instead of incurring the waste of war as in the present day when old guns are sold as junk, and entirely new guns are made at a cost of millions of dollars. These Snider Enfield rifles are now getting scarce, especially the carbines. We offer this rifle carbine in second hand, serviceable order, with side arm sword bayonet; price $12.00.

**No. 2270. SHARP'S CIVIL WAR COFFEE MILL CARBINE.** During the Civil War a workman, employed at the St. Louis Arsenal, devised a plan to incorporate a coffee mill on the butt stock of the gun. Sharp's carbine was selected. The grease box on the butt stock was retained as one of the side plates; the handle was detachable, and easily carried in the pocket. Several models of the carbines were altered in this way. It was intended to issue one of these carbines to each company; they are now very scarce; sold to museum.

**No. 1107A. OLD ENGLISH BLUNDERBUSS,** altered from flintlock, fitted on top of barrel with 13 inch spring bayonet. Lock marked: NOCK. Brass trigger guard, butt plate and side plate. Silver monogram plate. Barrel 15¼ inches, bore 1⅛ inches. Price, $28.00.

**No. 1107C. OLD ENGLISH BLUNDERBUSS,** altered from flintlock. 16 inch BRASS barrel, muzzle 1⅜ inches. Barrel marked: NICHOLSON, with three proof marks. Checkered grip, back action lock. Price, $28.00.

We wish to call special attention to pages 66, 67, 68, 69 and 366, where we show drawings and full description of all the World War guns. This information is not to be found in any book on the war. We have obtained this from first hand sources having access to all of the captured arms brought to this country by our government after the war. The drawings are all to scale and show every detail of guns. The different styles of bayonets are also shown. This information alone if in book form would readily sell at one dollar per copy, whereas we include this in our catalog and charge only 50c for all.

**EUROPEAN BREECH-LOADING RIFLE.** Charrion system; about Calibre 43; trigger guard forms the operating lever, which throws back the hammer and opens the chamber; full length 50 inches; barrel 29½ inches; weight 9 pounds; in good, second hand, serviceable order; with sword bayonet and steel scabbard; price $7.50.

**No. 2296.** Swinburne & Son, London, DOUBLE BARREL PERCUSSION LOCK RIFLE, about 58 Calibre, for hunting large game; four leaf sights ranged for 1,400 yards; fine curly walnut stock, 24-inch barrel; fine, easy working locks; price $12.00.

Note pages 367 and back cover where we show photographs of our place of business. These are included in the catalog for our new customers and for those who buy by mail who do not have an opportunity to call and see us. We wish customers to call and look over our collections of guns, relics and any other item that may interest them. We have been in business since 1865, and we endeavor to give entire satisfaction to every customer, and to give a little more value than the prices indicate.

**No. 1107D. OLD ENGLISH BLUNDERBUSS,** converted from flintlock. This style used by mail coach drivers. 5½ inch ornamented lock, BRASS barrel marked: LONDON, with three proof marks. Total length 31 inches, barrel 15½ inches, muzzle 1¼ inches. Checkered grip, brass butt plate, fancy brass trigger guard with acorn end. Price, $27.50.

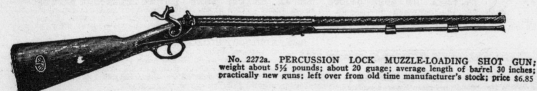

**No. 2272a. PERCUSSION LOCK MUZZLE-LOADING SHOT GUN;** weight about 5½ pounds; about 20 guage; average length of barrel 30 inches; practically new guns; left over from old time manufacturer's stock; price $6.85

**2297. U. S. NAVY LEE-REMINGTON CALIBRE 45 MAGAZINE RIFLE,** with U. S. N. label attached, marked as having come from the DeLong. Price, $15.00.

**2238. CHARLEVILLE FRENCH FLINTLOCK MUSKET;** 35-inch barrel; lock bears the French Charleville Arsenal marks. It was this pattern musket adopted by the U. S. Government when guns were first made at Springfield Armory. Serviceable order. Price, $48.00

**2232. FRENCH FLINTLOCK MUSKET;** 40-inch barrel; stamped B. D. 1811; stock has marks on the butt, which in olden times were blessed by the French clergy, and which the soldiers called "The Holy Water Mark"; gun in serviceable order. Price, $15.00.

**U. S. SPRINGFIELD CIVIL WAR MODEL 1855 RIFLE;** altered to breech-loader by Snider's patent, 1866; found in Europe. No doubt a model gun, as we understand the British Government bought from Snider all rights to his invention, and only the Military Enfield Muzzle-loading Rifles were altered. Price, $15.00.

**2226. ANCIENT TURKISH FLINTLOCK WALL GUN;** silver-inlaid barrel; Turkish Arsenal marks on the lock; ivory butt, inlaid with pieces of ivory (some missing); 34-inch barrel; marked as having been presented by the Sultan to Mr. Sutton, member of the British Diplomatic Corps. Price, $60.00.

**2227. DOUBLE-BARREL** (one over the other) **REVOLVING GUN,** similar to No. 1370, page 12 of our 1907 catalogue; fine percussion lock; silver inlaid; inscription on the barrel, "JOSEPH PROLICH IN BAMBERG"; carved walnut stock. Price, $35.00.

**No. 1107E. IRISH PERCUSSION BLUNDERBUSS,** with back action lock marked: TRULOCK & HARRISS. Checkered grip, engraved lock, tang and trigger guard. Half octagonal barrel, 18½ inches, marked: DUBLIN. Bore 1¾ inches. Some say that this is the style used by the landlords when they called to collect rent. Price $23.00.

**No. 1107F. OLD ENGLISH BLUNDERBUSS,** converted from flintlock. Brass butt plate, extra long brass guard, finely shaped BRASS barrel, 14¼ inches, marked: LONDON, with two old proof marks. Muzzle 1¼ inches. 6-inch flat lock marked: JOYNER. Unusual flat hammer. This is a fine specimen. Price, $26.00.

**0.764. ANCIENT BRITISH ARMY BAKER RIFLE, ORIGINALLY FLINTLOCK, ALTERED TO PERCUSSION.** Is complete, with the original sword bayonet, brass hilt with single guard. Brass-covered box on the stock for flints. British Crown, W. R. (King William Reign) Enfield stamped on the lock. About 7.10-inch calibre. Folding leaf rear sight. Hammer safety. Price, with bayonet, $20.00.

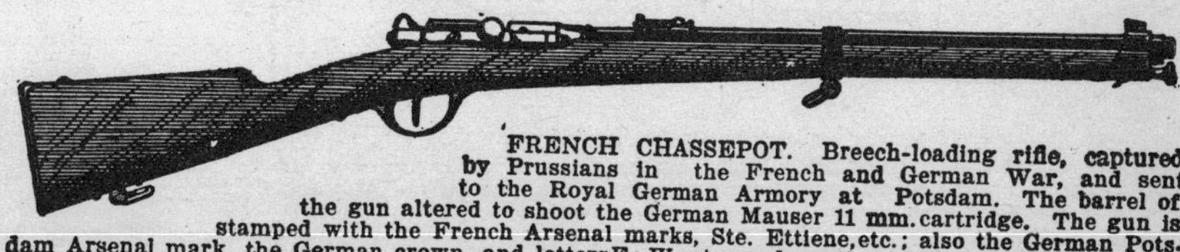

**FRENCH CHASSEPOT.** Breech-loading rifle, captured by Prussians in the French and German War, and sent to the Royal German Armory at Potsdam. The barrel of the gun altered to shoot the German Mauser 11 mm. cartridge. The gun stamped with the French Arsenal marks, Ste. Ettiene, etc.; also the German Potsdam Arsenal mark, the German crown, and letters F. W. stamped on the metal parts and over the "holy water mark" on the stock. Rare guns, in fine, serviceable order, with box of 20 centerfire reloading ball cartridges. Price, $8.50.

**800 U. S. Springfield Muzzle Loading Rifles,** 58 calibre, made at Trenton, New Jersey, during the civil war, to arm volunteer regiments. Have been used; are in good second-hand serviceable order, complete with bayonets. Barrel is 40 inches long; total length from butt to muzzle is 55½ inches; bayonet is 18 inches. These guns had been stored in New Jersey State Arsenal until Jan., 1905 (when we became the purchasers) along with five carloads of old military goods. Price $5.00 each.

**MILBANK'S BREECH-LOADING ALTERATION OF CIVIL WAR SPRINGFIELD MUSKET.** Patented in 1867, by I. M. Milbank and submitted to the Government along with some others as a means of utilizing the thousands of muzzle-loading arms then on hand. Some of these rifles found their way into Canada, in 1870 and were used by the Fenians in their raid. The breech block swings to the right and forward exposing the chamber; the point of the hammer acts as a lock upon discharge. An interesting American weapon. Price, $25.00.

**Illustration showing inside mechanism of all U. S. Springfield Rifle Locks.** We can supply all parts for Springfield locks as listed in our Catalogue.

**No. 1886. 10 GARABALDI MUSKETS,** purchased in Italy during the civil war period, to arm the U. S. Volunteers. Large bore, full length 48 inches, with sword bayonet, 26½ inches long, with leather scabbard and frog. Just as turned in by the U. S. soldiers at the close of the civil war. Guns have the under pin fastening with ramrod. (Sling swivels lost in service.) Offered as relics of two wars. In Italy with Garabaldi and with the Union soldiers in the civil war. Price $20.00.

**No. 1885. 20 AUSTRIAN MUZZLE LOADING** civil war percussion cap rifles with four-sided bayonet, with scabbard with attaching hook. In good second-hand serviceable order. Part of the lot purchased by order of President Lincoln, in Europe at the beginning of the civil war. Full length 52½-inches bayonet 20½-inches, Price, $5.60.

**No. 1887. 20 FRENCH RIFLES,** purchased in 1861 by order of President Lincoln to arm the U. S. volunteers. Full length is 56 inches. Complete with bayonet, 19-inch blade. In good second-hand order. Many thousands of these rifles were purchased. They have now become scarce. Price $5.60 each.

**No. 1884. CIVIL WAR SHARPSHOOTER'S LONG RANGE RIFLE.** Heavy rifle barrel; muzzle loading; fired with percussion cap. Used by the Union war soldiers attached to Gen. Berdan's regiment of sharpshooters. The guns are in poor order, owing to the heavy weight of the barrels, and careless handling. Hammers have been broken off the locks, ramrods missing. On receipt of order would select the best we have in stock and ship. Price $6.80 each. *Asare.*

**No. 1884A. SHARPSHOOTER'S, EXTRA HEAVY, LONG RANGE TELESCOPE RIFLES.** Such was the catalogue description of these famous rifles at the Government auction. On examination we found that they were without telescopes, and in very poor order. Many without hammers. Some of the barrels will weigh upwards of 20 pounds each. We offer as are, best selection with first offer, at $6.80 each.

**1884B. KENTUCKY MUZZLE LOADING RIFLE.** 32½ inch barrel. Full length 48½-inches. Brass bands, guard and butt plate, with brass covered cap box, on walnut stock. Round heavy rifle barrel, 54/100-inch in diameter with front and rear sights, with sling swivel. Made under contract, for use of the Government, by Eli Whitney, and other gun makers, patterned after the Harper's Ferry 1841 model rifle. We have these guns in two classes; the 1st class are those that are complete ready for shooting, requiring slight cleaning. Price, $10.00.

**No. 1883. GREEN'S PATENT CIVIL WAR RIFLE.** Bolt action, fired by percussion cap. Ring finger hammer strikes nipple UNDER the barrel. Patented 1857. Full length 52 inches. Rare relic. In serviceable second-hand order. Price $6.50.

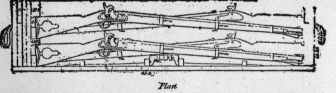

Plan.

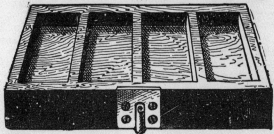

**VIEW OF ARMS CHESTS.** Made at the Government Armory, of well seasoned pine wood, with double ends, with partitions at each end, for keeping the guns from chafing. With compartments for holding spare parts, with rope ends. Bayonets are held in place at bottom of the case. These packing cases cost over $4.00 each to make. The lot of 40,000. Springfield B. L., Cal. 45 rifles are packed in these cases, and guns are offered free of charge for cases or New York down-town cartage.

**View of bottom of Gun Rack for holding butt of Gun.** These two parts form a fine walnut wood gun rack for holding 4 guns, any length desired; with two screws the tongue parts can be placed against wall, the rack parts fitting in at pleasure. 500 set. Price, complete set as per illustration. 75 cents set.

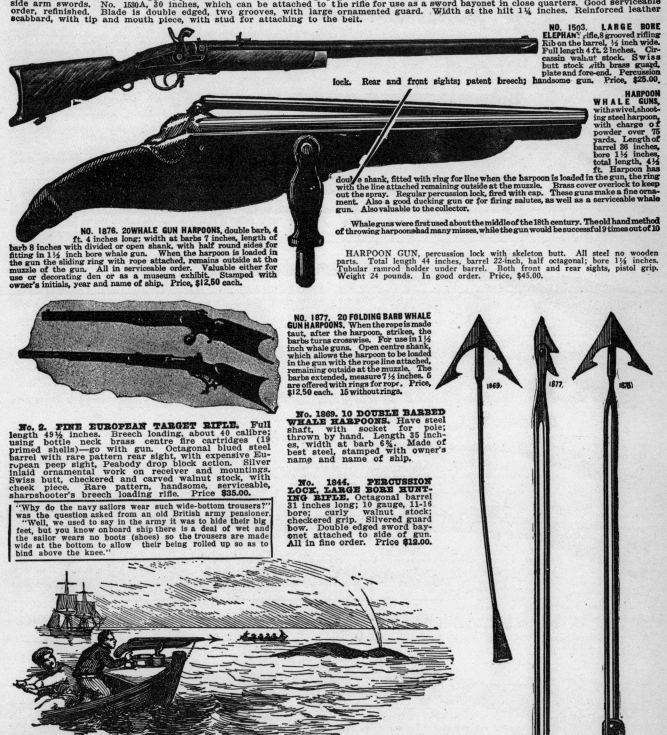

**No. 1530. 17 DOUBLE BARREL ELEPHANT RIFLES,** Jacob's patent, engraved on lock as being made by Swinburne & Son, 1860 and on the cover of the cap box in butt stock "Jacobs Rifle." Fine, well made, high class English rifle, for use of sportsmen in hunting elephants, lions and tigers. Blued steel barrel and mountings, with rib; with three short rear sights, and one long sight for 2,000 yards. With double hammers and triggers; percussion lock. With hand grip guard; with sling swivels. With these rifles we have five handsome side arm swords. No. 1530A, 30 inches, which can be attached to the rifle for use as a sword bayonet in close quarters. Good serviceable order, refinished. Blade is double edged, two grooves, with large ornamented guard. Width at the hilt 1¼ inches. Reinforced leather scabbard, with tip and mouth piece, with stud for attaching to the belt.

**NO. 1503. LARGE BORE ELEPHANT** rifle, 8 grooved rifling. Rib on the barrel, ½ inch wide. Full length 4 ft. 2 inches. Circassin walnut stock. Swiss butt stock with brass guard, plate and fore-end. Percussion lock. Rear and front sights; patent breech; handsome gun. Price, $25.00.

**HARPOON WHALE GUNS,** with swivel, shooting steel harpoon, with charge of powder over 75 yards. Length of barrel 36 inches, bore 1½ inches, total length, 4½ ft. Harpoon has double shank, fitted with ring for line when the harpoon is loaded in the gun, the ring with the line attached remaining outside at the muzzle. Brass cover overlock to keep out the spray. Regular percussion lock, fired with cap. These guns make a fine ornament. Also a good ducking gun or for firing salutes, as well as a serviceable whale gun. Also valuable to the collector.

Whale guns were first used about the middle of the 18th century. The old hand method of throwing harpoons had many misses, while the gun would be successful 9 times out of 10

HARPOON GUN, percussion lock with skeleton butt. All steel no wooden parts. Total length 44 inches, barrel 22-inch, half octagonal; bore 1⅛ inches. Tubular ramrod holder under barrel. Both front and rear sights, pistol grip. Weight 24 pounds. In good order. Price, $45.00.

**NO. 1876. 20 WHALE GUN HARPOONS,** double barb, 4 ft. 4 inches long; width at barbs 7 inches, length of barb 8 inches with divided or open shank, with half round sides for fitting in 1½ inch bore whale gun. When the harpoon is loaded in the gun the sliding ring with rope attached, remains outside at the muzzle of the gun. All in serviceable order. Valuable either for use or decorating den or as a museum exhibit. Stamped with owner's initials, year and name of ship. Price, $12.50 each.

**NO. 1877. 20 FOLDING BARB WHALE GUN HARPOONS.** When the rope is made taut, after the harpoon, strikes, the barbs turns crosswise. For use in 1½ inch whale guns. Open centre shank, which allows the harpoon to be loaded in the gun with the rope line attached, remaining outside at the muzzle. The barbs extended, measure 7½ inches. 5 are offered with rings for rope. Price, $12.50 each. 15 without rings.

**No. 2. FINE EUROPEAN TARGET RIFLE.** Full length 49½ inches. Breech loading, about 40 calibre; using bottle neck brass centre fire cartridges (19 primed shells)—go with gun. Octagonal blued steel barrel with rare pattern rear sight, with expensive European peep sight, Peabody drop block action. Silver inlaid ornamental work on receiver and mountings. Swiss butt, checkered and carved walnut stock, with cheek piece. Rare pattern, handsome, serviceable, sharpshooter's breech loading rifle. Price $35.00.

**No. 1869. 10 DOUBLE BARBED WHALE HARPOONS.** Have steel shaft, with socket for pole; thrown by hand. Length 35 inches, width at barb 6¾. Made of best steel, stamped with owner's name and name of ship.

**No. 1844. PERCUSSION LOCK, LARGE BORE HUNTING RIFLE.** Octagonal barrel 31 inches long; 10 gauge, 11-16 bore; curly walnut stock; checkered grip. Silvered guard bow. Double edged sword bayonet attached to side of gun. All in fine order. Price $12.00.

"Why do the navy sailors wear such wide-bottom trousers?" was the question asked from an old British army pensioner. "Well, we used to say in the army it was to hide their big feet, but you know on board ship there is a deal of wet and the sailor wears no boots (shoes) so the trousers are made wide at the bottom to allow their being rolled up so as to bind above the knee."

1869    1877    1876

Illustration showing Harpoon Gun in action.

**No. 1041. TIGER RIFLE,** shooting 12-gauge rifled ball. Twist steel rifled barrel, octagonal shaped, ramrod rib, fine walnut stock, checkered grip and fore-end, guard and lock plates engraved with tigers. Percussion lock. In fine order, like new. Front sight missing. Price $10.00.

# Sharpshooter's Rifles, Etc.

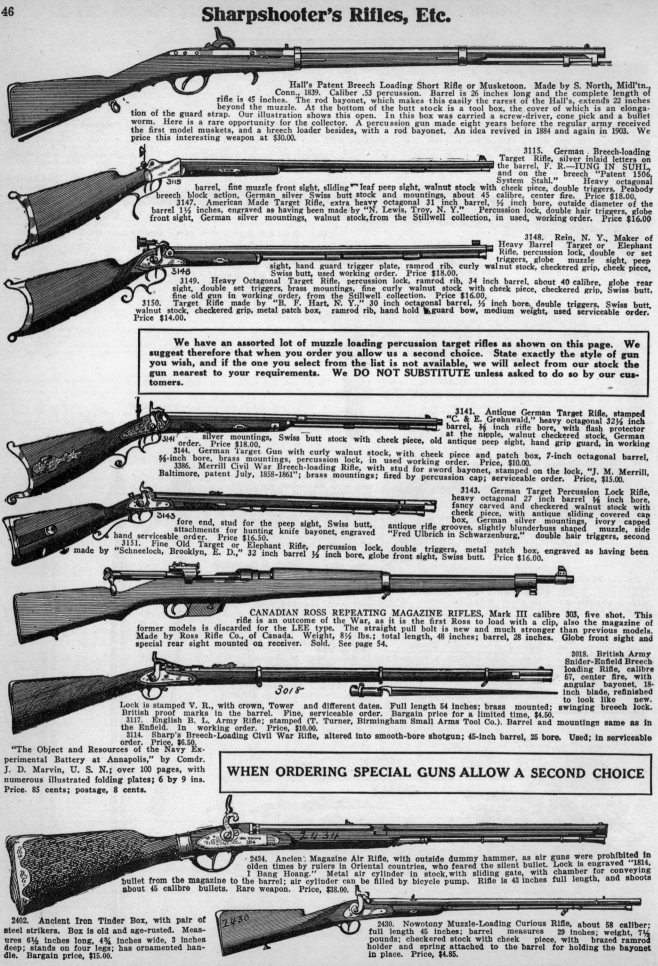

Hall's Patent Breech Loading Short Rifle or Musketoon. Made by S. North, Midl'tn., Conn., 1839. Caliber .53 percussion. Barrel is 26 inches long and the complete length of rifle is 45 inches. The rod bayonet, which makes this easily the rarest of the Hall's, extends 22 inches beyond the muzzle. At the bottom of the butt stock is a tool box, the cover of which is an elongation of the guard strap. Our illustration shows this open. In this box was carried a screw-driver, cone pick and a bullet worm. Here is a rare opportunity for the collector. A percussion gun made eight years before the regular army received the first model muskets, and a breech loader besides, with a rod bayonet. An idea revived in 1884 and again in 1903. We price this interesting weapon at $30.00.

3115. German Breech-loading Target Rifle, silver inlaid letters on the barrel, F. R.—IUNG IN SUHL, and on the breech "Patent 1506, System Stahl." Heavy octagonal barrel, fine muzzle front sight, sliding leaf peep sight, walnut stock with cheek piece, double triggers, Peabody breech block action, German silver Swiss butt stock and mountings, about 45 calibre, center fire. Price $18.00.

3147. American Made Target Rifle, extra heavy octagonal 31 inch barrel, ½ inch bore, outside diameter of the barrel 1½ inches, engraved as having been made by "N. Lewis, Troy, N. Y." Percussion lock, double hair triggers, globe front sight, German silver mountings, walnut stock, from the Stillwell collection, in used, working order. Price $16.00.

3148. Rein, N. Y., Maker of Heavy Barrel Target or Elephant Rifle, percussion lock, double or set triggers, globe muzzle sight, peep sight, hand guard trigger plate, ramrod rib, curly walnut stock, checkered grip, cheek piece, Swiss butt, used working order. Price $18.00.

3149. Heavy Octagonal Target Rifle, percussion lock, ramrod rib, 34 inch barrel, about 40 calibre, globe rear sight, double set triggers, brass mountings, fine curly walnut stock with cheek piece, checkered grip, Swiss butt, fine old gun in working order, from the Stillwell collection. Price $16.00.

3150. Target Rifle made by "B. F. Hart, N. Y.," 30 inch octagonal barrel, ½ inch bore, double triggers, Swiss butt, walnut stock, checkered grip, metal patch box, ramrod rib, hand hold guard bow, medium weight, used serviceable order. Price $14.00.

We have an assorted lot of muzzle loading percussion target rifles as shown on this page. We suggest therefore that when you order you allow us a second choice. State exactly the style of gun you wish, and if the one you select from the list is not available, we will select from our stock the gun nearest to your requirements. We DO NOT SUBSTITUTE unless asked to do so by our customers.

3141. Antique German Target Rifle, stamped "C. & E. Grøhnwald," heavy octagonal 32½ inch barrel, ⅜ inch rifle bore, with flash protector at the nipple, walnut checkered stock, German silver mountings, Swiss butt stock with cheek piece, old antique peep sight, hand grip guard, in working order. Price $18.00.

3144. German Target Gun with curly walnut stock, with cheek piece and patch box, 7-inch octagonal barrel, ⅝-inch bore, brass mountings, percussion lock, in used working order. Price, $10.00.

3386. Merrill Civil War Breech-loading Rifle, with stud for sword bayonet, stamped on the lock, "J. M. Merrill, Baltimore, patent July, 1858-1861"; brass mountings; fired by percussion cap; serviceable order. Price, $15.00.

3143. German Target Percussion Lock Rifle, heavy octagonal 27 inch barrel ⅝ inch bore, fancy carved and checkered walnut stock with cheek piece, with antique sliding covered cap box, German silver mountings, ivory capped fore end, stud for the peep sight, Swiss butt, attachments for hunting knife bayonet, engraved antique rifle grooves, slightly blunderbuss shaped muzzle, side "Fred Ulbrich in Schwarzenburg," double hair triggers, second hand serviceable order. Price $16.50.

3151. Fine Old Target or Elephant Rifle, percussion lock, double triggers, metal patch box, engraved as having been made by "Schneeloch, Brooklyn, E. D.," 32 inch barrel ½ inch bore, globe front sight, Swiss butt. Price $16.00.

CANADIAN ROSS REPEATING MAGAZINE RIFLES, Mark III calibre 303, five shot. This rifle is an outcome of the War, as it is the first Ross to load with a clip, also the magazine of former models is discarded for the LEE type. The straight pull bolt is new and much stronger than previous models. Made by Ross Rifle Co., of Canada. Weight, 8½ lbs.; total length, 48 inches; barrel, 28 inches. Globe front sight and special rear sight mounted on receiver. Sold. See page 54.

3018. British Army Snider-Enfield Breech-loading Rifle, calibre 57, center fire, with angular bayonet, 18-inch blade, refinished to look like new. swinging breech lock. Lock is stamped V. R., with crown, Tower and different dates. Full length 54 inches; brass mounted; British proof marks in the barrel. Fine, serviceable order. Bargain price for a limited time, $4.50.

3117. English B. L. Army Rifle; stamped (T. Turner, Birmingham Small Arms Tool Co.). Barrel and mountings same as in the Enfield. In working order. Price, $10.00.

3114. Sharp's Breech-Loading Civil War Rifle, altered into smooth-bore shotgun; 45-inch barrel, 25 bore. Used; in serviceable order. Price, $6.50.

"The Object and Resources of the Navy Experimental Battery at Annapolis," by Comdr. J. D. Marvin, U. S. N.; over 100 pages, with numerous illustrated folding plates; 6 by 9 ins. Price. 85 cents; postage, 8 cents.

## WHEN ORDERING SPECIAL GUNS ALLOW A SECOND CHOICE

2434. Ancient Magazine Air Rifle, with outside dummy hammer, as air guns were prohibited in olden times by rulers in Oriental countries, who feared the silent bullet. Lock is engraved "1814, I Bang Hoang." Metal air cylinder in stock, with sliding gate, with chamber for conveying bullet from the magazine to the barrel; air cylinder can be filled by bicycle pump. Rifle is 43 inches full length, and shoots about 45 calibre bullets. Rare weapon. Price, $38.00.

2402. Ancient Iron Tinder Box, with pair of steel strikers. Box is old and age-rusted. Measures 6½ inches long, 4¾ inches wide, 3 inches deep; stands on four legs; has ornamented handle. Bargain price, $15.00.

2430. Nowotony Muzzle-Loading Curious Rifle, about 58 caliber; full length 45 inches; barrel measures 29 inches; weight, 7½ pounds; checkered stock with cheek piece, with brazed ramrod holder and spring attached to the barrel for holding the bayonet in place. Price, $4.85.

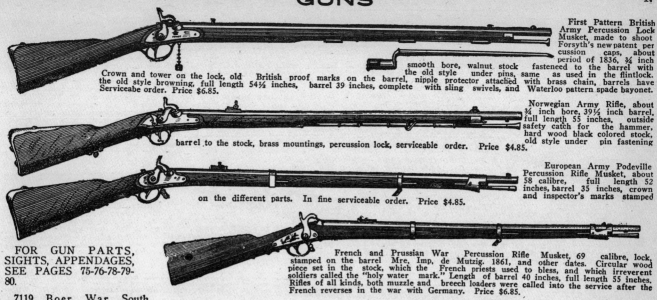

First Pattern British Army Percussion Lock Musket, made to shoot Forsyth's new patent percussion caps, about period of 1836, ¾ inch fasteneed to the barrel with the old style under pins, same as used in the flintlock.

Crown and tower on the lock, old British proof marks on the barrel, nipple protector attached with brass chain, barrels have the old style browning, full length 54½ inches, barrel 39 inches, complete with sling swivels, and Waterloo pattern spade bayonet. Serviceabe order. Price $6.85.

Norwegian Army Rifle, about ¾ inch bore, 39½ inch barrel, full length 55 inches, outside safety catch for the hammer, hard wood black colored stock, old style under pin fastening

barrel to the stock, brass mountings, percussion lock, serviceable order. Price $4.85.

European Army Podeville Percussion Rifle Musket, about 58 calibre, full length 52 inches, barrel 35 inches, crown and inspector's marks stamped

on the different parts. In fine serviceable order. Price $4.85.

French and Prussian War Percussion Rifle Musket, 69 calibre, lock, stamped on the barrel Mre. Imp. de Mutzig. 1861, and other dates. Circular wood piece set in the stock, which the French priests used to bless, and which irreverent soldiers called the "holy water mark." Length of barrel 40 inches, full length 55 inches. Rifles of all kinds, both muzzle and breech loaders were called into the service after the French reverses in the war with Germany. Price $6.85.

FOR GUN PARTS, SIGHTS, APPENDAGES, SEE PAGES 75-76-78-79-80.

7119. Boer War South Africa Captured Mauser Rifle, 7 M/M, in serviceable order, from London collector no doubt brought to England from South Africa by returning soldier as captured trophy. Price, $15.00.

C R R. COLT'S REVOLVING PERCUSSION RIFLE with full length stock. Round barrel 31 inches, caliber 54, full length 49½ inches. This is a MILITARY model. Raised front sight, two leaf folding rear sight. The standing rear sight is marked: 100, the short leaf: 300, the long front leaf: 600. The lower band has sling swivel, and there is also a sling swivel in butt stock. The frame is marked: COL. COLT, HARTFORD, CT., U. S. A. The butt plate has rod opening. Price, $150.00.

C R R-1. COLTS REVOLVING RIFLE, altered to take metallic cartridges. Full length 42 inches, round barrel 23¾ inches, caliber 38. This has full length stock without sling swivels. It is a military model. Frame is marked: COL. COLT, HARTFORD, CT., U. S. A., with one British VIEW MARK, and two Belgian proof marks. The barrel has these same marks also. Raised brass front sight, two leaf folding rear sight for 100, 300, and 600 yards. The trigger guard and butt plate are made of white metal. The butt plate has rod opening. Price, $100.

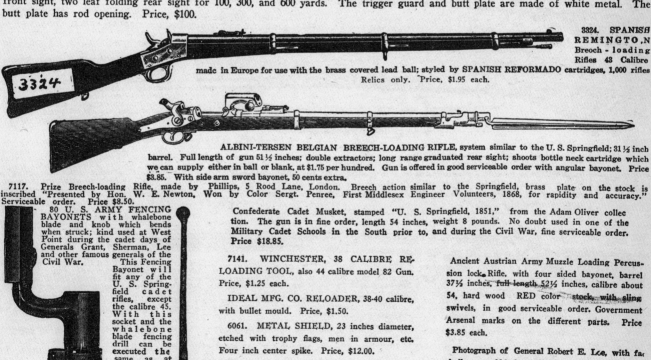

3324. SPANISH REMINGTON Breech-loading Rifles 43 Calibre

made in Europe for use with the brass covered lead ball; styled by SPANISH REFORMADO cartridges, 1,000 rifles Relics only. Price, $1.95 each.

ALBINI-TERSEN BELGIAN BREECH-LOADING RIFLE, system similar to the U. S. Springfield; 31½ inch barrel. Full length of gun 51½ inches; double extractors; long range graduated rear sight; shoots bottle neck cartridge which we can supply either in ball or blank, at $1.75 per hundred. Gun is offered in good serviceable order with angular bayonet. Price $3.85. With side arm sword bayonet, 50 cents extra.

7117. Prize Breech-loading Rifle, made by Phillips, 5 Rood Lane, London. Breech action similar to the Springfield, brass plate on the stock is inscribed "Presented by Hon. W. E. Newton, Won by Color Sergt. Penree, First Middlesex Engineer Volunteers, 1868, for rapidity and accuracy." Serviceable order. Price $8.50.

80 U. S. ARMY FENCING BAYONETS with whalebone blade and knob which bends when struck; kind used at West Point during the cadet days of Generals Grant, Sherman, Lee and other famous generals of the Civil War. This Fencing Bayonet will fit any of the U. S. Springfield cadet rifles, except the calibre 45. With this socket and the whalebone blade fencing drill can be executed the same as at West Point. Socket and whalebone blade. Price, $1.00 the set.

Confederate Cadet Musket, stamped "U. S. Springfield, 1851," from the Adam Oliver collection. The gun is in fine order, length 54 inches, weight 8 pounds. No doubt used in one of the Military Cadet Schools in the South prior to, and during the Civil War, fine serviceable order. Price $18.85.

7141. WINCHESTER, 38 CALIBRE RELOADING TOOL, also 44 calibre model 82 Gun. Price, $1.25 each.

IDEAL MFG. CO. RELOADER, 38-40 calibre, with bullet mould. Price, $1.50.

6061. METAL SHIELD, 23 inches diameter, etched with trophy flags, men in armour, etc. Four inch center spike. Price, $12.00.

7121. Braendlin-Albini Army Rifle, with bayonet. Price $3.50.

Ancient Austrian Army Muzzle Loading Percussion lock Rifle, with four sided bayonet, barrel 37½ inches, full length 52½ inches, calibre about 54, hard wood RED color stock with sling swivels, in good serviceable order. Government Arsenal marks on the different parts. Price $3.85 each.

Photograph of General Robert E. Lee, with fac simile copy of his farewell order to the Confederate army, April 10, 1865. Size 7x14 inches with border for framing. Price 25 cents.

0-769. SCHULOFF AUSTRIAN MODEL MAGAZINE RIFLE. High-power military weapon, with revolving magazine mechanism; forerunner of the Savage. Handsome, well made model gun, about 30 calibre. Straight pull-back breech bolt. Cartridges are inserted one at a time into the revolving carrier, and by the action of the bolt are fed up and into the chamber of the barrel. Schuloff was, in our opinion, the original inventor of the revolving high-power rifle. (In 1884 we were requested to become stockholders in a company organized for the manufacture of Schuloff's revolving high-power rifle.) The rear sight leaf is graded with the front sight up to 1700 yards, and by a sight on the middle band for 2500 yards. The finest, lightest gun mechanism made. New blued steel, 30-inch barrel. No proof marks on the gun. Valuable gun to rifle manufacturers. In fine order. Rare prize. Price, $50.00.

Jenks Breech-loading Rifled Carbine, made in 1847 by Ames of Chicopee, Mass., for the U. S. Navy fired with percussion cap; hammer is on the right side of the gun; opening in top of the barrel for the insertion of the cartridge; about calibre 54; full length 41 inches; barrel 24 inches; price $12.85.

Early American Breech-loading Rifled Carbine; medium length for use of either Infantry or Cavalry; invented by Colonel John Hall of Yarmouth, Mass. The first Hall guns were made to be fired with flint; later the guns were made to be fired by percussion cap, as in the above model. The U. S. Government had a separate armory at Harpers Ferry, Va., for the manufacture of the Halls patent guns. It was the Halls Armory at Harpers Ferry that John Brown captured in order to obtain rifles to arm the negroes to fight for freedom. The gun is in second hand, shooting order; no doubt has been used in the Mexican, Indian and Civil Wars; price $15.00.

**2235.** Brigand Guns, sold by the Italian Government as captured from the Brigands; assorted lot, no two alike; all are rare old pattern percussion lock guns; some have part of paper label pasted on the stock, no doubt the court record of some bad man; all in working order; price $3.85.

80 U. S. Springfield Muzzle-loading Rifles; stamped as having been made by E. Remington, 1865; found in London in 1907; no doubt this was the last lot of muzzle-loading Army rifles, Springfield pattern, made by contractors, and possibly and probably these guns formed part of the lot sold to the French Government during the French and German War; 3 band guns in serviceable, second hand order with both the U. S. and British proof marks; price $3.75 each.

**1212.** Gibbs Patent Carbine, made by William F. Brooks, New York, during the Civil War; 1052 of these carbines were purchased by the U. S. Government from 1861 to 1865 at an average cost of $24.00 each; full length is 38 inches; barrel 22 inches; 54 calibre; barrel tilts up to load; the trigger guard is the operating lever, which on being depressed moves the barrel forward and tilts it up to receive the cartridge; price $10.00.

**1883.** Green's Patent Civil War Breech-loading Rifle; bolt action, with under hammer, which strikes the cap on the under side of the barrel; serviceable second hand order; full length 52 inches; relic; price $50.00.

**2249.** Louis XVIII. of France Gar de Corp Flint-lock Musket with Bayonet. The flash pan instead of being covered by the hammer is covered by a brass tube, opening into the vent, preventing the priming from getting wet, also preventing premature discharge. The gun bears French Arsenal marks; full length 56 inches; barrel 41½ inches; bore 11-16 inches; weight 7½ pounds; brass guard and butt plate; rare gun; price $25.00.

**2235-A.** U. S. Navy Plymouth Civil War Rifle, made by Ely Whitney of New Haven, Conn., for U. S. Navy in 1862 and 1863; calibre 69; in second hand, serviceable order. For Dahlgren Knife Bayonets, see No. 1270-A, page 126, with scabbards, price $10.00; very scarce.

General Roberts U. S. V. Patent Breech-Loading Rifle. The Enfield Civil War Rifle supplied to the South during the Civil War by British blockade runners; altered to breech-loader under General Roberts's patent. Many of the Roberts rifles were purchased and used by the Fenians in the raid on Canada; calibre 58; full length of rifle, without bayonet, 49 inches; offered in good second-hand, serviceable order, with bayonet. Price, $20.00.

**0-765.** BRITISH RIFLE, MADE SPECIALLY BY POWELL & SON, BIRMINGHAM, for a Boer whose name and address is engraved on the barrel, "Jan Strydon, Dordrette," captured in the Boer War. From the sale of Lady Palmer's collection. Calibre is about 45; octagonal barrel, 31 inches. Percussion lock. Matted sighting rib, with sliding bar, leaf sight and three small folding sights; globe front sight. Walnut stock. Checkered grip and fore end. Patch box in the stock. Ramrod ribbed. Easy working lock. Fine, high-class rifle, as well as serviceable relic. Price, $15.00.

> This Catalog besides being a list of what we have for sale is offered as a reference book for collectors and museums and for that reason many special articles interesting to them are shown though sold. Some of the articles marked off may be in stock later or we may have something similar.

**0-760.** ANCIENT MUSKET WITH CARVED LION HAND HOLD. Originally flintlock, has been converted to percussion. Twist barrel shows great age and usage. Blunderbuss muzzle. Bronze mountings. Stock is slightly worm-eaten. The full length is 61½ inches. This gun is from the Lawson-Johnston, Kingswood collection sale, which contained only the finest and most historical weapons. One of the best private collections in Europe. My agent said the place was leased after Mr. Johnston's death to some one who did not like to see guns and weapons around, so had them taken down from the walls and stored in a stable, where they got "A JOLLY GOOD LOT OF RUST." Later the estate offered the collection at auction. There was such a demand for catalogues that 6d. each was charged. The sale contained the famous Stuart relic, the Culloden Bedstead, in which Prince Charles slept the night before the battle of Culloden-Moor. Our buyer was unable to obtain the history of this relic gun. We offer it at the bargain price of $22.50.

Maynard's first tape primer. Submitted to the U. S. Government Board at West Point, Jan. 29, 1845. Maynard's first proposition to the U. S. was to utilize the tape primer in connection with the alteration of thousands of flintlock muskets then on hand. The primer magazine is a box with a movable lid, placed on the outside of an altered flintlock plate. In the drawing, the cover of the magazine is open, showing the tape coiled up ready for use. A slot in the lower part of the hammer (see cut) worked the piece was cocked, and the knife-like edge of the lips of the hammer cut off the tape when exploded. 300 flintlock muskets were altered on this principle at Springfield Arsenal during 1848; they were of the latest model of the flintlocks then on hand. The original cone did not admit of the use of the regular percussion cap. This, however, was changed at the suggestion of the board of army officers soon after. Between 1845 and 1854 Dr. Maynard received $76,000 for the use of his invention.

**0-757.** "JOHN MANTON & SONS, DOVER STREET, LONDON," ENGRAVED ON A FINE TWIST-STEEL DOUBLE-BARREL PERCUSSION RIFLE. 30-inch barrels, 12-gauge rifle bore. Knife-blade front sight. Double leaf folding rear sight. Ribbed top. Gun sling swivels on barrel and butt. Chased mountings and lock, engraved "John Manton & Sons." Fine checkered fore end, grip and butt-plate. Silver vent plugs. Fine curly walnut stock. Easy working locks; well preserved gun. Famous Manton guns are now rarely found in the sales market. Double-barrel RIFLED gun of these famous makers is extremely rare. Bargain price, $65.00.

**2300.** Prize Rifle, similar to No. 2299, with silver plate, engraved as having been won by William Fuller, Victoria Rifles, at Wimbledon, 1865. Price, $10.00.

## BAYONETS

Nearly all authors of encyclopaedias and dictionaries, from the habit of copying one another, have repeated that the bayonet (Bajonnet in German) was invented and manufactured at Bayonne by Puysegur, who died in 1682. Nevertheless this sort of dagger or sword has not been carried at the end of a fusil only, it had been already adapted to the arquebus, and even perhaps to the earliest portable firearms. The bayonet was already known in France about 1570, but was not universally adopted until about 1640, when it replaced the pike in certain regiments. At the present day the bayonet is composed of the blade and socket with collar, which latter invention has been wrongly attributed in England to Mackay, in 1691, and in France to Vauban; but it was at first a simple handle in wood, iron, or horn, intended to fix into the barrel. Subsequently the bayonet was fixed at the end of the gun by means of the socket, which was sloped so as to turn on the collar. This was the side-arm joined to the firearm, called musket-gun or fusil-musket, and attributed to Vauban, which Couhorn, his rival, introduced among the Dutch infantry about 1680.

**No. 257.** Wesley Richards Breech Loading Army Rifle as furnished by this well-known gunmaking firm to the Portuguese Army in 1867; lock is engraved with name of firm with 1867 in triangle; rifles (we have 12) are in good, second-hand order; barrel is 32 inches long; total length, 49 inches; has the top-lever action; no cartridges; valuable to collectors; fine rifled barrel. **Price $5.85** each.

30 U. S. Ward-Burton Springfield Armory-made Breech Loading Rifles, 50-calibre, centre fire; model guns. Bolt action, in good condition. Price $15.00 each.

Collection 40 Assorted Rifles and Muskets; all in fine order. Price $400.00.

Wanzle B/L Rifles; fine order. Price $4.80.

Bennet Repeating Rifle, 26 shots, relic only. Price $20.00.

Fenian Raiders' Brown B/L Rifle. Price $8.75.

Canadian Army B/L Rifle. Price $5.50.

German B/L Rifle, altered from muzzle loader. Model gun. Price $8.50 each.

Enfield M/L Rifle, altered to breech loading; inventor's model; good order. Price $25.00.

2 Girkinet Patent Breech Loading Percussion Lock Rifles, ½-inch bore; safety lock; Springfield pattern breech lever action; fancy guard. Price $15.00.

1 Antique Breech Loading Musket with bolt; forerunner of the German Needle Gun; in serviceable order. Price $9.50.

German Needle Gun, stamped as being made at the Imperial Armory, Spandau, 1862; complete with bayonet. Price $8.75.

1 Old Military Musket, stamped 1829. Percussion lock, with hammer in center (no lock plate); rare pattern; serviceable order. Price $8.85.

Remains of a number of old British Guns fused together in the fire at the Tower of London in 1840; mounted on board. Price $15.00.

U. S. Springfield M/L, altered to Peabody B/L system. Price $10.00.

Inventor's Model, Tower Enfield, model 1870, altered to the Springfield breech loading system. Price $25.00.

German Mauser Magazine, small bore, high-power rifle. New. Price $25.00.

Army Drill Guns, with spring bayonet. Price, $3.80.

Whitney Repeating Rifle, 44 calibre, equal to new. Price, $15.00.

Inventor's Model Magazine Rifle with magazine in the butt, only one ever made; purchased from the inventor. Price $28.00.

**1780. 3 SNYDER ENFIELD BREECH LOADING RIFLES,** altered from percussion lock into breech loading rifled Snyder action. Used; serviceable. $4.85 each.

**1781. 2 EUROPEAN REMINGTON BREECH LOADING RIFLES.** In working order. $5.00 each.

**7107. ANCIENT FLINTLOCK SPORTING RIFLE,** 28-inch octagonal steel barrel, ¾-inch rifle bore; walnut stock, checkered grip; brass guard plate, with hand-hold; brass patch box in stock; leather covered cheek-piece; weight, 6 lbs. 7 oz. Serviceable order. Price, $25.00.

**8001. FLINTLOCK BLUNDERBUSS GUN,** 29½-inch barrel, 2 inches diameter; bell mouth; antique walnut stock, with relief ornamented brass butt plate. Fine old gun, in serviceable order. Price, $38.00.

## BEECHER'S RIFLES

To the *New York Herald Tribune:*

Both "The Topeka Capital" and W. F. J. are correct in stating that Henry Ward Beecher assisted in raising funds for the purchase of Sharpe's rifles. The first meeting at which Beecher advocated the purchase of rifles was one which had been called by Yale students and instructors at the Congregational Church in New Haven, Conn., in February, 1856. The primary idea of the meeting was simply to assist the Kansas pioneers in a general way, and while it was said that arms might be necessary for self-defense, it was urged that no aggressive use of them would be made. In Beecher's speech he said: "I do not doubt that the people of New Haven will not permit a band of their fellow citizens to become victims (for the lack of a few rifles) of attacks that their defenselessness may invite. They have a right to protect their property and to protect themselves."

A collection was taken up and subscriptions of $25 each for the rifles were made by Professor Moses Tyler and Benjamin Stillman, of Yale. Mr. Beecher then said: "If sufficient for twenty-five rifles is raised on the spot, I will pledge twenty-five more from Plymouth Church." The next Sunday morning he was back in Brooklyn and notice was given out that those who wished to aid the emigrants might subscribe in the lecture room. George H. Day, a friend of mine, told me that he was one who then and there contributed $25 for the cause. These rifles were packed in boxes and marked "Bibles" and forwarded to various points in Kansas. There were seventy-seven of them in all.

WILLIAM E. DAVENPORT.

Brooklyn, July 28, 1925.

---

**10938. RUSSIAN RIFLE** captured in Crimea War, Alma, 1854. Lock and side plate stamped as having been made in 1846. Muzzle loading, smooth bore, percussion. lock from Lord Wolsley. Price $18.50.

**11042. E. ROBINSON, NEW YORK** 1863–1864 with U. S and Government eagle stamped on the lock of Springfield muzzle loading rifle. This gun is one contracted for by the U. S. Government during the Civil War at a cost of $25.00 each, and is valuable beyond the ordinary Springfield rifle to those who are making a collection of Civil War Contract Springfield guns. The gun is complete with bayonet, in good condition. Price $4.85.

**MERRILL-JENKS, BREECH-LOADING CIVIL WAR CARBINE.** The Merrill breech action was based on the original Jenks patents, although twenty years separated their introduction (1838-1858). At the outbreak of the Civil War, a few of the old Jenks carbines were improved by the addition of the side-hammer and "Merrill" method of securing the breech. This arm is one of the rarest of carbines of the period, very few found outside of Government collections. Barrel is 24 inches long and calibre is .54. Price, $35.00.

**10571. ALLENS U. S. PATENT 1855 BREECH LOADING PERCUSSION LOCK RIFLED CARBINE.** Full length 40 inches, barrel 26 inches Top lever forms the breech, opened up exposing entrance to the cartridge chamber within the barrel. about40 calibre. Curly walnut stock. Rare weapon. Price $30.00.

**11040A. SHARP'S CARBINE, 18-INCH BARREL, CALIBRE 52,** equipped with the famous Maynard Primer. This carbine was made at Hartford, Conn., for the British Government and is stamped in several places with the English proof marks and the "Broad Arrow" denoting government ownership. On the tang of the brass buttplate is the following:

E
2
D G
62

Evidently a regimental mark and number. A number of American breech-loading systems were tried by the English in the 50's among them the Sharps, this is one of them, the peculiar thing about this gun is that it was afterward sold by the English to the U. S. and used by the North with others during the Civil War and in 1900 when the government sold all the remaining Civil War arms this piece was among the lot. The peculiar leaf sight common to English percussion carbines is on the barrel. A rare and interesting weapon.

**10937. FAMOUS RIGBY MATCH RIFLE,** 50 calibre, 36-inch heavy fine steel barrel. Pistol grip. Cap lock, Checkered grip and fore end. Base for rear peep sight. Buck horn muzzle sight. Lock engraved "John Rigby & Co." Good order, price $12.50.

**10933. TERRYS PERCUSSION LOCK BREECH LOADING RIFLE CARBINE,** issued to the British Army in 1860 and known as the "DOOR BOLT MECHANISM." shipped to the South by blockade runners. Carbine is in working order. This carbine is fac-simile of one in Confederate Museum, Richmond Va., used by General J., E. B. Stuart, the great cavalry leader. Price $25.00.

**10566. HEURTELOUPS SELF PRIMING PERCUSSION LOCK MUZZLE LOADING ARMY RIFLE.** under hammer, primer fed by grooved wheel in the stock and inserted on the nipple. Full length 55 inches. Price $14.50.

**10722. LARGE BORE ELEPHANT GUN,** heavy twist, steel 31-inch barrel, about 1 INCH SMOOTH BORE complete with bullet mould. The barrel is 2¼ inches wide at the octagonal barrel end. Polished dark colored hard wood stock. Checkered grip. Carrying sling Swivel ramrod extends under the stock. Fine order like new. FINE SERVICEABLE DUCKING GUN; has front and rear sights. Price $18.85.

**10934. INTERESTING MODEL CONVERTED ENFIELD, BREECH LOADING CAP & BALL RIFLE.** Evidently gun before Board prior to the adoption the Snider musket. Name indistinct (worn off). Price $25.00.

**11025. MONT-STORMS PATENT BREECH LOADING RIFLED CARBINE,** altered from the Enfield muzzle oader for competition before the British Board of Officers selected for the purpose of inspecting and testing guns for troops in the British Army service. This carbine has the two British broad arrow proof marks, one showing the arrow pointed to the RIGHT FOR SERVICE, the other arrow pointing to the LEFT shows DISMISSAL FROM SERVICE. Full length is 36½ inches. The lock has the Royal Crown Enfield marks. The breech block swings over on the top of the barrel for the insertion of the cartridge. Recess cup shaped projection to prevent the escape of gas. Gun has the swivel ramrod. Mont Storm claimed that the U. S. Springfield 1866 model infringed his patents. Price $17.50.

Mont Storm Rifle with 30½-inch barrel $15.00.

**11002. CONFEDERATE ALTERED HALL'S RIFLE,** made up from gun parts captured in 1862 by the Confederates at Harper's Ferry Arsenal, removed to Confederate Armories in Richmond, Va., or Fayetteville, N. C., where they were assembled into complete guns. Illustration shows plainly the Hall swinging block with brass plug and nipple screwed into the breech; the Hall safety hammer, guard bow, bands and other parts all assembled into a complete gun, which was used in service by the Confederates until captured by the Union troops near the close of the Civil War. Illustration is intended to show the breech mechanism. The barrel and stock is full length. The only breech loading gun on record, to our knowledge, which was altered back into muzzle loaders for army service. Rare relic in serviceable order. Price $50.00.

**0-930A. MARTINI ENFIELD 303 RIFLED CARBINE WITH KNIFE BAYONET AND SCABBARD.** In good order. Captured by the Boers, and recaptured by the British. From sale of Lady Palmer's collection. Price, $17.50.

Wolcott, N. Y.,
July 29, 1924.

Sirs:—

Herewith I enclose post office order for fifty cents for which kindly send me your catalog. Notwithstanding the agitation for the suppression of the sale of arms, things have come to such a pass that every honest man needs a gun to protect himself against thugs and highwaymen.

Very respectfully yours,
F. H. EVERHART,
(Attorney & counselor at law.)

**10565. FARQUHARSONS PATENT BREECH LOADING MILITARY RIFLE,** patent gun submitted to British Army officers appointed to select army service rifles at time the Martini-Henry was adopted. Rifle barrel made of Medford steel. Under lever action, 43 calibre. Working order. Price $12.85.

**No. U 3-6. A NEW MANUAL OF THE BAYONET FOR THE ARMY AND MILITIA OF THE UNITED STATES.** By Lieut. J. C. KELTON, SIXTH REGT. U. S. INFANTRY. Illustrated with 30 double page plates. Chapters AGAINST CAVALRY, AGAINST THE SWORD, BLOWS WITH THE BUTT, ETC. Published in 1861. A RARE BOOK. Size 4½x6½ inches, 108 pages of reading matter. Price $2.00.

**No. U 3-7. GUNNERY & EXPLOSIVES** for Field Artillery Officers. Issue of 1911. 100 pages and many diagrams. Size 4½x5½ inches. Price 60 cents.

**0-763. BOER MAUSER RIFLE,** captured at the battle of Modder River. From Lady Palmer's collection sale. The magazine attachment is missing. Price, $8.50.

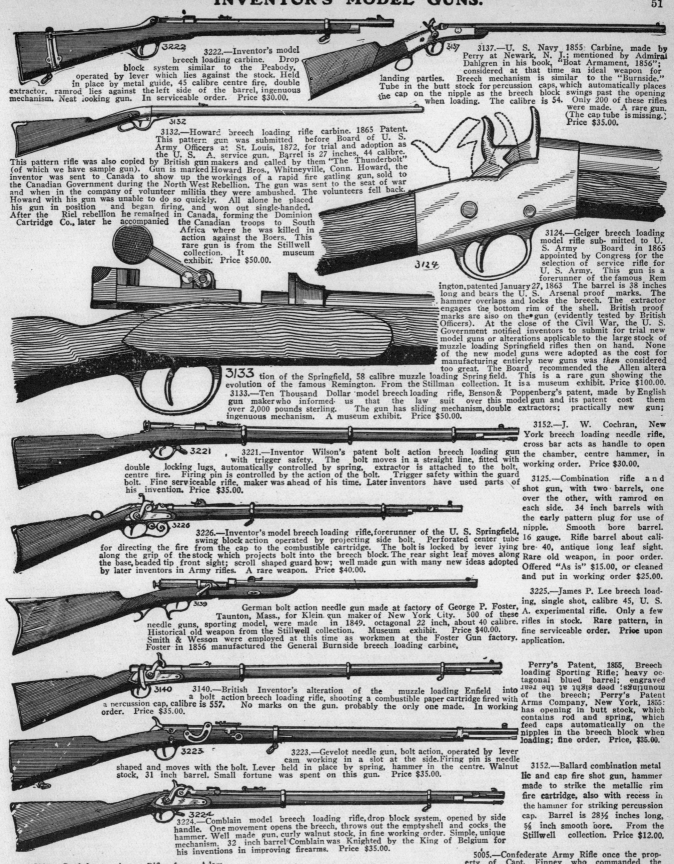

**3222.**—Inventor's model breech loading carbine. Drop block system similar to the Peabody, operated by lever which lies against the stock. Held in place by metal guide, 45 calibre centre fire, double extractor, ramrod lies against the left side of the barrel, ingenuous mechanism. Neat looking gun. In serviceable order. Price $30.00.

**3137.**—U. S. Navy 1855 Carbine, made by Perry at Newark, N. J.; mentioned by Admiral Dahlgren in his book, "Boat Armament, 1856"; considered at that time an ideal weapon for landing parties. Breech mechanism is similar to the "Burnside." Tube in the butt stock for percussion caps, which automatically places the cap on the nipple as the breech block swings past the opening when loading. The calibre is 54. Only 200 of these rifles were made. A rare gun. (The cap tube is missing.) Price $35.00.

**3132.**—Howard breech loading rifle carbine. 1865 Patent. This pattern gun was submitted before Board of U. S. Army Officers at St. Louis, 1872, for trial and adoption as the U. S. A. service gun. Barrel is 27 inches, 44 calibre. This pattern rifle was also copied by British gun makers and called by them "The Thunderbolt" (of which we have sample gun). Gun is marked Howard Bros., Whitneyville, Conn. Howard, the inventor was sent to Canada to show up the workings of a rapid fire gatling gun, sold to the Canadian Government during the North West Rebellion. The gun was sent to the seat of war and when in the company of volunteer militia they were ambushed. The volunteers fell back. Howard with his gun was unable to do so quickly. All alone he placed his gun in position and began firing, and won out single-handed. After the Riel rebellion he remained in Canada, forming the Dominion Cartridge Co., later he accompanied the Canadian troops to South Africa where he was killed in action against the Boers. This rare gun is from the Stillwell collection. It museum exhibit. Price $50.00.

**3124.**—Geiger breech loading model rifle sub- mitted to U. S. Army Board in 1865 appointed by Congress for the selection of service rifle for U. S. Army. This gun is a forerunner of the famous Remington, patented January 27, 1863  The barrel is 38 inches long and bears the U. S. Arsenal proof marks. The hammer overlaps and locks the breech. The extractor engages the bottom rim of the shell. British proof marks are also on the gun (evidently tested by British Officers). At the close of the Civil War, the U. S. Government notified inventors to submit for trial new model guns or alterations applicable to the large stock of muzzle loading Springfield rifles then on hand. None of the new model guns were adopted as the cost for manufacturing entierly new guns was *then* considered too great. The Board recommended the Allen altera tion of the Springfield, 58 calibre muzzle loading Springfield. This is a rare gun showing the evolution of the famous Remington. From the Stillman collection. It is a museum exhibit. Price $100.00.

**3133.**—Ten Thousand Dollar model breech loading rifle, Benson & Poppenberg's patent, made by English gun maker who informed us that the law suit over this model gun and its patent cost them over 2,000 pounds sterling.  The gun has sliding mechanism, double extractors; practically new gun; ingenuous mechanism. A museum exhibit. Price $50.00.

**3221.**—Inventor Wilson's patent bolt action breech loading gun with trigger safety.  The bolt moves in a straight line, fitted with double locking lugs, automatically controlled by spring, extractor is attached to the bolt, centre fire. Firing pin is controlled by the action of the bolt.  Trigger safety within the guard bolt. Fine serviceable rifle. maker was ahead of his time. Later inventors have used parts of his invention. Price $35.00.

**3152.**—J. W. Cochran, New York breech loading needle rifle, cross bar acts as handle to open the chamber, centre hammer, in working order. Price $30.00.

**3125.**—Combination rifle and shot gun, with two barrels, one over the other, with ramrod on each side. 34 inch barrels with the early pattern plug for use of nipple.  Smooth bore barrel. 16 gauge.  Rifle barrel about cali- bre 40, antique long leaf sight. Rare old weapon, in poor order. Offered "As is" $15.00, or cleaned and put in working order $25.00.

**3226.**—Inventor's model breech loading rifle, forerunner of the U. S. Springfield, swing block action operated by projecting side bolt. Perforated center tube for directing the fire from the cap to the combustible cartridge. The bolt is locked by lever lying along the grip of the stock which projects bolt into the breech block. The rear sight leaf moves along the base, beaded tip front sight; scroll shaped guard bow; well made gun with many new ideas adopted by later inventors in Army rifles. A rare weapon. Price $40.00.

**3225.**—James P. Lee breech load- ing, single shot, calibre 45, U. S. A. experimental rifle. Only a few rifles in stock.  Rare pattern, in fine serviceable order. Price upon application.

German bolt action needle gun made at factory of George P. Foster, Taunton, Mass., for Klein gun maker of New York City. 500 of these needle guns, sporting model, were made in 1849. octagonal 22 inch, about 40 calibre. Historical old weapon from the Stillwell collection. Museum exhibit. Price $40.00. Smith & Wesson were employed at this time as workmen at the Foster Gun factory. Foster in 1856 manufactured the General Burnside breech loading carbine,

Perry's Patent, 1855, Breech loading Sporting Rifle; heavy oc- tagonal blued barrel; engraved mountings; deep sight at the rear of the breech; Perry's Patent Arms Company, New York, 1855; has opening in butt stock, which contains rod and spring, which feed caps automatically on the nipples in the breech block when loading; fine order. Price, $35.00.

**3140.**—British Inventor's alteration of the  muzzle loading Enfield into a bolt action breech loading rifle, shooting a combustible paper cartridge fired with a percussion cap, calibre is 557.  No marks on the gun. probably the only one made. In working order. Price $35.00.

**3223.**—Gevelot needle gun, bolt action, operated by lever cam working in a slot at the side. Firing pin is needle shaped and moves with the bolt. Lever held in place by spring, hammer in the centre. Walnut stock, 31 inch barrel. Small fortune was spent on this gun. Price $35.00.

**3152.**—Ballard combination metal lic and cap fire shot gun, hammer made to strike the metallic rim fire cartridge, also with recess in the hammer for striking percus-sion cap.  Barrel is 28½ inches long, ⅝ inch smooth bore. From the Stillwell collection. Price $12.00.

**3224.**—Comblain model breech loading rifle, drop block system, opened by side handle.  One movement opens the breech, throws out the empty shell and cocks the hammer. Well made gun, curly walnut stock, in fine working order. Simple, unique mechanism. 32 inch barrel Comblain was Knighted by the King of Belgium for his inventions in improving firearms.  Price $35.00.

**5004.**—Confederate Army Rifle from Adam Oliver's Collection made up from different parts of Army guns. No doubt captured by the Con- federates and sent to the Augusta Arsenal, Ga., where Oliver was Master Armorer during its occupation by the Confederacy. The barrel is marked Proove, no doubt French; the balance of the gun is Springfield except the lower band which is of brass. Price $20.00.

U. S. GOVERNMENT CLEANER, 6 m/m on cord, to pull through barrel.  Brush made of heavy bristles.  Slot for cleaning rag on end of brush. Packed in cardboard box. Reduced to 15 cents each. Postage, 4 cents. WILL FIT ANY GUN FROM CALIBER 23 to 32.

**5005.**—Confederate Army Rifle once the prop- erty of Capt. Finney who commanded the Augusta Arsenal, Ga., for the Confederacy dur- ing Civil War. This gun is vouched for and came from the estate of Adam Oliver. It is stamped, "London Armory, 1862," and is a facsimile of the gun now in the National Armory Museum, as having been captured from JEF- FERSON DAVIS, PRESIDENT, C. S. A. Price $45.00.

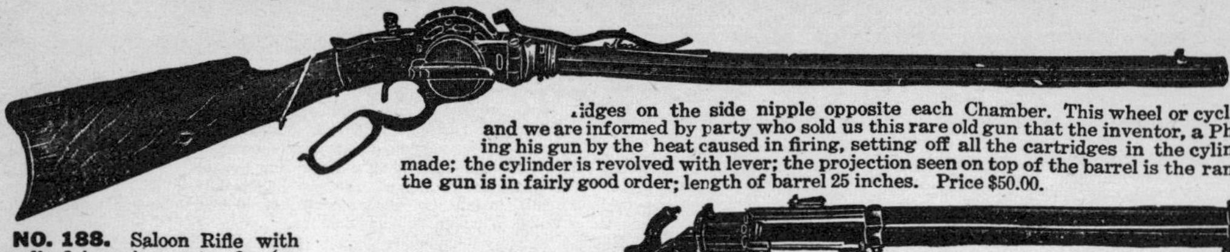

**NO. 262.** Revolving 8-Shot Rifle brought out during the Civil War period; mechanism consists of cylinder about ¾ in. thick and 3¼ in. in diameter; chambered to hold 8 cartridges on the side nipple opposite each Chamber. This wheel or cyclinder revolves in line with the barrel, and we are informed by party who sold us this rare old gun that the inventor, a Philadelphian, was killed while exhibiting his gun by the heat caused in firing, setting off all the cartridges in the cylinder. Only a few model guns were made; the cylinder is revolved with lever; the projection seen on top of the barrel is the rammer for ramming in the lead bullets; the gun is in fairly good order; length of barrel 25 inches. Price $50.00.

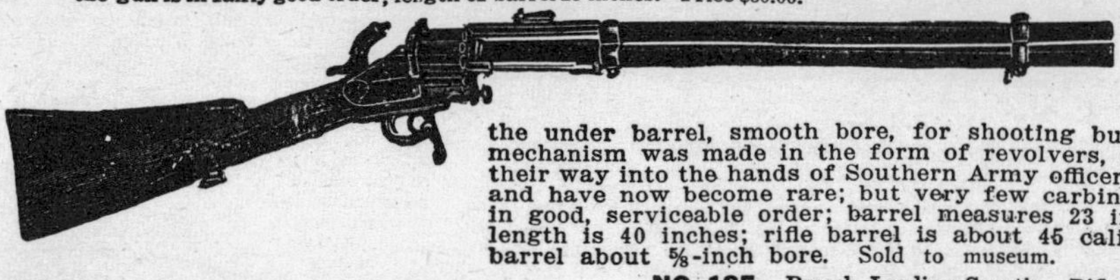

**NO. 188.** Saloon Rifle with needle firing pin, centre fire (no cartridges); blued steel, octagonal barrel, 25 in. long; about 44-calibre; finely chased; checkered walnut stock; almost new. Price **$10.00.**

**NO. 189.** Shot Gun, altered from musket, extra long, well made; 29-in, smooth bore barrel, about 12 gauge, percussion lock; fine order. Price **$4.00.**

**No. 261.** Le Mat Revolving Rifled Carbine, 6-shot, with large chamber in cylinder connecting with the under barrel, smooth bore, for shooting buckshot. This pattern mechanism was made in the form of revolvers, many of which found their way into the hands of Southern Army officers during the civil war and have now become rare; but very few carbines were made; gun is in good, serviceable order; barrel measures 23 inches in length; total length is 40 inches; rifle barrel is about 45 calibre; the smooth bore barrel about ⅝-inch bore. Sold to museum.

**NO. 185.** Breech Loading Sporting Rifle; chamber is about 50 calibre, for bottleneck cartridges: rifle barrel is about 44 calibre; 28-inch barrel, Swiss pattern stock, in good order. **$12.00.**

**NO. 186.** Trick Shot Gun; no visible trigger; about 20 gauge, extra light weight, breech mechanism, handsome carved curly walnut stock; trick in opening to load and fire; rare gun. Price **$18.00.**

**NO. 187.** 44-Calibre Breech Loading Centre-fire Lightweight Shot Gun; rare pattern, 26-inch barrel; total length 41 inches; positive extractor. Price **$6.85.**

**NO. 1838. WESTLEY RICHARDS' PATENT BREECH LOADING CARBINE,** with Whitworth polished steel rifle barrel; stamped on lock "1867" (in a) triangle," Top lever, which opens for the reception of the cartridge in the chamber of the rifle barrel, with brass knob handle which, when the lever is pressed down, pushes the cartridge in the gun. In working order. Requires cleaning. Price **$10.00.**

**No. 1373. 10 KROPATCHECK REPEATING RIFLED CARBINES,** with bolt mechanism; long range sight; with hand grip guard; with crown OE WC St 82. Length of barrel 22 inches; about 43 calibre. This carbine somewhat resembles model 71 Mauser. Price **$8.50.**

**NO. 190.** Pistol Grip Shot Gun, percussion lock; ⅝-bore, 32-inch barrel; good order; equal to new. Price **$5.00.**

**No. 209.** Fine Flint Lock, barrel only, 52½ inches long; beautifully chased with figures and scrollwork; also relief ornamented; about ½-inch bore; fine order. **$7.50.**

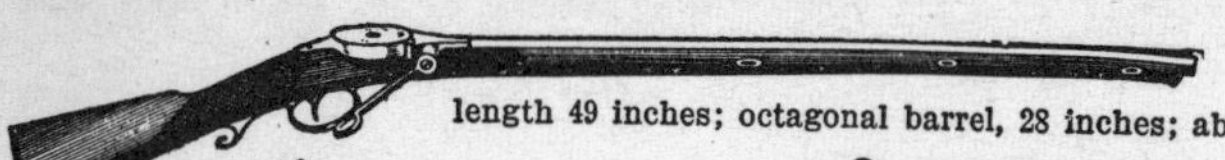

**2248.** Inventor's Model 10-Shot Monitor Rifle, with revolving cylinder situated on horizontal line with the barrel, operated by hand lever. Gilt inlaid figures, similar to dial on watch, over each cartridge chamber. Full weight 7 pounds. Price, **$50.00.**

length 49 inches; octagonal barrel, 28 inches; about calibre 44; brass receiver.

**10103.** FRENCH MUSKETOON, STAMPED 1853. Manufactured at the Imperial Arsenal, St. Etienne. Complete, serviceable order, with white leather gun-sling; used by famous artist in illustration. Price, **$8.50.**

**10103A.** FRENCH MUSKETOON. Stamped 1840. Price, **$10.40.**

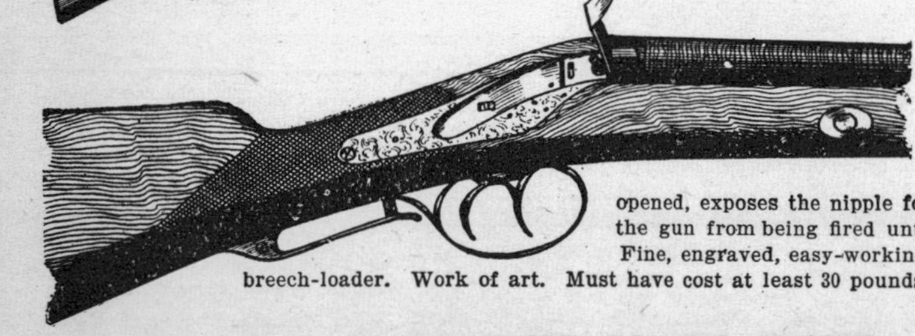

**7143.** Young's Patent Double-Barrel Shotgun, 14 bore, muzzle-loading, 32½-inch twist-steel barrels and rib, with fine Circassian curly walnut stock, checkered grip; folding side-lever attachment on the lock, which, when opened, exposes the nipple for capping; also cocks the hammer. Metal safety at the grip, which prevents the gun from being fired until held in position, the weight of the gun, held in the hand, releasing the safety. Fine, engraved, easy-working locks; evidently model gun. In appearance the gun looks like a high-grade breech-loader. Work of art. Must have cost at least 30 pounds ($150.00). Our bargain price, $45.00.

**No. 1409. BRITISH ENFIELD BREECH LOADING PEABODY.** Old muzzle loading Enfields, altered to Peabody mechanism. Full length 50 inches. Lock is stamped 1863. Breech marked "Peabody

Patent, 1852, Providence Tool Co." Price $20.00.
**No. 1410.** One very much similar, with sword bayonet, but imperfect breech. Price **$20.00.**

**No. 180.** Handsome Saloon Rifle; about 32 calibre, with centre fire needle as firing pin, with breech block opening to the right; fine curly, polished walnut, finely checkered with cheek piece; chased lock and mountings, octagonal blued steel barrels; almost new gun; beautiful workmanship. Price **$10.00.**

**No. 181.** Cadet Drill Gun; 30-inch barrel; total length 43 inches; ½-inch bore, 3 bands, percussion lock; good, second-hand, serviceable fair order. Price **$2.75.**

**No. 182.** Percussion Lock, Octagonal Barrel, Sporting Rifle, with double trigger; end of guard forms hand grasp; sling swivels; fine polished walnut stock, with cheek piece; almost new gun. Price **$10.00.**

**No. 183.** Smooth Bore Lightweight Shot Gun; blued steel barrel, 26 inches long; engraved mountings, walnut stock, with cheek piece; weight about 5 pounds; pin fire, 12mm. Price **$5.75.**

**KROPATSCHEK CARBINE.** Used by Portugal, about 1885 to 1890. The illustration shows the breech open ready to receive cartridges. The magazine is in the fore end underneath the barrel. The cartridges were .31 calibre (8 m/m.), and were placed in the magazine singly. The long rifle of this pattern was used about the same time by the French to arm the marine forces. Price, $20.00.

**No. 184.** Cadet Breech Loading 32-calibre Rim-fire Rifle; European-Remington action, 28-inch barrel; total length 43 inches; blued barrel and mountings; weight about 5 pounds. Complete, with bayonet; fine gun; superior to the common make guns. Price **$6.25.** Made as samples for us, but cost seemed too high to warrant us placing large order.

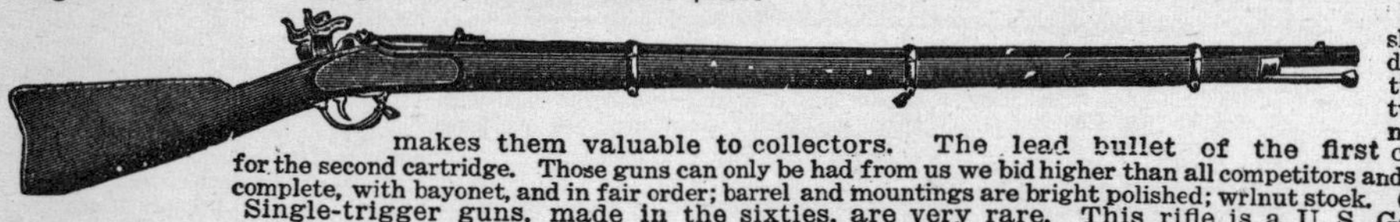

**United States Muzzle Loading Repeating Rifle** (two shots from one barrel), made at the United States armory during the Civil War. Intended for use of troops firing two balls without reloading. Rifle is 58 calibre; has two hammers, two nipples, only one trigger. Gun did not prove a success, so only a few were made, which makes them valuable to collectors. The lead bullet of the first cartridge is intended to act as the breech for the second cartridge. Those guns can only be had from us, complete, with bayonet, and in fair order; barrel and mountings are bright polished; wlnut stock. Single-trigger guns, made in the sixties, are very rare. This rifle is a U. S. Government gun, made at Springfield. we bid higher than all competitors and secured the lot. Our price is $15.00 each. Gun is (The stocks have a slight check, hardly noticeable

Inventor's Model Rapid-fire Gun, with hopper and crank; 20-inch blued-steel rifled barrel, about ½-inch calibre. Price, **$50.00.**

Inventor's Model Magazine Rifle, with box magazine; crude affair, in serviceable order; small bore. Price **$10.00.**

Inventor's Model Breech Loading Rifle, with hinged breech block worked by side lever; stamped "Realan Comblain's Patent"; in fine order. Price **$15.00.**

Schuloff's Patent Magazine Rifle, forerunner of the Savage; new gun, with fine checkered stock, blued barrel and mountings; model guns only were made; the bolt is missing in this gun.

French Gras Breech Loading Rifle. Fine order, with dagger bayonet. **$4.85.**

Spanish Officers' Remington Breech Loading 43-Calibre Rifle. Extra light weight. Serviceable order. Refinished. **$12.00.**

3 Double-barrel Percussion-lock Shotguns; about 16 gauge; have been in use; require cleaning; complete. Price **$4.85.**

V. V. English Tower, 2-Groove Rifles, made in 1834. **$8.50.**

Sharp's Breech-Loading Rifle from Malvern Hill battlefield. **$10.00.**

Inventors' Model Breech-Loading Rifle, rare pattern. **$22.00.**

Enfield Muzzle Loading Rifle, facsimile of one captured with Jeff Davis. **$10.00.**

Carter & Edwards' Patent London Breech Loading Rifle; about 50 calibre; has side-handle lever; fine, well-made gun; like new; believed to be inventor's model, over which there was a great English lawsuit that cost upward of $30,000. Price **$50.00.**

Benson & Poppenberg's Patent Breech Loading Rifle; about 50 calibre; has sliding breech bolt; fine gun; like new. Price **$50.00.**

T. Wilson's Patent Breech Loading Rifle; about 50 calibre, with breech block, which slides back from the breech to open somewhat similar to the modern Lee U. S. Navy straight-pull rifle; handsome, fine, well-made gun; believed to be inventor's model; like new. Price **$50.00.**

Double Barrel Flint Lock Sporting Gun; 30-inch barrel; about 20 gauge; fine polished walnut carved stock; carved fore-end; fine, well-made gun; like new. Price **$50.00.**

European Inventor's Magazine Rifle, with Lee magazine. **$18.00.**

Rare Pattern Percussion-lock Musket; hammer and lock is on the inside of the wood stock (no outside lock plate as in ordinary army muskets); gun requires cleaning.

6 Sample Percussion-lock Guns; retiring manufacturer's samples; fancy carved stock; octagonal barrel; about ½-inch bore; new; shop-worn. Price **$3.50.**

Snyder, or Zulu, Breech-mechanism Breech-loading Rifle; requires cleaning. Price **$4.50.**

Steven's Patent (Dutch) Alteration of Percussion-lock Rifle into Breech-loader; similar to the U. S. Springfield system; good condition; requires cleaning. Price **$12.50.**

Matthew's Patent Breech-loading Rifle; forerunner of the U. S. Springfield; in good condition; perhaps inventor's model gun. Price **$12.50.**

Bronsart's Pin-fire Breech-loading Rifle; under-lever action; about 36-calibre octagonal barrel; checkered grip; walnut stock. Price **$5.00.**

Inventor's Breech-loading Gun, with under-lever action, with device for tightening up the wear; about 20 gauge. Price **$6.00.**

Inventor's Model B.-L. Rifle; outside hammer, on being cocked, pulls back the firing pin; hair-trigger attachment; fine gun. Price **$25.00.**

**REMINGTON-KEENE MAGAZINE RIFLE.** Model of 1880. Army Model. 30-inch barrel. Magazine is tubular and is situated under the barrel holding eight .45 calibre cartridges. Mentioned in the U. S. Navy Manual of 1881. This is the first and only rifle used by the U. S., that employed this type of magazine. Carbines (the Ball and Henry) were used, however in Civil War days. A longer model was used in the Navy taking 9 cartridges. A unique feature of this gun was that it could be loaded either from the top or bottom of the breech. Takes the regulation .45 calibre. Triangular bayonet. Last patent date, July 31, 1877.

French Chassepot Breech-Loading Rifle. Relic of war with Germany. A few years ago the French Government sold a million of these old arms with their sword bayonets, a great many of which found their way to this country and were sold for use as decorations. Cartridges cannot be had as we have not found a ship that will accept them as frieght, on account of powder being incased in paper. We mention this fact as some unscrupulous dealers, in order to sell these guns, have told their customers that they could obtain cartridges from Bannerman the Gunman. We have these guns. Price $2.95 each.

**No. 60.** Joslyn Breech-Loading 50 Calibre Centre-Fire Rifle. Made at famous U. S. Springfield Arsenal for use of U. S. troops, and superseded about the beginning of the French and German wars. These guns found their way to France and eventually were captured by the Germans, who sold them at auction to Belgium gun dealers, from whom we purchased the lot. The guns are all in fine, clean and serviceable order, complete with bayonets, shooting the standard Government 50-70 centre-fire cartridge. Breech block is fitted with screw ejector which extracts the empty shell. Price $15.00 each.

**No. 1826.** European Army Sharpshooter's Breech-Loading Rifle, with Swiss Butt Stock; in working order; full length, 51 inches; 30 inch barrel; about Calibre 40. No cartridges. Valuable to collectors. Price $8.50.

GUEDES BREECH-LOADING RIFLE. Used by Portugal. Model of 1885. Made by the Austrian Small Arms Co., at Steyr. Calibre, 8 m/m. This rifle has a breech-loading system evidently copied after the English Martini of 10 years before. The specimen is new and very rare in this country as few Portuguese weapons have found their way into American collections. Price, $50.00.

**No. CA.** EUROPEAN CANDLE SNUFFERS, made of iron, in different shapes and sizes. We have 18 in this lot at $2.50 each.

**German Mauser Infantry Breech-Loading Rifles,** shoots the 43-calibre center-fire cartridge; serviceable order. We can offer the rifles for export in quantities at very low prices, together with the cartridges. Shipment from European port, in order to avoid the heavy American custom duties, or we can offer New York delivery in bond for export. Prices and terms to bona fide buyer on application.

**1850. SPORTING RIFLE.** Marked on lock, "J. G. Zuzer, Arnheim." Octagonal FLUTED STEEL BARREL, with front and rear sights; about 40 calibre. Large hand hold grip guard, curly walnut stock, with checkered and engraved mountings. Price, $18.00.

**No. 193.** Same Rifle, stamped 1838, the first year of Queen Victoria's reign; good, serviceable order. Price $7.00.

**No. 195.** U. S. Navy Lee Magazine 6mm. Rifles, relics of the Spanish War; barrels and stocks are damaged beyond repair; battle relics for decorating. Price $5.00.

**No. 197.** Austrian Breech-Loading Rifle, stamped 1869; mechanism similar to that in the old German Needle Gun; barrel,

German Sharpshooter Rifle with hair trigger; Swiss stock. Price $8.50.

Werder's Lightning Rifle. Price $8.50.

Harper's Ferry Musket, 1848-1852. Price $3.50 each.

Model 1842 Cadet Gun, the kind used at West Point during Grant's, Sherman's and Sheridan's school days; 15 in lot. Price $3.80 each.

35 inches; total length, 52 inches; good, serviceable order. Price $10.00.

**No. 199.** India Mutiny British Army Gun, Muzzle-loading Smooth-bore Musket, ¾-inch bore; has lion holding crown on lock; old proof-marks and the pattern of gun used in India by British Army at time of mutiny; good order. Price $5.00.

**No. 200.** French Cavalry Carbine; fine order. Price $6.50.

**No. 201.** Polish Breech-loading Rifle; in fine order. Price $7.50.

**No. 222.** Albini Sporting Breech-loading Rifle, about 40 calibre; 28-inch barrel; fine order. Price $8.50.

**No. 204.** British Enfield Percussion-lock Cavalry Carbine, with swivel ramrod; about ¾-inch bore; fine order. Price $5.00.

**No. 205.** Remington Carbine, fitted with bayonet; 43 calibre; Spanish cartridge; 23-inch barrel; total length, 38 inches; fine model gun. Price $6.00.

**No. 206.** German Needle Gun with octagonal barrel with double trigger, intended for sword bayonet, stamped with the German Eagle, Spandau B. B. Model, 1865, numbered 1063. Stocks and mountings are all stamped with Royal German marks. Fine gun for officers' use. Price $10.00.

**No. 207.** Blunderbuss-shaped Rifle, about 3¾-inch bore at the muzzle; percussion lock with safety catch; 30-inch octagonal barrel; total length, 45 inches; cap box in butt with old sliding wood cover; good order. Price $12.00.

**No. 212.** Heavy Percussion-lock Wall Guns, weight about 30 pounds; about 1-inch rifle bore; octagonal barrel; 1⅜-inch diameter across the muzzle; 50 inches long; good order. Price $17.50.

Albini Braendlin Model Breech Loading Rifle. Improved U. S. Springfield, the forward action of the hammer locking the breech. Price $15.00.

1 Model Breech Loading Gun, forerunner of the Peabody, with falling breech lock, with long side lever projecting along the butt of stock. Rare piece. Price $20.00.

**$19.50**

### SPRINGFIELD RIFLE, Model 1903

These rifles assembled and refinished, and offered in good order at special price of **$19.50** each. **No Bayonets.**

ARMY BALL CARTRIDGES, without clips. $3.50 per 100

.30 SPRINGFIELD MODEL 1906

We have a number of parts for the German Mauser Rifle and will quote prices upon receipt of description of the parts wanted.

CANADIAN ROSS RIFLE, caliber 303, five-shot, with concealed magazine. Model 1905. This is the type of gun with which many of the U. S. National Guard units were trained before going overseas. Guns are in good order. Price, $8.50 each.

U. S. DOUBLE HOOK GUN SLINGS, used, 30 cents each.

CARTRIDGE BELTS from 50 cents up.

ROSS RIFLE CARTRIDGES, Caliber 303, Mark VII, in fine order, with pointed bullets. Will fit any of the Ross rifles. Price, $2.50 per 100 in clips.

SPRINGFIELD REMINGTON RIFLE, for the Smith & Wesson calibre 32 CF revolver cartridges, $5.00 each. Packing charge, 45 cents. Ball cartridges, $2.00 per 100. This makes a fine small calibre gun for all round use.

We have also a number of the SPRINGFIELD REMINGTON RIFLES, altered to take the U. S. Army calibre 30, Model 1906 cartridge. Used with a reduced load, this makes a fine hunting rifle at a very low price, only $7.50.

New Orleans, La.
April 30th, 1924.

Francis Bannerman Sons,
501 Broadway, New York City.
   Dear Sirs:—
   The rifle and cartridges and primers I ordered from you on the 22nd inst. came today by express, in first class condition, and I wish to thank you for your promptness in sending them. The gun (U. S. A. Mod. '17 Rifle) is in better condition, and in fact it is a better gun in every way than I expected it to be. Please let me thank you for your very fair dealing, and if I can be of any service to you in any way please let me know.
      Very respectfully,
         EUGENE E. DICK,
           1026 Vallette St.

3383. U. S. SPRINGFIELD COMBINATION INFANTRY AND CAVALRY BREECH-LOADING CALIBRE 45 RIFLE. 26½-inch barrel, full length 47 inches, curved gunsling swivels, wind gauge rear sight. Experimental service rifle. Price, $4.85.

CADET QUAKER GUNS, made with wood barrel, for use of cadets in military schools and the Boys' Brigades. Weight is about 3 pounds; length, 42 inches. Gun has serviceable lock which fires percussion caps; has cast-iron bayonets; has tin covering over the end of barrel at the muzzle to stand wear of bayonet. We have these guns with barrel finished in imitation of bright steel, and our price is $2.25.

Krag-Jorgensen Rifle or Carbine main springs, new, price 20 cents each.

**$12.50**

U. S. A. KRAG JORGENSEN RIFLES, calibre 30-40, as used by the U. S. Army and Militia before the change to Springfield calibre 30 rifle. These rifles have been used but are offered in good condition WITHOUT EXTRAS at $12.50 each.

Krag Knife Bayonets and Scabbards, $3.50 each.

No. 500 KRAG JORGENSEN RIFLES in fine order. We offer one rifle with knife bayonet and scabbard, sight cover, screw driver, russet sling, double row gray web cartridge belt, pull through cleaner, and 20 service BALL cartridges at bargain price of $20.00 PER OUTFIT.

EMPTY BRASS SHELLS, caliber 30, model 1906, without primers or powder, with bullets. Price, $1.20 per 100.

2,000 cal. 32 solid head center fire cartridges for BULLARD rifle. 40 grains black powder, 150-grain grooved bullet, with No. 1½ U. M. C. primer. Packed 10 in paper carton. Price, $1.20 per 100.

10737. NEW REGULATION GUN SLING. Made at the Government Rock Island Arsenal, 1903-1907. Russet leather, with bronze loop in the centre, with double hook claw adjusting hooks at each end. Full length of the sling, 4 feet. Offered in good, serviceable order. Price, 75 cents each.

300 U. S. ARMY GUNNERS' RUSSET LEATHER POUCHES, with waist belt. Complete. Good as new. Size of box is 6x7 inches, 2 inches wide at the top. Price of box and belt, 60 cents.

10732. U. S. A. SOLDIER'S BLACK LEATHER WAIST BELT. Made at Government Rock Island Arsenal, complete with cast brass U. S. belt plate, hook for adjusting length, used a short time, offered in good serviceable order with brass plate. Price, 60 cents

20,000 SPANISH REMINGTON OR MAUSER 43 CALIBRE LEATHER CARTRIDGE BOX, fine serviceable order, 20 loops for holding either of the above cartridges, will also hold 20 rounds of any of the Springfield or any high power rifle cartridges, loops on back for waist belt, side strap fastening, small, neat cover. Presents dressy appearing front, edges are bound with soft leather, hand sewed, size of box is 7 inches long, 4 high, 2 inches wide, weight 14 ounces. Price, 20 cents. Bargain price for the lot.

On one occasion a buyer representing a large well-known, responsible firm, attended a Government Auction Sale and had the audacity to present his firm's card when the call was made for a deposit on his bid. For once he realized that his card was presented in the wrong place, as the auctioneer informed him that he could get such cards printed for 75 cents a 1000. (What we want is the CASH, and QUICKLY at that.)

**RUSSIAN SPRINGFIELD RIFLE,** caliber 30, for U. S. Army Model 1906 cartridges. This is the Russian Mouzin action with 22-inch caliber 30 NEW barrel. Total length 42 inches. This is the best sporting gun on the market at this figure. Price, $10.45 each.

For Russian Springfield Rifles.
**U. S. ARMY CARTRIDGES,** calibre 30. Model 1906, with 150 grain Spitzer bullet and Government load of powder. Packed in cartons of 20 cartridges (not on clips). Price, $3.50 per 100. Case of 1000, $25.00.

**KRAG SPORTER,** caliber 30/40 with 22 inch barrel, five shot. Military sights for 2000 yards. All in good condition. Special price, $11.85 each. Canvas breech cover, new, $0.10 each.
**NEW BALL CARTRIDGES,** hard or soft nose, 20 in box, $1.70.

1 **MANNLICHER SCHOENAUER RIFLE,** 9 m/m, .335 calibre, Full length 41 inches, Length of barrel 20 inches, Weight 6¾ pounds.

This is one of the best known sporting rifles in the world. The stock is of light wood, beautifully finished, and contains the circular magazine which is easily removed. Butt stock contains cleaning rod and space for two cartridges. This is a 1905 model, in unused condition. Price, $85.00.

**RUSSIAN SPRINGFIELD MILITARY RIFLE,** five shot, with box magazine. ALTERED TO USE THE AMERICAN ARMY CARTRIDGES, caliber 30, Model 1906. Rifles in good order. Length, 48 inches; barrel, 31 inches; weight, 8½ lbs. Made by the REMINGTON ARMS CO. Suitable for use in schools, military companies, Spanish American, or American Legion firing squads. NO BAYONETS. Price, $14.00 each.
**U. S. ARMY BALL CARTRIDGES,** $3.50 per 100. $25.00 per 1000.
See other pages for belts, slings and cartridge boxes.

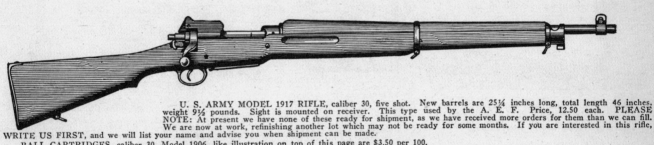

**U. S. ARMY MODEL 1917 RIFLE,** caliber 30, five shot. New barrels are 25¼ inches long, total length 46 inches, weight 9½ pounds. Sight is mounted on receiver. This type used by the A. E. F. Price, 12.50 each. PLEASE NOTE: At present we have none of these ready for shipment, as we have received more orders for them than we can fill. We are now at work, refinishing another lot which may not be ready for some months. If you are interested in this rifle, WRITE US FIRST, and we will list your name and advise you when shipment can be made.
BALL CARTRIDGES, caliber 30, Model 1906, like illustration on top of this page are $3.50 per 100.
Leather gun slings, used, Model 1907 are 50 cents each.
Leather gun slings, earlier model, used double hook pattern 30 cents each.

**SPARK PHOTOGRAPH BY PHILIP P. QUAYLE.**
30 Caliber, Armor Piercing Boat Tailed Bullet. Speed, 2600 Feet per Second.

Washington, D. C.
Sept. 17, 1923.

Francis Bannerman Sons,
501 Broadway, N. Y. City.

Dear Sirs: Enclosed I am sending you a photograph which I have taken of a 30 caliber bullet in flight. The two lines radiating from the nose and base are sound waves and clearly illustrate the origin of the sharp cracking sound which one experiences when such a high velocity bullet passes close to the head. The turbulent air composing the wake and the effect of the so-called "boat-tailing" is clearly shown by this method of photography.

The apparatus is suitable for investigating unstable bullets having a tendency to tumble or "keyhole." The effectiveness with which the bullet seals the powder gases that are driving it through the barrel could be easily shown by photographing the gun muzzle just before the emergency of the bullet.

Having been a customer and an ardent student of your catalog for twenty years, it occurred to me that this photograph might possibly be of interest to you.

Sincerely,
PHILIP P. QUAYLE.

200 Buffiington's Windgauge Rifle Sights as used by U.S. Army sharpshooters; equal to new. Price, $1.75 each.

Springfield Sharpshooter's Windgauge. Rear Sight for use on 45-calibre rifles; has screw attachment whereby leaf sight can be gauged to allow for windage—new. Price, $1.50 each.

Springfield Buckhorn Windgauge Rear Sight, for use on 45-calibre rifles sighted for 1,200 yds. Price, $6.00 doz.; 75c. each.

U. S. Krag-Jorgensen Rifle Sights; sighted for 2,000 yards; used by U.S. Navy Marines on rifles in late war; are in fine order. Price, $1.75.

**54 U. S. Army Screwdrivers**, with handles; serviceable order. Price, 10 cents each.

**Machine for Bushing Cannon**, from New York Arsenal; is in serviceable order. Price, $35.00.

**Set of Armorer's Tools** in walnut case, with forge. Price, $38.00.

**Set U. S. Brass and Steel Shell Gauges**, in fine walnut case 27 inches long, 8 inches wide, 2½ inches deep, for measuring thickness of cannon shells. Price, $6.00.

Side view Krag-Jorgenson Wind Gauge Rifle Sight, sighted for 2,000 yards, with wind guage attachment, allowing for drift of bullet with binder lever to hold in place; serviceable order. Price, $2.50 each.

30,000 Krag Jorgensen Magazine Rifle Covers. Made of drab canvas, with rawhide leather fastening thongs. Useful to cover the breech of any bolt action rifle. Not a very nice looking fit, but very serviceable. Made at the U. S. Rock Island Arsenal. Price, 10 cents each; $1.00 per doz.

400 Antique Steel Oil Cups, with screw metal tops and plunger used for holding gun oil and applying to fine guns in olden times; just as useful now for modern guns; every sportsman should have one; are in good, serviceable order; must have cost originally $2.00 each; our price is 25 cents each; $2.50 dozen.

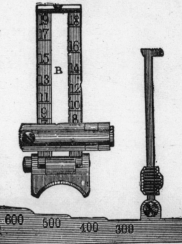

Front and side views of Krag Jorgensen U. S. Army rifle sights. NEW. We have 14,000 of these fine sights, which we offer, as illustration, at the bargain price of $1.00 each.

**Gun Cleaner**—Made of stiff bristles, brass wire fastened attached to leather thong for use in any carbine, 45 to 53 calibre. Price, 25c. each. Fitted to wood rod for use in any rifle, from 50 to 58 calibre. Price 35c. each.

British Enfield Rifle Tool; contains 7 tools in one; handy and useful tool. Price, 50c.; $5.00 dozen.

**1878.**—5,000 Steel Ram Rods for rifles. With end for cleaning rod. Length is 32¼ inches, with small neat knob handle ½-inch in diameter. In good second hand serviceable order. Useful rifle cleaning rod: also when covered, as a spring steel walking cane. Price 30c. each; $3.00 per dozen.

**1,000 Remington Breech-loading Rifle Ramrods**: fine spring steel, with slit for cleaning rag; will answer for 43, 45 or 50 calibre rifles. New, bright, polished. Price, 30c. each.

**1315.**—Wood covered Steel Ram Rods, for use in high power small bore rifles. The wood covering over steel rod, prevents injury to the rifling in the barrel, has small brass end piece for holding cleaning rag. Length 40 inches. Price, 30c. each.

**Steel Rod**, fitted with special spring steel wire brush for cleaning Mauser or any 30-calibre high power rifles: kind used at U. S. Government Armory for cleaning Mauser and Krag-Jorgensen rifles: specially made for us. Do not confound these cleaning brushes with the cheap brass-wire brushes, which fail to work in high-power rifles. Price, $1.50 complete rod and brush.

**1307.**—Spanish Remington 43 calibre rifle brass cleaning brush. Fitted on end of ram rod. Price, 10c. each.

1308    1306    1305

**1308.**—German Army Rifle Cleaning Rod, calibre 30 with slot in the head. With grooves on side for holding the cleaning rag. Fits on end of ram rod. For those made of steel 15c. each. In brass, 25c. each.

**1306.**—European Army Screw Driver, with metal cap : slit in the handle for inserting either end of the blade as desired, for large or small screws. With knurled head tightening screw. Price, 15c. each.

**1305.**—German Army Screw Driver, with iron cap, with slot for tightly holding the steel blade. One end of the blade is for small screws and the other end for large screws. Price, 15c. each.

British Army Steel Burnishing Pad; double rows of wire chain joined together; attached to heavy buff-leather pad; for cleaning rust from sabres and guns, and the buff-leather part for polishing. Useful to horsemen, cleaning bits, buckles, etc.; size, 5x5 inches. Price, 95c. each; $10.00 dozen.

**New Sharp's Heavy Octagonal Rifle Barrel**, with breech threaded to fit Sharp breech-loading rifles or carbines: are 30 inches long, chambered for 45-90 cartridge: weight about 10 pounds: fine rifling, no sights or extractor cuts: intended for big game shooting before the small bore rifles came into use, and were formerly sold at $200.00 each. We have about 50 in stock. Price, $2.75 each.

**30-calibre Fine Steel Rifle Barrels**, same as in the United States Krag-Jorgensen rifle. United States Government charged inventors $15.00 each; we will sell barrels at $5.00 each.

**Sharp's Breech-loading Rifle and Carbine, 50-calibre parts.** Price upon application, stating part wanted.

**European Army Nipple Wrenches**, with wood handles. Price, 40c.

Gun Sling Swivel, with base and screw holes, ready for fitting into stock of gun: good as new. Price, 40c.: $4.00 doz.

Black Walnut Gun Stock, well seasoned; large enough for any ordinary gun. Price, 45 cents; $3.50 per doz.

## STEEL-BLUE ENAMEL.

An enamel for use on any metal and which will keep so long as it is tightly corked is made as follows: Dissolve 1 part of borax in 4 parts of water. Macerate 5 parts of bleached shellac in 5 parts of alcohol, saving out a small portion of the alcohol for dissolving methylene blue of sufficient amount to give the color desired. Heat the watery solution to boiling, and constantly stirring, add the alcoholic solution. Stir out all lumps and add the blue solution. Before applying, clean the metal bright with an emery cloth. Apply enamel with a soft brush.

# BULLET MOULDS, GUN APPENDAGES

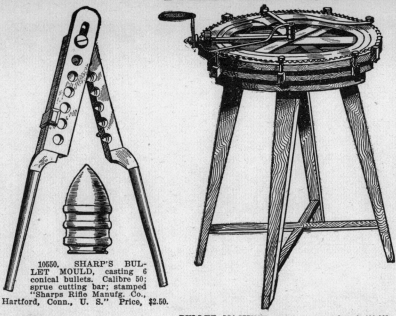

**10550. SHARP'S BULLET MOULD**, casting 6 conical bullets. Calibre 50; sprue cutting bar; stamped "Sharps Rifle Manufg. Co., Hartford, Conn., U. S." Price, $2.50.

For other gun parts, locks moulds screw drivers and ramrods, see pages 75, 76, 78, 79 and 80.

We have some parts for the old style army guns, also an assorted lot of musket main springs. Send us an exact outline and description of what you need. Please note that we have no mould smaller than caliber 40.

**No. 1815. ANCIENT STONE MOULD.** For casting buckshot bullets. In two parts, joined together by two round pins. Five holes in top side for round bullets ⅜ inch diameter. Six holes in bottom side for ¼ inch bullets. Size 4 inches long, 1¼ inches high, 1⅝ inches thick. Mould of stone are rare, and moulds casting two sizes are found only in museums. This mould was made by early settler for his own use. Price, $8.85.

**No. KR1. U. S. A. ARMY KRAG SUB-CALIBER CHAMBERS** for using caliber .32 Smith & Wesson cartridges in the Krag rifle for indoor or short range target practice. By using this chamber, it is possible at low cost to become familiar with the shooting and working of the rifle, and at a very low cost for cartridges. Made for use of the Army and Militia when the Krag rifle was Army Regulation. Price, 50 cents each.

We can furnish musket nipples of various sizes at 10 cents each. Also smaller sizes for percussion pistols or cap and ball revolvers at 15 cents each. Musket caps 25 cents per box of 100. Percussion caps, smaller, at 20 cents per 100. Caps cannot be mailed.

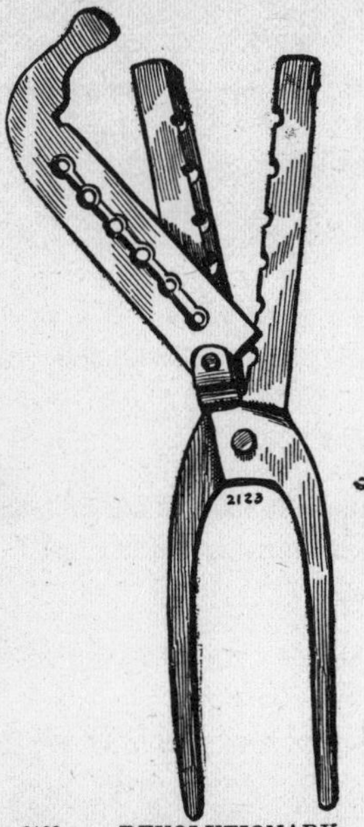

**3407. FIRST AMERICAN B/L FLINTLOCK HALL'S PATENT RIFLE BULLET MOULD.** Casting calibre 52 smooth bore bullets, with sprue cutter. Stamped on handle. "Hall's Rifle." No doubt made at Harper's Ferry Government Arsenal, 1831. Rare old relic. Price, $2.75.

**10707E. BULLET MOULD.** For casting 54 calibre round ball; sprue cutting pincher handles; locking tip; length 6½ inches, weight 5½ ounces. Price, 65 cents; 7 cents extra for mailing.

**BULLET MACHINE,** casting upwards of 100,000 bullets a day. Used by U. S. Army. Has 8 moulds, 10 balls each. Is operated by handle and casts upwards of 300 balls a minute, as quick as a man can pour in the lead and man can turn the handle. Is complete with doubled sprue cutting knife, which removes the surplus lead. Is complete with moulds for casting 69 calibre bullets. Offered to War Department, fitted with moulds casting their regulation size bullet. This mould, with our three million lot of new fresh-made cartridge primers, together with 50,000 new Springfield B/L rifles, with seven millions of ball cartridges, makes this a good opportunity for War Department to obtain at bargain prices a stock of rifles and ammunition with machines and primers for reloading.

**10704H. GERMAN ARMY MAGAZINE CAP SNAPPER.** Furnished to soldiers in old times for holding percussion caps. Hollow brass centre for holding caps, with follower for pushing the caps toward the side springs end for the soldier to quickly place the cap on the nipple of his gun. Complete with brass loading hook. Rare relic. Price, $2.50.

**No. A1.** Antique iron powder measure, length 3 inches. Rod slides up in tube showing charge of powder. Price $5.00.

**No. A2.** Antique brass powder measure, 3 inches long, with graduated rod, same style as No. A1. Price, $4.50.

**2123. REVOLUTIONARY WAR BULLET MOULD.** Brass, casting six (calibre 69) round balls at one time. Found in ruins of Fort Ticonderoga. Full length 10 inches, weight 2 pounds 5 ounces. In serviceable order. From Brooks collection. Price, $20.00.

**200 U. S. STEEL CLEANING RODS.** For pistols and revolvers. Length 11 inches, with hole in end for cleaning rag; will fit any pistol from calibre 22 up. Price, 10 cents each.
**3 CALIBRE 58 BRASS BULLET MOULDS,** casting 4 conical bullets for Civil War Springfield rifle musket. Price, $4.00 each.
**4 CALIBRE 45 BRASS ROUND BALL BULLET MOULDS,** casting 4 round bullets. Price, $3.74 each.
**1 CALIBRE 50 BRASS BULLET MOULD,** casting 6 round and 2 conical bullets. Price, $5.00.

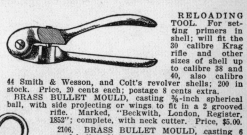

**RELOADING TOOL.** For setting primers in shell; will fit the 30 calibre Krag rifle and other sizes of shell up to calibre 38 and 40, also calibre 44 Smith & Wesson, and Colt's revolver shells; 200 in stock. Price, 20 cents each; postage 8 cents extra.
**BRASS BULLET MOULD,** casting ⅜-inch spherical ball, with side projecting or wings to fit in a 2 grooved rifle. Marked, "Beckwith, London, Register, 1852"; complete, with neck cutter. Price, $5.00.
**2106. BRASS BULLET MOULD,** casting 6 round bullets ⅜ inch diameter, with two wings for use in 2 grooved rifle; full length 10 inches; has neck cutter. Price, $8.00.
**NEW SPRINGFIELD MAGAZINE RIFLE LONG RANGE SIGHT.** Adjustable wind gauge front lever, indexed for 2,000 yards. Have been used. Offered in good serviceable order. Price, $3.00.
**3 CALIBRE 45 STEEL MOULDS** for casting 6 conical 500-grain bullets for use in Springfield B/L calibre 45 rifle. Price, $5.00 each.

On the last pages of the catalog, we show interesting information of the various parts of the flint-lock, also various types of magazines used in army rifles, showing their development.

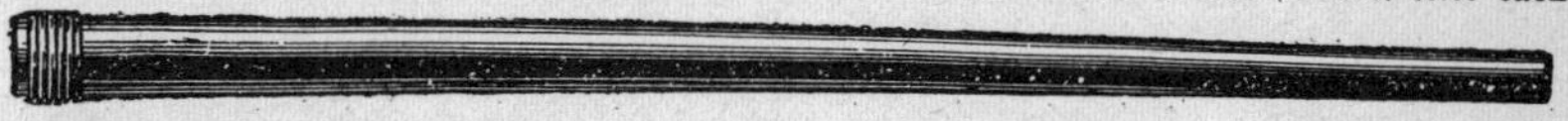

**MAUSER RIFLE BARRELS,** caliber 8 m/m, 28 inch, in used condition, suitable for use on any high power rifle. Reduced to $1.30 each.

**No. R. F. NEW RIFLE BARRELS,** length, 24 inches, without sights. Will fit any Krag rifle, carbine or sporter. Special price, $5.00 each.

**10286. BRASS BULLET MOULD.** Casting five calibre 30 round bullets for gallery target practice. Mould is of heavy bronze, with hard wood handles, weighs 1¾ pound; practically new. Price, $1.45 each.

**10172. U. S. AIMING STAND, CUSHING'S MODEL.** For teaching U. S. Army recruits how to aim and shoot; adjustable wood tripod with bronze fittings; new, with reflecting glass, etc. Price, $12.00.

**0-651. ENGLISH RIFLE SPRING STEEL RAMROD.** Finest quality. 33¾ inches long, tapered from 5/16 to 3/16-inch diameter. Screw thread for attaching ball removing worm. Slit in the head for cleaning rag. Cup-shaped rammer. ½ inch diameter. Bright, polished, new. 2,000 in stock. From retiring London gun manufacturer's stock. Price singly, 40 cents each; by the dozen, $4.00.

During the skirmish at Lexington, it was Major Pitcairn who ordered the British regulars to open fire on the minute men, April 19, 1775. The British were soon forced to retreat, and during which, on the afternoon of the 18th of April, Major Pitcairn's horse was wounded. The horse bolted and threw the Major. Later the horse with all equipment was captured by the minute men. The pistols were presented to General Putnam, and one of his descendants presented them to the town of Lexington, April 18, 1875.

Lexington is 12 miles northwest of Boston, was settled in 1642 and was long known as Cambridge Farms. It was the scene of the first conflict of the colonists and the British troops in the Revolutionary War. The British destroyed the colonists' stores but lost 273 men. (We are indebted to the Lexington Historical Society for Photograph.)

This photograph and the story with it shows the early date at which these Scotch pistols were first used, and by what character of men. We believe they were made for use of Scotch officers in the British army service. See special page 16-d, where we show 2 Scotch pistols, with full description and prices. We regret that we cannot give their history, but we do know that they were highly prized by the collector who formerly owned them. They are now becoming scarce.

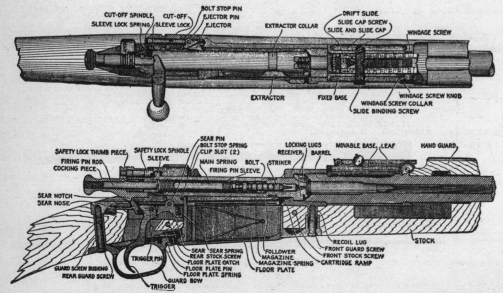

We show two views of the working parts of the SPRING-FIELD ARMY RIFLES, MODEL 1903, caliber 30. The rifle is shown with price on page 54.

These drawings are those issued with book of DE-SCRIPTION AND RULES FOR THE MANAGEMENT OF THE UNITED STATES RIFLE, caliber 30.

This diagram will be very useful to any owner of one of these fine rifles, as it will enable him to take the proper care of his gun, and to locate any trouble of operation.

**U. S. SPRINGFIELD BREECH LOADING RIFLES,** Calibre 50, centerfire. model '68. Made at the close of the Civil War. Its mechanism is somewhat similar to the Springfield calibre 45, the late regulation militia rifle, the difference being that of 5-100 of an inch larger in the size of the ball, for the calibre 50 takes a ball ½ inch in diameter, while the calibre 45 is a trifle smaller. These rifles are same as illustration, in good serviceable order, complete with bayonets. The rifle is 55½ inches long, weighs about 9 lbs., and the bayonet has 18 inch blade and weighs 12 ounces. 2-click tumbler, extractor flips the empty shell clear out of the gun. Made at the U. S. Arsenal at Springfield, and so stamped, these rifles were used to arm the soldiers, but on the adoption of the Springfield, calibre 45 they became obsolete and were sold off. We can recommend them as good serviceable guns. Packed in arm chest of 20 guns each. Price, $3.50 each.

20,000 Ball Cartridges for use in the Springfield-Remington and Sharps centre-fire calibre 50 rifles and carbines, copper shell inside centerfire primer, non-reloading. $2.00 per 100.

**NEW U. S. GOVERNMENT RIFLES,** caliber 50, center fire, with bayonets. Weight 9 pounds, barrels 36 inches long, full length 52 inches. These guns are new, and are suitable for drilling and target practice, by private military companies. Price $9.50 each.

CADET AND SCHOOL COMPANIES. We have an assorted lot of military guns and carbines, that need repairs, which are suitable for drilling, where it is desired to have a real gun, but one which the cadets cannot possibly use with cartridges. This avoids the possibility of anyone inserting a cartridge and causing trouble to others. Write us your requirements, stating the ages of the cadets, and we will quote prices with full description.

REMINGTON BREECH-LOADING 50 CALIBRE RIFLE CARBINES, made to order for the New York State Cavalry, used by Squadron A. All in fine, serviceable order with bright steel barrels; special locking devices, preventing accidental discharge; shoots the same centre-fire ball cartridges as the rifle. All we have written about the rifle applies to this carbine. Price, $4.50 each.

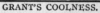

1411. 75 U. S. REMINGTON, ARMY BREECH LOADING, 58 CALIBRE CENTRE FIRE RIFLES, 3 band gun, from the U. S. Arsenal, patent 1865. This is the first pattern Remington breech loading rifle adopted by the U. S. Government. Full length 54½ inches. Complete, with sling swivels. Rare guns. Price, $7.75.

71ST REGIMENT SHARPSHOOTER'S TEAM, engraved Nos. 2, 3, 4, 5, 6, 7, 9, 11; special Remington Rifle; with 34½-inch blued steel barrels; good, serviceable order; 50-calibre centre fire. Price $9.00 each.

ONE REMINGTON RIFLE as above, with 33-inch barrel, and special wind gauge; rear sight. Price $9.00. sight is worth the price alone.

FOR GUN PARTS, SIGHTS, APPENDAGES, SEE PAGES 75, 76, 78, 79 and 80.

**GRANT'S COOLNESS.**

An instance of great presence of mind was narrated to me by John Russel Young, says a writer in the Grand Magazine. Once, during the Civil War, when Grant was in subordinate command, he was reconnoitering alone near the enemy's lines. Suddenly he found himself confronted by one of the Confederate's pickets, who was for arresting him.

"Sho! Sho!" said Grant, with the utmost coolness; "can't you see I am reconnoitering in the enemy's uniform? Don't make a noise. I shall be back directly."

And he walked quietly away until out of the picket's sight; then ran as nimbly as he could.

4,000 CAPTURED SPANISH REMINGTON BREECH LOADING RIFLES, 43 Calibre, centre fire, with bayonets; sold to us by the U. S. Govt. as "Captured Spanish Arms." A great many of the guns had leather sling straps, in which were cut notches representing the Spanish soldier's record of the number of the enemy (Cubans or Americans) who had fallen from the fire of his gun. Many of these guns must have been used by sharpshooters, as nearly all were more or less marked. These slings are for sale at 25 cents each. Some have names cut in the wood. These rifles were used by the guerrilla sharpshooters (Spanish-Cuban volunteers), "who, hidden in the trees above the stream, added a fresh terror to the wounded. Their bullets came from every side, sparing neither the wounded nor recognizing the Red Cross. The surgeons dressed wounds with one eye cast aloft at the trees. It was not the Mauser bullets they feared, but the bullets of the sharpshooters. The sound of the two bullets was as different as the sharp pop of a soda-water bottle from the buzzing of an angry wasp."—Extract from Richard Harding Davis' account of Battle of San Juan, in *Scribner's.*

AS IS—POOR. PRICE, $1.95 EACH

800,000 SPANISH REMINGTON 43 CALIBRE CENTRE FIRE BALL CARTRIDGES, made at Spanish Arsenal in Havana; offered cleaned and repacked; nearly all will shoot. Bargain price, $1.45 per 100; $12.00 per 1,000.

10122. RIFLE FROM U. S. S. WARSHIP KEARSARGE, Springfield, Cal. 45, from League Island Navy Yard auction, with department tag attached, marked "Kearsarge;" evidently relic of the famous old ship wrecked on Roncador Reef. Price, $15.00.

Two Thousand Calibre 45 Breech-loading Rifle-primed cartridge shells, new in factory cases; ready for insertion of powder for use as blanks; price $1.00 per hundred.

6 U. S. Springfield Breech Loading 45-calibre Rifles recovered from the wreck of the U. S. S. Maine. Purchased from the U. S. Navy Department by sealed proposals paying double the price offered by all competitors, (six only), U. S. Springfield breech loading rifles, were recovered from the wreck and offered for sale. Rifles show the working of the guns and have General Buffington's wind guage, 2,000-yard sights. They are not suitable for target practice, the rifling of the barrel having become rusted while under the water in Havana harbor. We will offer for sale only four of these rifles at $40.00 each, the other two are reserved for our museum. As to Authenticity, we will give buyer a copy of the bill we received (from the Navy Department together with statement of the officers who, under order of Commandant of New York Navy Yard, Admiral Philip delivered to us these guns (statement gives the arsenel numbers which are on each gun), so there can be no doubt of their being genuine. Our statement under notary's seal if you wish it. See other page for copy of bill of sale. No bayonets were recovered with these rifles.

Here is an incident in regard to the sale of rifles to the French Government during the German War. It is told among the trade how the French agent in quest of guns tried to purchase Springfield, Calibre 50 B/L rifles from a German firm in New York City. Being patriotic the first consulted Count Bismarck. His reply was: "Sell them all the guns they can pay for. We will have them eventually." And they did. France purchased them, Germany captured them, sold them to Spain, from whom our European agent purchased them. We sold them to a party who sold them to a Western State. Some years later the State turned them in, to the U. S. Government in exchange for Krag-Jorgensen Magazine Rifles. Last year the U. S. Government put the rifles up for sale and we became the owners for the second time.

Note pages in back of catalog where we show photographs of our place of business. These are included in the catalog for our new customers and for our mail order customers who do not have an opportunity to call and see us. We have been in this business since 1865, and we endeavor to give entire satisfaction to every customer, and to give a little more value than the prices indicate.

2,000 U. S. SPRINGFIELD BREECH LOADING RIFLES, obsolete on change to the Krag Calibre 30 Magazine Rifle. Many prefer the Springfield calibre 45, which shoots the 500 grain bullet, (¾ of an ounce) with its *certain stopping power*, rather than the small light-weight calibre 30 *Lead Pencil Bullet* of the repeating rifle; which as shown in the Japan-Russian war does not stop the enemy from fighting. Many incidents are on record when the soldier did not know that he was hit. Recently the U. S. Government changed form calibre 38 revolver to the calibre 45. This lot of rifles are in the original arm chests, in good *sure fire condition*, all are oiled, ready for prompt shipment from our storehouse. They cost upwards of $14.00 each to make. Price, $4.25.

No charge for cases or cartage to freight depots in New York City. The *finest, best* and *largest* lot of rifles for sale with cartridges today. All ready for prompt shipment. All made at the National Armory, each rifle bearing the "SPRINGFIELD" PROOF MARKS, THE HALL MARK OF PERFECTION.

No charge for cases or cartage to freight depots in New York City. The *finest, best* and *largest* lot of rifles for sale with cartridges today. All ready for prompt shipment. All made at the National Armory, each rifle bearing the "SPRING-FIELD" PROOF MARKS, THE HALL MARK OF PERFECTION.

REGULATION DOUBLE LOOP GUN SLINGS. Used, serviceable. Price, 60c each.

Buffington Wind Gauge Rifle Sights as used on U. S. Army Springfield Rifles.

Two Thousand Calibre 45 Breech-loading Rifle-primed Cartridge Shells, new in factory cases; ready for insertion of powder; price $1.50 per hundred.

.45—70—500
U. S. GOV'T.

600,000 Calibre 45 Blank Cartridges, $30.00 per M.

1,750,000 Calibre 45 Ball Cartridges, for use in the Springfield Breech Loading Rifle, or in the calibre 45 Gatling Machine Guns. These fine Cartridges became obsolete when the U. S. Gov't adopted the calibre .30 Magazine Rifle. The Cartridges are sure fire, 70 grains of powder, 500 grains lead ball. $3.00 per 100.

Illustration of 150,000 U. S. ARMY LEATHER GUN SLINGS for Springfield Army Rifle, made at Government Arsenal of finest quality leather, fitted with brass studs and the double claw brass adjusting hooks, in used serviceable order. Price, 30c each.

10122. RIFLE FROM U. S. WARSHIP KEARSARGE, Springfield, Cal. 45, from League Island Navy Yard Auction, with department tag attached, marked "Kearsarge;" evidently relic of the famous old ship wrecked on Roncador Reef. Price, $15.00.

6 U. S. SPRINGFIELD BREECH LOADING 45-CALIBRE RIFLES recovered FROM THE WRECK OF THE U. S. S. MAINE. Purchased from the U. S. Navy Department. Only six U. S. Springfield breech loading rifles were recovered from the wreck and offered for sale. Rifles show the working of the guns and have Buffington's wind gauge, 2,000-yard sights. They are not suitable for target practice, the rifling of the barrel having become rusted while under the water in Havana harbor. We will offer for sale only four of these rifles at $40.00 each, the other two are reserved for our museum. As to Authenticity, we will give buyer a copy of the bill we received (from the Navy Department together with statement of the officers who, under order of Commandant of New York Navy Yard, Admiral Philip, delivered to us these guns, statement gives the arsenal numbers which are on each gun), so there can be no doubt of their being genuine. Our statement under notary's seal if you wish it. See other page for copy of bill of sale. No bayonets were recovered with these rifles.

U. S. SERVICE EQUIPMENT, blue, gray or khaki color; web cartridge belt, with U. S. brass buckle, with swivel frog steel scabbard. All in good second hand serviceable order. Price, 95 cents per set.

Illustration of the adjustable Wind Gauge Long Range Sight on the Springfield triangular bayonet Rifles.

CAPTURED AMERICAN REVOLUTIONARY WAR FLINT LOCK MUSKET. The lock is marked 1780, and on the barrel, "9th Va. Regt. Bedford." On the stock, "Cowpens, Guilford C. H., King's Mt." In serviceable order, from a London collection. Price, $50.00.

1770 REVOLUTIONARY WAR PERIOD FLINT LOCK MUSKET. Lock marked "Clark 1770." Brass plate with initials J. H. C. Rare pattern spade bayonet with spring. Price, $35.00.

1744 BROWN BESS FLINT LOCK MUSKET with spade bayonet. Lock stamped "Tower G. R. with crown 1774." Butt plate marked D. V. 12. Tradition says that this gun was used at Battle of Preston Pans, Scotland. Price, $35.00.

1759 FLINT LOCK MUSKET. Lock marked Grieve 1759 with crown G. R., with broad arrow and small crown, full length 4 feet. Price, $25.00.

1770 REVOLUTIONARY WAR PERIOD FLINT MUSKET. Barrel stamped London, the Lock 1770. This pattern was made up for the American Colonists Trade. Price $30.00.

1776 FLINT LOCK MUSKET, lock stamped Lacy & Co., 1776, with crown and the old G. P. proof marks on the barrel. Gun has the spade bayonet. This pattern gun with shorter barrel was usually carried by British Sergeants. Price, $25.00.

EARLIEST TYPE MATCH LOCK GUN, taken by European soldiers at the looting of Pekin. Nearly 5 feet long, in working order. Perhaps 500 years old, as the Chinese were the first to use powder guns. Price, $25.00.

AFGHAN NATIVE FLINT LOCK GUN with curved dented butt, with old British Tower lock. Curious sling strap. Price, $25.00.

BATTLE OF QUEBEC FLINT LOCK MUSKET. The lock marked 1745, from Col. Surman's Collection, used by the British against the French. Full length, 58 inches, complete with spade bayonet, in fine order. Price, $35.00.

FLINT LOCK MUSKET FROM ADMIRAL NELSON'S FLAGSHIP VICTORY, from ancient Ipswich's Museum. Lock is stamped 1774 G. R. Royal crown; the bottom of the butt plate stamped VICTORY. Smooth bore 13-16 inch, full length 44 inches, rare gun. Price $40.00.

2 BRITISH ARMY MARTINI CARBINES, stamped with two broad arrow marks denoting Government ownership and release, with condemned saw cut in the barrel, the first method used to render condemned guns unserviceable. Shortly after a sale of these condemned guns, the British Government was at war with some of the Hill tribes in India, and found that the natives had neatly repaired the saw cut in the barrel by inserting and brazing a silver coin, thus putting the gun in serviceable order. After this experience, the British Government order is to break up all condemned guns under a hammer. These guns are now relics. Price, $6.85 each.

MARTINI CARBINE with original sling strap and brass stamped plate. $8.85.

MARTINI B/L RIFLE stamped as having been made special by Westley Richards for Z A R. Plate is lettered "In grateful recognition of the fact—that at least one parcel found its way to the front." This rifle was taken by Capt. Gilbert from a Boer whom he shot. Gun is in good serviceable order, sporting model. $12.85.

STEYR M 1885 MILITARY BREECH-LOADING RIFLE, taken from Boer Farm House during South African War; serviceable order. $20.00.

1771 FLINT LOCK MUSKET. Lock marked "Wheeler 1771," from the Col. Surman Collection, complete with spade bayonet, good order. Price, $25.00.

CELEBRATED BAKER FLINT LOCK RIFLE, The first rifles issued to the British troops succeeding the old Brown Bess smooth-bore muskets which were in army use for over 100 years. The Baker Flint Lock Rifles are extremely scarce. The fire 1847 in the Tower of London destroyed many of the Baker rifles. Gun is complete, but the stock is worm eaten. Price, $35.00.

BROWN BESS FLINT LOCK MUSKET, marked G. R. Tower, full length 4 feet, with spade bayonet. $15.00.

BATTLE OF PRESTON PANS FLINT LOCK MUSKET, full length 3½ ft., marked Tower G. R., complete with spade bayonet. $18.50.

5 BRITISH YEOMAN'S FLINT LOCK MUSKETS. Period 1776, full length under 4 ft., in good serviceable order. $13.85 each.

1 FLINT LOCK MUSKET, stamped Barrett 1795. $15.00.

Here is an incident in regard to the sale of rifles to the French Government during the German War. It is told among the trade how the French agent in quest of guns tried to purchase Springfield, Calibre 50 B/L rifles from a German firm in New York City. Being patriotic they first consulted Count Bismarck. His reply was: *"Sell them all the guns they can pay for. We will have them eventually."* And they did. France purchased the guns, Germany captured them, sold them to Spain, from whom our European agent purchased them. We sold the lot to a party who sold them to a Western State. Some years later, the State turned them in to the U. S. Government in exchange for Krag-Jorgensen Magazine Rifles. Last year the U. S. Government put the rifles up for sale and we became the owners for the second time.

A writer who opposed the organization of "Boys Brigades" on the ground that they inculcate a spirit contrary to Christianity and the teaching of the Bible, is effectively answered by a correspondent of the New York Evening Post, who says in part: "In the Bible no figure is used more often or more emphatically than that of the fighter. Christ himself speaks of the kingdom of heaven suffering violence, and the violent taking it by force. St. Paul employs no more striking imagery than that of the warrior and his armor, and in the Apocalypse we read that the armies which were in heaven followed Him—the word of God—upon white horses, and out of his mouth goeth a sharp sword, that with it He should smite the nations and rule them with a rod of iron. In what better way can the idea of fighting the good fight—St. Paul again—be impressed on the minds of growing lads than by forming them into organizations like the 'Boys' Brigades' and 'Knights of Temperance' and training them to march in columns of companies singing that soul-stirring battle song—'Onward Christian Soldiers, Marching as to War'? The statement has been made that there never has been, is not, and never will be a 'Christian Soldier.' What of Oliver Cromwell, of 'Chinese Gordon, of Sir Henry Havelock, of Captain Phillip, of our own Navy, and a host of other God-fearing men, who did not and do not think it inconsistent with their duty to their Maker to take service in the ranks of their countries' fighting machines?"

**1546.** Inventor's Model Magazine Rifle, engraved on lock "A Francotte Liege, Brevete." Bolt action. Clip magazine underneath the barrel. Wood jacket over the barrel. Sling swivels; in working order. Guard bow is missing. Believed to be the only gun of its kind. Price, $12.50.

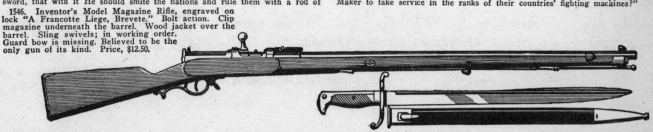

**No. JC71. Prussian Needle Gun.** The invention of Johann Nicholas Von Dreyse in 1836. This rifle, the first bolt gun, is the grand daddy of all the present day military rifles and is without doubt the most interesting military gun for collectors today. This rifle was tried in Warfare as early as 1848 in the first Scheleswig-Holstein war and again in 1866 in the war with Austria. It was the principal weapon of the Germans in the France-Prussian War of '71. A number of different improvements were made causing several models to be brought out, some have rod bayonets, some the old time triangular and yet a number with the long saber bayonet. Although a crude, heavy weapon as it appears to us, it was a great advance over the old muzzle loaders in spite of the fact that an enormous amount of gas escaped at the breech. The cartridge used was quite unique as it had the fulminite in front of the powder charge and in the center of the paper container. The long "needle" or firing pin extended so far from the head of the bolt that it went entirely through the powder charge to ignite the primer. The bullet was oval shaped and encased in a wooden "sabot" or covering. The rifles we offer are in excellent complete order. Complete with saber bayonet with a 20-inch blade and brass handle and equipped with a scabbard. Marked "1861," caliber .60, weight with bayonet complete 12½ pounds. Effective range 600 yards. Number of aimed shots per minute 5. No collection is complete without a specimen of this historical rifle. Price, $8.50.

**1830.** Modern Magazine Rifle with New Principle in Bolt Action. Steel cover over lock and breech serves as lever to operate the mechanism, assisted by left hand lever movement. Barrel about 30-calibre, intended for clip magazine, plain walnut stock. From gun manufacturer's collection. Valuable to inventors, to aid in inventing new fire-arms. Price $100.00.

**1833.** Inventor's Model Six Shot Revolving Rifle, cylinder chambered for bottle necked cartridges, under lever action revolves the cylinder and cocks the hammer. No name or marks, no fore-end, 28 inch barrel, full length 49½ inches, in working order, not quite complete. Price $40.00.

**1834.** Somewhat similar to 1833, with lever which revolves the cylinder and cocks the hammer, 28 inch barrel model guns, more complete than 1833. Price $50.00. (Model rifle gun at Spencer gun armory, cost upwards of $1,000 each.)

Snyder Sporting Model Rifle, breech-loading, with ring swivels for sling; fine European curly walnut checkered stock, handsomely finished, checkered fore-end, beautiful piece of workmanship. Price $15.00.

Snyder Breech-loading Mechanism Tower Enfield Rifle, good condition. Price $3.85.

Smooth-bore Musket, ¾-inch bore; 40 inches, length of barrel; good condition. Price $4.50.

Early Model Bolt Breech-loading Rifle; ½ in bore; European invention; in fine order; like new; rare pattern. Price $10.00.

3 Sporting Rifles, percussion-lock with rib for ramrod; fine-working lock, with sword attachment; fine order. Price $6.00 each.

Sporting Model Enfield Muzzle-loader Rifle; good condition. Price $4.50.

Twist Steel-barrel Breech-loading Smooth-bore gun; engraved. Price $7.00.

**1837.** Sporting Rifle, with nipple safety on percussion lock, retaining the old style flint flash pan; octagonal barrel; cap box in butt stock with the wood slide cover; complete working order; requires cleaning. Price 6.50.

Purdy Sporting Rifle—special 15-inch crooked stock of fine curly walnut (curves to the right about ½ inch); finely checkered; octagonal Damascus barrel, 24 inches; 32 calibre, chambered for center-fire needle cartridge: with fine special case. Price for the outfit. $10.00.

**1037.** Single Shot Vetterli Model Rifle with Swiss Butt, in fine order. Price $6.85.

**1038.** Antique Single Barrel Sporting Shot Gun, muzzle-loader; made by Turner, London; 12 gauge, twist steel barrel, fine walnut stock, checkered grip rib ramrod holder; good second-hand order. Price $10.00.

**1039.** Antique Sporting Rifle, made by W. Greener; about 6/10 inch bore; flat sighting rib; fine walnut stock; checkered grip, ramrod rib; engraved lock, hammer and mountings; silver name plate. Price $10.00.

**1536.** Allen & Wheelock Sporting Rifle, made in Worcester, Mass. Long barrel pistol, with extension stock, for use as a carbine; barrel is octagonal shaped, 17 inches long, 32 calibre; fired by percussion cap; with front and rear sights; with peep sight; beautiful curly walnut stock; checkered, with silver name plate, and cap box in butt stock; with Swiss butt; rare old weapon. Price 18.00.

**1547.** Inventor's Model Magazine Rifle, engraved on lock "A Francotte Liege, Brevete." Bolt action; clip magazine underneath the barrel; wood jacket over the barrel; sling swivels; in working order; guard bow is missing, believed to be the only gun of its kind. Price $12.50.

**1548.** Inventor's Model; High Power Repeating Rifle, cal. 765, for rim head cartridges; bolt action, with ingenious locking mechanism, which locks the bolt in three places; 30 inch barrel, 46 inches full length; magazine is in front of and in continuity of the guard; rare gun, valuable to any inventor studying out other inventions. Price $17.50.

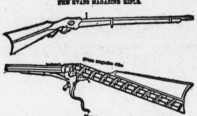

THE EVANS MAGAZINE RIFLE.

Evan's Magazine Rifle, 26 cartridges carried in the magazine in the butt stock; on the Archimedean Screw principle; loaded by operating the lever; rifle needs repairs; we offer as is; relic, $25.00.

50 Spencer Civil War Magazine Rifles, calibre 50, rim-fire; second-hand, in serviceable order. Shoots the 50-calibre rim-fire ball cartridge. These guns sold during the French and German War at $36.00 each; upwards of 100,000 were made, they were counted in those days the best repeating rifle. Of the older model Spencer General Grant said in 1864: "That they are the best rifles now in the hands of the troops, both as regards simplicity and rapidity in firing and superiority of manufacture." The magazine is contained in the butt of the stock; by opening the gate in the butt plate the magazine can be loaded with 7 cartridges, while one can be inserted in the chamber, making 8 balls ready for firing without reloading. Blank cartridges can be used for saluting and also bird-shot cartridges for shooting at birds. We offer these fine repeating rifles singly at $12.00. Blank or ball cartridges, $1.50 per 100.

## Bannerman Army Equipment

Of the various qualities ascribed to Uncle Sam in popular imagination there is one that has been more or less overlooked, and that is that Uncle Sam is a careful buyer.

When Uncle Sam buys anything and O. K.'s the bill for payment it is a safe bet that whoever the seller is he is delivering the goods as to quality and specifications in every respect. And if it is not of the best Uncle Sam does not buy.

Thus whenever any army goods are offered for sale their quality is always beyond question.

Perhaps the best known dealer in army goods is Francis Bannerman Sons, of 501 Broadway, 2625 Canal, a concern established in 1865 just after the close of the Civil War. They deal in rifles, army tents, cots, ponchos, blankets, saddles, outing suits and in fact every sort of army goods and have been doing so these sixty years. With this record back of them the purchaser may feel confident of fair treatment and satisfactory service. They are issuing at present a special catalogue sent for a 2 cent stamp, on Army Tents, cots, etc., which it would pay anyone to send for who is interested in such goods. At this season of the year an Army Tent out in the woods has charms that your apartment palace with its marble halls can by no means rival.—From a New York Trade Paper.

The Spencer Carbine was invented by Christopher M. Spencer, now living at Windsor, Conn. He is considered one of America's greatest inventors. He is also the inventor of the Spencer Repeating Shot Gun, of which we were the makers. The carbine bearing his name, was invented when he was only 19 years old. When the Civil War broke out Spencer went to Washington to show up his gun and try to obtain an order for its manufacture. But army officers were very busy and were overrun with inventors and had no time to see "the young man with his gun." While waiting around the corridors of the War Office Spencer made the acquaintance of one of the doorkeepers or messengers, to whom he showed his gun and related his disappointment, and that he was discouraged and was about to return home. The doorkeeper said, "You come here after I am through for the day and I will take you to a man who will examine your gun." His friend took him direct to the White House and introduced him to President Abraham Lincoln. Young Spencer showed the workings of the gun with the dummy cartridge, when the President said, "It works all right, but the proof lies in the shooting; let's go out and shoot it. So they started for the grounds attached to the White House. On the way the President noted that the pocket of his coat was torn and asked for a pin, remarking, "This is a nice dress for the Chief Magistrate to appear in public." Setting up a shingle against a tree a few shots were fired by Spencer, who handed the gun to the President, who fired a few shots, not making quite as good target as Spencer, gave the gun back for further shooting, saying, "When I was your age I could do better." The target shingle is now at the State House in Indianapolis, presented by Mr. Spencer after the death of the President. Needless to say that Mr. Spencer returned home with an order for all the guns he could furnish. A company was formed and 94,000 guns were delivered for use in the Civil War. Jas. G. Blaine was a stock holder in the Spencer Arms Company: Fisher, to whom Blaine wrote "Burn these letters," was its treasurer.

# RELIC RIFLES RECOVERED FROM U. S. S. MAINE
## SUNK IN HAVANA HARBOR,

**RIFLE RECOVERED FROM THE WRECK OF THE U. S. S. MAINE** in Havana harbor, Cuba, by U. S. Navy Department, and sold to Francis Bannerman, as shown by copies of the correspondence, together with the bill from the U. S. Navy Department. Price of rifle, $40.00.

Five U. S. Springfield Breech-loading 45-calibre Rifles received from the wreck of U. S. S. Maine. Price, $25.00 each.

*Cable Address, "Bannerman"*    ESTABLISHED 1865.    TELEPHONE, 1764 SPRING.

CANNON WAREHOUSE, 1356-1363 BERGEN ST., BROOKLYN.

## Francis Bannerman,
### ORDNANCE,
### WAR RELICS,
**OFFICE.**    **MILITARY GOODS.**
### 579 BROADWAY.

*New York, Jan 24 1900*

Rear Admiral John W Philip USN
Comdt New York Navy Yard

Sir: We understand that Gunner Joyce has the numbers of the Rifles lately sold to me as recovered from the USS Maine. Will you kindly have him mark the numbers on my bill enclosed. So that they will not get mixed up with others in our store

Would it be asking too much to have the names of the ships sent me from which the cartridge shell (as per enclosed bill) came from - i e vessels which turned in cartridge shells since last sale

We wish to give our customers the correct honest report of these old relics and thank you very kindly for aiding us

Yours respectfully Francis Bannerman

**No. 1.**

Navy Yard, New York, _JAN 2 1900_ 189

Mr. Francis Bannerman
### To U. S. NAVY DEPARTMENT, Dr.

| LOT NO | QUANTITY MORE OR LESS | SALE OF CONDEMNED STORES BY SEALED PROPOSALS @ | Dolls. Cts. | Dolls. Cts. |
|---|---|---|---|---|

**DEC 27 1899**

60   54 Rifles, 6 m-m
   6 Springfield Rifle, Cal. 45
   (From USS Maine)

6 m/m rifles, Lee straight pull. Numbers of -
9978 - 7178 - 8582 - 6525 - 5994 - 7380 - 7760 - 6868
6479   4694   8464   7281   7850   73   6174   8138
8486   6943   7131   8267   3867   8527   8873   8808
5808   9582   6938   9332   8333   6917   7151   7680
6483   5399   5960   2357   9076   9820   6472   6547
7027   6455   6799   8409   8700   6107   9622   4957
6627   7367   8586   7825   9722   8328 —
Springfield Rifles cal. 45 Numbers of :
472841 - 472941 - 322599 - 311218 - 322634 —
472927

M Joyce Gunner USN

**No. 2.**

75. ORDNANCE OFFICE, NEW YORK NAVY YARD, RECEIVED JAN 26 1900

1st Endorsement
NAVY YARD,    NEW YORK.
**JAN 26 1900**

Respectfully referred to the Inspector of Ordnance for the information necessary to enable Commandant to reply to writer.

J

REAR ADMIRAL, U. S. N.
Commandant Navy Yard & Station.

No. 3.

75    **2nd ENDORSEMENT**    RECEIVED JAN 27 1900 NAVY YARD, NEW YORK

NAVY YARD, NEW YORK.

Jan. 27, 1900   1898
*Respectfully returnd, Contents noted.*

Information asked for written in on face of bills as requested.

Commander, U. S. N.,
Inspector of Ordnance.

No. 2.

Navy Magazine Rifles, relics from U. S. S. Maine. These rifles were offered for sale by the United States Navy Department at New York Navy Yard, December 27, 1899, by sealed proposals publicly advertised as the identical rifles taken from the wreck after the explosion in Havana harbor. Our bid being the highest, the rifles were delivered to us. Each rifle has the factory number stamped on it, also the United States Navy Inspector's stamp, and the navy mark—an anchor. The officer delivering these rare and valuable relics has the number of of each gun on his books. We mention all this to show the proofs we can furnish with each gun. We will give every purchaser a copy of the bill we received from the Navy Department, with the number of each gun marked on the bill over the signature of United States Navy Officers—Admiral Philip kindly ordered the numbers of each gun marked on our bill,—with our statement under notary's seal if desired. Only a limited number were saved. One of the naval officers who obtained one of these relics refused to part with it, although offered $75.00. We will, for a short time, offer them at $40.00 each. They are valuable in our estimation only as relics. We have no doubt some of them could be cleaned up and put in serviceable order. The gun is complete with rifle breech bolts, sights and sling straps, just as they were placed in the gun racks on the evening of the explosion. Even the front sight protector is still on the gun. They were under water and were brought up by the divers employed. No bayonets were recovered. The calibre is 256-1000. Point-blank range was over 600 yards. At five feet from the muzzle the penetration would be through 60 boards ⅞ of an inch in thickness, or through a steel plate ⅛ an inch thick. The action is bolt straight pull, and was made for the United States Navy by the Winchester Arms Company. A rapid fire, repeating, small bore, high-power rifle. The most powerful rifle known. No collection of rifles will be complete without one of these fully authenticated rifles, which will increase in value as the years roll on. To start them, our price for the present, for a limited number only. is $40.00 each.

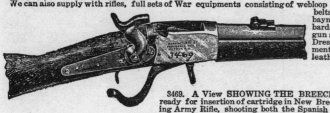

**3468. NEW BREECH LOADING ARMY RIFLE,** SHOOTING Ball and Blank SPANISH REMINGTON and GERMAN MAUSER 43 CALIBRE CARTRIDGES; 2,000 IN STOCK; made by the Providence Tool Company, famous for securing the contract away from the European gun makers for supplying the Turkish Government with 600,000 army rifles. These rifles have the under lever action, the lever forming a guard for the trigger, depressing the lever opens the breech for quick and easy insertion of cartridge; also flips the empty shell after firing clear out of the gun. Long range graduated rear sight, 32 inch barrels, full length 52 inches; complete with side arm angular bayonet. The Turkish Government Officer's inspection was so strict, that it was necessary to make GAUGES OF CRYSTAL to avoid changes in temperature. EVERY PART INTERCHANGEABLE. These Peabody rifles are all new in original zinc-lined army packing chests. Price of a single rifle. $5.85; a BARGAIN PRICE QUOTED FOR THE LOT.

We can also supply with rifles, full sets of War equipments consisting of webloop cartridge belts, steel bayonet scabbards and gun slings, or Dress equipment sets in leather.

**3469.** A View SHOWING THE BREECH OPEN ready for insertion of cartridge in New Breech-loading Army Rifle, shooting both the Spanish Remington and the German 43 Calibre Cartridge.

**JC20. FRENCH, LEBEL RIFLE.** The standard rifle of the French. Gun is factory new and has the original sling attached. Full description and illustration given in our history of World War Weapons. Very rare in this country. Price, $35.00.

**V-12. HIGH GRADE ENGLISH MADE DOUBLE BARREL PERCUSSION SHOT GUN, IN CASE.** Twist steel barrels 30 inches long, 11/16-inch bore, marked: E. & W. BOND, CORN-HILL, LONDON. Hardwood ramrod with metal tips. Front action locks, marked: E. & W. BOND. All parts including screw heads finely engraved. Stock is highly polished, with checkering at grip. Set includes one leather shot flask with brass measuring top, one heavy powder flask 8 inches with top measure, one powder flask, 6 inches, with top measure, one combination heavy copper flask, brass bound with measure with compartments for both shot and powder. Also steel oiler, small ivory box with extra nipples, mould, 2 boxes caps, wad-cutter, jointed rod, nipple wrench with hardwood handle, ball worm, steel brush and spring vise. In brass bound hardwood case with name plate marked: HENRY W. ANDREWS, NEW YORK, 1844. This outfit was evidently made to order, and is still like new. A rare bargain for some one. Price, $35.00.

500,000 Captured Spanish 43-Calibre Lead Ball Cartridges. Intended for use in the Remington rifles. In good serviceable order; packed in paper boxes, 1,000 to the case. Our price for these cartridges is $1.75 per 100. Bargain price quoted for large lots.

500,000 Spanish Remington Brass Covered Lead Ball Cartridges, made for use in European made Spanish Remington rifles, classified by the Spanish as Reformado Cartridges, the brass covered bullet giving longer range. These cartridges are packed 20 each in paper cartons, 2,000 in each wood case. Price $2.20 per hundred. Bargain prices quoted for quantity lots.

**3389A. INVENTOR'S MODEL BREECH-LOADING RIFLE,** "Milanois," Sharpe(brevete)system drop breech-block operated by lever in front of the guard. Appearance is similar to the Remington, about 50 calibre, center fire, 33 inch barrel, handsome gun. Price $25.00.

removed, and used with flat Springfield bayonet with leather cover and padded point. *full length 44 inches;* weight 8 pounds. We have 200 of these fencing practice rifles in stock. We offer these fencing rifles "as are," with spring steel bayonet, at $3.45.

**0-823A. ARMY FENCING BAYONET.** Flat spring steel, 18-inch blade, covered with russet leather, double stitched, with paddle leather-covered end. Steel socket will fit 58-calibre barrels. Complete with locking clasp. Stamped "Rock Island Arsenal, 1906." The spring bayonet blade will bend almost double. These are the bayonets offered with 0-823 Springfield Rifles. Price of the bayonets, separate, $1.25 each.

**No. 0-762. WESTLEY RICHARDS' BREECH-LOADING CAPTURED CARBINE,** found in Boer War farmhouse during South African War. From Lady Palmer's collection sale. Price, $7.85.

**10029.—SPRINGFIELD REMINGTON BREECH-LOADING RIFLE.** Made of Civil War Sprinfield rifle parts, with the famous Remington breech action known among collectors as the *"Remington alteration."* Extremely rare gun, with the possible exception of some experimental arms these are the first Remingtons used by the United States. Rifles offered to collectors in second hand serviceable order at price of $15.00 each.

**ITALIAN CARCANO** Breech-loading Bolt Action Army Rifle. This rifle is known as the second model improved by Italian Ordnance Officer Carcano, whose name is attached to Italian Army rifles for the last 20 years by reason of improvements. Rifles are in second hand working order, in two sizes, long and short, $6.85.

**CAPTURED SPANISH REMINGTON BREECH-LOADING RIFLES** from the Philippines with history labels pasted on the gun stock by U. S. Army officers. Rifles are in poor order; valuable only as relic trophies.

Rifle labeled, "Captured by Lieut. Cortier, 5th Infantry, Nu Maguila, April 5th, 1902."

Rifle labeled, "Surrendered April 5th, 1902, at San Juan de Rocboc, P. S. (Philippine Scouts), Q. M. San Juan de Rocboc."

Rifle labeled, "Captured January 21st, 1902, at Mt. Alacan, Marinduque, P. I., by Capt. Stegswall, 30 Infantry Commanding Company A." Buyer can have the choice of these relic trophies vouched for by U. S. Government labels. Price $20.00 each.

**3412. BENJAMIN BREECH-LOADING RIFLE,** Enfield barrel bolt cocks the hammer and operates the extractors, full length 40½ inches, calibre 56. No. marks, evidently inventer's model. practically like new. Price $30.00.

**0-823. U. S. A. FENCING RIFLE.** This is the regular Springfield breech-loading rifle, cut down to cadet size for fencing practice. Hammer sling swivels, ramrod and sight

**3389. PARIS MADE MODEL BREECH-LOADING RIFLE.** Falling breech system similar to that in the Sharps operated by side lever, the end of the lever striking the extractor flips out the empty shell; unique rear sight; with RIBBON SPRING; sighted for 1,200 yards. New rapid twist rifling about 45 calibre. full length 44½ inches, inscribed L. Volasse, Paris. Price $45.00.

**7116. BRITISH OFFICER'S MARTINI HEAVY SPORTING RIFLE,** made by "Patstone, 215 High Street, Southampton" Fine curly walnut stock, checkered grip and fore end, 31 inch blued steel rifled barrel, 45 calibre, with sling swivels. Price, $14.85.

# GUNS AND CARBINES

**3113. SHARP'S LONG NAVY BREECH-LOADING RIFLE**, with sword bayonet. Used on board Navy War Ships and by Army Sharp Shooters in Civil War. Has the Lawrence patented rear sight. Brass handle sword bayonet. Fired by percussion cap; also by Maynard's Patent Tape Primer. Price, $10.00.

**NEW SHARP'S HEAVY OCTAGONAL RIFLE BARRELS**, with breech threaded to fit any of the Sharp breech loading rifles or carbines; are 30 inches long, chambered for 45-90 cartridge; weight about 10 pounds; fine rifling, *no sights or extractor cuts;* intended for big game shooting before the small-bore rifles came into use, and were formerly sold at $20.00 each. We have about 50 in stock. They will require aid of gunsmith to put in extractor cut and sights for use in Sharp's carbines. Price, $2.75. each "AS ARE."

**20 U. S. ARMY MUSKETOONS**, with bayonet. Relic of the Mexican and Civil War periods. Calibre 58. In good second hand, serviceable order. Some of the Union cavalry were armed with musketoons during the Civil War. Rare serviceable relic. Price, $10.00 each.

**R. F. NEW RIFLE BARRELS**, length 26 inches, without sights, for Krag guns, cal. 30/40. Price, $5.00.

**R. F. 1. NEW RIFLE BARRELS**, 26 inches, without sights, for Springfield Mauser rifle, cal. 30, 1906. Price, $5.00.

**R. F. 2. NEW RIFLE BARRELS**, 26 inches, without sights to fit the Springfield rifle, Model 1903, cal. 30/06. Price, $5.00.

In the year 1848, Christian Sharp invented the rifle which bears his name, and the manufacture of the same was begun in Hartford in 1851, three years after the Colt company had located there. The company removed to Bridgeport in 1875, and, although the action is the strongest and safest ever devised, their manufacture was abandoned at the beginning of October, 1881. It was the Sharp's carbines that were used by John Brown's men in the historic raid at Harper's Ferry.

## THREE U. S. ARMORY MODEL SPRINGFIELD RIFLES.

**3017 MODEL RIFLE.** Made at Springfield Armory and submitted to the Board of Army Expert Officers appointed by Congress to examine and test Rifles for the purpose of selecting Army Service Rifle. Armory tag on the Rifles states history and that gun was fired 1,000 times. It was by the successful trial of this gun that the U. S. Army adopted the breech-loading Springfield Rifle.

**3021. SPRINGFIELD COLT'S M/L RIFLE.** Calibre 58. Stamped 1862, with letter M on the breech. MODEL RIFLE made by Colonel Colt, the *first of the Civil War Contract Guns* which served as the standard for the U. S. Inspectors.

**3021A. ALLEN-SPRINGFIELD B. L. RIFLE.** Made in 1865 at the Springfield Government Armory by altering the Civil War Muzzle - Loading Rifle into Breech-Loading by inserting rifle tube in the barrel, reducing the calibre from 58 to 50. This gun has a ratchet pinion side extractor, with short breech block. These three rare guns, representing Civil War and U. S. history from 1862 to 1884, are museum exhibits. Price for the three, $500.00.

**LEE, CALIBRE 45, U. S. ARMY SINGLE-SHOT BREECH-LOADING RIFLE.** Unique gun mechanism that puzzles experts to operate. A limited number of these rifles was made for trial by U. S. Army soldiers. From Rock Island Arsenal auction. Collector's Rifle, with full working instructions. Price, $36.00.

**0-931. ENGLISH BREECH-LOADING NEEDLE FIRE SPORTING RIFLE.** Patterned after the German needle gun. Made by Wilkins, London. Slide lever turns to the left for unscrewing the short breech, which allows the barrel to tip up for insertion of the cartridge. The face of the breech block screws into a recess in the barrel to help prevent escape of gas. Firing pin needle 1 inch long is attached to hammer. Rare gun; serviceable. Price, $14.85.

**ALLEN-SPRINGFIELD BREECH-LOADING RIFLE.** First transformation of the Civil War M/L Musket into breech-loader. Calibre 50. Springfield Master Armorer E. S. Allen's system ratchet extractor tube in barrel. Forerunner of the Springfield system, 1865. In use by U. S. Army for 30 years. Rare gun.

**FRANKLIN MAGAZINE RIFLE.** Calibre 45. Made by Colt's Armory in 1881. This is one of the systems invented by Gen. W. B. Franklin, then president of the Colt Company, and submitted to the U. S. for experiment. The gun is bolt action and the magazine, which is detachable, is slipped into a flat catch at the left side of the receiver. It holds 9 45-70 cartridges and one can be placed in the chamber, making a 10-shot rifle. The cartridges are fed into the breech by gravity only and the empty shell falls out through an opening at the bottom. It was intended for the soldier to carry a number of these magazines already loaded and when empty to throw them away.

**PALMETTO ARMORY, CALIBRE 69, MUSKET.** Altered to Breech-loader under the Merrill system. Rare gun. The U. S. has only one of these guns in all its collections. Lock plate is stamped with the South Carolina emblem, the Palmetto tree, Columbia S. C., 1852, Palmetto Armory. Price, $45.00.

**No. JC1. SHARP'S CARBINE**, designed in the '50s for use by express messengers. Barrel is 16 inches long and very heavy. Caliber .44. This is Sharp's second model breech action and is fitted with the famous Maynard primer. Also made in regular military model with longer barrel and larger caliber. This is no doubt the rarest type of Sharp's Carbine in existence. Note that the hammer is inside of the lock plate. Price, $25.00.

**No. 217.** Sharp's Civil War Percussion Lock Rifled Carbine, calibre 52; breech loading; shooting linen-covered combustible cartridge, used by the Union cavalry; one of the best of the breech-loading Civil War carbines; 22-inch barrel; total length, 38 inches; weight, 7¼ pounds; lever action, firing the regular cap; can be loaded with powder and shot, or ball, and fired with cap. (We have bullet moulds at 50 cents each.) Carbine has slide and ring for carrying by shoulder sling when mounted on saddle. Offered complete, somewhat rusty, "AS IS" at $3.50 each. Boxing 50 cents extra. NO CARTRIDGES.

## Collection of Rare Historical American Rifles and Carbines

1. SHARP & HANKINS B/L U. S. Navy Rifle. Caliber .54. Civil War Period..$15.00
2. MILBANK'S patent alteration of Springfield Rifle. Patent of 1867. One of the many Breech Loading Alteration of the Period ....................Price, 10.00
3. WARNER-GREENE B/L Carbine. Date 1864. Caliber .50. Late Civil War Weapon ........................ 25.00
4. WARD BURTON B/L Carbine. Date 1871. .50 caliber. One of the Earliest Bolt-Action Weapons .......................... 20.00
5. FRANK WESSON B/L Carbine. Caliber .44. A few of these were used during the Civil War.................... 20.00
6. PALMER Bolt-Action Carbine. Caliber .50. Civil War Period. Only six pounds in weight. A bolt-action with a side lock, very odd................... 14.85
7. HARPER'S FERRY F/L Rifle, model of 1819 with the peculiar oval patch-box cover. Caliber .54................ 36.00
8. WHITNEY, Model 1822. Musket altered in the 50's to percussion lock. A few were used in the early days of the Civil War ........................... 18.00
9. JENKS full length B/L Navy Rifle. Used in the 50's. Long rifles are rare....... 10.00
10. HARPER'S FERRY "1845" Rifle. This is the model of 1842. A famous rifle in its day .......................... 10.00
11. WHITNEY Model 1855 Musket. One of the very few private contract guns of this model ..................... 7.00

12. REMINGTON-ANNAPOLIS "Cadet" Rifle. Very rare as few were made.......... 10.00
13. PEABODY B/L Rifle. Style used in the '70s by the Connecticut State Troops.. 6.00
14. FRENCH Percussion Musket. One of the many purchased abroad for the U. S. at the outbreak of the Civil War......... 8.00
15. BRIDESBURG Civil War Musket. Private contract weapon of Civil War..... 10.00
16. AUSTRIAN Percussion Lock Musket. One of the many purchased at the outbreak of the Civil War............... 8.00
17. SPENCER'S Patent B/L Rifle. Civil War weapon. Long rifles of this make are rare ....................... 8.00
18. SHORT ENFIELD. English Percussion Rifle of 1858. Civil War purchase for U. S. Troops. Rare................. 8.00
19. REMINGTON-SPRINGFIELD Model 1870 Rifle. One of the few made at the Government armory ................. 6.00
20. MILLER'S Alteration of Springfield Rifle. Patent date, 1865. A breech loader of the '70s ..................... 12.00
21. JOSLYN RIFLE. Made at Springfield in 1865. Caliber .50. Rare....... 8.00
22. REMINGTON 1871 Navy Rifle. One of the rare types of this make........... 9.00
23. SPRINGFIELD 1877. One of the Civil War Muskets altered to breech loader and caliber reduced to .50......... 6.00
24. WHITNEY ENFIELD. This is one of the rarest of Civil War guns as it is a copy of the English musket made in this country ..................... 8.00

25. SPRINGFIELD Cadet Rifle. Type used after Civil War........................ 8.00
26. SPRINGFIELD "Artillery" Rifle. Caliber .58. Several inches shorter and heavier than regular model. Rare.............. 8.00
27. SPRINGFIELD "Artillery" Rifle. Caliber .50. Same particulars as No. 26........ 8.00
28. C. D. SCHUBARTH'S Civil War Musket. Caliber .58. Selected by the contractor as the finest specimen of the many he made for the U. S. in 1863-65. New, special stock ................... 40.00
29. SHARP'S Metallic Cartridge Carbine. A peculiar alteration from the percussion system. Very rare .............. 12.00
30. STARR'S Patent B/L Carbine. Civil War type ................... 12.00
31. JENKS' Muzzle-Loading Carbine. The only specimen we have seen. U. S. Navy gun ................... 15.00
32. JENKS' B/L Carbine. Pre-Civil War type ................... 12.00
33. JOSLYN B/L Carbine. Used in the '70s by U. S. Cavalry ................. 4.00
33. BALLARD'S Patent B/L Carbine. Caliber .50. A few were used just after the Civil War. Rare today.............. 9.00
34. LINDNER'S Patent B/L Carbine. Percussion. Civil War gun. Rare........ 10.00
35. SHARP'S Carbine. This is the type used by John Brown and his men. Very early model. Percussion................. 15.00
36. MAYNARD Percussion Carbine. First model. Has the famous primer lock. Very rare ..................... 20.00

ENFIELD CAVALRY CARBINE, kind used to arm the Confederates during the Civil War, 1861-1865. Some of the Union Army mounted men were also armed with the Enfield. Swivel ramrod attached to the gun allows the horseman to load without danger of losing the ramrod. Gun has British Army proof marks, V. R. Crown, 1858 (and other dates), with broad arrow showing one time Government ownership. Brass mountings, side bar ring for carbine sling. Walnut stock, calibre 577, full length, 36 inches, perfect order, rare serviceable relic. $6.85.

NORTH "HALL" CARBINE. This interesting weapon has the side lever to operate the breech. Invented by Savage and North (two famous names) in July, 1844. This method was considered a great improvement over the original method as the hook was liable to catch in the soldier's clothing. Caliber is .53. Barrel is 21 inches long and the arm weighs 8 pounds. Fine order and priced at $20.00.

Full sized illustration of muzzles of Elephant Rifles 3954a and 3395.

3459. ELEPHANT RIFLE, made by J. S. T. Botha, Cape Town, South Africa. ⅞-inch Rifle bore, Twist Steel, octagonal barrel, 28 inches long. Ramrod, 3-leaf folding rear sight. Percussion lock, curly walnut stock, checkered grip, maker's name engraved on barrel and lock. German silver mountings and name plate. We have these rifles in two sizes. See illustration showing the full size at the muzzle. Price, buyer's choice, $10.00 each.

3195. WERDER LIGHTING CARBINE, BREECH-LOADING, front trigger within the guard operates the breech block for loading and ejecting, the thumb piece works the hammer, protected front sight, 15½ inch barrel, ring swivel for carbine sling, calibre 44. No cartridges. Collector's gun. Price, $15.00.

FINE SMALL-BORE TWIST STEEL PERCUSSION LOCK SPORTING RIFLE, with rib forming part of the barrel, silver front sight, adjustable rear sight, ramrod rib, walnut stock, checkered grip, sling swivels, beautifully engraved. Price, $14.85.

1—58. FRENCH ARMY CHASSEPOT BREECH-LOADER MUSKETOON. Lock stamped "Mfg. Imperial Mutzig Mfe. 1866." French Government marks on the stock; practically like new gun, blued steel barrel complete with sling swivel, polished walnut stock. Price, $6.85.

3126. BALLARD RIFLE, calibre 44, rim fire, 20½-inch barrel. Second hand working order. Price, $6.50.
3129. ROBBINS & LAMSON U. S., CALIBRE 54, contract M/L Rifle, made at Windsor, Vt., 1851, brass-bound, fitted with stud for sword. Good working order. Price, $7.50.

5001. Triplett and Scott, patent 1864, Repeating Carbine, made by Meriden Mfg. Co. (now Parker). Stamped "Kentucky." New gun, never issued, stored for over 30 years at the U. S. Ordnance Arsenal, New York. Magazine is in the butt stock; contains 6 cartridges, rim fire, as used in the Spencer, barrel turns and opens gate to magazine, spring pushes the cartridge into the chamber of the gun. Full length is 30 inches, barrel is 19½ inches. Price, $15.00.

5002. Ball's 1864 Patent 7-shot Repeating Combination Carbine and Rifle, calibre 50, rim fire. shoots the Spencer Cartridge, made by E. G. Lamson & Co., Windsor, Vt. 1002 guns purchased by the U. S. Government; 7 cartridges contained in the magazine under the barrel, inserted through opening inside of the receiver, operated by under lever which also forms guard for the trigger; ram rod is a rod connected with the magazine spring and compresses the spring for loading; case-hardened frame. Blued steel barrel 22 inches, full length 38 inches. Price, $15.85.

5003. Civil War Carbine, from the collection of Adam Oliver, Master Armorer, Augusta, Arsenal, Ga.; Austrian Carbine Pattern, kind used in equipping Union Cavalry in 1861. No doubt a gun captured by the Confederates. Price, $7.85. See story of Adam Oliver.

No. 2276. Peabody Martini Sporting Rifle, small bore; practically new; price $15.00.

5006. Confederate Army Enfield M/L Civil War Rifle. One of the lot sent to the South by British blockade-running steamer. From Adam Oliver's collection. Price, $20.00.

Calibre 43 Spanish Remington Rifle captured by the Philippine Constabulary from Filipino native insurgent. The original stock has been replaced by Filipino home-made bamboo stock and fastened to barrel with bamboo fibre bands. The original tag attached to this rifle by the constabulary officer at the time of its capture and which goes with the gun, states that this rifle was "Captured from Filipino named Baloga, in Pampanga, Aug. 10, 1908, by Lieut. E. H. Walton, Philippine Constabulary." Price, $20.00.

*Continued on page 366*

**FIG. A. (GERMANY) MAUSER RIFLE,** the infantry arm of the German Army. Stamped on the left of the receiver "GEW 98" meaning Gewehr (weapon) of the year, 1898. The rifle is shown with the action open and bolt withdrawn to the rear, equipped with the breech-cover, designed to keep wind and dirt out of the mechanism while in use in the trenches. It will also be noticed that the extra magazine, made to hold 20 cartridges, is attached. A muzzle cover is in its proper place as well. The bayonet shown is the model brought out with the gun in '98, but during the War over forty different designs were made; these are shown in a book we have on sale, see notice elsewhere. The calibre of GEW '98 is .31 and the magazine holds five shots.

**FIG. B. CARBINE OR SHORT RIFLE,** stamped KAR '98, the Germans use a K in spelling Carbine. This rifle has the full wood protection for the barrel and takes a bayonet. The long hook shown at the muzzle-end is for use in stacking. The rear sight is of different design than that of the long rifle and much simpler. The bolt handle is turned down, out of the way, similar to the U. S. Springfield. There are no sling swivels, the sling passes through a loop on the left of the lower band and is fastened on the right side of the butt-stock, after passing through the recess just back of the pistol-grip. Calibre is the same as the long rifle.

**FIG. C. THIS IS FAMOUS "SNIPER" MODEL** of the long rifle, it will be noticed that the arm has a telescope with the bolt of the rifle turned down. Otherwise it is the same as Fig. A.

**FIG. D. THIS IS THE REAL CARBINE OF MODEL 1898.** The barrel is but 18½ inches in length and the rear sight although similar in pattern to the rifle is smaller. The gun takes a bayonet. Same calibre and number of shots as the upper three.

**FIG. E. MONDRAGON AUTOMATIC RIFLE.** Calibre, 7 m/m.; 10 shots in the magazine which is the same general principle as the Mauser. This arm is gas operated. The trigger must be pulled for each shot. The inventor of this rifle is a Mexican Army officer, who first offered his invention to France, but it was refused; he then went to Switzerland where he started making them. Germany later adopting the system and using them in aeroplanes in the early days of the War.

**FIG. F. MANNLICHER MAGAZINE RIFLE OF THE MODEL OF 1888.** The magazine of this differs from the Mauser in that it is necessary to insert both clip and cartridges to operate. When the last of the five shots are fired the empty clip falls out of the bottom of the magazine. Near the end of the War, however, they were altered to load with the Mauser clip and the aperture at the bottom was closed. This gun and the carbine (Fig. G.), have no wood protection for the barrel but instead a thin steel tube is used which leaves an air space all around the barrel. The muzzle end of the gun shows the tube very plainly. Calibre is .31, but the cartridges were round pointed. Five shots.

FIG. A

FIG. B

FIG. C

FIG. D

FIG. E

FIG. F

EIG. G

FIG. H

FIG. I

FIG. J

FIG. A. (FRANCE) LEBEL MAGAZINE RIFLE, MODEL OF 1886. This weapon is distinguished by the fact that it was the first small-bore (8 m/m.) ever used and also, the first to use smokeless powder. The French were evidently satisfied with the two innovations for the arm remains unchanged today. The magazine, holding eight shells, lies in under the barrel, being simply a hole bored in the fore-end, the cartridges being fed into the magazine by the action of a long spiral spring. The Lebel is the standard arm of the French Army, it takes the bayonet shown between Figs. C and D.

FIG. B. MANNLICHER MAGAZINE CARBINE. Model of 1890. This rifle has the well-known Mannlichers' type of magazine in which the clip and the cartridges are fed into the mechanism, the empty clip falling out when all the cartridges are fired. Before the war, the capacity was but three shots but during the conflict, the extra piece shown on Fig. C was added thus increasing the weapon to five shot capacity. These carbines were made in several styles, some with a hand-guard, some with stacking hooks and some with longer fore ends, this latter model did not take a bayonet. Takes same cartridge as the Lebel.

FIG. C. MANNLICHER MAGAZINE RIFLE. Model of 1907-'15. This is simply the carbine mechanism with a longer barrel. Made in several styles, some were only three-cartridge capacity, other five. Also made with and without a hand guard. Some had the long turned-down bolt of the carbine. They took on some models, the carbine bayonet and on others, the Lebel bayonet. Many were made in this country in early part of the war. It is interesting to note that the rifle bayonet has also been found designed so as to fit the carbine, a fact not generally known.

FIG. D. THIS IS THE FAMOUS AUTOMATIC RIFLE, Model 1917. It uses the regulation cartridge in the magazine which lies directly under the receiver. The weapon is gas operated and resembles the Lebel very much except at the breech. Takes the same bayonet and has the same rear-sight. The cut shows the bolt drawn back and the mechanism open. It is said that the French are experimenting with this rifle in shorter form with a view of adopting it as the regular weapon of all its forces.

Continued on page 366

3

FIG. A.

FIG. B.

FIG. C.

FIG. D

FIG. E

FIG. F.

FIG. G.

FIG. H

FIG. I

FIG. J

FIG. A. ENGLISH ENFIELD MAGAZINE RIFLE. Pattern 1914. Caliber, .303; five shots. The British government was experimenting with this rifle when the war broke out, it was however to be of a smaller calibre, i. e. .27. Thousands were made in this country for England in the early part of the War and as is well known, the U. S. adopted it in view of the fact that so many armories could produce it while but one could make the Springfield. This model differs from the U. S. in that it has a long range sight on the left side and the calibre being .303 instead of .30. Bayonets for both countries are the same. It will be noticed that there are 2 ribs cut into the wooden grips of the bayonet, this was done as a means of distinguishing this model from the model that fitted the 1903 short Lee-Enfield, the bayonets were very similar in looks. The rear sight being placed directly over the receiver and near the eye of the soldier is a new idea. The Ross of Canada, Mark III copied it. (See Fig. D.) In all the photographs of war scenes, the writer has never seen one of these rifles in the hands of an English "Tommy."

FIG. B. ENGLISH SHORT LEE-ENFIELD MAGAZINE RIFLE. Model of 1903. Calibre, .303; ten shots. The cut illustrates the Mark III*, issued in 1916 embodying all the improvements made on the rifle since its first introduction. There have been eight different patterns issued, some radical changes being made during the War as the elimination of the cut-off and the long range (auxiliary) sight. The peculiar hump over the receiver is the clip guide, a cumbersome feature but necessary as the body is open at the top all the way back on account of the bolt locking device. The bayonet shown is an earlier model, as the hooked cross-piece was abolished in 1913. The present pattern is the same but with a short straight cross-piece.

FIG. C. ENGLISH LEE-ENFIELD MAGAZINE RIFLE. Officially known as "Charge-Loader." Converted from early models of the long rifles, dated from 1889 to 1903. These guns are all 10 shot magazine and .303. A front sight guard has been added and an improved rear sight. The old short hand guard and old type bayonet have been retained. The gun (Fig. C) is a Lee-Metford (1892) converted.

There was also found among the captured arms, specimens of Lee-Metfords and Lee-Enfields, unchanged since their issue 1889-1899.

Continued on page 366

# THE PRINCIPAL WEAPONS OF THE WORLD WAR—Continued

This arm has a stacking hook on the left side of the end band which does not show in the illustration. Takes the bayonet as the rifle, except that guard was curved on the upper side.

FIG. A. AUSTRIAN STRAIGHT PULL MANNLICHER MAGAZINE RIFLE. Model of 1888-'90. Calibre, 8 m/m., five shots. On this rifle the cartridge clip, which is rather large, forms part of the magazine mechanism. On the middle band will be seen an extension point, this forms the foresight of the long distance sight, the rear being a slide on the right. Some of these rifles were provided with a hand guard of canvas, that was laced on (see illustration) other models, had a wooden hand guard and a different pattern rear sight. Bayonet blade is 10 inches in length.

FIG. B. AUSTRIAN STRAIGHT PULL MANNLICHER MAGAZINE RIFLE. Model of 1895. The principal infantry arm of the Austrians during the War. Takes same cartridge and clip as Fig. A. This rifle was the first weapon designed with the complete hand guard protection to the barrel. This model is lighter and stronger than the model of '88-'90, although of the same length. Bayonet has a blade of 10 inches in length, with this peculiar feature; the back is one, the lower side when fixed just opposite to other models. No carbines of the model '88-'90 were made, although some of the rifles cut down to carbine length were found.

FIG. C. AUSTRIAN STRAIGHT PULL MANNLICHER MAGAZINE CARBINE. Model 1895. Takes same clip and cartridges as rifles A and B. Barrel is 19½ inches long. Made both, with and without bayonet lugs.

FIG. D. ITALIAN MANNLICHER MAGAZINE RIFLE. Model of 1891. Known officially as the "Carcano," named after an ordnance expert of Turin Arsenal, who introduced some features in the breech mechanism. The calibre is .256 or 6.5 m/m., the clip holding 6 cartridges. No improvements have been made on the arm since its introduction. The swinging arm of the rear sight folds over to the front to prevent it catching in the soldiers' clothes. The cleaning rod is full length and very thin and light. Bolt is the usual quarter turn to the left and back pattern. The rifle is distinguished for its few parts and lightness being but 8½ pounds in weight.

FIG. E. ITALIAN MANNLICHER MAGAZINE (CARCANO) CARBINE. Model of 1891. Practically the same as the rifle, but with an 18½-inch barrel. The bayonet however is different, as it is attached by a circular motion using the barrel as a pivot. Six shots, calibre .256 or 6.5 m/m. The original model of the Italian carbine had a spring bayonet, which was attached permanently to the muzzle of the gun, it folded back and was held in place by a groove in the band which was placed about 6 inches in front of the rear sight. None of this model, however, seem to have found their way to this country.

FIGS. D and E take the same pattern bayonet with the slight change in method of adjustment to the pieces. Continued on page 366

Since our last catalogue was issued, the gun market has undergone quite a change, by reason of the United States Government selling off guns to the highest bidder that formerly had been held at high-limit prices. We purchased the largest lot, and at once interested some of the large department stores, to whom we sold many thousands at about a quarter of our former prices, realizing a fair profit for a quick turn of the money invested. We reserved a number of the choicest and rarest of these carbines, which will now be found on this and following pages. The low prices at which many of these carbines were sold by the department stores throughout the country induced many to start a collection. To such this catalogue will be valuable, enabling them to add further specimens.

FRUWIRTH MAGAZINE CAR-BINE. This is an historical piece as it represents the first magazine arm used for military purposes in Europe. Austria adopted this system in 1869 and they were in use a year later. Magazine is under the barrel and holds eight 11 m/m. cartridges. What looks like a hammer in rear of breech is really a cocking piece as in modern rifles. This is a remarkably up-to-date weapon despite its age. Stamped No. 599. Price, $50.00.

**The Society of American Military Engineers**

Capt. L. R. Lohr, *Executive Secretary*

Washington, D. C.

Deecember 9, 1925.

Francis Bannerman Sons,
    501 Broadway, New York, N. Y.
    Dear Sirs: Your bound catalogue was received and I have taken much pleasure in going over it. It is a liberal education in military equipment, and I appreciate your courtesy in sending it to me.
        Very truly yours,
            L. R. LOHR.

Gallagher Breech-loading Rifled Carbines, 50 calibre. Rim fire. Shooting same cartridges as the Spencer and Peabody rifles. New guns. Rare relics, as only a few were made to take metallic cartridges. Lever action with patch box in stock. Price, $6.50 each.

Merrill Breech-loading Rifled Carbine. For use with percussion cap. Used in Civil War, 1861-65. In serviceable order. Calibre 54. Price, $6.95 each.

Sharp & Hankins Breech-loading Rifled 50-calibre Rim fire Rifled Carbine. Shoots the rim fire cartridge. Lever slides the barrel forward, leaving the empty cartridge shell impinged on stationary extractor in the breech. Novel and rare mechanism. These guns are now very scarce. Price. $10.00 each. In serviceable order.

500 Burnside Breech-loading Rifled Carbines. Calibre 54. Shooting special metallic cartridge with the percussion cap. We can furnish these cartridges at $1.50 per 100. Guns are in good serviceable order. Price, $5.00 each.

Joslyn Breech-loading Cap and Ball Rifled Carbine. Calibre 54. Used in latter part of the Civil War. Good serviceable second-hand order. Price, $5.85 each.

Maynard Breech-loading Rifled Carbine. Calibre 50. Light, neat, serviceable. Metallic cartridge fired with percussion cap. We have large quantity of these cartridges. Cost the Government $18.00 each. Invented by Dr. Maynard, the originator of the patent primer bearing his name. Gun is operated by the lever. Chiefly valuable as relic of Civil War period. Guns, price $5.90 each.

100 Sharp's Heavy Octagon-barrel Breech-loading Cap and Ball Rifled Carbines. Used by Civil War sharpshooters. In good serviceable order. Calibres are various, from 40 to 50. Have the lever action. Weight about 10 pounds. Valuable relics. Finest kind of shooting has been done with these guns. We have no cartridges. With bullet mold from the Ideal Co., New Haven, sportsmen could, with little expense, make their own cartridges. Price, $6.80 each.

0-1321. CONFEDERATE PERRY CARBINE, captured, and sold after the Civil War as "REBEL." The lever is hinged to the frame at its forward end, connected to breech block by a link pressing the lever pushes up the mouth of the breech block for loading; fired by percussion cap. Made in the South during the Civil War; calibre 52,7 grooves. Price, $35.00.

0-1323. CONFEDERATE MUSKET, stamped B. & B., ALA., 1864, on the lock and barrel. The musket is the Mississippi pattern, kind with which, during the Mexican War, Col. Jeff Davis' Regiment was armed. Heavy steel barrel, brass band and mounting. Full length is 48½ inches. In serviceable order. Price, $30.00.

0-1321A. GREENE BREECH-LOADING CARBINE, with Maynard primer magazine box made by the Massachusetts Arms Co., 1856. By pressing the forward front trigger the barrel can be turned and moved forward for loading with powder. A sharp, hollow tube on the base of the breech tears the paper cartridge. Toothed wheel in the primer box moves forward the primer at the cocking of the hammer. Gun has been used by the British Government, as it is marked with the British mark, V. R., and the two Broad Arrows; evidently the second arrow was put on when the carbine was released from government service, no doubt during the Civil War, in order to obtain the high price prevailing during 1861 to 1865. The gun is in good condition. Price, $38.50.

No. 1519. 300 GERMAN ARMY CARTRIDGE BOXES. Size 4½ inches long, 2 inches deep, ⅝-inch wide. Fine leather, hand sewed, with loop for 1⅞ inch belt. Inside loops for holding cartridges. A number of these boxes can be carried on the waist belt if desired. Fine order; like new. Suitable for cade companies. Price, 25 cents each.

The Colonel who represented the Southern Confederacy in Europe during the Civil War, purchasing arms and war material to be shipped to the South by blockade running steamers, while in our store related an incident that may interest our readers: That after the Civil War was over he was in France trying to sell to the French Government some of the large quantities of arms left over from the war and had met with poor success getting through the red tape which surrounded the French War Minister, when meeting Mr. Slidell, he whose forcible removal from a British ship while on his way to Europe to represent the Southern Confederacy came near bringing on a war between the United States and Great Britain, Slidell suggested that the Colonel go and see the Emperor (Napoleon III.). So the Colonel wrote to the Emperor and received an invitation to call at the palace at Versailles. On showing the Emperor the Spencer Repeating Carbine and working through the mechanism 7 dummy cartridges a few seconds, the Emperor exclaimed, "Why, no army could carry sufficient cartridges to supply such quick-firing guns." The Colonel had his answer ready and replied: "Emperor, you have seen the gentle, lingering summer shower, also the sudden, destructive hail storm, which lasts but a short time but does great damage? The ordinary breech-loading gun is like the summer rain, the Spencer Repeater like the destructive hail storm." The Colonel was sent to the Minister of War, who in order to relieve the Emperor gave Colonel —— a small order, as he seemed provoked that he had not first been consulted. We believe this was the same War Minister who prior to the Franco-Prussian War assured Emperor Napoleon that the French army was all equipped ready for war even down to the soldier's shoe strings. No doubt had the French army been armed with Spencer Repeating Rifles the map of Europe would have been changed.

# CARBINES AND RIFLES.

71

Smith Breech-Loading Carbine. New Guns. Made for use during the Civil War, but held in reserve. Are now obsolete. ½-inch bore. Finely rifled. Many thousands of guns were sold by us to department stores last year. This kind has now become rare and price has advanced. Fired with the ordinary percussion cap. Price, $5.75 each.

Starr Carbine—Civil War relic. These Starr carbines were made at Starr's Armory Yonkers, N. Y., during the Civil War; afterwards moved to Binghamton, now occupied by Lt.-Govenor Jones' Scale Mnfy.—"Jones he pays the freight." Carbine has the falling breech-block somewhat similar to the Sharp Guns; are in second-hand service-able order; made to shoot combustable cartridges; fired with percussion cap. Price for gun with 10 cartidriges and caps. $8.00.

Brooks Patent Breech-Loading Rifled Carbine. Made by Gilb Arms Co. Shoots cap and ball cartridge. Very rare guns. Chiefly prized by collectors. This lot was obtained at one of the United States arsenals. Prior to this lot we obtained $25.00 each for a few we had. Our price now is $10.00 each.

30 European Breech-Loading Centre Fire Large Bore Rifled Carbines. Full length 33 inches; about 12 guage bore; chambers for Cartridges, 2¾ inches. Could be altered by buyer to shoot 12 guage Cartridge. Handy saddle rifle. Has ring swivel for carbine sling. In serviceable order, offered as is. Stamped on gun DELFT. Crown W. R. and year of manufacture. Bargain price $3.85.

1A. EUROPEAN AIR GUN, with full length hardwood polished stock. 18½ inch octagonal barrel, which pulls ahead to load. Air chamber 7 inch. Air compressed by winding handle at side. Brass mounted, with wood ramrod. This is an early type. Price, $6.50.

Cosmopolitan or Union Breech-Loading Carbine. New guns. Limited number only were made for use of the Union soldiers during the Civil War. ½-inch bore. Finely rifled. Breech block is hinged and worked by lever, similar to Sharps and Winchesters. Fired with percussion cap. This is the first and only lot sold by United States War Department. Price, $5.50 each.

Lindner Breech-Loading Rifled Carbine, ½-inch bore. Fired with ordinary percussion cap. Breech block is hinged at end, with sliding cover. Only few were made during Civil War period. This is the first lot offered for sale. New guns. Price, $10.00 each.

Ward-Burton Breech-Loading Carbine. United States Army Model guns. Shooting 50-calibre centre-fire metallic standard Government cartridge. In serviceable order. Bolt action, which flips the empty shell clear out of the gun automatically. Price, $25.00 each.

First Winchester Volcanic Repeating Rifled Carbine. Made by Henry, of New Haven, who sold out to the Winchester Arms Co. A few of these rifles were used in the Civil War. No cartridges can now be obtained. Rifles are as good as new. Valuable only as relics to collectors.

COLT REVOLVING CARBINE, like illustration is sold. See pages 38 and 47 for Colt revolving sporting and military patterns. Colts revolvers are shown on page 114 with prices, from the Dragoons up to the later types. Description of the various Army and Navy models is given with illustrations and all details on page 251.

**"Relics of the Civil War."**

Bargains!—in army rifles,
  Shown in a city store;
Piled up high on a counter,
  Stacked on the polished floor.
Rusty and old and clumsy,
  Battered and scratched and marred,
They are bought like slaves at market,
  Placed under a "bargain" card!
—Boston *Transcript.*

---

TP. LOT OF RELIC RIFLES AND CARBINES. Unserviceable weapons from collectors who made his own repairs. NOT IN WORKING ORDER. Offered AS ARE, NO SELECTION, at $1.00 each. If shipped alone add 50 cents extra for boxing.

5 Sharp's Breech-Loading Rifled Carbines. Captured by Confederates while unfinished from Harper's Ferry Arsenal; taken to Richmond, Va.,

After the fall of Richmond these arms were found buried and were turned over to United States Marshal Hayes and sold at auction. The Virginia soil is still attached. Rare relics that tell their own history. Price, $10.00 each.

2 Jenks United States Navy, 1847, Breech-Loading Rifled Carbines. Made by Oak Ames, founder of Union Pacific Railway. Fired with cap, by hammer placed on right side of the gun. Rare guns. Valuable only to collectors. Price, $16.50.

10 ENFIELD MUZZLE-LOADING PERCUSSION LOCK MUSKETOONS, with sword bayonet, quill back, double edged point sword bayonet; marked on lock, TOWER, 1862, with British crown. Brass butt, guard plate and nose cap. Full length of gun, 39 inches. Length of gun with sword bayonet attached, 63 inches. This arm is now quite scarce, and seldom to be found with sword bayonet, especially this pattern. Price, $5.50.

English Tower Musketoons, with swivel ramrod. Price, $4.00 each.

Tower Carbine. Percussion Lock. Price, $3.00 each.

French Musketoon. Price, $4.00.

Palmer's Breech-Loading Carbine. Relic. Price, $14.85.

Cuban Relics. Purchased from Governor of Spanish Arsenal at Havana Old relics. Supposed to have been captured from Cubans and stored in arsenal at Havana. Evacuation Day these guns were sold to us. Miscellaneous lot, upward of 20 different kinds of guns—long, single-barrel fowling pieces, old double-barrel guns, breech-loading carbines, rifles (Winchester system), Remington sporting rifles with owner's name inlaid in gold. Incomplete and valuable as relics only. Price, $5.00 each.

Collection of 50 different kinds of carbines, many of the systems brought out by inventors during the Civil War. This lot is duplicate of the lot collected by Hon. Amory Edwards for the United States Government at close of Civil War, and will be offered as a lot only. Price, $650.00.

English Musketoon, Lacy & Co., London. Price, $7.50.

Greene Breech-Loading Carbine, 1854. Rare relic Price, $25.00.

Inventor's Model Breech-Loading Carbine. Unique system. Price, $22.00.

Volcano Magazine Rifle. Rare. Price, $40.00.

5 Sharp's Breech-Loading Rifled Carbines that, we believe, were used in the Civil War, afterward sold to the Indians and used by Sitting Bull's warriors at Custer massacre. These carbines are all marked with Indians' record of scalps taken by brass-head tacks nailed in the stock. The authenticity of record is kept by Indian medicine man, who acts as historian. These carbines were sold to us by the United States Ordnance Department as Indian relics surrendered to United States Army officers by Sitting Bull's band on their return to the United States from British Columbia, whence they retreated after the Custer massacre. Guns are in fair order only. Stocks are worn, as if rubbed against rocks. Price, $18.00 each.

Double-Barrel Flint-Lock Gun, with polished steel engraved barrels, with figures of game, with black ebonized carved stock with old-fashioned cheek piece; decorated with ornamental scrollwork, beautiful piece of work; ½-inch bore, 36-inch barrels; in fine order, new. Price, $60.00.

Double-Barrel Flint-Lock Gun, with fine walnut stock, ½-inch bore, 36-inch steel barrels, plain finished; stock has split in it, otherwise in fine order, like new; will sell as it is for $28.75.

Inventor's Model Rapid-Fire Gun, with hopper and crank; 20-inch blued-steel rifled barrel, about ½-inch calibre. Price, $50.00.

United States Army Fencing Musket, with flexible bayonet for use in bayonet drill; in serviceable order. Price, $3.75.

**0-663. JOHN BROWN'S RIFLED CARBINE.** The kind used on his raid to capture the U. S. Arsenal at Harper's Ferry, Va., to obtain guns to arm the negroes to fight for freedom. These carbines are stamped on the barrel, "Sharp's Rifle Manufacturing Hartford, Co., Conn.," and on the lock, "Sharp's Patent, 1852." The paper or linen cartridge was fired by percussion cap placed on the nipple; also by copper disk primer inserted in the lock and worked by the cocking of the hammer. The barrel is 20 inches in length. This pattern Sharp's carbine is known among collectors as the John Brown Sharp's and is exceedingly rare. Is the first model Sharp's carbine with the slanting breech block. Price, $15.00.

200 Sharp's Breech-Loading Carbines were purchased in 1857 at a cost of $25.00 each by the Kansas Aid Committee of Massachusetts, with monies voluntarily subscribed by New England Abolitionists, for arming the Kansas Free State men in their fight at the polls in defence of freedom against the Border Ruffians from the Slave States, who wished to force the new State of Kansas into the Union as a Slave State.

These carbines were shipped to Kansas, but for some reason were held up en route at Tabor, Iowa. Later they were turned over to John Brown, with authority to sell 100 to individual worthy free State Kansans at reduced price of $15.00 each. The remaining 100 to be held for arming any companies that might be organized. John Brown, unknown to the committee, had part of the lot removed to the neighborhood of Harper's Ferry, Virginia, for use in his attack on the U. S. Harper's Ferry Armory to obtain guns to arm the negroes.

104 Carbines were captured from Brown together with 160 boxes "Sharp's Patent Pellet Primers." They were stored in the Harper's Ferry Arsenal (unclaimed by the Massachusetts committee) and later when the Civil War broke out were captured by the Confederates, taken to Richmond and used to arm the Confederate Cavalry.

**10034. BUCK BREECH-LOADING RIFLE.** Made by H. A. Buck & Co., West Stafford, Conn., about 1880. One motion cocks the gun, opens the breech, and ejects the empty shell. 28 shots have been fired by this piece in one minute. A gun made by Buck & Co. was submitted to a board of officers at Springfield Armory, and judging from a careful examination of this piece, regular Springfield parts have been used in its construction. It is safe to say that this is the model the inventor submitted to the U. S. Government. The gun did not meet with approval, and the Buck concern soon went out of business. The calibre is 45. Price, $65.00.

**0-662. BETHEL BURTON BREECH-LOADING PERCUSSION LOCK CARBINE.** Shoots paper cartridge, calibre 52. The nipple is attached to a sleeve on the bolt and slides back when the breech is open. The interrupted screw, which is familiar on the altered model of the Ward-Burton guns, is easily seen directly in front of the bolt handle. The action was patented December 20, 1859. Full length 39½ inches, barrel 21½ inches. Bethel Burton was an inventor ahead of his time, later inventors using many of his inventions. The interrupted screw is now used on modern navy breech-loading cannon. The spiral main spring in bolt is used on all high-power bolt action guns also. The screw movement for locking, which pushes the bolt forward, making a tight joint at the breech of the barrel to prevent the escape of gas. A rare weapon. Price, $30.00.

**0-661. U. S. SPRINGFIELD MUZZLE-LOADING CARBINE.** Stamped, "1855." Calibre 54, rifled. Carbines of this model were made as early as 1848. These first-made, however, were smooth bore, and the swivel for the rod was slightly different in shape. The barrel is 22 inches long; full length of gun 37 inches. The ring attached to the rear end of trigger guard is familiar to these arms. Lock is stamped with "Eagle, U. S. Springfield, 1855." The barrel has the V. P. and Eagle head proof marks. Brass nose cap. We have three patterns of these carbines. Buyer's choice. Price, $10.00 each.

**0-775. EUROPEAN MUSEUM EXHIBIT ENFIELD MUZZLE-LOADING RIFLE, WITH MAGAZINE PRIMER ATTACHMENT IN ADDITION TO THE REGULAR HAMMER AND NIPPLE.** Stamped "L. R. Chester Patent." Disk primers are contained inside tube and forced upwards by spiral spring, and in connection with the hammer is a two-pronged flat steel lever, which pushes the disk primer from the magazine opening and places it on the nipple. The detachable magazine screws into place. This is a rare gun from a famous museum collection. Price, $45.00.

**0-761. METFORD BREECH-LOADING RIFLE.** Made by Westley Richards. Taken from an old Dutch farmhouse in South Africa during the Boer War and brought to England and given to Lady Palmer for her collection. Name of the Boer owner, H. J. Lombard, is stamped on the barrel. The stock had been broken; repaired by the owner with rawhide thong and screw. Fine, easy working lever mechanism; about 50 calibre. Serviceable relic. Price, $15.00.

**0-929. WESTLEY RICHARDS' MODEL 1873 CAP-SHOOTING RIFLE.** Captured at Boer farmhouse during war in South Africa. Serviceable relic from sale of Lady Palmer's collection. Price, $9.85.

**TWENTY-SEVEN OLD SPRINGFIELD CIVIL WAR MUSKETS SECOND-HAND SERVICEABLE ORDER.** Made by different contractors, 1861-1865. Price for the collection of 27 guns is $500.00.

**3019. U. S. SPRINGFIELD-COLT'S MUZZLE-LOADING CIVIL WAR CONTRACT RIFLE MUSKET.** Stamped "U. S. Colt's Pt. F. A. Mfg. Co., Hartford, Conn. (1863)." Full length 55½ inches. In used serviceable order. Price, $6.50.

Colonel Samuel Colt's name appears *first* on the list of gun contractors when on July 5, 1861, he agreed to furnish the U. S. Government with 25,000 Springfield Model calibre 58 Rifle Muskets at the price of $20.00 each. First delivery to be made January 1, 1862, and all to be shipped by March, 1863. On later contract Colt received $25.00 for each gun. Those old guns are now scarce. In 1900 we shipped 50,000 of the Colt's guns to Europe to be altered into flintlocks, sold to African traders. We reserved a few for collectors who are making collections of guns manufactured by Colt.

We have in our collection one each of the following Civil War Contract 58 calibre Springfield Rifle Muskets, stamped as having been made at:

Trenton, N. J.,
Philadelphia, Pa.,
Norwich, Conn.,
E. Robinson, N. Y.,
Milbury, 1864,
Windsor Locks,
Remington Ilion, N. Y.,
Union Arms Co., N. Y.,
Wm. Moore, Windsor, Ct.,
Colt's, Hartford, Conn.,
L. G. & Y., Windsor, Ct.,
William Muir, Taunton, Mass.,
Providence Tool Co., Prov., R. I., Providence,

Amoskeag Mfg. Co., Manchester, N. H.,
Parker Snow & Co., Meriden, Conn.,
S. N. & W. T. C., Manchester,
R. F. A. Savage, Middletown, Ct.,
Whitney, New Haven, Ct.,
G. D. Schubarth, Providence,
Jas. D. Mowry, 1864, Norwich, Conn.,
Manton, New York,
Norfolk, Ct.,
Watertown, N. Y.,
Bridesburg, Pa.,
Whitneyville, Conn.,

A few duplicates. Price on application.

**1790. PERIOD PILL LOCKS.** Used on guns after the flint and percussion locks came in use. The old side spring for the front striker was retained on the lock and made to operate a steel covered part containing the firing pin, and fitting over the vent piece, in which was inserted the small round pill, containing fulminate, the hammer striking the firing pin, explodes the pill fulminate in the vent, firing the charge. These locks are in good working order. Price, $5.00 each.

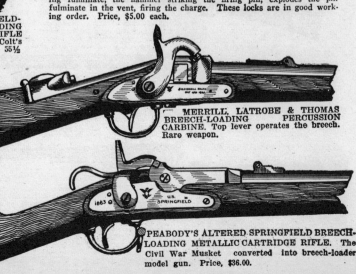

**MERRILL, LATROBE & THOMAS BREECH-LOADING PERCUSSION CARBINE.** Top lever operates the breech. Rare weapon.

**PEABODY'S ALTERED SPRINGFIELD BREECH-LOADING METALLIC CARTRIDGE RIFLE.** The Civil War Musket converted into breech-loader model gun. Price, $36.00.

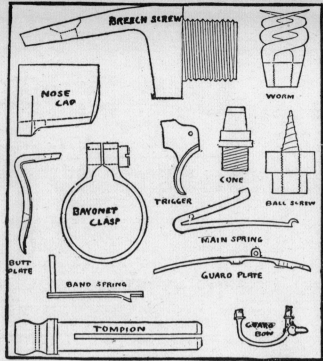

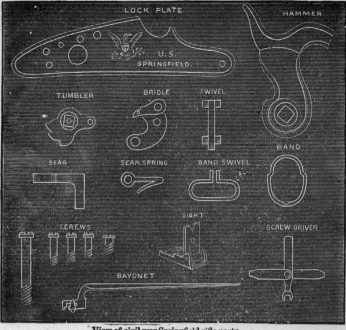

View of civil war Springfield rifle parts.

| | Each |
|---|---|
| Bayonet clasps | $ .08 |
| Nose caps | .12 |
| Lock plates | .40 |
| Hammers | .50 |
| Ramrods | .50 |
| Bayonets | .75 |
| Receivers | 1.50 |
| Breech blocks | 1.50 |
| Cam Latches | .25 |
| Cam shafts | .25 |
| Cam springs | .04 |
| Extractors | .25 |
| Ext'r springs | .05 |
| Firing Pins | .20 |
| Firing springs | .04 |
| Rear sights | .75 |
| Screwdrivers | .25 |
| Stacking swivels | .40 |
| Hinge pins | .30 |
| Wiping rods | .15 |
| Butt plates | .35 |
| Ramrod stops | .10 |
| Band swivels | .10 |
| Breech block cap | .15 |
| Breech block screws | .03 |
| Headless shell ejectors | .25 |

| | |
|---|---|
| Globe sights | .20 |
| Spring sights | .20 |
| Tompions | .10 |
| Metallic pistol grips | .30 |
| Wood pistol grips | .20 |
| Carbine swivel bars | .65 |
| Carbine stocks | 1.00 |
| Rifle stocks | 1.00 |
| Stock in rough | .75 |
| Ejector spring spindles, doz. | 1.00 |
| Round ball bullet moulds | .50 |
| Carbine barrels, 45 calibre | 1.00 |
| Carbine barrels, 50 calibre | 1.45 |
| Rifle barrels | 1.25 |
| Guard bows, complete | .80 |
| Bridles | .20 |
| Sears | .12 |
| 3-notch tumblers | .36 |
| Main springs | .25 |
| Thumb pieces | .36 |
| Band springs | .15 |
| Wind-gauge sights | 1.75 |
| Worms | .10 |

Calibre 58, Springfield Musket Parts.

| | |
|---|---|
| 25,000 Springfield lock plate and hammers, doz. | $4.00 |
| 20,000 tumblers, assorted kinds, doz. | 2.50 |
| 20,000 Lock screws, assorted kinds, doz. | .60 |

Side view of front sight cover.

End view, showing front side spring cover for Springfield breech calibre 45 B. L. rifle. 25c. each.

U. S. Springfield calibre 45 or 50 breech-loading rifle screwdriver, 2 blades, for large or small screws; tumbler punch, with wrench for taking out main spring. Price, 25 cts each; $2.75 per doz.

Brass sectional ramrods for Krag and Mauser rifles, 3 pieces which screw together. Price, 75c. per set.

| | |
|---|---|
| 20,000 Ramrod heads, doz. | $1.00 |
| 20,000 Screwdrivers, assorted kinds, doz. | 1.50 |
| 10,000 Ball screws, assorted kinds, doz. | 1.00 |
| 5,000 Rifle stocks, each | 1.50 |
| 5,000 Side screws, assorted kinds, doz. | .60 |
| 5,000 Tang screws, assorted kinds, doz. | .75 |
| 5,000 Butt plate screws, assorted kinds, doz. | .60 |
| 5 000 Guard plate screws, assorted kinds, doz. | .40 |
| 5,000 Bayonets, assorted kinds, each | .35 |
| 5,000 Cones or nipples, assorted kinds, doz. | .50 |
| 5,000 Sears, assorted kinds, doz. | 2.00 |
| 5,000 Sear springs, assorted kinds, doz. | 1.50 |
| 2,000 Rifle barrels, assorted kinds | 1.00 |
| 2,000 Main springs, assorted kinds, doz. | 3.00 |
| 2,000 Upper bands, assorted kinds, doz. | 1.00 |
| 2,000 Ramrods, assorted kinds, doz. | 3.50 |
| 2,000 Breech screws, assorted kinds, doz. | 3.50 |
| 2,000 Triggers, assorted kinds, doz. | 1.50 |
| 2,000 Guard plates, doz. | 3.50 |
| Bows, doz. | 3.50 |
| 2,000 Rear sights, each | .25 |
| 2,000 Nose caps, doz. | 1.50 |
| 5,000 Enfield rifle sights, doz. | 3.50 |
| 5,000 Springfield Tompions, brass, doz. | 2.50 |
| 5,000 Springfield Tompions, wood, doz. | .60 |
| 5,000 Springfield tumbler punches. | 1.00 |
| 58 calibre bullet moulds, each | 4.50 |
| Side screw washers, doz. | .80 |
| Band swivels, doz. | 1.00 |
| Butt plates, each | .30 |
| Enfield locks, complete, each | .95 |
| Springfield locks, complete, each | 2.50 |
| Band springs, each | .15 |
| Bayonet clasps, doz. | 1.25 |

Illustration showing Globe Sight Cover for sharpshooter's use on Springfield Breech-loading rifles, either 45 or 50 calibre. Price reduced to 35 cts. each, or $3.00 per dozen.

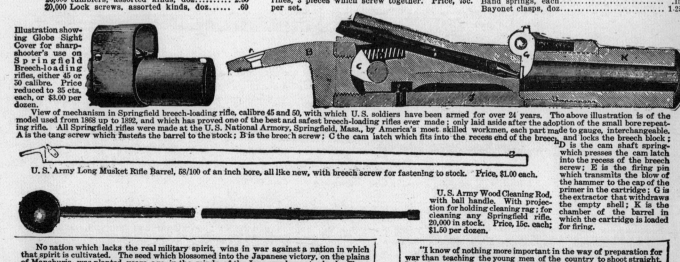

View of mechanism in Springfield breech-loading rifle, calibre 45 and 50, with which U. S. soldiers have been armed for over 24 years. The above illustration is of the model used from 1868 up to 1892, and which has proved one of the best and safest breech-loading rifles ever made ; only laid aside after the adoption of the small bore repeating rifle. All Springfield rifles were made at the U.S. National Armory, Springfield, Mass., by America's most skilled workmen, each part made to gauge, interchangeable. A is the tang screw which fastens the barrel to the stock ; B is the breech screw ; C the cam latch which fits into the recess end of the breech, and locks the breech block ; D is the cam shaft spring which presses the cam latch into the recess of the breech screw ; E is the firing pin which transmits the blow of the hammer to the cap of the primer in the cartridge ; G is the extractor that withdraws the empty shell ; K is the chamber of the barrel in which the cartridge is loaded for firing.

U. S. Army Long Musket Rifle Barrel, 58/100 of an inch bore, all like new, with breech screw for fastening to stock. Price, $1.00 each.

U. S. Army Wood Cleaning Rod, with ball handle. With projection for holding cleaning rag ; for cleaning any Springfield rifle. 20,000 in stock. Price, 15c. each; $1.50 per dozen.

No nation which lacks the real military spirit, wins in war against a nation in which that spirit is cultivated. The seed which blossomed into the Japanese victory, on the plains of Manchuria was planted years ago in the minds of the Japanese boys at school. Those boys were taught every day of their lives that military service was manly, honorable and ennobling: they were brought up to believe that obedience, cleanliness, sobriety and love of country were solemn obligations. The army was the nation, and when it went to war it was ready, not alone in organization, method and equipment: but in spirit, and with a determination that the spiritless, ignorant Moujiks could not withstand.

"I know of nothing more important in the way of preparation for war than teaching the young men of the country to shoot straight. It is of especial importance to the efficiency of our volunteer armies in the future, that the individual citizen-soldier should be a good marksman. It is of no use to pay, equip, subsist, and transport a soldier to the battlefield unless he can hit an enemy when he shoots at him."

ELIHU ROOT,
Secretary of War.

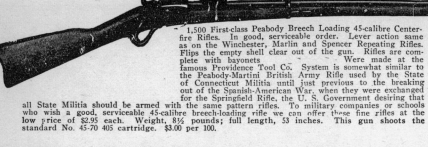

1,500 First-class Peabody Breech Loading 45-calibre Center-fire Rifles. In good, serviceable order. Lever action same as on the Winchester, Marlin and Spencer Repeating Rifles. Flips the empty shell clear out of the gun. Rifles are complete with bayonets. Were made at the famous Providence Tool Co. System is somewhat similar to the Peabody-Martini British Army Rifle used by the State of Connecticut Militia until just previous to the breaking out of the Spanish-American War. when they were exchanged for the Springfield Rifle, the U. S. Government desiring that all State Militia should be armed with the same pattern rifles. To military companies or schools who wish a good, serviceable 45-calibre breech-loading rifle we can offer these fine rifles at the low price of $2.95 each. Weight, 8½ pounds; full length, 53 inches. This gun shoots the standard No. 45-70 405 cartridge. $3.00 per 100.

View of the Peabody B/L Rifle with lever down, breech opened.

**11332. EUROPEAN HEAVY SPORTING RIFLE.** 29 inch octagonal barrel, with rear and front sights. 4½ inch percussion lock. Set triggers. Long guard bow, case hardened. Highly polished wood stock with two sling swivels. Cheek piece 6½ inches. In fine order. Price, $15.00.

1D. SECOND-HAND WEB GUN SLINGS, recent model with snap fasteners for quick adjustment. Price, 35 cents.

2D. WEB SLING, old regulation, of very heavy webbing. Fitted with two brass hooks. Can be used on gun or as shoulder sling on bag. Price, 38 cents each.

COLLECTION OF 500 GUNS, all different patterns, representing all types of guns in the history of the world. Beginning with the metal tube fired by fuse, commonly called the cannon lock, match lock, snaphaunce, flint lock, tube pill and percussion locks. The various breech-loading and magazine cartridge types up to and including the latest automatic guns, all in good serviceable order, with tags and book containing descriptive history. Many of the guns in the collection are of types found only in the HIGHEST CLASS MUSEUMS. Singly we value some of the guns at $1,000. The collection is offered for sale at $10,000. Six months' time required to write up history. A rare chance for some citizen to perpetuate his name and town by securing this museum collection.

Seven-shot Spencer Repeating Rifle Carbines. 50-caliber rimfire. Made under the supervision of Inventor C. M. Spencer. Magazine is in the butt stock and holds seven cartridges, while one can be inserted in the magazine. An effective rifle for hunting or defense. Short cartridges can be used in this gun as made by all the cartridge companies. Barrel is 22 inches long. Weight about 7 pounds. Sighted for 900 yards. Has Stabler's patent cuff-off, whereby gun can be used as a single-loader, holding the magazine in reserve. Edward Stabler was the inventor, a peace-loving Quaker, who took to hunting to recover lost health. His home was in Maryland. Is worked by a lever, same as in the Winchester or Marlin—simplest, safest and best mechanism in repeating gun. Fine walnut stock. Has a record of 7 shots in 20 seconds. Second hand, in working order. Price, $4.50 each. Cartridges, $1.50 per 100.

**REMINGTON SHARPSHOOTERS RIFLES.** We have several in stock in large calibers, not complete with sights. We offer these only to customers who can call here and make selection.

Martini-Henry Breech Loading Rifle used by British Army; serviceable, second-hand order. Limited number in stock.

These rifles have only of late years been discarded in favor of the small bore high power rifles. Gun makers still have calls for these well-known pattern guns, for so long a time the regulation British Army rifle. Price $7.50.

**10737. NEW REGULATION GUN SLING.** Made at the Government Rock Island Arsenal, 1903-1907. Russet leather, with bronze loop in the centre, with double hook claw adjusting hooks at each end. Full length of the sling, 4 feet. Second hand 50 cents. Selected 75 cents.

150,000 U. S. ARMY LEATHER GUN SLINGS for Springfield Army Rifle, made at Government Arsenal of finest quality leather, fitted with brass studs and the double claw brass adjusting hooks, in used, serviceable order. Old regulation WIHOUT center loop. Price 30 cents each; $2.50 per dozen.

**258. WERNDL BREECH LOADING AUSTRIAN RIFLES.** Total length 51 inches, barrel 34 inches. All in good order WITHOUT bayonets. Gun uses a caliber 43 European cartridge, which we CANNOT furnish at present. We offer the guns for drilling, or stage purposes. Many cadet companies wish to use a gun for which no cartridges are obtainable to avoid any danger from accidental discharge. We have 150 rifles left at $2.50 each. Packing charge is 45 cents extra.

Antique European Armory Target Rifle, short range, for use with reduced charge. The barrel is the usual length. The ball enters only half way. The hammer strikes a rod which fires the percussion cap. Only valuable to collectors of rare patterns or types of guns. Price, $4.85.

Alphonse Chassepot, inventor of the famous French rifle which bears his name, died recently in Paris, France, at the age of 72 years. He was the son of an armorer of Mutzig and followed his father's trade, entering the French Government factories and being transferred to Paris in 1858, where he soon became head of the establishment. He invented the Chassepot Rifle, which was used by France in Franco-Prussian War in 1870-71. Chassepot received the cross of the Legion of Honor in 1866.

**No. 1277. A BRITISH ENFIELD,** altered into Peabody system. Lock is Tower, 1863. Breech end of barrel is cut off and Peabody breech loading mechanism fitted; otherwise gun is old Enfield muzzle loading rifle. In good, serviceable order. Inventor's model. Price $22.00.

**No. 1402. 20 KYNOCH BREECH LOADING ACTION RIFLES.** Full length, 52 inches. Blued steel finish, about 43 calibre. No cartridges to be had. In good, second-hand order, Price, $2.95.

**No. 1372. 10 EUROPEAN MARTINI-HENRI BREECH LOADING RIFLES,** with long-range rear sight, blued steel rifle barrel, hardwood stock. Lock stamped "M, 1885, OE WG Steyer, 1886." Smooth bore, about 30 calibre. Price $8.75.

**No. 1590. 6 EUROPEAN ARMORY TARGET GUNS.** Full length, 49½ inches. Used in armory at short range. The hammer is in the usual place on the stock. Barrel loads only half way, a rod extending along the side of the gun, fires the cap when struck by the hammer. Stock is in poor order; worm eaten. Price $3.50 each.

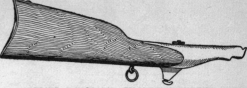

**U. S. ARMY STACKING SWIVELS.** By the use of which guns can be stacked by interlocking in the open swivels without the use of bayonet. Polished steel. Price 25 cents each.

**3172. U. S. ARMY SERVICE RIFLE MAIN SPRING,** piano wire quality spring steel, new. 20 cents each.

**U. S. ARMY SCREW DRIVERS,** Model 1890. 25 cents each.

**COLT'S AUTOMATIC PISTOL SEARS,** 15c each.

**47 U. S. MODEL 1903, INDEX CYLINDERS** for Telescopic Sights, 10c each.

**BURNSIDE CARBINE WALNUT GUN STOCK,** new, ready for attaching to rifle. Length, 15 inches; width at the butt, 4 inches. Price, $1.00 each.

**COLT'S REVOLVER SHOULDER-STOCKS.** Made in several different patterns. These detachable stocks enabled the soldier to convert his revolver into a repeating carbine. The pattern we have fits the "Old Model Army Revolver," model 1848, commonly called the "Dragoon" type. These stocks were first used in the early fifties. Very few of these to be had at any price today as they are more rare than the revolvers. Price, $15.00 each.

**3369. U. S. ARMY ANTIQUE FLINT-LOCK BRUSH AND PICK,** issued with old-time flint-lock guns, to enable the soldier to brush the pan and clean the burnt powder out of the vent. Spring chain with loop for attaching to the button on the coat. Ready for instant use when in action. Rare. Prize for collectors. Price, $1.00 each.

**3291. U. S. SPRINGFIELD FULL LENGTH STEEL ROD BAYONET.** Made for use on experimental rifles, at Government Arsenal. Length, 35½ inches. 3-16. Used in some parts of the country. Diameter, with screw thread for cleaning appendage. New and in perfect order. Made of the best tempered steel, as spring center for walking canes. We have 500 in stock. Price, 35 cents each.

**3025.** Rod Bayonet for U. S. Springfield Magazine Rifle. Made at Government Arsenal, for the new service Rifle discarded after the Japanese-Russian War when the knife bayonet was adopted by order of President Roosevelt. These Rod Bayonets are new, of the best tempered steel. Length 23½ inches. Diameter .30. The raw material cost 6c a pound. The finished Rod Bayonet 39c each. We have 60,000 in stock. Price, singly, 35c each; $3.50 a dozen. Order wanted for quantities.

**3173. U. S. ARMY RIFLE WIND GAUGE REAR SIGHT** with base ready for attaching to rifle. Side leaf graduated for 2000 yard range, with wind gauge, width, ⅝ inches; length of leaf, 3½ inches; complete with base spring and screws. Blued steel finished. Made at U. S. Government Arsenal at a cost of $1.49 in 50,000 lots. Our bargain price, $1.35.

**ANTIQUE GUN WORM AND BALL REMOVER,** with screw thread for attaching to the ramrod for removing bullet and powder charge in calibre 69 muskets, with slit for cleaning rag. Price, 25 cents each.

**SCREW DRIVER AND PUNCH.** Large and small size steel screw driver with punch used in taking apart and assembling. Ancient pattern army rifles. Price, 15 cents.

For several years we have been supplying steel ramrod to makers of bamboo canes, who use the rods to stiffen them and make them heavier, without increasing the size. We can still supply ramrods for this purpose at 30 cents each.

**3015. ANCIENT METAL OIL CUP,** with screw top and oil dropper. Made of iron with broad base. Cannot easily tip over. One drop of oil at a time directly on the spot where needed. Usually found in box sets of old high class Duelling Pistols. Old time serviceable relic. Useful household article. Price 25 cents each, $2.50 per dozen.

**U. S. Springfield Calibre 45** bullet moulds, casting 4 round calibre 45 bullets. Mould is of bronze. Length 10½ inches, weight about 3½ pounds, has wood handles also spruce cutters. Price $4.85.

**U. S. ARMORERS NEW STEEL PUNCH** for use in taking apart Springfield Rifles. Made at Government Arsenal. Average length, 4 inches; in small, medium and large sizes. Choice, 10 cents each.

**NIGHT SIGHT** for use on double barrel shot guns, with white enameled sight and light deflecting arms. Will fit any double gun. The slanting position of the white enameled arms reflects the light on the white enameled sight. Spring steel fits over any double barrel shot gun. Price, $2.50.

**GUN MAKERS' SPANNERS** for holding gun barrels in ordinary vise, with copper jaws so as not to injure guns. Length of jaw is 3¼ inches. Price, $3.50 each.

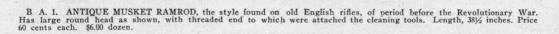

**B. A. 1. ANTIQUE MUSKET RAMROD,** the style found on old English rifles, of period before the Revolutionary War. Has large round head as shown, with threaded end to which were attached the cleaning tools. Length, 38½ inches. Price 60 cents each. $6.00 dozen.

**3089. SPRINGFIELD MAGAZINE RIFLE STOCK,** which buyer can with slight alteration make fit the 7 m/m. Spanish Mauser Repeating Rifle. Captured in Cuba. Price, $2.85 each.

We have in the past few years refused many orders for the Mauser Rifle Stocks. There are no more to be had. Any gunsmith can alter these Springfield Stocks to fit the Mauser, as the new Springfield Service Rifle is an adaption of the Mauser. These Stocks are fine selected walnut, rejected for some almost imperceivable imperfection. A fine curly walnut Stock is often rejected as not being straight grained, as required.

# Gun and Pistol Locks.

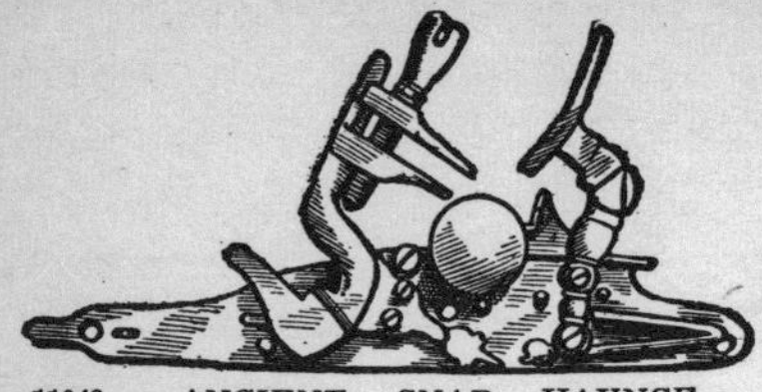

11049. ANCIENT SNAP HAUNCE FLINTLOCK, with automatic flash pan cover, automatic lever that uncovers the pan as hammer descends on the striker. LENGTH 8 inches, weight 14 ounces. Price, $20.00.

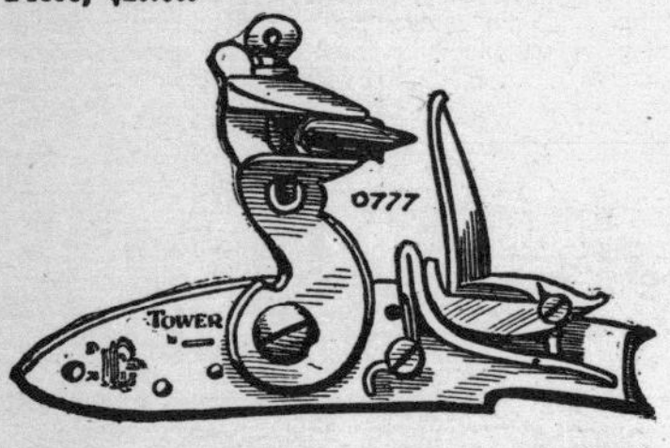


0-777. ADMIRAL NELSON SEVEN-SHOT FLINT-GUN LOCK. Stamped Tower, G. R. and British Crown. Used for firing flint guns with seven barrels at one time. We have one of these rare guns such as was used by the famous admiral at the battle of the Nile, Trafalgar and other great sea battles. We offer lock only. Price, $6.50.

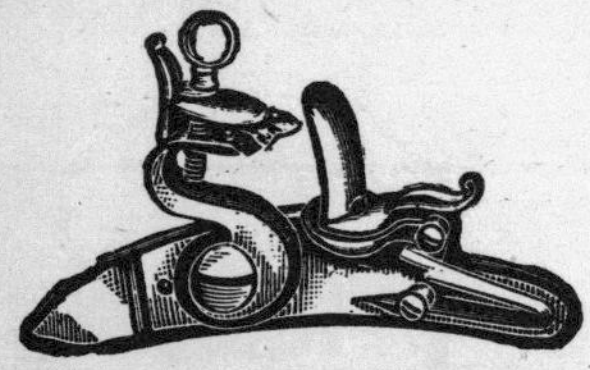

1747. BRITISH FLINTLOCK. Engraved, "G. R. Crown, Toldan, 1747." Length 5¼ inches. Price, $3.50.

BRITISH LOCK FOR FLINT GUNS. Engraved, "G. R. Tower Crown, 1729." Length 6¾. Price, $4.50.

FLINTLOCK. 5¼ inches long. Engraved with "Tower Crown, G. R., Tanner, 1745." Price, $4.00.

FLINTLOCK. 5¼ inches long. Engraved, "Egg, 1750, G. R. Crown. Price, $3.50. (Many of the Flintlock Muskets used during the American Revolutionary War were made by Egg.)

FLINTLOCK. 7½ inches long. Engraved, "Vernon, 1759, G. R. Crown." Price, $3.85.

Another by the same maker, 5¼ inches long. Engraved, "1760." Price, $3.50.

Another FLINTLOK. Made by Vernon. 7 inches long. Date, 1759. Price, $3.85.

FLINTLOCK. 7¼ inches long. Marked, "Price," with Crown Tower, dated 1762. Price, $3.85.

2419. METAL HELMET, with opening visor. Made of heavy metal; good facsimile of ancient helmet; used centuries ago. Price, $18.00.

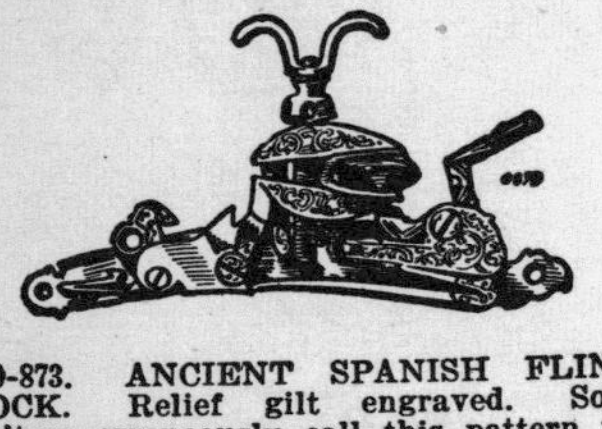

0-873. ANCIENT SPANISH FLINTLOCK. Relief gilt engraved. Some writers erroneously call this pattern the Snaphaunce. Rare outside lock construction. One lock is 6½ inches, the others 7 inches. Buyer's choice of either. Price, $5.00.

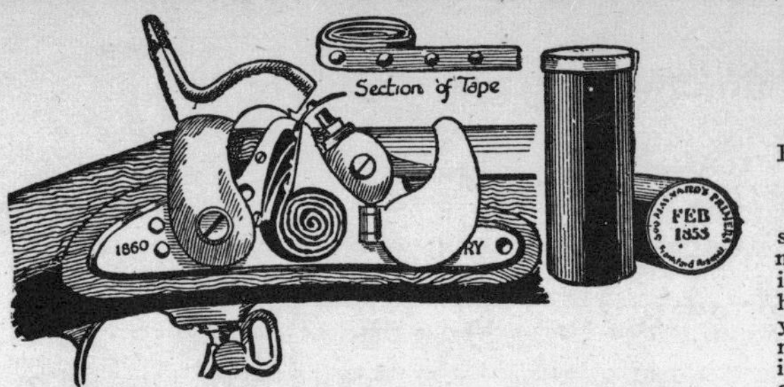


MAYNARD TAPE PRIMERS. Made for use in Civil War army muskets. Tape containing 50 charges of fulminate, was inserted in the lock, and each time the hammer was pulled back the feed finger spring mechanism pushed a section of the tape containing cap over the nipple, the hammer in descending simultaneously out off the tape and exploded the cap, which fired the charge in the gun. Serviceable relics for use on Maynard lock muskets (see our Springfield model 55). Price is 10 cents a roll of 50 caps. These tapes gave the soldier a double chance. He could use either tape or percussion cap.

0-868. PAIR D. EGG FINE FLINT PISTOL LOCKS. Rare early pattern. Fine, easy working locks with safety. Length 3½ inches. Price, $12.00 the pair.

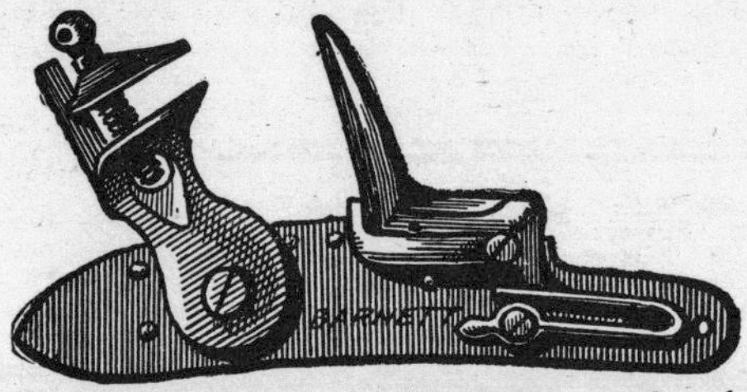


OLD CASTLE RAMPART GUN LOCK, as used on large sized old flint lock guns in defending castles. Length of lock plate is 8 inches; width of striker, 1½ inches; main spring ¾ inches wide. Old time English gun maker's name on lock plate. Rare old flint lock. Price, $6.00.

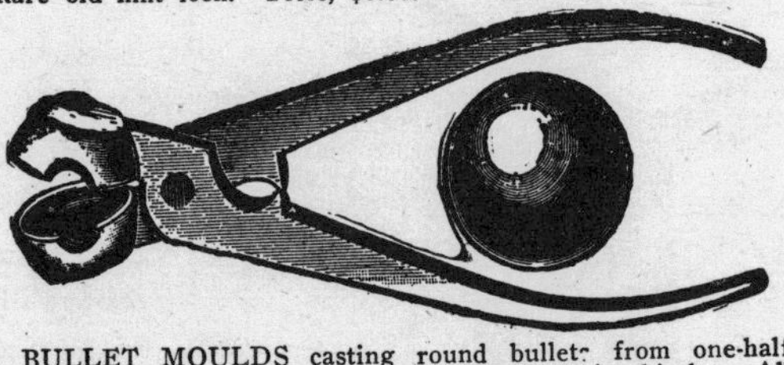

BULLET MOULDS casting round bullets from one-half inch upward. Both U. S. and Foreign moulds in this lot. All in serviceable order. Price, 85 cents each.

0-810A. NEW MOULDS casting one bullet 45/100 of an inch in diameter. Can be used for any calibre, 45 rifle or pistol. Price, $1.25 each.

0-653. CIVIL WAR NIPPLE PROTECTOR. Kind attached to Enfield guns used by both North and South 1861 to 1865. Leather covering for inserting on the nipple when not in use and attached to gun by brass chain. We offer the protector without the chain at 5 cents each. Price, 50 cents dozen; old-time make.

0-973. ANCIENT NIPPLE WRENCH FOR OLD-TIME GUNS. Six-sided with small screw driver blade fitted into handle. Price, $2.50.

0-864. ANCIENT HORSEMAN'S PISTOL RAMMER. Octagonal iron, brass end, ivory head with swivel. Price, $4.85.

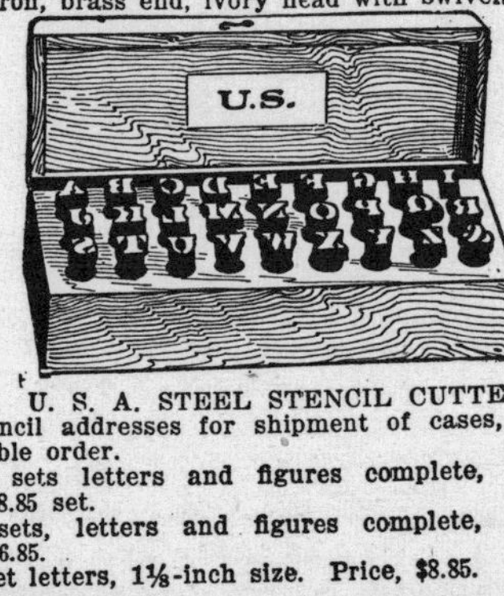


10058A. U. S. A. STEEL STENCIL CUTTERS. For cutting stencil addresses for shipment of cases, etc., in used serviceable order.

Three sets letters and figures complete, size ¾ inch. Price, $8.85 set.

Two sets, letters and figures complete, size ½ inch. Price, $6.85.

One set letters, 1⅛-inch size. Price, $8.85.

May 23, 1924.

Francis Bannerman Sons
New York.

I received the pistol I ordered of you some days ago in fine shape and am more than pleased with it. It certainly is a pleasure to deal with such an honorable and fair dealing house as yours is. I would thank you to place my name on your mailing list. Thanking you for such good value as you gave me, I am yours truly,

CHAS. HOOPER,
Danville, Va.

10422. LOCK. Engraved, "Albany S. N. Y." from London collection; perhaps taken from captured flintlock musket carried by New York State soldier in the War of 1812. Lock is in serviceable order. Price, $5.75.

0-870. ANCIENT ITALIAN FLINTLOCK. Gun size. Found in excavating near the barracks of Carracolla, Rome. The lock is a mass of rust; a relic only. Price, $3.85.

0-871. ANCIENT ITALIAN RELIEF CARVED FIGURES, MASKED FACE AND ORNAMENTAL WORKING ON RARE OLD-TIME FLINTLOCK. In good serviceable order. Fine specimen of ancient decorative gun work. Length 4¾ inches. Price, $8.00.

0-872. H. KNOCK PISTOL FLINTLOCK, with battery spring and striker on the inside of the lock plate, commonly called box lock. Fine working order. Length 4½ inches. Price, $4.50.

1841. REVOLUTIONARY WAR BRUSH AND PRIMING WIRE. Used in brushing burnt powder out of the flash pan and clearing the touchhole in flintlock gun. Once the property of Indian chief, Abraham Antone, Stockbridge. Hair brush is set in ivory with wire attachment. Rare relic. Price, $10.00.

11049A. ANCIENT SNAPHAUNCE GUN LOCK. 9½-inch plate. Price, $18.50.

11049B. ANCIENT SNAPHAUNCE GUN LOCK. 6¾-inch plate. Price, $17.50.

0971. ANCIENT BULLET MOULDS WITH LONG BORE NECK, casting 11/16-inch round bullet. Mould has the sprue cutter. Price, $1.75.

0-972. PISTOL MOULD FROM CASE OF DUELLING SET, casting ⅜-inch round bullet. Price, 75 cents.

0-973. ANCIENT WRENCH FOR UNSCREWING OLD-TIME FLINT PISTOL BARRELS. Price, $1.50.

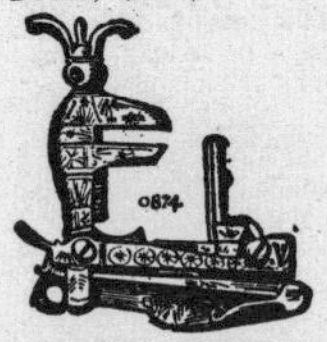

0-874. LOCK FOR ANCIENT SPANISH FLINTLOCK GUN. The lock parts are attached to the OUTSIDE of the lock plate. Some collectors and writers of books on arms erroneously call this lock the Snaphaunce. This is the well-known early Spanish lock attached to flint guns. We have a number of these locks in good working order. One illustrated is extra fine, gold chased; another gold chased, very slightly different style. Price, $6.00. Similar locks without gold ornation, price $3.50. Length of lock plate 3 to 3 1-3 inches. Large size Spanish lock for use on ship or castle wall gun, 6 inches long, weight 2¾ pounds. Price, $5.00.

0-869. FLINT PISTOL LOCK. Perfect order; 2¾ inches long. Price, $5.00.

For three solid hours the captain had been lecturing his men on "the duties of a soldier," and he thought it was time to see how much they had understood of his discourse. Casting his eyes round the room, he fixed on Private Murphy as his first victim.

"Private Murphy," he asked, "why should a soldier be ready to die for his country?"

Private Murphy scratched his head for a moment, and then a smile of enlightment crossed his face.

"Sure, captain," he said pleasantly, "you're quite right. Why should he?"

BRONZE LOCKS FOR CANNONS, used during Civil War; from U. S. Arsenal in Augusta, Ga., which was extensively used in making ordnance supplies for Confederate Army until captured by Sherman's Army. Many lots of goods at Augusta were sent there from Charleston during the war. These locks weigh about three pounds and are in second hand, serviceable order. Price, $3.00 each.

170B. WHEELOCK. Size 7¾x2⅛; engraved. Price, $22.50.

1702A. WHEELOCK. Size 8x2⅛; not engraved. In good working order. Price, $18.00.

1702. WHEELOCK'S FOR ANTIQUE GUN. Engraved with hunting scene, hunter in old time dress, with scroll work size lock plate 7¼x2½ inches. Complete working order. Price, $25.00.

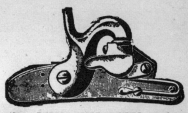

1790. PERIOD PILL LOCKS, used on guns after the flint and percussion locks came in use. The old side spring for the front striker was retained on the lock and made to operate a steel covered part containing the firing pin, and fitting over the vent piece, in which was inserted the small round pill, containing fulminate, the hammer striking the firing pin, explodes the pill fulminate in the vent, firing the charge. These locks are in good working order. Price, $5.00 each.

FLP-1. PAIR FRENCH FLINT POCKET PISTOLS, with BRONZE frames. 2¾ inch barrel, made to unscrew for loading, flat wood butt, trigger guards, center hammers. In fine order. Price, for pair, $18.00.

FLP-2. PAIR LOUIS XVI FLINT POCKET PISTOLS, flat wood grips, checkered, trigger guards with ornament, center hammers with safety catches, engraved frames, round barrels, 2½ inch, to unscrew for loading. It is unusual to find pairs in such small sizes. Price, for pair, $17.50.

FLP-3. BELGIAN FLINT POCKET PISTOL, with center hammer, guard, flat wood butt, safety catch, octagon barrel 3½ inch with proof mark. Price, $6.50.

FLP-5. BELGIAN FLINT POCKET PISTOL, with BRASS frame. 2½ inch barrel to unscrew, flat butt, guard, center hammer and safety catch. Price, $7.50.

1 BRITISH FLINT LOCK PISTOL, with 8-inch round barrel with two British proof marks. Lock marked REDFERNS. Brass mask butt, brass trigger guard and name plate. Price, $10.00.

1 FLINT LOCK HOLSTER PISTOL, period 1740, with tapered round barrel, 8-inch, with three proof marks and word LONDON. Lock marked G. BAUSSART. Price, $15.00.

1 FRENCH FLINT LOCK PISTOL, period of French Revolution. Barrel half octagon, 7 inch, with front sight. Carved wood stock with heavy ornamented brass butt, brass trigger guard and side plate. Hard wood ramrod is brass tipped. A fine specimen. Price, $17.50.

1 BRITISH FLINT LOCK PISTOL, period of 1760, with 7½-inch round barrel. Maker's name COLLUMBEL marked on lockplate. Three proof marks on barrel. Heavy oval butt brass mounted, with brass trigger guard, and name plate. Price, $14.00.

1 SHORT DUELLING FLINT LOCK PISTOL, with 5¼-inch heavy octagon barrel, marked 104 STRAND LONDON, with front and rear sights, and two proof marks. Lock plate is 3½ inch, marked BROWN. Wood butt checkered. Ornamented trigger guard and tang. Wood rod horn tipped. Price, $13.50.

No. 6633. 1 PAIR FINE FLINT LOCK HOLSTER PISTOLS, in hard wood case. Made by GATEHOUSE with name on locks. Barrels are heavy octagon, 9 inches long. Round wood butts are finely checkered. Ornamented guard, tang, and screw heads. Wood ramrods horned tipped. Set is complete with extra flints, round balls, copper flask, round mould, combination loading hammer with rammer and ball screw. A fine set. Price, $65.00.

No. 6634. 1 PAIR DUELLING FLINT LOCK PISTOLS IN CASE, with HAIR triggers. OCTAGON barrels, 9½ inch with front and rear sights. Gold breeches and touch holes. Horned tipped rods, silver escutcheons for barrel pins. Locks marked S. BRUNN. Barrels marked No. 55 CHARING CROSS, LONDON. Round butts finely checkered with ornamented butt plates. Silver name plates, ornamented side screws and trigger guards. Guards marked with cross like St. ANDREWS. Set complete with extra flints, round bullets, small copper powder flask, long wood rammer with FIVE attachments. Price, for set, $72.00.

FLP-6. FRENCH FLINT POCKET PISTOL, 3 inch barrel, frame and barrel in one piece. Flat butt, trigger guard, center hammer with catch. Ramrod under the barrel. Rods are seldom found on this type. Price, $8.00.

FLP-7 FRENCH FLINT POCKET PISTOL, length 7 inches, barrel 3 inches, center hammer with catch, trigger guard. Price, $7.50.

FLP-8. FRENCH FLINT POCKET PISTOL with frame marked: VELU. 2¼ inch removable barrel, center hammer, guard, flat butt. In fine order. Price, $9.00.

FLP-10. BELGIAN FLINT POCKET PISTOL, engraved frame, checkered butt, with silver monogram oval, center hammer with catch, 2¼ inch round barrel with proof mark. Price, $7.75.

FLP-11. BELGIAN FLINT POCKET PISTOL, with finely checkered grip studded with fine silver wire tacks. Engraved frame, 2¼ inch round removable barrel. Full length 5¾ inches. Price, $8.00.

FLP-12. FRENCH FLINT POCKET PISTOL, length 6 inches, round removable barrel 2¼ inches, center hammer with catch. Flat wood stock. Price, $7.50.

FLP-13. BRITISH FLINT POCKET PISTOL, made by JOYNER, LONDON, and so marked on frame. Plain flat stock, guard. Center hammer with half cock safety catch, 2 inch removable round barrel. Full length 5¾ inches. Price, $8.50.

FLP-14. BRITISH FLINT POCKET PISTOL, with frame marked: WILSON, LONDON. 2 inch barrel, round, removable, center hammer, flat stock. Price, $8.75.

FLP-15. BRITISH FLINT POCKET PISTOL, marked on frame with maker's name: H NOCK, LONDON. Frame is on brass with Birmingham proof and view marks. 2 inch removable barrel, flat stock with silver monogram plate, center hammer with safety lock for hammer and pan. Price, $11.00.

1 ENGLISH FLINT LOCK HOLSTER PISTOL, with half octagon barrel, 9-inch, with front and rear sights, ornamented guard. Lock marked TOW. Barrel marked TOW LONDON, with three proof marks. Plain wood butt, slightly flattened. Price, $18.00.

1 EARLY FLINT LOCK HOLSTER PISTOL, period 1750, with 8-inch tapered round barrel marked LONDON, with proof marks. Lock marked WILSON. Name plate, guard and butt ornamented and silver plated. Price, $15.00.

1 FLINT LOCK HOLSTER PISTOL, made by COLLINS of London. Barrel is 9-inch round. Heavy brass butt plate and trigger guard. Price, $12.00.

1 ENGLISH PISTOL, period of 1790, made by BUNNEY. Barrel is half octagon, 8½ inch, marked BUNNEY LONDON. Has rear sight only. Lock is 4½ inch, marked BUNNEY. Flat wood butt, ornamented guard and horn tipped rammer. Price, $16.50.

**10904A. FIVE BALL ARMY BULLET MOULD**, 50 caliber. Price, $4.85.

**BRITISH ENFIELD RIFLE BRASS MOULD**, casting conical bullet, with the MINNIE PATTERN CAVITY at base. Calibre 57-100 will answer for the Springfield 58 rifle. These moulds are in fine order, with automatic neck cutter. Price, 95 cents each.

**1583.** 4 Ancient Armory Brass Bullet Moulds, used in casting 5 conical bullets at a time, with square cavity in the base casting ball over ⅝-inch diameter 1-inch long. Handle has cross bar which locks the mould. The square cavity is formed by two guide rods. Relic of the days when armorors were learning how to do things. Price, $25.00 each.

**OLD TIME FLINT LOCK**, attached to cannon for igniting charge. Relic. Captured cannon in Washington Navy Yard Museum shows where flint lock was attached. Rare locks. $6.50. Have ten in stock, each different. Option reserved to supply the best we have when ordered.

**No. 7. ANTIQUE WHEEL LOCK OR ARQUEBUS GUN LOCK.** View shows inside of lock. This kind of lock was wound upon a spring wheel with a key. In use about 1560. Lock is incomplete; is offered to collector as relic. Price, $15.00.

**1701.** 3 WHEELOCKS FOR PISTOLS, in working order; cleaned; size 6½ inches in length; width, 2 inches. Price, $15.00 each.

1906

**1909.** Antique Brass Bullet Mould, casts 18 round bullets of a size about 12 to the pound, 2 rows of holes, 9 each, with iron handles. Length over 2 ft. Old time mould such as would have been used in Ancient Castles. Price, $15.00.

**1912A.** 3-6-ball brass bullet moulds, casting two round balls, cal. 50, and 4 round balls, cal. 69. Brass metal old time mould, used, serviceable. Price, $3.85.

**1912A.**

**1912B.** Similar mould, in iron, price, $2.85.

**1910.** 69 Calibre Round Ball Bullet Mould, casting 6 balls at one time, wood handle. Price, $4.85.

**1912.** Rare Pattern 6-Ball Brass Bullet Mould, casting 6 round balls about 12 to a pound. Odd pattern sprue cutter. Price, $5.75.

**1912A.** Large Mould, with long wood handles, casting 6 round balls about ⅝ inch. marked "A Gallway, London." Price, $5.00.

**Bullet Mould**, with neck cutter, for old style army rifle bullet. Price, $1.25 each.

**1576B.** Antique Bullet Mould, for casting *square* shaped ball. Rare old mould. Price, $5.50.

**No. 2. OLD CAPTURED FLINT LOCKS** from Guns taken by the British Government from the Irish during the rebellion of 1798. Stocks and barrels were destroyed. The locks sold at auction, upwards of a century ago to a company now giving up business, whose forbears were one of the original Guild of 13 chartered gun makers, and whose proof mark was the old G. P. monogram. These locks are rusty but are complete with parts. The buyer can clean and put in working order. Length of the lock plate is from 5 to 7 inches; some have old marks. We offer as are, $2.00 each.

**1577.** 71 Iron Bullet Moulds, Rare pattern, serviceable, though somewhat rusty. Length, 7 inches. A few are slightly different in the outside shape, casting, however, the same bullet. Price 9c each.

**30-Ball Confederate Brass Bullet Mould**, stamped "C. S. A., Fayetteville, N. C." Used by Confederates for casting pistol balls until Sherman captured Fayetteville armory. This bullet mould was thrown into Deep River to escape capture by one of the operatives who worked in the arsenal. Price, $25.00.

**8-Ball Civil War Bullet Moulds**, with attachment for making cavity at the base of bullet, known as the Minie bullet; made of bronze and steel, with neck cutter; calibre 69; in good order. Price, $8.00.

**1 Rare Old Confederate 2-Ball Bullet Mould.** 70 calibre, with lever attachment. Price, $18.00.

**1576.** 21 Brass Bullet Moulds, casting 69 cal. bullet 1-inch in length with sprue cutter length 2-inches. Fine order. Price, $1.25.

**1577A.** Rare Old Bullet Mould, casting 3 round balls for old-time musket, complete with wood handle and sprue cutter for cutting off the neck formed on the bullet in casting. Price, $3.85.

**Rifle Bullet Moulds**, cal. 52. By putting paper patch around the ball it will fit large size rifle up to cal. 58. Price, 5c.

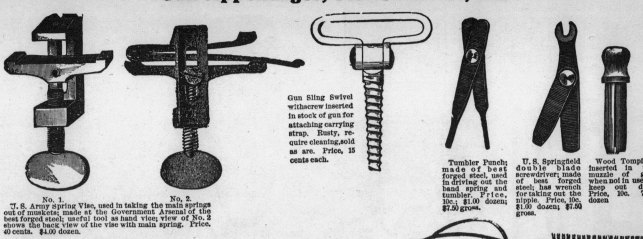

**No. 1.**      **No. 2.**

U. S. Army Spring Vise, used in taking the main springs out of muskets; made at the Government Arsenal of the best forged steel; useful tool as hand vice; view of No. 2 shows the back view of the vise with main spring. Price, 40 cents. $4.00 dozen.

**Gun Sling Swivel** withscrew inserted in stock of gun for attaching carrying strap. Rusty, require cleaning, sold as are. Price, 15 cents each.

**Tumbler Punch;** made of best forged steel, used in driving out the band spring and tumbler. Price, 10c.; $1.00 dozen; $7.50 gross.

**U. S. Springfield double blade screwdriver;** made of best forged steel; has wrench for taking out the nipple. Price, 10c.; $1.00 dozen; $7.50 gross.

**Wood Tompion;** inserted in the muzzle of gun when not in use to keep out dirt. Price, 10c. 75c. dozen.

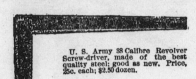

**U. S. Army 38 Calibre Revolver Screw-driver,** made of the best quality steel; good as new. Price, 25c. each; $2.50 dozen.

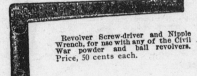

**Revolver Screw-driver and Nipple Wrench,** for use with any of the Civil War powder and ball revolvers. Price, 50 cents each.

**U. S. Government Rifle Cleaning Brush,** stiff hair bristles on brass wire with leather thong, for cleaning any rifle from calibre 40 up to calibre 50; new. Price, 25 cents each. $2.00 dozen.

**RIFLE BULLET MOULD** for 52 calibre rifles; casts conical ball with nipper cutting end piece. Suitable for Sharp's and other rifles. Price, 50 cents each; $5.00 dozen.

**Armorer's Forge Bellows,** circular-shaped. 15 inches in diameter; in serviceable order. Price, $3.00.

**Army Forge Bellows,** for use of armorers; size, 12 inches wide, 18 inches long; closed, 6 inches; expanded, 15 inches; in good serviceable order. Price, $3.00.

**Brass Nose Caps,** for Enfield Musket Stocks. Second hand serviceable order. 18c. each; $2.00 per dozen.

**KRAG-JORGENSEN SCREW-DRIVER.** The large blade is used for butt-plate and upper hand screws; the small blade for all other screws, except rear sight; joint screw, the pin serves as a drift in removing the butt-plate. Cap trigger and lower hand. Price, 30 cents each.

**OLD BRASS BULLET MOULD** from Augusta, Ga., Arsenal, used for casting musket balls for Confederacy. Bench size. Weighs about 25 pounds. Price, $35.00.

**No. 5. 100 CONFEDERATE GUN LOCKS.** These locks were made at Harper's Ferry Arsenal, Va. Intended for use on primer-lock musket. Just before completing the Confederates captured the arsenal and removed the gun parts to Richmond, Va., where these locks were completed and assembled on guns stamped "C. S., Richmond, Va.'" These locks fit Springfield M.-L. rifle; are complete. Price, $25.00 each.

**Brass Wire Cleaners for Small Bore Rifles.** New Price, 50 cents each.

**MODEL '92 KRAG-JORGENSEN RIFLE REAR SIGHT,** considered one of the best and by many sharpshooters superior to some of the later model rear sights, 2000 yards sight, marked on base for 300 to 600 yards range, marked on the leaf by 100 up to 1900 yards top of the sight making 2000 yards range. Slide leaf operated by pressing in the sides of the slide block, which is held in place by catch at each 100 yards. We have 14,000 of these fine rifle sights, and for a limited time will offer brand new complete rear-sights for $1.00 each.

**1806A** Flint, 10 cents each.

**2,000 Old Flint Army Pistol Barrels** with breech screw, stamped with old British proof marks, showing that they have been used on old guns, about 5-8 inch bore, rusty. Can be used on block of wood for single firing, or a number placed together, for firing a volley. Length of barrel is from 6 to 9 inches. Valuable to theatrical property men. Offered as are, at 68c. each.

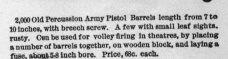

**2,000 Old Percussion Army Pistol Barrels** length from 7 to 10 inches, with breech screw. A few with small leaf sights, rusty. Can be used for volley firing in theatres, by placing a number of barrels together, on wooden block, and laying a fuse, about 5-8 inch bore. Price, 68c. each.

**F. M. 5. ARMY CONDIMENT CANS,** containing two compartments, with openings at each end. One top has extra compartment for salt or sugar. Length of can only is 5 inches. Price, 15 cents.

Adam Oliver, the most unique character in the service of the U. S. Army. A Scotchman who came to the United States when a boy, enlisting in the U. S. Ordnance Department at Springfield, Mass., learning the trade of Armorer at the National Army. About the period of the Mexican War he was transferred to Augusta Arsenal, Ga., as Master Armorer and Assistant Ordnance Storekeeper. When the Civil War broke out, Augusta Arsenal was captured by the Confederates, who forcibly detained and impressed Oliver into their service, assigning to him the same duties that he had been performing for the Federal Government. Four years later, when General Sherman captured Augusta, Adam Oliver alone stood at his post of duty in charge of the Arsenal, ready to return his trust to its original owners, the U. S. Ordnance Department. General Sherman continued Oliver in charge and until Oliver's death, 30 years after Lee's surrender, he served at Augusta Arsenal as MASTER ARMORER the only man who CONTINUOUSLY SERVED THE UNITED STATES AND THE SOUTHERN CONFEDERACY ALL IN ONE AND THE SAME POSITION, forced by circumstances to become a repetition of the "Vicar of Bray."—Extracts from Gen. J. W. Reilly, U. S. Ordnance Department. Article in the Military Service Bulletin.

**CONFEDERATE BULLET MOULD.** Used at Augusta Arsenal, Georgia during the Civil War, to cast lead bullets for Confederate Army. Vouched for by U. S. Army Officer, complete; serviceable order. Price, $100.00.

300 U.S. Army brass-jointed cleaning rods for 12-gauge shotguns, folding steel-wire scratch brush with screw thread with hole for wiping-rag. Full length 23 inches; folded, measures 10 inches. Made of fine hard red wood. Bargain price, 50c. each; $5.00 a dozen.

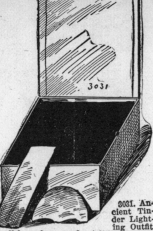
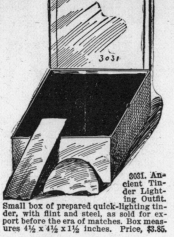

**3031.** Ancient Tinder Lighting Outfit. Small box of prepared quick-lighting tinder, with flint and steel, as sold for export before the era of matches. Box measures 4½ x 4½ x 1½ inches. Price, $3.85.

**ANTIQUE GUN WRENCH,** with screw-driver, nipple wrench, tumbler punch and vent cleaner. Price, 20c.

**6 LARGE SIZE FLINT LOCKS,** used in ancient times on cannon or rampart guns for the defense of castles. Length of lock plate 8½ inches. Complete in parts, with large size flint, maker's name marked on locks; rusty requires cleaning. Price, $6.00 each.

**Walnut Revolver Stock for Colt's Army Revolver.** Double stock, with inletting cuts for the metal parts. Price, 95 cents.

**12-GAUGE SHOT-GUN LOADING TOOL.** Brass tube, with inside lining to hold the mouth of the shell in position while loading, with hardwood rammer and stand. Length of tube 4¾ inches. Price, 20c.

**LARGE ASSORTMENT FLINT HAMMERS,** 95 cents each.

**FLASK STRIKERS,** 35 cents each.

NONE for American guns or pistols.

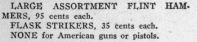

**0-655. BRITISH SNIDER-ENFIELD RIFLE BREECH MECHANISMS.** Complete with tang for stocking. All in fine order, like new. Taken from dismounted rifles. We have 10,000 in stock. Price, singly, 50 cents each. Will consider a low offer for the lot.

**0-652. SNYDER-ENFIELD GUN APPENDAGE.** Fine quality steel screwdriver for large and small screws, firing pins, nipple wrench, main spring vise, oil holder in the hollow handle, with thumb-screw and stopper. *Five parts in one.* Useful with any gun. Price, 20 cents each; $2.00 per dozen.

---

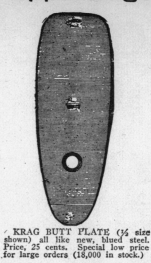

**KRAG BUTT PLATE** (½ size shown) all like new, blued steel. Price, 25 cents. Special low price for large orders (18,000 in stock.)

**British Army Soldier's Gun Appendage;** 6 tools in one — screwdriver, oil cup, worm, pick, rifle wrench, etc. 38 cents.

**0-767. ENFIELD RIFLE LOCK STIRRUP, CONNECTING MAIN SPRING AND TUMBLER.** Price, 15c. each; $1.00 per doz.

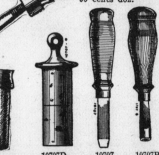

**10707D**    **10707**    **10707B**

Civil War Tompion, used for inserting in gun barrels to keep out moisture; 2½ inches, with knurled-brass screw-top for expanding the cork to fit the barrel. Price, 10 cents each.

**10707D.** Brass Tompion, used in the muzzle of antique guns. Length 1¾ inches. Fit any gun 45 calibre or over. Tompions help keep gun from rusting. Price, 15 cents.

**10707.** GERMAN ARMY SCREWDRIVER; fine tempered steel, detachable blade; screwdriver pointed at each end for use on large and small gun screws. Price, 15 cents each.

**10707B.** GERMAN ARMY NIPPLE WRENCH. For use on gun nipples; old-time tempered-steel gun tool. Price, 18c. ea.

**10707C**

**10707C.** European Army Soldier's Spring Vise for removing springs from the gun. Main spring jaws ¼ inch, tumbler spring 3-16 inch. Handy tool that formed part of old-time gun equipment. Rare. Price, 25 cents.

**10904. FIVE BALL ARMY BULLET MOULD,** casting conical lead bullet 1 1-16 inches long for 40 caliber rifle. Price $4.85.

**Enfield Musket Nipples;** 10 cents each; 90 cents doz.

**10866. LEAD LADLE.** Note that the ladles now in stock do NOT have the pouring lip, and have flat end handle instead of eye as shown in cut. Price, 65 cents each.

**10867. LEAD-STRAINING LADLE.** New. Furnished with U.S.A. breech-loading outfits. Ladle is 13½ inches in length; diameter of the bowl 33½ inches; depth 1¼ inches. Strong and useful strainer. Price, 15 cents.

**10707A.** European Army Soldier's Steel Worm for removing load from antique percussion guns, used on end of ramrod. Length 3¾ inches. Brass ball on the shank to prevent injury to rifling. Price of the worm, 15 cents.

**Confederate Army Nipple Protector.** Kind used on Enfield muskets supplied the South during Civil War. Brass chain attached to leather plug for fitting over nipple, to prevent hammer from injuring nipple when snapped. Found in Europe, 1910. Price, 10c. each, mailed.

**SPRING STEEL RAMROD,** for the Krag rifle, 29¼ inches long, with slit in head for wiping rag, with screw thread for attaching tool to remove obstruction in the barrel, all new, polished and blued. Price, 38 cents each.

**HAND CANNON PISTOL, FIRST PATTERN FIRE ARM MADE.** While roaming around in a city in the Orient, we discovered this ancient weapon. The high price the owner asked made us hesitate, but realizing that **powder was first known in the Orient,** and that this was no doubt among the **very first made powder shooting weapons,** we paid the price, and secured this old timer. We showed the weapon to expert collectors in the Far East, and they informed us that they had never before seen anything like it. We left some money on deposit with collectors, as a guarantee that we would buy other similar specimens they might find, but that was nearly two years ago, and none have yet turned up. Large powder shooting weapons, without lock, fired with fuse, are to be found in a number of museums in Europe, but **hand fired pistols** are very rarely ever met with. Length is 3½ inches. Ornamented bronze. We value this small ancient pistol at **$500.00.**

**RARE OLD JAPANESE PISTOL,** bronze barrel, with nipple for paper cap on barrel. Fired by pressing down the lever acting as hammer; with safety catch, with Japanese emblem. Length is 5½ inches.

**F 1. EARLY PATTERN JAPANESE BRONZE HAND CANNON,** fired with paper cap, which is exploded by pressing down long handle on top of cannon. These are now very rare. Price **$25.00.** Length 6½ inches.

**F 2. HAND CANNON** like F 1, plain finish, bronze, length 6½ inches. Has one arm of hand lever missing. Price **$20.00.**

ANCIENT MATCH-LOCK PISTOLS. Very seldom seen outside of museums or in the more costly collections. While in Japan in the fall of 1904 on business with Japanese Government, we employed experts in rare arms to travel through the country and buy up rare old military arms. On this page will be seen the result. Many are inlaid with silver ornamentation, and no doubt have belonged to the old Samuria nobility and are considered rare, even in Japan.

**No. 56.** Old Match Lock Pistol with inlaid silver ornamental work; cannon-shaped muzzle; has front sight; is fired with fuse; one of the earliest types of powder guns made; **is in fine serviceable order. Price $25.00.**

10999. PAIR FLINTLOCK HOLSTER PISTOLS, with BRASS barrels, 7-inch round. Brass tipped wood butts, long brass guards and side plates. 4½-inch locks marked: TOWER NOCK, with CROWN over G R. Barrel has two proof marks. Price for pair $32.00. See page 92.

FL-1. FRENCH FLINTLOCK PISTOL, with 6½-inch BRASS barrel, cannon shaped. Fish tail butt with heavy brass plate. 3¾-inch BRASS lock plate, long brass guard with acorn tip, fancy brass side plate. Price, $18.00.

FL-2. FRENCH FLINTLOCK PISTOL with 7½-inch round barrel marked: ENT SE BOUDET. 4-inch lock marked: MANUF RE A VERSAILLES. Long brass guard with plume end. Half length stock, iron ramrod. Price $14.00.

ANTIQUE MATCH LOCK PISTOL, with bronze barrel, raised ornamental decorating. Fine order, about 8½ inches long. Price $22.50.

**When ordering special articles allow a second choice when possible.**

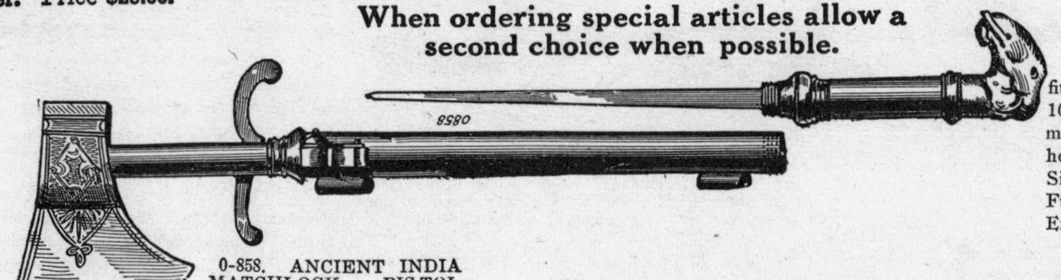

0-858. ANCIENT INDIA MATCHLOCK PISTOL, HAND BATTLE-AXE AND DAGGER. Three in one combination, from the Lawson-Johnston collection. Full length 20½ inches, weight 3¼ pounds. Axe 3¾-inch face. Pistol barrel 9 inches, ½-inch smooth bore, 8-inch square-shaped dagger, with head of elephant in bronze. Rare combination of ancient weapons. Museum exhibit. Bargain price, $100.00.

FL-3. FLINTLOCK PISTOL FROM INDIA, fitted with British lock marked: PARTRIDGE. 10¼-inch part octagon barrel, with four ornamental wide silver bands, grooved wood grip with heavy silver butt plate with sash or sling swivel. Silver side plate, brass guard with finger stud. Full length 15¾ inches. From British Museum Exhibition at Wembley, 1926. Price $20.00.

10926. SWIVEL RAMROD FLINTLOCK ARMY PISTOL, dated 1800. Figure of lion rampant on lock plate. London gun maker's proof mark on the barrel. Full length 15¾ inches in working order. This is one of the earliest swivel ramrod pistols made for use of mounted soldiers. Price $12.00.

0-913. MANTON & CO. SMOOTH-BORE PERCUSSION LOCK PISTOL, with 6-inch twist-steel barrel. Swivel ramrod; flatted top for sighting. Rear sight, gold breech band. Silver front sight. Name-plate engraved with Unicorn crest. Polished walnut stock, checkered grip. Chased mountings. Barrel engraved "Manton & Co., London"; 11/16-inch smooth bore. In fine order. Beautiful specimen of famous gunmaker's work. Price, $25.00.

11021. ANTIQUE FLINT HOLSTER PISTOL, with swivel ramrod with Rampant Lion engraved on lock; relic of Old East India Company troops. Ivory inlaid on the stock and brass ornamented by the natives. Pistols such as these were traded in olden times to the natives for ivory. Full length 15 inches. Working order. Stock trifle the worse for age and service. Price $20.00.

Flintlock Pistol, stamped as having been made in 1837 at Millbury, Mass., by A. Walters; used by Major Biff Haddox in Mexican and Civil Wars. He had the pair, but lost one at the first Manassas battle; serviceable order. Price, $20.00.

1243. Pair of Flint Duelling Pistols, made by P. Bond, London; practically new; old brown finish; octagonal barrel, 9-16 bore; engraved lock and mountings; fine curly walnut stock; checkered grip; in case with screw driver, powder flask, cleaning rod, bullet mould, extra flints, balls and wads; with gold inlaid vent; with Bond patent powder chamber, most perfect set of old flintlock duelling pistols we have ever seen. Price, $85.00.

2 Portuguese Pistols, stamped 1817, with crown and I. R. Port—. Swivel ramrod; full length, 15 inches; barrel, 9 inches; brass bound; serviceable order; requires cleaning. Price, $7.00 each.

FL-4. BRITISH FLINTLOCK HOLSTER PISTOL, with half octagon barrel, 9 inches long, marked: BENNET, ROYAL EXCHANGE, LONDON. 4½ inch BRASS lock with safety catch. Ivory tipped wood rod, brass mounted fish tail butt, long brass guard with acorn end. Lock plate is marked: BENNET, and barrel has three proof marks. Period 1780. Price $18.00.

FL-6. SPANISH FLINTLOCK PISTOL, with half octagon barrel, 7½-inch, cannon shaped, with ARMOURER'S MARK (Crown SIR BEN) with inlaid silver designs. 3½-inch outside Spanish lock, fish tail butt with heavy ornamented brass plate, brass side plate with silver inlay, long brass guard with urn end. Lock is marked: SALA. Price $20.00.

1477B. One with steel barrel, 2½ inches long. Full length, 7½ inches. Engraved, "Smith," surrounded by arms and flag trophies. Price, $12.00.

1477C. With 3½-inch steel barrel; full length, 8 inches. Engraved, "Simmons & Howell." Working order. Price, $12.00.

1477A. Same as above. Made by Bennet Royal Exchange, London. Price, $12.00.

1423. Antique Flint-lock Pistols, full length, 18½ inches; barrel 11½ inches; ⅝ smooth bore. Stock handsomely ornamented with inlaid silver wire, ornamented steel mountings. Handle of stock, raised discs of polished steel for hand hold. Barrel has raised ornamented work; ivory tip ramrod. Working order. Price, $30.00.

Spring Bayonet Flint Lock Pocket Pistol, made by H. Nock, London, who made so many guns and pistols, as were used during the American War of Independence. Has been a handsome weapon; now needs cleaning and putting in working order. Price $15.00.

Pair of Ketland Flint Duelling Pistols, in mahogany case, ½-inch octagonal barrel; full length 14½ inches; engraved brass mountings; lock engraved "Ketland & Co." guard has finger grip extension; walnut stock; mane plate S. F. S; monogram engraved on side plate and on handle of the mahogany case; barrel engraved London. Price of the pair $50.00.

Scotch pattern Flint Lock Pistol; stock, lock and barrel all of steel, finely engraved; screw breech rifled barrel, concealed trigger; round hole in metal stock for use as wrench operating screw barrel; full length, 10 inches, barrel is 5 inches, ½-inch rifle bore; serviceable order, $25.00.

Pair of Antique Flint Pistols claim to have been purchased at Athens, Greece, 38 years ago, from a party connected with the palace of King Otto. That they (at one time) belonged to and were used in battle by the Greek chieftain Athanasius Diaco during the Greek War of Independence. With this pair of pistols are two antique metal cartridge boxes ornamented with silvered metal, show three Turkish soldiers capturing a Greek soldier. Full length of pistols is 16 inches, silvered relief ornaments, gold and silver inlaid wire work; about 58 calibre. Price for the pair, of pistols, $45.00.

10899-A. PAIR ARCHER, LONDON, POCKET FLINTLOCK PISTOLS, with concealed triggers, which spring into position at the cocking of the hammer. Walnut stock, 1¾-inch barrels, full length 6 inches. Good working order. Price the pair, $15.00.

10539. DOUBLE BARREL FLINTLOCK PISTOL. Silver mounted, engraved with ancient castles. Barrels are side by side. Lock and flash pan to each barrel. Checkered walnut stock, seal stamped. Full length 10 inches. In good working order (fore end faulty). Price $22.50.

Two cartridge boxes for pistols, silvered metal, measure 4x5½ inches, ½-inch deep. Price for the pair, $15.00.

Two cartridge boxes for the above pistols, silvered metal, measure 4x5½ inches, ½-inch deep. Price for the pair, $15.00.

3 French Flint Lock Horse Pistols, supposed to be relics of Napoleon the First Army. Full length is 15 inches; ⅝-inch bore; length of barrel 8 inches. Maker's name on lock. Price $8.00.

Pair Double Barrel Superposed Flint Locks, with lock for each barrel; made by Wilson, London; silver name plate on stock, "TTA". 3-inch octagonal barrels; ½-inch smooth bore; rib for ramrod; checkered stock; engraved mountings; front and rear sight; fine locks. Price, 68.00 pair, all contained in fine box.

Pair Wallis Hull (England) made fine Flint Lock Duelling pistols; finely checkered; engraved mountings; full length, 9-inches; 4½ inch barrels ⅝ smooth bore; one hammer shows repairing, good condition. Price $20.000.

Pair of French Flint Lock Duelling Pistols, ⅝ bore; 8½ inch barrels; fine inlaid gilt decorated on lock plate "As Carlat, St, Etienne"; fine curly walnut, carved stock, with octagonal butt, with engraved metal cap, in fair condition. Price for pair, $50.00

A son of a military man, a little fellow about eight, had to write as a school exercise a composition on George Washington. Carefully writing what he knew about the General, he concluded with "General George Washington was married but had no children so, in order to save his feelings the people called him the father of his country.

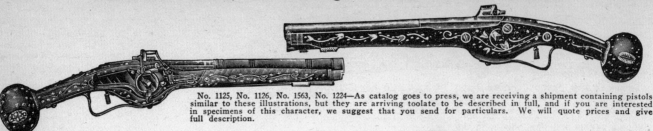

No. 1125, No. 1126, No. 1563, No. 1224—As catalog goes to press, we are receiving a shipment containing pistols similar to these illustrations, but they are arriving too late to be described in full, and if you are interested in specimens of this character, we suggest that you send for particulars. We will quote prices and give full description.

**1365B. LOUIS XIV FLINTLOCK POWDER TESTER,** shape of flint belt pistol, 10 inches long, 3½-inch lock. Powder chamber is mounted at breech with metal wheel marked with figures to show different strengths of powder. Spring to release tester wheel is depressed by screw through stock fore end. This is a very old piece. Price $22.00.

**1125. WHEELOCK PISTOL,** from European collection. 25¾ inches long, 17½-inch octagonal barrel, full length black wood stock. Price $50.00.

Scoth Type Double Barrel Flint Lock Pistol, in good second-hand order. Price **$18.00.**

Antique Rifled Flint Lock Pistol, with spring bayonet, engraved lock, old London maker, full length, 8 inches, in serviceable order. Price $16.00. Sold only to museums or vouched for collectors.

**1224.** Wheelock pistol 24½ inches long, 16½-inch barrel. Dark brown wood stock. From collection in Europe. Price, $50.00.

**D-25. COMBINATION PISTOL, STOCK & HOLSTER.** This is fitted with attachments for the old style European horse pistol. There is an iron frame so that the pistol may be carried in this as a holster. Fitted with one stud for belt. Price $3.50.

**34. ANTIQUE POWDER TESTER OR EPROUVETTE:** shaped like a small pistol without the barrel and having its powder chamber closed by a flat indexed plate; fire with cap; the force of the powder charge turns an indexed wheel, which is held by a spring brake, thus showing the strength of the powder. Price $10.00.

**1355. ANTIQUE FLINTLOCK LIGHTER.** Walnut pistol lock. Carved and checkered. Fine lock, with receptacle for catching spark. Price $10.00.

**1342. FLINTLOCK FIRE LIGHTER** with well hole for catching spark, with oil cup. Length, 7½ inches. In good order. Price $12.00.

**573. ANCIENT FIRELOCK** used in the olden times for obtaining fire. Rare pattern, with the outside hammer and lock springs, all of metal, complete. Price $14.00.

**3A. ANTIQUE FLINTLOCK FIRE LIGHTER,** with old out-side hammer and springs; has iron box with partition for holding tinder; mounted on 3 legs. Very old and has been rusted; is now in serviceable order. Relic. Price $10.00.

**3B. FLINT PISTOL FIRE LIGHTER,** with old-style leg-shaped stock; circular-shaped metal tinder box with separate compartment for holding tinder; small metal oil cup attached. All in fine, serviceable order. Price $12.00.

Rare old Spanish Flintlock Fire Lighter; outside lock; engraved on frame, "Ipansamis"; oil cup receptacle at the side; hard walnut round stock. Price $12.00.

**OLD TIME FLINT AND STEEL,** with Tinder for striking light; from sale of ancient N. Y. Exporter's stock. Price $5.00.

**573A. ANTIQUE FLINTLOCK TINDER LIGHTER.** Pistol shape with offset hammer to strike battery directly over the tinder chamber. Battery spring is mounted on fore end. Full length 8½ inches. Outside lock, two front legs, round butt. Candle holder or oil cup at side. Chamber for extra tinder. Price $20.00.

**DBF-1. LOUIS XVI FLINT POCKET PISTOL,** with double barrels. Flat butt silver wire inlaid. Case hardened frame and barrels, two hammers, and trigger guard. Cannon shaped barrels, 2¾ inches, notched at muzzle to screw. In fine order. Price $22.00.

**DBF-2. ANTIQUE FLINT POCKET PISTOL,** with double barrels. Round ball butt, trigger guard, 4½-inch cannon barrels, to unscrew to lead. Full length 9¼ inches. Price $20.00.

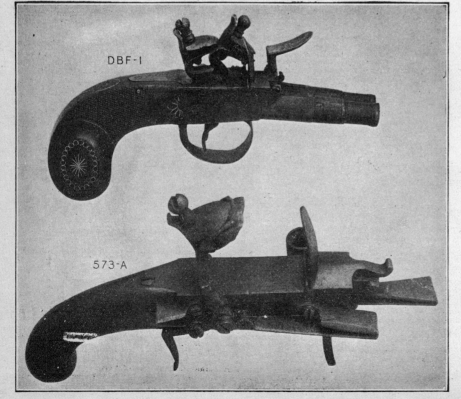

DBF-1

573-A

Present & give Fire

Illustration of armored soldier in ancient times shooting pistol.

**0-1120. TURKISH FLINTLOCK PISTOL,** highly ornamented with gold plated, full length stock in filigree work, with heavy butt stock and 5 inch muzzle band. Hand grip silver wire wrapped. Heavy trigger guard with urn end, ornamented trigger guard. 4¾ inch lock with Turkish marks. Total length 20½ inches, barrel 12¾ inches. A very fine and showy piece. Price $50.00.

**0-1120A. TURKISH FLINTLOCK PISTOL,** with carved wood stock, ornamented trigger guard and lock strap, heavy knob style butt covered with silver. Hand hold wire inlaid with dagger designs, with silver name plate with daisy design. 5½ inch muzzle band of silver. Total length 19 inches, barrel 12 inches, with crescent design and number 63. 4¾ inch lock. Price, $30.00.

**0-1120B. TURKISH FLINTLOCK PISTOL,** 22 inches long, cannon shaped barrel 14¼ inches, 5 inch lock with flower designs. Heavy brass butt with scale pattern, ornamened brass trigger guard and lock strap, brass monogram plate. Wood carving on stock. Price, $20.00.

**0-1120C. TURKISH FLINTLOCK PISTOL,** 20 inches long. Floral ornaments set in metal at handhold and at tang. 6 silver barrel bands with 3 inch muzzle band. Ramrod is an imitation and made of silver. Heavy ball butt, brass covered. Full length 20 inches, barrel 13½ inches, cannon shaped and with two armourer's marks. 4¼ inch lock with stars and crescent marks. Ornamented brass side plate and trigger guard. Price, $25.00.

**0-1120D. TURKISH FLINTLOCK PISTOL,** with wood carved stock, with brass embossed butt, ornamented brass guard and lock strap. Length 20½ inch, cannon shaped barrel 13¼ inches, 5 inch etched lock. Price, $22.50.

**0-1120E. TURKISH FLINTLOCK PISTOL,** similar to No. 0-1120D, with 11½ inch barrel. Both these pistols are very old. Price, $22.00.

**0-1120F. TURKISH FLINTLOCK PISTOL,** with BRASS barrel, with stars and crescent, with three proof or armourer's marks. Brass barrels are very rare in Turkish or Oriental pistols. Full length 17½ inches, barrel 11¼ inch, cannon shape. Heavy butt with ornamented metal cover. Lock strap ornamented with military designs, fancy trigger guard with urn end. 4½ inch lock marked: F. M. Price, $25.00.

**0-1120H. TURKISH FLINTLOCK PISTOL, WOOD CARVED STOCK IN FLOWER DESIGNS.** Lock strap and guard of brass, ornamented with figures of animals and men. Hand grip inlaid with wire in designs of dagger, star and horse shoes. Silver name plate in diamond pattern. Extra heavy brass butt plate. 12¼ inch cannon shaped barrel with short top rib. 4¾ inch heavy lock. Price, $15.00.

**0-1120J. TURKISH FLINTLOCK PISTOL,** plain stock, brass butt, 4½ inch lock. 9½ inch cannon barrel, inlaid full length with gold plated metal, with Turkish inscription. Price, $9.00.

**0-1120K. TURKISH FLINTLOCK PISTOL,** with silver wire inlaid stock, brass trimmed throughout. 14 inches long, 8¼ inch inlaid barrel. Price, $9.50.

**FL-13. POWDER TESTER,** very early pattern, lighted with fuse. Brass frame, long wood butt. This type exceedingly rare. Length, 6¾ inch. Price, $20.00. See illustration No. 2116, page 84 catalog. No. 2116 sold.

**FL-16. ANTIQUE BRITISH TINDER LIGHTER,** steel frame, rounded wood butt. Compartment or spill box on side for extra tinder. Flint lock with outside hammer and mechanism. Hammer of curious shape. Small candle holder, also leg rest to stand upright. In good order. Price, $20.00.

**FL-19. DUTCH TINDER LIGHTER,** with flint lock center hammer, extra compartment in front for surplus tinder. Small candle holder at side. No trigger guard. Flat wood butt, and leg rest. Price, $18.00.

**FL-21. BRITISH TINDER LIGHTER,** similar to FL-20. Price, $20.00.

**FL-22. ANTIQUE TINDER LIGHTER,** British, with outside flint lock and parts. Wide leg rest, extra compartment for tinder, flat wood butt, steel frame. Price, $24.00.

**FL29. WHEEL LOCK GUN,** with heavy octagonal barrel, 34 inches long, ½-inch bore with 7 grooves. Marked on top: JOHANN BAUER, in WIRTZBURG. Lock plate 7½-inch, finely engraved, with boar hunting scene. Rear and front sights. Large butt plate exending along comb in fancy design. Heavy wood stock

with 7-inch cheek piece, with box with sliding wood cover. Long trigger guard with hand hold. Price, $165.00.

**FL-30. ALBANIAN FLINTLOCK PISTOL,** with lock mechanism on outside. Lock 3½ inches long, barrel part octagonal, is 13¾ inches long, with proof marks and maker's marks. Almost straight stock ending in pike point, covered entirely with chased brass, inlaid with silver. Total length, 22½ inches. Price, $28.00.

**FL-31. ALBANIAN FLINTLOCK PISTOL,** similar to FL-30, with 3¾-inch lock, 12¼-inch barrel; full length, 20½ inches. Price, $24.00.

**FL-32. PAIR FLINTLOCK PISTOLS, GREEK,** with gold inlaid Damascus barrels, 10¾-inch octagonal, with front and rear sights. 5-inch locks with name of maker. Round wood butts, checkered, with ornamental round butt plates and trigger guards. Total length, 16½ inches. Greek pistols of this style are rare. Price, per pair, $38.00.

**FL-33. TURKISH FLINTLOCK PISTOL,** with 4½-inch engraved lock, with 9-inch ornamented tapering round barrel. Fancy trigger guard engraved. Wood stock studded with fine silver nails and inlaid with silver wire. Flat rounded butt stock, with heavy silver butt plated, ornamented with military equipment, including axes, drums, flags, etc. Price, $20.00.

**FL-34. TURKISH FLINT LOCK PISTOL,** with 13½-inch round tapered barrel, with 5¾-inch silver muzzle ornament, 5-inch lock, total length 20½ inches. Round wood butt stock. Silver trigger guard. Silver butt plate, side plate and stock ornaments in military designs, showing cannons, shells, flags, etc. Price, $25.00.

**FL-35. TURKISH FLINTLOCK PISTOL,** total length 19½ inches, barrel 12 inches, round, with 5¼-inch silver muzzle ornament, 4¾ inch-lock. Hand carved wood stock with silver side plate, trigger guard and butt plate. Price, $17.00.

**FL-36. PAIR TURKISH FLINTLOCK PISTOLS,** with 4¼-inch locks, with 12½-inch tapered round barrels, showing marks of maker. Hand carved stocks, with rounded flat butt plates. Long silver trigger guards and butt plates, with silver name plates and side plates. Total length 19 inches. Price for pair, $30.00.

**FL-45. FLINTLOCK PISTOL FROM INDIA.** 12½-inch octagonal barrel, ornamented in cut in scroll. 4¾-inch lock. Hardwood stock inlaid with triangular designs in ivory. Grip inlaid in silver wire. Heavy brass band on barrel, and brass butt plate. Total length 19½ inches. Price, $17.00.

**FL-46. FLINTLOCK PISTOL FROM INDIA.** 4¼-inch lock marked with LION, and dated 1801. 13-inch round barrel with top rib. Grip set with ivory squares. Fore end of stock has 1¾-inch ivory tip. Full length 18 inches. Made for the EAST INDIA TRADING COMPANY. Price, $20.00.

**FL-47. TURKISH BLUNDERBUSS,** with 9 inch, gold inlaid barrel, with 1 5/16-inch bell muzzle. Total length 17½ inches. Fancy stock inlaid throughout with gold and silver wire. Double cheek pieces, and carved pistol grip. Heavy brass trigger guard and butt plate. 4¼ inch lock with maker's name. Sling swivel on left side for shoulder sling. Price, $27.00.

**FL-49. INDIA MATCHLOCK GUN** from Central Asia. Total length 68 inches, heavy round barrel is 49½ inches, with five ornamental brass bands. Heavy polished brass frame and butt plate. Both front and rear sights. Two sling swivels. Hardwood stock. Price, $48.00.

**FL-50. INDIA MATCHLOCK GUN,** length 68½ inches. Barrel 49 inches, Damascus, with oak or similar leaf, inlaid full length in gold. Barrel ornamented at breech and muzzle. Six brass bands. Stock of dark red wood. Two sling swivels, with native two-piece leather sling. Price, $52.00.

**FL-51. INDIA MATCHLOCK GUN,** full length 68 inches, heavy round barrel 50¼ inches. Five metal bands. Heavy brass frame. Two sling swivels, rear and front sights. Price, $45.00.

**FL-42. TURKISH FLINTLOCK PISTOL,** with hand carved wood stock, 4-inch lock with name, 9¼-inch round tapered barrel, inlaid with silver. Round knob butt with heavy silver butt plate. Price, $21.00.

**FL-43. TURKISH FLINTLOCK PISTOL,** with 11¼-inch round barrel with four proof marks, and maker's insignia, 4½ inch lock with maker's name. Hand carved wood stock with ornamental trigger guard, and heavy silver butt plate. Total length, 18 inches. Price, $18.00.

**FL-44. FRENCH MADE TURKISH PISTOL,** with hand carved wood stock with 11½ inch barrel with silver band and 4¾-inch silver muzzle piece, 4½-inch lock marked: NORTIER & CO. French type silver trigger guard, round wood butt with silver butt plate. Full length 17½ inches. Price, $22.00.

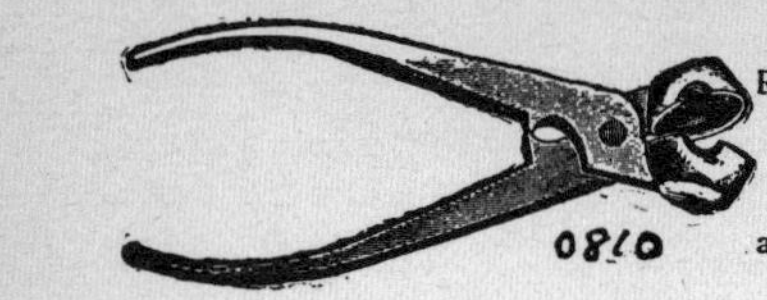

No. 0810 NEW MOULDS FOR ONE ROUND BULLET CALIBRE 36. $1.50.

No. 0810A CALIBRE 44. $1.25.

No. 0810B CALIBRE 45. $1.25. Postage 10 cents extra.

Swiss Army Revolver, marked "Bern", with Swiss Cross on handle, six inch barrel, blued steel finish, in good second-hand serviceable order. Price $12.00.

Belgian Army Revolver, with six inch barrel, nickle finish, in second-hand serviceable order. Price $12.00.

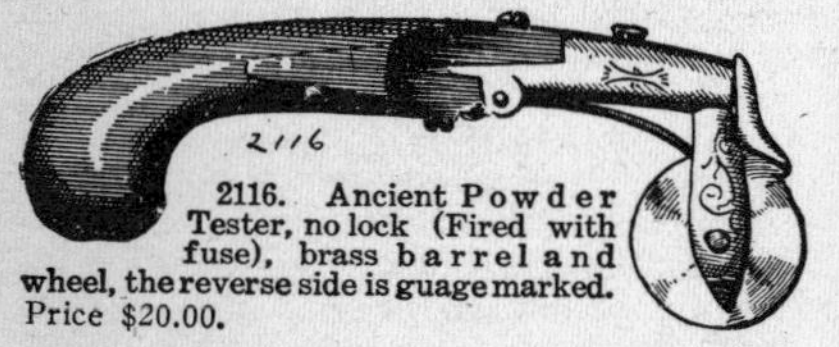

2116. Ancient Powder Tester, no lock (Fired with fuse), brass barrel and wheel, the reverse side is guage marked. Price $20.00.

2139. Pair of Captain John Smith type Flint-lock Pistols, with barrels that unscrew at the breech for loading and cleaning, made by Joyner, London, similar to the pistols now in the Virginia Historical Society, as having been carried by Captain Smith at the founding of Jamestown. Length of barrel seven inches about 25 guage, cannon shaped muzzle; hammer in the center; full length 12½ inches, in working order; price $40.00 the pair.

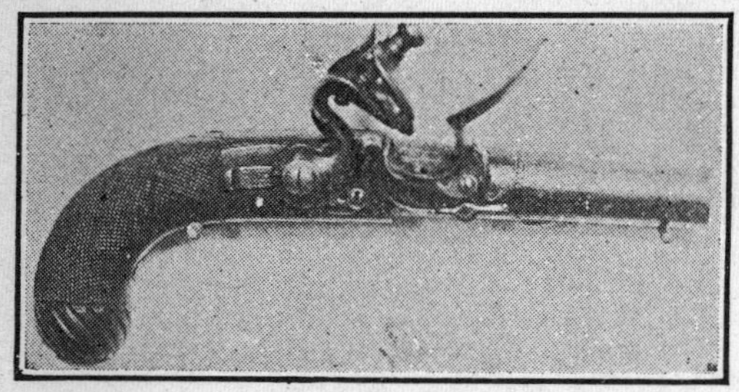

2100. Early model Single Barrel Flint-lock Pistol, unscrews at the breech, checked stock: used, serviceable order. Price $18.00

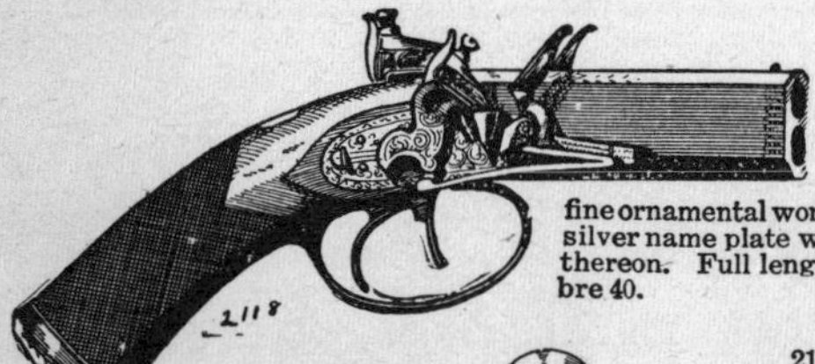

2118. Double Barrel (One over the other) Flint-lock pistol, with outside locks, gold inlaid letters Smith & Company, London, with fine ornamental work; checkered walnut stock, silver name plate with letters W. M, engraved thereon. Full length eight inches, about Calibre 40.

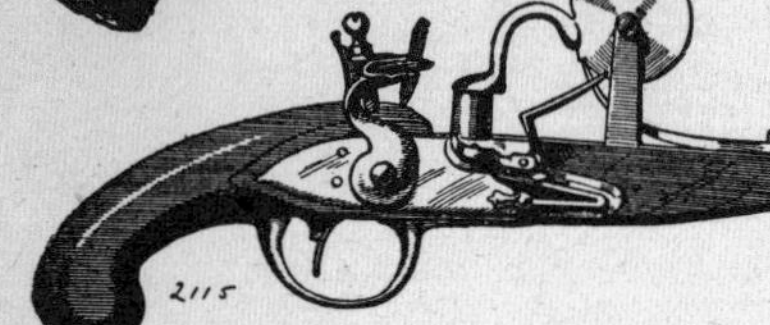

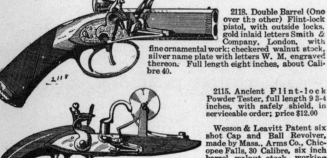

2115. Ancient Flint-lock Powder Tester, full length 9 3-4 inches, with safely shield, in serviceable order; price $12.00

Wesson & Leavitt Patent six shot Cap and Ball Revolver, made by Mass., Arms Co., Chicopee Falls, 30 Calibre, six inch barrel, walnut stock, working order, price $15.00.

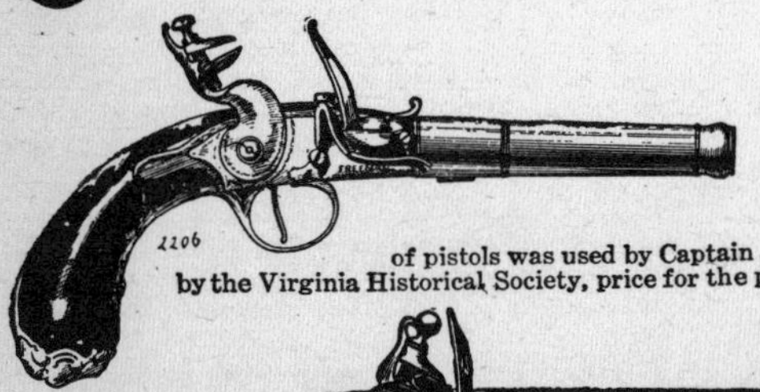

2206. Pair of Old English Dueling Pistols, made by Freeman, London; silver mounted old proof marks, cannon shaped barrels, which unscrew near the breech r loading. This type of pistols was used by Captain John Smith, as preserved by the Virginia Historical Society, price for the pair $60.00; singly $35.00.

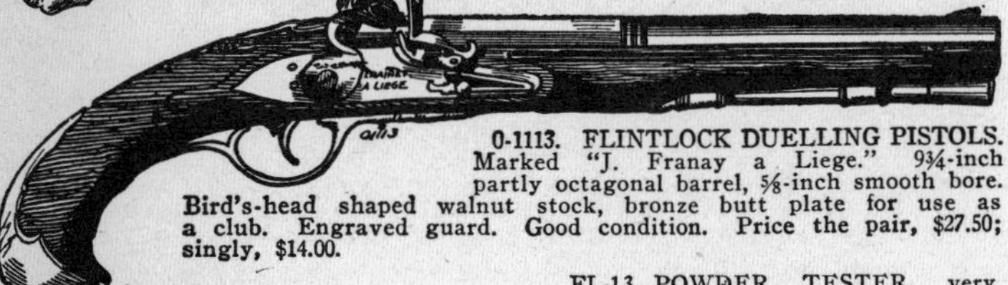

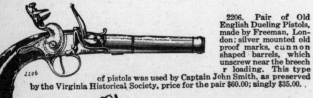

0-1113. FLINTLOCK DUELLING PISTOLS. Marked "J. Franay a Liege." 9¾-inch partly octagonal barrel, ⅝-inch smooth bore. Bird's-head shaped walnut stock, bronze butt plate for use as a club. Engraved guard. Good condition. Price the pair, $27.50; singly, $14.00.

FL-13. POWDER TESTER, very early pattern, lighted with fuse. Brass frame, long wood butt. This type exceedingly rare. Length, 6¾ inches. Price $20.00. See illustration No. 2116.

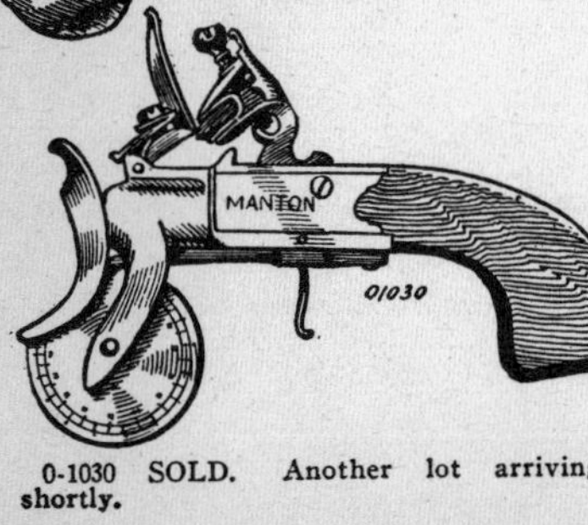

0-1030 SOLD. Another lot arriving shortly.

2206A. QUEEN ANNE CANNON BARREL PISTOL, FLINTLOCK, with 7-inch removable barrel, marked: JOYNER, LONDON, with 3 proof marks. Silver monogram plate, heavy silver butt plate with figure of victory sitting on draped flags, silver side plate. Price $28.00.

10881. LIEUT. GENERAL HONORABLE SIR JAMES LINDSAY, K. C. M. G., ENGRAVED ON NAME PLATE ON OAK CASE containing Colts revolver; 7½-inch barrel, made at Colts London factory, with powder flask, lead bullets and iron nipple cup. Size of the case, 14½ by 6½ by 3¾. Good order. Price, $20.00 the outfit.

10439. PAIR OF HEAVY BARREL DUELLING PISTOLS with hair triggers, made by Deane, London. Percussion locks. Figured Damascus barrel, octagonal, ½-inch smooth bore. Carved walnut fore end. Checkered grip. Silver name plate. Chased mountings. Working order. Price the pair, $22.50.

10984. PAIR PERCUSSION LOCK DUELLING PISTOLS, by J. Blanch, London, in Oak Case with Outfit. The pistols are in fine order like new; have the swivel ramrod, silver name plate and escutcheons; engraved mountings. Polished walnut stock; checkered grip; 8-inch octagonal twist-steel barrel; ⅝-inch smooth bore. Rear and front sights. Price the outfit, $35.00.

BRASS BARREL FLINTLOCK PISTOL, British maker, "Weston"; good second-hand, serviceable order. Price, $7.85.

ANTIQUE FOUR-BARREL FLINTLOCK PISTOL; brass barrels; ⅜-inch bore. Rare piece. London dealer sold similar weapon for 30 guineas ($150.00). Price, $150.00.

FLINTLOCK POCKET PISTOLS with rifled, cannon-shaped barrel, which unscrews at the breech for quick loading. Steel frame (no wood), finely engraved; serviceable order; 3-inch barrel, ⅜ bore. Price, $12.00.

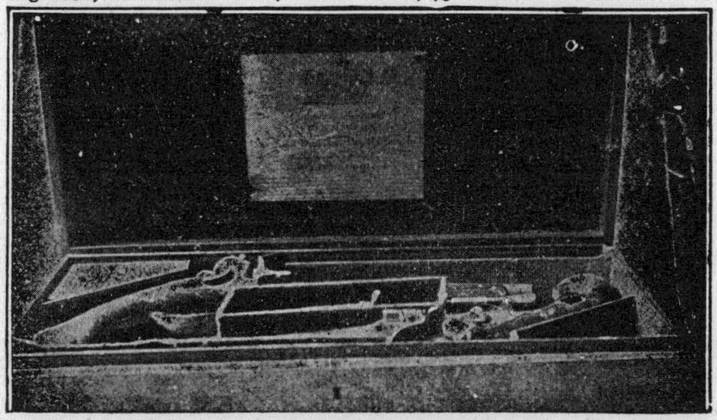

FLC-10. PAIR FLINTLOCK OVERCOAT POCKET PISTOLS, in case with tools. Rounded butts, ribbed, checkered grips, full length stocks. 6½-inch case hardened octagon barrels, with front and rear sights, marked: H. W. MORTIMER & CO., LONDON, GUN MAKERS TO HIS MAJESTY. Engraved guards with pine apple ends, and extra finger spurs. 4¼-inch engraved locks, with safeties, marked: H. W. MORTIMER & CO. Full length 11½ inches, bore ⅝ inches. Set includes rammer, oilcup and mould. Touch holes are gold bushed. Hair triggers. Price for set $80.00.

D75. ONE PAIR FLINTLOCK PISTOLS, locks marked BARNETT. Half octagon BRASS barrels are marked CUSTOMS. Used by Revenue Service. Both pistols brass mounted, with heavy round butt and ornamented brass trigger guards. Price for pair, $35.00.

D77. TURKISH FLINTLOCK PISTOL, extra long pattern, with 14-inch round barrel. Heavy silver butt with crest, and brass name plate. Lock needs adjustment. Price $14.50.

D78. 1 SPANISH FLINTLOCK PISTOL with carved wood stock and gold inlaid 7-inch barrel with flat top rib and front sight. Heavy brass butt plate, with scroll ornaments. Trigger gold inlaid. Lock is 4 inch with gold inlay, and marked D. ZANONI. Trigger guard missing. Price $14.50.

D79. 1 FRENCH FLINTLOCK PISTOL with 7½-inch barrel, with flat top rib and brass front sight. Carved stock, round iron butt with heavy iron butt plate. Price $11.00.

D80. 1 FLINTLOCK HOLSTER PISTOL, English make. Lock marked JOHN RICHARDS. Eight inch, is octagon for 3 inches, then round to muzzle. Plain brass trigger guard, with heavy brass ball butt. Brass name plate with crest of two flags over crown. Price $17.50.

2100. OLD ENGLISH FLINTLOCK PISTOL, Queen Anne type, full length 12 inches, barrel 6¾-inch removable, with 3 proof marks, and marked: WALKER, LONDON. Round ball butt with silver mask butt plate, silver side plate in flag design, silver monogram plate with design including helmet, cannon and flags, and bearing a crest. Plain trigger guard. Period 1750. Price $26.00.

2100A. QUEEN ANNE TYPE FLINTLOCK PISTOL, full length 8 inches, removable cannon barrel, 4¾ inches, with 3 proof marks and makers name: LOWE, LONDON. Round butt with silver mask butt plate, plain guard, silver monogram plate. This size carried in overcoat pocket. Period 1760. Price $22.00.

0-1008. FRENCH FLINTLOCK RIFLED PISTOL. Engraved, "Antoine Demarest." 7-inch twist steel, slightly blunderbuss-shaped barrel, about ¾-inch bore, with fine rifle grooves. Rear and front sight. Checkered grip. Walnut stock. Engraved mountings. Flat shaped butt. Fine weapon in good condition. Price, $25.00.

0-1007. Extra LARGE BORE FLINTLOCK PISTOL. Hinged ramrod. Lock engraved, "Osborne & Gundy, London"; 9-inch barrel, nearly ¾-inch smooth bore. Engraved mountings. Walnut stock. Price, $14.50.

# FLINT-LOCK PISTOLS

VSF. ITALIAN FLINTLOCK POCKET PISTOL, made after the pattern of the horseman's pistol, with full length wood stock, fishtail butt with heavy metal butt plate, fancy side plate, and engraved guard. 3¼-inch engraved lock, at side. 3⅛-inch RIBBED barrel. Full length only 7½ inches. Price $13.00.

VSF-1. PAIR ITALIAN FLINTLOCK POCKET PISTOLS, with 3-inch RIBBED barrels, fish tail butts, iron mounted, 3-inch engraved locks, long trigger guards. Full length 7¼ inches. Price for pair $22.00.

VSF-2. PAIR FRENCH FLINTLOCK PISTOLS, with 2¾-inch octagon barrels, slightly BELLED at muzzle. Fitted with REAR sights only. Checkered grips, flat butts with engraved plates, fancy side plates, ornamented guards with urn ends. French pistols in this size are rare. Price for pair $25.00.

M-3. FRENCH FLINT BLUNDERBUSS PISTOL, made of cannon bronze with plain wood grip, with monkey head bronze butt plate. Frame and barrel in one piece. Barrel 4½ inches long, bore at muzzle 9/16th inches, cannon shaped. Engraved frame, center hammer with safety catch and powder pan lock, engraved trigger guard. Price $18.00.

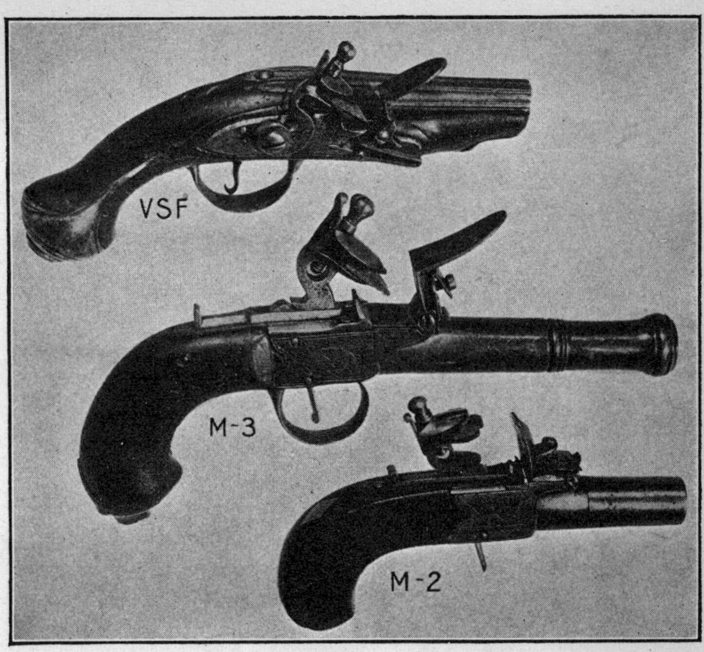


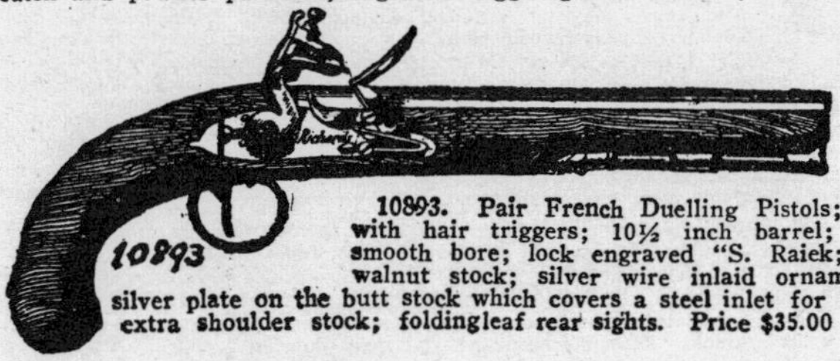

10893

**10893. Pair French Duelling Pistols; flintlock with hair triggers; 10½ inch barrel; ⅝ inch smooth bore; lock engraved "S. Raiek;" carved walnut stock; silver wire inlaid ornamentation; silver plate on the butt stock which covers a steel inlet for attaching extra shoulder stock; foldingleaf rear sights. Price $35.00 the pair.**

M-2-STF-1. PAIR FLINTLOCK POCKET PISTOLS, full length 5¾ inches, cannon shaped barrel, 2¼-inch, removable. Flat wood butts with silver monogram diamond shaped plate, center hammers with safety catches, secret triggers, no guards. Barrels have 3 proof marks, frames engraved with war trophies, and marked: NEVILL. Price for pair $20.00.

M-2-STF-2. PAIR FLINTLOCK POCKET PISTOLS, made by WHEELER, LONDON, and so marked on frames. Full length 5¾ inches, removable cannon barrels, 2 inches, with 2 proof marks. Flat wood butts, secret triggers, center hammers with safeties. Silver oval monogram disks. Price for pair $19.00.

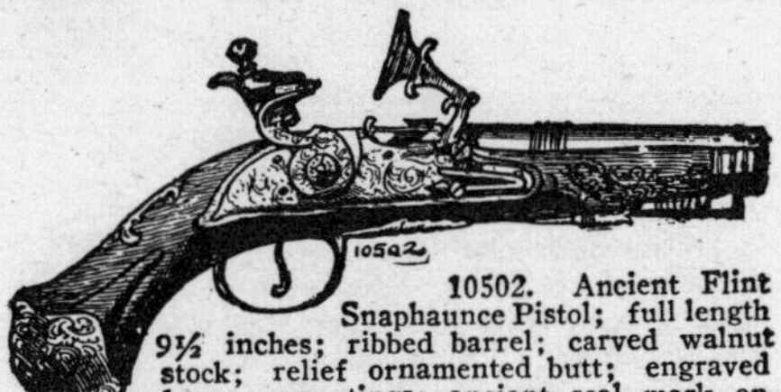

10502

10502. Ancient Flint Snaphaunce Pistol; full length 9½ inches; ribbed barrel; carved walnut stock; relief ornamented butt; engraved brass mountings; ancient seal mark on the barrel; in working order; cover on the flash pan opens auto-matically as hammer strikes the battery; ancient Italian or French work.

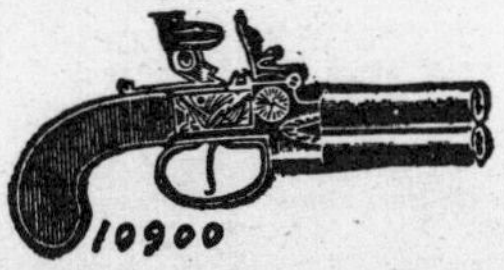

10900

10900. PAIR OVER AND UNDER POCKET FLINTLOCK PISTOLS, with plain flat butts, center hammers with safety catches, 3¼-inch barrels with 2 proof marks. Frames marked: P. BOND, LONDON. Fire is directed to lower barrels by turning lever on side of frame. Price for pair $38.00.

**10900-A. A Similar Double Barrel Over and Under Flintlock Pistol; French make; silver points in the diamond checkering on the walnut stock. Price $17.50.**

**10900B. Extra Long Barrel Over and Under Flintlock Pistol; made by Simmons, about the period of 1790; old proof marked barrel, 6⅝ inches in length; rifled at the muzzle. Price $20.00.**

**10901. Gun Metal Barrel Flintlock Pistol of period about 1750; carriage size, full length, 11 inches; old G. P. (London gun makers) proof marks; center hammer, with safety; good order. Price $17.50.**

10205. PAIR OF EARLY PERCUSSION FRENCH DUELLING PISTOLS IN CASE, with flask, mould, cleaner, mallet caps and extra nipples; 11-inch octagonal twist-steel barrel. Engraved German silver mountings. Pollard walnut stock, checkered grip. Cap box in the butt. Hair or set triggers. Muzzle rifling. Contained in mahogany case. Size of the case 20x10x2½ inches. Price the outfit, $28.00.

10855. ANCIENT EUROPEAN FIRE LIGHTER. Pistol grip; center hammer; two-legged stand; spark catcher with wick holder; full length 5 inches. Price, $12.85.

Brass Barrel Flint-Lock Side-Arm Pistol; 9-inch barrel; made by Rawson, Norwich; walnut stock; full length 15 inches. Price, $18.00.

10855B. Flint Fire Lighter, engraved "B May"; pistol shaped; walnut handle; spark catcher and wick holder; full length 7½ inches. Price, $14.50.

10998. Pair London Brass Barrel Holster or Duelling Pistols; flintlock engraved "Nock 1786"; full length 13 inches; in good order. Price, $36.00 the pair.

10530. Cossack Flint-Lock Pistol; IVORY BALL BUTT; decorated silver 12-inch barrel; wood stock covered with leather and ornamented in engraved silver; OUTSIDE SPANISH LOCK; ball trigger. Price, $18.85.

10531. Cossack Flint-Lock Pistol with decorated gold barrel, inlaid "VOTAGVVE"; old POLLARD WALNUT stock; IVORY BALL BUTT; ball-shaped trigger; barrel decorated with relief figures; full length 21 inches; OUTSIDE SPANISH LOCK. Price, $22.50.

Flint-Lock Pistol, ½-inch bore, light weight, twist-steel; serviceable order. Price, $6.50.

Double-Barrel Flint-Lock Pistol; full length 6½ inches; old style rifling at muzzle; in fine order. Price, $18.00.

Two French Army Flint-Lock Pistols, 7¼-inch barrel; serviceable order. (French name on locks.) Price, $8.75 each.

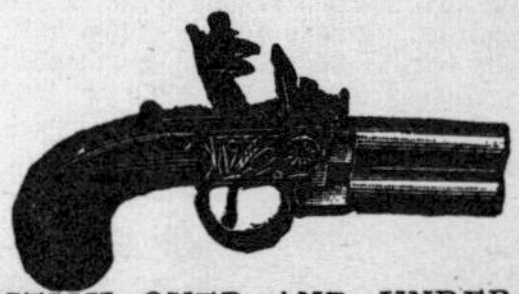

9. BRITISH OVER AND UNDER FLINTLOCK POCKET PISTOL, full length 7½ inches, barrels 3 inches with proof marks. Flat wood butts, center hammers with safety catches, plain guard. Frame marked: WILMOT & ROBERTS, and engraved with battle trophies. Price $20.00.

**10421. BRITISH DOUBLE BARREL FLINTLOCK PISTOL, by Layben. Bird head walnut butt stock. Barrels are side by side, 3½ inches long, ½ inch smooth bore; side locks. In working order. Price $14.85.**

**10421-A. OLD ENGLISH DOUBLE BARREL SIDE LOCK PISTOL, by Javor, London. Checkered Grip. Walnut stock. Double triggers. Double locks. Barrels are side by side, 7 inches long, ⅝ inch smooth bore. Rare type. $18.85.**

10584A. PAIR OF OVER AND UNDER PERCUSSION-LOCK PISTOLS, made by J. W. Edge, Manchester. About 8½-inch barrel; in fair order; complete in Walnut Case with ball and powder flask, screw driver, etc. Price the outfit, $35.00.

***Extract Battle of Kingston, N. C., 1862:***

**Early on that Sabbath morning,
Soon as 'twas fairly light,
The enemy began the game
Right lively from the right.**

**Out from the old church on the hill
There burst a sheet of flame,
And round about our battery fell
A shower of leaden rain.**

**Our guns soon woke the echoes,
As we worked them with a will,
And sent our iron compliments
To those upon the hill.**

**And our gunner laughingly remarked,
As he glanced along his gun,
"I guess the exercises
In the church have just begun."
—MORGAN SENNETT, N. Y.**

**10539. DOUBLE BARREL FLINTLOCK PISTOL. Silver mounted, engraved with ancient castles. Barrels are by side. Lock and flash pan to each barrel. Checkered walnut stock, seal stamped. Full length 10 inches. In good working order (fore end faulty). Price $22.50.**

**10540. FRENCH DOUBLE BARREL FLINTLOCK PISTOL, side locks engraved "F. Bon, Monte Lunai". Silver name plate, engraved steel mountings. In working order. Full length 12 inches. Price $22.50.**

# ANCIENT PISTOLS

10207. PAIR "BLISSET LONDON" NAVAL OFFICERS PERCUSSION LOCK PISTOLS, in Case with bullet mould, screw wrench, screw driver, rammer, bullets, etc. 6-inch octagonal twist-steel barrel with ramrod rib, swivel rammer, with belt hook. Silver name plate and mountings. Walnut stock, checkered grip; engraved mountings. Good workmanship. Oak case 14½x8x2¾ inches. Price the outfit, $27.00.

BRONZE BARREL CAP AND BALL PISTOL, captured from Italian Brigands; 7-inch barrel; working order. Price, $4.85.

10861. FRENCH PERCUSSION-LOCK POWDER TESTER, engraved mountings, walnut stock. Fine order. Price, $12.50.

8748.—SPANISH FLINTLOCK PISTOL. With maker's gold seal inlaid on the barrel "Joan Par." Cannon shaped 7½ inch barrel, ⅝ inch smooth bore. Inlaid silver scroll work, curious outside antique lock with projecting safety at half and full cock, which engages the hammer until released by a pull on the trigger. Engraved brass mountings and name plate. Carved walnut stock, full length 13¼ inches. Price, $25.00.

8749.—FRENCH FLINTLOCK PISTOL. With 8 inch octagonal barrel, 11/16 inch smooth bore. Steel mountings. Price, $16.50.

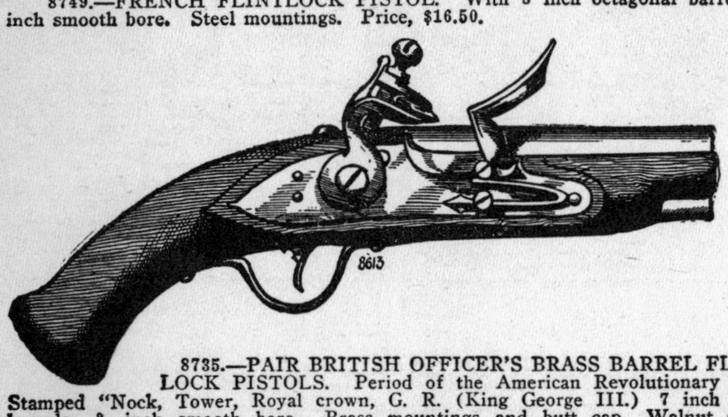

8735.—PAIR BRITISH OFFICER'S BRASS BARREL FLINTLOCK PISTOLS. Period of the American Revolutionary War. Stamped "Nock, Tower, Royal crown, G. R. (King George III.) 7 inch brass barrels, 7/16 inch smooth bore. Brass mountings and butt cap. Walnut stock. Serviceable order. Price, $32.00 the pair.

8710.—"H. DELANEY, LONDINI." With initials and mark of the maker. With old proof marks on the barrel. Early make flintlock pistol. 10 inch barrel, ⅝ inch smooth bore. Maker's name on the lock, "H. DELANEY." Solid silver guard, thimbles, name plate, and the ball shaped butt cap and front sight. Walnut stock. Full length 16 inches. Serviceable order. Price, $35.00.

8711.—PAIR BRASS BARREL FLINTLOCK DUELLING PISTOLS. Engraved "Henshaw, Strand, London," about the period of 1770. Elephant head crest on the name plate. Old proof marks. 8 inch barrel. Walnut stock. Masked butt cap. (Stock slightly cracked.) Full length 15 inches. Price the pair, $40.00.

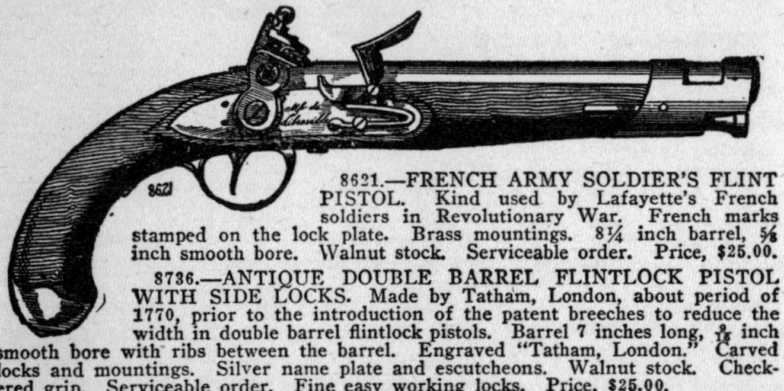

8621.—FRENCH ARMY SOLDIER'S FLINT PISTOL. Kind used by Lafayette's French soldiers in Revolutionary War. French marks stamped on the lock plate. Brass mountings. 8¼ inch barrel, ⅝ inch smooth bore. Walnut stock. Serviceable order. Price, $25.00.

8736.—ANTIQUE DOUBLE BARREL FLINTLOCK PISTOL WITH SIDE LOCKS. Made by Tatham, London, about period of 1770, prior to the introduction of the patent breeches to reduce the width in double barrel flintlock pistols. Barrel 7 inches long, 7/16 inch smooth bore with ribs between the barrel. Engraved "Tatham, London." Carved locks and mountings. Silver name plate and escutcheons. Walnut stock. Checkered grip. Serviceable order. Fine easy working locks. Price, $25.00.

8712.—PAIR FLINTLOCK DUELLING PISTOLS. Engraved as having been made by "Twig, London.". 10 inch octagonal twist steel barrels with original browning, 7/16 inch smooth bore. Safety lock attachment. Walnut stock. Checkered grip. Engraved mountings. Silver name plate. Period of about 1788. Serviceable order. Price, $40.00 the pair.

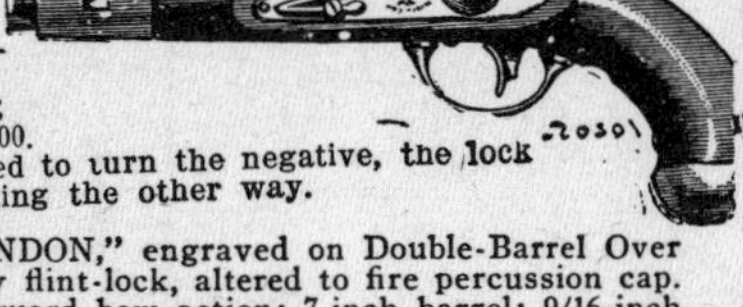

10263. U. S. ARMY FLINTLOCK Model 1816, made by S. North, Middletown, Conn. by contract for U. S. War Dept., between years 1816 and 1818, calibre 54, barrel 9 inches, iron mounted, wood ramrod, weight three pounds; in used serviceable order. Price, $20.00.

NOTE.—10263, our engraver has failed to turn the negative, the lock is on the right side, the pistol pointing the other way.

10902. "RICHARDS STRAND, LONDON," engraved on Double-Barrel Over and Under Revolving Pistol, originally flint-lock, altered to fire percussion cap. Barrels are revolved by hand-locked guard bow action; 7-inch barrel; 9/16-inch smooth bore. Side lock, single hammer, side rammer, knob shaped butt curly walnut carved stock, engraved frame. Has been an extra fine gun, worthy of its famous maker. If not altered would be worth $75.00. We offer as it is for $18.00.

8738. ANCIENT ORIENTAL FLINT-LOCK PISTOL. 8-inch cannon shaped barrel, ⅝-inch smooth bore. Square shaped fore end. Gilt inlaid mountings with verses from the Koran. Period of about 1770. Full length 15 inches. Price, $15.00.

8739. OLD SPANISH FLINT-LOCK PISTOL. "J. H. Deop" in raised letters on the gold seal on the lock. Two old seal proof marks on the barrel. Silver lettering on the barrel almost worn off. Ornamented 11-inch barrel; 11/16-inch smooth bore. Handsome silver mounted guard, thimble, side plate, name plate, and mask butt cap. Carved walnut stock. Full length 18 inches. Price, $40.00.

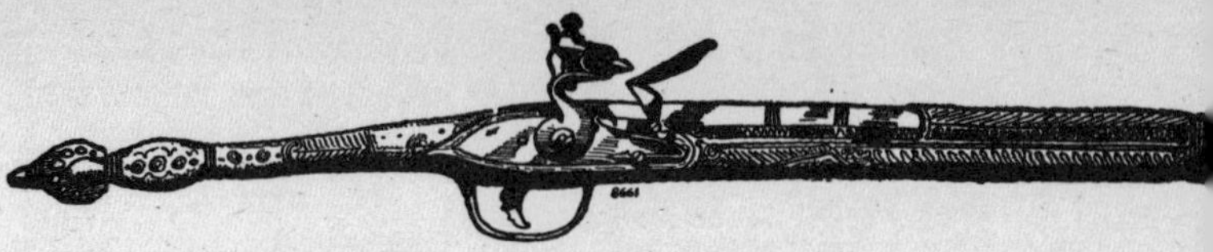

8661.—ALBANIAN FLINTLOCK 18th CENTURY PISTOL. With native chased *met stock*, relief ornamented pike butt. Full length 33 inches. Passed by the New York Custo House Appraisers as a work of art. Price, $75.00.

8740.—OLD INDIA FLINTLOCK PISTOL 18th century. Silver inlaid scroll work o the barrel. Name on the lock plate in ancient letters. Brass mounted. Full length 17 inches. Price, $12.50.

8715.—PAIR RIFLED FLINTLOCK PISTOLS. 6 inch steel barrels, ½ partly octagona ½ inch bore, 8 rifle grooves. Ornamented lock plate engraved and ornamented "J. W. Lier Carved walnut stock. Iron mountings. Bird head butt. Full length 12 inches. Rifled fli pistols are rare. Price, $60.00 the pair.

8716.—PAIR FLINTLOCK TRAVELING PISTOLS. Made by R. Outridge; 6 inch octa onal barrels. ¾ inch smooth bore. Engraved mountings. Artistic shaped hammer. Waln stock. Checkered grip. Silver name plate. Full length 12 inches. Price, $38.00 the pair.

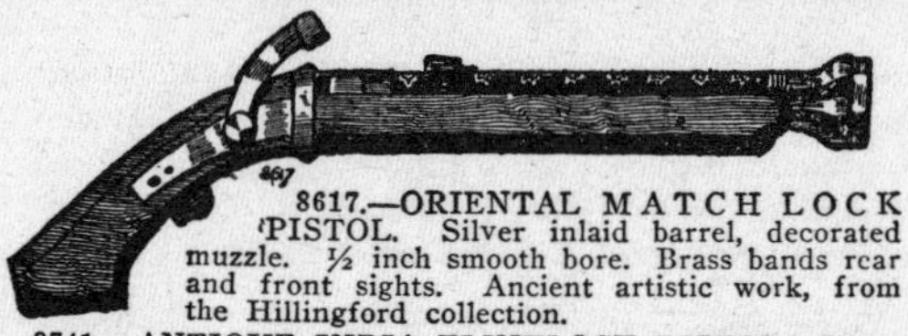

8617.—ORIENTAL MATCH LOCK PISTOL. Silver inlaid barrel, decorated muzzle. ½ inch smooth bore. Brass bands rear and front sights. Ancient artistic work, from the Hillingford collection.

8741.—ANTIQUE INDIA FLINTLOCK PISTOL. Silver inlaid ornamentation on the fluted barrel. Hollow brass rib for the ramrod. Walnut stock. Pearl inlaid ornamentation. Full length 18 inches. Price, $18.00. Orientals pay more attention to the outside decoration, whereas the European makers excel in mechanism workmanship.

8742.—EARLY ENGLISH FLINTLOCK PISTOL. With 6½ inch cannon barrel, which unscrews near the breech for quick loading. ⅝ inch smooth bore. Outside lock. Silver mask butt cap. Price, $15.00.

8743.—TURKISH FLINTLOCK PISTOL, 18th CENTURY. 11 inch ribbed barrel, 7/16 inch smooth bore. Checkered walnut stock. Maker's name on the lock plate in Greek letters. German silver, engraved mountings. Price, $15.00.

10206. PAIR DOUBLE BARREL PERCUSSION LOCK PISTOLS, IN CASE WITH OUTFIT, bullet mould, nipple wrench, powder flask, bullets, wads, etc.; 6-inch twist-barrels, ⅝-inch smooth bore. Ramrod attached by swivel for use in both barrels. Silver name plate and front sight. On the lock T. E. Mortimer, Princess St. Edinburgh, on the lock Mortimer. Polished walnut stock, checkered grip, fine order. Oak case (in poor order). Size of case 15x10x2¾ inches. Label in the case reads "Thomas Elsworth Mortimer, Gun and Pistol Manufacturer, 97 George St., Edinburgh, late 34 St. James, London," with British coat of arms. This rare outfit of one of the best of the old time gun makers. Price, $37.50.

8744.—FRENCH FLINTLOCK PISTOL WITH HINGED RAMMER. 11½ inch octagonal twist steel barrel; ½ inch smooth bore. Checkered grip, walnut stock. Brass mountings. Price, $16.50.

8744A.—FRENCH FLINTLOCK PISTOL. With polished walnut stock. Relief ornamented brass mountings. Full length 17½ inches. Flat shaped butt stock. Price, $15.00.

8717.—AMERICAN R VOLUTIONARY WA PERIOD OFFICER' FLINTLOCK HOLSTE PISTOL. Engraved on th barrel "Double Birmingha proof marks, with crown an H. N." Made by H. Noc 9 inch barrel 11/16 inch smoo bore. Full length 15 inche Brass mountings. Waln stock. Serviceable orde Price, $38.00 the pair.

8717B.—SIMILA FLINTLOCK PISTOL Single, for mounted office with hinged rammer, No. carved on the guard bo Price, $17.00.

8718.—PAIR BRAS BARREL FLINTLOC CARRIAGE PISTOLS Barrels unscrew near th breech for quick loadin Hammer and flash pan the center of the stoc Silver name plate. Inla silver wire ornamented scro work on the walnut stoc Old proof marks engrave "Bunney, London." F length 12 inches. Cann shaped muzzle. Price, $38 the pair.

8718A.—SIMILAR PA OF BRASS BARRE FLINTLOCK PISTOL Made by "Joyner, London Full length 9¼ inches, inch smooth bore. Pric $30.00 the pair.

A sailor had just shown a lady over the ship. In thanking him, she said, "I am sorry to see by the rules that tips are forbidden on your ship." "Lord bless, you, ma'am," replied the sailor, "so were apples in the Garden of Eden."

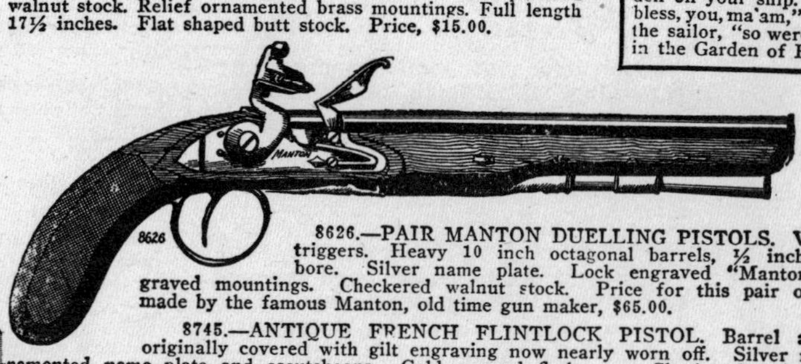

8626.—PAIR MANTON DUELLING PISTOLS. With ha triggers. Heavy 10 inch octagonal barrels, ½ inch smoo bore. Silver name plate. Lock engraved "Manton." E graved mountings. Checkered walnut stock. Price for this pair of pisto made by the famous Manton, old time gun maker, $65.00.

8745.—ANTIQUE FRENCH FLINTLOCK PISTOL. Barrel and lo originally covered with gilt engraving now nearly worn off. Silver relief o namented name plate and escutcheons. Gold covered flash pan. Checkered walnut stoc Relief ornamented military trophy mountings. Price, $20.00.

10826. FRENCH MODEL NAVY PISTOL, 7¾-inch barrel, ⅝-inch smooth bore, mark, in working order. Price, $4.85.

8747. HOLSTER FLINTLOCK LARGE BORE PISTOL. Made by "I. Egg, London about the period of the American Revolutionary War. 9-inch barrel; over ¾-inch smoo bore. Maker's name on lock and barrel. Checkered walnut stock. Engraved ste mountings. Price, $17.50.

8713. PAIR FRENCH FLINTLOCK DUELLING PISTOLS. 7¼-inch blued steel ba rels; 9/16-inch smooth bore. Polished curly walnut stock. Checkered grip. Engrave brass mountings. Square shaped butt cap; ebony top fore end. Full length 12¾ inche Price, $38.00 the pair.

10584. PAIR WILKINS DOUBLE-BARREL PERCUSSION LOCK PISTOLS. Barre are over and under. The hammer on the left is broken. Outfit is IN THE ORIGINA WALNUT CASE in perfect order. Fine point checkering on the stock. Silver nam plate, hinged rammer. Engraved on the barrel, "Wilkins, Pall Mall, London." Fu length 8 inches; about 40 calibre smooth bore. Case contains bullet mould, ramme wrench, etc. Price the outfit, $40.00.

# FLINT LOCK PISTOLS AND BLUNDERBUSSES

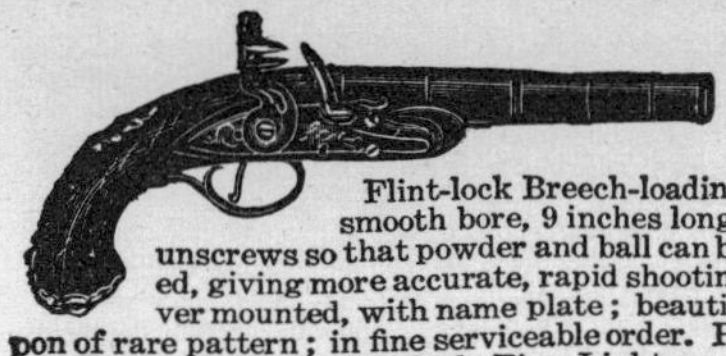

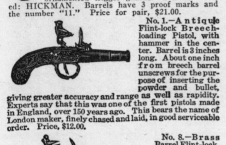

Flint-lock Breech-loading Pistol, smooth bore, 9 inches long; barrel unscrews so that powder and ball can be inserted, giving more accurate, rapid shooting; is silver mounted, with name plate; beautiful weapon of rare pattern; in fine serviceable order. Price $28.

No. 3A.—Antique Flint lock Fire Lighter, with old outside hammer and springs; has iron box with partition for holding tinder; mounted on three legs; very old and has been rusted; is now in serviceable order. Price $10.

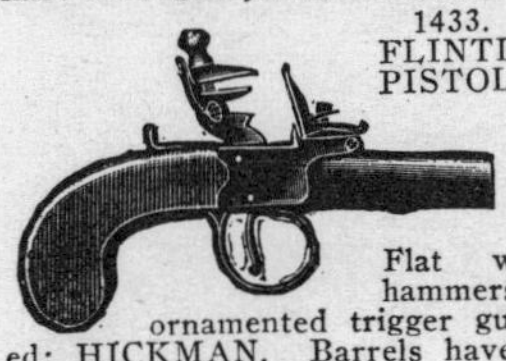

1433. PAIR BRITISH FLINTLOCK POCKET PISTOLS, with brass frames and barrels. Barrels are of the removable type, 2¾ inches long, full length of pistols 6½ inches. Flat wood butts, center hammers with safety catches, ornamented trigger guards. Frames marked: HICKMAN. Barrels have 3 proof marks and the number "11." Price for pair, $21.00.

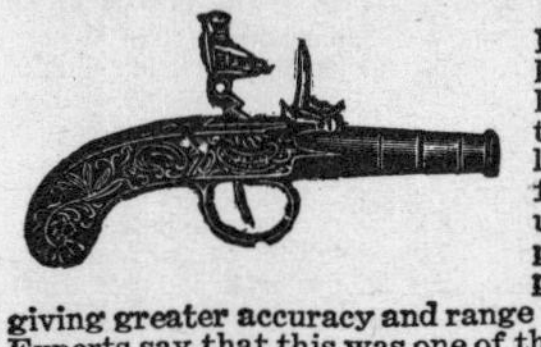

No. 1.—Antique Flint-lock Breech-loading Pistol, with hammer in the center. Barrel is 3 inches long. About one inch from breech barrel unscrews for the purpose of inserting the powder and bullet, giving greater accuracy and range as well as rapidity. Experts say that this was one of the first pistols made in England, over 150 years ago. This bears the name of London maker, finely chased and laid, in good serviceable order. Price, $12.00.

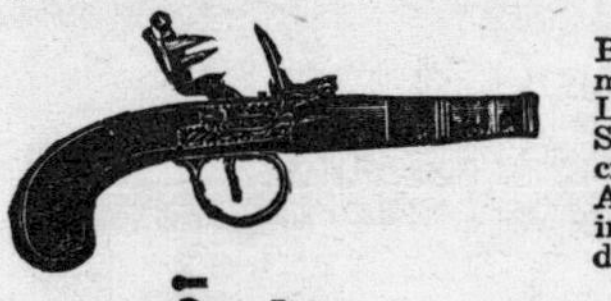

No. 8.—Brass Barrel Flint-lock, made by old-time London gun man. Similar to description No. 1. About 40-calibre, in serviceable order. Price, $10.00.

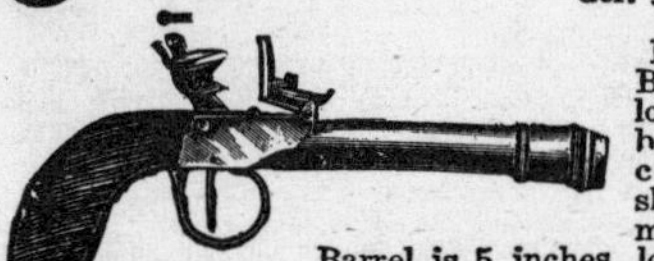

No. 4—Brass Barrel Flint-lock Blunderbuss, with cannon-shaped bell-mouth barrel. Barrel is 5 inches long, ¾-inch diameter at the flash pan; 1⅛-inches diameter at the muzzle. Found in an old gun factory in Europe that made guns and pistols over 100 years ago. Looks like new; in splendid order; polished. Price, $15.00.

R73. 1 Queen Anne Flint-lock Pistol, with half octagon barrel, marked Lowe, London. Lock-plate marked Lowe. Heavy brass butt and trigger guard. Price, $25.00.

R89. 1 Flint-lock Holster Pistol, with 8-inch brass barrel, round butt. Brass trimmed. Style used in Revolutionary War. Price, $21.00.

R57. 1 French Flint-lock Holster Pistol, with swivel ramrod. Octagon barrel 8½ inches, checkered grip and square butt. In fine order. Price, $17.40.

10900. BRITISH DOUBLE BARREL FLINT POCKET PISTOL, with SUPERPOSED barrels. Frame marked: SMITH, LONDON. Full length 8¼ inches, barrels 3 inches, flat butt, trigger guard. Price $22.00.

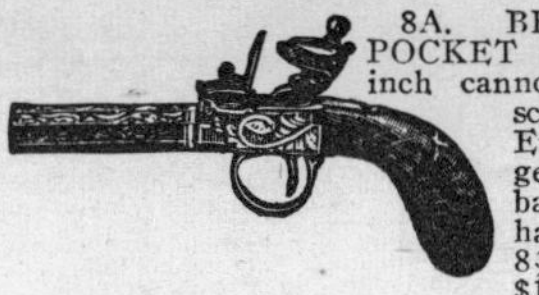

8A. BRITISH FLINT POCKET PISTOL, with 4-inch cannon barrel, to unscrew to load. Etched frame, trigger guard, round ball butt. Center hammer. Full length 8¾ inches. Price $10.00.

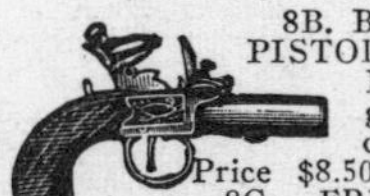

8B. BELGIAN FLINT POCKET PISTOL, with 4-inch cannon barrel. Full length 8 inches, engraved frame, flat wood butt, center hammer, trigger guard. Price $8.50.

8C. FRENCH FLINT POCKET PISTOL, ball butt, trigger guard, center hammer, cannon barrel 2¾ inches, full length, 6¾ inches. Three proof marks on barrel. Price $7.50.

Flint-lock Blunderbuss, barrel is 7 inches long, the muzzle is bell-mouthed and is 1¾ inches in diameter; butt of stock is shaped like gun stock and checkered; carved ivory ramrod; in good condition. Price, $25.00.

Flint-lock Blunderbuss, 10-inch barel, 1½ inches at muzzle; gun-shaped stock; found in India; in fair order, barrel is engraved. Price, $20.00.

Ornamented Flint-lock Blunderbuss, 11-inch barrel, 2¾-inch muzzle; relief work on barrel; carved and engraved stock; as the stock is in bad order, partly broken, we will sell for $22.00.

10475. PARKER FIELD & SON, LONDON, PERCUSSION-LOCK PISTOL. Octagonal 4-inch barrel. Checkered grip. Walnut stock. Silver name plate. Platinum vent plug, swivel ramrod. Engraved mountings. Used a short time; fine, serviceable order. Price, $8.50.

1433A. PAIR EUROPEAN FLINTLOCK POCKET PISTOLS, with center hammers with safety catches. 3-inch removable barrels with proof mark. Plain guards, checkered wood butts. Full length 7 inches. Price for pair $16.00.

1433B. PAIR BRITISH FLINTLOCK POCKET PISTOLS, with brass frames marked: H. NOCK, LONDON, with 3 proof marks. 2½-inch blued steel removable barrels, marked: A-N4353-4. Flat wood butts, center hammers with safety catches, ornamented frames, plain guards. Price for pair $23.00.

10517. NAPOLEON IMPERIAL ARSENAL CHARLEYVILLE LOCK HORSE PISTOL. Originally flint, now altered to percussion lock. Barrel stamped 1810. Found in America; perhaps a relic of the War of 1812. In good order. Price, $12.50.

10405. CURIOUS SHAPED PERCUSSION REVOLVER FROM LONDON collection, evidently French gun with enclosed sliding ramrod. Relief engraving. About calibre 36, six shot. 6¼-inch octagonal barrel. Working order. Price, $11.85.

R128. 1 Pair Brass Bound Flint-lock Pistols, with small round butt. Barrels are 7 inches round with swivel ramrods. Made by W. Bond, London. Price, $25.00.

R1. 1 Antique French Flint-lock Pistol, with heavy brass octagon barrel, 6 inch. Square butt with brass plate. Fancy brass trigger guard and brass flash pan. Price, $21.00.

R50. 1 French Iron Mounted Holster Pistol, with heavy butt, half octagon barrel, fancy trigger guard and side plate. Price, $17.10.

R75A. 1 British Flint-lock Holster Pistol, by Adams. Has 7-inch round barrel, fancy brass trigger guard and brass cap with curious face on round butt. Ramrod has ivory tip. Price, $32.00.

KING GEORGE III PERIOD OLD FLINT-LOCK, stamped with tower, crown, G. R. (George's reign), with broad arrow, with old proof marks. Full length 15 inches, ⅝ smooth bore, swivel ramrod, brass butt cap. In shooting order. Price, $10.00.

1457. BRASS BARREL FLINT-LOCK HOLSTER PISTOL, hexagonal barrel for half its length, cannon-shaped muzzle, ⅝ smooth bore, 13 inches full length. Polished walnut stock, fancy guard, steel knob-shaped butt for use in emergency as a club. In working order. Price, $14.00.

4A. LOUIS XVI BRASS BLUNDERBUSS POCKET PISTOL, flintlock with center hammer, safety catch to keep hammer at half cock, also to hold powder pan shut. 3½-inch barrel. Barrel and frame in one piece. Flat butt. Price $7.50.

1453.—Flint-lock Brass Barrel Blunderbuss Pistol, with short gun stock. Engraved on barrel "London," in scroll work, two old proof marks. On lock engraved "T. Hanshaw." Barrel is 9¼ inches, 1⅛ at the muzzle. Full length is 20½ inches. Fore stock partly broken and needs repairing. Brass mountings, name plate. We offer at bargain price of $15.00.

1454.—Old London Flint-lock Pistol; barrel is 11/16 smooth bore, 9 inches long. Full length 15 inches. Engraved brass mountings. Engraved on barrel "London." Breech part of the barrel flat for sighting. In working order. $10.00.

1436.—Brass Barrel Flint-lock Blunderbuss, cannon-shaped barrel, 7 inches, 1 inch diameter at bell-mouth muzzle. Made by "Mewis & Co., London." In working order; ramrod and guard missing. Safety lock at the flash pan. Price, $15.00.

2473.—Aubron Nantes engraved on lock of fine old French Bronze Barrel Rifled Duelling Pistol. Octagonal barrel, 8½ inches; 11/16 bore, rifled. Handsome engraved ornamented bronze mountings. Silver name plate on left side of pistol. Front and rear sights. Row of silver ornamented discs on stock; iron breech. Polished and checkered walnut stock—handsome pistol. Offered in working order. Flint rifled pistols are rare. Price, $30.00.

1334.—Old Flint-lock Carriage Pistol. Lock is in working order; rusty; complete. Full length 9½ inches, ⅝-inch smooth bore, walnut stock. Price, $10.00.

1496.—Tharmey Flint-lock Carriage Size Pistol, 5-inch octagonal barrel; 11/16 smooth bore, engraved mountings; polished walnut stock; in order. Price, $12.00.

1753.—French Flint-lock Pistol, engraved on the barrel "Rheims." Fine working lock. Barrel 5¼ inches long; ½-inch smooth bore; polished walnut ornamented handle. In fine serviceable order. Price, $15.00.

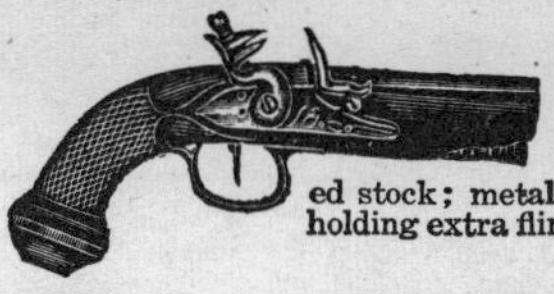

No. 2.—French Flint-lock, stamped St. Etienne. Octagonal barrel, about ½-inch bore; checked stock; metal box on butt for holding extra flint. Fine order. Price, 15.00.

Flint-lock Cannon-shaped Screw Barrel Pistol, smooth bore, silvered wire ornamented stock; engraved system, "S. Kingdon, Exeter"; full length is 8 inches; barrel is 3½ inches; ½-inch bore. Price, $9.50.

No. 0-1014. BRITISH GRENADIER GUARDS, OFFICERS' PAIR FLINTLOCK DUELLING PISTOLS IN CASE. Engraved as made by Wogdon and Barton, London, 10¼-inch steel octagonal barrel, 9-16-inch smooth bore. Fine, easy working locks. Hammer safety. Engraved mountings. Polished walnut stock. Silver name plate, with monogram. Front and rear sight. In good order, contained in mahogany case, 18-8-¼-2-¾ inches, with ramrod cleaner, wrench, spare flints and bullet moulds. Price the outfit, $60.00.

8D. LOUIS XV FLINT POCKET PISTOL, with flat wood butt, silver wire inlaid. Center hammer, trigger guard, cannon barrel 2¾ inches, full length 6½ inches. Price $8.00.

Pair 1812 Holster Flint-lock Pistols, with the old saddle holster used by old Long Islanders in 1812-1814; vouched for; name given to buyer; total length is 15 inches, brass barrels 8½ inches, smooth bore 11-16, brass butt and mountings. Engraved on lock T. Ketland & Co., on the barrel London, with the old proof marks. Price for the two pistols, with holster, $38.00.

Tower Flint-lock Pistol. Fine order. Rare relic. Price, $18.00.

Ball's London-made Brass Barrel Flint-lock Pocket Pistols, with breech-loading screw barrels, full length 7 inches, barrels 3 inches, about ½-inch mouth bore, good order. Price singly, $9.50. Price for the pair $18.00.

Flint Blunderbuss Pistol, gold and silver inlaid, ornamented in relief work. Oriental characters. Engraved lock and mountings; 1-inch diameter barrel, increasing in diameter towards the muzzle to 1¼ inches. Fine walnut stock, beautiful piece of work; full length, 20½ inches. Price, $40.00.

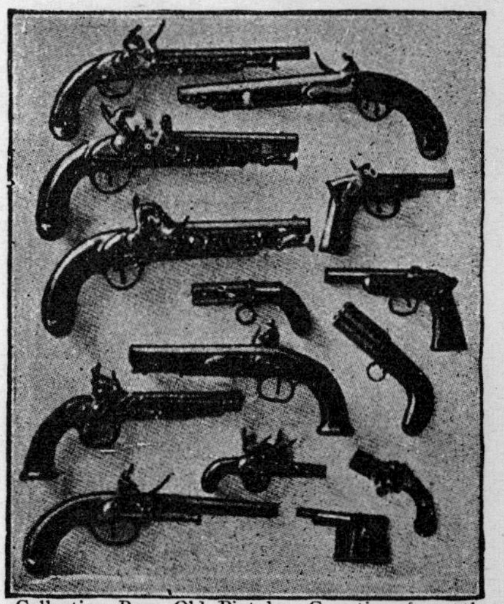

Collection Rare Old Pistols. Counting from the top down those that have the butt to the left, Nos. 1 to 7. Those that have the butt pointing to the right from top down, Nos. 8 to 14.

No. 1.—Officer's Old Flint-lock Pistol, in good serviceable order. Price, $15.00.

Nos. 2 and 4.—Pair Mounted Officer's Pistols, altered from flint to percussion lock, and retaining the part of the old flash pan mechanism as safety nipple device. Rare specimen. Price per pair, $18.00; singly, $10.00.

No. 3.—Leg Handle Pistol, percussion lock, good order. Price, $10.00.

No. 5.—Flint-lock Dragoon Pistol, hat-shaped butt, fine order. Price, $12.00.

No. 6.—Double-barrel Flint-lock Pistol. Price, $22.00.

No. 7.—Rare Pattern Flint-lock Marine Pistol, with metal lock. Price, $15.00.

No. 8.—Flint-lock Sporting Pistol, checkered stock, in fine order. Price, $14.00.

No. 9.—Leg Handle Percussion-lock Pistol, fine stock. Price, $10.00.

No. 10.—European Pepper Box Revolver. Price, $12.00.

No. 11.—Officer's Flint-lock Pistol, fine order; checkered walnut stock. Price, $17.00.

No. 12.—8-barrel Pepper Box Revolver. Sold.

No. 14.—Hand Repeating Pistols; by the pressing back of the finger loads and fires. Price, $15.00.

**3003A. Assorted lot of fine FLINT-LOCK PISTOLS ALL OVER A CENTURY OLD.** Our illustration shows but one of the several styles, some have stocks down to the muzzle and with several styles of bands both in brass and iron. Principally French types in the lot. They are all in A No. 1 cleaned condition and supplied with flints. The type illustrated was copied by Evans, an armorer, at Valley Forge, Pa., to enable him to make a lot for the U. S. Navy in 1812. We price this fine lot at $8.95 each, our selection. Extra flints at 10 cents each.

**10992-A. QUEEN ANNE FLINTLOCK POCKET PISTOL,** full length 7½ inches, removable cannon barrel 3¾ inches, round ball butt, ball or stud trigger without guard. Outside lock 3 inches long. Price $12.00. (See page 92.)

**3204-A. PAIR FRENCH FLINTLOCK PISTOLS, PERIOD LOUIS XIV,** undoubtedly made for some member of the royal household. Wood carved stocks, cannon barrels, part octagonal, 10½ inches long with large brass front sights. Heavy round butts with brass plate ornamented with floral designs and heads of man in two circles with large face on tip. Fancy brass ramrod tips (one ramrod missing) brass guard with head of man in circle, and with urn ends. Fancy lock straps with moon faces, and man in armour. 4½-inch etched locks, oval shape, swan neck hammers. Name plates are brass with long haired man in oval. Price $75 for pair.

**3204. PAIR TURKISH OFFICERS SIDE ARM FLINT LOCK PISTOLS.** Engraved barrels; with gold seal, with maker's name, with crest and star, silver engraving around the lock; carved and checkered stock. Gilt inlaid ornamentation work on the lock. Cut steel open work butt stock; handsome weapons; fine order. Price, $35.00 the pair.

**PAIR LONDON FLINTLOCK DUELLING PISTOLS,** 10-inch octagonal barrels, ⅝-inch smooth bore; full length, 16 inches; silver name plate and sidepin escutcheons. Ornamented pineapple guard plate and scroll work checkered grip stock; engraved mountings, "London," engraved on the barrels. Price, $45.00 the pair.

## SCOTCH PISTOLS WON FAME.

Before the advent of the American revolver the Scottish cities of Perth, Stirling and Dundee were great centers of the pistol-making industry. Scottish pistols were famous as far back as 1515, and were exported to many countries. There were at one time nearly one hundred concerns in Scotland engaged in the industry. —*N. Y. Tribune.*

**3233. ANCIENT SCOTCH TYPE FLINTLOCK POCKET PISTOL.** All metal; no wood used in its construction; loads from the muzzle. Rifle barrel; unscrews at the breech for quick loading; full length, 6½ inches; weight, 10 ounces; perfect order. Price, $25.00.

### MILITARY GOODS APPRAISERS.

We herewith tender our services to those who wish to have valuations placed upon second hand military goods, ancient or modern. We have frequently been called upon to serve in this capacity by the U. S. Treasury, Customs, Transportation Companies, Private Collectors and Others. Terms quoted on application.

**PFL. PAIR BRITISH PISTOLS.** One is FLINTLOCK, other altered to percussion. 6½-inch octagon barrels, with front and rear sights, maker's name set in silver: STAUDENMAYER, LONDON. Long checkered stocks, with very slight drop. Silver escutcheons, engraved guards with pineapple ends. 4-inch engraved locks marked: STAUDENMAYER, LONDON. Price for pair $25.00.

**PFL-1. PAIR BRITISH FLINTLOCK PISTOLS,** with 7-inch half octagon barrels, with 2 proof marks and maker's name: W. HENSHAW, STRAND, LONDON. 4½-inch BRASS locks marked: W. HENSHAW. Brass monogram ovals with initials: R.H.C. This type of pistol used by the British Naval officers. Fish tail butts, with heavy brass plates, all stock brass mounted. Brass guards with acorn ends. Price for pair $60.00.

**3249. PAIR FACSIMILE OF CAPT. JOHN SMITH'S, FOUNDER OF JAMESTOWN, SIDE ARM PISTOLS.** Ornamented butt plate; cap and name plate; ornamented silver mountings. Silver inlaid ornamentations on the stock; full length, 12½ inches; barrel, 5¼ inches; weight, 22 ounces. Old proof marks and seal of the maker, "R. Willoughby," with flag, antique cannon and other military decorations. In fair working order. Barrel unscrews for quick loading. Pistols are facsimile to those now in Virginia Museum as relics of Capt. John Smith. Price, $60.00 the pair.

**3249-A. PAIR BRITISH FLINTLOCK POCKET PISTOLS,** with barrels and frames of brass. Barrels are cannon shape, removable with 3 proof marks, frames marked: BUMFORD, LONDON. Round ball butts with silver mask butt plates, center hammers, brass guards. Large silver monogram plates. The unusual part of this pair of pistols is that the trigger guards slide FORWARD to act as safety catch. Period of 1760. Price for this fine pair is $34.00.

**3274. ANTIQUE FLINTLOCK POCKET PISTOL,** with antique outside lock. Concealed trigger which springs into position for firing upon cocking of the hammer. Engraved "H. W. Mortimer, 98 Fleet Street, gun maker to His Majesty." With military ornamentation of flags etc.; walnut checkered stock; in fine order. Price, $15.00. Mortimer was not only maker to the King, but was considered the king of old time gun makers.

**REVOLUTIONARY WAR DRAGOON LONG BARREL SIDE ARM FLINTLOCK PISTOL;** brass but; metal side belt hanger; full length, 20 inches; stamped with crown, tower, G. R., and broad arrow; ½-inch bore; serviceable order. Price, $20.00.

**3202. PAIR KETLAND FLINTLOCK ARMY PISTOLS,** in original leather holsters; locks stamped M. Ketland & Co.; barrel marked London. Brass mountings; full length, 15 inches; about 20-gauge smooth bore. No doubt relics of the British-American War of 1812. Hard wood used; stocks; serviceable order. Price for the outfit, $20.00.

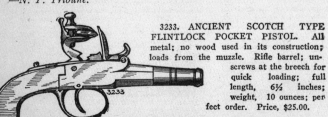

**PAIR 1760 REVOLUTIONARY WAR FLINTLOCK DRAGOON PISTOLS,** stamped Grice; 1760; crown G. R., and broad arrow marks; brass butt; 9-inch barrels; full length, 15½ inches; in serviceable order. Price, $30.00 the pair.

**3236. A BELGIAN MADE FLINTLOCK PISTOL,** facsimile of 3236, stock slightly split. Price, $

**MOUNTED DRAGOON FLINTLOCK PISTOL,** with swivel ramrod, ¾-inch smooth bore. Barrel made by J. Sampson. Easy working locks; scroll work stock; checkered grip; silver name plate; good order; full length, 12½ inches. Price, $17.50.

**1437.** Dragon Holster Pistol, American Revolutionary War Period. Made by D. Egg with British crown and "G R" on lock with three old proof marks on barrel. Brass mountings, with steel belt holder 7½ inches long, 11½ inch barrel, full length 19½ inches, working order. Price

**1437.** PAIR DRAGOON FLINTLOCK PISTOLS, with 13¼-inch barrel with flat top and large brass sights. Metal tipped wood rods, fish tail butts, fancy guards with acorn ends, 5½-inch locks. Full length 21 inches. Price for pair $19.00.

**8614A.** BRITISH YEOMAN'S FLINTLOCK PISTOL, with 12-inch barrel with three proof marks. Heavy round ball butt with brass plate. Stock and rod brass mounted. 5½-inch lock marked: R. WATKINS. Stock has opening for butt stock which is missing. Price $25.00.

**1420.** Pair New Flint Lock Brass Barrel Duelling pistols, made by "Henshaw Cambridge, England." Polished walnut carved stock with name plate, ⅝ smooth bore, 8 inch barrels, full length 14 inches, working order. Price the pair $32.00.

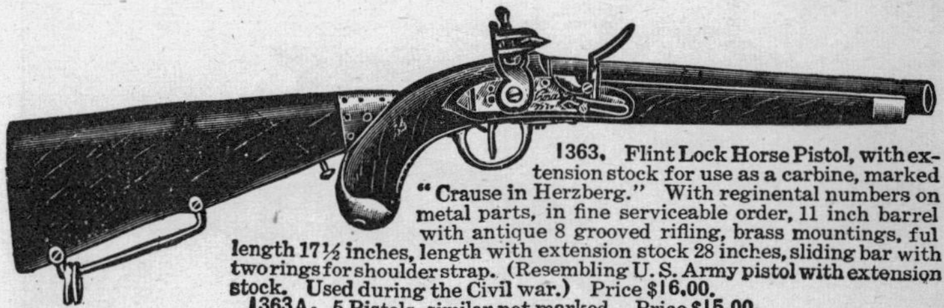

**1363.** Flint Lock Horse Pistol, with extension stock for use as a carbine, marked "Crause in Herzberg." With reginental numbers on metal parts, in fine serviceable order, 11 inch barrel with antique 8 grooved rifling, brass mountings. ful length 17½ inches, length with extension stock 28 inches, sliding bar with two rings for shoulder strap. (Resembling U. S. Army pistol with extension stock. Used during the Civil war.) Price $16.00.
**1363A.** 5 Pistols, similar not marked. Price $15.00.

Flint-lock Pistols, with brass butt in working order with flint. Some have maker's name on lock plate. Price, $14.00 each.

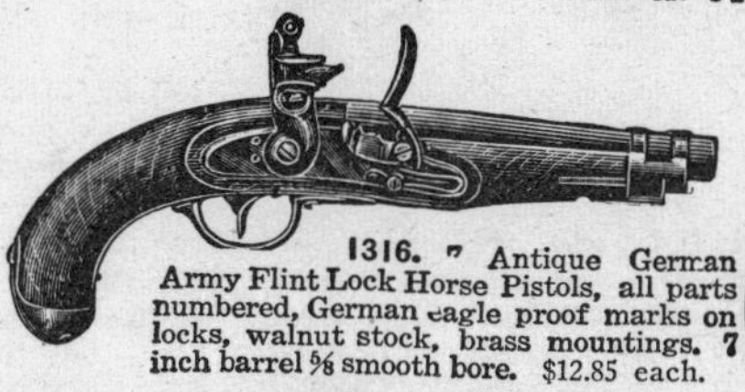

**1316.** ⁊ Antique German Army Flint Lock Horse Pistols, all parts numbered, German eagle proof marks on locks, walnut stock, brass mountings. 7 inch barrel ⅝ smooth bore. $12.85 each.

66 Aatique Flint Lock Army Pistols, in good working order, not cleaned. Price $14.85 each.

**No. 500.** Revolutionary War Fint-lock Brass Barrel Pistol, army size engraved "D Egg," with British crown; G R on barrel with two old British proof-marks; length of barrel 6½ inches, 9/16 inch smooth bore full length, 12½ inches, weight 1½ pounds. Many of Egg's makes of pistols were used by both British and American armies during the Revolutionary War. This lot came from the tower of London over half a entury ago. Price $15.00. Also some as above, stamped on lock Tower-Nock, on barrel H. N., with two old proof marks. Price $15.00.

Large Flint-lock Pistols, with ring in butt for lanyard. Complete with flint, in working order. Price, $10.00.

**1336.** French Flint Lock Dragoon Pistol with bronze frame, serviceable order: full length 13½ inch ⅝ smooth bore. Price, $10.00

**R85A.** 1 Short Flint-lock Pistol, with 5-inch heavy octagon barrel of large bore. Made by Eadon. Has round butt. Price, $12.40.

**R15.** 1 Pair Flint-lock Pocket Pistols, made by Twigg, London. Brass barrels and frames, center hammers. Barrels unscrew for quick loading and cleaning. Rare. Price, pair, $25.00.

**R15A.** 1 pair as above, with steel barrel, made by Wing, Braintree. Price, pair, $22.00.

**R42.** 1 Pair Flint-lock Pocket Pistols, by Moody. Cannon shaped barrels to unscrew. Wood butts are silver wire inlaid. Has combination tool used to unscrew barrels and also as rammer. Price, pair, $35.00.

**R40.** 1 pair as above, with tool, made by Richards. Price, pair, $35.00.

**No. 1251. PAIR EARLIEST TYPE FLINT LOCK PISTOLS,** made by Robert Harvey. With old proof marks on barrel. Barrel gradually increases from the muzzle to the breech, somewhat after the pattern of the late built up cannon. Barrel is 8 inches long, ⅝ smooth bore. Steel butt cap and side plate. Shows great age, but is in good order. Price a pair $35.00, singly $18.50.

**No. 1478. A PAIR OF OUTSIDE FLINT LOCK PISTOLS,** made by Ryan & Watson, with old G. P. gunmaker's proof mark; 3-inch barrel; concealed trigger. Full length, 8 inches; ½-inch smooth bore. Price the pair $18.00.

**10947.** PAIR JOSEPH EGG & SON, LONDON, ENGRAVED HOLSTER PISTOLS, percussion lock; octagonal twist steel 5-inch barrel; ⅝-inch smooth bore. Walnut stock; checkered grip; engraved mountings. Full length 10 inches. In working order. Price the pair, $11.50.

**10993K.** FLINTLOCK POCKET PISTOL, with 2-inch removable cannon barrel blued finish, center hammer with safety, secret trigger, round butt, finely checkered grip. Frame engraved with military trophies, and marked: HARCOURT, IPSWICH. Silver monogram plate. Pistol is like new. Price $13.00. (See page 92.)

British Flint Lock Tower of London Pistol, engraved on the lock "Tower and Crown, G. R.," which means "George's Reign as King of England"; in fine serviceable order; length, about 14 inches. Price $15.00.

One of King George's Soldier's Army Flint Lock Pistols. Has marked on the lock "G. R.," which means George's Reign. The British crown and broad arrow, which denote Government ownership. Tower, which shows that this pistol was proved at the old London Tower. Bore is ⅝ inch; full length, 16 inches, weight 1¾ pounds; barrel, 9 inches. $8.50.

**1502A.** A Turkish Army Flint Lock Holster Pistol, with swivel ramrod, with Turkish marks on locks, brass butt with ring, brass tip and guard, cleaned and polished, in working order, with flat walnut stock, smooth bore, full length 16 inches. Price $8.50.

**1364.** Flint Lock Horse Pistol, altered to percussion lock by adding the patent breech, the kind adopted by the U. S. in altering flint lock guns to percussion lock in 1842. These pistols have no extension stocks. Price $8.50. With name on locks $10.00.

**1461.** Ancient Flint Lock, with serpentine shaped hammer for holding the flint, barrel, ½ inch smooth bore, 10¾ inches long, full length, 17½ inches, old pattern hard wood, curly walnut stock, slightly worm eaten; in working order, one of the oldest flint lock pistols, hammer is patterned after the kind used in wheellocks, engraved butt, ornamented guard. Price $25.00.

**15. REVOLVING FLINTLOCK PISTOL DOUBLE BARREL,** single hammer. Note that this is the shape of illustration, but smaller size, length 11 inches, barrels 5½ inches, lock 2½ inches. Each barrel is fitted with striker and flash pan. Catch fitted in trigger guard is released to turn barrel for second shot. Oval butt, iron mounted. Revolving pistols are seldom found in this small size. This is a FRENCH pistol, period of LOUIS XIV. Price $75.00.

**R41.** 1 Pair Flint-lock Pocket Pistols, by Fermer, London. Cannon shaped barrels, 2 inch, to unscrew. Round butts have engraved brass caps and silver wire inlay. Price, pair, $25.00.

**R86.** 6 Flint-lock Pocket Pistols, with round removable barrels, center hammers and concealed triggers, without guard:
1 by Parsons-Salisbury, $6.00.
1 by Edridol-Bingdon, $6.00.
1 by Reynolds-Coventry, $6.00.
1 without name, $5.50.
1 with brass frame, by Palmer-Rochester, $7.50.
1 by Nock-London, $6.00.

**R19.** 1 French Flint-lock Pocket Blunderbuss Pistol, with 6-inch brass barrel, brass frame, side ramrod and 5-inch Spring-dagger bayonet. Price, $35.00.

**R29.** 1 as above, with 4-inch barrel and 3½-inch spring bayonet. No ramrod. Price, $30.00.

**1465.** Pair of Old Flint Duelling Pistols Geo. III period, stamped on lock in triangle, MBR, flatted on top barrel, for quick sighting. 11/16 smooth bore, 7¼ inch barrel full length, 13¼ inches, polished hard wood curly walnut stock; knob shaped club butt, brass covered with extended straps on side, ornamented brass mountings, fine locks, original hammer replaced on one pistol, steel horn tip, ram rod and fore-end; in working order. Price $30.00. the pair.

**2425.** PAIR FLINT-LOCK DUELLING PISTOLS in Case, with 9-inch Round browned barrels, with three British proof marks. 4½-inch locks, marked "W. Allport." Highly polished hardwood stocks, plain finish, with silver name plates. Brass trigger guards, ornamented. Set has 4-inch copper powder flask. Price for pair, $65.00.

**1474.** H. Nock, London, engraved on barrel and lock of Officer's model flint lock Holster Pistol, pattern used by King George III Officers in war of the American Revolution, barrel 9 inches in length, ⅝ inch smooth bore, three old British proof marks on barrel, length 15 inches, walnut stock, working order. Price $14.00.

**1418.** Pair of Flint Lock French Duelling Pistols. full length 14 inches, 8 inch barrel, carved walnut stock, silver name plate, with scroll ornamented border, steel cap butt, Engraved side plate, makers name on lock "Papier Raris," ramrods. missing. Price $40.00, similar to No. 1420.

**1418.** Ancient Flint Lock Brass Barrel Duelling Pistol, made by D. Moore London, with old proof mark on barrel, ornamented brass mountings and name plate, brass butt plate with man's face on butt cap, length of barrel 8 inches, full length 14 inches, offered in working order. Price $18.00, similar to No. 1420.

Antique Flint Lock Brass Barrel Duelling Pistol made by Heylen, Cornhill, London. 7½ inch, barrel ⅝ inch bore, brass mountings, carved walnut stock, has had considerable wear, fair working order. Price $14.50.

**1421.** Brass Barrel Flint Lock Duelling Pistol, London, old proof marks on barrel, silver guard and rod holder, full length 14 inches, 8¾ inch barrel, working order, guard needs repairing, offered as is $26.00.

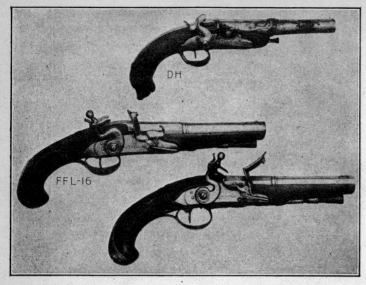

DH. PAIR FRENCH PERCUSSION PISTOLS, altered from flint-lock. 6-inch barrels, 3½-inch locks, one marked: ROUSSELY, the other: PERIGUEUX. 3½-inch side straps fitted with 3¾-inch belt or sash hooks. Long buttstocks carved in shape of DOGS HEADS. Small trigger guards fitted on strap which ends in barrel band over half length stocks. This is a very fine pair. Price for pair $30.00.

FFL-1. FRENCH FLINTLOCK PISTOL, EARLY TYPE, FULL LENGTH 21½ inches, cannon barrel 14½ inch, etched, oval butt, brass mounted, brass guard and strap. 4½-inch lock marked with stars and letters: M M. Period LOUIS XIV. Price $20.00.

FFL-2. FRENCH FLINTLOCK PISTOL, wood carved stock, brass mounted butt, cannon barrel with flat top rib marked ONTONRDU, length 13¼ inches, full length 20½ inches. 5-inch lock with name partly erased. Period LOUIS XIV. Price $19.50.

FFL-5. LOUIS XIV FRENCH FLINTLOCK PISTOL, evidently carried by Army officer. Light weight, with narrow butt with etched German silver butt plate. Black wood stock elaborately carved with fleur de lis designs. Hand grip inlaid with silver wire in spiral, circle and diamond shaped designs. 9¾-inch cannon barrel, with raised flat rib, with inscription. 4¼-inch etched lock. This is a very fine speci-men. Price $25.00.

FFL-6. LOUIS XV FRENCH FLINTLOCK PISTOL, with carved wood stock, cannon barrel 9½ inch, 4¼-inch engraved lock, round brass butt. Full length 15 inches. Price $14.00.

FFL-7. LOUIS XIV FRENCH FLINTLOCK PISTOL, with 5¼-inch curved lock with swan neck hammer, iron butt, trigger guard with urn end, scroll design lock strap. Brass ramrod guide and wood ramrod with brass tip. 8½-inch cannon barrel with short top rib. Full length 15½ inches. Price $15.00.

FFL-8. FRENCH FLINTLOCK PISTOLS, with heavy brass butt, plain brass side plate and ornamented guard with urn end. Half octagonal barrel 10½ inch with brass front sight. 4¾-inch lock. Wood chipped out near lock. Price $10.00.

FFL-10. LOUIS XIV FLINTLOCK PISTOL, with SPANISH type, out-side lock, 4¼ inch, etched. Brass butt ornamented with fleur de lis, brass lock strap with military designs, wide brass guard with urn end. 8¾-inch part octagonal barrel, slightly belled at muzzle. 2 armourers marks on barrel, also fluer de lis inlaid in silver. Brass ramrod guides, with wood ramrod brass tipped. This is a very fine piece. Price $28.00.

FFL-11. LOUIS XV DOUBLE BARREL FLINTLOCK PISTOL, length 13 inches, barrels 7¾-inches, brass front sight, 4-inch lock, right and left, flat oval butt brass mounted. Very wide trigger guard, brass ramrod guides. Double barrel pistols of this size at this period are rare. Price $30.00.

FFL-12. LOUIS XV FLINTLOCK PISTOL, with 4½-inch SPANISH outside lock, cannon barrel 9½ inch, bore 11/16th inches. Checkered grip, flat butt with heavy brass ornament. Wide guard of brass with urn end. Brass ramrod. Price $18.00.

FFL-13. FRENCH FLINTLOCK PISTOL OF FIRST EMPIRE. Length 15 inches, barrel octagon, 9¾ inches, with slight bell at muzzle, two leaf rear sight. (Front sight missing.) Barrel pin escutcheons are of silver. Brass tipped wood rod, checkered grip, round butt with carved wood rose. Wide guard, 4½-inch lock marked: FORIR. Swan neck hammer, extra heavy battery. Price $27.50.

FFL-14. PAIR LOUIS XVI FLINTLOCK PISTOLS, 3½-inch flat lock, 6¼-inch octagon barrel, with rear sight, not made with front sight, checkered grip, flat butt with metal plate, guard with urn end. Full length 11¼ inches. Barrel has maker's mark. Price for pair $40.00.

FFL-15. FINE FLINTLOCK PISTOL, with 9¾-inch octagon barrel, inlaid in silver with maker's name: I. CHRISTOPH KUCHENREITER, with silver wire inlaid, with armourer's mark in gold, with gold touchhole. All metal parts gold plated. Oval butt very thin with heavy butt plate, fancy guard and ramrod guides, checkered grip, with attachment opening for shoulder stock. 4-inch flat lock with SAFETY catch, swan neck hammer, and marked: JOP CHRISTOPH KUCHENREITER in script. This is a very fine piece. Price $50.00.

FFL-16. PAIR LOUIS XIV FLINTLOCK PISTOLS, in fine order, very handsome pair. Length 13½ inches, 7-inch barrels, part octagonal barrel, with front sight of silver, horn tipped wood ramrods, carved wood stock, grips inlaid with silver wire with owner's mark, round knob butts, with metal plates, 5-inch locks, one marked: LAMBERT, the other marked: DIT BIRON. Swan neck hammers, extra heavy batteries, long guards with acorn ends. Wood stocks horn tipped. Price for pair $100.00.

FFL-17. PAIR LOUIS XVI FLINTLOCK PISTOLS, length 9¾ inches, barrels half octagonal 4⅞ inches, bore ⅝ inches. 3½-inch locks, round butts with brass plates, steel rods, long guards with acorn ends. See No. 01039 on page 99 for shape and style. Price for pair $24.00.

FFL-18. PAIR LOUIS XIV FLINTLOCK POCKET PISTOLS, 8¼ inches long, 4-inch, octagonal barrels, with etched designs that have been gold plated, grooves in tangs for sighting, silver wire inlaid grips, round butts with plates, 3½-inch locks, wide trigger guards with urn ends. Shape and style of No. 01039 on page 99. Price for pair $32.00.

FFL-19. FRENCH FLINTLOCK PISTOL, FIRST EMPIRE, with 4-inch lock marked: M. BERLEUR. 6¾-inch octagonal barrel with bell muzzle. Checkered grip, flat butt with ornamented plate, rear and front sights, silver monogram oval, wide guard with urn end. Price $14.00. See No. 2, page 87.

FFL-20. FRENCH FLINTLOCK PISTOL, RENAISSANCE PERIOD, in fine order, length 11¾ inches, octagonal barrel 6⅛ inches with bell muzzle. Checkered grip, flat butt with plate, wide guard with urn end. Ornamented lock screw escutcheons. 4¼-inch flat lock. Similar to No. 2 on page 87. Price $10.00.

FFL-21. LOUIS XVI FLINTLOCK PISTOL, similar to No. FFL-19 and 20. Length 9 inches, octagonal barrel 4¾ inches with bell muzzle, front and rear sights. Price $13.50.

FFL-22. FRENCH FLINTLOCK PISTOL, RENAISSANCE PERIOD, similar to No. FFL-21 with 4¼-inch octagonal barrel, marked: CANON inlaid in gold, two, proof marks, 3¼-inch lock. Price $9.00.

FFL-23. LOUIS XV FLINTLOCK BELT PISTOL, with 4¾-inch cannon barrel, half octagonal barrel, round butt with brass plate, long brass guard with acorn end. 4¼-inch lock, iron rod, brass lock strap. Price $8.00.

FFL-23. LOUIS XIV FLINTLOCK PISTOL, with stock of Circassian walnut with WOOD trigger guard in same piece. Half octagonal cannon barrel, 4½-inch marked: GREZEPATH DYCK. Wood rod horn tipped. Price $12.50.

FFL-25. FRENCH GENDARMERIE FLINTLOCK PISTOL, with muzzle band, musket type, short round butt with plate, long trigger guard, 5-inch round barrel marked: 1812. Guard, lock strap and stock marked with crown and other marks including date: 1812. 4-inch lock with maker's name, brass flash pan. Full length 10 inches. Price $7.50.

FFL-26. FRENCH FLINTLOCK POCKET PISTOL, with large oval butt with brass plate. Brass guard with urn end, 3¾-inch barrel with flat top. 4¼-inch flat lock. Price $8.50.

FFL-27. LADY'S MINIATURE FLINTLOCK PISTOL, FRENCH, style of horse pistol, with 4¾-inch cannon barrel with front sight, 3½-inch lock with outside safety catch, oval butt. Price $10.00.

FFL-29. LOUIS XV FLINTLOCK POCKET PISTOL, with wood carved stock, oval butt with pointed plate, 4-inch cannon barrel with one proof mark, ornamental lock strap and guard, silver name plate with crown, 3-inch lock marked: MA GIVRATT. On account of stock cracks we offer this at low price of $9.00.

FFL-28. FRENCH FLINT POCKET PISTOL, with cannon shaped barrel, 3¼ inches, 3-inch lock, round wood stock, silver wire inlaid, trigger guard with acorn end. Price $6.50.

# FLINTLOCK PISTOLS

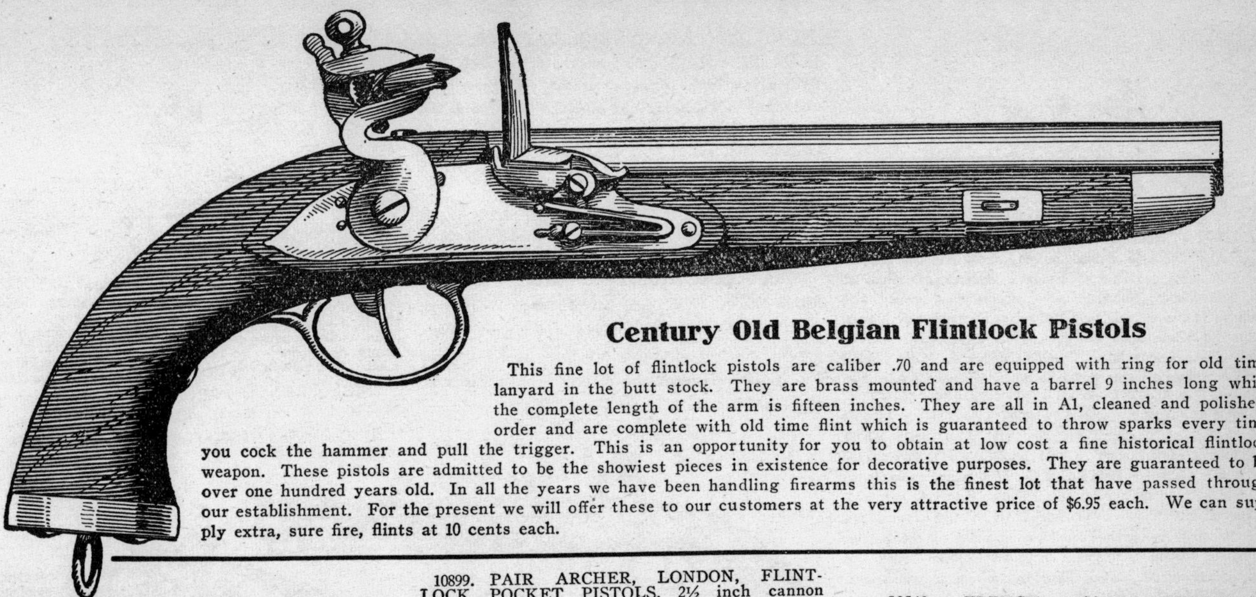

## Century Old Belgian Flintlock Pistols

This fine lot of flintlock pistols are caliber .70 and are equipped with ring for old time lanyard in the butt stock. They are brass mounted and have a barrel 9 inches long while the complete length of the arm is fifteen inches. They are all in A1, cleaned and polished, order and are complete with old time flint which is guaranteed to throw sparks every time you cock the hammer and pull the trigger. This is an opportunity for you to obtain at low cost a fine historical flintlock weapon. These pistols are admitted to be the showiest pieces in existence for decorative purposes. They are guaranteed to be over one hundred years old. In all the years we have been handling firearms this is the finest lot that have passed through our establishment. For the present we will offer these to our customers at the very attractive price of $6.95 each. We can supply extra, sure fire, flints at 10 cents each.

---

10897. PAIR FLINTLOCK TRAVELING PISTOLS, stamped "Wibraham, London." Hinged ramrods. Smooth top, 6-inch barrel, 11-16 inch bore. Silver name plate. Walnut stock. Checkered grip. Fine easy working locks. Engraved mountings. From the Brett collection. Price $25.00.

8625-B. PAIR ANCIENT SPANISH FLINT-LOCK PISTOLS, with OUTSIDE LOCK. Silver medallion on butt and guard. Cannon shaped 7½ inch barrels, 11/16 inch smooth bore. On the lock is engraved "Torrento," and on the barrel the maker's seal, "Leo Torren." Period about 1750. Price the pair $3[illegible].00.

10130A. LEG HANDLE PISTOL, with under hammer, from London collection. In fine order. Price, $6.85.

10438. PAIR CURIOUS SHAPED FLINT-LOCK CANNON BARREL HOLSTER PISTOLS. ornamented silver butt plate, Birmingham goldsmith's hall mark of the year 1776. Made by Binney, of London; 5½ inch barrel, ⅝ inch smooth bore. Barrel unscrews for quick loading. Silver inlaid wire on stock. Silver name plate engraved with Squirrel R. P. C. Rare old weapons The pair $55.00.

10173. TWELFTH ROYAL LANCERS B SQUADRON No. 30 FLINTLOCK HORSE PISTOL. Lock stamped with Royal Crown G. R. (George III.) Tower and British broad arrow marks, regimental number on brass butt. Swivel safety ramrod. In good serviceable order. Battle relic of the Twelfth Lancers. Price $15.00.

10533. LONDON MADE FLINTLOCK PISTOL, with gold inlaid ornamental crescent and nine stars. Stock and fore end covered with inlaid silver wire; ornamental work silver side plate. Lock engraved in script letters, "Clarke, Cheapside, London." Full length 15 inches, ⅝ inch smooth bore. Very fine gun, evidently made for some Oriental chieftain. Price $25.00.

10534. PAIR FLINTLOCK BRASS CANNON SHAPED BARREL POCKET PISTOLS. Checkered walnut stock. Center hammer and flash pan. Full length 6½ inches. In working order. Price the pair $18.50.

10544. BRONZE BLUNDERBUSS BARREL, WITH ELEPHANT SHAPED BELL MOUTH. Length 17½ inches; smallest diameter at the breech 1½ inches. The bell is 3⅛ inches by 1⅞ inches. Barrel is complete with tang for fastening to stock. In fine order. Price for this rare old barrel, $14.00.

10535. FRENCH FLINTLOCK POCKET PISTOL. Lock engraved "L. Hostandois, a Paris." Engraved silver name and butt plate, cap and side guards. Carved walnut stock. Gilt engraved barrel. In working order. Full length 7 inches. A little beauty. Price $18.50.

**When ordering special articles allow second choice when possible.**

10428. CURIOUS PATTERN POCKET FLINTLOCK PISTOL, with gun metal bronze blunderbuss barrel. Used about period 1760; somewhat similar to illustration No. 557, page 68. 3 inch barrel, 11/16 inch diameter across the bell mouth, safety hammer. Price $9.85.

10993J. PAIR FLINTLOCK POCKET PISTOLS, with 2½-inch cannon barrels, removable, round wood butts, finely checkered grips, center hammers, with safety catches, secret triggers, engraved frames, marked: WOOD, YORK. Price for pair $27.00. (See No. 10993, page 92.)

10899. PAIR ARCHER, LONDON, FLINT-LOCK POCKET PISTOLS, 2½ inch cannon shaped barrels, ½ inch smooth bore, center hammer, period about 1770. Good order. Price the pair $17.50.

HC. SWISS FLINTLOCK HAND CANNON, pistol shape, weight 7½ pounds. 15½ inches long, octagonal barrel 8¼ inches, bore half inch, outside measurement 1½ inches. Wood stock, two 1½-inch brass bands over barrel, 6¾-inch lock strap, 6¾-inch lock, no trigger guard, oval butt with brass plate, with opening for extension stock Pistol probably used on wall or through loop slot in fort. Price $20.00.

10524. FLINTLOCK NAVAL PISTOL, engraved "Anode 1814" on the outside lock mechanism, with GOLD SEAL, CROWN AND FLEUR DE LIS, with belt hanger as used by naval officer. Silver front sight. Decorated barrel. Full length 12 inches. Checkered walnut stock. Price $18.50.

18894. PAIR FRENCH FLINTLOCK PISTOLS, with elaborate relief. Silver ornamented markings, French Hall silver proof marked; 6½ inch barrel, 9/16 inch smooth bore. Silvered wire inlaid ebony stocks, etched gilt ornamented barrels. Price the pair, $30.00.

2165. 1730 period silver-mounted Flintlock Duelling Pistols, made by Tatham, London. 9-inch octagonal barrel, smooth bore; ramrod rib engraved lock and mountings; checkered walnut stock. No doubt these are old historical pistols, as they show evidence of having been extensively used during the hundred years in which flintlocks were in vogue. Bargain price, $40.00.

10890. PAIR HOLSTER FLINTLOCK PISTOLS, probably French made, 7 inch barrels, ½ inch smooth bore. Brass ball butt plate. Guard bow on one pistol missing, otherwise in good working order. Price the pair, $14.00.

10891. PAIR FLINTLOCK POCKET PISTOLS with concealed triggers. Center hammer, 2 inch barrels. Silver name plate with monogram "C. B. M." Curly walnut stock. Brass frame engraved "P. Bond, 45 Cornhill, London." Good condition. $15.00 the pair.

10892. EAST INDIA CO. FLINTLOCK PISTOL, dated 1810, with the company's insignia on the lock plate; 9 inch barrel. Used by the mounted troops in India. In working order. $8.85.

11000. BRASS BARREL FLINT LOCK HOLSTER PISTOL, full length 15 inches, made by Barber, London, period 1760. Officers' model, perhaps used by British officer in the American Revolutionary War. Brass mounting. Walnut stock. Good order. Price $20.00.

11001. ARMY OFFICER'S MODEL FLINT BRASS BARREL HOLSTER PISTOL, engraved "H. W. Mortimer & Son, Gun Makers to His Majesty" (George III). Full length 14½ inches. Extra heavy round barrel, about ⅝ inch smooth bore. Brass mountings. Hammer safety. Fine easy working lock. Walnut stock. Similar to No. 8630, page 348. Price $25.00.

11002. BRASS BARREL FLINT LOCK HOLSTER PISTOL. Hall marked silver mountings. AMERICAN REVOLUTIONARY WAR PERIOD; made by Grice, London. Full length 13½ inches. Silver name plate, rose ornamentation. Silver guard plate and bow; ornamented thimbles and side plates. A beauty, as well as a RARE WEAPON, with BRASS BARREL AND LOCK. Price $40.00.

10540. FRENCH DOUBLE FLINTLOCK PISTOL, side locks engraved "F, Bon, Monte Lunai." Silver name plate, engraved steel mountings. In working order. Full length 12 inches. Price $22.50.

10541. DOUBLE BARREL FLINTLOCK PISTOL, side locks. Carved walnut stock. Steel mountings. Engraved barrel. Full length 14½ inches; ⅝ inch smooth bore. Working order. Price $20.00.

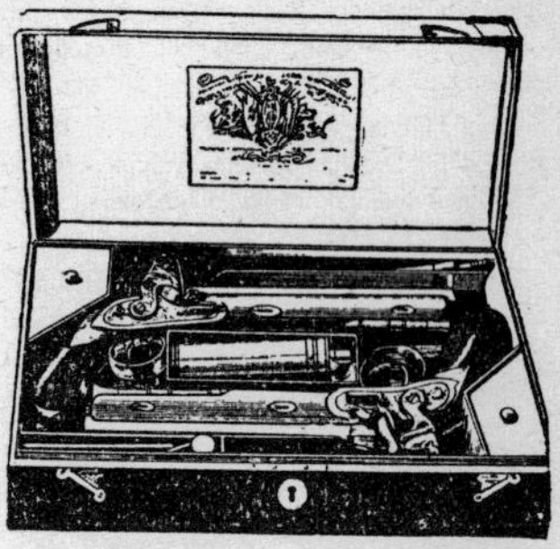

FB6. FINE PAIR FLINTLOCK DUELLING PISTOLS. Once owned by member of Royalty, as shown by inlaid silver crown and three stars. Total length 15½ inches. Barrel half octagon with front and rear sights. Muzzles slightly BELLED. Marked with two early British proof marks and word: Manchester is script. Lock marked: Aston, and has safety catch. Hard wood rammer with ivory tip. Ornamental trigger guard with acorn end, and decorated with scroll of drum, flags and lances. Heavy round butts with face of man with parted hair and ruffed collar, with military scrolls at sides. Silver name plates, Shield form, with letter C. Stocks of hard wood, partly inlaid with silver wire. All metal parts ornamented. Price, $150.00 for the pair.

Pair of French Duelling Pistols, with percussion lock, fluted steel engraved barrel, 9 inches in length, about ⅝-inch smooth bore; fine, easy working locks, relief hammer, locks and guards, carved stock. Good, second-hand, serviceable order. Price, $28.00.

10421. BRITISH DOUBLE BARREL FRENCH FLINTLOCK PISTOL, by Layben. Bird head walnut butt stock. Barrels are side by side, 3½ ins. long, ½-inch smooth bore; in working order. Price $14.85.

10421A. OLD ENGLISH DOUBLE BARREL SIDE LOCK PISTOL. By Jovar, London. Checkered grip, walnut stock, double triggers, double locks; barrels are side by side, 7 inches long, ⅝-inch smooth bore. Rare type. Price $18.85.

The United States Flag, adopted June 14, 1776, is claimed to be the oldest National Flag.

| | |
|---|---|
| Spain, 1785. | Portugal, 1830. |
| France, 1794. | Italy, 1840. |
| Great Britain, 1801. | Germany, 1870 |
| Norway and Sweden, 1817. | China, 1872. |

—Prebles' History U. S. Flag.

# Assorted Pistols

11038. CULLODEN BATTLEFIELD 1746 PISTOL. Double barrel side by side with 2 hammers, 2 secret triggers. Barrels are rifled at the muzzle for unscrewing from the frame. Hammer safety. Walnut stock, checkered grip. Engraved mountings. Made by Clemson Salof. Silver name plate engraved "CULLODEN MOOR 1746." Card attached to this pistol in noted English Collection says: "THIS PISTOL WAS USED IN THE BATTLE OF CULLODEN MOOR, FOUGHT ON THE 31ST OF JANUARY, 1746, BETWEEN THE ENGLISH AND SCOTCH, THE LAST BATTLE FOUGHT ON THE SOIL OF GREAT BRITAIN." This pistol came from the Mark Field collection. Full length 8 inches. In well preserved order. This pistol no doubt found its way to an English collection as a relic of the battle, taken by some victorious English soldier from the body of some Highland Chieftain, whose blood stained the heather fighting in defense of Scotland and "Bonnie Prince Charlie." Only an officer of high rank would carry such a weapon. Had it been offered at the sale in 1897 of Culloden House relics, it would have brought over 200 guineas ($1,000). Before sending it back for sale in Scotland we offer it to our American customers at the bargain price of $500.00.

R67. 1 BRITISH FLINT-LOCK HOLSTER PISTOL with 6-inch extra heavy large bore round barrel, marked Smith, London. Swivel ramrod, checkered butt. Price, $17.40.

R72. 1 QUEEN ANNE FLINT-LOCK PISTOL with large brass butt and brass trigger guard. Round barrel 8½ inches, marked London. Made by B. Brooks. Price, $25.00.

R74. BRITISH FLINT-LOCK HOLSTER PISTOL with extra long round barrel, marked London. Large brass butt, brass trigger guard and brass name plate. Made by Hadley. Price, $30.00.

10993. PAIR HIGHLY FINISHED FLINT POCKET PISTOLS, by Bailey, London. Full lengsh 6½ iuches. Center hammer and flash pan. Hammer safety. Silver name plate. Fine checkered grip. Walnut stock. Frame engraved with battle trophies. Blued steel barrel. Secret triggers. Price the pair, $25.00.

1537D. CONCEALED TRIGGER PERCUSSION LOCK PISTOL, 3 inch twist steel barrel, 7-16 RIFLED BORE, engraved frame. Trigger folds under the lock and springs out into position at the cocking of the hammer. Fluted walnut stock. Ornamented metal butt cap. Good order. Price $5.00.

1537B. SIMILAR PISTOL, with plain stock. Price $5.00.

1537C. CONCEALED TRIGGER PERCUSSION LOCK PISTOLS, barrels are of different lengths. All are in working order, but rusty, stocks marked showing much wear. Captured by Italian Government Troop from Brigands. Price $3.25 each.

10999. PAIR FLINTLOCK HOLSTER PISTOLS with BRASS barrels, 7-inch, round, marked: D. EGG, LONDON. Round butt with brass plates. Long brass trigger guards and side plates. 4½-inch locks marked: D. EGG, with CROWN over G. R. Price for pair $35.00.

11040. U. S. A. FLINTLOCK PISTOL marked U. S. R. Johnson, Midddleton, Conn., 1841." Swivel ramrod for mounted service. In goodorder. Price $20.00.

At U. S. auction sales held in January 1886 at Benicia Arsenal, Calif., we purchased 800 of these flintlock Dragoon pistols entirely new, in the original cases, having been sent to California when Benicia Arsenal was first established in 1851. We began the sale of these pistols at 78 cents, later at $1.50, then $5.00, $20.00, and now at $15.00. They are getting very rare.

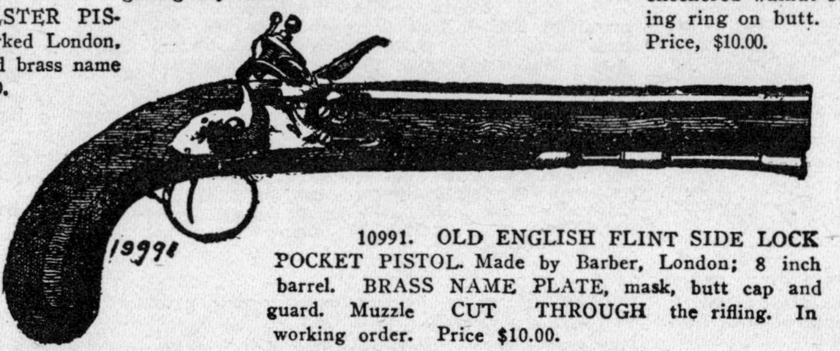

10991. OLD ENGLISH FLINT SIDE LOCK POCKET PISTOL. Made by Barber, London; 8 inch barrel. BRASS NAME PLATE, mask, butt cap and guard. Muzzle CUT THROUGH the rifling. In working order. Price $10.00.

10434. OLD ENGLISH FLINT PISTOL, 13-inch barrel. Fine chased ornamented barrel, lock, butt and guards in relief steel mountings. About the period 1750. In working order. Price $22.50.

10993H. BELGIAN FLINTLOCK POCKET PISTOL, similar to No. 10993E, with 1½-inch barrel, 4¾ inches long. Price $8.50.

11036. SINGLE FLINT HAMMER DOUBLE BARREL PISTOL, Barrels, are smooth bore, about 40-calibre are side by side. Sliding cover on the left side shuts off the left pan. Center hammer which throws the flint sparks into both pans. Polished walnut stock inlaid with ornamental silverwire. Silver mask butt cap. Engraved frame. Old English proof marks period about 1750. Full length 9¾ inches. Rare type. Price $35.00.

10432. FRENCH FLINTLOCK POCKET PISTOL. Engraved on the barrel 1766. Ornamented metal ball shape butt plate. 3¼-inch cannon shaped barrel. Working order. Price $16.00.

10992. PAIR SIDE LOCK FLINT POCKET PISTOLS. Full length 8 inches. Old London gun maker's proof mark. Cut rifling at the muzzle. Polished walnut stock. Engraver lock and mountings. Cannon shaped barrel. Fine order. Price $33.00 the pair.

10824. CAPTURED BRIGAND ITALIAN PISTOL, with nipple at base of the barrel, center hammer, evidently home made. Working order; rusty. Price, $3.85.

10611. "GOBERINO DE NICARAGUA" marked on officer's model flint-lock army pistol; 5-inch barrel; checkered walnut stock. Large front sight. Carrying ring on butt. About 40 calibre. In fine order. Price, $10.00.

10433. FRENCH FLINTLOCK HOLSTER PISTOL. Rifled. Chased brass mountings. Birds head shaped butt stock. Ornamental brass mask plate on the butt and guards. Carved walnut stock. 8¼-inch barrel, ⅝-inch rifle bore. Working order. Rare old weapon. Price $22.00.

10499. DOUBLE BARREL FLINTLOCK POCKET PISTOL with CONCEALED TRIGGERS. Barrels are side by side. Hammer and flash pan in the center. Engraved frame, ornamented ebony butt (plate missing). Full length 7 inches. In working order. Price $17.50.

10714B. DOUBLE BARREL PERCUSSION LOCK PISTOL, fluted steel 7-inch barrel, 32 calibre smooth bore; silvered finish lock and mountings; name plate; gilt cap box. Beautifully carved stock with hunting scene. Fine order. Price, $17.00.

1071C. DOUBLE BARREL PERCUSSION LOCK PISTOL, similar to 10714B, but with very fine twist-steel barrel marked "Troados de Aco." Price, $17.00.

10714. PAIR DOUBLE BARREL PERCUSSION LOCK PISTOLS, 8-inch fluted steel barrel. Full length 13 inches. Relief engraved silvered finish lock and mountings. Gilt letters on the barrel "Ac Tino." Silver name plate; ebony stock handsomely carved with metal point checkering. Gilt metal covered cap box and butt plate. Fine order. Bargain price for this pair of double barrel pistols, $32.00.

10822C. SINGLE BARREL CAP AND BALL PISTOL, 7½-inch octagonal barrel. Price, $2.85.

10825. PAIR ARMY SIDE ARM PISTOLS, percussion lock; 7½-inch barrels; ⅝-inch smooth bore; brass mountings; walnut stock; brass butt cap. Used, serviceable order. Price the pair, $8.00; singly, $4.50.

1537D. CONCEALED TRIGGER PERCUSSION LOCK PISTOL, with curious pattern hammer. Captured from Italian Brigand. Price, $5.00.

10820. DOUBLE BARREL PERCUSSION PISTOL, with Single Hammer Trigger and Nipple; 3-inch twist-steel barrel; engraved frame and mountings; walnut stock; checkered grip; silver name plate; cap box in this butt. Side lever controlling the fire from the cap to the lower barrel. In good working order. Price, $12.50.

10500. PAIR FRENCH FLINTLOCK CARRIAGE PISTOLS, full length 9 inches. CORONET and cross stamped on the barrel. Engraved mountings. Coronet and coat of arms on the stock. Relief ornamented butt cap and mountings. Carved walnut stocks, working order. For this pair of fine BEAUTIFUL pistols that have evidently belonged to some French Nobleman entitled to use coronet, price $45.00.

10430. FLINTLOCK HOLSTER PISTOL by R. Clark, period 1765. Somewhat similar to 8671, page 347, but with ramrod thimbles under the barrel. Old Birmingham proof marks. 7-inch barrel, ⅝-inch smooth bore. Walnut stock. In working order. Price $17.50.

10993A. BRITISH FLINT POCKET PISTOL, flat stock with silver monogram plate, 2¼-inch removable barrel, full length 6¼ inches, frame decorated with flag designs and marked: POOD CONWAL. Center hammer with safety catch for hammer and pan. Price $10.00.

10993B. BRITISH FLINT POCKET PISTOL, similar to No. 10993A, with 3-inch barrel, decorated frame marked: CALVERT LEEDS. Price $10.00.

10993D. FRENCH FLINT POCKET PISTOL, with bronze frame and barrel. 2¼-inch barrel, frame marked: IEAN GUIOTS, ABLEIGNE. Full length 6 inches. Center hammer, safety catch, secret trigger. Flat wood stock repaired. Price $12.00.

10993E. BELGIAN FLINTLOCK POCKET PISTOL, with proof mark on 2¾-inch round barrel. Full length 6½ inch, checkered flat stock inlaid with fine silver tacks. Flower decorated frame, center hammer with catch, secret trigger. Price $7.75.

10993F. BELGIAN FLINT POCKET PISTOL, similar to No. 10993E, with 2-inch barrel, full length 6¼ inches. Price $8.50.

10993G. BELGIAN FLINT POCKET PISTOL, like No. 10993E, with checkered stock without silver inlay. 1¾-inch barrel, 5½ inches long. Price $7.50.

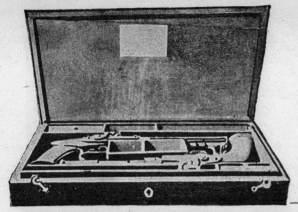

**R44.** 1 OLD ENGLISH FLINT-LOCK PISTOL with double barrels superposed. The lever on side turns one vent in the pan together with priming powder for shooting second barrel. Made by H. W. Mortimer & Co., London. Price, $25.00.

**R45.** One as above, with brass barrel and frame, by Jones & Co., London. Price, $25.00.

**R46.** One like R45, made by P. Bond, Cornhill, London. Price, $30.00.

No. 119. DAGGER KNIFE PISTOL, in good order. Can be sold only to museum or vouched for collector. $8.00.

**R127.** 1 PAIR PERCUSSION DUELLING PISTOLS in case with mould and flask. Octagon barrels 9 inches; saw-handle grip. Made by Richardson, London. Price, $65.00.

**R85B.** 1 PAIR FLINT-LOCK DUELLING PISTOLS in case with combination flask. Round barrels 7 inches. Plain round butts. Made by I. Barton, London. Price, $55.00.

**R131.** 1 PAIR PERCUSSION PISTOLS with 10-inch octagon barrels. Engraved locks and trigger guards, checkered. Made by H. Nock, London. Price, $30.00.

**R130.** 1 PAIR PERCUSSION PISTOLS with 8-inch octagon barrels, back action. Engraved locks, checkered grips, flat butt, swivel ramrods. Made by Gillett, Bristol. Price, $25.00.

**R129.** 1 PAIR PERCUSSION PISTOLS with 8½-inch round barrels, swivel ramrods, checkered grips. Made by Collins, London. Price, $25.00.

**R70.** 1 PAIR FLINT-LOCK PISTOLS with 6-inch brass octagon barrels. Engraved locks, swivel ramrods, checkered grips, lion head brass butts. Locks marked BOSTON; barrels marked WAKEFIELD. Price, $50.00.

**R68.** 1 PAIR FLINT-LOCK PISTOLS, by Inland Revenue Officer. Brass barrels 5½ inches; one marked I. R. 84; other I. R. 86. Have swivel ramrods. Made by Barnett, London. Price, $45.00.

**R81.** 25 BRITISH ARMY FLINT-LOCK HORSE PISTOLS, with marks on locks, brass trimmings, round barrels with average length 9 inches. All in good order with flint. Each, $15.00.

**R83.** 8 BELGIAN FLINT-LOCK PISTOLS with 9-inch round barrels, brass trimmed with ring in butt; in good order. Each, $9.50.

**R82.** FRENCH ARMY FLINT-LOCK PISTOLS. Brass mounted, ring on butt stock, 8-inch barrel. Average full length, 14 inches; weight, 2½ lbs.; used; serviceable order; rare old relics. Price, each, $8.85.

**R64.** 1 FLINT-LOCK PISTOL, made by Clark. Octagon barrel 7 inches with swivel ramrod, marked London. Grip is finely checkered. This is an officer's pistol. Price, $17.40.

**R66.** 1 BRITISH FLINT-LOCK HOLSTER PISTOL with 6-inch round barrel, marked Harcourt. This name is also on lock-plate. Butt is checkered. This is an officer's pistol. Price, $17.40.

**R67.** 1 BRITISH FLINT-LOCK HOLSTER PISTOL with 6-inch extra heavy large bore round barrel, marked Smith, London. Swivel ramrod, checkered butt. Price, $17.40.

**R72.** 1 QUEEN ANNE FLINT-LOCK PISTOL with large brass butt and brass trigger guard. Round barrel 8½ inches, marked London. Made by B. Brooks. Price, $25.00.

**R74.** 1 BRITISH FLINT-LOCK HOLSTER PISTOL with extra long round barrel, marked London. Large brass butt, brass trigger guard and brass name plate. Made by Hadley. Price, $30.00.

**R75.** 1 FLINT-LOCK PISTOL made by Adams. Barrel is 8 inches round, marked London. Round butt is brass trimmed, with brass trigger guard, brass name plate and brass side plate. Price, $32.00.

**R13.** 1 FRENCH FLINT-LOCK POCKET PISTOL with French octagon barrel, under ramrod, center hammer, silver wire inlaid butt. Price, $14.00.

**R82A.** 4 FLINT-LOCK PISTOLS with long round barrels; total length, 17 inches. In fair order. Each, $9.25.

**R85.** 14 ASSORTED SHORT HEAVY FLINT-LOCK PISTOLS; average length, 11 inches. All have maker's name on locks. A few brass mounted. Some have swivel ramrods. This size is now scarce. Each, $12.80.

**R84.** 17 BRITISH FLINT-LOCK HOLSTER PISTOLS; average length, 14 inches. A few are brass mounted. Many have octagon barrels. All with maker's name—Mortimer, Twigg, Gill and others. All have round butts; some checkered. Each, $14.75.

**R69.** 1 FLINT-LOCK HOLSTER PISTOL with swivel ramrod and round butt, brass mounted. Total length, 14½ inches. Made by Andrews, London. Price, $17.40.

**R27.** 1 FLINT-LOCK BLUNDERBUSS PISTOL with brass barrel, marked "London." Total length, 11 inches; in good order. Price, $25.00.

**R17.** 1 FLINT-LOCK PISTOL with 7-inch brass barrel, marked W. R., London. Brass guard and butt. Price, $21.00.

**R33.** 1 FRENCH FLINT-LOCK PISTOL with 7-inch heavy octagon barrel, checkered grip and round butt. Evidently used by an officer. Price, $25.00.

**R73.** 1 QUEEN ANNE FLINT-LOCK PISTOL with half octagon barrel, marked Lowe, London. Lock-plate marked Lowe. Heavy brass butt and trigger guard. Price, $25.00.

**R89.** 1 FLINT-LOCK HOLSTER PISTOL with 8-inch brass barrel, round butt. Brass trimmed. Style used in Revolutionary War. Price, $21.00.

**R57.** 1 FRENCH FLINT-LOCK HOLSTER PISTOL with swivel ramrod. Octagon barrel 8½ inches, checkered grip and square butt. In fine order. Price, $17.40.

**R92.** 1 BRASS TRIMMED BRITISH HOLSTER PISTOL, made by Freeman. Large brass butt. Period of 1740. Price, $25.00.

**R128.** 1 PAIR BRASS BOUND FLINT-LOCK PISTOLS with small round butt. Barrels are 7 inches round with swivel ramrods. Made by W. Bond, London. Price, $25.00.

**R1.** 1 ANTIQUE FRENCH FLINT-LOCK PISTOL with heavy brass octagon barrel, 6 inch. Square butt with brass plate. Fancy brass trigger guard and brass flash pan. Price, $21.00.

**R50.** 1 FRENCH IRON MOUNTED HOLSTER PISTOL with heavy butt, half octagon barrel, fancy trigger guard and side plate. Price, $17.10.

**R75A.** 1 BRITISH FLINT-LOCK HOLSTER PISTOL, by Adams. Has 7-inch round barrel, fancy brass trigger guard and brass cap with curious face on round butt. Ramrod has ivory tip. Price, $32.00.

**R78.** 1 BRITISH FLINT-LOCK HOLSTER PISTOL, made by Cullum, London. Brass mounted with large butt. Price, $20.00.

**R85A.** 1 SHORT FLINT-LOCK PISTOL with 5-inch heavy octagon barrel of large bore. Made by Eadon. Has round butt. Price, $12.40.

**R15.** 1 PAIR FLINT-LOCK POCKET PISTOLS, made by Twigg, London. Brass barrels and frames, center hammers. Barrels unscrew for quick loading and cleaning. Rare. Price, pair, $25.00.

**R15A.** 1 pair as above, with steel barrel, made by Wing, Braintree. Price, pair, $22.00.

**R42.** 1 PAIR FLINT-LOCK POCKET PISTOLS, by Moody. Cannon shaped barrels to unscrew. Wood butts are silver wire inlaid. Has combination tool used to unscrew barrels and also as rammer. Price, pair, $35.00.

**R40.** 1 pair as above, with tool, made by Richards. Price, pair, $35.00.

**R41.** 1 PAIR FLINT-LOCK POCKET PISTOLS by Fermer, London. Cannon shaped barrels, 2 inch, to unscrew. Round butts have engraved brass caps and silver wire inlay. Price, pair, $25.00.

**R86.** 6 FLINT-LOCK POCKET PISTOLS with round removable barrels, center hammers and concealed triggers, without guard:

1 by Parsons-Salisbury, $6.00.
1 by Edridol-Bingdon, $6.00.
1 by Reynolds-Coventry, $6.00.
1 without name, $5.50.
1 with brass frame, by Palmer-Rochester, $7.50.
1 by Nock-London, $6.00.

**10993N.** FLINTLOCK POCKET PISTOL, with 2½-inch removable barrel, plain wood butt with silver monogram plate, shield shape, center hammer with catch, folding trigger. Engraved frame marked: P. BOND, No. 15, CORN HILL, LONDON. Price, $12.00. (See cut page 92.)

**R7.** QUEEN ANNE FLINT-LOCK POCKET PISTOL with 5-inch cannon shaped barrel, center hammer and trigger guard. Stock wire silver inlaid with silver name plate. Silver mask head on butt. Made by Bunney, London. A rare specimen. Price, $30.00.

**R86A.** 2 FLINT-LOCK POCKET PISTOLS with round barrels, center hammers and trigger guards, 2-inch barrel. Price, $6.00.

**R58.** 1 ITALIAN FLINT-LOCK PISTOL with half octagon barrel, 5½ inch. Checkered stock, round butt, brass mounted. Ramrod has ivory tip. Price, $17.40.

**R59.** 1 BRITISH FLINT-LOCK HOLSTER PISTOL with 8-inch round barrel, checkered grip, round butt. Made by Twigg. Price, $21.00.

**R60.** 1 SHORT BRITISH FLINT-LOCK HOLSTER PISTOL with swivel ramrod. Heavy 4½-inch long barrel, large bore, marked London. Plain round butt with ring. Made by J. Egg. Price, $15.00.

**R87.** 1 PAIR PERCUSSION POCKET PISTOLS with round detachable barrels, center hammer and folding triggers. Price, pair, $9.50.

**R87A.** 7 ENGLISH PERCUSSION PISTOLS with 2-inch round barrels, center hammer and folding trigger. Some made by Cooper, Baker, Egg and Calvert. Price, each, $4.75.

**R87B.** 3 as above, with octagon barrels, engraved frames, in fine order. Price, each, $6.50.

**R76.** 1 LONG FLINT-LOCK PISTOL made by P. Clarke, London. Barrel is 10 inches with silver inlaid sight. Large brass butt, trigger guard and side plate. Price, $25.00.

**R88.** 1 BRITISH FLINT-LOCK PISTOL with 8-inch round brass barrel, marked London. Large brass butt and trigger guard. Wood ramrod is ivory tipped. Price, $25.00.

**SPB. PAIR SPANISH FLINTLOCK BLUNDER-BUSSES,** with outside Spanish locks, very short butt stocks, only 5½ inches from hammer to butt. 2½-inch locks, 9-inch barrels, bore 1¼ inches, ball triggers without guards, pistol grips wrapped with fine silver wire, two ornamental silver bands on each barrel, ivory butts, stocks inlaid with ivory and metal discs in curious designs. Lock straps made with loops to which are attached metal chains with rings. This is a very handsome pair. Price for pair $80.00.

**SPB-2. ORIENTAL FLINT-LOCK BLUNDERBUSS,** with short stock, inlaid with mother of pearl daisies in brass circle. Checkered grip studded with fine brass tacks, 9½-inch barrel, silver inlaid, bore 1½ inch. 4½-inch ornamented lock, brass butt and trigger guard. Full length 17¼ inches. Price $24.00.

**SPB-3. ORIENTAL FLINT-LOCK BLUNDERBUSS,** similar to No. SPB-2, except with 10½-inch inlaid barrel, ball trigger, 5-inch hand carved lock with encased battery spring. Price $26.00.

**SPB-4. TURKISH FLINT-LOCK BLUNDERBUSS,** with 12¾-inch barrel with bell muzzle, silver inlaid with name in Turkish letters. Full length 21 inches, wood carved stock, silver inlaid, 5-inch ornamented lock. Price $23.00.

**SPB-5. TURKISH FLINT-LOCK BLUNDERBUSS** with 9-inch silver inlaid barrel, wood carved stock inlaid with small brass studs, heavy brass butt plate, brass trigger guard with star and crescent design. 4½-inch ornamented lock. Price $24.00.

**SPB-6. TURKISH FLINTLOCK BLUNDERBUSS** with very heavy inlay of silver on 11-inch barrel. Stock wood carved throughout and inlaid with silver. Metal butt and guard inlaid with silver in various designs. 4½-inch silver inlaid lock. A very fine specimen. Price $27.00.

**PER-1. PERSIAN FLINT-LOCK PISTOL** with curved grip, fitted with ROUND wood ball, wood stock highly polished, looks like horn, two polished metal barrel bands, 13-inch barrel, decorated with floral designs, on which the gold plating is worn. Ball trigger, no guard, 2½-inch gold decorated SPANISH outside lock. Price $40.00.

**PER-3. ORIENTAL FLINTLOCK PISTOL** with leather covered wood stock, 2½-inch gold plated lock, outside Spanish, 12-inch cannon barrel inlaid with gold designs, THREE proof or armourers' marks and one Turkish mark. 1¾-inch ornamented barrel band in silver. Ball trigger round butt, silver covered, wide silver stock strap. This is a very showy piece. Price $60.00.

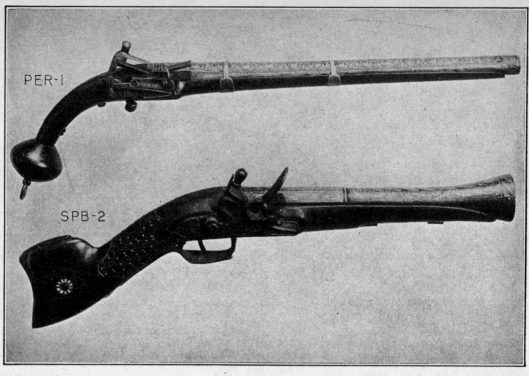

**PER-4. CIRCASSIAN FLINTLOCK PISTOL** with leather covered wood stock, gold inlaid barrel with top rib, length 13 inches, full length 18 inches. Gold inlaid outside Spanish lock, white ivory ball butt, gold inlaid ball trigger, no guard, gold ornamented stock strap. Hand grip trimmed with red plush. Price $42.00.

**PER-5. CIRCASSIAN FLINTLOCK PISTOL** with 11½-inch barrel, full length 16½ inches, wood stock leather covered, round wood ball butt, Spanish outside lock with armourer's mark, ball trigger. Price $35.00.

**INB. AFGHAN FLINTLOCK PISTOL** taken from bandits on Indian frontier. Blunderbuss barrel 10½ inches long, inlaid with gold and silver in designs. Heavy silver ball butt, 5½-inch gold inlaid lock. Stock inlaid throughout with silver studs in various designs. Price $22.00.

**INB-1. AFGHAN FLINTLOCK BLUNDERBUSS PISTOL** with 10¾-inch barrel. This has been inlaid with silver but is much worn. Hook shaped wood butt. 6-inch lock. Wood stock inlaid with small silver wire tacks in arrow head designs. Price $20.00.

**INB-2. AFGHAN FLINTLOCK BLUNDERBUSS PISTOL** inlaid with silver wire nails, 11¾-inch silver inlaid barrel, 6½-inch ornamented flat lock. Hooked stock with bird head butt. Price $21.00.

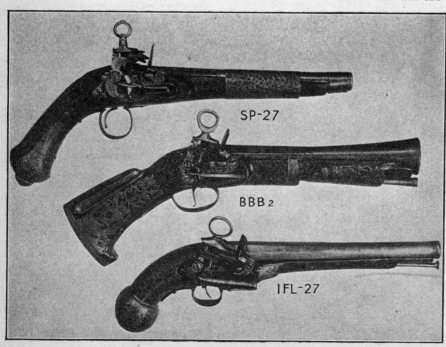

**BBB-2. SPANISH FLINTLOCK BLUNDER-BUSS PISTOL,** period 18th century. Full length 15¼ inches, barrel 8½ inches, bore at muzzle 1⅜ inches. Barrel is part octagon and inlaid with 9 brass ornaments. 7½-inch belt or sash hook on left side. 3-inch OUTSIDE Spanish lock, short grip, flat butt 3 inches long, with brass butt plate engraved. The ENTIRE stock covered with ornament brass designs, showing two headed bird in full plumage, trees, vines and serpents. A very handsome piece. Price $40.00.

**ILF-27. FINE ITALIAN FLINTLOCK PISTOL** with OUTSIDE Spanish lock, 3 inches long. Part octagon barrel 9 inches, bore ⅝ inch. 7¼-inch belt hook on left side. Full length 14 inches. Entire wood stock covered with embossed brass in floral designs, round ball butt, also brass covered. Pistol probably came from Sardinia. Price $40.00.

**SP-27. SPANISH FLINTLOCK PISTOL** with 3½-inch outside lock, mounted with gold plated, engraved ornaments. Full length 14½ inches, part octagon barrel 9 inches, bore 9/16 inch. Long grip, round butt with heavy engraved gold plated butt plate, engraved steel trigger guard, 8½-inch flat belt hook on left side. 3-inch oval monogram plate bordered by brass wire inlay. 3-inch brass barrel band, engraved barrel. Price $30.00.

F L C-A. PAIR BRITISH FLINT-LOCK HOLSTER PISTOLS, in case. Cannon barrels, 7 inch, made to unscrew for quick loading. Center hammers, trigger guards, belt hooks for left and right sides, round flat wood butts. Frames marked: BRAZIER. Barrels have two old proof marks. Case contains 4½-inch round copper flask, barrel wrench, extra flints and extra balls. Period of 1770. Oval silver monogram plates set in stocks. Price for set, $55.00.

F L C-2. PAIR FLINTLOCK PISTOLS, in case. 10¼ inch octagon barrels, gold inlaid at breech, silver front sights. Barrels case hardened and marked: H. W. MORTIMER, GUN MAKER TO HIS MAJESTY. Wood rods, horn tipped, round ball butts, checkered hand grips, guards with large urn ends. Gold touch holes, 4 inch locks marked in oval: H. W. MORTIMER. Set includes 3½ inch combination flask with three compartments, wad cutter, round mould, wood cleaning rod, leather wads, balls, and flints. This is a very fine set. Price, complete, $90.00.

F L C-3. PAIR BRITISH DUELLING FLINTLOCK PISTOLS, in case. 10 inch octagon barrels, with gold front sights, and gold inlaid breeches. Silver escutcheons at barrel pins. Round ball butts with finely checkered hand grips. Ornamented guards with urn ends. Barrels inlaid with makers' name in gold under gold crown: TWIGG & BASS, LONDON. 4¼ inch locks marked: TWIGG & BASS. Gold touch holes. Safety catches lock both hammers and pans. Set includes three part leather covered flask, wood cleaning rod with tools and sample bullet. Original label in cover of case. Price, for set, $100.00.

F L C-5. PAIR GEORGIAN OFFICER'S FLINTLOCK PISTOLS, in case. 7¾ inch barrels, half octagon, bore 9/16 inch, marked: LONDON. Ball butts flattened at sides, checkered grips, wood rods with horn tips, brass guards with acorn ends. 4½ inch locks marked: DAWES. (Doubtless the ancestors of our vice president.) Screw driver, round mould flints and bullets included in set. Price, complete, $60.00.

F L C-6. PAIR BRITISH DUELLING PISTOLS, FLINTLOCK, in case. Highly polished wood stocks with round ball butts and checkered grips. Guards have pineapple ends with extra spurs to steady the aim. Brass tipped wood rods, silver stock tips, silver escutcheons at barrel pins. 4¼ inch locks with name in gold: P. BOND. 10 inch octagon barrels, silver front sights, raised rear sights, gold touch holes, reinforced breeches, silver oval monogram plates. Name set in barrels in gold near breech: P. BOND. LONDON. Wood cleaning rod, mould, flints and bullets included with set. Price, complete, $98.00.

PAIR OF FRENCH DUELLING PISTOLS, percussion lock; fine rifling (upwards of 50 grooves); octagonal 7-inch barrel, twist steel; checkered stock; carved butts; case hardened locks; one hammer missing; full length 13½ inches. We offer the pair "as are" at $12.50, which will include old hammer not fitted.

2111. PAIR ANTIQUE SPANISH FLINTLOCK PISTOLS, gold inlaid seal of the maker, crown surmounting letters A. A. H. S., silver inlaid crown lion rampant, etc.; relief ornamentation on barrels; engraved lock; ornamented brass mountings; with medallion on the butt cap; ornamented name and side plate; handsome pair of old pistols; barrel 9½ inches; full length 14½ inches. Price the pair, $45.00.

0-1011. PAIR FLINTLOCK PISTOLS IN CASE WITH OUTFIT. Lock engraved, "W. Parker"; 6-inch octagonal barrel engraved, "W. Parker, Holburn, London"; ⅝-inch smooth bore. Checkered grip. Walnut stock. Engraved mountings. Rare old ornamented fine hammers. Silver name plate and front sight. Gold breech band. Platinum vent. Fine, easy working lock. Good order. Mahogany case with key lock, 15x8x3 inches. Case contains powder and shot flask, bullet mould, rammer, cleaners, screw drivers and parts. Price, $60.00.

SET MANTON & SON DUELLING PISTOLS. Octagonal barrels 7 inches long; about 46 calibre, smooth bore; full length 12 inches; engraved on the lock, "Manton & Son," on the barrel, "London"; percussion lock; altered from flintlock; in fine case; size of case, 17½x6¼x2⅛. Pistols are in good order. Price, $30.00.

PAIR DUELLING PISTOLS in Walnut Case; percussion locks; total length 12 inches; twisted steel barrel with bullet mould, flask, ball screw, etc., in good second-hand serviceable order. Price, $30.00.

1447. TURKISH ARMY FLINTLOCK HORSE PISTOL, British marks on barrel and lock; full length 14 inches; ring on butt; brass mountings; working order. Length of barrel 7¾ inches. Price, $6.50.

PAIR OF FLINTLOCK DUELLING PISTOLS, made by Clarke; in mahogany case, with swivel ramrod (one missing), with shot, wads, cleaning rod, etc.; total length 11 inches; octagonal barrels. Price, $35.00.

No. 1491. PORTUGUESE FLINTLOCK HOLSTER PISTOL, engraved on lock, "Barnett," with Portuguese crown, "P. R." Swivel ramrod, ring in butt, polished walnut stock; British proof mark. ⅝ smooth bore; full length 15½ inches. Price, $10.00.

No. 1497. "WILSON, LONDON," FLINTLOCK DUELLING PISTOL; 7-inch barrel, 11/16 inch smooth bore. Full length 13 inches; knob club butt; brass cover with figure of grotesque head; 2 old British proof marks; old engraving; working order. $14.50.

**No. 1455. FRENCH FLINT LOCK DUELLING PISTOL;** full length, 14 inches. Top part of the barrel, flat, and engraved brass mountings, carved walnut stock. Good working order. Price $17.00.

**No. 1456.** C. Lowe, London, **FLINT LOCK DUELLING PISTOL;** with engraved scroll work. Old British proof marks. Fine lock; 8-inch barrel. Full length, 13 inches. Engraved brass mountings. Good working order. Price $23.00.

**No. 1341. FRENCH FLINT LOCK PISTOL, OCTAGONAL BARREL.** Cannon-shaped muzzle; ornamented and engraved mountings. Full length, 11 inches; 9-16 smooth bore; carved walnut stock. $12.00.

**No. 1494. OFFICERS' MODEL FLINT LOCK REVOLUTIONARY WAR PERIOD HOLSTER PISTOL.** 9-inch barrel; ⅝ smooth bore. Full length, 15 inches. Polished walnut stock. In working order. Price $10.00.

**No. 1463. ANCIENT FLINT LOCK PISTOL;** 9¾-inch barrel; ½-inch smooth bore. Full length, 17 inches. Ornamented iron guard and butt cap and name plate. Carved walnut stock. In working order. Price $18.50.

**No. 1466. LONDON BRASS BARREL FLINT LOCK PISTOL.** In working order. Length of barrel, 8 inches. 11-16 smooth bore. Full length 13¼ inches. Engraved London on barrel. Also two old British proof marks. Hexagonal-shaped breech end. Price $14.00.

**No. 1489. BRASS BARREL FLINT DUELLING PISTOL.** Engraved on barrel, "W. Hanshaw, Strand, London," with 2 old proof marks. German silver guard. Ornamented butt plate and rod holder. Checkered walnut stock, with inlaid flower design on stock. Working order. Price $28.00.

**No. 1490. MANTON BRASS BARREL FLINT LOCK DUELLING PISTOL.** Length of barrel, 8 inches; 11-16 bore; full length, 13½ inches. Engraved on lock "Manton." Fine easy working lock. Silver front sight. Checkered stock; working order. Price $35.00.

**No. 1487. FLINT DUELLING PISTOL.** Finely ornamented with gold and silver trimmings on butt; name plate, guard, side plate, rod holder and lock. Length of barrel, 8½ inches; 11-16 bore. Full length, 14½ inches. Working order. $23.00.

**No. 1492.** Colt and Webber **FLINT LOCK DUELLING PISTOL;** engraved name plate; British proof marks; 8-inch barrel. 11-16 bore. Full length, 14 inches; brass mountings; in working order; walnut stock. Old timer. Price, $16.00.

**No. 1448. ANCIENT ITALIAN FLINT LOCK PISTOL,** engraved on lock "Griva Bastia." 6½-inch octagonal barrel; 11-16 smooth bore. Full length, 12 inches. Ornamented iron checkered walnut stock. Front and rear sight. Proof marks on barrel; working order. $14.00.

**F L C-1. PAIR BRITISH POCKET PISTOLS IN CASE.** 2½ inch cannon barrels to unscrew; secret triggers, checkered wood grips, center hammers with safety catch. Frames engraved with military designs, flags, shields etc. MARKED: WOOD YORK. Set includes barrel wrench, ivory pan-brush, mould, flints, combination copper flask for powder, shot and wads. Price for set is $30.00.

**"JOHN NICHOLLS, OXON,"** engraved on barrel of Flint Lock Duelling Pistol; 7½-inch barrel, ⅝ smooth bore. Full length, 14 inches. Same working engraved on lock as on barrel. Carved walnut stock. Ornamented brass side plate, rod holder, guard, butt plate, and name plate. Fine easy-working lock. Working order. $17.50.

**No. 1448A. FLINT LOCK DUELLING PISTOL,** maker, "Desrse." Barrel is flatted on top for sighting. Engraved ornamental scroll work in relief on side plate and trigger guard. Flat hexagonal butt stock with ornamental brass relief work. Handsome old relic; serviceable order. $17.50.

**No. 1101.** Handsome pair of Flint Lock Duelling Pistols. Brass barrel; flatted top for sighting; carved stock. Made by Henshaw, London, England. Engraved lock and mountings. Name plate with "B. O.," with ornamented figures in silver work. Guard plate, butt plate; in fine order. Found in Paris. Price $40.00.

**No. 1445. ANTIQUE FRENCH FLINT LOCK DUELLING PISTOL.** Octagonal twist steel barrel 10 inches long. Full length of pistol, 17 inches; 11-16 bore; rifled at muzzle; fine locks; engraved "Roe Lant." Ornamented guard and mountings; silver front sight, 5 leaf rear sight. Stock at breech carved with rose and leaves. Price $25.00.

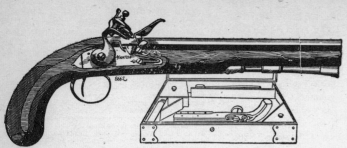

**FLC-7. PAIR BRITISH FLINTLOCK DUELING PISTOLS,** in case. Round ball butts, checkered grips, full length stocks, guards with urn ends, metal tipped ramrods. 9¼-inch octagon barrel marked: LONDON. 4¼-inch locks marked: WHEELER. Safety catches. Shield shaped silver monogram plates. 4¼-inch heavy copper flask, flints and bullets included with set. Price complete $70.00.

**8724. OLD WORM-EATEN FLINTLOCK PISTOL.** From the Middleboro Museum sale, 1908, at the time the captured flag of the American frigate Chesapeake was sold. This old relic was found hidden in roof of house in Ireland. Full length 15 inches. Octagonal barrel, ¾-inch smooth bore. Price, $15.00.

**8733. PAIR FRENCH FLINTLOCK PISTOLS.** Carried in olden times by stage coach travelers, 5-inch octagonal barrels, 9/16-inch smooth bore, carved mountings, flat-shaped butt cap, walnut stock, checkered grip, "A. R." branded on the fore-end stock. Full length 11 inches. Price, $19.50 the pair.

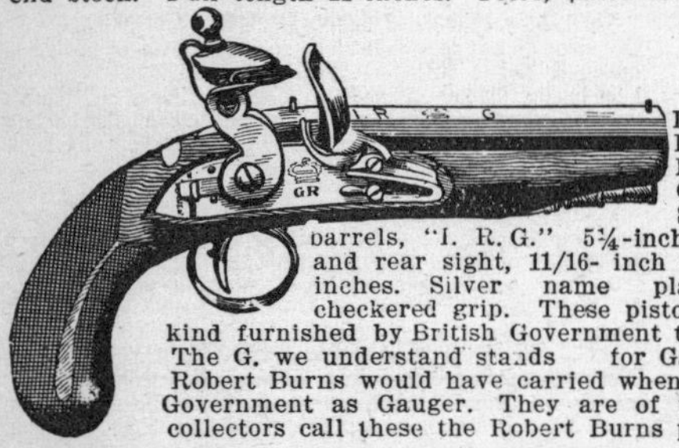

**O-1033. PAIR BRITISH INLAND REVENUE OFFICER'S FLINTLOCK PISTOLS.** Marked, "G. R., British Crown, Tower, Broad Arrow, Small Crown," and on the barrels, "I. R. G." 5¼-inch octagonal barrels, with front and rear sight, 11/16-inch smooth bore. Full length 10½ inches. Silver name plate, fine walnut stock with checkered grip. These pistols were of the period and the kind furnished by British Government to collectors of Inland Revenue. The G. we understand stands for Gauger. The pistols are such as Robert Burns would have carried when in the employ of the British Government as Gauger. They are of that period—1780 to 1800. Some collectors call these the Robert Burns pistols. Price the pair, $50.00.

The famous Scotch poet was from 1789 to 1794 in the employ of the British Government at a salary of £70 pounds a year as collector of Inland Revenue, or as he himself called it, a "Gauger." It is a matter of record that in 1792 Burns boarded and seized a brig that was engaged in smuggling in Solway Firth. The vessel was confiscated and Burns received quite a sum as his share of the price on sale of the vessel at Dumfries, together with her arms and cargo.

"Searching auld wives' barrels, och, hon, the day! That clarty barm should stain my laurels!"

**1 POCKET PISTOL,** with center hammer percussion, by Nock, London. This has one of Nock's early patent nipple protectors. Pistol has 2-inch cannon shaped barrel to unscrew, folding trigger, safety catch, and checkered grip. A rare specimen. Price, $15.00.

**8726. AMERICAN DERRINGER PERCUSSION PISTOL.** Found in London collection. Engraved, "Slotter & Co., Phil." German silver mountings and shield name plate. This pistol is similar in appearance to the one used by J. Wilkes Booth in the assassination of President Lincoln. Full length 5¼ inches. Price, $8.85.

**1A. PAIR FLINTLOCK POCKET PISTOLS,** with flat wood butts inlaid with fine silver wire. Full length 7½ inches, cannon barrels 3¾ inches, with 2 proof marks. Center hammers, plain trigger guards. Frames engraved and marked: CHATER, RINGWOOD. Price per pair $21.00. (See No. 1, page 87.)

**1B. PAIR BRITISH FLINTLOCK POCKET PISTOLS,** full length 8¼ inches, cannon barrels 3¾ inches, center hammers, flat wood butts with fine silver wire inlay. Frames marked: WILKINSON, BRISTOL. Trigger guards slide forward to act as safety catches. Price for pair $20.00.

**1C. PAIR BRITISH FLINTLOCK POCKET PISTOLS,** flat wood butt, silver wire inlaid, center hammers which are locked by pushing trigger guard forward. Full length 8 inches, cannon barrels 3½ inches, with proof marks. Frames engraved and marked: LAUGHER. Price for pair $19.00.

**1D. FLINTLOCK POCKET PISTOL,** with BRASS barrel and frame. Full length 8 inches, cannon barrel 3½ inches, removable, with 2 proof marks. Center hammer with sliding guard for safety. Silver inlaid butt. Frame marked: MORTIMER, LONDON. Period 1765. Price, $15.00.

**R68. I PAIR FLINTLOCK PISTOLS,** by Inland Revenue Officer. Brass barrels, 2½ inches; one marked "I. R. 84"; other, "I. R. 86." Have swivel ramrods. Made by Barnett, London. Price, $45.00.

**R81. 25 BRITISH ARMY FLINTLOCK HORSE PISTOLS,** with marks on locks, brass trimmings, round barrels with average length 9 inches. All in good order, with flint. Each, $15.00.

**R83. 8 BELGIAN FLINTLOCK PISTOLS** with 9-inch round barrels, brass trimmed with ring in butt; in good order. Each, $9.50.

**R82. FRENCH ARMY FLINTLOCK PISTOLS.** Brass mounted; ring on butt stock; 8-inch barrel. Average full length 14 inches; weight 2½ lbs.; used; serviceable order; rare old relics. Price, each, $8.85.

**R27. 1 FLINT-LOCK BLUNDERBUSS PISTOL,** with brass barrel, marked "London." Total length, 11 inches; in good order. Price, $25.00.

**R17. 1 FLINT-LOCK PISTOL,** with 7-inch brass barrel, marked W. R., London. Brass guard and butt. Price, $21.00.

**R33. 1 FRENCH FLINT-LOCK PISTOL,** with 7-inch heavy octagon barrel, checkered grip and round butt. Evidently used by an officer. Price, $25.00.

**8729. KETLAND & CO. ARMY FLINTLOCK HOLSTER PISTOL.** Engraved, "C. R. Ketland & Co." Brass mounted, ⅝-inch smooth bore. Full length 16 inches. Price, $15.00.

**R64. 1 FLINTLOCK PISTOL,** made by Clark. Octagon barrel 7 inches, with swivel ramrod; marked "London." Grip is finely checkered. This is an officer's pistol. Price, $17.40.

**PAIR ANTIQUE BRASS-BARREL DUELLING PISTOLS;** were originally flintlock, but altered to percussion. Made by D. L. Moore, London; handsome guns; German silver inlaid decorations; old London proof mark; have been roughly used; hammer, part of guard and ramrod missing; bargain for gunsmith who could repair them; worth $100.00. Price for the pair, $20.00.

**8734. PAIR FLINTLOCK OFFICER'S HOLSTER PISTOLS,** by H. Nock. In fine order. Original browning on the 9-inch twist steel barrel; ⅝-inch smooth bore. Gold vent hole, engraved, "H. Nock, London." Polished walnut stock; engraved mountings. Full length 15 inches. Price, $32.00 the pair.

**R70. 1 PAIR FLINTLOCK PISTOLS,** with 6-inch brass octagon barrels. Engraved locks, swivel ramrods, checkered grips, lion head brass butts. Locks marked "Boston"; barrels marked "Wakefield." Price, $50.00.

**1452. TOWER G. R. AND BRITISH CROWN STAMPED ON FLINTLOCK PISTOL,** with swivel ramrod, for use in hunting trips. Fine order, like new. Original browning on barrel, with 2 old British proof marks; polished walnut stock; full length, 15½ inches. Price, $7.50.

**1439. LARGE SIZE FLINTLOCK DRAGOON PISTOL,** 13-inch barrel, full length 20½ inches; in serviceable order. Brass front sight, brass mountings; ⅝ bore. Price, $10.00.

**1440. W. Parker, Holburn, London, Flintlock Pistol;** 9-inch barrel; ⅝ smooth bore; full length 16 inches; walnut stock, brass mountings. In serviceable order. Price, $12.00.

**1441. OFFICER'S PATTERN HOLSTER FLINTLOCK PISTOL,** 12-inch barrel; full length 19 inches; ⅝ smooth bore; flat top barrel; rib-shaped for quick sighting, with brass mountings. Offered in working order. Small part of stock at muzzle broken. Price, $10.00.

**10993L. FLINTLOCK POCKET PISTOL,** with 2½-inch cannon barrel, plain wood butt, center hammer with safety catch, folding or secret trigger, engraved frame, marked: BURNIE, BERWICK. Price $12.00. (See page 92.)

**10993M. BRITISH FLINTLOCK POCKET PISTOL,** with engraved frame, marked: HARCOURT, IPSWICH. Plain wood butt, with silver monogram oval. 2½-inch cannon barrel, center hammer with safety, secret trigger. Two proof marks. Price $11.00.

**1247. PAIR ANTIQUE FLINT PISTOLS,** with Belt Hanger attachment. Main spring on outside of lock plate. Ornamented silver name plate, with face on butt plate and ramrod holder; carved stock. Maker's seal on breech of barrel, with letters; ring hammer; fair order. Price, the pair, $45.00; singly, $25.00.

**MOORE'S PATENT REVOLVER.** For metallic cartridges. 7-shot. Marked on the barrel, "D. Moore's Patent, Sept. 18, 1860." By pressing a spring in rear of frame the barrel and cylinder swing out to the right for loading; the ejector is detachable rod held in place by a spring under the barrel. Engraved on the lock strap is, "Stephen Monks, Co. B, 34th Regt Mass. V." Evidently carried by him during the Civil War. Full length of revolver 9½ inches, about calibre 32; engraved, nickel plated. Rare relic. Price, $25.00.

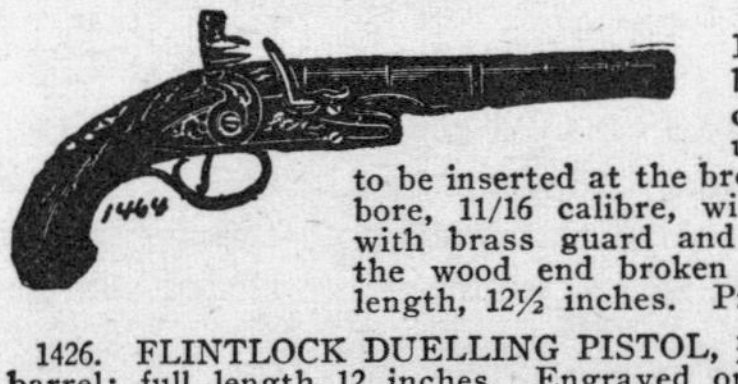

**1464. OLD SCOTCH TYPE FLINTLOCK PISTOL.** Made by Blyth, London, with early cannon-shaped barrel, which unscrews, allowing the charge to be inserted at the breech. Barrel is 7-inch smooth bore, 11/16 calibre, with ancient outside hammer, with brass guard and name plate. Small part of the wood end broken off; in working order; full length, 12½ inches. Price, $28.50.

**1426. FLINTLOCK DUELLING PISTOL,** ½-inch smooth bore, 6¾-inch barrel; full length 12 inches. Engraved on barrel "London," with old proof mark; on lock, "Wilson." Ornamented brass mounting, walnut stock; in working order. Price, $14.00.

**2102. DOUBLE BARREL PERCUSSION LOCK PISTOL.** Made by Southold, London. Ramrod rib, with swivel ramrod for use in both barrels, engraved mountings, checkered stock. Full length 8½ inches. Price, $12.00.

**8730. FLINTLOCK PISTOL MARKED 1778, "WHATELY."** Perhaps used in the Revolutionary War. 11¾-inch barrel, 11/16-inch smooth bore. Brass mountings. Price, $18.85.

**8731. ENGLISH FLINTLOCK PISTOL.** Tower. Royal Crown, G. R. and broad arrow, with date of *reissue* marked on the stock. 1786, Crown, G. R. 9-inch barrel, 11/16-inch smooth bore. Brass mountings. Knob butt. Brass cap. Fine order. Price, $18.85.

**8731A. REVOLUTIONARY WAR PERIOD OFFICER'S FLINTLOCK HOLSTER PISTOL.** Made by Tatham. Brass mounted. 9-inch barrel. 11/16-inch smooth bore. Price, $17.00.

In olden times the announcement of a Government auction always brought a large attendance of bidders, also those who had no cash, but relied on their wits and a general knowledge of values to pick up an odd dollar or two at the sales. These speculators, as they styled themselves, made up for a lack of capital in a good pair of lungs. The bona fide dealers called them *windy bidders*. These men attended the sales not for the purpose of purchasing, but for the sole purpose of being bought off by the dealers. If they did not succeed in that, they would bid up the goods, running no risk until the auctioneer knocked down the lot to them, then with brazen effrontery they would claim it was a mistake; they did not bid, etc. There was also a chance that the dealers would combine to buy the goods at the lowest limit prices. In this event the speculator was in clover, as he had to be taken into the combination and have an equal share in the dividends, viz., the difference between the prices paid at the sale and that paid by the dealers in reselling among themselves.

**1475. — 12-INCH SMOOTH BORE BARREL FLINTLOCK PISTOL,** octagonal barrel, 6¾ inches long, ¾ smooth bore. Full length 13 inches. Checkered walnut stock, brass mountings, in working order. Price, $15.00.

**1484.** —⅝-inch barrel, 11/16 smooth bore, engraved "H. Delaney" on lock and on barrel "Lundini." Ornamented iron mountings, silvered name plate and butt plate. Delaney was the maker of the earliest type of flint-locks. Small crack in stock, otherwise in working order. Price, $30.00. Rare old weapon.

**1248.** —PAIR OF LONDON BRASS-BARREL FLINTLOCK DUELLING PISTOLS, 8-inch barrel, ⅝ smooth bore, walnut stock, 2 old London proof marks on barrel. Engraved "Bass, London." Ramrod missing; needs repairs. Price, the pair, $30.00.

**1428.** —OLD LONDON MADE FLINTLOCK HORSE PISTOL, checkered stock, ornamented steel mountings, full length 15 inches. Kind carried by officers in olden times. Price, $14.00.

**8707.** —ALBANIAN FLINTLOCK PISTOL WITH PIKE BUTT STOCK. 18th century outside pattern lock. Brass stock, with hammer decoration. The pike shaped butt was used in close quarters, somewhat similar to the bayonet or the musket. Price, $9.85.

**8622.** —PAIR SILVER MOUNTED ENGLISH FLINT PISTOLS. Made by "Probin." With solid silver engraved guard, butt cap, ramrod, thimbles, name and side plates. 8 inch brass barrels ½ inch smooth bore. The silver mountings are hall proof marked the period of 1788. Name plate is engraved "F. S." Handsome pair of weapons. Price, $70.00 the pair.

**8708.** —TURKISH FLINTLOCK PISTOL. 18th century brass mounted. 8½ inch barrel. Curious weapon. Price, $8.85.

**8709.** —ORIENTAL FLINTLOCK PISTOL. 14 inch barrel. Chased lock. Relief ornamented brass mountings, name plate, handsome butt cap in brass relief. Walnut stock. Price, $14.50. Oriental locks lack the fine finish and easy working of those made by English gun makers.

**8614.** —ENGLISH YEOMAN'S 1760 FLINTLOCK PISTOL. From sale of Lord Sheffield's effects at Sussex. Used in army by troop of yeomanry under Lord Sheffield. The lock is marked with Royal Crown, Tower, G. R. Broad Arrow, 1760, brass mountings, name plate, 1—73. The barrel is engraved "Royal Foresters," with King's crown marked on the butt showing that this old weapon was used in protecting the King's deer. 10 inch barrel. Price, $45.00.

**8673.** —PAIR FLINTLOCK PISTOLS. In mahogany case, made by "R. Clarke & Son, London." 9¾ inch octagonal barrels, No. 62, Cheapside, London. Lock engraved, "R. Clarke & Son." Walnut stock. Checkered grip. Engraved mountings. Ivory tipped rammer. Case measures 18 by 9¾ by 3 inches, in fine order. Price, $55.00 the pair.

**8616.** —PAIR EARLY ENGLISH FLINTLOCK PISTOLS. 6 inch cannon shaped barrels which unscrew at the breech for loading. The guard bow can be pushed forward locking the hammer when at half cock; ½ inch smooth bore, "Clemens, Slug Lane, Picadilly, London." Engraved mountings walnut stock, serviceable order. Price the pair $30.00, singly $16.50.

**8674.** —PAIR FLINTLOCK PISTOLS. In quartered oak case, by "Theor. Richards." 9 inch octagonal twist steel barrels, ⅝ inch smooth bore. Silver name plate, engraved mountings. Barrel and lock engraved "Theor. Richards." Walnut stock, with checkered grip. Belt hanger; safety lock attachment. Case measures 19 by 8½ by 3 inches, complete with powder flask. Price the outfit, $65.00.

**8609.** —ANCIENT AIR PISTOL. By Crewfe in Herzberg, sharkskin covered butt air chamber, shot magazine in tube on the side, cocking the hammer opens the air chamber, bullet feeds into the barrel in the magazine by gravity, through the breech carrier; engraved frame, side safety, folding leaf rear sight, silver front sight, walnut stock, engraved mountings, 10½ inch barrel rifled at the muzzle, rare weapon, prohibited in olden times.

**8675.** —PAIR FLINTLOCK DUELLING PISTOLS. Octagonal twist steel 10 inch barrels, "Wogdon & Barton" inlaid gold letters on the barrel. Gold touch hole, breech band and flash pan. Silver name plate and escutcheons. Ramrod rib. Engraved mountings. Walnut stock. In mahogany case 20 by 9 by 3 inches. Price, $75.00 the pair.

**14A. FLINTLOCK HOLSTER PISTOL,** with fine wood stock inlaid with silver wire. 4¼-inch lock, 10-inch barrel with flat top rib, inlaid with silver and with makers name in silver: I. CRISTOPH KUCHENREITER. Barrel makers mark of horse and rider stamped on rib. Ornamented trigger guard with acorn end. Flat wood butt, checkered, with attachment for shoulder stock. Price, $20.00.

**1475A.** BRITISH HOLSTER FLINTLOCK PISTOL, with 8¾-inch round barrel, round butt, brass trimmed, with brass monogram plate, steel rod. Lock marked: T. KETLAND & CO. Price $15.00.

**8623.** —PAIR FRENCH FLINTLOCK PISTOLS. Richly ornamented with gold and silver work. Solid silver engraved fore end, guard plate, butt cap and name plate. Walnut stock with silver pointed diamonds in the checkering on the grip and fore end. 8½ inch tapered barrel inlaid gilt ornamented; ⅝ inch smooth bore. This pair of pistols was passed by the U. S. Government appraisers as a work of art. Price the pair, $150.00.

**8671.** —PAIR ANCIENT BRASS BARREL FLINTLOCK BREECHLOADING PISTOLS. Made by Sheppard, London. Fine silver wire inlaid ornamentation. Silver name plate, butt and cap, ancient British proof marks. Barrel unscrews near the breech for quick loading. Full length 12 inches. Rare weapons. Price, $60.00.

**8671A.** —QUEEN ANNE TYPE FLINTLOCK PISTOL, with 5-inch removable cannon barrel, with 2 proof marks. Round ball butt with silver mask butt plate. Ornamented trigger guard, center hammer, oval silver monogram plate. Frame marked: VERNCOMBE, BRISTOL. A very handsome pistol. Price, $30.00.

**8677.** —PAIR ALMOST NEW CONDITION FLINTLOCK PISTOLS. In mahogany case. Made by "Hamburger." Fine twist steel 8½ inch, octagonal barrels, with the original browning. Silver breech band and vent, lock engraved "Hamburger & Co., London." Silver name plate and escutcheons. Engraved mountings, curly walnut stock. Checkered grip, hinged rammer. Ebony fore end. Fine easy working locks. Mahogany case in good order. Size 19 by 9 by 2¾ inches, brass hinges, handle, lock and key. Price, $80.00.

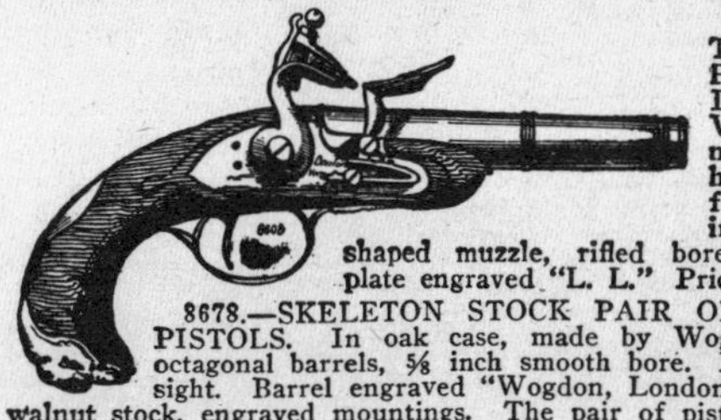

**8608.** — ANTIQUE FLINT POCKET PISTOL. By Boulon Vernius, silver mounted bird head butt stock, full length 9 inches, cannon shaped muzzle, rifled bore, silver name plate engraved "L. L." Price, $18.00.

**8678.** —SKELETON STOCK PAIR OF DUELLING PISTOLS. In oak case, made by Wogdon. 10 inch octagonal barrels, ⅝ inch smooth bore. Front and rear sight. Barrel engraved "Wogdon, London." Gold vent; walnut stock, engraved mountings. The pair of pistols weighs 3½ pounds. The case measures 17 by 7½ by 3 inches. Has brass carrying handles. Much used, in serviceable order. Easy working locks. Price, $50.00 the pair.

**8624.** —PAIR OLD ENGLISH PISTOLS. Converted from flint to percussion lock. Made by James Freeman, London, about the period of 1764. Silver mask butt cap, name plate and breech ornamentation. Cannon shaped barrels which unscrew at the breech for quick loading. Length 5½ inches, ⅝ inch smooth bore, full length of pistols, 12 inches. Price the pair $18.50, singly $10.00.

**1437A.** PAIR DRAGOON HOLSTER PISTOLS, like illustration, No. 1437 on page 89, except there are no belt hooks. Length 20 inches, barrels 13 inches. Round flat butts with heavy brass butt plates. Brass trigger guards, lock straps, and ramrod guides. Issue number marked on barrel: 791. Initials of various owners cut in stocks. Pistols of this size and weight are rare. Price for pair $22.50.

**8624A.** QUEEN ANNE PERCUSSION PISTOL, altered from flintlock. Similar to illustration No. 8624 on page 97, except that this pistol has steel ramrod under the barrel. The frame, lock and barrel are all in one piece. Heavy round butt trimmed in brass. Small brass monogram plate marked: I L L. Name of maker marked on frame: WYNN LONDINI. Price $12.00.

# Flint Lock Pistols

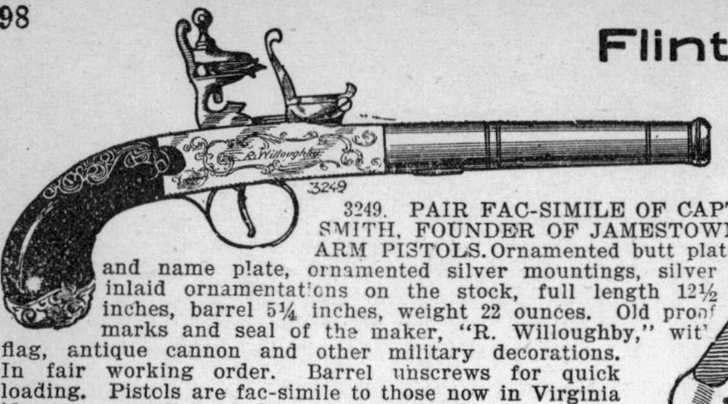

3249. PAIR FAC-SIMILE OF CAPT. JOHN SMITH, FOUNDER OF JAMESTOWN, SIDE ARM PISTOLS. Ornamented butt plate, cap and name plate, ornamented silver mountings, silver inlaid ornamentations on the stock, full length 12½ inches, barrel 5¼ inches, weight 22 ounces. Old proof marks and seal of the maker, "R. Willoughby," with flag, antique cannon and other military decorations. In fair working order. Barrel unscrews for quick loading. Pistols are fac-simile to those now in Virginia Museum as relics of Capt. John Smith.

3249A. PAIR ANCIENT FLINTLOCK PISTOLS. Centre hammer engraved "W. Guy, London," with silver mask butt, old G. P. London proof marked barrel, which unscrews for loading at the breech if desired; 6½-inch cannon-shaped barrels. Ornamented silver side and name plates. Full length 12 inches. Fine, curly walnut stock. Knob-shaped butt similar to illustration No. 3249. Fine order. Price the pair, $50.00.

3249B. ANCIENT FLINT HOLSTER PISTOL. Griffin, Bond Street, London. Similar to No. 3249. Cannon-shaped barrel. Full length 12 inches. Silver mask face butt. Silver wire inlaid ornamented stock. Price, $20.00.

3249C. SIMILAR FLINTLOCK PISTOL TO NO. 3249 PISTOL. Full length 12 inches. Engraved "Nickson, Bolsover." Curly walnut stock. Price, $18.00.

3249D. FLINTLOCK PISTOL SIMILAR TO 3249, by Buchmaster, London. Silver wire inlaid, ornamented stock. Cannon-shaped barrels. Full length — inches. Price, $20.00.

3249E. SIMILAR PISTOL to 3249. Made by Griffin, Bond Street, London. Curly walnut stock. Full length 12 inches. Price, $17.50.

3249F. SIMILAR PISTOL, by Thomas. Full length 13 inches. Price, $18.50.

3249G. SIMILAR FLINTLOCK PISTOL, by Archer, London. Full length 9½ inches. Price, $14.50.

3249H. SIMILAR PISTOL, by Joyner, London. About 1765. Full length 9 inches. Price, $14.00.

COLLECTION OF FINE, OLD BRITISH ARMY FLINTLOCK PISTOLS. CARRIED BY TRAVELERS IN OLD-TIME COACHING DAYS. OFTEN REFERRED TO AS TRAVELER'S OR COACH-SIZE PISTOL. FROM 100 TO 200 YEARS OLD.

0-1039. FLINTLOCK TRAVELING PISTOL, 5-inch octagonal steel barrel. Engraved "Clark, Holburn, London." Front and rear sight, ½-inch smooth bore. Fine, easy working lock. Checkered grip. Walnut stock. Rare pattern. Fine hammer, with safety. Engraved mountings. Fine order. Price $17.50.

0-1039A. ANCIENT FLINTOCK TRAVELING PISTOL. 5-inch octagonal steel barrel, ⅝-inch smooth bore. Engraved "W. Mills, London." Walnut stock. Hammer safety. Engraved mountings. Silver name plate, with engraved monogram, "H. P." Good order. Fine, easy working lock. Price, $15.00.

0-1039B. "McDERMOT, DUBLIN," ENGRAVED ON FLINTLOCK TRAVELING PISTOL. 4½-inch octagonal barrel, ¾-inch smooth bore, checkered grip, walnut stock. "D. C., 1902" stamped on the barrel. The date of permit showing that the British Government officials still require antique flintlocks to be licensed. Silver name plate. Fine, easy working lock. Swivel ramrod. Price, $17.50.

0-1039C. "N. WASHAM" ENGRAVED ON BARREL OF ANCIENT FLINTLOCK TRAVELING PISTOL. "Manning" engraved on the lock. 5¼-inch octagonal barrel, ⅝-inch smooth bore. Hammer safety. Easy working lock. Walnut stock. Silver name plate. Price, $14.50.

0-1039D. "E. BOND, LONDON, GUNMAKER TO THE HON. EAST INDIA CO.," engraved on barrel of TRAVELER'S ANCIENT FLINTLOCK PISTOL. 4½-inch octagonal barrel, ½-inch smooth bore. Silver side and name plate, engraved with eagle and crest. Checkered grip. Hammer safety. Engraved mountings. Fine, easy working lock. Price, $14.00.

0-1039E. TWIGGS, LONDON, ANCIENT TRAVELER'S FLINTLOCK PISTOL. 5-inch octagonal barrel, ⅝-inch smooth bore. Hammer safety. Engraved mountings. Fine, easy working lock. Walnut stock. Good condition. Price, $14.00.

0-1039G. "WHEELER, LONDON," ENGRAVED ON ANCIENT TRAVELER'S FLINTLOCK PISTOL. 4½-inch barrel, 9/16-inch smooth bore. Walnut stock. Fairly good order. Price, $10.00.

0-1039H. "BARNETT, LONDON," ON TRAVELER'S FLINTLOCK PISTOL. With swivel ramrod. The pistol is only in fair order. Price, $9.50. Barnett is one of the oldest London gunmakers. It was a Barnett who was the first president of the Gunmakers' Guild, chartered 1680 in London, and whose proof mark was the G. P. monogram. The firm has just retired from active business, having in 1912 sold to us the balance of their immense stock, which included over 12,000 of one kind of guns.

0-1039J. "TOWER, G. R., BRITISH CROWN, BROAD ARROW, T. W. RICHARDS," ENGRAVED ON FLINTLOCK TRAVELING-SIZE PISTOL. 6½-inch barrel, ⅝-inch smooth bore. Evidently made for a British Government official. Checkered grip. Walnut stock. Fine, easy working lock. Good condition. Price, $15.00.

8618. ENGLISH ARMY FLINTLOCK PISTOL, 1779 with hinged rammer. Lock marked with Royal Crown, Tower, G. R. and broad arrow. 9-inch barrel, over ⅝-inch smooth bore. Walnut stock, stamped "1779." Brass mountings. This is one of the EARLIEST DATE HINGED RAMMER ARMY PISTOLS. Price, $20.00. Similar pistol, marked 1785; price, $18.00.

8676. REVOLUTIONARY WAR PERIOD OFFICER'S HOLSTER PISTOLS. In oak case. Made by "H. Nock, London." Old British proof marks. 9-inch barrel, ⅝-inch smooth bore. Brass mountings, walnut stock. Nock pistols were used by both British and American officers during the War of the Revolution. Seldom are holster pistols found nowadays in pairs in original cases. Size of the case 17½x9½x2¾ inches. Powder flask. Case needs repairs. Price, $48.00 the pair.

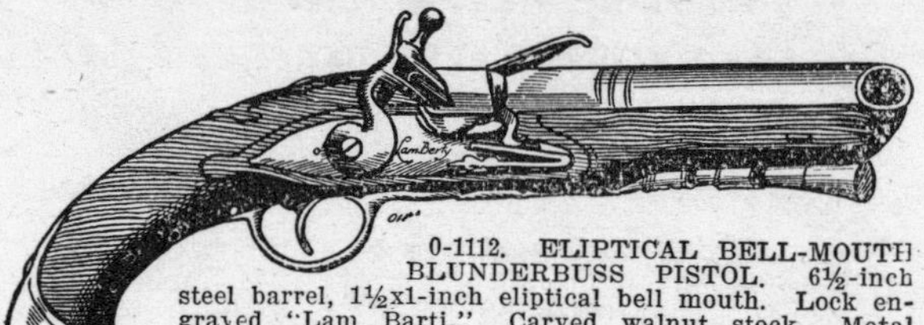

0-1112. ELIPTICAL BELL-MOUTH BLUNDERBUSS PISTOL. 6½-inch steel barrel, 1½x1-inch eliptical bell mouth. Lock engraved "Lam Barti." Carved walnut stock. Metal covered butt for use as a club. Full length 12½ inches. Rare weapon. Made to scatter shot horizontally. Price, $28.75.

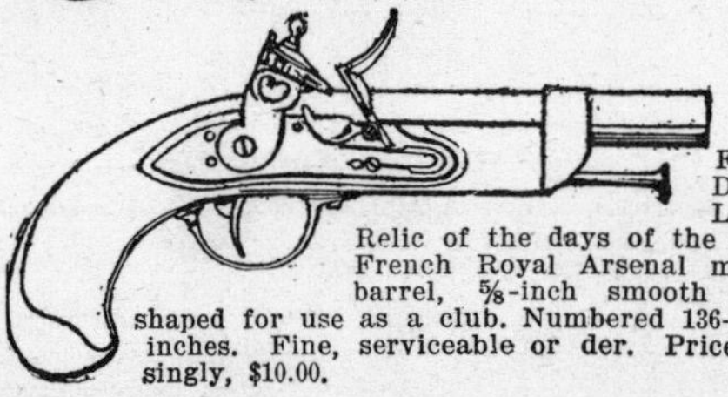

0-1111. PAIR FRENCH GENDARMIE FLINTLOCK PISTOLS. Relic of the days of the French Revolution. French Royal Arsenal marked lock, 5-inch barrel, ⅝-inch smooth bore. Butt plate shaped for use as a club. Numbered 136-79. Full length 10 inches. Fine, serviceable or der. Price the pair $19.00; singly, $10.00.

0-1041. FLINTLOCK POCKET PISTOL. Engraved "H. W. Montgomery, Gunmaker to His Majesty." With silver name plate, eagle crest and motto, "Pro Brusso et Patrea." Silvered monogram "C. F." Price, $12.50.

2105. PAIR OF TOWER FLINTLOCK HOLSTER PISTOLS. Engraved with Crown, surmounted by Cross. Evidently made in England for some foreign government. Full length 16 inches, barrel 9 inches, with swivel ramrods. Price, $15.00 per pair; $8.00 single.

0-1040. POCKET FLINTLOCK PISTOL, WITH HINGED RAMROD. London make. Polished curly walnut stock. Silver name plate. Octagonal 3½-inch barrel, ½-inch smooth bore. Fine, well-made handsome weapon. Price, $12.50.

0-1826D. "G. R." (George Rex) AND BRITISH CROWN STAMPED ON THE LOCK PLATE OF ANCIENT FLINTLOCK ARMY SOLDIER'S PISTOL. 9-inch barrel, ⅝-inch smooth bore. Brass mountings. Good condition. Price, $14.50.

10412. BATTLE OF WATERLOO FRENCH SOLDIER'S FLINTLOCK PISTOL. Found in a ditch near the battlefield. Pistol is the regular French Army model. Is rusted and valuable only as a relic of the famous battle. From London collection. Price, $15.00.

10432. FRENCH FLINTLOCK POCKET PISTOL. Engraved on the barrel 1766. Ornamented metal ball-shaped butt plate. 3¼-inch cannon-shaped barrel. Working order. Price, $16.00.

10403. QUEEN ANNE FLINTLOCK PISTOL. Cannon-shaped barrel. Oval butt stock. Pollard walnut stock. Old London proof marks. In working order. Curious shaped, rare, old pistol; about the period of 1700. Price, $18.85.

0-1026F. REA & SON, LONDON, MAKERS OF FLINTLOCK BRITISH ARMY HOLSTER PISTOL. 9-inch barrel, ¾-inch smooth bore. Period of about 1770 to 1780. Crown, 1 stamped on the lock plate. Brass mountings. Knob butt stock slightly worm-eaten, otherwise in fine order. Price, $15.00.

0-1026E. ANCIENT YEOMANRY FLINTLOCK HORSE PISTOL. Furnished by the British Government to company of yeomanry. The guard bow is marked "BUCKS," the lock Crown, Tower, G. R., and broad arrow. 9-inch barrel, ⅝-inch smooth bore. Brass covered knob butt. Fair order. Price, $15.00.

0-1026H. ANCIENT ROYAL MAIL COACH FLINTLOCK PISTOL. TOWER, G. R., CROWN, marked on the lock. Full length 14½ inches. In repaired order, some parts not original. Price, $10.00.

0-1034. ANCIENT YEOMANRY FLINTLOCK HOLSTER PISTOL. No. 42 stamped on the guard bow. Lock has the Crown with the cross. Pistol is ancient London proof marked, and English make. Cross on rare-shaped crown. Perhaps made for Government use in the reign of some English Catholic king or queen. 8½-inch barrel, ⅝-inch smooth bore. Brass mountings. Knob butt. Well preserved order. Price, $18.50.

0-1035. ANTIQUE FLINTLOCK PISTOL, WITH HINGED RAMMER. 8-inch twist steel barrel, with ½-inch flat sighting rib. Silver front sight, platinum touchhole, gold breech band, with maker's name in gold seal, inlaid, "Thomas Reynolds." Silver side and name plate. Engraved lock and mountings. Walnut stock. Checkered grip. Fine locks. Well-made gun in good condition. Price, $25.00.

0-1036. ANCIENT SPANISH FLINTLOCK HOLSTER PISTOL, WITH RARE OUTSIDE LOCK. "1790" stamped on the barrel. Pistol locks appear to be of much earlier period. Knob butt brass covered. Brass mountings, 8-inch barrel. ¾-inch smooth bore. Brass name plate. Fine condition. Price, $15.00.

8618A. ENGLISH ARMY FLINTLOCK PISTOL, dated 1787, similar to illustration No. 8618 but WITHOUT the swivel ramrod. This has steel rod with large flat end. Price $15.00.

8618B. 2 ENGLISH ARMY FLINTLOCK PISTOLS as above dated, 1800. Price $14.50 each.

8720A.—BRASS BARREL 1740 FLINTLOCK PISTOL. Full length 20½ inches. Brass lock and mountings. Date engraved on the barrel 1740. Side plate has classic subject in relief. Ball shaped knob butt. Gilt capped carved walnut stock. Price, $30.00.

8721. — GERMAN FLINTLOCK 18th CENTURY RIFLED PISTOL. Engraved on the lock "T. Goffart." 10¾ inch octagonal barrel with front and rear sight. ½ inch bore, with over 50 small rifle grooves. Ornamented and engraved mountings. Finger hold guard bow. Name plate. Silver mask butt cap. Steel points in the checkered hand grasp. Full length 16½ inches. Fine order. Price, $35.00.

8722.—"NEWTON, GRANTHAM," FLINTLOCK SIDE ARM PISTOL. 8 inch barrel, ⅝ inch smooth bore. Brass name plate and mountings. Walnut stock. Full length 14 inches. Swan shaped hammer. Price $17.00.

8723.—OVER AND UNDER FLINTLOCK DOUBLE BARREL RIFLED PISTOL. Made by "Wheeler, London." 4 inch barrels. Full length 9½ inches. Safety lock attachment. Spring lever shuts off the flash pan of the upper from the lower pistol as desired. Silver name plate. Price $16.00.

0-914. PAIR EXTRA LARGE BORE ENGLISH PISTOLS, nearly ¾ - inch smooth bore; 4-inch octagonal barrels. Percussion lock; swivel ramrod; double silver breech band; chased mountings; engraved: "Wm. Jones." Walnut stock, checkered grip; back-action locks; full length 10 inches. In good working order; fine condition; a few minor parts missing. Price, the pair, 12.50.

1000. PAIR OLD ENGLISH STAGE-COACH GUARDS' FLINTLOCK PISTOLS. Carried on the Royal Mail Coach between Leeds and Grantham, England. Lock is stamped with "British Crown, G. R. Calvert," one barrel marked "Leeds." Full length 15 inches, 11-16-inch smooth bore. Brass mountings, in good order. Price the pair, $22.00.

**0-1039. PAIR FLINT-LOCK. FINELY MADE TRAVELING PISTOLS.** By Clark, Holborn, London. Octagonal barrels 5 inches long, full length 9½ inches. Gold bushed vents, checkered stock, 9/16-inch bore. Price for pair, $30.00.

**0-1037. ANTIQUE ITALIAN FLINTLOCK TRAVELING PISTOL.** Gilt inlaid, ornamented and lettered barrel, "Torchione" name on the lock, 4½-inch barrel, ½-inch smooth bore, flat butt, knob ornamented. Steel covered, silver inlaid, ornamented stock. Inlaid pearl shield, oval name plate. Full length 9½ inches. Fine specimen of ancient Italian gunsmith's work. Bargain price, $17.50.

**1422. SCOTCH OFFICER'S FLINT LOCK PISTOL,** polished bronze metal stock. Engraved cannon-shaped muzzle and lock, twist steel barrel, 9 inches. Full length, 14 inches. In ancient Scotch pistols the stock and fore-end was entirely of metal. No wood was used. Offered in working order. Price, $25.00.

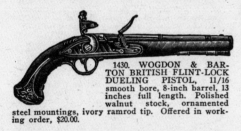

**1430. WOGDON & BARTON BRITISH FLINT-LOCK DUELING PISTOL,** 11/16 smooth bore, 8-inch barrel, 13 inches full length. Polished walnut stock, ornamented steel mountings, ivory ramrod tip. Offered in working order. $20.00.

**10598A. PAIR OF FLINTLOCK PISTOLS** similar to No. 10595; made by Simmons, but without belt hanger; full length 12½ inches; checkered walnut stock; in fine order; in rosewood case, 16x9x3½ inches. Price $85.00.

**R85B.** 1 PAIR FLINTLOCK DUELLING PISTOLS in case with combination flask. Round barrels 7 inches. Plain round butts. Made by I. Barton, London. Price. $55.00.

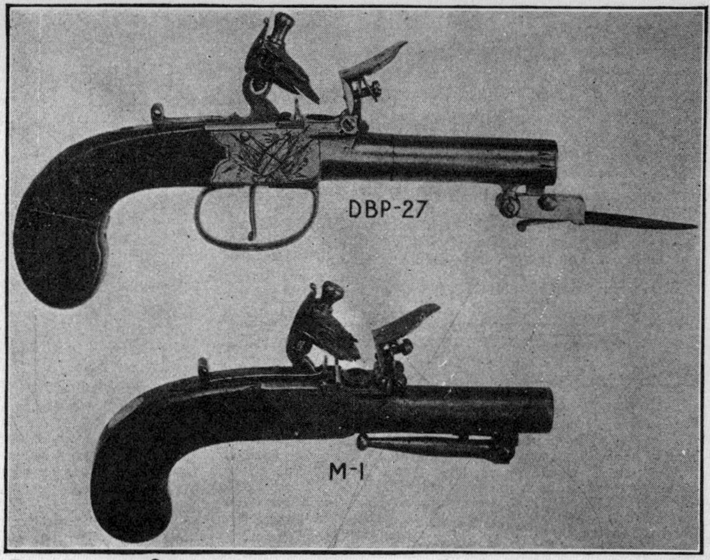

**1425. PAIR OF ITALIAN FLINTLOCK DUELING PISTOLS.** Engraved on barrels, "Pietro Moreta." Engraved lock, "Landi." 6-inch barrel, about 44 calibre. Full length, 11 inches. Carved walnut stock, ornamented brass mountings. Top of barrel flatted for sighting. One rod missing; one name plate missing. Stock in one pistol needs repairing. Offered in working order, as are. $30—pair.

**10986. PAIR FLINTLOCK PISTOLS;** in mahogany case, with bullet mould and powder flask; made by Essex, London; holster size; silver name plate is engraved G. G. N.; smooth bore barrels, octagonal shaped, 9 inches long; engraved mountings; polished curly walnut stock; checkered grip; fine easy working locks; old time proof mark on barrels; hammer safety; outfit in good order. Price $50.00.

**10987. COL. I. MAYNE PAIR FLINTLOCK DUELLING PISTOLS,** in mahogany case; engraved name plate; octagonal smooth bore 9 inch barrels engraved "Wogdon, London;" engraved mountings and butt cap; old English pineapple pattern guard plate; hair triggers; used considerably; in working order. Price $50.00 the pair, with case.

**10536. SPANISH NAVAL OFFICER'S FLINTLOCK PISTOL;** gold seal in crown on the barrel, "V BAR ZARAL;" steel belt hanger; 6 inch relief engraved cannon shaped barrel. Checkered walnut stock; engraved mountings; OUTSIDE LOCK mechanism. Price $16.50.

**1240. PAIR OF FLINTLOCK DUELING PISTOLS,** made by Myers Bruxelles. Octagonal twist steel barrels, reinforced at the muzzle; finely engraved walnut stock, with fish scale carving, with extension finger grip guard. All the mountings engraved with figures of animals; has been a handsome gun; original hammer broken. Price, with extra hammer, $30.00 the pair.

**DBP-27. BRITISH FLINTLOCK POCKET PISTOL WITH SPRING BAYONET.** Full length with bayonet extended 9½ inches, with bayonet shut 7½ inches. Bayonet is on the UNDER side and is released by drawing back the trigger guard. Flat wood butt, center hammer with safety catch, frame engraved with military trophies and marked: PALMER. Barrel has 2 British proof marks. Price $16.00.

**M-1. PAIR FLINTLOCK POCKET PISTOLS,** fitted with permanent attachment for removing the barrels for quick loading. The usual method of removing barrels was by wrench to fit over stud on barrel, or by special tool to fit in the grooves in the muzzle. These tools and wrenches were easily mislaid or lost, when most needed. By the attachment on this pair, there is no such danger. These handles could also be used to steady the aim when fired from wall or parapet. Full length 6½ inches, round barrels, 2¾ inches, with 3 proof marks. Flat wood grips, with oval monogram plates of silver, center hammer with safety catch and pan lock, secret triggers. Locks marked: RICHARDS, LONDON. Frames engraved with military trophies. Prices for pair $38.00.

**AM-272. PAIR LONG FLINTLOCK DUELLING PISTOLS,** made by H. NOCK. Ten-inch octagon barrel, long butt stock entirely checkered. 4½-inch lock with safety catch, marked: H. NOCK. Barrel marked: H. NOCK, LONDON. Fittings all engraved. Fancy trigger guard, with acorn ends, and FINGER GRIP. Wood stock half length with horn tip. A fine pair in unusual length. Price for pair $48.00.

**0-1030. ANTIQUE POCKET FLINTLOCK BAYONET PISTOL.** 3-inch rifled barrel, about 40 calibre; 8 old-time deep muzzle rifle grooves; 3-inch angular bayonet attached to the right side of the pistol. Has centre hammer with safety, concealed trigger. Engraved, "Potts, London." Walnut stock. Silver name plate. Full length 7¼ inches. Good order. Flintlock rifled pocket size pistols with side bayonets and concealed triggers are very rarely met with. Price, $20.00.

**0-1031. PAIR ANTIQUE FLINTLOCK TRAVELING PISTOLS,** by Mace, London. 4¼-inch twist steel barrels, ⅝-inch smooth bore, with wide flat tops for sighting. Front and rear sight, lock engraved, "T. Mace, Reading." Silver side and name plate. Engraved steel mountings. Fine, easy working locks. Fine, well-made pistol in well preserved serviceable order. PRICE THE PAIR, $30.00.

**2167 HANDSOME PAIR OF ORNAMENTED, SILVER-MOUNTED PERCUSSION-LOCK DUELING PISTOLS,** in case, with implements. Twist-steel, 10-inch octagonal barrel, small bore, with silver ball front sight, with small rear sight; with silver touch-hole, with silver-ornamented fore-end tip and side plate; silver name plate has the words, "S'Peo Durat Avorum," in half circle above lion; hammers are low hung, out of the way of sighting. Engraved lock and guard; ramrod rib; ebony-tipped ramrod; guard has extra finger grip; butt stock is flat shaped; silver engraved mountings on butt cap; easy working hair trigger. Made by James Wilkinson & Son, Pall Mall, London; case contains extra ramrod, powder flask, etc., all in serviceable order. Price, $40.00.

**1430-A. BRITISH OFFICER'S FLINTLOCK PISTOL,** similar to illustration No. 1430 on page 99. 8-inch tapered round barrel marked: LONDON. Brass trimmed with wood ramrod. 4¾-inch lock marked: W. HENSHAW. Price $15.00.

**1430B. BRITISH ARMY OFFICER'S FLINTLOCK PISTOL,** with 9-inch round barrel, brass trimmed, wood ramrod. 5-inch lock marked: BARBAR. Price $14.50.

**1430D. BRITISH ARMY OFFICER'S FLINTLOCK PISTOL,** with 9½-inch round barrel, marked: BLISSETT, LONDON. Ornamented brass butt and guard. Brass monogram plate marked: I. R. 4½-inch lock marked: BLISSETT. Price $14.50.

**1431A. FLINTLOCK BLUNDERBUSS,** with ring hammer, with outside lock. Twist steel barrel, gun stock butt, brass guard and butt plate. Fine order, like new. 2 inches across bell muzzle. Full length, 22 inches. Price, $15.00.

**1429. FLINTLOCK HORSE PISTOL,** same description as 1427, but with octagonal rifled barrel. Engraved on barrel "British standard proof," and on lock "Richards." In working order; required cleaning, $14.00.

**1470. BARTHOLEMY ROUSSETT FLINTLOCK DUELING PISTOL,** barrel 8½ inches, 11/16 smooth bore, full length, 16 inches. Trophy of arms and cannon engraved on side plate; engraved ornamented guard, bow and rod holder; carved walnut stock, inlaid with silvered wire. Flatted on top side of barrel for quick sighting. In good order. Price, $17.50.

**10597. PAIR OF ANTIQUE FLINTLOCK PISTOLS;** cannon shaped barrels; chased brass mountings; made by T. Richards about the period of 1750; 8½ inch barrels; ⅝ inch smooth bore; walnut stock; in working order; walnut case, 19½x7¾x3 inches. Price 45.00 the pair.

4

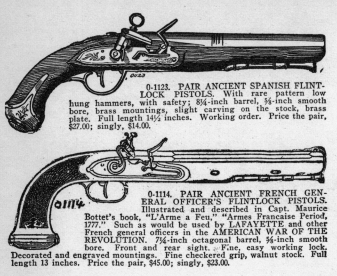

**0-1123. PAIR ANCIENT SPANISH FLINT-LOCK PISTOLS.** With rare pattern low hung hammers, with safety; 8¼-inch barrel, ⅝-inch smooth bore, brass mountings, slight carving on the stock, brass plate. Full length 14½ inches. Working order. Price the pair, $27.00; singly, $14.00.

**0-1114. PAIR ANCIENT FRENCH GENERAL OFFICER'S FLINTLOCK PISTOLS.** Illustrated and described in Capt. Maurice Bottet's book, "L'Arme a Feu," "Armes Francaise Period, 1777." Such as would be used by LAFAYETTE and other French general officers in the AMERICAN WAR OF THE REVOLUTION. 7¼-inch octagonal barrel, ⅝-inch smooth bore. Front and rear sight. Fine, easy working lock. Decorated and engraved mountings. Fine checkered grip, walnut stock. Full length 13 inches. Price the pair, $45.00; singly, $23.00.

**7105.** Ancient Brass Sun Dial, 3 inch square base. 2¼ inch protractor engraved with half and quarter hours with the points of the compass, with motto, "Early to Rise." From London collection. Price $5.00.

**0-1114A. FRENCH FLINTLOCK PISTOL,** holster size, length 15½ inches, barrel 9¾ inches, part octagonal, slightly belled at muzzle, DAMASCUS. Flat butt plate, checkered grip, trigger guard with urn end. All trimmings of cannon bronze. Price $15.00.

**7103.** Dragoon Officer's Flintlock Side Arm Pistol, with hinged rammer made by "James Wilkinson," 9 inch barrel, ⅝ inch smooth bore, engraved brass mountings, curly walnut stock, serviceable order. Price $15.00.

French Army Flintlock, long barrel pistol, stamped on the lock, "Mr. R. le de Tulle," 14½ inch barrel, ⅝ smooth bore, full length 21½ inches, brass guard and butt. Price $12.50. Similar pistol, not stamped, $10.00.

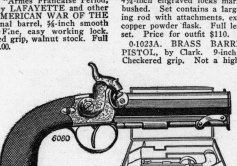

**6080.** Pair Wilkinson London Travelling Pistols, percussion lock, 31½ inch octagonal barrel, ½ inch smooth bore, ramrod rib, hinge swivel rammer, engraved hammer and mountings, silver name plate, curly walnut stock, with fine checkering, with safety lock attachments, belt hook attachment, serviceable order, with mahogany case, labeled "James Wilkinson & Son, Gun and Sword Manufacturer to Her Majesty, London." Size of case 11x7x2½ inches, brass name plate and handle, copper powder flask, bullet mould, cleaning rod wrench with bullets, etc.

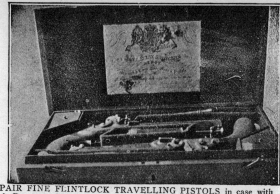

**FLC-8. PAIR FINE FLINTLOCK TRAVELLING PISTOLS** in case with tools. 8-inch Damascus barrels, octagon with front and rear sights, two gold inlay bands at breech, marked: LONDON. Half length stock with silver fore ends and silver escutcheons. Round ball butts, checkered grips, silver monogram squares marked: T. S. to G. L. Engraved guards with acorn ends, 4¼-inch engraved locks marked: DAVIDSON. The touch holes are platinum bushed. Set contains a large number of round lead balls, 11-inch wood cleaning rod with attachments, extra flints, mould for one round bullet, 4-inch oval copper powder flask. Full length of pistols is 14¼ inches. This is a very fine set. Price for outfit $110.

**0-1023A. BRASS BARREL ENGLISH FLINTLOCK, PERIOD 1775, PISTOL,** by Clark. 9-inch barrel, ⅝-inch smooth bore. Brass mountings. Checkered grip. Not a high-class pistol. Price, $17.50.

**C. S. A.** Officer's Pistol. Made by Sharpe, London, with concealed trigger, which springs into position for firing on the cocking of the hammer, checkered walnut grip. German silver band, flat-shaped butt stock. From Adam Oliver's collection, master armorer at Augusta Arsenal, Ga., 1861-65. Price, $10.00.

**FLC-9. PAIR FINE FLINTLOCK DUELLING PISTOLS,** in case with tools. Round ball butts, plain grips, full length stocks. 9¾-inch octagon barrels made by J. CHRISTOPH KUCHENREITER and so marked on barrels in silver inlay. His own private mark also inlaid in GOLD. Silver front sight, raised rear sights. Silver monogram plates, shield shape. Engraved guards with pine apple ends. 4¼-inch locks marked: RICHARDS, with safety catches. Horn tipped wood ramrods. Set contains extra lead bullets, round ball mould, screw driver, extra flints and leather covered brass flask with compartments for powder, shot or balls, and wads. Full length 14¾ inches. Price for set $75.00.

**6025. Pair Westly Richards London Duelling Pistols** in case, about ⅝ calibre, percussion lock, 8 inch octagonal twist steel barrel, silver name and side plate, engraved lock and mountings, curly walnut stock, safety attachments on the lock, full length 14 inches, mahogany case with brass handle and name plate, corner brasses, lock and catches, all in serviceable order. Size of case 16¾x8¾x2½ inches. With bullet mould, etc. Price the outfit, $40.00.

**6026.** Pair Duelling Pistols, twist steel octagonal 9 inch barrels. ½ inch smooth bore, ramrod rib, 2 silver bands at the breech, silver name and side plate, barrel engraved "J. C. Rielly, Holborn Bars, London. Walnut stock, checkered grip, oak case 17¾x8½x2¾ inches. With brass name plate, catches, lock and key, powder and shot flask, etc. Fine serviceable order. Price $40.00.

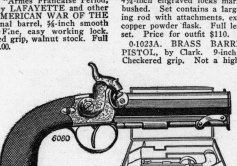

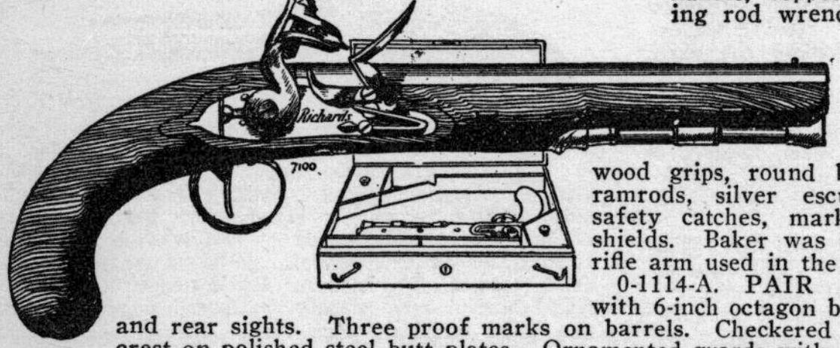

**7100-A. PAIR BRITISH FLINTLOCK PISTOLS,** with 9-inch round tapering barrels, marked: E. BAKER, LONDON. Brown finish. Checkered wood grips, round ball butts with silver plates. Swivel ramrods, silver escutcheon plates, 4¼-inch locks, with safety catches, marked: E. BAKER. Silver monogram shields. Baker was the gun maker who designed the first rifle arm used in the British Army. Price for pair, $70.00.

**0-1114-A. PAIR FRENCH FLINTLOCK PISTOLS,** with 6-inch octagon barrels, slightly belled at muzzle. Front and rear sights. Three proof marks on barrels. Checkered wood grips, flat butts with nobleman's crest on polished steel butt plates. Ornamented guards with urn ends. Wood rod with white ivory tips. 3¾-inch locks marked: LOUE AU MANS. Price for pair, $35.00.

**0-1106A. PAIR FLINTLOCK BRASS BARREL SPRING BAYONET PISTOLS.** Similar in size and description to No. 0-1106, with FLUTED walnut stocks, with the exception of a slight difference in the decoration of the stock. Price the pair, $25.00; singly, $12.85. This kind was furnished by French Government to naval officers up to 1763. The bayonet for use in hand to hand attack in boarding.

**0-1026. ARMY OFFICER'S FLINTLOCK HOLSTER PISTOL.** Made by Egg, London. Length of barrel 9 inches, full length 15 inches. Price, $17.50.

**6008. BAILEY, PLYMOUTH (ENGLAND), PEPPER BOX REVOLVER.** 6 shot, 3½-inch fluted steel barrels, engraved German silver frame and butt strap. Serviceable order. Price, $12.00.

**6027. PAIR EBONY STOCK DUELLING PISTOLS,** twist steel 10 inch barrels, ½ inch smooth bore, silver front sight, name and side plates, silver fore end, ramrod rib, safety attachments to the lock, engraved mountings, finger grip guard bow, ebony case, checkered grip, full length 16 inches, fine serviceable order, mahogany case 19x9x3 inches, brass name plate and handle, lock and catches, bullet mould, powder and shot flask, cleaning rod and rammers. Price, the outfit, $50.00.

**0-1122. PAIR FRENCH FLINTLOCK PISTOLS.** Size carried by travelers in ancient days. 4¼-inch rifled barrels, cannon muzzle, ornamented and engraved mountings. Walnut stock engraved butt cap. Full length 9 inches. Eight-grooved riflings, ½-inch bore. Price the pair, $26.00; singly, $13.50.

**0-912. LARGE BORE ENGLISH PERCUSSION RIFLED PISTOL.** Engraved, "John Lord"; 8-inch twist steel barrel. Silver sight, breech band, side plates, vent plug and name plate. Swivel ramrod. Nearly ¾-inch rifle bore, walnut stock, checkered grip. Well-made pistol. Price, $9.85. Another similar pistol by Hamburg, London, not in quite as good order. Price, $8.85.

**1007. JOHN BLANCH & SON REVOLVER,** made under Adam's patent, in case with wad cutter, metal cap box and cleaning rod. Six shot 6¾-inch barrel, checkered walnut stock, fired by pull on the trigger. In serviceable order. Oak case size 14x8x2½ inches. Price, outfit, $9.85.

# FLINT PISTOLS

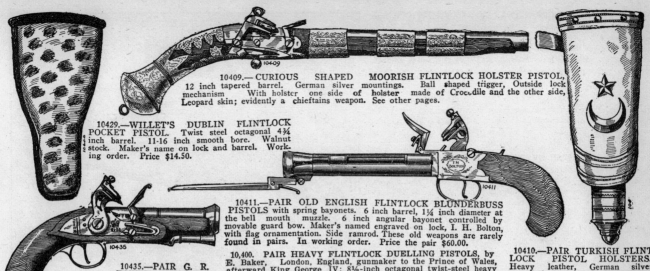

**10409.—CURIOUS SHAPED MOORISH FLINTLOCK HOLSTER PISTOL,** 12 inch tapered barrel. German silver mountings. Ball shaped trigger, Outside lock mechanism. With holster one side of holster made of Crocodile and the other side, Leopard skin; evidently a chieftains weapon. See other pages.

**10429.—WILLET'S DUBLIN FLINTLOCK POCKET PISTOL.** Twist steel octagonal 4¾ inch barrel. 11-16 inch smooth bore. Walnut stock. Maker's name on lock and barrel. Working order. Price $14.50.

**10411.—PAIR OLD ENGLISH FLINTLOCK BLUNDERBUSS PISTOLS** with spring bayonets. 6 inch barrel, 1¼ inch diameter at the bell mouth muzzle. 6 inch angular bayonet controlled by movable guard bow. Maker's named engraved on lock, I. H. Bolton, with flag ornamentation. Side ramrod. These old weapons are rarely found in pairs. In working order. Price the pair $60.00.

**10435.—PAIR G. R. TOWER FLINTLOCK BLUNDERBUSS HOLSTER PISTOLS.** Side locks. 4½ inch brass cannon shaped barrel. 1¼ inches in diameter across the bell mouth muzzle. Stamped with British crown, G. R. and Tower on the lock. Brass mountings. Walnut stock. British Government broad arrow marks; about the *period of 1775*. Blunderbusses are rarely found in Government service. This outfit perhaps furnished to British army officer for service in America during the Revolutionary War. See other pages.

**10,400. PAIR HEAVY FLINTLOCK DUELLING PISTOLS,** by E. Baker, London, England, gunmaker to the Prince of Wales, afterward King George IV; 8½-inch octagonal twist-steel heavy barrels. Silver shield name-plate, fore-end tip and escutcheons, engraved seal on the lock-plate, with maker's name; engraved on the barrel, "gunmaker to H. R. H. Prince of Wales." Barrels are ½-inch smooth bore, checkered walnut grip stock. In fine, serviceable order, in mahogany case, with copper powder flask and ramrods. (Case needs repairing.) Price, the outfit, $60.00.

FLINTLOCK DUELLING PISTOLS, SINGLE WEAPONS, ORIGINALLY IN CASES IN PAIRS. FINE, WELL-MADE, HIGH-CLASS PISTOLS NOW OFFERED SINGLY AT BARGAIN PRICES.

**10410.—PAIR TURKISH FLINT LOCK PISTOL HOLSTERS.** Heavy leather, German silver engraved mountings. Cloth fronts with gilt lace borders (tarnished). With crescent and star ornaments. Length 13½ inches. Price the pair $8.85.

AMERICAN REVOLUTIONARY WAR PERIOD ARMY HOLSTER PISTOLS BY DELANEY, EGG, NOCK, WILLIAMS AND OTHER GUNMAKERS OF THAT PERIOD, WHOSE PISTOLS WERE USED BY OFFICERS IN BOTH BRITISH AND AMERICAN ARMIES.

**0-1017.  FLINTLOCK DUELLING PISTOLS, WITH HAIR-TRIGGER, MADE BY BATES, LONDON.** 10-inch octagonal barrel, ⅝-inch smooth bore. Front and rear sight. Maker's seal E-B in barrel. Lock chased and engraved, "Bates, London." Polished walnut stock. In fine order. If in pair and case they would be worth $60.00. For the single pistol our bargain price is $20.00.

**LR-1. 10 EARLY FRENCH FLINTLOCK PISTOLS,** with 7½-inch round barrels. Heavy brass frame, trigger guard and round butt. Some have holder for use in sash or belt. A few are marked on frame ST. ETIENNE, with CROWN AND A LETTER. Some have stamped on stock AVRIL D 1783. We offer them without selection, in fine order at $11.00 each.

**0-1019. T. RICHARDS ENGRAVED ON FLINTLOCK DUELLING PISTOL.** 8½-inch barrel, with maker's seal, T-R, and with rare proof mark crown P and crown V; ⅝-inch smooth bore. Carved walnut stock. Ball butt, brass mounted. Mask face butt. Brass name plate. Pistol is in good condition. Fine easy working lock. Price, $18.50.

**0-1021. SILVER-MOUNTED FLINTLOCK DUELLING PISTOL.** 9-inch barrel, 11-16-inch smooth bore. Lock engraved, "Helley & Co." Hammer safety. Silver shield, name and side plates. Hall marked for 1796 on the silver guard. Walnut stock. In fair order. Price, $25.00.

**0-1023. BRASS BARREL FLINTLOCK PISTOL,** made by Brooks, London, about 1760; 8¾-inch barrel, ⅝-inch smooth bore, engraved brass mountings. Walnut stock. Knob butt. Engraved brass butt and name plate. Fair order. Price, $18.85.

**1 BRITISH FLINTLOCK PISTOL,** holster size, with 9-inch round barrel, brass trigger guard and plain round butt. Wood ramrod has horn tip. Lock marked H NOCK. Barrel marked LONDON, with proof marks. Price, $12.00.

**1 BRITISH ARMY HOLSTER FLINTLOCK PISTOL,** with 9-inch round barrel, brass trigger guard and steel ramrod. Lock marked W. PARKER. Plain round wood butt. Price, $13.50.

**1 BRITISH YEOMANRY FLINTLOCK PISTOL,** with 9-inch round barrel. Brass butt plate and guard. Wood ramrod is brass tipped. Lock marked PROBIN. Barrel has British proof marks and initials W. F. Price, $12.50.

**1 BRITISH HOLSTER FLINTLOCK PISTOL,** 9-inch barrel, with front and REAR sights. Ornamented steel trigger, and guard. Lock marked PROSSER. Barrel marked CHARING CROSS LONDON. Narrow wood stock with large checkering. Price, $14.50.

**1 BRITISH ARMY FLINT LOCK PISTOL,** with 9-inch round barrel, brass guard and butt plate. Lock marked H NOCK TOWER and CROWN. Barrel has English proof marks. Price, $12.50.

**0-1025. OFFICERS' FLINTLOCK HOLSTER PISTOL,** by D. Egg, London.  10-inch barrel, 9-16-inch smooth bore. British proof marked. Lock stamped, "D. Egg." Walnut stock. Ball butt. Brass mask face butt plate. Period 1775. Good order. Price, $17.50.

**0-1026. BRITISH ARMY OFFICERS' FLINTLOCK HORSE-PISTOL.** 9-inch barrel, 11-16-inch smooth bore. Engraved, "D. Egg, London." Lock has the British Tower and Crown marks, also the Government Broad Arrow mark. Guard is marked, "D No. 42." Much used, fair order. Price, $17.50.

**0-1027. OFFICERS' FLINTLOCK PISTOL.** 8-inch barrel, about ¾-inch smooth bore. Engraved London, with the old G. P. London proof marks, seal L. D. Lock is engraved, "Delaney." Brass covered knob butt. Brass mountings, name and side plates. About period 1750 to 1765. Many of Delaney pistols were used by American Revolutionary War Officers. Good working order, shows much usage. Price, $25.00.

**0-1028. TWO ARMY OFFICERS' FLINTLOCK HOLSTER PISTOLS,** by H. Nock. 9-inch barrel, 11/16-inch smooth bore. Lock marked H. Nock, period about 1770. Brass mounted. Walnut stock. Plain butts. Price, $14.50 each.

**0-1022A. 1750 PERIOD ENGLISH FLINTLOCK PISTOLS,** 9¾-inch barrels, ⅝-inch smooth bore. Muzzle end of the barrel now very thin. Name "Dafte" on the lock. One of London's early flint gunmakers. Engraved ball butt. Walnut mountings. Fair order. Price, $16.00.

**0-1025B. PAIR BRITISH FLINT-LOCK HOLSTER PISTOLS,** with 6¾-inch cannon barrels, with 3 proof marks. Fish tail butts with mask designs on brass plates. Brass guards, side plates and ramrod guides. Brass name plates. 4½-inch locks marked: WILSON. He was gunmaker in London about 1770. Price for pair $30.00.

**0-1026A. OFFICER'S FLINTLOCK HOLSTER PISTOL,** 9-inch barrel, ⅝-inch smooth bore. Brass-covered knob butt. Walnut stock. Lock stamped "Williams." Price $17.00.

**0-1026B. ENGLISH FLINTLOCK HOLSTER PISTOL,** 9-inch barrel, ⅝-inch smooth bore. Lock marked with Tower, G. R., British Crown and broad arrow with small crown. Brass-covered butt plate marked 19, broad arrow and B. O. "Board of Ordnance" marked on the butt stock. Hinged rammer. Good order. Price, $16.50.

**0-1026H. FLINTLOCK HORSE PISTOL,** stamped 1786 on the lock-plate; 9-inch barrel, ⅝-inch smooth bore. Hinged rammer. Traces to be seen of Crown and Tower markings. Price, $14.50.

**0-1026C. 1802 EAST INDIA CO. VOLUNTEER'S FLINTLOCK HOLSTER PISTOL.** Veil stamped in heart-shaped shield. Barrel and lock stamped "Wright, 1802." Brass-covered knob butt. Brass mountings. Crown and figure 2 on the lock. Good condition. Scarce type. Price, $16.50.

**0-1026E. 1786 and CROWN STAMPED ON FLINTLOCK HORSE PISTOL,** 9-inch barrel, ⅝-inch smooth bore. London proof mark E; 25, G. R., Crown, Tower and Broad Arrow 1786. Brass-mounted knob butt. Fair order; stock is somewhat worm-eaten. Price, $15.00.

**10427. PAIR OLD FLINTLOCK BRASS-BARREL POCKET PISTOLS.** ½-inch smooth bore. 3-inch octagonal barrel. Checkered grip. Walnut stock. English and Belgian proof marks. Full length, 8 inches. Hammer safety. Working order. Price the pair, $14.85.

# FLINT LOCK PISTOLS AND BLUNDERBUSSES

SFL. PAIR BRITISH GREAT COAT FLINTLOCK PISTOLS with 4-inch round barrel with flat top, marked: CHARING CROSS, LONDON. Bore ¾ inch. Full length 8 inches. Round butt with checkered grips, silver monogram plate, ornamented trigger guard with pine apple end. 3¼-inch locks marked: BRUNN, with safety catches. Front and rear sights, platinum touch holes, brass tipped rods. Price for pair $28.00.

SFL-1. PAIR BRITISH GREAT COAT POCKET FLINTLOCK PISTOLS with 5¾-inch round barrels with flat top, marked: LONDON. Round wood butts with checkered grips. Brass trigger guards, ramrod tips and side plates. Metal rods. 3¾-inch locks with safety catches, marked: BRUNN. Price for pair $33.00.

SFL-2. PAIR BRITISH OVERCOAT POCKET PISTOLS, FLINTLOCK, with 3¾-inch octagon barrels, with silver front sights. Barrels marked: LONDON. Round wood butts, engraved tangs and guards, which are with pine apple ends. Brass tipped wood rods. 3½-inch locks with safety catches, marked: H. NEW, Bore ¾ inch. Price for pair $30.00.

SFL-3. FLINTLOCK POLICE PISTOL with 4½-inch round barrel with flat top, marked: LONDON. Bore 11/16 inch. Round wood butt, checkered. Long brass guard with acorn end. 3¾-inch lock marked: W. PARKER. Horn tipped wood rod. Parker was a Government Contractor. Price $11.00.

SFL-4. PAIR ALTERED FLINTLOCK PISTOLS with round wood butts, all checkered, 4-inch octagon barrels, with front and rear sights, bore 9/16 inch, marked: 51 LONDON WALL. Silver monogram ovals, brass tipped wood rods, engraved guards, old type with square backs and pine apple ends. 3½-inch locks marked: E. LONDON. Price for pair $25.00.

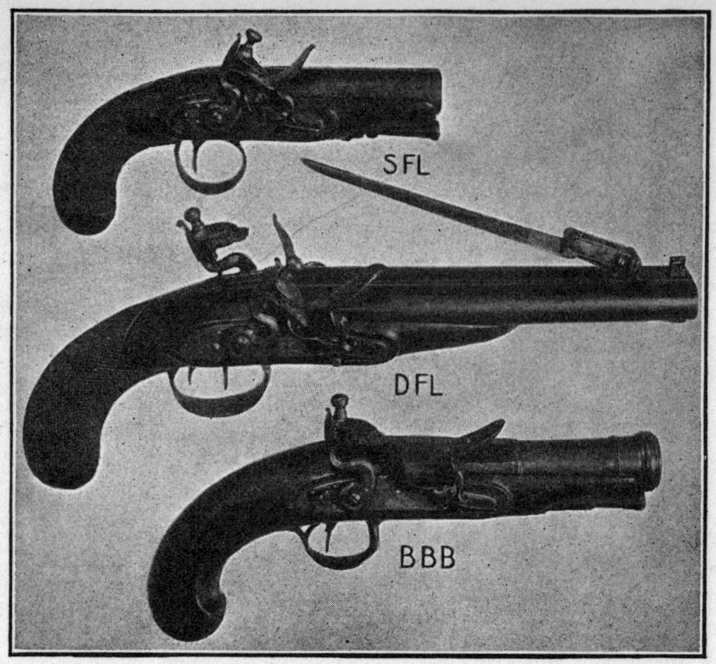


SFL-5. FLINTLOCK POCKET PISTOL with 4-inch barrel, marked: LONDON, C B-419. The initials and number are the IRISH permit mark as required by law at that time. Round wood butt, checkered, engraved guard with pine apple end. Silver monogram plate, diamond shape. 3½-inch lock marked: ADAMS. Brass tipped wood rod. Price $12.00.

DFL. DOUBLE BARREL FLINTLOCK PISTOL WITH TOP SPRING BAYONET. Full length 14 inches, round wood butt with finely checkered grip, 8½-inch round bronze trigger guard, engraved, with URN end. Ivory tipped wood rod, 8½-inch round barrels with 7-inch spring bayonet mounted on TOP. 4½-inch locks marked: SHARPE. This piece is in very fine condition. Price $40.00.

BBB. BRITISH BRONZE BARREL FLINT BLUNDERBUSS. Bird's head wood butt horn tipped wood rod, part octagon barrel 5½ inches long with two old English proof marks, with LONDON on top. Bore at muzzle ⅞ inch. 4¼-inch bronze lock with bronze pan. Lock has safety catch and is marked: BLAIR. Engraved bronze trigger guard with ACORN end. Blunderbusses in this pistol type are rare. Price $35.00.

BBP-1. FRENCH FLINT POCKET PISTOL with brass barrel and frame in one piece. Full length 7½ inches, barrel 3½ inches, with reinforced cannon muzzle. Flat wood stock, center hammer with catch, trigger guard. Price $8.50.

BBP-2. FRENCH FLINT POCKET PISTOL, period LOUIS XVI, similar to No. BBP-1, length 7½ inches. Price $8.00.

BBP-3. FRENCH FLINT POCKET PISTOL, like No. BBP-1, length 7¼ inches, no safety catch. Belgian proof mark. Price $7.50.

BBP-4. BRITISH FLINT POCKET PISTOL with brass frame and barrel in one piece. Frame marked: LONDON, barrel marked with Belgian proof mark. Length 6¼ inches, round wood stock, center hammer with catch, trigger guard, cannon shaped barrel with reinforced muzzle. Price $8.50.

BBP-5. FRENCH FLINTLOCK POCKET PISTOL, brass barrel and frame, checkered wood stock inlaid with fine silver tacks, cannon barrel, center hammer with catch, frame decorated with draped flags. Price $8.25.

FFL-30. LOUIS XVI FLINT POCKET PISTOL, length 7½ inches, lock 3½ inches, cannon barrel, half octagonal, 3½ inches. Oval butt with plate guard with acorn end, iron rod. Price $6.00.

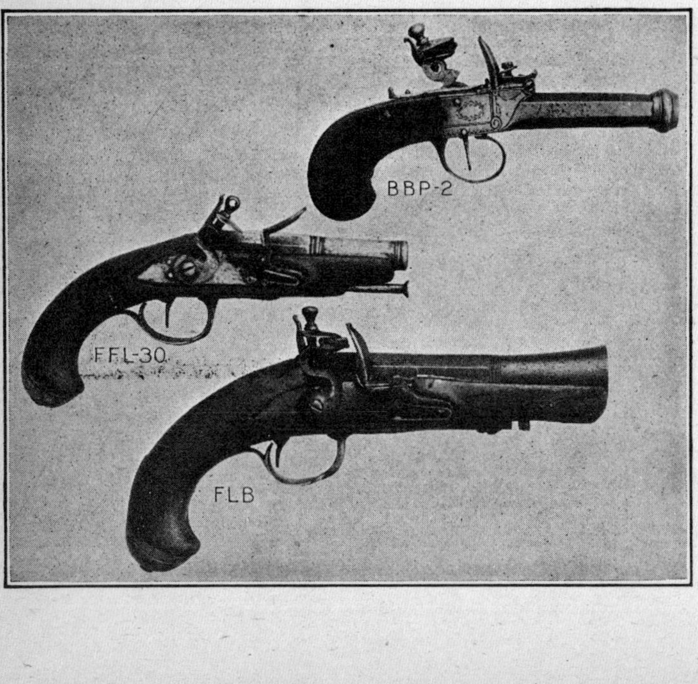


FFL-31. LOUIS XV FLINT POCKET PISTOL, with brass guard, butt plate and lock strap. Length 8 inches, half octagonal barrel 3½ inches, 3½-inch lock. Price $7.00.

FFL-32. FRENCH FLINT POCKET PISTOL, similar to No. FFL-31, with 3¾-inch barrel, 3¼-inch lock, all brass trimmed, full length 8 inches. Price $8.00.

FFL-33. LOUIS XV FLINT POCKET PISTOL, with wood carved stock, silver wire inlaid grip cannon barrel 3¼ inches, 3⅛-inch lock, full length 7⅛ inches. Ornamented metal trimmed, guard with acorn end. Price $10.00.

FFL-35. PAIR LOUIS XVI FLINTLOCK POCKET PISTOLS, with cannon barrels, 2¾ inches, round butts, 2¾-inch locks, stock reaches only to front end of lock. Pistols of this type in such small size are rare. Price for pair $25.00.

FFL-36. LOUIS XV FLINTLOCK POCKET PISTOL in very fine condition. Wood carved stock, all trimmings of bright metal, 2⅞-inch barrel with gold plated etching. Oval butt with plate, long guard with urn end, 3-inch lock. Full length 6¾ inches. This pistol is a miniature of the regular army horse pistols. Price $18.00

FLB. PAIR FRENCH BLUNDERBUSS FLINTLOCK PISTOLS, with 5-inch half octagon barrel with 1 1/16th-inch bell muzzles. Bird head butt with brass plates. Early pattern French guards of brass with acorn ends. 4-inch locks. These are period of Louis XV, and are a rare type, as blunderbusses are seldom found in paris, and in such small size. Price for pair $30.00.

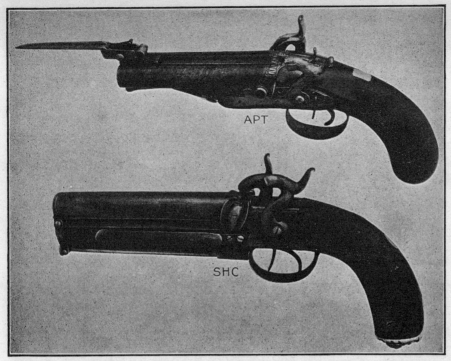

APT

SHC

**A P T. ALTERED DOUBLE BARREL PISTOL WITH SPRING BAYONET.** Originally flintlock, altered to percussion, fitted with SPRING bayonet on top, with release on tang between the hammers. Finely checkered wood grip, round barrels. Sold to Albert Payson Terhune for his collection.

**S H C. PAIR SHIP CAPTAINS SUPERPOSED PERCUSSION PISTOLS.** These are the same style as used by the British Sea Captains for the early days. In a previous catalog we offered a pair of similar shape, the style used by Captain Cook on his explorations. Finely checkered pistol grips, silver butts with LION heads. Engraved hammers, trigger guards, frames and tangs. 4¼-inch sash or belt hooks, 6-inch barrels with front and rear sights, swivel ramrods under lower barrel. Full length 11½ inches. Price for pair, $60.00. Single pistol, $35.00.

**0-727. PAIR SMITH LONDON PERCUSSION PISTOLS.** 4-inch twist steel barrels, with flatted sighting rib, ½-inch smooth bore. Silver front sight, name and side plates. Chased lock and mountings. Hammer safety attachment. Polished walnut stock, checkered grip. Full length 9 inches. Silver vent plugs. Fine, easy working locks. A pair well-made pistols in good serviceable order for $20.00.

**0-726. PAIR PARKER FIELD & SON PERCUSSION PISTOLS.** 4½-inch octagonal twist steel, ½-inch smooth bore barrels. Chased lock and mountings. Maker's name and address engraved on the lock and barrel. Polished walnut stock. Checkered grip. Silver vent plugs and name plate. Full length 9 inches. Easy working locks. Well-made pistols, in good, serviceable order. Price the pair, $25.00.

**H S P-1. PAIR OLD ENGLISH FLINT LOCK PISTOLS,** with 7-inch cannon barrels, marked: LONDON, with 3 proof marks. Barrels are removable for quick loading. Key is included with pair. Fish tail butt with metal plates, long guards with urn ends, fancy side plates in scroll designs, large monogram plates with floral tips, 4-inch locks marked: HAWKINS. He was a LONDON gunmaker about the time of 1760. Price for pair, $55.00.

**H S P-2. FLINT LOCK POCKET PISTOL, QUEEN ANNE TYPE,** with 3¾ inch removable cannon barrel, with 3 old proof marks. Round ball butt, long brass trigger guard, brass side plate. 3¾-inch lock marked: T. HENSHAW. With the pistol is a mould for one round bullet and the plug end for unscrewing the barrel. Moulds of this type are rare. Price for pistol with mould is $12.00.

**No. 2-26-1 (lower). EUROPEAN CAVALRY PERCUSSION PISTOL,** in fine order, with polished hard wood stock, long brass trigger guard, and round brass butt plate. Very early pattern altered from flintlock. Full length 12 inches, barrel 5¾ inches. Some pistols marked on barrel and butt with early dates. Price, $4.85.

**No. 2-26-2 (center). GENDARMERIE PERCUSSION PISTOL,** the type used in 1822 to 1842, now altered from flintlock. All metal parts of steel, bright finished. Full length 9½ inches, barrel 5 inches. Nose band attached to side plate. Front action 4-inch lock plate with name. Heavy round butt plate. Price, $5.25.

**No. 2-26-3 (top). DOUBLE ACTION FRENCH TYPE PIN FIRE PISTOL,** with rounded butt stock, two hammers, two triggers, with guard, 4-inch barrels with flat top rib with front sight. Full length 8½ inches. Caliber is 12 m/m. In good order. Price, $4.50.

**R.P. RARE PATTERN PELLET PISTOL,** Inventor's model, with 6½-inch octagon barrel, with front and rear sights. Wood carved grip, flat butt. 3-inch back action lock with outside hammer. Threaded steel plug similar to that used on the FERGUSON rifle, is taken out to insert the pellet, which cannot get lost or made unserviceable by rain. This is only the second one of this type that we have had in twenty-five years. Price, $20.00.

**V-2. ONE PAIR OLD COPPER POWDER FLASKS,** made by J. MATTHEWMAN. Came to us from NEW ENGLAND. Eight inches long, 4 inches wide at bottom. Plain backs, fronts show stag and fox heads with two fox hounds, surrounded by oak leaves and acorns. Spring tops with measuring necks. Price for pair, $7.00.

**V-3. BELGIAN PERCUSSION PISTOL,** with 3½-inch octagonal twist steel barrel, center hammer, and round wood butt. Has 3½-inch pointed spring bayonet released by drawing back sliding trigger guard. Price, $8.00.

**V-4. BELGIAN PERCUSSION PISTOL,** with 4-inch octagonal barrel, plain steel, with 3½-inch pointed spring bayonet held in place by sliding trigger guard. Center hammer, round wood butt. Engraved frame. Price, $7.50.

**V-6. EUROPEAN PERCUSSION PISTOL,** Navy type, with heavy octagonal barrel, 4¾ inches, bore 11/16 inch. Outside hammer, brass trigger guard and butt plate. Total length 9½ inches. Has 3½-inch belt attachment for carrying in belt or sash. Price, $8.00.

**V-7. PERCUSSION PISTOL,** with 3½-inch octagonal barrel, looks like Damascus, with outside hammer and folding trigger, no guard. Frame of German silver, marked: LONDON, with Belgian proof mark. Black wood grip, saw hammer type, without protection, with silver name plate, and small cap box in butt. Price, $6.00.

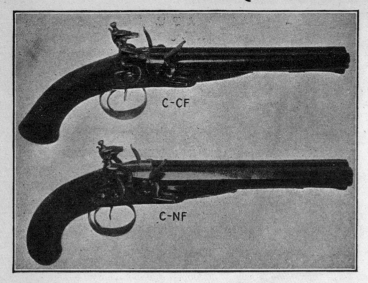

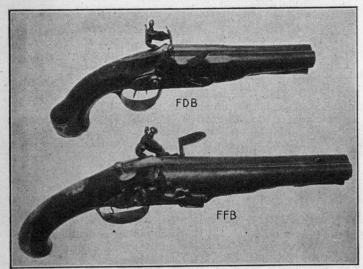

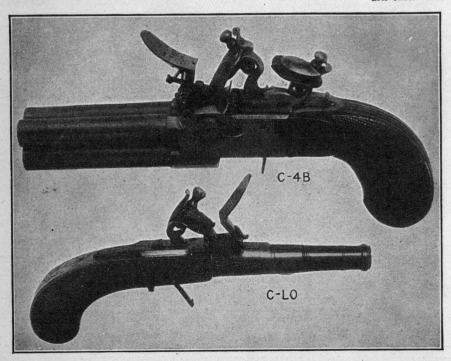

C-C F. BRITISH FLINT PISTOL, DOUBLE BARREL, full length 15 inches, round barrels, side by side, 9 inches, bore 9/16 inch. Silver front sight. Barrels marked on center rib: CLARK, HOLBORN, LONDON. Narrow wood butt, checkered grip, engraved guard with pineapple end. Wood rod with horn tip, engraved rod guide, and tang. 3¾-inch locks marked: CLARK, with GOLD touch holes. This style of pistol made for officer's use in the INDIAN SERVICE. Price, $75.00. (From British Collection.)

C-N F. PAIR FINE BRITISH FLINTLOCK PISTOLS, DOUBLE BARREL. Full length 15 inches, octagon barrels, side by side, 9¾ inches. These have gold lined breeches, with maker's name on each barrel in gold with CROWN over S. NOCK. On top rib between barrel is marked: S. NOCK, LONDON, GUNMAKER TO HIS MAJESTY. Round wood butts, finely checkered grips, ornamented guards with pineapple ends. 3¾-inch engraved locks with safety catches, marked: S. NOCK. Touch holes are platinum lined. These pistols in fine condition. Price for pair, $200.00. (From British Collection.)

F D B. FRENCH DOUBLE BARREL FLINTLOCK PISTOL, with RIFLED barrels, cannon shaped, 6½ inches long, bore 9/16 inch. Full length, 12 inches. Wide engraved trigger guard with urn end, ivory tipped wood rod, round ball butt with metal plate. 3½ inch locks. PISTOL CAPTURED FROM FRENCH OFFICER AT BATTLE OF WATERLOO. Price, $60.00.

F D B-1. FRENCH DOUBLE BARREL FLINTLOCK PISTOL, with polished wood stock, fish tail butt with plate, early pattern guard with urn end, 4½ inch round barrels, with center groove for sighting, bore 9/16 inch, full length 9½ inches. Wood rod white ivory tipped. 3¾ inch locks. French pistols of this type are rare. Price, $28.00.

F F B. PAIR DOUBLE BARREL FLINTLOCK PISTOLS, full length 15 inches, barrels 8¾ inches, bore 9/16 inch, carved wood stocks full length, bird's head butts with engraved plates. Ornamental trigger guards, engraved, with urn ends. Steel front sights with cut out tank for sighting. 4½ inch locks, marked: CLAUDE NIQUET, A LIEGE. Engraved monogram plates. A rare pair. Price for pair, $100.00.

C-4B. FRENCH FOUR BARREL FLINTLOCK PISTOL, with TWO hammers and ONE folding or secret trigger. Rounded wood butt, finely checkered, 3½ inch round barrels, full length 9 inches. Safety catch on tang to lock BOTH hammers at once. Catch at side to cut off the lower barrels while the upper ones are being fired. In fine condition. Price, $65.00. (From British Collection.)

C-L O. ALL STEEL FLINTLOCK POCKET PISTOL made by LOWE, LONDON, and so marked on engraved frame. Full length 7¾ inches, cannon barrel, 3-inch, removable, with stud for barrel wrench. Center hammer folding or secret trigger with stud safety. Butt engraved with floral decorations. This is a rare type. Price, $50.00. From British Collection.

## $3.20

AM-24. 200 PERCUSSION PISTOLS with center hammer, 3¼-inch octagonal barrels, large trigger guard, round wood butt stock. All in working order. Total length 8 inches. Price $3.20 each.

1207. ELLIOTT FOUR - BARREL PISTOL, caliber .32, with 3⅜-inch barrels. Ring trigger, hammerless, double action. Barrels tip up to load and eject, by releasing small catch in front of trigger. Barrels marked: MANUFACTURED BY REMINGTON & SONS, ILION, N. Y. ELLIOTT'S PATENTS. Blued finish. Price $18.00.

AM-27-A. 100 assorted percussion pocket pistols, similar to No. AM-27 but with fancier trimmings and of finer workmanship. Price $4.95 each.

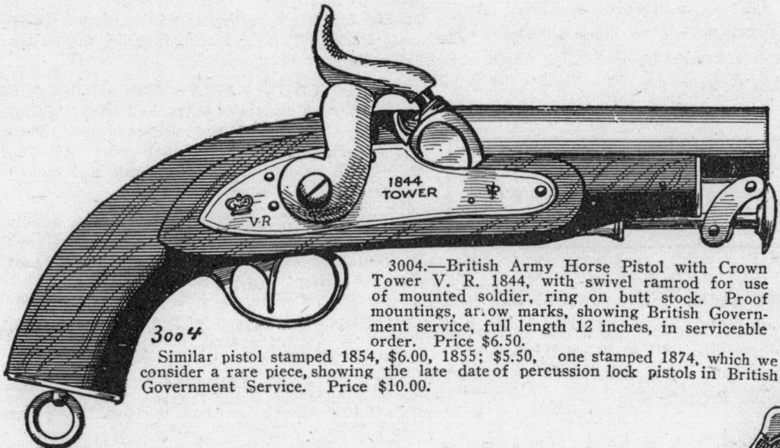

3121.—Pair of first U. S. Navy Percussion Lock Pistols, made under contract, one by N. P. Ames, Chicopee Falls, Mass.; the other by Henry De ringer, Philadelphia, Pa. Calibre 54, muzzle loading with swivel ramrod stamped on the lock 1844 with name of maker and U. S. Navy. Brass mountings, hammer on the inside of the lock plate, and the only arm so made and adopted by the U. S. Government. Price for these 2 rare pistols, one of each make, $55.00, or singly $30.00.

6088. Pair Westley Richards Travelling Pistols in Mahogany Case; 6-inch octagonal twist steel ⅝ inch smooth bore barrels, hinged swivel rammers, engraved mountings. On barrel "Westley Richards, 170 New Bond St., London." Curly walnut stock checkered grip, silver name plate and escutcheons, fine order, percussion locks. Case measures 14¼x8½x2¾ inches, brass, name plate and handle contains copper powder flask, etc. The outfit $14.00.

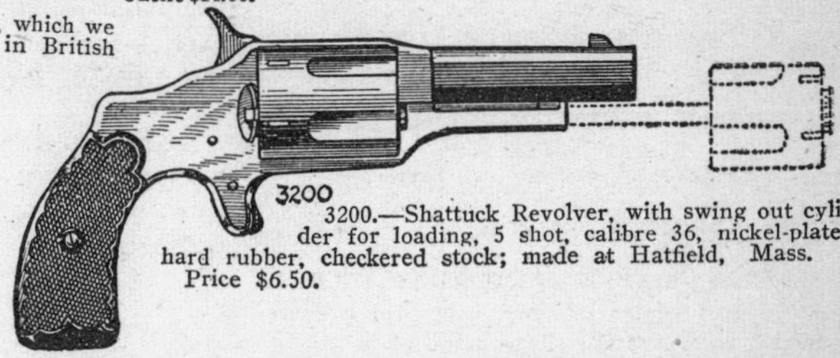

3004.—British Army Horse Pistol with Crown Tower V. R. 1844, with swivel ramrod for use of mounted soldier, ring on butt stock. Proof mountings, arrow marks, showing British Government service, full length 12 inches, in serviceable order. Price $6.50.

Similar pistol stamped 1854, $6.00, 1855, $5.50, one stamped 1874, which we consider a rare piece, showing the late date of percussion lock pistols in British Government Service. Price $10.00.

3200.—Shattuck Revolver, with swing out cylinder for loading, 5 shot, calibre 36, nickel-plated, hard rubber, checkered stock; made at Hatfield, Mass. Price $6.50.

JC12. BRITISH WEBLEY MARK VI. REVOLVER. Caliber .44. This is the latest model of the regulation English Army side arm. Barrel is 7½ inches long. Cartridges can be bought for the gun in this country. Fine order and exceedingly scarce outside of England. $20.00.

DUPLICATE of above but with original holster and cartridge box just as turned in by the officer who used it in the war. Priced at $25.00. Complete. Fine Shooting order.

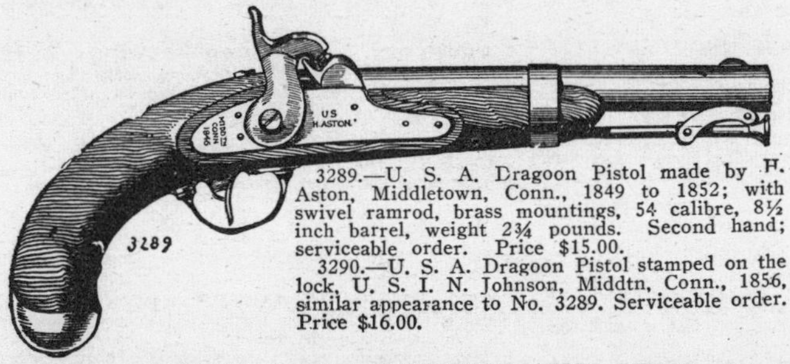

3201. KNUCKLE DUSTER, or MY FRIEND, REVOLVER. Caliber .22, 7 shot, with cylinder entirely enclosed in heavy brass frame. Pin at muzzle end is withdrawn to remove cylinder for loading and ejecting. Butt has finger hole. These pistols were used in the fist after the seven shots had been fired. Price $17.50.

3289.—U. S. A. Dragoon Pistol made by H. Aston, Middletown, Conn., 1849 to 1852; with swivel ramrod, brass mountings, 54 calibre, 8½ inch barrel, weight 2¾ pounds. Second hand; serviceable order. Price $15.00.

3290.—U. S. A. Dragoon Pistol stamped on the lock, U. S. I. N. Johnson, Middtn, Conn., 1856, similar appearance to No. 3289. Serviceable order. Price $16.00.

1000K. D. D. Cone Patent Revolver; 6 shots; rim fire; 31 calibre; 5-inch barrel. Made in Washington, D. C. One of the earliest of the cartridge revolvers. Called by some J. P. Lower's Patent. No name or date on the piece. Price, $17.50.

PP-27. BRITISH YEOMANRY PERCUSSION ARMY PISTOL with 9-inch round barrel, swivel ramrod, brass guard, and flat brass butt plate. 5¼-inch flat lock, marked: BEALE, LONDON. Price $6.50.

PP-27-A. BRITISH ARMY TOWER PERCUSSION PISTOL with 9-inch round barrel, swivel ramrod, brass butt and brass trigger guard. Lock marked with CROWN, V. R. TOWER 1845. Butt plate marked: 16th L. A. 20. Price $7.50.

PP-27-B. BRITISH VOLUNTEER'S PERCUSSION PISTOL with lock marked: LACY & CO. Round brass butt, brass guard, and swivel ramrod. 9-inch round barrel. Price $7.00.

3102-B. PAIR AMERICAN PERCUSSION PISTOLS, Derringer type, with 3¾-inch round barrels with flat top marked: A. R. MENDENHALL. Barrels fitted with front and rear sights, back action locks, 2¾ inches, checkered grips, bird head butts, also checkered, silver monogram ovals. Full length 7¼ inches. Price for pair $20.00.

0-924. Pair Navy or Tiger Pistols by "Fray, Leicester, England." 9-inch octagonal steel barrels. Front and rear sight; ⅝-inch smooth bore. Ramrod rib. Double breech band, silver fore-end, side plate, name and butt plate. Belt hanger as furnished on pistols for naval service and for use in hunting tigers in India. Beautiful curly walnut, polished stock, with checkered grip. Contained in rosewood case, size 17¾x8¾x3¼ inches, with brass plate and handle. Price $27.50.

3102A. London Derringer Pocket Pistol once owned by candidate for the presidency, S. A. Douglas in 1860 against President Abraham Lincoln, and which later became the property of J. M. Tenney of the National Hotel, Washington. "London" is stamped on the barrel and the name "Perkins" engraved on the lock. Fully vouched for, name and address will be given of the party from whom we purchased, will be furnished to the buyer. This pistol is a trifle larger than No. 3102 and in period of 1860 would be carried in the coat pocket. Price $25.00.

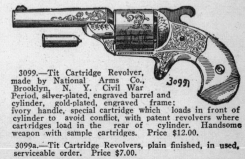

3099.—Tit Cartridge Revolver, made by National Arms Co., Brooklyn, N. Y. Civil War Period, silver-plated, engraved barrel and cylinder, gold-plated, engraved frame; ivory handle, special cartridge which loads in front of cylinder to avoid conflict, with patent revolvers where cartridges load in the rear of cylinder. Handsome weapon with sample cartridges. Price $12.00.

3099a.—Tit Cartridge Revolvers, plain finished, in used, serviceable order. Price $7.00.

The origin of the name pistol seems to be in doubt. Some writers claim that the name was derived from the first pistols having been made at Pistoia, Italy; others that the weapon was first carried in the pommel—or *pistallo*. Boutelle, the British writer, gives another origin, viz., that the pistol derived its name from the fact that its calibre corresponds with the diameter of the coin Pistole. The pistole, or miniature arquebus, was common in Germany about 1512. It was adopted by the French in 1550 and reached England a few years later.

**NORTH BERLIN FLINT LOCK U. S. PISTOL.** FIRST MODEL made by Simeon North at Berlin, Conn. Known as the MODEL 1808; copied after the British Tower Pistol, with the wood fore end extending to near the muzzle, the barrel fastened to the stock with metal pins. Lock plate stamped with American "EAGLE U. STATES, North Berlin, Conn." Brass guard bow and butt cap, polished; full length 16½ inches; in fine order. North was one of the earliest official U. S. pistol manufacturers. Similar pistol in not as fine order at recent auction sold for over $90. Our Bargain Price, $85.00.

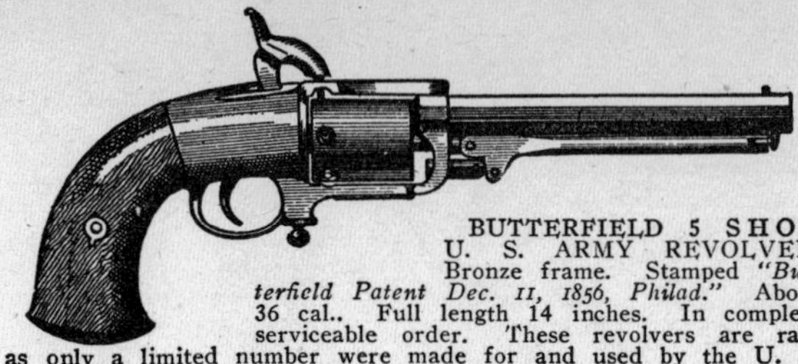

**NORTH FLINTLOCK DRAGOON PISTOL,** barrel stamped U. S. P. (proof). On the lock is stamped NORTH with American EAGLE, MIDLN, CONN. Made with front band for use about the period of the Mexican War. Has the long iron strap and heavy butt plate (for use in hand to hand fight as a club). Full length 15½ inches, about 52, smooth bore. In serviceable order. Price, $35.00.

**5 CENTER HAMMER FLINT LOCK POCKET PISTOLS,** with center hammers, trigger guards, flat wood handles, and detachable barrels, as follows:

1 by PEACOCK, LONDON, 2-inch barrel.

1 by DUNDERDALE MABSON & LABRON, 2½-inch barrel.

1 by HAYWARD & GOODWIN, LONDON, 2½-inch barrel.

1 by HIGHAM WARRINGTON, 3-inch barrel.

1 by WESTON LEWES, 3½-inch barrel.

YOUR SELECTION at $8.00 each.

**1 CANNON SHAPED FLINT LOCK POCKET** PISTOL, with center hammer, concealed trigger, no guard, safety catch, silver name plate, round wood butt, neatly checkered. Detachable barrel 2½ inches. Made by H. NOCK, LONDON. Price, $8.50.

**INDIAN MUTINY FLINTLOCK PISTOL,** relic of Siege of Delhi. Barrel stamped with East Indian Co., insignia. Carried by the Company's Volunteers through the Indian Mutiny. Was made by T. Potter & Co., London. Full length, 15 inches. Price, $14.85.

**BRITISH YEOMANRY'S FLINTLOCK HORSE** PISTOL, made by Wheeler. Full length 15 inches. Serviceable. Price, $12.85.

**BRITISH YEOMANRY F. L. PISTOL,** by Powers about 1780. Serviceable. Price, $12.65.

**BRITISH ORDNANCE BOARD FLINTLOCK** PISTOL, with swivel ramrod, stamped "Tower 1780" with B. O. and arrow marks on the butt stock. Full length 15 inches. Serviceable. Price, $14.65.

**BRITISH NAVY FLINTLOCK PISTOL,** with belt hook. P. H. C. G. stamped on the brass guard. serviceable. Price, $12.65.

**ANCIENT STRIKE A LIGHT TINDER BOX,** used by cottagers in olden times. Iron, square shaped, 4¼ inches in diameter, 1¾ inch high. Top part has place for candle, inside box contains the flints and steel. Rare pattern. Price, $4.85.

**No. LR8. 1 FLINT LOCK TRAVELLING** PISTOL, with extra long barrel, 12-inch, half octagon, with three proof marks. Wood ramrod is copper tipped. Lock is 4¼ inch, marked W. PERKS. This is period of 1790. Price, $19.00.

**No. LR6. 1 CANNON BARREL FLINTLOCK** HOLSTER PISTOL, with center hammer. Made by KING LONDON and so marked. Flat wood grip, detachable barrel, 6½ inch, and frame and guard. Price, $15.00.

---

**When ordering special articles allow a second choice when possible.**

---

**1 SPANISH FLINT LOCK PISTOL,** with half octagon, half round, 9½-inch barrel, which has eight inlaid marks. Curious ornamented trigger guard, heavy brass butt with scroll, and wood ramrod tipped. Price, $18.00.

**1 PAIR OF HEAVY BARREL FLINT LOCK** HOLSTER PISTOLS, full length 13 inches, octagonal twist barrels, engraved locks, silver mountings. $45.00.

**PAIR OF FLINT LOCK TROOPER'S PISTOLS,** broad arrow and crown mark, lock is dated, G. R. Tower, 1759, American Revolutionary War Period. Full length, 15 inches; regimental marks, 44-106; price, $30.00 the pair.

**PAIR OF FLINT LOCK TROOPER'S PISTOLS,** dated 1759 Tower G. R. Crown, full length 19 inches. Price, $35.00 the pair.

**2 PAIRS OF OFFICER'S FLINT LOCK** HORSE PISTOLS, American Revolutionary War Period, made by the famous H. Nocks, London; full length, 15 inches. Price, $35.00 the pair.

**PAIR OF FLINT LOCK NAVY PISTOLS,** stamped Tower G. R. Royal Crown, broad arrow, full length, 19 inches. Price, $35.00.

**1 PAIR FLINT LOCK POCKET PISTOLS,** by GILLS LONDON. Detachable barrels, 2¼ inch, center hammer, trigger guard and flat wood butts. Price for pair, $16.50.

**J. W. RICHARDS FLINT LOCK TROOPER'S** PISTOL, Royal Crown G. R., maker's name; 11-16 inch smooth bore, full length 15 inches, Revolutionary War Period. Price, $15.00.

**ANCIENT TOWER FLINT LOCK VOLUNTEER OR YEOMAN PISTOL.** ¾ inch smooth bore, full length 15 inches, masked butt, rare design. Price, $16.00.

**PAIR OF FOUR BARREL SILVER MOUNTED FLINT LOCK FRENCH PISTOLS,** full length 8½ inches. 7-16 smooth bore. Each pistol has two center hammers and flash pans, with safety lock attachment, side attachment for shutting off the lower set of barrels. Rare French weapons. Price, $250.00 the pair; singly, $140.00.

**1 DOUBLE BARREL REMINGTON ACTION** B/L PISTOL, about 40 calibre, nickel plated, checkered hard rubber handles engraved, made by F. T. Baker, London, complete with original velvet-lined case. Price, $10.00.

**BUTTERFIELD 5 SHOT** U. S. ARMY REVOLVER. Bronze frame. Stamped "Butterfield Patent Dec. 11, 1856, Philad." About 36 cal.. Full length 14 inches. In complete serviceable order. These revolvers are rare as only a limited number were made for and used by the U. S. Army during the Civil War. Price $27.50.

**1 ENGLISH FLINT LOCK TRAVELLING** PISTOL, with heavy round BRASS barrel, 6 inch. Brass butt plate, brass trigger guard, and brass tipped wood ramrod. Lock marked TINDALL & DUTTON. Barrel marked LONDON, with THREE proof marks. This is a rare type, in fine order. Price, $19.50.

**PAIR OF SCOTCH EARLY PERCUSSION LOCK** PISTOLS, with ramshorn butts, ball triggers, German silver steel frame and fore end, with thistle and shamrock engraving, 6¼-inch twist steel barrel, ½-inch smooth bore, full length 10½ inches, fine weapons. Price, the pair, $75.00.

**1 FLINT LOCK PISTOL,** with 8-inch highly ornamented Damascus barrel, and swivel ramrod. Wood stock inlaid with mother of pearl. Flat butt plate with ring. Price, $15.50.

**WATERLOO PERIOD FLINT LOCK PISTOL,** marked E. Parker, swived ramrod, full length 15 inches; 11-16 inch smooth bore. Price, $15.00.

**BRITISH NAVY FLINT LOCK PISTOL** from the Newton Manor House Dorset. Lock is stamped with the Royal Crown, and the lock 1770; full length 19½ inches. Price, $18.50. Similar pistol dated 1759. Price, $18.50

**SINGLE FLINT LOCK DUELING PISTOL,** made by Trigg, London. Octagonal twist tapered barrel, walnut stock, fine easy working pistol, silver escutcheon plate, full length 16½ inches, ⅝-inch, smooth bore. Price, $20.00.

**BRITISH FLINT LOCK PISTOL** by Harcourt, from the Rosting Collection. Octagonal steel barrel, checkered grip, walnut stock, silver name plate, full length 15 inches, ¾ inch smooth bore. Price, $17.50.

**REVOLUTIONARY WAR PERIOD OFFICER'S FLINT LOCK PISTOL** by Bass, London. Walnut stock, full length 15 inches, 11-16-inch smooth bore. $17.50.

**ANTIQUE FRENCH FLINT LOCK CARRIAGE PISTOL,** silver wire inlaid ornamentation. 6-inch octagonal twist steel barrel. Price, $17.50.

**GUN METAL BARREL FLINT LOCK CARRIAGE PISTOL,** by Parsons Salisbury Wilks, full length 8 inches, octagonal barrel, ½-inch smooth bore. $12.00.

**1802 EAST INDIA CO. FLINT LOCK** TROOPER'S PISTOL, made by Henshaw, used in the Indian Mutiny by the E. I. C. Volunteers, full length 15 inches, 11-16 inch smooth bore. Fore end of stock has been neatly repaired, in good order. Price, $16.85.

**7 ARMY FLINT LOCK PISTOLS,** 9-inch round barrels, brass trigger guards. In good order. Price from $9.00 up.

**PAIR OF HEAVY BARREL FLINT LOCK** HOLSTER PISTOLS, engraved J. Harding, Boro, London, No. 344-231, fluted muzzle; has inscription, "For His All;" fine working order. The pair, $25.00.

**PAIR OF DUBLIN CASTLE FLINT LOCK** TROOPER'S PISTOLS, full length 15½ inches long; lock engraved with Royal Crown G. R. Dublin Castle; 11-16 inch smooth bore. brass mounted. In working order; rare weapons. Price, $35.00 the pair.

**PAIR OF LARGE BORE ANTIQUE FLINT** LOCK OFFICER'S PISTOLS, made by Williams, from the late Col. Surman's Estate Sale, ¾-inch smooth bore, full length 12½ inches, fine order. The pair, $25.00.

At the outbreak of the great European War in 1914 when the German Army invaded Belgium we wrote to the Secretary of State to instruct the American Consul at Liege, Belgium, to inform the invading German commander to respect our war material stored in our Arsenal at 79 Rue Lairesse, Liege, as belonging to a citizen of the United States stored there for the purpose of supplying gun parts to the Liege gunmakers for making up into our cadet guns for the Boy Scouts of America. The answer we received from the Secretary of State was that he was then unable to communicate with the American Consul at Liege. That if any of our property was taken we would receive remuneration." What has become of our Liege Arsenal or our agent and workers we do not know. We were fortunate in receiving a shipment of 3,000 cadet guns which were on the way, or as our agent declared, "were swimming." Our Arsenal at Liege was well filled, for only a short time before the war we bought out the old gun manufacturing firm of Barnett & Sons, of London, a firm that was chartered in 1628 as the Chief of the Gunmakers' Guild, and which had the earliest corporated proof mark, the old G. P. (gunmaker's proof). Their factory situated in the Whitechapel district in London was lying idle, used only for the storage of rifles and hundreds of tons of gun parts. The factory property had become valuable for rebuilding and so the entire contents were sold to us. Some of the material was shipped to New York, but the larger part was sent to our Liege Arsenal, in order to save paying the expensive U. S. Customs Duties. Also to be near to the workmen's home shops where the gun parts could be utilized in making up into our wood barrel Quaker and other guns, such as we have supplied to the cadets of military schools, churches and the Boy Scouts for over half a century. A business in which all acknowledge Bannerman to be the founder (April, 1865).

PP-1. PAIR PERCUSSION POCKET PISTOLS, made by WALKER, and so marked on frames. Two British proof marks on removable barrels, center hammers, dolphin shape, trigger guards, flat wood butts, 3½-inch round barrels. Pistols of this type in pairs are rare. Price for pair $14.00.

PP-2. PAIR BRITISH PERCUSSION POCKET PISTOLS. Engraved frames. Round removable barrels, 3½ inch, with two British proof marks. Round wood butts, finely checkered, with silver ovals with monogram I. A. T. Center hammers, dolphin shape. Secret triggers. Price for pair, $13.00.

PP-3. BRITISH PERCUSSION POCKET PISTOL, with 2¼-inch barrel, removable. Engraved frame marked: W. P. Parker, 233 HOLBORN, LONLON. Finely checkered stock with silver monogram disk. Center hammer with safety. Secret trigger. Price $6.50.

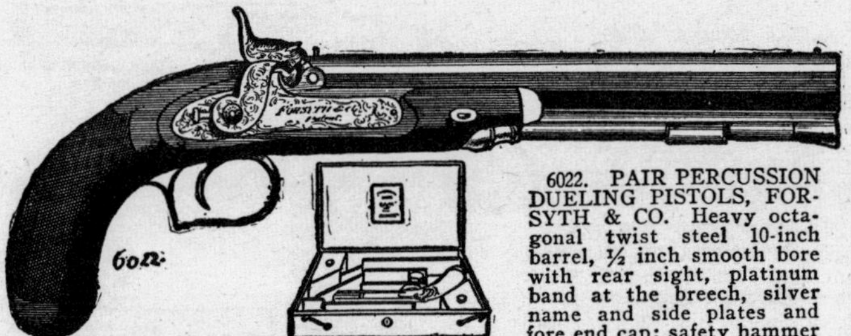


6022. PAIR PERCUSSION DUELING PISTOLS, FORSYTH & CO. Heavy octagonal twist steel 10-inch barrel, ½ inch smooth bore with rear sight, platinum band at the breech, silver name and side plates and fore end cap; safety hammer attachment, engraved lock and mountings; barrel is inscribed "Forsyth & Co., Patent Gun Makers, London." Curly walnut stock, checkered grip, fine easy working locks. Mahogany case with brass catches, ring handle and name plate. Size 18½ inches, 9¼ inches, 3 inches. Pistols are in fine serviceable order.

Forsyth was a Scotch clergyman fond of shooting, who discovered the idea of the copper cap in 1805, in 1807 patent granted. Forsyth refused Napoleon's offer of 20,000 pounds for his invention. The British government assigned him room in Tower of London to perfect the percussion cap. Year later, on change of administration, he was ordered to "clear out his rubbish." In 1809, to introduce cap weapons, he joined with London gun makers to make nipple guns when this set was made. First official government test took place 1832. Historical pistols, forerunner of all modern weapons. Price $100.00.

2 BREECH-LOADING 12 M/m., METALLIC CARTRIDGE REVOLVERS; checkered stock, engraved; self-cocking; barrel, 6¼ inches; fine order. Price, $10.00 each.

RARE PATTERNS GOLD-PLATED REVOLVER, European make, with concealed trigger; self-cocking, 5 shots, inside hammer, sighting rib, centre fire; calibre, 44; proof-marked crown and star R. P.; weighs 2 pounds; handsome weapon; pearl handle. Price, $18.50.

No. 37. SINGLE BARREL RIFLED PISTOL, with 10½-inch barrel, with breech-loading mechanism, operated by a bolt, part of the barrel opening to allow the insertion of cartridge; when opening is closed looks like regular barrel with bolt knob projecting. Valuable only to collectors as showing the evolution of the modern breech-loading gun; in order. Price, $10.00.

PAIR PERCUSSION LOCK, FLUTED BARREL POCKET PISTOLS, with ornamental silvered wire inlaid stocks, lion's head butt plate, engraved frames, concealed trigger. Price single, $8.00, or $15.00, the pair.

No. 2251. MANTON, LONDON, PERCUSSION PISTOL, with engraved lock and mountings; fine checkered grip; walnut stock; swivel ramrod; 4½-inch octagonal barrel; good working order; bargain price for this pistol, $15.00.

No. 2152. INVENTOR'S MODEL, SINGLE TRIGGER, DOUBLE BARREL PERCUSSION LOCK; SELF-COCKING PISTOL; British workmanship barrels, one over the other; engraved lock and mountings, cap box in butt stock; walnut stock, 6-inch barrel, 7-16 inch smooth bore; no name or proof marks; found in London collection, probably only one made with such rare combination mechanism; prize for any collector. Price, $35.00.

No. 2153. PAIR OF AMERICAN REVOLUTIONARY WAR PERIOD SIDE LOCK PISTOLS, made by H. Nock, London, with silver name plate, fine checkered walnut stock; engraved lock and mountings; 4-inch barrel, over ½-inch bore; in good working order (ramrods missing). Flint side lock pistols were very rare when these pistols were made; price, $25.00.

No. 2154. AMERICAN REVOLUTIONARY WAR PERIOD DOUBLE BARREL FLINT-LOCK DUELLING PISTOLS, made by H. Nock, London; 10-inch smooth bore barrels; ½-inch bore. The barrels are side by side; easy working locks, old fashioned browning still on the barrels; walnut stock, full length 16 inches, one hammer tube repaired, price, $45.00.

No. 2155. BRITISH NAVAL OFFICERS FLINT LOCK SPRING BAYONET BRASS BARREL PISTOL. Made by Barnett, London; in working order; 8-inch octagonal shape barrel, 1⅝ inch smooth bore; 7-inch bayonet, released by finger catch; ideal arrangement for use when loading, walnut stock, brass ornamented; price, $25.00.

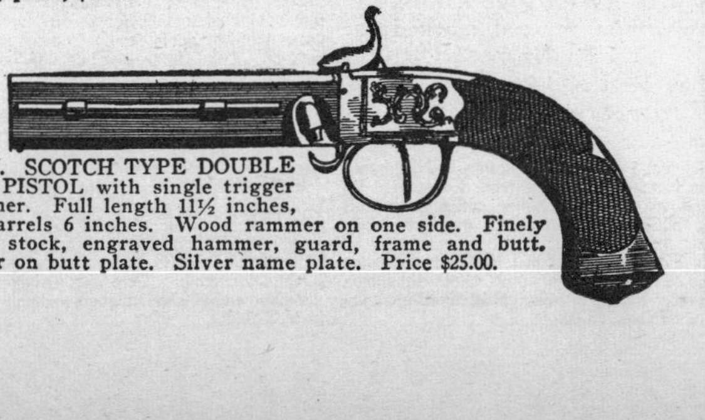

No. DB1. SCOTCH TYPE DOUBLE BARREL PISTOL with single trigger and hammer. Full length 11½ inches, octagon barrels 6 inches. Wood rammer on one side. Finely checkered stock, engraved hammer, guard, frame and butt. Cap holder on butt plate. Silver name plate. Price $25.00.

PP-4. BRITISH PERCUSSION POCKET PISTOL, with 2½-inch octagon removable barrel, case hardened. German silver engraved frame, marked: henry elwell. Barrel has proof marks. Silver monogram oval, round wood butt, secret trigger. Dolphin hammer in center with safety catch. Price, $6.00.

PP-5. BRITISH PERCUSSION POCKET PISTOL with finely checkered stock, silver monogram disk, secret trigger, engraved frame. 3¼-inch removable barrel with two British proof marks. Price $5.50.

PP-6. BRITISH PERCUSSION POCKET PISTOL with very short barrel, 2 inch, removable, with 2 proof marks. Flat wood butt with silver monogram oval, engraved frame, center hammer, round trigger guard. Price $5.00.

PP-7. BRITISH POCKET PISTOL, PERCUSSION, with extra long barrel, 4¼ inch, octagon, with brass front sight. Bronze engraved frame, with outside hammer, rear sight, checkered wood grip, flat butt bound in German silver, with silver monogram disk. Round trigger guard. Price $7.00.

BREECH-LOADING DOUBLE-BARREL PIN-FIRE METALLIC CARTRIDGE PISTOL; nickel-finished barrels; under-lever breech action double triggers; engraved mountings; checkered ebony stock; 4¾-inch barrels; fine order, new; 9 m/m. Price, $7.50.

2 same as above, with 4-inch barrel; 7 m/m. Price, $6.00.

1 with 7-inch barrel; 7 m/m.; under-lever action for opening the breech and extracting shells; engraved on frame with dog's head; carved and checkered stock; fine order, new. Price, $10.00.

LEG-HANDLE SINGLE-BARREL PERCUSSION-LOCK PISTOL; octagonal barrel; 3¼ rifle; patent breech case hardened; front and rear sight; concealed trigger; full length, 7 inches; weight, ¾ pound; old curly walnut stock; handsome old-time specimen. Price, $7.50.

OLD PERCUSSION PISTOL, with crown and coat-of-arms stamped on the barrel; ornamental name plate; full length, 9 inches; barrel, 4¾; weight, ¾ pound; gold inlaid breech; carved curly walnut stock; serviceable order. Price, $9.50.

6018. PAIR PERCUSSION DUELLING PISTOLS, made by W. Child, London. Twist steel 8½ inch octagon barrels, ½ inch bore, silver front sight, engraved lock and mountings, "W. Child, 280 Strand, London." Silver name and side plate, silver fore end, ramrod rib, walnut stock, checkered grip, low hung-hammers, serviceable order. Price, $32.00.

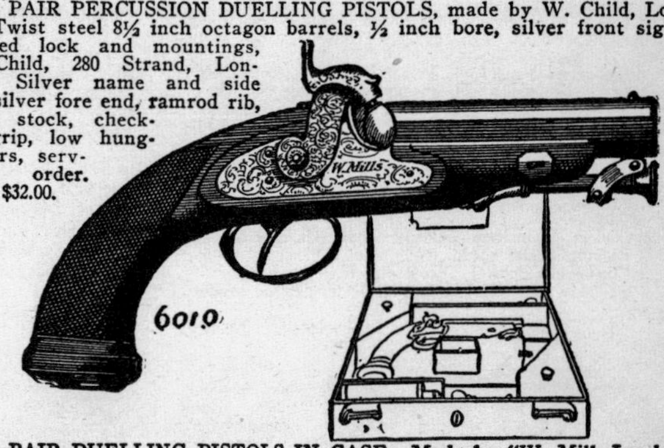


6010. PAIR DUELLING PISTOLS IN CASE. Made by "W. Mill, London, Imperial Gun Maker to His Majesty"; 4 inch octagonal barrel, ½ inch smooth bore, engraved band, lock and mountings, silver name plate, checkered grip, curly walnut stock, engraved metal cap butt with cap box, seasonable order. Mahogany case, 12½, 9½, 2½ inches. Brass, name plate, handle and catches with combination powder and ball flask, screw wrench, etc. Price the outfit $28.00.

6020. PAIR DUELLING PISTOLS, engraved H. James, London, 9 inch flat ribbed barrels, smooth bore, almost ¾ inch; hinge rammer, engraved lock and mountings, flat butt metal cap with ornamented cap box with side hinges for belt or sash, curly walnut stock, checkered grip, silver name and side plate, percussion lock, serviceable order. Price the pair; $40.00.

2 NICKEL-PLATED BREECH-LOADING PISTOLS, 9 m/m.; same pattern as illustration No. 47; 2 barrels are 3½ inches long; has the under-lever breech-opening action; fluted stock, metal butt; fine order; new. Price, $7.00.

2 same as above, in 7 m/m. calibre. Price, $6.75.

1 same action as above, 15 m/m., with 7¾-inch barrel. Price, $7.50.

No. 2104. FRENCH FLINT-LOCK CHARLEVILLE PISTOL, holster size; brass mounted; 7 inch barrel; full length 13½ inches; about 70 calibre, smooth bore; in working order; the same as illustration No. 1336. Price, $14.00.

No. 2114. TWO BRITISH ARMY ENFIELD REVOLVERS marked with the Crown V. R. Enfield, 1894, with broad arrow marks, showing Government ownership, used and in serviceable order; no doubt relics of the Boer War, 5¾-inch barrel. Price, $12.50 each.

No. 2101. PAIR OF SMALL FLINT LOCK POCKET PISTOLS, with side hammers and springs; concealed trigger; barrel unscrews at the breech. Fine carved and checkered stock, made by Mortimer, London; full length, 7 inches; rare pattern now very scarce. Price, singly $16.00.

DOUBLE BARREL FLINT LOCK PISTOL, one barrel rifled ½-inch bore, 6 grooves, the other ½-inch smooth bore, engraved lock, marked "Dirdorff"; groove for sighting between the two barrels, front sight parrot head shaped stock; in working order, price, $45.00.

No. 2132. ANTIQUE FLINT LOCK PISTOL, made in London, kind carried in carriage when traveling in preparation for Highwaymen of the Jack Shepherd or Dick Turpin type; octagonal barrel, nine inches long; 21 gauge; polished walnut stock, with flatted side; full length, 15 inches; fine working order. Price, $14.00.

No. 2134. 1810 PERIOD LONG BARREL FLINT LOCK PISTOL, with knob trigger and butt stock length of round barrel 13½ inches, full length 20 inches; cannon shaped muzzle; relief ornamentation, about 14 gauge, smooth bore. Price, $15.00.

No. 2135. 1815 PERIOD FLINT LOCK PISTOL, kind used by Napoleon's troops at the Battle of Waterloo, in working order; brass mountings; name on plate is worn off, full length 14 inches; barrel, 7½ inches; about 16 gauge, smooth bore. Price, $9.75.

6021. PAIR OF PERCUSSION DUELLING PISTOLS with hair trigger attachment, engraved on the barrels, "George Sturman, Islington, London." Twist steel engraved 9 inch barrels, ½ inch smooth bore, gold band at breech, silver name and side plate and fore end, ramrod rib, engraved lock and mountings, walnut stock, checkered grip, safety attachment to lock. Price the pair $38.00.

# PISTOLS AND REVOLVERS

No. 521.

Pill-lock Army Pistol. Percussion capsule is placed in the old flint pan; hammer strikes a plunger which ignites the percussion pill and fires the gun. Rare old mechanism, invented after the flint-lock, prior to the universal adoption of the guns fired with percussion caps. Before the Civil War many of these old pill-lock guns were to be had. The American Civil War demand for guns led to nearly all this kind of guns being altered into cap guns, by placing the nipple on the barrel. They have now become very rare. Full length is 18 inches; barrel is 9¾ inches; smooth bore, 70-100 calibre, brass mounted, fine order; was formerly used in Austrian Army. Price, $40.00.

Illustration of the Lock in the Pill-lock Pistol.

D B 1. COLT'S DRAGOON REVOLVER WITH SHOULDER STOCK. Has rear sight and is in perfect condition. This fine specimen was picked up after the first BATTLE OF BULL RUN, by Col. Henry G. Staples of the 3rd Maine Regiment, and has remained in the possession of the family until this year, 1924. "DRAGOONS" with the rear sight and in such fine condition are scarce today. We price this remarkable fine specimen, complete with the shoulder stock, at $75.00. See our historical pages on SMALL ARMS, also pages 114 and 251.

R124. 1 Scotch Over and Under Percussion Pistol, with center hammer, made by Robertson, Glasgow. Engraved frame, checkered grip. Barrels 2½ inch, revolve for second shot. Note nipple guard in front of folding trigger.

R123. 1 as above with 2-inch barrels, made by Smith, Braintree. Engraved frame, plain grip. Price, $12.00.

8A. 1 short Flint-lock Pistol by T. Lane, $21.00.
8B. 1 short Flint-lock Pistol by Barker, $21.00.
8C. 1 short Flint-lock Pistol by Webb, $25.00.
8E. 1 short Flint-lock Pistol by T. Lane, $15.00.
43. 1 large Flint-lock Pistol by Probin, $30.00.
62. 1 pair large Flint-lock Pistols by Ketland, $70.00.
53. 1 Silver Mounted Pistol, Flint-lock by Barker, $25.00.
2 Pocket Flint-lock Pistols with BRASS barrels by Richards, $8.25 each.
1 Flint-lock Pocket Pistol by Innes, $6.00.
23. 1 pair fine Flint-lock Pistols by Italian maker, $40.00.
49. 1 Flint-lock Holster Pistol by C. Moore, $22.00.

No. 5.—Percussion Lock Blunderbuss Pistol; formed part of maker's collection of old and rare arms; barrel is of polished steel; hammer and nipple is in the centre; 5-inch barrel, 1⅛-inch diameter at the bell mouth; fine order, as new. Price, $6.00.

No. 1539.—Damascus Barrel Percussion-lock Pocket Pistol. Barrel is of fine Damascus, neatly ribbed. When hammer is cocked, trigger which is concealed appears in place; ebony-colored stock; fine order, like new; about 45 calibre. Price, $5.00.

We have in stock ENTIRELY NEW FACTORY MADE CAPS for percussion pistols. Most horse pistols take the musket size at 25 cents per box of 100. Smaller pistols, pocket and holster size, take the regular pistol caps at 20 cents per box of 100. CAPS CANNOT BE MAILED.

0-916. BRITISH NOBLEMAN'S PISTOL, with naval officer's belt hook, the kind used in India hunting tigers, Lock engraved with CROWN and LION RAMPANT; 7-inch Damascus barrel, full length 13 inches, about ¾-inch smooth bore. Engraved lock and mountings. Swivel ramrod. Silver side plates, front and rear sight. Polished dark-colored walnut checkered grip. Engraved metal cap box in the butt; in good order, evidently used by some Scotch nobleman entitled to a Crown and as his crest the National Scottish emblem, "Lion Rampant." Price, $25.00.

1539A.—8 Twist Steel Percussion Lock Pistols, rifled at the muzzle. Concealed trigger; ½-inch bore: in working order. Price, $3.85.

1539B.—5 Twist Steel Barrel Percussion lock Pistols with octagonal barrel; with 4 grooved muzzle rifling. Engraved breech 3¼-inch barrel. Price, $4.00.

1540.—3 pistols with fluted stock, Damascus barrels, with steel cap, ornamented butt, ½-inch bore, rifled at muzzle. Price, $4.25.

1541.—Pair Concealed Trigger Twist Steel Barrel Rifled Pistols. Engraved hammers and breech. Walnut stock, 3-inch barrel, ½-inch bore. The pair, $10.00.

R124. FAIR SCOTCH OVER AND UNDER PERCUSSION PISTOLS, with single center hammer, 3⅛ inch octagon barrel, made to revolve by hand, each barrel fitted with its own nipple. Each barrel has two proof marks. Side ramrod, secret trigger, finely checkered wood grips, round butts with silver plates with lion head design. Finely engraved frames, marked: D. MORTIMER, LONDON. Price for pair, $25.00. Price for one pistol only, $13.00.

S H C-A. BRITISH SHIP CAPTAIN'S DOUBLE BARREL PISTOL, over and under type. 6-inch round barrels, with flat top, front and rear sights, swivel rod to fit each barrel, round ball butt fitted with engraved plate containing cap box, finely checkered grip, side hammers with safety catches, engraved frame, silver monogram oval. Maker's name on top of barrel: WILKINSON & SON, LONDON. Price $20.00.

S51. EUROPEAN INVENTOR'S MODEL CAP PISTOL. 6½-inch octagonal barrel, total length, 13 inches. Wood stock with flat wood butt. Back action lock with outside hammer. There is an attachment which screws through the under side of barrel at place usually occupied by nipple. On the top end of this attachment there is a nipple shape projection on which the cap is placed. The hammer strikes above this in firing. By this method the cap cannot be lost. A rare type. Price $8.50.

CR-D. 3 COLT DRAGOON REVOLVERS, WITH BRITISH PROOF MARKS, on 7½-inch part octagon barrel. Proof mark on each cartridge chamber. Barrel marked: ADDRESS SAML. COLT, NEW YORK CITY. All three have very low numbers which might indicate that these were sent to England when the model was first issued. All in good order, blued finish. Price $70.00 each. See No DB-1.

CR-D1. COLT DRAGOON REVOLVER, same size as No. CR-D without the British marks. ALL METAL PARTS NICKEL-PLATED. Serial number is 18095. Price $60.00.

CR-362. 2 COLT NAVY REVOLVERS, caliber 36, one with 7½-inch barrel, another with 5¼-inch barrel. BARRELS ROUND, marked: ADDRESS COL. SAML. COLT, NEW YORK, U.S. AMERICA. Cylinders engraved with Navy battle scenes. Price $21.00 each.

CR-H. COLT HOUSE PISTOL, also known as the CLOVER LEAF model, on account of the shape of the cylinder which fires four shots. 2¾-inch round barrel, marked: COLT'S HOUSE PISTOL, HARTFORD, CT. U.S.A. Stud trigger guard which is part of frame. Bird's head butt, bronze frame. Price $18.00.

CR-LD. 2 COLT REVOLVERS, known as the "LITTLE DRAGOON", caliber 31, 5 shot, similar to illustration No. 7 on page 251. 4-inch barrels, octagon without ramrod, marked: ADDRESS SAML. COLT, NEW YORK CITY. Cylinder has ROUND openings for the stop, back of trigger guard is square. Price $120.00 each.

1542—Fluted Damascus Barrel Pistol, with concealed trigger, ebony stock, engraved steel butt cap, frame and hammer. In fine working order. Percussion lock, 8 grooved rifling, 8 small ribs on outside of barrel. Fine neat pistol. In good working order. Price, $9.00.

1359.—French Pistol with Firing Pin. Fine looking weapon. Valuable only for decorating or for collector as no cartridges can be had. Has Damascus barrel. Ebony stock. Engraved mountings. Full length, 7 inches. Price, $3.00.

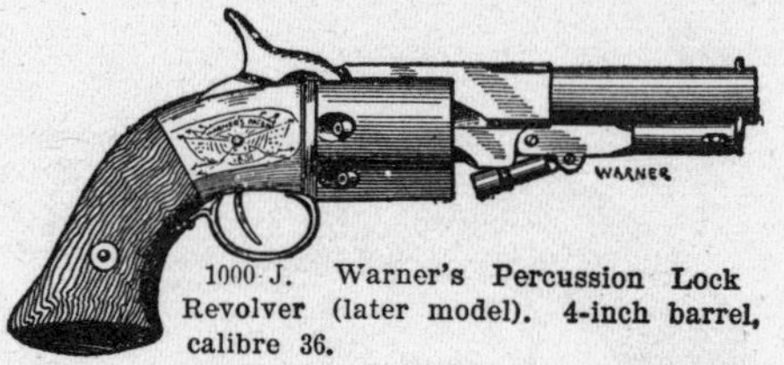



1000-J. Warner's Percussion Lock Revolver (later model). 4-inch barrel, calibre 36.

No. 1537.—Damascus Barrel Percussion Lock Pistol, with concealed trigger, which springs into position for firing, by the cocking of the hammer. Octagonal Damascus barrel, rifled at the muzzle ⅝ calibre. Fluted stock, engraved butt cap and breech. In good working order. Price, $5.00.

No. 1538.—6 Twist Steel Percussion Lock Pistols, same as 1537, only with twisted steel barrels instead of Damascus. Price, $3.85.

**This catalog besides being a list of what we have for sale is offered as a reference book to collectors and museums, and for that reason many special items interesting to them are shown though out of stock at present. Some of the articles may be in stock later, or we may have something similar.**

0-733. IRISH PERMIT STAMPED ON DOUBLE-BARREL RIFLED PERCUSSION LOCK PISTOL. 4½-inch steel barrels, ⅝-inch smooth bore. Walnut stock. Checkered grip. Full length 10 inches, 2½ pounds weight. Fine, serviceable order. Lock is engraved, "Rich & Hollis." Well made pistol. Price, $10.00.

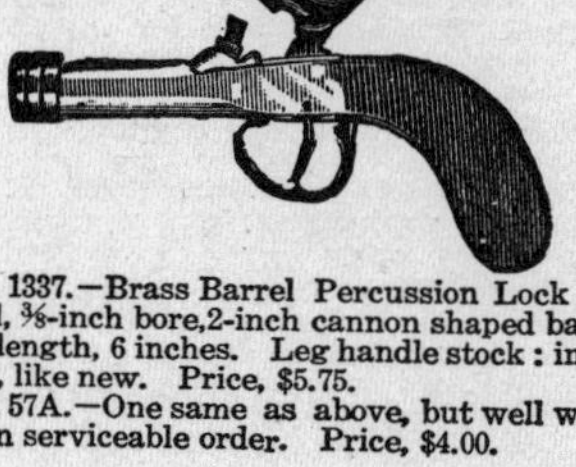

No. 1337.—Brass Barrel Percussion Lock Cap Pistol, ⅜-inch bore, 2-inch cannon shaped barrel; total length, 6 inches. Leg handle stock: in fine order, like new. Price, $5.75.

No. 57A.—One same as above, but well worn; still in serviceable order. Price, $4.00.

No. L-8. FRENCH PERRIN REVOLVER made in Paris, and sample submitted for use of Federal Forces in the Civil War. One of the early type using metallic cartridges. Six-shot, caliber .44, with 5½-inch barrel. Rare type. Price, $20.00.

No. 1331.—Large Flint Lock Side Arm Pistol. 11½-inch barrel, with top of barrel flatted like rib, for sighting. Ornamented bronze mountings. Fine lock, serviceable order. Price, $10.00.

1332.—Norwegian Army Pistols, Percussion Lock, with swivel ram rod, bronze mountings, crown, marked K, 1850. Price, $5.00.

1337A.—Pair of Bronze Cannon Barrel Pistols, bell mouth ¾-inch bore, full length 9½ inches, percussion lock. One cap cover in butt stock missing, otherwise in good order. Price for the pair, $12.00.

2130. FOUR AMERICAN REVOLUTIONARY WAR PERIOD HORSE PISTOLS, with crown, tower, G. R., and broad arrow marks on the lock; length of barrel, 9 inches; full length, 15½ inches; 16 gauge; brass mountings; swivel ramrod, cleaned and in working order. Price, $12.50.

2168. TRANTERS PATTERN REVOLVER, part of trigger extending below the guard, used to cork the hammer, to which the firing pin is attached. Six shot, about calibre 44; octagonal 5-inch barrel. Stock has projection to prevent hammer from striking; has ramming lever on the side. Case contains cartridges; ball screw **rod, oil cup and** powder flask, rare weapon. Price, the outfit, $30.00.

No. 12A. DOUBLE BARREL PIN-FIRE PISTOL, with fine twist steel barrels with top extractor; finely carved stock; under lever action for opening. Price, with box of cartridges, $10.00.

No. 13. FOUR BARREL RIFLED PISTOL, with top break for opening the breech, similar to Sharps, wherein the firing pin revolves at each cocking of the hammer. Valuable only as type. In fine order. Price, $8.50.

HALL'S PATENT LEG HANDLE PISTOL, single barrel with hammer underneath the barrel; about 30-calibre; stock is in poor order. Rare pistol which has been allowed to get rusty. From Southern gentleman's collection of battlefield relics; offered as is, $8.50.

PEPPER-BOX REVOLVER in poor order; relic for decoration. Price, $3.00.

2 NICKEL PLATED BREECH-LOADING PISTOLS, 9 m/m., same pattern as illustration, No. 47, barrels are 3½ inches long; has the under-lever breech-opening action; fluted stock metal butt; fine order; new. Price, $7.00.

2 same as above in **7 m/m.** calibre, $6.75.

Same action as **above**, 15 m/m., 7¾-inch barrel. Price, $7.50.

**0-719. PAIR FRENCH DUELLING RIFLED PISTOLS, P/L by Baucheron, Paris, in mahogany case with outfit. Pistols have octagonal 9-inch twist steel barrels, with fine front and rear sights; many groove rifling. Easy working locks. Engraved with ornamental work and maker's name and address, gold breech band and name plate. Mahogany stock, finely checkered. Carved base round the butt. Carved mask fore-end. Pistol grip guard. Full length 15 inches. Compartments in the case contain graded brass powder charger, nipple wrench, round bullet mould with pinchers, rosewood mould-cleaning rods and rammers, powder flask, with graded charging cup, carved miniature wood barrel for holding caps, bullets, etc. Handsome specimen of old-time French gunsmiths' art. In well preserved order. Price the outfit, $65.00.**

**0-720. PAIR PERCUSSION DUELLING PISTOLS, by Collins, London. 9-inch octagonal twist steel, smooth bore barrels. Ramrod rib, silver breech band and name plate. Patent breech, with barrel-shaped nipple plug, kind first used in altering from flint to percussion lock. Steel mountings. Barrel engraved, "Collins, 12 Vega Lane, Regents Street, London." Polished walnut stock, checkered grip. Full length 15 inches, about 54 calibre. In serviceable order. Mahogany case. Price, $35.00.**

**R85. 14 ASSORTED SHORT HEAVY FLINT-LOCK PISTOLS; average length, 11 inches. All have maker's name on locks. A few brass mounted. Some have swivel ramrods. This size is now scarce. Each, $12.80.**

**R84. 17 BRITISH FLINT-LOCK HOLSTER PISTOLS; average length, 14 inches. A few are brass mounted. Many have octagon barrels. All with maker's name—Mortimer, Twigg, Gill and others. All have round butts; some checkered. Each, $14.75.**

**R69. 1 FLINT-LOCK HOLSTER PISTOL with swivel ramrod and round butt, brass mounted. Total length, 14½ inches. Made by Andrews, London. Price, $17.40.**

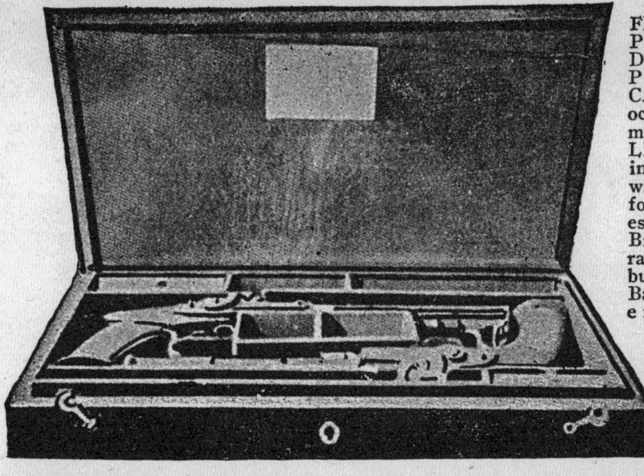

PPC-1. PAIR FINE IRISH PERCUSSION DUELLING PISTOLS in CASE. 8½ inch octagon barrel marked: DUBLIN, bore 11/16th inches, bald stock with silver tip at fore ends, silver escutcheon plates. Brass tipped wood ramrods, round butts, checkered. Back action locks, engraved, and marked: CALDERWOOD. All metal parts engraved, including hammer. Guards have urn tips. Set includes hard wood cleaning rod, nipple wrench, and combination leather covered brass trimmed flask with compartments for powder, shot and percussion caps. Price for set is $35.00.

PPC-2. PAIR BRITISH PERCUSSION DUELLING PISTOLS IN CASE. 10¼-inch heavy octagon barrels, marked: CHAMPION-CHICHESTER. Bore 7/16th inches, silver front sight, raised rear sight. Front action locks marked CHAMPION. 2 silver escutcheon plates, also rectangular name plate in silver. Round wood butts, checkered. Locks, hammers and guards engraved. Safety catches on hammers. Set includes long hard wood rammer with cleaning attachments, extra bullets, and 4-inch copper flask. The set is in the original case with the maker's label in it. Price for set is $32.00.

PPC-3. PAIR PERCUSSION DUELLING PISTOLS, in case, altered from flintlock. 9¼-inch octagon barrels, inlaid with gold in designs at breech and muzzle ends. Silver ramrod guides and escutcheons. Slightly curved butt stocks, with silver lion head plates, checkered grips. Silver monogram plates. 3¾-inch engraved locks marked: H. TATHAM, LONDON. Highly polished wood stock, full length. Total length of pistols is 16 inches. Engraved guards with pine apple ends. Set contains wood cleaning rod with attachments, screw driver, nipple wrench with cleaner, small round bullets, also large ones, 4-inch heavy copper powder flask. Pistols and tools in fine condition. In original case. Price for outfit $45.00.

PPC-4. PAIR ARMY OFFICER'S PERCUSSION PISTOLS, in case, altered from flintlock. 7¾-inch octagon barrels, marked: J. BLANCH, LONDON. Front and rear sights. Swivel ramrods, round ball butts, plain, checkered grips, engraved guards with pine apple ends, silver monogram plates, 4-inch engraved locks, marked: J. BLANCH. Polished wood stocks. Full length 12½ inches. Set contains extra balls, wood cleaning rod with attachments, screw driver, round ball mould. Locks have safety catches, with dolphin shaped outside hammers. Price for outfit $42.00.

PPC-5. PAIR PERCUSSION DUELLING PISTOLS in case, altered from flint lock. Round ball butts, checkered grips, half stocks fitted with silver tips and escutcheons. 8¾-inch octagon barrels, with front and rear sights, gold inlay at breech end. German silver guards with extra finger spurs. Silver monogram ovals, engraved tangs. Locks, 4¼-inch with safeties, marked: CONWAY, MANCHESTER. Polished wood stocks. Full length 14 inches. Set contains iron rammer, eley cap box. Price for outfit $40.00.

PPC-6. PAIR PERCUSSION HOLSTER PISTOLS, in case, altered from flint lock. Swivel ramrods, round barrels, 9 inch, with flat tops, marked: W. BOND, 50 LOMBARD STREET, LONDON. Full length stocks, round butt with engraved plates, checkered grips, silver monogram plates, 4¼-inch locks, with safeties, marked: W. BOND. Engraved guards with pine apple ends. Dolphin shaped hammers, with platinum touch holes. Set includes extra balls, ball head rammer with attachments, and wad cutter. Price for outfit $45.00.

PPC-7. PAIR OFFICER'S PERCUSSION PISTOLS, in case, altered from flint lock. Fitted with swivel ramrods, 4½-inch belt or sash hooks, engraved guards, and butts, flat, checkered grips, silver escutcheons at barrel pins. 9-inch barrels with flat tops, front and rear sights, engraved tangs. Barrels marked: WESTLEY RICHARDS, 170 NEW BOND ST. LONDON. 3¾-inch engraved locks with safeties, platinum touch holes, marked: WESTLEY RICHARDS. Set contains cleaning rod with attachments, nipple wrench with cleaner, round ball **mould, extra balls, wads, and 4½-inch copper powder flask. Price for outfit $50.00.**

**1222. 2 REVOLUTIONARY WAR DRAGOON PISTOLS, made in England, altered from flint to percussion lock, by screwing a tube on the side of the barrel. Full length, 15 inches. Used by the British army soldiers. Price, $6.50.**

**1224. GERMAN ARMY DRAGOON PISTOL. Percussion lock, marked on lock plate 1849, with swivel ram rod. Full length, 12½ inches. ⅝-inch bore. Patent breech end; in good order; requires cleaning. Price, $8.00 each.**

**1225. GERMAN ARMY DRAGOON PISTOL, 17 inches in length. Low-shaped stock. Lock marked H. O. with German crown, 1846. Brass mounted; complete order; requires cleaning. $8.00.**

**1443. KETLAND & CO. LONDON FLINT LOCK DUELING PISTOL. 10-inch barrel. Barrel, full length, 15½ inches. 11-16 smooth bore. Brass mountings. Offered in working order. 2 old British proof marks on barrel. Price, $14.00.**

**1543. PAIR OF FINE ENGLISH PERCUSSION LOCK DUELING PISTOLS, in case, made by Kitching Darlington; twist steel octagonal barrels. ½-inch smooth bore. Ram rod rib. Engraved lock and mountings. Carved walnut stock. All in fine order, like new. Contained in hardwood case, velvet lined, with comparts for the two pistols. With copper powder flask, bullet moulds, cap box. Size of the case, 12¾x7x3 inches. Price of the outfit, $25.00.**

R127. 1 PAIR PERCUSSION DUELLING PISTOLS in case with mould and flask. Octagon barrels 9 inches; saw-handle grip. Made by Richardson, London. Price, $65.00.

> Bannerman is an appropriate name for a man in the business of military equipment, flags and supplies. Think you?—*Editor of "Chat" Magazine.*

No. 2129. RARE OLD SPANISH PISTOL, barrel with gold seal, crown with letters "G. Sofi Antim," with relief ornamentation, with sighting rib fitted to percussion lock; beautiful weapon, which no doubt has had a history; is in fine order like new; fine easy working engraved lock and mountings; silver lion's head butt cap in relief; checkered walnut stock; silver name plate on the side; length of barrel 10½ inches; about 20 guage smooth bore; ramrod rib. Price, $20.00.

0-919. FINE PAIR ENGLISH PISTOLS, P/L in rosewood case, with gunner's implements. Lock engraved, "R. Braggs." The barrel engraved, "57 High Holburn, London"; 3¾ octagonal twist steel barrel. Silver front sight, gold breech band. Fine rear sight. Swivel ramrods. Chased lock and mountings. Silver side plates and name plate, engraved with Unicorn crest. Fine walnut stock. Diamond checkered grip. Complete in good order. Size of the rosewood case, 9x12x2½ inches, with bullet mould, rammer **and nipple wrench.** Price the outfit, $27.50.

**Pair Derringer Dueling Pistols, fine twist-steel octagonal barrel; 4 inches long, about 38 calibre; percussion-lock; fine chekered polished walnut stock, with cap box in the butt, with coat-of-arms in relief work; German silver mountings. Price for the pair, $13.50; singly, $7.50.**

**Pair Troxado Damascus Percussion-lock Dueling Pistols: polished and checkered walnut stocks, with German-silver mountings; fine barrels, with alternate light and dark damaskeen etching, with matted rib for quick sighting; total length, 15 inches; 10-inch barrel, ½-inch smooth bore. Price, $20.00 the pair; singly, $11.00.**

**No. 77.—Henson, London, Pair Dueling Pistols; percussion locks; chased lock and mountings; with maker's name, London; ⅝-inch bore; 7-inch octagonal barrels; swivel ramrod; name plate, polished, and checkered old English walnut stocks; contained in oak case; sizes 16x8½x2½; all in serviceable order, $24.00.**

**Pair Old English Dueling Pistols, made by Sutherland; altered from flint locks; octagonal barrels; found in Porto Rico directly after the close of the Spanish War by U. S. officers; ⅝ bore; in fair order; valuable pistols, as well as Spanish war relics. Price, $20.00 per pair.**

**Revolutionary War Army Pistol from Virginia; brass barrel, used as flint-lock at Yorktown, afterward converted into percussion lock; is in good order. Price, $10.00.**

**1348. FRENCH PERCUSSION LOCK DUELING PISTOLS. Carved walnut fine checkered stock and fore-end. Ornamented case hardened mountings. Ivory ram rod tip. Octagonal twist steel barrel. Fine rifling. Barrel encased in wood at muzzle, with front sight; two leaf folding rear sight. Full length, 14 inches. Handsome weapon. Perfect order. Fine, easy lock. Price, $25.00.**

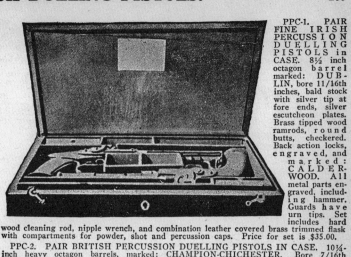

**1338. PAIR FRENCH DUELING PISTOLS. Octagonal twist steel barrels with 16 rifled grooves. Full length, 16 inches. Engraved stock and mountings. Cap box in butt of stock. Silver name plate. Extension guard for finger grip. In shooting order. Price, per pair, $18.00; singly, $10.00.**

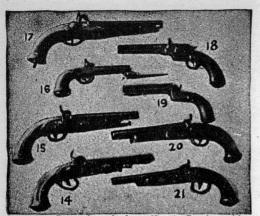

**No. 579.** Single-barrel Percussion Lock Pistol, with extra fine Turkish Damascus barrel, 9 inches long. Price; $9.00.

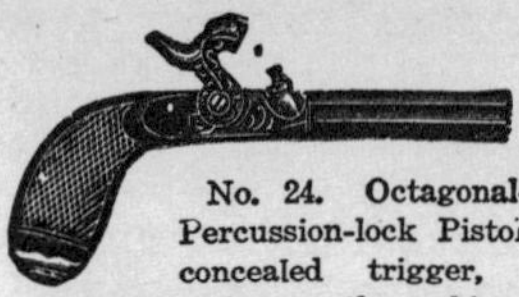

**Arabian Horseman's Flintlock Pistol.** Captured from Arabians and sold at auction by Turkish Government at Constantinople. Serviceable trophies. $15.00 each.

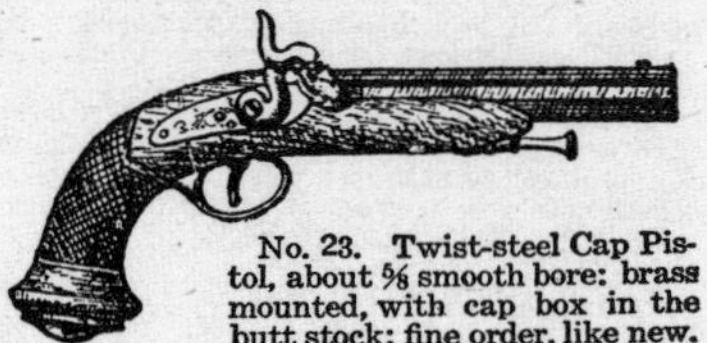

**No. 24.** Octagonal-barrel Percussion-lock Pistol, with concealed trigger, which springs into place at the cocking of the hammer; plain stock, not checkered stock as shown in the illustration; check stock pistol was sold before proof was ready for the printer; in fine serviceable order, like new; with 3-inch barrel; smooth bore. Price, $7.50.

**No. 23.** Twist-steel Cap Pistol, about ⅝ smooth bore; brass mounted, with cap box in the butt stock; fine order, like new. Price, $8.00.

**No. 28A.** Fine Damascus Octagonal-Barrel Cap Pistol; smooth bore, 8½-inch barrel; ½-inch bore; checkered stock; cap box in butt stock; gilt-etched barrel; engraved mountings; fine order, like new. Price, $7.00.

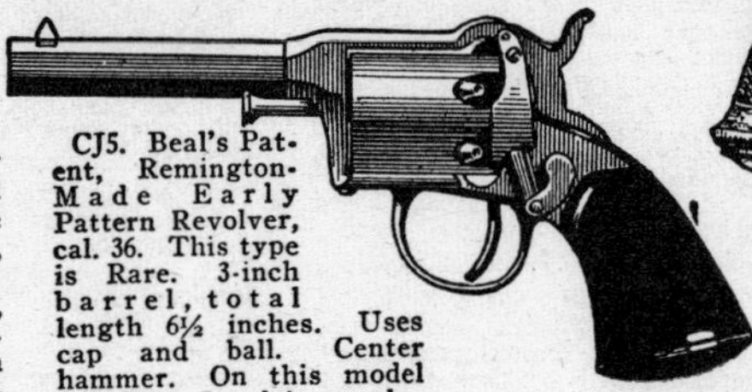

**CJ5.** Beal's Patent, Remington-Made Early Pattern Revolver, cal. 36. This type is Rare. 3-inch barrel, total length 6½ inches. Uses cap and ball. Center hammer. On this model the finger used in revolving the hammer is on the *Outside*, so as not to infringe the Colts Patents. Handle seems to be of Horn. A fine specimen. Price, $35.00.

**No. CJ2.** Allen & Wheelock Early Model Revolver, calibre 36 for metallic cartridges. 4-inch barrel, octagon, total 8 inches. Outside hammer, brass front sight. Barrel marked Allen & Wheelock, Worchester, Mass., Allen's Pat's, Sept. 7, Nov. 9, 1858, July 3, 1860. Uses rimfire cartridges. In good order. Price, $20.00.

**No. 17.** Percussion Lock Dragon Pistol. Price, $6.00.

**No. 19.** Pistol with Spring Bayonet. P/L. Price, $10.00.

**No. 14 and 15.** Octagonal barrel, P/L Sporting Pistols. Price, $7.50 each.

**No. 20.** Sporting Pistol, walnut checkered stock. Octagonal blued steel barrel. Price, $8.00.

**No. 21.** Sporting Pistol, fancy framed checkered stock, fine order. Price, $8.50.

4 Leg-handle Ebony Stock Single-barrel Percussion-lock Pistols, with concealed trigger, about 36 calibre; good as new. Price, $6.00 each.

Pair Rifled Percussion-lock Pistols, leg-handle walnut stocks, checkered; engraved lock and mountings; fancy pistols. Price, for the pair, $10.00; singly, $6.00.

Ebony colored Stock Pistol, with bright metal studs at the intersection of the diamonds in the checkering, making pretty effect; German silver mountings, engraved frame; octagonal barrel 8½ inches long; 45-100 calibre; percussion lock; Spanish model; cap box in the butt stock; fine order; like new. Price, $7.50.

One same as above with 5-inch double barrels, marked on the plate "Rio de Janeiro." Price, $9.50.

Pair Percussion-lock Target Pistols. Full length, 18 inches; 8¾-inch barrel, ⅜-inch smooth bore, carved stock, fine Damascus barrel, hat-shaped butt stock, fine order. Price, $20.00 pair.

Pair Twist Steel Octagonal Barrel Percussion-lock Pistols. Full length, 16½ inches; ⅝-inch smooth bore; fine order. Price, per pair, $15.00.

Pair Ebony-colored Wood Stock Percussion-lock Pistols. Octagonal shape, finely blued barrels; full length, 17 inches; ⅝-inch smooth bore. Engraved locks, hat-shaped butt stock. Price for pair, $12.00.

**No. 24A.** Ivory-Handled, Damascus Barrel, Percussion-lock Pistol. Handsome fluted barrel in *finest Damascus, beautifully chased*, with *concealed trigger*, which springs into position when the hammer is cocked. Total length, 6½ inches; in fine order, like new. Price, $10.00.

**No. 65.** Dickinson Cap Revolver; has British proof marks stamped London; chased frame, checkered stock, self-cocking; breaks down with thumb screw attachment; in serviceable order. Price, $8.00.

**No. 503.** Percussion-lock V. R. Pistol, 1849, with swivel ramrod; Victoria's reign; serviceable order; marked with crown and broad arrow; made by Holland & Son. Price, $10.00.

Another similar to 503, V. R. Tower, 1874. Price, $5.50.

Percussion-lock Pistol, with spring bayonet; full length is 12 inches; length of bayonet is 3½ inches; curly walnut stock, octagonal barrel, engraved. Sold only to museums and vouched-for collectors. Price, $15.00.

Single-barrel Army Percussion-lock Pistol; old style 5-inch bore; total length, 16 inches; smooth bore; brass mounted. Price, $6.00.

Single-barrel Percussion Pistol; length is 15 inches; the hammer and nipple are placed on the side instead of on the top of the barrel; the calibre is about ⅜ of an inch; heavy barrel, engraved; checkered stock; this odd gun was found in India; in serviceable order. Price, $15.00.

**No. 1,288.** Pair of German Army Rifled Horse Pistols, percussion lock, marked 863 and 864, with German crown and W and proof mark on the barrel; also letters J and C in a circle; well made, serviceable pistols; 10½-inch barrel, 9/16 bore; hardwood stock; ring in butt with safety catch is for holding back the hammer from rising on the nipple; full length, 16½ inches. Price, the pair, $15.00.

**PL-27-C.** 10 LIGHT-WEIGHT PERCUSSION PISTOLS, single barrel, average length 12 inches, barrels average 7 inches. Back action locks, metal ramrods, some with checkered grip, round and flat butts assorted. All have cap boxes of brass in various patterns in butt. Trigger guards and other trimming of brass. Twist steel barrels, some with marks inlaid in gold as: DAMAS TORR. TROXADO DE ACO. All in good working order. Price $6.00 each.

**PL-27-D.** 10 PERCUSSION PISTOLS, similar to No. PL-27-C but with finer stocks and more ornamentation. These barrels range from 9 to 12 inches in length, bore about ⅞ inches. Many with engraved trigger guards and lock plates, nearly all with checkered grips. Pistols in this size now rare. Price $8.75 each.

**PL-27-DD.** 3 PERCUSSION PISTOLS, similar to Nos. PL-27-C and D, with 15-inch barrels, octagonal, with proof marks on barrel. Back action locks, flat butts with cap boxes, steel ramrods. Pistols with such extra long barrels are scarce. Price $10.00 each.

**PL-27-E.** 10 DOUBLE-BARREL PERCUSSION PISTOLS, very finely made, resemble double barrel shotguns. Assorted lengths of barrel from 6 to 10 inches long. Rounded butts with cap boxes, all metal parts engraved, mostly twist barrels, wood ramrods, metal tipped. Hand grips checkered, back action locks with two hammers and two triggers. Very showy pieces in working order. It has been several years since we have been able to offer any pistols of this type and quality. Price $14.50 each.

**PL-27-EE.** DOUBLE BARREL PERCUSSION PISTOLS with flat butts with caps boxes, checkered grips, back action locks, length of barrels run from 7½ to 10½ inches. Top ribs with brass sights. All in working order. Price $14.00 each.

**DOUBLE-BARREL DAMASCUS PERCUSSION-LOCK PISTOL;** barrels are side by side; 13 inches long with Damascus rib, engraved in gilt with figures; checkered stock with cap box in the butt; fine, serviceable order; like new. Price, $12.00.

**PAIR PERCUSSION-LOCK, FLUTED BARREL POCKET PISTOL** with ornamental silvered wire inlaid stocks, lion's head butt plate; engraved frames, concealed trigger. Price, $9.00, or $15.00 the pair.

**588.** MINIATURE WATCH-CHARM PISTOL. Breech loading; shoots small cartridge; has ring for attaching to watch chain; makes good, loud report. Price, $1.00.

**1329.** 30 ASSORTED EUROPEAN PERCUSSION AND FLINT PISTOLS, various lengths, in poor order and requiring repairs. Will sell as are, the lot, for $60.00.

**1,329.** 30 ASSORTED EUROPEAN PERCUSSION AND FLINT PISTOLS, various lengths, in poor order and requiring repairs. Will sell as are, the lot, for $60.00.

20 FLINTLOCK PISTOLS, some with brass, some with bright iron mountings; antique; cleaned and in working order. Price, $10.00 each.

**CJ1.** French Percussion Pistol, altered from flint-lock. Handsome piece. 4-inch patered Brass barrel, with 3¼-inch Brass lock marked Duval a Nantes. Heavy brass butt, ornamental brass trigger guard and side plate. Goose neck hammer. Total length, 8½ inches. Price, $12.50.

**PAIR PERCUSSION - LOCK POCKET PISTOLS**, engraved as having been made by Hewson, London; engraved lock and hammer, concealed triggers, extra fine-checkered stocks; full length 6 inches; 2-inch barrels, ½-inch bore, silvered name plate. Price, singly, $6.50; $11.50 the pair.

**CJ4.** Pettingills Patent, In Small Size Which Is Now Very Rare. Calibre 36 with 4½-inch barrel, total length 10 inches. Double action. Frame, barrel and rammer all engraved. Barrel marked Pettingill's Patent, 1856. Frame marked Raymond & Robitaille, Patented 1858. Price, $45.00.

---

**A LONG SHOT.**

Just after the international match at Creedmoor in 1874, when Col. John Bodine fired the last shot at 1,000 yards, making a bulls-eye and saving the match to the American team by a lead of three points, I was telling an interested Hibernian about the match and Col. Bodine's fine shot, when he commented as follows: "Yis, that was very fine shooting; but do you know we had in our country a gentleman who once shot, on a wager, an egg off his son's head with a rifle just a mile away!" It's pretty hard getting the start of Pat in any stories of remarkable feats.—*Correspondent.*

**PP-271. BRITISH HOLSTER PISTOL,** percussion lock, altered from Flintlock. 9-inch round barrel marked on top: E. BAKER, GUN MAKER, H.R.H. THE PRINCE OF WALES. Brass trimmed, and fitted with swivel ramrod. Trigger guard ornamented with military design of flags and drums. Price $10.00.

**PP-272. BRITISH HOLSTER PISTOL,** percussion lock, altered from flintlock. 9-inch octagonal barrel with silver front sight, steel rear sight. Barrel marked: IPS-WICK. This probably made by BATES. Plain round butt with fine checkering, wood ramrod horn tipped. Silver monogram plate marked: T F C. Price $11.00.

**PP-273. BRITISH HOLSTER PISTOL,** medium size, percussion lock, altered from flint. 7¾-inch cannon shaped barrel. Brass trimmed with large butt. Wood ramrod brass tipped. Price $9.50.

**1 Waterloo Period Horse Pistol** found among lot of Emperor Napoleon's First Arms, supposed to have been originally flint lock. Ring hammer is quite a rarity; full length 15½ inches, stamped on the barrel "1815." ⅝ bore, 8¼-inch barrel; note nipple screwed into the barrel; good working order, slightly rusty. Price, $6.85.

**No. 569.** Rare old-fashioned French Dragon Pistol, each with safety catch for the hammer; old hardwood stock; metal trimmed; in working order. Price, $10.00.

British Tower V. R. 1855 Dragoon Pistols, with swivel ramrod; V. R. crown, tower and date stamped on lock, with British broad arrow; good serviceable, second-hand order. Price, $8.00.

**Cooper Double-Action Percussion Revolver.** Patented by James M. Cooper of Pittsburgh, Pa., September 22, 1863. Resembles the Colt, except that it is double action. Made at Frankford, Pa. Price, $17.50.

0-736. W. and Jno. Rigby Five-shot Revolver. Adams patent. 6½-inch octagonal barrel, nearly ½-inch rifle bore. Checkered grip, walnut stock. Low-set hammer below the sighting line. Rare pattern front sight. Revolver has two triggers, one extending below the guard which cocks the hammer, the second trigger which fires. Considered in olden times an improvement. In working order. Full length 12 inches. Rosewood case contains gun-metal double ball bullet mould, German silver oil bottle, copper powder flask, rammers, cleaners, etc. Price the outfit, $20.00.

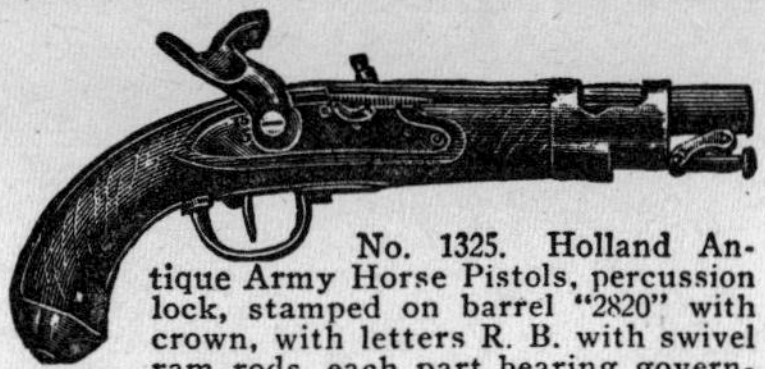

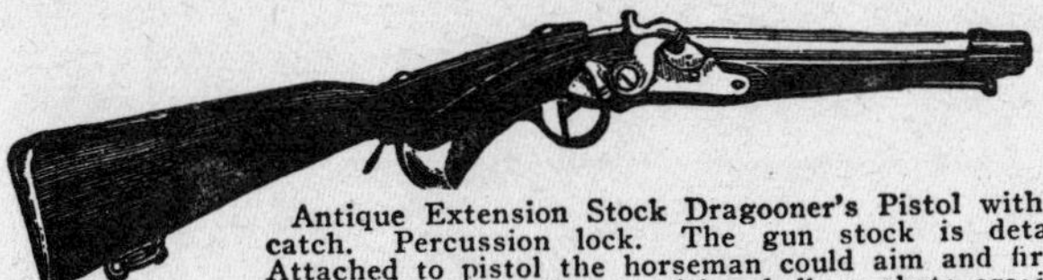

**Antique Extension Stock Dragooner's Pistol** with safety catch. Percussion lock. The gun stock is detachable. Attached to pistol the horseman could aim and fire same as with carbine. Shoots either ball or shot; are in good working order; cleaned and polished. Price, $10.00.

**No. 1339.** Pair of large size pistols, full length 17 inches, ⅝-inch smooth bore. Percussion lock, bronze mountings. Brown finish barrel. Walnut stock. The pair, $18.00.

**No. 48.** Rare Pattern, self-cocking, with top hammer; carved and engraved; ⅜-inch bore; valuable to collectors as showing improvement over the pepper-box; rare. Price, $10.00.

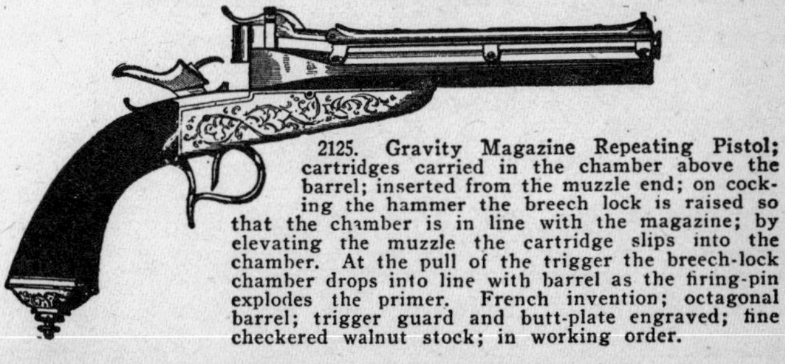

**No. 1325.** Holland Antique Army Horse Pistols, percussion lock, stamped on barrel "2820" with crown, with letters R. B. with swivel ram rods, each part bearing government marks; ⅝-inch smooth bore. Walnut stock. Brass mountings. Lock looks as if had been altered from flint-lock. Well made pistols. Price, $6.50.
No. 1326. Same size and detail as 1325, but hammer and ring for finger, same as shown on ring hammer carbines. Price, $8.00.

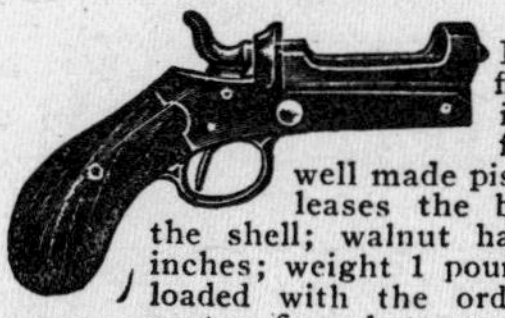

**No. 570.** Signal Pistol. Centre fire breech-loading, 12-gauge fine blued steel; well made pistol. Spring releases the bolt and ejects the shell; walnut handle; length 5 inches; weight 1 pound. This pistol loaded with the ordinary 12-gauge centre fire shot-gun shell with red or blue colored powder, with upper part of shell cut open; can be used for signaling or giving Fourth of July fireworks exhibition. Price, $2.75.

Illustration of 12-gauge paper gun shot shell, cut away for use in signal pistol with colored fire for Fourth of July celebration.
Pair Army Horse Pistols, altered from flint to percussion lock with part of the flash pan mechanism used to protect the nipple. Curly walnut stock; full length 15½ inches, ⅝-inch smooth bore. Price, $12.00 pair.
10 Percussion Lock Army Horse Pistols, with safety hammer striker; full length 15½ inches; ⅝-inch smooth bore; steel bound butt stock with carrying ring; nipple at side (model 42 pattern). Good working order; requires cleaning. Price, $7.50.

0-1009. Sharps' Four-Barrel, Calibre 36, London-Made. Presentation Pistol. Manufactured by Tipping & Lawden, under Sharps' patents. 3-inch blue steel barrel. London proof marked. Ivory stock, gilt frame. Rare pattern. Price, $15.00.
3 Double-Barrel Percussion-Lock Fine Twist-Steel Barrel Pistols. Ebony carved stock, ornamented with small metal discs; German silver mountings, engraved lock; full length 12¼ inches; handsome pistols. Price. $10.00 each.
Antique Double Superposed Barrel Percussion-Lock Pistol with one concealed trigger which operates both hammers independently. Which shows that single trigger guns are old. Fluted stock; good order. Price, $10.00.
Fine Twist-Steel Double Barrel Percussion-Lock Pistol, made by Wilkinson, London. Engraved on brass plate "Chas. D. Reich, Esq., 9th Lancers," with mahogany case and gunner's outfit. Price, $20.00.

Kerr's Patent Army Revolver, made by London Armory Co.; proof marked "London" on the cylinder opposite each nipple. This revolver has once belonged to some one whose armorial bearings are engraved in the silver name plate—Deer on Crown. Revolver is in fine order, new; in oak case, with 2-ball bullet mould, cleaning rod, with printed circular. Price, $12.00.
0-735. Fair Naval Officers' Percussion Lock Pistols. Engraved on lock and barrel, "John Probin, London," in original mahogany case, with gunner's outfit; 4-inch octagonal twist barrel, about 40 calibre, smooth bore. Chased lock and mountings. Silver vent plug, breech band, name and side plates. Walnut stock with checkered grip, naval officer. Full length 8½ inches. Price the outfit, $22.50.

**No. 31.** Old Dragon Horse Pistols with swivel to prevent mounted soldiers losing ramrod while loading; cap lock; ⅝-inch bore; 10-inch barrel; sure fire; checkered stock; fine serviceable pistol in good second-hand order; used about sixty years or more ago. Price, $6.00.

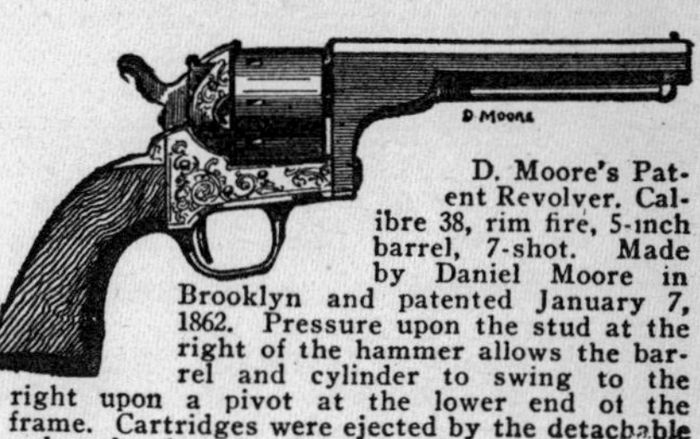

**D. Moore's Patent Revolver.** Calibre 38, rim fire, 5-inch barrel, 7-shot. Made by Daniel Moore in Brooklyn and patented January 7, 1862. Pressure upon the stud at the right of the hammer allows the barrel and cylinder to swing to the right upon a pivot at the lower end of the frame. Cartridges were ejected by the detachable rod under barrel. Price, $17.50.

**PL-27-B. DOUBLE BARREL PERCUSSION PISTOLS,** with blued steel barrels, with heavy ribs, with top rib with brass front sight. Barrels 7¾ inch, bore 11/16th inch. Brass tipped wood ramrod. Front action lock 4½ inch, two outside hammers, double triggers, checkered grip, brass guard, brass cap box in butt, with lion's head cover. In fine order. Price $12.50 each.

**No. 1211.** 6 Old British Army Dragoon Pistols, percussion lock, walnut stock, brass guard and butt cap. Full length 16 inches, 12 gauge smooth bore, in working order; requires cleaning. With tower and crown marks. Price, $6.50 each.
No. 1218. 2 British Army Dragoon Pistols, with swivel ramrods, full length 15 inches. With tower and crown marks, in fair order; requires cleaning. Price, $7.50 each.
No. 1220. 2 British Army Dragoon Pistols, 15½ inches full length. Percussion locks, made by Yeoman. With side hanger, $7.50 each.
R87. 1 Pair Percussion Pocket Pistols with round detachable barrels, center hammer and folding triggers. Price, pair, $9.50.
R87. 7 English Percussion Pistols with 2-inch round barrels, center hammer and folding trigger. Some made by Cooper, Baker, Egg and Calvert. Price, each, $4.75.
R87B. 3 as above, with octagon barrels, engraved frames, in fine order. Price, each, $6.50.

2125. Gravity Magazine Repeating Pistol; cartridges carried in the chamber above the barrel; inserted from the muzzle end; on cocking the hammer the breech lock is raised so that the chamber is in line with the magazine; by elevating the muzzle the cartridge slips into the chamber. At the pull of the trigger the breech-lock chamber drops into line with barrel as the firing-pin explodes the primer. French invention; octagonal barrel; trigger guard and butt-plate engraved; fine checkered walnut stock; in working order.

**No. 1778. Double-Barrel Revolving Pistol.** Single hammer; nipple on each barrel. After firing the upper barrel, the lower barrel is revolved by hand, bringing the nipple of the lower barrel opposite the hammer. Length of barrel, 5 inches; full length, 10¼; rusty. With guard. Rare. Price, $10.00.

**No. 1778B. Double-Barrel Revolving Pistol, with 7¼ inch barrel;** 14 gauge. Working order. Needs cleaning. Price, $12.00.

**R131. 1 PAIR PERCUSSION PISTOLS** with 10-inch octagon barrels. Engraved locks and trigger guards, checkered. Made by H. Nock, London. Price, $30.00.

**R130. 1 PAIR PERCUSSION PISTOLS** with 8-inch octagon barrels, back action. Engraved locks, checkered grips, flat butt, swivel ramrods. Made by Gillett, Bristol. Price, $25.00.

**R129. 1 PAIR PERCUSSION PISTOLS** with 8½-inch round barrels, swivel ramrods, checkered grips. Made by Collins, London. Price, $25.00.

**R60. 1 SHORT BRITISH FLINT-LOCK HOLSTER PISTOL** with swivel ramrod. Heavy 4½-inch long barrel, large bore, marked London. Plain round butt with ring. **Made by J. Egg.** Price, $15.00.

**FLD-1. FLINT-LOCK DAGGER BAYONET PISTOL.** 5¼-inch round barrel, to which is attached on the right side, a dagger spring bayonet 5 inches long, released by catch on side of frame. Flat wood butt, secret trigger, center hammer with catch. Total length 9¾ inches. Price, $15.00.

**1 FLINT-LOCK HOLSTER PISTOL** by Sharpe. Has heavy brass barrel marked Sharpe, extra proof. Price, $28.00.

**1 PAIR CENTER HAMMER PERCUSSION PISTOLS,** by I. Richards, Strand, London, with 2¾-inch cannon shaped barrels. Price for pair, $13.00.

**Assorted lot of CENTER HAMMER PERCUSSION PISTOLS** with cannon shaped barrels, iron trigger guards and flat wood handles. Price, from $4.75 up.

**No. 548. FINE DOUBLE SUPERPOSED BARREL PISTOL,** with polished maple stock, finely carved and checkered; fine old twist steel barrels, in which the twist stands out in relief; 8-inch barrels, ½-inch smooth bore; full length 13½ inches; weight 1¾ lbs.; German silver mountings; ramrod on side. $14.00.

**R76. 1 LONG FLINT-LOCK PISTOL** made by P. Clarke, London. Barrel is 10 inches with silver inlaid sight. Large brass butt, trigger guard and side plate. Price, $25.00.

**R88. 1 BRITISH FLINT-LOCK PISTOL** with 8-inch round brass barrel, marked London. Large brass butt and trigger guard. Wood ramrod is ivory tipped. Price, $25.00.

**No. 583. DOUBLE-BARREL PERCUSSION-LOCK, SMOOTH BORE PISTOLS,** new with top rib, blued barrels; odd shaped walnut stock; ⅝ bore; metal frame. Price, $12.50.

**DOUBLE-BARREL FINE TWIST-STEEL PERCUSSION-LOCK PISTOL;** barrels are 10¾ inches long, with four ribs along the sides of each barrel; ⅝-inch bore; checkered stock with German silver cap box in the butt; wire-twist-steel rib between the barrels, which are side by side, as in the ordinary double gun of today; fine order; like new. Price, $10.00.

**No. 1738. DOUBLE-BARREL PISTOL,** one over the other, with one centre fire hammer, with two nipples; slide in the head for hammer, whereby the lower barrel can be either fired or reserved. Has sash fastener; in working order; rusty; about 12 gauge; 8-inch barrel; full length 12¼ inches. Valuable to collectors to show the evolution in fire arms firing more than one shot. Price, $12.75.

**No. 1412. DOUBLE-BARREL FRENCH PISTOL,** with concealed trigger, about 32 calibre; full length 4 inches; length of barrel 3 inches; rifled; in cleaned and polished order. Price, $15.50.

**R7. QUEEN ANNE FLINT-LOCK POCKET PISTOL** with 5-inch cannon-shaped barrel, center hammer and trigger guard. Stock wire silver inlaid with silver name plate. Silver mask head on butt. Made by Bunney, London. A rare specimen. Price, $30.00.

**R86A. 2 FLINT-LOCK POCKET PISTOLS** with round barrels, center hammers and trigger guards, 2-inch barrel. Price, $6.00.

**R58. 1 ITALIAN FLINT-LOCK PISTOL** with half octagon barrel, 5½-inch. Checkered stock, round butt, brass mounted. Ramrod has ivory tip. Price, $17.40.

**R59. 1 BRITISH FLINT-LOCK HOLSTER PISTOL** with 8-inch round barrel, checkered grip, round butt. Made by Twigg. Price, $21.00.

**No. 1001. DOUBLE-BARREL PERCUSSION LOCK RIFLED PISTOL,** one over the other; 2 hammers; 2 triggers; gun maker's proof; also V. P. proof mark. Good second hand order. $14.00.

**No. 1778A. DOUBLE-BARREL REVOLVING PISTOL.** Needs gunsmith to repair. In poor order. Price, $6.85.

# SCHEDULE OF GUN PROOF MARKS

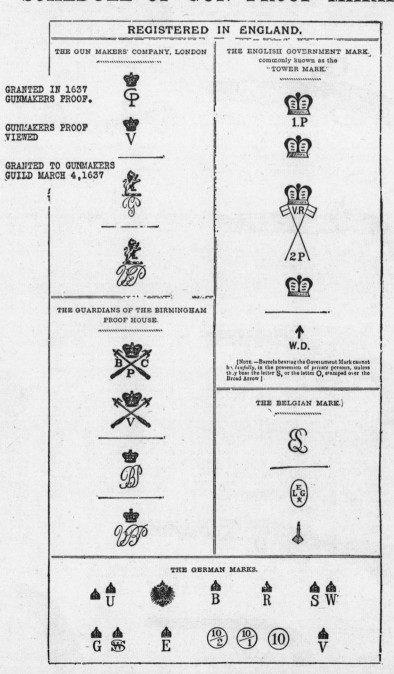

Issued by Order of the Authorities of the London and Birmingham Proof Houses. September, 1891.

No. 531.

No. 532.

No. 533.

No. 534.

No. 535.

No. 536.

No. 537.

No. 538.

400 Rare Old Pattern Pistols, Captured from Italian Brigands and sold by the Italian Government in 1903 to European gun manufacturer, from whom we purchased the entire lot. 400 Single-barrel Pistols, *no two alike*; all old-pattern percussion lock; many have the mainspring on the outside of the lock plate, and have the metal attachment whereby the pistol can be carried in the sash or belt, as shown by illustration No. 538. The illustrations are from photographs and are correct, except that the engraver has failed to show the worn stocks and metal parts, resulting from long, hard usage. We have shown illustrations, all of which are numbered, as before stated, no two are exactly alike. We reserve the right, in filling orders, to select the pistol nearest the kind ordered as per above numbers. All are in working order, requiring cleaning. All show extensive use. All are genuine relics. Many in the lot are brass mounted, checkered and engraved, although the checking and engraving has been almost worn off. The gunman from whom we purchased this lot said that there were many pistols in the lot for which, if he would select, he could obtain 30 marks each from Berlin antiquarian dealers, equal to $7.50 each, or, with American customs duties, about $10 each. The locks alone on some of these old relics are worth more than we ask for the complete pistol. Coming from the Italian Government, and the pistols not being uniform pattern, together with their worn appearance, prove them to be genuine weapons carried by famous brigands. No doubt, from all the stories published by captured travelers held for ransom, these pistols have played a most important part. The bore of these brigand pistols is nearly ¾ of an inch; weight, from 1½ to 2¾ pounds. Some have round and some octagonal barrels; all have ramrods and are, with a little cleaning, ready for business. The full length is from 12 to 15 inches; barrels are from 8 to 9 inches long. We offer you your choice of these single-barrel pistols at $3.65 each.

**BFL-1. BRITISH FLINTLOCK HOLSTER PISTOL,** made by PARKES, 8-inch round BRASS barrel marked: LONDON. BRASS lock marked: PARKES. Oval butt with brass plate, brass guard, with acorn end, brass ramrod guides. Top of stock inlaid with silver wire, two proof marks on barrel, oval brass monogram plate. Price $17.50.

**BFL-2. BRITISH FLINTLOCK HOLSTER PISTOL,** with BRASS barrel and lock. Length 14½ inches, barrel 9 inch, half octagon, with FOUR proof marks and marked: LONDON. Oval butt with brass plate, brass guard with acorn end, brass lock plate marked: GRICE. Wood ramrod horn tipped. Brass monogram plate. Price $18.00.

**BFL-3. BRITISH FLINTLOCK HOLSTER PISTOL,** with 8-inch cannon barrel marked with two proof marks and: HEYLIN, CORNHILL, LONDON. Full length 14 inches, oval butt with brass plate with mask, lock strap of brass in designs of flags and cannon, brass guard with urn end, 4½-inch lock with makers name partly erased. Price $16.00.

**BFL-4. BRITISH FLINTLOCK PISTOL,** length 12 inches, BRASS barrel, half octagon, re-inforced at muzzle, with marks: E C 462. BRASS lock 4 inches, oval butt with plain brass plate, wide guard with urn end. Price $15.00.

**BFL-5. BRITISH FLINTLOCK HOLSTER PISTOL,** length 12 inches, with 6¾-inch round BRASS barrel with 2 proof marks and: D. EGG, LONDON. 4½-inch lock marked: D. EGG. Small oval butt with brass plate, brass lock strap and plain guard marked: No. 4 Small brass oval monogram plate marked with CROWN over letter B. Price $16.50.

**BFL-6. BRITISH FLINTLOCK HOLSTER PISTOL,** with 9-inch BRASS barrel with 3 proof marks and slightly belled at muzzle. 4-inch etched lock marked: D. EGG. Round butt, etched guard with pine apple end, wood ramrod with horn tip. Price $18.00.

**BFL-7. BRITISH FLINTLOCK PISTOL,** known as a TRADE pistol, as traded with natives of India and other British colonies. 7-inch octagonal BRASS barrel, marked with two proof marks and figures 22. Round butt, brass guard, 5¼-inch lock. Stock heavily studded with large brass tacks, to show standing of owner according to his wealth. Price $12.50.

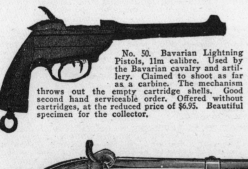

**No. 50. Bavarian Lightning Pistols,** 11m calibre. Used by the Bavarian cavalry and artillery. Claimed to shoot as far as a carbine. The mechanism throws out the empty cartridge shells. Good second hand serviceable order. Offered without cartridges, at the reduced price of $6.95. Beautiful specimen for the collector.

**561. FRENCH PERCUSSION PISTOL,** altered from flintlock. Army model, with 7¾-inch round barrel with raised front and rear sights, bird's head butt with heavy grass plate. Full length 14 inches. Brass side plate to which is attached the combination barrel band and fore end. Heavy brass guard. 5-inch flat lock with marks which appear to be ST. ETTIENNE M. J. DAJADS. Barrel marked: 1819. C. D. 17.6 A. Stock stamped: ST. ETTIENNE, with numbers. Price $9.75.

**PBD. HEAVY PERCUSSION DOUBLE BARREL PISTOL.** This type made up for use of officers in the INDIAN SERVICE in the British Army. Round barrels, 7¾ inches long, with top rib and front sight. Fitted with swivel ramrod. Short butt stock, checkered with flat butt plate. Narrow guard with pine apple end. 3¼-inch back action locks, silver monogram oval. Price $15.00.

**No. 46. DOUBLE BARREL METALLIC CARTRIDGE PISTOL;** 4-inch barrel, rib in centre; breech block opens to the left; pin-fire, 12mm, cartridges. In good, serviceable order. Price $4.50.

**No. 575. TWIST-STEEL, OCTAGONAL BARREL, PERCUSSION-LOCK PISTOL,** with old-fashioned rifling at the muzzle; has front sight, also notch in frame for rear sight; beautifully etched barrel, showing light and dark shades of the twisted steel; barrel screws into frame; German silver mountings; silver name-plate stamped with crown which shows Government ownership; length, 8 inches; weight, 14 oz. $4.85.

**No. 561A. 5 SINGLE-BARREL, PERCUSSION LOCK PISTOLS,** same pattern as 561, with 8-inch barrel; stamped on lock "M. R., St. Etienne"; good, second-hand, cleaned. Price $11.00.

**PAIR OF FLINTLOCK DUELLING PISTOLS,** made by Richards; total length, 14 inches; octagonal barrels, about 14 guage, smooth bore, engraved lock and guard; fine English walnut stock, barrels have the old British proof marks; walnut case with brass handle and name plate, with flask, etc. Price $45.00.

**PAIR PERCUSSION LOCK DUELLING PISTOLS,** made by Hewson, London; octagonal barrels ⅝ smooth bore, checkered stock, in hardwood case, with name plate, mould and flask. Price $18.50.

**FRENCH LEFAUCHEAUX REVOLVER,** calibre 40, for centre-fire cartridges; purchased during the Civil War for use of Army Officers; Civil War relic. Price $5.00.

CR-Cl.

**CR-P. COLT DRAGOON PRESENTATION REVOLVER,** with 7½-inch round barrel marked: ADDRESS SAM'L. COLT, NEW-YORK. The cylinder is marked with battle scene between Soldiers and Indians, and marked: MODEL U.S.M.R. COLT'S PATENT. The barrel has silver sight, with engraving at muzzle. The breech end of barrel is deeply engraved with leaf designs and shows wild boar. The frame, hammer and rammer swivel are also engraved. The back strap, and trigger guard are of silver, engraved. The trigger guard has the American shield engraved on it. The wood grips are highly polished. See illustration No. DB-1 on page 108. Price $85.00.

**CR-P1. LONDON COLT PRESENTATION REVOLVER,** Navy pattern, caliber 36, with 7½-inch octagon barrel marked: ADDRESS COL COLT, LONDON, with two British proof marks. Cylinder shows Naval Battle, is marked: COLTS PATENT, and each cartridge chamber has British proof mark. All metal parts are deeply engraved in leaf and flower designs. The back strap and trigger guard are of silver, also engraved. This revolver is similar to No. 9 on page 251. Price $38.00.

**CR-P1A. LONDON COLT PRESENTATION REVOLVER,** Navy pattern, similar to No. CR-P1, but with less engraving, and with steel back strap and trigger guard. Price $35.00.

**CR-P2. LONDON COLT PRESENTATION REVOLVER, "OLD MODEL"** BELT type, with 5-inch octagon barrel, engraved at muzzle and breech ends. Barrel has two British proof marks, and is marked: ADDRESS COL. COLT, LONDON. The cylinder shows stage coach hold-up, and is marked: COLT'S PATENT. The frame is engraved and marked on left side: COLT'S PATENT. The trigger guard with strap, also back strap are of silver, engraved. This revolver is similar to illustration No. 8 on page 251. Price $33.00.

**CR-P3. PRESENTATION COLT REVOLVER,** cal. 31, "OLD MODEL," belt type, similar to No. CR-P2, with 6-inch octagon barrel, marked in old English: SAM'L COLT. Barrel, frame, hammer and trigger guard engraved. Guard and strap of silver, back strap, silver plated but much worn. Price $26.00.

**CR-P4. PRESENTATION COLT REVOLVER, NAVY MODEL,** cal. 36, with 7½-inch octagon barrel, heavily engraved on breech end, frame and butt plate. Trigger guard and strap silver, back strap silver plated but much worn. Price $25.00.

**CR-44. COLT REVOLVER,** caliber 44, ARMY MODEL, similar to No. 5 on page 251. 8-inch round barrel, marked: ADDRESS COL. SAML. COLT, NEW-YORK, U. S. AMERICA. Brass trigger guard and strap, hard wood grips. This is the style used by most of the soldiers in the Civil War. Price $22.50.

**CR-36. COLT REVOLVER, NAVY PATTERN,** similar to No. 9 on page 251. 7½-inch octagon barrel marked: ADDRESS SAML. COLT, NEW YORK CITY. Brass trigger guard with strap, also brass back strap. Price $20.00.

**CR-31. COLT REVOLVER, "OLD MODEL"** belt type, caliber 31. 4 and 6-inch octagon barrels, marked: ADDRESS SAML. COLT, NEW YORK, U. S. A. Brass trigger guard with strap. Back strap of brass has been silver plated but this is almost all worn off. Similar to No. 8 on page 251. Price $18.50.

**CR-361. 2 COLT REVOLVERS, "NEW MODEL"** belt type, cal. 36, one with 3½, one with 4½-inch round barrel, marked: ADDRESS COL SAML. COLT, NEW YORK, U. S. AMERICA. This model has FLUTED CYLINDER. Brass guard with strap and back strap. Brass front sight. Price $19.00 each.

**CR-NM. COLT REVOLVER, "NEW MODEL,"** caliber 31, with solid frame, as used on the Remington revolver. 3½-inch octagon barrel, marked: COLTS PT. 1855. ADDRESS COL COLT, HARTFORD, CT. U.S.A. This model is 5 shot with 1½-inch cylinder, with OUTSIDE HAMMER, as used on the Colts rifles. Stud trigger guard, in which the trigger is protected when hammer is not cocked. Price $30.00.

**CR-C. PRESENTATION COLT REVOLVER IN CASE, "OLD MODEL" BELT PATTERN.** All metal parts deeply engraved with grape vine ornament, with hard rubber grips embossed in leaf design. Caliber 31, with 4-inch barrel, marked: COLT PATENT. Cylinder has the BELGIAN proof mark. This is similar to illustration No. 8 on page 251. Set is in mahogany case with brass inlaid cover. 3½-inch copper flask, round oilcup, mould for one round and one conical bullet, cleaning rod with brass ball handle, extra caps and extra bullets included with the set. Revolver and each piece set in its own compartment. This is a very handsome set, like new. Price $50.00.

**CR-C1. COLT LONDON REVOLVER, "OLD MODEL" BELT PATTERN,** in case with implements. Barrel is 4-inch octagon, marked: ADDRESS COL COLT, LONDON, and has two British proof marks. The cylinder shows stage coach hold-up and is marked: COLTS PATENT. Each cartridge chamber has British proof mark. Set includes 4½-inch round copper flask with bottom ring, two ball mould, screw driver with nipple wrench, steel cleaning rod with wood ball end. The revolver is cal. 31. This is the ORIGINAL CASE and the directions for use are pasted in lid. Directions for loading Colt's pistols. Directions for loading Colt's foil cartridge. Directions for Cleaning. To take the lock to pieces, clean and oil. To put together. Price for set $45.00.

**CR-C2. COLT LONDON NAVY REVOLVER,** in case, caliber 36, with 7½-inch octagon barrel, marked: ADDRESS COL. COLT, LONDON. 2 British proof marks on barrel, and one British proof mark on each cartridge chamber. Cylinder marked: COLTS PATENT, with Naval battle scene. Set includes 6-inch round copper flask with bottom ring, two ball mould. Full instructions for use and care are pasted in lid, as described with revolver No. CR-C1. Price for set with oak case $42.00

**V-1. PRESENTATION COLTS REVOLVER,** caliber 31 with 4-inch octagonal barrel, marked in old English letter: SAML COLT. Hold-up of prairie schooner engraved on cylinder. Revolver richly engraved throughout, with stock strap and trigger guard silver plated, now partly worn off. Solid ivory grips, polished smooth. A very handsome piece, and such as were made up only for presentations. This is offered in coffin shaped hardwood case, 14 inches long, complete outfit for $38.50.

**V-9. COLT'S PERCUSSION REVOLVER,** caliber 31, 5-shot with 6-inch barrel. In hardwood case (looks like walnut) made out of solid block. Set complete with BRASS mould for one round and one conical bullet, 4-inch copper flask with American eagle on each side, wood rammer, extra bullets, round and conical. Fitted with lock, no key. This is a fine set. Barrel marked: ADDRESS SAML COLT, NEW YORK CITY. Cylinder marked with holdup of Prairie Schooner. Price $40.00.

**V-10. COLT'S PERCUSSION REVOLVER,** caliber 31, with 5-inch octagonal barrel, marked: ADDRESS COL. SAML. COLT, NEW YORK, U. S. AMERICA. Cylinder shows hold up of Prairie Schooner. In case with the original 4½-inch copper flask with American Eagle on each side. Sample round and conical bullets. Price $30.00.

**C-26A. LONDON COLTS REVOLVER** in ORIGINAL case with tools. Caliber 36 with 7½-inch octagonal barrel. Round cylinder shows naval battle. Barrel marked: ADDRESS COL. COLT, LONDON and has two British proof marks. Cylinder has six proof marks. Set includes mould for one round and one conical bullet, combination screw driver and nipple wrench, old style oiler with dropper in cap. The original label is pasted inside of cover, giving the London address, and full directions for using the Colts revolvers. Price for set, $48.00.

**C-26B. LONDON COLTS REVOLVER** in ORIGINAL case with full instructions for loading, cleaning and dismantling. Caliber 31, with 4-inch octagon barrel with under rammer. Barrel proof marked: ADDRESS COL. COLT, LONDON, and has two British proof marks. Cylinder shows stage coach hold-up, also five proof marks. Equipment in set includes Colt Patent mould for one round and one conical bullet, screwdriver with nipple wrench attachment, 4½-inch plain copper flask with ring in end. Price for set with case, $44.00.

**C-26C. LONDON COLTS REVOLVER** in case. Caliber 31 with 4-inch proof marked barrel, marked: ADDRESS COL. COLT, LONDON. Similar to C-26B. Four-inch metal flask, Colt patent mould, combination screwdriver and nipple wrench, cleaning rod with heavy iron handle are included in case with revolver. Price for outfit $42.00.

**C-26D. LONDON COLTS REVOLVER** in case. Caliber 31, five shot with 6-inch barrel, marked: ADDRESS SAML. COLT, LONDON. Number of revolver is No. 63, showing it was one of the first of this type. Set includes 4½-inch round copper flask, two ball BRASS mould, and combination screwdriver.

**CR-L. COLT "NEW MODEL" REVOLVER,** belt type. Caliber 36, with 5½-inch round barrel, marked: ADDRESS COL. SAML. COLT, NEW YORK, U. S. AMERICA, with TWO British proof marks. Cylinder has one British proof mark on each chamber. CYLINDER IS FLUTED. Price $23.00.

**CR-L31. LONDON COLT REVOLVER,** caliber 31, with barrels 4, 5, and 6 inches long. Marked: ADDRESS COL COLT, LONDON. With two British proof marks on frame, and one proof mark of each chamber. Cylinders are engraved with stage coach hold-up. Some revolvers have silver trigger guards, others have been silver plated, and still others are brass. Similar to illustration No. 8 on page 251. Price $28.50 each.

**CR-L31A. COLTS REVOLVER,** caliber 31, with 4-inch barrel marked: ADDRESS COL SAML. COLT, NEW YORK, U. S. AMERICA, with 2 BRITISH proof marks on barrel, and each chamber with proof mark. Brass trigger guards with strap, and brass stock strap. Price $25.00.

**CR-L36. LONDON COLTS NAVY REVOLVERS,** caliber 36 with 7½-inch barrels, stamped with 2 British proof marks, and: ADDRESS COL COLT, LONDON. Each cartridge chamber stamped with British proof mark. Similar to No. 9 on page 251. Price $29.00 each.

**CR-L36A. BRITISH GOVERNMENT OWNED COLT REVOLVER,** caliber 36 with 7½-inch barrel with 2 British proof marks, and: ADDRESS COL. SAML. COLT, NEW YORK, U. S. AMERICA. Each chamber has British proof mark. On the left side of butt is stamped the British Government mark: A CIRCLE WITH LETTERS R M WITH CROWN BETWEEN, and inside the circle: CROWN OVER LETTERS G S M. Price $32.00.

**0-713. ANTIQUE BRITISH SIGNAL PISTOL,** gun-metal barrel and frame. Walnut stock. Side attachment for naval officer's belt. Stamped, "W. D. British Broad Arrow, Crown, E, 12", 2½-inch barrel, full length 8 inches. Rare specimen. Price, $10.85.

**No. 1333. 4-Barrel Rifled Pepper-box Pistol;** each barrel is full length and is attached to the frame separately: 4-grooved rifling. Under lever, which revolves the barrel to the left, the hammer is attached to operating lever. In fine order. Finely engraved. Ebony handle; rare piece. Price, $20.00.

**No. 0-23. FINELY MADE ENGLISH PEPPER BOX REVOLVER** with six barrels, in one piece made to revolve when trigger is pulled. German silver frame, engraved, and marked with maker's name: Bailey, Plymouth. Plain hardwood handles, engraved trigger guard. Full length 8 in., barrels 3½ in. Each barrel marked with British proof marks. Price, $16.50.

**No. 0-23A. 1 BRITISH SIX SHOT PEPPER BOX REVOLVER,** about cal. 40, a rare size. Engraved German silver frame and trigger guard, hardwood handles. Each barrel stamped with British proof marks. Made by Williams & Powell, Liverpool. Full length 8 in., barrels 3½ in. Price $17.50.

**No. 0-23B. BRITISH PEPPER BOX REVOLVER,** about cal. 44, six shot, engraved German silver frame, stock strap, and butt plate. Finely checkered hard wood handles. Size 7½ inches, barrels 3¼ inches, marked with British proof marks. Frame marked with maker's name: H. MARSH, PONTEFRACT. Price $17.00.

**0-728B. ENGLISH IMPROVED REVOLVER,** similar to illustration No. 0-728 on page 115, but without knife bayonet. 6 shot, cal. 44, with 4¾-inch barrel. Checkered grip, with flat butt. Frame and stock straps engraved. Cylinder proof marked. Barrel marked: F. BARNES & CO., LONDON. Price $9.50.

**0-728C. ENGLISH IMPROVED REVOLVER,** similar to No. 0-728B. 6 shot, cal. 38. Frame marked: SMITH LONDON. Barrel marked: IMPROVED REVOLVER. Price $9.00.

**0-713A. BRITISH ARMY SIGNAL PISTOL,** similar to illustration No. 0-713 on page 115. This is doubtless the first of these pistols made as breech loaders. Brass frame and trigger guard in one piece. The end of barrel unscrews to insert the rocket or flare. Wood grips, with lanyard ring in butt. This model now rare. Price $8.50.

**023-27. WESTLEY RICHARDS PEPPERBOX IN CASE WITH TOOLS.** 3½-inch barrels, case hardened and fluted. Marked with British proof mark on each barrel, engraved at muzzle. Frame, hammer and butt plate case hardened and etched. Frame marked WESTLEY RICHARDS, LONDON. IMPROVED REVOLVING PISTOL. Flat butt plate with cap box. Wood grip very finely checkered. Silver monogram plate. Tools include nipple wrench, round mould with rammer end, combination ball screw and cleaner. SET COMPLETE WITH CASE, $25.00.

Burglar Alarm Pistol; percussion-lock, with screw attached for holding in position against door; in poor order. Price, $3.00.

Sharp's Four-barrel Breech-loading Pistol; in unserviceable order; fit only for decorating or gunsmith who might repair. Price, $8.00.

6-Shot British Pepperbox Revolver, top hammer, fluted barrels, engraved frame, finely checkered stock, serviceable order; self-cocking. Price, $16.00.

6-Barrel Pepper-box Revolver, self-cocking under hammer; shoots pin-fire cartridges, about 32 calibre; full length, 7 inches; centre fire, which by moving the cylinder can be removed. Engraved frame; fine order. Price, $20.00.

8-Barrel Pepper-box Revolver, self-cocking twist steel barrels, 8 barrels joined together in one. Rifled; full length, 8 inches; fine order; cleaned. Price, $25.00.

**See special pages, No. 16-a, b, c, d, e, f, g, and h, for collection pieces.**

**No. 119. DAGGER KNIFE PISTOL,** Rogers patent, in good order. Can be sold only to museum or vouched for collector. Price, $15.00.

**R66. 1 BRITISH FLINT-LOCK HOLSTER PISTOL** with 6-inch round barrel, marked Harcourt. This name is also on lock-plate. Butt is checkered. This is an officer's pistol. Price, $17.40.

**S1. BRITISH PERCUSSION COACH PISTOL,** made in London. Lock marked Parker, Field & Sons. Barrel marked 233 Holborn, London. 4¼-inch octagon barrel with swivel ramrod, with three proof marks. Round wood butt, checkered. Ornamented trigger guard, lock and tang. Price, $10.00.

**S2. BRITISH HOLSTER PISTOL,** 12 inches long, with 7¼-inch heavy barrel with tapered rib, and inlaid in silver. Has rear sight on tang. Round wood butt, finely checkered. Hammer, guard and lock engraved. Has safety catch. Price, $8.50.

**S4. EUROPEAN DOUBLE BARREL HEAVY PISTOL,** with leg handle wood butt. Round barrels are 9 inches, with steel ramrod underneath. Two inside percussion hammers, and large trigger guard with extension. Price, $9.00.

**S3. PAIR BRITISH DUELLING PISTOLS,** made by W. Spies, London, and so marked. Round wood butts, brass mounted. Brass barrels, 7¾-inch octagon. Ornamented brass trigger guards. Altered from flint lock. Price, $18.50 for pair.

**1353A. 5-BARREL PEPPER BOX REVOLVING PISTOL,** old style muzzle cut rifling, 2¾-inch barrels, full length 7½ inches. Finger ring trigger cocks and fires; unique hammer situated under the barrel. Barrels are full length. In working order; requires cleaning. Price, $12.00.

1353A

20 Shot Revolver found in old shop in Paris, bore is about ⅜, length, 15 inches, weighs about 6 pounds. Rare piece. Sold to collector.

**0-728A. FINE ENGLISH, WELL-MADE REVOLVER.** Similar to 0-728, but without spring bayonet, in rosewood case, with bullet mould, screw driver, nipple wrench and copper powder flask, German silver box for holding caps, ramrod, cleaner, bullets and rods. Six-shot; in fine order; like new. Price, $17.50.

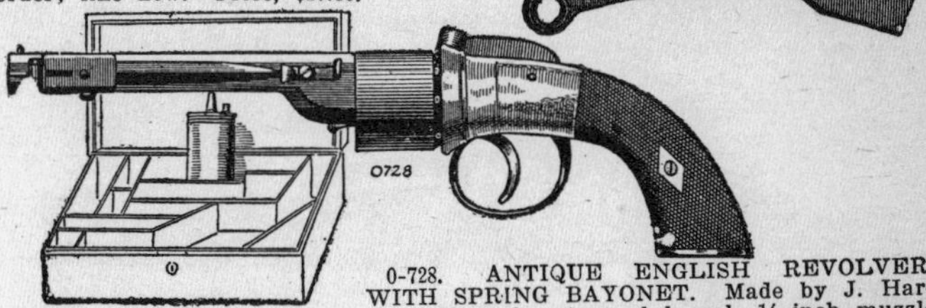

0728

**0-728. ANTIQUE ENGLISH REVOLVER, WITH SPRING BAYONET.** Made by J. Harper. 5¾-inch octagonal barrel, ½-inch muzzle. Six-shot cylinder. rifling. Double action, with pepper-box pattern top hammer. German silver chased frame, with powder charger and butt cap. Fine diamond checkering. Full length 12 inches. In quartered oak case, size 14x 7½x2½ inches, with combination powder and shot flask, engraved letter H. Price the outfit, $20.00.

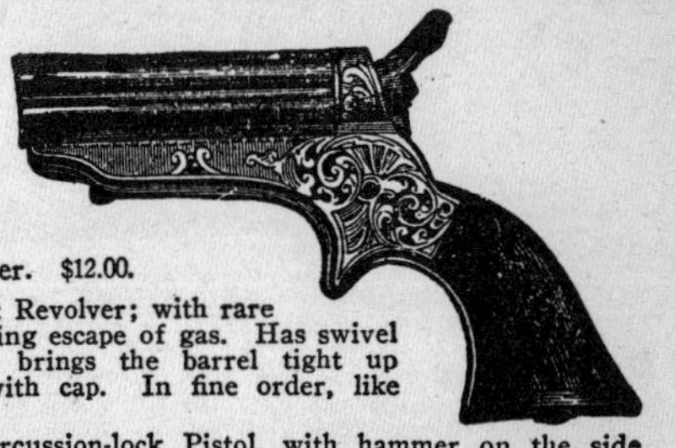

**23. SHARPS 4 BARREL PISTOL,** engraved frame 2½-inch barrels. Firing pin revolves each time hammer is cocked. Safety catch, hard rubber checkered grip. Marked: C. SHARPS, PATENT 1859. Price $15.00.

**No. 59.** Connecticut-Arms Co. Rim-fire Single-barreled Pistol. Patent 1864. Good order. $12.00.

**No. 60.** Mack's Patent 6-shot Revolver; with rare mechanism for preventing escape of gas. Has swivel extension that when operated brings the barrel tight up against the cylinder. Fired with cap. In fine order, like new. Price, $10.00.

**No. 62.** Single-barreled Percussion-lock Pistol, with hammer on the side (right); length of barrel, 8 inches; total length, 15 inches; checkered stock. Found in India. Rare relic. Serviceable order. Price, $10.00.

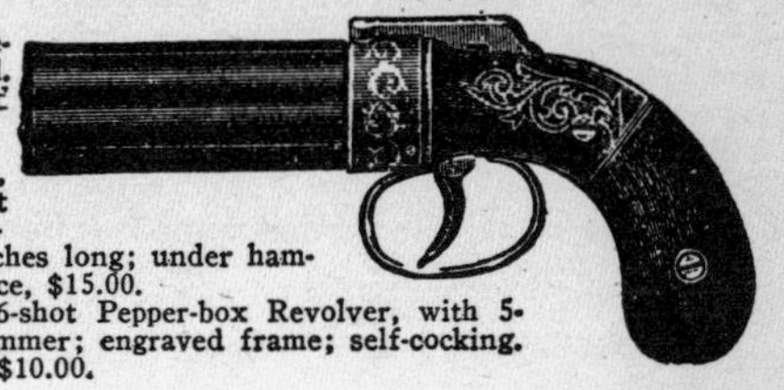

**No. 22.** Pepper-box Revolving Barrel 6-shot Pistol, Top hammer. Engraved frame. In order. $12.00.

**No. 22A.** Pepper Box, with 6 separate and distinct barrels joined together. Barrels are fine Damascus, 3 inches long; under hammer. Fine order; rare. Price, $15.00.

**No 22B.** 6-shot Pepper-box Revolver, with 5-inch ribbed barrels. Top hammer; engraved frame; self-cocking. Guard lock missing. Price, $10.00.

**23A. SHARPS 4 BARREL PISTOL,** like No. 23, plain finish, wood grips. Large size with 3-inch barrels. Price $14.50.

**23B. FRENCH MODEL SHARPS 4 BARREL PISTOL.** Hard wood butt, 3-inch barrels, nickel frame and barrels, all etched, flat trigger. Price $14.00.

**23C. BELGIAN MODEL SHARPS 4 BARREL PISTOL,** blued finish, 3-inch barrels, hard wood grips, fitted with ramrod. The originals were all made without rods. Price $12.00.

**No. 1873. PEPPER-BOX PISTOL,** 5 shots, in rosewood case; 3¼-inch fluted barrels; curly walnut stock; finely checkered; with name plate engraved with swan; handsome case hardened metal lock engraved "Parker, Field & Son, 233 Holborn, London." Top hammer, double action. Case contains bullet mould and hammers. Ivory box, with extra nipples and powder flask. Cleaning rods, wrench, wads, etc. Price for this handsome outfit, $25.00.

**0-1191. PILL LOCK PISTOL.** Barrel stamped "Rogers and Hearst, Utica, N. Y." About 26 calibre, full length 11½ inches. Evidently changed from flintlock by insertion in the side vent of the early pattern barrel-shaped plug with nipple. Steel barrel 7¼ inches long with 8 deep rifle grooves; ramrod rib. Silver name and side plates. Polished walnut stock. Engraved mountings. Silver tip in butt and side. Fixed rear sight on the barrel. In the face of the hammer is a small pin made to enter the nipple and explode fulminate priming. This was the earliest form from the flint to the percussion cap. Price, $17.85.

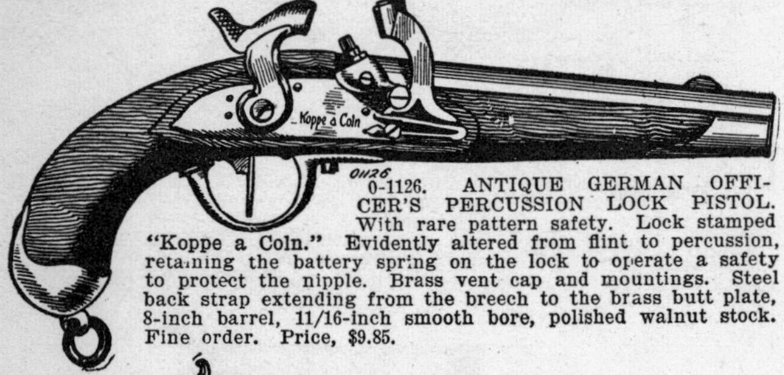

**0-1126. ANTIQUE GERMAN OFFICER'S PERCUSSION LOCK PISTOL.** With rare pattern safety. Lock stamped "Koppe a Coln." Evidently altered from flint to percussion, retaining the battery spring on the lock to operate a safety to protect the nipple. Brass vent cap and mountings. Steel back strap extending from the breech to the brass butt plate, 8-inch barrel, 11/16-inch smooth bore, polished walnut stock. Fine order. Price, $9.85.

**0 - 1 1 2 7. TROMBLON PERCUSSION LOCK BLUNDERBUSS PISTOL.** Barrel is ⅝ inch diameter at the breech and nearly 1 inch wide at the muzzle, centre hammers, engraved mountings. Good working order. Not high grade. Price, $6.50.

**R44. 1 OLD ENGLISH FLINT-LOCK PISTOL** with double barrels superposed. The lever on side turns one vent in the pan together with priming powder for shooting second barrel. Made by H. W. Mortimer & Co., London. Price, $25.00.

**R45.** One as above, with brass barrel and frame, by Twigg, London. Price, $25.00.

**R46.** One like R45, made by P. Bond, Cornhill, London. Price, $30.00.

**0-1107. DOUBLE BARREL SPRING BAYONET PERCUSSION PISTOL.** 4-inch octagonal barrels, 7/16-inch smooth bore. Full length 8¾ inches, 2½-inch bayonet blade, operated by removable guard bow. Walnut stock. Two outside hammers. Barrels are side by side. In working order. Not high-class weapon. Price, $12.85.

**1854A. PERCUSSION LOCK SPRING BAYONET PISTOL.** 4¼-inch octagonal barrel, ½-inch smooth bore, 3¼-inch bayonet blade controlled by movable guard bow. Walnut stock. Good order. Not a high-grade pistol Price, $6.50. Sale restricted to known collectors and to customers in New York State a license permit is required.

**0-1124. EIGHT-BARREL REVOLVING PISTOL.** Eight separate fine Damascus barrels, 3 inches long, attached to revolving frame. Each barrel numbered from 1 to 8. Engraved frame and mountings. Black oak wood stock. Ring trigger, which revolves trigger to the left. Under hammer, self-cocking. All in fine serviceable order. Proof marked. Was on exhibition in European museum when purchased.

**0-1124A. EIGHT-BARREL REVOLVING PISTOL.** Similar to No. 0-1124 except that the barrels are twist steel and 2¾ inches in length. From European museum.

**0-1190. SEVEN-SHOT REVOLVER.** Stamped "Whitneyville Armory, Conn., U. S. A." About calibre 22. Walnut stock. 3-inch octagonal barrel. Price, $12.00.

**DBC-27. PAIR DOUBLE BARREL PERCUSSION PISTOLS in CASE.** 4-inch round barrels with front and rear sights, fitted with swivel ramrod under the barrels. Flat wood butts with engraved cap boxes, entire grips finely checkered. Engraved trigger guards and frames. Silver monogram ovals, outside hammers, engraved, dolphin shaped. Frames marked: C. LANCASTER. He was London maker, at 151 New Bond Street. Set contains cleaning rod with hammer head, round ball mould, extra balls, nipple wrench, 3-inch oval copper powder flask, steel oil cup. Fine steel cleaner for nipples contained in head of nipple wrench. Price for outfit $35.00.

**SHC-1. SHARPS FOUR BARREL PISTOL,** in case with combination rod and cleaner. 2½-inch barrels, BRITISH PROOF MARKED, and engraved, blued finish. Fancy hard rubber grips, silver plated engraved frame and stock strap. This was evidently a presentation piece, as SHARP pistols seldom come in cases. Price for outfit $25.00. See No. 23, page 115.

**SHC-2. SHARPS FOUR BARREL PISTOL,** caliber 32, in case, 3-inch barrels, blued with BRITISH PROOF MARKS. Hard rubber grips, nickel finished frame. Full length 5¾ inches. Set contains combination rod and cleaner, and screw-driver. Case has two covered compartments for cartridges. Price for set complete $22.00.

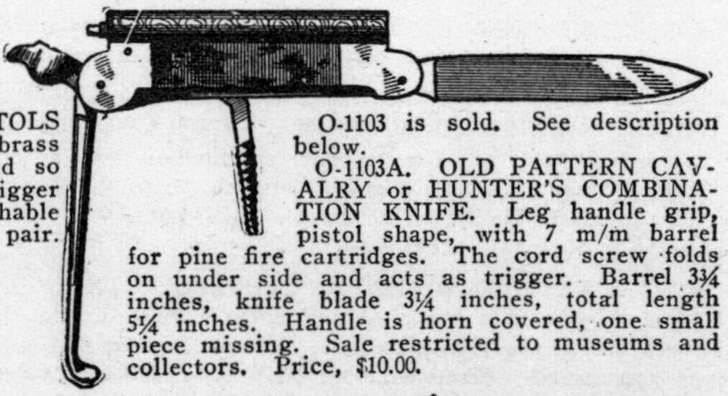

**D99. PAIR FLINT LOCK POCKET PISTOLS** with brass cannon shaped barrels and brass frame. Made by JOYNER, LONDON, and so marked on frame. Center hammers, with trigger guards. Wood butt silver inlaid. Detachable brass barrels are 5 inches. This is a fine pair. Price, $25.00 pair.

**0-1092. ANCIENT CAP CHARGER.** Steel box, with compartment, which slides out for refilling; by pressing side spring the cap is pushed forward to the opening ready for placing on the nipple of the gun. Size 4½x1¾ inches. Rare pattern. Price, $5.00.

**0-1132. WATCH CHARM BULLET MOULD.** Full length three-fourths of an inch. Complete miniature mould. Price, 85 cents.

**S-5. ALLEN SIX SHOT PEPPER BOX REVOLVER,** caliber 36, like illustration No. S-1 on page 117. Top hammer, engraved frame, hard wood handle. Total length 10 inches, barrels 5½ inches. Barrels in this length are rare. Large trigger guard with extra spur or spud for second finger, to steady the aim. In fair condition. Price, $12.00.

**0-1146. ANCIENT COPPER POWDER FLASK WITH SPRING - CATCH MEASURING TOP.** Length 6 inches. Tube-shaped for convenience in the hand while loading. Used; serviceable order, with carrying rings for cord. Price, $3.50.

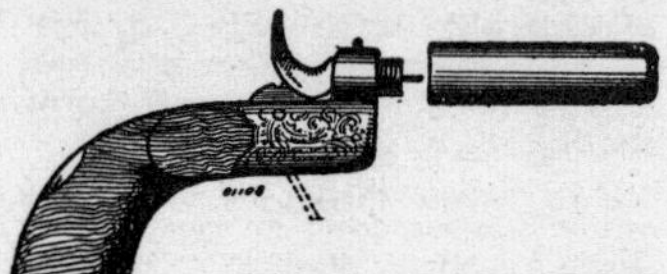

**O-1103 is sold.** See description below.

**O-1103A. OLD PATTERN CAVALRY or HUNTER'S COMBINATION KNIFE.** Leg grip, pistol shape, with 7 m/m barrel for pine fire cartridges. The cord screw folds on under side and acts as trigger. Barrel 3¾ inches, knife blade 3¼ inches, total length 5¼ inches. Handle is horn covered, one small piece missing. Sale restricted to museums and collectors. Price, $10.00.

**0-1108. PAIR CONCEALED TRIGGER NEEDLE-FIRE SINGLE-BARREL PISTOLS.** Fine rifled barrel 2½ inches long, which unscrews for the insertion of special made cartridge. Centre-fire hammer. Needle firing pin. Engraved frame. Metal name plate. Full length 6¼ inches. Price the pair, $8.00; singly, $4.50.

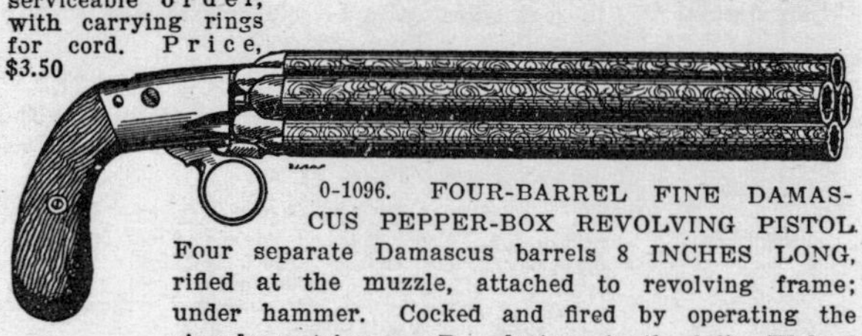

**0-1096. FOUR-BARREL FINE DAMASCUS PEPPER-BOX REVOLVING PISTOL** Four separate Damascus barrels 8 INCHES LONG, rifled at the muzzle, attached to revolving frame; under hammer. Cocked and fired by operating the ring lever trigger. Barrels turn to the left. Walnut stock. This fine weapon was on exhibition in a gunnery school museum in Europe when we induced the owner to let us have it for some of our American collectors. This is a rare piece in fine condition. Full length 12 inches

**0-1125. FOUR-BARREL REVOLVING RIFLED PISTOL.** 2⅞-inch twist steel separate barrels, attached to revolving frame, numbered from 1 to 4. Engraved frame and mountings. Fine checkered walnut stock. Ring trigger revolves the barrels to the left. Under hammer self-cocking. In good working order.

**0-1124B. FIVE-BARREL REVOLVING PISTOL.** Five Damascus separate barrels 2½ inches long, attached to revolving frame. Four-muzzle rifle grooves. Engraved frame and mountings. Walnut stock. Ring trigger revolves barrel to the left. Self-cocking under hammer. Working order. Price, $22.50.

**0-1121. FRENCH MAJOR GENDARMIE DOUBLE-BARREL PERCUSSION LOCK PISTOL.** Period 1855. 7-inch barrels, one over the other; 1½-inch smooth bore. Two hammers, one on each side. Two triggers. Brass mountings. Walnut stock. Long back strap. Cap box in the butt. Rib between the barrels. Full length 12 inches. Price, $9.85.

No. 507-22. LANCASTER BRITISH FOUR SHOT PISTOL, caliber .455, with 6½ inch barrels, total length 10½ inches, weight 2½ pounds. Double action, with lanyard swivel in butt. Side lever releases barrel catch, barrels, hinge downward to load. Four empty shells ejected simutaneously. Barrel marked: CHARLES LANCASTER PATENT, 151 NEW BOND ST., LONDON. Pistols of this type now rare. Price, $23.00.

D-27. IMPROVED MARIETTE REVOLVER PEPPER BOX. Cylinder revolves by hand. SIX shot, about caliber 22, but will not take an American cartridge. Cylinder 2¾ inches long, finely engraved. Hard wood, highly polished grip, engraved frame. The improvement consists in the application of a center hammer which strikes a firing pin, which is made to strike the head of shell straight across, thus avoiding any chance of misfire. This type is rare. Price, $20.00.

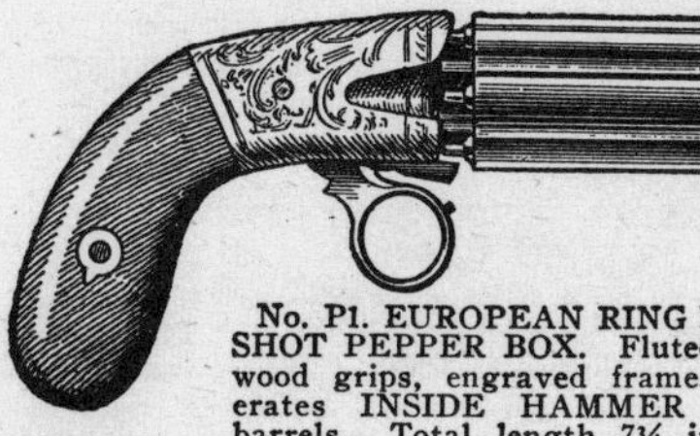

No. P1. EUROPEAN RING HAMMER SIX SHOT PEPPER BOX. Fluted barrels, hard wood grips, engraved frame. Trigger operates INSIDE HAMMER and revolves barrels. Total length 7¾ inches, barrels, caliber 32, 3½ inch. In fine order. Price $15.00.

No. P-2. 1 PEPPER BOX REVOLVER LIKE No. P-1. Caliber .32; full length 7½ inches; barrel 3¼ inches. Price $14.50.

No. P-3. BRITISH FIVE-SHOT PEPPER BOX, CALIBER .44. ENGRAVED FRAME, wood grips, under lever ring trigger. Heavy FLUTED barrels, 3½ inch, with each barrel marked with BRITISH PROOF MARK. Pepper boxes in this caliber are rare. Price $18.00.

MARIETTE REVOLVING PEPPERBOXES. We list below several of these in different sizes. They all have four barrels, which revolve when the combination ring hammer-trigger is pulled. Barrels revolve to the LEFT. Each barrel is grooved at muzzle for removal by the special tool used for that purpose. See illustration No. 1333 on page 117 of 1925 Anniversary Catalog.

1333C. 2½ inch plain steel barrels, engraved frame, polished wood grip. Price, $15.00.

1333D. 2½ inch Damascus steel barrels, engraved frame, checkered grips. Price, $15.00.

1333E. 2½ inch TWIST steel barrels, engraved frame, polished wood grips, diamond shaped stock screw escutcheons. Price, $16.00.

1333F. 3¼ inch plain steel barrels, plain wood handles, engraved frame. Price, $17.00.

1333G. 2½ inch DAMASCUS steel barrels, black wood handle, engraving on frame and stock straps. Price, $17.00.

1333H. 2½ inch plain steel barrels, black wood grip, frame engraved. Price, $16.00.

1333J. 2⅜ inch plain steel barrels, engraved frame, plain wood grips. This is in fair condition, but in good working order. Price, $13.00.

1333K. 3 inch Damascus barrels, black wood handle, engraving on frame, also proof mark. Price, $19.00.

1333L. 2¾ inch Damascus steel barrels, engraved metal parts, black polished wood grips. Price, $20.00.

1333M. 2¾ inch Damascus steel barrels, engraving on frame and other parts, plain wood grips. Price, $14.00.

1333N. 3¼ inch Damascus barrels, with two proof marks, polished black wood handles, top of frame engraved, stock strap marked: HAAKENPLOMDEUR, FRT D'ARMES, A LIEGE. Price, $25.00.

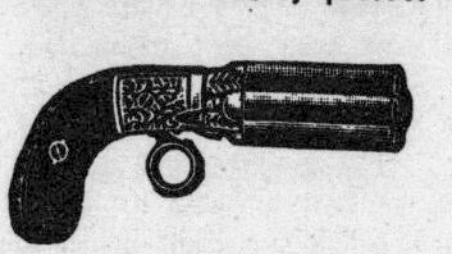

No. 1333. FOUR-BARREL PERCUSSION PEPPER BOX with Damascus barrels about caliber .40, with engraved frame, operated by under lever ring which operates the hammer and revolves the four barrels. Full length 7¼ inches, barrels 2¾ inch, DETACHABLE. European make. Price, $20.00.

No. 1333A. FOUR-BARREL PERCUSSION PEPPER BOX REVOLVER with engraved frame and stock strap, with hard wood handles with fine fine checkering. Under lever ring trigger. Full length 6¾ inches, plain steel barrels, detachable, 2⅞ inches. Price, $12.00.

No. 1333B. 1 FOUR-BARREL PERCUSSION PEPPER BOX REVOLVER, with 2¼ inch DAMASCUS detachable barrels, engraved frame and stock strap, HARD WOOD HANDLES. Under lever ring trigger. This is a fine specimen of European gunmakers' work. Price, $25.00.

R. L. 2. FIVE-SHOT AMERICAN PEPPER BOX made by ROBBINS & LAWRENCE CO., WINDSOR, VERMONT. This type has barrels hinged to frame at BOTTOM, and the HAMMER REVOLVES inside the frame, instead of having the barrels revolve as in all other styles. Two openings in frame give view of hammer to show which barrel will be the next to fire. Extra long frame with saw handle grip, hard wood handles, ring trigger operating hammer. About caliber .32. The ring trigger cocks hammer, but a regular trigger is also provided to make for more accurate shooting. Top catch holding barrels in place is grooved for rear sight. This pistol also has brass front sight, very rare on this style. Full length 7¾ inches. Barrels 3⅝ inch, are detachable for cleaning. Price, $23.00.

R. L. AMERICAN PEPPER BOX BY ROBBINS & LAWRENCE LIKE No. R. L. 2, in good order. Price, $21.00.

10401. PAIR PERCUSSION FLINTLOCK DUELLING PISTOLS. By Perrins, Windsor, England, gunmaker to his majesty. 8-inch octagonal twist steel barrels, 9/16-inch smooth bore, with silver name plate on comb, also on the butt stock, engraved with lion rampant on castle tower, silver fore-end and escutcheons, engraved mountings; on the lock "T. Perrins," on the barrel "T. Perrins Gun Maker to His Majesty." Curly walnut stock, checkered grip, gold breech band, ramrod rib, in mahogany case, in fine order, with brass-mounted hinges, handle, catches and lock. A pair of fine pistols in serviceable order, fit for a king's use. Price, $45.00.

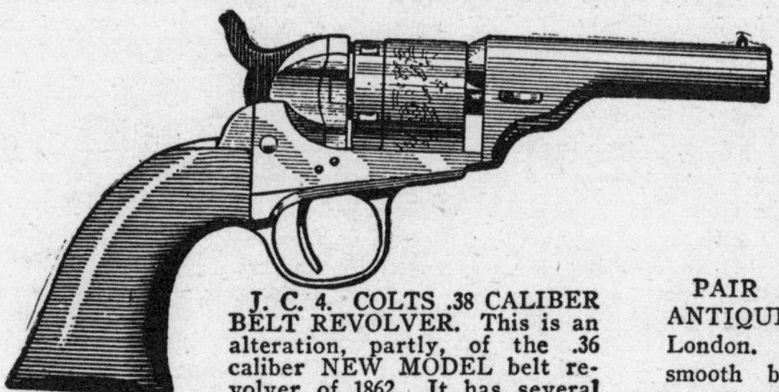

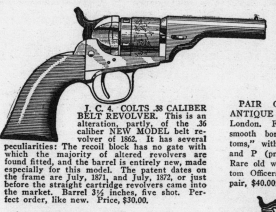

J. C. 4. COLTS .38 CALIBER BELT REVOLVER. This is an alteration, partly, of the .36 caliber NEW MODEL belt revolver of 1862. It has several peculiarities: The recoil block has no gate with which the majority of altered revolvers are found fitted, and the barrel is entirely new, made especially for this model. The patent dates on the frame are July, 1871, and July, 1872, or just before the straight cartridge revolvers came into the market. Barrel 3½ inches, five shot. Perfect order, like new. Price, $30.00.

6002. REVOLVING PISTOL. Six-shot. Engraved. "Made by J. Beattie, 223 Regent St., London," about the period of 1846. Serviceable order. Price, $12.00.

10423. REVOLVING PEPPER POT PISTOL. Six-shot Cooper's British patent. Under hammer, ring trigger, walnut stock. Full length 8 inches. Working order. Price, $11.85.

No. S-1. ALLEN SIX-BARREL PEPPER BOX REVOLVER. About caliber .32, with engraved frame, hard wood handles, with small silver name plates. Top hammer marked: ALLEN'S PATENT. Trigger raises hammer and revolves barrels. Total length 7 inches, barrels 3 inches. Price $15.00.

No. S-2. ALLEN'S PATENT SIX-SHOT PEPPER BOX, about caliber .32, with engraved frame, and hard wood handles. Like No. S-1. Barrels marked: Allen & Thurber, Worcester, patented 1837. Full length 8 inches, barrels 3½ inches. Price, $16.50.

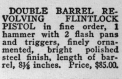

DOUBLE BARREL REVOLVING FLINTLOCK PISTOL in fine order, 1 hammer with 2 flash pans and triggers, finely ornamented, bright polished steel finish, length of barrel, 8⅜ inches. Price, $85.00.

No. 2138. PAIR OF FLINTLOCK POCKET PISTOLS, made by H. Nock, London, American Revolutionary War period gun makers; octagonal barrel 4 inches long; smooth bore, ⅝ inches; engraved lock and mountings; guard has the Pineapple engraving peculiar to the last century; checkered walnut stock; silver name plate; handsome pair of pistols, in fine working order. Price, $26.00.

No. 2128. OLD ENGLISH FLINTLOCK HORSE PISTOL, made by Reeve & Greaves, London; octagonal barrel, 8½ inches long; 16 gauge; smooth bore, checkered walnut stock; engraved lock and mountings; silver name plate; full length, 15 inches; in working order. Price, $14.00.

PAIR PERCUSSION LONDON CARRIAGE PISTOLS. R. S. Clarke, maker. Twist barrels, centre hammer, silver engraved mountings; full length 8 inches. Concealed trigger. In walnut case with flask for shot and powder, bullets, wrench, caps, etc. Serviceable. Price, $11.85.

PAIR OF CUSTOM OFFICERS' ANTIQUE PISTOLS. Made by Barnett, London. Flintlock, brass barrel, ⅝-inch smooth bore, barrel engraved. "Customs," with Crown and V and Crown and P (probably viewed and proved). Rare old weapons, used by British Custom Officers in older times. Price the pair, $40.00.

1486. BREECH LOADING POCKET PISTOL with spring dagger. Percussion lock, bronze frame, blued steel rifled barrel marked "Pinder Sleaford." Full length, 7 inches, 7/16 rifled. Length with dagger extended, 9½ inches.

D-27-A. IMPROVED MARIETTE REVOLVER PEPPER BOX. Five shot, about caliber 38. No American cartridge fits. Plain steel cylinder, engraved frame, hard wood handle with fine carving. Cylinder 3 inches long. By unscrewing button at muzzle the cylinder is removed to load, and the cylinder pin is pointed to us as rammer in unloading. This is similar to D-27 except in size and caliber. Price, $25.00.

No. S-3. FIVE-BARREL ALLEN'S PATENT PEPPER BOX, MARKED: ALLEN & WHEELOCK. About caliber .32. Engraved frame, plain wood grips. Full length 6½ inches, barrels 3 inches. Hammer marked: ALLEN'S PATENT 1845. Price, $12.00.

No. S-4. AMERICAN SIX-SHOT PEPPER BOX REVOLVER, caliber .32 with 2½ inch barrels; full length 6¾ inches. Has trigger guard, top hammer, wood grips. In FAIR condition only. Price, $9.50.

AM-27. LE MAT REVOLVER, 12 m/m, TEN shot, 9 cartridges from cylinder, one shot gun size from center barrel, located under the regular barrel. Attachment on hammer is moved to use special firing pin on center barrel. Cylinder is loaded through side gate, and cartridges ejected by side lever. Wood grip is polished, and of saw handle type. Small ring on frame to carry revolver on lanyard. Barrels 4½ inches, total length 10½ inches, weight 3 pounds. Revolvers of this style were supplied to officers of the Confederate States through blockade-runners. Barrel marked: LE MAT. Price $50.00.

AM-27A. LE MAT REVOLVER, 7 m/m, TEN shot, similar to No. AM-27, with 4-inch barrels, total length 9 inches, weight 2 pounds. Price $50.00.

DPC-28. FOUR BARREL REVOLVING PERCUSSION PISTOL, with 3¼-inch barrels, made to revolve by hand. Two outside hammers, engraved, dolphin shape. Each barrel has its own nipple, each set proof marked. Rounded butt into which is screwed the ramrod. Checkered grip, engraved guard and frame. Maker's mark: CHS. JONES, 32 COCKSPUR STREET, LONDON. Oval monogram plate. Each hammer has safety catch. Price $48.00.

FL-7. PAIR FLINTLOCK DUELLING PISTOLS IN CASE. Made by WOGDON, LONDON, and so marked on locks and barrels. Wogdon was famous as a maker of fine duelling pistols. Barrels 10 inch octagonal with slight bell at muzzle, front and rear sights. Four-inch lock plates. Ornamented butt plate and trigger guard. Round butt, slightly flattened at sides. A very well made pair. Set includes extra flints, extra bullets, steel rammer with worm, 3-inch copper powder flask miniature bottle with gun oil. Hardwood case has brass name plate in top with old style eagle, and letters C.W.G. Case measures 18½ inches long by 8½ inches deep by 2¾ inches high. Price for outfit $80.00.

FL-8. PAIR TRAVELLER'S FLINTLOCK PISTOLS, IN CASE. Made by TWIGG, LONDON. Locks 4¼ inch marked TWIGG, with safety catch. Nine-inch octagonal barrels with front and rear sights, marked LONDON. Round wood butt, with checkered grip, and silver name plate. Set includes 3-inch metal flask, round ball mould, wood wiping rod with metal tip, several extra flints, and extra round bullets. Case is of hardwood, size: 17½ inches long, 8½ inches wide, 3 inches high. Price of complete outfit, $75.00.

FL-10. PAIR FLINTLOCK DUELLING PISTOLS, in case, 4½-inch locks, with safety catches, marked: ESSEX. Heavy octagonal barrels, 9 inch, with front sights, browned finish, marked: LONDON. Ornamented trigger guard with fancy tip. Round wood butt, with flatted sides, finely checkered, with silver name plates. Set includes extra bullets, extra flints, round ball mould, and 2-inch bristle brush for cleaning pan. Polished wood case has top brass handle with lock and side hooks, and measures 18 inches long by 8½ inches deep by 3 inches high. Price for outfit, $75.00.

FL-26-A. PAIR MORTIMER FLINTLOCK PISTOLS, in case. Full length 12 inches. Round barrels, extra heavy, 7 inch, with flat top, marked: LONDON. Front and rear sights. Highly polished stock, full length, finely checkered butt with round end. Four-inch flint locks with safety catches, marked: H. W. MORTIMER. Engraved trigger guards with acorn tips. Pistols in fine condition. Set includes extra flints, extra round balls, extra wood rammer with tools, round mould, 4-inch flat copper powder flask. Price for set, $100.00.

BELGIAN FLINTLOCK PISTOLS, CALIBER 70, with lanyard ring in flat butt. Barrel 9 inch, total 15 inch. Brass trimmed. Sure fire. Complete with flint, $6.95. Extra flints 10 cents each.

PL-26-F. PAIR RARE SAW HANDLE PERCUSSION PISTOLS, in case with equipment. Full length 11½ inches, with 5½-inch octagonal barrel, with word LONDON inlaid in silver. Front sight silver, rear sight silver with peep. Swivel ramrod fitted in silver groove on under side of barrel. Frame, trigger guard and ramrod guides all silver. Finely checkered polished wood stock, with flat butt fitted with silver ornament. Trigger guard and frame engraved. Tang marked with maker's name: WESTWOOD. Set includes extra ramrod with tools, mould, oilcup, combination nipper wrench and oildropper, bullets, and barrel shaped copper flask with three compartments for bullets, caps, and powder. This is a very handsome set. Price, $60.00.

PL-26-G. PAIR PERCUSSION BELT PISTOLS, in case. Full length 14 inches. Twist steel round barrels with flat top, marked: J. D. DOUGALL, GLASGOW. 3¾-inch locks marked: J. D. DOUGALL. Swivel ramrods. Full length stock horn tipped. 4¼-inch blued steel belt hooks on left side. Engraved trigger guards with acorn ends, engraved lock, hammer and tang. Checkered grips, oval ends with engraved butt plates containing cap boxes. Oblong silver monogram plates. Set includes oilcup with dropper, mould, horn tipped extra wood ramrod with tools, 4-inch copper flask and extra round bullets. Price for outfit, $50.00.

PL-26-H. PAIR BELT PERCUSSION DOUBLE BARREL PISTOLS, in case. A rare type. Round barrels, 6-inch with center groove containing sights. Marked: MANTON, LONDON. Made for use in INDIA. Full length 11 inches. Swivel ramrod on under side. This type of rod rare on double barrel pistols. Four inch flat blued steel belt hooks on left side. Trigger guards, frames and hammer finely engraved. Checkered stocks with engraved butt plates with cap boxes. Silver monogram plates have the crest, gauntleted hand holding rose. Set complete with extra hardwood rod with tools, mould, wad-cutter, extra bullets, 3½-inch barrel shaped copper flask for powder and bullets. Flask loads from the BOTTOM. Price for the set, $47.00.

PL-26-J. PAIR PERCUSSION DOUBLE BARREL PISTOLS, in case. Full length 14 inches, barrels round, twist steel, 8-inch, marked: LONDON. Center top rib. Silver front sight, swivel ramrods, 9/16-inch bore. Back action, engraved locks, marked: WILSON. Ornamental trigger guards with acorn ends. Dolphin head hammers, engraved. Flat round butt with finely checkered hand grips. Oval monogram plates of silver. Set contains extra ramrod with tools, bullets, three compartment tub shaped 3¾-inch copper flask. Price for outfit, $36.00.

## "Sitting Bull"

The people in the East are always interested in anything pertaining to the Old West. Anything concerning Buffalo Bill, "Wild Bill" Hickok, California Joe, Old Jim Bridger or any of those old sports. Particularly interesting are items relating to the Injuns of those days—now gone forever.

Injuns such as Sitting Bull, Red Cloud, Gall, Crazy Hoss, Rain-in-the-Face, Little Wolf, (the Cheyenne who licked the United States Cavalry three times running), Spotted Tail, American Hoss, Geronimo, Cochise, and as the law wolves say, "et al."

My attention was called last week to the article in *The Star*, "Sitting Bull a Cadet at West Point," and Sunday I noticed in a paper an item which explained Bull was not a Mason, as credited. The old-timers West must laugh when they read this bit, for Sitting Bull was so crooked he couldn't lie straight in a round tent. And, figuring how the Injuns never knew what was going on inside of him, you can push in all your chips that Masons marked him "Bad Medicine" before the deal.

### BULL AN UNKPAPA

A few real true facts regarding Sitting Bull may interest readers. He was a Unkpapa, which is the name of one of the tribes of the Sioux nation. His Injun name was Te-a-tonka-e-a-tonka. He was an implacable enemy of all white men and made more trouble than any other redskin who ever wore mocassins.

Sitting Bull was not a chief, (and let me say in parenthesis, no photos of him may be found in a chief's feathers and regalia.) He frequently stuck an eagle feather in his scalp lock, which even the squaws had a habit of doing when being photographed, and after joining Cody's Wild West show in 1883 and touring the East, finding he could sell his picture for four bits, making forty-five cents a time, he got to dolling up and putting on a lot of dog, as we say West.

It has been erroneously supposed that Bull was in command of the Injuns in the fight known as the battle of the Little Big Horn, (erroneously called the Custer Massacre.) Such is not the case. In fact, while present among that great gathering of redskins at the time, he had no authority and as soon as the scrap started he packed off north with two or three of his wives and the kids and was all of ten miles away when overtaken by a messenger who informed him that Custer and his entire command, (five companies of the Seventh Calvary) were killed, and then he returned for the dance held by the Sioux and Cheyennes that night.—HENRY CODY BLAKE, in Greenpoint, N. Y., *Star*.

**We wish to call special attention to pages 66, 67, 68, 69 and 366, where we show drawings and full description of all the World War guns. This information is not to be found in any book on the war, as we obtained it from first hand sources, having access to all of the captured arms brought to this country by our government after the war. The drawings are all to scale and show every detail of gun, and the different styles of bayonets are also shown. This information alone, if in book form would readily sell at $1.00 per copy, whereas we include this in our catalog and charge only 50 cents for all.**

**On the last pages of the catalog, we show interesting information of the various parts of the flint-lock, also various types of magazines used in army rifles, showing their development.**

3238. COLT'S REVOLVER, with extension stock; Civil War relic. Pattern issued to U. S. Cavalry for use as a side arm revolver, and with the extension stock. Fired from the shoulder as carbine. In working order. Price, $50.00.

EMPEROR NAPOLEON 1810 FLINT-LOCK HORSE PISTOL. Stamped as having been made at the Imperial Arsenal, St. Etienne (France). The barrel stamped 1819, in ample time to have been used at the Battle of Waterloo. Pistol is from an English collection. No doubt a captured relic. Club butt protection. Parts proof marked. Price, $12.50.

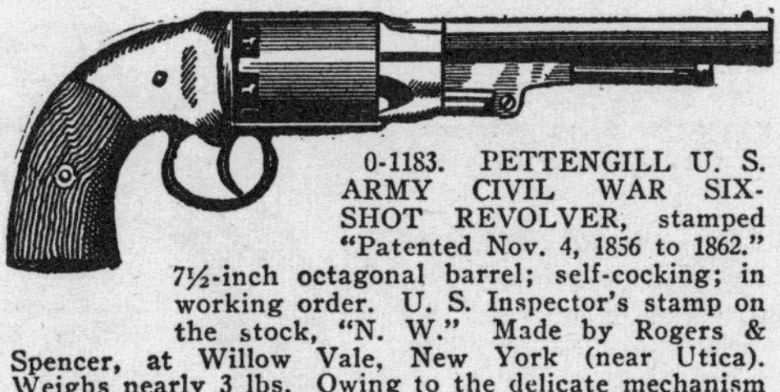

0-1183. PETTENGILL U. S. ARMY CIVIL WAR SIX-SHOT REVOLVER, stamped "Patented Nov. 4, 1856 to 1862." 7½-inch octagonal barrel; self-cocking; in working order. U. S. Inspector's stamp on the stock, "N. W." Made by Rogers & Spencer, at Willow Vale, New York (near Utica). Weighs nearly 3 lbs. Owing to the delicate mechanism they did not prove serviceable weapons. Only a few were used toward the end of the Civil War. Rare guns. Price, $15.00.

PP. FINE PAIR NOCK PERCUSSION PISTOLS IN CASE. 9-inch octagon barrels marked LONDON, with front and rear sights. Hard wood rammers, with horn tips, one plain end, one with ball screw. Lock, hammer, and guard finely engraved. 4¼-inch lock with safety catch marked: H. NOCK. Oval silver name plate on grip. Round ball butt with flattened sides. Blued finish trigger guard with pine apple end. Total length of pistols is 14 inches. Set is in hard wood case, with wads, caps, round bullets, 4-inch copper powder flask, 2 wad cutters, round ball mould, and four gun tools. Price $75.00.

PP1. WESSON & LEAVITT NAVY REVOLVER IN CASE. Caliber 36 with 5-inch barrel and extra cylinder. Has MAYNARD type attachment for caps. Side hammer, brass guard. THESE PISTOLS ARE NOW RARE. Set contains small copper flask, with old style American eagle embossed on one side, with maker's name on other. Pistol barrel marked: MASS. ARMS CO., CHICOPEE FALLS. Price for outfit, $65.00.

10179. FIVE-SHOT ENGLISH REVOLVER, Adams Patent, stamped Adams Revolver Arms Co., New York; made by Massachusetts Arms Co., Chicopee Falls, Mass., patented 1853, 1855, 1857. Many of the Adams revolvers were in use during the Civil War; 31 calibre was the size carried by officers. Octagonal barrel is 3½ inches long. Checkered walnut grip, in new condition. A rare weapon. Price, $15.00.

10180. BACON POWDER AND BALL FIVE-SHOT REVOLVER, altered to shoot metallic rim fire cartridge; 4-inch round barrel, engraved cylinder; good working order. Price, $8.50.

10826B. GERMAN NAVY CAP AND BALL PISTOL, marked Potsdam, with Royal Crown and letters S. S. Side attachment for the belt; 9½-inch barrel; ⅞-inch smooth bore. Brass mountings require cleaning; in working order. Price, $5.85.

0-1150A. ANCIENT LEATHER POWDER FLASK, with revolving charging cup-funnel, same as 0-1150. Length 8 inches. Stamped "B" in circle. Used; serviceable order. Price, $4.85.

0-1152. ANTIQUE COPPER POWDER FLASK. Circular-shaped, 3¾ inches, with GLASS WINDOW in each side to see the contents of the flask. Brass graduating, measuring cup-funnel. Full length 5¾ inches. Serviceable curiosity. Price, $6.50.

0-1153. ANTIQUE POWDER FLASK, with graduated funnel measuring cup hinged to side post, whereby the cup can be turned to receive the charge of powder from the flask and then turned away from the flask for pouring the charge into the gun. Likely an inventor's model. Price, $7.50.

3034. CIVIL WAR WHITNEY NAVY REVOLVER, engraved on the butt strap "taken of George Dent of Mathias Point, Nov. 11, 1861." This came from the Stillwell collection. It is in good second-hand order. It is a curious coincidence that we offer for sale No. 500, Smith & Wesson revolver, that has the same identical engraving, and that now after 50 years' separation these two weapons should come together. Price for the pair, Nos. 508 and 3034, is $25.00.

10178. BEALS PATENT SEVEN-SHOT REVOLVER, made under contract by Eli Whitney and stamped on the revolver, "address E. Whitney, Whitneyville, Ct." Ring trigger, 6-inch octagonal barrel, calibre 31. Curly walnut. Ornamented stock. Side plate on the cylinder encloses part of the revolving mechanism. The revolver is in ROSEWOOD CASE, velvet lined. Size of the case 13 by 5½ by 2 WITH OUTFIT of mould casting round and conical ball, RARE PATTERN BRASS MAGAZINE CAP HOLDER and mould whereby revolver could be quickly capped, copper powder flask with EAGLE COAT OF ARMS, nipple wrench, brass ball setting tool, rare type with outfit. Price, $25.00.

R75. 1 FLINT-LOCK PISTOL made by Adams. Barrel is 8 inches round, marked London. Round butt is brass trimmed, with brass trigger guard, brass name plate and brass side plate. Price, $32.00.

R13. 1 FRENCH FLINT LOCK POCKET PISTOL with French octagon barrel, under ramrod, center hammer, silver wire inlaid butt. Price, $14.00.

R82A. 4 FLINT-LOCK PISTOLS with long round barrels; total length, 17 inches. In fair order. Each, $9.25.

10819. CURIOUS CAP AND BALL REVOLVER. 6-shot, about 30 calibre, 6¼-inch octagonal barrel. Walnut stock, engraved frame. Cylinder and mountings firing by pressing spring in front of the cylinder. Barrel tips up, allowing withdrawal of the cylinder for loading. Good working order. Price, $16.50.

10186. UNION ARMS CO., NEW YORK CITY, CIVIL WAR OFFICERS' MODEL 5-SHOT REVOLVER, 3-inch octagonal barrel, 31 calibre. Resembles the Colts. Price, $9.85.

10185. BEAL STUD TRIGGER. Early model 5-shot cap and ball revolver. Stamped on the barrel, "Beal's Patent 1856-57-58. Manufactured by Remington, Ilion, N. Y." Outside revolving mechanism. 31 calibre 4-inch barrel. Price, $12.85.

AUTOMATIC PISTOL CASE, green silk and velvet inside lining, outside lining black imitation morocco leather covered, nickel fasteners. Size 7¼x5¾x1⅜ inches. Price, $2.85.

MERWIN & BRAY PEARL HANDLE 5-SHOT REVOLVER, calibre 30, nickel finished in *walnut case* with cartridges, etc. Length 8½ inches; neat, serviceable outfit. Price, $10.00.

10181. MORSE 7-SHOT REVOLVER. Metallic rim-fire cartridge (original Morse made in cap and ball for use in Civil War); 4-inch barrel, nickel plated, engraved. Thumb attachment at the base for cylinder frame for side swing opening of the cylinder. Rare weapon. Fine order. Price, $10.00.

10182. REVOLVER. Marked, "Wm. Cooper Fire Arms Mfg. Co., FRANKFORD, PHILADELPHIA, PA., PATENT 1851 TO 1863." Cap and ball, 4-inch barrel, double action, 31 calibre. This model used by Union Army officers during the Civil War. Price, $8.85.

10183. RAYMOND & ROBITARE, Patent 1858, Hammerless, Cap and Ball, Civil War Revolver in working order. 44 calibre, 6½-inch octagonal barrel, PETTINGILL PATENT, 1850-1858. Double action, Civil War relic, in working order. Price, $15.00.

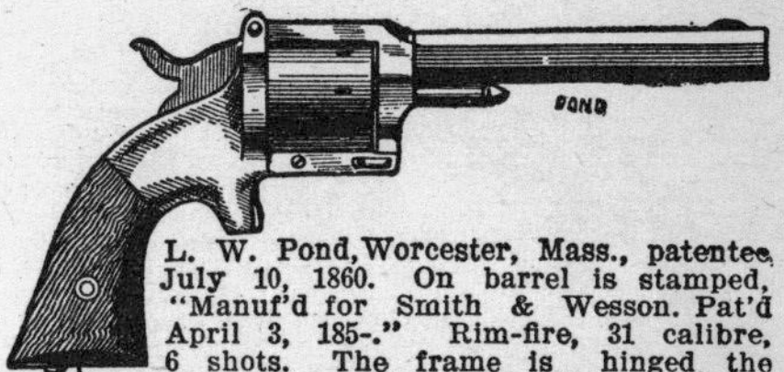

L. W. Pond, Worcester, Mass., patentee, July 10, 1860. On barrel is stamped, "Manuf'd for Smith & Wesson. Pat'd April 3, 185-." Rim-fire, 31 calibre, 6 shots. The frame is hinged, the barrel and the forward part of the frame open upwards, being released by pressure upon a flat spring upon the left side. This method of opening was employed by Smith & Wesson in their first pistols, they having bought out Pond's patent. Price, $17.50.

LF-1. FRENCH FLINTLOCK PISTOL, with large flat butt iron bound, ornamented lock strap, long trigger guard with urn end. Cannon shaped barrel, 8¾ inches, marked DAUID. Front and rear sight. 5-inch lock marked: ARNOLD DAVID. Period of Louis XV. Plain metal monogram plate. Price $20.00.

LF-2. FRENCH FLINTLOCK PISTOL, like No. LF-1 with 4¾-inch lock marked: ASKALL. 10-inch cannon shaped barrel, slightly belled at muzzle. Three armourer's marks on barrel. Price $22.50.

LF-3. FLINTLOCK PISTOL, evidently made to order for gentleman's use. Length 15½ inches, barrel 8¾ inches, part octagonal, marked in silver on top: DAMASCO FINISH, with two narrow silver strips set in near touch hole. 4½-inch engraved lock marked in silver: SCHOLBERG GADET A PELOTAS. Engraved German silver butt plate, trigger guard and ramrod guide. Brass tipped wood ramrod. Price $14.50.

TFL-2. TURKISH FLINTLOCK PISTOL, with long pointed butt, with ornamented brass butt plate. Wood carved stock, ornamented brass trimming, with brass barrel bands. Length 24 inches, barrel 16½ inches, with armourer's mark in gold. Price $12.00.

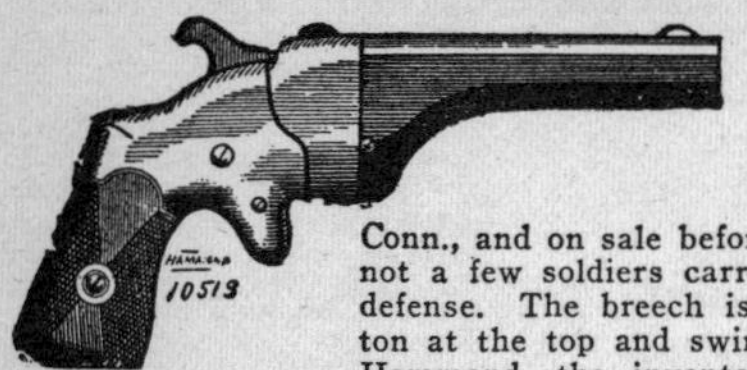

**10518. HAMMOND BREECH-LOADING PISTOL.** Calibre 41 rim-fire, 4-inch barrel. These pistols were patented October 25, 1864. Manufactured by the Conn. Arms & Mfg. Co., Natick, Conn., and on sale before the end of the Cival War and not a few soldiers carried them as pocket weapons of defense. The breech is released by pressing the button at the top and swings to one side. In 1866 Henry Hammond, the inventor, submitted a carbine, which worked on the same principle, to the board then in session at Washington on breech-loading arms. The weapon contains few parts, is very simple to manipulate and is exceedingly strong. Price, $12.85.

**0-724. "BOALEN, NEWARK," ENGRAVED ON PAIR OF PERCUSSION LOCK POCKET-SIZE PISTOLS.** In quartered oak case, with combination nipple and barrel wrench. Full length of the pistols 6 inches, ½-inch smooth bore, centre hammer, chased lock, concealed trigger, silver name plate, walnut stock with fine diamond checkered grip. Price the outfit, $16.50.

**PEP-1. BRITISH PEPPER BOX REVOLVER,** with engraved frame marked: J. R. COOPER, PATENTEE. Polished hard wood grips, ring trigger. Six shot, about caliber 38. Each barrel has the Birmingham proof mark. Set includes 3¾-inch copper powder flask, mould and CASE. Price for set $15.00.

**508. CONFEDERATE OFFICER'S CAPTURED REVOLVER.** Old pattern Smith & Wesson 22-calibre. Either silver or nickel-plated. Engraved on the pistol, "Captured at Matthias Point, Va., Nov. 11, 1861: Once Rebel now Loyal." Purchased from New York Policeman. Price $15.00.

> **See page 114 for Colt revolvers in various models and calibers. Also page 251 for HISTORY OF COLT REVOLVERS.**

**5007. CONFEDERATE OFFICER'S PEPPER BOX REVOLVER,** 6 shot, ivory handle, engraved frame, under lever action. No name or stamp thereon, from the collection of Adam Oliver, Master Armorer, 1861-1865, Augusta Arsenal, Ga. Fine weapon, full length, 7¾ inches. This revolver may have been made in Augusta, as some of the rich men in the South escaped being drawn into the service of the Confederate Army by becoming stockholders in fire arms factories. Price, $25.00.

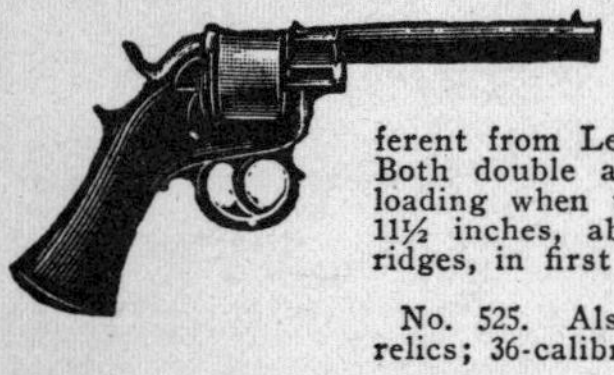

**No. 1856. 20 CIVIL WAR REVOLVERS,** part of the lot purchased by order of President Lincoln, from the New York Arsenal sale in 1900, are in working order. Slightly different from Lefaucheux, in that they are centre fire. Both double and single action. Cylinder turns for loading when the hammer is let down. Full length 11½ inches, about 40-calibre. Offered without cartridges, in first class order. Price $15.00

**No. 525.** Also one of Colt's Civil War battlefield relics; 36-calibre. Price, $10.00.

**Deane, Adams & Deane's Army Officer's Revolver** in case which bears the maker's name and states that they were gun makers to H. R. H. Prince Albert, His Royal Highness (Queen Victoria's husband). Revolver is fired with percussion cap; has checkered stock; engraved mechanism; London proof marks on the cylinder opposite each nipple. About 45-calibre: quantity of expansion bullets go with the revolver: all contained in one case. Price, $10.00.

**No. 66.** Springfield Arms Company Cap Revolver; 6-shot; calibre, 36: chased frame nipples are set in the top of cylinder on an angle: serviceable order. rare arm. Price. $15.00.

**No. 63.** Walsh Firearms Company. 10-shot Revolvers: double hammers: single trigger, long cylinder with 5 chambers, each holding 2 shots, fired separately: rare arm: patented 1859: relic. Price. $20.00.

**No. 64.** Butterfield 5-shot Cap Revolver: patented 1855. Philadelphia; lacks stock and small parts. Price, $20.00.

**Nickel-Plated Colt's Revolver** and Outfit in Case, with mould, flask screwdriver: percussion lock. Price, $8.00.

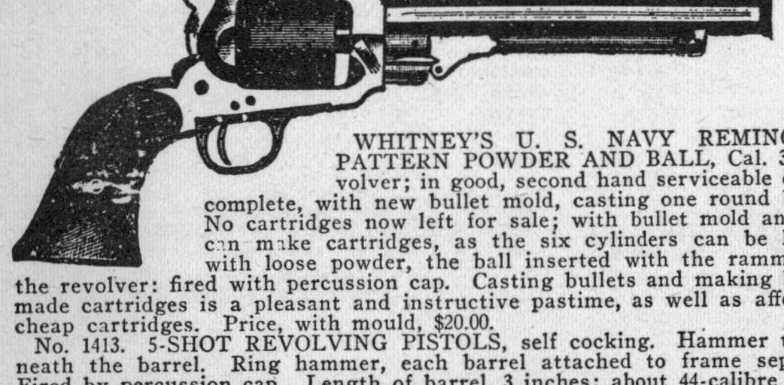

**WHITNEY'S U. S. NAVY REMINGTON PATTERN POWDER AND BALL,** Cal. 36 Revolver; in good, second hand serviceable order; complete, with new bullet mold, casting one round bullet. No cartridges now left for sale; with bullet mold any one can make cartridges, as the six cylinders can be loaded with loose powder, the ball inserted with the rammer on the revolver: fired with percussion cap. Casting bullets and making home-made cartridges is a pleasant and instructive pastime, as well as affording cheap cartridges. Price, with mould, $20.00.
**No. 1413. 5-SHOT REVOLVING PISTOLS,** self cocking. Hammer underneath the barrel. Ring hammer, each barrel attached to frame separate. Fired by percussion cap. Length of barrel, 3 inches: about 44-calibre rifled. Engraved frame. Serviceable order; requires cleaning. Price, $12.00.

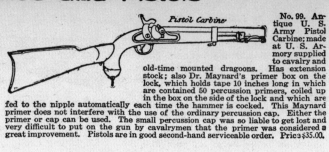

*Pistol Carbine*

**No. 99. Antique U. S. Army Pistol Carbine;** made at U. S. Armory supplied to cavalry and old-time mounted dragoons. Has extension stock; also Dr. Maynard's primer box on the lock, which holds tape 10 inches long in which are contained 50 percussion primers, coiled up in the box on the side of the lock and which are fed to the nipple automatically each time the hammer is cocked. This Maynard primer does not interfere with the use of the ordinary percussion cap. Either the primer or cap can be used. The small percussion cap was so liable to get lost and very difficult to put on the gun by cavalrymen that the primer was considered a great improvement. Pistols are in good second-hand serviceable order. Price $35.00.

**10878. BREECH-LOADING PIN-FIRE PISTOL.** For European cartridge, 6¾-inch octagonal barrel. Engraved frame; blue finish; good working order; dark-colored hard wood stock. Offered without cartridges. Valuable only to collectors. Price, $3.65.

**10878A.** Same pistol with 4½-inch barrel. Price, $2.95.

**EARLY PERCUSSION REVOLVER,** between the Pepper Box and Revolver type made in Britain. German silver engraved frame and butt. Mahogany stock, double acting, 6 chambers; 6-inch octagonal blued steel barrel. British proof marks on the cylinder over each chamber. Fine order, like new. In mahogany case, 2¼x6¼x2½ inches, with loading implements, powder flask, bullet moulds, powder measure, bullets. Price $17.85.

**V-11. W. TRANTER'S PATENT PERCUSSION REVOLVER,** caliber 36, IN CASE. Five shot, double action, with extension grip below the trigger guard. This model has bullet rammer attached to the left side, instead of underneath as on the various American revolvers. Set includes mould, brass, for two conical bullets, steel oil cup, small wood box for patches, nipple wrench with wood handle, screw driver, wood rammer with metal tip, 4¾-inch heavy copper barrel, extra nipples, caps and lead bullets. Cylinder has 5 British proof marks. Barrel marked: H. BECKWITH, SKINNER ST. LONDON. Price $25.00.

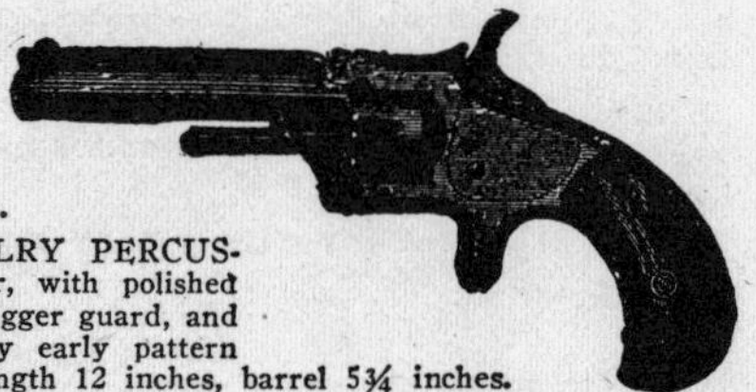

**32. OLD STYLE SMITH & WESSON METALLIC CARTRIDGE REVOLVERS.** One of the first patterns made. No cartridges. Valuable only as a relic. Sold as are. Captured by N. Y. City Police and sold at auction.

**2-26-1. EUROPEAN CAVALRY PERCUSSION PISTOL,** in fine order, with polished hard wood stock, long brass trigger guard, and round brass butt plate. Very early pattern altered from flintlock. Full length 12 inches, barrel 5¾ inches. Some pistols marked on barrel and butt with early dates. Price $4.85.

**No. 7.** Allen & Wheelock Civil War Revolver, purchased by President Lincoln's agents in Europe for arming Union Army Volunteer Officers, 1861-1865. Marked, Patent 1859. The guard forms the lever for ramming the cartridge: fine order; blued: with one of our bullet moulds at 50 cents, you can cast your own bullets: load cylinder with powder same as with army cap gun and you have fine, big, accurate army 6-shooter. Price for revolver, $10.00.

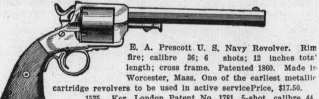

**E. A. Prescott U. S. Navy Revolver.** Rim fire; calibre 36; 6 shots; 12 inches total length; cross frame. Patented 1860. Made in Worcester, Mass. One of the earliest metallic cartridge revolvers to be used in active service. Price, $17.50.

**1535.** Ker. London Patent No. 1781, 5-shot, calibre 44. Revolver, fired by percussion cap. British proof mark over each chamber cylinder. Second-hand, serviceable order. Price, $5.00.

> **THE COLT ARMS.**
> The manufacture of the now world-famous "Colt" revolving firearms, embracing at the outset carbines and rifles as well as pistols, all made on the revolving principle, was begun on a systematic scale in the year 1836, in Paterson, New Jersey. Their first employment by the U. S. Government was in the Seminole Indian War, where they at once established the efficiency of the repeating principle in firearms for military use. In 1848 the factory was established in Hartford, Conn., where the arms have since continued to be manufactured.

**No. 82. SAVAGE REVOLVER** with blued barrel and mountings, walnut stock; in perfect order; for which we want $16.00 each; beautiful specimens of Civil War period revolver. We sold hundreds of old, rusty Savage revolvers about twenty years ago at 25 cents each; now they are rare.

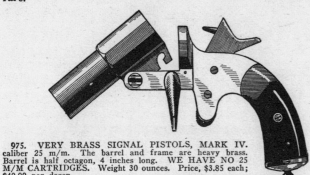

**975. VERY BRASS SIGNAL PISTOLS, MARK IV.** caliber 25 m/m. The barrel and frame are heavy brass. Barrel is half octagon, 4 inches long. WE HAVE NO 25 M/M CARTRIDGES. Weight 30 ounces. Price, $3.85 each; $40.00 per dozen.

**No. 17. ADAMS REVOLVER,** stamped "Adams, London," purchased during the Civil War. We cannot find out if they were purchased by the North or sent to the South by blockade-running steamers. They were sold along with a lot of other revolvers at U. S. Government auction in 1900. They are in serviceable order now and are fired with percussion cap, loaded with powder and ball. Limited number only. Price, $10.00.

**No. 3029. MINIATURE WATCH CHARM PISTOL,** nickel plated, full length 1¾ inch, illustration full size. Breech loading, for pin fire cartridges. Ring on butt for attaching to chain. WE HAVE NO CARTRIDGES. Price for pistol, $1.00.

**AIR GUN SHOT,** selected for size and put up in tubes of 4 ounces. Price, 10 cents per tube. Allow postage on 1 pound.

**BRITISH ARMY SAM BROWNE TAN HOLSTERS,** almost new, with top flap. Length of top is 9 inches. These will carry most any revolver, also the Luger Automatic Pistol. Special price, 85 cents each.

**BRITISH ARMY TAN OPEN HOLSTER.** This is without flap, but has top strap to keep the pistol from coming out. There is holder on back for ramrod. Small end is open, so that any revolver may be carried. Almost new. Price, 55 cents each.

**No. 552. U. S. NAVY STARR WAR REVOLVER;** self-cocking; 36 calibre; kind used on Navy warships; are in good, second-hand serviceable order, steel screw driver with wrench for taking off nipple. All for $9.85. Round mould, $1.25 each. Caps, 20 cents.

**U. S. ARMY STARR REVOLVER** with 8-inch barrel, single action. Altered to take the Colt's calibre 44 cartridge (same as the altered Remington on this page), in second hand, serviceable order. Have quick take-down system. Price, $8.75.

COLT'S CARTRIDGES, calibre 44, NEW, $4.00 per 100.

**No. 540. STARR ARMY REVOLVER;** calibre 44; Center-Fire.

View of the Starr Army Revolver, showing how the cylinder can be quickly removed for loading or cleaning.

**U. S. ARMY STARR, 5-SHOT, CALIBRE 44, SELF-COCKING REVOLVER.** Altered from the cap and ball to shoot the Regular Colt's 44 Calibre, Center-Fire Cartridges. These revolvers are with fine walnut stocks; have quick take-down system. They weigh a trifle over 2 pounds. The barrel is 6 inches long; range is 300 yards. Price, $9.65.

**U. S. NAVY GREEN AND RED NIGHT SIGNALS.** These signals are loaded in 10-gauge brass center fire shells and are intended to be fired in the Very's Signal Pistol. They can be fired in any 10-gauge breech-loading shotgun. Price, 20 cents each.

**WANTED COLT'S TEXAS REVOLVER,** calibre 34, concealed trigger thrown out by the cocking of the hammer. No guard, no lever attachment, stamped, Paterson, N. J.

**WANTED COLTS - WALKER REVOLVERS,** made at Colt's factory, calibre 44.

**WANTED COLT'S 8-SHOT REPEATING RIFLE,** under lever action, made by Colt at Paterson, N. J. 36 calibre, stamped on barrel, Colt's Patent Arms Manufacturing Co., Paterson, N. J. Four horse heads in white metal set in the check piece on the stock. Full length 47 inches, lever revolves the cylinder, cocks the inside concealed hammer. Rammer lever for pushing the cartridge in the cylinder.

We have customers who desire to purchase any of the above. Colt's guns, also Colt's or Remington Army, size cap revolvers made in the South during the Civil War, usually with brass frame, stamped C. S. A. We have a large stock of Colt's revolvers and will *only be* interested in the three weapons as *illustrated* and *described* above. Will be pleased to hear from anyone who may have any of these guns for sale. Please *state price* and *condition*.

For sale, photograph of Colt's gun factory at Paterson, N. J., 1834 to 1842. Where Col. Colt, first started to make guns in 1834 and failed for upwards of $150,000, as he stated in address in 1851, "Gaining experience in gun manufacturing." The old factory building on the banks of the beautiful Passaic Falls, Paterson, N. J., was destroyed by fire in 1861. We have the photograph negative. Size, 8x10 inches, and will furnish mounted copy at $2.50.

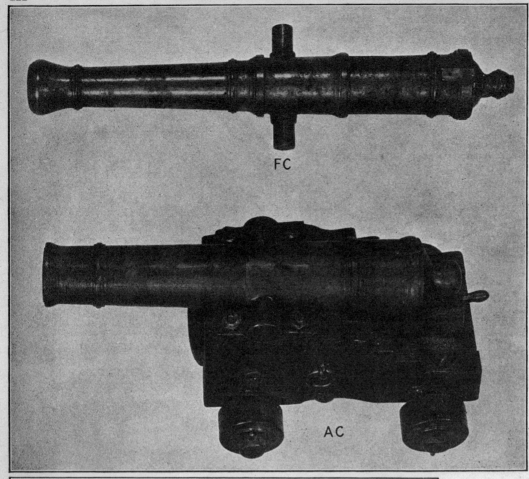

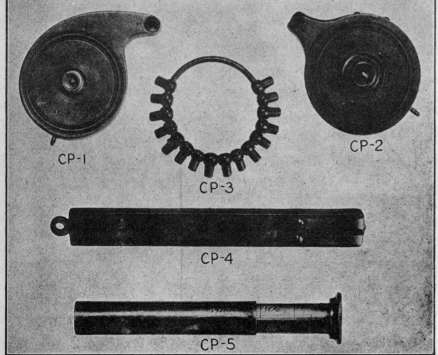

**AC. ENGLISH MODEL BRONZE CANNON ON NAVAL CARRIAGE.** This is the Model 1755 as used in the British Navy, and the same as the American Navy used during the Revolutionary and 1812 Wars. It is a 32 pounder. Length of model cannon is 7¼ inches, bore ½ inch. Weight of cannon and carriage is 3 pounds. This is a very popular companion to go with ship models. Price, $24.00.

**F.C. FRENCH MODEL BRONZE CANNON,** Army type as used prior to 1800. This has the low trunnions and heavy muzzle. Length, overall, is 9⅜ inches, bore 5/16 inches. Weight 1¾ pounds. Offered unmounted. Price, $9.75 each.

**C P-1. BRASS CAP CHARGER,** British, made by Sykes, and so marked. Made for use with percussion caps for shot guns or pistols. The caps are fed to opening by magazine spring. To use, the tip end is placed over nipple, and charger withdrawn. To reload, the screw fastening on top is undone. Charger measures 2 inches across, 2⅞ inches long. Price, $4.00.

**C P-2. BRASS CAP CHARGERS,** BRITISH, marked IMPROVED. These are similar to No. C P-1, but different shape. Size 2 inches wide, 2⅝ inches long. Price, $3.50.

**C P-X. ANTIQUE BRASS CAP CHARGER,** GERMAN, size 2¼ inches wide by 3⅛ inches long. This charger was originally a holder for SLOW MATCH as used with MATCHLOCK GUNS, and has been altered to use percussion caps. Top is held in place by revolving disc which engages center stud. This charger secured from a collector who purchased it from NEUMANN, of NURNBERG, in 1912. It is a very rare piece. Price, $8.00.

**C P-3. RARE CAP CARRIER.** 16 brass cap holders are fitted over steel ring, and were carried on sash, belt or in cartridge box. Diameter of ring is 1¾ inches. This is a unique cap holder. Price, $5.00.

**C P-4. GERMAN CAP CHARGER,** with DOUBLE MAGAZINE. Marked: WEBER & SCHULTIES, IN FRANKFURT. Ring in butt end to attach to cord. Caps are loaded by pushing down against inside spring, and are held in place by 2 external springs, as shown in illustration. Length 5½ inches, width ⅝ inches. Cap chargers in this shape are rare. Price $4.00.

**CP-5. COMBINATION POWDER AND SHOT MEASURE.** Illustration shows measure open to one ounce of shot. On the opposite side are the marks for drams of powder. A knurled button works on center screw to get different charges. Length closed 3½ inches, open 6 inches, bore ½ inch. A very odd piece. Price, $4.50.

**U3-3. INFANTRY FIRE TACTICS,** by Lieut. C. B. MAYNE, ROYAL ENGINEERS. Published at CHATHAM, ENGLAND, in 1885. Many sketches and tables. Size 5x7¼ inches, 441 pages. Price, $1.50.

**U3-4. SUBMARINE WARFARE, OFFENSIVE AND DEFENSIVE,** including a discussion of the OFFENSIVE TORPEDO SYSTEM, its effects upon iron-clad ship systems, and influence upon future naval wars. By LIEUT. COMMANDER J. S. BARNES, U. S. N., WITH ILLUSTRATIONS. Published in New York in 1869. Size 6x9 inches, 233 pages. Price, $1.50.

**U 3-5. ABSTRACT OF INFANTRY TACTICS,** including EXERCISES AND MANEUVERS of LIGHT-INFANTRY AND RIFLEMEN, for use of the MILITIA of the United States. Published at BOSTON in 1830. Profusely illustrated with sketches and drawings. 137 pages, size 4½x7¼. Price, $3.00.

# Cartridges

The New York City Fire Laws limit the storage of cartridges. We purchased so many cartridges since the close of the Spanish War (over 30,000,000), that it was necessary for us to find a magazine outside of any city limits. Fortunately, we found an island of about ten acres, in the Hudson River, 55 miles from New York, which we secured, and have erected thereon storehouses for our cartridges. Orders under 5,000 will be delivered from New York warehouse. Large lots from the island direct, unless special agreement is made. Erie, New York Central, West Shore and New York, Ontario and Western Railways are from ½ to 3 miles distant. Single cartridges are charged 10 cents each. All cartridges are offered AS ARE.

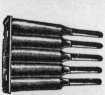

Illustration of Clip of 7.65 mm. Mauser Cartridges, all bright and new, just as when they left the makers. They cost in Germany over $30.00 per 1,000. These cartridges are offered LOOSE, WITHOUT CLIPS at $1.45 per 100.

Calibre 30 U. A. Magazine rifle smokeless powder pointed ball cartridges on clips for use Model 1903 U. S. A. Rifle, new Spitzer steel bullet. $3.50 per 100.
Blank Cartridges, caliber 30, Model 1906, in clips. All in fine order. Special price, $1.90 per 100.
Empty Brass Shells, caliber 30, model 1906, without primers or powder, with bullets. Price $1.20 per 100.

831. Center Fire Ball Cartridges, for 58-calibre rifle, Springfield, Remington, Needham, Peabody and Roberts breech-loading calibre 58 rifles. Single cartridges, 10 cents each; box of 20, 50 cents; $2.00 per 100.

30.-Calibre United States Army Smokeless Powder Nickel-covered Lead Ball Military Cartridges. Good, sure-fire, serviceable cartridges. We have 50,000 for sale; not in original paper boxes. Price, $6.00 per 100.

2,000,000 Captured Spanish 43-Calibre Lead Ball Cartridges. Intended for use in the Remington rifles. In good serviceable order; packed in paper boxes, 1,000 to the case. Many of the cartridges were made in Spanish arsenals and are so labeled. Our price for these cartridges is rate of $12 per 1,000; $1.50 per 100.

Captured Spanish Brass-covered Ball Cartridges, called by United States soldiers the "Poison Bullet," from the fact that brass covering over the lead bullet corroded and became covered with verdigris. We have 1,000,000 of these cartridges. Valuable relics. Packed 10 in box, with the Spanish label: "Pirotecnia Militar de la Habana, 10 Cartuchos de Guerre, Mod. 1871-84. Para Fusil B. F. O. O. de 11 mm. Varnia, 1896. Langa, 1890." Price, 25 cents per box of 10 cartridges, or $16.50 per 1,000, $1.75 per 100.

Burnside's Brass Case Lead Ball Cartridge, for use in Burnside carbines; fired with percussion cap. Packed 10 in case, 1,000 in box. Price, rate of $16.50 per 1,000. $1.75 per 100.
Snider Breech-loading Rifle Cartridges. 10 cents each.

200,000 Letaucneaux Pin-Fire 12-mm. Metallic Cartridges. All in first-class condition, in tin-lined cases in paper boxes of 25 each. Made in Paris. Price, 90 cents per 100; $7.50 per 1,000.

United States 50-Calibre Standard Government Ball Cartridges, for use in all 50-70 calibre center-fire rifles. Packed in paper boxes, 20 each; 1,000 in wood case; total weight, 115 pounds. Sold off by United States Army when 50-calibre guns were displaced by the 45-calibre a few years ago. Cartridges will target almost as well as those direct from the factory. Price, $2.50 per 100.

10,000 Reduced Charge Blank Cartridges, calibre 50 centre-fire, in serviceable order. Price $3.00 per 100.

Springfield 45-Calibre Rifle Cartridges. We have sold a great many thousands, all of which were sure fire and gave good satisfaction. Cartridges are packed 20 in a paper box, 1,000 in wood case. $3.00 per 100.

7,000,000 United States Army Standard Springfield Rifle Cartridges, 45 calibre. Cartridges are packed 1,000 to case; are sure fire; are the 500-grain ball cartridge, $3.00 per 100.

Springfield Civil War Musket Powder-and-Ball Paper Cartridge. Kind the soldiers had to bite to load in the gun properly. For use in Springfield or Enfield muzzle-loading rifles. Price, 10 cents each.

Gallager's Ball Cartridge; linen covered; fired by percussion cap. Relics of Civil War. Price, 10 cents each.

Sharp's Linen Calibre 54 Ball Cartridge. For use in percussion lock calibre 54 Sharp's and other rifles. Powder is contained in linen case with lead ball; fired with percussion cap. Price, 10 cents each.

100,000 Spencer Rim-fire Ball Cartridges, 56-50 calibre. Packed 7 in pack, 6 packs in paper box, 1,000 in case. These are copper-shell lead-ball cartridges, with the fulminate contained inside the rim. Used in Spencer, Peabody, Palmer, Ball's, Scott, Triplett, Ballard and Joslyn rifles and carbines. To all whom we have sold they have given fairly good satisfaction. Our price is $13.75 per 1,000. $1.50 per 100. Offered as are.

2000 Calibre 44 Bird Shot Cartridges for use in the Evans Magazine Rifle, model 1877; centre fire, loaded with No. 9 shot; price $1.35 per hundred.
50 U. S. Army Regulation Steel Cannon Shot, new, with bronze sabot and fuze plug for the new 32/10 inch breech-loading cannon. Price $2.00 each.

Maynard Brass-Shell Ball Cartridge, for use with percussion cap in Maynard carbine, calibre 50. The brass head has small hole which admits the flame (when fired) from the cap into the powder charge contained within the brass case. Price, rate of $15 per 1,000. $1.65 per 100. Packed 10 in a package, 1,000 in a case. We have also some Maynard cartridges that have paper covering over the brass case. These were first kind made. Price, rate of $15 per 1,000. $1.65 per 100.

50,000 Spencer 50-Calibre Blank Cartridges. Made at United States Frankford Arsenal. Packed in paper box; 1,000 in wood case. Rim fire, giving good loud report. Price, $13.75 per 1,000. $1.50 per 100.

A. U. S. Army Civil War Powder and Ball 36-Calibre Revolver Cartridge, package of 6 for $1.00.

25,000 Reduced Charge Blank Cartridges, for calibre 45 center fire rifles. All in good order. Price $3.00 per 100.

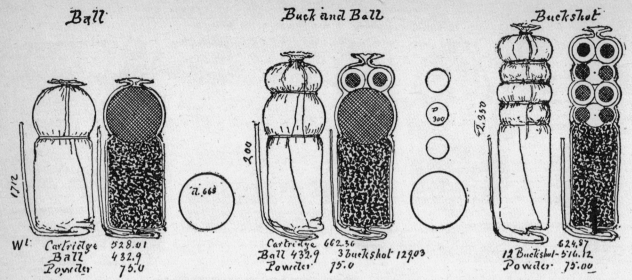

*Ball*      *Buck and Ball*      *Buckshot*

Wt. Cartridge 528.01
Ball 432.9
Powder 75.0

Cartridge 662.36
Ball 432.9
3 buckshot 129.03
Powder 75.0

.624.87
12 Buckshot 516.12
Powder 75.00

**Detail Drawings Showing Construction of Calibre .69 Ball, .69 Buck and Ball and .58 Calibre Buck-Shot Cartridges of Civil War Days**

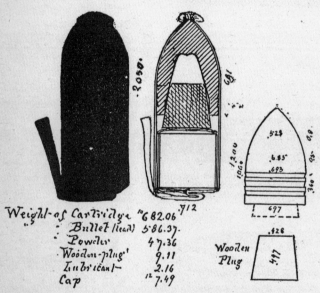

Weight of Cartridge 682.06
Bullet (lead) 586.37
Powder 47.36
Wooden plug 9.11
Lubricant 2.16
Cap 7.49

Wooden Plug

**Detailed Drawing Showing (full size) Construction of the Famous "MINIE" Bullet and Cartridge Used in the Model 1842 U. S. Rifles, Calibre .69. Many Used in Civil War Time.**

24,000 CALIBRE 38 REVOLVER BALL CARTRIDGES, center fire, made at Frankford Arsenal, smokeless powder. In original packages. Price $1.50 per 100. $12.00 per 1,000.

21,000 CALIBRE 38 REVOLVER BLANK CARTRIDGES, center fire, made at Frankford Arsenal, smokeless powder. Price, $1.00 per 100. $8.00 per 1,000.

13,000 CALIBRE 22 SHORT RIM-FIRE, U. S. GALLERY BALL CARTRIDGES, made by U. S. Cartridge Co. Smokeless powder. Price, 40 cents per 100. $3.50 per 1,000.

AIR GUN SHOT, selected for size and put up in tubes of 4 ounces. Price, 10 cents per tube. Allow postage on 1 pound.

There were several types of German cartridges, among them being the "high explosive" variety, the "armor piercing" and the "tracer" models, the famous copper-covered drawn-iron-case pattern. This cartridge-case is made of iron so prepared that it can be drawn similar to brass. (It was the shortage of brass that brought out this new idea.) Within a few days after the armistice an American Ordnance Officer began a tour of the munition works and soon learned the formula. Machine gun used another type of dummy and the blanks had wooden bullets stained blue. (From German Mauser rifle book, price 45 cents.)

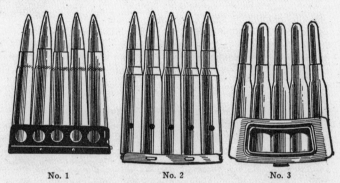

No. 1      No. 2      No. 3

No. 1. BRITISH BALL CARTRIDGES, calibre 303, for ROSS or other British rifles. Mark VII, with pointed bullet. Price $2.50 per 100 in clips.

No. 2. DUMMY CARTRIDGES ON CLIPS for the calibre 30 Army rifles, Models 1903, 1906, 1917, or Enfield. Full size cartridge without powder. Used for drilling or testing the mechanism of rifle. Price, $2.00 per 100.

No. 3. MANNLICHER BALL CARTRIDGES IN CLIPS, 6.5 m/m or .256 caliber. Made for the Model 1895 Mannlicher rifle of Holland. Can also be used in the Roumanian rifle if loaded singly, as the clip, which is intended to be placed fully charged in the magazine, will not function in the Roumanian rifle. Price, $6.50 per 100.

RUSSIAN RIFLE BALL CARTRIDGES, caliber 7.62, for any of the Russian model guns. Price, $2.50 per 100.

2,000 cal. 32 solid head center fire cartridges for BULLARD rifle. 40 grains black powder, 150-grain grooved bullet, with No. 1½ U.M.C. primer. Packed 10 in paper carton. Price, $1.20 per 100.

2,000 REMINGTON SPECIAL BALL CARTRIDGES, calibre 44, for MATCH RIFLE. Shell is 2½ inch bottle neck, with patch lead bullet. Packed 6 in paper box. Price, $1.35 per 100.

**The following Cartridges we have in stock and offer subject to prior sales at prices given.**

|  | Per C |
| --- | --- |
| Colts Auto. Cartridges, cal. 45 | $ 5.00 |
| 333. Jeffrey Mauser, Soft Pointed | 15.00 |
| 12.7 M/M. French Revolver, center fire | 6.00 |
| 303. Savage M. P. | 5.50 |
| Mauser 8 M/M. soft nose | 9.50 |
| Mauser 7 M/M soft | 9.50 |
| Pistol Caps | Per Box .20 |
| Musket Caps | Per C .25 |

SEE PAGES 123 AND 125 FOR AMMUNITION AT SPECIAL BARGAIN PRICES. WRITE US WHAT YOU NEED. OUR PRICES ARE THE LOWEST

C. S. A. Cannon Primers, made at Selma, Ala., 1863, and so stamped; relics..Price, $1.50 a package

Frankford Arsenal Make Cannon Primers, 1864; relics only......................20 cents a package

4,000 Peabody-Martini Ball Cartridges, Price, $1.50 per 100

4,000 U. S. Exploded Brass Cartridge Shells, 45 and 50 calibres................Price, $4.00 per 100

20,000 Musket Flints..........Price, 10 cents each

5,000 Pistol Flints............Price, 10 cents each

4,000 Starr's Carbine 52-Calibre Ball Cartridges, linen wrapped, similar to the illustrated Sharp's Linen Cartridges. Price, $1.75 per 100; $15.00 per 1,000.

PRIMED RIFLE SHELLS.

9,000 calibre 40, 1⅞-inch primed Brass Shells, Price, $7.00 per 1,000

4,000 calibre 38, 1¾-inch primed Brass Shells, Price, $7.00 per 1,000

4,000 calibre 44, 2¼ to 2 7-16 inch primed Brass Shells ..................Price, $7.00 per 1,000

Prussian Army Musket Caps; relics of Civil War .................Price, 50 cents per box of 250

2142. Crispin Rim Fire Cartridges, valuable only to collectors showing the evolution of the present day metallic cartridge; copper shell with projecting rim near the center in which is contained the explosives fulminate; the rim also serves as a gas check; Calibre 50; made for use in the Smith improved B-L Civil War Rifle; as shown in the above illustration; price for Cartridges, $1.00 ea.

5,000 Winchester New Rival 16 gauge Primed Empty Paper Shot Gun Shells, 2½ inches long; made to stand heavy charge of black powder; our bargain price 45 cents per hundred.

Maynard Tape Primers, made for use in Civil War army muskets. Tape containing 50 charges of fulminate, was inserted in the lock, and each time the hammer was pulled back the feed finger spring mechanism pushed a section of the tape containing cap over the nipple, the hammer descending simultaneously out off the tape and exploded the cap, which fired the charge in the gun. Serviceable relics for use on Maynard lock muskets; (see our Springfield model 55). Price is 10 cents a roll of 50 caps. These tapes gave the soldier a double chance. He could use either tape or percussion cap.

Civil War Cannon Primers, cup-shaped; unserviceable; relics only..........Price, 20 cents each

Collection of 10 Cartridges taken from captured Boer soldier's bandolier; some with sharpened points; relics..... . .....Price, $5.00 for the lot

Lee-Metford Cartridges with British broad arrow mark, taken from Boer soldiers, Price, 50 cents each

Collection of 12 Cannister Shot and Cartridges from South Africa..........................Price, $3 50

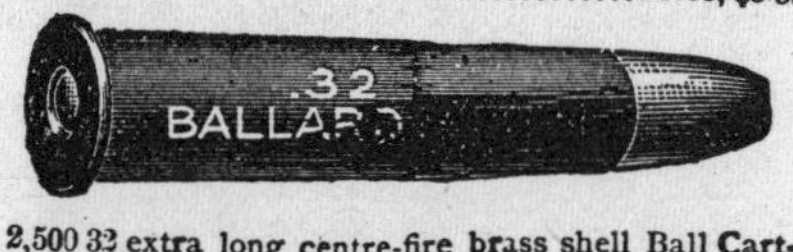


2,500 32 extra long centre-fire brass shell Ball Cartridges for Ballard rifle. Price, 75 cents, box of 50.

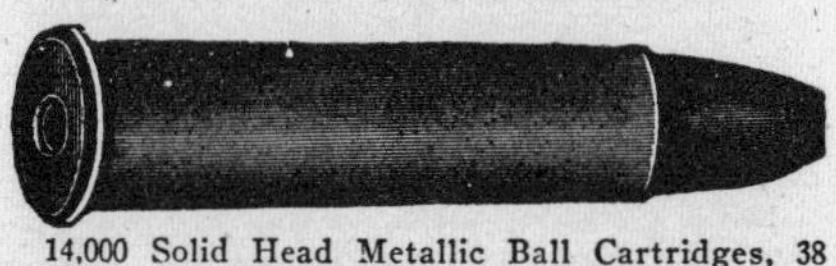

14,000 Solid Head Metallic Ball Cartridges, 38 calibre Straight Shell, 40-grain powder, 1¾ length of shell; primed with No. 3½ Remington primer. Packed 25 in box. Price, 40 cents per box; $1.40 per 100.

Cannon Trunnion Steel Gauge, engraved "U. S., Frankford Arsenal, 1859"; in neat walnut case; total length 47 inches, 7 inches wide, 3 inches deep; used for measuring cannon axles or trunnions for all sizes of U. S. cannons at that period, Price, $5.00

Percussion Caps for our Cadet Drill Guns, Price, 20 cents per box of 100

Civil War Musket Caps; relic. Price, 30 cents per box of 250

Eley Best-Quality Caps for Revolvers, 100 in box........................Price, 10 cents per box

Cartridges.—Civil War Set of Cartridges, loaded with powder and ball; some are very scarce, all were made for use during the Civil War. Sharp's linen, calibre 52; Spencer, metallic, calibre 56; Billinghurst and Requa Mitrailleuse metallic cartridge, calibre 58, powder and ball, paper; calibre 58, powder and ball, paper; calibre 36 combustible revolver cartridge; Maynard metallic cartridge, calibre 50; Smith metallic cartridge, calibre 50; Gallagher metallic cartridge, calibre 51; Martin metallic cartridge, calibre 50; Springfield metallic cartridge, calibre 58; Ballard metallic cartridge, calibre 44; Union Army cannon primer, metallic; musket and revolver caps. Set of 29 cartridges and gun primers by express, prepaid, to any part of the U. S., Price. $3.50

SIX SPANISH WAR CARTRIDGES, with powder packed in box. Price, $1.50 per set. Springfield 45-calibre, with which the Volunteers were armed; this lot was wrecked while on the way from the factory to Government Arsenal, so they fell into our hands. Krag-Jorgensen Ball Cartridges, kind used by U. S. Regulars; these cartridges came to New York in shipment of old brass gathered up in the vicinity of and shipped from Santiago, Cuba; they have the galvanized-color shell and the U. S. Army cartridge factory marks and we have reason to believe that they were picked up on the Santiago Battlefield. U. S. Navy Ball Cartridge, made by W. R. A. Co. factory under contract for U. S. Navy; these cartridges were on the U. S. cruisers Harvard and Columbia; those on the Harvard got wet somewhere around Cuba or Porto Rico, and those on the Columbia were damaged while the ship was looking for the Spanish fleet by a collision while cruising with all lights out off the coast. The damaged cartridges were turned into the Navy Yard and sold by sealed bids. We were the only bidders; other dealers could see no value in them until we got them. Spanish 7-65 millimeter Mauser Smokeless Ball Cartridge, from lot sold to us by U. S. Ordnance Department as part of lot captured in Cuba and Porto Rico, used by Spanish Regulars. Spanish Remington Lead Ball Cartridges, as used by Spanish Volunteers captured at Santiago. Spanish Remington Reformado brass-covered ball cartridges, usually called the "Poisoned Bullet." These cartridges are real relics.

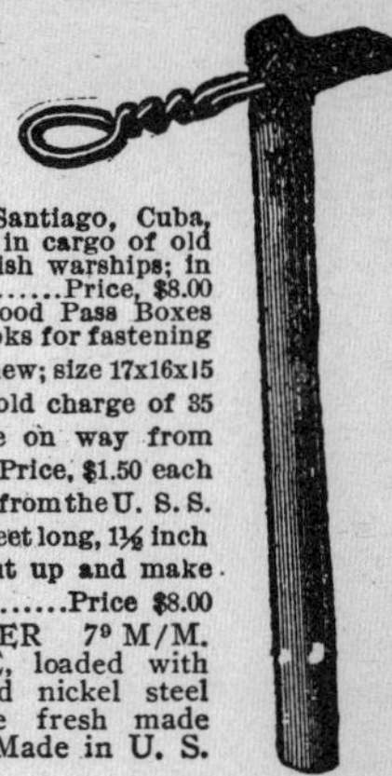

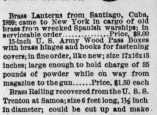

Cannon Primers. Made at U. S. Government Arsenal. Fit any Army Cannon. $3.00 for box of 50.

Brass Lanterns from Santiago, Cuba, 1899; came to New York in cargo of old brass from wrecked Spanish warships; in serviceable order..............Price, $8.00

15-inch U. S. Army Wood Pass Boxes with brass hinges and hooks for fastening covers; in fine order, like new; size 17x16x15 inches; large enough to hold charge of 85 pounds of powder while on way from magazine to the gun......Price, $1.50 each

Brass Railing recovered from the U. S. S. Trenton at Samoa; size 6 feet long, 1⅛ inch in diameter; could be cut up and make good relic napkin rings........Price $8.00

GERMAN MAUSER 7 M/M. RIFLE CARTRIDGE, loaded with smokeless powder and nickel steel covered bullet. Fine fresh made sure fire cartridges. Made in U. S. Price, $9.50 per 100.

Hotchkiss Bottle-Neck Primed Brass Cartridge Shells; new; in fine, serviceable order; will fit the 50-calibre Springfield B/L rifle. Price, $1.00 per 100 or $8.75 per 1,000.

Prussian Needle Gun Primed Paper Cartridge Cases; ready for the powder and ball, Price, $5.00 per 100, or 10 cents each

U. S. Navy 6-Pounder Brass Dummy Shell, with wood in place of steel projectile; used on warships for practice drill in loading quick-firing cannons, Price, $5.00

250 Hotchkiss Gun Cartridge Cases; first kind made for use in cannons; size, 8 c/m., with tin side, iron base, primed with cap; are new, empty; rare relics.....................Price, 50 cents each

U. S. Army Hot Shot Furnace; used at the forts for heating spherical shot to be fired at enemy for purpose of setting fire to ships or buildings; weight about 2 tons, size 3½x2½ feet, Price, $50.00

Antique Bullet Mould with part of handle forming a circular wrench for unscrewing the old flint lock barrel in the pocket pistol, thereby making Pistol Breech-loading. Price, $2.50.

RIFLE CARTRIDGES MADE BY THE REMINGTON ARMS CO., ILION, N. Y.

2,000 38-calibre extra long ball cartridges for Remington Sporting Rifle, in original cases, Price per 1,000, $12.00

0-833A. 58-Calibre Center-Fire Blank Cartridges, for use in altered Civil War rifles. Price, singly, 10 cents each; box of 20, 50 cents; $2.00 per 100.

14,000 38-40 Ball Cartridges, with patched bullets for the Ballard and Remington midrange Sporting Rifles. Price, $12.00 per 1,000.

3,000 Calibre 32 Extra Long Ball Cartridges for Ballard and Remington Sporting Rifles. Price, $12.00 per 1,000.

80 Dynamite Gun Brass Shells from Cuba, intended for use in the Sims-Dudley gun, now empty; shells are 6 inches long and 2 inches in diameter; new; fine decoration; have safety caps, which consist of brass cup-shaped shells, which covered the mouth of the real shells; this cover is 2 inches in diameter and about 2½ inches long. Price, complete, $1.00 each.

0834. 50-Calibre Center-Fire Carbine Ball Cartridges, for use in center-fire Springfield Remington, Whitney and Peabody 50-calibre carbines. Price, singly, 10 cents each; box of 20, 50 cents; $2.00 per 100.

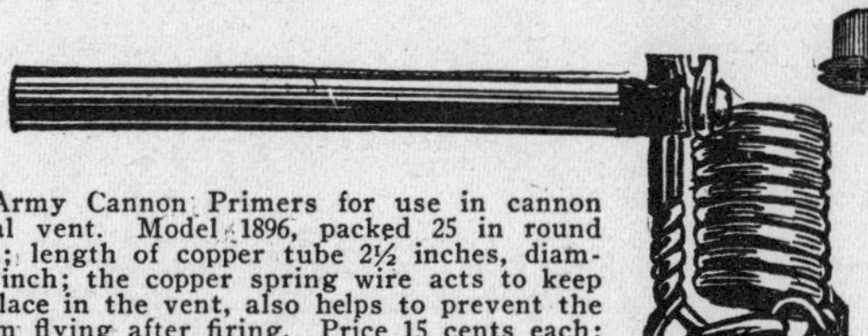

U. S. Army Cannon Primers for use in cannon with axial vent. Model 1896, packed 25 in round tin boxes; length of copper tube 2½ inches, diameter 2-10 inch; the copper spring wire acts to keep tube in place in the vent, also helps to prevent the parts from flying after firing. Price 15 cents each; $1.00 per box of 25; $3.00 per hundred.

Calibre 50 Carbine Cartridges; center-fire; inside primer; not reloadable; made at U. S. Armory; have 100,000; Government test gave average of 95 per cent. sure fire; for sale at $1.00 per 100, less 10 per cent. in case lots of 1,000; will answer for Sharp's or any center-fire carbine of 50 calibre.

MUSKET CAPS, for army muskets and large size percussion horse pistols. All new direct from factory. Packed 100 to a box. Price, 25 cents per 100.

3388. U. S. ARMY PRIMERS, 3,200,000 for use in Springfield breech-loading calibre 45 cartridges shell and shot, gun ammunition. Also for use in calibre 30 Krag gallery practice cartridges. Made at U. S. Government cartridge factory; all new and only sold by reason of change from the 45 calibre black powder to the 30 calibre smokeless cartridge. Primers are packed 500 in a tin box with screw top; each primer is in a seperate hole in cardboard with flannel lining between each of the layers; 30,000 primers packed to each wood case. Useful to all who have purchased Springfield breech-loading rifles and desire to reload the brass cartridge shells. The Trust price is $2.00 per 1,000, our price is 50 cents per box of 500, 90 CENTS PER THOUSAND, $25.00 for a box of 30,000.

166,000 U. S. GOVERNMENT FLINTS; finest quality, just purchased at the late auction sale at the old arsenal in Augusta, Ga. Boxes have the old-time manner of lettering as used over a hundred years ago. These flints are assorted sizes. Price, 10 cents each; $1.00 a dozen. These quantity prices strictly adhered to in order to protect customers who purchase at wholesale.

U.S.A. Colt's Revolver Blank Cartridges, made at U. S. Government Cartridge Factory; copper shell; inside center-fire primer, sure fire; non-reloading, price $1.50 per hundred.

Calibre 45 Revolver Ball Cartridges, with inside primer, black powder, non-reloading. Made for Colts revolver. $1.50 per 100.

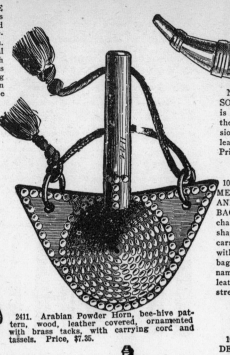

**1876. 1 ANTIQUE FLASK**, made of brass and highly ornamented with scroll work of flowers and border designs. Neck 2½ inches, total length 9 inches. Width 4½ inches. Two brass side lugs for carrying sling. This type used in 17th century. Price $14.00.

**No. 8. 1 NATIVE POWDER HORN FROM SOMALIA.** Total length 20 inches. Horn part is covered with leather including opening. To the end of cow horn is attached a wooden extension, tapered to point, and all covered with leather. A very curious specimen. Like cut. Price $10.

**10515B. ORNAMENTED ANCIENT POWDER HORN**; wood, leather covered, long steel charge cup; belt hanger and caps; length 14 inches, width 5 inches. Price $20.00.

**10515C. SIMILAR SHAPED POWDER HORN**; with brass capped steel powder charger and cut-off; ornamented with ancient battle scenes. Price $25.00.

**10515D. SIMILAR SHAPED ANCIENT POWDER HORN**; length 16 inches, width 5 inches; without metal fixtures; black mottled color; needs repairing; offered as is Price $4.85.

**10515E. SIMILAR SHAPED POWDER HORN**; wood frame, leather covered; steel charge cup and cut-off; with steel belt hanger; wood bottom and cap missing; in poor order from GREAT AGE. Sold as is, $9.85.

**10515F. SIMILAR SHAPED POWDER HORN**; wood body; with curious steel charging cup and cut-off; complete with steel cap covering; top and bottom, hardwood; rough at the edge from great age; relic of 16th century; length 13 inches. Price $25.00.

**10516A. WHEELOCK SPANNER**, with holes for measuring powder charges in the hollow iron handle; screw driver and hammer end formation; three wrench holes for winding up the wheel spring in the gun. Price $15.00.

**1 EXTRA LARGE POWDER HORN**, almost black, with ornamented leather butt and leather slide. Butt is 4¾ inches in diameter, and length 23 inches. Price, $6.00.

**No. 2411. 2 ARABIAN OR MOORISH POWDER FLASKS**, bee hive pattern, wood covered with leather and ornamented with brass tacks. Complete with carrying cord and tassels. Price, $7.35 each.

**1 SPANISH POWDER FLASK**, leather covered, with real horn tip. This is a curious model, and rare. Price, $6.00.

**10514. ANCIENT BRASS POWDER HORN**; boat shaped (similar to No. 8637, page 129); engraved and ornamented; length 5x2½ inches. Price $8.85.

**10514A. BOAT SHAPED ANCIENT POWDER HORN**; pistol size; brass ornamented; 4x2 inches. Price $6.85.

**10514B. BOAT SHAPED WOOD POWDER HORN**, with ornamental wrought steel attachment; with metal cap. Price, $6.85.

**2411. Arabian Powder Horn**, bee-hive pattern, wood, leather covered, ornamented with brass tacks, with carrying cord and tassels. Price, $7.35.

**10508. ANCIENT NAVAL POWDER HORN**; ribbed horn, length 10 inches; steel mountings with belt hanger attachment; width 3 inches; from French Nobleman's collection; rare specimen. Price, $35.00.

**No. 4. 1 CHASED BRASS MOORISH POWDER FLASK** of 19th Century. Total length 9¼ inches, diameter at largest part 4 inches. Scroll work on both front and back. Long neck with small loops for attaching stopper. Larger loops to attach shoulder cord for carrying. Price $10.

**0-976. ANCIENT JAPANESE POWDER FLASK.** Dark-colored hard wood, covered with ornamental woven fibre, with gilt seal, detachable carved top, 5-inch bronze engraved belt hanger. Length of the flask is 8 inches, widest width 3¾ inches, cover 1½ inches long. Rare piece. Price $14.85.

**SUDANESE NATIVE FANCY MARTINGALE**, leather decorated with tassels. Price, $4.85.

**SUDANESE NATIVE WOVEN FIBRE HAVERSACK**, 10½ inches by 12 inches. Serviceable relic. Price, $3.50.

**KAFFIR NATIVE MAN'S DRESS**, or gee cloth, decorated with small brass rings, a bunch of tassel cords and beads. Price, $5.75.

**AFRICAN KAFFIR NATIVE WOMAN'S DRESS**, waist girdle, made of hide, bead ornamented, with tanned beaded fringe 12 inches long. Price, $8.75.

**10513. ANCIENT POWDER HORN**, beautifully covered with gilt carving, silver rings and charging cup; length 6¾ inches, width 3½ inches; work of art as well as ornamental relic. Price $22.50.

**10413. MOORISH POWDER FLASK**; beehive pattern, with brass bands and studs; loading handle with carved stopper; with native woven red carrying cord; 18th Century period, from the Kyble Tribe. Price $9.85.

**10414. QUEEN ANNE PERIOD ENGLISH POWDER FLASK**; horn with brass rim; with unique oval charging cup; serviceable order. Price $7.85.

**10414A. QUEEN ANNE POWDER FLASK**; transparent horn with copper bottom and bands; with spring charging cup. Price $7.85.

**10414B. EARLY ENGLISH HORN POWDER FLASK**; about the period of 1740; wood bottom; metal top; screw charging cup. Price $5.85.

**L9. 2 VERY OLD HOME MADE SICKLES** with rough wood handles and 27-inch inch blades. Rusty. Relics. Price $2.50 each.

**SUDANESE NATIVE HEAD PIECE** for the horse, with decorated slings. Very showy. Price, $3.50.

**2 NUBIAN WAR SHIELDS**, 22 inches in diameter (see page 238, No. 1801, for illustration). Made of hippopotamus hide with 5-inch cone center, with arm hole and strap. Fine specimen of African native work. From the late Walter Behren Collection. $18 each.

**10415. EARLY MOORISH METAL POWDER FLASK AND LEATHER BULLET BAG**; curious shaped; finely chased brass metal circular shaped flask, with sling for carrying over the shoulder; with pair of small leather bags for bullets; finely ornamented with colored leather; with long leather streamers. Price $14.85.

**10511. ANCIENT STAG WHEELOCK POWDER HORN**, crudely carved, horn powder charger with wood stopper, Fifteenth Century period; yellow with age. Length 9 inches, with 5½ inches. Price $25.00.

**11003. 1 ANTIQUE BRASS POWDER FLASK** without chain. Both sides ornamented. Has lizard shaped stopper. Price, $16.00.

**10511-B. ANCIENT STAG POWDER HORN** with steel cap and charging cup, carved. Price $25.00.

**10512. ANCIENT ROUND SHAPED POWDER HORN.** Carved with cross cannon, iron bound; 5¾ inches in diameter, 2½ ins. through the center. Price $22.85.

**10512-A. ANCIENT CIRCULAR SHAPED WOOD POWDER HORN.** Ivory inlaid ornamentation. Length 3½ inches, diameter 1½ inches; poor order. Price $8.85.

**No. 9. 1 ANTIQUE POWDER FLASK** of wood, covered with hide and ornamented with iron nails. Diameter of flask 6 inches. Price, $7.00.

**No. 14. 1 EXTRA HEAVY POLISHED BLACK POWDER HORN**, outside length 14 inches. Style used by hunters. No stopper. Price, $6.50.

**10420. RARE OLD LEATHER POWDER FLASK**, made about the period 1800. Carried by gamekeeper for refilling sportsmen's flasks. Size 6½x10x1½ inches. Metal top with hasp for locking. Rare specimen. Price $8.50.

**Why does a Presidential or National Salute consist of 21 guns?**
The United States follows the mother country in a great many things. In 1776 twenty-one guns was the British National Salute, made up of seven guns for each of the three countries, Ireland, Scotland, England and Wales counting as one. Three sevens, twenty-one guns on their uniting as a kingdom. Twenty-one was also the age of majority.
Some seem to believe that the figures in the date of the year of Independence, 1-7-7-6—twenty-one—have given the number of guns.

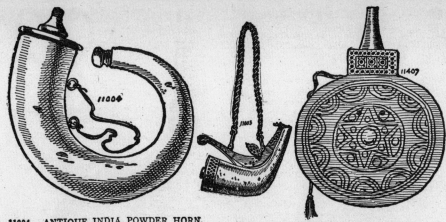

**11004. ANTIQUE INDIA POWDER HORN,** CAPTURED from native on the battlefield by PRIVATE FINDLATER, to whom QUEEN VICTORIA AWARDED the honor of the VICTORIA CROSS. Length around the outside 22 inches. diameter at the butt 2½ inches. Made from the horn of some wild animal; dark colored with age; inlaid ivory ornamentation. From Lady Stewart's collection. Price $25.00.

**11004A.** FACSIMILE OF NO. 11004 POWDER HORN; in fine order, but without history. Price $15.00.

**11004B.** POWDER HORN with ivory inlaid butt cap; dark colored; 3½ inch diameter at the butt, 16 inches around the outside edge; in fine order; made from the horn of some wild animal. From Lady Stewart's collection. Price $15.00.

**11005.** ANTIQUE PERSIAN POWDER HORN, made in the form of pistol; of boiled leather; decorated; length 9 inches, diameter at the ball shaped butt 3 inches. Attached is small steel hammer; pick and screw driver. With swivel loop for strap, all neatly ornamented in relief. Price $8.85.

**11006.** QUEEN ANNE PERIOD POWDER HORN, with horn screw measuring cup; length 7½ inches, width 2¾ inches. Price $6.00.

**10416.** OLD ENGLISH HORN POWDER FLASK, with metal bottom and top; spring charging cup; period about 1800. Price $6.00.

**10417.** REVOLUTIONARY WAR PERIOD small Leather Powder Flask, with brass charging cup. Price $6.85.

**10418.** FLINTLOCK POWDER PRIMING HORN, pocket size (3 inches). Price $4.85.

**10417A.** OLD ENGLISH POWDER HORN, about period 1750; with leather bottom; horn charging cup. Price $6.85.

**10419.** OLD MOORISH POWDER FLASK, chased brass and copper ornamental mounting, with carrying rings; with charging cup; about the 17th Century period; similar flask is now in the South Kensington Museum, London. Price $14.85.

**10520.** 17TH CENTURY OCTAGONAL POWDER HORN; leather covering over this horn; with protecting corner irons; with carrying rings; removable sliding cover at the base for insertion in receptacle of loaded charges; spring measuring cup on cover; length 8½x6 inches. Price $22.50.

**10520A.** 17TH CENTURY POWDER HORN, similar in shape to No. 10520; wood, with cover; iron spring controlling charging cup; 11x8 inches. Price $20.00.

**10520B.** 17TH CENTURY ANCIENT WHEELLOCK POCKET POWDER HOLDER made of wood covered with leather; strengthened by corner iron plate formation; size 4x3 inches. Price $8.85.

**10521.** ANCIENT POWDER HORN, made of ornamented leather; horn shaped handle; rare specimen; from French nobleman's collection. Price $14.85.

**11003. ANTIQUE STEEL POWDER HORN;** Persian; cut steel ornamented; complete with chain; lizard shaped stopper; good order; rare old relic; length 5 inches. From Lady Stewart's collection. Price $16.00.

**11407—1** ANTIQUE POWDER FLASK, made of heavy metal with various curious designs. Pierced steel ornamented neck. Complete with carrying rings for shoulder sling. Price $15.00.

**11407A.** 3 RARE BRASS POWDER FLASKS, about 4 inches in diameter, 1¼ inches thick. Both front and back covered with unique ornamental scroll designs. Like cut 11407. Price, $9.00 each.

**10473.** ANCIENT POCKET FLINT AND STEEL; polished steel; silvered case with flint. Price $2.50.

**10508A.** NAVAL HORN with smooth surface; blued mountings, with belt hanger with wrench, similar to 10508. Price $18.00.

**10509.** ANCIENT STAG POWDER HORN, carved with figures of women with executioner's sword and man's head; metal charging cup and cap; length 9½ inches, width 4¾ inches. Price $27.50.

1 INDIAN HORN PRIMING FLASK with ivory butt. Has brass lizard shaped stopper. Price, $10.00.

1 LARGE POWDER HORN with brass stopper. Used in priming cannon in British Navy in time of Nelson. In fine order. Price $6.50.

No. 19. OLD-TIME U. S. ARMY POWDER HORN from Pittsburg Arsenal. Purchased in the general cleaning up sale. All in fine order; with strap; large size. Price, $6.75.

**10612.** ANTIQUE SPANISH CIRCULAR SHAPED WOOD WATER BOTTLE; 7½ inch diameter, 4 inch top; wood stand and mouth piece; decorated; leather strap. Price $8.85.

**10163.** OLD ENGLISH POWDER HORN, about the period 1760; cone shaped SEMI-TRANSPARENT ivory bottom; screw thread detachable measuring cup; top 6½ inches long, 2¾ inches wide; fine order. Price $8.85.

**10164.** OLD ENGLISH FISH SHAPED WOOD POWDER HORN; length 7¾ inches, width 3 inches; rare dark colored mottled wood; brass measuring cup. Price $7.85.

**10165.** OLD ENGLISH POWDER HORN, beautifully engraved with British coat of arms, flags, cannons, drums and inside PLAN OF FORTIFICATIONS; with British Union Jack; the original bottom has been replaced; length 12 inches. Price $16.00.

**10880.** ANTIQUE SILVER MOUNTED POWDER HORN; translucent horn, with swivel socket charging cup; silver hall proof marked; with carrying chains; size 9x5¼x3 inches. Price $15.00.

1 EARLY INDIAN POWDER HORN from North West Frontier. Butt 3¼ inches in diameter. This is the short thick pattern, and loads from butt. Ornamented in brass with small crosses and other odd designs. Price $9.85.

1 EXTRA LARGE POWDER HORN. Length 19 inches, butt 3¾ inches, made of wood and marked with owner's name W. CAPEL. Price $6.50.

No. 6. QUEEN ANNE POWDER HORN. Rare size, only 6 inch, complete with stopper measure. Price $4.50.

1 PAIR LIGHT COLORED POWDER HORNS, ornamented with birds, snakes, animals and fish. Tip of one horn is missing. Price for pair, $11.00.

**PF1.** SET LEATHER POWDER FLASK WITH PRIMER, 18th Century. Flask is of leather, brass bound, 6½ inches long, 4½ inches wide, with 4 leather loops for sling. Priming flask is triangular shaped, brass bound, 3½ inches long. Combinations of this kind are rare. Price for set $8.00.

**PH.** EXTRA LARGE POWDER HORN. Outside length 31 inches, diameter at base 5 inches. The base is mounted with wood carved head of short horned bull. Color of horn dull white with black tip, which unscrews to fill with powder. A rare specimen. Price $12.00.

**0-945.** ANCIENT SPANISH POWDER HORN FLASK. Engraved on the steel belt attachment, "Hilario Matheo en Madrid." The horn flask is 7 inches long, shaped to conform to the body; 2-inch detachable measuring stopper. Rare pattern. Price, $20.00.

**10197.** PAIR OF HORNS FROM AFRICA, each about 2 feet long; unmounted; dark colored; from London auction. Price $7.80 the pair.

**10198.** PAIR LARGE SIZED DARK COLORED HORNS, taken by British sportsman in hunting trip in Africa; unmounted; length of each measured around the outside, 3 feet, width 6 inches at the base. Price $15.00.

**10194.** ELEPHANT TOOTH, 9 inches long 2¾ inches wide, showing 18 rows of teeth. Price $7.50.

**10194A.** SECTION OF ELEPHANT TOOTH, sawn through the center, showing full length of the tooth formation; the main ones 5½ inches long; size of the section 6½x5½x1 inches. Price $6.00.

**10896.** CURIOUS KIDNEY SHAPED POWDER PRIMING HORN; translucent horn; brass bound sides; has top and charge cup; spring load regulator; length 4¾ inches, width 2 inches. Price $6.85.

No. 3. 1 ANTIQUE POWDER FLASK from Afghanistan. Copper with hide holder for use on saddle. Period of 1790. (Like cut No. 8634, Page 129.) Price $25.00.

No. 12. 1 EXTRA LARGE LEATHER POWDER FLASK, with copper top and measure. Hunting model. Price $3.00.

No. 10. 1 LEATHER POWDER FLASK from the Soudan. Solid leather with three inch neck. Body of flask decorated with inlaid shells. Leather loop for carrying on belt or saddle. Price $8.50.

# Antique and Hand Carved Powder Horns

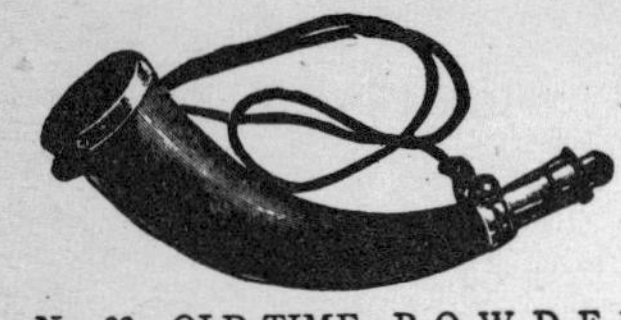

No. 22. OLD-TIME POWDER HORN, with detachable brass measuring charger; brass top and bottom, with ring and white leather strap. Military kind used period 1740 to 1812. Price, $8.50.

Old-time powder horn, $2.50.

Hunters' Old-time Leather Powder and Shot Pouch, with shoulder strap; fair state of preservation. Price $4.75.

Small-size Powder Horn. Four-square, carved with land and water scenes. Price $4.50.

Medium sized Old Powder Horn; plain, $3.50.

MOROCCO NATIVE'S LEATHER BULLET POUCH, decorated. Price, $2.85.

SOMALI NATIVE WAR SHIELD, 21 inches in diameter, raised center. $16.00.

SUDANESE NATIVE MADE CURIOUS MUSICAL INSTRUMENT. Resembles banjo with two winding pegs. The back is of turtle shell. Price $6.85.

AFRICAN NATIVE'S BEAD COVERED NECKLACE. Full length 20 inches. Covered with beads artistically arranged. Price, $2.50.

AFRICAN NATIVE MAN'S GIRDLE, colored beads neatly arranged with shell covered straps with two tufts of fiber. Native artistic work. Price $6.85.

AFRICAN NATIVE'S GIRDLE, three row belt 32 inches long, 1½ inches wide covered with blue beads with fringe. Two rows of white beads, square center of beads 7¼ inches by 4¼ inches. Artistic native work. Price $9.85.

RARE ANTIQUE POWDER HORN, with finely chased brass mountings. Rare old relic, length 22 inches. Price $16.85.

ANTIQUE STEEL POWDER MEASURE. Scoop shaped steel top, ⅝-inch bore with graduated center bar for measuring charge. Kind used with early powder gun. Price $9.85.

No. 7. 1 OLD ENGLISH COW HORN POWDER FLASK, light color, with copper butt and neck, with measuring top. Length, 8 inches. Price $5.50.

No. 6D. 1 AFRICAN HORN POWDER FLASK, 14 inch, with thong sling, and wood fetish. Native made. From Curtis collection. Price $10.00.

No. 21. 1 ANTIQUE INDIAN HORN POWDER FLASK, with finely ornamented brass butt, and long brass neck. Stopper attached by long brass chain. Woven ornamented shoulder sling. Price $15.00. Length 18 inches.

WF1. ARABIAN POWDER CHARGER, made of hard wood, black, in shape of pineapple. Resembles ancient stone water jar. Top half lifts up to use in filling charger or loading gun. A neck is on lower part to fit in muzzle of gun for quick loading. Height 3½ inches, diameter 2½ inches. These chargers are very old and rare. Price $4.50.

WF2. ARABIAN POWDER CHARGER, similar to No. WF1, height 3¼ inches, diameter 2¼ inches. Price $4.25.

WF3. ARABIAN POWDER CHARGER like No. WF1, 3 inches high, diameter 1¾ inches. Price $4.75.

WF4. ARABIAN POWDER CHARGER, pistol size, ornamented, 2¾ inches high, 1¾ inches wide. Price $5.00.

WF5. ARABIAN POWDER CHARGER like No. WF4, 2½ inches high, 1¾ inches wide. Light colored hard wood, ornamented. Price $5.50.

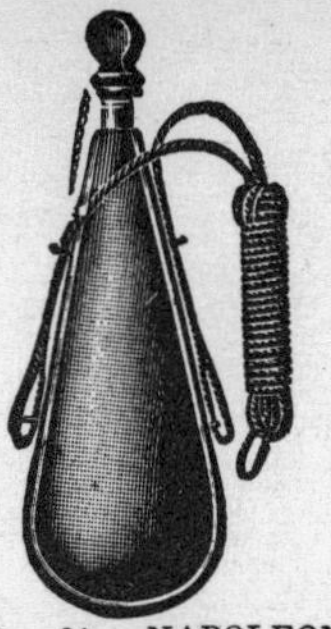

No. 24. NAPOLEON FIRST SOLDIER'S POWDER FLASK, 10¼ inches long; 3¾ inches in width. Serviceable order, complete with carrying cord. Genuine old relic; (metal). Price $3.50.

0-854B. CAMEL HIDE POWDER FLASK, hand sewn native work, length 8 inches, diameter at large end 3 inches. Price $6.50.

0-854C. 3 INDIA HIDE FLASKS of embossed hide, native hand sewing, length 6 inches, diameter 2¾ inches. Price $6.25 each.

No. 12. 1 OLD ENGLISH KIDNEY SHAPED POWDER FLASK of horn, brass bound with measuring neck. Rare style. Price $5.50.

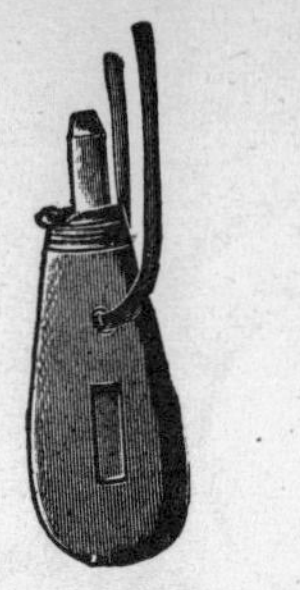

No. 27. ADMIRAL NELSON POWDER HORNS. Powder Flask, kind used on board Admiral Nelson's Battleship, Royal British Navy; transparent horn, leather covered, with a slit for examining contents. Price $3.85.

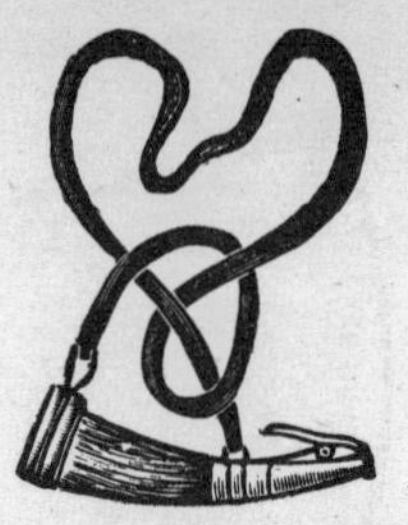

No. 24. ANTIQUE POWDER HORN for priming the old-time cannon; kind used 1740 to 1820; brass charger and can. Price $4.50.

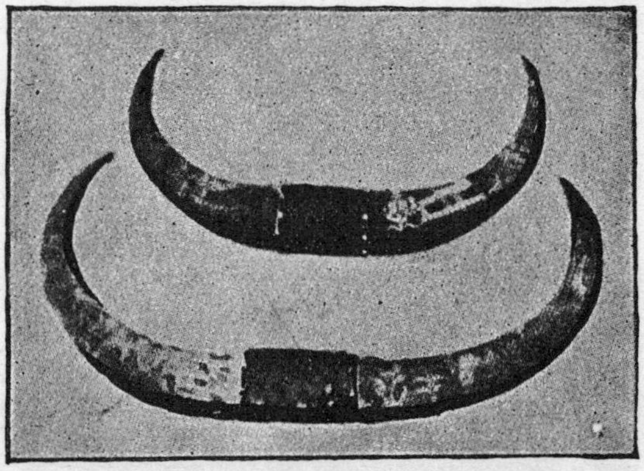

No. 10. CARVED PHILIPPINE CARIBOU HORNS. Lot exhibited by the U. S. Government at the St. Louis Exposition, and which were so much admired. The above illustration is from photograph, wherein will be seen the carving of houses, trees, flowers, etc., drawn by Filippino artists. We obtain $20.00 a pair, Caribao horns purchased from returning soldier, but having purchased the entire Government lot, we offer them at a bargain price, for $6.50 per pair.

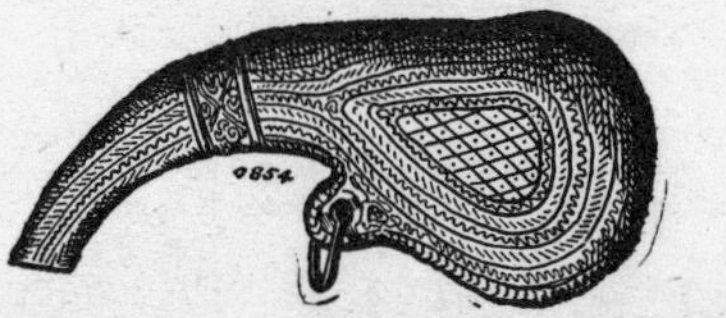


0-854. ANTIQUE INDIA HIDE POWDER FLASK, from sale at Queens Gate, London, the effects of the late F. G. Souter, India officer. Leather steamed into shape and profusely decorated with native relief ornamental work, with carrying swivels; length 8 inches, 3-inch diameter, weight 4½ ounces. Price $6.85.

0-854A. 1 CAMEL HIDE SKIN powder horn, small size as used for priming guns. 18th century period. Complete with short leather sling. Full length 5½ inches, a rare size. Price $6.25.

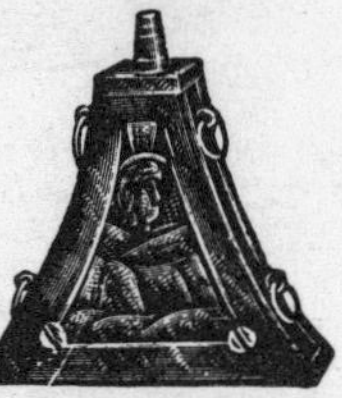

No. 21. 17TH CENTURY POWDER HORN, wood, covered with hammered iron in relief decorated work; triangular shape, 4½ by 6 inches. Price $18.00.

No. 20. 1 HEAVY IRON POWDER FLASK from India, early pattern, with lizard shaped stopper, and two rings for sling. Like No. 11003, Page 127. Price $7.50.

No. 21R. 1 EARLY PATTERN INDIAN POWDER FLASK, made of heavy horn or bone, with native made lizard shaped stopper with carrying rings. Price $9.00.

ERIC XII NORVEGER VIKING KING 1360 POWDER HORN beautifully carved in relief showing coat of arms, eagle with open sword in claws, with ornamented helmet showing shield, torch, battle axe, old Norse ship, etc. This horn is also the work of an artist, length 14 inches. Price $38.00.

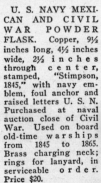

U. S. NAVY MEXICAN AND CIVIL WAR POWDER FLASK. Copper, 9½ inches long, 4½ inches wide, 2½ inches through center, stamped, "Stimpson, 1845," with navy emblem, foul anchor and raised letters U. S. N. Purchased at naval auction close of Civil War. Used on board old-time warships from 1845 to 1865. Brass charging neck; rings for lanyard, in serviceable order. Price $20.

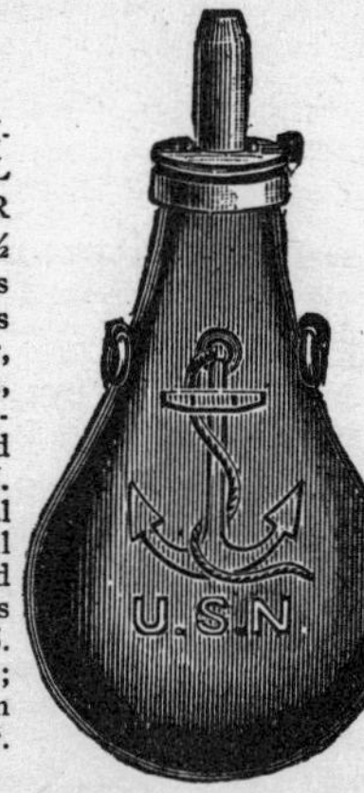


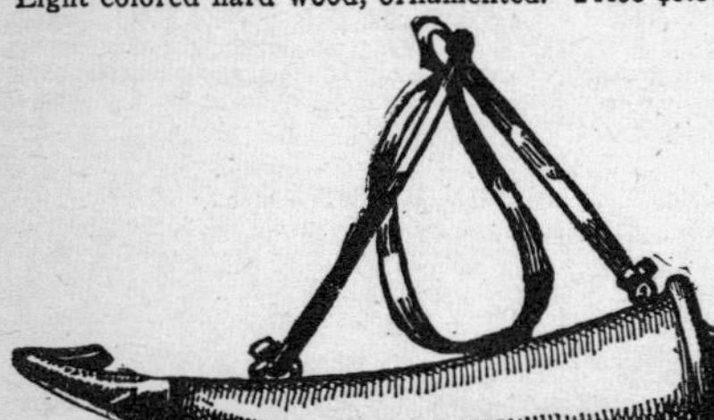

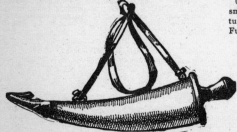

No. 17. ANTIQUE POWDER HORNS, with brass stopper; with rawhide strop; with opening for filling in the butt. All as shown in the above photograph. Length averages about 10 inches. Are all in good state of preservation. This pattern was in use over 100 years ago. Price $6.00 each.

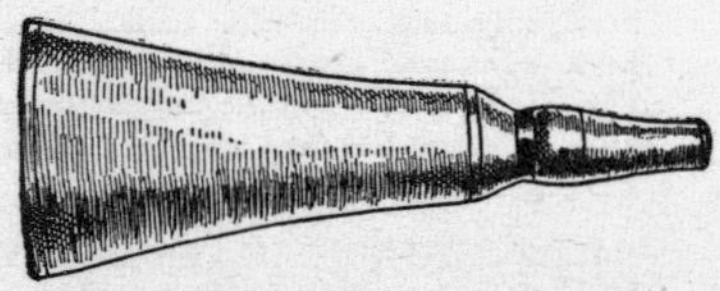

R176. 11 QUEEN ANNE POWDER FLASKS, average length, 6½ inches. These are oval shape with screw top, which also acts as powder measure. Rare type. Price $7.50 each.

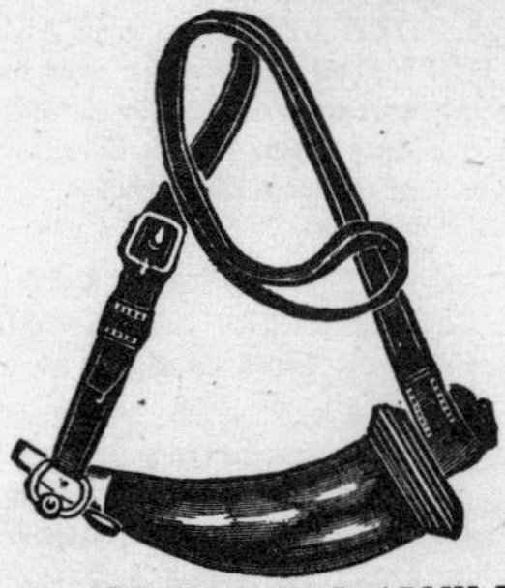

No. 19. OLD-TIME U. S. ARMY POWDER HORN from Pittsburg Arsenal. Purchased in the general cleaning up sale. All in fine order; with strap; large size. Price $6.75.

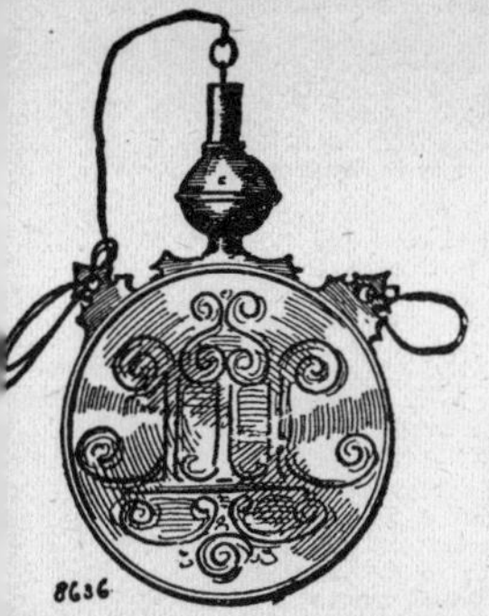

8636.—BRASS PILGRIM
OWDER FLASK. Square shaped.
4 inches in diameter, width 1¾
ches. Raised scroll ornamental
ork with ring for carrying sling;
½ inch mouth piece. From Lon-
n collector; weight 18 ounces.
rice, $25.00.

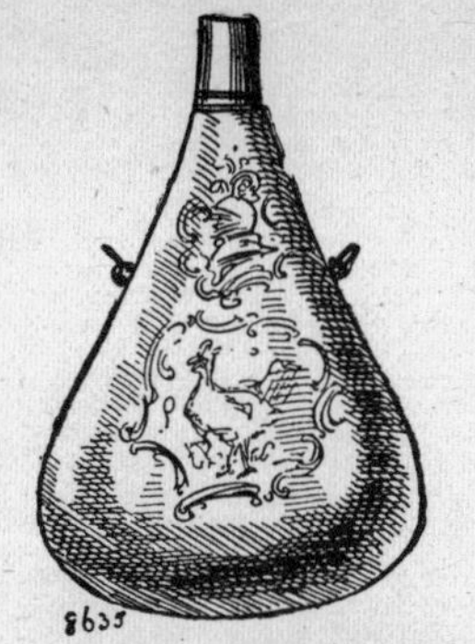

8635. — ANCIENT WHEELLOCK BRASS POWDER FLASK. Engraved with Gallic cock coat of arms, with scroll work. Inscribed "de Julio Ges In Pestagallo In Campbo bethes; Duce 1690." Size 7 by 4½ by 2½ inches. Rare piece from the Christie sale, London. Price, $35.00.

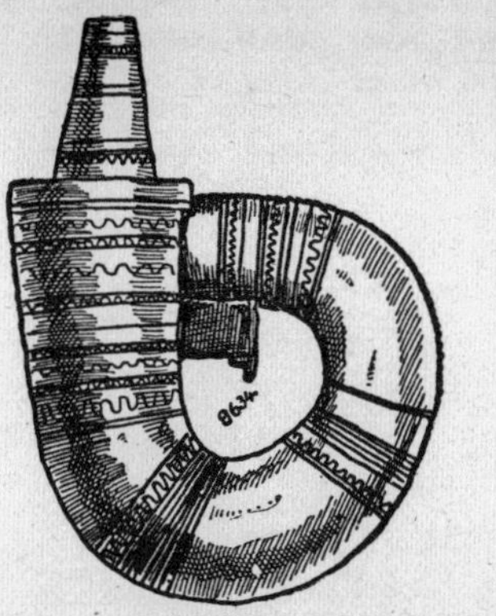

8634.—ANCIENT SILVER MOUNTED POWDER FLASK. From India about the period of 1790; with attachment for measuring charge. Price, $22.00.

No. 75F. 1 FRENCH COLONIAL POWDER HORN, made from horn of water buffalo, very wide and flat. Length outside 16 inches, width at bottom 5½ inches. Wood bottom, carved neck, leather carrying thong. Price $10.00.

No. 76F. 1 EUROPEAN ANTIQUE POWDER FLASK, made of wood, with heavy black leather covering, with iron butt and iron hinge top fitted with 3½ inch measure, with long iron sash attachment for wearing on belt. This is a rare military type. Price $22.00.

No. 2. 1 OLD ENGLISH BLACK POWDER HORN, with copper butt, copper band with ring and copper mouth piece and neck. Price $5.75.

1 BRITISH NAVY POWDER HORN, about 11 inch, with wood loading stopper and copper neck. Smaller than the regular issue. Price $6.00.

No. 15. 1 AFRICAN NATIVE POWDER FLASK, of black horn with wood bottom. Braided hide sling for attaching to saddle. Price $7.00. Length 18 inches.

10277. OLD POWDER HORN. Rudely carved, George I., with row old-time buildings engraved around the base of the horn, in poor order. Price, $6.85.

10276. REVOLUTIONARY WAR PERIOD POWDER HORN. Carved with sloop flying British pennant and owner's name. "Nathan Pease." Price, $8.75.

10116.—OLD NEW YORK VOLUNTEER FIREMAN'S LEATHER HELMET. With eagle holding in its beak red leather shield, design with figure 3, No. 777. Relic from a noted artist's collection. Price, $5.00.

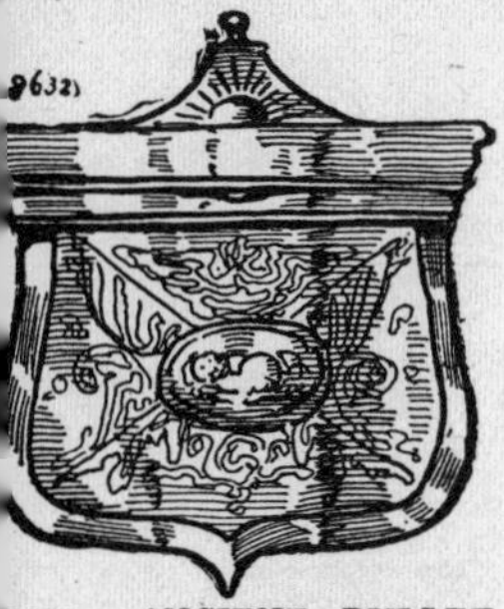

8632. — ANCIENT BULLET
OX. Brass shield shaped. Size
by 3½ by 1½ inches. Hinged
ver with relief figure of eagle,
n, flags, etc.; with attachment
r the waist belt. Assorted
tterns. Price, $10.00.

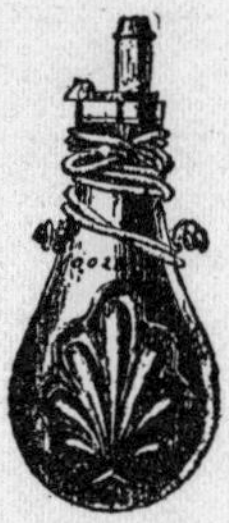

METAL POWDER FLASKS, assorted sizes and patterns, ranging in price from $1.50 upwards.

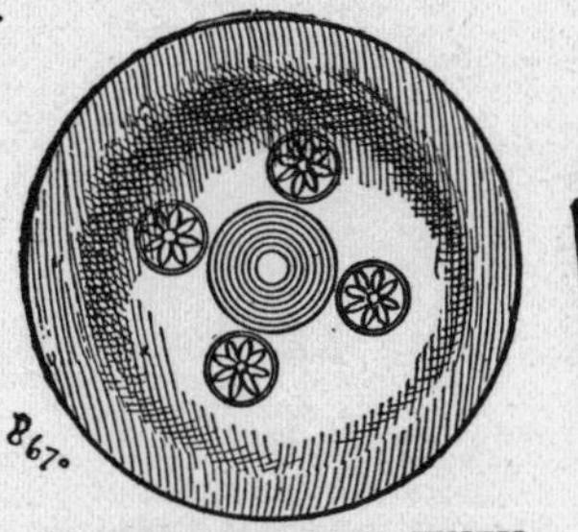

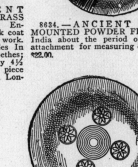

8670.—EIGHTEENTH CENTURY INDIA SHIELD SEMI-TRANSPARENT. ⅜ inch thick, 11½ inch diameter. Gilt ornamented with 4 metal bosses. This shield when held up to the light is semi-transparant, finely mottled. Price, $15.00.

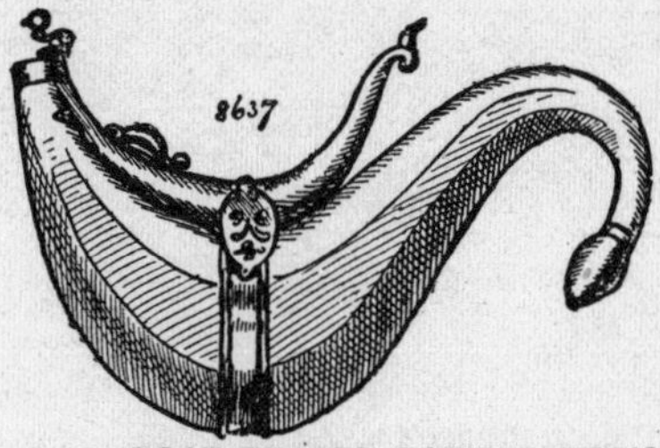

8637.—BOAT SHAPED POWDER HORN. From the Bidwell collection. Gold inlaid cut steel ornamental work. 6 by 3½ by 1½ inches. Used in priming old time flint weapons. Price, $10.00.

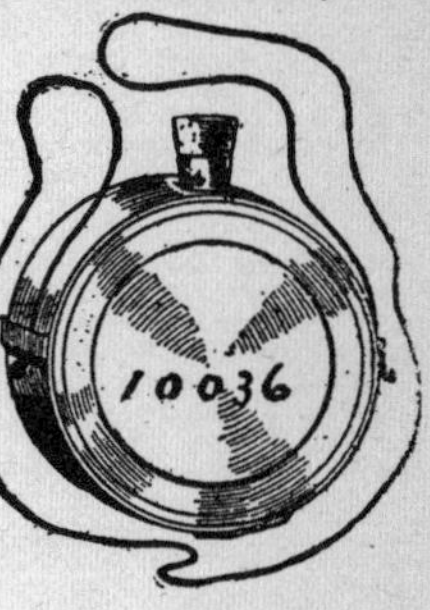

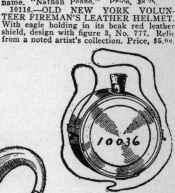

10036.—CANTEEN LABELED "FIRST CALL FOR TROOPS IN REBELLION, 1861." Found in New Jersey State Arsenal as sample of the canteens issued to three months' soldiers; 7½ inches in diameter, 2½ inch. deep, flat at the back, oval shaped in the front, worsted sling guard, historical relics. Price, $1.00 each.

10107.—BRITISH ROYAL LANCERS OFFICER'S HELMET. With gilt ornamented plate. Price, $8.85.

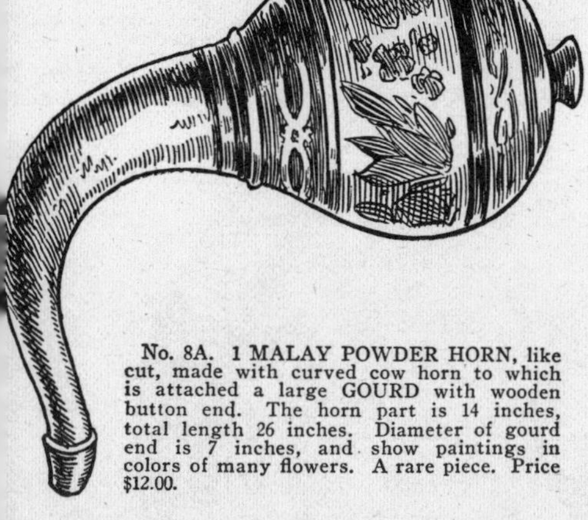

No. 8A. 1 MALAY POWDER HORN, like cut, made with curved cow horn to which is attached a large GOURD with wooden button end. The horn part is 14 inches, total length 26 inches. Diameter of gourd end is 7 inches, and show paintings in colors of many flowers. A rare piece. Price $12.00.

8637A. MOORISH PRIMING FLASK, made of heavy
namented brass, boat shape, similar to illustration No.
37 on page 129. Two swivels for carrying sash. Price
0.00.

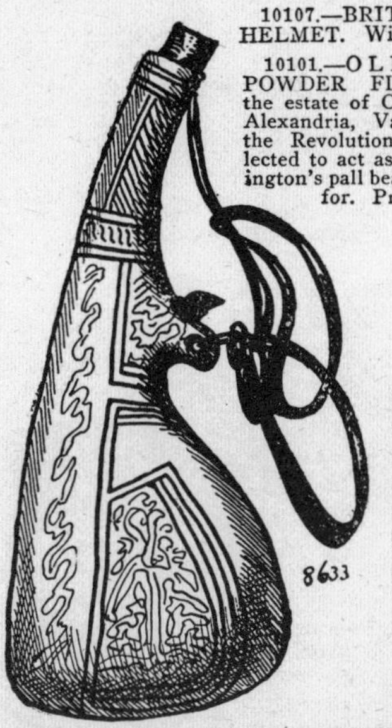

10101.—OLD BRASS POWDER FLASK. From the estate of Col. Simmes of Alexandria, Va. Colonel in the Revolutionary War; selected to act as one of Washington's pall bearers; vouched for. Price, $10.00.

8633.—CAMEL HIDE SKIN ANCIENT POWDER HORN.—Native embossed ornamentation of flowers and scroll work, 18th century period. Size 12 by 5 by 4 inches, with shoulder straps. Price, $15.00.

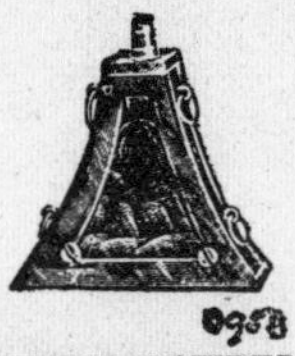

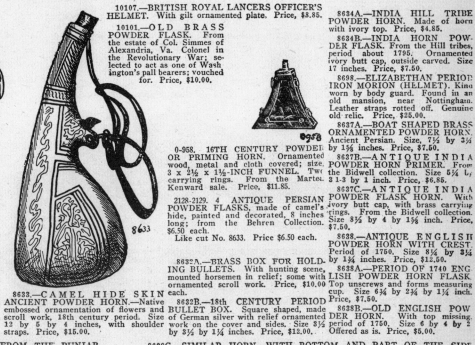

0-958. 16TH CENTURY POWDER OR PRIMING HORN. Ornamented wood, metal and cloth covered; size, 3 x 2½ x 1½-INCH FUNNEL. Two carrying rings. From the Martel Kenward sale. Price, $11.85.

2128-2129. 4 ANTIQUE PERSIAN POWDER FLASKS, made of camel's hide, painted and decorated, 8 inches long; from the Behren Collection. $6.50 each.

Like cut No. 8633. Price $6.50 each.

8632A.—BRASS BOX FOR HOLDING BULLETS. With hunting scene, mounted horsemen in relief; some with ornamented scroll work. Price, $10.00 each.

8632B.—18th CENTURY PERIOD BULLET BOX. Square shaped, made of German silver with relief ornamented work on the cover and sides. Size 3½ by 3½ by 1¼ inches. Price, $12.00.

8634A.—INDIA HILL TRIBE POWDER HORN. Made of horn with ivory top. Price, $4.85.

8634B.—INDIA HORN POWDER FLASK. From the Hill tribes, period about 1795. Ornamented ivory butt cap, outside carved. Size 17 inches. Price, $7.50.

8698.—ELIZABETHAN PERIOD IRON MORION (HELMET). Kind worn by body guard. Found in an old mansion, near Nottingham. Leather straps rotted off. Genuine old relic. Price, $25.00.

8637A.—BOAT SHAPED BRASS ORNAMENTED POWDER HORN. Ancient Persian. Size, 7½ by 3½ by 1⅝ inches. Price, $7.50.

8637B.—ANTIQUE INDIA POWDER HORN PRIMER. From the Bidwell collection. Size 5¼ by 3 1-3 by 1 inch. Price, $6.85.

8637C.—ANTIQUE INDIA POWDER FLASK HORN. With ivory butt cap, with brass carrying rings. From the Bidwell collection. Size 8½ by 4 by 1⅝ inch. Price, $7.50.

8638.—ANTIQUE ENGLISH POWDER HORN WITH CREST. Period of 1750. Size 8¼ by 3¼ by 1¾ inches. Price, $12.50.

8638A.—PERIOD OF 1740 ENGLISH POWDER HORN FLASK. Top unscrews and forms measuring cup. Size 6¾ by 2¾ by 1¼ inch. Price, $7.50.

8638B.—OLD ENGLISH POWDER HORN. With top missing. period of 1750. Size 6 by 4 by 2. Offered as is. Price, $5.00.

8697.—ANTIQUE INDIAN DECORATED SHIELD FROM THE PUNJAB.
th century period, face of the shield is nearly covered with paintings of tigers,
elopes, fish, etc., 4 metal bosses, 16½ inches in diameter. Price, $9.85.

8639.—AFRICAN BEE HIVE SHAPED POWDER CARRIER. Made of wood,
ass ornamented with tube handle, with carrying ring. Size 11½ by 5½ by 9 inches.
ice, $8.85.

8640.—ANTIQUE IVORY POWDER HORN. For priming flint weapons, steel
ing and ring. Size 3¾ by 2 by ⅞ inches. Price, $7.50.

8641.—ANTIQUE BONE POWDER PRIMER. With steel spring. Size 3 by 2
hes. Price, $4.85.

10978.—FRENCH SOLDIER'S TIN CANTEEN. With air vent tube, leather
oulder sling, used, serviceable order. Price, $1.50.

8750.—CARVED WOOD CHERUB HEAD AND OUTSTRETCHED WINGS.
om old London (City Church), by Grinley Gibbons. Length 10½ inches, height 5¼
hes, width 2¼ inches. Price. $5.00.

8638C.—SIMILAR HORN, WITH BOTTOM AND PART OF THE SIDE MISSING. With ancient top, with spring for measuring. With brass bands. Price as is, $5.00.

10098.—ANCIENT LEATHER HELMET. With large brass front plate, with Royal Crown surmounting Eagle, with sword in one talon, with sceptre and crown in the other. Metal chin strap, large black horse hair crest; rare specimen. Price, $17.50

10118.—ANTIQUE BRASS HELMET WITH BLACK HAIR ON CREST. With metal plate stamped with bursting bomb, crossed battle axes, Gallic cock. (Et Devourment S ro Pompiers De Roilot.) Very showy decorations. Price, $12.50.

10100.—BRITISH ARMY WHITE HELMET WITH HAVERLOCK. Scale chain, chin strap, with brass spike; used, serviceable. Price, $1.50.

10100A.—FRENCH SOLDIER'S HAVERSACK. Relic. Price, 85c.

10115.—TURKISH ARMY SOLDIER'S FEZ. Red felt with blue tassel. Price $1.50.

# Ancient and Historical Powder Horns.

## COLLECTION OF OLD CARVED POWDER HORNS FROM THE FRENCH AND INDIAN WARS, THE REVOLUTIONARY WAR AND WAR OF 1812.

Total of 45 horns used by men who helped make American history. The collection is the life work of Mr. A. E. Brooks, Hartford, Conn., who started collecting early in the last century and spared neither time nor money in gathering together the greatest and best collection of powder horns in the United States. (His collection of firearms is now in the National Museum of Washington, D. C.) Before retiring from business, knowing our interest for old powder horns, he turned the collection over to us. We offer the lot as described above, also described in Brooks' catalogue, pages 183 to 187. The collection is worthy of a place in some of our public museums. Price, $3,000.00.

No. 2037.—Inscribed "His Horn David Willson Derefeld the 18th 1747, February, David Willson of Holles." Also ornamented with deer, snakes, turtles, etc.

No. 2038.—Inscribed "Old Fort at Oswego 1755." Facsimile of the old fort at that time, also the old bridge across the river, with two large trees at the end of the bridge. This horn has a finely carved mouthpiece.

No. 2039.—Inscribed "Hacob Hooper. This horn made in the year of April the 5 day 1758." Also trees, etc. On the under bottom of this horn are the initials A. H. W. Probably Hooper carried this horn in the French and Indian Wars.

No. 2040.—Inscribed "Zaphin Dodge His Horn made in 1760." Also ornamented with trees, leaves, etc.

No. 2048.—Inscribed "Cesar Bacgdon His Horn the year of Kin H." Also ships flying the British flag; Fort Mermaid, etc. This horn was a fine one in its day; some one has cut and spoiled it before it came into Mr. Brook's possession.

No. 2043.—Inscribed "Asa Smyth 1865" and the initials A. S. Also ornamented with ships, fancy work, etc.

No. 2044.—Inscribed with large British man-of-war, 70 gun frigate, with flag flying, marked "The Sea Horse." Fishes, snakes, etc. On under bottom is letter H. Fine old horn (no date), probably made during or before Revolutionary War.

No. 2045.—Inscribed "Lieut. Joshua Bushwell, Saybrook, January ye 29, 1765. I powder with my brother ball. Hero-like do conquer all." With drawing of old Saybrook fort, flowers, etc.

No. 2046.—Inscribed "Mihl Waben City of New York," and the whole length of the Hudson River with its many forts and noted houses and villages, with the City of Albany, sailing vessels, etc., of Revolutionary War period.

No. 2057.—Inscribed "Henry Wallton 1768." Marked on bottom, "L. L." Fine ornamental work, reduced from original size.

No. 2048.—Inscribed "David Prior His Horn, Boston," with ships, forts, running vines, etc.; used as a priming horn.

No. 2049.—Inscribed "M. Steadman Berlin, Ct. 1773-1776." On under bottom is inscribed M. Steadman, Berlin, Conn., 1773. In 1776 Steadman was captain in Colonel Douglas' regiment, which served in Boston, 1776.

No. 2050.—Inscribed "Made at Roxbury in the year of our Lord 1775." It has also fine drawings of the town of Roxbury at that time. It has houses, churches, forts, barracks, river, fish, trees, etc.

No. 2052.—Inscribed "J. Marsh 1774." This horn belonged to John Marsh, Sturbridge, Mass., who was a Revolutionary War soldier from Sept. 17, 1775, to Sept. 27, 1776.

No. 2053.—Inscribed "Isaac Harrington Horn 1774," with town of Camden, Maine, houses, church, river, with signboard "Walk In," with deer, sheep, lambs, pigs, dog, unicorn, and man leading horse; glass on the under bottom.

No. 2051.—Inscribed "Apl. J. S. L. B. M. H. D. A. T.," with trees, leaves, flowers and many other kinds of work—Revolutionary War period.

No. 2041.—Inscribed "E. D. 1756." Also fleet of eight vessels; some of the vessels are ship-of-war flying the British flag; also other ornamental work.

No. 2054.—Old Carved English Powder-horn. Inscription on this horn: "This is the Priming Horn of H. B. M., 5th Artillery, Fort Niagary May 10th 1796. Made by Sarjent Armstrong." The British flag is up, and the American flag is down. Under the flags he says: "Where waves the British flag the sun shall never sett. Yankee Doodle be damd. God save the King and dam the Yanks." The drawing on the horn is Fort Niagara and round-house. An American eagle is perched on the flagstaff of American flag. The lion is grasping the flagstaff of the British flag. There are also a cannon, wild ducks, etc. Finely carved mouth-piece. The wooden bottom is a carved lion's head.

No. 2055.—Old Carved Powder-horn. Inscription on this horn: "J. P. Denman." With gun, dog, deer, snake, trees, fish, heart and hand pointing to C. A., also young lady, a cross, and five stars, etc.

No. 2056.—Old Carved Powder-horn. Inscription on this horn: "The Chase," a beautifully engraved landscape or hunting scene, with huntsmen on horseback with two greyhounds, having the frightened hare in sight. "The horn of a Australian ox. Engraved with a penknife by C. W."

No. 2057.—Old Carved Powder-horn. Inscription on this horn: "Aaron Osborn's horn, made at Lake George Nov. 10th, 1756. I powder with my brother ball. A hero like do conquer all. Hidelum fistelo margelo gig." Drawing of a road. "The road from Albany to Lake George," also "Fort William Henry," with its barracks, and a flag flying from flagstaff on the fort; an eagle is perched on one end of the fort. The words "Lake George," cannon mounted on wheels, eagle standing by the side of the cannon. Indian chief in his war dress with tomahawk in his right hand and a rifle in his left hand, under which is marked "Saratoga." Militiaman with gun in his hands at present arms, under which is marked "Still Water." Mermaid, snakes, running vines, flowers, etc. It also has the square and compasses with letter "G" in its center; Masonic apron, all-seeing eye, hour-glass, and sprig of cassit. All the work on this horn is fine.

No. 2058.—Old carved Powder-horn. Inscription on this horn: "Essex 1634. French Wars 1755, 1759, 1765. Last, 1777." Also marked "Amos Riggs horn. Indian and French Wars 1755, 1759, 1765. Enock Riggs, son of Amos Riggs, War of 1777."

No. 2059.—Old Carved Powder-horn. Inscription on this horn: "Robert Avery. His horn 1757. Stonington, Conn., Sept. 8th to Nov. 17th, 1776." Also a duck, snake, etc. On the wooden bottom of this horn is marked "R. A. 1757." Probably this horn was carried in the French and Indian Wars by Robert Avery, who was in the Revolutionary War. He enlisted September 8, 1776, in Captain Stoddard's company, Colonel Wells, regiment; discharged November 17, 1776.

No. 2060.—Old Carved Powder-horn. Inscription on this horn: "Isaac Thomas. His horn Haddam, Conn. Cap Pecks Company Fifth Battalion. Dec. 25th, 1776." Also female figure, Indian with goose and fox, turkey and peacock, tree, two bears, snakes, etc. On the wooden bottom of this horn is marked "W. B. 1788." Isaac Thomas was a Revolutionary soldier who was in Captain Peck's company, Fifth battalion Wadsworth brigade. Colonel Douglass, 1776; afterwards enlisted in Captain Horton's company in regiment of "Artificers."

No. 2061.—Old Powder-horn. Inscription on this priming horn: "Uriah Howland. Ticonderoga, 1776." Uriah Howland was a gunner in Bigelow's artillery company. The first artillery company raised in Connecticut during the Revolution was an independent organization, commanded by Captain John Bigelow of Hartford. It was recruited early in 1776, stationed during the summer and fall of 1776 at Ticonderoga and vicinity.

No. 2062.—Old Carved Powder-horn. Inscription on this priming horn: "E. B. R. 1807." It has a decanter, tumbler, and goblet, under which is marked "Help yourself to grog I hope God will forgive me for passing away my time so foolishly." It also has a gun, powder-horn, birds, ship, anchor, fish, etc.

No. 2063.—Old Carved Powder-horn, with carving of the town or village of Stanford, marked "Stanford 1809," also houses, churches, ships in the harbor, trees, wild ducks, etc. The words "Custom House" and inscription "Yankee Doodle cum to town. Wareing linen breeches. He made the Red Coats leave the sound and filled up all his ditches. 1812."

No. 2064.—Old English Powder-horn, with fine carvings. Inscription on this horn: "Captain Hatt. Horn. H. B. MS 49th Grenadiers. Lewiston Heights. Queenstown. 1812 Glengary. Cap. McNeal Newfoundland Lake Ontario, Ft. Toronto, Harbor." Also log house, trees, Indian tepee, bows and arrows, and the British Crown with G. R. in the crown, etc. Finely carved mouthpiece on this horn.

No. 2065.—Old Carved Powder-horn. Inscription on this horn: "S. B. M. S." Has the American flag under which is marked "U. S. A." Also eagle, ships, female figure, heart, two trowels, square, compass, etc.

No. 2066.—Old Carved Powder-horn. Inscription on this horn: "The Red Coat that steals this horn will go to hell so sure as he is born. Simeon Coe 1814 Fort Ontario Oswego." Also drawings of Fort Ontario and barracks, ships, fish, wild ducks, etc. On the wooden bottom of this horn is marked "Sim Coe, Oswego. His horn. 1814."

No. 2067.—Old Carved Spanish Powder-horn, marked "Sept. 18, 1818." It has the Spanish coat-of-arms finely engraved on it, man-of-war and other vessels, mermaid, fish, and running vines with flowers, etc.

No. 2068.—Old Carved Powder-horn. Inscription on this horn: "Dr. Burr and Lieut. Smith, 2d Infantry Madison Barracks, Sackets Harbor 1820." Also flag and staff, log house, shade trees, dragon, etc. Priming horn.

Etc., Etc. Total 45 horns, in the collection.

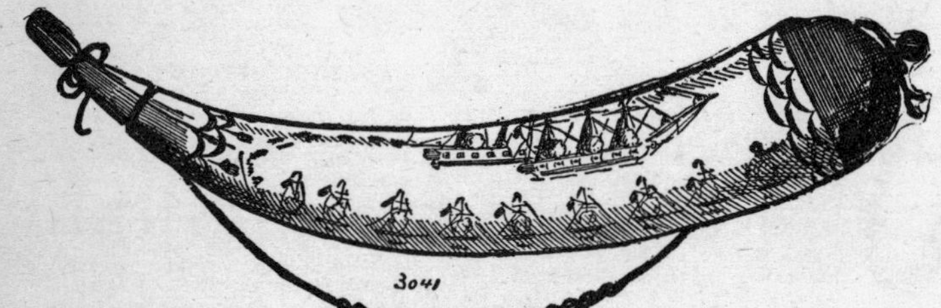


1812 AMERICAN WAR WITH ENGLAND POWDER HORN, engraved, showing engagement June 29, 1813, between the British frigate, Junon, 30 guns, Capt. Sanders, and the Martin, 18 guns, Capt. Senhouse. The Martin grounded while in Delaware Bay on Crown Shoal, and was attacked by Lt. Samuel Angus, commanding the American force of 8 small sloops, assisted by a fleet of cutters with armed men. This is the only illustration known showing the engagement. We learned this official history by writing to the War Record Department, U. S. Navy, Washington, D. C. The history of the horn as we learned from the party who sold it to us, was that it was pawned by the descendants of the owner, who had taken part in the battle, and correctly gives the position of the vessels and cutters in the engagement. The powder horn was never redeemed and was sold to us by the pawnbroker's heirs. We value this old horn, which furnishes the only illustration of Naval Battles in the War of 1812, at $250.00.

0-944. ANCIENT BRASS POWDER FLASK. Square-shaped, 4 inches by 1¼ inches, covered with engraving, 2 carrying rings, long funnel. Price, $17.50.

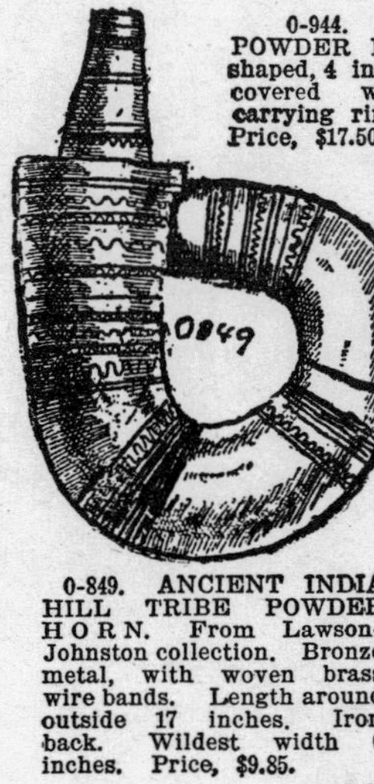


0-849. ANCIENT INDIA HILL TRIBE POWDER HORN. From Lawson-Johnston collection. Bronze metal, with woven brass wire bands. Length around outside 17 inches. Iron back. Wildest width 6 inches. Price, $9.85.

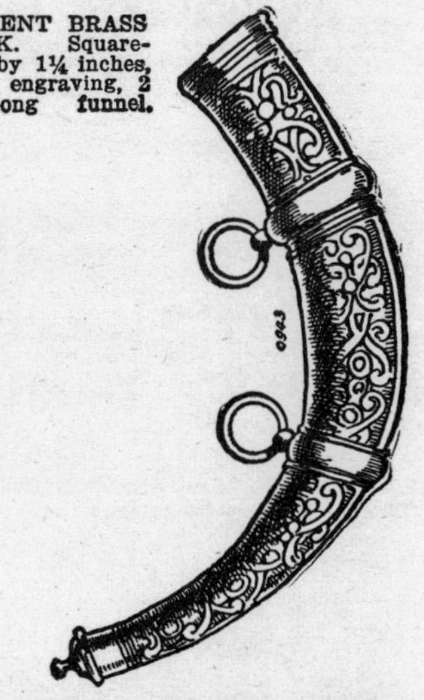

0-943. ANCIENT NORWEGIAN POWDER HORN. Brass relief, ornamented. Length 11 inches, 2-inch rings for shoulder sling, measuring stopper. Price, $14.50.

0-903. COMBINATION POWDER SHOT AND CAP FLASH. Old antique English, THREE IN ONE, from duelling pistol case sets. Price, $4.85.

0-973B. ANCIENT STEEL OIL BOTTLES AND STOPPERS. From case of flint duelling pistol sets. Fine workmanship. Valuable to complete missing sets. Price, $2.50 each.

0-991. SMALL POWDER FLASK. From broken up sets of duelling pistols in cases. Ancient pattern. Price, $3.50 each.

0-978. ANCIENT CURIOUS CAP CHARGER. Pocket size, stamped "S. Alport." Government proved. For holding and inserting caps on the nipple of the percussion pistol, 2 inches square, 1½-inch brass neck. Price, $3.50.

0-959. CIRCULAR-SHAPED ORNAMENTED COPPER POWDER FLASK, American Revolutionary War period. Pocket size, 4-inch diameter, 1-inch thick, 1½-inch funnel. Spring top. Price, $11.85.

On this page will be seen 17 different systems of breech-loading weapons. These were made as carbines only. On another page where the single shot breech-loading rifles are pictured will be found other systems made in both rifles and carbines. These details are clearly set forth in the reading matter descriptive of the rifles.

No. 1. The U. S. experimented with two flintlock carbines, the Hall and the Jenks. In 1841 a trial was held at Carlisle Barracks of Jenks carbines. These were .69 caliber. At the Museum in Fairmount Park, Philadelphia, will be found one of the rare carbines. It is stamped "U. S. Wm. Jenks, 1839." The chief of ordnance in those days, Geo. Talcott, says in a report, "A prejudice against all arms loading at the breech is prevalent among officers, especially the Dragoons, and they are not worth the storeroom they occupy." But that was in 1841.

Although the flintlock Jenks was a breech-loader, the first percussion arm of this system was a muzzle loader, then came the common model which was later followed by one with the Maynard primer magazine. All these three had the well known side hammer which cocked to the right instead of backwards. During the Civil War Merrill of Baltimore altered a number to the regulation size hammer and breech-lever. The Jenks system was the fore-runner of the Merrill, both alike in principle.

No. 2. SYMMES BREECH-LOADING CARBINE. Caliber .54. Patented 1858. One of the early experimental pieces, 200 only purchased. The breech-block rotates upward. Has the famous Maynard magazine primer.

No. 3. GIBBS BREECH-LOADING CARBINE. Although patented in 1856 it was not until 1863 that any were made. W. F. Brooks of New York was given a contract in '61 for 10,000. He completed and delivered only 1,052. The barrel slides forward and tilts up at breech to load. Caliber .52. Paper cartridge.

No. 4. U. S. SCHROEDER CARBINE. Caliber .53. Patented in 1856. This is a needle gun, the charge being fired by a long firing pin which penetrates the powder charge and ignites the fulminate, which in this case, is in front end of cartridge and at base of bullet. Barrel slides forward. Several in government collections. They are marked with an eagle and U. S. on the tang. Used about 1858. Very rare.

No. 5. J. D. GREENE'S BREECH-LOADING CARBINE. Patented June, 1854. 700 of these issued for trial, 1856-57. Caliber .53. By pulling on forward trigger barrel is revolved one-quarter turn. Barrel is then pulled forward to clear the receiver. Sleeve and barrel then revolve to right to insert cartridge. Arm has the Maynard primer. One of the rare U. S. arms.

No. 6. JOSLYN BREECH-LOADING CARBINE. Patented 1855. Caliber .54. Made at Stonington, Conn., by B. F. Joslyn. This is the first of the Joslyn systems used, the rest, however, being cartridge arms. When ring on top of butt is released the strap on small of stock lifts up and uncovers the breech.

No. 7. COSMOPOLITAN BREECH-LOADING CARBINE, also called Union. Caliber .50. 9,342 purchased during the Civil War. Made at Hamilton, Ohio. There were three models, the one shown being the last and common model. Note the extreme length of the hammer, caused by the fact that it spans the entire breech-block. This carbine weighed slightly less than seven pounds.

No. 8. STARR BREECH-LOADING CARBINE. Caliber .54. Made at Yonkers, N. Y. 25,603 purchased 1861-65. The breech-block is in two pieces, one of which falls back disclosing the breech. Patented in 1858 by E. S. Starr who also invented and made the famous Starr revolvers. These carbines were later altered to take metallic cartridges.

No. 9. SMITH BREECH-LOADING CARBINE. Caliber .52. The cartridge was encased in a rubber shell. By pushing up the catch in front of the trigger the lever on top of the tang is released, this allowing the barrel to drop like a shot gun. 30,062 purchased during the Civil War at a cost of $24.00 each. They were evidently put to use as over 13 million cartridges were purchased to use in them. Some were altered later to take a metallic cartridge, the invention of Silas Crispin. It had the rim near the middle so as to fit the peculiar breech action.

Continued on Page 235

**0-660. BOOK ILLUSTRATING U. S. ARMY SOLDIER'S UNI-FORMS.** From 1774 to 1888. Made for the U. S. Government by celebrated artist. 44 colored lithographed plates. Size of each plate 14x16¾ inches. Only limited number made and the lithograph plates destroyed. We have these pages of uniform plates framed and on free exhibition in our museum salesroom, where they attract the attention and study of artists, publishers, costumers and others who visit our store. These 44 plates are works of art, as showing the U. S. Army uniform of the different periods from 1774 to 1888. Made under the authority of the U. S. Government. Not only are the soldiers shown in uniform, but artillery, cavalry, tents, barracks and fortifications, which form part of the life of the soldier of the period, with descriptive key and illustration showing the general orders regarding the uniform from the earliest records to 1888.

WE HAVE IN STOCK AT OUR ISLAND MAGAZINE, ready for immediate delivery, and we mention immediate delivery, as manufacturers only make to order, which sometimes requires months of waiting, the following LOADED PROJECTILES for HOTCHKISS MOUNTAIN CANNONS. Each explosive projectile consists of brass shell case, in the head of which is the centre-fire primer, in the shell case is the powder charge. Securely packed in the mouth of the cartridge case is the STEEL SHOT or EXPLOSIVE SHELL in which is the fuse, either at the point or base of the shell, for bursting by time or percussion.

The ONE POUNDER HOTCHKISS projectiles measure ½ inch in diameter and is 6¾ inches long, weighs 22 ounces.

The two pounder Hotchkiss projectiles measure 1.65 inch in diameter. The full length is 8 inches, weight 2 pounds 7 ounces. The firing charge is 5¾ ounces. The bursting charge in the shell is 1 4/5 ounces.

The two pounder cannister shot is 6¾ inches long and weighs 2½ pounds, and contains 30 one ounce metal bullets in a brass cylinder-shaped shell case.

OUR STOCK CONSISTS AS FOLLOWS:

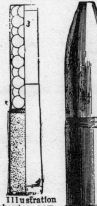

Canister Shot, Hotchkiss Mountain Cannon. — Explosive Steel Shell Hotchkiss Cannon. — Illustration of Solid Shot, with copper ring sabot. — Illustration showing powder and balls in shrapnel shot. — 12 Pounder Explosive Shell.

### ONE POUNDER PROJECTILES.
2,279 Rounds of Canister Shot, filled and fixed.
2,000 Rounds of Explosive Shells, filled and fixed.
1,000 Empty Shells, 50 cents each.
### TWO POUNDER PROJECTILES.
5,100 Rounds of Canister Shot, filled and fixed.
9,000 Rounds of Explosive Shells, filled and fixed.
### THREE POUNDERS.
132 Brass Cartridge Cases, filled with powder for saluting.
### SIX POUNDERS.
5,000 Empty Explosive Shells, with copper rotating band. 85 cents each.
### THREE-INCH OR TWELVE POUNDER.
1,433 Rounds of Shrapnel Shot, filled and fixed.
198 Rounds of Canister Shot, filled and fixed.
1,580 Rounds of Explosive Shells, filled and fixed.
491 Rounds of Blanks, for saluting.
### THREE AND TWO-TENTH-INCH PROJECTILE.
1,200 Cartridge Bags, fitted with service charge of smokeless powder.

### 40 CIVIL WAR ILLUSTRATIONS.

**0-669. "THE LIFE ILLUSTRATIONS OF THE GREAT ARMY."** By Edwin Forbes, official artist with the armies of the Union. 40 copper etched plates, illustrating the life of the Union armies during the years 1862-3-4-5. Full size of the plate 18x42 inches. In fine order. Very suitable for framing. Bargain price, $40.00.

**0-789. ANCIENT ILLUSTRATED BOOK OF BATTLES.** Published in 1725. "Batalies Gagnees, Par le Prince Francoise Eugene de Savoye," by Jean Huchtenburg. Size 16x22 inches. Double page plate 16x44 inches, showing plans, description and locations, with fine engravings of the battle scenes of the Princes' battle in Hongeri, 1697, Italy, Bavaria, Piedmont from 1697 to 1717, with ancient map, 19x33 inches. Size of the book 21x13½ inches. In fair state of preservation. Price, $35.00.

**499. FRENCH-ENGLISH MILITARY TECHNICAL DICTIONARY,** by Col. C. DeWitt Wilcox, U. S. A., Professor of Modern Languages at West Point. Published by Harper & Brothers, New York. It contains all the latest terms of aviation, trench warfare, artillery and camouflage, military slang, etc. 584 pages on glazed paper, size 6x9 inches. 1917 edition. Regular price was four dollars. Our bargain price $1.00 each. Allow postage on three pounds.

ARMSTRONG STEEL ADAPTER FOR SHELL FUSES. Length 1¾ inch, diameter at the head 1¼ inch, diameter at the thread ⅞ inch. New. Price, 18 cents each.

NEW MOUNTAIN HOWITZER PACK SADDLE HARNESS EQUIPMENT for transporting small cannon over mountainous country, complete as above illustration. Price $40.00 per horse.

Have a few extra Saddles only. Price $20.00 each.

CANNON FLINT LOCKS, used for firing cannons in olden times. Size 6x5 inches. Price $15.00.

ARMY WHEELS, with axles, in second-hand serviceable order. Price $22.00 pair.

CANNON RAMMERS and SPONGES, 6-pounder, $2.75; 3-inch, $3.00; 12-pounder, $3.00; 20-pounder, $4.50; larger sizes upon application.

THREE ASSORTED ROCKET STANDS, from Charleston Arsenal, S. C. Fine ornament as well as valuable relic. For shooting war rockets. Price $20.00 each.

"JAMES" IRON RIFLE CANNON BORE, 4.62; weight 3,050 lbs.; fine order; relic Civil War; unmounted; length, 10 feet. Price, $280.00.

TWO 20-POUNDER BREECH-LOADING RIFLES, almost new; length 10 feet; bore 3⅝ inches; weight of gun 1,700 lbs. $500.00.

CANNON WORMERS for withdrawing defective charge. $4.50 each.

**0-804A. CIVIL WAR HAND GRENADE.** Known as the "Excelsior," N. W. Haynes patent, August 26, 1862. Made of cast iron. An inner and outer shell. The inner shell is 2½ inches in diameter and contains the powder. On the outside of the inner shell 14 nipples are screwed for to take the regular musket percussion caps. The outer shell is in two halves, in which is inserted the inner shell, the two halves screwing together. Before firing, percussion caps are placed on the nipple; when the shell strikes, some one of the 14 caps is sure to receive the compact and thus explode the shell, which, being in two parts, would break up into many small destructive pieces. This projectile was considered so dangerous that we understand its use was prohibited. Only a few were made. Sale restricted to public museum. Price, $50.00.

**0-1074. STONE CANNON BALL.** Found near old castle near the River Meuse at Liege, Belgium, near where the great Mans-Meg cannon, now at Edinburgh castle, was built. The original size was 8½ inches in diameter. Small part broken off. Ancient artillery manual provided for the use of cannon balls of stone in the absence of metal, "that the ball be placed in a basket resting on a wooden bottom for placing in the cannon near the powder charge." Price, $15.00.

Illustration of ancient soldier with bag of small explosive shells thrown by hand from castle walls or fortifications. Shell measures usually about 2½ inches in diameter, with short fuse ignited by soldier before throwing. Later this gave name to regiment of British soldiers, "Grenadiers."

Breech Loading 32 2-10 inch bore Rifled Steel Cannon, Krupp Breech Mechanism. Purchased by U. S. Government for testing purposes. Gun is like new, fine serviceable order; mounted on steel carriage, with bronze elevating mechanism with seats for gunners; length of gun over 5 feet, weight about 900 lbs., weight of carriage about 1,000 lbs. Must have cost originally upwards of $3,000. Offered complete with gunner's implements. Bargain Price, $675.

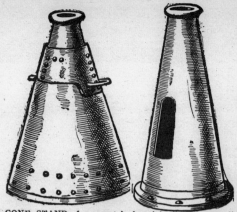

U. S. NAVY CONE STAND, for mountain breech-loading cannon, diameter at the base 24 inches, height 37 inches, brass socket, chest, flange, handle and base; riveted steel frame, English pattern purchased for use on the American Warships during the Spanish War. Offered at bargain prices.

BRITISH NAVY CANNON MOUNT STEEL BODY with brass socket and deck flange with opening door for gunner's small tools, diameter at the base 23 inches, height 38 inches. Offered either singly or mounted with breech-loading cannon at bargain prices.

When the Spanish War broke out, international law prevented open sale of arms by European manufacturers to the United States. To get around the law, a large steamship was loaded with boxes of cannon, ammunition, etc., the boxes covered with coal. When the steamer was within a short distance of the American coast, the crew abandoned the ship. Singularly it was an American Warship that discovered the abandoned ship and towed her to the Navy Yard. We believe these British Naval Cones formed part of the cargo of the Steamer Scipio.

War of 1812 Cannon, 5 feet long, 3¼ inch bore, weight about 1,000 pounds. For many years has stood as Hitching-Post on Delaware Avenue, Philadelphia, Pa. Could be cleaned up and made serviceable. We offer it as it is. Historical relic. Price $150.

**Hotchkiss 5-Barrel Rapid Fire Revolving Machine Gun.** Calibre 1.46 inches (37 m/m.) Mounted on naval steel carriage. Weight of projectile 1½ pounds. 60 rounds a minute may be fired, effective at 3,000 yards range. Brass cartridge cases can be reloaded a dozen times. Length of gun from muzzle to end of shoulder bar 57 inches. Price of the gun mounted as is or on naval pedestal mount, or on army field carriage, with projectiles, given to those who may wish to purchase.

**20 Gatling Rapid Fire Machine Guns.** Illustration shows side view of the 10-barrel gun with Accles drum feed, quick firing guns. Mounted on field carriage with ammunition chest complete with limber. Gun is calibre 45. Steel barrels are encased in polished brass jacket. Gun is operated by turning crank; as many as 1,000 shots a minute may be fired. These guns can be offered with naval pedestal mounts or mounts for ships' fighting top. All in good serviceable order, used only a short time.

10,000,000 ball cartridges for these guns are in stock at our Island Magazine at bargain prices.

CONFEDERATE ROCKET STAND, from Charleston, S. C., used to signal to Fort Sumter, Moultre and other forts in the harbor during the Civil War. Height is 3½ feet; has gauge for setting the angle; weighs about 75 lbs.; serviceable relic for lawn decoration or museum. Price, $18.00.

**10 New Three-inch Steel Muzzle Loading Rifled Cannons.** Made for use of U. S. Army Field Artillery. Gun weighs 815 pounds. Length, 60 inches. Diameter of shot, 3 inches. Mounted on serviceable second-hand army field carriages, with gunners' tools, price $350.00 for each gun with outfit. Shot, shell or cannister can be furnished at $1.50 each.

**Breech Loading 3²⁄₁₀-inch Rifled Cannon,** altered from 3-inch muzzle loader. Illustration is from photograph. Shows the screw breech mechanism. Gun is in good 2nd-hand serviceable order, mounted on army field carriage, and is offered complete with limber and gunner' stools for $600.00. 100 shrapnel with time fuses for this cannon, at $3.00 each.

**GERMAN BREECH LOADING HAND CANNON.** Rare old relic; supposed to have been used in war with Austria and France. Screw plug breech closing mechanism; curved part goes over the shoulder and spring takes up the shock of recoil; rifled. Price, $25.00. Length of barrel, 40 inches; 1 inch diameter of bore. Full length, 67 inches; weight about 40 pounds.

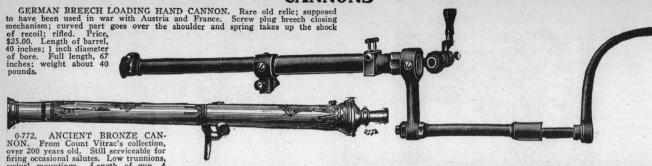

**0-772. ANCIENT BRONZE CANNON.** From Count Vitrac's collection, over 200 years old. Still serviceable for firing occasional salutes. Low trunnions, swivel mountings. Length of gun, 4 feet 9 inches; weight, 137 pounds; 1¾ inch smooth bore. Outside diameter at the muzzle 5 inches, at the breech 6 inches, width at the trunnions 3½ inches. Rare old relic, early model cannon. Ornamental cascabel, with socket for directing pole. For lawn decoration. Concrete stand can be easily and cheaply made for this gun, with pipe for the swivel socket to rest in. Bargain price, $100.00, including gunner's tools for firing.

**CALIBRE 45 LOWELL BATTERY RAPID-FIRE GUN.** Mounted on Army Field Carriage, with 5-foot wheel, all in fine, serviceable order, with feed cases. Bronze-covered mechanism with automatic turning movement, operated by the crank. Cost, upward of $2,500.

**6 GATLING RAPID-FIRE GUNS.** Calibre 50, shooting the standard government centre fire cartridge. 6 long barrels; breech mechanism encased in bronze jacket; mounted on Army Field Carriage, with 4-foot wheels, with feed cases. All in good, serviceable order.

Limber, if desired, price $90 each. Caissons, if desired, price $85 each.

Illustration of Cannon used in the Fifteenth Century—From Bannerman's book, "Weapons of War."

**MORTAR CANNON** from Kennebec Arsenal, Augusta, Me. Made in Washington, 1828. Has been well cared for and will make good cannon for firing salutes. Is complete, with base and gunner's tools, primer and powder bags for firing 25 rounds. **Price,** $65.00.

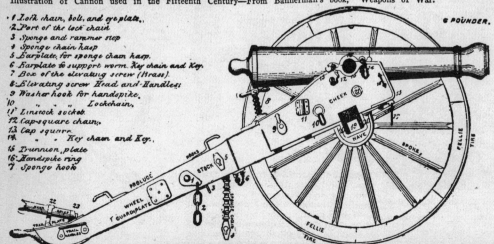

1 Lock chair, bolt, and eye plate.
2 Port of the lock chain
3 Sponge and rammer stop
4 Sponge chain hasp
5 Earplate for sponge chain hasp.
6 Earplate to support worm. Key chain and Key.
7 Box of the elevating screw (Brass).
8 Elevating screw Head and Handles.
9 Washer hook for handspike.
10       Lockchain.
11 Linstock socket.
12 Cap-square chain.
13 Cap square.
14      Key chain and Key.
15 Trunnion plate
16 Handspike ring
17 Sponge hook

6 POUNDER.

ILLUSTRATION SHOWING EACH AND EVERY PART OF THE 6-POUNDER CIVIL WAR CANNON, WITH PROPER NAME OF EACH PART.

SEE OTHER PAGES FOR THESE GUNS AND EXTRA PARTS AND IMPLEMENTS WITH PRICES.

18 Axle body (Wood)    9 } Are also the extremities of    22 Large pointing ring     Stock { Head, groove, trail and the
19 Axle tree (Iron).     10 } the assembling bolts       23 Small                 rounding of the trail
20 Under strap.         21 }

**12 Pounder Hotckkiss Mountain Gun on Carriage with Limber.**

2 Hotchkiss 12 Pounder Mountain Guns, Calibre 3 inch, mounted on field carriages, complete with 4 ammunition limbers, with 1580 explosive shells, 1,433 shrapnel, 198 canister shot, 491 brass cartridge case blanks for saluting, with 1,200 rounds service charges of smokeless powder, contained in cartridge bags, with complete pack outfits, all U. S. standard. Carriage and limbers are of reinforced steel; four chests on each limber, each chest has compartment for holding 8 complete rounds of ammunition. Length of gun is 45 inches, 24 rifle grooves; weight of projectile, filled and fused, 14 pounds; range upwards of three miles; weight of gun 218 pounds; weight of carriage body 205 pounds; each wheel weighs 62 pounds; all parts light enough to be drawn by men, or mounted on the pack saddle of the mule for Mountain transportation. Guns and outfits are offered in fine, serviceable order, packed in original army cases, with gunners appendages and spare parts, at about half the original cost. These fine guns and outfits should be particularly desirable to South American Government War Departments or to any government for service in mountainous countries.

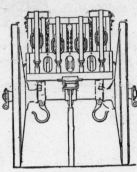

**Complete Shell with brass case.**

**Common Shell**

**Steel Shell**

**Canister**

**Front view 12 Pounder Hotckiss Limber.**

Length of brass case, 5⅜ inches.

Charge of powder for propelling the shell, 14 ounces.

Bursting charge of powder contained in the steel shell, 6 ounces.

Length of steel or cast iron shell, 10½ inches. Weight of shell, 12 pounds. Weight of the shell complete with brass case, filled and fused, 14 pounds.

Penetration at muzzle through 1½ inches of steel.

Extreme range nearly 3 miles.

100 Sets U. S. A. Pack Saddles and Harness for Mountain Guns, 2 Pounder, and 12 Pounder. Pack saddles fitted with steel frames on heavy leather saddles for carrying the gun, the carriage, the ammunition, and accessories; complete with breechings, bridles, halters, blinders, drag ropes, cinches, paulins, lash ropes, girths, harness sacks, cruppers, neck yokes, shafts jointed poles, double and single, with splinter bars, etc.; all in fine, serviceable order, in original armory packing cases, every part inspected and accepted by U. S. Government Officer. Gun Pack Saddle Harness outfit weighs 69 pounds, carriage pack, 69 pounds; ammunition, 58 pounds; Artillery Outfit at less than half the manufacturer's price.

Shrapnel is similar to the shell except that the walls are thinner in order to break up more readily, and to scatter over the enemy the 16 hardened lead balls, which it contains; exploded either by time fuse, or percussion fuse. The bursting charge is 1¾ ounces of fine powder with central tube connecting to the fuse.

Canister shot is thin brass shell of nearly the same shape as the explosive shell, in which is contained 125 small balls.

**Percussion Fuses.**

Fuses are of three kinds made of brass containing fulminate, either screwed into base or point of the shell, which explodes the charge on striking. Time fuse explodes the charge in the shell at the time set by the gunner before firing.

12 pounder Mountain Gun Ammunition, Calibre 3 inch. The complete cartridge consists of three parts; the brass case, in which is contained the firing cap or primer, and the charge of powder for propelling the shell; the cast iron or steel shell with soft copper band securely attached for rotating the shell; inside of the cast iron or steel shell is contained the charge of powder, which bursts the shell into fragments on striking, or at set time, by the brass fuse filled with explosive fulminite screwed into the point or the base of the shell.

**Pack Outfit, with Gun.**

**Pack Outfit with Gun Carriage.** pack for wheels and shafts, 60 pounds; offered with Mountain Gun

**Outfit, with Ammunition liber Chests.**

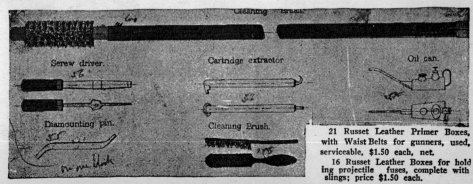

Screw driver.

Cartridge extractor

Oil can.

Dismounting pin.

Cleaning Brush.

21 Russet Leather Primer Boxes, with Waist Belts for gunners, used, serviceable, $1.50 each, net.

16 Russet Leather Boxes for holding projectile fuses, complete with slings; price $1.50 each.

**Illustration of Gunners tools and implements with Hotchkiss B-L Mountain Gun Outfits.**

No. 1706-A. Illustration of Pack Saddle with frame for Mountain Gun. Made for the Hotchkiss Gun Company by best Paris maker. Price, $35.00 per horse.

IN THESE PAGES OF BREECH-LOADING ARTILLERY CANNON, WILL BE FOUND ON SALE NEARLY THE ENTIRE OUTFIT OF THE U. S. ARMY LATE REGULATION MOUNTAIN CANNON, TOGETHER WITH THIS OUTFIT OF SHOT, SHELL AND CANISTER.
50 Hotchkiss 2-pounder Cannon.
12 Hotchkiss 12-pounder Cannon.
15 Hotchkiss 1-pounder Revolving Cannon.
Offered for sale, mounted on field carriage, for army or on cone-stands for navy. At bargain prices, with prompt delivery.

SEE SADDLE PAGES AT THE BACK OF THIS CATALOG FOR OTHER STYLES OF PACK SADDLES AND RIDING SADDLES FOR ARTILLERY USE.

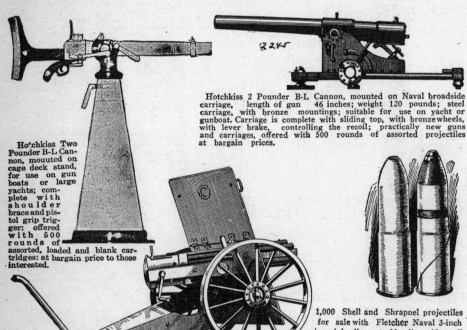

Hotchkiss Two Pounder B-L Cannon, mouuted on cage deck stand, for use on gun boats or large yachts; complete with shoulder brace and pistol grip trigger: offered with 500 rounds of assorted, loaded and blank cartridges: at bargain price to those interested.

Hotchkiss 2 Pounder B-L Cannon, mounted on Naval broadside carriage, length of gun 46 inches; weight 120 pounds; steel carriage, with bronze mountings; suitable for use on yacht or gunboat. Carriage is complete with sliding top, with bronze wheels, with lever brake, controlling the recoil; practically new guns and carriages, offered with 500 rounds of assorted projectiles at bargain prices.

38 U. S. Army Hotchkiss Two Pounder Breech-loading Mountain Cannons, Calibre 1.65; made at the Hotchkiss Armory, Paris, for the U. S. Government; sliding wedge breech block mechanism, operated by side lever; empty brass cartridge case is automatically ejected after firing; requires only two men, one to feed cartridges, and the other to aim and fire. Gun barrel is made of Whitworth steel, compressed when in fluid state; length of gun 46 inches; weight 120 pounds; number of rifle grooves, 10. Reinforced steel carriage, which can be hauled by hand with drag ropes, supplied with the gun, or by shafts for single horses or tandem, or horses side by side by use of jointed pole. Carriage weighs 120 pounds, wheels 51 pounds each; tracks 2½ feet. All parts can easily and quickly be dismounted, and of size and weight that can be drawn by men. Outfit includes harness pack for horse to carry the gun, and two chests of accessories; with other harness packs for the carriage and wheels, and packs for carrying ammunition. Our purchase included the guns complete with everything necessary that the U. S. Army had in stock. With these guns are offered:
11,460 rounds filled and fused ammunition.
5,534 rounds filled and fused ammunition, with base fuses.
1,965 rounds filled and fused ammunition, with point fuses.
5,700 rounds filled Canister Shot.
132 rounds Saluting Blanks.
Each projectile consists of brass cartridge case, with 5½ ounce powder charge; 14-5 ounces; bursting charge, with percussion fuse with two pound iron or steel explosive shell
Canister Shot contains 30 one ounce balls.
Weight of Shell complete, 2 pounds, 7 ounces.
Weight of Canister, 2 pounds, 8 ounces.
Length of Shell complete with brass case, 8 inches.
Length of Canister complete with case, 6¾ inches.
For war service in mountainous countries or where transportation is difficult these fine guns and outfits cannot be excelled. Many of the guns and outfits are entirely new, still in the original cases, all are in serviceable order. To Government War Ministers we can offer complete outfits, gun carriages, spare parts, ammunition, etc., at bargain prices. Offer solicited for the lot.

12 Hochkiss Field Artillery Revolving 5 Shot Cannons, Calibre 1.5, shooting 80 projectiles a minute; operated by turning a crank, which automatically feeds loaded projectiles from the trough into the gun, and extracting the empty brass cartridge shells; only three men necessary, one to insert cartridges in the feed trough, one to aim and fire the gun, and one to carry cartridges from the ammunition chest; gun has automatic adjustment giving a lateral motion to the gun when firing; the operating mechanism is located in chamber at the breech, readily opened and easily accessible. Gun barrels are made of the best oil tempered steel, mounted on frame and trunnions, which absorbs greater part of the recoil. Range 3 miles, penetrating through one-inch metal plate at ½ mile; length of gun 46 inches; full length from muzzle to end of trail, 7 feet 2 inches; outside width of carriage 4 feet 10 inches; heighth of wheel, 45 inches; size of shield 41 x 64 inches; thickness 3-16 inch. Shield can be folded up and provides seats for the men. Weight of gun 225 kilos. Carriage is made of steel with tool compartments in the trail; with limber holding 200 rounds of ammunition. These fine guns are offered with 10,000 rounds of shells and canister shot, filled and fused, at bargain prices to those who are seriously interested.

1,000 Shell and Shrapnel projectiles for sale with Fletcher Naval 3-inch breech-loading steel landing rifles, all packed in original factory cases, filled and fused, ready for service.

U. S. Navy 12 Pounder Steel Rifle Cannon. Mounted on Navy Field Howitzer Carriages with either wood or iron wheels. Gun has two amunition chests, one on each side of gun. Front wheel serves in place of limber. Suitable for Cadets or Campaign Clubs to parade with. Serviceable gun for use, or an everlasting gun for lawn decoration, with iron wheels. Nothing to deteriorate.
Price $200,00. Shot, Shell, Grape, Cannister, $2.00 per round.

U. S. Civil War Army Cannon. Relics of Civil War battles; used by the Government after the war to ornament the Allegheny Arsenal grounds; sold to us at the disbandment of the arsenal. The history of these cannons given to us by Ordnance Sergeant at the arsenal was that they were Union Army guns and were captured by the Confederates, and spiked before being recaptured. For such relic guns, unmounted, spiked, our price is $150.00. For guns mounted on Army Field Carriage, with gunner's outfit, useful for firing occasional salutes or decorating lawn, our price is $300.00. If limber is wanted, the price is $75.00 extra; caisson, $95.00 extra.
U. S. Army Bronze Six Pounder Smooth Bore Cannon. Relic of war, 1861-65. Weight 880 pounds. In serviceable order. Mounted on Field Carriage. Complete with gunners' utensils. Price, $500.00. Handsome gun.

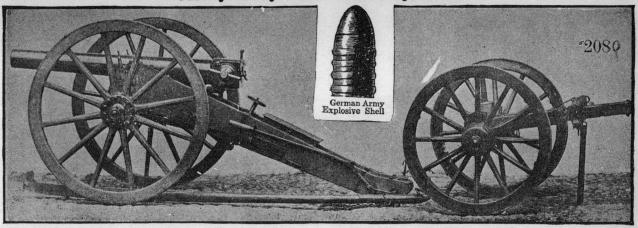

German Army Explosive Shell

2080

**2080. GERMAN ARMY FIELD CANNONS, THREE BATTERIES OF 6 CANNONS.** Each 3 2/10 inch bore. BREECH-LOADING STEEL LONG RANGE RIFLE GUNS mounted on FIELD CARRIAGES for use either in FIELD or SIEGE service, and mounted on NAVAL CARRIAGES, can be used either on WARSHIPS or in fortifications for COAST DEFENSE. Guns were made at ROYAL PRUSSIAN ARMORY SPANDAU and by the famous FRIED KRUPP at ESSEN. The German calibre is 7.85 C/M, the Range is upwards of FOUR MILES. Rifle cannons are as good as new, certified by the German War Department to the purchaser as being in "The very best serviceable order for war." Cannon barrel measures 6 feet 4 inches, average weight is about 1,000 pounds, outside diameter at the muzzle 5¾ inches, Trunnion and rear sights adjustable to 30 degrees with wind gauge. Engraved on the barrel German Eagle "Pro. Gloria Patria," with Emperor's monogram, "WR Eagle Ultima Ratio Regis." One turn of the handle opens the breech for quick insertion of shell or cannister shot with the economical always obtainable powder bag, fired by friction primer and lanyard. Extra gas check with each gun together with full outfit of gunner's tools and implements.

FIELD CARRIAGE has 5 foot wheels for quickly getting over rough roads, spokes are bolted into brass hubs, bolted tires, round axle, 5-foot tread, double trail, with gunner's implement steel box which also serves as seat, steel manœuvering bar attached to the carriage. Length from the muzzle of the gun to end of the trail 10 feet 4 inches.

LIMBER has 4-foot wheels, steel pintle for quickly attaching to the field carriage double whiffletrees, pole has hook for attaching lead teams.

HARNESS. We can furnish for either 2, 4, 6 or 8 horses, wheel and lead, either the American plan or German custom where gunners ride full horse. All new and complete as may be desired. canister sample shell $2.65

PROJECTILES. 2,000 rounds explosive shells, each weighing 9 pounds, 6½ inches long, 3⅛ inches diameter with four ribbed lead bands for expanding into the rifle grooves. All new and packed in German Army Ammunition Chests. With either the percussion fuses which explodes charge of powder in the shell on striking, or the old reliable time fuse which the gunner sets before firing and which is ignited by the firing charge and burns until the time set for exploding. We have over a million fuses timed from 5 to 30 seconds (1 to 4 miles), and which can be set to any fraction of time desired. We can furnish the mould for making explosive shells. Sample Shell $2.65

CANISTER SHOT. 2,400 rounds each weighing 8¼ pounds, 9 inches long, 3⅛ inches diameter, filled with 47 zinc balls, ⅞-inch diameter, packed in canister between 2 zinc plates with outside soft copper ring band for expanding into the rifling with wood sabot for attaching the powder bag firing charge. The entire outfit is stored at our Island Arsenal, all packed, the cannons in boxes, the carriages and limbers taken apart and wrapped in burlap bagging ready for immediate delivery to National War Departments at bargain prices. Five minutes' time for telephoning to our Island and delivery will begin—no red tape delay with our quick deliveries.

German Navy Breech-loading Siege Cannon, 5-inch bore. Wedge shaped breech block with copper ring gas check, mounted on naval carriage, all guaranteed by the German War Department to the purchaser as being in "The very best service for war." Gun is offered complete with gunner's outfit and 1,000 ROUNDS of explosive shells, each weighing 29 pounds, 9¼ inches long, 5-inch diameter, with 6 inch lead band with four ribbed projections for expanding in rifling, with percussion and time fuses at bargain prices to war departments. (Price of single shell free from powder to collectors is $4.85.)

**BANNERMAN'S ISLAND ARSENAL ON THE HUDSON.**
Francis Bannerman, of 501 Broadway, New York, is the present owner. "Dealer in Military Goods from Government Auctions" is the way he describes the goods he has for sale in the illustrated 372 page catalogue of which he claims to sell over 25,000 copies a year at 50 cents a copy. Military men in Europe, as well as America, keeping on file Bannerman's catalogue, not alone for the purchase of his goods, but for reference, as the author is recognized as an authority on ancient Military weapons. On this island he has erected storehouses, built after the style of Old Scotch baronial castles, utilizing in building the waste stone paving blocks in the worn out streets of New York City. In these castellated buildings are stored large quantities of guns, swords, cannons, ammunition, equipments — war material enough to fit out a government.
"From many a battlefield where cannons thundered,
Where charging squadrons swept the lines of steel;
From many a camp and port, dismantled, plundered
War's trophies numerous these stores reveal."
The small castle seen from the south is the summer home of the owner, appropriately called "Crag-inch," the Scotch for Rocky Island. Red flags and danger signs warn the stranger that landing is prohibited. European dealers in military goods, who are under government restrictions in the storage of explosives and who know of the freedom enjoyed by the owner of this Island, call him "King of Bannerman's Island." To distinguish this from his arsenals in other places, he calls it his "Island Arsenal." Asking if it was true, as stated in so many guide books of the Hudson, that the Island was alive with snakes, the owner said: "If ever there were snakes here it must have been before St. Patrick's time, for none have ever been seen."
No visitor to New York should fail to call at No. 501 Broadway and view the Bannerman free exhibit of war relics. The New York Herald says: "A numerous collection of ancient and modern arms, covering every country and age since the Crusades." Over a thousand different kinds of guns, of pistols, of swords; battle flags used in every war in America; no museum in the world exceeds in the number of exhibits, free to see; to buy if you wish, with some exceptions in case of weapons of a character that might endanger the public safety, when references as to identity and responsibility are required. Cash with the order is required from all, even Governments have to send Treasury Draft in advance.
The view from West Point north presents one of the most beautiful panoramic scenes on the surface of the earth, and the beholder does not wonder that the Indians were so impressed that they called the mountain after the name of their Great Spirit, Manitou; or that the grandeur and sublimity of the river and the mountains attracted and inspired so many of our great poets and literary men to reside within its borders.
N. P. Willis never seemed to tire of the grandeur of the scenes presented from the summits of the rocky crags, and much of his literary work was done on his frequent visits to the island. William Cullen Bryant's beautiful lines dated Cornwall, seem to refer to his visit to this island:
"All, save this little nook of land,
Circled with trees on which I stand;
All, save that line of hills which lie,
Suspended in the mimic sky."
—Hudson River Day Line Bulletin.

**U. S. ARMY BRONZE 6 POUNDER SMOOTH BORE CANNON.** Relic of war, 1861-65. Weight, 880 pounds. In serviceable order. Mounted on Field Carriage. Complete with gunners' utensils. Price, $500.00. Handsome gun.

**GERMAN NAVY NEW BREECH LOADING STEEL RIFLED CANNON,** 12.7 c/m, about 5-inch bore, with double wedge breech mechanism, with copper gas ring checks. Mounted on steel naval carriage, with elevating screw, manouvering bars, ratchet shifting levers. All in fine order. (See bottom of the page for front view of the carriage,) We can also mount this cannon on siege carriage if so desired. We offer this fine large powerful cannon at bargain price. Weight of the cannon two tons. Carriage weighs over a ton. We have a model sample shell, and can furnish as may be desired in a short time.

End view of steel carriage for German Navy, 5-inch bore, breech loading cannon.

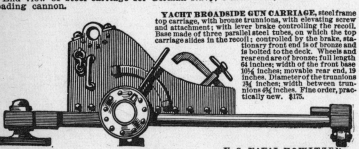

**YACHT BROADSIDE GUN CARRIAGE,** steel frame top carriage, with bronze trunnions, with elevating screw and attachment; with lever brake controlling the recoil. Base made of three parallel steel tubes, on which the top carriage slides in the recoil; controlled by the brake, stationary front end is of bronze and is bolted to the deck. Wheels and rear end are of bronze; full length 64 inches; width of the front base 10½ inches; movable rear end, 19 inches. Diameter of the trunnions 1¾ inches; width between trunnions 4¾ inches. Fine order, practically new. $175.

**U. S. NAVAL HOWITZER,** mounted on field carriage, with ammunition chest, used in launch on broadside carriage, or for operating on land, mounted on field carriage. Gun is of medium size, 4½ feet long, made of steel; weight 750 lbs. Suitable for artillery company or decorating lawn. This type of cannon is now used at the navy yards for decorating. We offer the gun complete, in second-hand order, with 50 powder bags, 50 primers, with lanyard. thumb stall, gunner's haversack, tube pouch, sponge rammer, sponge bucket, with U. S. Navy Ordnance instruction book, in which found illustration and drill manual showing stations and duties of the twelve men required to form the gun crew. We can furnise projectiles if desired. Our bargain price for the outfit, $185.00.

FIG. 234.

The Captain of the "Montezuma" was telling his boys about the great difference in the people of Ireland, how that the north of Ireland, the Province of Ulster, a little tract of about 75 miles square, had furnished from its descendents nine Presidents and Vice-Presidents to the United States, that the people were a mixed race, composed of the native Irish with Scotch colonists, who settled in the North of Ireland after Cromwell's Irish campaign, together with French Huguenots, who were brought to Ireland to teach the Irish the linen industry, and how their intermarriage had produced such an intelligent, progressive people, when he was interrupted by one of his young hopefuls, remarking that it was a *sort of Irish stew.*

G.SP.12.

No. 1521

**1521. 600 KRUPP EXPLOSIVE SHELLS FOR BREECH LOADING CANNON.** Length 7½ inches, diameter 3⅝ inches, 4¾ lead band with 4 rings for taking the rifling. With each shell we can furnish either U. S. Ordnance time fuse from 5 to 25 seconds, or Krupp percussion fuse, enclosed in brass case, with exploding primer, causing the shell to explode on striking. Also with zinc screw safety cap. These shells are fired with Krupp cannon. To collectors we can furnish sample shell at **$3.00** each.

**1522. KRUPP EXPLOSIVE SHELL,** for breech loading cannon. Length 15½ inches, diameter 5 inches, lead band 9½ inches, with 4 enlarged ring bands for taking the rifling. Furnished with either light regulation U. S. Ordnance time fuse, or Krupp percussion fuse, which causes the shell to explode on striking. Price on application.

**1740. U. S. NAVY CANNON DRILL CARTRIDGE** for 1 pounder, rapid firing cannon. Wood case contains 45 cal. steel rifle barrel 9 inches long. Chambered to take 500 grain, centre fire, rifled ball cartridge, with brass head and nose cap. Used in practice gun firing pointing. The firing pin of the cannon strikes the primer of the cartridge, and saves the immense cost of firing the regular service cannon projectile. In good serviceable order. Barrel can be easily dismounted and used for other purposes if desired. Cost price upwards of $15.00 each. Our bargain price **$4.75.**

**GATLING MACHINE GUN CAISSONS** in good serviceable order. Copper covers on the ammunition chests. Offered with the Gatling Guns and Limbers.

**TWO EXPERIMENTAL STEEL BREECH-LOADING CANNONS,** cost the U. S. upward of $20,000; one rifled 3-inch bore, other one is 12-pounder smooth bore, unmounted, good as new. $250.00 each.

**COLLECTION 10 SHOT AND SHELL GAUGES,** mostly for spherical projectiles now obsolete. $25.00.

**U. S. NAVY SHOT TONGS,** for spherical and conical projectiles. $3.00 each.

**U. S. ARMY 8-INCH GRAPE SHOT.** Make fine decoration for gate posts. Consist of a number of 4-inch iron balls, held in place on stand by circle of rings; weight 80 lbs. $6.50.

**POWDER MEASURE.** Large bronze powder measure used at Morro Castle to measure charge for antique mortars; is marked "Decalitro de Maltabouche Valencia"; shot went through one side and made deep indentation on the opposite side. This rare relic came from Santiago in cargo of old brass; weight 20 lbs., 10 inches across top, 10 inches deep. $100.00.

**FR. KRUPP 9 c/m BREECH LOADING STEEL CANNON,** practically new, with wedge breech block, fired with friction primer. This fine gun is mounted on steel carriage, Marsilly type, with elevating screw. Offered with powder bags, friction primers, sponge, rammer and gunner's implements. Ready for immediate delivery, at bargain price, to those interested.

Front view of Steel Carriage with German Navy 5-inch Heavy Rifled Cannon.

# CANNONS, ETC.

**U. S. Artillery Folding Canvas Water Bucket,** made at the Government Rock Island Arsenal; of heavy drab color water repelling canvas; 12 inches high, 11 inches in diameter, weighs 26 ounces; used, good serviceable order; Price, 85 cents each.

**Bronze Yacht Cannon,** Breechloading, from the Yacht "White Heather", (Scotch for Good Luck). Yates patent breech mechanism, opened by under-lever, mounted on handsome rose wood carriage; shoots the U. M. C. 2⅛ diameter brass shell; length of gun 3 feet; weight, complete, upwards of 200 pounds: offered with 10 empty primed brass shells, with 1000 primers. Price $150.00.

**Bronze Cannon,** mounted on small size U. S. Naval Field Carriage, with gunner's outfit. Cannon is 3¼ feet long, 2¾-inch bore; weight about 150 pounds. Carriage is in fine order; wrought-iron trail; bronze mountings; good, serviceable gun. Price, $150.00.

**U. S. ARMY CANNON SPONGE COVERS,** for sizes up to 12-pounders, $1.50 each; other sizes, price upon application.

**U. S. NAVY WOOD CARRIAGES.** For 12-pounder smooth bore, $65.00; for 20-pounder rifle, $100.00; for 30-pounder rifle, $150.00; for 32-pounder smooth bore, $150.00; for 42-pounder, smooth bore, $150.00; for 8-inch smooth bore, $150.00.

**YACHT GUN CARRIAGE,** rosewood, on 4 wheels. Almost new. Price $25.00.

**32-Pounder Smooth-Bore Cannon** in good serviceable order, mounted on navy carriage with bronze trimmings, weight 6,000 lbs. From the Wabash. Price $850.00.

**TWO BULLETS** that met in mid air, found on the battlefield of Chickamauga. Price $10.00.

**2244-A. Brass Cannon** unmounted, made from old Revolutionary War relics, contributed by Philadelphia citizens to Sons of Veterans' Camp. The S. O. V. Camp finally disbanded and their guns were sold at public auction; length 3 feet; bore 1½ inch; weight 150 pounds, offered unmounted for $72.00.

**2268. U. S. Navy Breech-loading Rifled Steel Cannon;** mounted on Naval steel carriage; used on board of U. S. S. Revenue Cutter; length of gun 5 feet; weight 487 pounds; three inch bore, can be fired with powder bag, which makes it very desirable as an economical breech-loading saluting gun as well as serviceable for war, bronze; mountings. Our artist has drawn the gun with the top carriage run back so as to show the slide, which takes up the recoil or jump. Price $385.00.

**U. S. Artillery No. 8 Field Gun Bucket,** made of wrought iron, used for holding grease for oiling the axles. No. 9 for holding water to wet the cannon sponge. Height is 7 and 9 inches. Diameter 9 and 7 inches. Make handsome souvenir flower pots. Price, $2.00 each. We have 1,000 in stock.

No. 8

No. 9

**4 U. S. NAVY 12 POUNDER STEEL RIFLE CANNONS.** Almost new guns. Mounted on Navy Field Howitzer Carriages with either wood or iron wheels. Gun has two ammunition chests, one on each side of gun. Front wheel serves in place of limber. Suitable for Cadets or Campaign Clubs to parade with. Serviceable gun for use, or an everlasting gun for lawn decoration with iron wheels. Nothing to deteriorate. Price, $200.00. Shot. Shell. Grape Canister. $2.00 per pound.

**No. 1. Collection of Relic Spanish War Cannon Shot** with the brass cases. As shown in photo. Size of case is 21½x15½ inches. Price for the collection cleaned and polished, $35.00.

**2208. Antique Model Minature Brass Cannon,** on field carriage, full length 10 inches; width 9 inches; length of gun 19 inches; ⅝ths inch bore; all of polished brass except the axle, which is of iron; serviceable order, has been proved at the British Government Proof House; handsome model, price $20.00.

**2421. Breech-loading Iron Cannon**-rifled barrel; one inch bore, early model. European Machine Gun; 40 inches long; bolt action, with bolts for fastening to frame. Price $20.00.

**U. S. A. OFFICERS' HAND-BOOK, AR-TILLERY 3-INCH FIELD GUN,** with instruction for its care. 32 illustrated plates, 1911 edition. 184 pages. 6x9 inches. Price $1.00.

**U. S. A. VICKER'S MAXIM DESCRIPTIVE HANDBOOK,** 2.95 inch Mountain Gun, 27 plates. Size, 6x9 inches. Edition of 1904. Price, 95 cents each.

**UNION REPEATING GUN,** called by soldiers at siege of Petersburg, "The Coffee-Mill"; unmounted. Valuable as relic only. Price, $350.00.

**GATLING GUN CAISSON,** with limber in fine order, with poles, etc. Price $150.00.

**2247. Ancient Bronze Cannon;** beautifully ornamented in relief with Arabic inscriptions. The metal when struck rings out like a bell, which contains silver composition; weight 270 pounds; length 6 feet; diameter of the bore, 2¼ inches. Price $350.00.

**No. 12. Old Time U. S. Navy Quill cannon-primer.** Relic. $3.00.

**No. 3. Ancient Pattern U. S. Artillery Fuse Plug,** made of wood, inserted in the mouth of bomb shell with time fuse, ignited by the charge and bursting at timed distance. Price, with time fuse, 50 cents.

**No. 6000. U. S. ARTILLERY MOGUL SPRINGS,** for relieving strain in starting. Can be used for towing autos, or other heavy work. Attached by any connecting shackle. Bargain price, $1.95 per pair.

**No. 16. U. S. Army Metal Jack Screws.** In good serviceable order, with slot for quickly placing in position; brass bound, made in the best manner, as per U. S. Army requirements. Not to be considered with the made-to-sell cheap jack screws in the market. In good second hand serviceable order. Price, $1.75 each.

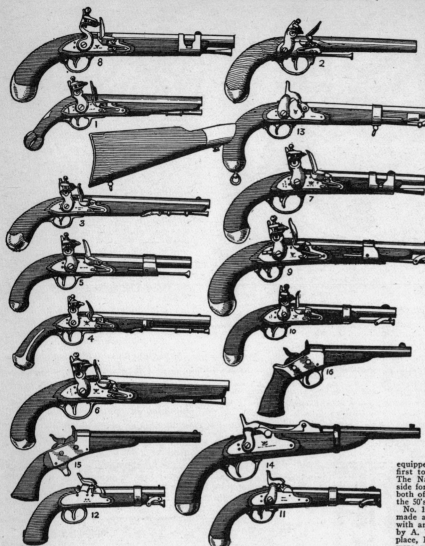

No. 1. RAPPAHANNOCK FORGE FLINTLOCK PISTOL. Date, 1775. The first authentic American pistol, the lock, however, being imported from England. The forge, established by an act of the Virginia legislature, was destroyed in the early days of the Revolutionary War.

No. 2. NORTH AND CHENEY FLINTLOCK PISTOL. Earliest known of the famous North pistols. Copied from the French army pistol of 1777. Made at Berlin, Conn., in 1794. Caliber .69. The frame is brass and the only wood on the weapon being the two grips of the handle. Rare.

No. 3. HENRY DERINGER FLINTLOCK PISTOL. Army type. Made in Philadelphia. This represents the style of pistol made for the government at the various private armories in the east, especially Pennsylvania. Deringer lived until 1868 and was the manufacturer of the famous pistol which bore his name, one of which was used by Booth to assassinate President Lincoln. This Deringer flintlock supposed to have been used in War of 1812.

No. 4. U. S. HARPER'S FERRY FLINTLOCK PISTOL, 1804, caliber .54. The barrel is rifled and it is the earliest military pistol made by our government. These pistols were made to conform to the design of the rifles of the same date made at the same armory. Note the half stock, rib under barrel and brass tipped ramrod. Highly prized by collectors for their beautiful lines and balance.

No. 5. VALLEY FORGE (Pa.) FLINTLOCK PISTOL. About 1809-10. Made in several models and copied from the French model of 1805. Brass mounted. Caliber .69. Very rare.

No. 6. NORTH "BERLIN" FLINTLOCK PISTOL. Made in several styles by S. North under contracts dating from 1798 to 1812. Specimens have been found with eight and ten-inch barrels, pin fastened as illustration. Also nine-inch barrel with double band as on the 1816 model. All are caliber .69. No collection is complete without a specimen of this product of Simeon North's famous Berlin armory.

No. 7. NORTH, MODEL 1816, FLINTLOCK PISTOL. Made in two calibers, .54 and .69, smooth bore. These are the most familiar of the early types and are quite common even today. In the early 50's many were altered to use percussion caps, being brought up to date by the addition of swivel ramrods. Intended for use of mounted troops and issued in pairs.

No. 8. U. S. SPRINGFIELD MODEL 1818 FLINTLOCK PISTOL. Caliber .69. Barrel is nearly twelve inches long. 1,000 made, 1818-19. The locks were imported from England, being made by Dale, his name, however, upon request, was stamped upon the inside of the plate. Note the goose-neck hammer, a rare thing on an American weapon. These pistols are very rare.

No. 9. NORTH, MODEL 1819, ARMY AND NAVY FLINTLOCK PISTOL. Caliber .54. The first to be equipped with a safety catch in rear of the hammer. Also the first to have the rod attached by a swivel. Ten inch barrel. The Navy pattern was shorter and had a hook on the left side for insertion in the belt. Also made by Evans and Henry, both of Pennsylvania. Many were converted to percussion in the 50's.

No. 10. U. S. FLINTLOCK PISTOL. Model 1836. The last made and the first to have a fence on the pan. Caliber .54 with an eight and one-half inch barrel. Made under contract by A. Waters at Milbury, Mass., A. H. Waters & Co., same place, R. Johnson at Middletown, Conn. The original models were made at Springfield Armory. Made until 1844. Many converted to percussion in the 50's.

No. 11. U. S. PERCUSSION PISTOL. Model 1842. Very similar to the 1836 Flintlock in appearance. Made by H. Aston at Middletown, Conn., I. N. Johnson also at Middletown, Springfield Armory, and the rarest of the lot at the Palmetto Armory, "Wm. Glaze & Co.," Columbia, South Carolina. The original pattern pistols, although designated as Model 1842, were not made until 1844 and issued from Springfield Armory early in 1845. The Navy model had an anchor stamped at the rear end of the barrel. Caliber is .54.

No. 12. U. S. NAVY PISTOL. Model of 1843. Caliber .54. Brass mounted. These are the first percussion pistols issued as they appeared prior to the Model 42. The hammer is on the inside of the lock plate and the only arm so made, as it was thought they would function better in the belts of the sailors than with the outside hammer. Made by N. P. Ames at Springfield, Mass., and Deringer at Philadelphia. They are found both rifled and smooth bore.

No. 13. U. S. SPRINGFIELD, MODEL 1855, PISTOL CARBINE. Caliber .58. First issued in 1856 to take the place of the Model 1842 Musketoons, the manufacture of which was stopped at that time. Equipped with the famous Maynard primer. The shoulder stock is detachable. Pistol has a 12-inch barrel and is 3½ pounds in weight. A few of these were made at Harper's Ferry Armory. They were intended to use but one-half the quantity of primers in the Maynard magazine that the Model '55 Rifle used, as the lock and its parts were smaller. When originally designed this pistol was intended to have a 10-inch barrel and no shoulder stock.

No. 14. U. S. SPRINGFIELD BREECH-LOADING PISTOL. Caliber .50. Although none of this particular model was ever issued, it is included to show what some experts in the ordnance department considered suitable weapons for our soldiers in spite of the fact that revolvers were common in those days. This arm has a regulation musket lock of 1868 with the barrel shortened and lightened. It is difficult to see how a man could hold this in one hand and fire it without personal injury. It was 18½ inches over all and weighed 5 pounds.

No. 15. REMINGTON NAVY BREECH-LOADING PISTOL. Caliber .50. Model of 1867. Barrel is 8½ inches long. Also made with 7-inch barrel and a trigger-guard. The arm shown is one of the rarest of pistols.

No. 16. REMINGTON ARMY. Caliber .50. Model of 1871, breech-loading pistol. Barrel is 8 inches long. These pistols are famous for their wonderful shooting qualities and balance.

## The Evolution of the Bolt-action Rifle in the U.S. Service

The parent of all bolt-action arms was the Needle-gun of Nicholas Dreyse, invented in 1838. It was adopted by Prussia in 1841 and used with success in the wars of 1848-1866 and 1871. A paper cartridge was used. The first bolt action rifle used by the U. S. was the GREENE, invented by J. D. Greene, an Army officer, in 1857. This weapon had a bolt handle at the extreme rear, same being released by pressing down a spring catch on the tang. It was a percussion arm with the nipple underneath with a hammer of peculiar design. The cartridge had the bullet in the rear. A number of these were used in the Civil War as was also the PALMER action. This was the first system to employ a metallic cartridge. The arm had an ordinary side lock and hammer. The next rifle of this type was the Ward-Burton invented in 1869 and adopted and manufactured by the government in 1870. This arm was caliber .50 and took a center fire cartridge. It was the first bolt gun to have the firing pin in the bolt.

The Ward-Burton system was considered dangerous by the troops and was in use but a short time. About this time a number of the Merrill alterations were used by some of the states. This arm was caliber .58, the bolt having a hammer in the rear.

In 1873 a board of officers, convened to test and adopt a breech loading system for the Army, had twelve bolt action rifles submitted to them but adopted the familiar 1873 model Springfield, a rifle with a swinging breech block. Another board, 1877, had eight bolt-action systems submitted and adopted one, the Hotchkiss, the first bolt magazine arm. This rifle was followed in 1880 by the Lee and Remington-Keene. In 1882 another board tested eight different bolt systems and adopted the Chaffee-Reece and an improved Hotchkiss, both magazine rifles.

1885 saw the improved Lee in use in the Navy, the first to have the bolt handle turned down close to the stock, in use until 1900 in various branches of the service.

The Krag Jorgensen was the next arm of this type to be adopted, being our first small caliber weapon, caliber .30, and the handle made to lie close to the stock. There were 34 systems tested in 1892 and but two were not of the bolt action type.

The Navy decided in 1895 to use the Lee Straight-Pull, a caliber .23 magazine rifle with the familiar Lee magazine not detachable. The same year the Army purchased a quantity of the Model 1895 Winchester rifles. This was a bolt action arm but manipulated by an under lever. It was not a success and was soon discarded. Various models of the Krag were issued, 1892-1900, when an arm was tested to take the caliber .30 cartridge, but with the Lee magazine and an improved Mauser bolt, it was not approved.

In 1901 what is now known as the Model 1903 first appeared, having a 30-inch barrel and a ramrod bayonet.

VIEW IN OUR ORDNANCE YARD, BROOKLYN, N. Y.

Note Cannons No. 117 and 340 marked "Hartford." These two cannons, which are 9-inch smooth bores and weigh over 9,000 pounds each, are vouched for by U. S. Navy Department as having been part of the battery of the U. S. Frigate Hartford, under Admiral Farragut at the battles of New Orleans and Mobile Bay. See page 44 for illustration of the battle showing these guns in action. Price, $1,250 each. Also Guns No. 176, 177, the only 2 Rifled Cannons on the U. S. Frigate Brooklyn at the battles of New Orleans and Mobile Bay, which fired 100-lb. rifle shot. These guns were made at Parrot Foundry, Cold Spring, N. Y.; they weigh nearly 10,000 lbs. each, and are vouched for by letter of Admiral Sampson while Chief of Ordnance, U. S. N., as bearing record that these rifled cannons formed part of the battery of the old Civil War Frigate Brooklyn. These Rifles are for sale at $1,250 each. Note also the 20 and 80 pounder Parrot Breech-loading Rifle Cannons, of which we will give particulars and prices to intending purchasers. Note also the boxes of cannon shot and shell: the Limber Chests, Cannon Carriage, etc.

UNION BATTERY GOING INTO ACTION CIVIL WAR PERIOD 1861-1865.

"When banners are wav-
ing,
And lances a pushing;
When captains are shout-
ing,
And war horses rush-
ing;
When cannons are roar-
ing,
And hot bullets flying,
He that would honor win
Must not fear dying."

No. 2. 12 COLT'S AUTOMATIC, caliber 30, Rapid Fire Machine Gun Ammunition Boxes. Steel frame, covered with russet leather; with swivel locking clasp; with brass fastener; with compartments for holding the ammunition. In good as new order. Price, $4.50 each.

No. 11. ARCHIBALD PATENT GUN CARRIAGE WHEELS, height is nearly 5 ft. We have 200. We now offer to wheelwright at bargain price the lot minus one part of the axle box. We furnish pattern casting; wheels originally cost $20 each. Our price as described $3 each the lot.

U. S. A. ARTILLERY STEEL SNAP COLLARS, adjustable, fitted with tugs for traces. Price, $3.90 each.

Calibre 45 Gatling Gun Feed Cases, complete, in fine order, like new; for use or decoration, $2.75 each.

No. 4. U. S. Army Target Plates, for use in armory at target practice. Made of heavy, tough metal, ¾-inch thick, 30 inches high, 20½ inches wide. The bull's eye consists of a hole in the center, with an 8-inch bell. Weighs upwards of 100 pounds. Splendid for indoor practice and cadet schools. Price, $3.85 each.

U. S. ARMY MORTAR CANNON. 8-inch bore; made of old-time cast-iron gun metal. Length of cannon, about 3 feet; weight, over 1,200 pounds. Mounted on wrought-iron carriage weighing over 900 pounds; complete as per illustration. Handsome ornament that will stand all kinds of weather, being made of iron; nothing to deteriorate; with gunner's utensils, ready for firing salutes; from Pittsburg Arsenal, Pa. Price, $350.00.

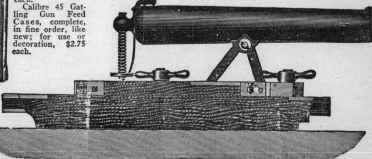

12 Pounder U. S. Navy Steel, Muzzle-Loading Rifled Cannon, mounted on U. S. N. Broadside Carriage. Gun is of forged steel; Wiard's patent; throws a 12-pound shot; bore is about 4 inches; length, 4½ feet; weight, about 750 pounds. Carriage is the Civil War regulation carriage with elevating screw, compressor slide screws, with bronze fittings; in good, serviceable order. Price, $300. Shot, Shell, Grape or Canister or Case Shot to fit these guns. Price, $1.75 each.

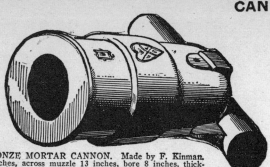

**1816. BRONZE MORTAR CANNON.** Made by F. Kinman. Length 23 inches, across muzzle 13 inches, bore 8 inches, thickness of metal at the muzzle 2½ inches, length of trunnions 23 inches, diameter 5 inches. Has British East India Co. heart-shaped monogram cast on the gun, with letters V. E. I. C. surmounted with figure 4; also weight, 6 cwt., 0 quarter 4 pounds (676 pounds). In fine order. Handsome, ornamental old relic. Price, $3.85.

Before the new charter went into effect consolidating the city of Brooklyn with New York, it was our good fortune to obtain at one of the naval auction sales a pair of large rifled cannons, weighing upward of about 10,000 pounds each, and one smooth bore cannon which weighed over 9,000 pounds and fired a nine inch shot—historical cannon that U. S. Navy records vouched for as having formed part of the battery of the old Civil War Frigate Brooklyn in the world-renowned battle under Farragut at New Orleans and Mobile Bay. A few years previous the old ship had been sold and broken up for the scrap metal, and there was nothing left to commemorate. Having resided in Brooklyn since 1858, the year the Brooklyn was built, we thought it would be fitting to have placed at the soldiers' monument, at the entrance to the park, a pair of these old cannons, suitably mounted on iron carriages with bronze fittings, etc., and so made offer to the mayor of the city, offering to present and mount the guns as a free gift. About a month after our offer was made, we received answer that the gift was declined, as the city had no place for them. These historical cannons are now for sale at $1,200 each.

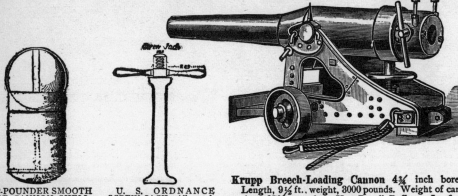

**Five-inch Brass Shell Case**, used on board U. S. S. Brooklyn in battle of Santiago de Cuba on July 3, 1898; from officer on the Brooklyn during the fight. Name given to purchaser. Shell is 5 inches in diameter. stands 2 feet high; polished brass. Price, $18.00.

Also **6-pounder Polished Brass Shell Case**, same ship, used at battle of Santiago, July 3, 1898. Price, $8.75.

Also **1-pounder Hotchkiss Shell Case**, same ship, same battle. Price, $5.00.

Old Revolutionary War Period Carronade from Pittsburg Arsenal Sale, we sold to Mr. Pell of N. Y. City who used it with other cannon from us in restoring the famous Fort Ticonderoga in N. Y. State.

Old 1812 Period 6-pounder small cannon; 4½ feet long; weight about 700 pounds; from Pittsburg arsenal; no doubt mounted on the old Fort Duquesne. Price on field carriage, $220.00.

**12-POUNDER SMOOTH BORE CANNON SHELL.** Fitted to sabot. Charge of powder in bag can be furnished if desired. Price of shell attached to sabot. Each, $1.50.

**U. S. ORDNANCE SCREW JACK.** All metal, with brass screw box, in 2nd hand serviceable order, from the late Government Arsenal fire sale. Price, $1.85.

**Krupp Breech-Loading Cannon** 4¾ inch bore. Length, 9½ ft., weight, 3000 pounds. Weight of carriage 2700 pounds. Has Recoil Buffer. In fine order, equal to new. Now in Europe. Ready for quick delivery. Price upon application for gun with projectiles.

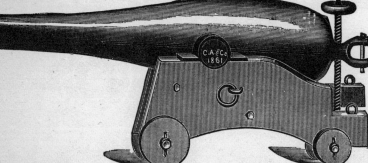

**U. S. Navy Muzzle Loading Rifle Cannon**, (Dahlgren Patent.) Shoots 12-Pounder Shot. In serviceable order. Mounted on Navy Carriage. Gunners implements. 20 Powder Bags, 50 Primers go with the gun. Length, 5 feet, weight, 1000 pounds, bore, 4 inches. Price, $1250.00.

**Old-Time U. S. Navy 12-Pounder Smooth Bore Cannon**, for saluting purposes. Mounted on Ship Carriage. Complete with gunner's implements. 20 Powder Bags, 50 Cannon Primers. Handsome ornament for lawn; useful for firing salutes. Weight, 900 pounds; bore, 4 inches. Price, $200.00.

**VICKERS - MAXIM AUTOMATIC MACHINE GUNS,** Cal. 30, complete with Tripod and Equipment. This is the type used by U. S. Army. We have Cartridges in larger quantities.

**COLT AUTOMATIC MACHINE GUNS,** Cal. 30, with Tripod and full Equipment. U. S. Army pattern. Large stock of Cartridges to fit.

Please note that we quote on these and other war materials only to responsible parties, and subject to approval of U. S. Government.

**2 U. S. Navy 9 inch Smooth Bore Muzzle Loading Cannon.** Vouched for by U. S. Navy Department, (Admiral Sampson), as having been part of the battery on board the U. S. S. Frigate Brooklyn, during the Civil War engagements at New Orleans and Mobile Bay Battles. Navy records show that these guns have been fired about 500 times. Weight, 9000 pounds. Rare and valuable authenticated relics. Mounted on Iron Carriages. Complete with gunners implements. Price, $1,250 each.

**2 U. S. Navy 100 Pounder Parrot Rifles.** The heaviest rifles on board the old Frigate Brooklyn during the Civil War, taking part in engagements at New Orleans Forts and Mobile Bay. Weighs nearly 10,000 pounds. Mounted on iron carriages. Price, $1,250 each. Shot and Shell furnished for these guns $6.00 each.

**45-500 GOVERNMENT SMOKELESS**

1,200,000 Smokeless Powder Machine Gun Ball Cartridges, for use in the Calibre 45 U.S.A. Gatling and Lowell Machine guns: 500 grain lead bullet; range upwards of 2 miles; all new in the original paper cartoons, 20 cartridges each, 50 cartoons in each wood case of 1,000 cartridges. sold only by reason of change of calibre: made by U.M.C. Cartridge Company under contract for the U. S. Government.

**45 GOVERNMENT BLANK SMOKELESS**

45 Calibre Smokeless Powder Blanks, altered from ball cartridges, made by the U. M. C. Cartridge Company for the U. S. Army.

**250 U. S. A. RAPID FIRE MACHINE GUNS;** famous Colts Gatlings, with 8,000,000 rounds of ball cartridges; all models U. S. calibre 45 service guns, sold on account of change in regulation. Many of the guns are New, never out of the factory chests. We can offer this lot of fine recent regulation U. S. Army Machine Guns, ALL MODELS WITH THEIR OUTFITS. ALL STYLES OF FEED, WITH SPARE PARTS; IN SERVICEABLE SURE FIRE ORDER, MOUNTED ON FIELD CARRIAGES, TRIPODS, CAVALRY CARTS OR CASEMENTS, WITH LIMBERS AND AMMUNITION CHESTS, BOTH IN WOOD AND IN STEEL; WITH HARNESS, SHIELDS, ETC; GREAT BARGAIN PRICES TO ANY GOVERNMENT WAR DEPARTMENT DESIRING TO EQUIP THEIR ARMY WITH A FIRST-CLASS MACHINE GUN OUTFIT. WE HAVE FOR SALE NEARLY THE WHOLE U. S. A. ENTIRE OUTFIT OF 45 CALIBRE MACHINE GUNS.

**4 Lowell Battery Machine Guns, New.** The four barrels are arranged in circle, firing one barrel at a time at the rate of 600 shots a minute. When the barrel gets heated it can by, by a simple movement, be moved aside and another barrel brought into action, thus giving time for the barrel heated in firing to cool off. The working parts are strong and simple, and can be dismounted in a few seconds. Gun can be operated by men of ordinary capacity without previous extensive training. Loaded cartridges when inserted into the hopper are automatically loaded into the gun, fired, and the empty shell extracted, all by the simple operation of turning the crank. Two men can work and fire steadily 400 shots per minute; with a third man to help in feeding, 600 shots per minute can be fired continuously. Gun is mounted on new improved carriage, with swivel yoke that allows the gun to be turned into any position without moving the carriage. The chests on each carriage, in easy reach of gunner's will, contain 4,000 cartridges. These new guns have passed the U. S. Army officers inspection, are still in the original factory cases, and are offered at bargain prices with either black or smokeless powder ball cartridges at less than half the manufacturer's price.

**FOR PACK SADDLE MACHINE GUN OUTFITS,** see illustration and description, page 19.

**8 U. S. Naval Deck Mounts** for Machine guns, made of wrought iron, strongly braced and bolted top measure 9 1-2 by 10 inches bottom 23 by 24 inches weight 100 pounds Swivel yokes and mounts with machine guns at bargain prices.

**Colt's Brass Cover-ed Machine Gun,** mounted on Naval style Cage Deck stand; for use on board gun boats, yachts or fortifications; with yoke, which turns in any desired direction, elevating adjustment, illustrations shows the height of steel stand 34 inches full length from top of gun, 48 inches, length of gun 36 inches. Naval cage stands can be furnished in either polished brass or steel in any desired heighth. Handsome, serviceable outfit; offered with blank or ball cartridges at bargain prices.

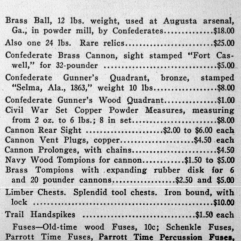

**U. S. A. Tripod,** with 10 barrel short Gatling, barrel encased in brass frame: (looks like brass cannon), swivel yoke with attachment with elevating screw.

**U. S. A. Machine Gun Harness;** practically new: for sale with gun outfits at bargain price.

Brass Ball, 12 lbs. weight, used at Augusta arsenal, Ga., in powder mill, by Confederates ............$18.00
Also one 24 lbs. Rare relics ........................$25.00
Confederate Brass Cannon, sight stamped "Fort Caswell," for 32-pounder ................................$5.00
Confederate Gunner's Quadrant, bronze, stamped "Selma, Ala., 1863," weight 10 lbs .................$8.00
Confederate Gunner's Wood Quadrant...............$1.00
Civil War Set Copper Powder Measures, measuring from 2 oz. to 6 lbs.; 8 in set........................$8.00
Cannon Rear Sight ......................$2.00 to $6.00 each
Cannon Vent Plugs, copper.....................$4.50 each
Cannon Prolonges, with chains........................$4.50
Navy Wood Tompions for cannon...........$1.50 to $5.00
Brass Tompions with expanding rubber disk for 6 and 20 pounder cannons..................$2.50 and $5.00
Limber Chests. Splendid tool chests. Iron bound, with lock ...................................................$10.00
Trail Handspikes ........................$1.50 each
Fuses—Old-time wood Fuses, 10c; Schenkle Fuses, Parrott Time Fuses, **Parrott Time Percussion Fuses,** Boerman Time Fuses, Hotchkiss Percussion Fuses.

A party called in our store one day and offered to sell us an old tattered and worn American flag, which, he claimed, his grandfather had found floating in the waters of Lake Erie the day after Commodore Perry's victory, September 13, 1813. The flag at first glance seemingly confirmed his claim, but upon further examination we found the stripes were SEWED BY MACHINE and that the heading on the flag lacked the old-time hand-made grommet holes and was fitted with BRASS GROMMETS, stamped "PATENTED, 1884."

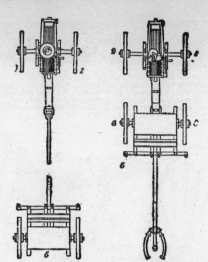

Illustrations showing stations of the 5 men forming Rapid Fire gun squad, both in action and the march.

**25 U. S. Army Fortification Rapid Fire Machine Guns.** New, shooting one inch cartridge, size as shown in illustration. We have these guns with 6 also with 10 barrels. Gatling's invention, made at the Colt's Armory. New guns, offered mounted on good second hand army field carriage, fitted with gunners accessories, with ball or shrapnel cartridge. Guns are still in original factory cases, new, never used. Can be mounted for use in fortifications, for flank defense. Complete with feed cases. Rapidity, 200 large size balls a minute, by simply turning the crank. Each barrel has its own independent lock and firing mechanism. Bargain price quoted upon application.

We have a number of 1 inch Gatling machine guns, that are in unserviceable order *rusty*. We can offer these guns, mounted on field carriage, for lawn decoration, at bargain prices.

BRONZE CAN-NON, 3¼-inch bore, 4 feet long, weight 345 lbs.; smooth bore. Good, serviceable order—ARMY PATTERN. Offered unmounted. Price, $150.

10 Calibre 50 Colt's Gatling Machine Gun, 6 revolving barrels, shooting ½ inch lead bullets at rate of upwards of 400 a minute. Mounted on field carriage with 2 ammunition boxes attached. All in serviceable order; used a short time. Complete with feed cases. Price upon application.

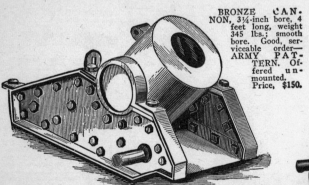

**4 U. S. ARMY MORTAR CANNONS,** 10-inch bore, mounted on iron carriage bed. Weight of gun, 1,900 lbs.; carriage, weight about 1,200 lbs.; height, 27 inches; length 5 feet; length of gun, 29 inches; outside diameter, 19½ inches; length of carriage about 4 feet. Used and now at Military State Sea Coast camp grounds, at Fort Pitt, N. J., 1863. Price $465.00 each.

**2 10-INCH RODMAN CANNONS,** smooth bores. Mounted on wrought iron carriage with chassis at Military Sea Coast camp.

GUN is 120 inches length of bore. Full length, 136 inches; outside muzzle diameter, 16 inches; outside diameter at the breech, 32 inches. Weight of gun, 15,000 lbs.

TOP CARRIAGE. Length, 75 inches; weight, 1,900 lbs.

CHASSIS. Length, 173 inches; weight (exclusive of circular tracks), 3,000 lbs. Each gun with carriage and outfit weighs a total of 20,000 lbs.

Bargain prices quoted to those interested.

BATTERY OF 2 HOTCHKISS ONE-POUNDER BREECH LOADING GUNS, mounted in field carriages with limber and ammunition chests or on Naval Pedestal Mounts with quantity of shell and canister shot. All in fine serviceable order, offered at Bargain Price, subject to inspection and testing.

BRONZE CANNON FROM COMMODORE ELBRIDGE T. GERRY'S YACHT ELECTRA, used for many years in firing the signal gun for starting the International Yacht Races off New York Harbor. Bore, 2¾ inches; length, 38½ inches; mounted on four-wheel mahogany carriage; 30 inches long, 21 inches high; heavy rubber tires on the wheels; bronze mountings. All in fine polished serviceable order. Price, $130.00.

MOUNTAIN HOWITZER OR GATLING GUN PACK HORSE EQUIPMENT, consisting of saddle with frame for holding the cannon, with collar, breeching, bridle, etc. All in good as new order used only a few times. Bargain price quoted upon application.

View of Derrick Lighter taking 6-inch naval cannon from our Island dock for delivery to U. S. Government for use in World War.

**U. S. ARMY SMOOTH BORE STEEL CANNON.** Altered to short 6 pounder round shot, taking the place of the 6 pounder cast iron cannons (which have all been sold). These fine guns are superior in strength, neater in appearance and nearly 200 pounds lighter in weight. They are offered mounted on Army Field Carriage with Rammer, Sponge and Gunner's outfit at $300.00 each.

**U. S. NAVY FRIGATE WABASH CIVIL WAR CANNON.** 8 inch smooth bore, mounted on Naval carriage; weight of cannon 6,550 lbs. A serviceable cannon as well as an interesting historical relic of the Naval battles of the Civil War on the famous old warship. Price, $900.00.

**10151.**

**10172. — CAPTURED SPANISH NORDENFELT NAVAL MACHINE GUN** that came from Manila and was part of the War Department exhibit of captured Spanish and Philippine arms and weapons at the St. Louis Exposition in 1904. This gun was evidently taken from one of the Spanish warships sunk by Admiral Dewey at the battle of Manila Bay, 1898. The firing mechanism is not in order. The elevating and traversing gear is in working order; the gun is calibre 45. Five barrels laid side by side; the cartridges are fed in through hopper placed over the gun and the operating mechanism withdraws the bottom and allows the cartridges to drop into the barrels. The firing pin and loading mechanism is worked by a handle which is moved backward and forward by the gunner; one hand only is required to work the firing handle, leaving the other at liberty to adjust the elevation and direction. The gun can be efficiently worked by one man. We offer gun as it is a *relic of the Spanish War*. Rare exhibit for museum. Price, $285.00.

**10151.** This is the famous DYNAMITE GUN used by the ROOSEVELT ROUGH RIDERS IN CUBA IN 1898. It is the finest relic of the famous regiment and is viewed here by many men who were members of that regiment. Before our purchase of this gun we told the officer in charge of sale that it should be retained as a rare relic of the SPANISH-AMERICAN WAR. However, it was sold to us. Guns of this type used a dynamite filled projectile, which was driven from the gun by a charge of compressed air generated by discharging a BLANK cartridge in the lower barrel. The projectile has screw propeller similar to a torpedo, to steady it and give it direction. In Scribner's Magazine, General Funston says of its use in Cuba: "When it gave its characteristic cough, we saw the projectile sail through the air and strike the block house squarely in the center, the shell penetrated and burst inside, killing the sixteen defenders, the structure was all demolished, portions of the roof being blown a hundred feet in the air." See notice from N. Y. Tribune on bottom of this page.

**50 U. S. ARMY LATE REGULATION STEEL CANNON SHOT,** new, with bronze sabot and fuse plug for the 3 2/10 inch Breech-loading Cannon. Price, $2.00 each.

**10166. — U. S. A. BLACKSMITH'S FORGE CART.** New, sold only by reason of change in regulations from wood to steel. Forges are offered with the limber as shown in illustration whereby the cart becomes a wagon, drawn by 2 horses, Col. Laidley's patent. Very suitable for contractors or any outdoor work that changes from place to place which requires blacksmith outfit. The forge is hard wood covered with heavy sheet copper top containing blacksmith's bellows, forge with tuyer, vise, anvil attached to block, etc, with compartment for tools, coal, etc. All ready for immediate use. Cost upwards of $500.00 to make at U. S. Armory, our bargain price for the outfit, forge cart, limber and outfit, $185.00.

**10173. 3-INCH BREECH-LOADING CANNON WOOD SPONGE HEAD.** Hard wood, with two copper bands with hole for pole. Will answer also for six pounder muzzle-loading cannon. Price, $1.00 each.

**No. 15. U. S. ARTILLERY VISES.** Used on Field Carriage Forge. Size of Jaw 4 inches, weight about 40 lbs., made of wrought iron, not to be compared with cheap cast iron vises. Size of opening 4½ inches. These are rusty and will need new spring to make them work. We offer these sewed in burlap for shipment at $1.40 each.

**1836. BRONZE CROWN.** Found on old cannon raised from the wreck of vessel in the Harbor of Quebec. Length 3¾ inches, height 2½ inches, ⅝-inch relief. Evidently British. Weight 5 ounces. Price, $7.50.

**10170A. STUDEBAKER SET TWO WHEELS.** 46 inch high, with 2¼ inch axles. The outfit for $8.00.

**10170B. FIFTEEN NECK YOKES FOR STUDEBAKER ARMY WAGON.** In serviceable order. Price, $1.50 each.

**U. S. NAVY ORDNANCE POCKET MANUAL.** Pocket size. Manual of exercise for great guns and small arms, equipment of boats, progressive instruction for gun and powder divisions, and directions for target practice with machine guns, small arms, etc. 484 pages, size 4x5½ inches. Red binding. Price, $1.00.

**12-POUNDER** Shrapnel or Case Shot, light cast iron shell filled with 3½ lbs. of round lead bullets, with just enough powder to burst the shell and allow the bullets to scatter over a wide area at a long distance. Offered with powder bags and time fuse complete, $3.00. Shot is free from powder.

**Fig. 339**

**Civil War Mitraleuse Ball** Cartridge, made for use in the Billinghurst and Requa guns. Fired by percussion cap igniting the charge through small opening in the head of the cartridge. Price, 20 cents.

**Civil War Mitraleuse,** Billinghurst and Requas Invention, 24 steel rifled barrels fired by one movement of firing lever. Cartridges are carried in limber chest fixed in metal clips, inserted for firing in gun by one movement. Gun is in splendid serviceable order, mounted on field carriage, and was found in old New Jersey State Arsenal. Rare relic of the days in '61, when the writer saw the inventors with the gun on exhibition in front of the old Stock Exchange, Broad and Wall Streets, seeking to interest financiers to capitalize their invention. Price, $500, with limber and complement of cartridges and metal holders or clips.

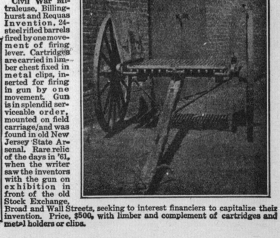

The historical dynamite cannon used with such good effect by Roosevelt's Rough Riders against the Spanish in Cuba, '98, is on exhibition at the military museum of Francis Bannerman, 501 Broadway, New York City.

The Rough Riders who came to New York to welcome Roosevelt on his return from Africa, wanted the loan of their cannon for parade, but Mr. Bannerman was afraid that after such long disuse the wheels might not stand the strain, but agreed to display it over the balcony from his Broadway museum salesroom.

President Roosevelt recognized the famous old gun, and enthusiastically joined his comrades in saluting and cheering it as the parade passed up Broadway. Some of Bannerman's neighbors on the opposite side of Broadway, said: "Roosevelt's eyes remained spiked on that old gun."—Extracts *N. Y. Tribune*.

**U. S. A. TWO-POUNDER CANNON PACK HARNESS OUTFIT.** Illustration shows mule with pack saddle loaded with the cannon carriage for mountain transport. We have 100 pack outfits for carrying cannon-carriages and ammunition. Also suitable for mountain transporting of all kinds of materials. All new. Price, $40.00 each outfit.

**Brass Mortar**, with date 1676 and figure of hunters in Puritan dress cast in relief. Diameter at mouth, 11 inches; length, 9 inches; weight, 100 lbs.............................$100 00

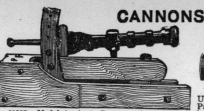

**01207. Model Ancient Cannon**, planned after one of the earliest Powder guns now in famous European Museum. As is well known the first cannons included among their number, breech loaders. The barrel of this model cannon is 9¼ inches long with reinforced muzzle band, 2¼ inches, ⅞ bore, two iron strengthening bands with large band in the center to which is attached the mountings for swivel. Detachable breech which contains the powder charge. Breech is held in place by back plate and top bolt. Gun has directing handle. Mounted on hard wood, light colored frame 18 inches long, 9 inches wide, well made museum exhibit. Price $50.00.

**Twenty-pounder United States Navy Parrott Muzzle-loading Rifle Cannons.** In serviceable order, almost new. Weight, 1,760 pounds; bore, 8⅝ inches. Mounted on navy Marsilly carriage, as per illustration.................................$350 00
We can furnish twenty of these cannons, unmounted, at $250 each.

**2 Revolutionary War Period Bronze Mortars**, with seal of George the Third and British crown; maker's name Verbrigger, London, 1780-1782, all cast in gun; fine specimen; weight marked as 1 cwt., 1 qr., 9 lbs.; 5½-inch bore. Handsome ornament. Old-time flash pan. Price, $500. each.

Engraving, "August Morning with Farragut, Mobile Bay." We have these fine pictures for sale, nicely framed in oak; size, 2½ feet square; $15.00 We have the gun shown in the engraving. Authenticated by records of United States Navy Department as gun in battery of the old frigate Hartford at battle of Mobile Bay. Size, 9-inch bore; fired over 500 times. Still in serviceable order; valuable relic. Length, about 14 feet; weight, 9,000 pounds. Mounted on navy carriage.........................$1,500 00

**Pair of Revolutionary War Period Bronze Cannons**, with seal of His Majesty George the Third and the British crown mark; maker's name, Walter Gilpin, date 1770 cast on the guns; weight 2.3 pounds. We found these guns in Hanover, Germany, perhaps carried there by Hessians on return from American Revolutionary War. Infantry howitzer. Rare guns. Four-inch bore. $1000. each.

**300 U. S. ARMY GUNNERS' RUSSET LEATHER POUCHES**, with waist belt. Complete. Good as new. Size of box is 6x7 inches, 2 inches wide at the top. Price of box and belt, 60 cents.

Side view.

**High Power Machine Gun.** 6m/m Accles' quick feed, shooting smokeless powder, nickel steel rifle ball cartridges, six revolving barrels encased in aluminum covering, mounted on tripod with training bar and swivel socket, whereby the gun can be quickly elevated or depressed, or fired in any desired position. New Gun, never used since tested by the U. S. Navy Dept. Offered with a limited number of ball cartridges and spare parts. Cartridges will be furnished in quantities by the U. M. C. Cartridge Co.

Rear view.

**Two British Saluting Cannons**, iron, from London. Weight about 150 lbs.; length, 32 inches; bore, 1¾ inches; serviceable order. Price, $30, or $50 the pair, unmounted.

**United States Army 6-Pounder Iron Cannon**, smooth bore. In serviceable order; from sale at Augusta Arsenal, Maine, September, 1901. Mounted on Army field carriage; for firing salutes; handsome decoration; cannon is made of old-time United States Army gun metal. Length, 5 feet; bore, 3½ inches; weight, 800 pounds. Complete, with gunners' accessories......

**Relics from Cuba** at close of Spanish-American war. Handsomely engraved cannon with Spanish crown, coat-of-arms, name, date and place of manufacture; over 5 feet long, 3½-inch bore. Made in Seville, Spain, 1793; weighs over 700 pounds; named Juno, duplicate named Ceres. Forty-five per cent. duty was paid in 1899 on arrival from Cuba as serviceable guns. Price, $585. each.

**U. S. ARMY CIVIL WAR RELIC. 6 Pounder Bronze Cannon.** Used in many of the battles of the period 1861-1865, captured and recaptured. This gun has an interesting history. It has been all over the United States with Shenandoah Theatrical Co. It is in good second-hand serviceable order and is offered mounted on Army Field Carriage, complete with gunner's implements, for $500.

**No. 400. ELEMENTARY NAVAL ORDNANCE AND GUNNERY.** Includes Close-order Infantry with 1918 Drill Regulations. By Lt. M. C. Ramsey, in charge of Naval Ordnance and Gunnery at U. S. N. Officer's Training School at Harvard University. 412 pages, size 5 by 7¼, on heavy glazed paper. Many drawings of cannon, machine guns, projectiles, etc. Large detail sketch of 12 inch 2 gun turret. Chapters on NAVAL GUNS, BREECH MECHANISMS, TURRETS, PROJECTILES, FIRE CONTROL, TORPEDOES, BATTLE DRILLS, ETC. A fine text book for individuals or schools. Price, postage paid in U. S., 65 cents.

**U4-13. THE NAVAL HOWITZER ASHORE.** By Foxhall A. Parker, Commander U. S. Navy, 1865. Contains many charts and full page illustrations. 64 pages. Price, $1.00.

**Forty United States Army Limbers** for 6-pounder, smooth-bore, 12-pounder and 3-inch Rifle Cannons. Complete, with ammunition chest, pole and irons. Wheels, 5 feet high. In serviceable order. $85 each.

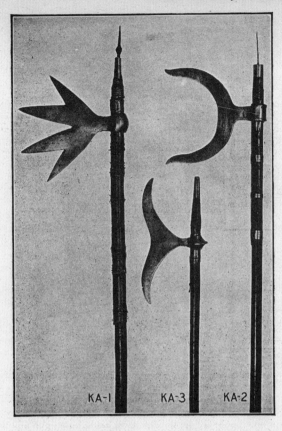

KA-1     KA-3     KA-2

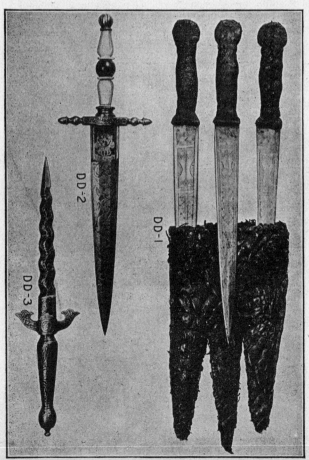

**K A. INDIA KHOMD AX,** with 36 inch wooden shaft, brass wire bound, brass ferrule, and brass bound tip with iron arrow point. Three pronged ax head, 7 inch by 6 inch. Price, $5.85.

**K A-1. INDIA KHOND AX** wth 34 inch wooden shaft, brass tipped at each end and bound with fine brass wire. Four pronged ax head, size 7 inch by 7½ inch. Price $6.00. (See illustration.)

**K A-2. INDIA KHOND AX** moon shaped head, size 7 by 7 inches, wooden shaft 33 inches, brass bound at each end, with steel arrow point, with 3 brass bands. Price, $6.00. (See illustration.)

**K A-3. 7 INDIA KHOND AXES,** all with wooden shafts, average length 36 inches, brass bound, some tipped with arrow points in steel. Long flat heads, average length 8½ inches. Some are brass wire bound. Price, $6.50 each. (See illustration.)

**K A-4. INDIA KHOND AXES** with wood shafts, brass wire bound, and steel arrow tipped. Average length, 35 inches. Long flat ax heads, average length 10 inches. Price, $5.75 each.

**353. SCHLAGER FENCING SWORD OR HAUTE RAPIER.** With large basket guard handle with ribbed cord grip; guard surrounds the hand; straight oval-shaped blade, 34 inches long. This kind of foil used by German students. Price each, $3.75.

**24-4. AFRICAN DAGGER,** with 5¾-inch flat blade. Handle made from antelope horn, with iron guard. Evidently native made. Price $4.50.

**24-5. MOROCCAN POCKET DAGGER,** with 3¾ inch blade to fold up in handle. Horn handle is corrugated and ends in shape of horse's foot. Price, $4.85.

**24-3. SUDANESE DAGGER,** 5½ inch wide blade, with scroll. Horn handle ornamented with ivory disks, mounted in silver. Plush covered scabbard has silver throat and tip. Price, $4.95.

**1225. JAPANESE OFFICER'S SWORD,** with steel scabbard with two rings for slings. Total length 29 inches. Polished sharp steel blade 21½ inch. Brass pommel and guard, which has small piece to turn down to keep scabbard from slipping off. In good order. Price, $9.50.

**1225-B. JAPANESE SWORD,** similar to No. 1225, with hilt pommel missing. Otherwise in good condition. Price, $8.00.

**24-1. JAPANESE SHORT SWORD,** without scabbard. Blade is 11 inch, slightly curved at tip. Short hilt with copper pommel and guard. Handle is fibre wrapped. In good order. Price, $7.50.

**24-2. ASIATIC SHORT SWORD,** with 11 inch blade slightly curved. Wood hand grip with iron pommel in shape of lion's head, with mouth partly open to hold wrist cord. In fair condition. Price, $5.00.

**D D-1. SET OF THREE DAGGERS** from the FAR SOUDAN. The scabbard has three compartments, made of crocodile skin, with the roughest part on the front, and the finest skin on the back. Each dagger handle is covered with the fine grain skin. Blades all 7¾ inches long, with native crude engraving or markings. A most curious set. Price, $25.

**D D-2. MODEL SPANISH DAGGER** in morocco leather scabbard, with chased metal tip and throat. Handle is 3½ inches long, with ball metal stud pommel, with white and black ivory. The blade is embossed and gold inlaid. On one side (as shown in illustration is the Spanish coat of arms), on the other: FABa, DE TOLEDO, 1856. The 8 inch blade has chiseled steel designs of flowers and hunting scenes. Daggers of this style were presented to notable visitors to the famous Toledo factory. Price, $17.00.

**D D-3. OLD TOLEDO DAGGER** with chased handle and blade. Note wavy blade, 6¼ inches long. On one side the head of a man, on the other: FABca DE TOLEDO. All metal scabbard of chased steel. Sold.

**D D-4. SPANISH DAGGER or STILLETO,** with 5 inch wavy blade similar to No. D D-3, with very sharp point. Ebony handle, ribbed, with 2 inch cross bars with metal ball ends. No scabbard. Price, $8.00.

# GATLING GUNS, ETC.

50 Calibre Gatling Machine Gun mounted on Special Naval carriage. Mounted on this carriage gun can be quickly wheeled to any part of the deck to repel attack of enemy. Very suitable to enterprising yachtsmen cruising among waters infested with pirates. Price of Gun, mounted on this carriage, All in good serviceable order.

U. S. Army 50-Calibre Gatling Machine Gun. Mounted on Cavalry Gun Cart for use in company with mounted troops. Two ammunition boxes are attached to the cart—one each side of the gun. Wheels are high, strong and light. All in good, serviceable order.

At the beginning of the war with Spain in the Spring of 1898, American officers in the East approved of contracts given by the Filipinos for the purchase of guns to help them fight the Spanish. Afterwards, when the Filipinos turned against the Americans, the German firm who took the contract were blamed. While in China last winter, we learned that this firm felt provoked at being censured, and said it was a case of getting damned both ways.

Some of the guns supplied were the German 11 m/m or 43 Calibre Mauser Model 71-84, obsolete guns from the German army; the American soldiers captured about 1,500 of these guns, which we bought.

U. S. Army Steel Caisson with Steel frame, two steel ammunition chests, patent brass hub wheels, with shoe brake, with extra spare wheel. All practically as good as new. Price for Limber and Caisson, $300.

Original Volcanic Repeating Rifle Pistol Cartridges, 35 cents each.

U. S. Army Steel Limber for Gatling Machine Guns. Patent brass hub wheels. Metal whiffle trees. Steel ammunition chests. In fine serviceable order, practically as good as new. Offered complete with Caisson.

1,200 U. S. Artillery Iron Buckets, with ring and chain for attaching to artillery carriages; used for carrying grease or other lubricants for axles. All in good serviceable order, painted black, height 7 inches; diameter, 7 inches; Make useful decorative flower pots. Price $2.00 each.

While having a friendly cup of tea last Summer with a friend who was a pastor of a Covenanter Church, in Ireland, and touching upon the short sermons in America, compared with the 2½ hours sermon in North of Ireland, our friend made reply: "Do you know what a farmer in my Church, who comes 7 miles to services, said to me lately: "Mon but I wad nae think it wurth me while yoking up me horse to gang for anything less than twa and a half oors."

Wind Guage Cannon Sight for Modern B-L Rifled Cannons, with spirit level attachment, with leather holder. Price, $12.50

Limber for One Inch Gatling Machine Gun, with ammunition box, with pole, whiffletrees, all complete for attaching to the gun carriage. In good second-hand serviceable order. Price, $150.

125 U. S. Artillery Sponge Buckets, with handle and toggle. All as good as new. Made of iron plates riveted together; height is 9 inches; diameter, 7 inches. Price $2.00 each.

0-788. CONFEDERATE FIELD CANNON, illustrated on page 56 Brady's photos, "History of the Civil War." Cast-steel jacketed barrel. Length 4¼ feet, smooth bore 2½ inches. Weight of the gun 715 pounds; diameter of the trunnions 3 inches, length of the trunnions inches width between the trunnions 10 inches; mounted on field carriage, now in repaired order; full length of the carriage 78 inches; height of the wheel 35½ inches, truck 50 inches. Offered in serviceable order, suitable for firing an occasional salute. At the bargain price of $250.00 for the outfit.

0-773. ANCIENT BRONZE BOAT OR WALL GUN, with swivel for mounting on pedestal or castle wall. Length of gun 32 inches, 1⅞-inch smooth bore, outside diameter at the muzzle 4 inches, at the breech 6 inches, weight 130 pounds. Serviceable for firing occasional salutes. From the estate of French nobleman. Price, with gunner's outfit, $75.00

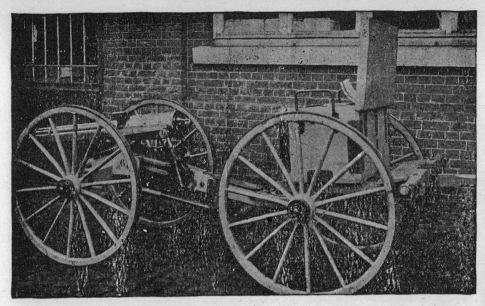

Illustration showing **GATLING RAPID FIRE GUN,** mounted on field carriage, attached to limber (with cover of limber chest open). We can furnish these famous guns in all calibres, from the high power modern calibre 30, shooting Krag smokeless powder cartridge, up to the large guns used in coast fortifications, for flank defense, shooting a cartridge 1 inch in diameter. All in serviceable order at bargain prices. With either Straight, Accles or Bruce feeds. Complete with gunners' accessories. We have a large stock, purchased at *right prices,* and *can meet any legitimate competition.*

**Illustration showing SHORT BARREL GATLING MACHINE GUN,** mounted on camel's back, for use in desert countries, by Arabian Governments. We can furnish guns, saddles, gunners' accessories, and ammunition. Practically as good as new. Only used a short time. For sale at bargain prices, either with of without saddle mounts.

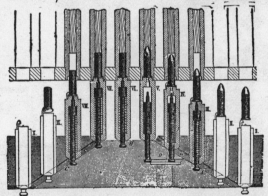

**ILLUSTRATION SHOWING LOCK MECHANISM OF COLTS GATLING MACHINE GUNS.** Note the five locks to the left have fired the cartridges, and are shown in the act of extracting the empty shells, while the five locks to the right are in the act of firing.

Illustration showing Colt's Gatling Gun, frame, barrels, lock and operating mechanism. Barrels are revolved by turning the crank around the central shaft, which projects beyond the muzzle, and also extends behind the breech. The locks have forward and backward motion of their own. By the forward motion, the loaded cartridge is placed in the barrel and closes the breech, ready for firing. The backward motion extracts the empty cartridge case. The loading and firing is all done by turning the crank handle from left to right. A continual firing can be kept up. The cartridges are fed into the gun through the feed case, placed in the hopper on top, each revolution of the barrels around the shaft, fires ten shots. The number of shots depends on the rapidity of the operator turning the crank handle. If the gun is well served, as many as 1200 shots a minute can be fired. Naturally a fire of such rapidity could not be kept up very long, as the gun would soon become too hot. 63,000 cartridges have been fired at one time, without ever cleaning the barrels. Range is over a mile, depending on the elevation. The Colt's Gatling is by many officers preferred to the new automatics which are so apt to get out of order.

Canvas Covered Hair Cushion for U. S. Army Limber Chest. Used as seat by artillerymen. Size, 27 x 46 inches, 2¼ inches thick. Practically new. Made at U. S. Government Rock Island Arsenal. Hair, covered with drab canvas; used as seats for artillerymen on the ammunition chests. $4.50 each.

Late model Calibre 45 U. S. Army Colt's Gatling Gun, with limber. With large size ammunition chest. All in fine serviceable order. Used only a few times. Large stock at reduced price. Offered complete with gunners' accessories, with millions of long range ball cartridges, at bargain prices.

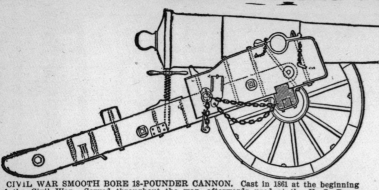

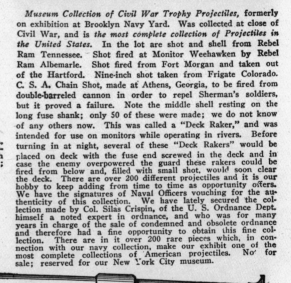

**CIVIL WAR SMOOTH BORE 18-POUNDER CANNON.** Cast in 1861 at the beginning of the Civil War. Served throughout the war, afterwards used at the U. S. Barge Office at the Battery as mooring posts for the U. S. revenue cutters. Length of the gun is 9 feet 8 inches, 5-4-inch smooth bore, weight 4,900 pounds. Newspaper item of April 13, 1912, stated that these cannon were of the Revolutionary War period, buried many years ago when the river front was filled in. We purchased the lot and from the marks on the guns are able to give correct history as stated above. We can furnish the guns at $450.00 each.

**174. ANCIENT ORNAMENTAL BRONZE CANNON,** with under pin studs for fastening to wood frame in addition to the regular trunnion or axle. Cascabel has projection for socket, directing bar; rear and front sight studs. Length 34 inches, 1¾-inch smooth bore. Outside diameter at the muzzle 4½ inches, at the breech 5½ inches, weight 126 pounds. From the Count Vitrac estate. Suitable for firing occasional salutes. Bargain price, with gunner's outfit, $75.00.

*Museum Collection of Civil War Trophy Projectiles,* formerly on exhibition at Brooklyn Navy Yard. Was collected at close of Civil War, and is *the most complete collection of Projectiles in the United States.* In the lot are shot and shell from Rebel Ram Tennessee. Shot fired at Monitor Weehawken by Rebel Ram Albemarle. Shot fired from Fort Morgan and taken out of the Hartford. Nine-inch shot taken from Frigate Colorado. C. S. A. Chain Shot, made at Athens, Georgia, to be fired from double-barreled cannon in order to repel Sherman's soldiers, but it proved a failure. Note the middle shell resting on the long fuse shank; only 50 of these were made; we do not know of any others now. This was called a "Deck Raker," and was intended for use on monitors while operating in rivers. Before turning in at night, several of these "Deck Rakers" would be placed on deck with the fuse end screwed in the deck and in case the enemy overpowered the guard these rakers could be fired from below and, filled with small shot, would soon clear the deck. There are over 200 different projectiles and it is our hobby to keep adding from time to time as opportunity offers. We have the signatures of Naval Officers vouching for the authenticity of this collection. We have lately secured the collection made by Col. Silas Crispin, of the U. S. Ordnance Dept. himself a noted expert in ordnance, and who was for many years in charge of the sale of condemned and obsolete ordnance and therefore had a fine opportunity to obtain this fine collection. There are in it over 200 rare pieces which, in connection with our navy collection, make our exhibit one of the most complete collections of American projectiles. Not for sale; reserved for our New York City museum.

Six-pounder Mexican War Cannon, in serviceable order for saluting purposes; mounted on field carriage; with gunner's outfit; length, 4½ feet; weight, 350 pounds. Price, $200.00.

Illustration showing Mexican War Cannon and gunners, from *Bannerman's book "Weapons of War."*

*Mann's Steel Breech-Loading, Smooth-Bore Howitzer,* shooting 12-pound shot; mounted on Naval Howitzer Carriage, with 4-foot wheels; all in serviceable order, like new. Make fine breech-loading saluting cannon, fired with ordinary primer and powder bag. The arms attached to the trunnion hold breech block in place; depressing the muzzle end opens the breech for fresh charge. Price on carriage, $375.00.

**Mann's Steel Breech-Loading Rifled Howitzer,** shooting 12-pound rifle shot; all in fine order, like new, mounted on field carriage. Price, $400.00. Projectiles, $1.50 each. These two experimental guns cost upward of $20,000 to build.

**Wingate's Armory Tripod,** with clamp and ball socket to allow the adjusting of the rifle in any desired position. Used in armories to give recruits practice in aiming. Clamp will fit any gun. Some theatrical men have used these tripods on stage to represent Rapid-Firing Gatling or Colt's Machine Gun; worked with sliding lever rifle. Price of tripod in serviceable order, $18.00.

Spanish Bronze Cannon, 12-pounder, made in Seville, Spain, 1796; weight, about 800 pounds; 5 feet long, with the old style handles over the trunnion; handsomely decorated with Spanish crown and King's monogram; named the "Juno." In serviceable order. Rifled, which shows that the Spanish were, at the time this gun was made, in advance of all other nations, who did not have rifled guns until many years later. Price, $450.00.

Another one the same as above, engraved as having been made at Barcelona, 1792, and named the "Cerezo." Price, $450.00.

The above Spanish Gun can be mounted on Army Field Carriage for $100.00 extra, or on Navy Carriage for $65.00 extra.

Spanish Bronze Cannon, 12-pounder, Mountain Howitzer, rifled, from Cuba, 1899. Handsomely engraved as named "Entero," Seville, with Spanish crown and other scroll work; length is about 3 feet; the weight, about 200 pounds. Price, $140.00.

Another one of the same with engraved name "Arqujas." Price, $140.00. We can mount these guns on Naval Carriages without wheels or cap squares; answers for decorative purposes. Price of the Carriage, $10.00.

Spanish Bronze Cannon made in 1860, 12-pounder; length, 5 feet; 4-inch bore, rifled; in serviceable order; weighs over 800 pounds; came from Cuba, 1899. Price for gun, $350.00.

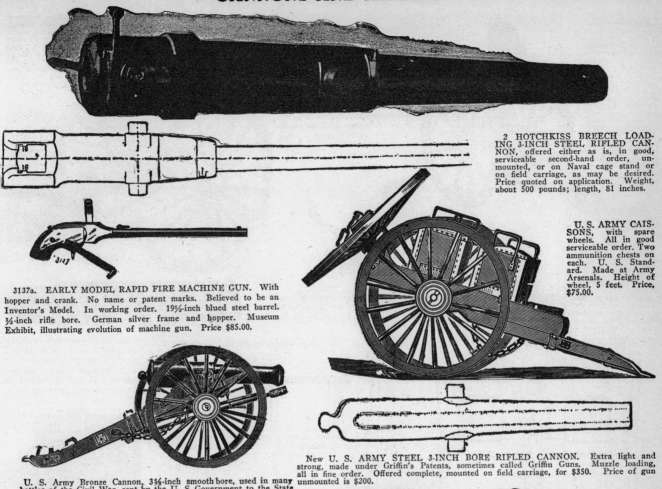

**2 HOTCHKISS BREECH LOAD-ING 3-INCH STEEL RIFLED CANNON,** offered either as is, in good, serviceable second-hand order, un-mounted, or on Naval cage stand or on field carriage, as may be desired. Price quoted on application. Weight, about 500 pounds; length, 81 inches.

**U. S. ARMY CAIS-SONS,** with spare wheels. All in good serviceable order. Two ammunition chests on each. U. S. Stand-ard. Made at Army Arsenals. Height of wheel, 5 feet. Price, $75.00.

**3137a. EARLY MODEL RAPID FIRE MACHINE GUN.** With hopper and crank. No name or patent marks. Believed to be an Inventor's Model. In working order. 19½-inch blued steel barrel. ½-inch rifle bore. German silver frame and hopper. Museum Exhibit, illustrating evolution of machine gun. Price $85.00.

**New U. S. ARMY STEEL 3-INCH BORE RIFLED CANNON.** Extra light and strong, made under Griffin's Patents, sometimes called Griffin Guns. Muzzle loading, all in fine order. Offered complete, mounted on field carriage, for $350. Price of gun unmounted is $200.

**U. S. Army Bronze Cannon,** 3⅝-inch smooth bore, used in many battles of the Civil War, sent by the U. S. Government to the State of New Jersey to be cast into the Bronze statue of General Kilpatrick. The cannon not arriving in time, the State used other bronze guns on hand in the Armory at Trenton. Later this old relic was sold to us. We offer it mounted on Civil War Field Carriage, complete with limber, in second-hand serviceable order, with Gunners' utensils. Price $700.00.

**6063. Ancient Steel Target or War Shield** (copy) 12½ inch diameter, 3 inch, centre crown. Price $4.85.

**Battery of U. S. Steel Muzzle Loading Rifle Cannon,** used at the close of the Civil War, and sold by us to General Gilmore for firing salute in connection with his Band Performance at Manhattan Beach, Coney Island. The Guns are in serviceable order, mounted on Army Field Carriages, complete with sponge, rammer, sponge bucket and gunners' implements. The length of the gun is 5 feet, the bore 3 inches, the weight is 880 pounds. Offered in cleaned serviceable order, the outfit, for $350.00.

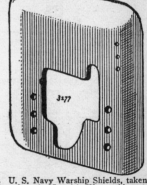

**3277. U. S. Navy Warship Shields,** taken from the ships after the Spanish War, sold at auction New York Navy Yard. Length 3 feet 3 inches, width 4 feet 2 inches. Opening 12¼ by 18 inches. ¼-inch thick armored steel; weight 170 pounds, in serviceable order for use on Hotchkiss gun. We have 8 Shields

15 Nordenfelt.
2 Shields, 1-pounder Hotchkiss.
8 Shields, 3-pounder, Mark 111.
7 Shields, 6-pounder, Mark 11 D. S.
15 Shields, 6-pounder Hotchkiss.
All for sale at bargain prices.

**3278. U. S. Navy Steel Cannon Armor Shield,** removed from Warships after the close of the Spanish War. Used in front of the gun to protect gunners from enemy's fire. 3278 size is 4 feet high, 2 feet wide, opening is 10 by 19 inches. ¼ inches thick, weighs 292 pounds. Price $30.00. We also have the following Shields:

2 Shields for Nordenfelt 6-pounder.
6 Shields for 7 M. M. Gun.
2 Shields for 9-pounder Gun.
9 Shields for 6-pounder Driggs-Schroeder Cannon. For sale at bargain prices.

**500 U. S. ARMY GUN-NERS' LEATHER HAVERSACKS.** Made of russet leather, with shoulder sling; size, 12½x13 inches. Good, serviceable, second-hand. $2.50 each.

**Loading Machine for Hotchkiss Breech-Loading Cannon:**
1 Set for Calibre 1.50 m. m.    1 Set for Calibre 47 m. m.
4 Sets for Calibre 1.65 m. m.    1 Set for Calibre 53 m. m.
**Heavy Steel Barrels for Automatic Machine Guns.** Length of barrel 28 inches. Weight 6 pounds.
4 Colt's, Calibre 30, Model 1898. $6.50.
25 Maxim's, Calibre 30. U. S. A. $6.50.

Spain holds the record for placing the greatest obstacles in the way of bona fide bidders pur-chasing at Government Auction sales. Just be-fore the evacuation of Cuba in 1898, the Spanish Government by its officers in Havana, offered at Auction, hundreds of tons of old Bronze Can-nons. The hour at which the bid was to be opened was TWELVE O'CLOCK MIDNIGHT. Bidders were required at this unseemly hour in those troublesome days to deposit with his bid the sum of $25,000.00 IN GOLD. It was an American who took the risk, and outbid the Spanish favorite, and was awarded the prize, on which he made a large profit.

For illustration of the old cannons, see other pages.

# High Power Gatling Machine Guns

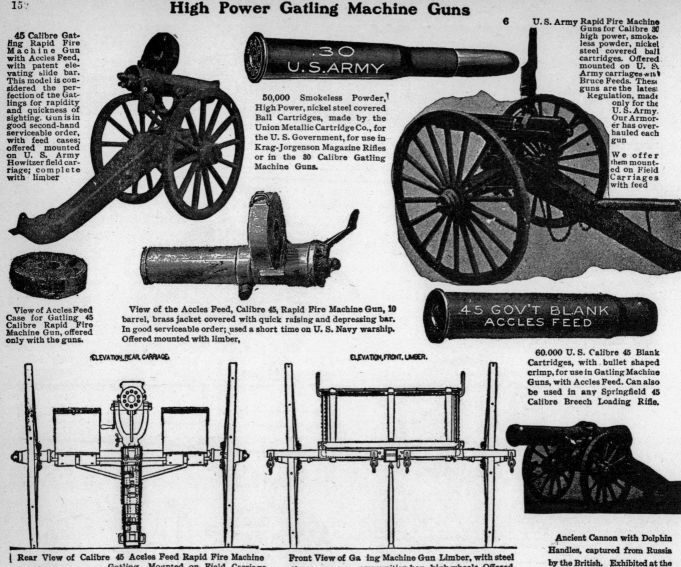

45 Calibre Gatling Rapid Fire Machine Gun with Accles Feed, with patent elevating slide bar. This model is considered the perfection of the Gatlings for rapidity and quickness of sighting. Gun is in good second-hand serviceable order, with feed cases; offered mounted on U. S. Army Howitzer field carriage; complete with limber

50,000 Smokeless Powder, High Power, nickel steel covered Ball Cartridges, made by the Union Metallic Cartridge Co., for the U. S. Government, for use in Krag-Jorgenson Magazine Rifles or in the 30 Calibre Gatling Machine Guns.

**6** U. S. Army Rapid Fire Machine Guns for Calibre 30 high power, smokeless powder, nickel steel covered ball cartridges. Offered mounted on U. S. Army carriages with Bruce Feeds. These guns are the latest Regulation, made only for the U. S. Army. Our Armorer has overhauled each gun

We offer them mounted on Field Carriages with feed

View of Accles Feed Case for Gatling 45 Calibre Rapid Fire Machine Gun, offered only with the guns.

View of the Accles Feed, Calibre 45, Rapid Fire Machine Gun, 10 barrel, brass jacket covered with quick raising and depressing bar. In good serviceable order; used a short time on U. S. Navy warship. Offered mounted with limber,

60.000 U. S. Calibre 45 Blank Cartridges, with bullet shaped crimp, for use in Gatling Machine Guns, with Accles Feed. Can also be used in any Springfield 45 Calibre Breech Loading Rifle.

ELEVATION, REAR, CARRIAGE.

ELEVATION, FRONT, LIMBER.

Rear View of Calibre 45 Accles Feed Rapid Fire Machine Gatling. Mounted on Field Carriage with the two ammunition boxes. Special price will be quoted on application for this style mounting.

Front View of Gatling Machine Gun Limber, with steel ammunition box, high wheels. Offered with Gatling Gun outfit.

Ancient Cannon with Dolphin Handles, captured from Russia by the British. Exhibited at the Woolwich Arsenal, England. The early made bronze cannon had lifting handles, in the form of the dolphin fish. In cannon of a later period, the handles were cast in the form of caterpillars. Bronze cannon with plain handles were used during the Civil War, the lifting handles still retaining the name of "dolphin." From Bannerman's Book on "Weapons of War."

An Editor in days of '63, announced that he had been drafted as follows:
Why should we mourn conscripted friends,
Or shake at draft alarms?
'Tis but the voice that Abram sends
To make us shoulder arms.

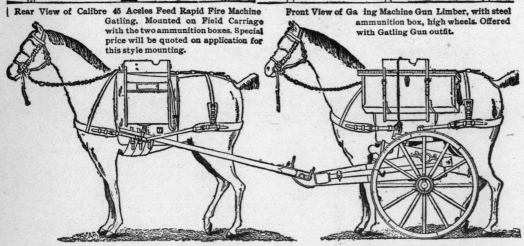

U. S. Army Harness, with Pack Saddle for Packing Gatling Machine Guns over mountains. Complete harness as per illustration. For two horses. Price, $80.00.

From *N. Y. Sun*, March 26, 1923.
## LAST REMARKS OF THE IOWA

"This being shot at is no novelty for me. In that I have the advantage of these big young ships that are going to finish me. I was first to see Cervera when he came out of the bottle at Santiago twenty-five years ago. I was first to fire at the Spaniards and I gave and took more than any other ship in our fleet.

"In this battle I can't shoot. I can run away, but that isn't to my fancy. I'm glad old Bob Evans isn't here to see me run from these newfangled ships. He would want to turn my twelve inch guns against the sixteens of the Maryland and the fourteens of the Mississippi and have it out with anybody who shot at me.

"There's quite a crowd here for my last rites.

The Secretary of the Navy, some Admirals, a lot of experts and one man who was on board me the day we chased the Teresa down the Cuban coast.

"Well, they've been trying those fancy thin walled projectiles on me and they won't do. Now the Mississippi is going to use the real thing at nine miles. My wireless steering outfit is broken and I'm glad of it. Flight is unbearable, even when it's for your country's good.

"They've got me. Those service shells are all right, especially when the gunners are so good that they can hit almost every time at nine miles. I could stand the first five hits—nothing gone but the upper works; but that sixth took me at the water line. That means the end.

"Yes, it's the finish. I can hear the band play and they're firing a salute. Twenty-one guns sounds good to a tired old battler, after all. And

this Pacific water is warm; not as hot as it was at Santiago that third of July, but comfortable. Deep too; seventy fathom; nobody ever to bother me again.

"There's only one thing I regret about it all. I'm not flying the flag. But of course I couldn't, because they wouldn't shoot at me if the flag was there. Everybody has to make some sacrifices. This is for the good of the service.

"There's one of those airplanes buzzing overhead. Twenty-five years ago, when I was the finest ship in the American navy, we never saw an airship. And twenty-five years from now, when they take the Mississippi and the Maryland out to sea to use as guinea pigs, the airplane will be the boss of the ocean.

"Down by the stern and—sinking. I wonder if anybody will tell the Oregon?"

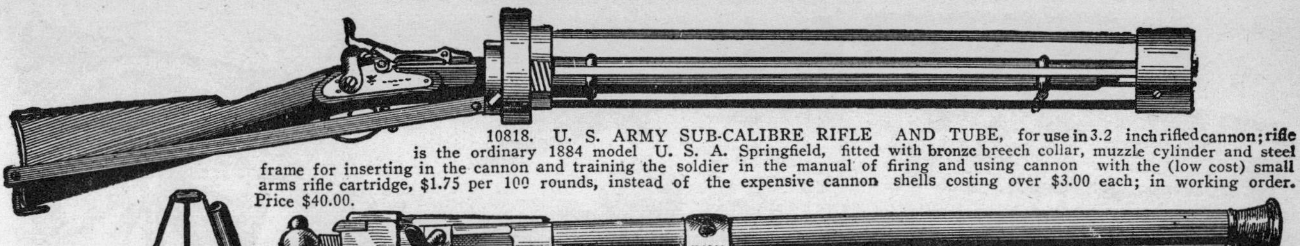

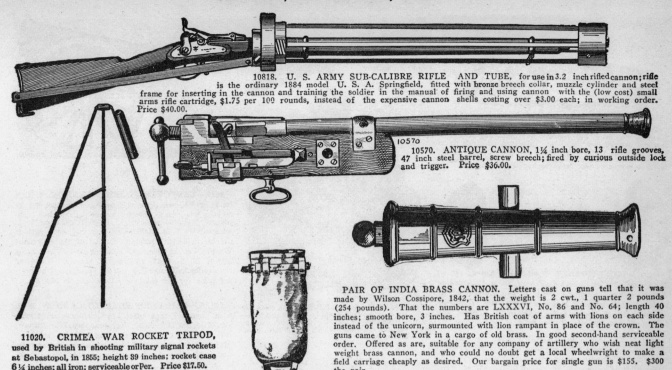

10818. U. S. ARMY SUB-CALIBRE RIFLE AND TUBE, for use in 3.2 inch rifled cannon; rifle is the ordinary 1884 model U. S. A. Springfield, fitted with bronze breech collar, muzzle cylinder and steel frame for inserting in the cannon and training the soldier in the manual of firing and using cannon with the (low cost) small arms rifle cartridge, $1.75 per 100 rounds, instead of the expensive cannon shells costing over $3.00 each; in working order. Price $40.00.

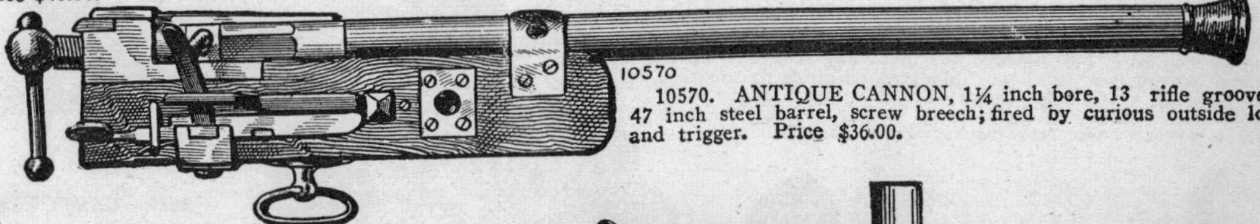


10570. ANTIQUE CANNON, 1¼ inch bore, 13 rifle grooves, 47 inch steel barrel, screw breech; fired by curious outside lock and trigger. Price $36.00.

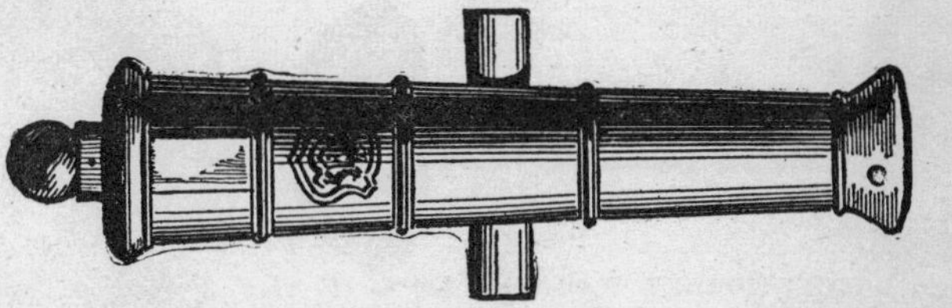

PAIR OF INDIA BRASS CANNON. Letters cast on guns tell that it was made by Wilson Cossipore, 1842, that the weight is 2 cwt., 1 quarter 2 pounds (254 pounds). That the numbers are LXXXVI, No. 86 and No. 64; length 40 inches; smooth bore, 3 inches. Has British coat of arms with lions on each side instead of the unicorn, surmounted with lion rampant in place of the crown. The guns came to New York in a cargo of old brass. In good second-hand serviceable order. Offered as are, suitable for any company of artillery who wish neat light weight brass cannon, and who could no doubt get a local wheelwright to make a field carriage cheaply as desired. Our bargain price for single gun is $155. $300 the pair.

11020. CRIMEA WAR ROCKET TRIPOD, used by British in shooting military signal rockets at Sebastopol, in 1855; height 39 inches; rocket case 6¼ inches; all iron; serviceable or Per. Price $17.50.

10812. GERMAN CANNON SHOT BULLET MOULD, for casting lead rifling band on the shot or shell for 7.85 C-M Rifled Cannon; brass mould, iron reinforced, fitted with handle 2 ft. long attached with screw bolt; mould forms part of the Krupp 6 gun battery. Price separate from the battery, $100.00.

10832. MICROMETER ADJUSTER FOR BRITISH CANNON SIGHTS; relics of the Spanish War;; 2 inch jaws knurled screw head; full length 3 inches. Price 50 cents.

10193. ANCIENT ITALIAN MODEL BRONZE CANNON; 16½ inches in length; 11-16 inch smooth bore; finely ornamented with bands and scroll work, hunting scenes; with antique coat of arms (three legged pot, armor, etc.), with letters "G. G." in border; Dolphin handles; ornamented cascabel and breech. We offer this old cannon with nipple inserted in the vent (for firing salute with percussion cap). Museum exhibit. Price $65.00.

10910. GERMAN ARMY RUSSET LEATHER BAG for covering the wool sponge rammer; 3⅝ inch diameter, 12 inches long; with hand hold strap and with short strap and buckle for fastening on the pole; new. Price $2.85.

10942. U. S. N. PRACTICE DRILL SHELL, for use in 6 pounder Hotchkiss quick firing cannon; steel rifled barrel for firing the 45 calibre Springfield small arms cartridge; encased in wood conforming to the regular shaped cannon shell; used on U. S. Navy war ships for drill purposes. Price $2.50.

10911. GERMAN ARMY CANNON BREECH COVER; waterproof canvas; leather bound, with strap and buckle for fastening over the breech; complete with separate cover for projecting breech block. The set $3.85.

U4-21. TREATISE OF ARTILLERY, or the Arms and Machines used in war since the invention of gun powder, being part of LeBlond's Elements of War. Illustrated with Above Fifty Representations, Beautifully Engraved on Copper Plates. Published in London in 1746. 134 pages, size 7½x9½ inches. Price, $5.00.

10939. PAIR OF FRENCH AND GERMAN RIFLE CANNON SHELLS (free from powder), with marks of the rifle grooves on the sabots made in firing. The German shell has lead covered sabot, is 3½ inch diameter, 10½ inches long. The French shell is 3½ inch diameter and 11 inches long; fitted with brass fuse plug. Supposed to have been found on the French and German War battlefields. Pair came to us from sale of a French nobleman's collection. Price $25.00 the pair.

10543. ANCIENT FRENCH MODEL CANNON; submitted by contractor to the government in olden times; miniature model of the 12 pounder Napoleon cannon used by the French at Waterloo. This model cannon is made of silver and copper, beautifully ornamented with Dolphin handles and engraved cascabel and breech; length 8½ inches, 1¾ inch diameter, ⅝ inch smooth bore; low hung trunnions; perfect order; weight 3 pounds. Price $18.50.

**U. S. ARMY 12 POUNDER NAPOLEON CANNON.**

10941. COLLECTION OF ANTIQUE CANNON SHELL, FROM FRENCH NOBLEMAN'S ESTATE; 3 inch spherical shell; empty. $3.00.

10941A. 4¾ inch spherical shell. $5.00.

10941B. 9 INCH SPHERICAL SHELL with ANCIENT SIDE LUGS, 2 fuse noles; evidently used in olden times for setting fire to buildings. Price $10.00.

10941C. CONICAL SHELL; 6 inch diameter, 12 inches in length, with lead studs set in spherical form on the outside of the shell to rotate the shell; studs have RIFLE MARKS MADE IN FIRING; similar shells were used prior to 1790; as witness of the fact that we have a number of Spanish brass cannons dated 1790, RIFLED for firing similar studded shells. Price $20.00.

10940. FRENCH RIFLE CANNON SHELL, empty, with marks of the rifle grooves, made in firing, on the copper sabot rotating band; shell is 3 inch diameter, length 11 inches. From French nobleman's estate. Price $12.00.

U. S. ARMY 12-POUNDER NAPOLEON CANNON, used through Civil War; offered mounted on field carriage with limber, complete with gunner's equipment. This pattern smooth-bore gun was adopted from the French and in use by U. S. Artillery prior to and during the Civil War. As the Government had no cannon, foundry guns were supplied by contractors, Alger of Boston and Ames of Chicopee. The bronze composition was composed of 90 per cent. copper, 10 per cent. tin, and cost the Government 46 cents a pound. General McClellan and Meigs advocated that two-thirds of all field artillery should be light 12-pounder Napoleons, which shooting a large charge of canister was terribly effective in destroying, breaking and repulsing infantry and cavalry charges. Gun weighs about 1,250 pounds, carriage and limber 1,950 pounds. Gun is in serviceable order as no Napoleon cannon burst, or wore out during the entire war. Civil War Bronze Cannon are extremely rare owing to their high value as bronze nearly all were broken up and remelted. Cannon and outfit. Price $1,000.

U. S. A. AUTOMATIC GUN SIGHT; 5-inch base, fitting over barrel 1½-inch diameter, 4-inch leave indexed for 2,000 yards, with adjustable wind gauge. Blued finish, fine order. Price $4.85.

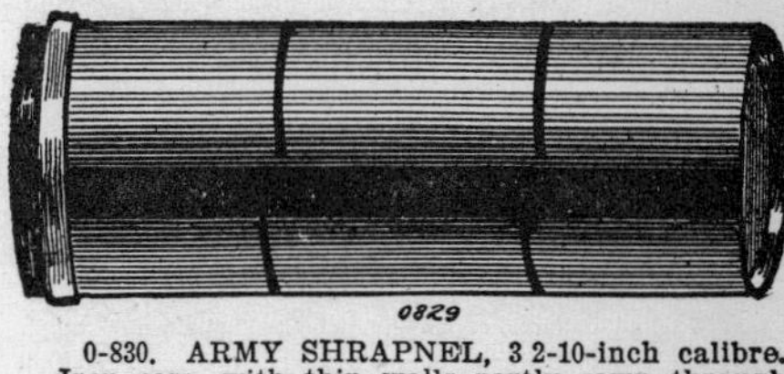

0829

0-830. ARMY SHRAPNEL, 3 2-10-inch calibre. Iron case, with thin walls partly sawn through in order to facilitate breaking when discharged from the cannon and scatter the small metal bullets with which the shell is filled. Diameter is 3 2-10 inches, height 9¾ inches, copper band to take rifling, 3 holes in the bottom plate for powder gas; 100 in stock. Weight 11¼ pounds. Price, $1.85 each.

What deeds our fathers wrought,
What battles we have fought.
Let fame record.
Now vengeful passion, cease;
Come victories of peace;
Nor hate, nor pride's caprice,
Unsheath the sword.
*—Geo. Huntington.*

2214

**2214.—CAPTURED FILIPINO CANNON,** 2 ft. 5 in. long, ¼-inch bore, 4½ diameter at muzzle, 5½ at breech. Ancient pattern low trunnions. Mounted on crude naval style carriage 4 ft. long, wheels 10 inches high. Made of plank and tired with sheet iron. Vouched by U. S. Govt. as captured war relic trophy. Price, $500.00.

**Rare** antique **Highly Carved Bronze Cannon,** over 300 years old, length, 33 inches; bore 1⅛ inches. From some Rajah's Indian palace. Price $500.

2212

**642. REVOLUTIONARY WAR BAR SHOT.** Fired from the British warship Huron while bombarding New London, Conn. Resembles two halves of 4-pounder shot joined together by iron bar. Diameter of the balls, 3 inches space between 6½ inches; the bar is ⅝-inch square. Price, $25.00.

**0-659. CANNON POWDER BAGS.** Made to order of U. S. Navy pongee silk, any size up to 5-inch breech-loading rifle cannon; sewed with silk or woolen thread. Bargain price submitted on receipt of sample pattern.

**Captured Spanish Bronze Rifled Cannon,** reported as having been made in Spain in 1794; weight upward of 800 pounds; 5 feet long; 3 3-4 bore. Eighteenth century museum exhibit. Price $500, with stand $100 extra.

**2215.—CAPTURED FILIPINO CANNON,** 2 ft. 9 in. long, 2¼-inch bore, 4½-inch outside diameter at muzzle, 6½-inch at breech; ancient pattern; low trunnions. Mounted on crude field carriage 4 ft. long, wheels 2 ft. 7 in. high. This cannon formed part of the U. S. Govt. Philippine Exhibit at the St. Louis World's Fair in 1904. All vouched for and sold to us by the U. S. Govt. as captured cannon. They are rare relics and *some day will be priceless.* Our present price for this museum relic trophy is $500.00.

**2215A.—CAPTURED FILIPINO CANNON,** 3 ft. 2 in. long, 2¼-inch bore; 5½-inch diameter at muzzle; 8 inches at breech. Revolutionary War pattern; low trunnion cast-iron gun (one trunnion missing). Mounted on crude field carriage wheels 2 ft. 7 in. high. No doubt hundreds of years old. Price, $450.

Native Filipino-made Brass Cannon; patterned after the old model guns of 150 years ago; length is 19 inches; weight, about 30 pounds; ⅞-bore; in serviceable order. Illustration is from photograph. Captured in attack on Filipino fortifications by U. S. A. Scout. Price, $100.

2220

**2220.—HANDSOMELY ORNAMENTED BRONZE CANNON, CAPTURED BY U. S. TROOPS IN THE PHILIPPINE ISLANDS.** On exhibition in 1904 at the St. Louis World's Fair as part of the U. S. Govt. Philippine Exhibit. The handsomest gun in the lot; length, 3 ft.; bore, 1-inch; 3-inch outside diameter at muzzle, 4 inches at breech; with yoke and pivot for use on wall or on boat. Filipino star in circle inlaid in silver, with other letters. Among all the captured guns this is admitted to be the best. Price, $375.00.

Antique Spanish Brass Saluting Cannons brought from Philippines by U. S. A. Captain; sold to us on account of inconvenience in transporting to different stations assigned him. One shown on the left weighs 24 pounds, is 9 inches long, 2-inch bore, 6-inch base, brass handle; still serviceable for firing salute as well as historical relic. Made and used hundred years ago; kind still used by firework manufacturers in shooting bombs; fired with fuse. Price, $65.00. Cannon shown on the right is 10½ inches long, 7½-inch base, 1½-inch bore, marked on the muzzle; 50 pounds; serviceable order. Price, $80.00. One Cannon, marked 49 lbs. Price, $75.00.

1841

**1841.—BREECH LOADING BRASS CANNON,** shooting No. 4 shot cartridges. The breech end is closed with screw knob. When opened the breech part of the gun turns downwards, operating a lever to draw out the cartridge. Fired by trigger attached to bolt. Full length, 28 inches; width of cannon barrel at the trunnion, 5 inches: with 50 primed empty shells. Price, $50.00.

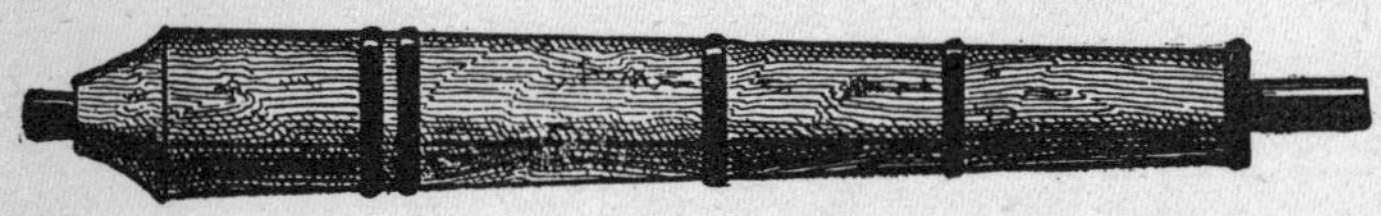

**2214A.—CAPTURED FILIPINO CANNON,** 2 ft. 7 in. long, 2-inch bore, 4-in. outside diameter at muzzle, 6½-inch at breach. Ancient low trunnions. Mounted on naval carriage 4½ feet long, with two 10 inch wheels, made from plank with sheet iron tires. Price, $450.00.

**2244B.—CAPTURED FILIPINO CANNON,** 2 ft. 9 in. long, 2-inch bore, 4½-inch outside diameter at muzzle, 6½ at breech; low trunnions; unmounted. Price, $250.00.

**2200G.—CAPTURED FILIPINO GAS PIPE CANNON,** 6 ft. long, 2½-inch bore; reinforced at breech end by larger pipe, and wound the entire length with telegraph wire. Price, $150.00.

**2200H.—CAPTURED FILIPINO CANNON,** 3 ft. 2 in. long. Made from iron gas pipe, with flange at *breech end,* and plate bolted close to opening. *Double wound* with *telegraph wire* at *breech end.* Price, $150.00.

**2200F.—2 CAPTURED FILIPINO CANNON.** Barrel made of pipe, wrapped with *telegraph wire,* partly covered with wooden jacket; 3¼ ft. long. One similar 2 ft. 10 in. long, 2-inch bore. Price, $100.00 each.

**2200D.—CAPTURED FILIPINO CANNON,** 4¼ ft. long, 2-inch bore. Made from gas pipe, reinforced at breech with iron bands close together. Price, $75.00.

**2200D.—CAPTURED FILIPINO CANNON,** 2-inch bore, 2 ft. 8 in. long; made with 2-inch pipe wire wrapped at muzzle end. Breech end has a larger pipe with cap over it. Here in this old crude weapon, made by Filipino natives, is shown the principle of reinforced and wire wrapped guns, with which the leading nations of the world are now experimenting. Price, $100.00.

2200

**2200.—CAPTURED FILIPINO GAS PIPE CANNON.** Length, 4 ft. 4 in.; 2-inch bore. Pipe is inserted in wood log, held together by iron bands, similar to bands on hub of wheels; wood trunnions. This and other guns mentioned on this page formed part of the U. S. Govt. Philippine Exhibit at the St. Louis World's Fair in 1904. Diameter at the breech is 7 inches; at the muzzle 4 inches. Rare relic for museum exhibit. Sold to us as captured war relic. Price, $100.00.

**2200A.—CAPTURED GAS PIPE CANNON,** 4 ft. 8 in. long, 2-inch bore, with wood jacket covering; 6-inch diameter at breech, 5 inches at the muzzle; iron bands. Price, $75.00.

**2200B.—CAPTURED FILIPINO CANNON,** 3 ft. long, with wood jacket and iron bands covering the gas pipe cannon barrel. Reinforced by small iron bands. Tube is burst at the muzzle and the explosion has split open part of the jacket covering, which is missing. No trunnions. Rare cannon. Patterned after the first made 14th century cannon. This is a museum exhibit. Price, $150.00.

**2200C.—3 CAPTURED FILIPINO CANNON,** 4¼ ft. long, 1½-inch bore, with wood jacket cover; 3-inch diameter at the muzzle, 6 inches at the breech, with iron bands. Price, $100.00.

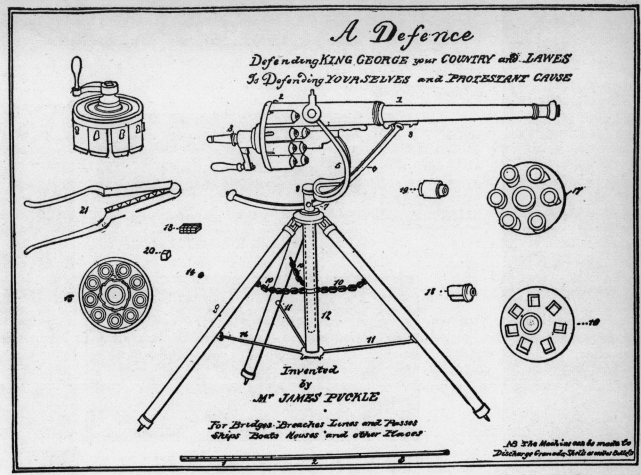

*A Defence*

Defending KING GEORGE your COUNTRY and LAWES
Is Defending YOUR SELVES and PROTESTANT CAUSE

*Invented by
Mr JAMES PUCKLE*

For Bridges Breaches Lines and Passes
Ships Boats Houses and other Places

NB The Machine can be made to
Discharge Granado Shells at once Bullets

*Whereas our Sovaaign Lord King George by his Letters patents bearing date the Fifteenth day of May in the Fourth Year of his Majesties Reign was Graciously pleas'd to Give & Grant unto me James Puckle of London Gent my Exors Admors & Assignes the Sole priviledge & Authority to Make Exercise Work & use a Portable Gun or Machine (by me lately Invented) called a DEFENCE in that part of his Majesties Kingdom of Great Brittain call'd England his Dominion of Wales Town of Berwick upon Tweed and his Majesties Kingdom of Ireland in such manner & with such Materials as should be ascertain'd to be the sd New Invention by writing under my Hands & Seal and Inrolled in the High court of chancery within Three calendar Months from the date of the sd patent as in & by his Maj: his Letters Patents Relacon being thereunto had Doth & may amongst other things more fully & at large appear NOW I the said James Puckle Do hereby Declare that the Materials whereof the sd Machine is Made are Steel Iron & Brass and that the Trepied whereon it Stands is Wood & Iron And that in the above print (to which I hereby Refer) the said Gun or Machine by me Invented is Delineated & Described July the 25th 1718.*

AB 180

## The Forerunner of the Gatling Gun

This is not a picture of some new-fangled notion in firearms, but represents a very old-fangled idea in that direction—a revolving gun, mounted on a tripod, the whole an invention of one James Puckle away back in 1718, or more than two centuries ago.

On the 15th of May, 1718, James Puckle, a citizen of London, was granted a fourteen-year patent, numbered four hundred and eighteen, by King George, "Defender of the Faith." The inventor, who was evidently a staunch royalist as well as a "gentleman," placed at the head of his application these words:

Defending King George, your Country and Lawes,
Is Defending Your Selves and Protestant Cause,

and declared that his invention consisted of "A portable Gun or Machine called a Defence, that Discharges soe often and soe many Bulletts, and can be soe Quickly Loaden as renders it next to Impossible to Carry any Ship by Boarding." He also explained that one of the most important features of the invention was its adaptability for "shooting square bullets against Turks and round bullets against Christians." This machine-gun was mounted on a tripod and, in general appearance, strongly suggests the Gatling gun.

Prior to Puckle's time, and for nearly one hundred years after, progress in the improvement of this form of weapon was slow and uncertain.

Long before the flintlock was invented, revolving firearms of various forms were in use, and harquebuses with from three to eight chambered cylinders were made in the first half of the sixteenth century.

**This illustration is an exact reproduction of the original patent claim.**

Spanish Torpedo with War-head, Air-chamber, Engine, Propellers and Rudders. Rare and valuable relic recovered from the Almirante Oquendo. Over 10 feet long, made of copper and gun metal, weighing about 500 pounds; cost originally upwards of $5,000. Torpedoes of this large size are propelled by compressed air, which starts the machinery as it is shot out of the gun, which attain a speed of 20 miles an hour and carry explosive enough to wreck the largest battleship; now free from powder. Price, $385.00.

This story is told to us as true. An admiralty clerk was giving luncheon to a brother official from the war office. "Black coffee?" asked the admiralty clerk.

"Good heavens, no!" cried the other. "Why, if I were to drink a drop of coffee at this hour of the day, I shouldn't get a wink of sleep all the weary afternoon."—London Globe.

Spanish Bronze 12-Pounder Mountain Howitzer Cannon. Smooth bore, used in Cuban war, brought to New York in 1899. Handsomely engraved with Spanish crown and named the "Rondo." In fine, serviceable order, safe for firing salutes; complete with gunner's implements, sponge, rammer, etc., etc. Weighs about 200 pounds; 3 feet long. Price, $150.00.

Drag Ropes for U. S. Army Gatling Gun. Fine manila rope, about one inch diameter, with wood handles. In good, serviceable order, like new, $2.50 each.

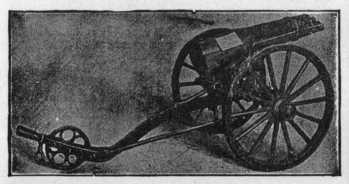

— Spanish Rapid-Fire Machine Gun from the Almirante Oquendo, sunk off Santiago, July 3, 1898. Made by the Hotchkiss Company in Paris. Was mounted on the mast, and when the ship took fire fell into the hold. All vouched for by the captain of schooner Chase, who received the gun. The breech mechanism was not found. We have mounted the gun on naval carriage and offer it for sale as per illustration for $450.00.

Spanish Bronze Torpedo recovered from the wreck of the Spanish warship Almirante Oquendo, sunk off Santiago, Cuba, July 3, 1898. This torpedo was lying on deck ready for attaching the war head with the guncotton explosive. The holes shown in the illustration were made by shots from United States war ships and exploding projectiles. It is 6 feet long, made of copper and bronze. Price, $275.00.

United States Army Pass Box. Made of wood neatly painted, with brass hinges and hook fastener; size 15 inches, 8½ inches wide, 3½ inches high; used to carry the powder charge from the caisson to the cannon. When covered with carpet by the buyer will make neat (hinged) hassock, as well as handy box (with cover) for holding small things. Real relic of the Civil War. In fine order, like new. Price, 45 cents each.

Antique Cannon Flintlock, used in shooting old-time cannon; was fitted on the side of the cannon at the touchhole and threw the fire spark into the fuse hole. Rare relic. Price, $6.50.

133. SWEET'S DOUBLE ACTION, Marked 11, 12 second fuses. Bronze-zinc capped. Made by the American Ordnance Co. for use in exploding charge of powder in projectiles. New; weight 18 ounces. Price, $1.85 each.

120. PERCUSSION LOADED FUSES. For use in base of 1-pounder explosive shells. Bronze, weight 2 ounces; new; made by American Ordnance Co. Price, 65 cents each.

100 SPRING CLIPS FOR TWO-WIRE ELECTRIC FUSES. Made of bronze and hard rubber, with knurled head adjusting screws. Length 3 inches, front width ⅞-inch, rear 1⅝ inches; weight 2½ ounces. New. Price, 85 cents each.

Six 30-pounder U. S. N. Parrott Rifle Cannons, all in serviceable order; weight, 3,500 lbs. each; bore, 4 inches; $285.00. Mounted on navy carriage, $500.00. One of these fine guns with mahogany carriage, $600.00.

Antique German Mortar Cannon, iron; length 18 inches; bore, 2 inches; weight, 90 lbs.; serviceable order for saluting on Kaiser's Birthday; unmounted. $28.50.

Five Antique Saluting Cannons, found in London; length, 15 inches; bore, 1⅛ inches; weight, 20 lbs. $5.00 each.

U. S. Navy Cannon Carriages, large stock suitable for mounting large cannons, both in the two wheel marsilly and four wheel truck pattern. Old veterans of the Civil War that have been in many a battle if interested send us measurement of the cannon you wish to mount and we will advise you size we can furnish with the price.

Mahogany Navy Carriage for 30-pounder Parrott Rifle with bronze mountings. $250.00.

Rosewood Pivot Carriage (navy) for 30-pounder Parrott rifle. $350.00.

8 Armory Limber Poles, suitable for use in drill-room, with limbers and caisson. $5.00 each.

8-inch Smooth-Bore Cannon in good order from U. S. S. Wabash; complete with carriage. $800.00.

100-pounder Rifle Cannon from the Civil War gunboat Pawtuxet, vouched for by U. S. N. records; in serviceable order; weight, 9,000 lbs. $800.00.

Two 80-pounder Breech-Loading Rifles, almost new; length, 14 feet; bore, 6 inches; throws shot weighing 100 lbs. upward of five miles, according to elevation; weight of gun, 9,000 lbs. $1,000.00 each.

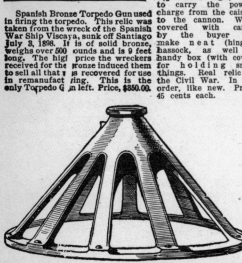

J. S. NAVY CAGE STAND.

Spanish Bronze Torpedo Gun used in firing the torpedo. This relic was taken from the wreck of the Spanish War Ship Viscaya, sunk off Santiago July 3, 1898. It is of solid bronze, weighs over 500 pounds and is 9 feet long. The high price the wreckers received for the bronze induced them to sell all that was recovered for use in remanufacturing. This is the only Torpedo Gun left. Price, $350.00.

10561

10562

**10561. FRENCH CONTRACTOR'S MODEL BRONZE CANNON**, as submitted to EMPEROR NAPOLEON. The cannon which was made from this model is now in the British Artillery Museum, and from the notes taken for our book on Weapons of War it reads, "French Dolphin handles;

Cannon, Bronze, Captured at the BATTLE OF WATERLOO," nearly 7 feet; smooth bore, 4¾ inches; weight 1,940 pounds; name and date engraved on the gun, "Voltaire, L'an3, de la republique Francaise.. (the third year of the French Republic, 1795); maker, "A Douai Bouquers, 29 Burmaise." The car- riage has double trunnion holds, the front ones for use in firing, the rear for use in trans portation to prevent the muzzle from trailing, also helping to distribute the weight. Iron drag hooks and chain attached to the front of the carriage for use in retreating without taking time to turn. This pattern of wheels was copied from the Madras India Gun Carriage wheels. Each set of felloes is spanned with tire irons in sections bolted through, with square head projecting above the tire to prevent slipping in transportation and jumping in firing. The HAND BARROW is portable magazine chained on limber and usually contained about six rounds of powder and shot for emergency use before arrival of the ammunition wagon or caisson, THE ABOVE ARE THE NOTES ABOUT THE REAL GUN IN BRITISH ROYAL ARTILLERY MUSEUM, BEFORE WE HAD THE GOOD FORTUNE TO PURCHASE THE CONTRACTOR'S MODEL. The model cannon which we offer for sale is 23 inches long; 13-16 smooth bore' Dolphin handles; flash pan; touch hole; engraving in relief with oval shield in quarters fleur de lis, with raised moulding band; ¾ inch iron axle (wood cov ered); all complete, passed by the U. S. Customs as over 100 years old. Handsome antique for any high class museum. Rare prize.

In olden times contractors and inventors had to submit WORKING MODELS together with their specifications. Of late years models are not required. It was the presence of models in the U. S. Patent Office in Washington that induced British officers, Admiral Cockburn, in the War of 1812 to give orders to spare that building, that Yankee inventions may benefit the world. Price for Model Cannon, $350.00.

U. S. Civil War Army Cannon, Relics of Civil War battles; used by the Government after the war to ornament the Allegheny Arsenal grounds; sold to us at the disbandment of the arsenal. The history of these cannon given to us by Ordnance Sergeant at the arsenal was that they were Union Army guns and were captured by the Confederates, and spiked before being recaptured. For guns in serviceable order, mounted on Army Field Carriage, with gunner's outfit, useful for firing occasional salutes or decorating lawn, price $3.50. If limber is wanted, the price is $75.00 extra; caisson, $95.00 extra.

U. S. Army Bronze Six Pounder Smooth Bore Cannon. Relic of war, 1861-65. Weight 880 pounds. In serviceable order. Mounted on Field Carriage. Complete with gunner's utensils. Price $500.00. Handsome gun.

**10562. FRENCH MODEL BRONZE MORTAR CANNON**, mounted on swivel carriage, with elevating screw, with hooks, rollers and position notch irons; trunion caps; length 6½ inches, width 3⅜ inches; smooth bore, 2⅛ inches; mask face forms flash pan; powder chamber 1½ inches wide by ⅝ inch diameter; trunions 5 inches by 1⅜ inch diameter; length of the base of the carriage 11½ inches, width 8 inches. Model no doubt submitted by cannon maker in olden times to secure order from Emperor Napoleon. It is only in the last 50 years that the U. S. Patent Office agreed to accept SPECIFICATIONS instead of WORKING MODELS. Rare museum antiquity. Price $150.00.

We have in our Book of War Weapons a copy of an engraving of a French arsenal showing shelves filled with models of cannons, mortars, etc.

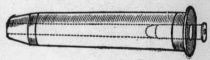

**10908A. GERMAN ARMY BREECH LOADING CANNON GAS CHECK;** ⅜ inch diameter, ½ inch thick; polished steel grooved rim; in velvet lined case brass mountings; size of the case 6x6x1½ inches. Price $8.50.

**10545. FRENCH MODEL ANCIENT CANNON;** full length 22 inches; diameter at the breech 3 inches, at the muzzle 1¾ inches; low hung trunnions; Dolphin handles; breech finely engraved with lion's head in act of swallowing mace. Model gun no doubt submitted for government approval and test, as was the custom in olden times (same as the U. S. Patent Office in olden times required inventors to submit models). This old relic is facsimile of some of the ancient large size cannons now in the King's Museum, Berlin, captured from France. Price $18.50.

**10905. DR. GATLING'S EARLY MODEL MACHINE GUN FEED CASE**, made of stamped tin; size 13x2½x⅞ inches; like new; relics. 18 cents each.

**11041. U. S. NAVY DRILL SHELL**, made of hardwood, polished to fit into one-pounder Hotchkiss naval cannot; rifle barrel in the center of shell for shooting 45 calibre cartridges. These drill cartridges are used in the navy to train gunners in the manual of aiming and shooting rapid fire cannon, at the reduced cost of 2 cents for small arms rifle cartridge. as against $3.00 if the real shot is used.

To seaside resorts we would suggest the purchase of cannon shooting these drill shells, shooting at target placed out at sea, say one-half or three-fourths of a mile away. In our opinion visitors would gladly pay 10 cents a shot for the rare privilege of FIRING A SHOT OUT OF A CANNON AT A TARGET. Drill shells for one pounder gun $3.00 each. Three pounder gun $4.50 each.

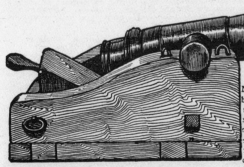

**10808. PAIR OF ANTIQUE CANNON HOWITZERS**, period prior to the War of 1812; mounted on wood carriage (not original carriage); length 16 inches, bore 3 inches; Fired with flash pan; iron is 1¾ inches thick at the muzzle; suitable for decoration or firing an occasional salute; weight of each cannon 112 pounds. Price, the pair, $65.00; singly $35.00.

**10909. GERMAN ARMY BREECH LOADING CANNON MUZZLE COVER**, hand sewed russet leather, new; 6 inch diameter, 2¼ inches deep; 3 foot double strap. Price $2.50.

**10908. GERMAN ARMY BREECH LOADING CANNON GAS CHECK;** polished steel; 4¾ inches in diameter; ⅝ inch thick; recessed copper rim. Price $8.50.

**U. S. ARMY BRONZE 12 POUNDER, SMOOTH BORE, MUZZLE LOADING, CIVIL WAR CANNON**, weight 1,275 pounds, offered in used serviceable order, mounted on field carriage; complete with limber and gunner's equipment. Price $1,000.00.

**U. S. A. 30 TON HYDRAULIC JACK**, used for mounting heavy cannon at fortifications. Offered in serviceable order. Price $30.00.
Fifteen Ton Hyrdaulic Jack, price $20.00.

## HOPE SPRINGS ETERNAL IN THE HUMAN BREAST.

A number of young men meeting an elderly Scotch-Irish lady, who was well known for her skill at repartee, and who, at the age of nearly 80 was still a Miss, thought they would have a little fun with her. "Morro, geed Aunty," "Morro yoursels, ma bonny laddies." "Aunty, cud you tell us how auld a wuman must be ere she gies up hope of getting a mon?" Without a moment's hesitation they received her reply, "Ye maun spier (ask) at some yen aulder than me."

**10733. U. S. A. GUNNER'S LANYARD**; newfine flax rope, 35 feet long, with russet leather covered hand grip with snap hook for fastening to the primer; the extra length of the lanyard helps prevent accidents from pieces of the flying primer; serviceable for any gun. Price 90 cents each.

No. 7. 2,000 Felt Gun Wads for 9 pounder projectiles, ⅝-inch thick, 2½ inches diameter, 6½ ounces each, light weight. Will be made to fit smaller shells if ordered in quantity. Price, 10 cents each.

3,000 One pounder Felt Gun Wads, for 3 inch projectile, ⅝ inch thick, 3 inch diameter, ½ ounce each, light weight, price as are, 15 cents each.

Shell Ignition Bag, brass guard, cardboard wad, ¾ inches thick, 3⅞ inch diameter with 1⅝ inch center hole, covered on both sides with light open scrim cloth pocket, weight 2 ounces. Price 20 cents each.

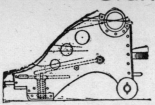

No. 3.—U. S. Navy Iron Gun Carriage; bronze mountings; used during later years of Civil war; are in good, serviceable order. Price. $150.

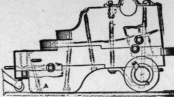

No. 4.—U. S. Navy Wood Gun Carriage; Marailly pattern; made of hard wood, bolted and ironed. Have been in use on board of navy warships during the Civil War. Are offered in serviceable order in different sizes.

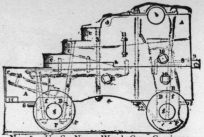

No. 5.—U. S. Navy Wood Gun Carriage; ancient style 4-wheel truck. Made at Navy Yard of hard wood securely bolted and ironed. These old carriages have been in use on board navy warships and are valuable as relics as well as serviceable for mounting cannon for lawn decoration.

Boerman Time Fuse used in Civil War shells fired from smooth bore cannon, with one mile range. Relics. Price, $3.

No. 7.—Old Revolutionary War Cannon that formed part of the battery of the British 44-Gun Frigate Charon, set on fire and sunk by a red hot shot fired by the American battery at Gloucester Point at the Battle of Yorktown, 1781. Gun was recovered by diver at the Yorktown Centennial after 100 years submersion. Large hole eaten through near the muzzle. Fully authenticated. We only succeeded in purchasing after waiting 20 years. We would like to keep it for our museum, but cannot hold all the good things. It will take $1,000 to tempt us to part with it.

WE HAVE IN STOCK A LARGE ASSORTMENT OF LARGE AND SMALL CANNON, BOTH BRASS AND STEEL. WE HAVE SOLD MANY FOR USE AS ORNAMENTAL NEWEL POSTS FOR CLUBS, AND FOR OUTDOOR DECORATION. WRITE US WHAT YOU NEED AND WE SHALL QUOTE PRICES AND GIVE FULL PARTICULARS.

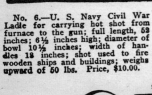

No. 6.—U. S. Navy Civil War Ladle for carrying hot shot from furnace to the gun; full length, 52 inches; 6½ inches high; diameter of bowl 10½ inches; width of handles 18 inches; shot used to fire wooden ships and buildings; weighs upward of 50 lbs. Price, $10.00.

U. S. Navy Spar Torpedoes, in sizes to contain 100 and 200 pounds of high explosive gun cotton. Torpedo is attached to spar, and on approach of enemy's vessel the spar is lowered under the side and exploded by battery. Length of cylinder, about 3½ feet, 1 foot diameter. Serviceable order; practically new; complete. Price, $35.00.

No. 8.—GARDNER RAPID FIRE MACHINE GUNS, MOUNTED ON FIELD CARRIAGES, FOR SHOOTING CALIBRE 43 SPANISH, 43 MARTINI-HENRY OR 45 SPRINGFIELD BALL OR BLANK CARTRIDGES. IN SERVICEABLE ORDER AT LOWEST POSSIBLE BARGAIN PRICES.

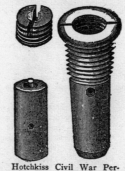

No. 17

No. 18

Hotchkiss Civil War Percussion Fuse which explodes charge in cannon shells by impact. Relics. Price, $3.

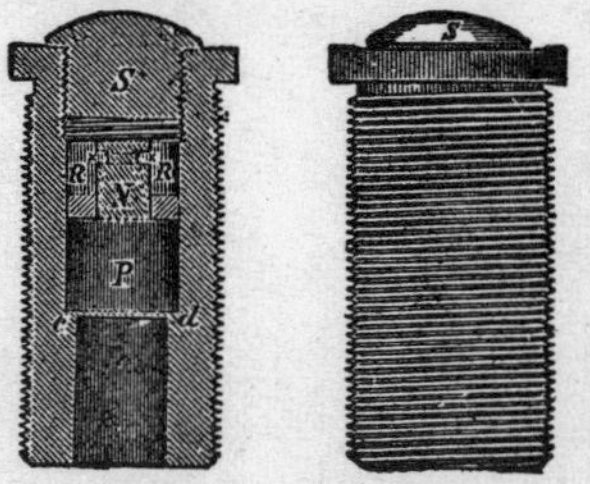

Parrott Civil War Percussion Fuse, used in exploding the powder charge in shells fired from Parrott Rifled Cannon. Relics. Price, $3.00.

10174. THREE-INCH BREECH-LOADING RIFLE CANNON WOOL SPONGES. Woven wool, also in fleece. Price, $1.50 each.

10175. CANVAS COVERS FOR THREE-INCH RIFLE CANNON SPONGES. New. Price, 45 cents.

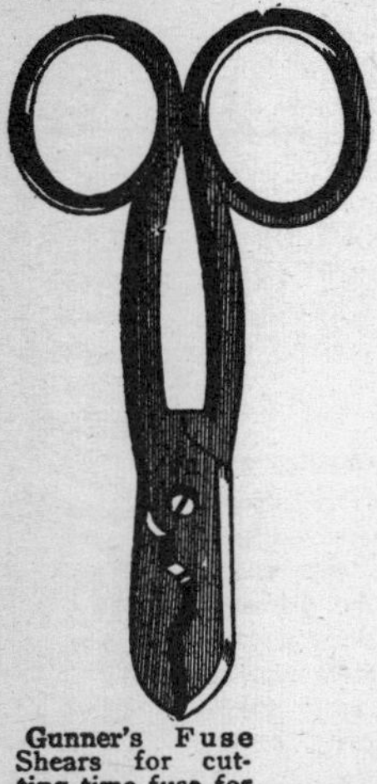

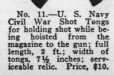

Gunner's Fuse Shears for cutting time fuse for bombshells; steel; 7-inch U. S. Price, $6.00.

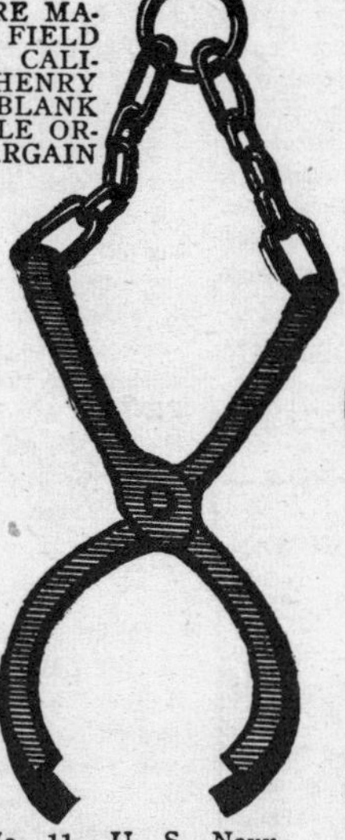

No. 11.—U. S. Navy Civil War Shot Tongs for holding shot while being hoisted from the magazine to the gun; full length, 2 ft.; width of tongs, 7½ inches; serviceable relic. Price, $10.

Ancient Shot Gauges, used in olden times for measuring round shot and shell; from U. S. Navy. We have seen handsome decorations made with these old steel gauges at the Norfolk Navy Yard. Assorted sizes. Price, from $2.75 upwards.

Historical cannon were on sale at the old Allegheny Arsenal yesterday. Twenty-two sealed proposals were received for condemned ordnance and ordnance stores, including cannon, ammunition and equipments. The highest bid was made by Francis Bannerman, of New York. The cannon number 46. Among them are several bearing dates prior to 1840 and used in the Mexican War. Others bore dates ranging on to 1861, and having seen service in the Civil War. These will be shipped to New York, and from there some will find their way to other lands and possibly serve a warlike purpose again.

Many of the guns, especially the smaller cannon, find their way to the lawns of country places, not for the purpose of scaring away burglars, but to give the grounds an attractive appearance.—*Extract from Pittsburg Newspaper.*

Antique U. S. Govt. Port Fire Staves, used in olden times by gunner to hold port fire, with which the charge was fired. No. 17 has sliding copper tightening ring; also spear point. No. 18 has thumb screw and loop for belt. Choice of these old Govt. Arsenal relics, $1.50 each.

*All Projectiles are offered free from Powder.*

Conical Shot.  Conical Shell.  Grape Shot. 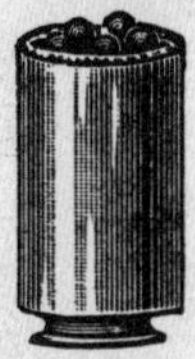  Cannister Shot.   Breech Loading Conical Shell.   Exploded Brass Cannon Shell.   Massage Ball.   Hand Grenade.

**Nickel Steel Projectiles** 1896. Model from the U. S. Navy. Fired through Armor Plate in testing at the Navy Proving Ground, Annapolis, Maryland.

Same as used by Admiral Dewey, Schley and Sampson in the Spanish American War.

6 inch Shell, $15 00 Shot, $20 00
8 " " 30 00 " 35 00
10 " " 35 00 " 38 00
12 " " 40 00 " 50 00
13 " Shot .............. 50 00

The 13 inch Shot weighs 1,100 pounds. At 2,000 yards the penetration is 22 inches. The range 13 miles; leaves the gun at speed of 2,000 feet a second. Rapidity 1 shot every two minutes.

Diameter 13 in., height nearly 4 ft.

### Conical Projectiles.
**For Rifled Cannon.**

1,200 3 inch U.S. Army Shell, $1.50 ea.
3 inch Armstrong Shrapnel Confederate ................... $3 00
3 inch Dahlgren ............... 2 00
500 3 inch Hotchkiss ......... 1 50
1,000 3 inch Parrott .......... 2 00
3 inch Confederate ........... 5 00
8 inch Absterdam Shot or Shell ........................ 2 00
12 Pounder Hotchkiss ........ 2 50
Confederate 12 Pounder ... 3 50
500 20 Pounder Parrott Shell.. 2 50
500 20 " " Solid Shot 2 50
500 20 " Absterdam Shell 2 50
500 30 Pounder Parrott Shell. 3 00
500 30 Pounder Parrott Breech Loading Rifle Shell. ..... 3 00
Schenkle 30 Pounder Shell with Paper Mache Sabot ........ 3 00
Schenkle 20 Pounder Shell with Paper Mache Sabot.........
   as used early part of Civil War ...................... 3 00
U. S. Navy Experimental 30 Pounder Shell ............... 3 00
Confederate 30 Pounder Shell (Lead Bands) ................ 00
50 Pounder Rifle Shells........ 5 00
100 80 Pounder Breech Loading Rifle Shell ................. 6 00
100 100 Pounder Parrott Shot, Civil War Style .............. 6 00
100 100 Pounder Parrott Shot, Late regulation ............. 6 00
200 100 Pounder Parrott Shell, Late regulation ............. 6 00
100 Pounder Parrott Shrapnel .................... 6 00
6 inch U. S. Navy Steel Shot, broken in firing ............20 00
32 Pounder Shrapnel Shot .. 2 50
8 inch Shrapnel Shot...... 3 25

**San Juan Spanish Brass Shell,** with case, total length 2½ feet, diameter case 4½ inches. Relic. ................................ $22 50

**Spanish Explosive Shell** from San Juan, free from Powder. Snell has lead studs to take rifle grooves. Rare pattern, Price, $7 00.

### Grape Shot.
15 inch Monitor Shot....$20 00
11 " Stands for Grape Shot ...............Each 2 00

**Canister Shot** free from powder. Very destructive when used against troops. Filled with small balls that scatter over wide area.
6 Pounder .................$1 00
3 inch Rifle............... 1 50

**BK-3. Army Brass Cartridge Case,** empty, **without Base.** Length 19¼ inches, diameter at bottom 4 inches, weight 4½ pounds. Price, $3 00 each.

One 200 Pounder Parrott, Rifle Shot, weighs 280 lbs.. kind Gen'l Gilmore threw into Charleston from Morris Island, (5 miles.) Price. $25 00.

### Hand Grenades.
**With Arrow and Fuze.**
1¼ lb. Grenade ..........$1 00
3 lb. " ............... 1 50
5 " " ............... 2 00
Sold only to responsible parties.

### U. S. Navy Exploded (Brass) Cannon Cartridge Shells
removed from the gun after shot has been fired. In 5 sizes.
2 Pounders........$ 50 cents each.
3 " ......... 75 " "
6 " .........1 50 " "
4 inch diameter shells........$5 00
Few 5 inch diameter shells..... 8 00
Handsome and ornamental relics.

**U. S. Navy Breech Loading Cannon Explosive Steel Shell,** (free from powder.) Has Copper band, polished up, makes handsome relic. 10 Pounders. Price, $1 80 ea.

**100 Pounder** Civil War Armstrong Confederate Shell. Rare relic. $30 00.

**Spanish Cartridge Shells (Brass)** from San Juan. 20-Pounder, $8 00

**Spanish 12 Pounder Shell** with lead studs to take rifle grooves; from Santiago. Relics. $7 00.

**Spanish Rifled Cannon Shell** with brass case, found at San Juan, Cuba, for high power cannon from Spanish Battleship, Reine Mercedes, used by Spanish land force against Genl. Shafter. Shell is 4½ in. diameter, foot long; the brass shell is 20 inches. Handsome relic. Price, $20 00.

**Also Steel Shot** with brass shell from same place. Price, $20 00.

**Pongee Silk Powder Bag,** Spanish, from San Juan. $2 00.

**Safety Cap** for Spanish 20-pound Shell. $1 50.

**U. S. Navy Experimental Breech Loading Rifle Shell,** 30 Pounder. $4 50.

### Spherical Projectiles for Smooth Bore Guns.
6 Pounder Solid Shot....$0 75
12 " Shell ......... 1 50
18 " Solid Shot.... 2 00
7 inch Shell ............. 3 00
8 " Shell ............. 3 25
8 " Shrapnel ......... 3 00
8 " Solid Shot........ 3 25
Peavy 9 in. Shrapnel Shell 5 00
Crane 9 in. Shrapnel Shell 5 00
11 inch. Original size of Shot used by U. S. S. Monitor engagement with Merrimac ................16 00
15 inch Shell (later Monitors) ................20 00
15 inch Shrapnel (later Monitors) ..............20 00

### Torpedoes.
12 inch Spar Torpedoes from Washington Naval Park Collection. $20 00.

**Stone Cannon Ball** from Old Scotch Battlefield, 7 inches in diameter. $25 00.

**Collection Spanish Shot and Shell,** from the Arsenal in Havana, Cuba. Purchased in December, 1898, previous to the evacuation.

Sawyer Canister Shot, $2 50.

6 Pounder Shell with wood Sabot. Price, $1 00 each.

**Part of Iron Shell,** fired from Admiral Sampson's fleet at Morro Castle, Santiago. Found near the Fort. $3 50.

**U. S. N. Russet Leather** Cartridge Box for carrying Rapid Fire Cannon Shells. Holds 20 three Pounders. Price, $6 00.

No. 5. U. S. NAVY LEATHER POWDER BUCKETS. Relics of the Civil War. Assorted sizes.
XI inch, as illustration..........$3.75
IX inch .......................... 3.40
VI inch .......................... 2.00
12 Pounder ...................... 2.70
6 Pounder ....................... 4.25
XIII inch Mortar................12.00
Makes good waste paper holder as well as relic.

We have had frequent calls from Physicians for iron cannon balls for their patients to use in massaging (by rolling on the abdomen) for constipation. We can now furnish in two sizes. 3 inches in diameter, weighing 3 pound, price 40 cents. Leather covered, 70 cents. 3¼ inches in diameter, weighing 5½ lbs., 75 cents.

"Massage in all its forms has been recommended by Prof. Dujardin-Beaumetz; especially for constipation, and advises to kneed or roll, with an iron ball, the epigastrium or abdomen, in order to restore the tone of the abdominal muscles and to stimulate the vermicular motion of the intestines and peristalsis of the stomach.

These cannon balls avoid any undue exertion as they produce massage by simply rolling them on the abdomen."

Broken half 15 inch Monitor Shell ......................$10 00
Broken half 15 inch Shrapnel with small balls .......... 12 00
Broken half 8 inch Shrapnel with balls.................. 5 00
Broken half 8 inch Shell....... 3 00
" " 10 " " ....... 3 50
" " 3 " " ....... 2 00
" " 12 Pounder ........ 1 50

One half part of Spanish 10 inch steel core Shot from Havana Arsenal. $30 00.

### 15 inch Spherical Case Shot.
U. S. Navy Civil War relic filled with 1,000 iron balls, 1 inch diameter. Price, $20 00.

Broken Half part of one of these 15 in. case shot with 500 bullets, $12 00

**BK1. Army Brass Cartridge Cases,** empty, size 2½ inches by 9¼ inches, weight 1½ pounds. Price, $1.95 each.

**Canister Shot** 1½ inches in diameter, flatted on one side to answer for desk use as paper weight. Relics. 20 cents each.

**Broken Part Crane 9 inch Shell,** showing two parts. $5 75.

**Broken Part Peavey 8 inch Shell,** showing construction. $5 75.

**10 inch U. S. Navy Shell,** fired and which has point end fuzed by impact. Rare relic. $50 00. Weighs 700 lbs.

**Spanish Shell and Brass Cartridge Case** from wreck of Viscaya. 6-inch shell, total length of shell and case nearly 6 feet, fine relic. $38.00.

**Spanish Sighting Bar** from the 11-inch Turret rifle, on the Viscaya, 2 feet long, covered with sight marks. Price, $12.00.

**Spanish Shells** for rapid fire guns, 1-pounders. Price, $1.80 each.

**Mitraileuse Brass Cartridges.** Relics. 20 cents each.

**BK-2. Army Brass Cartridge Cases,** empty size 5 inches by 16¾ inches, weight 7 pounds. Price, $5.00 each.

Brass Cannon Shells recovered by divers from the wreck of Spanish warship Cristobal Colon, sunk off Santiago; height of 29¼ inches; diameter 6 inches. Souvenir, relic, umbrella stand. Price, $12.00.

Spanish Cannon Shells, 6 in. diameter conical, with lead studs to take rifle grooves; very old pattern; partly broken. Price, $5.85.

Carved Walnut Headboard, from the U. S. Ordnance Cutter, used in olden times as ferry to Governor's Island. Size, 38x16 inches. With crossed cannons, 10 piles of shot; fine piece of decorative work. Price, $12.00.

**Cannon Shells.**

**United States Navy Rapid-fire Brass Cannon Shells that contained the powder and the shot fired at the Spanish fleet in Manila Bay and at Santiago. These shells are placed in the cannon; when fired the shot speeds on its mission, the shell is removed from the gun and packed away to be sent to the Navy Yard shops where each shell is carefully examined for flaws developed in firing. If found perfect the shell is reswedged and sent to the magazine to be refilled with powder and fresh shot; if imperfect (the least little flaw) it is condemned and sold. These shells we offer have been found slightly imperfect. They were turned in from nearly all the warships. U.S.S. Massachusetts, U.S.S. Indiana, U.S.S. Detroit, etc., from the U.S.S. Olympia by way of Boston Navy Yard and from the United States warships at Manila by the transport Buffalo. The small shell is the 1 pdr., 4 inches long, 1⅛ inches diameter, and the price, unpolished, just as taken from the gun, is 50c. each;** The medium is the 3 pdr., 14¾ inches long, 2⅜ inches dameter. Price, $1.25. The large shell is the 6 pdr., 12 inches long, 3 inches diameter. Price, $1.50. A few 28½ inches long, 4 inches diameter, long enough for table legs, $8.00. Some 35 inches long and 5 inches diameter, $12.00. We have the following brass cannon shells that came from the Spanish warships at Santiago.

**3¾ in. long, 1⅛ in. diameter, $0.75 unpolished.**
**6⅛ " 3 " 1.25 "**
**12 " 2⅝ " 1.75 "**
**14½ " 2¼ " 1.75 "**
**18 " 4 " 3.75 "**

**We have sold many of these for use as vases, steins, decorations, etc.**

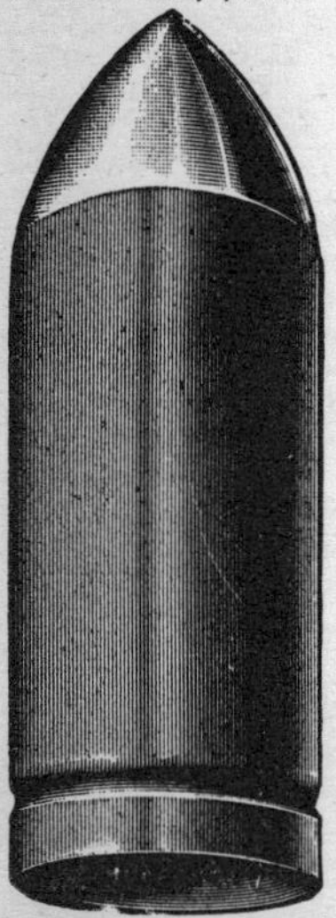

5,000 Captured Spanish Shot, brass covered (full size), taken by the U. S. Navy Warships. Cartridge Case was unloaded and the shot, all free from powder, sold to us. Makes trophy, paper weight or ornament, brass covered. Price, 25c ea.

**Confederate Powder Bags**

Made of Scotch plaid flannel, captured during the Civil War, sent to the South by blockade steamers. Size, when opened up, 15x20 inches; assorted color plaids; new. Price, 45c each.

**No. 2.**

Confederate **Army relic. Steel cannon ball made by Whitworth Armory in England, for use in Confederate Army during Civil War; Whitworth steel, hexagonal bolt, weighs over 10 lbs., 9 inches long. Price, $1.00 each.**

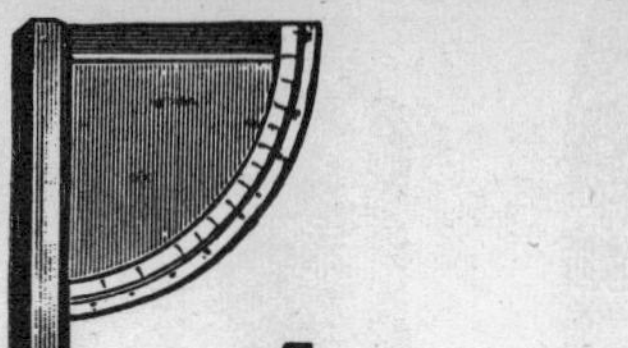

**No. 3.**

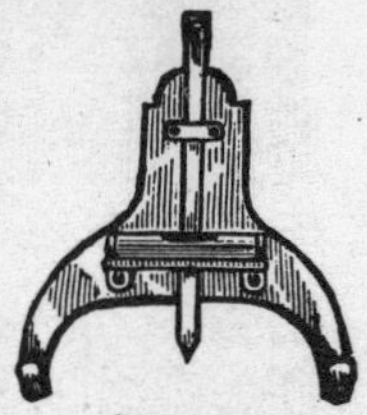

**No. 4.**

**No. 3. United States Army Civil War Gunner's Quadrant, made of polished mahogany, with brass cap, 18 inches long, 7-inch radius, marked with degrees, 50c. each.**

**No. 4. United States Army Gunner's Level, polished brass, with spirit level and gauge; new; useful article; fine decoration. Price, $2.50 each.**

Confederate Powder Bags, made of paper; rare relic. Price, 25c.

**United States Artillery Cannon Sponges and Rammers, in serviceable order, like new. 8 inch, 6 and 12 pounder, 7½ feet long, price, $3.00; 20 and 30 pounder, 10 feet long, price, $4.50.**

**Civil War 12-pounder Shell Clock. Small clock set in the fuse hole of the shell, with gilt bronze flag-pole eagle on the top. Handsome desk ornament. Price, $12.00.**

**U. S. Navy Bronze Cannon Lock, relic of Civil War, $5.00.**

**C. S. A. Cannon Sponge Bucket, made of leather, with brass hoops. Relic, $4.75.**

**Spanish Torpedo Propellers and Rudders, 22 x 14 inches, weight 60 pounds. Relic from sunken Spanish battleships. Price $50.00.**

**Spanish Torpedo Engine, recovered from Santiago wrecked warships; relic; $40.00.**

Boer Shell, with brass fuse. Relic from South Africa. Shows rifle groove marks on the copper band. Price, $7.85.

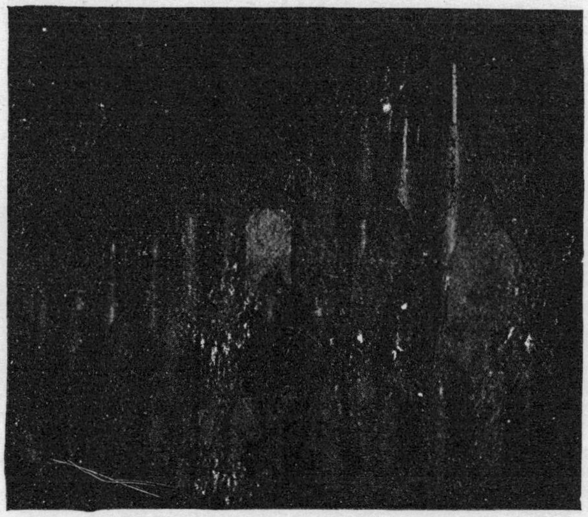

**Collection of Spanish War Shot and Shell.**

**Sixty different kinds, ranging in size from the 1-pounder rapid-fire shot up to the 1,300-pound steel armor-piercing shot with its range of thirteen miles. Collected from soldiers and sailors returning from Cuba and the Philippines, from United States Government auction sales and from the Spanish Governor of the Arsenal in Cuba, taking delivery direct from the maestranza. This illustration fails to show the large 6, 8, 10 and 13 inch projectiles. Some of the brass shell cases stand 4 feet high; some show the coral deposit, as when recovered from the wrecked Spanish warships off Santiago. Price for the lot, $2,500.**

**U.S A. Civil War Fuses for use in cannon shells. Placed in the fuse hole, ignited by the fire that starts the shell out of the gun, it burns the desired time, then ignites the powder in the shell, which causes shell to burst. Made at Frankford Arsenal during the Civil War.** Now very rare, 50 cents each.

Hemp Rope Cannon Shot Slings to hoisting the shot from magazine to the gun deck on men-of-war. Price, $1.00 each.

Copper Vent Plugs, pure copper. Price, $4.75.

**Spanish Torpedo War Head, 28 x 14 inches. Conical shaped, copper, $35.00.**

**Piece Boer Shell from South Africa. Price, $1.00.**

**Piece of Philippine Shell, with rifling marks on the head band, $4.75.**

**200 U. S. Army Gunners' Pincers made of forged steel with nail claw. Price, 30c.**

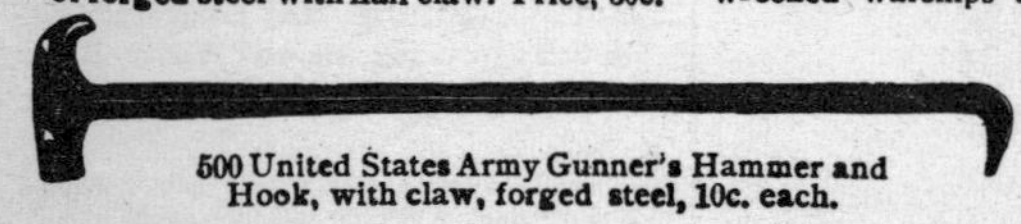

**500 United States Army Gunner's Hammer and Hook, with claw, forged steel, 10c. each.**

**Olympia Gunners' Magazine Shoes. Price, $2.00.**

**300 U. S. Army Gunners' Russet Leather Pouches, with waist belt. Complete. Size of box is 6x7 inches, 2 inches wide at the top. Price of box and belt, 60c.**

**Leather Fire Bucket, from the U. S. S. Olympia. Relic. Fine waste-paper receptacle. Price, $5.00.**

**80-pounder Parrott Civil War Battering Shot, with the copper disk sabot. Rare pattern. Price, $8.00.**

**Civil War Monitor 15-inch Cannon Tompion. Price, $3.75. 15-inch Cannon Wad, $2.50. 20-inch Cannon Tompion for t e gun exhibited at Centennial Exposition. Largest gun ever made in America. Price, $5.00.**

**Spanish Powder Tanks from one of the wrecked warships at Santiago, Cuba; hold 300 pounds. Price, $60.00. Spanish Powder Charger for 11-inch breech-loading rifle, copper, 3 feet long. Price, $65.00.**

**6-pounder Solid Shot, strapped to wood sabot. Price, $1.00 each.**

Tin Cannon for window display; facsimile of 6-pounder, unmounted. Price, $18.00.

**United States Gunner's Pendulum Hausse, in russet case, like new. Stamped Washington, 1865. Price, $3.50.**

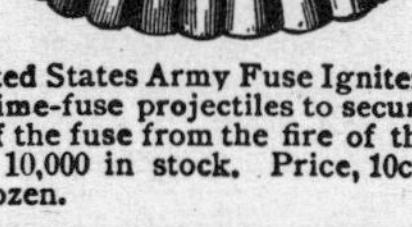

**United States Army Fuse Igniters, used with time-fuse projectiles to secure ignition of the fuse from the fire of the gun. New; 10,000 in stock. Price, 10c. each; 75c. dozen.**

**Gunner Liedle's (of U.S.S. Texas) collection of Spanish War bursted shot and shell from Morro Castle, Santiago, Cuba; 12 pieces. Price, $15.00.**

**6-inch Steel Shell from the U.S.S. Maine. Only one offered for sale by United States Navy Department. Labeled U.S.S. Maine. Stands 20 inches high, weighs 80 pounds. Rare relic. Price, $75.00.**

**Cannon Powder Bags.**

| | |
|---|---|
| 6 pounder | 15c. each |
| 10 " | 20c. " |
| 12 " | 20c. " |
| 20 " | 35c. " |
| 30 " | 40c. " |

| | |
|---|---|
| Priming Wire | $ .25 each |
| Gunner's Gimlet | .30 " |
| Gunners' Boring Bit | .50 " |
| Gunner's Thumstall | 1.50 " |
| Gunner's Haversack | 2.50 " |
| Gunner's Fuse Cutter | .75 " |
| Gunner's Lanyard | 1.00 " |
| Gunner's Fuse Wrench | 1.50 " |
| Spanish Fuse Wrench | 2.50 " |
| Artillery Manual Regulation | 1.00 " |
| Gunner's Fuse Picker | .25 " |

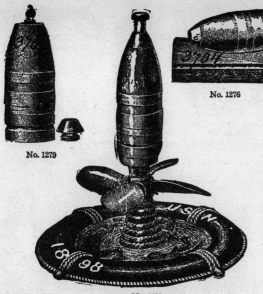

No. 1276

No. 1279

No. 1898

No. 1275.

No, 1278

No, 1277

**1276a.** 1 Pounder Steel Projectile, highly polished, mounted on marble stand, for use as desk weight, length, 4¾ inches; width, 8 inches; height, 2¼. Price, $3.00.

**No. 1998.** U. S. N. Cigar Cutter, neatly gotten up, 7 inch base resembles life buoy, painted red, engraved U. S. N. 1898, with imitation coil of rope, propeller wheel on stand, surmounted with polished steel shell with copper bands, fitted with cigar cutter. Neat, showy useful novelty for cigar store. Price, $4.85.

**No. 1279.** Polished Steel 1 Pounder Projectile Lamp. Brass bushing, which screws into fuse hole, fitted with wick, whereby the projectile can be filled with oil and used as lamp. Brass top, which can be screwed on, when not in use, making it look like a real projectile. Price, $3.00.

**No. 1275a.** Polished steel 1 pounder shell, with two copper bands fitted as cigar cutter, for cutting off the ends of cigars. Mounted on polished copper ash tray, with holder for box of matches; diameter 5 inches, height of projectile and tray 5¾ inches. Price, $3.50.

**No. 1278.** Polished Steel Projectile Cigar Cutter, fitted on polished brass, shell cartridge case 10¼ inches diameter, length 7½. Placing end of cigar in tapered hole of projectile and pressing down the spring cuts off the end off cigar. Price. $3.00.

**No. 1277,** A polished steel 1 pounder shell projectile, fitted with cigar cutter, mounted on polished copper base, resembles "Light House," diameter 2 inches; height, 7 inches. Price, $5.80.

No. 1287

**No. 1287.** 1 Pounder Steel Projectile, with brass fuse plug cutter altered into spring knife, with hole in side of the projectile, for use as cigar cutter. Price, 1.95.

Brass Medallion of Duke of Wellington; solid brass casting. Size, 7 inches; weight, 20 ounzes. Price, $3.50.

U. S. Navy Civil War Sand or Log Glass. Used in heaving the log on board war ships. Relics. Price, $2.00. Few large size Sand or Log Glasses, $5.00 each.

Relic U, S, S. Oregon; gate removed from the ship after the famous battle of Santiago, Size, 18x28 inches; marked U. S. S. Oregon; purchased from Navy Department. Price, $2.50.

Kearsage Relics. Cannon Lock, $7.50. Bronze Lock cover, $10.00.

Ericson's U. S. Civil War Monitor, Dictator Glass Deck Light, relic. Makes good Paper Weight for desk; size, 3 inches in diameter, ¾ inch thick. Price, 35 cents each.

U. S, Navy Shaving Box, with mirror in cover, Engraved on the cover of box is the Lawrence motto, "Don't give up the ship." Price, 45c.

Fast Steam Yacht Gunboat.

Second-Hand Steam Yacts are always to be had in the Ports of New York and Liverpool. On receipt of notice from Government Minister of Marine, we will advise what can be obtained and will quote bargain price for steamers fully armed and equiped, delivered if desired. In one week we furnished from our stock Rapid-fire Cannons, Machine Guns, Small Arms, etc., equipping a 3,000 ton passenger ship into a Man of War for South American Government.

At the close of the Civil War the U. S. Navy Department offered for sale many of the old war ships. A story is told of unprincipaled speculators who bought one of the old ships and sold it to a South American government. On arrival of the ship at its destination, it was arranged to give the President of the Republic a grand salute, so the large 15 inch gun was loaded with 30 pounds of powder and 450 pounds solid shot, and just as the President reached the deck of his new purchase the lanyard was pulled, the primer cracked out its report, but instead of the charge that should have blazed out and rended the air, only a sputtering report was heard, while the ball merely rolled out of the gun instead of leaving at the speed of over 1,000 feet a second. All were surprised, and the President was alone equal to the occasion, as he said to the Yankee crew in broken English, "Must have usa afore." The powder was principally sand.

Leather Match Holders, made from Civil War carbine sockets; used on cavalrymen's saddles to hold gun; fitted with wood bottom, make neat military ornament as well as useful match safe. Price, 20c. each. We have 5,000 of these new sockets and will close out this entire lot at 5c, each as they are without the wooden bottoms.

Revolutionary War Relic Desk Weight, made from a section of the great chain used by Gen. Geo. Washington, placed across the Hudson at West Point in 1778, to prevent the passage of British war ships. This chain was stored at West Point until loaned to the Sanitary Fair, held in New York City to aid the wounded soldiers of the Civil War. After the Fair it was sent over to the Brooklyn Navy Yard, where it lay until 1887, when Bord of Naval Officers, Commodore R. W. Mead, president, ordered it sold as of no further use to the Navy Department. We have sold some of this chain to the decendants of the makers, who inform us that they have in their possession the original contract signed by Gen. Washington and the Sterling Iron Furnace owners. Each link is four sided; 3½ inches in diameter, 3 feet long, weighing over 300 pounds—a gigantic work at that time. Made up into desk weights, as above illustration, ¼ to ⅜ inch thick, 3½ inches wide, sarmounted with small grape shot as handle (relic of the Civil War), 1¾ inch diameter, all finely polished. Genuine relic that any decendant of Revolutionary War patriot should feel proud to possess. Price $20.00 each. With each Desk Weight we give pamphlet giving history of the chain, copy of contract, etc.

Revolutionary War Relic Gavel, made from piece of the above chain, with hardwood handle taken from the Oregon after the famous voyage and after the battle of Santiago, July 3, 1898. Price, $30.00.

No. 27. 6-Pounder Cannon Ball, covered with leather for massaging the stomach to relieve constipation; recommended by New York physicians. Price, 75 cents each. 3-Pounder Cannon Ball, leather covered, 70 cents.

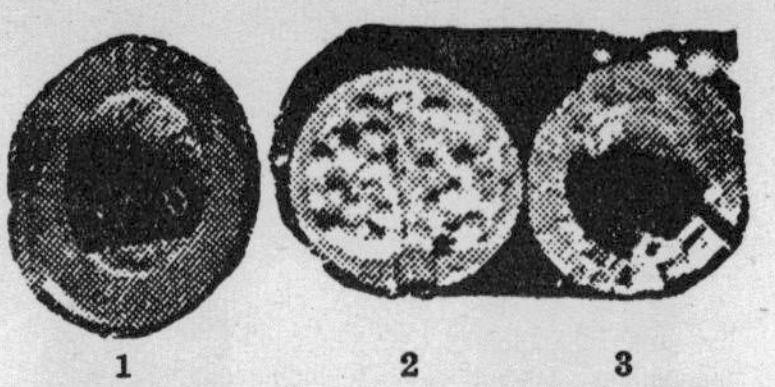

No. 40. Revolutionary War Solid Shot, supposed to have been fired from British warship on Long Island Sound while bombarding town on Connecticut shore; size originally about 6 inches; badly corroded; weight, about 35 lbs. Price, $5.

No. 17. Canister Shot for 6-Pounder. Price, $0.75.

No. 19. Canister Shot for 12-Pounder, Price, $1.50.

No. 18. James Rifle Shot, civil war relic, 12-Pounder. Price, $3.00.

No. 16. 80 Dyer Projectiles for use in 3-in. rifled cannon; lead base. Price each, $2.50.

No. 20. Rifled Shell for 3 2-10 B-L cannon. Price, $1.50.

No. 1. Half part of broken 8-inch shell. Makes souvenir card receiver for military man's den. Price, $4.75.

No. 2. Half part of 8-inch Case Shot, showing small shot (no powder). Price, $5.50.

No. 3. Half part of 8-inch Case Shot. Price, $4.00.

Three-inch U. S. Navy Cannon Shot, with the copper ring with the groove marks made by the rifling when fired. Shot is 15 inches long; free from powder. Price, $3.85.

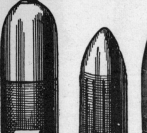

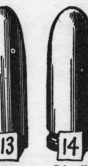

No. 43

No. 15. Schenkle Projectile, 30-Pounder, with Sabot. Price, $7.50.

No. 23. Confederate Projectile with lead Sabot, with rifle groove marks of firing; about 12-Pounder; rare relic. Price, $25.00.

No. 31. Hollow Steel Projectile, relic of Spanish war, 1½ inch diameter, 3½ inches long, with 1¼ inch brass band. Price, 75 cents each.

No. 32. Hollow Steel Projectile, relic of Spanish war, with two copper bands; diameter of steel shell 1½ inches, length 3½ inches: price, 85 cents. Either of above projectiles (31-32) will fit in brass cartridge case we have for sale. Relic of Manilla Bay. Length of brass case 3¾ inches, 1⅝ diameter. Price of brass case $1.00.

No. 12. Hotchkiss 10-Pounder Rifle Shot or Shell. Price, $2.50.

No. 13. Parrott 30-Pounder, Civil War Shot. Price, $3.00.

No. 14. Confederate 30-Pounder Projectile: rare relic. Price, $15.00.

No. 21. Parrott Rifled Shot for 20-Pounder, Civil War M-L Cannon, Price, $2.50.

No. 43. U. S. Armor Piercing Steel Shot, fitted with armor-piercing plug; free from powder: fitted with composition band to take the rifling; height 18 inches, diameter 6 inches, weight 70 pounds. Price, $4.00.

> The Good Book says that in the millenium days swords shall be turned into plough shares, and spears into pruning hooks. We are helping to hasten along the glad time by selling cannon balls to heal the sick.

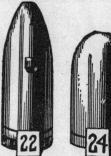

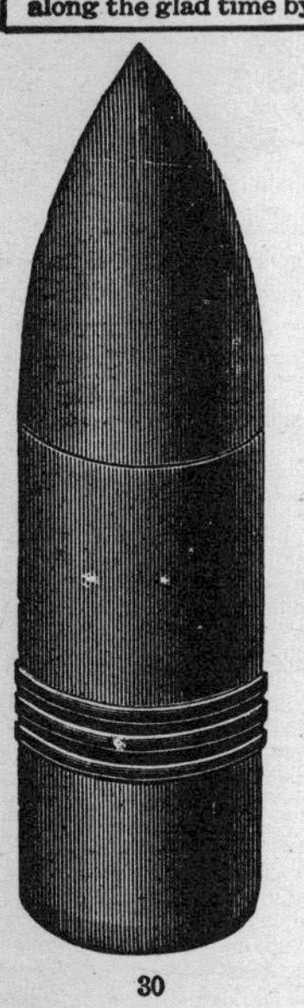

No. 25. Confederate Rifled Projectile from Norfolk Navy Yard. We have duplicate, otherwise we would not offer this one for sale. Price, $100.00.

No. 26. Rare Confederate Rifled Projectile, with brass studs for rifling; from Norfolk Navy Yard. Price, $100.00.

No. 30. Six-Pounder Steel Projectile, with two grooves, copper bands, shell 2¼ diameter, length 8 inches. Free from powder; relic of Spanish war; price for steel shell $1.25. We can also furnish brass cartridge case—3-inch rim, 2¾-inch base, 12 inches long; price $3,85, with steel shell and cartridge case, polished. Price, for the pair complete shells, for andirons, $7.50.

No. 29. Spanish War Steel Projectiles, free from powder, purchased from the Ordnance Deparm't Brooklyn Navy Yard after the Spanish War. Steel shell, 2-inch diameter, 5⅜ in. long, with 1½ inch copper band; price for steel shell, $1.00 each. We also have from a previous sale, brass shells (empty) that will hold this projectile. It is 2¾ inches at the rim, 2½ base, 15 in. long. Price of steel shell with brass cartridge case, complete, polished, suitable for decoration; makes a beautiful andiron, $3.50: the pair, $6.75.

No. 45 Balloon Gun Shot Relic French-German War. Used in balloon gun. Makes handsome deskweight. Size 2 inches by 5 inches. Price, $1.75.

U. S. Army Grape Shot: 8-inch stand of grape purchased from Ft. Wadsworth, New York harbor, after the Spanish War; 8 in. in diameter: 10½ in. high: contains 3½-in. ball, held in place by two rings, top and bottom plate and iron bolts: breaks apart when it strikes: considered very destructive: used against ships: contains no pow er We have 50 in stock, Price, $5.00 each.

No. 44. Captured Spanish Shell, now free from powder: 3⅝ in. in diameter: fitted with white metal studs which take the rifle grooves. This is the only lot of Spanish projectiles that came from Cuba sold by the U.S. Government; 6½ inches high; weight, about 10 pounds; fine old relics. Price, $4.25 each.

No. 28. Confederate Relic. 24-Pounder Smooth Bore Shot, altered for use in rifled cannon. Rare relic from Norfolk (Va.) Navy Yard. Relic of "Monitor" and "Merrimac" days. Price, $75.00.

15 10-inch Parrott Solid Shot, from Augusta, Ga., Arsenal. Supposed to have been made for use in Confederate rifle cannon during the Civil War and captured by Gen. Sherman. Complete with bronze sabot. Price, $10 each.

No. 22. Armstrong 20-Pounder Projectile, with lead studs for rifle grooves. Price, $5.00.

No. 24. Confederate Rifle Projectile from Norfolk Navy Yard. Price, $20.

2,500 Rapid Fire Cannon Cartridges; calibre, 25 mm., about 1 inch; from U.S. Navy Dept. at Mare Island Navy Yard. Loaded, price, $1.00 each; $75.00 per 1,000.

Confederate Torpedo removed after the battle of Mobile Bay; 165 lbs. Was attached to sunken spar; height, 2½ ft. Price, $ each.

No. 41. 6-inch Civil War Parrot Solid Shot, with large copper disc scabot: rare pattern: supposed to be confederate. Stands 12½ inches high; weight, about 80 pounds. Price, $5.00.

No. 42. Parrott Solid Shot, weighing nearly 300 pounds: kind fired by Gen. Gilmore's Swamp Angels at Charleston during Civil War. Price, $18.00.

In 1865 the U. S. Government conducted a series of experiments at Springfield Armory of breech-loading systems with a view of adopting an arm for use in the Army. In all, 65 different weapons were submitted by inventors and manufacturers. On this and the opposite page will be found twenty-three of the principal ones copied from photographs still preserved at the Armory.

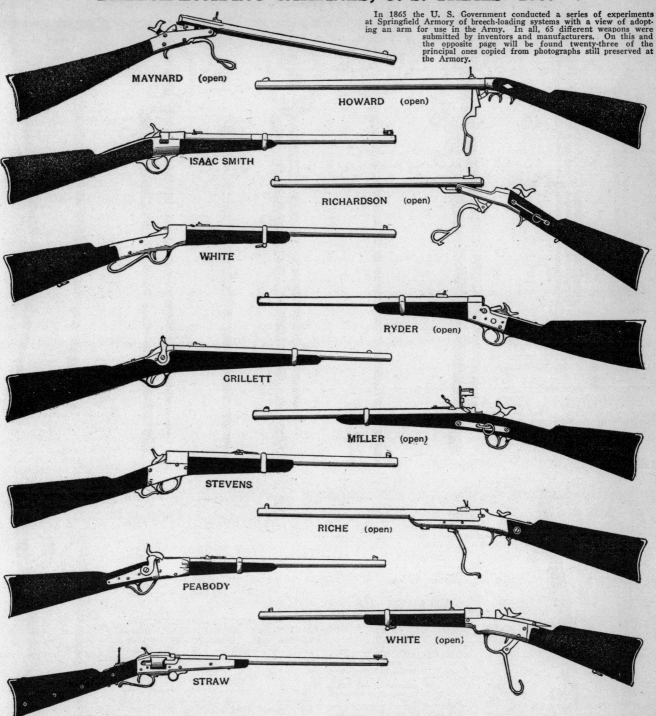

A number of these systems will be familiar to the collectors of firearms as they were in actual use, some before, during the latter part of the Civil War and some in the late sixties.

The Board after weeks of experiments finally recommended —May 2, 1866—five systems for trial, as follows: Allin, Berdan, Yates, Roberts and Remington. It was proposed to alter fifty muzzle-loading arms on each plan. When, however, the recommendation of the Secretary of War was received, the list was changed to Allin, Peabody, Laidley, Remington and Sharps.

The Allin alteration became the best known as it was the forerunner of the Springfield breech-loader, famous until the adoption of the Krag Jorgensen in 1892.

Among the guns shown will be found several weapons used in the Civil War: the Maynard—this one altered, however, to take a rim fire cartridge; the Richardson, formerly the Gallagher; the Starr, Peabody, Warner, Palmer, and the English arm, the Snider. It will be noticed that in some cases the breech of the guns are shown open ready to receive the cartridge, thus enabling the reader to understand readily how the action worked. On those shown "closed," we find first: the Smith—the breech-block on this one swings to the left. Patented by J. S. Smith, 1864. The White carbine had a large block which contained the hammer; this, upon the manipulation of the lever, swung to the rear. Patented by L. S. White, 1863. The Grillett action drops down and back by manipulation of trigger-guard, the hammer is for cocking only. No patent date shown.

The Stevens is an adoption of the familiar Remington system, worked by the lever in rear of the trigger-guard. Patented 1864, by W. X. Stevens. The Peabody, patented in July, 1862, by H. O. Peabody, employed a block which dropped at the front end, worked by the guard-lever. This was a familiar weapon for many years, especially in long rifles, the militia regiments of several states being armed with them. (Continued on page 193)

1914B

**1914B. LARGE SIZED VIEW, SHOWING HANDLE AND GUARD OF U. S. ARMY OFFICER'S NEW SABRE WHICH WE SELL AT THE BARGAIN PRICE OF $11.85 each.**

**1914A. NEW ARMY OFFICER'S SABRE.** For all U. S. A. officers, excepting the Chaplain. Polished steel blade, slightly curved, etched with letters U. S. surrounded with ornamental scroll work. Polished steel guard and handle, polished black horn finger hilt grip, 30 or 32-inch blade. Nickeled steel scabbard, with two rings. NEW SWORDS. Our bargain price, $11.85 each.

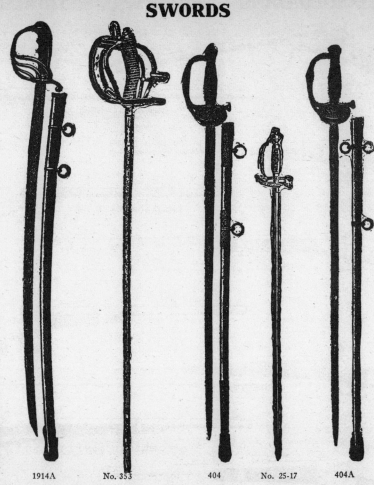

1914A     No. 353     404     No. 25-17     404A

515     516

**515. GERMAN SCHLAGER FENCING SWORD.** Nickel plated basket handle, handsome colored steel etched blade; full length, about 42 inches. Price, $10.75; with plain steel blade, $9.50.

**516. NEW CURVED STEEL BLADES** for the fencing sword. Price, 95 cents each.

**353. SCHLAGER FENCING SWORD OR HAUTE RAPIER.** With large basket guard handle with ribbed cord grip; guard surrounds the hand; straight oval-shaped blade, 34 inches long, ⅝ inch at hilt, tapering to ⅜ inch at point; blade is fastened with screw nut. This kind of foil used by German students. Price, $3.50 each, or $6.85 pair.

**510. PRACTICE SWORD,** 11/16 polished blade, with large guard, with screw nut on pommel whereby the blade can be taken out; black leather covered grip. Price, $3.50 each.

**No. 25-17. ANTIQUE COURT SWORD** with 26-inch blade, engraved with military ornaments and flowers, hardwood handle, brass pommel and cross bar with acorn ends. PRICE, $7.00.

**404B. LATE REGULATION U. S. A. COMMISSIONED OFFICER'S SWORD.** Polished steel etched U. S. blade, with gilt bronze ornamented handle; gilt wire wrapped hilt, with leather scabbard; with ornamented gilt bands and rings, mouth and tip piece; practically new swords. Price, $9.75 each.

**404D. U. S. CAVALRY OFFICER'S LATE REGULATION SABRE.** Polished steel etched blade; bronze handle and guard; wire wrapped hilt, nickeled steel scabbard, with bronze bands, two rings, mouth and tip; fine order, practically new. Price, $10.00.

**404A. COMMISSIONED OFFICER'S SWORD.** With sharkskin grip; bronze handle and guard, with cast eagle in relief; diamond shaped steel blade; beautifully etched, with letters U. S. and ornamental scroll work. Price, $10.00.

**No. 10A. PRESENTATION SWORD** made by the sword maker of English Kings. This sword made for presentation to foreign notables calling at the English Court. Similar to No. 10, p. 188. Price, $55.00.

**No. 10B. SWORD** similar to No. 10, page 188, fitted with plain blade, marked SOLLINGTON. Price, $50.00.

**404C. U. S. ARMY OFFICER'S OLD PATTERN ARTILLERY SABRES.** Polished steel etched blade, ornamented bronze handle, wire wrapped hilt, two ringed nickel plated steel scabbard; in good serviceable, refinished order. Price, $6.75 each.

**398. ANTIQUE RAPIER.** With 32-inch triangular blade, ¾ inch wide at the hilt, tapering to the point, ornamented with metal bosses that look like jewels set in the handle and guard; rare old relic. Price, $20.00. Pair of German Student's Fancy "Schlagers," good serviceable, second-hand order. Single, $6.00; pair, $11.00.

**No. 3091A. SPANISH OFFICER'S CAVALRY SABER** with nickel plated scabbard and long blade. Brass hilt with sharkskin grip. Lot purchased in Cuba 1898. Similar to No. 3091, page 191. PRICE, $10.00.

**No. 1619. OFFICER'S ANTIQUE SWORD** with quill shaped plain blade; leather scabbard with brass ring, throat and tip. Light brass guard. Wire wrap grip. Price, $6.85.

**No. 25-5. WEST POINT CADET SERGEANT'S SWORD,** old pattern, with 26-inch blade, blued steel scabbard, with stud for frog. Brass guard with American eagle on each side. Price, $12.00.

**No. 8993. U. S. ARMY LIGHT CAVALRY SABRE.** This sabre has 35-inch slightly curved blade; total length with scabbard is 42 inches; weight 3¾ lbs. Offered at REDUCED PRICE of $1.95 each. Special price for lot of 3,000.

We have a large assortment of assorted swords and sabres, both U. S. and foreign, and offer these at $100.00 per 100, to dealers or others for decoration. The selection will be made by us.

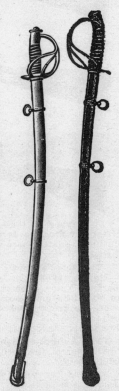

404B     404C              8993     404D

# Swords and Sabres.

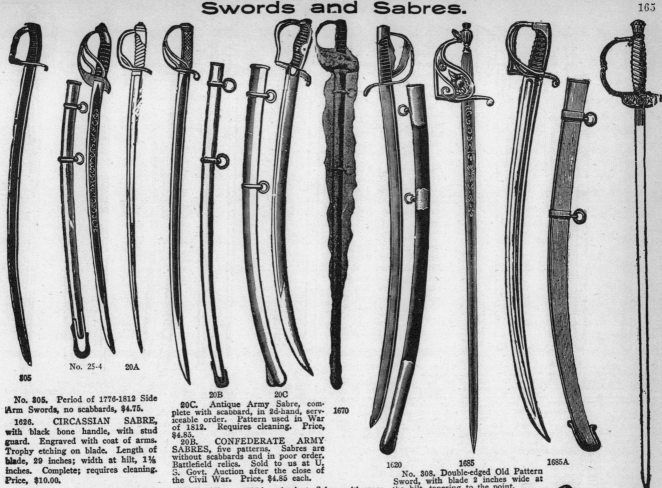

No. 25-4     20A     20B     20C     1670     1620     1685     1685A     1620B     1626     1607

305     1589

**No. 305.** Period of 1776-1812 Side Arm Swords, no scabbards, $4.75.

**1626. CIRCASSIAN SABRE,** with black bone handle, with stud guard. Engraved with coat of arms. Trophy etching on blade. Length of blade, 29 inches; width at hilt, 1⅛ inches. Complete; requires cleaning. Price, $10.00.

**1589. 10 FRENCH LIGHT ARTILLERY SABRES.** Engraved on back of blade, Mrle de Chatellezault, with old proof mark, 1834. Blade 32 inches; widest width, 1 5-16, with brass hilt, with number, proof and inspector's marks; 2-ring, polished steel scabbard. All in fine order. $4.65.

**25-4. EUROPEAN OFFICER'S SWORD,** with 30½ inch etched blade, with brass guard and eagle head. Sharkskin grip. Blade made by W. Clauberg of Sollington. No scabbard. Price, $7.50.

**1669. ANTIQUE BRITISH OFFICER'S SABRE,** with lion head pommel, ornamented gilt cross guard, shark skin grip. Ornamented scabbard guide, 2-ring steel scabbard; blued etched steel blade, 30½ inches in length, 1⅜ wide, 2¾-inch curve. Price, $10.00.

**1670. OFFICER'S SABRE,** fine blued steel etching with scroll flowers, "Presented by friend" on blade; ornamented Persian style brass hilt. Good order, no scabbard, blade 28½ inches in length, 1¼ wide, 3-inch curve. Price, $10.00.

**1671. IVORY HILT ANTIQUE SWORD,** made by "S. Brown, 55 Charing Cross, Sword Maker to His Royal Highness, the Prince of Wales," engraved on gilt mouth piece of scabbard. Gilt cross guard and handle; etched steel blade, 32 inches in length, 1⅜ in width at hilt, 1¾-inch curve. Good condition. Price, $15.00.

**1607. OFFICER'S SCOTCH CLAYMORE,** buck skin lined basket hilt, ball pommel with dark red silk tassel, 33 inch double grooved blades, finely etched with CROWN over V R, also three plumes, the crest of the Prince of Wales. Star design with circle of gold, marked: PROVEN. Marked name on blade: LECKIE & CO., 60 STOCKWELL ST., GLASGOW. No scabbard. Sword in very fine condition. Price, $35.00.

**20C.** Antique Army Sabre, complete with scabbard, in 2d-hand, serviceable order. Pattern used in War of 1812. Requires cleaning. Price, $4.85.

**20B. CONFEDERATE ARMY SABRES,** five patterns. Sabres are without scabbards and in poor order. Battlefield relics. Sold to us at U. S. Govt. Auction after the close of the Civil War. Price, $4.85 each.

**1685A.** Ancient Sabre with rare pattern square shaped handle guard; grooved blade. With two-ring scabbard. From European collectors' museum exhibit. Price, $15.00.

**1620. ANTIQUE SWORD WITH LARGE BRASS GUARD,** 35-inch blade, 1⅜ inches in width at the hilt. Brass mounted, with 2-ring leather scabbard. Rare pattern. $12.50.

**No. 1620B.** 112 OFFICER'S SWORDS, 30-inch oval steel blade, brass guard; with letters A. O. H. on guard. Nickeled steel scabbard, all in good second-hand order; taken in exchange for other goods. Offered at the bargain price of $3.45 each.

## When ordering from this page please allow a second choice when possible.

**20A. EXTRA LIGHT CADET CAVALRY SABRES;** weight, 2½ pounds; used; refinished; 34-inch blade; width, ⅞ inch. $2.95.

**20AA. 52 CADET CAVALRY SABRES;** weight, 2½ pounds; second-class order; scabbards dented and rusty; 34-inch blade; width, ⅞ inch. Price, $1.75.

**Copper Powder Knife,** from Dewey's flagship Olympia; 10½-inch blade. Vouched for. Price, $5.00.

**U. S. Navy Yeoman's Axe.** Guillotine pattern, 5-inch blade, iron handle, fine order. Polished, decorative. $3.75.

**U. S. Cavalry, Mexican War Sabres,** with quill back, double-edged, steel-pointed blade. Complete with scabbard, $2.85 each.

**No. 343. German Artillery Officer's New Sword;** gold-finished handle and mountings; nickeled steel, silvered scabbard, with gold-plated mountings; crossed cannon in relief on the guard; lion's head pommel; etched blade. Beautiful new sword. Price, $12.50.

**No. 375. German Cadet Officer's Sword,** small handle, German silver wire-wrapped grip; silvered eagle coat of arms of Germany on the guards; straight-grooved blade, 33½ inches long, etched with German eagle, crown and ornamental design; leather scabbard with bronze mountings, with sword hook as side arm; used; in serviceable order. Price, $8.50.

**No. 308.** Double-edged Old Pattern Sword, with blade 2 inches wide at the hilt, tapering to the point.

**No. 349.** Spanish Model Cadet Side Arm Sword, with russet leather scabbard; German silver mouth and tip piece; crown stud for belt fastener; ebony guard; Eagle pommel; 13¾-inch blade; 1 inch wide; total length, 22½ inches; fine, neat, serviceable sword. Price, $3.50.

**No. 400.** German Officer's Sabre, blade slightly curved, with German silver handle, inlaid with gilt decorative work; shark skin grip; etched steel blade, 30½ inches long, 1 inch wide at the hilt, tapering to double-edged point, with German sword knob, with steel scabbard with one loose ring; length over all, 37 inches; fine order. Price, $8.50.

**No. 401.** Belgian Officer's Sword, straight, diamond-shaped, double-edged blade with turn-down guard; total length, 38 inches; Belgian coat of arms on handle guard with lion rampant; shield and wreath; no scabbard; fair order. Price, $7.50.

**No. 402.** One of Emperor William II.'s Officer's Sword, with German eagle cast in the guard, with scroll crown and II. on the shark skin hand grip; triple wire wrapped; with sword knot; 2-grooved straight, narrow blade, 29½ inches long, ¾ inch wide at the hilt; nickel-steel scabbard; two loose rings with hook for use as side arm; serviceable order. Price, $10.00.

Pair of Antique Sabres with etched blade, showing mounted horseman wearing Russian hat; leather scabbard. Full length, 3 feet, brass handle. Price, $8.00 each.

German Sabre with large brass handle and guard, with scabbard, in fine order. $3.75.

British Army Officer's Sword V. R. in scroll work on the hilt. (Victoria's "Fran se" engraved on blade; brass Reign.) $8.50.

4 French Side Arm Sabres, with hilt; full length, 3 feet; with antique leather scabbard, brass topped; serviceable order. Price, $6.00 each.

**No. 4.** Rare pattern Sabre Bayonet for attaching to gun; scimetar-shaped blade; serviceable, second-hand order. $2.65.

Antique Model Sword, straight blade; total length, 4 feet, with scabbard. Basket handle, fine order, good steel blade, $8.50.

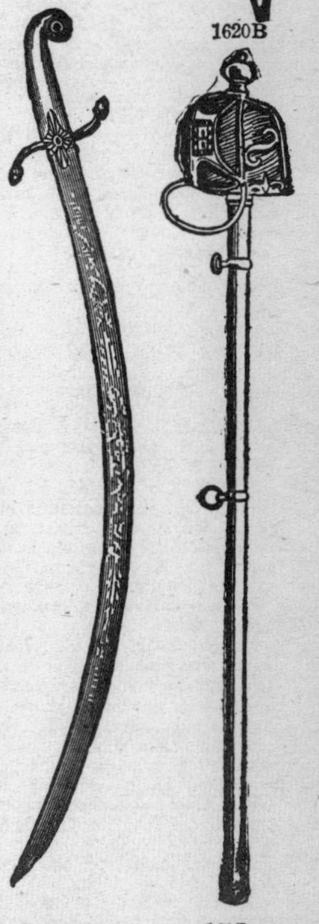

**Garibaldi Sabres,** imported from Italy during Civil War for use of U. S. Cavalry. Rare. Price, $8.50 each.

Antique Sword, 40 inches long, handsome ornamental handle and guards; representing fifteeenth century period; leather scabbard. Price, $12.00.

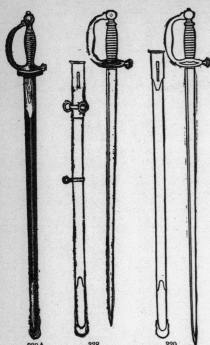

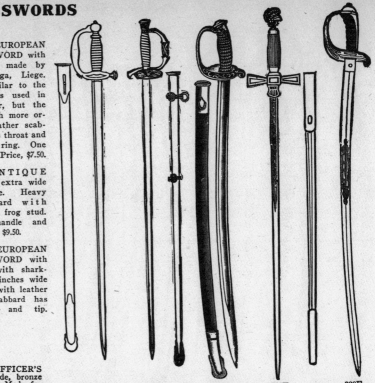

**No. 25-6. EUROPEAN OFFICER'S SWORD** with 30-inch blade, made by Lassence Ronga, Liege. Somewhat similar to the officer's swords used in the Civil War, but the handle is much more ornamented. Leather scabbard with brass throat and tip, and one ring. One ring missing. Price, $7.50.

**No. 25-21. ANTIQUE SWORD** with extra wide 34-inch blade. Heavy leather scabbard with metal tip and frog stud. Brass flat handle and guard. Price, $9.50.

**No. 25-1. EUROPEAN ANTIQUE SWORD** with flat handle, with sharkskin grip, 24 inches wide curved blade with leather scabbard. Scabbard has brass throat and tip. Price, $5.00.

338A     338     320

**No. 338A. CIVIL WAR PERIOD NON-COMMISSIONED OFFICER'S SWORDS;** new, complete with leather scabbard, 28-inch steel blade, bronze handle and guard. No side guard extension. Neat, light swords. Made for use of Government. All have passed Government officers' inspection. Black leather scabbard, with brass tip and mouth piece. With hook for sword frog. 3,000 in stock. Left over after the Civil War. All new, but may require a slight cleaning from long storage. Were never out of the original cases. 28-inch blade, and flat guard, makes these fine Government-made swords very desirable for Cadet officers' swords. Cost the Government upwards of $7.00 each. Made for use of non-Com. and musicians, Civil War officers. Our bargain price, $3.50 each.

**No. 338. COMMISSIONED OFFICER'S CADET SWORD;** rings on scabbard for use of commissioned officers, with sling strap attached to the waist belt; 28-inch blade; total length, 34 inches; bronze handle, wire grip; new sword; also fitted with hook on scabbard for use with frog, for use by non-commissioned officers. Price, $4.85.

**No. 320. NON-COMMISSIONED OFFICERS' SWORDS** with 32 inch blades and steel scabbards. These were new, but have been in fire and the handle, blade and scabbard are tarnished. Can be cleaned and repolished. Will answer for cadet companies or for decoration. Our bargain price is $1.30 each; $13.00 per dozen.

**No. 338B. CIVIL WAR NON-COM. OFFICERS' SWORDS;** with 32-inch steel blade and extension guard. New swords, never out of original cases. May require slight cleaning from long storage. Bronze hilt and guard. Black leather scabbards, with brass mouth and tip. With frog hook, for attaching to waist belt. Only a limited number of these fine swords are now for sale. They cost the Government originally upwards of $8.00 each. We have 200 in stock. Our bargain price, $3.50 each.

**No. 320A. U. S. NAVY SERGEANT MAJOR'S CIVIL WAR MARINE CORPS SWORD.** Polished steel blade, slightly curved, with ornamented bronze handle and guard; black shark skin wire-wrapped grip; black leather scabbard. With bronze mouth and tip; with hook for sword frog. New swords. Bargain price, $6.00 each.

Some of the theatrical companies have purchased these swords for their Naval Officers' characters.

**No. 25-22. CADET OFFICER'S SABER** with finely etched blade made by CLAUBERG OF SOLLINGTON, for sale in the U. S. Brass guard, sharkskin grip, and eagle head pommel. Scabbard has been nickel plated. Price, $6.50.

**No. 320 G. U. S. ARMY CIVIL WAR PERIOD STAFF OFFICER'S SWORDS;** fine polished steel blades, etched with letters U. S., surrounded with scroll work. Bronze guard and handle, with black shark skin grip, gilt wire wrapped hilt; with black leather scabbard; with gilt bronze bands, rings, mouth and tip. New swords, left over after the Civil War. Never issued. In fine serviceable order. Only a limited number left. Price, $8.50 each.

A few Swords, somewhat similar to No. 320G, battle field relics, poor order, price, $6.50 each.

**No. 320I. U. S. ARMY LIGHT CAVALRY SABRE,** complete with scabbard; in fine refinished, serviceable order, polished steel blades; brass guards and handle; wire wrapped hilt; 1,000 in stock; weight of sword and scabbard, about 3½ pounds. Price, $2.00 each. We also have a lot that have been used extensively, and while the blade and handle are in fairly good order, the scabbards are dented, and in poor order. This lot we offer at $1.45 each. We also have a lot without scabbards at $1.25 each.

**No. 320J. WEST POINT CADET SWORD.** Kind in use after the Civil War; diamond-shaped steel blade, with copper bronze handle and cross-guard. With liberty cap pommel; with letters M. A. (Military Academy) on the guard. With steel scabbard. In good second-hand serviceable order. Souvenir relic of the school days of famous Army officers at West Point. Price, $15.00 each.

**No. B1. CADET OFFICER'S WAIST BELTS** fitted with detachable leather sling, fitted on large brass hook to slip over the waist belt when sword or saber is to be carried. Black leather, with brass studs on slings and heavy brass eagle belt plate. Belt second hand, slings and plate NEW. Price, $1.35.

**No. B2. CADET OFFICER'S RUSSET WAIST BELT WITH HEAVY RUSSET SLINGS,** detachable. Similar to No. B1, but with bar buckle in drab finish. Second hand in good order. Price, $1.45.

**No. 320H. 30 EXTRA LIGHT CADET ARTILLERY SABRES;** brass guard; full length, 37 inches. In good second-hand serviceable order; weight, 3 pounds 2 ounces. Price, $3.50 each.

**No. 320 HH. 500 U. S. ARTILLERY LATE REGULATION SABRES,** complete with scabbard; in fine order; practically new; curved pattern polished steel blade; brass handle; wire-wrapped grip; polished steel trimming nickeled. Artillery sabres are now quite rare. We have been buying up all the U. S. Government has offered for sale for many years. Our bargain price, $2.75.

338B     320C     320A     320E     320F

**No. 320C. COMMISSIONED OFFICER'S SWORD;** with diamond-shaped polished, etched steel blade. With bronze handle and guard. With nickeled steel scabbard, with bronze bands, rings, tip and mouth piece. Fine new serviceable swords, at bargain price of $4.25 each.

**No. 25-18. ENGLISH MADE RAPIER,** with 31-inch triangular blade, marked Wilkinson, Pall Mall, London. Large iron guard with long hand grip and leather finger hold. Price, $5.50.

**No. 320E. NON-COM. OFFICER'S SWORD,** with white bone handle, with bronze liberty cap pommel, with cross guards. Polished steel blades. Black leather scabbard, with hanger, mouth and tip. New swords. Kind used by Society organizations.

**No. 320F. U. S. ARMY OFFICER'S SWORD,** from Government Arsenal auction, after the close of the Civil War. Practically new swords. Never used. Foreign made; polished steel, etched blade; shark skin grip; steel guard. With steel scabbard and rings. Only a limited number left. Bargain price, $8.85 each. A few swords in poor order, battle field relics, somewhat similar to No. 320F illustration; price, $6.50 each.

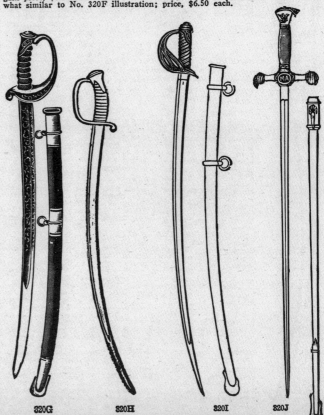

320G     320H     320I     320J

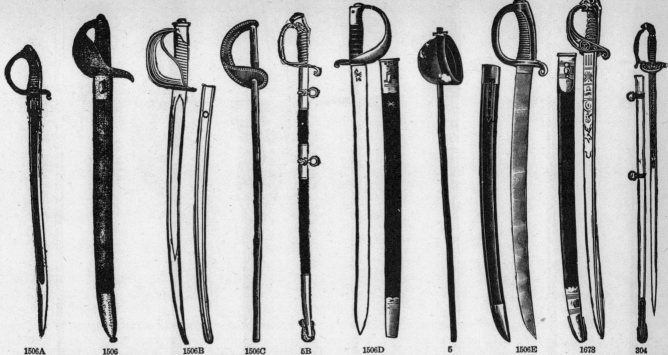

1506A      1506      1506B      1506C      5B        1506D      5      1506E      1678      304

**1506A. IMITATION CUTLASS,** made in Germany, to represent old pattern Navy cutlass. 22 inch steel blade, cast metal handle. Offered without scabbard, as are, rusty. Price, $1.40.

**1506. FRENCH NAVY CUTLASSES, WITH LARGE STEEL GUARD,** for protecting the hand. With leather scabbard. Large brass tip and mouth piece. With loop for attaching frog to the belt. Anchor engraved on each side of the blade. Also Arsenal of Manufacture, Chatellerault, with date, 1846, and other years. Wood hilt steel capped; blade 1½ inches wide; length 26¾ inches. Full length 32 inches. Price, $2.75.

**1506D. BRITISH NAVY CUTLASS** with large polished steel guard, wide blade, grooved hand hold, with opening in guard for sword knot. British proof marked steel blades, complete with leather scabbard. With polished steel mouth and tip. All in fine order, practically new, never used. May require slight cleaning from long storage. They were made for the Sultan of Morrocco, but owing to financial difficulties, were not delivered. We procured the lot of 500. Offered at bargain price of $1.95 each.

**1506B. U. S. NAVY CUTLASS,** with large brass guard handle, polished steel blade; with leather scabbard, with brass stud for attaching to belt by sword frog. U. S. N. cutlasses, have now become very rare. Recently we secured a small lot of 150, that we have put in cleaned, repaired and polished order. For sale at $12.00 each.

**5B. NAVAL OFFICER'S SWORD,** gilt plated handle, white sharkskin grip, etched steel blade. Leather scabbard, with U. S. Navy knot bands and rings. With scorpion scabbard tip. All in serviceable order.

**1506E. GERMAN NAVY CUTLASSES.** Fine steel blade, 23½ inches long, with bronze handle and guard. Complete with leather scabbard, with bronze mouth and tip. With loops and strap for attaching to waist belt by sword frog. All in good second-hand serviceable order. Full length, 30 inches. Bargain price, $1.75 each.

We have a number of these cutlasses without scabbards, at $1.60. They make very handsome decorations, by reason of their curved blade and flat shaped handle.

**No. 705.**—18 Captured Spanish Navy Cutlasses, sold by U. S. Navy Department. This is the only lot of captured Spanish cutlasses taken during the Spanish War, offered for sale. We understand that these trophy relics were taken out of the cutlass racks on the sunken Spanish Warships. Genuine relics, vouched for by a sale record. Price, $15.00 each.

**No. 304.**—Spanish Officer's Sword. Length of blade, 25 inches; on the handle guard, in relief scrollwork, are crossed anchors and flags, surmounted with Spanish crown; bronze gilt handle, nickel-steel scabbard; in fine order. Price, $22.50.

**5A. CIVIL WAR PATTERN OFFICER'S SIDE ARM CUTLASS,** with letters U. S. N. cut in brass handle guard. We have had a limited number of these cutlasses put up in this way. Will make handsome decoration for library or den. Price, $25.00.

**1678. BRITISH NAVAL OFFICER'S SWORD,** with crown, and foul anchor, in relief, on basket-shaped guard. White sharkskin grip; turned down side guard. Etched blade with crown, anchor and British coat-of-arms. Quill back blade, 1⅜ wide, double edged at near the point. 31⅝ inches in length. Leather scabbard with gilt mouth and tip, with frog fastening stud. Good condition. Price, $18.50.

**No. 5.** British Sailor's Fencing Stick, as used in King Edward's Warships; heavy rawhide handle; limited number only in stock. Price, $2.85 each.

**No. 705A.** 5 Spanish Navy Toledo Blade Cutlasses. 29-inch blade; 1⅜ wide; double edged point. Full length 34½ inches. In fair order. Steel guards, partly broken at hilt. Fac-simile of lot sold to us by the U. S. Navy Dept., captured from Spanish war ships. Price, $6.00 each.

**1622. ANCIENT CUTLASS SWORD,** bronze handle, slightly ornamented leather scabbard, with old style stud for fastening to the belt by frog. Length of blade, 26 inches; width, 1⅜ inches. Requires cleaning. Price, $8.00.

**1639. BRITISH NAVAL OFFICER'S SWORD,** with anchor and lion, in relief on guard. Lion head pommel, white pebbled, sharkskin grip, gilt brass mounted leather scabbard. In fine order. Price, $12.00.

**1681.** BRITISH NAVAL OFFICER'S SWORD, with lion head pommel, white sharkskin grip, with anchor in relief on gilt basket guard. Turned down guard. Quill back etched blade. Doubled edged near point. 31 inches length. 1⅜ width. Leather scabbard, with gilt mountings. Price, $16.00.

**1683. REVOLUTIONARY WAR PERIOD BRITISH NAVAL OFFICER'S SWORD,** ivory hilt, gilt guard, with lion head, scabbard guide, with anchor. Scabbard with gilt trimmings, with stud for frog. With place for rings. Blued etched blade, with crown, G R coat-of-arms, and trophy. 32½ inch. Almost straight blade. In fair order. Price, $18.00.

**1679. BRITISH NAVAL OFFICER'S DRESS SWORD,** white sharkskin grip, lion head pommel, with sword knot. Gilt mounted, Lion and anchor in relief on guard. Etched blade with Lion, foul anchor, British crown and coat-of-arms. Quilled back, with double edge cutting point. With leather scabbard, gilt mountings. 28-inch length, 1 inch width. Price, $16.00.

**1506C. U. S. NAVY SINGLE OR FENCING STICK.** Hard wood stick, with russet leather guard handle. Used for fencing drill on board war ships. Second-hand serviceable order. Price, $1.00 pair.

U. S. Navy Cutlass from U. S. S. Rhode Island, used at assault on Fort Fisher, January, 1865. Given Mr. Dimmock by Edward Trenchard, son of Admiral who commanded the ship. Leather scabbard. Price, $12.50.

1376      705                5A

## CAPTAIN PHILLIP OF THE TEXAS.

### By A. M. Boyle.

The fight was won. The Spanish fleet
  In wreck and ruin lay
With battered hulls and flaming sides
  Off Santiago Bay.

A glorious victory it was
  Our ships had won that day!
Then Phillip of the Texas
  Off Santiago Bay

Said to his men, "There is a God!
  Bare every head and pray
With grateful hearts to Him who gave
  Us victory to-day."

The bravest men that ever fought
  Uncovered then and there,
And from each manly seaman's heart
  Arose a silent prayer.

The reverent duty quietly done,
  Then burst the ringing cheers
For Phillip of the Texas,
  Who said through manly tears—

"Don't cheer, my lads; our fellow-men
  Are dying over there;
The anguish of their dying groans
  Is on the summer air."

Hushed every cheer, while tender thoughts
  Went out for those who fell
Enshrouded on the burning ships
  And torn by shot and shell.

"The bravest are the tenderest,"
  And none will ever say
More tender words than Phillip said
  Off Santiago Bay.

Hurrah for all our gallant men,
  Columbia's bravest sons;
America has naught to fear
  While heroes man her guns.

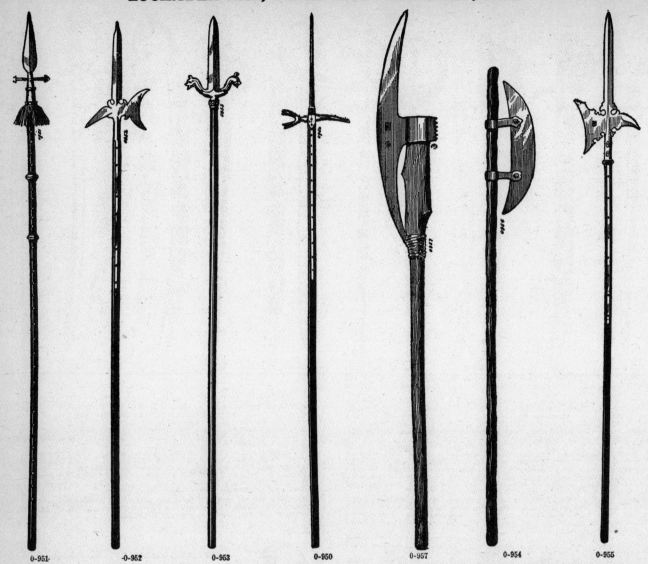

0-951·    -0-952    0-953    0-950    0-957    0-954    0-955

**0-951. ANCIENT BRITISH ARMY SPONTOON, OR HALF PIKE.** Carried by British and French infantry sergeants up to the year 1800. Used now in the Tower of London also at coronation ceremonies. by the Boufitieres (called by the London Cockney "Beef Eaters") Length of spear 12 inches, width 2¼ inches; double edge, pointed, cross guard 5¼ inches, 7-foot shaft, covered with maroon colored velvet, ornamented 4-inch tassel. Full length 8 feet 3 inches. Perhaps this old spontoon formed part of the equipment of British infantry regiments sent to subdue American colonies. Price, $25.00.

**0-952. 17TH CENTURY SCOTCH HALBERD.** From the sale of Toddington Manor collection. 11-inch double-edged, pike-pointed steel spear, with 4-inch half moon shaped battle axe; four sharpened falcon-shaped points; four recessed spaces for catching and breaking the enemy's spear. Socket and tang 1 foot long to fasten to pole. Full length 7 feet 3 inches. Price, $25.00.

**No. 25-19A. ANTIQUE RAPIER** with 29-inch wide triangular blade with sharp point. Heavy brass handle, evidently a reproduction. Price, $7.50.

**No. 25-20. ANTIQUE RAPIER** with 28½-inch triangular blade, ornamented with military insignia. Small iron handle with iron guard and urn shaped pommel. This is a rare type. Price, $20.00.

**0-953. 16TH CENTURY VENETIAN BRONZE AND STEEL HAMMER AND SPEAR.** Originally ceremonial. The bronze spear has 5-inch steel blade, double edged; 7-inch cross guard; full length over 8 feet. Price, $25.00.

**0-950. ANCIENT STEEL BATTLE HAMMER PIKE.** Full length about 7 feet. Quadrangular pike 16 inches long; four-clawed steel hammer extending 4 inches out from the centre of the pike. Square-shaped socket and shaft. Similar hammer pike is to be seen in the Artillery Musee, Paris, and dates from the 16th century. This rare old pike is from the Lawson-Johnston collection and is offered at the bargain price of $40.00.

**0-957. ANCIENT RUSSIAN SOLDIER'S BATTLE POLE AXE HAMMER.** Armorer's seal marks. Length of axe 27 inches; 6-pointed hammer 1⅞ inches, full length 7 feet 2 inches, similar to the axe shown in the Musee of Artillery, Paris, having the name of Bardiche. Used in ancient times. Price, $65.00.

Native-Made Steel **ARROW AND SPEAR** for throwing: 16 inches long... ...........Price, $1.75

**No. 25-11. CRUSADER'S SWORD WITH** 31½-inch blade, blued finish, marked with British Royal Coat of Arms, on each side, with other ornaments. And each side marked "For My Country and King." Wide flat guard with ivory grip. Leather scabbard complete with frog stud. This is a rare piece. Price, $20.00.

**10261. SWORD COLLECTION,** Six swords, Queen Victoria, inclusive.
No. 1—RAPIER. Officer's: period of George I.; leather scabbard. Full length 42 inches.
No. 2—GEORGE II. PERIOD. Officer's sword. Steel wire grip, brass scabbard. Full length 40 inches.
No. 3—GEORGE III. and British coat of arms pommel, curved blade, leather scabbard. Full length 38 inches.
No. 4—G. R. IV. monogram in relief on hilt of on the blade. "Prosser, Mfr. to the King," leather scabbard. Full length 40 inches.
No. 5—WILLIAM IV. marked on the blade and arms and king's monogram W. Leather scabbard.
No. 6—V. R. and British Crown on officer's Leather scabbard, brass mountings. Full length 38 inches.

**0-954. SCOTCH LOCHABER BATTLE AXE ON ORIGINAL POLE. SOLD.**

**10847D. ANTIQUE INDIA MARHATTA SWORD,** evidently used by high official. Wide, flat blade 26 in. long, slightly wider at tip to give extra force to blow. Handle similar to No. 10851 on p. 196. Wood seabbard covered with plush, with long red plush shoulder sling. This is a fine specimen. Price, $35.

**0-955. THREE ANCIENT EUROPEAN BATTLE HALBERTS,** with armorer's seal marks. From the Lawson-Johnston collection sale. Each spear has the centre ridge, the crescent-shaped battle axe and falcon-shaped hooks. The circular recesses for catching and breaking enemy's spear. Octagonal black hard wood shafts, with long tangs. Square-shaped metal sockets.

No. 1—Length of spear 16 inches, face of the axe 9 inches, length of hook 5 inches; full length 6 feet 11 inches.

No. 2—Length of spear 15 inches, face of axe 8½ inches, length of hook 5 inches; full length 7 feet 6 inches.

No. 3—Length of spear 14 inches, face of axe 10½ inches, length of hook 5 inches; full length 7 feet 2 inches. Buyer's choice. Price, $30.00 each.

English officer's, from the reign of George I. to open chased gilt mountings, silver wire grip with Marked with G. R. and British coat of arms. marked on the blade of officer's sword, lion head length 37 inches. officer's sword. Curved quill-shaped blade; etched guard of officer's sword, also British coat of sword. Early period of Queen Victoria's reign. Price for the 6 swords, $96.00.

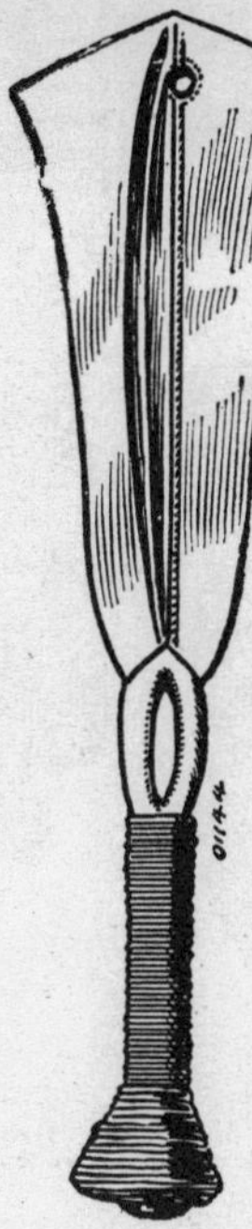

1209A.

0-1211. LODGE GAVEL TOMAHAWK AXE. 4½ inches long, 1⅞-inch face nickle plated. Disk-shaped head for use as gavel. Turned and mounted wood handle. Price, 85 cents.

0-1209A. BRASS TOMAHAWK AXE. With eagle stamped on blade. Disk-shaped hammer end for use as gavel in lodge room. Polished hard wood mounted turned handle. Price, 85 cents.

0-1144. AFRICAN NATIVE'S LILY-SHAPED SWORD. 7½-inch double-edged, pointed, sharpened sword blade. Curious blade, 1½-inch opening, 4¼-inch hilt, copper wrapped disk-shaped pommel. Full length 13¾ inches. Price, $7.50.

0-1212A. CHIEFTAIN'S PIPE TOMAHAWK AXE. Brass ornamented and nickle plated, 8 inches long, 2¾ inches wide, with turned wood handle. Price, $2.75.

0-1213. ARROW-SHAPED TOMAHAWK AXE. With figure of metal eagle cast on the blade. Length 8½x 4¾ inches. Red-colored hard wood pole. Price, 85 cents.

0-867. ANCIENT SWORD BLADE. Dated 1644. Scolloped shell-shaped guard stamped with the soldier's number—43. Double-edged blade 26½ inches long. Brass wire wrapped hilt. Iron pommel. Price, $18.85.

0-853. OLD-TIME HARPOON WITH LETTERS "H. H.," probably the initial name of the ship. 5-inch double barb, 3-foot steel shaft, with socket for pole with small piece of rope attached. Price, $4.85.

0-911. ANTIQUE SWORD HANDLE GUARD. The two side guards fold together for concealment. Ancient pattern. Price, $4.85.

358B. SAW SWORD WITHOUT SCABBARD. Price, $7.50.

1212. TOMAHAWK AXE WITH PIPE BOWL HEAD. Cast metal, with engraved head of Indian, arrow and wild boar cast in relief. Length 7⅜ inches, width of face 6⅜ inches, 1-inch socket hole for handle, 1¼-inch pipe bowl head, mounted on turned wood handle. Price, $1.00.

1212.

0-1210. TOMAHAWK AXE GAVEL. With flat hammer-like head for use as gavel in lodge room. Made of brass, nickle plated. Hard wood, dark-colored handle. Price, $1.00.

0-1214. COPY OF ANCIENT BATTLE AXE MOUNTED ON 7-FOOT ASH POLE. Large size, made for decoration. The metal head weighs 5¾ pounds, 6½-inch spear, 12-inch face, 5½-inch hook, 1¼-inch socket. In serviceable order (nickle plating worn off). Mounted on 7-foot hard wood pole. Price, $6.85.

0-1197. PAIR ANTIQUE LANCES. Each 9 feet 4½ inches long, 7½-inch spear and shank, with 1½-inch ball at the base of the spear. Long stud tang and shoe. Dark-colored hard wood. Price the pair, $12.00.

0-1198. PAIR LANCES, DOUBLE - EDGED 8½-INCH STEEL SPEAR. With long pole straps. Steel shoe full length 9 feet. Similar to illustration No. 81, showing the lances carried by Col. Rush's Pennsylvania Regiment in the beginning of Civil War. Price the pair, $15.00.

0-1199. ANCIENT PIKE, WITH 5½-INCH SHARPENED PIKE POINT. ⅝-inch wide at the base, metal shoe butt, heavy ash pole (slightly wormeaten with age). Old-time relic. Price, $6.75.

0-1079. ANCIENT FRENCH BATTLE AXE. Nickled finish steel blade, 8½-inch face, from the centre of the shaft to centre of face 8½ inches, length of the pick 11 inches, length of the shaft 38 inches, brass cap at the axe and butt ends. The best museums in Europe have these axes on exhibition. When crossed in connection with armor they are very decorative. Patterned after kind carried by ancient Roman Lictors in FASCES. Bargain price, $25.00 each.

0-1143. AFRICAN NATIVE'S SPEAR-SHAPED SIDE ARM SWORD. 14-inch double-edged sharpened blade, 1½ inches wide at the hilt, increasing to 4 inches wide and ending in ½ inch at the point; 3¾-inch hilt handle, wrapped with copper wire. Ornamented groove through the centre of the blade. A curiosity. Price, $7.50.

0-1209. LODGE TOMAHAWK AXE GAVEL. Nickle-plated brass, with polished wood handle. Length of axe 6¼ inches, 2⅛-inch face. Flat disk-shaped axe head for use as a gavel. Like new. Price, $1.00.

DA-2. ITALIAN DAGGER. With 4½ inch narrow sharp pointed ornamented blade with small hole. Hard rubber checkered grip inlaid with 2 mother of pearl ovals. Short cross bars and stud pommel. Steel scabbard with sash ring. Price, $6.00.

0-1136BB. SWORD BAND. Gilt brass with ring, 4½ inches long, relief ornamented. Fits over 11/16-inch scabbard. 150 in stock. Plain and with letters "P. M."; buyer's choice. Price, 10 cents each, or $1.00 dozen.

U. S. CAVALRY FENCING HELMET. Made of heavy re-inforced wire, with inside pads for chin, head and ears, heavy quilted neck and shoulder protector. Made at U. S. Government Rock Island Arsenal. Good as new. Price, $3.85.

0-1130. SWISS ARMY ENGINEER CORPS SIDE ARM SAW SWORD. Blade stamped "S. M. Neuhasen," with soldier's numbers on the guard. 18¾-inch blade with deep groove, flat on the reverse side, 10 inches of the back of the blade has saw teeth. Tapered edge thrusting point. Black checkered bone hilt, flat guard. Full length 23½ inches. Complete with black leather scabbard. Polished steel tip mouthpiece. Loop with small strap for attaching to waist belt. In fine, serviceable order, cleaned and polished. Price, 75 cents each.

0-1216. SOCIETY OFFICER'S SWORD BELT. Buff colored patent leather, with red velvet and gold lace scolloped edges, with 2 short sling straps and one long strap, gilt snap hooks and sword hanger. Gilt brass plate triangular-shaped, with the letters "R. A.," also other assorted pattern job lot of buckles. Good, serviceable order. Price, $3.50.

SCOTTISH VOLUNTEER'S EQUIPMENT. Russet leather shoulder belt 2⅛ inches wide, with cartridge box 6 inches long, 4 inches wide; metal coat of arms on the belt and box, British crown, with wreath surrounding the Scottish Lion rampant. Stamped "London Scottish Volunteers." Used. In fine order. Price, $3.50 each set.

10741. U. S. INFANTRY FENCING MASK. Steel wire mask with quilted cover for neck and shoulders, inside chamois leather head and chin pads, dark-colored quilted duck, with fastening straps. Like new. Made at Government Rock Island Arsenal. Price, $3.85 each.

10471A. U. S. INFANTRY FENCING PLASTERN. For protecting body in fencing practice. Dark-colored quilted cotton cloth, complete with slings. Good second-hand order. Made at U. S. Government Arsenal. Price, $3.85.

Bill Arp tells the following about the Confederate pikes: Illustrated on page 232.

"Early in the war Gov. Brown ordered 5,000 pikes to be made with a spear point and a side blade curved downward, like a reap-hook, having very long handles, so that our soldiers might take the Yankees going and coming. If our opponents did not run we were to spear them, and if they did run we were to overtake them and hook them back or jerk off their heads. Mr. Lewis, the master mechanic at C. S. A. Milledgeville Arsenal, who superintended the making of these terrible weapons, lives near me and in his 88th year. He is an Englishman. 'Why did the Georgia boys use those pikes?' I asked. 'Well, you see,' he replied, 'the old army officers who were drilling the Georgia recruits at Big Shanty looked at those pikes and said to the Governor: "What will the enemy be doing with their guns while our boys are rushing on them with spears?"' The Governor could not answer the question, and so much fun was made of the pikes that their manufacture was abandoned. Those that were made are scattered over the country and highly prized as war relics."

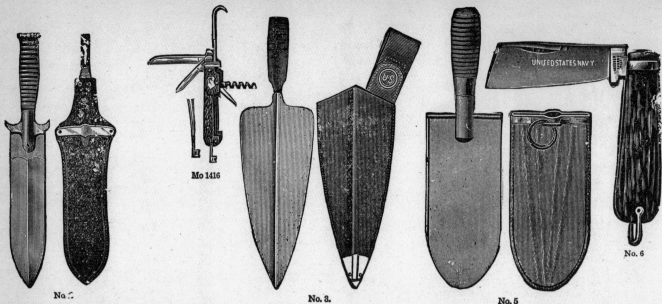

Mo 1416

No. 2            No. 3.            No. 5            No. 6

**No. 2.—United States Army Hunting Knife.** With leather scabbard and brass hanger for attaching to cartridge belt; fine tempered steel blades. Made at Government arsenal; brass guard, harness-leather scabbard. Length of blade, 8 inches; width, 3 inches. We have secured 5,000 of these handsome knives. Price, with scabbard, $1.25 each.

**No. 1.—Captured Spanish Mauser Hunting-knife Bayonet.** Fits either the 7mm. or 7.65 mm. Mauser. Price for those made in Germany, $1.20; for those made at famous sword armory and so stamped, Toledo, Spain, $2.50. In serviceable order, with scabbard.

**No. 1416.** Combination Knife with many different tools as shown. These are American make and are all guaranteed. Price, $1.65 each.

**No. 3.—United States Army Trowel Bayonet.** With harness-leather scabbard and swivel hook. Made at Government arsenal of best tempered steel, handsomely polished; makes fine decoration mounted on pole for cozy corner decoration, or fitted on the regular Springfield rifle it serves as it was intended for a useful bayonet or trowel for throwing up intrenchments; also makes a fine garden trowel. We have over 4,000. Price, 85 cents each; $9.50 per dozen.

**No. 5. U. S. Army** intrenching tool and scabbard, with ring for attaching to soldier's belt. Make fine tool for garden or for campers and hikers. Price, $1.15 each.

**No. 6.—United States Sailor's Jack Knife.** With brass hook for attaching to lanyard. "United States Navy" etched on each blade. New goods. 75 cents White Braid United States Navy Lanyards, 15 cents each; $1.60 per dozen. Five thousand in stock. Practically new goods.

No. 1385    No. 345    No. 244

**Cut 1385. EUROPEAN ARMY INTRENCHING STEEL SPADE,** with T-shaped handle, practically new; with maker's name; ½-inch foot rest, for forcing. Full length 25½ inches; width of spade, 6½ inches; 4½ inches across handle; strong, well made. A number of spades carried in each company of soldiers. Some of the U. S. crack military Cadet Schools have adopted these spades as part of the intrenching equipment. Perhaps it was this up-to-dateness that caused the U. S. Inspector to pass their schools as first-class. Price, $1.25 each.

**No. 345.—British Army Engineer Soldier's Saw and Shovel** combined in one tool and carried as part of soldier's intrenching equipment; total length, 20 inches; length of blade, 7½ inches; width, 5¾ inches; strongly made of good steel; fitted to ash-wood handle; the steel straps of the shovel encasing the handle from London, 1902, on return of British soldiers from South Africa. Valuable relic as well as fine, serviceable shovel and saw. Adopted by Military Schools. 500 in stock. Price, $1.25 each.

**No. 344.—British Army Engineer Soldier's Steel Shovel,** carried as part of his equipment; blade is 5¾ inches wide, 7½ inches long; total length, 20 inches; with pick-shaped handle. Purchased in 1902 on the return of soldiers from Boer War. Very strongly made; valuable to miners on prospecting trip or for gardening; fine steel. Adopted by Military Schools. 500 in stock. Price, $1.25 each.

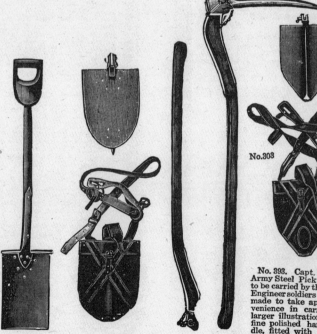

No. 2        No. 394        No.303

**200 New U. S. Army Steel Spades,** No. 2 size, made by Old Colony Co. D. Handle, 11½ inch; blade, 7 inches wide; full length, 36 inches. Price, 65 cents each, $6.50 dozen.

**No. 394.—Elliott's U. S. Army Steel Intrenching Outfit** for engineer soldiers to carry while on the march. Handle is of fine polished hardwood, fitted with steel eyebolt and straps for strength and lightness; pick is seen at the back of the shovel, thus giving greater strength to the shovel; the pick is also fitted to the handle separately as desired, as shown in No. 393. Invaluable to miners out prospecting. Whole outfit is conveniently carried in fine leather case slung over the shoulder. Price of outfit, $8.75.

**No. 393. Capt. Elliott's U. S. Army Steel Pick and Shovel,** to be carried by the U. S. Army Engineer soldiers on the march; made to take apart for convenience in carrying. The larger illustration shows the fine polished hardwood handle, fitted with strong steel straps, with the steel pick fitted on the eyebolt, securely held in place by the keybolt. The smaller illustration shows the handle, shovel and leather scabbard apart. Note the shape of the pick, with the rib on back, making it light and strong; also the rib on the shovel; shoulder slings on the scabbard, which is made of fine bridle leather. When assembled, the pick is at the back of the shovel. We have 10 sets; they are the finest and best made; valuable to geologists or prospectors. Price per outfit, $8.75.

No. 4

**200 U. S. Army New Round Pointed No. 4 Steel Shovels** with long handle with ring. 11 inch blade, 10 inches wide; full length, 56 inches. Made by Ames Company. Price, 65 cents each; $6.50 dozen.

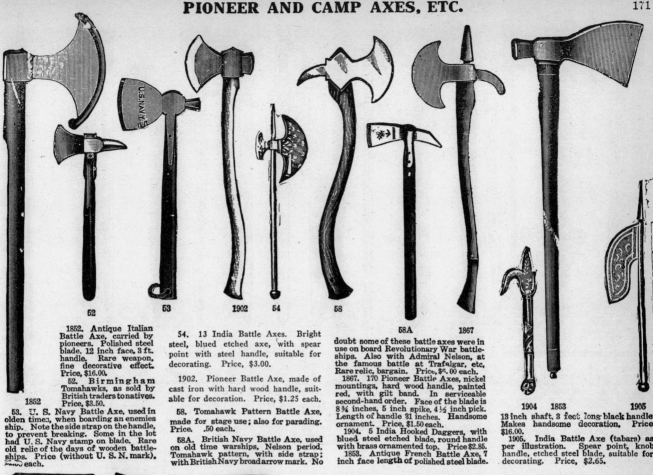

**52**      **53**      **1902**      **54**      **58**      **58A**      **1867**      **1904**   **1853**   **1905**

**1852**

**1852. Antique Italian Battle Axe**, carried by pioneers. Polished steel blade. 12 inch face, 3 ft. handle. Rare weapon, fine decorative effect. Price, $16.00.

**52. Birmingham Tomahawks**, as sold by British traders to natives. Price, $3.50.

**53. U. S. Navy Battle Axe**, used in olden times, when boarding an enemies ship. Note the side strap on the handle, to prevent breaking. Some in the lot had U. S. Navy stamp on blade. Rare old relic of the days of wooden battleships. Price (without U. S. N. mark), ____ each.

**54. 13 India Battle Axes.** Bright steel, blued etched axe, with spear point with steel handle, suitable for decorating. Price, $3.00.

**1902. Pioneer Battle Axe**, made of cast iron with hard wood handle, suitable for decoration. Price, $1.25 each.

**58. Tomahawk Pattern Battle Axe**, made for stage use; also for parading. Price, .50 each.

**58A. British Navy Battle Axe**, used on old time warships, Nelson period, Tomahawk pattern, with side strap; with British Navy broadarrow mark. No

doubt some of these battle axes were in use on board Revolutionary War battleships. Also with Admiral Nelson, at the famous battle at Trafalgar, etc. Rare relic, bargain. Price, $5.00 each.

**1867. 170 Pioneer Battle Axes**, nickel mountings, hard wood handle, painted red, with gilt band. In serviceable second-hand order. Face of the blade is 8¾ inches, 5 inch spike, 4½ inch pick. Length of handle 31 inches. Handsome ornament. Price, $1.50 each.

**1904. 5 India Hooked Daggers**, with blued steel etched blade, round handle with brass ornamented top. Price $2.85.

**1853. Antique French Battle Axe**, 7 inch face length of polished steel blade.

13 inch shaft, 3 feet long black handle Makes handsome decoration. Price $16.00.

**1905. India Battle Axe (tabars)** as per illustration. Spear point, knob handle, etched steel blade, suitable for decorating. Price, $2.65.

**368**      **368A**

**368. Tomahawk Steel Battle Axe**; width of blade 5 inches; with strong steel sides attaching to handle; with sharpened hook. Old relic. Price, $4.50.

**368A. Army Camp Axe**, medium size, without holster. Price, 85c.

**U. S. Army Camp Axe**, with carrying holster; fine steel bladed axe, with hard wood handle. Contained in russet leather holster, with sholder sling strap; with adjusting buckle, new. Price for the outfit, $1.85.

**U. S. Army Steel Picks**, sharp pointed; weight 3½ pounds, is 16½ inches in length, 50c.

**1265. Bayonet Candle Stick**, made from old Army bayonets. We can furnish the bayonets at the price of 15c. each and upwards, or made into neat candlestick like illustration, at $1.50.

**No. 321. Bayonet Candlestick** made up from old bayonets, blued, fitted to hardwood circular-shaped frame for attaching to a wall same as a picture; with German bronze Eagle across the center; with 3 colored wax candles in the sockets, making a beautiful serviceable military ornament for home decoration. Length, 22 in.; width at top, 10½ in.; Eagle is 6 inches in width. Price, for the set, $4.85.

**F D. FRENCH DAGGER** of the 18th Century from the Moppin sword collection. 8-inch plain blade, 4½-inch grip of white ivory, silver bound with silver pommel with small swivel. 4-inch silver cross bar, on one end the Gallic cock's head, on the other a silver knob with swivel. The wood scabbard is plush covered with wide silver tip, silver throat with ring, and silver middle band with ring. All the silver scabbard part engraved. This is a very showy piece, and is the style worn by French noblemen. Price, $20.00.

**L D. 17th CENTURY DAGGER**, hard wood grip with spiral grooves for sure hand hold. Large steel ball pommel, 4½-inch cross bar with special round ring for thumb. 13½-inch triangular blade with sharp point, all engraved. Probably French. Secured from the collection of SIR ARCHIBALD LAMB, Bart., of Beaufort Park Battle, Sussex, England. Full length 18 inches. Price, $12.00.

**S D. SPANISH DAGGER OR STILETTO**, of the 17th Century. 3¾-inch hard wood handle, brass bound and studded with small brass tacks. 4½-inch engraved blade, with wide back and sharp point. Price, $8.00.

**No. 25-10. EUROPEAN OFFICER'S SWORD**, with 29-inch plain blade and bronze handle, with acorn ends on cross bar. Price, $8.50.

**No. 25-14. CIVIL WAR OFFICER'S SWORD**, with nickel plated scabbard with ornamented brass ring holders; tip of scabbard missing. This is the regular Civil War sword. The pommel is marked O. G. which may mean OLD GUARD. Price, $8.00.

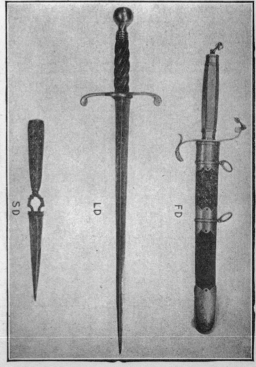

**S D**      **L D**      **F D**

# Side Arm Swords:

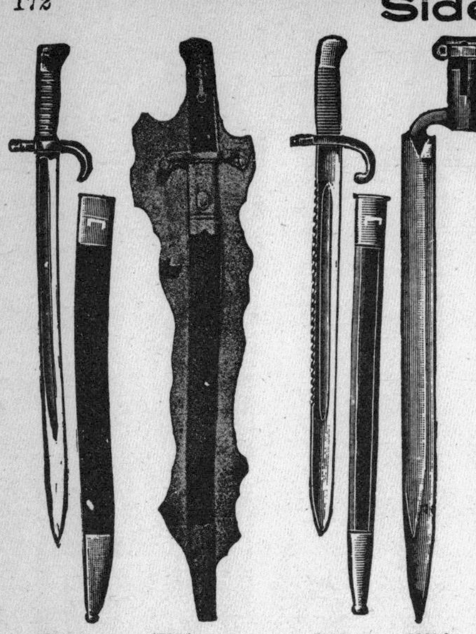

1504. 1528A. 1527. 1390A.

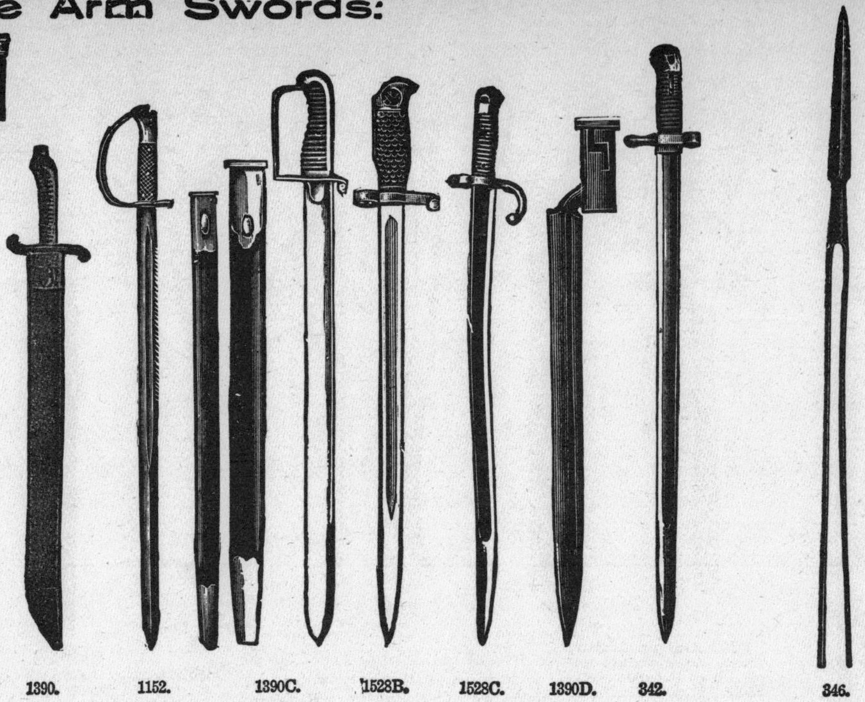

1390. 1152. 1390C. 1528B. 1528C. 1390D. 342. 346.

Cut 1504.—137 Rifled Bayonet Side Arm Swords, with scabbard, full length, 25½ inches, size suitable for Cadets; regular 20-inch sword-shaped blade with slight curve; width of blade, 1 inch; brass hilt, with ring groove on hand-hold; black leather scabbard with bronze tip and mouth-piece, with loop for sword frog. Price, $1.00 each. Some of the above without scabbard, 75c each.

1528A.—British Army Sword Bayonet with checkered bone hilt polished steel hand and guard; polished steel blade with leather scabbard with steel mouth and tip, with stud for belt-frog; kind used on Enfield Snyder Br. Army service Rifle; good; cleaned and polished order. Price, $1.50.

Small lot, not polished, rusty, without scabbard, 50c.

**1527A.—Antique Side Arm Saw Sword, blade 20 inches** long, 1¾ inches wide; full length 25 inches; bronze hilt and cross guard; with good second-hand serviceable leather scabbard; with brass mouth and tip piece; loop for attaching to belt by frog. Price, $3.65.

1390A.—European Side-Arm Sword, as per illustration. Not a sword bayonet. Fine steel blade, with leather scabbard, brass tip and mouth. Price, $1.75.

1390.—100 Antique Sword Bayonets, with socket, enclosing muzzle or barrel. *With blade parallel to the socket.* Blade 1⅜ wide; 20 inches long. Socket 3⅝. Made for use on ancient muskets; rare pattern. Price, $1.85.

1152.—British Side Arm Saw Sword, used in Engineer Corps. Many Govt. proof marks; checkered black bone handle. Bright steel grip guard and blade; at the point of the blade, double edged. Full length, 31 inches; weight, 2¼ pounds. Slot in the sword hilt for sword knot. Complete with scabbard. Second-hand serviceable order. No doubt a relic of the war in South Africa. Price, $3.45.

1390C.—European Army Side-arm Sword, bronze handles and guard with scabbard guide, steel blade, black leather scabbard with belt-stud mouth and tip. Second-hand, serviceable order. $1.95.

1528B.—U. S. Navy Roman Pattern Sword, bronze handle with U. S. N. ordnance insignia, crossed cummmm within circle on the hilt, fish-scale pattern grip, with cross guard double-edged steel blade, black leather scabbard, with brass and mouth-and-lip, with belt-frog stud, second-hand serviceable order; used in U. S. N. warship Honduras; decorative weapons.

These bayonets are equipped with a hole in the handle in which the ramrod is inserted when attached to gun, with the view of steadying it when in use. These are the only U. S. bayonets so made. Price, $2.50 each.

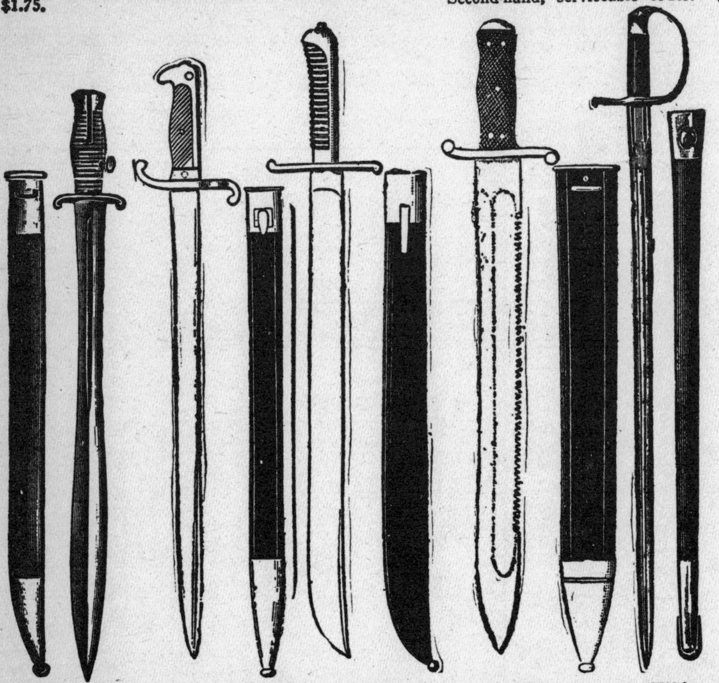

1659A. 1527. 1526. 1524. 1513A.

No. 342.—Bronze Handle Sword Bayonet; straight blade, 1⅛ inches wide, 24 inches long. Good as new. 100 in stock. Price, $1.20. If scabbards are wanted, 30 cents extra. Rare pattern.

**1659A:—Brunswick Army Musket Side-arm** Bayonet, marked as having been made at Enfield, 1840: attached to the British Army gun, called the Brunswick Rifle. Bronze handle, double-edged steel blade; second-hand order. Price, $1.50 each. New black leather scabbard if desired; 35c each extra.

1513A.—Elephant Rifle Sword Bayonet, made for use on Jacob's Rifles, Swinburne & Son, 1860. Double-edged steel blade, two grooved with large ornamented guard handle, leather scabbard with mouth and tip piece, with belt-stud; good second-hand serviceable order. Price, $5.00.

1528C.—European Army Sword Bayonet, brass handle and guard rusty; requires cleaning; no scabbard. Price, $1.00.

1504.—50 Gendarme Swords, cleaned and polished, with scabbard; blade shows old stains, marked "Charleville, 1833." Price, $3.75.

**1524.—24 Officers Side Arm Swords, fine steel** blade, 1⅝ inches wide, 20 inches long with sharpened blade and fine saw extending 13½ inches. with bronze guard and cap; checkered hilt: strong and neatly riveted; in fine order, equal to new; with leather scabbard: brass tip and mouth-piece, with loop and scabbard for attaching to frog on belt; useful weapon for prospectors. Price. $3.95.

**1526.—12 Side Arm Swords, 1⅜ width blade: 18½ inches long, full length 24½ inches, with** steel guard and hilt, made by old time Solingen sword maker; leather scabbard with iron mouthpiece and tip; with hook for attaching direct to belt from frog. In good second-hand serviceable order. Price, $3.25.

No. 346.—Old Pattern Lance Head, with long steel strap for fitting on pole. Four-sided diamond-shaped blade, 9 inches long. Length of blade and strap, 35 inches; width of blade at widest part, 1 inch, tapering to sharpened point. Price, $2.50.

1390D.—175 Flint Lock Side Arm Sword Bayonets, double-edged point, same kind of socket as the Revolutionary War spade bayonets. Found in old warehouse in London, established over 300 years ago. Full length, 23½ inches; socket, 4 inches; blade, 19½ inches ; slightly rusty; offered as are, $1.00 each.

1855.—First Napoleon Cadet Side Arm Roman Sword, with crowing cock cast in the pommel (which was Napoleon's insignia). Length of blade, 17¾ inches; 1¼ width. Leather scabbard, with brass mountings; good order. Price, $10.00.

1585.—6 French Gendarme Cadet Side Arm Swords, full length, 22¼ inches, 1⅜ widest width of blade; bronze hilt and guard. Price, $3.85 each.

1504A.—56 Gendarme Sword, brass handles, cleaned and polished, no scabbards; blade cleaned, but shows old stains; blade is marked 1832-1836. Price, $2.90.

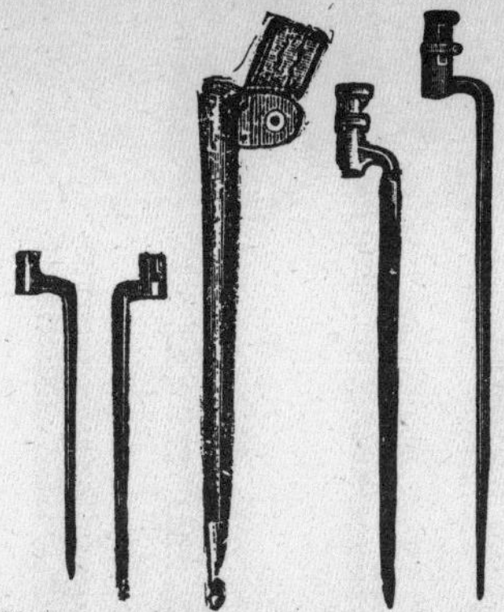

No. 10 No. 11 No. 1 No. 7 No. 8

**10-11.**—Cadet Bayonets for drill guns. Cast iron. Price, each, 15c.

1.—Black Leather Bayonet Scabbard, with swivel loop for attaching to belt, Cadet size, each, 30c.

8.—Confederate Enfield Pattern Civil War Bayonet. Serviceable order for Enfield or Snider Rifle. Price, each 45c.

9.—Model 1842 U. S. Musket Bayonet, same as the model 1822, with the addition of Clasp on the socket to lock to the gun, to prevent expert cavalrymen from detaching bayonets; each 35c.

1662A.—King George III. OFFICER'S SABRE, with black shark skin grip. Price, $18.00.

No. 3A.—Civil War Style Leather Bayonet Scabbard, with brass tip. Relics. Each, 25c.

**100 Leather Scabbards, for the Revolutionary War; wide Spade Bayonet in good serviceable order, with brass mouthpiece.** Relics. 60 cents **each.**

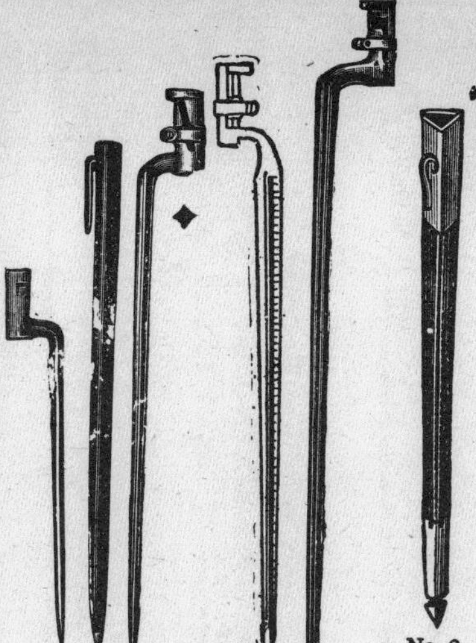

No. 9 No. 350 No. 22 No. 1103 No. 2

9.—Model 1822 U. S. Musket Bayonet, used on old American made Flint Locks. In serviceable order. Fine relics; each 35c.

No. 350.—Four-sided Bayonet, 18½-inch blade, socket 3⅛ inches long; outside diameter, ¾ inch; leather-covered wood scabbard; good, serviceable order; has been used. Price for bayonet and scabbard, 50 cents. 100 in stock.

No. 22.—EUROPEAN ARMY BAYONET, with small socket, for use on Cadet guns. Price, 75 cents each.

1103. 1,000 four-sided Steel Bayonets, sharp point, fine blued order; length of blade, 19 inches; inside diameter of socket hole, 11-16; length of socket, 2⅝ inches. European Armory proof mark on each, and also regimental numbers. Bargain price, 25 cents each.

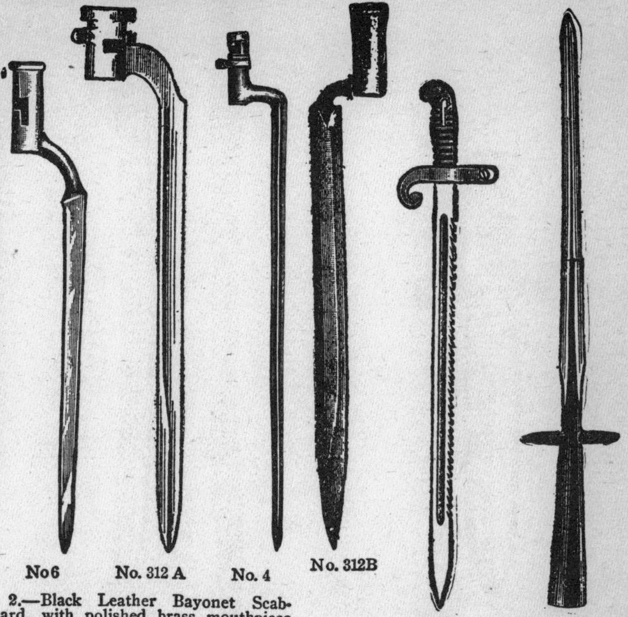

No 6 No. 312 A No. 4 No. 312B No 6 A No. 21

2.—Black Leather Bayonet Scabbard, with polished brass mouthpiece and tip, with hook attachment for dress, shoulder belt equipment; new goods. Each, 30c.

312A.—Antique Sword Bayonet, with circle socket for gun that muzzle measured 1¼ in. in width; quill back double-edged blade, 20 in. long; 1 in. wide; socket, 2½ in. long. Rare pattern, only seen in a few of the best museum collections; shows great age; relic only. Price, $3.75.

4.—Spanish Bayonettes. Made for the Spanish Remington Rifle. Used by Cuban Patriots, also by Spanish Volunteers. Quadrangular blades, rusty, damaged. Relics, each 50c.

6.—American Revolutionary War Period Old Tower Spade Bayonets, used on old Queen Bess Flint Lock Muskets. Rare relics. Each, $1.00.

No. 21.—PIKE BAYONET, with socket for pole, with cross guard. Made in the South during the Civil War. Rare relic. Price, $1.75 each.

3.—100,000 Steel Scabbards, with swivel frog; blued, 60c. each. Nickel-plated Steel Scabbards, 75 cents each. Large quantity of this pattern scabbard are just as turned in by the Spanish War soldier; second-hand, serviceable order. Price, 35c. each.

No. 20. U. S. Navy STEEL BAYONET SCABBARDS, in good second-hand, serviceable order. With swivel frog, with letters U. S. N. on brass swivel. Price, 40 cts. each.

13A.—U. S. STEEL SCABBARDS for Cavalry sabres; practically new. Price, 85 cents each. Lot rusty and dented, 40 cents each.

7.—Springfield Civil War Musket Bayonet. U. S. stamped on each blade. Polished. In serviceable order. Fit any 1861-1868 Springfield Rifle; each 45c.

No. 346.—Old Pattern Lance Head, with long steel strap for fitting pole. four-sided diamond-shaped blade, 9 inches long. Length of blade and strap, 35 inches; width of blade at widest part, 1 inch tapering to sharpened point. Price, $2.50.

No. 3 1. Antique Sword Bayonet, with handle socket, same as in the Revolutionary War pattern bayonet; rare pattern blade; measures 24 inches; 1⅜ inches at the hilt; handle is 4½ inches; history unknown; from old London collector; no scabbard. Price, $2.75.

Rare Old Bayonet, with large socket for big bore musket; with double-edged sword; like point; poor order; rusted and worn; relic. Price, $3.75.

No. 6A.—Yatagan Saw Sword, with leather scabbard, steel mountings, 18-inch blade; full length, 24 inches; weight, 2 pounds. Price, $3.85.

No. 715.—Old U. S. Army Pike Blade, in use prior to Civil War period. Length of blade, 10½ inches; full length of blade and steel straps for the pole, over 3 feet. In good order, ready for mounting. Price, $3.75.

No. 23B.—300 SPANISH REMINGTON BREECH LOADING RIFLE BAYONETS; American manufacture; blade, 21¼ inches; socket, 2¾ inches; blued; full length, 24 inches. These bayonets were made for Remington breech loading rifles; made at Ilion, N. Y. Polished and blued; look like new. Price 85 cts. each.

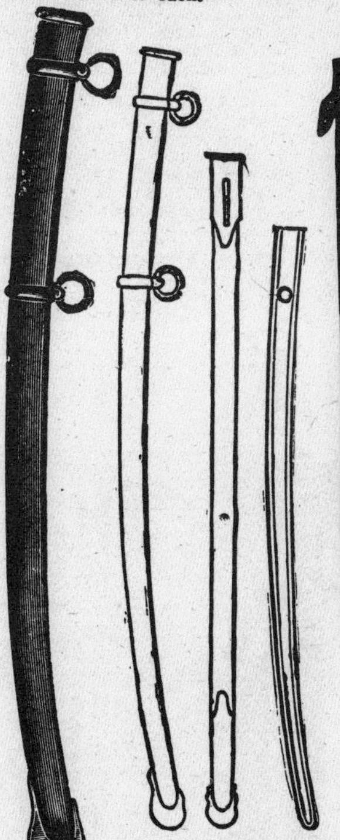

No. 13A No. 13 No. 14 No. 15

13A. U. S. Steel scabbard for cavalry sabres; new. Price, 85 cents each.

13.—U. S. Cavalry Steel Sabre Scabbard; second-hand, slightly rusted. 50 cents each.

14.—Non-Commissioned Sword Scabbard; leather; new, with hook attachment. 90 cents each.

No. 15.—U. S. Navy Cutlass Scabbards; heavy leather; serviceable order. Each, 40c.

OLD BATTLEFIELD RELIC BAYONETS, similar pattern to No. 3; rusty, require cleaning. Price, 15 cents each.

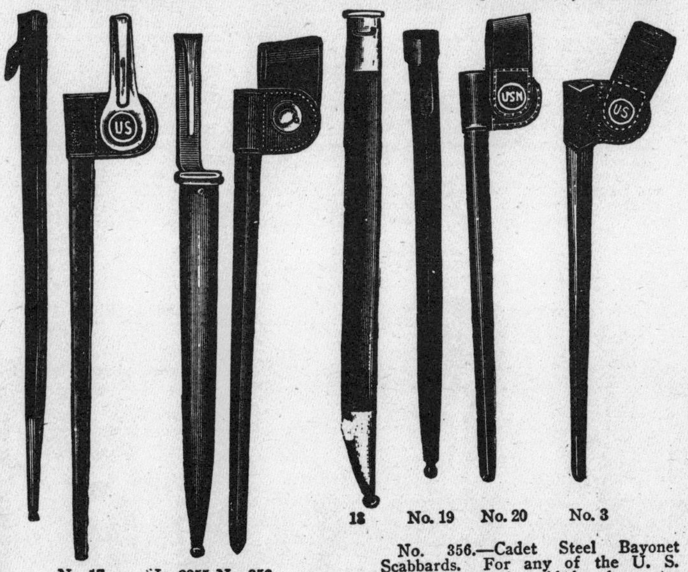

No. 17 No. 3355 No. 356 13 No. 19 No. 20 No. 3

12.—Captured Spanish Bayonet Scabbards, for holding the long bayonet used on the captured Spanish Remington Rifles; 5,000 in lot; in good, second-hand, serviceable order; made of leather, with brass tips. Price, 30 cents each.

No. 17.—6,000 U. S. ARMY STEEL BAYONET SCABBARDS, with brass hook, for use with any cartridge or waist belt; swivel frog. Made at U. S. Arsenal. In good, second-hand, serviceable order (not refinished). Price, 35 cents each. Some that are practically new, bluing slightly worn from long storage, 60 cents each.

No. 355.—Krag-Jorgensen Rifle Bayonet Scabbard, from U. S. Navy Department on return of marines from China and the Philippines. Relics of two wars. In serviceable order. 700 in stock; will fit captured Spanish Mauser bayonets. 95 cents each.

No. 356.—Cadet Steel Bayonet Scabbards. For any of the U. S. Springfield 16-in. blade bayonets; scabbards, with swivel leather frogs, either with U. S. on the brass swivel stud or plain, as desired. Price, 60 cents each.

No. 18.—Black Leather Scabbards for Sword Bayonets, 2,000 in stock. New goods. Will fit most any sword bayonet. Polished brass mouthpiece and tips. Special price for the lot. Price, each, 45c.

No. 19.—10,000 Leather Bayonet Scabbards, with steel lining that prevents breaking; will hold any calibre Springfield Bayonet; full length blade, 18 inches. Almost new. Price, 35c. each; $2.75 doz. Price, fitted with swivel frogs, 35c. each; $3.85 doz.

312B.—Antique Sword Bayonet, with socket, that fits a British Revolutionary War G. R. Musket; blade is 22 inches long, ¼ inch wide at the hilt; 26 inches total length. Rare old relic. Price, $2.00.

# SIDE ARM SWORDS

1270A

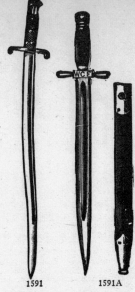

No. 1388

2          1570B

1523

1591     1591A

**1270A. CIVIL WAR ADMIRAL DAHL-GREN NAVY MACHETE-KNIVES,** used on the sharp and Hankins navy rifles on board U. S. Navy Civil War battleships. Now very rare. In fine order, equal to new, makes handsome decoration. Brass mounted handle. Polished steel blade ("Ames" make), leather scabbard, with polished brass mouth piece and tip. Price, $10.00 each. Length, 14 inches.

**1381. FRENCH GENDARME SIDE ARM SWORD;** double-edged blade, 19 inches; full length, 23 inches. Bronze hilt, marked as having been made at the French Arsenal. Price, $4.50 each.

**177A. FRENCH ARMY SIDE ARM SAW SWORD.** Saw teeth and cutting blade. Metal handle and cross guard, with black leather scabbard with tip and mouth piece, with loop for waist belt frog. Price, $3.00.

**339. ANTIQUE SWORD BAYONET,** with handle socket, same as in the Revolutionary War pattern bayonet; rare pattern blade; measures 24 inches; 1⅜ inches at the hilt; handle is 4½ inches; history unknown; from old London collector; no scabbard. Price, $3.75.

**1777. 50 ANTIQUE SIDE ARM SWORD BAYONETS.** Stamped on blade with crown, with letter P; bronze handle and guard with slit in guard for fastening to old style gun. Full length, 26 inches; width of blade, 1¼ inches. Price, $1.00 each.

**2. MACHETE,** as furnished by British manufacturer to the Colonies, wood handle, double edge quill back sword blade; second hand, serviceable. Price, $1.00 each.

**1570B. EUROPEAN ARMY SIDE ARM MACHETE;** fine steel blade; metal handle and cross guard; second hand order. Price, $1.85.

**OLD RUSTY SABRES,** collected by Southerners on Civil War battlefield, with scabbard, $3.50 each. Without scabbard, $2.85 each. Home-made Southern Confederate Sabre, with scabbard, $3.50.

**1388. EUROPEAN MACHETE BLADE,** as per illustration; requires cleaning. Price, 45 cents.

**342. BRONZE HANDLE MACHETE SWORD BAYONET;** straight blade, 1⅛ inches wide, 24 inches long. Good as new. 100 in stock. Price, $1.20. If scabbards are wanted, 30 cents extra. Rare pattern.

**1908. BRITISH ARMY MACHETE,** with British crown, V. R. stamped on blade; wood handle; serviceable relic; blade curved; 21 inches long. $1.85 each.

**No. JC2. ENGLISH ENFIELD KNIFE BAYONET.** Fits the early models of the LEE ENFIELD RIFLES. Many used in the World War. Blade is made of the finest Sheffield steel. On account of having no groove the blade can easily be shortened into a fine hunting knife. All have British Government Broad Arrow marks. A limited number left at low price of $1.95 each. NO SCABBARDS.

**No. 1523. 100 MACHETES** with steel blades. Hardwood riveted handle. 18 inches long; blade 1½ inches. Good condition. Price, 85 cents each.

**1591A. WORLD'S FAIR COLUMBIAN GUARD,** Chicago, 1893, used by Columbian Guards during time of the Fair. Sword like one in cut with the scabbard in good order. Price, $4.00. Swords with part of guard or hilt damaged, $3.00.

**1591. ENFIELD PATTERN SWORD BAYONETS,** with scabbards. Blade, 22¾ inches; scabbards are leather with iron throat and tip. All in good order. Price, $1.65 each.

**1540A. PRUSSIAN ARMY SIDE ARM SWORD.** Kind used during the Franco-German War. Complete with leather scabbard with fastening belt loop. Good second hand, serviceable order. Price, $1.85 each.

**6. YATAGAN SAW SWORD,** 19-inch blade, saw teeth on one side, cutting edge on other side of the blade; full length, 24 inches; weight, 1¾ pounds; brass handle; in serviceable order; no scabbard. Polished, $2.75.

**6A. U. S. CIVIL WAR SIDE ARM SWORDS,** bronze handle and cross guard. Steel blade, with leather scabbard, with brass mouth and tip; new, never issued. Will, however, require cleaning, on account of long storage. Length, 20 inches. Price, $1.25.

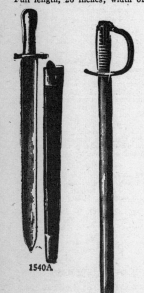

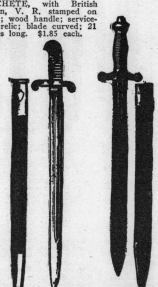

1540A

1777     1777A     339     6     6A     1381

**354A. RELIC SIDE ARM KNIFE BAYONETS,** used on Lee Navy Repeating Rifles on U. S. Navy warships. Purchased from Navy Dept. at close of Spanish War. Fair, serviceable order, without scabbard. Price, 60c

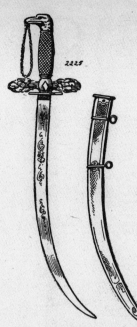

**2225A. OLD PATTERN BRITISH NAVY SCIMITER SHAPED DIRK** with 11-inch blade, ivory handle and lion claw pommel. Has metal trimmed leather scabbard. Price, $12.50.

**2225B.** One as above with wide blade, slightly curved, with ivory handle and lion head pommel, used as dress sword. Price, $10.00.

**ONE OLD STYLE BRITISH NAVAL DRESS SWORD** with 17½-inch straight blade, shark skin grip, lion head pommel, and leather scabbard. Price, $11.50.

One as above with 14-inch extra wide blade with one saw edge. Leather scabbard has coat-of-arms at throat. Price, $9.50.

**TWO BRITISH NAVY DIRKS** with 16-inch rapier blades, ivory handles. Leather scabbards are in fair condition. Price, $12.00 each.

**209B.** One as above with 12-inch blade without scabbard. Price, $9.00.

**209A. ONE OLD ENGLISH NAVAL DIRK** with 16-inch blade, an unusual length in this style weapon. No scabbard. The grooved blade is marked TOMASO on one side, and on other EN TOLEDO. Price, $15.00.

**RL-1. ANTIQUE COURT SWORD, OR RAPIER,** with 30-inch triangular blade, engraved, with fine tapering point. Cut out metal hilt, inlaid with small gold roses. Total length 36½ inches. Scabbard is of rawhide, but in poor order. Price, $13.50.

**RL-2. ENGLISH RAPIER,** time of George II, with triangular blade, 32½ inches long. Ornamented hilt and guard on which the gold plating has nearly worn off. No scabbard. Price, $8.50.

**RL-3. FIGHTING SWORD,** made about 1700, with 31-inch diamond shaped blade, with short deep blood gutters near hilt. Marked: EN TOLEDO. Heavy wide brass guard, wire wrapped grip. This is a rare piece. Price, $22.00.

**RL-5. ANTIQUE RAPIER,** time of Charles II, with triangular shaped blade 28½ inches long, 1 inch wide at hand guard. Small gold inlaid ornament. Hand guard, cross bar and pommel decorated with human figures. Price, $14.50.

**RL-7. SMALL COURT SWORD,** time of George II, with triangular blade, 26½ inches, cup hand guard, wire wrapped hilt. Price, $13.50.

**RL-8. ANTIQUE RAPIER,** time of George II, with early pattern triangular blade, 31 inches long, with deep blood gutter full length of blade. Cup hand guard, wire wrapped hilt. Price $11.00.

**RL-10. ANTIQUE RAPIER,** with pebbled steel hilt and hand guard. Engraved triangular blade 30½ inches. Price, $12.00.

**RL-12. ANTIQUE FIGHTING RAPIER,** time of 1700. Wide triangular blade, 29½ inches, with deep blood gutters. Wide hand guard, with wire wrapped grip. Marked with initials: T. N. Price, $16.00.

**RL-13. COURT SWORD,** time of George III. Belonged to SIR BENNETT GOLDNEY, MAYOR OF CANTERBURY. 34-inch narrow angular blade, inlaid with gold near guard. Heavy brass handle with oval hand guard. Has been gold plated. Scabbard in poor order, marked: R. JOHNSTON, late BLAND & FOSTER, Sword Cutler, Belt Maker to HIS MAJESTY, 68 St. James St., LONDON. Price, $20.00.

**CJX. U. S. ARMY WORLD WAR TRENCH KNIVES.** Model 1917 without scabbards. Knobbed handle with triangular shaped blade. Price, $4.50 each.

**CJZ. U. S. ARMY WORLD WAR TRENCH KNIVES WITH STEEL SCABBARDS.** Model 1918. Scabbard has two heavy wire attachments on back to hold on belt. Large brass handle, dull finish, as shown in cut. 7-inch blade, 1 inch wide, with two ridges in center.

PLEASE NOTE, THAT THE RESTRICTIONS REGARDING DANGEROUS WEAPONS APPLIES TO SALE OF THESE TRENCH KNIVES. WE MUST HAVE PERMIT FROM YOUR CHIEF OF POLICE WITH YOUR ORDER.

**1862. ORIENTAL SCIMITER,** 29-inch blade, 1/16 inch wide, 2-inch curve. Made up for theatrical or decoration. Richly polished gilt hilt, cross guard and chain. Handle represents ivory. Russet leather scabbard, with polished ornamental gilt mountings. Rich and handsome NEW Scimiter. Price, $15.00.

**No. 25-8. TURKISH OFFICER'S SWORD,** with 29-inch plain blade, heavy bronze handle with curved pommel and cross bars with acorn ends. No scabbard. Price, $8.00.

**No. 25-16. TURKISH OFFICER'S SWORD** with scimiter shaped blade with two Turkish inscriptions. Sharkskin scabbard, brass trimming, gold plated. White ivory handle with long cross bar. Ornamented with gold plated leaves. Price, $20.00.

**1866. RICHLY MOUNTED THEATRICAL SWORD,** polished gilt open work basket guard, with 10-inch cross guard, gilt and silvered wire wrapped hilt. Ornamented pommel and guard. Diamond shaped steel blade (dull edge), width ⅝ inch, length 34 inches. Russet leather scabbard, with polished gilt mountings, and belt attachment. This handsome new sword must be seen to be appreciated. One of the finest swords we have ever had for sale. Price, $25.00.

**1611. PAIR OF LONG FANCY SWORDS.** Full length 44¾ inches, 7½-inch cross bar at guard. Large cup shaped guards, wire hilt. Double edged blade, 37 inches long, 1¼ at hilt, gradually tapered to the point. Second hand, serviceable order. The pair, $11.85.

**No. 6032. TURKISH OFFICER'S SWORD,** presentation, with watered steel blade 34 inches long, curved, with 7-inch ornamented silver cross bar with bar ends. Rhinoceros horn handle, silver bound. Leather scabbard with silver mounted throat showing double headed axes, two silver ring bands with entwined serpents, 14-inch silver tip with designs showing serpents, double headed axes, etc. A very showy piece. Price, $40.00. (See also illustration No. 6032 on page 201.)

**No. 6032-A. TURKISH OFFICER'S PRESENTATION SWORD,** with watered steel blade, 34 inches, with 6-inch silver cross bar with ball ends, rhinoceros horn grip with ball end, silver bound. Leather scabbard with 8½-inch silver bound throat, two ring bands of silver, tip silver covered, 17 inches. All silver mountings are engraved. Price, $35.00.

**D-67-1. CEYLON PRIEST'S KNIFE,** with 7-inch narrow blade, silver inlaid black carved ivory handle. In wood scabbard is included a brass handle stylus used in writing on palm leaves. Price, $9.00. (See illustration on page 215.)

**D-67-2. CEYLON KNIFE,** with 7-inch blade overlaid with silver in scroll designs for almost entire length; 2-inch black ivory carved handle, wood scabbard, covered with blue plush. Scabbard contains 7-inch brass handle stylus. Price, $11.00.

**D-67-3. CEYLON KNIFE,** with 8-inch blade overlaid partly with heavy silver. Brown carved ivory grip with silver pommel. Corrugated wood scabbard, silver bound at throat. There is an opening for stylus which is missing. Price, $9.50.

**D-67-4. CEYLON KNIFE,** with silver bound 7-inch blade. Light wood scabbard, leather covered. There are three openings in scabbard besides the one for knife. Other implements missing. Price, $10.00.

**D-67-5. CEYLON SACRIFICIAL KNIFE,** with silver covered handle. Blade 7¼ inches, narrow. No scabbard. Price, $8.00.

**No. 6908-A. COSSACK DAGGER,** similar to illustration No. 5908 on page 192; 10-inch wide blade with one raised ridge on center of each side. Ornamented polished steel handle, inlaid with gold plated designs. Velvet covered wood scabbard, bound at tip and throat with steel in scroll designs. A very fine piece. Price, $10.00.

**No. 6908-B. RUSSIAN OFFICER'S KNIFE,** old style, as worn by Cossack of the Don River; 6½-inch blade with one groove on each side. Very sharp point. Hilt and scabbard covered with silver, the front side in carved scroll designs. Price, $8.00.

**No. 6908-C. SOUDAN KNIFE,** native made, with 15-inch long sharp pointed blade with moon and star designs, also writing. Blade and handle in one piece, grip covered with alligator skin. Embossed leather scabbard, bound at throat, center and tip with band of alligator skin. This is a very rare and curious piece. Price, $12.00.

**No. 2204-A. TOLEDO BLADE DAGGER,** with 5¾-inch blade with scroll design, and marked: FABRICA DE TOLEDO 1877. Handle is made of brass and is a figure of sailor standing bare footed on two large fish. Leather scabbard. Price, $7.50. (See illustration No. 2204, page 210.)

**No. 2204. TOLEDO BLADE DAGGER,** with 6¾-inch blade with scroll designs on both sides, and marked: TOLEDO, 1863. Heavy bronze handle, corrugated, with ornamental cross bars. Price, $9.00.

LARGE ASSORTMENT OF KNIVES, DAGGERS, BOLOS, KRISES, THROWING KNIVES, DIRKS AND DAGGERS from Asia and Africa. If you wish any special kind, send us your description, and we will send outline and price.

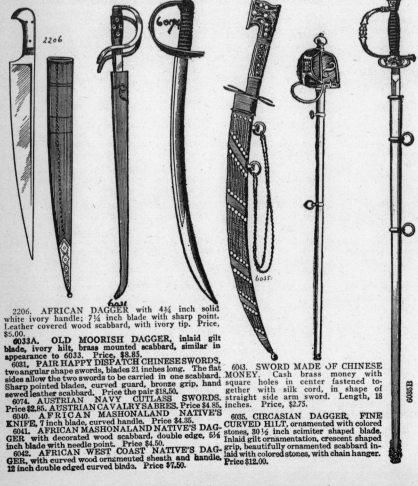

**AS A PICK.**

Elliott's Intrenching Tool as Hoe.

Elliott's Intrenching Tool as Pick.

**GENERAL ELLIOTT'S MILITARY INTRENCHING TOOL, COMBINING PICK, SHOVEL AND HOE.** The blade folds up against the handle when carried as part of soldiers' equipment. By use of a bolt attached, the handle can be removed, or by its use the blade can be set to any angle desired for use as a pick or hoe; blade is made of the best forged steel with strong center rib; handle is of hard wood with steel strap with socket. We have 400 in stock that have been used a short time, all in good serviceable order, for sale at the bargain price of $2.85 the set.

**2206-A. EARLY INDIAN STONE HANDLE DAGGER.** from Scinde. 11½ inch blade, ribbed back, sharp reinforced point. Heavy stone handle, copper bound. Wood scabbard, leather covered, with metal tip and metal band with ring. Price, $10.00.

**2206-B. INDIAN DAGGER** with heavy gray stone handle, metal bound; 10 inch blade with ridged back and sharp point. Price, $9.00.

**2206-C. INDIA DAGGER** with handle of stone and jade, brass bound; 9½ inch narrow blade, slightly curved. Price, $8.50.

**2206-D. INDIA DAGGER** with shell handle tipped with stone; 9½ inch narrow blade. Price $9.50.

**2206-E. INDIA DAGGER** with stone handle, brass tipped and brass bound; 8 inch pointed blade. Price $8.00.

**2206-F. INDIA DAGGER** with 8¼ inch blade, stone handle, ring stud, mountings gold plated. Price, $7.50.

**2206-G. INDIA DAGGER** with 7½ inch flat blade, pointed; heavy brass handle, embossed. Price, $6.50.

**2206-H. INDIA DAGGER** with wide flat blade, 6½ inch, with ornamental handle made of alternate disks of stone, gold and jade, silver pommel and band. A very showy piece. Price, $8.00.

**2206-J. INDIA DAGGER,** very old, with hardwood black handle, corrugated, short copper guard, marked: N Z K A 30; 8 inch wide flat blade with sharp point. Blade has various designs; rising sun, scythe, helmet, ladder, new moon, man with turban and plume, and letters B E R C. Engraved work has been gold plated, but mostly worn off. Price, $9.00.

**U. S. EXPERIMENTAL KNIFE BAYONET FOR FENCING,** calibre 30 model. Price, $2.50.

**CALIBRE 45 AND 58 ANGULAR BAYONETS FOR FENCING.** Price, $1.00.

**CIVIL WAR SPRINGFIELD MUSKET INTRENCHING BAYONET,** trowel shaped, 9 inches wide, with leather scabbard, rare old relic. Price, $8.50.

**6035A. U. S. ARMY LIGHT CAVALRY SABER,** Model 1906. This saber has 35-inch slightly curved blade; total length with scabbard is 42 inches. Weight 3¾ pounds. Handle and scabbard are bronze finish but this has worn off somewhat. Offered at REDUCED PRICE of $1.95 each. Special price for lot of 3000.

**6073. AUSTRIAN OFFICER'S SWORD,** with engraved blades. Price $6.50. A few with gilt inlaid engraving on the blades. $7.85.

**6074B. ROMAN MODEL CADET SWORDS,** similar to 6074A except that they are smaller and lighter; evidently made made for use of military school cadets. Price $3.50 each.

**1067. THE QUEEN'S OWN CAMERON HIGHLANDERS CLAYMORE SWORD,** used by British Officer; supposed to be relic of South African War in which the CAMERON HIGHLANDERS WON GLORY AND HONOR. Blade is double edged, 33 inches long, engraved "Frazer & Son., Church st., Inverness," with V.R. Crown, Thistle leaves and Flowers. "The Queen's Own Cameron Highlanders." Basket hilt lined with red cloth, sharkskin grip, steel scabbard. fine order. Price $35.00.

**6035B. CADET OFFICER'S SWORD,** second hand. Complete with scabbard. Some have letters A O H on hand guard, others with eagle or plain. Price, $3.45 each.

**6036. INDIA FEMALE DEITY HILTED DAGGER.** Curved steel double edged wide blade, etched with Koran characters. Full length 12¾ inches. Price $4.85.

**6037. INDIA GOORKA KNIFE,** with sword handle, Damascus etched, curved steel blade, serviceable weapon. Price $8.50.

**6038. DERVISH KNIFE,** Engraved 10 inch blade, curved decorated handle. Price $4.85.

**6039. INDIAN DAGGER,** wire silver inlaid hilt, 10¾ inches, curved double edged blade. double guard. Price $7.50.

**6074A. U. S. ARTILLERY ROMAN SWORD.** advertised on page 128, at $3.50 each, SOLD. We have similar ones as per illustration 6074A used as European side arm, with bronze hilt, double edged steel blade, bronze handle, complete with leather seabbard, with brass mouth piece. in polished serviceable order. Price $2.85 each.

**6034. SCOTCH HIGHLAND REGIMENT OFFICER'S DIRK.** Relic of the Boer War. Queen Victoria's crown on the pommel in relief; Ionic pattern hilt, 12 inch blade stoned with Thistle leaves and Flowers. Steel mouth piece and tip ornamented in relief with Thistle. Full length 18 inches, weight 21 ounces. In serviceable order. Price $25.00.

**2206. AFRICAN DAGGER** with 4¾ inch solid white ivory handle; 7¼ inch blade with sharp point. Leather covered wood scabbard, with ivory tip. Price, $5.00.

**6033A. OLD MOORISH DAGGER,** inlaid gilt blade, ivory hilt, brass mounted scabbard, similar in appearance to 6033. Price, $8.85.

**6031. PAIR HAPPY DISPATCH CHINESE SWORDS,** two angular shape swords, blades 21 inches long. The flat sides allow the two swords to be carried in one scabbard. Sharp pointed blades, curved guard, bronze grip, hand sewed leather scabbard. Price the pair $18.50.

**6074. AUSTRIAN NAVY CUTLASS SWORDS.** Price $2.85. AUSTRIAN CAVALRY SABRES. Price $4.85.

**6040. AFRICAN MASHONALAND NATIVE'S KNIFE,** 7 inch blade, curved handle. Price $4.35.

**6041. AFRICAN MASHONALAND NATIVE'S DAGGER** with decorated wood scabbard, double edge, 5½ inch blade with needle point. Price $4.50.

**6042. AFRICAN WEST COAST NATIVE'S DAGGER,** with curved wood ornamented sheath and handle, 12 inch double edged curved blade. Price $7.50.

**6043. SWORD MADE OF CHINESE MONEY.** Cash brass money with square holes in center fastened together with silk cord, in shape of straight side arm sword. Length, 18 inches. Price, $2.75.

**6035. CIRCASIAN DAGGER, FINE CURVED HILT,** ornamented with colored stones, 30½ inch scimiter shaped blade. Inlaid gilt ornamentation, crescent shaped grip, beautifully ornamented scabbard inlaid with colored stones, with chain hanger. Price $12.00.

**2206-K. INDIA DAGGER,** very short, full length only 7¼ inches. Stone tipped shell handle, brass bound; 4 inch pointed blade. This size usually worn concealed. Price, $7.00.

**SC-1. OFFICER'S SCOTCH CLAYMORE,** with leather scabbard; 32½ inch double grooved blade, etched, showing crown over V R. Large basket handle guard, copper plated. Price $37.00. (See other pages in this catalog for other Claymores.)

0-879A. SCOTCH CLAYMORE. Early pattern, with large steel basket hilt, with conical stud pommel. Guard ornamented with triangular shaped cut-outs. 37½ inch blade with ridge in top side. Wood grip wire wrapped. Price, $48.00.

0-879B. SCOTCH CLAYMORE. Antique pattern, with 31½-inch blade, large steel basket hilt, ornamented with triangular and circular cut-outs. Leather covered grip, stud pommel. This claymore supposed to have been used in the Battle of Culleden Moor. Opening in bottom of hilt for bridle fingers. Price, $50.00.

0-879C. SCOTCH CLAYMORE. Early pattern with extra large steel basket hilt, ornamented with heart shaped cut-outs. Shark skin grip, round flat stud pommel. 37-inch blade with one full length groove on each side, also on short groove. Price, $40.00.

0-879D. SCOTCH CLAYMORE. With heart shaped ornamented basket, shark skin grip, gilt wire wrapped, round flat pommel stud. Wide blade, 33 inches, with 10-inch deep center groove on each side. Blade etched in vine designs. On one side: WARRANTED, on the other: J. H. RIEDELL & COMPANY. Price, $42.00.

0-879E. SCOTCH CLAYMORE. With extra large steel basket hilt, heart shaped ornamental cut-outs, shark skin grip, gilt wire wrapped. Ball pommel stud. 35-inch wide blade with double grooves. On each side engraving of CROWN over what appears to be monogram G R. Price, $38.00.

0-879F. SCOTCH CLAYMORE. Medium size with smaller sized polished steel basket, hilt heart ornaments. Shark skin grip, gilt wire wrapped. 31½ inch blade with double center grooves. Price, $33.00.

0-879G. SCOTCH CLAYMORE. Very early pattern, period of 1740, with unusual shaped basket hilt, in iron work of 1-inch squares, with bridle finger opening at bottom, leather covered grip, round flat pommel stud. Blade 34 inches long, very wide, with 2 short grooves or blood gutters. In EACH groove is the word: TOLEDO. On each side also there is a shield with CROWN over D K. and on each side near the shield a roughly engraved FISH with open mouth. This piece secured from a collection at Templemore Abbey near Dublin. Price $90.00.

25-16. FRENCH OFFICER'S SWORD with 33½-inch straight blade with long blood gutter. Blade marked I. Giroult, Paris. Blade, scabbard and handle have been nickel plated. Guard handle and pommel are similar to the present regulation army officer's saber. Scabbard has one ring only. Price, $12.00.

0-781. SPEARMAN'S TOLEDO BLADE DAGGER. 7¼-inch double-edged relief etched and decorated blade, stamped "Fabrica De Toledo, 1884." Steel cross guard and pommel. Dark-colored hard wood hilt. Full length 12 inches. Serviceable order. Price, $6.85.

0-782. SCOTCH SKENE DHU KNIFE. Worn in the stocking. Silver-mounted, with relief carved monogram and motto 1865. Full length 7¾ inches, blade 3¾ inches. Fine order. Price, $6.85.

0-749A. U. S. N. REAR ADMIRAL'S CARVING KNIFE AND FORK. Steel polished, slightly curved, 15-inch blade. Silver plated ornamented handle with letters U. S. N. and Admiral's emblem, two stars. Silver plated guard rest; the fork to match the knife, with two stars and navy monogram, U. S. N. Fork is two tined, with guard with safety. Silver-plated. All in serviceable order. Needs repolishing. From recent navy yard auction sale. The set, $4.85.

0-911A. SPANISH BULL FIGHTER'S SWORD, WITH ENGRAVED SILVER-MOUNTED MOUTH AND TIP SCABBARD. Blade engraved, "Malgar Fa-Ca de Gabrielle Carrasco-M," and on the reverse side, "Rd-Maa, Lax El ce bre Diorto." 31½-inch double-edged sharpened steel blade, 8¼-inch cross guard, 2-INCH HILT, silver guard. Used by noted bull fighter or matador. Price $17.85.

0-963. EDMUND KEENE'S STAGE SWORD. Roman pattern 19½-inch grooved blade. Bronze ornamented guard and hilt. Red leather scabbard. Large brass mouth piece and ornamental tip. In used, serviceable order. From the sale of the Royal Artist Ernest Croft's collection. Price, $16.X.

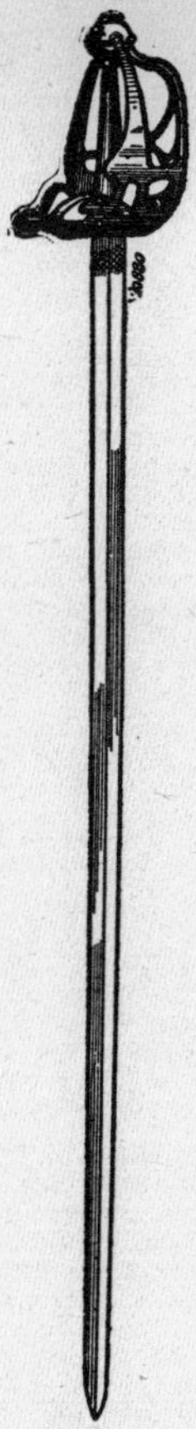
0-880

0-879

0-947

0-880. OLIVER CROMWELL'S CAVALIER'S *MORTUARY* SWORD. A relic from the battle of Worcester, 1651. King Charles I. head on the pommel was removed after his execution, and the sword hilt was blackened (Mortuary). 31½-inch double-edged blade, tapered steel, with 3-inch basket guard covering the hilt. Ball pommel with king's head ornament removed. The wood hilt is worn off, and small part of one of the guards is broken, otherwise sword is in good condition, considering it is over 260 years old. Rare sword. Price, $100.00.

0-879. BATTLE CULLODEN MOOR SCOTCH CLAYMORE SWORD. From the sale of the late Lawson-Johnston collection, which contained many historical Culloden relics, including the famous Stuart relic bedstead in which Prince Charles slept at Culloden House the night before the battle of Culloden Moor. Six pence was charged for catalogues, owing to the great demand. Special permits required to view the goods prior to day of sale. We mention the above facts as showing the authenticity of this historical sword. The blade is fine, double-edged tapered steel 35 inches long. Large ornamental basket guard, wire wrapped hilt. Cone-shaped metal pommel. Sword blade slightly pitted from battlefield exposure and age. BATTLE was fought January 3, 1746. This sword evidently was carried by some Scotch chieftain and was drawn in defense of Bonnie Prince Charlie. This sword, with Culloden Pistol No. 11038, should go together. Our price for this relic sword, $250.00.

8606J. FRENCH HUNTING SWORD, antique pattern, with leather covered grip, wrapped with twisted copper wire. Cross bar of brass has dog head gargoyle on each end. 23-inch with one large groove on each side, etched with scenes (dogs chasing wild boar, dogs chasing stag) with French fleur de lis. Price $9.00.

6072A. U. S. NAVY DESSERT KNIVES. Have been used on navy warships. Are stamped with the U. S. Navy monogram, anchor and rope. Handles are silver plated, 4-inch steel blades (need repolishing). Offered in used serviceable order. Visitors to navy warships often desire souvenirs; this is a splendid opportunity to get a genuine serviceable relic. Price, 50 cents.

0-785. FOLDING SIDE ARM SWORD. 9-inch Sheffield steel blade, width 1½ inches, dirk point. Checkered ivory or bone hilt. German silver guard and mountings. Contained in leather scabbard with belt loop. Price, $7.85.

8606C. 18th CENTURY FRENCH HUNTING SWORD, shark skin grip, copper wire wrapped. Ornamented strap and hand guard. 21½-inch narrow blade with grooves. Price $10.00. (See illustration page 195, No. 8606.)

8606D. 17th CENTURY HUNTING SWORD, with 4½-inch stag horn grip metal studded. 20½-inch wide grooved blade showing on one side ST. MARTINUS, and on the other the DUCAL coat of arms of owner with several inscriptions. Price $12.50.

8606E. QUEEN ANNE PERIOD ENGLISH HUNTING SWORD, with 4-inch stag horn grip, iron pommel; strap and hand guard. 27-inch blade with grooves. Price $9.00.

8606F. OLD GERMAN HUNTING SWORD, with 3½-inch stag horn grip, iron pommel and hand guard. 24½-inch blade with double grooves. Price $8.00.

8606G. OLD ENGLISH HUNTING SWORD with wood grip, brass pommel and fluted guard. 25-inch slightly curved blade with single long groove. Price $7.00.

8606K. FRENCH HUNTING SWORD, OLD PATTERN, with black hard wood corrugated grip, brass pommel with ball stud, brass cross bar with acorn ends. 21½-inch wide blade etched with hunting scenes. Price $8.00.

0-947. FRENCH OFFICER'S ANCIENT REVOLUTIONARY WAR PERIOD SABRE. With brass scabbard, 33½-inch steel blade, slightly curved. Traces of gilt and blue etching; single guard. Fine wire wrapped hilt brass scabbard with two rings. Lafayette's officers carried such a sword in helping American colonies to gain their independence. The sword has been much used. In serviceable order. Price $25.00.

8606L. ANTIQUE FRENCH HUNTING SWORD with 4½-inch grip covered with sharkskin and wrapped with flat copper wire. Brass pommel, brass cross bar. Flat blade 22 inches, with one full length groove on each side, and one shorter groove. Blade somewhat nicked. Price $7.50.

0-892. GEORGE II. NAVAL OFFICER'S DIRK. With ivory hilt, brass pommel, cross and centre guards. Double-edged tapered steel 13½-inch blade. From the Lawson-Johnston sale. Perhaps carried by British officer in British-American Revolutionary War. Price, $7.85.

0-891B. "G. R. III" ENGRAVED ON SABRE BLADE. British marked coat of arms and motto. 33-inch blade, single guard, gilt bronze guard, sharkskin grip wire wrapped. In serviceable order, with sword in British lion head pommel. Price, $12.85.

25-15. ANTIQUE AMERICAN SWORD with 31-inch blade. White ivory grip with ornamented cross bars with acorn ends. Pommel is brass eagle mounted on cannon ball. No scabbard. Price, $8.00.

0-664. U. S. NAVY RELIC CUTLASS. Stamped on the brass guard, "Philadelphia," and the blade stamped "1862." As it is contrary to naval regulations to stamp any name on service weapons these cutlasses must have had some important history—perhaps relics of Commodore Bainbridge at Tripoli. Price, $9.85.

0664A. REVOLUTIONARY WAR DAGGER. 4¼-inch double-edged tapering blade, ⅝-inch wide at the tang, 3¼-inch ivory hilt. Relic from the Brooks collection. Price, $17.50.

Illustration showing attack of tramps repulsed by use of sword cane.

No. 0756. SWORD UMBRELLA, with 23½-inch triangular Toledo blade, blued finish, with gold inlaid work. Marked T. PEARSON, PARIS, DEC. 1886. Long heavy bamboo handle with leather guard. The silk umbrella has been repaired and is in fair condition. Price, $10.00.

No. 1289A. SWORD CANE HANDLE WITH BLADE. Blade is square shaped, 17¾ inches long. Marked GOTTATAY. The handle is crooked. Price, $6.00.

No. 1758B. SWORD CANE WITH HANDLE ONLY. Blade is 25 inches long, flat with blood gutter on each side, and ornamented with scroll work, wire inlaid. Handle is heavy wood with large knob. Price, $6.75.

No. 1163. TAKE DOWN SWORD CANE. Shaft made of heavy bamboo handle made of black hard wood, crooked, with end to represent horse's foot. Bamboo shaft unscrews in center for packing. Triangular shaped blade is 11 inches. Price, $8.00.

No. 1267. SWORD CANE WITH LARGE CROOKED HANDLE, with 17¾-inch wide flat blade, with blood gutter. Silver band. In good condition. Price, $9.50.

No. 1162. LIGHT BAMBOO SWORD CANE WITH BRASS band and fitting. Top with stag horn handle, with silver band and silver name plate on top. The 27-inch blade is triangular and is somewhat ornamented. Price, $10.00.

No. 1161. LIGHT WOOD SWORD CANE, dark red color with handle of iron to represent Serpent. The blade is 34 inches, triangular shaped and is ornamented with scrolls. Sword canes with blades of this length are rare. Price, $9.50.

No. 25-2. SPANISH NON-COM. OFFICER'S SWORD, with 27½-inch straight blade, cross guard, horn handle, with eagle head, with slot for cord. Leather scabbard has metal throat and tip. Price, $5.00.

No. 25-3. EUROPEAN OFFICER'S SWORD, with rare style square cornered guard with duck head on cross bar. 27-inch blade with gold inlaid scrolls. Sharkskin scabbard with metal throat and tip. Trimmings on handle and scabbard appear to be silvered. Price, $18.50.

1758B

1289A

No. 25-23. ENGLISH OFFICER'S ANTIQUE SWORD with wide leather scabbard brass fittings, with two rings and one stud. Fittings were originally gold plated. Flat handle with white ivory grip neatly checkered. Extra wide curved, blued finish part way. Marked on the crown G. R. and Arms Trophies. Made by SALTER, 35 STRAND, LONDON. Blade is 30 inches. Price, $18.00.

No. 25-24. WATERLOO PATTERN SABER, as used by an officer of the 71st Highlanders, leather scabbard, steel trim, with flat handle and wire wrap sharkskin grip. Blade is 31½ inches and is marked as made by R. JOHNSTON, ST. JAMES STREET. Both sides of blade are etched with crown over horn scroll, marked 71 with the Scotch Insignia. Also marked for the following battles: PENINSULAR, ALMARAZ, PITORIA, AND WATERLOO. This is a rare sword. Price, $35.00.

No. 150K. FENCING SABERS, with corrugated grip, large iron basket guard, with 34-inch narrow blade. Can be used in any style of fencing. In good order, slightly rusty. Bargain price, $1.50 each.

No. 25-26. COURT SWORD RAPIER with 29½-inch triangular shaped blade ending in sharp point. Small ivory handle, brass top with short brass guard, representing the four suits in cards. Price, $14.00.

No. 25-27. EARLY PATTERN BRITISH OFFICER'S SABER, with 32-inch blade. This is marked as made by RUNKEL, of LONDON. Blued finish is nearly worn off. Eetching shows Dragoon on each side. Leather scabbard, brass, mounted with two rings and one stud. Flat brass handle with white ivory corrugated grip. Scabbard marked S. BRUNN, SWORD CUTLER, TO HIS ROYAL HIGHNESS, THE PRINCE OF WALES, 55 CHARING CROSS, LONDON. Price, $17.50.

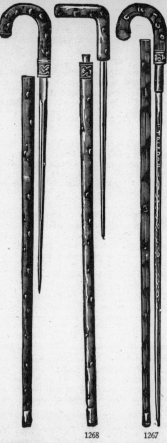

1268    1267

No. 25-28. TURKISH OFFICER'S SCIMITER, of early pattern. Blade is 31½ inches with much curve. Blade has been sharpened. Leather scabbard with brass tip and throat which have been gold plated. Heavy brass handle, ornamented but gold plating worn off. Pommel ends in Pigeon head. Hand guard ends in ornament to represent Tiger head. Price, $18.50.

IRISH BLACKTHORN SHILLALAH, with knot or crook, polished natural wood, imported, $4.85 each.

No. 357.—LONDON POLICE OFFICER'S TRUNCHEON with Queen Victoria's monogram and letters S. C. Length, 18 inches; width at butt, 1⅝ inches. Grooved handle, with wrist cord. Serviceable relic. Price $1.00 each.

357 A. CENTENNIAL POLICE CLUB, with cord and tassels. Souvenir relic of World Centennial Fair, Philadelphia, 1876. Sold only to authorized parties. Price $1.00 each.

24. OLD CLUBS, formerly used by police. Sold only to watchmen or authorized persons. Price 70c.

23. N. Y. POLICE CLUB OR BILLY. Locust wood. Sold only to watchmen who can show their police badge or other authority to carry club. Price 60 cents each.

## NOTICE.

The sword canes here advertised will only be sold to Curators of incorporated museums, under the seal of the museum, or to physicians or collectors, who will furnish us with an official letter, under seal, from the magistrate of their city, authorizing us to sell these weapons.

Collection of 100 Antique Swords and Sabres for $500.00. All cleaned and polished. Some very old patterns. Real genuine old swords, purchased by our agent at sale in London, no two alike. Collectors have desired to purchase part of this lot to complete their collection, but we offer the lot complete. Rare chance to obtain valuable collection. No doubt they represent the life work of some collector.

Collection of fifty different kinds of Daggers and Bowie knives. Some very rare patterns in the lot; no two alike; represents twenty years' labor of collector. Price $150.00.

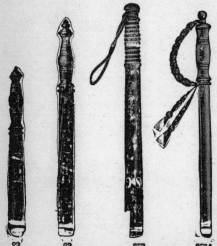

23    23    357    357A

**310-C.** SPANISH CLASP KNIFE or dagger. Full length, open, is 17 inches; 8 inch blade, very wide, with sharp point, marked: HAUDEVILLE EN ALBAGETTE. Handle is of red shell, brass bound, with long brass pommel. Price, $8.50. (See illustration on page 213.)

**310-D.** SPANISH DAGGER, similar to No. 310-C; total length 20 inches; blade 9 inches. Shell handle brass bound. Price, $9.00.

**310-E.** SPANISH DAGGER with horn handle inlaid with white ivory flower designs; full length 17 inches; blade 8 inches. Has ring for cord. Rare pattern. Price, $9.25.

**310-F.** SPANISH DAGGER with white bone handle inlaid with white ivory in vine designs, copper bound; full length 19½ inches; sharp pointed blade, marked: VALERO-JON, ZARAGOZA. Price, $9.50.

**D64.** ONE EXTRA LONG SOMALI KNIFE with native made leather scabbard. Handle is 8½ inches long, of horn, iron tipped and inlaid with white metal. Blade is 14 inches long, sharp on both edges. A rare specimen. Price, $8.00.

**D65.** ONE NATIVE KNIFE from Coastal Somalia; 6½ inch horn handle, iron bound at pommel; 10 inch wide blade, 2½ inches at widest part. Native made leather scabbard with crude leather shoulder sling, and buckle. Price, $7.50.

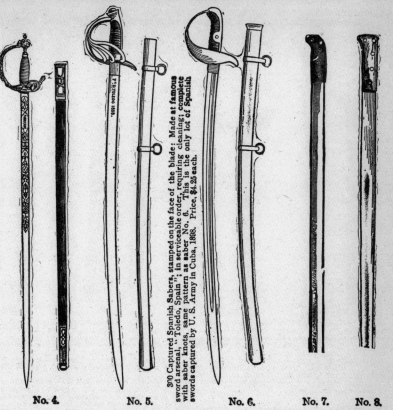

370 Captured Spanish Sabres, stamped on the face of the blade: Made at famous sword arsenal, "Toledo, Spain"; in serviceable order, requiring cleaning; complete with saber knots, same pattern as saber No. 6. This is the only lot of Spanish swords captured by U. S. Army in Cuba, 1898. Price, $4.25 each.

**No. 4.** **No. 5.** **No. 6.** **No. 7.** **No. 8.**

**No. 58.** U. S. A. PICK MATTOCK WITH RUSSET LEATHER HOLDER, 17-inch blade, with sharp pick and 2½-inch mattock; attached by different screw bolt to 31-inch hickory handle. The pick takes apart and is contained in holster with straps and attached to the waist belt. Fine serviceable order. Price, $1.50.

**No. 11.** U. S. A. 1908 MODEL HOSPITAL CORPS KNIFE, with russet leather scabbard; heavy steel blade stamped "U. S.—S. A. (Springfield Arsenal) 1908." Brass cross guard, walnut handle with finger hold grooves, with thong hole; fine serviceable order, $3.85.

**No. 4.** **Spanish Officers' Sword,** with gold-plated handle, with Spanish crown in relief work, etched blade in raised work, marked in on one side "Fabricade," and on the other side "De Toledo." Leather scabbard with crown insignia on stud. Rare relic. Spaniard reluctantly parted with this handsome sword—one of the best specimens of Toledo blade, famous for centuries for the finest swords . . . . . . . . . . . . . . . Price, $30 00

Handsome double-edged **Toledo blade Spanish Naval Officers' Sword,** marked, with steel handle engraved with insignia of Spanish crown. With leather scabbard; fine order. . . . . . . $25 00

**Spanish Engineers Officers' Fine Sword,** Toledo make, with castle surrounded by wreath on silver plated guard. Leather scabbard. Fine order. . . . . . . . . . . . . . . . . . . . . . . . . . . . . . . . . . . Price, $20 00

We secured a number of beautiful Swords a few weeks before the Spaniards evacuated Cuba—some fine enough for the Captain-General—nearly all of famous Toledo make and marked with year of manufacture, ranging from 1858 to 1896, and supposed to have been used in the different campaigns. Price ranges from $14 to $30. The intrinsic value of the swords is much greater than our price, not considering their value as choice relics, on which we have had to pay 35 per cent. duty.

**No. 5.** **Spanish Cavalry Sabre,** marked Toledo, years from 1842 up to 1878. Handsome polished brass guard, polished steel scabbard, fine order, equal to new. . . . . . . . . . . . . . . . . . . . . . . . . . . . . . . . . . . . . $4 75

**No. 6.** **Spanish Artillery Sabre,** marked on back " Art. de F. Toledo," (mostly year of) 1872. Polished steel guard, steel scabbard. Some in lot with only one ring. Fine order. . . . . . . . . . . . . . . . . . . . . . . . . . . . $3 50

**No. 7 and No. 8.** **Cuban Machetes.** Relics, showing effects of rough usage. This lot came from the Spanish Arsenal in Havana, and are different from the kind used by the Spanish. We have every reason to believe that these Machetes were captured from the Cubans and were stored in the Arsenal as relics and at the evacuation were sold to our agent. There are over 20 different patterns in the lot, some with names of American, German and English manufacturers. Some of the blades are worn quite thin, owing to frequent sharpening ; some have end of blade broken off—all sorts and sizes. Perhaps some poor Cuban patriot has parted from one of these Machetes before being taken to Cabanas to be shot at sunrise. They are not handsome looking, but fine specimens of the weapons that for years in hands of Patriots defied Spain's army. . . . . . Price, $1 00 each

**No. 9.** **Spanish Heavy Bush Machetes,** 6 different patterns; ornamental. . . . . . . . . . . . . . . . . . . . . . . . . . . . . . . . . . . . . . . . Price, $1 35

**No. 10.** **Spanish relics of the British occupation of Havana.**—Old Tower (Tower of London) Spade Bayonets used on the old-time flint-lock muskets same as were used during the Revolutionary War in 1776. Spaniards had used these bayonets as ornaments on top of railing in the Arsenal at Havana. . . . . . . . . . . . . . . . . . . . . . . . . . . . . . . . . Price, $1 00 each

**No. 11.** **Spanish Bayoneta,** 20-inch blade. Some angular and quadrangular blades, rusty—damaged in shank ; make fine decorations ; fine steel ; will polish up well. We have a large number, and will sell at 35c. each.

**No. 12.** **Spanish Machete Bayonet.** Used by Order Publico in Havana (Spanish Police) complete with Russet leather scabbard and frogs for attaching to belt. Some in the lot have the owner's name pasted on the back of the scabbard. Brass handles. Fine relics. . . . . . . . . . . . . . . . . . $1 75

**No. 13.** **Spanish Machetes.** Brass guard, brass-tipped handle, steel blade, leather scabbard with brass mountings. Fine order. Refinished. Fine relics. . . . . . . . . . . . . . . . . . . . . . . . . Price, $7.25 each

**No. 25-9A.** CUBAN OFFICER'S MACHETE, with 28-inch blade, brass cross bars, and horn handle. Complete with yellow sword knot, no scabbard. Price, $4.50.

**No. 25-7.** CAPTURED SPANISH OFFICER'S SWORD, with blade marked "TOLEDO," 28-inch, wood grip, brass wire wrap, duck head on end of cross bar. No scabbard. Price, $15.00.

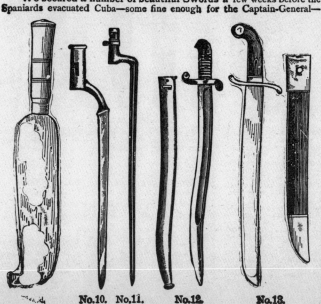

**No.10.** **No.11.** **No.12.** **No.13.**

SHOWING THE CHOICEST AND MOST BEAUTIFUL WORKMANSHIP. CAPTURED BY U. S. SOLDIERS FROM THE INSURGENTS IN THE PHILIPPINES. ALL HAVE DOUBLE-EDGED BLADES EXCEPTING No. 334. ALL SCABBARDS ARE FINE, DELICATE PIECES. THESE ARE IN FAIRLY GOOD ORDER. ALL NATIVE, FINE HANDMADE.

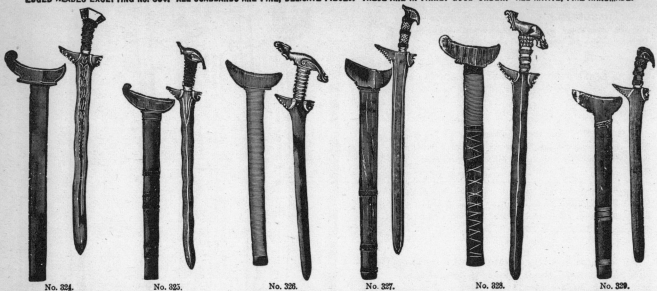

No. 324.     No. 325.     No. 326.     No. 327.     No. 328.     No. 329.

**No. 324.**—Silver-inlaid Kris with razor sharpened double-edge blade; 22¼ inches long, 1½ inches wide; beautifully inlaid, with two silver wires running parallel nearly the entire length of the blade, with silver wire inlaid ornamented scrollwork in between; serrated insignia work on each side of the blade at the hilt; silver bands with black caribou hair grip with handsome silver handle top. Kris is in fine order; scabbard is native hard wood resembling American curly walnut. Price, $30.00.

**No. 325.**—Kris with wavy-edged blade, 21½ inches long, 1½ inches wide; with very sharp double-edged blade; two silver bands with serrated insignia work at the hilt; black corded caribou hair grip with ivory-headed top; dark-colored native curly-wood scabbard. Price, $25.00.

**No. 326.**—Handsome large Ivory-head Kris captured from prominent insurgent leader; blade is very sharp and measures 22¾ inches long by 1½ inches in width; serrated insignia work at the hilt; silver handle with bands for grip surmounted with large solid ivory top which told the owner's high rank; (datto) dark-colored native curly-wood scabbard. Price, $100.00.

**No. 327.**—Rare pattern Kris with blade partly hollow, which when struck rings like bell; razor-sharpened edge; 22½-inch blade, 1½ inches in width; serrated insignia work at the hilt; woven silver-cloth-like grip with black caribou hair bands; solid ivory peculiarly shaped handle; dark curly-wood scabbard. Price, $70.00.

**No. 328.**—One of the most beautiful Kris that ever left the Philippines. We have examined many collections, but this is the finest we have ever seen, and must have belonged to prominent Datto leader; wavy, double-edged blade, 23 inches long, sharpened like razor, with the silver wires inlaid nearly the entire length; serrated insignia work at the hilt, bound by two silver bands; silver grip with caribou corded work with large silver top; beautiful workmanship which shows in the design the high rank of the owner; silver top measures 6½ inches long by 1¾ inches wide; scabbard is of native wood resembling American curly walnut. Price, $100.00.

**No. 329.**—Philippine Kris with sharpened double-edged blade which measures 21½ inches in length, with serrated hilt work joined to handle by two copper bands; copper wire grip, surmounted with head of peculiar design; light-colored native hard wood scabbard. Price, $22.00.

**No. 330.**—Philippine Kris with 23-inch double bevel-edged very sharp blade, 1⅝ inches wide, with insignia serrated work; steel band; hard wood handle, with three corded bands forming grip; dark-colored hard wood scabbard. Price, $20.00.

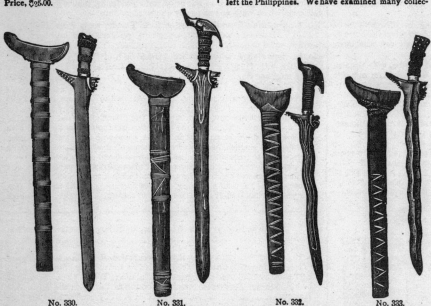

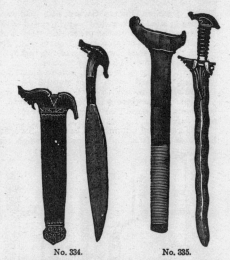

No. 330.     No. 331.     No. 332.     No. 333.     No. 334.     No. 335.

**No. 331.**—Philippine Leader Kris with double-edged razor-sharpened blade; 23 inches long, 1⅝ inches wide; beveled edges with serrated insignia work at hilt, with two silver bands with deep grooved lines in the blade; black corded caribou hair grip; silver band; scabbard is of dark-colored native hard wood. Price, $30.00.

**No. 332.**—Wavy-blade Kris, 19½-inch blade, with two long grooves nearly the entire length with four shorter deep grooves near the hilt; figured steel; silver ornamented with serrated insignia work; silver band wire grip with dark hard wood top; light-colored hard wood scabbard. Price, $30.00.

**No. 333.**—Wavy-blade Kris, 21-inch sharpened, double-edged blade; in fine order with the exception of number of stains and one small nick. Soldier from whom we purchased this weapon said the stains were caused by the owner who parted with it only after a fierce struggle; blade averages 1¼ inches wide and has the usual serrated insignia work at the hilt; caribou corded hair grip with silver band; caribou horn top

inlaid with ivory discs, and silver ornamental pommel; dark-colored native hard wood scabbard. Price, $30.00.

**No. 334.**—Philippine Borong, worn by Moros of Sulu, insignia of rank; oval-shaped blade, 16 inches long by 2¼ inches at widest part; razor-sharpened on one edge; sharp pointed; caribou horn grip surmounted by native hard wood handle resembling fine grained mahogany, with notched work denoting owner's high rank; hard wood light-colored scabbard with ornamented work. Price, $17.00.

**No. 335.**—Wavy-blade Kris, 21 inches; double-edged blade, razor sharpened; four deep grooves near the hilt; silver bound, serrated insignia work; caribou hair grip with hard wood handle top, with native work designating owner's tribe, station, etc.; with scabbard. Price, $27.00.

**No. 336.**—Philippine Moro Bolo; native made; taken from chief at Elegan, Mindanayo, July, 1901, by member of 10th U. S. Infantry (name given to the purchaser); 28-inch sharp blade; 2⅛ inches at widest point, with wicked looking projecting ripping point; crude; carved forked insignia handle; in serviceable order, no scabbard. Price, $20.00.

**D48.** 1 long knife from Bikanis, Northwest India. Heavy horn handle with 13-inch long tapered blade, with heavy ornamented back, and signed in gold. 18th century pattern. Price, $10.00.

**D49.** 1 long hunting knife from Nepal. Horn handle with 13-inch blade ornamented on one side with kings and queens, on other two tigers chasing antelope and rabbits. Price, $8.00.

**SCOTCH HUNTING SWORD,** with stag horn hilt and cross guard. Silver mounts on hilt and guard. Early 18th Century period. Full length 22 inches. Leather scabbard. Price, $7.85.

**AFRICAN SPEAR HEAD,** native work, inlaid with brass ornamental work, 24½ inches long. Price, $4.85.

**KAFFIR NATIVE MADE KNOB KERRY.** Price, $3.85.

**EARLY PLUG BAYONET-KNIFE,** period about 1700, with the rare King's Head Armor mark stamped on the blade. Brass pommel and guard with mask heads, ebony butt. Blade is slightly pit-marked from age. Length 11½ inches, width at the hilt 1½ inch. Rare pattern. Price, $15.00.

**NORTH AMERICAN INDIAN STONE AXE CLUB.** Rare pattern, stone is ground to adze shape, bound to hardwood curved handle by deer skin thongs. Length of axe 7½ inches, width 2¾ inches. From the Elliott Collection. Price $9.85.

**SET OF SUDANESE DAGGERS,** in native-made alligator skin scabbard. Scabbard is trident shaped. Center dagger is straight, the two side daggers are scimiter shaped. All the blades are covered with inscription. Bird beak hilts with talons. Fine specimens of native work. This set was the property of some great chieftain. Full length 12 inches. Price, $9.85.

**AMERICAN REVOLUTIONARY WAR OFFICER'S SHORT CURVED DRESS SWORD,** checkered ivory grip, lion head pommel, 13-inch blade. Price, $7.50.

**STEEL STRAIGHT EDGE,** nickel plated, stamped Kueffel & Esser Co., New York, Chicago; used at West Point Military Academy; offered in fine like new condition; 1¾ inch wide, 15 inches long. Price, 48c.
**U. S. A. STEEL STRAIGHT EDGE,** 30 inches long. Price, 98c.

**OLD ENGLISH SWORD OF OFFICE,** carried by King George II's master of the horse, 28-inch curved blade, carved ivory hilt, bronze horse head pommel, relief ornamented guard, bronze scabbard, from the Sir Richard Wallace Collection. Price, $20.00.

**GENERAL'S SWORD OF THE PERIOD OF GEORGE I.,** 31-inch blade engraved, ivory hilt with scabbard, from the Wallace Collection, $18.00.

**KING GEORGE II. PERIOD NAVAL OFFICER'S DOUBLE EDGED DIRK,** 6½ inch blade, carved ivory hilt. Price, $4.00.
Similar Dirk with 8-inch blade and scabbard, $6.00.
Similar Dirk with 10-inch engraved blade. $5.00.
Dirk with 14-inch blade (relic). $5.00

**NAVAL OFFICER'S DIRK, PERIOD OF KING GEORGE II.,** with engraved gilt bronze scabbard, with two rings with coiled snake head pommel and guard, ivory grip, handsome mountings. Price, $15.00.

**NAVAL OFFICER'S ANTIQUE DIRK,** with 3¾-inch blade, ivory grip, Revolutionary War Period; would make fine paper cutter for lady's desk. Price, $6.00.

**DIRK WITH 9-INCH BLADE,** with bronze scabbard, ivory hilt, gilt bronze mountings. $8.00.

**DIRK WITH 16-INCH DOUBLE EDGED GROOVED BLADE,** Revolutionary War Period. $8.75.
Another with 6½-inch blade. $6.50.

**STEEL TRIANGLE** 8 inches, stamped Kueffel & Esser, New York; nickel plated; from West Point Military Academy; fine order. Price, 48c.

**U. S. ARMY IN-TRENCHING STEEL SPADE;** carried as part of soldier's equipment; width of blade 7 inches; length 8¼ inches, with handle 85 inches. Lot of 600 without handles. Bargain Price, 25c each.

**ANCIENT HANOVERIAN OFFICER'S SWORD,** finely tempered 30-inch double edged blade with crown in relief on both sides of the pommel, with figure of horse on the guard, representing the "WHITE HORSE OF HANOVER." Silver wire wrapped hilt. This sword is from the Sir Richard Wallace Collection, who only accepted and retained the finest and choicest weapons. This is a rare sword. Price, $25.00.

**BRITISH NAVAL OFFICER'S SWORD,** used under Nelson at the Battle of Aboukar; curved blade, engraved with the Royal Arms of England, G. R., etc. Made by Tatham from the Wallace Collection; lion head pommel with scabbard, $18.00.

## Relics from the Philippines

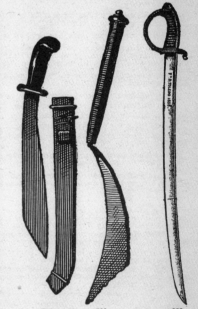

1    2    709    711    323

**1st on the right** is the Sword Scabbard, belonging to and offered with long Kampilan Filipino weapon, with 30 inch blade, with large carved Ebony handle, decorated with Manila blackfibre, and red, yellow and white colored strap; beautiful specimen. Price, $25.00.

Second and Third item is Filipino spears, with carved handle, 22 inch grooved metal steel blade. Price, $12.00 each.

Antique European Army Lance. Relic of First Emperor Napoleon. Price, $7.50.
Filipino Dagger, 10 inch blade, $4.50
"    "   11 "   "   3.50
"    "   15 "   "   4.00
"    "    9 "   "   2.75

Filipino Bolo Scabbard are bound together with thin bamboo cane. The natives fooled many an American soldier who thought the native must *first* draw the bolo out of the scabbard before he could attack. The tricky native just brought down the bolo, scabbard and all, on the soldiers, the keen blade of the bolo cutting through the slight cane binding.

Filipino Native Bolos and Barongs.
No. 1. Long Bolo with checkered
    handle............$12.00
" 2. Bolo with Scabbard... 8.00
" 3. Barong, fine weapon.. 15.00

**FILIPINO BOLOS.**
2 Bolos, Native Crude work; 19 in. long. Price, $5.00 each.
3 Bolos, 17 to 19 inches long. Crude native work weapon. Price, $3.85 ea.
Bolo, engraved on blade. "Kabbalankalan 14 4 de Novbre de 1896 Matteo Guanzin Villalra," full length 30 inches; horn hilt sword guard. Price, $15.00.

**SOLDIERS' FILIPINO COLLECTION.**
1 Long Moro Kris with red ribbon crown; record of killing 2 soldiers at Jolo. Price, $20.00.
1 Kris with red and yellow handle; taken by 12th Infantry mounted scouts. Price, $18.00.
1 Philippine Bolo; with bad record. Owner was hung. Price, $14.00.
1 Moro Spear, handle cut in two parts for transportation. Price, $8.00.
1 Spanish Stiletto. Price, $6.00.
1 Moro Kris Dagger. $7.50.

No. 1. 100 Brass Handled Cutlass, with steel scabbard, full length is 31 inches. All in good serviceable order, requiring cleaning; sold as are. Price, $1.75 each.

No. 2. Antique French Fauchars, double edged Lance, with wide blade, found among relics of Napoleon's (First Empire): 18 inches long, 3 inches wide, rusted. Handsome historical relic. Price, $4.50 each. Fited to pole and polished. Price, $7.50.

Collected Filipino Spears and Lances, by U. S. A. Captain. Lance, 12 inch blade, 5½ ft. pole; flat, double edged. Price, $9.50.

3 Lances with 13 inch blades, 5¼ ft. poles. Price, $8.00.

3 with 10 inch blade; poles 6 ft. long. Price, $6.85.

1 with 9 inch blade; 5½ ft. pole. Price, $6.00.

Native Spear made of *Bamboo.* 6 ft. pole. Price, $3.75.

Lance made of hard-wood. Pole and Spear all in one. Price, $4.25.

No. 709. Filipino Bolo, with wood scabbard, from lot collected in Philippines by U. S. A. Captain. Price, $10.00.

No. 711. Rare Pattern Filipino Weapon, long handle, scimietar scyth shaped bolo. Collected by U. S. A. officer while serving in the Philippines. Price, $16.00.

No. 323. Captured Spanish officer's Toledo Blade side arm sword, purchased from U. S. Govt. at Auction Sale in 1900. Only six swords were offered. We have purchased all the Swords captured by the U. S. Govt. which were sold at auction both by the Army and Navy. This weapon has stamped "Toledo 1872" on the blade; brass handle. Rare relic. Price, $15.00.

No. 323A. Captured Spanish Officer's Toledo Blade Side Arm Sword, purchased in Cuba, in 1898. Blade marked TOLEDO, 1887, heavy brass handle, leather scabbard. Similar to cut No. 323. Price, $12.00.

The war in the Philippines has brought to collectors of military weapons many new pieces, the names of which are very conflicting, hardly two persons calling a weapon by the same name. We think, therefore, that our readers will be interested in the following history and names applied to the collection of Philippine weapons now on exhibition at the National Museum, Washington:

**INSIGNIA OF THE BOLO.**—Every Filopino has his bolo. It enters into his life and marks his social and professional rank. A Filipino who has risen to the rank of an officer in the army preserves care fully the bolos he has acquired in his upward career. At home the bolo is kept in place sacred to itself, usually over the door of the main room. It enters into the religious life of the Moro, and before its home niche men and women perform sacred rites. The best are manufactured in Mindanao. The classification of the social and professional signignificance of the arms by the Moros of Mindanao is tacitly accepted all over the Phillipines as official, Officers and men of importance in the Filipino army and government accept this classification. The bolos are made by hand and the workmanship is so ornate and beautiful that it compares favorably with the best work of the European armorer. The bolo proper, with the handle cut from the horn of the caribou and blade hammered out of a piece of steel, has given the generic to all classes of the weapon.

In Luzon and the Northern Island, the type known as SUNDANG places the owner in the laboring class, as it is the implement of agriculture as well as the weapon of the private soldier.

The CAMPILAN is the arm of the private soldier: the HAIRY CAMPILAN, ornamented with a tuft of hair, that of the officer below the rank of major.

The KRIS, often with gold inlaid blade and jeweled handle, is the insignia of leadership.

The TERCIADA, similar in form, but not so ornamental, is the insignia of the non-commissioned officer.

The BARONG, like the Kris of the Moros, indicates rank, but rather of the forum and the council than of the field. Holders of political office carry the Barong. It is not for use. The original purpose has been forgotten. The Moro Sultans carry it.

The PIMAL DE KRIS is carried by all the women and children of any social pretensions. The blade and handle hammered from silver and inlaid with gold.

The QUINBASI is the blade of general utility to the private soldier.

The TALILONG, carrying with it social distinction, is a sort of headman's sword or ax from four to five feet long, weighing as much as eight pounds, generally used in the advance line of attack and also by the official headsman, who formerly decapitated the wounded enemy upon the field of battle.

Filipino Four-Pronged Spear; length of spear, 14 inches, ready for inserting on pole. Price, $8.50.

Central American Machete, with 24-inch blade; brass-mounted guard grip. Price, $5.00.

Spanish Sergeant's Sabre, taken at fall of Manila: stamped on the blade "Toledo, 1895;" light, neat sabre: checkered hilt. Price, $10.85.

Bamboo Cane Spring Stick, bent and set in buried trap. Price, $1.85.

Filipino Kris Scabbard; rare workmanship; wood is covered with caribou horn; silver mounted to represent the Phillipine coat of arms; with sunburst and silver rays; length, 21 inches; width, 2¾ inches. Price, $16.00.

Kris Scabbard; wood covered with caribou horn; ingenious piece of work; silver mounted. Price, $10.00.

Kris Scabbard, hardwood covered with caribou horn. Price, $6.00.

Bolo Scabbard for curved blade. Price, $3.50.

Pinal de Kris Scabbard, 12½ inch blade. Price, $2.00.

Spanish Bayonet found near Canta, May 2, 1899. Price, $1.00.

Spanish Orderly's Russet Leather Despatch Box, 6 by 5 by 1 inch; taken by Scout V_ amp. Price, $2.00.

Hide Case used by natives for carrying rice. Size 6 by 8 by 2 inches. Price, $2.75.

Bolo taken from Filopino Insurgents' intrenchments and fight at Balatong, P. I. October, 1899, by troops under command of Generals Carpenter and Hughes; length 21 inches. Price, $15.00.

1225. JAPANESE OFFICER'S SWORD, with steel scabbard with two rings for slings. Total length 29 inches. Polished sharp steel blade. 21½ inch. Brass pommel and guard, which has small piece to turn down to keep scabbard from slipping off. In good order. Price, $9.50.

Filipino Hollow-Headed Kris; silver-mounted, ebony handle, with serrated work at the hilt end of the blade; fine order. Price, $30.00.

Rare Pattern Filipino Double-edge Dagger, with diamond-shaped steel blade joined to brass guard. Price, $16.00.

Filipino Insurgent's Spear which killed one of Company M, 33d U. S. Volunt ees made of bamboo pole, cut in two parts for transportation to U. S. Van Camp collection. Price, $25.00.

No. 392. Captured Spanish Side-arm Swords from the Philippines; sold to us January 2, 1903, at the U. S. Springfield Arsenal auction sale as "Musicians' Swords, Spanish." The one shown in the illustration is complete, with cross guard, and the price is $6.85; for others which have been longer in service and the cross guards are broken off, the price is only $5.85. Only a few swords were captured in the Spanish war; they will soon became rare and prices advance.

No. 1320
1321    1322
1300 SPANISH SPEAR HEAD stamped "Toledo." Price, $8.75.
No.

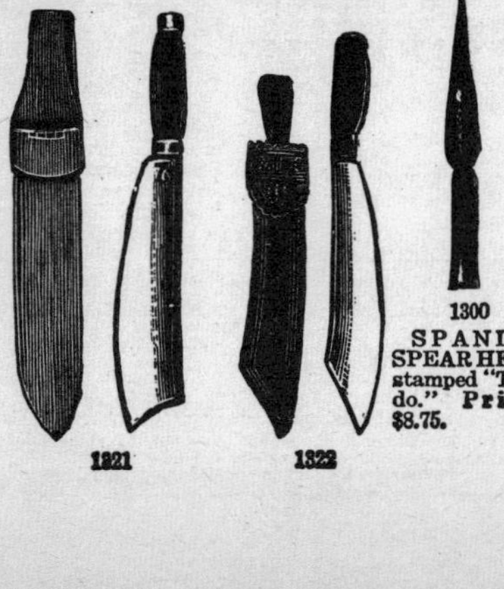

Filipino Battle Flag: also piece of U. S. Army Flag recaptured from Filipinos at Panay (in our museum collection.)

Filipino Bow with four arrows made of bamboo with spear points. Price, $

KRIS DAGGER, taken from the saddle of General Gidro Garcia; his horse was killed and he wounded in the arm; escaped at San Panay December 7, 1899; dagger is silver mounted, blood stained: full length, 17 inches. Vouched for by U. S. A. Scouts Vna Camp and Hike, of 2d Battery, 18th Infantry. Price, $18.00.

Filipino Bolo taken from intrenchments at Carlos Pili Colisa by soldiers under General Carpenter's command, October 23, 1899. Bolo has carved idol-head handle; full length, 22 inches; widest part of blade, 2⅛; fine order. Price, $17.50.

Filipino Kris, taken from body of dead Moro after fight and landing of 38th U. S. Volunteers at Cayagan, December, 1900; full length, 27 inches; has wavy blade with scabbard. Price, $32.00.

Filipino Insurgent's Bolo, with carved idol-head handle, taken from insurgent at Island of Panay, October, 1899; full length, 26 inches. Price, $20.00.

*Barong*, taken from wounded native after Gunboat Paragua had bombarded the coast of Jolo, October, 1900; full length, 24 inches; has silver-mounted carved wood handle; complete with scabbard. Price, $22.50.

Bolo, with handle guard; sharp point, beveled cutting edge; from Van Camp collection. Price, $18.00.

Dagger Bolo, with carved dragon-head handle; length, 14 inches; from Van Camp collection. Price, $8.75.

Handsome Bolo, with silver guard and ornamented idol-head handle, chased blade; full length, 26 inches; width, 2¼; rare pattern. Vouched for by U. S. A. Scout Van Camp. Price, $42.00.

*Officer's Bolo*, silver mounted, with handsome ornamented handle in shape of head with small red jewels for eyes; no scabbard; length 24½ inches; inlaid; widest width of blade, 2 inches. Price, $38.00. The jewel eyes may be very valuable; it belonged to General Garcia and was found in the saddle. Vouched for by Hike and Van Camp.

Ijeno Waniga, President of San Dimicia. Bolo used to behead ten natives; carved idol-head ebony handle; length, 28 inches; 2½ inches widest width. One side of blade has beveled cutting edge, the other side of blade is flat. From Van Camp collection. Price, $33.00.

Philippine Islander's Bolo, with sharp beveled cutting edge as on surgeon's knives; the other side of blade is flat; full length, 21½ inches; no scabbard. Van Camp collection; fine order. Price, $17.00.

Filipino Insurgent Officer's Dagger, silver-mounted ebony handle, handsomely decorated; taken from wounded officer, September 21, 1900, Tulunga; full length, 21 inches. Price, $25.00.

Seal of Spanish Justice of the Peace, Agoo de Union, Luzern. Price, $8.00.

Cartridge Reloading Outfit used by the Insurgents; crude. Price, $1.50.

Spanish Revolver of Capt. Vincinete Caspo, killed at Lunluwano, Panay, August 21, 1900; relic only. Price, $8.50.

Collection of Native Philippine Arms, collected by R. C. Croxton and Lieutenant Jno. W. Morrow, 23d U. S. Infantry; offered at auction in New York City; withdrawn and sold to us. Description is from their catalogue list:

1. Officer's Campilan; carried by Maharaja from Island of Tapul, South Archipelago; brought from Mindanao, where it is a favorite weapon. Our price is $20.00.

2. Barong from Island of Siassi; is a style used principally in Northern Mindanao. Price, $18.00.

3. Wavy Kris; carried by Moro from Topak, Siassi group; one of the types favored by the Moros; ivory handle. Our price is $45.00.

5. Ordinary Kris; very old; slightly wavy, with ornamental blade. Our price is $32.00.

6. Straight Kris; Moro pattern, from Pangduna, Siassi group; plain blade; very old; ivory handle; was carried by Hadji Ossmond, of Siassi, P. I. Price, $65.00.

9. Kris; peculiar type used by the Moros many years ago; laminated blade and old ivory handle; rare specimen; brought from the Island of Pandami, Sulu group. Price, $38.00.

11. Large Barong; principal weapon of the Moros; this specimen is the largest ever found in the islands; brought from Siassi, P. I.; 22-inch blade; originally from Jolo. Price, $38.00.

12. Very Old Ivory-handled Barong; procured from an influential Moro of the Island of Topak. Price, $22.00.

13. Ordinary Barong; from Island of Lugus, Sulu group; was taken from a native for wearing same in the market place, contrary to law. Price, $20.00.

15. Barong; from Siassi, P. I.; carved and checkered handle; peculiarly Moro. Price, $18.50.

17. Old Barong; brought from Tawi-Tawi Island; carried by follower of Amul Houssin, Dato of the Island of Lugus. Price, $30.00.

20. Barong Dagger; horn handle; from Tawi-Tawi, Sulu Archipelago. Price, $12.50.

Cut 1320. PHILIPPINE BOLOS; collected by Consul-General Williams, last U. S. Consul-General to the Philippine Islands, under the Spanish regime. Consul-General Williams at the declaration of war, hauled down the American flag, and sailed for Hong Kong, returning with Admiral Dewey on board the Flagship Olympia, and took part in the battle of Manilla Bay. At the fall of Manilla, he made a collection of old bolos, and other curios to distribute among friends. We bought the surplus bolos, and can now offer, vouched for by General Williams, as having been collected by him at the fall of Manilla. In order to start the sale, we will offer for a short time, at the BARGAIN PRICE OF $1.00 EACH. Average full length of the bolos, 22 inches, *with russet leather scabbards and frog for attaching to belt*. Average length of blade, 17 inches, widest width, 1⅝; width of scabbard, 2½ inches. Bolos are rusty, just as when captured.

Cut 1321. FILIPINO BOLOS, width of blade, 2½ inches; length of blade, 11 inches.

Cut 1322. Full length 16 inches; blade 2 inches; dirk shaped point. Length of blade, 10¾. Eancy scroll work on scabbard. Only limited number of pattern. Price, 50.

1743   1404   1505   1505-A

1235   1260   1236

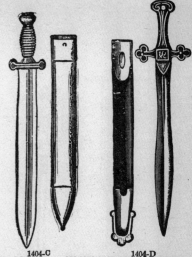

1404-C   1404-D

**1743. SCOTCH SKENE DHU**, with silvered St. Andrew's cross on hilt; blade, 4¼ inches; full length, 8 inches, with jeweled stone in hilt. Good second-hand order. $9.75.

**1744. SCOTCH SKENE DHU**, with silver bands, engraved with thistles carved on wood hilt. In poor order. $4.95.

**1404. BOLO DAGGER SHARPENED STEEL WAVY BLADE**, 5¼ inches long; full length, 9½ inches; horn hilt; German silver guard and mountings; black leather scabbard; German silver tip and mouthpiece, with belt hanger; new. Price, $2.50. Only sold to responsible parties.

---

**RESTRICTION NOTICE.**

DAGGERS, SWORD CANES, HAND GRENADES AND BAYONET PISTOLS WILL NOT BE SOLD TO ANY ONE WHOM WE THINK WOULD ENDANGER THE PUBLIC SAFETY. This has been the rule of our business for over forty years. These dangerous weapons are collected for sale to established Museums, or those who can furnish us with Magistrate's official letter under seal, authorizing the sale. Recently we refused to fill an order from a European revolutionist, who disputed our right to restrict the sale of catalogued goods.

---

**1505. BEAUMONT DAGGER BAYONET**, length 14 inches, double edged blade. These knives were made in Solingen, Germany in 1891 for use of the infantry regiments of Holland. Price, $1.50 each.

**1505A.** Hunting Knives made in Germany and called Arkansas Bowie Knives. (They are not facsimile of Col. Bowie's invention.) Fine steel blade, handsomely decorated. German hilt and scabbard. 7 to 8-inch blade. Price, $7.50 each.

**1235. SCOTCH HIGHLANDER'S SKENE DHU;** full length, 16¾ inches. The ornamental jewels on the two knives are missing. Top of pommel of the large knife broken. Kind formerly used by Scotch regimental pipers in the British Army. Price, $20.00.

**1260. KING'S SCEPTRE;** carved ivory; 25 inches long; beautifully carved ornamented silver top; rare piece from London collection. Price, $100.00.

**1236. SCOTCH HIGHLANDER'S SKENE DHU.** Steel cap for large knife lost. Old leather scabbard; length, 17 inches. Carved hilt studded with steel discs. Price, $19.00.

**1404C.** Illustration shows the complete Confederate Fort Artillery Sword, with scabbard. We offer for sale the blades only, which were bought from the U. S. Govt. directly after the Civil War, when swords were broken up for their scrap value. Price for blade only, without handle, relics sold by the Govt. as "Rebel," $1.00 each.

**1404D. BRITISH ARMY BAND SWORDS.** Bronze hilt and cross guard, with letters V. R. (Queen Victoria) on guard. Double-edged steel blade. Leather scabbard, with brass mouth and tip. Good second-hand order. Price, $2.85.

---

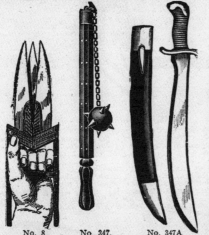

No. 8   No. 347   No. 347A

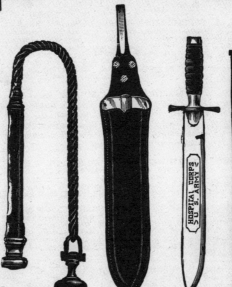

No. 00    347-B

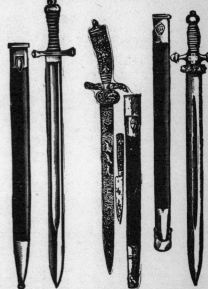

347-C   No. 319   347 D

**7. INDIA DAGGER KUTAR.** By pressing on handle bar three blades appear; length 14½ inches, width 3¾. Etched for use in decorating. Price, $6.85.

**8. ANTIQUE KNOUT OR MORNING STAR** Round metal ball with spikes, connected by chain to handle. Offered for sale only to reputable collectors for museum. Price, $10.00.

**347B. SPANISH WAR HOSPITAL CORPS SIDE ARM.** Made at U. S. Govt. Arsenal, furnished to members of U. S. Hospital Corps during the Spanish War. Good, second-hand order. Price, $5.50, with scabbard.

**347A. ANTIQUE EUROPEAN SIDE ARM SWORDS.** (The lot of swords now left have a straighter blade than shown in the illustration.) Good order. Complete with scabbard, $3.85.

**347C. EUROPEAN NON COM. OFFICER'S SIDE ARM SWORD,** complete with scabbard, in fine second-hand, serviceable order. Price, $2.75 each.

**347D. POPE'S SWISS BODY GUARD SIDE ARM SWORDS,** used by Vatican soldiers, in Rome. Fine, handsome swords, with cross on brass guard; also on leather scabbard; grooved blade. Rare relic. Price, $4.85.

**COLLECTION OF 100 ASSORTED DAGGERS AND KNIVES,** gathered by Lieut. Garvin. The assortment includes rare U. S. Rifleman's knife as issued to the troops about the Mexican War period. Each speciment has descriptive tag. The entire collection, $385.00.

**No. 347.** Sword, with basket handle; 17-inch blade. 2 inches wide; guard hand, curved rare old relic; fine steel good order; no scabbard; from London collection. Price, $4.85.

**No. 00** Antique British Knout; mahogany handle, 10 inches long, with 2-inch ivory ornamented head; rare pattern chain 18 inches long; knot shaped head. Genuine old relic. Price, $55.00.

**3 Swiss Poignards;** side arms, 27 inches; full length; fair order. Price, $3.50 each.

**No. 319.** German Hunting Knife, with the small dagger knife, both contained in the one scabbard, which is fitted with two compartments. The long blade is 16 inches in length, beautifully etched with hunting scenes, deer, etc. The small blade is 4 inches long; stag horn handle with deer-foot guard; leather scabbard, finely mounted, with acorn stud for attaching to waist belt, similar to the Scotch Skene Dhu, now obsolete. Price, $8.00.

---

**THE BOWIE KNIFE.**

The knife which made Col. Bowie famous in the early years of the past century was really the invention of a negro blacksmith who worked on the plantation of Rezin P. Bowie, a brother of James, in Louisiana. Manuel, such was his name, had much ability at the forge, and one day he fashioned the knife, with its peculiar point, from a large file in the shop; It had a length of fifteen inches with the handle, the blade being nine inches. This was the original Bowie knife and its purpose was for cutting the throats of deer. James Bowie, when he first saw it was attracted by it at once and afterwards took it with him to New Orleans. Here in a fight one night in a quadroon ball he killed a man with it literally disembowelling him. The wound was so terrible that it attracted expert attention, and George Wilkins Kendall, then editor of the *Picayune* wrote an article about it, also printing a picture of the weapon. Bowie, thinking the knife could be improved upon in some respects, gave an order to a celebrated cutler in New Orleans named Pedro, who modelled one for him after the Manuel knife but somewhat lighter, keener, with a thinner blade and longer point. This was the model of the Bowie knife which subsequently became so famed. Up and down the Mississippi and throughout the South it became so noted that no Southern gentleman was considered armed unless he had one within reach. The original knife, made from the file by Manuel, was on the plantation as late as 1864, in the hands of descendents of Rezin P. Bowie, but it was burned and lost in the ashes of the "big house" when Banks went through with his army of Federals in that year. Col. Bowie fell, with Crockett and the other daring spirits, at the Alamo. The bodies were incinerated on the spot where now stands the Post Office, at the intersection of Houston Street and Alamo Plaza. The president of the Texas Society in Washington, D. C., has a gavel made from the leg of the cot upon which Bowie was lying when slain. The "Pedro" knife was carried away by the Mexicans.

*Item contributed by D. Louis Bodge for Our Catalogue.*

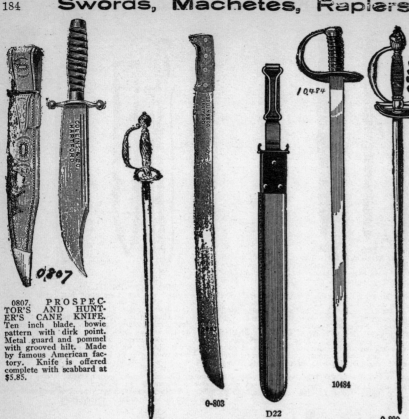

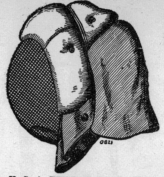

**O-821. U. S. A. FENCING MASK.** Blued steel wire, with chamois leather hair-filled pads on top and sides, with throat and back of the head protected by leather flaps; snap button fastenings. Chin pad inside the steel wire frame. Have been used; are in good serviceable order. Made at the Rock Island Arsenal. Price, $3.85.

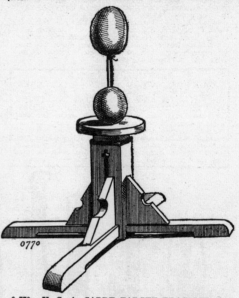

**0807. PROSPECTOR'S AND HUNTER'S CANE KNIFE.** Ten inch blade, bowie pattern with dirk point. Metal guard and pommel with grooved hilt. Made by famous American factory. Knife is offered complete with scabbard at $5.85.

**0-886. ANTIQUE GERMAN RAPIER.** Gold inlaid letters, "Potzdam," with head of King Frederick set in gold as a seal mark on both sides of the blade near the tang. 31¼-inch straight double-edged fine steel blade. Mounted bronze guard. Price, $12.85.

**0-886A. ANTIQUE FRENCH OFFICER'S RAPIER.** 31-inch steel blade, relief ornamented, bronze guard. Price, $6.85.

**0-886B. SIMILAR RAPIER SWORD,** with 26-inch blade. Price, $5.85.

**0-888A. FRENCH CADET OFFICER'S SABRE,** with pearl handle and ornamented brass scabbard. Lion head pommel holding chain guard. Mother of pearl shell covered hilt. Full length 28 inches. Price, $7.85.

**0-889. 17TH CENTURY GERMAN CROSS HILT SWORD.** Blued steel blade gilt inlaid. Marked, "Peter Raus, Solingen"; 30-inch double-edged steel blade, 7-inch steel cross guard, ball pommel. Dark colored hard wood fluted hilt, complete with metal scabbard. In good serviceable order. Price, $12.50.

**8689. AMERICAN REVOLUTIONARY WAR PERIOD OFFICER'S SWORD.** With checkered ivory grip; 30-inch curved steel blade. With ancient bluing; etched G. R.; with Arms trophy. Single guard, gilt mounted leather scabbard, with stud and rings, for belt and slings. Engraved on the mouth piece, "Salter & Co., Jewellers and Sword Cutlers." Price, $20.00.

**8690. NAVAL OFFICER'S ANTIQUE SWORD.** Made by "R. Ward, Goldsmith, Yarmouth." With ancient pattern steel rings for belt straps, single guard, with scabbard. Engraved with foul anchor, black sharkskin grip, 26-inch curved steel polished blade, kind used by U. S. naval officers in the War of 1812. Price, $18.50.

**8691. OLD ENGLISH NAVAL SWORD.** With chased gilt mountings. Scabbard engraved, "Prosser, Maker to the King and Royal Family, London." 30-inch curved steel blade. Two rings on the scabbard. Price, $18.50.

**8692. FRENCH HUNTING SWORD.** 17th century period, bronze hilt with classic subjects in relief, centaur, females, hounds, hunters, hunting trophies, etc., 23-inch blade. Engraving is indistinct. Leather scabbard. Chased gilt mountings, with small knife, with bronze gilt handles. With female figure in relief. Price, $20.00.

**105B. 1812 U. S. ARTILLERY SABRE.** With broad iron scabbard, curved steel blade, single guard, the shoe on the scabbard shows extensive wear. Also used in State militia after the Mexican War. Price, $7.85.

**U. S. SPRINGFIELD SWORD BAYONET SCABBARD,** stamped as having been made at the Government Rock Island Arsenal, 1909. Russet leather with swivel hanger for attaching to web cartridge belt. Length, 17 inches. In used, serviceable order. Price, 85 cents each.

NEW MACHETES from salvaged ship. Water stained with paper wrapping stuck to blade. These are made by famous American makers. Offered without scabbards at $1.25 each.

**0-803. NEW MACHETES,** made in United States by famous firm. These have 17-inch blades, no scabbards. We do not carry these in stock, but will buy for mail order customers. Prices will be quoted on application. We can obtain other styles with various lengths of blade, so advise us what you need.

**10484. BRITISH NAVY PRACTICE SWORD.** Large cutlass-shaped guard, handle engraved, iron pommel, 29-inch steel blade and rounded point. Used on British warships. Weight 2¾ pounds. Strongest and best practice swords to be had. Our bargain price, $1.65 each.

**0-890. GEORGE I. PERIOD ENGLISH OFFICER'S SWORD.** With very much earlier period blade, fitted to double guard gilt handle, silver wire wrapped, 33-inch double-edged tapered blade. Maker's name now indistinct from great age. Part of the letters show, "Ju-IIIi." From Royal Artist Ernest Croft sale. Price, $20.00

**0-890A. GEORGE II. PERIOD BRITISH OFFICER'S SWORD.** Straight 32-inch grooved blade, with three- branch steel guard. Ball pommel. From Ernest Croft's, Royal Artist, collection. Price, $12.50.

**0-891. AMERICAN REVOLUTIONARY WAR PERIOD OFFICER'S SABRE.** With carved steel 28½-inch blade, gilt ornamented with British Crown, G. R. and Coat of Arms; fluted ivory hilt, steel guard; complete with leather scabbard in good serviceable order. Price, $13.50.

**0-891A. GEORGE III. BRITISH OFFICER'S SWORD.** With blued gilt steel blade, etched with King George's monogram G. R., Coat of Arms, etc. Checkered ivory grip hilt, leather scabbard with gilt mountings. Price, $15.50.

**8693. GEORGE II. PERIOD SILVER MOUNTED SIDE ARM SWORD.** With green ivory handle grip. Ornamented silver mountings. Full length 27 inches. Price, $9.85.

**8695. ANCIENT SCOTCH SIDE ARM SWORD.** With stag horn hand grip. Thistle top pommel, relief ornamented with thistle flower and leaves; 17th century period; single guard, slightly curved steel blade, 20-inch; engraving worn off. Price, $15.00.

**8686. ANCIENT HUNTING SWORD.** With double guard, 20-inch blade (broken and repaired). The guard decorated with snake charmers in relief. Price, $8.85.

**0-770. U. S. A. SABRE TARGET PRACTICE OUTFIT.** Wood frame with hollow square centre in which weight operates to keep upright the hide-covered striking bags. The bags bend when struck and swing back into position by the centre weights inside of the frame. Most useful in any armory to teach sword practice. Width at the base 62 inches, height to the top of the platform 22 inches, height of pendulum 26 inches, diameter of the head 7½ inches, sliding ball 8 inches, full length 5 inches. Rock Island Arsenal make. Taken apart, packed in case for shipment. New. Bargain price, $12.85.

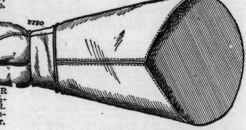

**0-882. U. S. A. GAUNTLET FENCING GLOVES.** With large russet leather cuffs, chamois leather hair-filled gloves, with 2-inch wrist space, with 12-inch fine russet leather cuff. Stamped as having been made at Rock Island Government Arsenal. Superior to the ordinary trade-mark fencing gloves. We have these fencing gauntlets in right or left hand as desired. In serviceable order. Price, $1.50 each.

**0-664. U. S. NAVY WAR RELIC CUTLASS.** Stamped on the brass guard, "Philadelphia," and on the blade, "1862." As it is against naval regulations to stamp any name on weapons in service this cutlass must have had some important history. Perhaps brass guard is relic of Bainbridge at Tripoli, 1803. With Civil War blade. Price, $9.85.

CIVIL WAR INFANTRY OFFICER'S PRESENTATION SWORD. Battlefield relic. Engraved. Presented to Lieut. L. Mosher by his Court House friends. Price, $8.75.

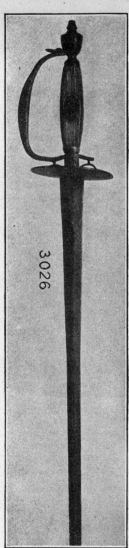

3026

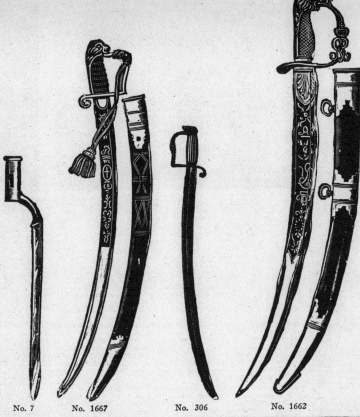

No. 7    No. 1667    No. 306    No. 1662

**1662. KING GEORGE III. OFFI-CER'S AMERICAN REVOLUTION-ARY WAR PERIOD SABRE,** with G. R. crown and coat of arms etched in gilt on the blued steel blade. Blade is 1⅝ inches in width at hilt, 33½ inches in length. Ivory hilt, lion head pommel holding guard. In good order. British crown and G. R. in open work on guard. Leather scabbard, with gilt mountings. 2 rings. Price, $20.00.

**306. REVOLUTIONARY WAR OF-FICER'S SWORD,** from Tilton collection; ivory handle, eagle pommel hand guard; fair order, only no scabbard. Price, $25.00.

**25-19. BRITISH NAVAL OFFICER'S SWORD,** old pattern, leather scabbard, brass, ornamented with two rings; 31-inch quill blade, ornamented with crown anchor and coat of arms. Marked as made by Gillott, 36 Strand, London. Large one-piece brass guard with anchor and crown with sharkskin grip and Lion head pommel. Price, $25.00.

**305. REVOLUTIONARY WAR PERIOD SABRE,** found on Winchester battlefield during the Civil War. Length of blade, 30 inches; total length, 35 inches; iron handle; no scabbard; fair order; relic. Price, $18.00.

**3026. SWORD WORN BY CAPTAIN BROKE,** commanding His Majesty's frigate Shannon when he captured the U. S. frigate Chesapeake, Captain Lawrence, off Boston Harbor, June 1, 1813—a battle made memorable by Captain Lawrence's dying words, which have been a rallying cry in the U. S. Navy ever since—"Don't give up the ship." The gentleman from whom we purchased this old sword along with a number of others, at his private residence near Hyde Park, London, wrote us after we received the swords: "Referring to the old swords you bought of me at my private house there is one I ought not to have sent—the one with an ivory handle. This sword was the one worn by Captain Broke of the British frigate Shannon, when he captured the U. S. frigate Chesapeake. It was unpatriotic of me to let this go to America." And in another letter, giving the history of it, ends with: "I should be glad to have it back. In fact, it was a mistake of mine parting with it." It will take $500 to induce us to part with this rare old relic. We will give letter from London gentleman to purchaser. Sword is fairly well preserved. The ivory handle is yellow with age. The gold plating is badly worn. Has oval plate set in ivory grip with British crown and anchor. Blade has double edge, 31 inches long, 1⅛ inches at hilt, tapering to point. Total length, 38 inches. Price, $500.00. See also illustrations on page 186, numbers 3376 and 3026.

**7A. AMERICAN REVOLUTIONARY WAR PERIOD MUSKET BAYONETS.** Commonly called the Spade Bayonet, owing to the wideness of the blade. This pattern bayonet was used on all guns during the Revolutionary War, by both American and British soldiers. Bayonets are not interchangeable; each bayonet fitted to its particular rifle. These are genuine relics of that period, and are offered at the bargain price of $1.00 each.

**1607. REVOLUTIONARY WAR PERIOD OFFICER'S SWORD;** blued steel blade, etched with crown and G. R. on one side; with trophy of arms decoration on the reverse side; ivory checkered hilt; gilt guard, with antique sword knot, with scabbard engraved, "Fuller, 2 Charing Cross." Blade, 31 inches long; 3-inch curve from hilt to point. Sword is in good order. Scabbard's rather the worse for age, but complete, with large gilt mouth and tip. One-ring scabbard, with frog button. Price, $18.50.

We have hundreds of assorted swords and sabers in stock, and if you wish any special style for decoration or theatrical use, please send us your sketch, and we will quote prices.

**BRITISH ARMY OFFICER'S SWORD,** 1776 period, lion head pommel; in fair order. Price, $12.00.

**REVOLUTIONARY WAR PERIOD OFFICER'S SWORD,** without scabbard; poor order. Price, $12.00.

**"SWORD OF CAPT. BENJAMIN CHURCH,** of Rhode Island (Colonial days) who conquered King Philip of the Pequits and Wampanoags at Mount Hope, Bristol, R. I., in 1677. Very curious sabre blade, bone grip, smooth brass hand guard obtained by Mr. Dimmock in Bristol, R. I., September 1677; no scabbard; genuine." Mr. Dimmock's son informs us that the Rhode Island Historical Society wished to purchase this interesting old Relic. It is now for sale. Price, $200.00.

**RES. 2 REVOLUTIONARY WAR OFFICER'S SWORDS,** with leather scabbards, with brass tip, with two brass bands, with rings and stud, for use with sword slings or a frog. Eagle head pommel, plain brass guard, white ivory grip, checkered. 28-inch blade with slight curve, old style bluing half length, with military designs engraved, and gold inlaid. Price $28.00, each.

Movable Tower, used against besieged cities, five story with ram in lower story. Aided by bowmen with Pavisors.

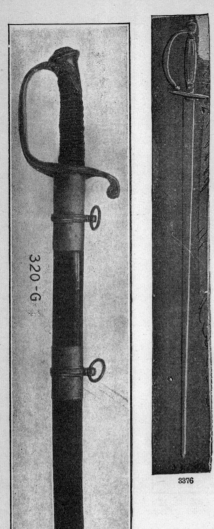

**3026.** Illustration from old book showing the sea fight between the American Frigate "Chesapeake," Captain Lawrence, and the British Frigate "Shannon," Captain Broke, off Boston Harbor, June 1st, 1813, in which the Chesapeake was captured; Lawrence was killed. His dying words having since been used by the U. S. Navy as motto—"Don't give up the ship." The sale of the captured flag of the Chesapeake in London last year brought the memory of the Battle before the Public. The flag was bought by a wealthy American residing in Europe, who presented it to the United Service British Museum, in the old St. James Palace, Whitehall, London. Our agent attended the sale and bid for us on the flag. We desired to have the flag to keep company with the sword, once carried by Commodore Broke commanding the victorious Frigate "Shannon." This sword, illustration No. 3376, we purchased some years ago from London Collector who included it along with a number of other weapons. This old sword is fully vouched for. It is of the period of 1800, has ivory hilt, well worn, stained with age, with British Crown and anchor inlaid in gold. Double edged, 31 inch blade, full length of the sword 38 inches. The sword is on free exhibition in our Museum Salesroom. It would take $500.00 to induce us to part with it.

**5007.** Revolutionary War Officer's Sword with Eagle Pommel, ivory hilt, showing extensive use. Full length 39½ inches, weight 21 ounces, from Master Armorer Adam Oliver's collection. Used no doubt not only in the Revolutionary War but in all the American Wars up to and including the Civil War. A relic that has helped make American History. Price $25.00.

**5008.** War of 1812 Artillery Officer's Saber from Adam Oliver's collection. Full length 32 inches. Weight 18 ounces. Price $15.00.

3376

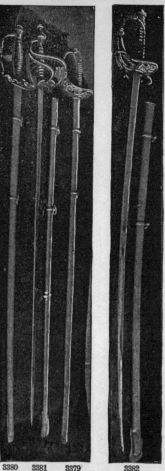

3380  3381  3379  3382

**3379 to 3382.** Photo. illustration of Spanish Officer's Sword from Cuba, 1898.

**3379.** Spanish Officer's Toledo Sword, 36 inch blade with Spanish Crown marks with raised relief etching, inscribed Fa. D., Toledo, Ano. D. 1858. Blade is double edged, large basket guard with open ornamented scroll work. Two ring nickel steel scabbard. Full length 41½ inches. Serviceable order. Price $35.00. Relic Spanish War, Cuba, 1898.

**3380.** Spanish Officer's Sword relief ornamented, 32½ inch blade, giltmounted. "F. A. D., Toledo," and on the reverse side "Ano. D. 1873." Three guard handle, with Spanish coat arms cast in relief on the guard, ivory hilt, gilt wire, wrapped, double edged nickel-plated blade; complete with scabbard. Fine serviceable order from Cuba, 1898. Price $65.00.

**3381.** Spanish Officers Toledo Blade Sword inscribed F. A. D., Toledo, Ano, D. 1873. Spanish coat of arms on the blade, and on the bronze guard. The blade is slightly curved. Price $25.00.

**No. 310B.** SPANISH FOLDING DAGGER, handle of mother of pearl and ivory with military figure of man with sword. German silver tips. Blade 9 inches with sharp point, length when open, 20¼ inches. Price, $8.50.

**5022.** Lord Darnley's Sword, old tag attached is inscribed, "This sword formerly belonged to Lord Darnley and was left by him to Sir John Bligh on whose demise it was sold by auction. Rare old ancient sword, 3 guard, full length 43 inches, complete with scabbard. Price $50.00.

**D56.** 1 long Persian knife like No. D55. Price, $6.00.

**5029.** Admiral Seymour British Navy Officer's Sword, used by him in the Baltic and Crimea Wars. Vouched for by London collector. Sword is similar to illustration No. 1678, page 121, in our 1907 catalogue. Complete with gilt sword knot, chamois leather lined sword bag. Gold plated, British lion pommel, turned down guard. Etched steel blade with anchor and coat of arms; fine order. Price $45.00.

**5023.** General Officer's Indian Sword, kind used by British Army Officers at the Siege of Lucknow. Full length 34 inches, scimetar shaped steel blade, brass hilt and guard, leather scabbard. Serviceable order. Price $19.85.

**5016.** Ancient Sword, 1664 inscribed in gold inlaid figures on the blade, square shaped guard, shark skin grip, full length 37 inches, rare pattern, old sword in serviceable order. Price $38.00.

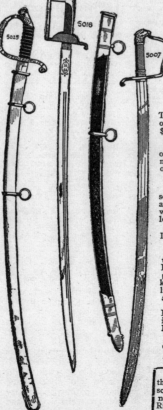

**320-G.** U. S. ARMY CIVIL WAR OFFICER'S SWORD, as used by STAFF officers. All new with 30-inch blade, etched half way in vine designs. Heavy leather scabbard with long brass tip, brass throat with ring, and middle band with ring. Hilt is brass with fine shark skin grip. All metal parts seem to have been gold plated as they are very bright. These swords were made and purchased by the U. S. Government in Europe as the American makers could not fill all the orders promptly. These swords are suitable for officers of private military organizations, or make a fine decoration, as a souvenir of the Civil War. Price $8.00, each.

**3378.** Revolutionary War Pay Master's Side Arm Sword used by Col. Philip Marsteller, Member of the Constitutional Convention, July, 1776. Prominent in raising troops in 1775-6 at Lebanon, Pa. Appointed Lieutenant-Colonel of the First Battalion and acted as Pay Master, superintending the purchase of army supplies, serving through the War. At the close of the War received letter from General Washington, thanking him for the faithful performance of his duties. Colonel Marsteller after the War removed to Virginia and long enjoyed the personal friendship of General Washington, and was one of the six Colonels who served in the Revolutionary War to act as Pall Bearer at Washington's Funeral. The sword has ivory handle, blade 25 inches long. The leather scabbard is in poor order. Engraved on the mouthpiece of the sword is the maker's name, "Cullin, Sword Maker to his Majesty." This sword is a Museum Exhibit. We value it at $500.00.

**5026.** Famous J. J. Runkel Solingen Sword, double edged, 31 inch blade with center groove inscribed, "J. J. Runkel Solingen"; large basket guard. Wire wrapped hilt. Original traces of heavy gold plating. Part of the mouthpiece on the scabbard engraved, Prosser & Cullin Sword Cutters to the King and H. R. H. Duke of York. Charing Cross Old relic. Price, $50.00.

The flag of Colonel Richard Henry Lee. the beau sabreur of the revolutionary war, whose flag crest was a HORSE HEAD inscribed "U. S. Light Dragoons." known as Light Horse Harry is now to be seen at Bannerman's Military Museum. Colonel Richard Henry Lee was the father of General Robert E. Lee.

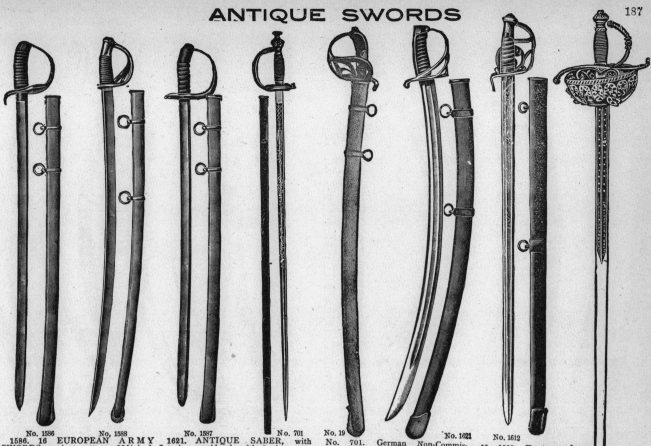

No. 1586    No. 1588    No. 1587    No. 701    No. 19    No. 1621    No. 1612    No. 1660

**1586. 16 EUROPEAN ARMY SWORDS,** ancient pattern; 35¼-inch blade; 1¼ inch widest width; brass guard basket handle. Full length, 40 inches. Almost straight blade; only ⅝-inch curve from hilt to point; 2-ring steel scabbard. In serviceable order. Price, $3.50.

**1621. ANTIQUE SABER,** with flat, iron scabbard, with 2 rings; 36-inch 2-grooved saber blade; 1⅝ inches in width at the hilt; rare pattern guard handle. Bright polished blade. Offered, cleaned and polished, $12.50.

**No. 701.** German Non-Commissioned Officers Swords; full length, about 37 inches; silvered wire wrapped hilt; leather scabbard; fine steel blade; have been used by German army officers; are in fair order. Price, $4.15 each.

**No. 1519.** European **Army** Saber; large bronze handle and guard with steel scabbard in good second hand **service. A** rare pattern. $4.85 each.

**1587. 18 ANCIENT EUROPEAN ARMY SABERS,** almost straight, 35½-inch blade; 1¼ inches in width at hilt. Large brass guard. 3½ inches widest width, with hole for sword knot; 2-ring steel scabbard. Bright, cleaned. Back of the scabbard is partly flat. Price, $3.95.

**1588. 25 EUROPEAN ARMY SABRES, 1821,** with quill back; polished steel, double edged at point of blade with polished brass hilt. Similar to U. S. late regulation cavalry sword, only slightly smaller hilt, and lighter blade. Marked on back of blade "Klingenthal, 1821," with 3 old proof marks on blade; width, 13-16 inches; length of blade, 36 inches; ⅞-inch curve from hilt to point; 2 ring polished steel scabbard. All in fine serviceable order. Price, $3.85.

**No. 19. EUROPEAN ARMY SABER,** with large bronze handle and guard; with steel scabbard; in good second-hand, serviceable order. Rare pattern. $4.85 each.

**1612. ANTIQUE FRENCH SWORD,** with one long and two narrow grooves, with bursting bomb cast on the guard. Blade is straight, double edged at the point. Length, 35½ inches; 1½ inches wide; well tempered. Grooved hilt etched with trophy of arms, mounted horsemen, etc. Scabbard leather and brass covered. Requires cleaning. Fair order. Rare weapon. $35.00.

**1660. SPANISH CAVALIER'S SWORD,** with large cup-shaped handsomely decorated guard, with double cross guard woven wire wrapped hand hold, with maker's mark, which resembles an inverted F. Large cup guard is worn so thin it is very fragile. Slightly crushed. Length of blade, 36 inches; 1 inch at hilt, with two grooves; blade is lightened near the hilt by seven series of small holes. 2 rows of lettering on each side of the blade, almost indistinct from age. Can make out "Viva Carlos III Rey 15— de E— Pmn." No doubt relic of the 14TH CENTURY. Price, $65.00.

**1610. ANCIENT SWORD WITH EAGLE AND CROWN IN RELIEF ON GUARD;** length of blade, 34 inches; widest width, 1 ⅜. Full length, 40 inches; rare old weapon.

**No. 405. 1814** French Officer's Sword, long, straight blade, grooved and etched with "Vive le Roi"; bronze handle with crown and fleur-de-lis in circle, with ornamented designs cast on the guard, with sword knot; leather scabbard with bronze mountings; handsome, serviceable sword; relic of the days when Napoleon was a prisoner and Emperor Louis XVII. reigned for 100 days. We found this fine sword in old collection in Europe and had to pay a tempting price to obtain it, on which price we have paid heavy import duty. For sale. $37.50.

**1277. BRITISH ARMY CAVALRY SWORDS,** no scabbards. Good, second-hand serviceable order. Guard each side of hilt, with leather loop for finger hold. With knurled cavity on hilt for thumb hold. 34-inch blade. Price, $1.85.

**1615. ANCIENT SWORD,** straight double edged blade, 37½ inches, 1⅜ at hilt, tapered to point, with heavy steel guard, wire wrapped handle. With leather scabbard rather the worse for age.

**No. 390. SCOTCH CLAYMORE SWORD** with 31-inch plain oval blade, steel scabbard with rings. Hilt is red leather lined, and is complete with red tassel. Price, $30.00. No scabbard.

**1645. SHOILE BRIDGE** stamped on blade of antique double edged sword, 1 inch at hilt; 31 inches long; tapered point; double guard, small part of the guard missing. British collector informed us that this make was of the period of 1710. Relic. Price, $10.00.

**1682. VICTORIA RIFLES OFFICERS' SWORD;** etched on blade, "British Volunteers," with coat-of-arms, Galley ship, Resnon Verva Em, with bugle, crown V. R.; handsome ornamental etching. Maker's inlaid proof mark seal. Large four-branched guard, with crown and bugle, in open work (the bugle on an officer's sword represents the Volunteers); leather scabbard, with 2 rings. Fine order. Price, $12.00.

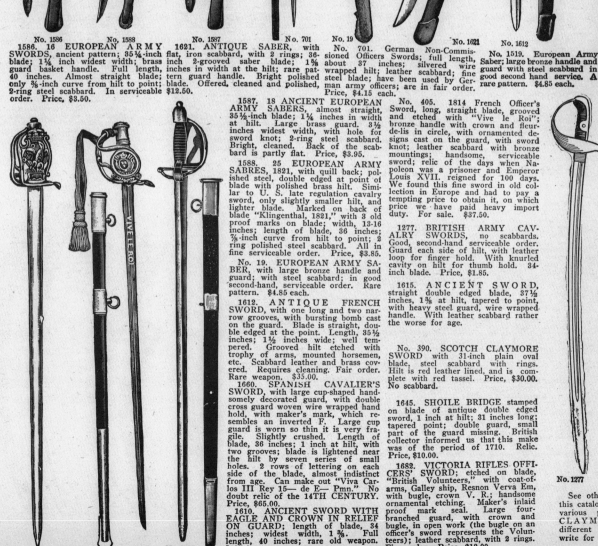

No. 1610    No. 405    No. 1615

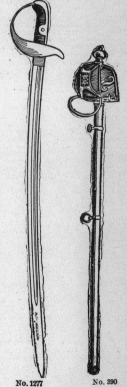

No. 1277    No. 390

See other pages **in** this catalog for many various patterns of CLAYMORES, of different periods, **or** write for prices.

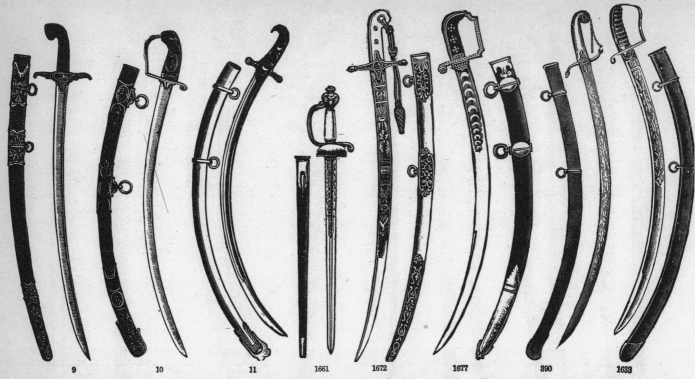

9     10     11     1661     1672     1677     390     1633

**No. 9. KING GEORGE OF ENGLAND PRESENTATION SWORD,** made by cutler to His Majesty, for presentation to officers and notables. Polished steel blade, with rich gilt hilt and cross guard; with scabbard guide. Leather scabbard, with large gilt ornamented rings and trimmings. From old time London collection. Cleaned and polished like new. Handsome sword. Price, $60.00.

French Scimetar; with ivory handle, brass mounted, beautifully engraved blade, German silver polished scabbard. Full length, 3 feet; fine order. Price, $16.00.

**No. 10.** Ancient Presentation Sword, made by sword maker to His Majesty the King of England, for presentation to foreign notables. Handsome sword; carved polished steel etched blade: rich gilt ornamented hilt, with lions head pommel. Black leather scabbard, with large gilt bands, rings and trimmings all restored to look like new. From old London collection. Price, $68.00.

**No. 1638.** 18th Century Officers Sword, poor order; relic. Price, $8.00.

**1661. DIRK,** "Pro Gloria et Patria," engraved on each side of the etched gilt blade pommel, with German eagle, cross and crown, with crown and shield with E. V. on white metal double guard hilt. Blade, 18 inches long, double edged, tapered to the point. Leather scabbard, with gilt bronze mountings, all in fine order. Price, $15.00.

**1672. HANDSOME IVORY HILT SWORD,** etched on blade, "Prince Albert's Own Hussars. Egypt, Salamanca, Penninsular, Waterloo, Bhurtport, Alma Balakalava, Inkerman, Savastopool," with trophy of arms, crown and other ornamental etching. With maker's name, "Sexton, Dawson St., Dublin;" blade 30 inches long, 1⅛ at hilt, 1¼ curve. Ivory handle with ornamented gilt mountings, with scabbard guide. With sword knot 2 ring steel scabbard, with rich gilt large ornamented mountings. All in fine order; almost new. Handsome presentation sword. Price, $20.00.

**No. 1674.** Antique Ivory Handle Sword; similar to 1673 with leather sword knot; Damascus etched blade. $16.50

**No. 390.** Damascus Scimiter Sword, with ivory handle. Blade shows the beautiful Damaskeen figure. Complete, with the scabbard, as illustrated. Fine relic. In good, serviceable order. Price, $20.00.

**No. 11. TURKISH SCIMETAR SWORD,** for stage use. Fine steel blade. Bronze Turkish pattern handle, with steel scabbard; good, serviceable order. Altered from U. S. Artillery curved sword. Price, $5.85 each.

**1677. OFFICER'S SCIMETAR SWORD,** blade 29½ inches, 1⅜ in width, 3½-inch curve, with row of crescents on gilt etched blade. With rare pattern guard and handle. With British officer's ranking stamped escutcheon on handle. Gilt trimmed scabbard. Fairly good order. Price, $18.00.

**No. 1623. SCIMETER SWORD,** ornamented eiched blade. Revolutionary War pattern handle; complete with flat steel scabbard. With two rings. Offered cleaned and polished, $15.00.

**U. S. GOVERNMENT CUSTOMS APPRAISER** recently requested our services in placing valuation on a lot of antique weapons that had been imported without invoice. We placed a valuation on the basis of the prices we had paid for similar goods in foreign countries, and agreed with the Appraiser that if the importer objected, we would stand by, and if necessary, would be willing to purchase the goods at our appraised valuation. The Appraiser expressed his opinion that we were all right on the valuation on guns, bows and pistols, but did not think our prices quite high enough on swords, as he had only a short time before passed a lot of swords for the Metropolitan Museum of Art, which were valued at hundreds of dollars each, whereas on nearly similar swords (in his opinion) we placed the valuation at about 1/10. This incident causes us to believe that our customers will see good bargains in the antique swords we have purchased and advertise for sale.

**1623.** 19th Century French Sword marked "Worthan Manon Suffolk.." Probably captured in the Mexican War. Fine copper wire wrapped hilt, with double guard, with liberty cap pommel; triangular shaped rapier blade, ¾ inch wide at the hilt, tapered to needle point; 34 inch blade. Good order. Leather scabbard, in fair order. Price, $15.00.

**No. 1673.** Antique Ivory Handle Sabre, with steel cross guard and mountings; with scabbard guide; blade, 32 inches in length; 1½in width and 2-inch curve; double edged; widest width, 10 inches from point. In order, to render cutting weight blow; rare pattern; flat triangular shaped steel scabbard, 2 bands for rings; with cross like extension; no projecting shoe at bottom: old pattern sword and scobbard: good order. Price, $18.50.

**No. 1675.** George IV Officers sword, with brass scabbard, ivory handle on blade, G R monogram and crown, with makers name, "Johnson Sabre Maker te the King, 38 St. James St:" gilt cross guard; length of blade, 30¼ inches; ⅞-inch hilt: 1⅜-inch curve; 2 rings on brass scabbard; all good condition. brass scabbard sabres are very rare. Price, $17.50.

**1687. CADET OFFICER'S SCIMETER SABRE,** etched steel blade with female figure carrying tropy of arms; with scroll work; with name "P. Angier." Width, 1 inch; length, 23 inches, 3¾-inch curve. Price, $14.00

**1327. PAIR ORIENTAL SCIMETERS.** Ornamented inlaid blade, gilt wire inlaid stock and scabbard. Full length, 25½ inches. Price, $7.00 each. 1 pair, full length, 21 inches, $6.00 each.

**1647. BATTLE OF WATERLOO DRAGOON OFFICER'S SABER,** old style blued steel etched blade, with trophy of arms 1⅜ inch at the hilt, 30 inches long, 3-inch grooved copper wire-wrapped hand grip; single guard; with Fairly good order; requires cleaning. scabbard guide; 2-ring steel scabbard. Price, $12.00.

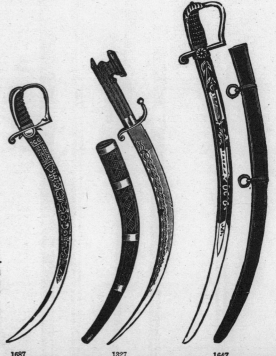

1623     1687     1327     1647

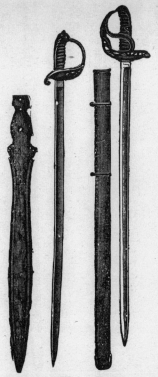

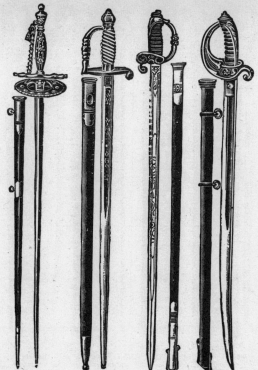

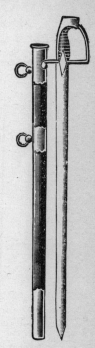

No. 1120. No. 1592.　　No. 383.　　　　No. 1630.　　　No. 1032.　No. 1640.　　No. 1649.　　　　　　　No. 1619.

No. 383. ANTIQUE STRAIGHT SWORD, with large, double guard, basket-shaped handle; total length, 42½ inches; width, 1½ inches; in fair order. Price, $4.50. Polished and put in serviceable order. Price, $5.50.

D522. 1 HEAVY NATIVE KNIFE, with large handle of antelope horn. 10-inch tapered blade with sharp point and edge, and heavy back. Both blade and back of handle ornamented. Leather covered wood scabbard with fancy metal end. Price, $7.50.

1630. OLD ENGLISH COURT SWORD, with scabbard, 32½-inch triangular-shaped highly polished steel blade, ⅝-inch at the hilt, tapered to needle point. Double guard ornamented with raised polished steel discs; with guard chain. In fairly good order. Price, $10.00.

1649. V. R. AND CROWN in relief on gilt brass guard officer's sword. Shark skin grip. Blade has been etched; gilt proof mark; length of blade, 31½ inches, with 2-ring steel scabbard. The shoe at the bottom of the scabbard has been worn through in service. Price, $8.50.

1592. 43 EUROPEAN OFFICERS' SWORDS, cleaned and polished order; 32-inch blade; 1-inch wide, with ornamental brass guard and handle; with hole for sword knot; blade has pair of scales as proof mark; full length, 37½ inches; without scabbards. $2.95.

1593. 3 TURKISH OFFICERS' SWORDS, with Star and Crescent on the guard; with gold proof mark; blade has been etched, now worn off; handle missing; untempered relics. $3.00 each.

D-89-2. MOORISH DAGGER, similar to No. D-89 with 9¾ inch narrow blade with embossed brass scabbard inlaid with silver ornaments, with heavy red sash cord or shoulder sling. Price, $10.00.

1120. OLD ROMAN BRONZE SWORD BLADE, found in excavation near London. In good state of preservation. The bronze blade rings like a bell when struck. No doubt a relic of the lost art of tempering. Length, 23½ inches. Widest width of the blade, 1⅞ inches. Price, $55.00.

1613. ANTIQUE LARGE BLADE STRAIGHT SWORD, with crown and large letter C on guard. Double-edged blade, 36½ inches. Width, 1½ inches. The old marks on hilt are indistinct. Price, $18.00.

1665. Same as 1649. BRITISH OFFICER'S SWORD, with V. R. crown in relief on gilt bronze guard. V. R. stands for Victoria's reign. Black shark skin grip. Quill back shaped sabre blade; no scabbard. Price, $6.00.

1032. REVOLUTIONARY WAR PERIOD OFFICER'S SWORD, with ivory grooved hilt; gilt bronze guard; old-fashioned blued gilt edged steel blade; all in good, serviceable, second-hand order, with leather scabbard, brass mountings; scabbard is in poor order. Price, $12.50.

1640. REVOLUTIONARY WAR PERIOD BRITISH OFFICER'S SWORD, straight blade; etched with monogram British coat-of-arms and scroll work. "Prater & Co., London," on blade, with bursting bomb in white metal relief work on gilt guard; shark skin grip: fine double edged blade, 33 inches in length, ⅞ inch at hilt, tapered to point; length at scabbard, with old style stud fastening; fine order. Price, $12.50.

1665. REVOLUTIONARY WAR PERIOD OFFICER'S SWORD, with ivory hilt, steel guard, pommel, with scabbard guide; somewhat similar to No. 1632; good order, no scabbard, $12.00.

ND1. BRITISH OLD STYLE NAVY DIRK, with 14¾-inch narrow blade with various designs including new moon, flags, etc. Gold plated brass guard with anchor, hardwood grip, corrugated, with anchor on band. Leather scabbard with place for rings and frog. Price, $12.00.

ND2. BRITISH NAVY DIRK, or dress sword, with 14-inch etched blade with scroll designs, with crown over anchor, and crown over V R. Cross bar with acorn ends, lion head pommel with ring in mouth for cord, shark skin pebbled grip. Leather scabbard with gold plated throat and tip with frog stud. Price, $13.00.

ND3. BRITISH NAVY DIRK or dress sword. Cross bar with acorn ends, with navy emblem at center, crown over anchor encircled by wreath. Lion head pommel, pebbled shark skin grip. 18¼-inch blade with gold inlaid designs. Leather scabbard with copper throat and tip, with 2 rings for dress belt. Price, $14.00.

ND4. BRITISH NAVY DIRK with plain cross bars, 4-inch white ivory hand grip, with stud pommel. 12 narrow blade with one deep groove on each side. Leather scabbard with brass throat and one brass band with sword ring. This type used in British navy at time of Nelson. Price, $15.00.

ND5. BRITISH NAVY OFFICER'S DIRK, style used at time of Nelson. Plain cross bars, white ivory grip, 14-inch narrow blade. Metal scabbard with 2 rings for belt. Scabbard marked: WOOLLEY, DEAKIN, DUTTON & JOHNSON, LONDON. Price, $16.00.

ND6. BRITISH NAVY OLD STYLE DIRK, with 14½-inch narrow blade, engraved in floral designs, acorn tipped cross bars, 3 inch white ivory grip with stud pommel. No scabbard. Price, $13.50.

No. 1619. EUROPEAN OFFICERS' ANTIQUE SWORD with scabbard. Long wide blade with same style hilt as on swords used in the Revolutionary War. Swords of this style are now becoming rare. Price, $20.00.

No. 1614.　　　No. 1612.

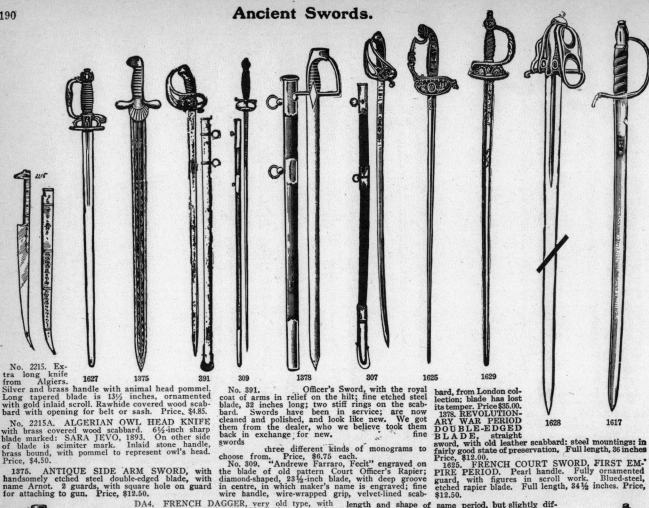

No. 2215. Extra long knife from Algiers. Silver and brass handle with animal head pommel. Long tapered blade is 13½ inches, ornamented with gold inlaid scroll. Rawhide covered wood scabbard with opening for belt or sash. Price, $4.85.

No. 2215A. ALGERIAN OWL HEAD KNIFE with brass covered wood scabbard. 6½-inch sharp blade marked: SARA JEVO, 1893. On other side of blade is scimiter mark. Inlaid stone handle, brass bound, with pommel to represent owl's head. Price, $4.50.

1375. ANTIQUE SIDE ARM SWORD, with handsomely etched steel double-edged blade, with name Arnot. 2 guards, with square hole on guard for attaching to gun. Price, $12.50.

DA4. FRENCH DAGGER, very old type, with 3½-inch white ivory handle ridged for firm grip. Silver cross bar and band, silver stud pommel. 6¼-inch pointed blade four sided. Leather scabbard with silver throat and tip. 18th Century. Price, $8.50.

No. 1628 SOLD. See other pages in this catalog for many patterns of CLAYMORES, of different periods.

No. 1617. ANCIENT SWORD with old time marks on long blade. Extra long hilt. Price, $20.00.

1616. ANCIENT SWORD, double-edged, straight blade, 33 inches in length, 1½ width, wire-wrapped brass handle, with rare pattern guard, as shown in illustration. Serviceable order. $17.00.

1377. ANTIQUE DOUBLE-EDGED BROAD SWORD. Fine steel blade engraved on one side "Nome en Baines Sin Honor," and on the other side "Nome saoutes sine Razon," which we understand as "Do not draw me without reason" and "Do not sheathe me without honor." Full length, 41 inches; widest width of blade, 2 inches; 3 grooves, rusty. Handle does not seem to be original. Price, $20.00.

1684. ANTIQUE IVORY HANDLE SWORD, with open ornamented work on guard. With three short pierced grooves. Etched blade, 33½ inches in length, 1¼ width. Scabbard in poor order. Price, $20.00.

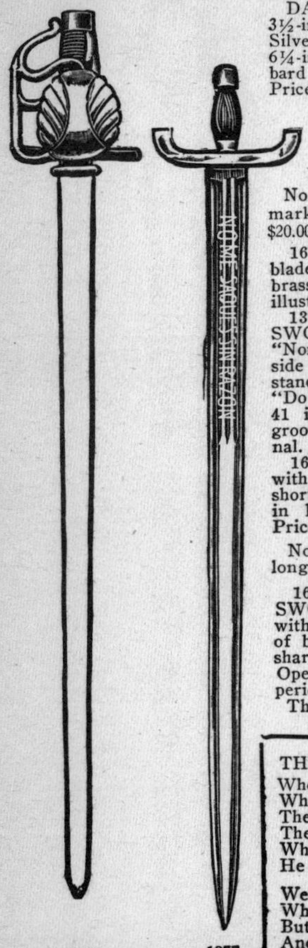

No. 1618 SOLD. We have somewhat similar extra long blade antique swords from $15.00 up.

1629. Set of 3 1750 period RAPIER DRESS SWORDS. "Recte Faciendo Neminen Timea" with other ornamentation engraved on blade. Length of blade, 32 inches, 1 inch at the hilt, tapered to sharp point. Guard and handle is a work of art. Open ornamented work, with flags, etc. Old time period double guard, pierced steel triangular blade. The other two swords are somewhat similar in

No. 391.    Officer's Sword, with the royal coat of arms in relief on the hilt; fine etched steel blade, 32 inches long; two stiff rings on the scabbard. Swords have been in service; are now cleaned and polished, and look like new. We got them from the dealer, who we believe took them back in exchange for new.    fine swords

three different kinds of monograms to choose from. Price, $6.75 each.

No. 309. "Andrewe Farraro, Fecit" engraved on the blade of old pattern Court Officer's Rapier; diamond-shaped, 23½-inch blade, with deep groove in centre, in which maker's name is engraved; fine wire handle, wire-wrapped grip, velvet-lined scabbard, from London collection; blade has lost its temper. Price $35.00.

1378. REVOLUTIONARY WAR PERIOD DOUBLE-EDGED BLADE, straight sword, with old leather scabbard: steel mountings: in fairly good state of preservation. Full length, 36 inches Price, $12.00.

1625. FRENCH COURT SWORD, FIRST EMPIRE PERIOD. Pearl handle. Fully ornamented guard, with figures in scroll work. Blued-steel, etched rapier blade. Full length, 34½ inches. Price,

length and shape of same period, but slightly different design. The third sword in the set has steel discs ornamented work, which looks like inlaid jewels. Price for the set of three, in original chamois bag, $70.

1650. SCOTCH CLAYMORE SWORD, with good blade. Handle has gotten crushed. Hand grip and cap missing. We offer at bargain price, to some one who can repair and put in good order. Price, $8.50.

1822H. PART OF ROMAN SWORD BLADE, 1¾ inches long, ⅝ wide. Price, $1.75.

D51. 1 heavy knife from Cabul, Afghanistan. Antelope horn handle with 14-inch grooved blade. Wood scabbard covered with ornamented leather. Price, $8.00.

D52. 1 knife like No. D51 with 10½ inch blade and wood-covered scabbard with fancy iron tip. Price, $7.50.

1822A. PART OF OLD ROMAN SWORD BLADE, 5¾ inches long, 1⅜ wide. Shows the double edge with diamond shape, with two centre lines. From London collection. Price, $6.50.

1822B. PART OF ROMAN SWORD BLADE, 4⅝ inches long, 1⅜ wide. $5.00.

1822C. PART OF ROMAN SWORD BLADE, 5½ inches long, 1⅜ wide. Price, $5.50.

1822D. PART OF ROMAN SWORD BLADE, 4½ inches long, ⅞ wide. Price, $3.85.

1822E. PART OF ROMAN SWORD BLADE, 3⅜ inches long, ¾ inches wide. Price, $3.25.

1822F. PART OF ROMAN SWORD BLADE, 2¾ inches long, ¾ wide. Price, $3.50.

1822G. PART OF ROMAN SWORD BLADE, 1¾ inches long, 1 inch wide. Price, $2.25.

307. European Officers Sword, finely etched quill back blade, 28-inch long, serviceable order with Prince of Wales 3 Plum emblem. Price, $10.00.

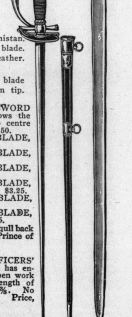

1686. GEORGE III. OFFICERS' STRAIGHT SWORD. Blade has engraved crown G. R.; large open work on basket-shaped handle. Length of blade, 35 inches; width, 1⅜. No scabbard. Good condition. Price, $15.00.

Scotch Officer's Sword, with silvered thistle on the guard, straight, oval-shaped etched blade; silvered wire wrapped hilt, ornamental brass guard; leather scabbard with highly decorated brass mountings; fine sword, good order; full length, 37 inches. Price, $15.00.

**THE WHITE MAN'S BURDEN—OTHERWISE THE SWORD.**

Wherever the flag is floating, wherever we push our trade,
Wherever we tinker an army, we find the British blade,
The useless pot-metal weapon, old as the trees and grass,
The implement Balaam sighed for, to slap his weary ass,
Which dates 'way back to Eden, where the Maker's wrath began,
He bade the angel shake it, in the face of the erring man.

We fail to count the ages, no scientist can trace,
When first this ancient weapon once adorned the human race.
But when some protoplasm was compounded from the air,
And developed after Darwin, to an ape without his hair,
The ancient writers tell us, and agree with one accord,
The first thing he constructed was the prehistoric sword.

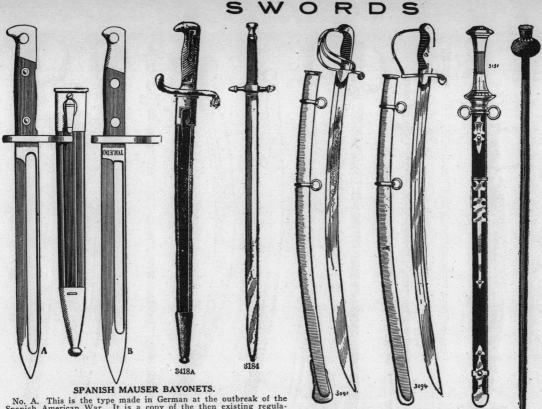

## SPANISH MAUSER BAYONETS.

No. A. This is the type made in German at the outbreak of the Spanish American War. It is a copy of the then existing regulation knife bayonet of Germany, the Model of 1888, and also similar to the Roumanian Model of 1893.

No. B. This is the Spanish made model and is marked: ARTILLERIA FBA. DE TOLEDO, the arsenal made famous by the TOLEDO BLADES of history. Both bayonets fit the Models 1891 and 1893 Mauser Rifles.

For No. A, German Model with scabbard, the price is $1.20 each.

For No. B, the TOLEDO MODEL with scabbard the price is $2.50 each.

3020. South Sea Savage War Club round stone, 3½ inch diameter with hole in the centre fitted with hardwood shaft. 4 feet long, row of teeth, holds stone in place. Price $10.00.

3020a. Similar War Club with stone cracked offered "as is." Price $5.00.

3091. Spanish Officer's Cavalry Sabre with BRASS SCABBARD, 34 inch engraved blade, 3 guards handle, polished brass hilt with scabbard guide attached to the cross guard, gilt polished. These Swords came from Cuba in 1898. Brass Scabbard Swords are rare. Fine serviceable order. Price $14.00.

3094. Spanish Officer's Artillery Sabre. Gilt finished hilt, wire wrapped, 34 inch polished blade. Two ring steel scabbard. Serviceable relic of Spanish War. Price $10.85.

3131. Large Two Edged Blade Sword 40 inches long, German silver *relief* ornamented Hilt and scabbard. Price $12.00.

3092. Spanish Officer's Sword, engraved 34 inch blade, 3 guard brass hilt, steel scabbard. Purchased from the Spanish Governor of the Havana Arsenal, Cuba, 1898. Serviceable order. Price $10.85.

5024. British Militia Volunteer Officer's Extra light weight sword (2 pounds), 32 inch polished steel blade, etched with V. R. (Queen Victoria's) monogram. Shark skin grip. In good order. Price $9.85.

3254. Officer's Sword stamped 1746 on the blade. Brass handle and cross guard, shell shaped side guard. 26 inch blade from the Pettingill Collection. Said to have been captured during the Revolutionery War and used in 1812. Serviceable order, no scabbard. Price $20.00.

3360. U. S. Rifleman's Knife. Kind used by Gen. Fremont's Troops. Blade stamped U. S., 1849. Inspector's mark W. L. Made for U. S. Government by Ames Mfg. Co., Cabotsville. 12 inch blade. Full length 19 inches. Brass guard wood handle with hole for carrying thong. Rare Weapon, Museum Exhibit. Price with scabbard, $20.00.

5033. Indian Idol Spear. German silver 3 pronged spear ornamented with socket for attaching to round iron shaft with sectional screw joint containing Elephant Spear. Price $7.85.

3000. Spanish Machete Steel Blade. Full length 21½ inches. Widest width 5¼ inches, 3 grooves at the blade, hardwood handle, 4 rivet fastenings. Used for cutting sugar cane, trimming hedges, etc.; like new. Price, 90c.

0-1291B. CONFEDERATE OFFICER'S SABRE AND BELT. Captured at Fort Walker, South Carolina, by Third Assistant Engineer John G. Bolander of the U. S. side-wheel gunboat Mercury, attached to Flag Officer Dupont's fleet, November, 1861. The Mercury before the war had been a Sandy Hook towboat. The sabre is the old pattern U. S. heavy cavalry three-branch guard. Black enameled, Scabbard with BRASS shoe tip. Enameled leather sword belt, with PALMETTO TREE and South Carolina motto. Black belt buckle. Rare relic. Vouched for by letter of relative, which goes with the outfit. Price, $20.00.

3360a. Similar Knife to 3360 with brass handle, marked Ames Mfg. Co., Chicopee, Mass., 1861. Price $16.00.

5017. British Revenue Officer's Antique Side Arm Cutlass Sword, with spring catch at the hilt to lock the scabbard. Single guard, full length 25½ inches, weight 2 pounds, etched quilt back Blade. Serviceable. Price, $4.85.

3184. Ancient side arm double edged sword with brass acorn end cross guard fluted hilt. Brass Pommel, Blade, 24 inches. Used, serviceable order. Price, $2.85.

3418A. German Army Side Arm Sword, relic of French and German War. Brass handle and guard, leather scabbard. Price, $2.50.

Two captured Spanish Non-Com. Officers' side Arm Swords, stamped Arta Fab De Toledo, 1889. Relic of the Spanish War. Purchased at the U. S. Government Arsenal auction sale January, 1910. Offered with scabbard. Price $9.85 each.

3253. War of 1812 Sword used by Captain Enoch Nichols as private in the War of 1812, sailing from Portsmouth, N. H. Blade is 3 feet long, stamped 1812, with figure of rabbit. Brass handle, leather scabbard with frog. Fair order. Price, $20.00.

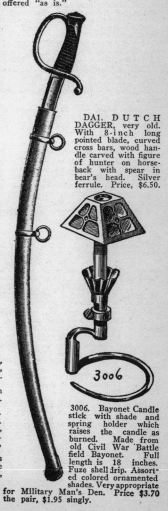

DA1. DUTCH DAGGER, very old. With 8-inch long pointed blade, curved cross bars, wood handle carved with figure of hunter on horseback with spear in bear's head. Silver ferrule. Price, $6.50.

3006. Bayonet Candle stick with shade and spring holder which raises the candle as burned. Made from old Civil War Battle field Bayonet. Full length is 18 inches. Fuze shell drip. Assorted colored ornamented shades. Very appropriate for Military Man's Den. Price $3.70 the pair, $1.95 singly.

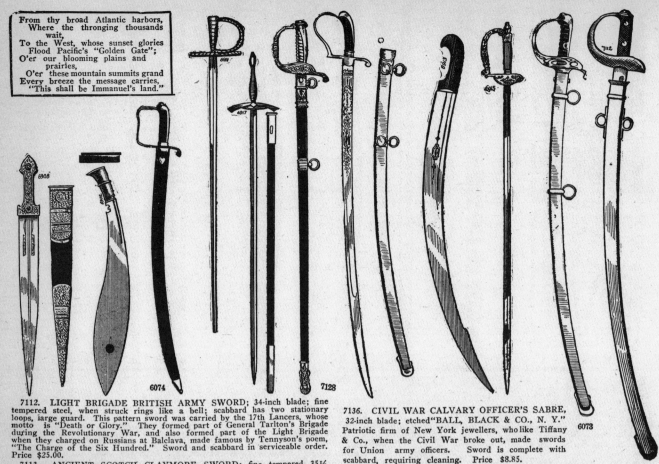

6908   6074   7128   6073

**7112. LIGHT BRIGADE BRITISH ARMY SWORD**; 34-inch blade; fine tempered steel, when struck rings like a bell; scabbard has two stationary loops, large guard. This pattern sword was carried by the 17th Lancers, whose motto is "Death or Glory." They formed part of General Tarlton's Brigade during the Revolutionary War, and also formed part of the Light Brigade when they charged on Russians at Balclava, made famous by Tennyson's poem, "The Charge of the Six Hundred." Sword and scabbard in serviceable order. Price $25.00.

**7113. ANCIENT SCOTCH CLAYMORE SWORD**; fine tempered 35½ inch double edged steel blade, 1¾ inches wide at the hilt; basket guard handle; serviceable order; no scabbard. Price $16.50.

**6902.** India Goorka Knife, sharp steel oval shaped blade with disemboweling notched hook near the hilt. Three in stock, average length of blade 14 inches, width 2¾ inches. Antique service knives, no doubt captured by British soldiers in the many engagements in Sepoy Rebellion, Lucknow, etc. Price $11.00 each.

Goorka Knife, with 12-inch blade, 2 inches in width, with leather scabbard, Price, $9.00.

Goorka Knife with small knife in scabbard. Price $8.50.

U. S. N. Steel Carving Knife, and Fork, silver plated, stamped with letters U. S. N. and two stars (Admiral's mark); full length of knife, 12 inches; fork, 10 inches; serviceable order. Price $6.85 the set.

**6045. INDIA GOORKA KNIFE**, ornamented etched blade showing mounted horsemen; full length, 21½ inches. Price $9.85.

**6046. ORIENTAL KNIFE**, 11½ inches, steel blade, with sharp point; cut brass hilt; ornamented scabbard. Price $4.85.

**6908. PERSIAN** Side Arm Sword, with 16¼-inch double edged blade, 1¾ inches wide at the hilt; bone handle; inscribed with verses from the Koran, inlaid in silver on the blade; richly decorated scabbard. Price $14.85.

**6909.** Seventeenth Century SWISS SWORD of State (copy), large TWO-HANDLED SWORD; length, 5 feet 2 inches; 16-inch iron ornamented cross guard; fluted iron pommel (handle rusted). Price $15.00.

**6910. CARVED WOOD PADDLE** from west coast of Africa (Benin); length, 57 inches; width of blade, 5 inches; ornamented with figurehead. Price $8.85.

**6911. SPANISH BULL FIGHTER'S SWORD**, used by noted Spanish Matador; from London collection; 32-inch double-edged blade; small iron handle with cross guard wrapped with red cloth. Price $16.85.

**6912.** India Native's Thrusting Dagger, double-edged, 9-inch blade; 9-inch handle; with double crossed bar; with shield for protecting the hand. Price $6.85.

**6913. RUSSIAN COSSACK'S SWORD**, curved steel 32-inch blade, double edged near the point, bone handle, divided pommel, inlaid gilt silver ornamentation on the blade. Price $9.85.

**6913a. RUSSIAN COSSACK'S SWORD** with ivory handle, 21½-inch blade. Price $6.85.

**6917. SEVENTEENTH CENTURY SWORD**, serviceable order; facsimile copy of original in European Museum; 32-inch double-edged steel blade. Price $6.85.

**D58.** 1 antique Persian knife with gold ornamented 7½ inch WAVY blade. Solid horn handle, silvered studded. Price, $4.00.

**6915a. EMPEROR NAPOLEON PERIOD COURTIER'S SWORD**; double edged blade, 31½-inch blade; wire wrapped guard, with figure in relief. Price $9.85.

**6037. ANTIQUE MOORISH DAGGER**, silver mounted hilt and pommel; 9-inch blade with curved point; inlaid gilt and silver ornamented scabbard. Price $12.00.

**7136. CIVIL WAR CAVALRY OFFICER'S SABRE**, 32-inch blade; etched "BALL, BLACK & CO., N. Y." Patriotic firm of New York jewellers, who like Tiffany & Co., when the Civil War broke out, made swords for Union army officers. Sword is complete with scabbard, requiring cleaning. Price $8.85.

**BRITISH OFFICER'S SWORD.** Bronze handle, with V. R. and crown monogram in guard. Handsome relief etched blade, with V. R. and crown. Made by Johnston & Co., Sackville Street, London; leather scabbard; in serviceable order. Price, $8.00.

**D57.** 1 ivory handled Persian knife, brass bound. Curved blade is 7½ inches, ornamented on both sides with birds and flowers. Price, $4.50.

**7140.** Civil War Officer's Sword, with fine old Toledo double-edged blade; fitted to ordinary bronze handle of the Mexican War period; no scabbard. Price $10.00.

**7141. BELGIAN ARMY OFFICER'S DRESS SWORD**, silver mountings. with lion head pommel; fluted wood hilt, with crown and letter "L" in relief on the guard; 31½-inch etched gilt blade; leather scabbard; silvered mountings. Price $7.85.

**7141a. MEXICAN OFFICER'S SWORD**, with eagle and serpent in relief on the brass guard. Sharkskin grip, 32-inch blade etched with Mexican coat-of-arms; German silver scabbard; fine order. Price $9.85.

**7141b. GERMAN ARTILLERY OFFICER'S** Grooved Blade Sword, with lion head pommel, sharkskin grip; 33-inch blade; no scabbard. Price $7.85.

**7141c. OFFICER'S SWORD WITH BLADE**, etched with U. S. coat-of-arms, engraved "W. H. Horstman & Sons, Philadelphia"; with TOLEDO SEAL, with bronze handle, with liberty cap and clasped hands ornamented on the guard (Kentucky emblem), with lion head pommel. This sword was found in Europe, perhaps used in Confederate service by Kentucky Militia Officer during the Civil War. Price $8.50.

**7141d.** Antique Naval Officer's Sword, double-edged, quill back, etched blade; with anchor and wreath on the guard, with stud on the scabbard for use with the old fashioned shoulder belt. Price $9.85.

**7142.** Side Arm Sword, with double-edged 18½-inch blade, with German Silver hilt; shell shaped guard; leather scabbard, with German Silver mountings; fine order. Price $4.85.

**7141e. FRENCH EMPIRE RAPIER SWORD**, with bronze double guards; no scabbard. Price $6.50.

**6073. AUSTRIAN CAVALRY SABRE**, 33-inch blade; double guard; iron scabbard, with stationary loop, for use with shoulder belt; in serviceable order. Price $4.85.

**6074. AUSTRIAN ARMY SIDE ARM SWORD**, single guard, leather scabbard, with stud for use on frog or shoulder belt; 26-inch blade; serviceable order. Price $2.85.

**6073a. AUSTRIAN OFFICER'S SABRE**, with 33-inch blade; handsomely etched with arms trophy ornamentation. "Erinnerung anden 13, 14, 15ten Marz, 1848." Single guard; steel scabbard; serviceable order. Price $6.00.

**6073b.** Similar Sword with gilt etched inscription. Price $7.35. 6073b, with plain etching without inscription. Price $5.00.

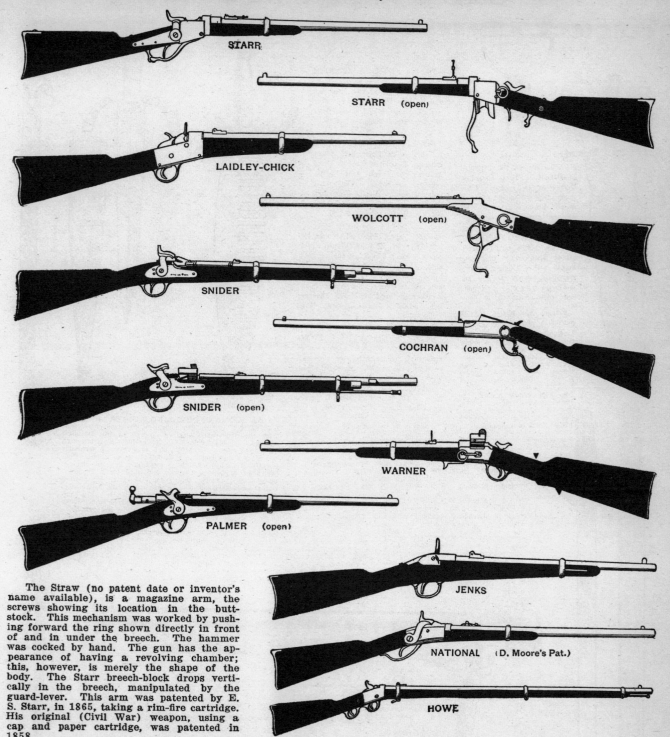

STARR

STARR  (open)

LAIDLEY-CHICK

WOLCOTT  (open)

SNIDER

COCHRAN  (open)

SNIDER  (open)

WARNER

PALMER  (open)

JENKS

NATIONAL  (D. Moore's Pat.)

HOWE

The Straw (no patent date or inventor's name available), is a magazine arm, the screws showing its location in the butt-stock. This mechanism was worked by pushing forward the ring shown directly in front of and in under the breech. The hammer was cocked by hand. The gun has the appearance of having a revolving chamber; this, however, is merely the shape of the body. The Starr breech-block drops vertically in the breech, manipulated by the guard-lever. This arm was patented by E. S. Starr, in 1865, taking a rim-fire cartridge. His original (Civil War) weapon, using a cap and paper cartridge, was patented in 1858.

The Laidley system—submitted by Colonel Laidley of the Army—is based on the Remington system. The story is told by an old ordnance officer that the Colonel was quite proud of his gun and affectionately named it "my chick," hence the name Laidley-Chick.

The Snider is the well-known alteration of the English Enfield. This was the standard weapon for the British army at the time, an invention, by the way, of an American.

The Jenks Carbine, patented in 1868, by B. H. Jenks, has a rotating block which dropped down and back, worked by the hammer at the top.

The National, patented in 1861, by D. Moore, had a falling block similar to the Peabody, worked by guard-lever.

The Howe rifle is an adoption of the Remington, employing the guard-lever which is released by pressure on the rear trigger, the inventor's name and date of patent unknown to the writer.

Other patentees and dates are as follows:

J. H. Howard, no date; G. J. Richardson, April, 1864; W. H. and G. W. Miller, May, 1865; L. S. White, January, 1863; H. H. Wolcott, November, 1866; J. W. Cochran, July, 1863; J. W. Warner, February, 1864; W. P. Palmer, December, 1863.

Among the Carbines not shown in our illustrations which were included in the tests spoken of, we find the Sharps, Ball, Triplett and Scott, Smith (a cartridge gun and not the percussion system weapon), Spencer (an improved Carbine), Union, (the Cosmopolitan) altered to take a metallic cartridge, and the famous Remington, using a side hammer.

Among the names not so well known as the above were: Hubbell, Gray, Roberts, Johnston, Morgenstern, Root, Burke, Fitzgerald, Robertson and Simpson, Hayden, Wilson and Flathers, Armstrong and Taylor, Coleman, Poultney, Berdan, Meig's, Norny, Mix and Horton, Underwood and Wright.

(Continued on page 242)

**0-844. INDIA OR PONNA DAGGER.** From Lawson-Johnston collection. 4¼-inch tapered and pointed steel blade, attached to chased silver curved 4¾-inch gilt guard. Cross guard measures 18½ inches. Made with chased silver ornamented discs on steel rod. Copper wire-wrapped hand hold. In well preserved order. Sold to museum.

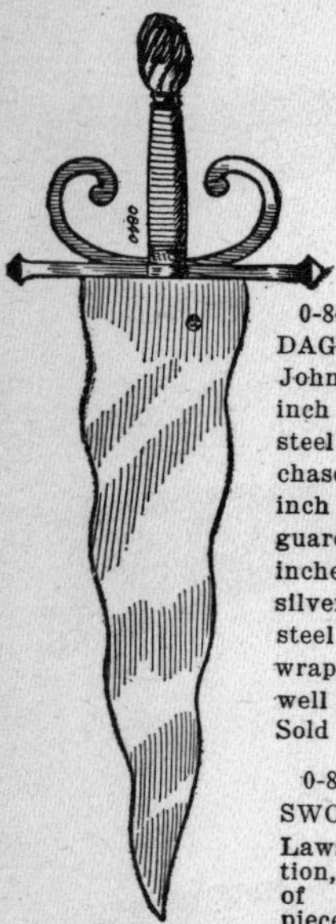

**0-840. ANTIQUE MACE SWORD.** From the famous Lawson-Johnston collection, which contained some of the most historical pieces. Money was no object when collection was being made. Has armorer's mark, "Three lions and ball." 4¾ inches wide, 9½-inch cross guard, 18-inch wavy steel blade, curved club-shaped pommel, copper wire wrapped hilt. Sold to museum.

**D99. 1 ANTIQUE SPANISH DAGGER.** Wide back 6-inch blade with one sharp edge and round tip. Horn handle silver mounted and inlaid with silver wire. Price, $8.00.

**6908A. 1 CIRCASSIAN LONG KNIFE** with horn and ivory handle. 15-inch blade has three grooves on each side, ornamented in scroll. Very long pointed tip. Width 1¾ inch. Leather covered scabbard has ivory ball tip. Price, $12.00.

**6908B. 1 CIRCASSIAN LONG KNIFE** with 15-inch blade which has one deep blood gutter on each side, two sharpened edges and long pointed tip. Handle has one side white ivory, the other horn. Leather covered scabbard has one iron band with hole for sling. Price, $10.

**6908C. 1 CIRCASSIAN LONG KNIFE** with 10-inch wavy blade, embossed full length with birds at rest and in flight. A rare blade with long point. Horn handle checkered. Leather covered scabbard with iron ball tip and iron band for sling. Price, $15.00.

**0-875. PAIR ANCIENT CHINESE SWORDS.** 17-inch double-edged blade, ornamented bronze guard and pommel, fluted hilt, relief ornamented mouth piece, band and tip. Imitation tortoise shell lacquered scabbard. Price the pair, $12.00; singly, $7.00.

**0-877. ANCIENT PERSIAN SWORD.** 32-inch double-etched straight sharpened blade, covered with relief ornamentation inscription and figures of Persians in ancient dress. Shows traces of original silver inlaid. Metal hilt, with sword-breaking guards. Inlaid ornamented. Rare old weapon. Price, $17.50.

**0-877A. A SIMILAR SWORD.** With 26½-inch blade. Price, $15.00.

**0-859. ANCIENT DUELLING DAGGER OR "MAIN GAUCHE."** From the Lawson-Johnston collection. Demmin illustrates similar dagger in the Dresden museum. Dagger is held in the left hand to ward off blows and to catch and snap the opponent's sword blade in the comb-like teeth steel blade. Full length 26 inches, weight 2 pounds 6 ounces, widest width of blade 2¾ inches, open space between the teeth 5/16 inch. Sharpened point and back edge. Length of blade 18 inches. Armorer's seal mark, "Crescent and ball." 7½-inch guard or quillions curved in inverse direction. Rare 16th century museum exhibit. Sold to museum.

**0-918. ANTIQUE DAGGER.** 10-inch double-edged, tapered steel blade with guard or quillions curved downwards with thumb ring, grooved hilt, complete with wood scabbard, metal relief ornamented. Loop for fastening to the belt. Full length 14¾ inches. This may be a COPY of ancient sword; if so it is perfect enough to pass for genuine. Price, $19.85.

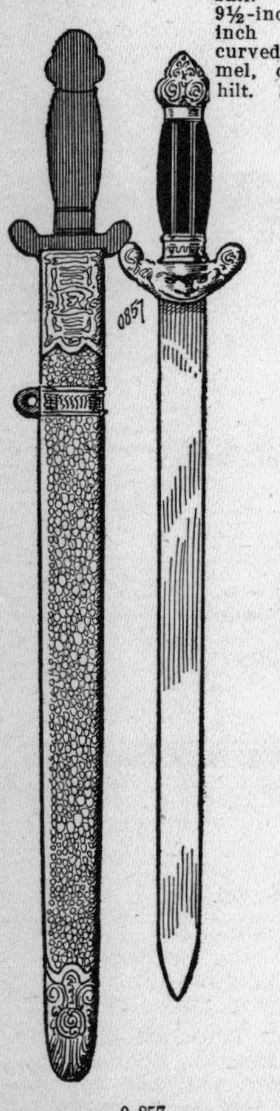

**0-847. INDIA BATTLE HAMMER PIKE.** Used by horsemen with 13½-inch dirk attached, contained in hollow handle. The pike extends 7½ inches below the bronze hand (width of the hand 2 inches). Top of the pike ends in bronze tiger head. 17½-inch handle. ⅞ inch diameter, left-hand screw, bell top silver-chased knob. Rare old weapon from the Lawson-Johnston sale. Price, $20.00.

**CHINESE SWORD.** With carved bone handle and scabbard, figures of Chinese women, flowers, etc.; total length is 18 inches; blade 11¼ inches. Price, $8.75.

**EAST INDIA SWORD.** With curved blade, leather scabbard. Price, $7.50.

**AFRICAN NATIVE-MADE DAGGER.** With ornaments, leather scabbard. Blade has needle point. Price, $6.85.

**SIDE ARM SWORD.** With imitation tortoise shell scabbard, bronze handle, with short, engraved guard; total length 18 inches. Price, $9.85.

**0-857. PAIR ANCIENT CHINESE DOUBLE SWORDS IN SHARKSKIN COVERED SCABBARD.** Double-edged 7½-inch steel blades. Chinese masked faces ornamented guards nd pommel. Black bone guard hilt. One side of the ilt is flat in order to allow the PAIR of swords to be contained in single scabbard. Ornamented bronze mask, bands and tip. Polished sharkskin covering over the wood scabbard. Weight of the two swords is 3 po nds. From the Lawson-Johnston sale. Price the pa r, $18.85.

**D-891. MOORISH DAGGER** with 9-inch slightly curved blade, 5-inch hard wood handle, copper bound, with wide copper pommel. Scabbard of very heavy brass embossed in various designs, flowers, leaves, scrolls etc. Scabbard has the usual Moorish curved tip, with two rings for sash cord. Price, $9.50.

**0-882. ANTIQUE DAGGER, WITH BRONZE FIGURE OF HUNTER HOLDING FUSE LOCK GUN.** From the Lawson-Johnston sale. 8-inch double-edged steel blade, pitted and rusted, but still in fair order, with bronze guard and figure of hunter and doe forming the hilt. About 300 years old. Price, $18.85.

**0-885. ANTIQUE NAVAL OFFICER'S DIRK.** With carved ivory hilt, relief ornamented bronze acorn end guard, 8-inch double-edged steel blade. Complete with bronze scabbard, two rings. Well preserved; relief ornamented. Price, $12.85.

**0-856. ANCIENT GERMAN BATTLE AXE.** "Fuss-Streight" axe, the old-time German soldiers' favorite weapon. Axe, handle and pole can be taken apart for concealment or convenience in carrying. The axe is steel or iron, 6⅝ inches long, 4½-inch face, fastened to iron handle by large thumb screw, 2-foot pole with square-shape socket for the wood shaft, ⅞-inch socket hole. Rare old weapon. From Nevinson sale, Stephens' auction rooms, London. Sold to museum.

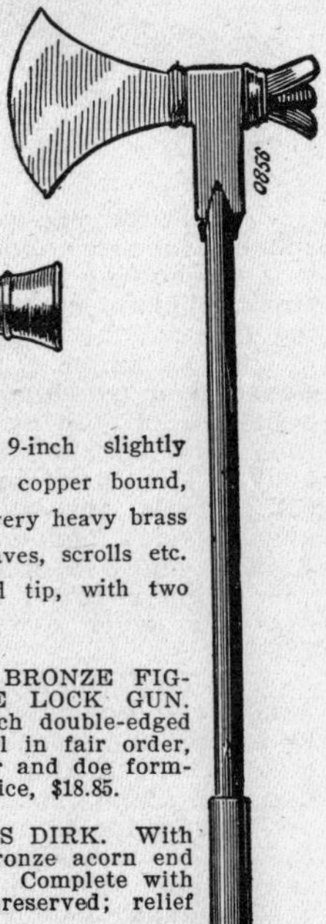

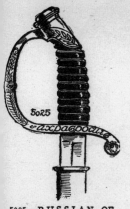

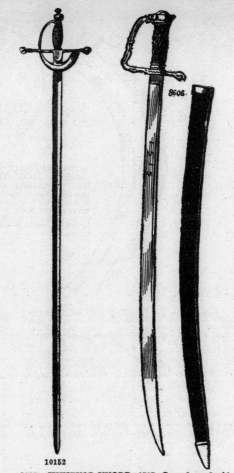

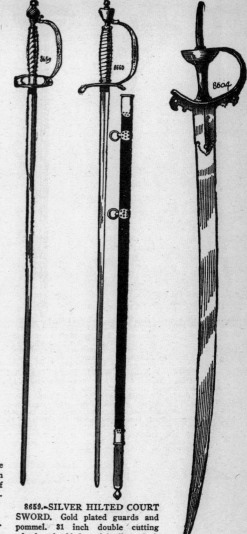

**5025.—RUSSIAN OFFICER'S SWORD.** Captured at Balaclava. Curved steel blade, brass guard inscribed A. x P. A. 6 P O C M 6. Rare relic of the battle made famous by Tennyson's Poem, "The Charge of the Light Brigade." Price, $50.00.

**8603.—** SCOTCH CLAYMORE. Basket hilt is of the 18th century, the blade is of a much earlier period, is 32 inches in length with center groove,

Width at the hilt 1½ inches. We believe this blade to be a genuine old word supplied by famous sword maker to Scottish Highland Chieftain. blades made by Farara in Shakespeare's time were considered worth their weight in gold. Bargain price, $100.00.

**8684.—LORD SHEFFIELD'S YEOMANRY SWORD FROM SHEFFIELD PARK SALE.** Used by armored troop, raised by Lord Sheffield in 1787. Old flint pistol that came with this sword is carved "Royal Foresters." Made is 30½ inches, hand forged steel. Three guard handle. Price, $17.50.

**8659.—SILVER HILTED COURT SWORD.** Gold plated guards and pommel. 31 inch double cutting edged rapier blade, originally etched, now worn off. Price, $15.00.

**8660.—GEORGE FIRST RAPIER.** Gold-plated chased mountings. 31 inch double cutting edged blade, original inscription worn off. Silver wire wrapped hilt. The leather scabbard is in poor order. Handsome gold etched mountings on scabbard. Price, $35.00.

**8606A.** 17th CENTURY GERMAN HUNTING SWORD, with 4-inch grip, inlaid with ivory strips. Brass pommel, strap shows hunting dog biting wild boar on nose. Cross bar ends in gargoyle. Small brass guard shows forest scene with dog and wild boar. 25-inch wide at blade. Price, $12.50. Similar to illustration No. 8606 on page 195.

**8606B.** OLD FRENCH HUNTING SWORD, with raised brass grip, strap and hand guard. 24½-inch flat blade with many grooves or blood gutters. Price, $11.00.

**8680.—GEORGE I. PERIOD OFFICER'S SWORD.** With hand wrought steel hilt, 32 inch slightly curved steel blade. Double cutting edge near the point. Engraved black bone handle, fine workmanship. Price, $18.85.

**8681.—GEORGE III. COURT SWORD.** Cut steel handle and guard, angular rapier shaped, 31 inch blade. Sword is work of art. Price, $17.50.

**8682.—MILITARY SWORD.** George III. period, kind used by non-commissioned artillery officers in the American Revolutionary War. Black bone grooved hilt, single steel square shaped guard. 31 inch slightly curved blade, rare pattern. Leather scabbard, iron mountings. Engraved "C. Bowns, Bank Top." With stud for shoulder belt, good order. Price, $12.50.

**8683.—EARLY GEORGIAN MILITARY SWORD WITH CROWN, G. R.** Military trophy, engraved on the inch blade, stamped Solingen. Rust has eaten two holes through the center of the blade. Antique pattern hilt and large flat shaped guard Old relic which shows extensive use. Price, $10.00.

7

**8606.—HUNTING SWORD, 1515.** Carved on the blade (from the Spiller collection); 22 inch ancient pattern blade, horn hilt, bronze single guard with relief figure of hunter with horn, gargoyle cross guard, old leather scabbard. Price, $35.00.

**8706.—ANTIQUE PERSIAN SIDE ARM SWORD.** 17½ inch double edged blade, with deep center channel. Both sides of the blade nearly covered with gilt inlaid and etched inscriptions. Width near the hilt 2 inches. Bone handle, scabbard inlaid with gilt and pearl shell. Iron band. Shoulder sling holder. Price, $18.50.

**10106.—BATTLE OF WATERLOO PERIOD FRENCH SIDE ARM SWORD.** Engraved on the blade Jackson & Tanvier, 1815. Length of blade slightly curved 25 inches, brass guards, leather scabbard, with brass knot for the shoulder sling. Price, $15.00.

**10152.—ANCIENT SPANISH RAPIER.** Blade stamped with old time maker's name, now indistinct from age, full length 44½ inches, blade 38½ inches; woven copper wire covered hilt, 8 inch cross guard; tempered blade that in olden times could be bent from the point to the hilt; cup guard; rare weapon, in serviceable order. Price, $25.00.

**10153.—ANCIENT SPANISH SWORD.** With double edge cutting blade, with wrought iron cross guard with large cup guard; evidently a fine sword in its time; kind that would be used by Spanish officers of the period of Columbus. Found in the Island of Santo Domingo; has been misused by negro natives. Blade is 35 inches in length; needs restoring, offered as is. Price, $18.00.

**10154.—ANCIENT SPANISH CAVALIER'S SWORD.** Double edge cutting blade 35 inches long, 7 inch cross guard, wood hilt (not original), cup guard. Kind of blade that could be bent from point to hilt. Found in Island of Santo Domingo; second hand, serviceable order, offered as is. Price, $15.00.

**10157.—HAITIAN ARMY SABRE.** 31 inch steel blade, bone hilt, iron cross guard; serviceable old relic that no doubt has helped to place some of the many colored men in President's office in Haiti. Price, $4.60.

**8659.—SILVER HILTED COURT SWORD.** Gold plated guards and pommel. 31 inch double cutting edged rapier blade, originally etched, now worn off. Price, $15.00.

**8604.—ANTIQUE INDIA MARATHA SWORD.** Of the 18th century period, extremely wide blade with pike pommel. Length of blade 30 inches, nearly 2 inches in width, with one large and two small grooves (blood gutters), basket handle with sword blade breaker guard. 5 inch pommel pike, full length of the sword 47 inches. Price, $38.00.

**10156.—CONFEDERATE CAVALRY OFFICER'S CIVIL WAR SABRE.** Letters C. S. cast in brass guard, surrounded with oak leaves: 32 inch blade, double edge at the point; iron scabbard with brass rings; kind made in the South during the Civil War; found in northern city, evidently captured. Price, $27.50.

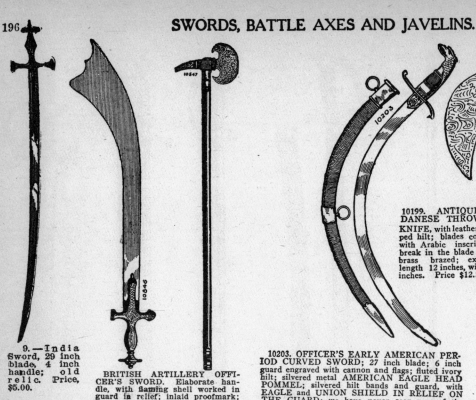

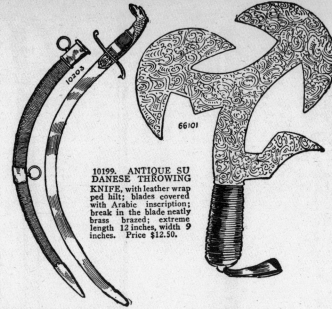

**10199. ANTIQUE SU DANESE THROWING KNIFE,** with leather wrapped hilt; blades covered with Arabic inscription; break in the blade neatly brass brazed; extreme length 12 inches, width 9 inches. Price $12.50.

**9.—India Sword,** 29 inch blade, 4 inch handle; old relic. Price, $5.00.

**BRITISH ARTILLERY OFFICER'S SWORD.** Elaborate handle, with flaming shell worked in guard in relief; inlaid proofmark; thin blade; etched, with crown and flaming shell; steel scabbard; serviceable order. Price, $12.00.

**10846. KORAH SWORD FROM NAPOUL, INDIA.** Inlaid silver hilt; scimiter sword blade, 2 feet long, 4 inches wide at the end. Price $15.00.

**10547. TRIPOLITAN PACHA TOMAHAWK BATTLE AXE;** gilt inlaid decorated scroll work on the blade and pike; size across the face 4¾ inches; length from the face of the blade to the end of the pike 8 inches; length of the handle 3 feet; old faded paper label is marked "Azza-Scure de Principe Josef Pacha Caramand de Regno in Tripoli de Barbaria." Price $20.00.

**10203. OFFICER'S EARLY AMERICAN PERIOD CURVED SWORD;** 27 inch blade; 6 inch guard engraved with cannon and flags; fluted ivory hilt; silvered metal AMERICAN EAGLE HEAD POMMEL; silvered hilt bands and guard, with EAGLE and UNION SHIELD IN RELIEF ON THE GUARD; we have never seen any of the 1776 or 1812 officers' swords with SO GREAT A CURVE; leather scabbard, with silvered metal war mountings. Price $50.00.

**10852. BURMESE DHA SWORD;** native artistic decorated metalwork 12½ inch hilt, 16½ inch blade. Price $9.85.

**8606H. OLD ENGLISH HUNTING SWORD,** with 3½-inch horn grip, brass pommel and strap. Brass guard in filigree work shows head of King with crown. 19-inch plain flat blade with armourer's mark set in. Price $10.00.

**10200. ANCIENT DYAK WAVY FLUTED KRIS,** with Damascene center; with side and hilt grooves; dark colored hardwood handle; fibre wrapped hilt; full length of blade 21½ inches; fine speciment of native made watered Damasck work. Price $17.40.

**10862 EUROPEAN ARMY OFFICER'S SWORD;** 30 inch steel polished blade; three guards (German silver); lion head pommel; polished hilt complete with single ring; leather scabbard. Price $6.75.

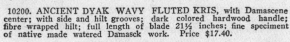

**10847. ANTIQUE INDIA MARHATTA SWORD,** wide guard, short grip, round pommel with 4-inch stud slightly curved. 40½-inch blade, a most unusual length except in two handed sword, braced at guard with ornamented metal, appears gold plated, with one deep wide groove on each side, and marked on both sides: ANDRIA FERRARA. He was a famous sword maker, and evidently sent blades to all parts of the world. A blade in an old sword of this type is rare. Price $65.00.

**10851. CURIOUS INDIA SAW BLADE SABRE;** 32 inch WATERED STEEL BLADE; silver inlaid ornamented work on blade and hilt. Sold to museum.

**11019. KORAH, OR EXECUTIONER'S SWORD,** from Nepaul, India; purchased at the sale of Arnold Museum, Milton Hall, Gravesend, England, 1911; the sword is polished steel; length 23¼ inches, width 6 inches; in fine serviceable order. Price $16.50.

**11019A. VERY OLD KORAH SWORD;** length 26 inches, width 3 inches; in fair order only. Price $8.85.

**10201. ANCIENT CHINESE SWORD,** with EXTRA HEAVY 18 inch blade; back of blade is over HALF INCH thick; COPPER GUARD and HILT complete with leather scabbard. Price $9.50.

**EARLY GEORGE III. PERIOD NAVY OFFICER'S DIRK;** ivory hilt with lion head pommel; gilt mountings; diamond shaped blade; full length 14 inches. Price, complete with scabbard, $8.50.

**1854D. 18th CENTURY GERMAN HUNTING SWORD,** with 5½-inch wood grip, wrapped with copper wire. 3½-inch brass cross guard. 22¼-inch wide flat blade. Price $8.50.

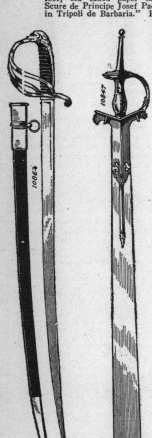

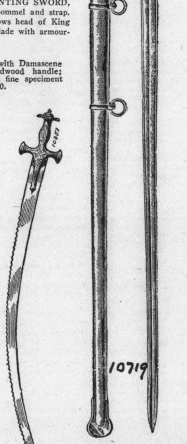

**10719. ANTIQUE DRAGOON SABRE;** straight 36½ inch two grooved blade; full length 46 inches steel guard; complete with scabbard. Price $15.00.

**10853. INDIA MUTINY RELIC JAVELIN;** 9 inch blade, 2 inches wide; relief engraving full length 38½ inches. Price $12.50.

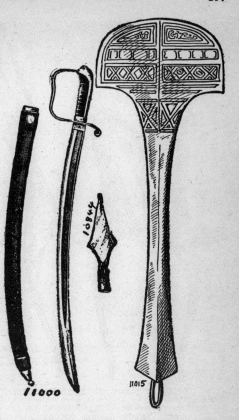

**11013. ANCIENT CARVED WAR CLUB,** from Samoa; native carved; heavy dark colored wood; length 30 inches; square butt 2¾ inches. From the Arnold Museum Collection. Price $12.00.

**11014. ANCIENT NEW GUINEA NATIVE'S SWORD SHAPED HEAVY WOOD CLUB;** dark colored, polished, carved; length 26 inches, width 23 inches. From Arnold Museum Collection. Price $10.00.

**11014A. SIMILAR CLUB,** 3¾ inches wide. Price $8.85.

**10476. GEORGE REX III. PERIOD PIKE AXE,** circular blade, 11 inch pike. Price $6.50.

**10836. PAIR OLD GERMAN SIDE ARM SWORDS;** heavy steel blade, 20 inches long, 1¾ inches wide; brass hilt and guard, with black leather scabbard; brass mountings; inspector's stamp 1839 (although swords are claimed to be much older). Price for this PAIR of rare old swords $15.00, singly $8.00.

**10837. ANTIQUE CHINESE SWORD,** with POLISHED FISH SKIN SCABBARD; relief ornamented guard and mountings; sling with belt hook; full length 29½ inches. Price $12.00.

**10849. REVOLUTIONARY WAR PERIOD NAVAL OFFICER'S SWORD,** with 31½ inch straight blade; with ivory grip; lion head pommel; single guard with anchor design; rare weapon. Price $16.50.

**10842. ANTIQUE FRENCH SWORD,** with finely curved wood hilt, with ancient GALLIC COCK POMMEL holding the guard in its mouth. On the guard is cast in relief a woman and child in grief over the dead body of a man. 31 inch blade; curved shaped watered steel, ENGRAVED WITH DATE 1713; rare old weapon. Price $20.00.

**10914. GAUNTLET SWORD OF THE 18TH CENTURY,** captured at Indian Mutiny; 31 inch straight double edge watered steel blade with strengthening guard joining the blade to the gauntlet. Length of the hilt gauntlet 12 inches, two round and one diamond shaped bosses. Ornamented in cut steel. Good serviceable order, from British collection. Price $25.00.

**10868. U. S. A. INTRENCHING SHOVEL,** new, as carried by U. S. soldiers; made of the best steel. Full length 31½ inches, the shovel blade is 8¼ inches long, width 6¾ inches, weight 27 ounces from New York Arsenal, 1910. Price 50 cents each.

**11020. IRISH CONSTABULARLY SIDE ARM SWORD BAYONET,** furnished to the Irish Police soldier with the B/L carbine, 25½ inch blade; on the back of blade next the hilt is 9 inches of heavy SAW BACK, in order no doubt to enable the soldiers to PARRY THE IRISH SHILALEIGHS. Single guard. Checkered black rubber hilt. In fine serviceable order, like new, complete with scabbard. Polished nickel mountings, stamped with the Royal Crown and the War Department broad arrow marks. (Facsimile of the one now on view in the Tower of London.) Price $2.85.

**10850. FRENCH OFFICER'S SWORD,** WATERLOO PERIOD; single brass guard; checkered ebony hilt; 26 inch gilt inlaid blade; leather scabbard. Price $10.00.

**11015. ANCIENT SAMOA CURIOUS WAR CLUB;** dark colored heavy wood, carved; length 27 inches, width 10 inches, 2½ inches thick. Price $14.50.

**10196. ANCIENT SOUTH SEA ISLAND SAVAGE'S THROWING CLUB,** similar to our No. 8663; length 16 inches, diameter 4¼ inches; called the Knob Kerrie; shaped by the natives with crude sea shell tools. Price $10.00.

**11016. OLD TIME DYAK WOOD SHIELD;** 10 rows of cross bars bamboo ornamentation with smaller row at each end; full length 48 inches, width 17 inches; fine ornament. Price $18.00.

**10843. ANTIQUE PLUG BAYONET,** of period about 1650, one of the earliest forms of bayonets made with round tapered handle for inserting plug fashion in the muzzle of the gun. Dirk shaped 12 inch blade, needle point, 1½ inches wide at the hilt. Brass guard (one end of guard broken), wood hilt, brass capped. From the Brett Collection. Price $16.50.

**10845. FRENCH GRENADIERS' SWORD,** PERIOD 1740. Engraved on the blade "Vive Le Roy," with French Coat of Arms, and on the reverse side "Grenadier de France," with etching of French Grenadier in the costume of period of 1740. Name engraved on the back of the blade, "B. Dominick Kirshbaum, Manufacturier des Sabres de la Marque au Raisin a Sohlingen." Five guards, leather hilt, 33½ inch blade. Rare old relic that tells its own history. Price $22.50.

**10831. ANCIENT COMBINATION SPADE BAYONET,** with adjustable socket for fitting on ALL THE OLD TIME MUSKETS; full length 27 inches; blade 16 inches; rare weapon. Price $10.00.

**10815. ANTIQUE SOUTH SEA ISLANDER'S WAR CLUB;** from collection of Capt. Roberts; length 34 inches; curved end with carved knob; work done with sea shells. Price $15.00.

**10860. FRENCH REPUBLIQUE BANNER TOP;** gilt metal harp with lion head, letters "R F.;" full length 16½ inches, width 6½ inches; 1½ inch socket hole; fine order. Price $8.85.

**10605. ANTIQUE ARTILLERY SABRE,** made LONDON, about the 18th century; BLADE ENGRAVED with crescent, flags and warriors; complete with scabbard. Price $14.85

**10208. CIVIL WAR OFFICER'S SWORD,** engraved on the scabbard, "Presented to Lt. Thomas Cummings, by the member of Co. H, 2nd Regt. N. Y. S. M., July 11th, 1861." Sword is the usual pattern carried by officer during the Civil War. Requires cleaning. Price $8.85.

**11000. AUSTRIAN CORPORAL SWORD;** slightly curved steel blade; steel hilt and pommel; single guard; leather scabbard; iron mouth piece and tip; average length O. M. 80; weight 1¾ pounds. Price $2.85.

**10844. REVOLUTIONARY WAR PERIOD BANNER TOP.** Brass metal (originally gilt) fastened to the top of banner pole. Length 9½ inches, width 2½ inches, ¾ inch socket. From London Collection. Price $10.00.

**11015. SAMOA OLD TIME NATIVE'S WAR CLUB,** made of dark colored heavy wood; cleaver shaped, carved, with hook on the back; length 26 inches, width 5¾ inches. From Arnold Museum. Price $12.00.

**10857. SWISS TWO HANDLED SWORD.** Double edged 46 inch wavy blade, 13½ inch relief ornamented bronze guard, 11½ inch bronze hilt fluted and ornamented. Made for use with armor. Facsimile of ANCIENT SWORD OF STATE. Full length 61 inches, weight 13 pounds' Price 18.00.

**10841. INDIA TULWER,** with extra wide blade; from London collection; inlaid silver decorated and ornamented; 30 inch curved blade, 2¾ inches wide; back rib ½ inch; single guard. Price $12.50.

Sounding "taps" over the grave at the burial of a soldier originated with Captain Tidball. On the retirement from the peninsula in August, 1862, Horse Battery A, Second artillery, was serving with the rear guard, and on reaching Yorktown one of the cannoneers died and was buried there. Not wishing to stir up the enemy by firing three rounds from the battery guns, as was customary, Captain Tidball substituted the sounding of taps ("lights out"), which impressive custom has since been observed at all military funerals at the conclusion of the ceremony.—*N. Y. Sun.*

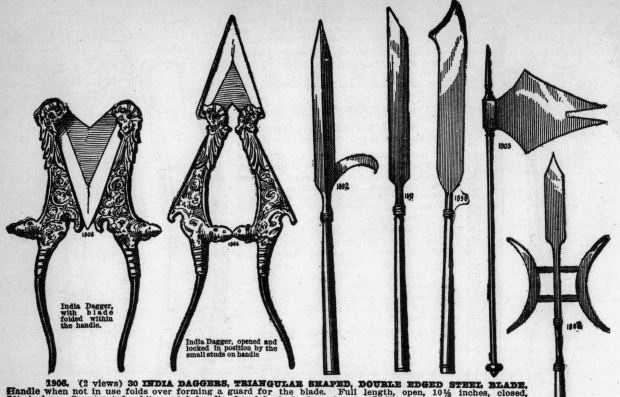

India Dagger, with blade folded within the handle.

India Dagger, opened and locked in position by the small studs on handle.

**1906.** '(2 views) 30 **INDIA DAGGERS, TRIANGULAR SHAPED, DOUBLE EDGED STEEL BLADE.** Handle when not in use folds over forming a guard for the blade. Full length, open, 10½ inches, closed, 7½ inches. Ornamented white metal handle. Intended only for decorative use. **$2.65 each.**

**1881. INDIA HAND GUARD SWORD.** Light steel etched guard. Useful only for decorating or the theatre. Price **$3.85.**

**1888. 8 DOUBLE EDGED SPEARS,** with double crescent-shaped side cutters; 34-inch steel shaft with socket for pole. Unique weapon. Price **$5.00 each.**

**1889. 5 LONG WAVY AND ETCHED SPEARS,** with two curved hook side cutters; length 34 inches. Steel shaft for socket of pole. Price **$6.00 each.**

**1890.** Similar to 1889, spear is quadrangular shaped, with two side curved hook cutters. Price **$5.00**

**1891.** 4 similar to 1889, with straight wavy edged centre spears, with two curved hook side cutters. Length of shaft, 34 inches, with socket for pole. Price **$5.00 each.**

**1892. 4 SPEARS** with curved hook side cutters, double edged blade; length, 33 inches. Price **$4.85 each.**

**1896. 8 ORIENTAL SPEARS,** full length, 35 inches; 16-inch cutting blade, with heavy back; double point. Price **$5.00.**

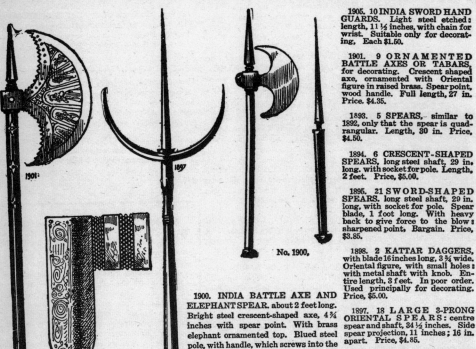

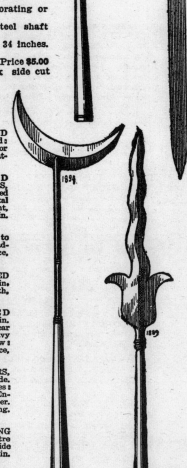

No. 1900.

**1900. INDIA BATTLE AXE AND ELEPHANT SPEAR.** about 2 feet long. Bright steel crescent-shaped axe, 4¾ inches with spear point. With brass elephant ornamented top. Blued steel pole, with handle, which screws into the pole and contains small spear. Suitable for decorating. **$3.50.**

**1905. 10 INDIA SWORD HAND GUARDS.** Light steel etched: length, 11½ inches, with chain for wrist. Suitable only for decorating. Each **$1.50.**

**1901. 9 ORNAMENTED BATTLE AXES OR TABARS,** for decorating. Crescent shaped axe, ornamented with Oriental figure in raised brass. Spear point, wood handle. Full length, 27 in. Price **$4.35.**

**1893. 5 SPEARS,** similar to 1892, only that the spear is quadrangular. Length, 30 in. Price **$4.50.**

**1894. 6 CRESCENT-SHAPED SPEARS,** long steel shaft, 29 in. long. with socket for pole. Length, 2 feet. Price, **$5.00.**

**1895. 21 SWORD-SHAPED SPEARS.** long steel shaft, 29 in. long, with socket for pole. Spear blade, 1 foot long. With heavy back to give force to the blow; sharpened point, Bargain. Price, **$3.85.**

**1898. 2 KATTAR DAGGERS,** with blade 16 inches long, 3¾ wide. Oriental figure, with small holes; with metal shaft with knob. Entire length, 3 feet. In poor order. Used principally for decorating. Price, **$5.00.**

**1897. 18 LARGE 3-PRONG ORIENTAL SPEARS:** centre spear and shaft, 34½ inches. Side spear projection, 11 inches; 16 in. apart. Price, **$4.85.**

**1903. 16 INDIA BATTLE AXES,** with double pointed axe, 6-inch face, with spear point; blued steel handle. **$3.00.**

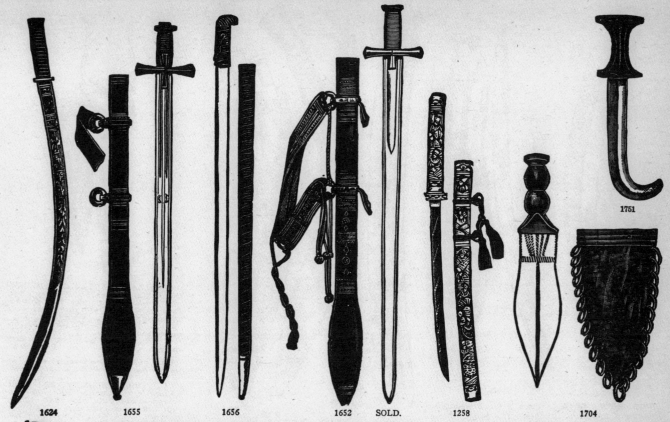

1624     1655     1656     1652  SOLD.     1258     1704

1751

D68

> Japanese Samurai Sword, must never be withdrawn from the scabbard without shedding blood. If accidentally withdrawn, the owner would prick his arm or hand so as to draw blood. Sword would be shown by withdrawing all but point of the blade.

**1624. LONG SWORD.** Finely etched steel blade, with trophy figures, flowers and other designs etched on both sides of the blade. Maker's name engraved on blade, "Thomas Gill, Birmingham. Warranted never to fail." Blade 1⅜ inches to the hilt, tapering to point; length of blade, 34½ inches; no guard; leather hilt, wire wrapped.

**1655. SOUDAN DERVISH'S SWORD,** 1¾ inches wide; 31½-inch double edged sharpened blade; leather pommel, and hand grip, iron cross guard and scabbard guides, with native made leather ornamented scabbard, with brass rings; with paper attached, stating the history of the capture of this sword, but writing is now indistinct. Price, $16.00.

**1656. AFRICAN NATIVE'S SWORD.** Straight blade, 34 inches in length, 1 inch in width, with cord wrapped hilt: woven cord pommel, with cord around scabbard; good order.

**D 68. 1 SACRIFICIAL KNIFE FROM CEYLON,** an early pattern, total length 11 inches. Carved ivory handle, brass bound, with ornamented inlaid blade. Very heavy. Price $8.00.

**D69.** 1 large sacrificial knife from Ceylon. Total length 12½ inches. Carved ivory handle, brass bound. Very heavy blade with thick back and large blood gutters. Evidently used in killing the larger animals for sacrifice. Price, $8.00.

**D 70. 1 EARLY SACRIFICIAL KNIFE FROM CEYLON.** Total length 12 inches. Carved ivory handle with silver top. Heavy blade brass mounted with two inlaid brass grooves, and inlaid brass scroll work. Shows actual use. Price $10.00.

**D 71. 1 SMALL SACRIFICIAL KNIFE,** small pattern from Ceylon. Carved horn handle, silver mounted. Total length 10 inches. Blade has heavy thick back, brass inlaid, with inlaid brass scroll work on blade and two grooves. Price $9.00.

**No. 11. OLD CANDLE SNUFFERS,** rusty, in poor order. Came to us with a lot of antique gun parts from Europe. Price, $1.50 each.

**No. 12.**

> It is only of late years that surgical instrument makers in this country began to put on the lances and other sharp cutting instruments, the same kind of cutting edge that the Japanese had on their swords for a thousand years back.

**1258. CHINESE SWORD AND SCABBARD.** Hilt measures 5 inches in length; 15-inch blade; full length in scabbard, 27 inches; practically new; handsomely carved with Chinese heads and figures; sold as are; made for show. Price, $3.90.

**No. 1704. AFRICAN NATIVE MADE DAGGER.** With scabbard covered with snake skin, and ornamented with brass rings; blade is polished, 7 inches long, 2¼ wide; ornamented polished wood handle; full length, 10½ inches; no doubt considered by the natives as a work of art. Price, $7.85.

**1751. TWO AFRICAN NATIVES' KNIVES.** With double edged hook blade, 7½ inches in length; full length, 11 inches. Price, $6.75 each.

**D 96. 1 SOMALIA KNIFE** with 9-inch trade blade. Horn handle has large leather knob at pommel. Leather scabbard has wood core, and is ornamented with circles resembling our bull's eyes. Price, $8.00.

**D 97. 1 INDIA THRUSTING KNIFE OR DAGGER.** 6-inch curved blade of plain steel. Oval open handle, wide on outer side for protection, with iron stud on end. Price, $6.00.

**1635. SOUDAN DERVISH'S NATIVE MADE SWORD,** without scabbard, otherwise similar to 1652; in good order. Price, $12.00.

**No. 12. U. S. NAVY SCISSORS.** From the Boston Navy Yard auction sale on change of regulation. Fine steel scissors, 7 inches long, made by York. Bargain price, 30 cents. Good value for 75 cents.

**1654. SOUDAN DERVISH'S SWORD,** blade 2 inches wide, 37½ inches long; full length, 43 inches; has one long and two short grooves, double edged, sharpened; brass cross guard and scabbard guide; no scabbard. Price, $14.00.

**No. 702. FIVE JAPANESE CAVALRY SWORDS.** The old Samurai blade fitted to modern handle with steel scabbard; relic of the Jap-Russian war, purchased in Nagasaki, Japan, 1904. All in good second-hand, serviceable order. Price $9.50 each.

**JAPANESE NAVAL OFFICER'S SWORD,** with white sharkskin grip; gilt handle, engraved hilt, fine old etched blade, fitted to modern hilt and scabbard. Purchased in Japan, December, 1904. Price, $20.00.

No. 1748      No. 2

**No. 1748. CENTRAL AFRICAN NATIVE DAGGER.** Crude steel double edged blade, with hollow on each side of the blade; from 3 to 5 inches long. Hilt is covered with fine woven brass wire, wood scabbard, with wire and cord fastening. From Zambesi. Price, $3.75 each.

**1748A.** Similar Dagger, not so finely ornamented, $3.75.

**No. 2. HUNTER'S BOWIE KNIFE.** With 6-inch blade, leather scabbard and open loops for belt. Please note that the knives now in stock do NOT have the cross bar on hilt as shown in cut. Price, 95 cents each.

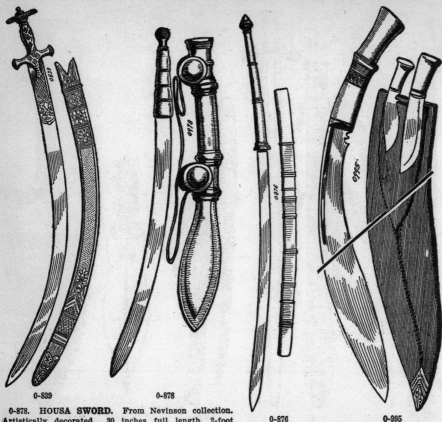

0-839   0-878

0-876   0-995

**0-878. HOUSA SWORD.** From Nevinson collection. Artistically decorated. 30 inches full length, 2-foot blade, 1½ inches wide, leather hilt, brass ball pommel. Scabbard at the bottom is bottle shaped. Illustration shows the leather ornamented disks for covering the belt fastenings. Ornamented leather hangers. Rare pattern; highly decorated. Price, $16.50.

**0-839. ANCIENT INDIA TULWER SWORD, WITH SCABBARD.** Damascus steel, 30-inch, curved blade. Gold and silver chased ornamentation work on the blade and hilt. Leather scabbard beautifully embossed and decorated. Ornamented silver tip. No doubt an historical sword.

**0-839A. PAIR ANCIENT HINDOOSTAN TULWER SWORDS.** Similar to 0-839, but without ornamentation. Label on scabbard states that they were sold in Calcutta in 1855 as loot taken from Lahore, 1848, the second Sikh War. From English officer's collection in 1911. 28-inch steel curved blade with iron handle, with dark-green colored velvet over the wood scabbard, red velvet shoulder belt, with SILVER BUCKLE AND SILVER BROOCH. Price for the two swords, with two silver buckles and two silver brooches, $35.00; singly, $18.00.

**0-994. ANCIENT PERSIAN SWORD.** In green sharkskin scabbard. Rich silver mountings, 17½-inch double-edged blade with very deep centre gutter, bone hilt with ornamented silver escutcheon. Scabbard has large mouth and tip in native silver, ornamented. Antique gilt inlaid ornamental work. Full length 2 feet. Price, $25.00.

**0-783. HANDSOME MINIATURE PERSIAN SCIMITER.** Handle and blade covered with gilt etching, 5½-inch curved blade, 4-inch curved hilt. Beautiful ornament for lady's desk as paper cutter. Price, $6.50.

**0-784. HANDSOME MINIATURE CRUSADERS' SWORD PAPER CUTTER.** 6½-inch straight blade, covered with gilt etching. Full length 8½ inches. Rare pattern. Price, $4.85.

**0-780. AFRICAN NATIVE'S CURIOUS KNIFE AND SCABBARD.** Crude ornamentation. Full length 7¾ inches. Price, $4.85.

**0-842. ZULU NATIVE HIDE SHIELD.** Captured at the battle of Rook's Drift. Has saber thrust cut. Length 3 feet, 21 inches wide, dark-colored, shows much usage. Price, $15.00.

**0-983. SAVAGE NATIVE'S IVORY TUSK TRUMPET.** Crudely ornamented. Length 10½x1¾ inches. Shows much usage. Price, $6.85.

**0-876. BURMESE DHA SWORD.** Ivory and silver hilt, 20½-inch sharpened steel blade, 12-inch solid ivory handle, with native ornamented silver band and pommel. Dark-colored hard wood scabbard with silver and fibre bands. Price, $18.85.

**0-995A. 1 INDIA NATIVE GOURKA KNIFE** with leather covered scabbard WITH TWO EXTRA SMALL KNIVES contained in pocket at mouth piece of scabbard. Heavy blade, 15-inch. Darl colored hard wood carved handle. Metal tipped scabbard. Price, $15.00. In stock Jan., **1927.**

**0-755. KAFIR NATIVE'S WAR WEAPON.** Artistic iron and brass wire woven around pole with knob, to which is fitted a British sword bayonet (no doubt captured). Full length is 4 feet. Rare specimen. Price, $7.50.

**0-755A. KAFIR NATIVE'S CLUB.** Hard wood pole with knob on the end. Woven around the pole is series of brass and iron wire, making a very artistic appearance. Full length 41½ inches. Price, $5.50.

**0-946. ANCIENT INDIA JAVELIN.** 8½-inch spear-head, 25-inch tapered steel ornamented handle, native-made. Fine order. Price, $7.85.

**0-961. CINGALESE NATIVE'S CARVED AND ORNAMENTED IVORY HILTED KNIFE.** Silver pommel, 7-inch native-made steel blade. Wood scabbard. Full length 12 inches. Fine specimen. Price, $12.50.

**0-858. DOUBLE BARBED IRON SPEAR,** with socket for pole. Full length 23½ inches, spear 2¼ inches. Two folding side barbs 3 inches long. Rare weapon. Price, $4.85.

**0-884. CARVED IVORY SWORD HANDLE.** From Bennim (Africa). Length 4½ inches, diameter 1¼ inches. Carved turtle pommel, 10 figures of Africans artistically carved by the natives on the hilt. Price, $8.85.

**0-708. ANCIENT FLAG POLE SPEAR HEAD.** Bronze, with steel fastening screws. Full length 3 inches, width 1 inch. Price, 55 cents.

**1712B. ANCIENT HEADSMAN'S AXE.** From European collection. Price, $14.75.

**0-855. ANCIENT WAR MACE.** Used by India horsemen, with guard handle highly ornamented. From the Lawson-Johnston collection sale. Full length 27½ inches, weight 3 pounds, 1½-inch ball mace. Pole is partly chased and silvered, deep ornamental line cuts. Silver hand guards, velvet lined. Very decorative. Disk-shaped pommel. We have two pairs. Price the pair, $12.00; singly, $6.50.

**21J. 1 EARLY KOTAR OR THRUSTING DAGGER** with 8-inch wavy blade with thick tip for palm leaf writing. Plain iron handle with two cross bars and extension sides. Price, $8.75.

**22J. 1 INDIA THRUSTING KNIFE** with 11-inch blade 2¼ inches wide. Heavy brass handle with two cross bars and 8-inch extension sides. Price, $8.00.

**When ordering allow a second choice, as we may have item similar to one ordered.**

**24J. 1 INDIA THRUSTING KNIFE OR KATAR** from Mahrattas Tribe. 6½-inch grooved blade with ribs. Iron handle with four cross grip bars and 6½-inch extension sides, all gold inlaid. Plush covered wood scabbard. Price, $8.25.

**25J. 1 EARLY INDIA THRUSTING DAGGER** from Nepal. 5½-inch blade, has two ribs and is 3 inches wide. Gold inlaid iron handle. Wood scabbard. Price, $8.75.

**26J. 1 CURIOUS SHAPED INDIA KATAR** with thick pointed 9-inch blade with two wide ribs. Handle has only one cross bar grip. Evidently an early pattern. Wood scabbard. Price, $9.50.

**SW27. FRENCH ARMY OFFICER'S SWORD,** period of 1848. 32-inch long narrow blade, the upper end blued, with gilt designs. Round pommel, hard wood checkered hilt, brass guard showing Gaelic cock between four draped flags, with foot on cannon ball. NO SCABBARD. Price $11.

1712B.     08;0

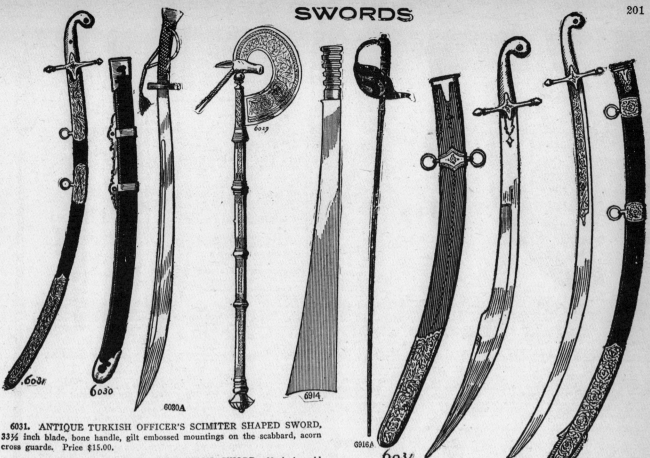

**6031.** ANTIQUE TURKISH OFFICER'S SCIMITER SHAPED SWORD, 33½ inch blade, bone handle, gilt embossed mountings on the scabbard, acorn cross guards. Price $15.00.

**6032.** ANTIQUE PERSIAN PRESENTATION SWORD, 29 inch gold inlaid blade with scroll work and hunting scenes, blood stain rust marks, ivory hilt, ornamented gilt metal scabbard mountings in relief. Price $30.00.

**6031-A.** ANTIQUE TURKISH OFFICER'S SCIMITER SHAPED SWORD, with rare pattern sword blade. Silver inlaid, embossed gilt ornamented guard, bone handle with scabbard guide, leather covered wood scabbard, brass mounted. Price $18.50.

**6914.** BURMESE EXECUTIONER'S SWORD, bone handle, with ribbed hilt, silver mounted, 19 inch watered steel blade 3 inch across the end, bevelled cutting edge blade. Price $15.85.

**6915.** ANTIQUE BURMESE SWORD called DHA, with long ornamented silver hilt, 17½ inch native made watered steel blade, with triangular shaped pointed wood scabbard. Price $12.85.

**6916-A.** U. S. N. BROAD SWORD, used on board navy war ships for fencing. Steel blade, large basket guard, shark skin grip, weight 27 ounces, length of blade 33 inches, slightly rusted. Serviceable order. Price $3.50.

**6030A..** CHINESE BOXERS' SWORD with Scabbard, 33½ inch grooved blade, 2⅛ inches wide, Mandarin hat shaped pommel, 7 inch hilt, wood scabbard ornamented brass mountings, full length 40½ inches. Relic of the Boxer War.

**6029.** ANTIQUE PERSIAN PROCESSIONAL AXE with circular blade, antelope head and horns, silver inlaid hunting scenes and scroll work, full length 21¾ inches. Price $14.85.

**REVOLUTIONARY WAR OFFICER'S ARTILLERY SWORD,** Scimiter Shaped, 4 inch curved single guard, gilt inlaid engraving of crown with shield, lion rampant and two castles (Spanish), "Plus Ultra" warranted with scroll ornamentation, weight 2¾ pounds, length of blade 29 inches. Fine serviceable order complete with two ring scabbard, the shoe of the scabbard shows much wear. From Adam Oliver's collection. Tradition, "found on Mexican battlefield and used by C. S. A. officer." Price $50.00.

**6087.** BRITISH ARMY SABRE stamped 1831 with crown, blade 33 inches, steel scabbard, fair order. Price $4.85.

**6069.** GEORGE III. PERIOD OFFICER'S SABRE, 36 inch blade engraved with monogram A. R. (Runkel), Solingen. Rare pattern, leather and iron scabbard. Price $9.85.

**6065.** TURKISH ARMY OFFICER'S SWORD, silver mounted, with star and crest in relief on the hilt and scabbard, 31 inch steel double-edged large quill back blade, bone handle. Price $12.50.

**6066.** TURKISH ARMY OFFICER'S SWORD, silver mounted guard and scabbard, proof marked, 31 inch steel blade with two large grooves, leather scabbard, bone hilt, serviceable order, weight 1 pound 9 ounces. Price $17.85.

**6066-A.** ANTIQUE TURKISH OFFICER'S SCIMITER SWORD, double edge quill back gold inlaid blade, with Turkish inscriptions, 7 inch silver cross guard, length of blade 31 inches, leather scabbard, silver bands and rings. Price $14.85.

**6066-B.** ANTIQUE TURKISH OFFICER'S SCIMITER SWORD, brass mounted, in good order. Price $7.85.

**6052.** DERVISH SPEAR HEAD with bullet hole through the blade, captured at Omdurman, from the Middlesex (Edinburgh Castle) Museum collection sale at the same time the famous Chesapeake flag was sold. The blade is 15 inches long, 4 inches wide, hole evidently made by bullet from British rifle in repelling attack of the native Sudanese. Price $50.00.

**6044.** SIXTEENTH CENTURY ITALIAN DAGGER (copy), pierced steel ornamental work on blade, ornamented hand guard, wire wrapped hilt, full length 15 inches. Price $6.50.

**6047.** EMPIRE PERIOD FIRST NAPOLEON DAGGER, double edged diamond shaped steel blade, gilt etched with gilt hilt and acorn hand guards, ornamented scabbard, full length 18 inches. Price $7.50.

**6048.** Oriental Knife 5¾ inch blade, black bone handle, brass mounted. Price $4.50.

**6048-A.** SMALL KNIFE with engravings on the blade. Price $5.50.

**6049.** SPANISH FOLDING KNIFE, with bone ornamented handle, 9-inch blade, folds into the handle as in the ordinary knife. Price $9.00.

**6049-A.** Ditto. Eight-inch Curved Blade, $8.50.

The above knives sold only to responsible collectors as we will not endanger the public safety by selling to any one who has the price.

**6050.** ANCIENT BATTLE AXE (copy), showing relief engraving as on the original now in King's Museum, length of blade 5½ inches. Price $4.50.

**6051.** Exact Copy of Seventeenth Century Halberd Head, showing relief engraving, same as on the original now in European Museum, length 21 inches, width 9½ inches. Price $6.85.

One day, seeing a number of Chinamen throwing their large umbrella-shaped hats into the Yangtze River, he inquired the cause of such seeming waste by the usually economical Chinamen. They said, "See that flock of ducks down the river. We throw our hats in the river so that they will float down among them. At first the ducks are alarmed, but by-and-by, when we see that they are no longer afraid, we get in the water and under cover of our hats swim down among the ducks and catch hold of them by the legs." This may seem like a fish story, but I can readily believe it to be true after seeing such immense flocks of ducks from the deck of our steamer.—New Yorker on the Yangtze. Copyrighted by Francis Bannerman.

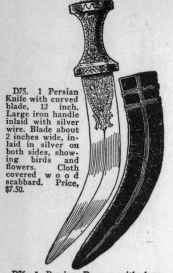

**D75.** 1 Persian Knife with curved blade, 12 inch. Large iron handle inlaid with silver wire. Blade about 2 inches wide, inlaid in silver on both sides, showing birds and flowers. Cloth covered wood scabbard. Price, $7.50.

**D76.** 1 Persian Dagger with home made bone handle and curved blade, 9-inch. Blade has thrusting point, two sharp edges, 2 wide blood gutters and raised scroll work of flowers on both sides. Wood scabbard covered with plush and bound with gilt lace. Price, $8.00.

**D27-15. ITALIAN STILETTO** with 5-inch three sided blade with sharp point. 1¾-inch cross bar, 3-inch handle. The whole dagger with handle is cross shaped. Price $4.50.

**D78.** 1 Arab dagger with silver mounted horn handle, embossed. 8-inch curved blade with two sharp edges, and large single ridge on each side, running to tip. Wood scabbard, leather covered. Price, $6.75.

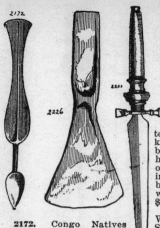

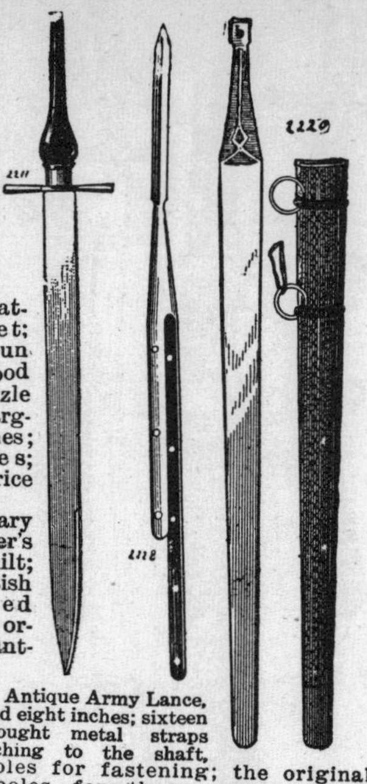

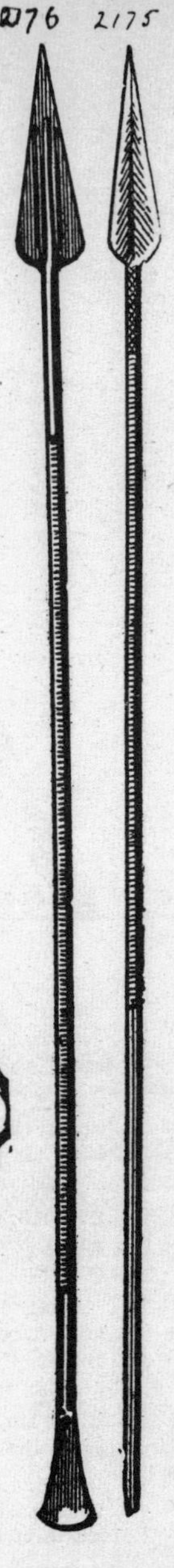

**2172.** Congo Natives Knife and Spoon, made by native; ornamented handle; full length 12 inches; from Belgian Army Officer's collection; price $4.75.

**2226.** Ancient Bronze Axe or Celt, from London collection, possibly and probably made and used thousands of years ago; deeply covered with green rust, and when struck the metal gives the ancient ring of the hardened bronze, in fine state of preservation; museum exhibit, price $18.00.

**2201.** Antique Pattern Plug Bayonet; double edged steel blade; 7 inches long, one inch wide at the hilt; with hard wood handle; tapered for use either as side arm or as bayonet when inserted in the muzzle of gun; cross guard hammer and screw driver ends; full length 11½ inches; plug bayonets are very rare; price $9.85.

**1090.** Extra light Weight New Cadet Sabres, three guard brass handle; fine steel blade, 28 to 30 inch; fine bright steel scabbard; sword and scabbard complete weighs under two pounds; price $3.25.

**2211.** Antique Pattern Plug bayonet; kind first used on gun by inserting the wood handle in the muzzle of the gun when charging; handle 7⅜ inches; blade 18½ inches; width 1⅜ inches; price $9.85.

**2199.** Revolutionary War Period Officer's Sword; with ivory hilt; with G. R. and British monogram engraved on the 30-inch blade; ornamented iron mountings; price $15.00.

**2228.** Antique Army Lance, spear head eight inches; sixteen inch wrought metal straps for attaching to the shaft, with holes for fastening; the original wood poles for these spears rotted away; mounted will make fine decoration; rusty, offered "as are," without pole, at $1.50 each; polished $2.45 each.

**2220.** Pair Captured Swords taken from slave "Dhow" near Lyanibar, 1873; from London collector; double edged 31 inch blade; iron pommel; leather covered decorated scabbard; shows extensive use; swords are not exactly alike; price the pair $20.00; singly $12.00.

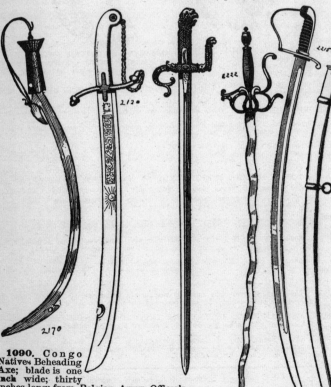

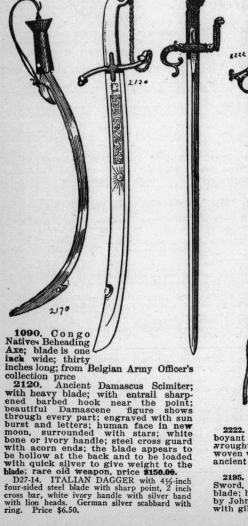

**1090.** Congo Natives Beheading Axe; blade is one inch wide; thirty inches long; from Belgian Army Officer's collection price

**2120.** Ancient Damascus Scimiter; with heavy blade; with entrail sharpened barbed hook near the point; beautiful Damascene figure shows through every part; engraved with sun burst and letters; human face in new moon, surrounded with stars; white bone or ivory handle; steel cross guard with acorn ends; the blade appears to be hollow at the back and to be loaded with quick silver to give weight to the blade; rare old weapon, price $150.00.

**D27-14. ITALIAN DAGGER** with 4½-inch four-sided steel blade with sharp point, 2 inch cross bar, white ivory handle with silver band with lion heads. German silver scabbard with ring. Price $6.50.

**FS1. LOUIS XVL RAPIER,** with gold plated pommel, strap and guard. Mother of pearl grip, ornamented pommel, guard shows three fleur de lis in circle in swords, guarded by two lion heads. Lion head on each side of handle strap. 32-inch triangular shaped blade, with very sharp point, with etchings of flags, crown, shield and words: VIVE LE ROY. This was evidently the fighting rapier of some French court attendant. Price $20.00.

**D27-2. ZANZIBAR DAGGER** with 5½-inch flat blade, black leather covered wood handle, ornamented leather scabbard, bottle shaped. Price $5.00.

**D27-3. ZANZIBAR DAGGER** with 5¾-inch BRASS blade, wood handle, bottle shaped scabbard, of russet leather with native ornamentations. Price $5.75.

**D27-4. ITALIAN LADY'S STILETTO** with 6¼-inch sharp pointed double edged blade marked: VENDETTA CORSA. 3¼-inch handle, silver bound, and inlaid with mother of pearl. Blue plush covered scabbard with fancy silver throat and tip. Silver chain to attach to belt. Price $6.50.

**D27-5. ITALIAN LADY'S STILETTO,** the same as No. D27-4 with 3½-inch blade and brown plush scabbard. Price $6.00.

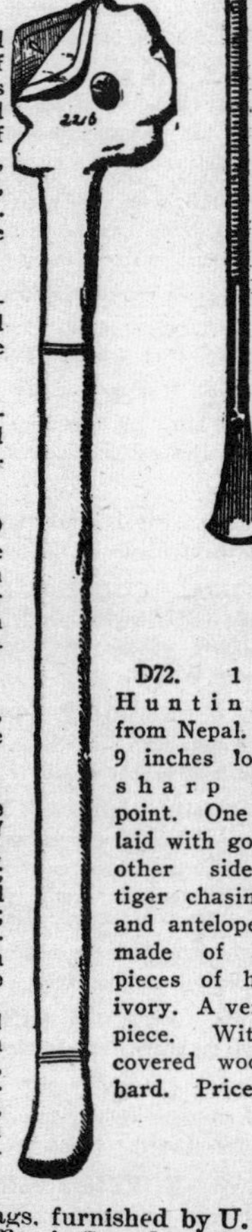

**2175.** African Congo Warriors Native made Spear and Pike; spear blade is 17 inches long; width at widest part 2¾ inches; grooved double edged blade; mounted on ornamented hard wood shaft, with polished bands of wire; metal wrapped; metal pike end polished; full length of spear 5½ feet; from Belgian Army Officer's collection; price $15.00.

**2176.** Congo Natives Spear; full length 6½ feet; rare pattern spear, with flat shaped pike; mounted on shaft, brass ornamented; vouched for by Belgian Army Officer, who took it from a native, and who said that his collection of 600 pieces did not cost him a d—— centime; price $15.00.

**D72.** 1 Native Hunting Dagger from Nepal. Blade is 9 inches long, with sharp thrusting point. One side inlaid with gold scroll; other side shows tiger chasing rabbit and antelope. Handle made of alternate pieces of horn and ivory. A very showy piece. With plush covered wood scabbard. Price, $6.00.

**2222.** 17th Century Sword with flamboyant or flaming blade, with hand wrought iron ornamented, double guard; woven wire wrapped hilt; head pommel; ancient German, rare old weapon.

**2195.** Victorian Period Officer's Dress Sword, Empire pattern; etched steel blade; helmet and plume pommel; made by Johnson & Sadler, London; scabbard with gilt mountings; price $8.85.

**2214.** Chamois Sword Bags, furnished by U. S. Government, with Artillery Officer's Swords; will fit most any sword or sabre; new; 85 cents each.

**2194.** Victorian Period British Officer's Sword, with brass scabbard; etched steel blade; made by Wilkinson, London; shark skin grip; "V. R." cast in relief scroll on guard; good second-hand, serviceable order; price $11.00.

**2196.** British Naval Officer's Sword of the American Revolutionary War period; white shark skin grip; Lion head pommel, used, in good order, with scabbard and sling strap; price $15.00.

# SWORDS AND SPEARS.

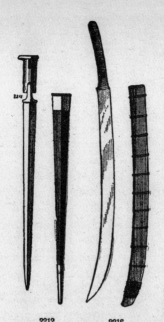

**2212    2216**

No. 2212. Battle of Waterloo Period Bayonet; length of blade 17 inches, 1¼ inches wide; similar to the bayonet used in the American Revolutionary War, with the addition of projection on the socket for fastening to the muzzle of the gun; price $1.00 each; with genuine old leather bayonet scabbard, price $1.50 each.

No. 2201. XV. Century Type Sword; 32-inch double edged blade; etched with British Coat of Arms, "G. R." (King George's reign); maker's name Osborne; ornamented with rose, thistle, female figures, etc.; etching is work of art; price $15.00.

No. 2202. Naval Cutlass, with 23-inch blade; engraved with crossed anchors, flowers, 1796, etc.; brass handle and guard; wire wrapped hilt, with leather scabbard; price $15.00.

Antique pattern Masonic Side Arm Sword; ivory hilt; brass pommel and guard; double edged 15 inch steel blade, engraved with rising sun, with compass enclosed in wreath, with skull and cross bones; ancient blueing; engraved V. R. Mancon; leather scabbard, with two gilt bands and rings, with tip; price $12.75.

60 Light Cavalry Sabres, with partially oxidized steel scabbards; bright steel blades, with polished brass handles; used, in cleaned and polished order; U. S. A. experimental sabres; price $3.00 each.

D84. 1 ARAB DAGGER from Zanzibar with horn handle, silver mounted. Curved 8-inch two-edge blade with raised ribs running to tip. No scabbard. Price, $5.50.

Congo Native made Banner or Flag; made of woven fibre with colored tufts of jute, with colored border; size 8x8 inches; rare piece; price $3.00.

No. 2206. Afghan Sword, with ivory hilt; 26 inch, partly double edged, dirk shaped blade; two grooves; India pattern ornamented handle wood scabbard; leather covered; price $12.00.

D53. 1 INDIA KNIFE with 9-inch blade sharpened on both edges at point. Solid ivory handle. Price, $4.50.

2225D. CONGO CALL TRUMPET made of elephant ivory tusk, 19 inches long, unpolished. Native work. Similar to illustration No. 2225 on page 206. Price $10.00.

2225E. 2 CONGO CALL TRUMPETS made of ivory from elephant's tusks. 14 inches long, unpolished. Price $8.50 each.

2225F. CONGO WAR TRUMPET made of highly polished elephant tusk ivory. All white. This is a fine specimen. Price $9.50.

---

**54**

D79. 1 ARAB DAGGER FROM ZANZIBAR. Horn handle, silver mounted and embossed. 8-inch double edge sharp blade with 2 large ridges running to tip. No scabbard. Price, $6.00. See illustration D75, page 202.

D27-8. BRASS DAGGER from Tunis. 7¾ inch double edged sharp pointed steel blade, black wood handle inlaid with strips of white ivory. Heavy brass scabbard, ornamented. Price $6.00.

D81. 1 ARAB TYPE INDIA DAGGER with heavy metal handle, heavily inlaid with gold scroll. 6-inch blade, curved with two ridges in center. Wood scabbard, plush covered, inlaid with heavy gold inlaid throat. A very handsome piece. Price, $8.00.

D27-7. ARABIAN DAGGER, with 6½ inch double edged blade, hard wood handle with brass tip, fancy leather scabbard. Price $4.50.

D83. 1 ARAB DAGGER with 8-inch curved blade, two sharp edges, and solid horn handle. No scabbard. Price, $5.00.

No. 54. LONG KNIFE BAYONETS, for use on the MAUSER RIFLES, both 7 m/m and 7.65 m/m. Blade 15½ inches, full length 20½ inches, weight with steel scabbard 20 ounces. These were made for the Boers but never delivered, owing to the British blockade. Very similar to the Serbian model in appearance. Price, $1.80 each.

No. 2410. African Quiver made of wood; covered with decorated leather; shows extensive use; length 22 inches; diameter 3 inches; price $5.00.

No. 2216. DhaSword from Mandalay; 25-inch blade; 9½-inch handle; round scabbard, with fibre bands; price $8.75.

---

**00000    0000**

No. 00000. Side Arm Sword Bayonet; blade marked with crown and letters P crossed; bronze handle and guard; 23-inch blade; 1¼ inches wide; black leather scabbard with brass mouth and tip; full length 30 inches; weight 2 pounds, 9 ounces; in second hand, used order; price $1.50.

No. 0000. Side Arm Sword Bayonet with brass cross guard and hilt; steel blade, leather scabbard, with brass mouth and tip; second hand, serviceable order; price, $1.20.

No. 2219. Scotch Officers Claymore Sword; engraved "London Scottish Volunteers"; 33-in double edged steel blade with two grooves; in fine used order; red cloth lined handle; shark skin grip; leather scabbard; price $25.00.

---

**4X**

4X. Mauser rifle side arm sword bayonet with SAW edge, with scabbard. Made for Boers in South Africa, but owing to strict British blockade were never delivered. Blade is 18½ inches long; brass handle, black leather scabbard with brass mouth and tip, with hook for belt frog. Full length 25 inches. Price, $2.35 each.

U. S. Cavalry Wood Fencing Sabre; about 34-inch blade; heavy iron guards, 4½ inches wide; made at Government Arsenal; price $2.40.

No. 2217. Kaid's Sword from Morrocco, with Spanish blade; bone hilt; ornamented iron guard; full length 41 inches; wood scabbard-leather covered; price $10.00.

---

**U. S. Cavalry Fencing Sabre**

---

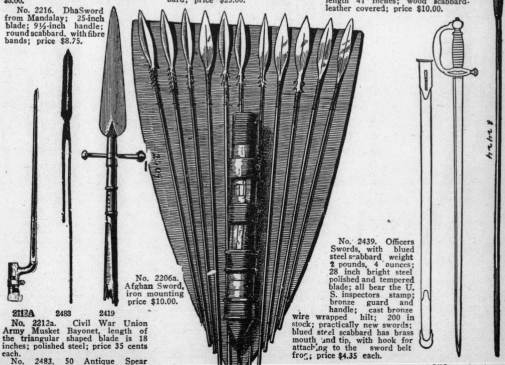

**2212A    2483    2419**

No. 2212a. Civil War Union Army Musket Bayonet, length of the triangular shaped blade is 18 inches; polished steel; price 35 cents each.

No. 2483. 50 Antique Spear Heads; eight inch spear blade; with long strap for securing to pole; rusty; price $2.45 each.

No. 2419. Napoleonic Period War Lance; metal blade that screws into socket; have all been mounted and used, part of the broken shafts remaining; real old relic; price

No. 2206a. Afghan Sword, iron mounting price $10.00.

**2409**
☞ Spears and Quiver.

No. 2439. Officers Swords, with blued steel scabbard weight 2 pounds, 4 ounces; 28 inch bright steel polished and tempered blade; all bear the U. S. inspectors stamp; bronze guard and handle; cast bronze wire wrapped hilt; 200 in stock; practically new swords; blued steel scabbard has brass mouth and tip, with hook for attaching to the sword belt frog; price $4.35 each.

**2439**

No. 2424. Congo Native made War Spear, full length 4½ feet; wrought metal double edged sharpened blade, with grooves; length six inches, width 1½ inches; from Belgian Army Officer's collection, captured from the Natives; price $5.85.

No. 2409. African Natives Barbed Spears, with quiver, mounted on shield, $10.00.

**1854B. OLD FRENCH HUNTING SWORD** with hard wood grooved grip, flat iron pommel, 4-inch cross guard. 27½-inch narrow blade. Price $7.00.

**1854C. GERMAN HUNTING SWORD,** 18th CENTURY, with wide black wood handle, iron fastened. 3-inch flat iron guard. 22¼-inch wide flat blade. Price $8.00.

**D40. 1 CURIOUS SHAPED KNIFE** with ivory handle and 9½-inch curved blade with wide back, sharp edge and long point. From Northwest India. Price, $5.85.

**D41. 1 LONG KNIFE** with ivory handle and 11-inch straight blade, with wide back and long point. Has ring in handle to attach to shouldersling. From Northwest India. Price, $6.25.

**D42. 1 KNIFE** like No. D41 with horn and ivory handle with 11-inch blade. From Afghanistan. Price, $6.00.

**8643.—EARLY AFGHAN (KYBER) KNIFE,** in sheath, silver mounted; white bone handle: 9½ inch blade. Price $8.85.

**8643A.—SIMILAR KNIFE.** With scabbard, with black bone handle, 11½ inch blade. Price, $4.85.

**8643B.—EIGHTEENTH CENTURY INDIA KNIFE,** with jade handle; 5 inch; partly double edged blade, with needle point. A dangerous weapon; sold only to responsible party. Price $6.85.

**8663.—SOUTH SEA ISLANDERS' THROWING CLUB,** from London collection; no history. Diameter of the knob 5 inches; carved handle; full length 16 inches. Price $16.00.

**8663A.—SIMILAR CLUB,** with round handle, wood knob. Price $14.

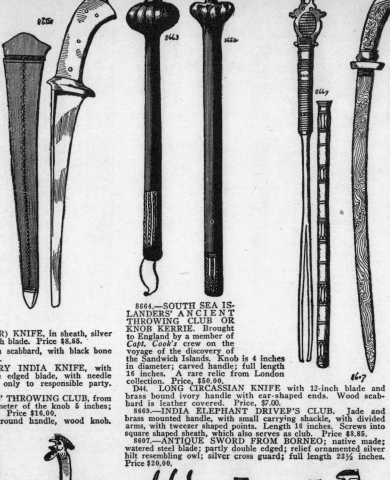

**8664.—SOUTH SEA IS- LANDERS' ANCIENT THROWING CLUB OR KNOB KERRIE.** Brought to England by a member of *Capt. Cook's* crew on the voyage of the discovery of the Sandwich Islands. Knob is 4 inches in diameter; carved handle; full length 16 inches. A rare relic from London collection. Price, $50.00.

**D44. LONG CIRCASSIAN KNIFE** with 12-inch blade and brass bound ivory handle with ear-shaped ends. Wood scabbard is leather covered. Price, $7.00.

**8669.—INDIA ELEPHANT DRIVER'S CLUB.** Jade and brass mounted handle, with small carrying shackle, with divided arms, with tweezer shaped points. Length 16 inches. Screws into square shaped sheath, which also serves as club. Price $8.85.

**8607.—ANTIQUE SWORD FROM BORNEO;** native made; watered steel blade; partly double edged; relief ornamented silver hilt resembling owl; silver cross guard; full length 23½ inches. Price $20.00.

**10161**

**10139**

**10160**

**10138**

**HOSPITAL CORPS KNIVES, made at** U. S. Springfield Arsenal for use of Hospital Corps attached to State militia. Offered in used serviceable order, complete with leather scabbard; with brass hook for attaching to the cartridge belt. Price $3.85.

**10038.—U. S. SPRINGFIELD CAL. 30 BARONG BAYONET;** only six in stock; made for Philippine experimental service, after the pattern of the Filipino Barong (side arm sword). Offered in serviceable order, with steel scabbard, with steel fastening loop for use on the web cartridge belt; rare relics. Sold to Museums.

**10,161.—U. S. A. TORMENTOR.** Used by cooks in army service; from recent fire in Medical Department, Army Building. New; slightly tarnished; all in serviceable order. Weight about 6 ounces; length 18 inches. Price 35c.

**10038**

**10,139.—FRENCH SWORD, WITH WARRIOR'S HEAD POMMMEL,** with eagle, cross guard ends, 33½ steel engraved blade, with quill back; also quill shaped point, with leather scabbard; brass mouth and tip, with double rings. Price $28.00.

**10,138.—ANTIQUE FRENCH SWORD, WITH GALLIC COCK,** brass pommel, with cross guard with lion heads; blade engraved Mftare de Klinginthal, with two government seal marks; 29 inch curved steel blade; leather scabbard, with long brass mouth and top, with frog for attaching to the old style shoulder belt. Rare even in France; serviceable order. Price $25.00.

**8696A.—ANCIENT HUNTING SWORD.** With hilt and guard ornamented with figures of warriors in hand to hand fight. 24 inch fluted blade, engraving worn off. Price, $7.85.

**8665.—ANCIENT DECORATED WAR CLUB,** shaped after the pattern of war canoe. Hard wood; 34 inches long, width 2½ inches. From Santa Cruz. Price, $12.50.

**8601.—ANTIQUE FIJI WAR CLU** rare specimen. Diameter of the knob head 5 inches; carved handle; full length inches. Price $17.50.

**8710.—SCOTCH SKEEN DIRK, w** engraved silver (thistle) bands, mouth a tip pieces; Ionic checkered black wood h Complete with silver knife and fork, silv capped. The jewel in the pommel of large blade is missing. Full length inches. Price $25.00.

**10,090.—MACHETES FROM GOVER MENT AUCTION SALE;** 25 inch bla bone handle; tan leather ornamented shea made by Collins & Co.; relics of service Philippines. Price for complete mach and scabbard, $2.50. Price for machete w broken blade with scabbard, $1.50.

**10,160.—U. S. N. TORMENTOR, lc** iron fork used by navy cook on board w ship; length about 3¼ feet; weight pounds; serviceable order, as good as ne Price 95c.

**8644.—EARLY INDIA GORRE KNIFE,** ivory handle, disemboweling kni at the hilt; 11 inch curved blade, with sc bard. Price $7.85.

**8645.—CIRCASSIAN KNIFE,** with tive silver, richly chased ornamented and scabbard; 7 inch blade; fish head bard tip. Price $15.00

**8646.—ANTIQUE INDIA KNIFE,** fin ornamented with native silver chased and silvered scabbard. Price, $15.00.

**8643AA.—KYBER KNIFE,** used by ghans; full length 17 inches; ornamen brass scabbard mountings; bone hilt. P $7.85.

**8647.—IVORY HILT DIRK;** period George III; gold plated mountings; 14 i double edged blade, leather scabbard, w rings for the belt slings. Price $12.00.

**8648.—ANCIENT STILETTO,** 9 ir six sided blade, needle point; ivory h (Part of the leather scabbard missin Sale restricted to responsible parties. P $12.00.

**8649.—BRITISH MIDSHIPMA ANCIENT DIRK,** similar to No. 2 page 21. With ivory carved hilt; with head pommel, much used. Price $15.00.

**8649A.—MINIATURE DIRK,** used British Navy midshipmen, Admiral Nelso period. Ornamented ivory hilt, gold pla cross guard and scabbard; 8 inch scim shaped blade. Price $12.00.

**8685.—FRENCH OFFICERS' MI TARY SWORD,** with silver lace sw knot, bronze pommel; single guard; bl bone hilt; 29 inch steel blade, engraved w arms trophies, etc.; letters I S and C the leather scabbard; brass mountings, w stud for the shoulder belt. Price $12.50.

**8686.—AMERICAN REVOLUTIONA WAR PERIOD OFFICER'S SWOR** with blade made by the famous J. J. Run Solingen. Engraved with "G. R.," 1 with arms, trophy, cannon and name of maker. Checkered ivory hilt; gilt mou ings; 31 inch blade; leather scabbard graved "Loxham, Royal Exchange," v stud for shoulder sling, also place for sw sling rings. This old relic shows excess use. Price, $20.00.

**8687.—BRITISH NAVAL OFFICE WAR OF 1812 PERIOD SWORD,** w silver plated mountings, 26 inch rib sharpened blade, with quill back poi basket handle, with turn down guard; lic head pommel, sharkskin grip; with f anchor and crown in relief; leather sc bard, with stud for shoulder belt; fine sword. Price $20.00.

**8688.—WAR OF 1812 PERIOD NAV OFFICER'S SWORD.** 31 inch curved s blade; ornamented gilt open guard; lion h pommel; Checkered black bone hand g leather scabbard, gilt mountings, with s and ring, tip missing. Price $15.00.

**8694.—ANTIQUE HUNTING SWO FRENCH.** 17th century period, w chased mountings representing hunting s jects. Tortoise shell and pearl ornamen hand grip. 21½ inch double cutting bla engraved with ancient cannon troph Work of art. Price, $14.85.

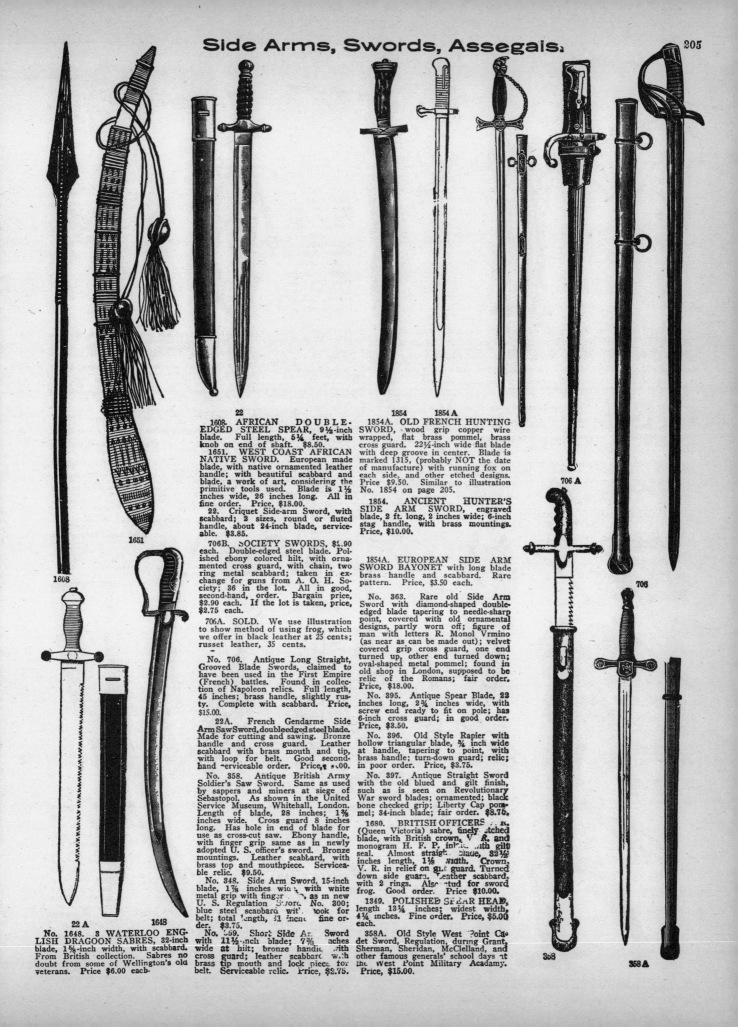

# Side Arms, Swords, Assegais.

**1608. AFRICAN DOUBLE-EDGED STEEL SPEAR,** 9½-inch blade. Full length, 5¼ feet, with knob on end of shaft. $8.50.

**1651. WEST COAST AFRICAN NATIVE SWORD.** European made blade, with native ornamented leather handle; with beautiful scabbard and blade, a work of art, considering the primitive tools used. Blade is 1½ inches wide, 26 inches long. All in fine order. Price, $18.00.

**22.** Criquet Side-arm Sword, with scabbard; 2 sizes, round or fluted handle, about 24-inch blade, serviceable. $3.85.

**706B. SOCIETY SWORDS,** $2.90 each. Double-edged steel blade. Polished ebony colored hilt, with ornamented cross guard, with chain, two ring metal scabbard; taken in exchange for guns from A. O. H. Society; 36 in the lot. All in good, second-hand order. Bargain price, $2.90 each. If the lot is taken, price, $2.75 each.

**706A.** SOLD. We use illustration to show method of using frog, which we offer in black leather at 25 cents; russet leather, 35 cents.

**No. 706.** Antique Long Straight, Grooved Blade Swords, claimed to have been used in the First Empire (French) battles. Found in collection of Napoleon relics. Full length, 45 inches; brass handle, slightly rusty. Complete with scabbard. Price, $15.00.

**22A.** French Gendarme Side Arm Saw Sword, double edged steel blade. Made for cutting and sawing. Bronze handle and cross guard. Leather scabbard with brass mouth and tip, with loop for belt. Good second-hand serviceable order. Price, $4.00.

**No. 358.** Antique British Army Soldier's Saw Sword. Same as used by sappers and miners at siege of Sebastopol. As shown in the United Service Museum, Whitehall, London. Length of blade, 28 inches; 1⅜ inches wide. Cross guard 8 inches long. Has hole in end of blade for use as cross-cut saw. Ebony handle, with finger grip same as in newly adopted U. S. officer's sword. Bronze mountings. Leather scabbard, with brass top and mouthpiece. Serviceable relic. $9.50.

**No. 348.** Side Arm Sword, 15-inch blade, 1⅞ inches wide, with white metal grip with finger grips, as in new U. S. Regulation Sword No. 300; blue steel scabbard with hook for belt; total length, 31 inches, fine order. $3.75.

**No. 359.** Short Side Arm Sword with 11½-inch blade; 7¾ inches wide at hilt; bronze handle with cross guard; leather scabbard with brass tip mouth and lock piece for belt. Serviceable relic. Price, $2.75.

**1854A. OLD FRENCH HUNTING SWORD,** wood grip copper wire wrapped, flat brass pommel, brass cross guard. 22½-inch wide flat blade with deep groove in center. Blade is marked 1315, (probably NOT the date of manufacture) with running fox on each side, and other etched designs. Price $9.50. Similar to illustration No. 1854 on page 205.

**1854. ANCIENT HUNTER'S SIDE ARM SWORD,** engraved blade, 2 ft. long, 2 inches wide; 6-inch stag handle, with brass mountings. Price, $10.00.

**1854A. EUROPEAN SIDE ARM SWORD BAYONET** with long blade brass handle and scabbard. Rare pattern. Price, $3.50 each.

**No. 363.** Rare old Side Arm Sword with diamond-shaped double-edged blade tapering to needle-sharp point, covered with old ornamental designs, partly worn off; figure of man with letters R. Monol Vrmino (as near as can be made out); velvet covered grip cross guard, one end turned up, other end turned down; oval-shaped metal pommel; found in old shop in London, supposed to be relic of the Romans; fair order. Price, $18.00.

**No. 395.** Antique Spear Blade, 22 inches long, 2¾ inches wide, with screw end ready to fit on pole; has 6-inch cross guard; in good order. Price, $3.50.

**No. 396.** Old Style Rapier with hollow triangular blade, ¾ inch wide at handle, tapering to point, with brass handle; turn-down guard; relic; in poor order. Price, $3.75.

**No. 397.** Antique Straight Sword with the old blued and gilt finish, such as is seen on Revolutionary War sword blades; ornamented; black bone checked grip; Liberty Cap pommel; 34-inch blade; fair order. $8.75.

**1680. BRITISH OFFICERS** (Queen Victoria) sabre, finely etched blade, with British crown, V R, and monogram H. F. P. inlaid with gilt seal. Almost straight blade, 32½ inches length, 1⅛ width. Crown, V. R. in relief on gilt guard. Turned down side guard. Leather scabbard, with 2 rings. Also suited for sword frog. Good order. Price $10.00.

**1349. POLISHED SPEAR HEAD,** length 13¼ inches; widest width, 4¼ inches. Fine order. Price, $5.00 each.

**358A.** Old Style West Point Cadet Sword, Regulation, during Grant, Sherman, Sheridan, McClelland, and other famous generals' school days at the West Point Military Acadamy. Price, $15.00.

**No. 1648. 3 WATERLOO ENGLISH DRAGOON SABRES,** 32-inch blade, 1⅝-inch width, with scabbard. From British collection. Sabres no doubt from some of Wellington's old veterans. Price $6.00 each.

# AFRICAN CONGO NATIVES' WEAPONS

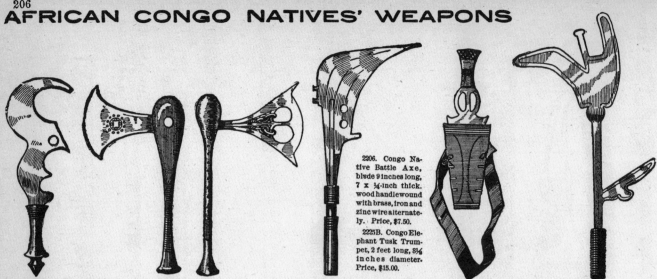

2217.

2203.

2204.

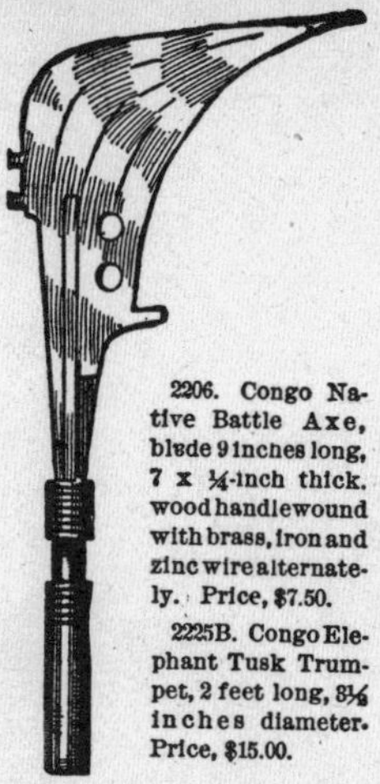

2206.

2206. Congo Native Battle Axe, blade 9 inches long, 7 x ¼-inch thick. wood handle wound with brass, iron and zinc wire alternately. Price, $7.50.

2225B. Congo Elephant Tusk Trumpet, 2 feet long, 3½ inches diameter. Price, $15.00.

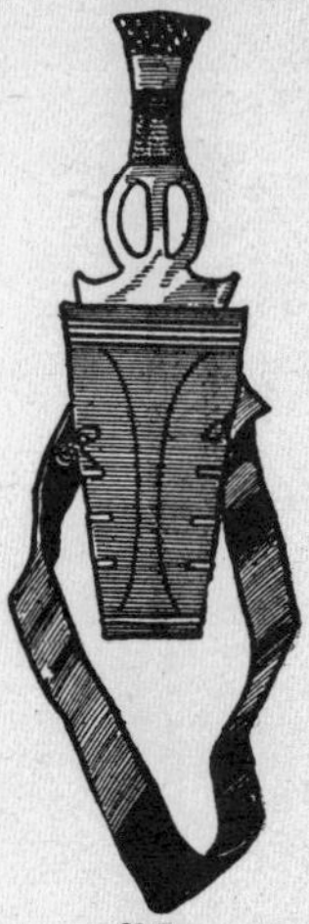

2207.

2205.

2229. WATER BOTTLE, made by covering soda water bottle with colored leather, 8½ inches long, 3 inches in diameter, Price $3.85.
2229E. CONGO NATIVES DRUM, 13 inches high, hoops 2 inches wide, 10 inch shell, heads are made of heavy hide, complete with crude sticks. Price $15.00.
2229F. NATIVE MADE HAMMERED COPPER DISH, 7 inch diameter, 1½ inch deep, Price $4.75
2229G. CONGO NATIVE WAR SHIELD, made of colored woven fibre, 18 inch diameter. Price $10.00.
2229H. CONGO NATIVE BROOM, made by sewing fibre or roots, to stick with raw-hide handle, 8 inches long, broom end 2 feet. Price $2.50.
2208A. 3 HAND BELLS, 8 inches long, 1½ inch wide, made of iron, shaped like pea pod, with wood handle. Price $4.50 each.
2208B. WOODEN BELL, 3½x4 inches, carved out of block of hard wood, with wooden tongue or clapper. Price $2.50.
2208C. NATIVE RATTLE, dumb bell shaped wicker basket on each end, containing small beans. Ends are 3 inch diameter, round bar is 7 inches long, 1½ inch diameter. Price $3.75.
2208D. MUSICAL BOX, carved from one piece of hard wood rose wood) size 8½x5x6, makes a musical sound when struck. Price $8.50.
2208E. CARVED HARD WOOD ORNAMENTED VASE, 5½ inch high 2⅝ inch diameter. Price $3.75
2208F. CARVED ORNAMENTED HARD WOOD VASE, 5½x5½ inches. Price, $4.50.
2208G. NATIVE MADE BELL, nut with three iron clappers, with loop 3½x7½x2. Price $5 90.
2208H. COW BELL FROM CONGO, 3½x2½x6½ inches, without clapper. Ha hide loop to fasten around animal's neck. Price $2.75.
2208I. CONGO COW BELL, 3½x3½x4 inches, with tongue, good tone. Price $2.50.
2226. TWO CONGO KNIVES, with handle of steel, copper and raw hide, 18 inch steel blade, 2 inches wide, hide covered scabbard. Price $15.00 each.
2226A. A CURIOUS BRASS BLADED KNIFE, wood handle 9 inches long, blade 9x1½ inches wide. Price $10.00. Same knife without handle, $7.50.

2210A. TWO CONGO KNIFE SCABBARDS, made of wood, 4½ inches wide, 14 inches long, with belt made in shape of braided rope, similar to 2210. Price $6.50.
2210B. CONGO NATIVE ORNAMENTED COLLAR, made from Elephant hide, covered round with copper wire, size 10½x9 inches. Open at one end, considered by natives a valuable personal ornament. Price $10.00.
2203. CONGO NATIVE WAR CLUB AXE. Handle is wound round with sheet copper, brass blade 6 inches wide by 3 inches long, handle 14 inches long. Price $3.50.
2203A. TWO CONGO NATIVE WAR AXES, copper wound handle, 14 inches long, steel blade 6 inches long, 1½ inches wide, with copper medallion in laid in blade. Price $10.00.
2204. CONGO NATIVE WAR AXE, wrought steel blade, artistic work, considering the crude forging facilities, blade 6 inches long 1½ to 7 inches wide, 15 inch copper wound handle. Price $10.00.
2204A. A similar war axe to 2204, but with handle covered with snake skin. Price $15.00
2212 CONGO NATIVE COPPER BLADE KNIFE with handle, blade measures 8 inches, handle 4 inches. Price $6.00.
2212A. CONGO NATIVE KNIFE, with steel blade, 9 inches long, with 9 inch copper handle. Price $6.00.
2211. CONGO NATIVE MASK, carved from piece of hard wood, with handle on the back, evidently intended for carrying. 10¾ inches long, 7 inches wide. Price $5.80.
2211A. MASK, 5½ inches wide, 9 inches long. Price $5.00.
2205. THREE CONGO NATIVE MADE FOUR BLADED BATTLE AXES, length of blade 10 inches, 18 inches long, fibre wound around handle. Price $8.50.
2217. FIVE CONGO NATIVE MADE WEAPONS, 16 inch blade with three side grooves, small decorative lines on edge, 7 inch wood handle, brass bound. Price $7.50 each.
2201. CONGO NATIVE KNIFE, 15 inch blade, 1½ to 3¾ inch wide, 5 inch handle with fancy carved wood scabbard No. 2202, price for the knife and scabbard, $10.00.
2207. SIX CONGO NATIVE MADE KNIVES, 14 inch blade 3½ inch wide, 4 inch handle, wound with copper, brass covered leather scabbard. Price $12.00. Two nearly similar knives without scabbard. $10.00 each.
2223. PAIR OF YOUNG ELEPHANT TUSKS, 12 inches long, 1¼ inch diameter. Price $10.00.

2225C. Congo Elephant tusk 12 inches long [has been much longer, but partly broken off], 2 inches at large end, stained light brown color. $8.50.

2224.

2202.

2232.

2201.

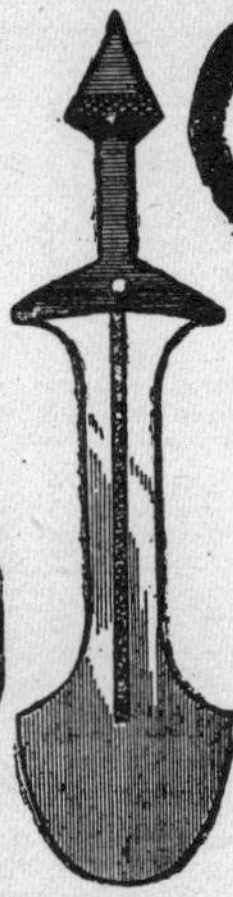

2213.

2210.

2223.

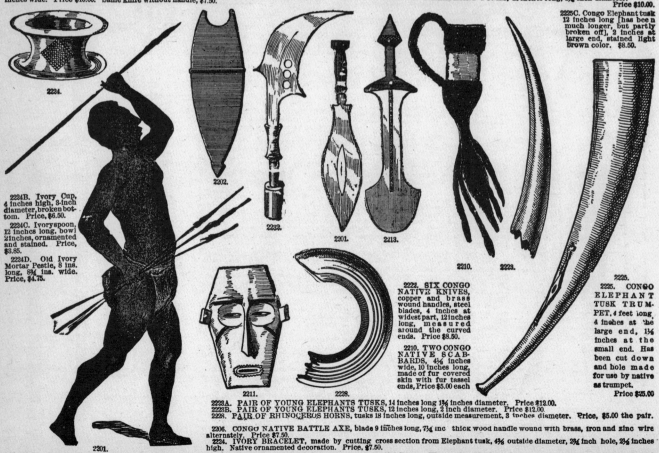

2224B. Ivory Cup, 4 inches high, 3-inch diameter, broken bottom. Price, $6.50.

2224C. Ivory spoon, 12 inches long, bowl 2 inches, ornamented and stained. Price, $3.85.

2224D. Old Ivory Mortar Pestle, 8 ins. long, 3¾ ins. wide. Price, $4.75.

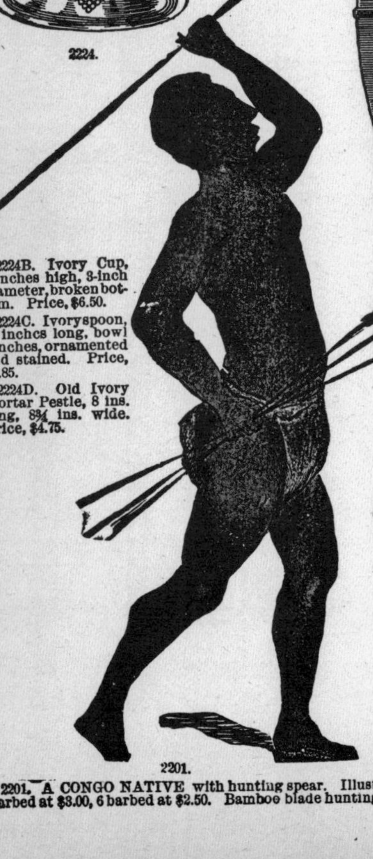

2201.

2211.

2228.

2222. SIX CONGO NATIVE KNIVES, copper and brass wound handles, steel blades, 4 inches at widest part, 12 inches long, measured around the curved ends. Price $8.50.

2210. TWO CONGO NATIVE SCABBARDS, 4½ inches wide, 10 inches long, made of fur covered skin with fur tassel ends, Price $5.00 each

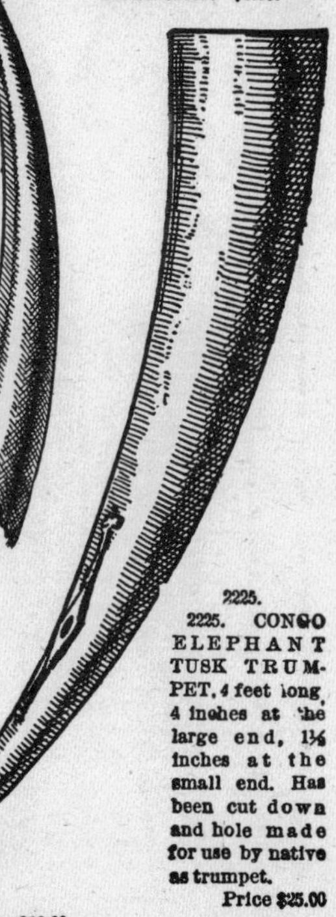

2225.

2225. CONGO ELEPHANT TUSK TRUMPET, 4 feet long, 4 inches at the large end, 1½ inches at the small end. Has been cut down and hole made for use by native as trumpet. Price $25.00

2223A. PAIR OF YOUNG ELEPHANTS TUSKS, 14 inches long 1⅜ inches diameter. Price $12.00.
2223B. PAIR OF YOUNG ELEPHANTS TUSKS, 12 inches long, 2 inch diameter. Price $12.00.
2228. PAIR OF RHINOCEROS HORNS, tusks 18 inches long, outside measurement, 3 inches diameter. Price, $5.00 the pair.

2206. CONGO NATIVE BATTLE AXE, blade 9 inches long, 7¼ inc thick wood handle wound with brass, iron and zinc wire alternately. Price $7.50.
2224. IVORY BRACELET, made by cutting cross section from Elephant tusk, 4⅜ outside diameter, 2¾ inch hole, 2½ inches high. Native ornamented decoration. Price, $7.50.

2201. A CONGO NATIVE with hunting spear. Illustration made by Official Belgian Government artist to the Congo. We can furnish these Congo native spears from 5 to 6 feet long, 9 barbed at $3.00, 6 barbed at $2.50. Bamboo blade hunting spears, $2.00.

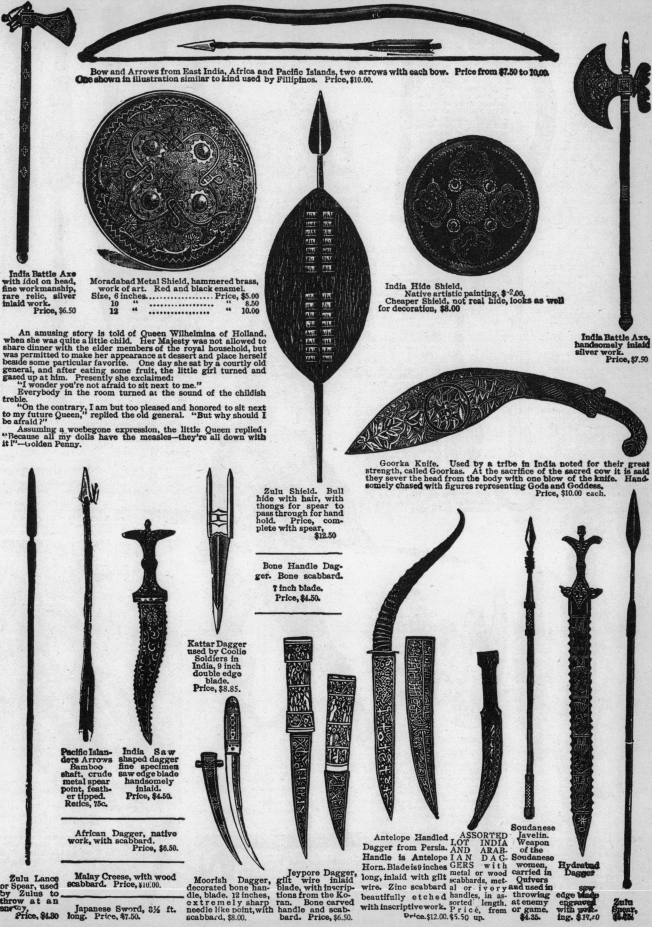

Bow and Arrows from East India, Africa and Pacific Islands, two arrows with each bow. Price from $7.50 to 10.00. One shown in illustration similar to kind used by Fillipinos. Price, $10.00.

**India Battle Axe** with idol on head, fine workmanship, rare relic, silver inlaid work. Price, $6.50.

**Moradabad Metal Shield,** hammered brass, work of art. Red and black enamel.
Size, 6 inches.................... Price, $5.00
10 " ................... " 8.50
12 " ................... " 10.00

**India Hide Shield,** Native artistic painting, $12.00, Cheaper Shield, not real hide, looks as well for decoration, $8.00

**India Battle Axe,** handsomely inlaid silver work. Price, $7.50

An amusing story is told of Queen Wilhelmina of Holland, when she was quite a little child. Her Majesty was not allowed to share dinner with the elder members of the royal household, but was permitted to make her appearance at dessert and place herself beside some particular favorite. One day she sat by a courtly old general, and after eating some fruit, the little girl turned and gazed up at him. Presently she exclaimed:
"I wonder you're not afraid to sit next to me."
Everybody in the room turned at the sound of the childish treble.
"On the contrary, I am but too pleased and honored to sit next to my future Queen," replied the old general. "But why should I be afraid?"
Assuming a woebegone expression, the little Queen replied:
"Because all my dolls have the measles—they're all down with it!"—Golden Penny.

**Goorka Knife.** Used by a tribe in India noted for their great strength, called Goorkas. At the sacrifice of the sacred cow it is said they sever the head from the body with one blow of the knife. Handsomely chased with figures representing Gods and Goddess. Price, $10.00 each.

**Zulu Shield.** Bull hide with hair, with thongs for spear to pass through for hand hold. Price, complete with spear, $12.50

**Bone Handle Dagger.** Bone scabbard. 7 inch blade. Price, $4.50.

**Kattar Dagger** used by Coolie Soldiers in India, 9 inch double edge blade. Price, $8.85.

**Pacific Islanders Arrows** Bamboo shaft, crude metal spear point, feather tipped. Relics, 75c.

**India Saw shaped dagger** fine specimen saw edge blade handsomely inlaid. Price, $4.50.

**African Dagger,** native work, with scabbard. Price, $6.50.

**Zulu Lance or Spear,** used by Zulus to throw at an enemy. Price, $4.30

**Malay Creese,** with wood scabbard. Price, $10.00.

**Japanese Sword,** 3½ ft. long. Price, $7.50.

**Moorish Dagger,** decorated bone handle, blade, 12 inches, extremely sharp needle like point, with scabbard, $8.00.

**Jeypore Dagger,** gilt wire inlaid blade, with inscriptions from the Koran. Bone carved handle and scabbard. Price, $6.50.

**Antelope Handled Dagger from Persia.** Handle is Antelope Horn. Blade is 9 inches long, inlaid with gilt wire. Zinc scabbard beautifully etched with inscriptive work. Price, $12.00.

**ASSORTED LOT INDIA AND ARABIAN DAGGERS** with metal or wood scabbards, metal or ivory handles, in assorted length. Price, from $5.50 up.

**Soudanese Javelin.** Weapon of the Soudanese women, carried in Quivers and used in throwing at enemy or game. $4.35.

**Hydrabad Dagger** saw edge blade engraved with setting. $17.50

**Zulu Spear,** $4.45.

**386. AFRICAN NATIVE CHIEFTAIN'S BATTLE AXE;** stone made into circular shape with sharp edges, with hole in center, mounted on pole with feather decorations (chieftains or leaders rank). Price, $15.

**7 BRONZE ANKLETS,** ranging from 1¾ to 2¾ inches in diameter, in different weights and with native markings from $1.00 to $3.00 each.

**No. 220. 1 PAIR NATIVE BRONZE LEG ORNAMENTS,** 3¾ in. in diameter, with acorn ends with native markings, Price $5 pair.

**No. 221. 1 PAIR BRONZE ANKLETS** with open ends and rings for thongs to tie on, 2 inches in diameter. Highly ornamented. Price, $3.50 pair.

**4 NATIVE ANKLETS** made from old ivory elephant tusk. Size about 1¼ inches wide, 2½ inches in diameter. Price, $1.50 each.

**D27-12. ITALIAN DAGGER,** with six sided 6-inch sharp pointed blade, 2½-inch cross bar, hard wood black handle with silver band. Scabbard of German silver, with ring. Price $7.00.

**D46. 1 INDIA SHORT KNIFE** with ivory handle, plush covered wood scabbard and 6½-inch sharp pointed blade. Price, $3.75.

**D47. 1 PAIR KNIVES in ONE** leather covered wood scabbard. Both have ivory handles with ear shaped ends. One knife has 8-in. sharp blade, the other 9-in. blade. This is a rare combination. Price, $12 for pair.

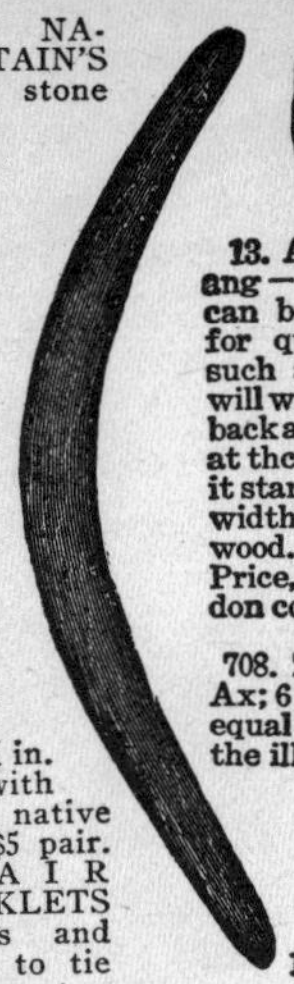

**13. Australian Boomerang**—native weapon—can be thrown forward for quite a distance in such a manner that it will whirl in the air, come back and strike with force at the place from which it started. Length, 22 in.; width, 2 in.; native hardwood. Fine specimen. Price, $7.85. From London collection.

**708. Zulu Natives Battle Ax;** 6 different kinds; all equal to or better than the illustration. $4.50 ea.

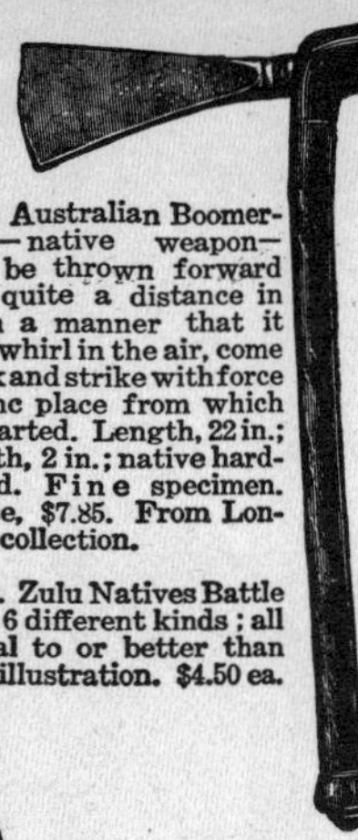

**z226. Native Hand Harp or Zither,** musical instrument with 8 steel rods attached to metal box; size, 6½x4½x½. Price, $6.50.

**2229. Native Musical Instrument,** made by stretching snake skin, while wet, around carved shell; 5 tightening keys; fibre strings; shell measures 8x4x2½; handle or finger board is 5x6x½ in. diam. $10.

**2229A. Musical Instrument,** similar to 2229, size 12x6x4, handle 5x 13x1¼; price, $12.00.

**2229B. Musical Instrument,** carved wood shell and finger board with skin fastening, with wooden pegs, 5 ivory keys: carved, ornamented heads; shell measures 6x8x4 inches; finger board is 25 in. long, 1½ wide. 1½ thick. Made by civilized natives Price, $15.00.

**2229C. Water Bottle,** made by covering beer bottle with colored leather; 10 inches long, 2½ diameter. Price, $3.89.

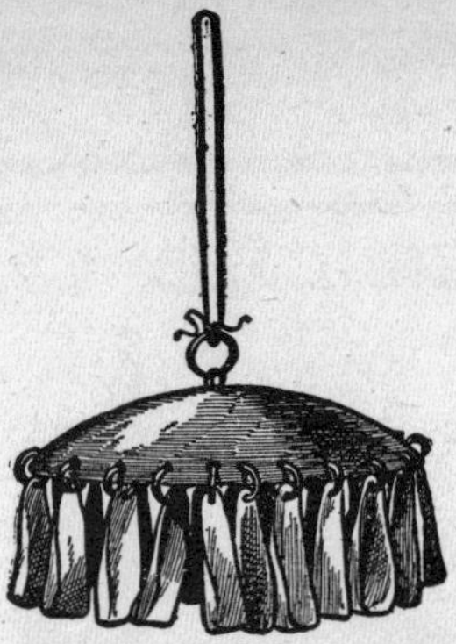

**2208. Set of Metal Bells,** inverted saucer shape, with 19 small iron bells attached by rings and suspended from the edge. Probably used in war dances. Price, $35.00.

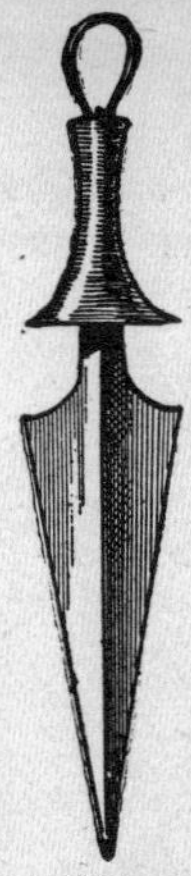

**2212B. 31 Knives Native Congo Make,** brass and wood handles from 8 to 18 in. long, blades from 2 to 3 in. wide. Price, from $2 to $6; depends on length and artistic workmanship. If you desire the cheapest pattern, send $2. If the best in the lot is wanted, send $6. If a medium knife is desired, send $4. Our reputation is guarantee that we will send you just what you order, and, if sold when order is received, we promptly return your money.

**65. South Sea Islanders' War Club,** made with crude native tools, presumably sea shells. Duplicate of the Peabody Collection; rare specimen, Price, $7.50.

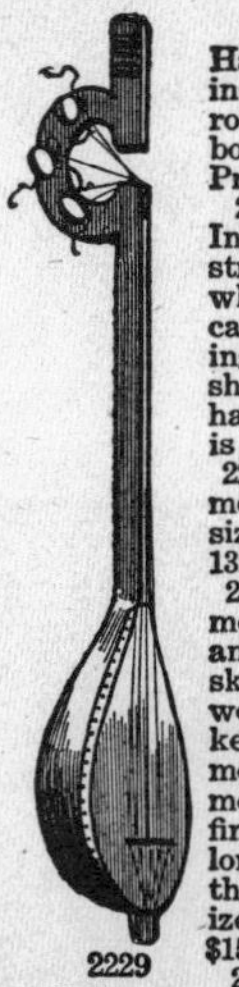

**66. South Sea Islander's War Club,** from the Peabody Collection. Price, $8.50.

**1838. West Coast African War Paddle,** 5¼ ft. long. 7¼ in. wide; carved figure with arms extended. Price, $7.80.

**1839. West Coast African Native War Paddle,** 5 feet long by 8¼ wide, with two carved figures on blade of paddle. Price, $10.00.

**1840. West Coast African Native War Paddle.** 5 1-3 ft. long. 6 in. wide; handsomely carved. Price, $10.00.

**1841. West Coast African Native War Paddle,** 4¾ feet long, 6 in. wide; handsomely carved. Price, $9.75.

**1837. West Coast African Native War Paddle,** 5¼ ft. long, widest part 7¾ in. with carved figure, hard wood resembling walnut, evidently made by native with crude tool, fairly sharp edge. Price $7.80.

**2219. Congo Native Water Bottle** made of heavy leather; 6 in. diameter, 16 inches long; rare pattern; price, $8.85.

**Native Woven Hat,** about size 6, 4 inches high, 3-inch brim; price, $3.85.

**2235. CONGO NATIVE WARRIOR WITH SPEAR.** — 88 Congo Native Made Spears, with steel blades, from 6 to 18 inches long, 1¼ to 5 inches wide; wood handle from 3 to 5½ feet in length; some are stained, others wound with copper. steel or brass; some have carved wood handles. Prices range from $3.50 to $12.00. If you wish one of the largest and finest spears, send us $12. If medium size, send $7.75, and if the cheapest spear, send us $3.50.

Our reputation is a guarantee that we will send what you order.

**2213A. 3 Congo Native Knives,** with 12-inch steel tapered blade, with 5-inch copper handles. Price, $7.50.

**1.** Filipino Warrior Shield; width, 7 inches, length, 33 inches; shows that it has been used; relic. $6.00.

**2.** Filipino Warrior Decorated Shield in different colored woods, inlaid with shells, hair ornamented. Length, 45 inches; width, 5½ inches. Price, $18.00.

**3.** Filipino War Shield, with handhold in back, carved centre; crude native work. Price, $6.00.

**Native African Dressed in White Duck Coat and Trousers** from lot of 170,000 suits we purchased from U.S. Government, a large part of which were sold to African traders. Only small lots of trousers are exported.

**Indian Stone Clubs,** made by American Cheyenne Indians; for decorative use; price, from $6.85 to $10.00.

**Native made Leather Cartridge Belt;** holds 29 cartridges; about 16 gauge; fancy hand stamping on flaps; length 24 in., width 4 in. Price, $3.85.

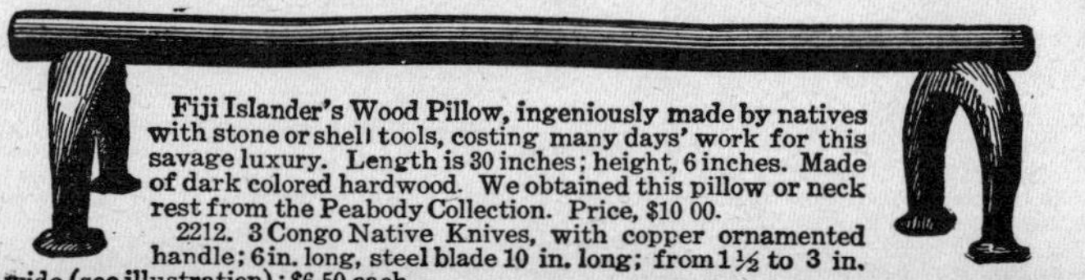

**Fiji Islander's Wood Pillow,** ingeniously made by natives with stone or shell tools, costing many days' work for this savage luxury. Length is 30 inches; height, 6 inches. Made of dark colored hardwood. We obtained this pillow or neck rest from the Peabody Collection. Price, $10 00.

**2212. 3 Congo Native Knives,** with copper ornamented handle; 6 in. long, steel blade 10 in. long; from 1½ to 3 in. wide (see illustration) ; $6.50 each.

**Antique British Javelin,** with fluted steel rib the entire 3 foot length; inlaid with ebony and ivory; rare. Price, $10.00.

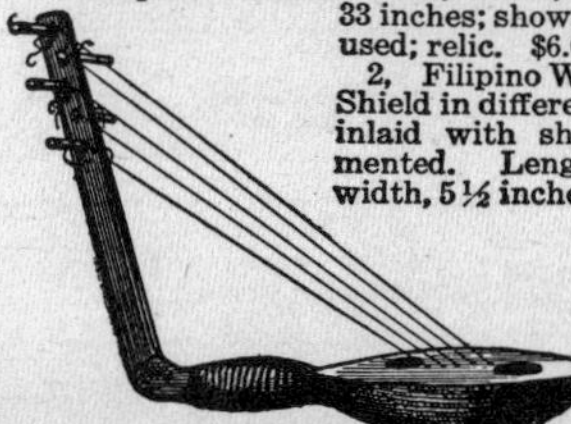

No. 2229

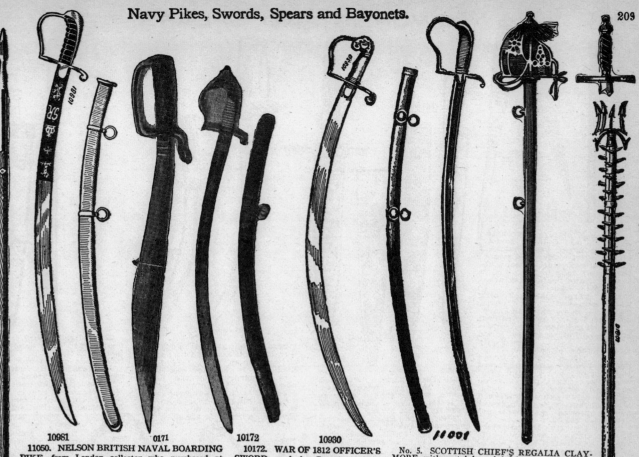

10981    0171    10172    10930    *11001*

**11050. NELSON BRITISH NAVAL BOARDING PIKE,** from London collector who purchased at old British dock yard auction sale. 4½-inch three sided pike blade with 10-inch iron straps, fastened to hard wood pole. Full length 7½ feet, diameter 1¼ inches. Some of the pikes have losenge shaped brass plate with number so that each sailor could identify his own pike. Price $3.85. Similar pikes used on board old wooden frigates of U. S. Navy. Price $3.85. Boarding Pikes were used in both British and American Navies during Wars of 1776 and 1812.

**10981. GEORGE THE THIRD OFFICERS SABRE,** kind used by British Officers during American Revolutionary War period. Blade engraved in gilt and blue, with Royal Crown, G. R. Made by the famous J. Runkel of Solgen. Sabre is complete with scabbard. All in good condition; full length 40 inches. Price $9.85.

**10171. FILIPINO BOLO,** brought to the U. S. by returning New Hampshire soldier. The blade is native made, flat on one side, razor sharp. Scabbard is bound with fiber thongs, which native in fight cuts through without drawing the bolo from the sheath. Many American soldiers suffered, thinking the native would have to draw the bolo out of the scabbard, unaware of this trick. Price $8.85.

**10172. WAR OF 1812 OFFICER'S SWORD,** used by Captain in New Hamsphire Regiment, 30-inch blade, blued steel, gilt etching, gilt guard with eagle head, ivory grip. Leather scabbard is in poor order. Sword is said to have belonged to Capt. Hanson Evans; used in the old time training muster. Price $15.00.

**10930. INDIA ELEPHANT HEAD COPPER POMMEL SWORD,** scimiter shaped 33-inch blade, single guard. Rare weapon. Price $14.50.

**11001. AUSTRIAN LIGHT CAVALRY SABRE,** military model, fine steel blade slightly curved. Single guard with scabbard guide; 2 ring steel scabbard. Length O. M. 98, weight 2¼ pounds. Price $3.85.

**11022. GEORGE II MIDSHIPMAN DIRK,** with ivory handle. Blue gilt etched, double edged 7-inch blade. Complete with scabbard. Price $7.85.

**No. 5. SCOTTISH CHIEF'S REGALIA CLAYMORE** with metal bound leather scabbard with two rings, and also frog stud. Fancy guard with thistle pommel, with silver band showing entwined THISTLES, and mounted by LARGE CAIRNGORM, PERIOD OF GEORGE III. Has been in same family for generations. Blade is 32 inches with three grooves in each side, also marker's mark CROSS IN CIRCLE. Made by ANDREA FERRARA. This is the most ornamental Claymore we have seen outside of a MUSEUM. Price, $45.00.

**10916. ANTIQUE ORIENTAL BARBED SPEAR.** Three rows of ¾-inch projecting spears, eight in a row, with combination hook and spear ends. Useful both for attack and defense. Full length 6 feet. Price $15.00.

**10886. ANTIQUE KNIFE** with bronze mount, 10-inch watered steel hand forged dagger blade; width 1¼ inches. Price $7.00.

**11017. GEORGE II OFFICERS SWORD,** made by Rea, Dublin; 31 inch straight blade etched with Royal Crown, coat of arms and small shield with CROWN SURMOUNTING HARP. Bronze hilt, leather scabbard. Price $18.50.

See other pages for Scotch Claymore swords, with prices.

10916

**D68-7. SACRIFICIAL KNIFE** as used in Ceylon. These are now rare even in that country. 7-inch blade, brown ivory handle silver pommel, corrugated wood scabbard with silver plated copper bound throat. Price $10.00.

**10828. FRENCH ARMY OFFICERS' SWORD WITH GALLIC COOK** cast in relief on the gilt finished brass guard; 30-inch steel blade. Engraved on the blade "Maunfre Rale de Clingenthal Juin 1832." Fine sword in good order. Price $10.00.

**D68-6. HIGH PRIEST CEYLON KNIFE,** similar to D68-5 with fiber bound wood scabbard. Black ivory handle, with silver on pommel and blade. Price $11.75.

**10949. OLD BRITISH ARMY OFFICER'S (GENERAL) CURVED SWORD,** engraved with motto "Sub Robore Virtus" surmounting tree with names of five battles on the reverse side including Delhi, Lucknow and others. Brass hilt with scales, with lion head pommel. Good order. Price $16.50.

**10931. ANTIQUE SWORD USED BY GERMAN OFFICER,** lion's head pommel, ornamented single guard, 32-inch steel blade DATED "1813-1814"; engraved "Fur Eigenes Wohl Frehe Hanseatische Burger Garde" with three castle insignia. Price $10.00.

**10927. GEORGE THE FIRST ARMY OFFICERS' SWORD,** six guard steel handle. Checkered grip; 39-inch straight blade. Engraved with monogram Royal Crown, G. R.; maker's name Bland. Rare old weapon. Price $18.50.

**10928. ANTIQUE INDIA SWORD** with wide blade covered with relief engravings of India animal life, Elephants, Tigers, Lions, Monkeys and Hunters. Full length 34 inches. Originally silver mounted. Blade 2 inches wide. Price $16.50.

**10924. SWORD BAYONET BAMBOO WALKING CANE,** three feet long containing a small bayonet which springs out when the handle part is jerked downward quickly. Sold only to responsible parties. Price $8.85.

**10848. GEORGE II PERIOD OFFICERS' SWORD** with fluted ivory hilt. Steel guard, 28½-inch curved blade, engraved with arms trophy, Royal Crown, G. R. Price $16.00.

**D68-1. SACRIFICIAL KNIFE** from Ceylon. White ivory handle, ornamented with silver, 7-inch heavy back blade over laid with silver in scroll designs. Corrugated wood scabbard. Similar to illustration No. D68 on page 199. Price $12.00. (See cut page 199.)

**D68-2. CEYLON SACRIFICIAL KNIFE** with heavy white ivory handle, silver and brass trimmed. 8-inch blade with heavy back. Wood scabbard with copper throat and fiber bound tip. Price $11.00.

**D68-3. SACRIFICIAL KNIFE** from Ceylon, with carved ivory handle with silver pommel. 7½-inch heavy blade, corrugated wood scabbard. Price $11.50.

**D68-4. SACRIFICIAL KNIFE** as used in Ceylon. Carved ivory handle, 8-inch heavy blade, brass bound. Corrugated wood scabbard copper bound at throat. Price $10.00.

**D68-5. HIGH PRIEST SACRIFICIAL KNIFE** from Ceylon, with brown ivory carved handle, silver pommel, 8-inch narrow heavy blade, inlaid with silver, brass bound and silver inlaid. Price $12.00.

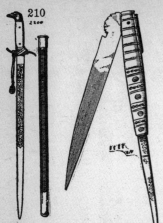

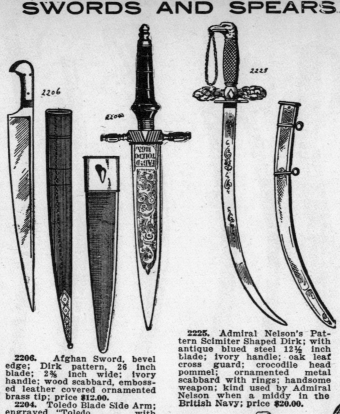

**2200.** Miniature Machete Paper Cutter; Officer's model, Eagle pommel; pearl handle; etched steel blade; gilt sword knot; leather colored steel scabbard; full length 10¼ inches; beautiful and useful desk ornament; price $2.35.

**2231.** Large Spanish Folding Knife; engraved, blade; 2⅝ inches in width; with sharpened needle like point; ratchet and spring holds blade in desired position; scabbard inlaid offered only to collectors; price $9.50.

**2180.** U. S. Naval Officer's Service Sword; with gilt sword knot; white shark skin grip; with black shark skin covered scabbard; etched steel blade; marked "Iron Proof"; engraved with anchors, etc.; handsome sword; in used, serviceable order; price $25.00.

**2200a.** Georgian Period (1740) British Officer's Sword; double edged 32 inch steel blade; marked with the name of "J. J. Runkel, Solingen," the famous sword maker; scabbard is engraved with names of Prosser and and Cullinan, sword cutlers and belt makers to the King and H. R. H. Duke of York, Charing Cross, London; fine old sword with cup and cross guard; wire wrapped hilt; price $20.00

**2206.** Afghan Sword, bevel edge; Dirk pattern, 26 inch blade; 2⅝ inch wide; ivory handle; wood scabbard, embossed leather covered ornamented brass tip; price $12.00.

**2204.** Toledo Blade Side Arm; engraved "Toledo, with ornamental scroll work; full length 13¾ inches; width of blade at hilt 1⅝ inches; ornamented German silver cross guard; wood hilt:

offered with scabbard, with hook for sword frog; price $10.00.

**2225.** Admiral Nelson's Pattern Scimiter Shaped Dirk; with antique blued steel 12½ inch blade; ivory handle; oak leaf cross guard; crocodile head pommel; ornamented metal scabbard with rings; handsome weapon; kind used by Admiral Nelson when a middy in the British Navy; price $20.00.

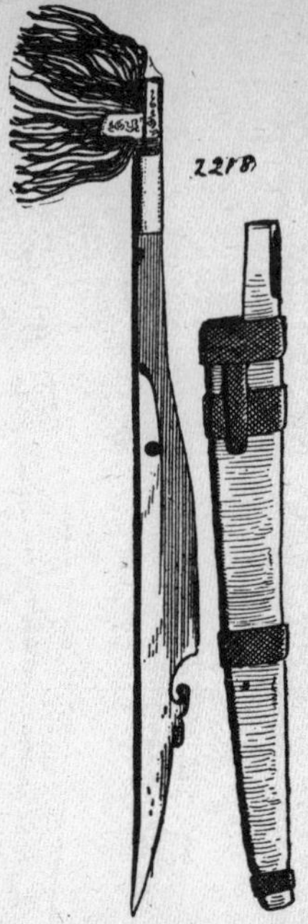

**2218.** Dyak Sword from Borneo; carved bone handle, ornamented with hair; 20 inch blade, ornamented with brass discs; with wood scabbard; price $10.00.

**2229-E.** Antique Indian Sword with recessed groove in the blade; originally silver wire inlaid ornamentation, only trace of which can now be seen; full length 31 inches; double edged point at the point; price $12.25.

**2229-D.** India sword with silver ornamented hilt and blade; full length thirty-four inches; no scabbard; price $9.85.

**2229-C.** India Sword, with decorated hilt; full length three feet; complete with scabbard; price $12.00.

**2229-B.** India Mutiny Captured Sword or Tulwar, taken from native; 33 inch sharpened blade; double edged to the point; from London collection; price $20.00.

**2229.** Ancient India Scimiter Sword; 30 inch blade; 3¼ inch curve; 1⅞ inches at widest part; sharpened double edged blade to ten inches from the point; quill or rounded back; blood gutter groove; wrought metal hilt and guard, with scabbard guides; hilt originally gilt ornamented, only trace of which can now be seen owing to extensive use and age; wood scabbard, leather covered; price $12.75.

**2239.** U. S. Army Officers' Chamois Sword Bags, made at U. S. Springfield Armory for officers' swords; new; price 85c. each.

**2239a.** Ornamental Steel Halbard, with socket for mounting on pole; gilt etched with antique blueing; full length 17 inches; width 8¼ inches; bright finish; price $6.00.

**2229-A.** Ancient India Scimiter, price $12.00.

**2240.** Italian Sword; 27 inch gilt etched blade, engraved "Viva Pio IX.," and on the reverse side of the blade, "Viva Italia"; brass guard and pommel; checkered hilt; price $12.50.

European Army Lance, 9¼ feet long, hard wood pole with steel spear, with iron loops for attaching small flag, with steel socket, in fine order, same as we furnished to the New York Hippodrome for the Cossacks; price $3.50 each.

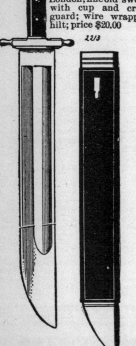

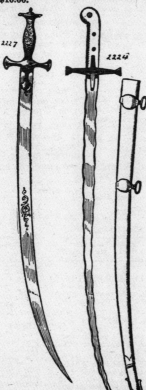

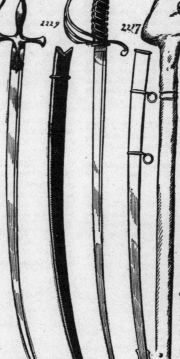

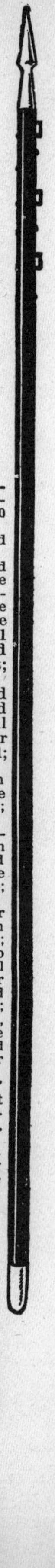

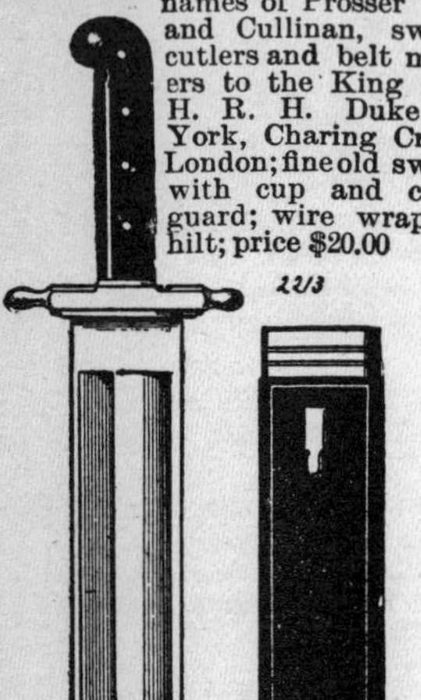

**2213.** 100 Antique Wide Blade Side Arm Swords; kind said to have been used by German Artillery men at Waterloo; length of blade 18½ inches; width 2 1-16 inches; black bone hilt; steel cross guard; wood scabbard, 2½ inches wide at the mouth; with hook; with tip; full length 26 inches. The wide blade in this sword makes it very desirable for use for decorating; offered in fine order; price $2.95.

**2224.** Ancient Scimiter, with flamboyant wavy edged blade; sharpened point and cutting edge; 34 inch blade; ivory handle; three inch curve; velvet covered scabbard, with wrought metal tips and bands; rare weapon; price $25.00.

**2227.** India Scimiter, with inlaid gilt ornamentation on the blade; silver wire ornamented hilt; 30 inch blade; 2¼ inch curve; cleaned and in serviceable order; blade is double edged to seven inches from the point; width of blade at hilt 1¼ inches; price $7.85.

**2217.** U. S. Army Officers Sword, as used in the War of 1812, Seminole Indian and Mexican Wars, and probably the Civil War; Eagle head pommel; 32 inch etched steel blade; German silver scabbard; purchased at U. S. Government Auction, Springfield Arsenal, 1907; in used, serviceable order; price $12.00.

**D94.** 1 ARAB DAGGER with 8-inch curved blade and solid horn handle silver mounted, also two native brass coins attached. Wood scabbard covered with cloth and leather with long shoulder sling and buckle. All shows native work. Price, $7.00.

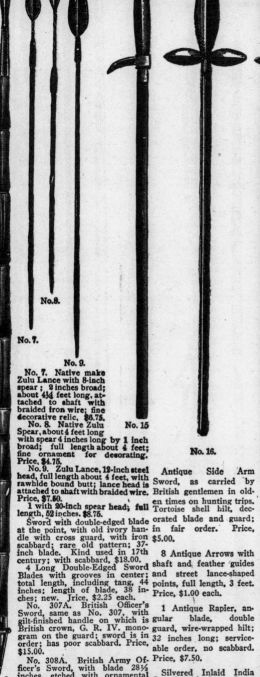

Long have you been in hiding,
Veterans of the war!
Many the shifts and changes
That have brought you where
you are.
Like poor old Rip Van Winkle,
You belong to another day,
To different scenes and duties,
To times that have passed
away.

Civil War Lance with red and white Guidon flag, with leather buckle; in fine, serviceable order. Price, $12.75

No. 50

No. 374. European Officer's Sword: en-
the guard handle shark skin, with black and yellow sword knot; very slightly curved quill back; 30½-inch blade, 7½-inch
**No. 4.** width; with leather scabbard; 2 rings; brass bands; mouth and tip pieces; in good, second-hand, serviceable order. Price, $6.50.

No. 376. Holland Officer's double-grooved straight blade Sword; with two rings,
31½-inch straight quill back blade;
*iem;* grooved handgrip with guard handle, steel scabbard; serviceable, second-hand order. Price, $8.75.

No. 377. Antique Pattern, Double-Edged Sword; 33-inch blade; 1¾-inch at hilt; with heavy brass 7½-inch handle; leather scabbard; 2 rings; firmly mounted in brass. Price, $10.00.

Revolutionary War Saber with carved ivory handle, brass guard; artillery pattern; engraved with British Coat of Arms and motto, and on the reverse side G. R. British crown. Dieu et mon droit; full length, 34½ inches; fine order. $11.50.

No. 7.

No. 8.

No. 9.

**No. 7.** Native make Zulu Lance with 8-inch spear; 2 inches broad; about 4¼ feet long, attached to shaft with braided iron wire; fine decorative relic, $6.75.

No. 8. Native Zulu Spear, about 4 feet long with spear 4 inches long by 1 inch broad; full length about 4 feet; fine ornament for decorating. Price, $4.75.

No. 9. Zulu Lance, 12-inch steel head, full length about 4 feet, with rawhide bound butt; lance head is attached to shaft with braided wire. Price, $7.50.

1 with 20-inch spear head; full length, 52 inches. $8.75.
Sword with double-edged blade at the point, with old ivory handle with cross guard, with iron scabbard; rare old pattern; 37-inch blade. Kind used in 17th century; with scabbard, $18.00.
4 Long Double-Edged Sword Blades with grooves in center; total length, including tang, 44 inches; length of blade, 38 inches; new. Price, $2.25 each.
No. 307A. British Officer's Sword, same as No. 307, with gilt-finished handle on which is British crown, G. R. IV. monogram on the guard; sword is in order; has poor scabbard. Price, $15.00.
No. 308A. British Army Officer's Sword, with blade 28½ inches, etched with ornamental scroll work and Royal Artillery and British Crown. The old-style 2-ringed scabbard; with sharkskin grip; 4-guard handle; sharp double-edged blade for about 6 inches from the point; in serviceable order. Price, $10.00.
John Brown Pike, one of the lot made to arm the negroes in their fight for freedom. Purchased from party in Maryland. Price, $65.00.
No. 15. Georgia Pike, with bridle cutter; made by workmen of Georgia, at the request of Gov. Brown during the Civil War period, to repel Sherman's troops, who were then "marching through Georgia." Rare relic. Price, $12.00
No. 16. Georgia Pikes, with double hook bridle cutter, called the "Clover Leaf Pattern." Price, $15.00 each.
No. 17. Georgia Pikes, as illustrated. Price, $3.00.
These Georgia Pikes were sold to us by the U. S. Ordnance Dept., we taking delivery direct from the U. S. Arsenal at Augusta, Ga.
No. 50. Antique War Lances, polished steel fluted spear head, with socket, fitted to hard wood pole. With metal shoe; length over 8 feet. Price, $2.50 each. With lance pennant flag, $3.00 each. With carrying strap, 80 cents extra.

No. 15

No. 16.

**No. 6.**

Antique Side Arm Sword, as carried by British gentlemen in olden times on hunting trips. Tortoise shell hilt, decorated blade and guard; in fair order. Price, $5.00.

8 Antique Arrows with shaft and feather guides and street lance-shaped points, full length, 3 feet. Price, $1.00 each.

1 Antique Rapier, angular blade, double guard, wire-wrapped hilt; 32 inches long; serviceable order, no scabbard. Price, $7.50.

Silvered Inlaid India Sword with large ivory handle, silvered inscription from the Koran on the blade. Price, $15.00.

6 Native-made Javelins, assorted patterns. For transportation to America the wood poles were cut off. All show scars from service. Price, $3.85 each.

No. 2.

No. 13.

No. 14.

No. 1.

No. 13. Napoleon long straight blade Sword; kind used by Napoleon's cavalry at Waterloo, 1815 and earlier dates are stamped on the blade so that it may have been possible for some of these swords to have been used at the Battle of Waterloo. All in good, serviceable, clean and polished order; full length, 45½ inches; brass handle, wire wrapped, with steel scabbard. Price, $15.00.

No. 14. Philippine Dagger Kris with native wood scabbard; blade is rusty; wood work broken; is a good relic. Price, $14.00.

No. 1. Spanish Navy Boat Hook, from Santiago.
No. 17. Gun metal, anchor pattern, 6-foot pole; $6.00.

No. 2. Spanish Arrows, from the Havana Arsenal, 1898; made of ¾-inch steel, 4 feet long, with 1-inch arrow point, supposed to have been furnished to the Cuban Indians hundreds of years ago; finely polished. Price, $1.75.

No. 3. Spanish Toledo Blade Lance, fitted to 8-foot ash pole, steel shod on bottom. Stamped on steel blade, "Habana Maestranza." Very few lances were captured. Price, $18.00.

Large Sword, 3-foot blade, double-handed, grooved handle is 10 inches long, 7½-inch cross guard with second cross guard lower down on the blade; blunt edges; intended for armoral figure; not polished; $6.50.

No. 6. Male Bamboo Lance; poles as required in the British Army Regulation Lances; only kind that will stand for tent pegging; rare quality, hard to obtain. Price of British Army Lance with male bamboo pole, $8.50.

A good story is told of a certain colonel in connection with an inspection of a crack rifle corps which he commanded. The inspection passed off satisfactorily; there were no complaints, and the regiment was evidently in good order. "But," said the inspecting general, "I am bound to tell you, colonel, that rumors have reached me of gambling being carried on extensively among your officers." "That may have been the case, sir," said the colonel, "some months ago; but I can assure you that nothing of the kind is in vogue now, because I've won all the ready money in the regiment, and I would not allow any gambling on credit."—Canadian Military Gazette.

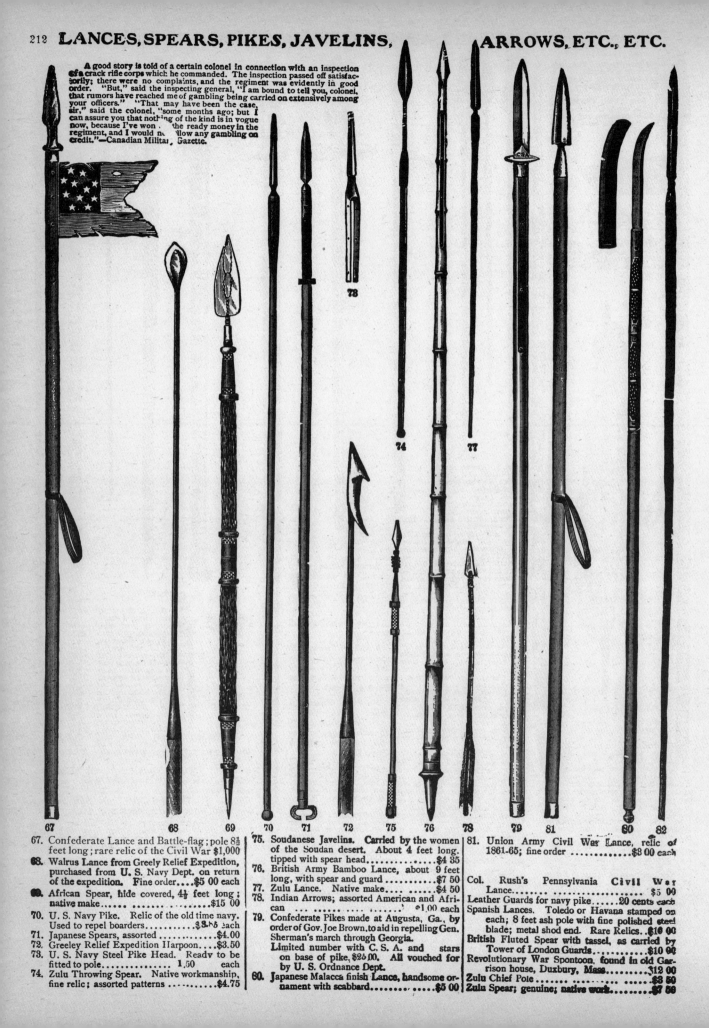

67. Confederate Lance and Battle-flag; pole 8½ feet long; rare relic of the Civil War $1,000

68. Walrus Lance from Greely Relief Expedition, purchased from U. S. Navy Dept. on return of the expedition. Fine order....$5 00 each

69. African Spear, hide covered, 4½ feet long; native make...... .........$15 00

70. U. S. Navy Pike. Relic of the old time navy. Used to repel boarders...........$3.75 each

71. Japanese Spears, assorted .............$4.00

72. Greeley Relief Expedition Harpoon....$3.50

73. U. S. Navy Steel Pike Head. Ready to be fitted to pole...............1.50 each

74. Zulu Throwing Spear. Native workmanship, fine relic; assorted patterns ..........$4.75

75. Soudanese Javelins. Carried by the women of the Soudan desert. About 4 feet long. tipped with spear head...............$4 35

76. British Army Bamboo Lance, about 9 feet long, with spear and guard ...........$7 50

77. Zulu Lance. Native make.... ......$4 50

78. Indian Arrows; assorted American and African ... ...............$1.00 each

79. Confederate Pikes made at Augusta, Ga., by order of Gov. Joe Brown, to aid in repelling Gen. Sherman's march through Georgia.
Limited number with C. S. A. and stars on base of pike, $25.00. All vouched for by U. S. Ordnance Dept.

80. Japanese Malacca finish Lance, handsome ornament with scabbard..............$5 00

81. Union Army Civil War Lance, relic of 1861-65; fine order ...............$8 00 each

Col. Rush's Pennsylvania Civil War Lance........ ...................... $5 00

Leather Guards for navy pike......20 cents each

Spanish Lances. Toledo or Havana stamped on each; 8 feet ash pole with fine polished steel blade; metal shod end. Rare Relics..$10 00

British Fluted Spear with tassel, as carried by Tower of London Guards............$10 00

Revolutionary War Spontoon, found in old Garrison house, Duxbury, Mass........$12 00

Zulu Chief Pole ...................$3 50

Zulu Spear; genuine; native work........$7 50

No. 502.

No. 504.

No. 505.

No. 506.

No. 508.

No. 509.

No. 500. No. 501. No. 502.

No. 310.

No. 506.

**No. 500.** Antique German Lance with 18-inch blade, 1¼ inches wide; total length, 8 feet; with leather hand grip, tassels and pennant, with socket. Price, $7.75.

**No. 501.** Spear; large polished steel blade, 20 inches long, 3¾ inches wide; blade rings out when struck; length, over 6 feet. Price, $12.00.

**No. 502.** Spontoon, with battle axe and bridle cutter; length of blade, 12 inches; width at the bridle cutter, 7½ inches; old black-colored pole. Price, $10.00.

**No. 503.** Halbard Battle Axe; real old timer, from London collection; has rose stamped on the blade; hand forged; in fine state of preservation; facsimile of piece in Tower of London which is upwards of 500 years old; length of blade, 28 inches; 12 inches at widest part; pole is square shaped, of old, hard, black-looking wood; total length, 7 feet 9 inches. Cheap at $25.00.

**No. 504.** Spontoon; polished steel; 19-inch blade; width, 7 inches; stamped 288 on steel, also on the shaft; in fine order; blade is double edged, sharp pointed, with axe; total length, 7½ feet. Price, $14.00.

**No. 505.** Antique Gisarm; antique weapon with double-edged cut and thrust blade, used against mounted horsemen; hook was used to cut the bridles; sharpened for serious business; blade is 11 inches long, 5 inches wide at hook; 7½ feet long; dark-colored hardwood pole with antique socket. We have pair of these rare old relics. Price, $20.00 the pair, or $11.50 singly.

**No. 506.** Rare Old Pike, polished steel blade, 12¾ inches long, 2½ inches wide at widest part, with metal socket; total length, 7 feet. Price, $6.75.

**No. 507.** Pair of Irish Pikes, captured by the British from the Irish revolutionists, one in 1798 and one in 1868 from Dublin Castle. Purchased from collector, who obtained them from London gentleman residing on Cromwell Road, whose address will be given to purchaser. Pole is rough and crooked; the metal pike no doubt made by country blacksmith; length is 8 feet, blade is 16 inches, fastened to pole by iron straps. Rare prize for collector. Price for the pair, $25.00.

**No. 508.** Tower of London Halbards, same as carried by the Boufitiers ("Beefeaters") in King Edward's coronation procession, acting as the King's body guard. Came from Tower of London over 50 years ago and are vouched for to us by the man who obtained them direct from the Tower; rare interesting relic; 12½-inch blade, 5¾-inch arm guard; old rosewood pole, 7 feet long. Price, $25.00.

**No. 509.** German Army Lance with three sided, hollow-shaped blade; total length of blade and pole strap, 2 feet; total length, 9½ feet; fine hardwood pole with metal socket, with metal rings for holding the pennant. Considered rare even in Europe. Price, $4.50 each, or $8.00 the pair. We can supply bunting pennants (made up, not original) at 50 cents each.

**No. 510.** Pair Antique Spears from British collection, over 6 feet long, 6-inch blade, with the old-time square pole with beaded edge. Price, $12.75 the pair.

Guidon Flags with poles; any design or color; made to order, either in all-wool standard bunting or silk. Price on application, with design and quantity wanted.

No. 310.

**310A. SPANISH FOLDING KNIFE** with 7½-inch pointed blade, held in place when open by heavy spring in handle. Length when open is 16¼ inches. Ornamented with brass bands and red shell. Price $6.50.

**310B. SPANISH FOLDING KNIFE** with 12-inch long pointed blade. Length when open 25 inches. Brass handle is ornamented with silver disks evidently made from old silver coins. Knives of this length are rare. Price $8.50.

**Old time British Midshipman's Side Arm Sword,** etched steel carved blade; ivory handle with lion head pommel; decorated cross guard; full length, 21½ inches; 2 rings in the scabbard for use with sling straps; leather scabbard. Price, $10.00.

**Antique Rapier;** shark skin grip, gilt wire wrapped; full length, 35 inches; in serviceable order. Price, $6.80.

**British Officer's Sword** with lion head pommel holding guard in mouth; gilt bronze, with G. R. and crown with hunting horn, showing that the owner belonged to the Volunteers while the G. R. looks as if it was made in time of King George the Third. The blade is gilt etched with figure of Britanna, G. R., spears, helmet, etc., decorating; on the reverse side of the blade the British Coat of Arms is etched with motto "Honi Soit Qui Mal y Pense." No scabbard. Price, $10.00.

**Antique Fluted Spear Head,** British —with screw, easy to fasten to pole. Polished malleable iron, will wear well, $2.50.

**XVII Lancers old Scimiter Shaped Saber** with steel scabbard, all in fine order; shark skin grip; wrapped and fluted steel handle; blade finely etched with British Crown, G. R. and P. R. R. with mounted horseman in act of charging; on the reverse side is etched skull and cross bones— "Death or Glory, XVII, etc." Price, $8.00.

**No. 310.—Spanish Dagger;** blade folds up in handle, with spring, which locks it when opened; 7½-inch blade; fine order. Price, $8.00.

**2 British Engineers' Saw Sword** stamped 1831; bronze handle, one side of the blade for cutting, the other with teeth for saw ing; 26 inches long; 2½ inches wide, with scabbard; brass mounted—sword in fine order. Price $6.75 each.

**Malay Spear—**Hammered Steel, $8.00.

**Captured Spanish Toledo Blade Sabers—**Vouched for by U. S. A.; stamped "Toledo"; rusty. Price, $3.85 each.

**Philippine Islander's Bolo—**Purchased from returned soldier; good order. Price, $12.50.

**British Army Sappers' and Miners' Sword Bayonet—**Brass handle, steel double-edged blade, $1.50.

**Pacific Islander's Stone Club—**With row of human teeth at the base, fair order. Price, $12.60.

**Brown Bess Spade Bayonet—**With leather scabbard, rare relic, $1.50.

**Old-Time Flint Locks—**Taken from guns captured by the British soldiers in Ireland, last century; guns were broken up, locks were sold at Enfield, England; rusty, complete, $1.50 each.

**British Army Officer's Sword—**With V. R. in metal ring on guard of handle, fair order. Price, $7.50.

**British Army Bamboo Lances—**With pennant, for decorating. Price, $6.50.

**Pair Combat Swords—**With 21-inch steel blade, with large basket-guard handle. Price, $6.50 pair.

**U. S. A. Officer's Sword—**Found in hospital, San Juan, Cuba. We are unable to find owner and now offer it for sale; rare relic; vouched for. Price, $20.00.

**Chinese Idol Swords—**One foot long. Price, $3.50.

**African Spears,** set 4, sold by New York Customs Officers. Spear and socket is native work; decorated with colored fibre at centre; rare specimens. Price, $40.00 the set; will sell singly if desired, $12.00 each.

No. 506.

No. 508.

No. 509.

**Antique British Halberd** — From original purchased in Edinburgh, Scotland. Malleable iron, polished like steel, with round screw set in ready to fasten to pole. Handsome cozy corner decoration. Price, $3.50.

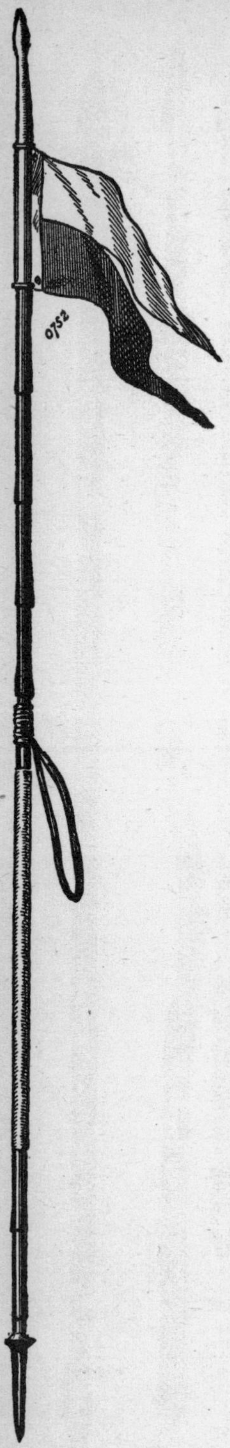

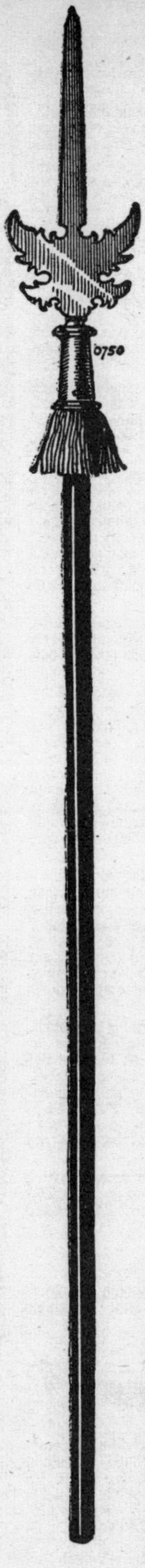

**ANCIENT CRUSADER.**

**0-752. PAIR OF BOER WAR BRITISH ARMY BAMBOO LANCES WITH FLAGS.** Brought back to England by general. Given to Lady Palmer's museum of weapons. Afterwards sold at auction room. These are the regular service male bamboo British Army lance with red and white pennants. Iron straps, with tangs, neatly covered with russet leather and stamped No. 103 and No. 466. Length of steel socket and blade 12 inches. Full length 9 feet. No doubt there is some interesting history with these lances. We offer the pair at $30.00; singly, $16.00.

**0-750.** Sold to collector. See other pages for lances and spears of similar style. We can furnish spears in different lengths for decoration.

**0-753. RARE ANCIENT PATTERN HALBARD,** with 13¼-inch thrusting wavy-edged steel blade; 6-inch ornamented battle axe; 5-inch hooked spear, and bridle cutter. Square socket, with long tangs mounted on octagonal poles. Full length 7 feet 3 inches. Price, $25.00.

**0-751. MORNING STAR SPEAR.** Triangular-shaped 19-inch blade, 11 quadrangular side spears, projecting 2 inches. Full length 7 feet 8 inches. From the Lawson-Johnston sale. Price, $20.00.

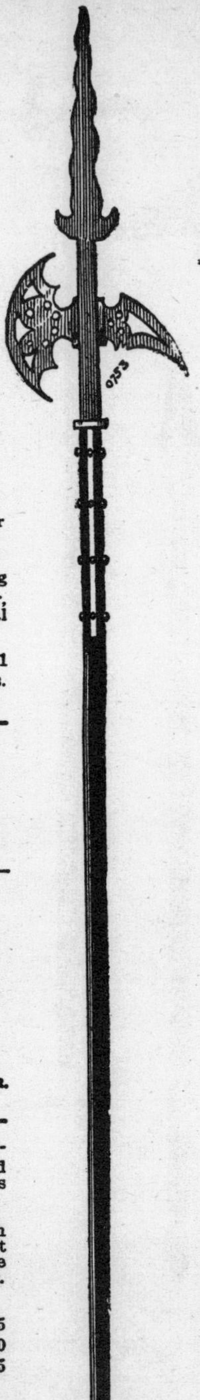

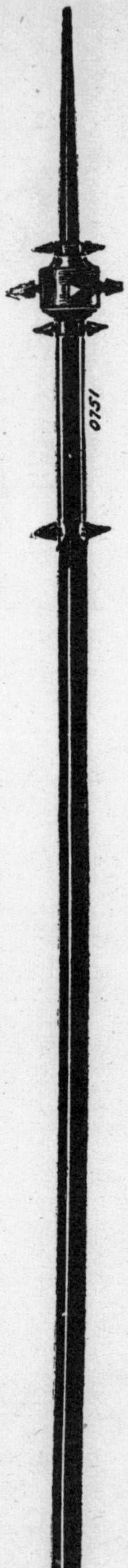

**GIVE THE MEN OF YESTERDAY THE WEAPONS OF TO-DAY**

We've got the men of yesterday—
  Red-blooded, staunch and true;
Ready to fight—by day or night—
  For the Red and White and Blue.

We've got the Public spirit,
  Yes, and the Public cash
To give and spend—for any end—
  Then hand our soldiers trash.

*     *     *     *     *

We've got the arms of yesterday—
  To give these men to fight
Clothes that leak, and arms antique—
  Too heavy or too light.

Wake up to-day—AMERICA
  And buy the things that PAY
Give the men of YESTERDAY
  The weapons of TO-DAY.

           F T Dexter.

**0-754. PAIR BRITISH ARMY OFFICER'S PIG-STICKING MALE BAMBOO LANCES.** India service spears. Full length 7 feet 8 inches. Loaded butt socket, 4-inch double edge sharpened steel thrusting spear. One is stamped, "Bodraj, Arungahad." Price the pair, $16.50.

**0-779. PAIR BRITISH ARMY PIG-STICKING SPEARS.** Used by British army officers on India service in hunting wild boars. From a sale at Queen's Gate, London. India officer's relics. Indian names stamped on the socket. Full length 9¼ inches, ½-inch socket. Good serviceable order. Price the pair, $9.85.

Philippine Harpoon-shaped Three-barbed Spear.................Price, $12.85
Malay Islander's Spear; native work.............................Price, 10.00
Philippine Native's Spear; wire wrapped.......................Price, 14.85
Philippine Native's Spear, with kris-shaped blade, wavy edges, native watered steel; decorated pole, fancy gilt ferrule, with service marks; rare relic.........................Price, 30.00
Philippine Islander's Spear, with 10-inch blade, mounted on pole..Price, 12.50
Assegai Spear, with long iron shank, wood handle...............Price, 8.50

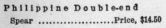

**Philippine Double-end Spear** ....................Price, $14.50

**Savage Chieftain's Wood Pole,** with ball-shaped top; rude native carving. Pole is scepter of authority.....Price, 8.50

**India Elephant Driver's Iron Spear,** with hook; 5-inch spear, 6-inch hook.......Price, 8.25

India Spiked Club, with spikes and spear point.................Price, $12.50
Cannibal Island Stone War Club, with two rows of pig's teeth set in pole around the circular stone club. Size of stone 2x3½ inches; length of pole, 42 inches..........................................Price, 10.00

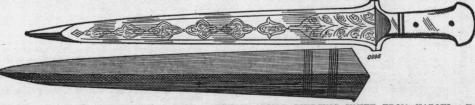

**0-996. AFGHAN ARMOR PIERCING KNIFE FROM KABOUL.** From the sale of the Nevinson collection. Double-edged 16-inch steel blade, with very sharpened reinforced steel point for puncturing through old-time armor. Engraved blade. Bone hilt handle; leather covered scabbard. Rare old weapon. Price, $16.75.

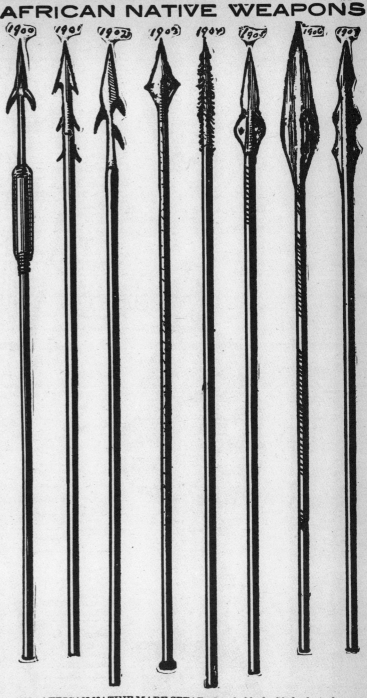
(1900) (1901) (1902) (1903) (1904) (1905) (1906) (1907)

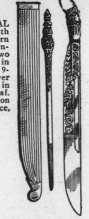

D67. 1.SACRIFICIAL KNIFE, 11 inch, with silver mounted horn handle, and silver inlaid blade with two grooves. Knife is in wood scabbard with 9-inch pencil, silver mounted, for use in writing on palm leaf. A rare combination from Ceylon. Price, $10.

O-917. ALGERIAN NATIVE'S DIRK. Pair of knives contained in single scabbard; ornamented steel blades and hilt all in one piece. Full length 9¼ inches. Sharpened blades. Wood scabbard. Brass metal inlaid. Rare pattern. Price, $7.85 the pair. Sale restricted to known collectors.

O-921. COMBINATION WAR CLUB AND DAGGER. 12-inch bamboo handle. Woven fibre covered, weighted oval-shaped club, 1¾-inch diameter, containing 5½-inch dagger blade, held in place by spring hilt and covered with woven fibre and cord. Sale of this antique weapon is restricted to high-class museums. Price, $8.75.

O-987. AFRICAN FETISH WORSHIP SACRIFICIAL BLOOD VESSEL. Used to hold the blood of the victim. From the Martyn-Kenard collection. Dried skin 5 inches high, 4¾ inches wide, 2½ inches thick. Bottle-shaped. Perhaps has held the blood of some missionary. Price, $12.85.

O-715A. SAVAGE WAR DRUM OR TOM-TOM, in serviceable order. 8 inches high, 9-inch head. Drum skin head, stretched across a kettle-shaped fibre pot, with rope tightening cords, attached to grommet. Native construction. Rare specimen. Price, $15.00.

O-846. ELEPHANT TAIL FLY WHISK. 13-inch flesh end, with about 12 inches of the coarse black hair of about the thickness of shoe laces; dried and hard. Price, $4.85.

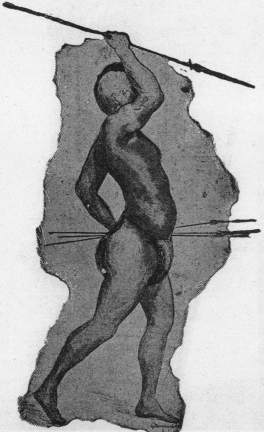

1900 AFRICAN NATIVE MADE SPEAR, detachable double barb steel spear, head 9 inches attached to pole by cords, which allows the shaft to come apart from the spear when it strikes. Full length, with shaft 5½ ft. price $7.00

1901 STEEL SPEAR HEAD, 20 inches. Full length, 5½ ft. price $6.00

1902 DOUBLE BARB SPEAR POINT, 11 inches. Full length 6 ft. 4 inches price $6.00

1903 18 inch DOUBLE EDGED BLADE, raised copper and brass work. Full length 5¼ ft. price $8.50

1904 DOUBLE ROW OF SMALL BARBS spear 35 inches in length. Full length with pole 5½ ft. price $10.00

1905 DOUBLE EDGED STEEL SPEAR 16 inches long with two holes, centre rib. Full length 5¼ ft.

1906 DOUBLE EDGED STEEL SPEAR, blade 23 inches, octagonal ornamented socket, centre rib, full length 4¼ft. $10.00

1907 DOUBLE RECESSED SPEAR SHAPED BLADE 2 feet long. Full length 5½ ft. price $10.00

712-713-714 South Sea Islanders War Clubs or Battle Axe, made of stone, they have made some round and some shield shaped, with hole formed in centre for pole, used as battle axe, Purchased from London collector. Choice of three patterns; circular, shield or egg shaped. Price $9.50 each.

Kava Bowls, made with sea shells, by natives of Samoa, Fiji, Santa Cruz, Islands in Pacific Ocean. Price $5.50

Illustration of Congo Native Hunter, Drawn for us by Belgian Government Artist from whom we purchased collection of weapons.

Captain to an Irish soldier, who has laid claim to a coat that had been found: "Why are you so positive that the coat is yours?" Soldier: "Bekase, sor, me name is in it," and promptly producing from a pocket two dried-up peas said, "there is me name, sor, P. for Pat and P for Powers."

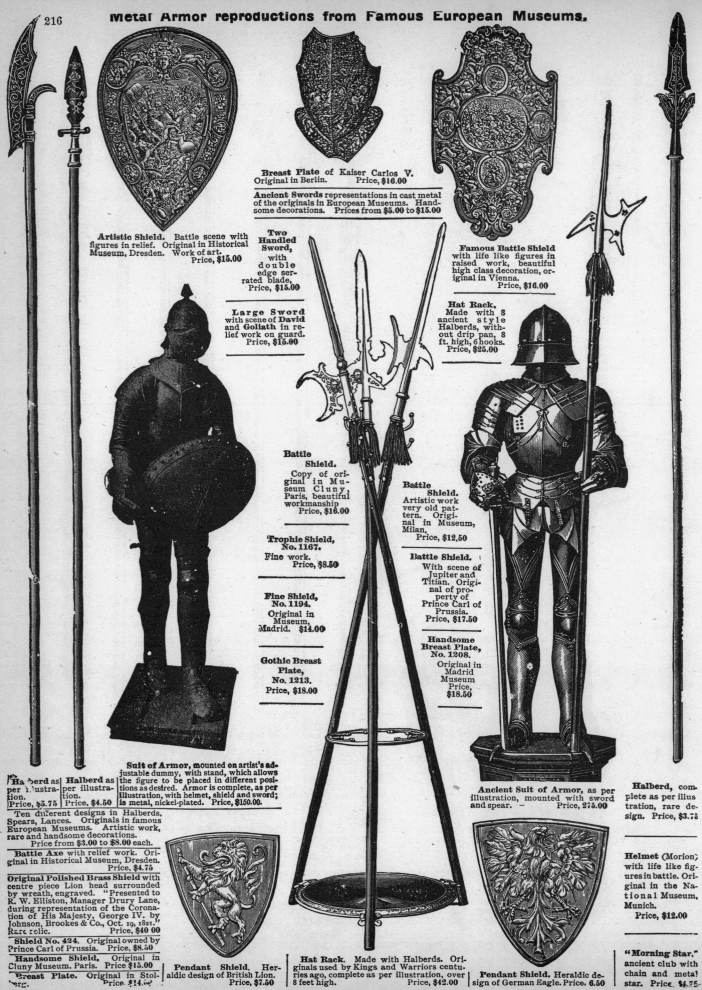

**Breast Plate of Kaiser Carlos V.** Original in Berlin. Price, $16.00

**Ancient Swords** representations in cast metal of the originals in European Museums. Handsome decorations. Prices from $5.00 to $15.00

**Artistic Shield.** Battle scene with figures in relief. Original in Historical Museum, Dresden. Work of art. Price, $15.00

**Two Handled Sword,** with double edge serrated blade, Price, $15.00

**Large Sword** with scene of **David and Goliath** in relief work on guard. Price, $15.00

**Famous Battle Shield** with life like figures in raised work, beautiful high class decoration, original in Vienna. Price, $16.00

**Hat Rack.** Made with 8 ancient style Halberds, without drip pan, 8 ft. high, 6 hooks. Price, $25.00

**Battle Shield.** Copy of original in Museum Cluny, Paris, beautiful workmanship Price, $16.00

**Trophie Shield, No. 1167.** Fine work. Price, $8.50

**Fine Shield, No. 1194.** Original in Museum, Madrid. $14.00

**Gothic Breast Plate, No. 1213.** Price, $18.00

**Battle Shield.** Artistic work very old pattern. Original in Museum, Milan. Price, $12.50

**Battle Shield.** With scene of Jupiter and Titian. Original of property of Prince Carl of Prussia. Price, $17.50

**Handsome Breast Plate, No. 1208.** Original in Madrid Museum Price, $18.50

**Halberd as per illustration.** Price, $5.75

**Halberd as per illustration.** Price, $4.50

**Suit of Armor,** mounted on artist's adjustable dummy, with stand, which allows the figure to be placed in different positions as desired. Armor is complete, as per illustration, with helmet, shield and sword; is metal, nickel-plated. Price, $150.00

Ten different designs in Halberds, Spears, Lances. Originals in famous European Museums. Artistic work, rare and handsome decorations. Price from $3.00 to $8.00 each.

**Battle Axe** with relief work. Original in Historical Museum, Dresden. Price, $4.75

**Original Polished Brass Shield** with centre piece Lion head surrounded by wreath, engraved. "Presented to R. W. Elliston, Manager Drury Lane, during representation of the Coronation of His Majesty, George IV. by Johnson, Brookes & Co., Oct. 19, 1821." Rare relic. Price, $40.00

**Shield No. 424.** Original owned by Prince Carl of Prussia. Price, $8.50

**Handsome Shield.** Original in Cluny Museum, Paris. Price $15.00

**Breast Plate.** Original in Stolberg. Price, $14.00

**Pendant Shield.** Heraldic design of British Lion. Price, $7.50

**Hat Rack.** Made with Halberds. Originals used by Kings and Warriors centuries ago, complete as per illustration, over 8 feet high. Price, $42.00

**Ancient Suit of Armor,** as per illustration, mounted with sword and spear. — Price, 275.00

**Pendant Shield.** Heraldic design of German Eagle. Price, 6.50

**Halberd,** complete as per illustration, rare design. Price, $3.75

**Helmet (Morion)** with life like figures in battle. Original in the National Museum, Munich. Price, $12.00

**"Morning Star,"** ancient club with chain and metal star. Price, $4.75

# MILITARY DECORATIVE TROPHIES.

**Made up with genuine historical weapons that have been used on many fields of battle, making the most interesting as well as the cheapest of decorations.**

Prices quoted on application.

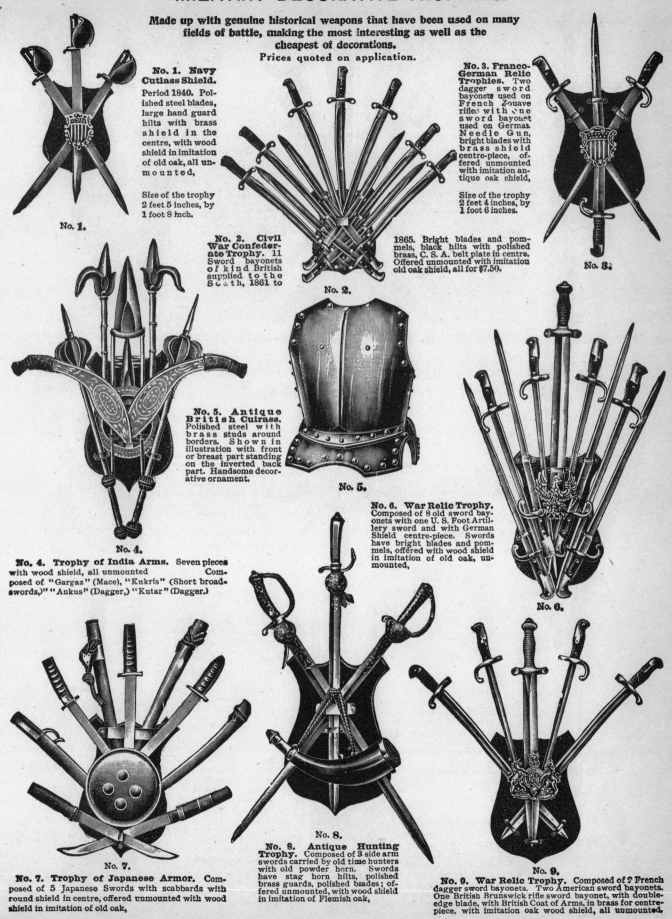

**No. 1. Navy Cutlass Shield.** Period 1840. Polished steel blades, large hand guard hilts with brass shield in the centre, with wood shield in imitation of old oak, all unmounted,

Size of the trophy 2 feet 5 inches, by 1 foot 8 inch.

**No. 1.**

**No. 2. Civil War Confederate Trophy.** 11 Sword bayonets of kind British supplied to the South, 1861 to

**No. 2.**

1865. Bright blades and pommels, black hilts with polished brass, C. S. A. belt plate in centre. Offered unmounted with imitation old oak shield, all for $7.50.

**No. 3. Franco-German Relic Trophies.** Two dagger sword bayonets used on French Zouave rifle with one sword bayonet used on German Needle Gun, bright blades with brass shield centre-piece, offered unmounted with imitation antique oak shield,

Size of the trophy 2 feet 4 inches, by 1 foot 6 inches.

**No. 3.**

**No. 5. Antique British Cuirass.** Polished steel with brass studs around borders. Shown in illustration with front or breast part standing on the inverted back part. Handsome decorative ornament.

**No. 5.**

**No. 4.**

**No. 4. Trophy of India Arms.** Seven pieces with wood shield, all unmounted Composed of "Gargaz" (Mace), "Kukris" (Short broadswords,)" "Ankus" (Dagger,) "Kutar" (Dagger.)

**No. 6. War Relic Trophy.** Composed of 8 old sword bayonets with one U. S. Foot Artillery sword and with German Shield centre-piece. Swords have bright blades and pommels, offered with wood shield in imitation of old oak, unmounted,

**No. 6.**

**No. 7.**

**No. 7. Trophy of Japanese Armor.** Composed of 5 Japanese Swords with scabbards with round shield in centre, offered unmounted with wood shield in imitation of old oak,

**No. 8.**

**No. 8. Antique Hunting Trophy.** Composed of 3 side arm swords carried by old time hunters with old powder horn. Swords have stag horn hilts, polished brass guards, polished blades; offered unmounted, with wood shield in imitation of Flemish oak,

**No. 9.**

**No. 9. War Relic Trophy.** Composed of 2 French dagger sword bayonets. Two American sword bayonets. One British Brunswick rifle sword bayonet, with double-edge blade, with British Coat of Arms, in brass for centre-piece, with imitation oak wood shield, all unmounted,

**No. 10. Indian Trophy of Arms.** Composed of long straight antique Nepalese sword. 2 "Tabars" (crescent shape battle-axes) with wood shield, unmounted

**No. 12. War Relic Trophy.** Size, 2 feet 10 inches, by 1 foot, 9 inches. Composed of 4 French Army dagger bayonets as used on the Grah rifles. 2 side arm sword bayonets as used on the French Chassepot rifles, relics of 1870. 1 double edge side arm sword bayonet as used on the British Army Brunswick rifle, all offered, unmounted, with wood shield

**No. 11. Trophies from many lands.** 1 U. S. A. Foot Artillery Sword. 2 French side arm sword bayonets. 2 sabres captured in the Spanish-American War. 2 Antique Sabres, Prussian Army helmet, eagle centre, with wood shield, all unmounted

### Prices Quoted On Application.

**No. 13. Handsome Trophy of Arms used in India.** Composed of one double-bladed dagger "Kutar." 2 Short swords "Kukris." 2 Mace or Bludgeons "Gargaz." 2 Battle-axes "Tabars," with wood shield, unmounted,

**No. 14. U. S. A. Civil War Relic Trophy.** Composed of 5 sword bayonets used during the Civil War, bright steel blades, brass handles, with imitation oak shield, all unmounted, Brass eagle shield for center, 30 cents extra.

**No. 15. Indian Trophy.** One celebrated India Gauntlet Sword "Pata" with 2 battle-axes "Tabars," surmounted with antique Japanese Helmet, all with wood shield, unmounted.

**No. 16. U. S. Army Trophy.** 3 Side arm sword bayonets, polished steel blades and bronze handles with wood shield in imitation of old oak, all unmounted,

**No. 17. War Relic Trophy.** Composed of 8 French Dagger Side-arm bayonets with one U. S. Army Foot Artillery Sword with scabbard, all polished blades, offered with imitation oak shield, unmounted,

**No. 18. Indian Trophy.** Center-piece double-bladed dagger "Kutar," right and left, hooked dagger "Ankus," curved daggers, "Pichangetti." For the above named 5 weapons with wood shield, unmounted.

No. 10.  No. 11.  No. 12.  No. 13.  No. 14.  No. 15.  No. 16.  No. 17.  No. 18.

# Military Decorations

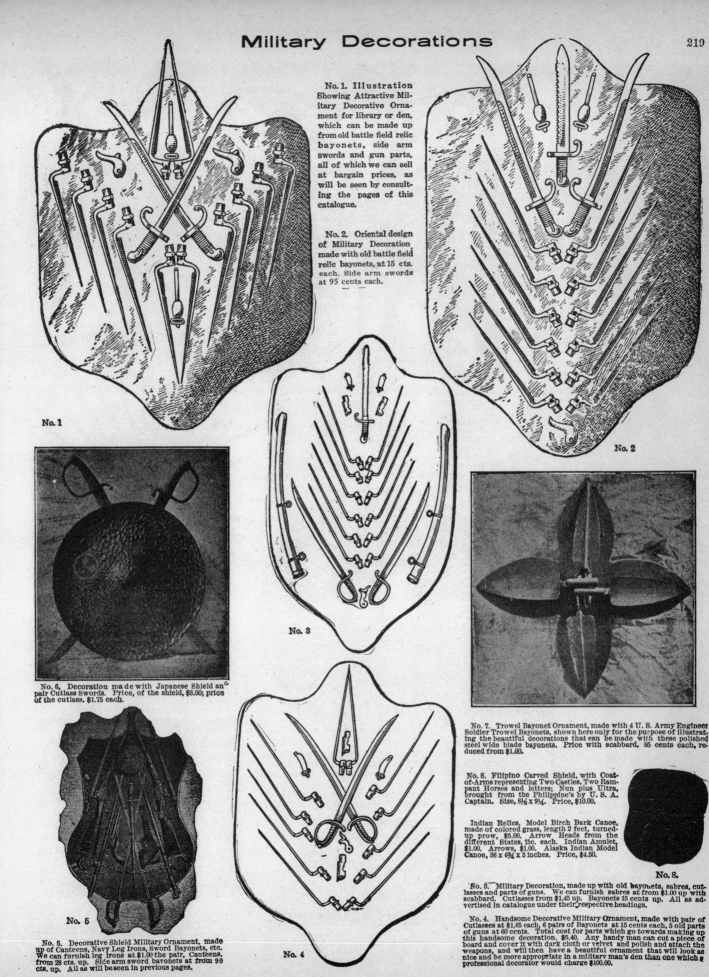

No. 1. Illustration Showing Attractive Military Decorative Ornament for library or den, which can be made up from old battle field relic bayonets, side arm swords and gun parts, all of which we can sell at bargain prices, as will be seen by consulting the pages of this catalogue.

No. 2. Oriental design of Military Decoration made with old battle field relic bayonets, at 15 cts. each. Side arm swords at 95 cents each.

No. 1

No. 2

No. 3

No. 6. Decoration made with Japanese Shield and pair Cutlass Swords. Price, of the shield, $8.00; price of the cutlass. $1.75 each.

No. 7. Trowel Bayonet Ornament, made with 4 U. S. Army Engineer Soldier Trowel Bayonets, shown here only for the purpose of illustrating the beautiful decorations that can be made with these polished steel wide blade bayonets. Price with scabbard, 85 cents each, reduced from $1.00.

No. 8. Filipino Carved Shield, with Coat-of-Arms representing Two Castles, Two Rampant Horses and letters; Nun plus Ultra, brought from the Philippine's by U. S. A. Captain. Size, 8½ x 9¼. Price, $10.00.

Indian Relics. Model Birch Bark Canoe, made of colored grass, length 2 feet, turned-up prow, $5.00. Arrow Heads from the different States, 15c. each. Indian Amulet, $1.00. Arrows, $1.00. Alaska Indian Model Canoe, 36 x 6¾ x 3 inches. Price, $4.50.

No. 8.

No. 5

No. 4

No. 3. Military Decoration, made up with old bayonets, sabres, cutlasses and parts of guns. We can furnish sabres at from $1.00 up with scabbard. Cutlasses from $1.45 up. Bayonets 15 cents up. All as advertised in catalogue under their respective headings.

No. 4. Handsome Decorative Military Ornament, made with pair of Cutlasses at $1.65 each, 6 pairs of Bayonets at 15 cents each, 5 old parts of guns at 60 cents. Total cost for parts which go towards making up this handsome decoration. $5.40. Any handy man can cut a piece of board and cover it with dark cloth or velvet and polish and attach the weapons, and will then have a beautiful ornament that will look as nice and be more appropriate in a military man's den than one which a professional decorator would charge $100.00.

No. 5. Decorative Shield Military Ornament, made up of Canteens, Navy Leg Irons, Sword Bayonets, etc. We can furnish leg irons at $1.00 the pair, Canteens. from 28 cts. up. Side arm sword bayonets at from 90 cts. up. All as will be seen in previous pages.

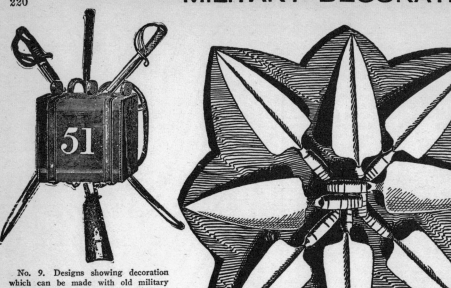

No. 9. Designs showing decoration which can be made with old military knapsack at 50 cents; 2 old sabers, at $1.00 each; 1 old carbine, at $2.00.

No. 10. Decoration made with two old sword bayonets and one leather cartridge box. Price, $2.35. Brass eagle ornament is 20 cents.

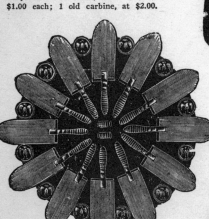

No 8, Decoration made with 8 U. S. Army Trowel Bayonets, broad polished steel trowel like blades, which can be easily formed into shape of flowers or leaves. Make a handsome ornament. We have upwards of 4,000 of these trowel bayonets for sale at 85 cts. each with eather scabbard, with brass mountings.

No. 11 Decoration formed with U. S. A. Intrenching Tools, with brass eagle belt plates. We have upwards of 5,000 of these broad steel bladed intrenching tools for sale at 65 cts. each. Eagle plate 15c each.

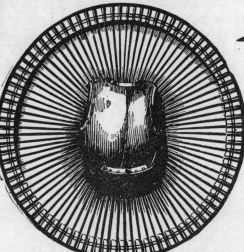

No. 12 Civil War Bayonet Decoration. 32 old bayonets polished and arranged as per illustration with brass Army buttons between, Eagle in centre. Very showy ornament. We can supply the bayonets at from 15 cents each upward. Brass Eagle 35 cents. Brass Cap Ornaments $1.00 doz. We have quantity of Spanish Bayonets that can be arranged same as above. Price $25.00. Mounted

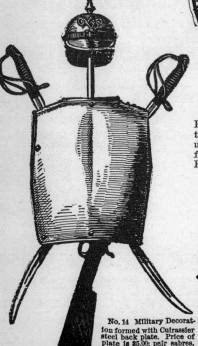

No. 15 Decoration made with Steel Armor Breast Plate and Bayonets. This makes a beautiful decoration. We can furnish bayonets at from 15 cents each upwards. Steel armor at $7.00 for back plate and $10 for breast plate. Breast plate is shown in illustration. Back plate is shown in decoration No. 14.

No. 14 Military Decoration formed with Cuirassier steel back plate. Price of plate is $5.00; pair sabres, $1.00 each; Old Military Carbine. $2.00.

No. 13 Rainbow Bayonet Decoration, made from old War bayonets. Make handsome decorative ornament placed over windows or door. We can furnish the bayonets at from 15 cents each upward. U. S. Belt Plate 25 cents. Any handy person can easily cut out board and mount the bayonets.

Carved Portrait of Admiral Dewey by U. S. Navy Sailor on the Olympia while at Manila. Walnut wood supposed to be some relic, ornamented with 28 polished steel Spanish dagger blades, forming a sunburst. Photo shows how well the work was performed. Size 14 inches long, 14 inches wide, Price $25.00

Picture of Admiral Dewey set in section of Ivory Tusk, with miniature field glass, with view of Manila. Size 3¾ inches. Price $10.00

Carved Whale Tooth, by U. S. Navy Sailor, length, 6½ inches. Price $10.00

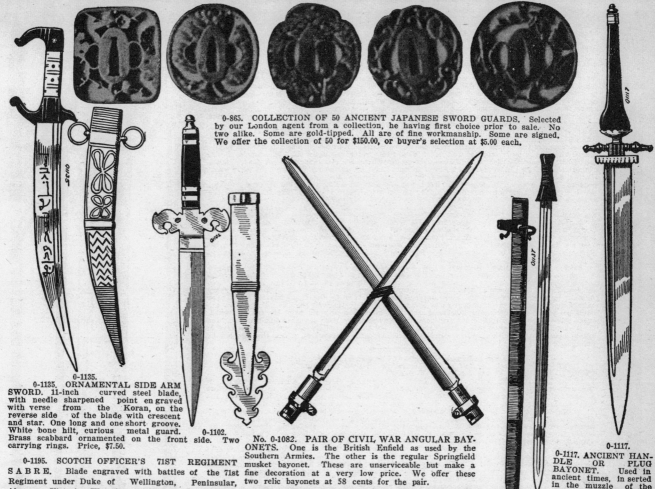

0-863. COLLECTION OF 50 ANCIENT JAPANESE SWORD GUARDS. Selected by our London agent from a collection, he having first choice prior to sale. No two alike. Some are gold-tipped. All are of fine workmanship. Some are signed. We offer the collection of 50 for $150.00, or buyer's selection at $5.00 each.

0-1135. ORNAMENTAL SIDE ARM SWORD. 11-inch curved steel blade, with needle sharpened point engraved with verse from the Koran, on the reverse side of the blade with crescent and star. One long and one short groove. White bone hilt, curious metal guard. Brass scabbard ornamented on the front side. Two carrying rings. Price, $7.50.

0-1195. SCOTCH OFFICER'S 71ST REGIMENT SABRE. Blade engraved with battles of the 71st Regiment under Duke of Wellington, Peninsular, Alamarz, Victoria, Waterloo, with Scotch thistle leaf and flower in centre of the shield with the Scotch motto, "NIMO ME IMPUNE LACESSIT" (No One Attacks Me With Impunity), 71 with the bugle (volunteer infantry emblem), with crown and sunburst. Sharkskin handle, but the rough edges of the sharkskin are WORN SMOOTH. Single guard. 31-inch blade. Leather scabbard with mouthpiece band and tip. Single ring mouthpiece on the scabbard is engraved "R. Johnson, Late Bland & Foster, Sword Cutlers and Belt Makers to His Majesty, 6 St. James Street, London." No doubt this old relic has been drawn on many a famous battlefield. Price, $25.00.

No. 0-1082. PAIR OF CIVIL WAR ANGULAR BAYONETS. One is the British Enfield as used by the Southern Armies. The other is the regular Springfield musket bayonet. These are unserviceable but make a fine decoration at a very low price. We offer these two relic bayonets at 58 cents for the pair.

0-1102. ANTIQUE SIDE ARM SWORD. With ornamental brass scabbard, 7¼-inch hand-forged double-edged steel blade, 3¾-inch brass cross guard. Black bone handle, with four rows of white bone ornamentation. Full length 15 inches. Price, $7.85.

0-1194. NAPOLEON BONAPARTE OFFICER'S RAPIER SWORD. With LETTER N on the side of the hilt pommel, with CROWN AND CROSS on the reverse side of the hilt; EAGLE with outstretched wings on both sides of the cross guards. Folding guard. 32¾-inch angular tapered steel rapier blade, engraved "COULAUX AND CIE, KLINGENTHAL." Woven silver covered hilt. Brass pommel. This is a rare sword even for France. Price, $35.00.

0-1117. ANCIENT HANDLE OR PLUG BAYONET. Used in ancient times, inserted in the muzzle of the gun after firing to repel cavalry charges. Some attribute its invention to the Scotch General MacKay, others to the French General Vauban. General Vauban in the reign of Louis XIV supplied the French infantry with flint muskets equipped with bayonets, with collar fitting over the outside of the barrel, which allowed the soldiers to shoot with bayonets fixed. Length of the sword blade is 12 inches; grooved. Artistic ornamental bands above and below the cross guard. 6-inch handle, tapered to insert in the muzzle of the old-time gun. Rare old weapon. Museum exhibit. Price, $17.50.

0-1137. AFRICAN NATIVE-MADE SWORD. 18-inch double-edged blade, recess rib in the centre, sharpened point, 3½-inch hilt, wire wrapped. Wood scabbard ornamented with iron and copper wire. A curiosity in the weapon line. Price, $6.75.

0-1137A. AFRICAN NATIVE-MADE SWORD. Similar to No. 0-1137, but slightly wider blade, plain wood scabbard, carved tip. Price, $6.25.

0-1194A. FRENCH OFFICER'S SIDE ARM RAPIER SWORD. 32½-inch tapered steel angular blade, ornamental cut work hilt, shell-shaped cross guard, rare ornamental open work pommel in gilt. Has been a handsome sword. Leather scabbard, with engraved brass tip (scabbard is in pieces). Sword and blade is in good order. Rare weapon. Price, $17.85.

D27-9. ARABIAN FLY WHISK DAGGER. The handle is 8¾ inches long, and leather tassel 5 inches long. The handle is of red leather into which is woven strips of colored reed. The dagger proper has a foursided steel blade set in the handle of whisk, and is one very good example of a "concealed weapon." Price $3.50.

U. S. N. ICE PITCHER. Engraved with American Eagle, U. S. N. Silver plated, porcelain lined; height 9 inches, diameter 6 inches. Price, $4.85.

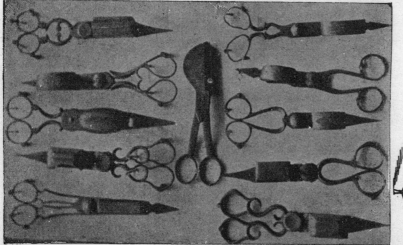

0-1099. COLLECTION OF ANCIENT CANDLE SNUFFERS. 11 different kinds in brass and iron, as shown in photograph. The average length is 6½ inches. Old-time European. To those who are making collection of ancient snuffers this offer will be a prize. Bargain for the 11 snuffers, $40.00.

0-1100. ANTIQUE BRASS CANDLE SNUFFERS. Used on the continent of Europe in ancient times. 1¼-inch snuffing box. Stands on three legs. Pointed end for stirring up the wick. Full length 6¾ inches. Spring snuffer. Price, $3.75.

0-1100A. SLIGHTLY SMALLER SIZE ANCIENT EUROPEAN CANDLE SNUFFER. Price, $3.50.

# John Brown and Georgia Pikes:

JOHN BROWN AND GEORGIA PIKES from leaf in our *contemplated book* on WEAPONS OF WAR, showing the general plan and scope of what we hope to accomplish in our book.

Many museums that we have visited in the United States have on exhibition, labeled "John Brown Pike" the pike made in Georgia during the Civil War and known as the Georgia, or Governor Joesph E. Brown Pikes. The following illustration and description and history will enable curators and collectors to distinguish and exhibit correctly:

520. JOHN BROWN PIKE, OR HANDLED SPEAR. Made by Charles Blair, edged tool maker of Collinsville, Conn., in 1857, on special order for John Brown, patterned after an 8-inch blade, double-edged dirk, submitted by Brown, which he claimed to have captured from Captain Pate, one of the border ruffians in the Kansas Free State war. One thousand pikes were contracted for at the price of $1.00 each. The blade was to be double-edged and to average 9 inches in length, 2 inches in width at the base, tapering to a point; to be made of tool steel, with cast malleable iron ferrule and guard, attached to a 6-foot ash pole with screw, fastening spear to the pole; the spears packed in boxes, the poles in bundles, which Brown claimed was for convenience in shipping and for quickly assembling. (Packed in this way their character would be concealed in transportation.)

**JOHN BROWN** in ordering these spears claimed that they were intended for WORTHY FREE STATE KANSAS SETTLERS, too poor to purchase firearms to have in their cabins for defense against the border ruffians from the Slave States, of whom it was a matter of public record had at the polls attacked and killed Free State voters. August 27, 1859, Charles Blair, the maker, received order to ship the pikes to Brown under assumed name of Isaac Smith, Chambersburg, Pa. Afterwards conveyed to the Kennedy farm that Brown had hired near Harper's Ferry, Va., where they were handled by Brown and his men (14 whites and 5 negroes), thence taken by wagon Sunday night, October 16, 1859, to Harper's Ferry Arsenal, which Brown and his men hoped to capture in order to obtain supply of firearms to arm the negro slaves in the South to fight for their freedom. History records the result of how Brown captured the Arsenal, how the U. S. Marines from the Washington Navy Yard under the command of Col. Robert E. Lee of the army recaptured the arsenal, taking Brown and some of his men. 483 handled spears and 175 broken handles were captured and stored at the Harper's Ferry Arsenal. After the execution of Brown some of the pikes were given as souvenirs by State officials to their friends. No. 520 pike was presented by Governor Wise of Virginia in 1859 to the Rev. Mr. Willey of Waterbury, Conn., while in attendance at an Episcopal convention in Richmond, Va. Eventually passing into the E. A. Brooks collection of Hartford, from whom we obtained it.

FOR ANOTHER JOHN BROWN PIKE, purchased from a Virginia collector, who obtained it from a farmer who resided near the Kennedy farm and who received it for his share in helping the soldiers load the pikes on the wagons sent to take them from the Kennedy farm to the Arsenal, our price is $65.00. The captured Brown Pikes remained at Harper's Ferry Arsenal until its capture in the early days of the Civil War by the Confederates, when they were sent further South to prevent recapture and in the last years of the Civil War, when the Southern ports were effectually blockaded and the importation of arms from Europe prevented, these pikes were given to a Texas regiment, from whom they were captured and stored at the U. S. Arsenal, Mt. Vernon, Ala. Afterwards destroyed by fire and the old metal in the arsenal ruins sent to the rolling mill at Rock Island Arsenal. Historical pikes that helped to precipitate the great Civil War.

## GEORGIA PIKE.

### Joseph E. Brown Governor of Georgia, in July, 1862,
after the fall of Fort Donelson, issued the following:

"PROCLAMATION! To the Mechanics of Georgia:

"The late reverses which have attended our armies show the absolute necessity of renewed energy and determination on our part. We are left to choose between freedom at the end of a desperate and heroic struggle, and submission to tyranny, followed by the most abject slavery to which a patriotic and generous people was ever exposed.

"Surely we cannot hesitate. Independence or death should be the watchword and reply of every freedman's son of the South. Our enemies have vastly superior numbers and the greater advantage in the quality and quantity of their army. Including those, however, which have been and will be imported in spite of the blockade, we have enough guns in the Confederacy to arm a very large force, but not enough for all the troops.

"What shall be done in the emergency? I answer, use the 'Georgia Pike,' with six-foot staff and the side knife, eighteen-inch blade, weighing about three pounds. Let every army have a large reserve, armed with a good pike and large, heavy side knife, to be brought upon the field with a shout for victory when the contending forces are much exhausted, or when the time comes for the charge of bayonets.

"When the advancing column comes within reach of the balls let them move in double-quick time and rush with terrible impetuosity into the lines of the enemy. Hand to hand the pike has vastly the advantage of the bayonet, which is itself but a crooked pike with shorter staff, and must retreat before it. When the retreat commences let the pursuit be rapid, and if the enemy throw down their guns and are likely to outrun us, if need be throw down the pike and keep close at their heels with the knife until each has hewed down at least one of his adversaries.

"Had five thousand reserves, thus armed and brought to the charge at the proper time, who can say that the victory would not have been ours at Fort Donelson.

"But it is probably important that I state here the use to be made of that which I wish you to manufacture. I have already a considerable number of these pikes and knives, but I desire within the next month ten thousand more of each. I must have them, and I appeal to you, as one of the most patriotic classes of our fellow-citizens, to make them for me immediately.

"Each workman who has the means of turning them out in large numbers will be supplied with a proper pattern by application at the Ordnance Office at Milledgeville.

"In ancient times that nation, it is said, usually extended its conquests furthest whose arms were shortest. Long range guns sometimes fail to fire and waste a hundred balls to one that takes effect, but the short range pike and the terrible knife, when brought within proper range (as they can be in almost a moment), and wielded by a stalwart patriot's arm, never fail to fire and never waste a single load. I am, very respectfully, your fellow-citizen,
JOSEPH E. BROWN."

About 2,500 Georgia pikes were made and turned into the arsenal and later given out to soldiers of Georgia to repel General Sherman's army as it came marching through Georgia. The workmen were no doubt glad of the call and opportunity to give a month's work making arms, for it was the rule in the South during war times, same as in the North, to exempt from military service workmen engaged in manufacturing war material. It seemed as if each workman followed his own idea in the large assortment of patterns and decoration.

These pikes were included among the weapons captured by General Sherman, stored at the Augusta Arsenal, where they remained until 1904, when the U. S. Ordnance Department included in an auction sale 1,200 rebel pikes. The writer attended the sale and made successful bid for a selected number, taking in all the rare and curious pikes as illustrated and described, now on exhibition at Bannerman's Military Museum, Broadway, New York City.

A few of the pikes are for sale and will be found advertised, with price, on other pages of this catalogue.

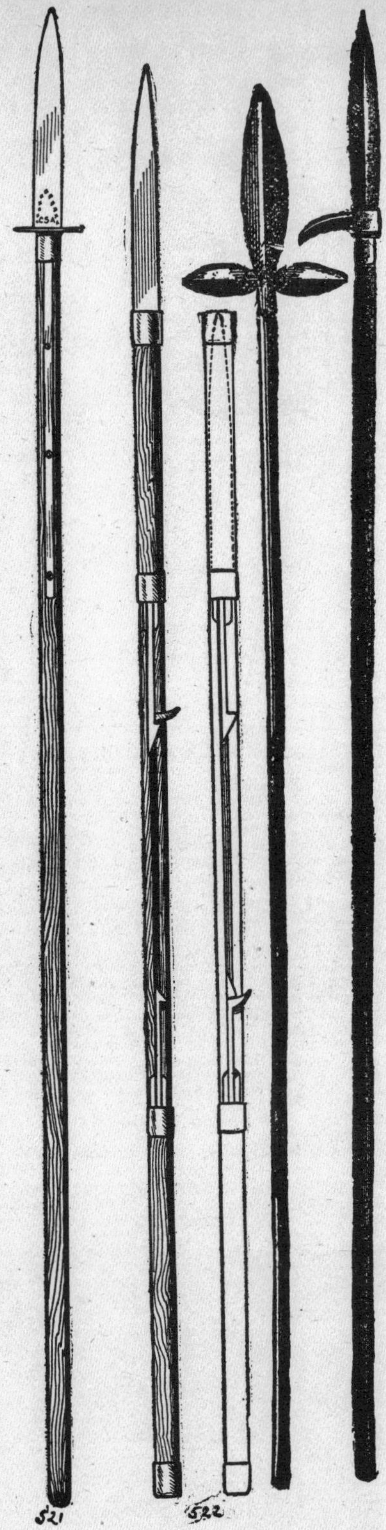

"John Brown, of Ossawatomie, spake
on his dying day:
'I will not have, to shrive my soul, a
priest in slavery's pay,
But let some poor slave mother whom
I have striven to free,
With her children from the gallows
stair, put up a prayer for me!'

"John Brown of Ossawatomie, they
led him out to die:
And lo! a poor slave mother, with her
child pressed nigh;
Then the bold blue eye grew tender,
and the old harsh face grew mild,
As he stooped between the crowding
ranks, and kissed the negro's child!"
—J. G. Whittier.

The long, straight, double-edged blade pike, while adhering perhaps to the Milledgeville sample in length of pole and blade, was ornamented in various ways, some with dotted outlines of the Confederate flag, some with letters C. S. A., with one star, and again with eleven stars, one for each State. The three-bladed pike, called the clover leaf, was also ornamented and finished in various designs. Pikes with the reaper like side knives were called the bridle cutting pikes; the side knife hook intended to catch in the bridles of the cavalry, the straight 12½-inch blade for attacking the rider. The most interesting was the folding blade pikes, No. 522. Whether this pattern was manufactured from the Milledgeville sample, or was evolved out of the brain of its maker, is not known. No old world museum contains such an exhibit. As a writer says: "It goes the ancients one better." The blade is double-edged, 14 inches long, 1⅝ inches wide, sharpened like a large stiletto. The handle is made of two half round pieces of Georgia pine recessed to contain the blade, which slips up and down, controlled by spring catches to hold the blade in position for use, scabbard, is 2½ inches in diameter. Brass and iron ferrule with iron knob capped butt and sharpened blade. Weight 6¼ pounds. Length, extended, 6 feet.

521. GEORGIA PIKE. 7 feet long, 1½-foot diameter, ash pole, the blade decorated "C. S. A." and eleven stars, 12-inch sharpened blade, 1¾ inches wide, 18-inch tang strap, weight 5 pounds.

523. GEORGIA CLOVER LEAF PIKE. 6 feet tapered ash pole, 1¾x1 inch diameter, 10-inch sharpened blade, 3¼-inch side blades, weight 3¾ pounds.

524. GEORGIA BRIDLE CUTTING PIKE. 7 foot ash pole, blade 12½ inches, double-edged sharpened point, 5½-inch curved side hook, weight 4½ pounds.

**U. S. SPRINGFIELD RIFLE BAYONETS.** With brass U. S. Coat of Arms Shield. Offered unmounted, without wood shield. Bayonets at 50 cents each; polished brass Coat of Arms, 35 cents.

**01115.**

**0-1115. ANCIENT FRENCH OFFICER'S SIDE SWORD.** With brass scabbard, illustrated and described in Capt. Maurice Bottet's book "L'Armes Blanche Period, 1777," 13-inch double-edged steel blade, with centre reinforced rib for use in piercing ancient armor. Blade engraved "Coulau Freres," and on the reverse side "Manufacture De Klingenthal." Dark-colored ribbed bone handle, scolloped-shaped brass guard; brass polished, with strap stud; polished scabbard. This is a rare weapon even in France. Price, $30.00.

**BRITISH ARMY BOER WAR SWORD BAYONETS.** Offered unmounted. Brass Coat of Arms centre shield. These swords were used on rifles by British troops in South Africa. We offer the swords at $1.50 each; Coat of Arms at 50 cents. Any carpenter will furnish the wood shield for about 50 cents.

**D90. 1 SOUDAN DAGGER** inscribed on handle, blade and scabbard with verses from the Koran. 10½-inch blade has two center ribs running full length. Iron handle has bird shaped pommel. Scabbard is wood covered with skin, with heavy metal throat and tip. In fair order. Price, $5.00.

**D91. 1 CURIOUS SHAPED INDIA DAGGER** from Tahore. 9½-inch curved blade with heavy tip for thrusting. Heavy brass handle is oval shaped, with upper half made wide as hand guard. Has large knob on pommel, evidently to be used the same as our "brass knuckles." Price, $12.00.

**D92. 1 CURIOUS INDIA DAGGER** from Sind. 9-inch double edge blade, slightly curved. Solid horn handle, pistol butt shape. Wood scabbard, plush covered with long silver tip. Price, $8.00.

**D27-11. CHINESE DAGGER** with 6-inch blade with bamboo handle ivory tipped. Bamboo scabbard, brass bound. Two 8½-inch chop sticks of ivory, also ivory tooth pick 5 inch. These are also carried in the scabbard. Price $5.00.

**ENFIELD BAYONETS.** With U. S. M. C. brass shield. Offered unmounted, 50 cents for each bayonet; 20 cents for the brass shield. All have been used. Are war relics. Buyer can make wood shield to mount the bayonets as desired. We merely illustrate suggesting the handsome ornaments that can be made at little cost.

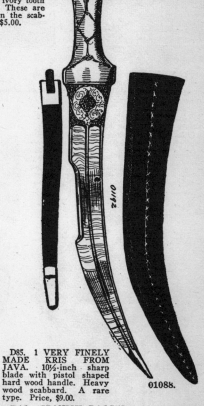

**01157. 01156.**

**0-1157. ANCIENT ITALIAN SABRE POIGNARD.** With box-like part on the under side of the hilt, with side spring for fastening to the gun. Early pattern sword bayonet. 18-inch blade, brass hilt, small neat cross guard. Complete with leather scabbard. Brass mouth and tip shows much usage. In serviceable order. Price, $6.50.

**0-1156. ANCIENT SAXON SIDE ARM SWORD.** 19½-inch blade, 1⅝-inch wide at the hilt, brass hilt, 4-inch cross guard, with square ends; full length 24½ inches. Complete, with leather scabbard, with brass mouth and tip. Shows much usage. Rare pattern side arm. $6.75.

**0-883. ANCIENT ROMAN DAGGER.** Found in Kent, England. Bronze hilt of Roman matron in ancient dress time of the Roman occupation of England; 9¼-inch double-edged straight blade badly rusted, with bronze cross guard and female figure. From sale of the late Lawson-Johnston Kingswood collection. Roman relic, as well preserved as this one is, scarce even in old England. Price, $100.00.

A gentleman, whose wife and daughter were starting for an extended trip in Europe, desired to know from father what they could bring back for him. His request was, "Bring me an old Roman sword for my collection." A few months later his daughter wrote him, "Why did you make such a hard request? We have hunted all over Europe and cannot find a Roman sword." In answer, he told her, "Never mind; I will go to Bannerman's on Broadway, New York, and get it," and, sure enough, we had it for him.

**3421. 01098.**

**0-1098. ANTIQUE SIDE ARM SWORD.** With ring for attaching to the hilt. Brass hilt and scabbard, covered with fine engraving, 7¾-inch double-edged blade, with centre groove 2¼ inches. Museum exhibit. Price, $8.75.

**3421. SCOTCH SKENE DHU.** Sword with small knife and fork. Thistle and Ionic relief mounted hilts, with ornamented yellow stone or glass tops, with black leather scabbard with thistle flower and leaf ornamented mouthpiece. Full length 19½ inches, weight 1 pound 13 ounces. Fine order; like new. Made for theatrical and ornamental use. Price, $18.85.

**0-1141. EUROPEAN POLICE OFFICER'S CLUB.** Heavy black-colored wood, with grooved handle, slightly larger at the butt, or club end. Length 18 inches. Sold "as is." Slightly cracked. Price, 75 cents.

**DA-3. SPANISH DAGGER** with hard wood handle, black, with very heavy ribbed blade, 4-inch sharp pointed. Price $4.50.

**D89. 1 MOORISH DAGGER** with 10-inch sharp blade. Horn handle is bound with figured brass. Scabbard has wood center, outside of heavy brass ornamented on one side. Has two large rings with shoulder cord. Price, $10.

**0-1131. ANCIENT CUTLASS.** Period American Revolutionary War. Single guard, grooved brass hilt, ball pommel, 23-inch curved blade. Brass hilt is corroded green, with rusty blade. Offered as a relic. Price, $7.50.

**D85. 1 VERY FINELY MADE KRIS FROM JAVA.** 10½-inch sharp blade with pistol shaped hard wood handle. Heavy wood scabbard. A rare type. Price, $9.00.

**01088.**

**DA5. SPANISH DAGGER,** with hard wood black handle, corrugated, with plain silver band. 6½-inch wide blade, with sharp point. Price $6.00.

**0-1192. KING'S ARMOR PIERCING SIDE ARM SWORD.** Blade, richly inlaid with gold ornamented scroll work, relief engraving, fine Damascene figured blade 13½ inches in length, double-edged, with sharpened curved point, with CENTRE RIDGE REINFORCING POINT FOR PIERCING through old-time armor. Part of the back of the blade is recessed and broadened to form place for the HAND TO REST IN to give weight to the armor-piercing point in giving the death thrust to the fallen enemy. This hand rest is inlaid with gold. The steel hilt with ornamental gold inlaying. The blade shows the ANCIENT FINE Damascus figure. Wood scabbard covered with king's purple velvet. This is a RARE and HANDSOME WEAPON. It will compare with Kensington Museum exhibit and a bargain at $100.00.

**HANDSOME SUIT OF ARMOR,** mounted with halberd. A St. Louis sporting paper published photos of this armor just previous to our purchase, as exhibited in a collector's store window in Antwerp, Belgium, commenting on what a handsome window display it made. Illustration is from photograph, and shows the the fine decorative ornamentation. Price complete, boxed, $275.00.

### FRENCH ARMORED MOUNTED SOLDIER

| | |
|---|---:|
| We can furnish the metal helmet | $12.00 |
| Long steel sword and scabbard | 8.50 |
| Saddle with steel stirrups | 7.50 |
| Blue coat and trousers, to order, each | 6.85 |

Saddle cloth made to order if desired.

### GERMAN ARMORED SOLDIER—

We can furnish metal helmet with ornamented front plate, with brass scale chin strap and spike, $6.50.

Steel breast and back plate, with bronze shoulder chains and waist strap, $20.00.

Long straight German sword with scabbard, $8.50.

Long boots with legs to knee, $3.50.

German sword knot, 75c.

Sword belt with sling straps, German belt buckle, $4.75.

1 Waterloo Cuirassier breast plate. Heavy steel with shot hole. Rare old relic. Price $15.00.

4 Waterloo Cuirassier back plates. Relics, poor order. Price $5.00 each.

**British Army Soldier's Steel Breast Plate.** Heavy polished steel, front part only. Old time bullet proof at 40 yards. Price $8.00 each.

Back armor plate $5.00 each.

**MINIATURE SUIT OF ARMOR,** on stand complete with shield, WITHOUT spear or helmet. An exact reproduction of the full size armor. Probably a maker's model. Movable joints. Price, $35.00.

**Mounted Knight,** time of King Henry II. of England, dressed in scale mail armor, with flat helmet, armored horse; from Bannerman's book on "Weapons of War."

**Suit of Metal Armor,** Helmet, Coat of Mail, Metal Leg Guards, full life-size, good representation of the real old armor, now very scarce and expensive. Looks as well as the original. Is offered complete with figure and battle axe. Boxed, for $100. Found in Belgium.

Mounted Knight time of King Henry II. of England.

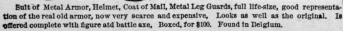

**No. 1020A.**

No. 1020A. FRENCH CUIRASSIERS STEEL ARMOR, front and back pieces, complete with shoulder chains, and leather belt. Both pieces brass studded. Front has French SUNBURST ornament 7½ by 6 inches, with smaller sunburst in center. Very early pattern, probably Waterloo. Similar to No. 1020, but doubtless used by different regiment, as the ornaments are not the same. Price, $30.00.

(In this cut is shown the half armour of a general officer, the costume and accoutrements of a pikeman, an archer, and a musketeer, of the Elizabethan period.)

No. 1766. French Cadet Suit of Half Armor, Helmet, with visor, with breast and back plate with stomach protector, with armor for arm and elbow, with double chain front skirt. Price, $46.00.

No. 1002. Light Steel Theatrical Armor Breast Plate with greaves as illustrated. Old, requires cleaning. Price, $18.50.

No. 1180, European Steel Armor front and back plate, with brass chains. Polished steel, genuine. Price per set as illustrated, $20.00.

FRENCH STEEL HELMET, nickle plated, but now dull finish. High brass ornamented comb, without hair plumes. Sunburst ornament in front surrounded by leaves and fruit. Heavy side buttons covered with leaf design. Leather chin strap, chain covered. We believe this to be one of the Waterloo helmets. In fair condition. Price, $12.50.

No. 1020. French Cuirassiers Polished Steel Breast Plate with eagle coat of arms and sunburst in polished brass. Complete with brass scale chains. Handsome decorations. Real article. Price, $35.00.

WATERLOO METAL HELMET, made of steel with heavy brass ornamented comb with head of woman with snakes, also flaming shell. Pompon and hair plumes missing. Bottom part of helmet covered with fur, laced at back. Metal chin strap, chain covered. This pattern helmet worn by French soldiers at Waterloo. In fair condition. Price, $13.50.

Filipino Antique Spanish Armor, made of Caribou horn, joined together with brass rings. Rare old piece; this kind said to be upwards of 300 years old. Bargain at $100.

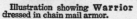

**Illustration showing Warrior dressed in chain mail armor.**

No. 1769. Ancient Chain Mail Shirt, formed of double metal rings, fastened to each other, with armlets, projecting about 3 inches from the body. Length of the body of the shirt 2 feet; size about 40 inch chest. Originally built for business. Slightly rusty. Price, $35.00.

No. 1775A. Chain Cap with small flatted discs, without plume holder. Price, $15.00.

No. 1773. Heavy Woven Chain Stomacher, iron rings joined closely together; width, 20 inches; length, 18 inches. Price, $20.00.

We have tried some of this chain mail armor, and find that a ball from a modern .38 caliber revolver, fired 10 feet will go clean through. An ordinary knife blade will have difficulty in penetrating. We offer as antique relics, as are.

We have many requests from SHERIFFS, CONSTABLES, and private police for armor to be worn under the other clothing. None of the armor shown on this page, either all steel, or chain, can be used for that purpose, and we do not know of any such article that would give proper protection.

No. 1281. German Army Skull and Cross Bone Cuirasseers Steel Breast Plate, with curved front, width, 13½ inches; length, 17 inches. Steel back plate, 14 inches, with leather strap and buckle for joining at the waist with steel scale brass mounted shoulder strap. Lined with burlap. Rare old Armor. Price, $35.00.

No. 1004. Light Steel Armored Hand Cover, scale formation for fingers and thumb, leather back. $12.50 the pair.

British Cavalry Shoulder chains: worn over the coat to stand blow from enemy's sabre; useful and ornamental; new, adopted by Lord Roberts in South African campaign. Price, $1.00 per pair.

No. 1002. Light Steel Cuirass or Breast Plate, with front protector, slightly rusted. Price, $20.00.

6056. SIXTEENTH CENTURY ENGRAVED HELMET. With visor. Fac-simile of priceless original. Full size. Serviceable order. Price, $17.50.

10512. CABASSET POT HELMET. Antique Spanish, period about 1600. Made of hammered iron, with one-inch turned edge, with brass ornamental disks. Price, $22.00.

GERMAN ARMY STEEL ARMOR, consisting of front and back of heavy steel with shoulder straps of scale chain with leather back, with leather waist belt. Also steel helmet with SUNBURST ornament with small eagle in center with inscription at edge: MIT GOTT FUR KONIG UND VATERLAND 1860. In center words, SUUM CUIQUE. Large bright metal EAGLE WITH CROWN on top of helmet in place of spike. Price of outfit, $45.00.

0-1075. ANCIENT BRASS AND LEATHER HELMET. With ventilating top and ornamental front. Artistic chin scales, metal rims, helmet plate, crossed battle axe's on the front plate. Price, $12.50.

FRENCH CUIRASSIER'S STEEL ARMOR. Consisting of polished steel breast and back plates, with polished brass eagle, wreath and sunburst on the breast plate, with leather waist belt, with leather shoulder straps, covered with brass scales, with metal helmet, with large plume, with polished brass chin strap, with Napoleon's insignia of bursting bomb on the helmet plate, all genuine armor that has been used in the French Army service. Price of the outfit, $50.00.

0-1077. FRENCH METAL HELMET. With black hair plume, with masked face front ornaments, with ancient castle battlements, with Fleur-de-Lys, with red plume. Price, $20.00.

No. 3. Very fine looking suit of armor, articulated scale plate, mailed gauntlet. Price, f.o.b. N. Y., boxed, $125.00.

0-1077A. FRENCH METAL HELMET. Nearly similar to 01077 with helmet plate marked with "GARDE DE PARIS." Price, $20.00.

SEVEN SUITS OF ANCIENT ARMOR, as per photographic illustration No. 1, 2 and 3 on this page Made of steel or iron plates, hammered into special shape. Each armor stands six feet in height and is large in size. The armor was on exhibition at the time of our purchase in a gunnery school MUSEUM IN EUROPE. Loaned by the owner, who was connected with the school as MANAGING DIRECTOR, and, being about to retire, sold the armor to us. This armor is patterned in every detail after the ANCIENT MAIL ARMOR worn by warriors in olden times. They are mounted on (concealed) wood frame and are offered as shown in photo illustration, together with Battle Axe No. 1214, illustrated on page No. 406. Each suit is complete with helmet, visor and neckguard, gorget, breast and back plate, shoulder, selbow and arm guards, with lance rest, waist plate and chain mail under armor apron, loin, thigh, knee and leg guards, mailed, articulated hand and foot covers.

1735. Period of 1812 SOLDIER'S HAT; rare old relic; fair order. Made of heavy black felt. Has crossed cannon ornamentation and artillery rosette; front flap, 8½ inches; back flap, 11½ inches in height. Price, $20.00.

No. 1. The helmet is cone-shaped at nose and arms, with slits for eyes and holes for breathing. Note the two small octagonal star-shaped shields, one on each breast. Price, boxed, f.o.b. N. Y., $145.00.

No. 2. The two parts projecting from the shoulders are 6 inches in width. Note the small round breast shield and the ribbed helmet. Price for this outfit of armor, boxed, f.o.b. N. Y., $150.00.

No. 1.

No. 2.

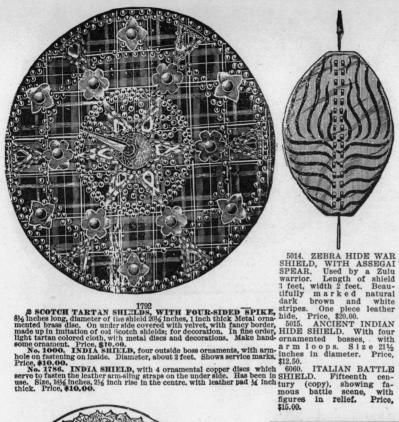

**1792**

**2 SCOTCH TARTAN SHIELDS, WITH FOUR-SIDED SPIKE,** 8½ inches long, diameter of the shield 20½ inches, 1 inch thick Metal ornamented brass disc. On under side covered with velvet, with fancy border, made up in imitation of old Scotch shields; for decoration. In fine order, light tartan colored cloth, with metal discs and decorations. Make handsome ornament. Price, $10.00.

**No. 1000. INDIA SHIELD,** four outside boss ornaments, with armhole on fastening on inside. Diameter, about 2 feet. Shows service marks. Price, $10.00.

**No. 1786. INDIA SHIELD,** with 4 ornamental copper discs which serve to fasten the leather arm-sling straps on the under side. Has been in use. Size, 18½ inches, 2½ inch rise in the centre, with leather pad ¼ inch thick. Price, $10.00.

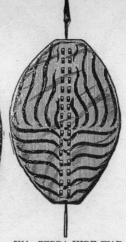

**5014. ZEBRA HIDE WAR SHIELD, WITH ASSEGAI SPEAR.** Used by a Zulu warrior. Length of shield 3 feet, width 2 feet. Beautifully marked natural dark brown and white stripes. One piece leather hide. Price, $20.00.

**5015. ANCIENT INDIAN HIDE SHIELD.** With four ornamented bosses, with arm loops. Size 21½ inches in diameter. Price, $12.50.

**6060. ITALIAN BATTLE SHIELD.** Fifteenth century (copy), showing famous battle scene, with figures in relief. Price, $15.00.

**1795A. CONGO NATIVE WAR SHIELD,** made of woven fibre, colored to make crude design. Re-inforced on inside by laying narrow strips sidewise. Hand hold cut from wood block and attached on under side. Length 40 inches, width 11½ inches, hand hold 3¼ inches. Similar to illustration No. 1795 on page 228. Price $10.00.

**1795B. CONGO NATIVE WAR SHIELD,** made from single layer of fibre, very tightly woven. Colored black and white in varied designs. Hand hold made from branch of bush. Similar to No. 1795. Length 38 inches, width 16½ inches. Price $12.00.

**1795C. CONGO NATIVE WAR SHIELD, MADE FROM SINGLE LAYER OF WOVEN FIBRE.** Black and white designs. Length 43 inches, width 18½ inches. Hand hold cut from block of wood, re-inforced with narrow fibre. Similar to No. 1795. Price $14.00.

**1795D. CONGO NATIVE WAR SHIELD,** made of woven fibre over light wood for stiffness. The outside edges bound with hide, with hair. The ends of the shield curve OUTWARD showing it is used in some peculiar way. Length 42 inches, width 12½ inches. Similar to No. 1795. Price $15.00.

**No. 1787. INDIA SHIELD,** similar to No. 1786, with 4 copper discs. Size, 19 inches in diameter, 2¼ inch rise in center, ¼ inch thick with velvet pad and arm hold. $10.00.

**No. 1788. INDIA SHIELD,** similar to 1786, with 4 brass discs, ornamental crescent, two decorated bosses. Has been in use. Size, 17 inches. Has 2 inch rise in centre, embossed pad and arm strap. Price, $10.00.

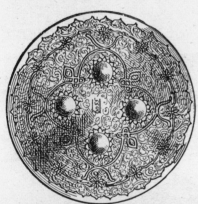

**6055A. INDIA INLAID ORNAMENTED SILVERED STEEL SHIELD.** 13½ inches in diameter. From Central India. Work of art. Price, $22.50.

**6901. ZULU WARRIOR'S SHIELD.** Taken by British soldier from Zulu warrior at the battle of Rookes Drift. Black colored hide, nearly 3 feet long, 20 inches wide, with 4½ feet carved ebony wood hand hold. Price, $20.00.

**SIMILAR HIDE SHIELD.** Without history. Price, $14.00.

**ZULU WARRIOR'S HIDE SHIELD.** 2½ feet in length, brown colored hide with fluted wood handle. Price, $12.50.

**YOUNG ZULU WARRIOR'S HIDE SHIELD.** 2 feet in length. Price, $10.00.

**6064. RELIEF ORNAMENTED IRON SHIELD.** Oval-shaped (3 boar's heads), length 17¾ inches, 14 inches. Handsome copy of old antique shield. Price, $7.50.

**No. 1803. ZULU NATIVE HIDE SHIELD,** with assegai spear. 22 inches wide, 40 inches long. Colored hide. Price, $15.00.

Oriental Metal Shield, with Decorations. Illustration is from photo. Size is 15 inches diameter. Price, $10.00.

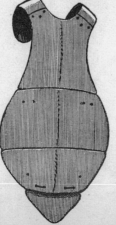

FM5

Hide Shield, with metal bosses of raised circular ornaments. Handsome decoration. Size, 15 inches. Price, $10.00.

One very much similar, but made of pressed fibre; hand painted. Size, 15 inches. Price, $7.50.

side as arm straps. Diameter, 18¼ inches, cleaning. Rows of letters around the rim, wh who can read it. Price, $20.00.

**FM5. U. S. ARMY WORLD WAR ARMOR,** designed for and used by the MACHINE GUNNERS. Joined throughout and padded on chest with heavy crude rubber. Sections fastened together by soft russet leather straps. Full length 30 inches, widest part 16¾ inches, weight 5¼ lbs. This can be worn under the clothing. Price $4.50 each.

8

**1797**

**TWO NATIVE AFRICAN SHIELDS,** oval shaped, woven colored fibre, with projecting rim, with circular steel shield and spike centre, with wood hand hold, neatly and artistically attached to under side of shield. Width. 15 inches. Length, 3 feet.

Good order. Price, $15.00 each.

**6057. WATERLOO BATTLE PERIOD ENGLISH BREAST PLATE.** Price, $14.50.

**6057A. ANCIENT BREAST PLATE.** Price, $16.50.

See pages 211, 212, 213, 214, 215 and 216, for LANCES, SPEARS and HALBERDS to go with these shields. Or write us what you want, and we will quote prices with full description and measurements.

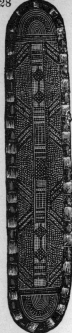

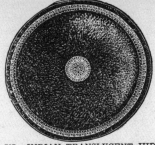

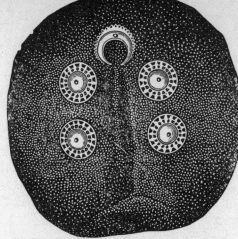

**0-707. INDIAN TRANSLUCENT HIDE SHIELD.** 20½ inches diameter, 5-inch crown, with ancient steel bosse centre, surrounded by four ornamental copper bosses, ornamental gilt painted border, arm pad on reverse side. This fine, large shield when held up to the light is translucent and is in demand for decoration. Hide is finely polished. Has wax-like appearance. Bargain price, $25.00.

**1785. INDIA WARRIOR'S SHIELD.** Black fibre, with four ornamented discs, with spear in centre 4 inches long, with ornamented crescent, 19½ inches diameter, 2½ inches crown, ¼ inch thick. Price, $12.50.

**1794.—** Turtle Shell Shield, made from back of a large turtle, size 15½ inches wide 15 inches long with ornamented brass discs, with ornamented brass crescent; fitted with pad and arm strap on under side, which is painted red; upper side has been shellaced over painted gilt border. Serves to show savage ingenuity as well as decorative ornamentation. Price, $15.00.

**1795.** Congo Native War Shield colored woven fibre, to form decoration. Reinforced inside with fibre. On under side is attached wood hand hold; width ½ inches; length, 4 feet. Taken from native by Belgian Government officials. Considering the primitive state of the Congo native, this decorated shield required artistic ability in the making. Price $15.00.

**1786. INDIA SHIELD.** With four ornamented copper discs, with carrying sling on the under side; 18 inches diameter, 2½-inch rise, ¼ inch thick. Handsome decoration. Price, $10.00.

*The 2ᵈ Palming motion.*

Ancient Pikeman from Bannaman's Book Weapons of War.

Guiana African Native Carved Shield hand-painted and Carved as in illustration. Price, $8.75.

**1796.—** Congo Native War Shield, size 12½ inches wide; 54 inches long; rounded ends. Decorated with woven colored fibre. Price, $15.00.

**1790.—** Similar to 1788; ¼ inch smaller in diameter with holes through the shield, evidently made by some high power bullet. No doubt this shield is a war relic. Price, $15.00.

**1791.** Similar to 1789, only slightly different style of decoration. Price, $12.00.

**1784.—** Rhinoceros Shield, translucent heavy hide, decorated in colors by native workman; size, 20½ inches; diameter ¼ inch thick; 3 inch rise in centre. In this order; handsome specimen, Price, $18.00.

**1885.** Warrior Shield, black fibre with four ornamental discs to which are fastened on the under side the leather straps for the arm, with double edged 4-inch spear shaped point; with ornamented handle; size, 19½ inches; 2½ inch rise in centre; ¼ inch thick. Price, $12.85.

**1789.** Two views 1789 Decorated Hide Somali Native Shield. heavy hide, bleached nearly white in color with turned-up hat, shaped rim With raised centre with circular row of indentations and decoration, as illustrated, which considering the primitive tools, are to be considered as a work of art, beautiful decorative ornament. Illustrated view of the under side, shows how the arm straps are attached and decorated, price $12.50 size 12½ in. diameter 1¾ in. rise in centre, ¼ in. thick. Price, $15.00.

**1801.** African Native War Shield, made of heavy hide, with circular shaped cone centre. With cuts in the edge for spear-strap, for carrying shield. With hand holdstrap, 25-inch diameter, ⅛ inch thick in centre. Looks like hipotamus hide. Evidently a war shield. It has marks of two small bore bullets, evidently .30 cal. shot through the edge of the shield, from some high power modern rifle. For this battle relic; price is $20.00.

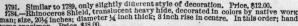

**1789**

**1801**

**1800—Abbysanian Native Shield,** made of heavy hide native decoration; with rawhide straps for hand hold; with fur covered centre knob size 22½ inches; 4½ inch elevation; turned up rim ¼ inch thick. Price, $12.00.

**1800A.—** Similar to illustration of 1800 slightly different in decoration with tuft of hair on centre knob; 20 inches in diameter. $12.00.

**1801A.—** Native War Shield, similar to 1801; size **21** inches; diameter with marks of three bullet holes. Price, $22.00.

**1801B.—** 2 War Shields, similar to 1801. 21-inch diameter; not bullet marked. Price, $18.00.

## ORIGINAL U. S. COAT OF ARMS
### Stars and Stripes
Price in iron...............$12.75

## ST. ANDREWS CROSS
Price in iron...............$15.50

**ORNAMENTAL METAL SHIELDS** for decorating buildings. Cast iron for exterior and plaster of Paris copper electro-plated for interior. Size is 2 feet square; base ½ inch thick, at the relief 1 inch thick.

Price    Made in bronze on request.

## U. S. COAT OF ARMS
### War Shield
### (Eagle facing the arrows.)
Price in iron...............$18.00

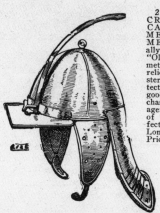

**2126. OLIVER CROMWELL'S CAVALIER METAL HELMETS.** Originally called the "Old Pot Helmet." Genuine old relics. With lobster tail neck protector. In fairly good order. Purchased by our agent at the sale of Whitely's effects (the great London Provider). Price, $40.00 each.

**SCOTCH SHIELD.** With lion rampant in bold relief, surrounded with Fleur de Lis border. This expensive pattern was made to obtain shields for ornaments for our island storehouses on the Hudson. We can now supply these fine ornamented shields in size 2 feet by ½ inch thick, weight about 80 pounds. **Price, $12.00.**

**6060. 15TH CENTURY SHIELD (copy).** Made in cast iron reproducing in relief ancient battle scene, circular shield, 22 inches in diameter. Price, $15.85.

**2418. ANCIENT METAL HELMET,** as per illustration. Outside shows numerous small dents; inside is rusted with age. From the appearance and make we believe it to be a genuine old helmet. It was sent to us from one of the European museums by a professor who had loaned it for exhibition. Price, $100.00.

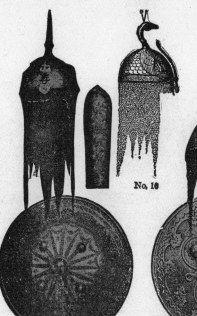

### No. 10

### No. 11

### No. 12

### No. 13

### No. 14

**15. PERSIAN SHIELD,** about 20 inches in diameter, etched and inlaid with metal wire, marked with curious designs. NOT LIKE ILLUSTRATION. Very fine workmanship, a handsome piece. Price, $45.00.

**9.—India** Sword, 29 inch blade, 4 inch handle; old relic. Price, $5.00.

**1352.—Antique Iron Door Knocker,** from London collection, lion's head, poor order; size 8x5; $6.85.

**1303.—Heavy Antique Ring Pattern Door Knocker,** shows great age; size, 6 inches diameter; offered complete; price $7.50.

**Native Zulu Hide** Shield, size used by women and children; decorative piece for library or den. Price, $7.50.

**12.—Oriental Shield Helmet** and Guard, etched and inlaid with native gold ornamental work; beautiful set. Price, $38.00.

**10.—Persian Helmet** peacock shaped top, with chain mail neck protectors, beautifully engraved, gold inlaid, with Sun God, with plume holder; 7½ inches diameter; 10 inches high; chain mail 15 inches long.

**13.—Persian Shield Helmet** and Guard, handsomely ornamented, pierced and etched steel overlaying crimson colored metal decorated with native gold ornamentation; Shield is 20 inches in diameter 3½ inches crown. This was considered the most beautiful set exhibited at the World's Fair; fit for a king's palace. Bargain Price, the set, handon set. $65.00.

**11. — Persian Metal Helmet,** beautifully ornamented with spear horns, with chain mail, neck protectors, 7½ inches in diameter. Price, $18.00.

**14.—Persian Shield, Helmet** and Guard; shield is 20 inches in diameter and has four ornamented gold bosses; the etching is a work of art; helmet has neck guard and shield; etched and inlaid in same pattern as the shield. The hand guard is gold inlaid and etched; needs to be seen to be appreciated; rare $100.00.

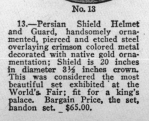

PK-1

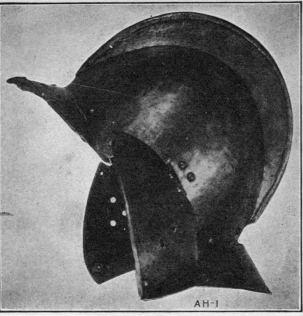

AH-I

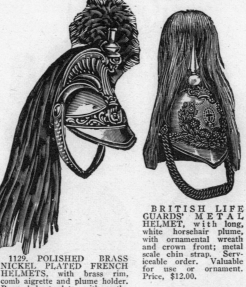

PK-2

**AH-1. OLD ENGLISH CASQUE or STEEL HELMET**, period of 1620. This type probably worn by the soldiers of early colonial times. This piece has high comb, 2½-inch visor, and MOVABLE ear pieces. These are 5 inches high, and 4½ inches wide, with perforations for air. This is a rare specimen. Price, $35.00.

**PK-1. OFFICER OF CHARLES I PIKEMEN ARMOR**, with breast plate, back plate and helmet. The three pieces painted black, with a gilt edging, which denote an officer. The breast plate has long point in front. Note the helmet with lobster tail back, and the curious face guard. This visor with guard is hinged so as to be pushed back when not in battle. This outfit was worn over a buff leather jacket. Price for the three pieces, helmet, breast plate and back, $60.00.

**PK-1A. SET PIKEMAN'S ARMOR**, similar to set above, three pieces. These are unpainted but otherwise the same in every detail. There is a deep dent on waist line at left side. Price for set of three pieces, $45.00.

**PK-2. SET PIKEMAN'S ARMOR**, with breast plate, back, and helmet. As used by the old English pikemen under CROMWELL. This set secured from the sale of duplicate at the TOWER OF LONDON. Combinations of this style are now rare. The breast plate has dent on left side. Price, for the three pieces, $50.00.

CUIRASS. The cuirass, as its name implies, was originally a jerkin, or garment of leather for soldiers, so thick and strong as to be pistol-proof, and even musket-proof. The name was afterwards applied to a portion of armor made of metal, consisting of a back-plate and breast-plate hooked or buckled together; with a piece jointed to the back called a culet or garde de reines. The French cuirass, represented in the drawing, is composed of a breast-plate, a, and a back-plate, b, joined together by straps. The thickness and form of the breast-plate are such as to ward off small-arm projectiles beyond a distance of forty yards; this distance is assumed under the supposition that within it the infantry soldier will be too busily engaged preparing to defend himself against the cavalry soldier, with his bayonet, to fire his piece. The back-piece is only made of sufficient thickness to resist the stroke of a sword; it is presumed this will induce the wearer to present his front rather than his back, when he arrives within a short distance of his enemy. The middle of the breast-plate is formed into a ridge, and the sides slope off to deflect projectiles coming from the front. The thickness at the ridge is 23 inch; from this it tapers to the edges, where it is .078 inch. The back-piece is .047 inch thick throughout, and the weight of the entire cuirass is about 16.75 lbs. The edges are turned up to prevent the point of a sword from slipping off against the body. The cuirass and helmet worn by the leading sapper in digging a siege-trench are thick enough in all their parts to resist a bullet at the distance of 40 yards.—From Farrow's Military Encyclopedia.

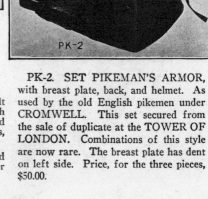

1129. POLISHED BRASS NICKEL PLATED FRENCH HELMETS, with brass rim, comb aigrette and plume holder. Brass helmet plate, with castle, tower, fleur de lis and ancient ship and scroll work, with liberty head. Leather band, red aigrette and plume, black horsehair comb; very showy. Price, $12.00.

1138. ONE DITTO, slightly discolored, without red aigrette, $8.50.

1098. WATERLOO PERIOD METAL HELMET; not refinished; slightly dented. Offered as is. $10.00.

**BRITISH LIFE GUARDS' METAL HELMET**, with long, white horsehair plume, with ornamental wreath and crown front; metal scale chin strap. Serviceable order. Valuable for use or ornament. Price, $12.00.

**BRITISH DRAGOON'S METAL HELMET**, with ornamental front, with long hair plume, with metal scale chin strap. In fair order. For use or decorating. Has been used. Price, $10.00.

**GERMAN CUIRASSIER'S METAL HELMET** or Picklehaut, with large eagle and with eagle ornament. Worn by Emperor's Guards. Rare relics. Probably used in the Franco-Prussian war. Price, $35.00.

Several of the articles shown on this page are museum pieces, especially numbers PK-1, PK-2 and AH-1. These articles are as fine as any shown anywhere. Through our agents in London and Europe we are able to secure some fine specimens of helmet and armor, and shall be glad to have you write us of your requirements.

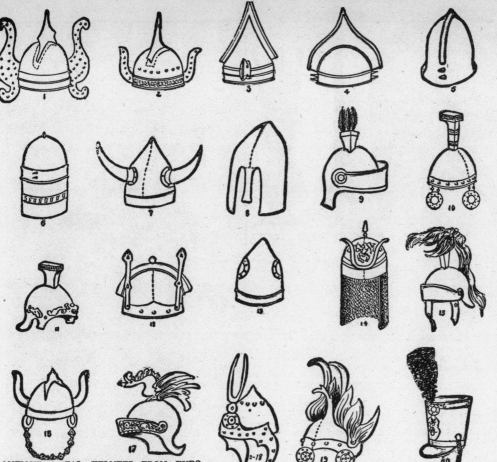

**1262.** European Army Chapeaux, 14½ inches high stiff hat, blue cloth, covered with patent leather visor and back, with red band around top, with red ball pompon with brass side chain, brass crossed cannon w.th bras shield, with red, yellow and black rosette; new. $5.00 each.

Brass Helmet with Visor, ornamented with shell in flames and pioneer axes with ridge in centre of crown. Supposed to be French fireman's; marked Pompiers de Vitry, Le E. S. Price, $10.00.

Old Leather Helmet, with ridge in centre; brass bound with ornamented shield on which is design of three scimitar-shaped swords. Price, $8.75.

2 Japanese large brim Metal Helmets. $6.75 each.

**ANTIQUE METAL HELMETS FROM EUROPEAN MUSEUM COLLECTION.** These helmets we purchased from the owner, who had loaned them to a leading museum in Belgium. They are mostly copies of originals. The owner said there were a few in the lot that were genuine.

No. 5. Size 7x9 inches. Light brass helmet with projecting rim. Price, $12.00.

No. 4. 7x8 inches. Light steel helmet with spike and projecting rings, supposed to be genuine old antique; offered as is $22.00.

No. 2. 7x7½. Light brass helmet, nickeled with ornamental trimmings and rings. Price, $7.50.

No. 1. 7x8 inches. Light copper helmet with wings. $8.00.

No. 10. 7x8 inches Light Brass Helmet with ear protectors with plume holder ornament. $12.00.

No. 12. 6½x8. Light steel helmet with spear, prongs, side pins. $10.00.

No. 8. Size 8½x8½. Light steel helmet with neck protector. Supposed to be genuine, offered as is. $25.00.

No. 15. 6½x7½. Light steel helmet, with side piece, ear protector, with chin straps for protecting the ears, with movable visor, with plume holder. $15.00.

No. 16. 6¾x7¼. Copper helmet, with wings, with chin chain, with rim. $15.00.

No. 18. 6¾x7. Oxidized brass helmet, with side protector, with forked spear, ornamented. $8.50.

No. 9. 6½x8. Light brass helmet with movable visor, with feather top. $15.00.

No. 6. 7½x9. Light steel helmet with brass band, with spike. Price, $12.00.

No. 19. 7x8 Brass Helmet, with ornamented ear protectors, with wings. $18.00.

No. 20. NAPOLEON THE FIRST FRENCH SOLDIER'S HELMET, with red plume, with liberty cock. Arms trophy ornamented plate with chin strap, with bursting shell, silver lace, top hand, with rosette, made of black fur. Old antique. Price, $20.00.

Helmets not described are out of stock. When ordering please allow a second choice when possible.

**1782. 2 BRASS HELMETS,** with large black fur crest, with chain scale, with chin strap, with plate engraved "Sapeurs Pompiers de la Ville d'Anvers"; with sign of open hand and ancient castles; with crossed battle axes. Price, $15.00 each.

**1855. ANTIQUE MILITARY LEATHER HELMET,** with large brass plate, with crown and cross, double-head eagle, with mounted horsemen on shield. In old style figures 26, with bursting shell in flames. Price, $12.00.

When the New York laid aside the helmets they had worn so long and adopted the bell-top cap, the following verses appeared in one of the daily papers.

"For they've killed the poor old helmet; you can hear the dead march play.
The force is sheddin' briny tears—the helmet's dead to-day.
They have taken off the leather and they've cut the badge away,
An' they've gone and knocked the helmet in the morning."

"The people thought it funny an' they passed him with a grin.
But grinnin' at a copper is the seventh deadly sin,
So he clubbed him in the midriff and he's runnin' of him in
For he's grievin' for his helmet in the morning."

British Army Lancers, Helmet with plume, brass plate ornament with names of the battles that regiment took part in "Glory Boys." Assorted sizes. Price $3.65.

**1853. OLD SCOTCH HIGHLAND SHAKO,** with St. Andrew's cross and bugle, with thistle ornaments. Leather frame. Dark blue cloth covered, with broad arrow, showing British Government ownership. Old relic. Price, $8.50.

**854. OLD ANTIQUE MILITARY LEATHER HELMET,** with brass crown, ornamented bugle, brass scales, chin straps, lion head side pieces. Black brooch ornamentation. Price, $12.00.

**1139. FRENCH OFFICER'S RED CAP,** gilt and silvered trimmed, made in Paris, used. In good serviceable order. Price, $5.75 each.

**FRENCH SOLDIER'S LEATHER SHAKO,** with brass military ornament (not French) assorted sizes, with pompon. Price, $1.50 each.

**2269. CHAUSSIER'S SHAKO.** Blue cloth, trimmed with white braid around bottom and top. Infantry side buttons, assorted sizes. Used. Offered in serviceable order. Price, $1.00 each.

**10170. WAR OF 1812 OFFICER'S LEATHER HELMET.** Used by military officer, New Hampshire Regiment, in war with Great Britain. Eagle button ornament has 16 STARS; silver chain seal and tassels. All leather. Fair order. Price, $12.50.

**6922. WATERLOO PERIOD HELMET.** British officer's, with gilt plate in the form of a Maltese cross, glass ornamented. Inscribed, "Queen's Own Royal Yeomanry." with crown, with feather plume, gilt and silvered lion, silver chain strap, gilt breast cord. Serviceable order. Worn in action in olden times. **Price, $18.50.**

**SCOTCH HIGHLANDER SOLDIERS' MILITARY BONNET,** with feather plumes, in secondhand serviceable order. Price $15.00.

**U. S. ARMY PLUME SOCKETS,** with screw rod for use on Military helmets for holding plumes; polished brass, new. Price 50c per set.

## NEW MOHAIR COLORED MILITARY BRAID

| | | |
|---|---|---|
| 120 yards Cream White, ⅜-in. width | ...Per yd. | .04c. |
| 350 yards Red, ⅜-in. width | ...Per yd. | .05c. |
| 150 yards Blue, ⅜-in. width | ...Per yd. | .05c. |
| 500 yards White, ⅜-in. width | ...Per yd. | .04c. |
| 2,000 yards Red Soutache, ⅛-in. width | ..Per yd. | .02c. |

**3000. NEW FULL DRESS COATS,** 31 inches long as formerly worn by the UNITED STATES MARINE CORPS. Fine dark blue cloth, trimmed around the collar, shoulder tabs, and cuffs with RED. High standing collar. Single breasted, padded and lined, with hook and eye fastening at collar. Made at Government uniform factory. ALL NEW. Price is $3.00 each in sizes up to and including CHEST 36. Sizes 37 to 40 are $3.50 each, sizes 41 to 44 are $3.95 each. Please note these prices in ordering.

**3000-A. HEAVY ARMY LIGHT BLUE TROUSERS,** second hand, serviceable, without stripes, in sizes not over waist 35 inches, price $2.75 pair. With white, yellow, or red stripes, put on, $3.50 per pair.

**3000-B. ARMY WHITE HELMETS,** NEW, in assorted sizes. We offer the helmets with ventilator top at 75 cents each. For helmet trimmed as shown in illustration, with brass helmet spike and brass base, the price is $1.00. If plume and holder are desired the outfit will cost $1.60 each.

Many customers in purchasing No. 3000, have their own tailors put on the special color trimmings desired, to match the colors of their organization. We cannot agree to do this work, and offer the dress coats, trousers, and helmets as described above. In ordering uniform outfits of this or other style, we suggest that you allow about one week for us to fill your order. We will accept a deposit of 25 per cent, when you send the order with sizes, and ship the uniforms by EXPRESS, C. O. D., for the balance and charges.

**1552C**

**1552C. British Army Fencing Masks. $2.85 each, or $5.50 pair.**

**British Army Officers Pill Box Cap,** with gilt lace band ornamented top, used, good serviceable order. Price, $2.85.

**BRITISH POLICE HELMET,** stiff body cloth covered with metal ornament, denoting station. Illustration is (Dock Dept.) genuine "Bobby's 'At." Second hand, assorted sizes. Price, $2.85 each.

**UNITED STATES ARMY HELMET BASE,** polished brass, new. Price 15 cents each. $1.50 dozen.

**U. S. ARMY HELMET,** side buttons. 15c. set, $1.50 doz. sets.

**3000**

**Our Bargain Band or Uniformed Rank Outfit**

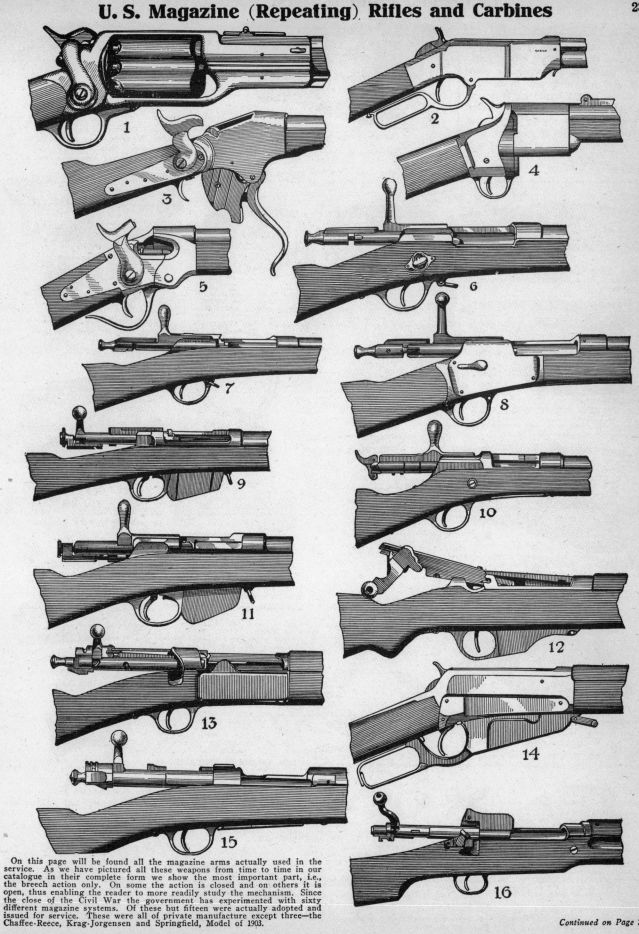

On this page will be found all the magazine arms actually used in the service. As we have pictured all these weapons from time to time in our catalogue in their complete form we show the most important part, i.e., the breech action only. On some the action is closed and on others it is open, thus enabling the reader to more readily study the mechanism. Since the close of the Civil War the government has experimented with sixty different magazine systems. Of these but fifteen were actually adopted and issued for service. These were all of private manufacture except three—the Chaffee-Reece, Krag-Jorgensen and Springfield, Model of 1903.

*Continued on Page 235*

We make up to order caps of various designs to go with any special uniform. These can be made in assorted colors and in different shapes. Many bands and theatrical companies want something different to make a showy appearance. Send us sketches of what you want and we will quote prices. Caps to order made in not less than one dozen at one time.

No. 2. NEW U. S. ARMY BLUE BELL TOP CAP, late regulation, in assorted sizes. This style worn by bands and military companies. Price, $1.80 each.

This cap made into officer's by putting on black braid, gilt lace strap, and gilt metal coat of arms.

OVERSEAS CAPS. These are olive drab wool and are in fine condition. This is the style of cap issued to the troops sent abroad, as it was found more practical than the felt campaign hat as used in this country. Price, 50 cents each.

No. 4. NEW ARMY CAP BANDS, in colors of the different branches of the service. Price, 50 cts. each.

Nos. 5 and 6. BLUE CLOTH PILL BOX CAPS, worn by hotel hall boys and military men. Very natty looking caps. This pattern is worn by the British Army soldiers on the side of the head, held in place with a small chin strap. Blue cloth cap, with black mohair band. Leather straps, with side buttons. All practically new. Price, 85 cts. each.

1853. SCOTCH OFFICER'S BLUE SHAKO, with tartan border and leather peak. Regimental ornament topped with silver THISTLE insignia. In good order. Price, $8.50.

No. 7. U. S. A. Officers' Caps, fine quality dark blue cloth, mohair braid band, leather visor, gilt wire lace chin strap, with coat of arms; new goods in assorted sizes. Price, $4.85. NOT REGLN.

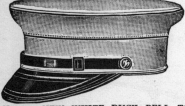

No. 8. NEW WHITE DUCK BELL TOP CAPS, for summer use, or in hot climates. Made of fine white cotton cloth, with leather straps and vizor; in assorted sizes. $1.85 each.

10164. NEW LINEN CAPS. Made for railroad trainmen in Central America; never used. Sold to us on account of change of style. Assorted sizes. Made of the finest unbleached linen. 177 in the lot. Mohair cloth stiffening with leather peak, flexible top with detachable cover for washing. Weight 4½ ounces. Maker's price, $19.00 dozen; our bargain price, 50 cents each; $4.00 per dozen.

1016A. LINEN CAP COVERS. New, detachable for washing; can be used over any square-top cap. Unbleached linen color. Price, 14 cents each.

U. S. ARMY HAT CORDS, red, yellow or blue colors, complete with tassels; made for use during the Civil War; new; never used. Price, 10 cents each; $1.00 per dozen.
GILT CAP CORDS with acorn ends for officer's Civil War Hats; new goods. Price, 25 cents.

British Army Officers' Caps, "Pill Box" and "Dice Box," as they are nick-named: made of fine cloth, gilt lace embroidered, in good second-hand, serviceable order. Price, $3.

MORO DATTO'S HAT, found near Palamayo after skirmish November 21, 1901, Island of Mindanao, Philippine Islands, by Corporal R. T. O'Brien, of 26th Volunteers, who told before the United States Senate of the water-cure business. The straw in this hat is made under water and takes from seven months to a year to make. Price, with signed statement, $10.00.
Also one which is supposed to be over 100 years old, used by natives at times to carry concealed despatches; fairly good state of preservation. Price, with signed statement, $7.50.

10168. ANCIENT AUSTRIAN SOLDIER'S LEATHER HAT. With double-headed eagle, "F 11" on brass front plate. In serviceable order. Price, $4.85.

10169. GERMAN FIREMAN'S LEATHER HELMET. With brass front plate, with axe decorations. In fine order. Price, $3.85.

No. 13. GRAY CLOTH CAPS, to be usew with the CONFEDERATE UNIFORMS. We make these to order only, and will quote price on application.

200 MARINE SHAKOS, stiff body blue cloth covered. New goods slightly soiled, assorted sizes, pom pon. Price, $1.50 each.

No. 11. NEW BELL TOP GRAY CLOTH CAPS. Fine quality gray cloth, with leather strap and vizor; assorted sizes. Price, $1.80 each.

No. 3. NEW BLUE CLOTH MILITIA CAPS, sizes 7⅛ up. Reduced to 50 cents each.

No. 3A. MILITIA BLUE CAPS, second hand, in assorted sizes. Price 38 cents each.

No. 19. GILT BRASS CAP WREATHS, with wire fastening on back. New. Price, 12 cts. each, $1.20 per doz.

No. 22, WEST POINT CADET GRAY CLOTH BELL TOP CAP, trimmed with black mohair, 1⅝-inch band, with small black piping around the top, with small leather vizor; silk lined. Have been used. Are offered second-hand Price, 65c each.

No. 11. 2,000 Blue Cloth Caps, 10 cents each, $1.00 dozen.
Old regulation used by soldiers of National Guard, second-hand, more or less moth eaten, buyer can repair. We offer as are without regard to sizes, 10 cents each, $1.00 dozen.

24 Band Caps, straight vizors. New; not regulation; bargain. Price, $6.00 per dozen.

No. 20. CIVIL WAR CAP ORNAMENTS. New, large size brass bugle, with wire fastenings, used on infantry soldier's cap. Crossed sabres, used by Cavalry, and crossed cannon, used by Artillery. Regulation during the Civil War period. Price, 10 cts. each, $1.00 a doz.

No. 21. GILT OR SILVER CAP CORDS. For use on any military cap. Used by many societies for improving the appearance of ordinary caps; usually worn by privates. New. Price, 50 cts. each.

FEATHER PLUME FOR HELMET OR SHAKOS; new; fairly good serviceable order. Price, $1.25.

No. 1. COLT'S REPEATING RIFLE. Model of 1855 and made at Hartford, Conn. This side hammer model was patented by E. K. Root. Government records show that a few of these were purchased in 1857 at a cost of $50 each. This would seem to prove that the Colt rifle was the first repeater adopted and used by the U. S. Made in several lengths of barrels for both Army and Navy use. The caliber was .56. During the Civil War the Navy purchased a number at $44 each. These had a saber bayonet with a blade 24 inches in length. The revolving cylinder held five cartridges.

No. 2. HENRY MAGAZINE RIFLE. The invention of Tyler Henry in 1860 and made at New Haven, Conn. The magazine of this rifle which is placed under the barrel, is loaded at the muzzle end. It took a metallic cartridge (one of the first) and was both rim and center fire. Caliber .44. Twelve hundred of these rifles were ordered for Baker's Washington (D.C.) Regiment of Cavalry in 1861 at a cost of $36 each. They saw service before the year was out and to the Henry belongs the honor of being the first magazine arm to be used in the Civil War.

No. 3. SPENCER MAGAZINE RIFLE AND CARBINE. Patented by C. M. Spencer in 1860 but not perfected and finally patented until July, 1862. The magazine, which was situated in the butt-stock, held seven shots. The butt plate had a sliding cover for insertion of the loaded tube of cartridge. Made at Boston, Providence and Bristol, R. I. All the Spencers used in the Civil War were not equipped with a cut-off, this feature being added in 1865. Next to the Springfield Rifle, the Spencer was the most famous weapon of the war. The 197th Ohio regiment used them for over three years and General Hooker stated in a report that several regiments in his army had asked for permission to purchase and arm themselves with Spencers. A leather box was later designed to hold ten tubes, each having seven cartridges enclosed, thus giving the soldier seventy shots. Spencers were used in great numbers in the west as late as the 80's.

No. 4. TRIPLETT AND SCOTT CARBINE. Patented by L. Triplett in December, 1864, and made in Meriden, Conn. The magazine is located in the butt-stock and loads from the front end, the barrel revolves until it opens the magazine, thus allowing the cartridge to slip into the chamber. The extractor is worked by the rotation of the barrel. Six shots. Caliber .50. Rimfire. These appeared too late to be used in the Civil War but they were adopted by some of the states later for arming the militia.

No. 5. BALL MAGAZINE CARBINE. Patent of Albert Ball, June, 1863. 1,002 of these were purchased near the end of the Civil War. The magazine, which was placed underneath the barrel, held eight shots and was loaded from the rear end. The ramrod pulled out the magazine spring to facilitate loading. Rim fire. Caliber .50, and made at Windsor, Vermont. The Ball was a remarkably fine shooting arm and it would have played an important part in the Civil War had it appeared sooner.

No. 6. HOTCHKISS MAGAZINE RIFLE AND CARBINE. Model of 1878. Patented by B. B. Hotchkiss, a well known name in ordnance material. The magazine, which held five cartridges, was situated in the butt-stock and was provided with a cut-off which shows clearly in our illustration at the side of the rifle. Hotchkiss rifles were used more by the Navy than by the Army. The bands, sights and bayonets were similar to the Model 1873 Springfield rifle. The Hotchkiss made its first appearance at the Centennial Exposition in Philadelphia in 1876. Made by Winchester at New Haven. Caliber of both rifles and carbines was .45.

No. 7. CHAFFEE-REECE MAGAZINE RIFLE. Patent of General J. N. Reece and R. S. Chaffee. Submitted to and recommended by the Ordnance Board of 1882. The first government made magazine arm. 1,000 were ordered made in 1884 at Springfield Armory. The magazine is in the butt-stock and holds five shots of .45 caliber. The mechanism was very complicated and the rifles were not a success in field trials. The fittings, bayonets, sights, etc., were similar to the Model 1884 Springfield.

No. 8. HOTCHKISS MAGAZINE RIFLE. Model of 1883. Second model of the famous Hotchkiss. Submitted to the Board of 1882 and recommended for field trials. The system was considered an improvement over the 1878 model. Army model only made. Caliber .45, 5 shots, also made at New Haven by the Winchester Company. The magazine, like the first model, was placed in the butt-stock, the last of this kind to be used by the U. S.

No. 9. REMINGTON-LEE MAGAZINE RIFLE. Caliber .45, 5 shots. This arm was given first place in the list of guns chosen by the Board of 1882. Principally a Navy rifle and used by some Naval Militia units as late as 1903. The fittings and bayonets identical with the model 1873 Springfield made by Remington at Ilion, N. Y. The first patent on this gun is dated 1879. This system used very extensively by foreign countries. The magazine was detachable and could be attached fully loaded in a second.

No. 10. REMINGTON-KEENE MAGAZINE RIFLE. Caliber .45. Model of 1880. Magazine is tubular and placed under the barrel. Holds nine cartridges. Patent of J. Keene, 1874. Can be loaded either at the top or bottom of the breech and can also be used as a single loader. Has a cleaning rod at the left of the fore end. Cocking piece is shown at the rear end of the bolt. Army model had a barrel 32 inches long as against the Navy model of 29½ inches. Made by Remington at Ilion, N. Y. This is the only full length rifle ever used by the U. S. that had the under barrel magazine.

No. 11. LEE MAGAZINE RIFLE. Patent of J. P. Lee, November 4, 1879. 5 shots. Caliber .45. U. S. Navy model. This is the first model of the famous Lee Central Magazine Rifle and upon which, with few exceptions, all modern military arms are patterned. The rifle, with the exception of the breech mechanism, resembled the 1873 Springfield, made at Bridgeport, Conn., by the Lee Arms Co. In 1880 the Navy had 300 of these rifles together with 2,500 Hotchkiss (Model 1878) and 250 Remington Keene for experimental purposes. This was 12 years before the Krag-Jorgensen was adopted for the Army.

No. 12. LEE "STRAIGHT-PULL" MAGAZINE RIFLE. Model of 1895. Also based on the patents of J. P. Lee. This rifle was adopted by a board of Naval officers sitting at Newport in May, 1895. The shape of the stock, fittings, sling strap and bayonet were all determined by the board. The Winchester Company got the contract to make the first 10,000. This rifle is distinguished by the fact that it was the first U. S. Clip Loader, it was also the smallest calibered military rifle ever made (i.e. 6 m.m. or .23 caliber), and also had the shortest knife bayonet, the blade being but eight and one-half inches long. The arrangement of the sling was copied from the Model 1888 of Germany. Great fault was found with the bolt in actual service. The length of service of this Lee was short as they were soon displaced by the Krag after 1900.

No. 13. U. S. KRAG-JORGENSEN MAGAZINE RIFLE. Caliber .30, 5 shots. Adopted by a board of ordnance officers in 1892. 53 different systems were submitted to this board, both of domestic and foreign manufacture. Even the Krag as first offered did not pass the rigid tests and the model accepted was the fifth one submitted. The cartridges are dropped in the magazine singly. It was originally intended to load the rifle with a charger or clip and many devices were tried but none adopted. The bayonet is a copy of the one used by Switzerland on the Schmidt-Rubin rifle. Many improvements were made and a number of models issued before the manufacture of the Krag was stopped in November, 1903. It is interesting to note that the first Krags had long cleaning rods and that the first model carbine had a long stock and was also equipped with a cleaning rod. In all there was 400,000 Krags made, one quarter of these were issued to the militia regiments of the several states. Denmark and Norway both use the Krag, but in a different form, the principle of the magazine, however, being the same.

No. 14. WINCHESTER, MODEL 1895, MAGAZINE RIFLE. Caliber .30, 5 shots. This rifle was chambered to use the Krag cartridge. Has the famous Lee magazine, the bolt action, however, being operated by a lever. The bayonet is the same as that used on the Lee "Straight-Pull" of 1895 and the sling and its fittings are also identical. On the recommendation of the commanding officer of the Army, General Miles, 10,000 of these rifles were ordered by the Secretary of War on May 3, 1898. This purchase was not approved by the Ordnance Department. None were issued until September, 1899, when 100 were ordered to San Francisco for the use of the infantry in the Philippines. The report from Manila was adverse in the extreme. The 100 were returned and sold to a Boston dealer and the remainder, 9,900, were sold in 1906 to M. Hartley Co., who immediately disposed of them to Cuba. Lever action rifles were never liked by the Army and especially ordnance officers. In spite of this, however, the Model 1895 is a great favorite on the target ranges and a fine shooting arm. Russia used some thousands in the World War.

No. 15. U. S. SPRINGFIELD MAGAZINE RIFLE. Model 1903. Caliber .30, 5 shots. Magazine system is based on the Mauser model of 1893, the U. S. paying the Mauser people a lump sum at the time of its adoption by a board of officers at Springfield Armory. The original model had a 30-inch barrel with a stock reaching to the muzzle, so designed to take care of a rod-bayonet. 5,000 of this model were ordered made for experiment in the fall of 1901. Before these were completed, however, the length of the barrel was reduced to 24 inches, thus producing a rifle suitable for both cavalry and infantry. The rod bayonet was retained, however. In 1905 several important changes were ordered, new rear and front sights were designed and the fore end was altered to take a knife bayonet with a blade 16 inches in length. This is the rifle practically as we have it today. The peculiar catch on the bayonet is copied from the handle of the Norwegian Krag bayonet.

No. 16. U. S. ENFIELD MAGAZINE RIFLE. Model of 1917. In 1914 the British government was experimenting with this rifle, with an idea of replacing the Lee Enfield. The caliber was to be .27. When the war broke out pattern rifles were sent to various contractors in the United States and orders soon followed for thousands to arm the British infantry in Flanders. When the U. S. entered the war the first great need was rifles and as Springfield Armory was the only place equipped to produce the service arm (Rock Island had a small plant, not worth while when quantity production was looked for). The ordnance experts found three large plants capable of producing the Enfield. Steps were immediately taken to adopt the Enfield to U. S. ammunition and modify the arm to our use. From September, 1917, until November 1, 1918, these three armories, Eddystone, Pa., Ilion, N. Y., and Winchester, turned out 2,193,429 Enfield Caliber .30 rifles. The bayonet is identical with the English model and exactly like the Lee Enfield bayonet with one slight difference. The idea of the rear sight being placed to the rear of the receiver was new and evidently a successful one as our crack marksmen today practically all have their rifles equipped with sights of this kind. The Enfield was withdrawn from service after the war and the two million rifles that did such signal service in the great struggle are laid away in government arsenals.

## U. S. Carbines—Continued from page 131

No. 10. WARNER BREECH-LOADING CARBINE. Patented in 1864. Rim fire. Caliber .50. Breech-block swings to the right like the Joslyn, the extractor, however, being worked by hand. 4,001 were purchased during the Civil War but few, however, used. Gun weighed less than seven pounds. Not popular on account of the extra movement to eject shell. The extractor handle shows at bottom of stock in front of the trigger guard.

No. 11. MAYNARD BREECH-LOADING PERCUSSION CARBINE. Uses a metallic cartridge the base of which filled the space between the barrel and breech. Patented by Dr. Edward Maynard, the inventor of the famous magazine primer. Date, 1859. Barrel tilts up to load like a shot gun. Twenty thousand purchased for use in Civil War. The first models of these carbines were equipped with the Maynard primer, only a few being made, however. Caliber .50.

No. 12. PALMER BREECH-LOADING BOLT ACTION CARBINE. Caliber .50. An interesting weapon as it was the first metallic cartridge bolt gun used in the U. S. Rim fire with an ordinary side lock. Patented in December, 1863. A contract was given for a quantity of these and 1,000 were delivered before the end of the war (1865). One of the lightest guns of the war as it weighed but 5¾ pounds. An interesting feature of the bolt of this carbine was the sectional locking screw similar to the breech-blocks of our modern cannon.

No. 13. GALLAGER BREECH-LOADING PERCUSSION CARBINE. Caliber .54. Cartridge was linen covered. Patented in 1860 and one of the principal carbines of the Civil War. Barrel tilts up to load like a shot gun. Made by Richardson & Overman of Philadelphia, who in 1865 altered a specimen to rim-fire, calling it the Richardson, and submitted it to the Hancock Board on breech-loading arms. As over $212,000 was expended for cartridges for this particular carbine (1861-1865) they must have seen considerable service.

No. 14. WESSON CARBINE. The invention of Frank Wesson in 1859. This breech-loading arm was more of a sporting arm but during the early days of the Civil War 150 were purchased by the U. S. Barrel tilts up like the Gallager and Maynard. The front trigger releases the catch holding the barrel. Cartridge was all metal and rim fire. Caliber .44. Gun weighs less than six pounds, which made it a great favorite with the Indians. Many specimens are to be found today with the well-known Indian ornamentation of brass headed tacks on the butt-stock. Wesson afterwards became one of the founders of the firm of Smith and Wesson.

No. 15. BURNSIDE BREECH-LOADING CARBINE. Percussion. Caliber .54. Invented by A. E. Burnside, afterwards General, in 1856. One of the principal carbines of the Civil War about 56,000 being purchased for use. This carbine used the first metallic shell cartridge designed for a military arm. The tapered end was open for the purpose of igniting the powder charge by the percussion cap. Made principally by George P. Foster at Providence, R. I., who brought out several improvements on the arm, in fact the carbine as shown above is vastly different in appearance from the original weapon conceived by Burnside.

No. 16. PERRY NAVY BREECH-LOADING CARBINE. Caliber .54. Patented in 1855 and made at Newark, N. J. Two hundred purchased for trial February, 1855, and in 1856 they were favorably commented upon by Admiral Dahlgren. The arm has a magazine primer, consisting of a tube which is inserted through the butt plate. The caps are fed by the action of a spring exactly like the cartridge in the Spencer carbines and rifles. This arm is the second model of Perry's breech action. The first is the so-called "Rebel" Perry. This name was applied on account of a few of the Newark made rifles finding their way down south in the early days of the war.

No. 17. MERRILL, LATROBE AND THOMAS BREECH-LOADING CARBINE. Caliber .54. The strap along the top of stock is brought up and forward to open breech, which is merely a circular piece of metal with a hole extending through it. This is Merrill's first patent and dated 1856. A peculiar feature of this weapon was the method of loading. The cartridge was pushed into place by a piston worked by hand against the action of a spring. As with nearly all arms of the period this carbine has the familiar Maynard primer. Made by Remington at Ilion, N. Y., but no records found as to quantity, so they can be called rare.

Black Cloth Covered Cork Helmet, with polished brass chain strap; eagle spike and base; assorted sizes. Good serviceable order. Original cost upwards of $5.00 each. Our bargain price, $1.10.

500 Black cloth-covered Cork Helmets, with horse-hair plumes, polished gilt brass spread eagle, chin strap and plume holder; all in good second-hand cleaned order; assorted sizes; very showy helmet. Price, $1.45 each.

600 white Cloth-covered Cork Helmets, as used by State Militia, with polished brass gilt spike, spread eagle and chin strap; all in good cleaned second-hand order. Price, $1.10 each.

5000 New York State Militia Black Cloth-covered Cork Helmets. with gilt brass spike and base and gilt front ornaments; assorted sizes; all in good, cleaned, second-hand order, like new. Price, 85 cents each.

8,000 Militia Helmets, cork body, covered with fine black colth; almost new goods, assorted sizes; gilt burnished ornaments, spike, chain and eagle; handsome, showy helmets; $1.10 each; with horse hair plumes, any color, $1.45 each.

U. S. Army Tan-colored Cotton Cloth Covered Cork Helmets; late regulation; cost the U. S. Government $1.24 each; assorted sizes. Our price for single helmets, 62c; by the dozen lot, $7.00.

British Army Helmet, fine black cloth, finished with gilt chain strap with spike and base. With any selection of British Army helmet plates advertised in our catalogue. Price, $3.45.

NAVAL OFFICER'S BLUE CAP, with gilt strap, black mohair braid. New, to order only.

U. S. NAVAL OFFICER'S CAP ORNAMENT, silvered and gilt metal finished foul anchors, shield and eagle, with pin fastenings. New. Price $1.00 each. With buckle loops for attaching to belt for lady. Price $1.25.

U. S. NAVY SAILOR'S BLUE CLOTH HAT, second hand moth-eaten, 48 cents.
Same hat fitted with white detachable cover, 65 cents each. The white covers are removable for washing.

WATCH CAPS, knitted blue wool. Price, 95 cents each. New.

6,000 U. S. ARMY NEW WHITE HELMET, made of selected long light cork covered with fine white drill, with ventilator in top that can be unscrewed, and gilt ornamented spike, used if desired, with sweat band ventilator; assorted sizes. Price, 75 cents each, special price for export quantities.

ARMY DRIVERS CAP. This style was used by drivers and soldiers in cold weather. It is made of heavy canvas with peak. The sides can be turned down and tied under the chin for protection against cold. Price, 95 cents each.

10165. NEW PATTERN U. S. N. WHITE DRILL HATS. Entirely new, with U. S .N. clothing factory labels attached. Made of fine twill, thoroughly shrunk white cotton cloth; rows of fine stitching around the brim to keep its upright shape, giving that natty dressy appearance to U. S. Navy sailors; inside tape binding, white cloth sweatband, weighs 3½ ounces. Entirely new. In assorted sizes. Price is 50 cents.

THEATRICAL OR POLITICAL CAMPAIGN HATS, with colored cord; no ornaments; 30 cents each, $3.00 dozen. New goods, assorted sizes.
SPANISH SOLDIER'S DRESS HATS; fine new goods; relics, $4.75 each.
HELMET PLUMES, U. S. Army, late regulation; yellow, 40c; red, 60c.
U. S. INFANTRY OFFICER'S HELMET, with white yak plume, gilt ornaments and cord; size 7; new. Price, $10.00. One slightly used, price $7.50.

C24. U. S. ARMY TRENCH HELMETS, as issued for use in France. Fine souvenir of the war. Allow postage on five pounds packed. Price only 85 cents each.

U. S. ARMY RELIC TRENCH HELMETS. Painted in various colors of camouflage by the soldiers. RARE RELICS. Price, $10.00 each.

No. 24. ARMY AIGULETTE of fine white wool, with brass tips. Second hand.
RED AIGULETTES, as used by Artillery privates, late regulation. Price 65 cents each.
WHITE AIGULETTES, for privates, with tassel ends, second hand in fair order, can be repaired. Price 35 cents each.

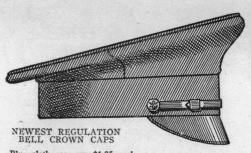

**U. S. A. OLIVE DRAB HEAVY WOOL CLOTH HOODS.** Fine for automobile riding. NEW. Cost upwards of $5.00 to make. Our bargain price, 50 cents.

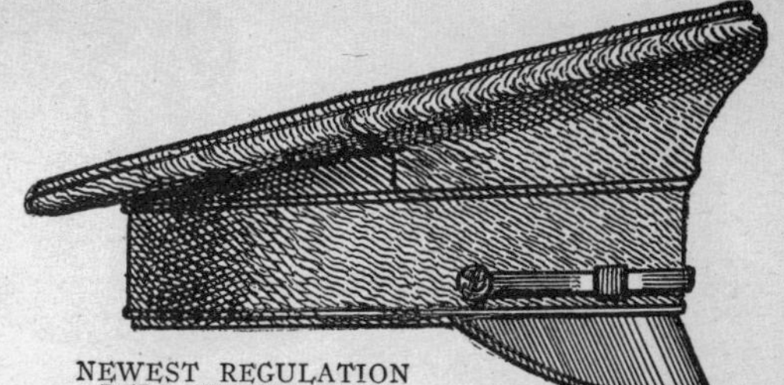

### NEWEST REGULATION BELL CROWN CAPS

Blue cloth caps are $1.85 each.
Gray cloth caps are $1.85 each.
Olive drab cotton cloth caps are $1.25 each.
We can supply brass eagle ornament and gilt lace chin strap to any of the above for officer's use at $1.25 extra per cap.

### NEWEST REGULATION BELL CROWN CAPS

Made of olive drab WOOL cloth, in assorted sizes. Can supply black or russet leather peak as desired. Price, $1.75 each. Brass cap eagle and gilt chin strap to change this into officer's cap will cost $1.25 extra per cap.

### HOW TO MEASURE FOR A HAT

Adjust tape as shown in cut. Number of inches around the head indicates size as per scale below.
Boys' sizes: 6½, 20¾ in.; 6⅝, 21 in.; 6¾, 21¼ in.; 6⅞, 21⅝ in.; 7, 22¼ in.
Men's sizes: 6¾, 21¼ in.; 6⅞, 21⅝ in.; 7, 22¼ in.; 7⅛, 22½ in.; 7¼, 23 in.; 7⅜, 23⅜ in.; 7½, 23¾ in.; 7⅝, 24 in.; 7¾, 24½ in.; 7⅞, 25 in.; 8, 25¼ in.

**3169B. NEW CAMPAIGN HATS,** finest quality, sold on change in Army regulation. These have the soft top, with two fine wire ventilations. Some have corrugated sweat band to keep the head cool. Price, $1.25 each. WE HAVE ONLY A SMALL QUANTITY LEFT IN STOCK NOW.

**1,500 U. S. ARMY CIVIL WAR HAT,** commonly called the "Jeff Davis Hat," adopted by Davis while Secretary of War in President Pierce's Cabinet; used by both North and South during the early years of Civil War; new goods, made during Civil War, slightly faded from age; black, stiff felt, with worsted hat cord in either yellow, red or blue, $5.00. Trimmed as in illustration.

**STATE MILITIA CAMPAIGN HATS.** Old regulation, second-hand, suitable for outdoor workers or sportsmen, in assorted sizes at low price of 50 cents each.

**No. 0-835. ARMY REGULATION CAMPAIGN HAT.** Offered now in assorted sizes at reduced price. These are all entirely new, fitted with tie string. Price, $1.65 each. Hat cord, 18 cents. We offer a cheaper quality hat of exactly the same style for Boy Scouts and Cadet companies in dozen lots at lower prices.

**500 FEATHER PLUMES,** second hand, serviceable order. Each with cardboard box. Price, 80 cents each.

**BRITISH ARMY SOLDIER SOUTH AFRICA CAMPAIGN HAT ORNAMENT,** red fluted silk with metal crown IV and plume ornament. Price, 25 cents.

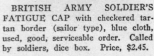

**TWO VIEWS, 1560, NEW BRITISH ARMY HEAVY FELT CAMPAIGN HAT.** With wide brim, 4¾ inches on one side, narrowing to the front, tapering to the crown, with ventilated sweat band, with two rows of small holes for ventilation around the rim. Sides can be fastened to spring button for rapid riding, or let down for use as sombrero. These hats were favored for the Boer war by the Prince of Wales (King Edward). We understand that the famous American hat maker, Stetson, made up a large number of these pattern hats for the British Army. Practically indestructible. Price, $1.50. New hats.

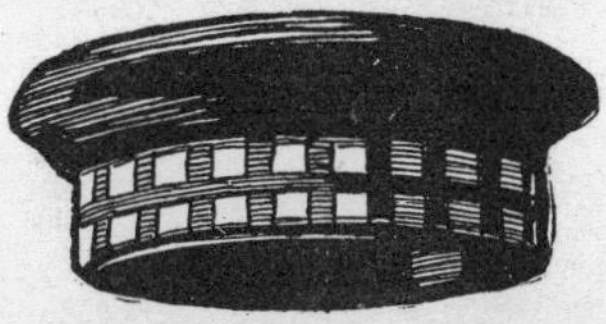

**BRITISH ARMY SOLDIER'S FATIGUE CAP** with checkered tartan border (sailor type), blue cloth, used, good, serviceable order. Called by soldiers, dice box. Price, $2.45.

**SCOTCH REGIMENT THISTLE AND LEAF EMBLEM,** silvered metal. Size, 2 inches. Price, 50 cents, with pin fastening.

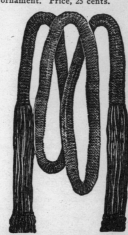

**1553. SCOTCH GLENGARRY CAP** with checkered border, bright blue cloth cap with white and red checkered squares, leather lined. Price $4.00 each.

**BLUE GLENGARRY SCOTCH CAPS,** plain with FEATHER, in assorted sizes, NEW. Price, $2.50 each.

**No. 1149. FRENCH SOLDIER'S BLUE CLOTH SHAKO,** with silver ornamental emblem, castle, fleur de lis ancient ship, etc. Price, $2.50.

**300 NEW U. S. ARMY LIGHT WEIGHT HELMETS** for use in tropical climates, made of fine light fibre, covered with light silver-gray cloth, with ventilated sweat band, all new, our bargain price, 75 cents each.

**No. 1. FEATHER PLUME** for Helmets or Shakos; assorted colors; new, shopworn; in fairly good serviceable order. Price, 95 cents each.

**SPANISH OFFICER'S GERMAN SILVER EPAULETTES;** new, not used. Price, $3.25 pair.

**No. 25. LONG SILK SASHES** in red, blue or green colors, with tassels, long enough to go twice around the waist; just what is wanted for Theatrical Buccaneer Plays, for holding Pistols in sash. Price of sash is $1.55 each or $18.00 a dozen.

10553.

**10553. BRITISH CONSTABLE'S HELMET.** With bronze front plate having the Royal Crown and monogram of King Edward VII, Devon Constabulary, with metal scale chin strap. Side buttons with English Rose and wreath. Used; serviceable order. Price, $1.85 each.

**LATE REGULATION BLUE CLOTH CAP.** With new khaki bell top cap cover. 8,000 U. S. Army late regulation blue cloth caps altered to the present regulation khaki bell top, by use of a detachable khaki cap cover, inside steel wire spring extender. Covers are new. U. S. Army specification, with buttonhole eyelet for chin strap. Can be used with blue cloth uniform, or as new regulation bell top khaki cap. Caps are in assorted sizes. Used a few times; with new cover look practically like new caps. Our bargain price for caps, with cover, 85 cents.

**5039. BRITISH ARMY BRODERICK BELL TOP CAP.** In blue cloth, with small red band around base. Price, $1.95.

**6070. OLD TURKISH MILITARY HELMET.** With arrow and crown, iron body, brass ornamented. Genuine old relic. Price, $15.75.

**0-1219. LODGE OFFICER'S CAP.** Brown cloth, with blue enameled velvet band, ornamented with silver lace and stars. Assorted patterns; job lot. Price, $1.65 each.

**2247. 2500 CIVIL WAR SOLDIER'S CAP.** Made by contract in 1864 for the Union Army Soldiers. New. Fine blue cloth, with leather band and peak, brass Eagle buttons. Very slightly moth eaten. Caps are not pretty looking, but very comfortable. This pattern cap was worn by General Sherman's soldiers on the march through Georgia, which gave occasion for the Confederates to call the soldiers "Sherman's Bummers." Price, $1.00 each.

**0-1243A. BEAD EMBROIDERED CAP.** For stage use to represent INDIAN CHIEFTAIN. Cloth cap, with colored feathers sewed in the band, which is ornamented with beads. Price, $3.50.

10557.

**SECOND HAND CAMPAIGN HATS,** old regulation, suitable to hunting, fishing or outdoor work. 50 cents each.

**10557. HELMET COVER.** In khaki. Adjustable for cleaning. New. Price, 35 cents each.

German Soldier's Chinese Campaign helmets. Back folds up. Price 85 cents each.

**GRAY CADET CAPS** similar to illustration No. 200 on this page, with red or light blue trimming to represent the GERMAN ARMY CAPS for movies or theatrical use. Price, 75 cents each.

We have many styles of caps and can alter or trim these to represent many different foreign caps. We also offer Army and Militia dress coats and blouses that can be altered or re-trimmed to answer for European uniforms. Prices quoted on application. Send us your lists of uniforms needed, and we will quote on entire production.

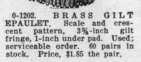

**0-1202. BRASS GILT EPAULET.** Scale and crescent pattern, 3¾-inch gilt fringe, 1-inch under pad. Used; serviceable order. 60 pairs in stock. Price, $1.85 the pair.

**200 ARMY CADET CAPES.** Heavy blue Kersey cloth. 21 inches in depth, 3-inch collars. Used, fine serviceable order. Price, $2.65.

**50 ARMY CADET CAPES.** Heavy blue cloth, bright red flannel lined, 3½-inch collar, 22 inches depth. Price, $3.00 each.

**50 DRUM MAJOR'S UNIFORM COATS.** No two alike. Frock coats made of fine dark blue broad cloth, elaborately trimmed. Handsome coats, very showy. NEW. Large assortment. Price $6.50 each.

**TAN LEATHER CHIN SCALE HELMET STRAP.** Length 17 inches, with buckle and eyelet for adjusting length. New. Price, 15 cents each; $1.50 a dozen.

**5041. HAIR PLUME.** White hair top, red hair base, mounted in ornamented shell holder, with whalebone rib for use on helmet shako, nickel ring around the base to keep hair in shape. Full length 7 inches. Price, 55 cents each.

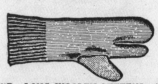

**61D. LONG WOOLEN MITTENS** with trigger finger for shooting or driving. Length, 16 inches. Price, per pair, 45 cents.

**U. S. ARMY REGULATION WHITE HAT CORDS.** With acorn ends. For use on campaign hats. Used; serviceable order. Price, 10 cents each.

**100A. U. S. A. OFFICERS' CAPS.** Late regulation, with gilt embroidered U. S. Eagle, wreath and stars, with gilt cord, with 1½-inch black mohair braid, with eyelet side ventilators. New; gilt slightly tarnished. Regular $4.00 cap; our bargain price, $1.00.

**10455. WATERLOO PERIOD BRITISH OFFICER'S HELMET WITH PRINCE OF WALES MOTTO,** "Ich Diem." In silvered metal, with gilt crown, with chains and front plate. Handsome old helmet; somewhat similar to No. 6922, page 310. Price, $20.00.

**OLD ARMY TROUSERS AND BLOUSES.** Moth-eaten. Useful to workmen working among acids, which would destroy good clothing; also suitable for property returns. Offered "as are" in small sizes. Price, $1.00 each.

**5,000 BRASS HELMET CHAINS.** ⅝ inch wide, 14 inches long, stitched to leather band. Used on New York State helmets. In second-hand, serviceable order. Price, 35 cents each; $4.00 per dozen.

**10458. LEATHER HELMET.** Revolutionary War period. Somewhat similar to No. 6922, page 310. Price, $15.00. Similar one in poor order, $8.85.

**10951. CROMWELLIAN BATTLEFIELD IRON HELMET.** Relic found on Naseby battlefield, where the Cromwellian and Royalist troops fought. Helmet has the triple bar nose guard. Shows for itself as a battlefield relic. Price, $15.00.

**10453. BRITISH OFFICER'S HELMET.** Marked "V. R. Suffolk Yeomanry Cavalry." Price, $14.50.

**10452. BRITISH OFFICER'S METAL HELMET.** Profusely ornamented; front plate marked "North Somerset," with "V. R." in the centre in relief. Price, $15.00.

**10454. BRITISH POLICE OFFICER'S HELMET.** Marked "Sheffield," with brass front plate. Price, $3.50.

**U. S. ARMY WORSTED HAT CORDS,** black and gilt with acorn ends; new, for officers, 40 cents.

**U. S. ARMY WORSTED HAT CORDS,** with acorn ends, in colors, dark blue, green, light blue, maroon red, white or black. 20 cents each, or $2.00 a dozen.

3400

3402

3250

### OFFICERS WHITE DUCK UNIFORM

Officer's Bell Top Cap, with white mohair band, with gilt chin scale strap, with gilt or bronze Eagle Coat-of-Arms. Price $2.85.

Fatigue coat with standing collar trimmed with white mohair braid around the collar, front and sides, with side openings for sword sling strap. Price $5.00.

Officer's White Duck Trousers with white mohair braid stripes 1½ inches wide. Price $2.20 the pair.

### NEW U. S. ARMY REGULATION FLANNEL OLIVE DRAB DRESS SHIRTS

with two outside breast pockets with place for pencil, etc. Turn down collar re-inforced cuff, full length all as per U. S. Government specification. Finest quality shirt made of which we have supplied to many Foreign Government officers. New Regulation Shirts. Price, $3.00 each.

**7139. U. S. NAVY SAILOR'S ANTIQUE RATING BADGES,** white cotton cloth, size 3½ by 3 inches, stamped in black with star, eagle and foul anchor, some with star and anchor, others with steering wheel, with marlin spike, marine glasses, rope knots, crossed anchors, crossed cannons. Buyer's choice, 10 cents; 60 cents a dozen. Can be used for sofa pillow decorations, etc.

**3400. ROUGH RIDER'S UNIFORMS,** the same style as used by officers and privates. We do not have the full outfit except in small sizes.

**CAMPAIGN HATS,** used, in serviceable order 50 cents each. NEW hats up to size 7 are $1.25 each.

**BLOUSES:** New, trimmed with blue or yellow in sizes 33 inch chest and smaller. Price 75 cents each.

**BREECHES:** NEW with fastenings at bottom of tape, lace or buttons, our selection, medium sizes at $2.50 each.

**SHIRTS:** New blue shirts, army style, but not army quality, to order only, in assorted sizes. Price $2.00 each.

**CARTRIDGE BELTS,** both double and single row, also with pockets as used by the NAVY in Spanish War. Price 65 cents.

We have also the various ornaments as used by officers and privates, also brass shoulder straps and chevrons. Write for price.

**LEGGINS,** Khaki Canvas, 14-inch length, used by State Militia, serviceable, complete with laces. Size 3, 38c a pair; size 1 and 2, 45c a pair.

**HANDKERCHIEFS,** either Navy Blue or Turkey Red color, kind worn around the neck by Spanish War soldiers. New. Price, 15c each.

**4 British Officer's Belt Buckles** with crown and coat of arms design in center; gilt background, silvered design in relief; size, 1¾x2 inches; have been in use. Purchased in London, 1903; probably relics of South Africa. Handsome buckle for lady. Price, $3.00 each.

**3402. CHAPLAIN UNIFORM** new, fine black felt hat, with leather sweat band. All sizes. Price $1.25.

Fine new black broadcoth coat, with standing collar, black cloth covered buttons. Full length skirts. Silk ined and padded, inside breast pockets. These coats are entirely new. Made by the best Military Uniform House in America, to sell for $25.00 each. We have 150 coats in stock. Assorted sizes. Anyone can use these fine dress coats, and our bargain price is $8.50 each.

75 Vests, new, assorted patterns and colors. Size 34 to 36 inch chest measure. Price $1.00 each. For larger sizes a trifle higher price. All new, salesmens' samples.

**Russian Cossack Overcoat** with wide skirts. From the late Fred Remington Collection. Price $10.00.

6087

**6087. Coat Chain Hangers,** 90000 in stock, new, in original boxes, 3½ inches long, double ring steel nickeled, 100 in box, contract price $1.00 hundred. Our bargain price 35 cents per 100.

**3250. SPANISH WAR MILITIA UNIFORM** for practical service and looks as good as new. Sold by reason of change from the blue to the olive drab colors.

**CAP:** fine blue cloth with side buttons. leather sweat band, and peak chin strap, with ventilating eyelets, silk lined with carrying loop. Weight 5 ounces, assorted sizes, 68c each. Some that have been crushed and much worn. Suitable for Theatrical use. Price 38c each.

**BLOUSE** fine dark blue cloth, turndown collar, 5 brass buttons, inside breast pockets. Lined body and sleeves. Average weight 2 pounds. Selected. Price $3.25. Some that have been much used are offered in cleaned and repaired order. Price $2.50

**TROUSERS** heavy blue Kersey cloth. Lighter shade of blue than the blouse as required in Militia Regulation. Side and hip pockets. Price $3.25. Some that have been much used. Offered in cleaned and pressed order. Price $2.50.

**OLD TROUSERS and BLOUSES** worn, moth eaten and torn, of which we have sold many to Manufacturing Companies, who employ laborers working among acids. Our selection as to the condition and sizes. No order for special sizes will be received. Price $1.00 each garment.

In 1861, when the Civil War broke out the Arsenals of the North were found to be nearly empty. Jefferson Davis, while Secretary of War, foreseeing the coming struggle, had ordered large quantities of arms and other war materials shipped to the Government arsenals in the South, which later on, when the South seceded, were used to arm the Southern troops. The commanding officer of one of the arsenals of the North is reported to have continued to ship arms to the South, even after Fort Sumter was fired on, and when remonstrated with said, that he was obeying the orders of his superiors. In order to procure arms for the volunteer soldiers of the North, President Lincoln gave contracts through Secretary of War Stanton to everyone who would sign a contract to make guns. Gunmakers in those days were looked upon as public benefactors. Springfield Muzzle Loading Rifles were furnished to contractors as models, the contractors marking on the lock-plate, name, place and date. A dealer in fire arms in New York City was commissioned by President Lincoln a Brigader General and sent to Europe to buy up arms, not only for arming the Northern volunteers, but also to prevent the guns from going to the South.

**BOYS' CLUB OUTING AT BANNERMAN ISLAND**

For many years Mr. Francis Bannerman, the founder of this business, found rest and recreation in evening games, and the study of the Bible with poor boys in Brooklyn, near the Navy Yards, where he spent several years of his early youth, especially when his father was in the Navy as engineer during the Civil War. Realizing what few opportunities they had for real recreation, he held annual outings at Bannerman Island. The boys went up the Hudson River on the Day Line boat to Newburg and were brought across in one of the motor boats. Here were held all sorts of water sports, swimming, boat racing, etc., with lots to eat, and ending off with the boys' favorite desert of ice cream in abundance. Mr. Francis Bannerman enjoyed it all as much as the boys. During the World War many former members of this club joined up, and saw service both in this country and in France.

## Story of the Krags

Many stories in the newspapers and magazines regarding the sale of the 300,000 Krag Rifles in the U. S. Armories have appeared since the present European war. We are about the only firm that had any legal right to purchase the Krags after the outbreak of the war, for according to the law as laid down by the U. S. Senate after the investigation of arms sold in 1870 and '71 during the French-German War, *"No arms belonging to the United States was allowed to be sold to any person or firms who had not previously to the outbreaking of the war been a purchaser."* Early in 1914 we were negotiating with the U. S. War Department for the purchase of the Krags together with their ammunition and we hold a bill showing the purchase from U. S. War Dept. of a sample case of Krag Rifles at a cost of $3.40 each. These samples were sent to our agent in Europe and negotiations were under way for the sale, and had proceeded so far that we made a visit to Washington and entered into an agreement with the War Department that when we returned to the Department the Landing Certificate of the arms and cartridges endorsed by the U. S. Consul at Antwerp (or any other European port) the export bond we were required to give at the time of purchase would be cancelled. The European War and the President's Neu-

trality Proclamation stopped the business. We never made any effort after the war began, to claim our sole right of purchase of the Krags.

Indeed it was against our public protest that the U. S. War Department should offer for sale any of the Krags (or even sell the old 45 calibre Springfields, which would make good drill guns) for history bears record that no great war has ever taken place that did not bring back into service, rifles and war material formerly discarded. Our May, 1910, catalogue supplement (written at the request of our customers) shows our position at that time: For on asking a retired army general in our store one day what was the rapidity test for the new Springfield service rifles, he replied, 35 shots fired from the hip, and 21 aimed shots; adding, "What do you want the information for?" I replied that customers had asked me to tell them how our nation stood for preparedness and that I was going to publish it. His warning reply was "Look out, young man, or you'll have somebody in your wool." So in face of warning, censure and derision we published in our May, 1910, supplement catalogue the following notice which we here reproduce. In the light of the past seven years it now makes interesting reading; showing our humble efforts to awaken the American people from living in a Fool's Paradise.

## Reprinted from our May 1910 Supplement

It is the wise policy of the U. S. Government to hold the Krag Rifles in reserve for seldom has any war taken place without calling into active service rifles formally discarded. According to the statements appearing in the public press:

THE UNITED STATES HAS IN ALL ITS ARSENALS AND IN THE HANDS OF REGULARS AND MILITIA ABOUT:

| RIFLES 300,000 Krags 600,000 Springfields | CARTRIDGES 70,000,000 | Rapidity of Fire, 20 Aimed Shots a Minute | TIME with all Rifles in Use to Exhaust all Cartridges 3½ Minutes | New Supply of Rifles Government Armories 1,500 Daily. Private Armories 6 Months to Produce the 1st U. S. Model Rifle. | New Supply of Cartridges Government and Private Factories 900,000 Daily | One Cartridge for each Rifle per Day |

This indifference to safeguarding the nation by having an adequate Army and Navy with proper reserve stock of War Material (a national insurance), is caused in a great measure by Peace Advocates who believe that every difference between nations can be settled at The Hague.

Was it not the Czar of Russia who called the first meeting of the Peace Congress at The Hauge, and like the boy who brought his teacher the rattan, was he not the first to get whipped?

The Empire of China is an example of the doctrine of peace.

The Hague, without the armed power of the Nations it represents as a Police Force, will always fall short of settling by moral suasion great differences between nations.

If I have read my Bible aright, Jesus Christ, the Son of God teaches me not only the sermon on the Mount—Blessed are Peace Makers (the GOD-GIVEN IDEAL RULE for the citizens of his kingdom), but He teaches me by His example that while striving to live the higher Ideal Life, it is also necessary to live and act to meet the conditions surrounding us in the world today. For did not He in the three years spent in teaching the people of Judea and training His twelve disciples, know that His Disciples carried swords. Necessary in those days, for did He not illustrate the story of the "Good Samaritan" by showing the necessity of travelers carrying weapons to defend themselves against the robbers, the BAD CITIZENS OF THOSE DAYS? Am I to take it altogether as an allegory when the Master on the night of the betrayal said in St. Luke xxii-36: "And he that hath no sword let him sell his garment and buy one," and in the 38th verse, "And they said, 'Lord, behold here are two swords'," and He said unto them "It is enough," and in the 49th verse when they which were about Him saw what would follow, they said unto Him, "Lord, shall we smite with the sword?" and one of them (Peter, did not give the Master time to answer) smote a servant of the High Priest and cut off his right ear and Jesus said, "Suffer ye thus far." Perhaps Jesus in rebuking Peter, for his haste in swiping off the ear of the foremost, rudest of the temple band, when He said: "PUT UP AGAIN THY SWORD INTO ITS PLACE, FOR ALL THEY WHO TAKE THE SWORD SHALL PERISH WITH THE SWORD," was predicting that the Jews who were then using the swords of the Romans against Him, would themselves perish with the Roman swords, and such would be the fate of all aggressors.

Two swords in company of eleven (Judas, the treasurer, who no doubt also carried a sword, was absent), gives a percentage of one sword to every sixth man. Does not Jesus state our case in Luke xi, 22-22.

"When a strong man, armed, keepeth his palace, his goods are in peace, but when a stronger, than he shall come upon him and *overcometh* him, he taketh from him all his armor wherein he trusteth."

Battle Ships and War Material wear out, Insurance Policies also run

out yearly, and yet he would be considered a poor business man who failed to renew.

Evidently A. D. 30 was not the time for the Son of God, the Prince of Peace, to put into practice the Ideals of His Sermon on the Mount.

### COMPULSORY MILITARY TRAINING.

When we are in need of salesmen we advertise in army papers for army men with good discharge references. We appreciate men who have had army training. (German manufacturers pay higher wages to men who have had military service), and yet army men who for three or more years the United States has spent time in training are discharged at the end of their enlistment, and no record is kept of them—men who would be invaluable in a war emergency, and there are discharged from the army and navy over 25,000 men yearly, the majority of whom are leaving the service without any record kept regarding their address or claim by the United States on their future services. The United States is the only nation who acts in this careless way.

For many years we have advocated that the trained army and navy veterans that hold good discharge records, should be retained on the rolls for war emergency and paid a small salary with a short annual attendance at advanced instruction schools or camp. We believe the only cure for the present spirit of "know-it-all," "I-don't-care" and "I'll-do-it-if-I-feel-like-it" now shown by employees, which every merchant knows is the cause of nearly all the trouble in business correcting the mistakes and errors, of *employees who do as they please*, not as their employer wishes, will be to enforce compulsory military service on the youth of the country so that they will be educated and trained in obedience, self discipline, cleanliness and order; to know how to care for themselves. The drill of the soldier giving him strength, endurance, gracefulness and a spirit of patriotism.

The greatest peace insurance the U. S. could have, will be for the youth of the land to be trained in military service schools so that OUR YOUNG MEN WILL BE A NATION OF WEST POINTERS.

The Russians thought it a great joke when the little brown monkeys, as they called the Japs, declared war, but soon found it was no joke. The great success of the Japs over China and Russia has fired their ambition, and made them so sensitive that they now demand treaty recognition by nations of the first-class, and woe be to that nation that fails to accord to her citizens all the rights of a privileged nation.

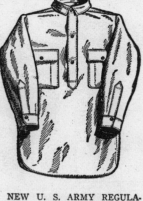

**3406.** Drum Major's Band Uniform. Fine blue cloth cap slightly Bell Top, with black mohair braid band.

With bronze metal Eagle Coat-of-Arms. Price $2.50.

Fine new Red Cloth Officer's Pattern Coat, with 8 buttons concealed by the black mohair braid fly, standing collar, black mohair braid trimmed, ornamented with small gilt braid with sword sling openings at the side. Ornamental fancy scroll designs in black cloth on the breast, sleeves and shoulder tabs, with gilt soutache braid trimmings. Full lined, inside pocket. Good value for $30.00 to make. One of the handsomest band leader coats made. Good value for $30.00. Our bargain price $12.50.

**3209.** U. S. Navy Shoe Brush Outfit. Brush, Dauber, Blacking. Per set, 35c.

Fine new white duck Trousers, Military Pattern passed U. S. Government Inspector. Two side and one hip pockets, in assorted sizes, small to medium. Price $1.50.

**3408.** Band Uniform Helmet, cork body. Fine black cloth covered with leather peak, front and rear, side buttons, sweat bands, inside lining, practically new helmets, with side ventilators, with polished chin scale straps with brass helmet eagle coat-of-arms. Brass metal oak leaf top with brass spike, holding hair plume either red, yellow or white color; would cost $7.00 to make. Our bargain price, $1.50, assorted sizes.

Fine red cloth Frock Coats, double breasted, 2 rows 7 buttons each. Standing collar with light blue trimmings, with small white cloth edging on shoulder tabs, cuffs and skirts. Padded and quilted breast lining. Inside breast pocket. Pocket in each skirt. From collar to the end of the skirt measures 31 inches. We have 80 of these fine coats. Have been used by a military band for a short time. Are offered in serviceable order at the bargain price of $4.85 each.

Cork Helmets covered with white cloth, with polished brass ornaments including brass scale chin strap and red, white or yellow hair plumes. Price $1.50, in small sizes only.

Sky Blue Kersey Cloth Trousers with 1⅛ wide cloth strap with pockets. Used, serviceable, cleaned and pressed order at $2.75 a pair.

**3401.** A BAND LEADER'S NEW UNIFORM COATS, 300 Assorted Patterns, salesman's samples, great variety in dark blue, green, red and white cloth, fancy trimmed, assorted sizes, good value for from $15.00 to $30.00. Our bargain price from $7.85 to $12.50.

Large Stock of Military Cloth Trousers, sky blue color, with 1⅛ inch white stripes, in second hand, cleaned and pressed order. Price $3.45.

Blue Cloth Bell Top Cap with gilt strap, with either gilt or bronze metal eagle coat-of-arms. Price $2.50.

**2417.** Japanese Metal Helmet, black enameled, with folding scale rim, fine order. Price, $7.85.

**3176.** French Non-Com. Officer's, size 36, sky blue cloth Coat, soutache trimmed, red cloth trousers with leather bottoms. Serviceable second-hand. From late Fred Remington. Price $12.00.

**3175.** FRENCH OFFICER'S UNIFORM. Size 36, red cap, gilt trimmed, red trousers with 2-inch black stripe, black cloth coat, soutache braid trimmed, plain leather leggins. Serviceable second-hand order. Purchased from the late Fred Remington. Price $18.00.

NEW U. S. ARMY REGULATION FLANNEL OLIVE DRAB DRESS SHIRTS with two outside breast pockets with place for pencil, etc. Turn down collar, re-inforced cuff, full length all as per U. S. Government specification. Finest quality shirt made of which we have supplied to many Foreign Government officers. New Regulation Shirts. Price $3.00 each.

NEW BLUE ARMY SHIRTS, offered in assorted sizes to order. This is the SPANISH WAR pattern, but is not of Government high quality. Two outside pockets, turn down collar. Price $3.00.

GRAY TROUSERS with BLACK stripes as used by the Spanish American War Veterans, with the blue shirt and gray cap. Trousers in used condition, up to waist 34 inches. Price $2.50 each.

NEW GRAY CAPS, bell top in assorted sizes. $1.85 each.

South African Republic (Z. A. R.) Military Button, relic from uniform coat of Officer who served in the Boer War. Price $2.00.

U. S. A. OLIVE DRAB WOOL CLOTH UNIFORMS. Olive drab cloth coat, four outside pockets, bronze button flaps. Used, cleaned, repaired, serviceable. Sizes, 34 to 38. Price, $1.95.
NEW OLIVE DRAB WOOL CLOTH BREECHES. All sizes. Price, $4.50.
OLIVE DRAB WOOL CLOTH BREECHES, used, cleaned, repaired, serviceable. Price, $1.95.
NEW U. S. OLIVE DRAB CANVAS PUTTEE. Price, 95 cents pair.
MONTANA PEAK HAT. Price, $1.75.
CAMPAIGN HAT, used, serviceable. Price, 35 cents.
OLIVE DRAB CLIP CARTRIDGE BELT. Price, 50 cents.
OVERSEAS WOOL CAPS, new, 50c each.
NEW OLIVE DRAB WOOL CAPS. Price, $1.75 each.
NEW OLIVE DRAB COTTON CAPS. Price, $1.50.
BRASS CAP ORNAMENTS without letters or figures, 10 cents each.
TAN KHAKI WEB BELT, single row, new at 75 cents each. Second hand, 40 cents each.

While the Japanese-Russian war was in progress, the writer made a hurried trip to the Orient in order to try and dispose of some of his immense stock of military goods. On arrival, and after passing the Yokohoma customs, wishing to get quickly to business, I asked the hotel runner what I should say to the Japanese rickshaw man in order to have him take me to my agent's place of business. He surprised me by saying, "Tell him number 21." I was about to remonstrate that the address was insufficient, but remembering that this was his busy day I called one of the baby carriages, gave the rickshaw man the number, and was trundled right to the agent's door. Later I asked the hotel man the reason. He informed me that all foreigners lived in districts set apart by the Japanese Government, which was divided into squares, and known by number to all Japanese.

And yet when the Japanese come to the foreigner's country, they demand the privilege of residing where they please.
New Yorker on the Yangtze.

FRANCIS BANNERMAN.

**2500.** Leather Sweat Bands, for use in army hats or caps, 2¼ inches wide, for 6¼ and 6½ hats or caps. New, surplus quantity, good value for $10.00 per gross. Our bargain price 10c each, $5.00 per gross.

# Breech-loading Carbines U.S. Trials 1865

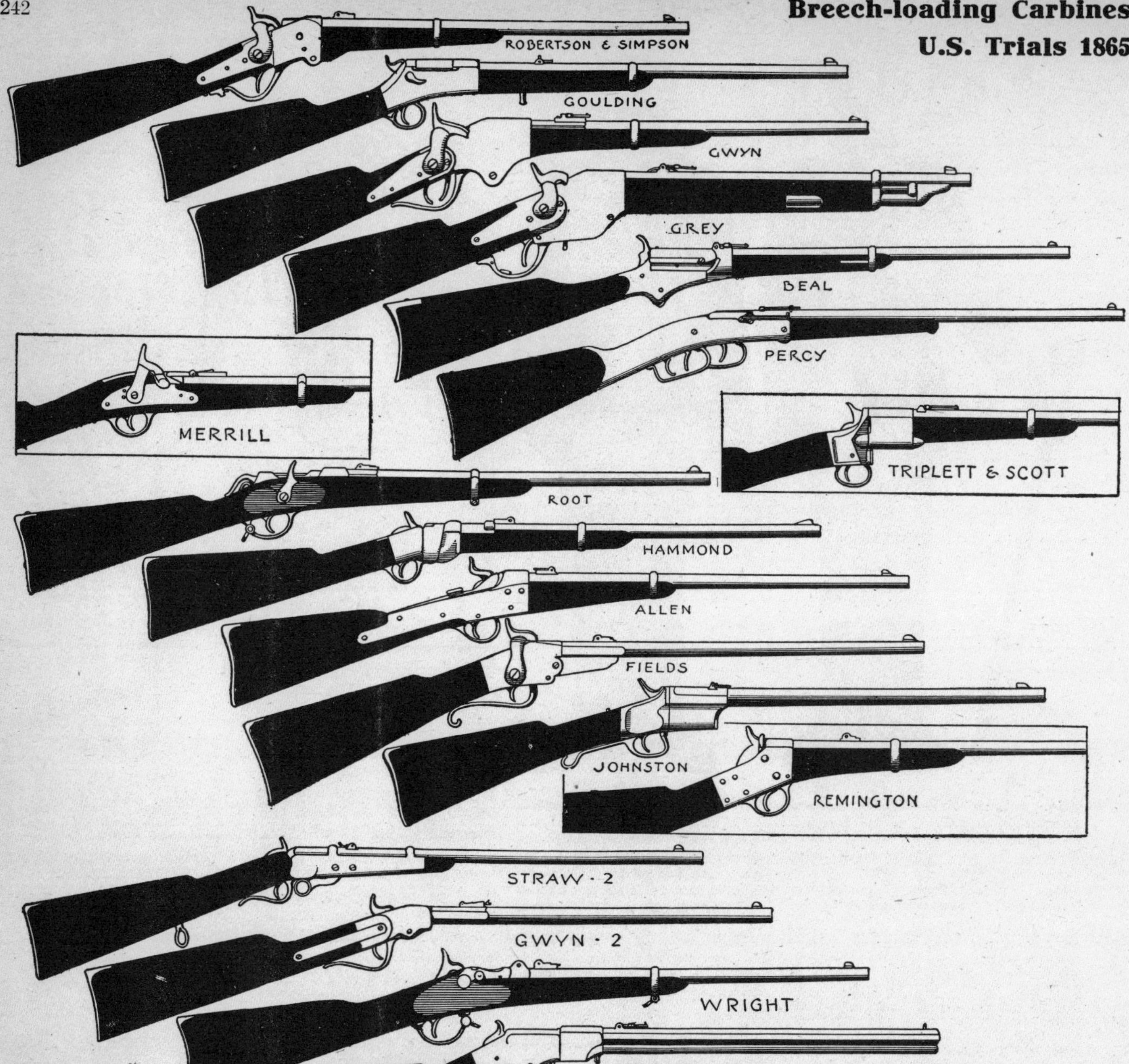
ROBERTSON & SIMPSON
GOULDING
GWYN
GREY
BEAL
PERCY
MERRILL
TRIPLETT & SCOTT
ROOT
HAMMOND
ALLEN
FIELDS
JOHNSTON
REMINGTON
STRAW · 2
GWYN · 2

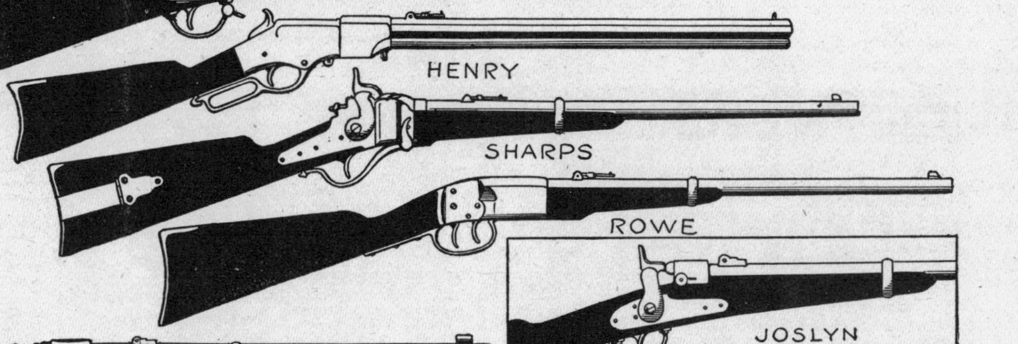
WRIGHT
HENRY
SHARPS
ROWE
JOSLYN

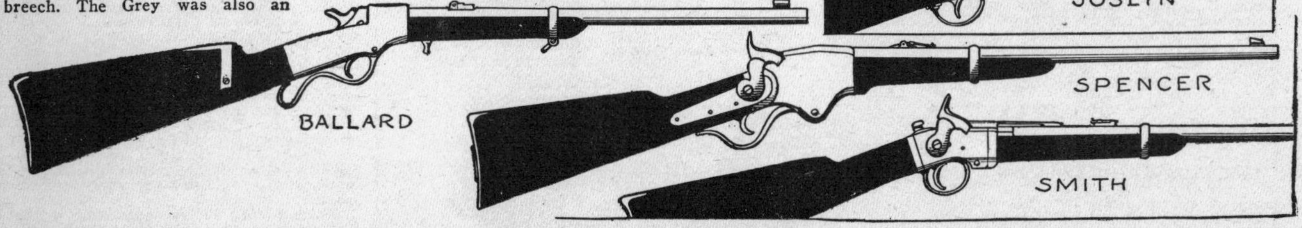
BALLARD
SPENCER
SMITH

**On the preceding two pages will be found 25 breech-loading systems illustrated. On this page** are 24, which completes the list of all those officially photographed at that time. Some familiar weapons are seen above, the Spencer, Joslyn, Smith, Sharp, Ballard, Remington, Merrill and the Henry. Several magazine carbines are included in the lot also. Among those not mentioned on the preceding pages are the Straw, Gwyn Nos. 1 and 2. No. 1 is evolved from the old Cosmopolitan percussion carbine and No. 2 is an adaptation of the Spencer breech. The Grey was also an adaptation of the famous Spencer action with the magazine in front under the barrel instead of in the butt-stock. The Robertson gun was made at the Sharp's Armory and parts of the Sharp's carbine plainly show in the drawing. The Hammond is exactly like the revolvers of the same maker, but of course on a larger scale. The Riche worked on the same principle as the old Sharp and Hankins, while the Beal was a copy of the breech system of the Warner. We consider these three pages, with their very clear illustrations, valuable data for the student of U. S. Military Arms history.

*See also pages 163 and 193.*

We have only the following parts for the Scotch Highlands Uniform:
GLENGARRY CAPS, used, red and white tartan, $2.00 each. THISTLES, 50 cents each.
KHAKI WOOLEN KILTS, NEW, $12.00 each.
PLAID HOSE TOPS, used, 75c per pair.
KHAKI SPATS, new, $1.20 per pair.
FEATHER BONNETS, used, $15.00 each.
HAIR SPORRANS, used, $3.50 each.
TARTAN KILTS, $15.00.

SCOTCH CLAYMORE SWORDS, without Scabbards, from $22.00 up.

**No. 3**

**3. Militia Officer's Fatigue Uniform;** Blue Cloth Cap, 60c; Fine Blue Cloth Blouse, mohair trimmed, standing collar, $7.85; Shoulder Straps (metal), any rank, 85c; Blue Cloth Trousers, white stripe, $3.50.

**300 UNITED STATES NAVY SAILORS' BLUE SUITS.** Blue flannel double breasted overshirt, with wide collar, braided and embroidered. Blue cloth trousers to match, new, assorted sizes, rows of white braid on collar, white embroidered stars, new regulation flap in front, with buttons in front to protect the throat; used by firemen and others who appreciate these fine goods. Shirt and trousers.

**NEW REGULATION U. S. OLIVE DRAB COLORED KHAKI UNIFORMS.**
New Coats with 4 outside pockets, button flaps, all sizes. Price, $2.25.
New Breeches, lace in front. Price, $1.95.
New Puttee Leggins, 95 cents pair.
New Munson Tan Shoes. Price, $5.00 pair.
Montana Peak Hat. Price, $1.75.
Officers' Gilt and Black Hat Cord. Price, 40 cents.

We carry in stock most of the new regulation Chevrons. We do not give prices here as these are changing and new regulations are being made. Write us with full description of rank, color of background and color of stripes and we will quote prices promptly.

**0-778. ARMY CADET GRAY CLOTH RAINCOAT.** With large cape. Used by cadets. Offered in repaired serviceable order. Regulation cadet gray rain cloth, heavy quality, complete, with 28-inch cape. Seams are sewed and lined —not stuck together as in the ordinary trade raincoats—46 inches from collar to bottom of skirt, has ventilation armholes, hook tightening straps, upright side pockets. Will answer for cadet gray overcoat as well as raincoat. Weight, over 4 pounds each. Waterproof, with best Para rubber. In used serviceable order. Bargain price, $2.65.

**POLISH SOCIETY UNIFORM.** Leather helmet, brass scale chain, hair plume, and silvered Eagle helmet ornament. Fine dark blue cloth dress coat, with buttoned front in white, red or any other colored trimmings desired, heavy blue cloth trousers, leather cross belt, brass buckle, pouch, waist belt, brass belt plate, red centre and Polish Eagle, leather sling straps with sabre, fine complete uniform outfit, as named above, $15.85.

37,00 in Khaki large.
1,600 Khaki small.
40,000 Cloth large.
21,000 Cloth small.
600 Cloth and Khaki Service Stripes.

**100,000 U. S. ARMY CHEVRONS—NEW.**

All new from the late Government Arsenal Auction, **on change** of regulations to Olive-drab. Silk embroidered designs on finest blue facing cloth; also on Khaki, both in large and in small sizes. It would take pages to enumerate all the different designs included in our purchase. We have bought *all the stock of the U. S. Arsenal*, which must have cost upwards of $50,000. We will gladly close out the lot at the rate of $1.00 a dozen. **OUR SELECTION.**

**No. 1. PRESCOTT NAVY REVOLVER.** Patented in 1860 by E. A. Prescott of Worcester, Mass. Caliber .36. Barrel is seven inches in length. Took a rim fire cartridge. Called a Navy revolver although there is no government record of any being purchased. Rare.

**No. 2. REMINGTON ARMY REVOLVER.** Caliber .44. Paper cartridge. 125,314 of this model purchased, 1861-1865. Next to the Colt, this revolver was perhaps the best known of the various Civil War types. Patent is dated September, 1858. Also made in .36 caliber for Navy use, 5,000 being purchased during the Civil War. There were several models, differing in slight details only. During the late 70's and the early 80's many were altered to use metallic cartridges. The .44 caliber arm had an eight-inch barrel and the .36 a seven and one-half inch. Made at Ilion and Utica, N. Y. The contract price of these revolvers was $12.50 each, while Colts averaged $18.00 to $27.00.

**No. 3. ROGERS AND SPENCER REVOLVER.** Caliber .44. Made at Utica, N. Y. Patented by Freeman (see No. 9). 5,000 purchased, 1861-1865, for Army use at $12.00 each. Barrel is seven inches in length. As many of the specimens of these revolvers in collections are quite new it is doubtful if the the Rogers & Spencers were issued in time to see much service. Noted for the remarkably fine grip and balance.

**No. 4. PETTINGILL ARMY REVOLVER.** Caliber .44. Patented in 1856 by Raymond and Robitaille. 6 shots. Percussion and double action, hammerless. Very complicated and easily put out of order. In 1861 Rogers and Spencer at Willowvale, N. Y., got a contract for 5,000 for Army use. But 2,001 were delivered. Made also in caliber .36 and pocket sizes. Army model had a 7½-inch barrel and weighed three pounds.

**No. 5. WHITNEY NAVY REVOLVER.** Caliber .36. Made at Whitneyville, Conn. Patent date not given. Barrel seven and one-half inches long. 11,214 purchased by the government during the Civil War. Made in several calibers and sizes. During 1862 these revolvers were copied by the Confederates both at St. Louis and Augusta, Ga. The frames of these being made of brass, and stamped C. S. on the left side.

**No. 6. SAVAGE NAVY REVOLVER.** Caliber .36. Made at the Savage Armory at Middletown, Conn. Patented by S. North in 1856-1859. 14¼ inches long. This arm has two triggers, the rear (ring) trigger to revolve the cylinder and cock the hammer, the front one to fire. A gas-tight joint was formed by the cylinder being drawn back from the rear end of the barrel each time it was cocked. The illustration shows the last model of this arm. Earlier models had several forms of triggers and were not provided with the trigger-guard. 11,284 at $19.00 each purchased for use in the Navy, 1861-1865.

*Continued on Page 254*

**3676.**  **11053.**  **11053A.**

1000 SUITS U. S. A. PAJAMAS. New slightly soiled by water at recent fire in Army Medical Building. Cost Government over $2. Are made of dark gray cotton cloth. Four-button coat, turn-down collar, white braid button loops, fly front trousers quickly fastened by draw lacing. Soldiers in Cuba enjoyed wearing these light weight suits while not on active duty. We offer the suit, coat and trousers, at the bargain price of 75 cents suit. SMALL SIZES.

11045. PAIR REVOLUTIONARY WAR PE-RIOD, Officer's Epaulettes from FRAUNCES TAVERN SALE, New York City, May 9th, 1909, previous to its transfer to the Sons of the Revo-lutionary War, who now maintain a historical museum in the old building made famous as the place where Washington took the last farewell of his troops. The epaulettes are tarnished and valuable only as Revolutionary War relics. Price $25.00 the pair.

10167. CIVIL WAR UNION ARMY CAP, found in London; evidently worn by some British soldier of fortune who fought in the northern army: blue cloth slouch cap, in used serviceable order. Price $1.50.

I knew him! by all that is noble, I knew
    This commonplace hero I name!
I've camped with him, marched with him,
        fought with him, too,
    In the swirl of the fierce battle-flame!
Laughed with him, cried with him, taken a
        part
    Of his canteen and blanket, and known
That the throb of this chivalrous prairie boy's
        heart,
    Was an answering stroke of my own.
            —H. S. Taylor, National Grange.

3676. NEW YORK STATE MILITIA SOL-DIER'S MILITARY OVERCOATS; blue cloth; had just been issued when the new olive-drab became the regulation. These fine coats were sent back to the State Arsenal. We secured the entire lot, 3,676. Our price for the selected is $3.50. Much used, $1.95.

11053. NAVAL MIDDIE'S TUXEDO JACKET; fine navy blue cloth; double breasted, with turned down collar, lapel front; full length sleeves, semi-silk lined and quilted; two double rows of brass gilt navy or plain buttons as desired; one inside pocket; used by naval militia; offered in fine serviceable order, like new. Price $3.85.

60 SOCIETY UNI-FORM DRESS COATS, made of the finest broad-cloth, silk and satin lined; some with quilted lining. The maker as-sured us that the cloth in some of these uni-forms cost upward of $5.00 a yard. His price was $40.00 each. Our price is $8.00 each, which does not pay for the em-broidered work. Assorted sizes; in single or double breast; some with one row of braid and some with four. All one price, $12.00 each.

SOCIETY DRESS COATS. Single breasted frock coats, made of finest broad-cloth. Black coats have standing collars, dark blue coats have rolling collars. All new in assorted sizes. No extra charge for coats with cross on sleeve. Our bargain price, $7.75.

11053A. NEW U. S. NAVY SAILOR'S WHITE WORKING DRESS, LATER REGULA-TION, BLOUSE SHIRT; made at the Navy Yard clothing factory of the FINEST QUALITY BLEACHED cotton drill, weighing 6½ to 7 ounces to the yard; made to descend from 2 to 3 inches below the hips: LARGE COLLAR, OPEN rolling flap AT THE THROAT; square cut sleeves; pocket on left breast; 2 gussets at each side of the bottom. Price $1.25.

THE NAVY BLOUSE SHIRT now worn by young ladies we offer as above illustration and de-scription at $1.25 each, or with the collar, neck front and cuffs covered with navy blue flannel (fast color), with 3 rows of braid on the collar; in assorted sizes; generally loose fitting). Price $2.50.

NEW U. S. NAVY WHITE HAT, made of well shrunken bleached cotton drill; navy pattern, 6½ to 7 ounces to the yard; stitched brim to retain shape; either pattern No. 200 or No. 10165. Price 50 cents each.

NEW U. S. NAVY WHITE DRESS TROU-SERS; some a little stained from shop worn; same fine material as the blouse; fly front; fit snugly over the hips and down the thighs to 2 inches above the knee, from which part downward cut bell shaped, full enough to be pulled over the thigh; seam on inside of leg; wide turn up at the bottom; gusset at center of the back, 2 inch open-ing at the top and from 4½ to 5½ inches deep, including the 2 inch waist band, with from 6 to 8 eyelets, with ⅜ inch wide lace. Price $1.50.

SILK NECKERCHIEFS, SLIGHTLY SHOP WORN, 36 inches square, to be tied in a square knot leaving the ends from 4 to 6 inches long, the knot to be directly under the neck opening of the shirt Price 1.50

NEW U. S. NAVY KNIFE LANYARD, bleach-ed white cotton, flat, ½ inch wide and long enough to go around the neck and to allow use with arm extended. Price 18 cents each.
NEW U. S. NAVY JACK KNIFE, as per illus-tration No. 6, $1.00

NEW SCOUTS WHIST LE. with lanyard. Price 40 cents.

3405

## 3405. MILITARY OF-FICER'S DRESS UNIFORM

Fine dark blue cloth bell top cap, with gilt and sil-vered lace band, with gilt embroidered N. Y. State Coat-of-Arms on the cap, with embroidered peak. Prac-tically good as new. Price $8.85.

Officer's Bell Top Cap with mohair braid with gilt chin strap with metal coat-of-arms, not full U. S. regula-tion. Price $2.45.

Fine new dark blue broad-cloth Military Cutaway Dress Coat, with 3 rows of polished brass buttons, with 9 double rows of gilt braid across the breast. Standing collar, 3 rows of gilt lace. 200 coats of different patterns. Sales-men's samples. Regular $25.00 quality. Price $9.85. Shoulder knots either in gilt cloth or white cloth mohair braid. Price $2.85 a pair.

## 1898. LATE REGULA-TION KHAKI CANVAS PUTTEE SHAPE CUFF LEGGINS, made of heavy canvas with brass eyelets with laces, open at side. Held to the shoe by lace at the back; double stitched, conforming to shape of the leg; length 11 inches. New. Price, 48 cents a pair.

3299

## 3299. DRUM MAJOR'S UNIFORM

Black Fur Hat, mounted on light willow frame 13 inches high, large tan leather cap shape, sweat band for keeping firmly on the head. Small leather peak, 4-inch gilt tassel. Average weight, 14 ounces. Used only a few times. Each hat packed in paper box. Brass scale chin strap.

Fancy Dress Coat, Cutaway Pattern, with rows of gilt braid across the breast. 3 rows of gilt buttons. Fancy cloth, colored facings on collar, cuffs and skirt. 300 different kinds in stock. Made as sales-man's samples, of fine broad-cloth, by leading Military Tailors. All new, never used. Regular $25.00 quality. Price $9.85 each.

Gilt Shoulder Knot, white cloth ground, with double row of gilt cord around the edges, double knot in the centre. Com-plete with gilt metal coat fasten-ings. Price $2.85 the pair.

White Duck Trousers, Military Style, with side hip and watch pockets. In small to medium sizes. Price $1.50 a pair.

**Customers will please take notice that on low price uniforms the price does not include the privilege of taking tailor's time trying on. A higher price will be charged than that named in this catalogue for low price suits when trying on or fitting is desired.**

We mention this as we have had fastidious custo-mers who took our tailor's time in fitting that cost us as much as we got for the suit.

UNITED STATES MARINE CORPS CHEVRONS, for Cuba, Philippines and China service. All ranks. First sergeant's, 60c; sergeant's, 50c; corporal's, 40c.

UNITED STATES MARINE SHOULDER SCALES, with world, eagle anchor designs. In good, serviceable order. Price, $1.00 per pair.

No. 3.

No. 3. Militia Soldier's Uniform, fine blue cloth, coat white trimmed with standing collar, used, cleaned, pressed; price $3.00. Sky Blue Cloth Trousers at $2.50. Cork Helmet, black cloth covered with gilt stripe and other trimmings, 95c. Leather waist belt with brass buckle at 60c.; all in sizes from 32 to 36 chest measure. We have few large sizes, but they are held to fill company orders.

No. 7.

Revolutionary War Style Officers' Dress Uniform, fine red cloth coat, silk lined, with blue and gold trimmings, with black cloth neck stock, with lace front, with fine cream colored cloth vest and breeches. Sold to museum.

No. 4.

KHAKI BLOUSES, MODEL 1898, as used in the Spanish War, with trimming on collar, cuffs and pockets. ALL SMALL SIZES. Price, 75 cents each.

No. 8.

8. U. S. NAVY BLUE PEA JACKETS, offered without price as supply is limited and coats not always in stock. Can quote on these in dozen lots only.

**Over one million dollars was paid into the U. S. Treasury for the year 1916 from the sale of obsolete and condemned Govrnm't stores. —Army-Navy Journal.**

No. 7.—U. S. Army Blue Rubber Cloth Raincoats; over-coat pattern with large de-tachable capes; new assorted sizes; good value for $12.00. Our bargain price, $5.00.

Military Overcoats, heavy blue cloth with flannel lined detachable large-sized capes. Price, $4.85.

We have OLIVE DRAB OVERCOATS, both new and second hand, but prices are omitted on account of the changing market. Write us for prices being sure to give chest measure over your jacket.

500 Military Overcoats, with capes. Heavy blue army cloth, lined with blue flannel, as per illustration; have been worn a few times; are now in cleaned, pressed order; cost originally upward of $15.00 each. 34 to 38 chest measure sizes. Our tailors require chest measure in order to select sizes required. We have fitted out a number of military bands with these fine warm coats. Price, $3.00.

**WEST POINT CADET OVERCOATS** with Cape; double breasted, 2 rows of Eagle Buttons, in assorted Cadet sizes. Made of finest quality heavy grey cloth, large collars, double breasted; they make a fine dressy appearance. In second hand, clean and pressed order, $3.50 each.

**300 CIVAL WAR OVERCOATS** in serviceable order, much used, complete with capes and buttons. Small and medium sizes. Will answer for any one wishing a serviceable storm coat. Price $2.50 each.

We have several thousand Militia Blue Overcoats in stock of different patterns. These have been used and are moth eaten from storage. To bands and others wishing a good article at a low price we can offer coats in dozen lots at very attractive prices. We offer the coats "AS ARE," all repairs to be made by purchaser. Price, $1.95.

Brass buttons will be supplied but will not be sewed on at wholesale price.

500 Military Band Uniform Dress Coats made of fine dark blue broadcloth (not to be confounded with light cloth finished flannel, or coarse kersey). Trimmed with straight rows of white braid, three rows of gilt-finished brass buttons; trimmed around collar and cuff with fine white cloth. These coats cost upward of $15.00 each to make. They have been worn only a few times; are in fine, serviceable, cleaned, pressed and perfect order; like new. Price, $3.50.

Leather shako, second hand with plain ornament. $1.50 each.

**NEW** Blue bell top caps, without ornament or braid. $1.80 each.

**NEW WHITE WEBBING BELT** with light brass belt plate. 50 cents each.

Brass shoulder scale epaulettes with catches. 50 cents pair.

Cloth epaulettes with fringe from 95 cents pair upwards.

**100 VESTS.** New goods. Large assortment in different patterns and colors. Fine cloth; well made. Regular price, $5.00. Our price, $1.75 each.

3,500 Military Uniforms Coat double-breasted, fine dark blue cloth, with white trimmings, two rows of gilt-finished buttons. Coats cost new upward of $12.00 each. We have 200 that are new, and our price is $4.75 each.

200 fine dark blue broadcloth double-breasted Dress Coats, trimmed with fine white cloth, two rows of gilt-finished brass buttons. Price, $3.00 each.

400 dark blue Dress Coats, single-breasted, trimmed with lighter shade of blue cloth, new, one row of gilt-finished brass buttons. Made to order for regiment in Massachusetts, costing $10.00 each. Price, $3.85.

Helmet Spikes for use on any of the Helmets, offered for sale in this Catalogue. Price, 15 cents each.

Engineer Corps dark-blue cloth chevrons; also U. S. Marine Corps chevrons, all ranks, from 40 cents pair upwards.

Blue and Yellow silk cord, 1/16 inch diameter, for edging. Price 5 cents per yard.

600 United States Navy Sailors' White Dress Suits. Fine white twilled canvas overshirt, with blue flannel collar and cuffs; collar trimmed with braid and embroidered stars. Trousers to match. Assorted sizes. Regulation kind worn by United States Navy sailors during Spanish-American war at battle of Santiago. Lady reporter for New York Sun, while visiting our museum, saw the above statement and promptly corrected us by informing us that history recorded the fact that sailors fought the battle with their shirts off. Price for dress shirt and trousers, $3.95. Dress shirt without trousers. Price, $2.50.

Blue Cloth Cap, with white linen adjustable cover, 60c.

Cap without the white linen cover, 45c.

500 new Caps that have small moth holes, price 30c; and 50 second-hand United States Navy white caps, with gilt embroidered letters, "2 Division," on black silk ribbon attached, 35c.

**U. S. NAVY FENCING MASKS,** padded; secondhand; serviceable. $1.75 each, $3.25 pair.

50 United States Army Overcoats, with capes. Heavy blue kersey cloth, flannel lined, with extra large capes, in cleaned, repaired order.

Sizes, 34 to 38-inch chest measure. $4.50.

200 Civil War pattern Army Overcoats, flannel lined, second-hand, serviceable order, slightly moth eaten, $2.50 each.

4 British Army Overcoats, no capes. Dark blue cloth; good, second-hand order; $3.50.

150 Military Overcoats, with capes; heavy blue kersey cloth, flannel lined; second-hand, cleaned and repaired order; worn by Militia; very nearly resembles United States Army style overcoat. Price, $3.00. Sizes, 34 to 38.

100 sky blue kersey cloth Overcoats, used by State of Michigan Militia; lined with blue flannel, complete with capes; assorted sizes; in serviceable order; $3.00 each; some lined with red flannel. Price, $3.50.

Fatigue Caps, new, 45c. each; good, second-hand, 10c. each.

U. S. A. Cavalry Sabers, second hand with steel scabbard at $1.95 each.

Saber Belts, black leather, second hand, consisting of waist belt with detachable saber slings, 95 cents each.

## Spanish Soldiers' Fatigue Uniform, $4.85

Complete Suit, consisting of hat, with rosette (real thing), blouse with Spanish buttons, trousers.

Blanket, Roll, $1.25.

Spanish Remington, B/L Rifles, with Gun Sling, $1.95.

## Spanish Officers' Fatigue Uniform

Complete Suit, consisting of Hat, Coat, Trousers and Sleeve Cuffs, denoting rank; new goods. Real Spanish lace and buttons, $14.75 per suit.

We found it necessary to personally visit Cuba before the Spanish evacuation in order to obtain lace, buttons and correct samples of uniforms. For Spanish War relics, see pages of Swords, Machetes, Buttons, Rifles, Cartridges, etc., etc.

We shipped from Havana to our European Agent over 5 million rounds of Ammunition and over 11,000 Rifles in December, 1898. Our Theatrical customers can be assured that we can furnish correct uniforms that will be above criticism. Purchase from us and avoid the frosts.

The import duty on military uniforms of foreign soldiers is so great as to be almost prohibitive. For theatrical customers we can offer fine dark-blue cloth uniforms used by American militia, trimmed in colors to represent very nearly the foreign soldier's uniform. We have books containing colored illustrations of British, French, Spanish, German, Italian, Russian, Austrian and Japanese soldiers' uniforms. State kind and quantity desired and we will name price.

## U. S. Army Officers' Fatigue Uniforms

These are late regulation and are offered to officers in private companies or for theatricals.

Fine blue cloth blouses with black mohair braid around the collar, down the front and around the bottom edge, in sizes up to chest 40, at $7.85 each. Second hand.

Lighter Shade Blue Trousers, with or without white stripe in sizes not over waist 35, at $2.75 each, second hand.

New Campaign Hat with officers gilt cord, heavy quality, $1.95 each.

Polished Brass Spurs with black straps, not regulation, $1.25 per pair.

Metal Shoulder Straps, in imitation of embroidery, in all ranks at 60 cents per pair. Prices on embroidered straps quoted on application.

Swords for officers range from $4.50 up.

Black Belts with slings, second hand from 95 cents up. Russet Belts from $2.25 up.

U. S. V. Collar set, 80 cents each. Other insignia will be found priced on ornament pages of this catalog.

## British Naval Officers' Dress Coat

Full Dress, made of fine dark blue cloth, with British Navy gilt plated buttons; almost new. $5.00.

## U. S. Naval Officers'

Fine White Duck Fatigue Coats, such as worn by petty officers, with gilt navy buttons. Price, $1.75.

Trousers, same material as coat, $1.00 pair.

## 50 Officers' Gray Blouses

Fine Gray Cloth, with black braid down the front and around the skirt, with slit for sword sling; new goods of finest material, well made, in assorted sizes. $5.50.

## Cuban Soldiers' Uniforms

No regulation, took what they could get, generally of white or tan duck. Hat with Cuban flag and star. Blouse Coat in white duck, white duck Trousers. Suit, $2.50.

Genuine Cuban B/L Rifles or Carbines; sure fire. $2.75.

Ball Cartridges, $1.80 per 100.

Machetes, part of lot sold us from Spanish Arsenal in Havana, December, 1898, believed to have been captured from Cubans; old relics that have seen considerable service. $1.00 each.

## Confederate Officers' Uniforms

For theatrical use. Gray Felt Hat with gilt cord and acorns; new goods. $1.00.

Gray Coat, small size (fatigue), with Southern State buttons, second-hand, serviceable order. $2.75.

Gray Trousers, fine cloth, with black stripe, second-hand, $2.00.

Confederate Soldiers' Uniform for theatrical use.

Gray Hat, 75 cents.

Gray Blouse, $1.75.

Gray Trousers, $1.75.

## 30 Society Fatigue Uniforms

Blue Cloth Blouse, with embroidered stripe unlined, $5.00.

## Union Officers' Civil War Uniform

DARK BLUE COAT. 9 buttons, trimmed with narrow colored braid (denoting branch of service) around the edges, rolling or standing collar. New goods. Size 36, $3.85.

TROUSERS, light Blue cloth. Second-hand. $2.00.

HAT. Soft felt, with ornament and feather, $1.65.

SWORD BELT. Leather, with Eagle belt plate, $1.50.

SWORD. Price, $7.50.

U. S. ARMORERS' STEEL THIMBLE. Practically new. From Government Rock Island Arsenal auction. Price, 10 cents each.

50 BLUE CLOTH BLOUSES. Made of fine blue cloth, in assorted sizes. Price, $2.50.

## 50 Gray Cloth Blouses

Made of finest gray Cadet Cloth, in assorted sizes; new goods.

Lined and braided, $5.00.

## 40 Gray Cloth Blouses

With narrow braid trimming, $5.00.

## Civil War Line Officers' Uniforms

Coat, fine Dark Blue Broadcloth, with gilt buttons, spaced to denote rank, full dress, with standing or rolling collar; new goods. $12.00. Small.

Trousers, light Blue Cloth, $2.75.

Hat, Soft Felt, with gilt cord and acorns, or with feather and ornament, $1.50.

Epaulettes. Per pair, $8.00.

Shoulder Straps, in Metal, 80 cents pair.

Sash, crimson, $5.00.

Sword, $8.00.

Sword Belt, Fatigue, $1.50.

Dress Belt, $6.50.

## 50 West Point Officers' Cadet Fatigue Uniforms

Blouse made of finest quality Cadet Gray Cloth, trimmed with fine black braid down the front and around the skirt, with opening for sword slings; assorted sizes. $3.50.

Some in second-hand, serviceable order. Cadet sizes, $2.50.

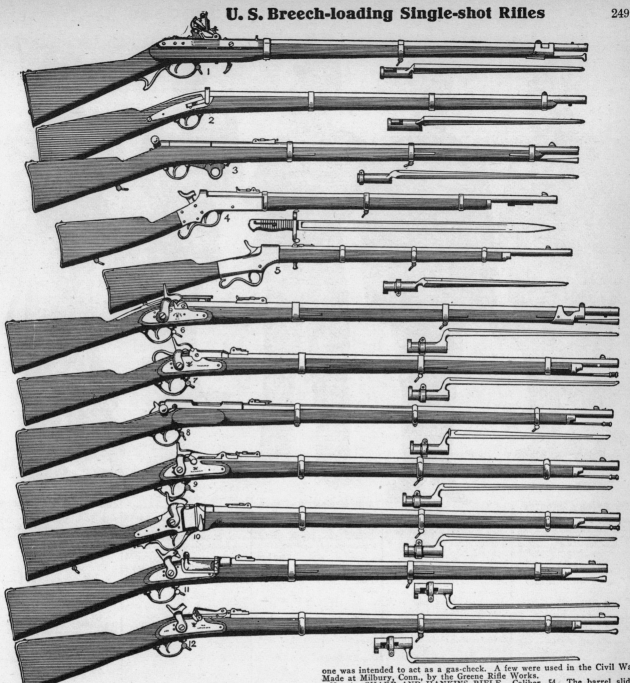

**No. 1. HALL FLINTLOCK RIFLE.** Invented by J. H. Hall in 1811, who also invented the idea of interchangeable parts. The first government breech-loader. Made both in flintlock and percussion and in use from about 1820 until the Civil War. Although an improvement over the existing muzzle-loaders, they were not favored by the soldiers. Made in many models including rifles, short rifles and carbines. The ramrod bayonet, an idea used later in 1884 and 1888, was first introduced on the Hall rifle. At West Point is a specimen of this model, the ramrod of which extends 32 inches beyond the muzzle. The Hall carbine has also the distinction of being the first percussion arm of the U. S. These were standard cavalry weapons of 1841-1850. Hall carbines, improved, were made by S. North in the early 50's, these finding their way into the hands of the troops at the outbreak of the Civil War. Among the captured Confederate arms were found a few Halls that had been altered to muzzle-loaders, this, however, may have been caused by the lack of parts to make complete guns as some Hall material was captured at Harper's Ferry in 1861 by the rebels. Caliber was .53.

**No. 2. JENKS RIFLE.** Invented by Wm. Jenks in May, 1838. Made both in rifle and carbine models. The Jenks was the forerunner of the Merrill of Civil War time. Used as early as 1841 by troops in Florida. The hammer, which operated horizontally, was the outstanding feature of these arms. A few were equipped with the Maynard primer. Made principally by N. P. Ames at Springfield and Remington. Caliber .54. See Jenks Flintlock Carbine elsewhere.

**No. 3. GREENE RIFLE.** The invention of J. D. Greene, an Army officer, in 1857. This was the first bolt action gun used by the U. S. The bolt handle was in the rear, same being released by pressing down a spring catch on the tang. It was a percussion arm and had the nipple underneath with a ring-shaped hammer. The cartridge (Caliber .535) had the bullet in the rear so that there were always two in the gun when loaded. The rear

one was intended to act as a gas-check. A few were used in the Civil War. Made at Milbury, Conn., by the Greene Rifle Works.

**No. 4. SHARP AND HANKINS RIFLE.** Caliber .54. The barrel slides forward to expose the breech. One of C. Sharp's inventions. Principally used in the Navy (1861-1865), both as carbines and rifles. One of the carbine models had the barrel covered with leather for protection to the enlisted men. Although made 60 years ago the rear sight is of the same principle as those in use today on some of the foreign arms. There was a safety catch provided on these rifles also. The saber bayonet had a blade 24 inches in length.

**No. 5. BALLARD RIFLE.** Invented by C. H. Ballard in 1861. Various calibers, .44 to .54. Made both in rim and center fire. The extractor had to be manipulated by hand, being pushed to the rear to eject the empty shell. The extractor shows in the cut just in front of the breech and at the underside of the stock. The block enclosed the hammer, same being brought to the rear and down by action of the lever. The Ballard was made in both rifles and carbines. The rifle took an ordinary triangular bayonet. As there were over three and a half million cartridges purchased for Ballard arms during the Civil War, they undoubtedly saw service.

**No. 6. MERRILL ALTERATION OF MODEL 1842 MUSKET.** Caliber .69, rifled. This is the famous Minie rifle, but a breech-loader. Some of these were made in the early days of the Civil War in Baltimore. On account of the large caliber the breech mechanism is heavy and clumsy, otherwise it is exactly like the Merrill carbine and rifle. The rear sight is the same as used on the Minie musket, even the original hammer being used.

**No. 7. PEABODY'S ALTERATION OF A MODEL 1861 SPRINGFIELD RIFLED MUSKET.** Caliber .58. Directly after the Civil War ended steps were taken to furnish the Army and Navy with breech-loading arms and the Peabody was one of the many experimented with. The breech mechanism is like the regular arm bearing the Peabody name, but the lever to operate is on top of the breech. The system was patented in December, 1867, and was center-fire. A new hammer was necessary, otherwise the arm was original. Also made of Model 1863 and 1864.

*Continued on Page 327*

## 200 Cavalry Uniforms

We offer dress coats with blue or white trimming, which customer can cover with yellow cloth for cavalry. Extra yellow cloth for one coat will cost 50 cents.

Trousers without stripes from $2.50 up. Stripes in yellow red or blue. $1.25 per pair.

Helmet, cork body, covered with fine black cloth; polished brass trimmings, spike, chains and eagle, with new yellow horse-hair plume. . Price, $1.50

Saber Belt, black buff leather, with sling straps, Price, 95 cents.

Sabers, with scabbards. Price, $1.00, $1.50, $2.00.

1,000 Black Leather Saber Belts, with eagle or "U. S."; regulation brass buckle, with sling strap. . . . Price, 60 cents.

500 second-hand black leather Saber Belts, with buckles and sling straps. Relics. . . . . . . . Price 75 cents.

Cavalry Aiguillette; new goods, fine worsted cord with tassel; late regulation. Price,1.00cents

White Aiguillette, 45 cents.

Set of Cavalry Equipments, consisting of leather waist belt with cartridge box and revolver holster, Price, $1.25 per set.

Regulation Web Cartridge Belt, with loops for holding 100 30-calibre cartridge, with sword hook. Price, 85 cents.

Regulation Web Belt for holding 50 45-calibre cartridges, with sword hook. Price, 75 cents.

3403. MILITIA OFFICER'S UNIFORM. Fine blue cloth bell top Cap, with inside leather sweatband, black mohair braid band with gilt leather re-enforced adjustable chin strap. With brass side buttons and gilt metal Coat of Arms. In assorted sizes. Complete, $4.85.

Kersey Blue Cloth Trousers, with 1⅛ inch white cloth stripe, with side and watch pockets. Trousers are of shade lighter than the blouse, as per Military Regulation.

In medium sizes.

For Trousers that have been used, cleaned, repaired and pressed, $3.25.

New Dress Coats; made of fine dark blue cloth, trimmed with red around collar, cuffs and skirt. Price, $3.50.

New Dark Brown Blouse; fine corkscrew cord cloth, with blue shoulder straps, with 5 rows of gilt braid across the breast; outside pocket. Price, $5.00 each.

Greeley Relief Expedition Blanket Insoles for keeping the feet warm in cold climates. Price, 20 cents per pair.

## 100 Mexican and Civil War Uniforms

Coat; close-fitting jacket, braid trimmed, new goods.
Price, $3.85.

Trousers; sky-blue kersey cloth, repaired and pressed, look good.
Price, $2.00 per pair.

Black leather carbine sling with brass buckle and swivel snap hook. Price $1.00 each.

Belt, leather, with U. S. plate. . . . . . . . . Price, 45 cents
Musket, U. S. Springfield, 1862, with bayonet. $3.75.

Mexican War Knapsack, with white buff leather strap; collapsible frame; new goods, in serviceable order.
Price, $1.50.

British Army Scarlet Tunics, unlined, Dress Coats, lightweight for summer wear.

Black Leather Carbine Sling 52 inches long, 3 inches wide, with brass buckle and swiveled snap hook; new.
Price, $1.00 outfit.

Fawn-colored heavy leather Gauntlets, with large cuffs, new; all sizes.

3,000 NEW FULL DRESS COATS, late Regulation, U. S. Marine Corps. Fine, dark blue cloth, trimmed with bright red cloth around the collar and edges, shoulders and sleeves—standing collar—single breasted, padded and lined, hook and eye for fastening at the collar, made at Government uniform factory—entirely new—in assorted sizes—32 to 36 inch chest measure. A few larger sizes at $3.50 each. Single orders for large sizes not accepted. (Retained for company's orders.) Coat measures 31 inches from the collar to the bottom of the skirt. These fine coats would cost upwards of $8.00 each to make. Our bargain price, $3.00 each.

NAVY MILITIA WORKING SUITS, from State sale, blouse, shirt, cap, trousers and lanyard, used. $1.50 the outfit.

ARMY BROGAN SHOES, new, good quality leather, in sizes, 5-12, only $1.65 per pair.

86. WEST POINT CADET BRONZE CANDLE STAND. 3¼-inch base; 1⅝-inch holder; serviceable souvenir; used by the cadets at West Point Military Academy. Price, $1.00.

BELGIAN SOLDIER'S SHAKO ORNAMENT. Sunburst star with wreath, 3¾ inches in diameter, made of brass with red circle center; with Belgium crown and Coat-of-Arms (Lion Rampart)— same as is used on the Belgian soldiers shako in the German War. Price, 50 cents each, mailed.

## 200 Civil War Uniforms

Blouse; loose-fitting blue cloth flannel, 5-button blouse, in good order, repaired and pressed. . . . . . . . . . Price, $2.50

Trousers, sky-blue kersey, slightly moth eaten. Price $2.50

Caps, the real thing, "Contract 1864," moth-eaten, poor order. . . . . . . . Price, 35 cents

Militia Caps, similar in looks; good order.
Price, 60 cents.

Canteens.
Price, 30 cents each.

Musket and Bayonet.
Price, $3.50.

Civil War Knapsacks in serviceable order, the real thing, new,
Price, 55 cents each.

British Army white buff leather Riding Breeches, 33-inch waist, heavy leather.
Price, $12.00.

Indian Leather Trousers, with fringed edges, second-hand, serviceable order.
Price, $8.00.

New Cutaway Dress Coats, trimmed with gilt braid, West Point style, assorted sizes, gilt and black trimmed; also some with gilt and scarlet trimmings. Price $6.00.

On this page will be found a concise pictorial history of the development of the Colt Military Revolver. The illustrations will show at a glance the development of the manufacture of all weapons of this class. First, the heavy, cumbersome weapons of the 50's which, while they were a great improvement over the regulation single shot pistol, were not received with favor by the troops. Then the lighter and more efficient Civil War types— still percussion. Following these came the alterations of the early 70's to use metallic cartridges. Then followed the straight cartridge revolver. All these weapons were single action, they had to be cocked by hand. Almost immediately came the first of the double action types still of large caliber. About 1890 a reduction of caliber to .38 came and then early in 1900 a return to the .45. We find the last word in revolver construction in the Model 1917 together with the famous Automatic of the World War. Colonel Samuel Colt started the manufacture of revolvers in 1836 at Paterson, N. J. The factory was situated at the foot of the falls of the Passaic River, the power to run the works being supplied by the falls. In 1842 the Colt Armory failed and it was not until 1847, at the outbreak of the Mexican War, that Colt received encouragement from the government. He was given a contract to make 1,000 revolvers similar in design to one of those made at Paterson, but as no specimen was available, the new weapon was made from memory (see No. 3). These arms were made at Whitney's Armory near New Haven, Conn. In 1855 the factory was started at Hartford, Conn., where it has been located ever since.

No. 1. COLT'S "TEXAS" REVOLVER. The first of the Paterson products, made in .28, .31 and .36 caliber. Authorities differ as to these various calibers, some claiming a range from .22 caliber to .50 caliber. The writer gives only those he has seen. Barrels varied in length from 4½ inches to 12 inches. All these arms had the folding trigger, no guard being provided. It is said that but 2,000 of these revolvers were made, 1836-1841. The cylinder pin had a cup-shaped end which was used as a ramrod. These revolvers were in great demand in the southwest and as high as $200 has been paid for specimens even in second hand condition.

No. 2. COLT'S TEXAS REVOLVER, caliber .28. This is a later make than No. 1. Note change in shape of handle. Also the arm has been equipped with a loading lever. Otherwise it is the same as No. 1. This type is very much rarer than the original model. This pattern was originally made without the loading-lever, in .31 caliber.

No. 3. COLT'S ARMY REVOLVER. Caliber .44, Model of 1847. This is the weapon made at Whitneyville, Conn., 1,000 in all being fabricated. It is familiarly known to collectors as the "Walker," but in reality it is but a copy from memory by Colt as no specimen of the original model could be found at the time (1847). These arms were 15½ inches long with a 9-inch barrel and weighed 4 lbs. 9 oz. Notice the similarity of the ramrod to No. 2. Colt's contract price for these revolvers was $28.00 each.

No. 4. COLT NAVY REVOLVER. With canteen shoulder-stock, caliber .36, six shots, Model of 1851. The U. S. Navy experimented with this model in 1852. A powerful and popular weapon and a great advance upon its predecessors as it contained several improvements. Made until 1865. The screw cap of the canteen is shown at the comb of the stock held in place by a small chain to prevent loss. A flat metal canteen is placed in the butt, held in place by the butt-plate. One of several styles of shoulder stocks made at this time.

No. 5. COLT'S ARMY REVOLVER. Model of 1860, .44 caliber, 6 shots, 8-inch barrel, total length, 14 inches. Also made in .36 caliber for Navy use. The principal revolver of the Civil War, over 200,000 being made. A very similar model had a fluted cylinder with the barrel ½ inch shorter and also .44 caliber. The shoulder stock on this weapon is the most familiar type as more were made of this pattern both to fit the Model 1860 and also the Model 1848 No. 6.

*Continued on Page 363*

**10 FIREMEN'S TAN-COLORED CLOTH DRESS COATS.** New goods. Made by one of America's leading uniform makers. Well made of fine cloth. Assorted sizes and patterns, with firemen's buttons. Made to sell for $20.00. **Price, $7.50.**

We carry in stock most of the new regulation Chevrons. We do not give prices here as these are changing and new regulations are being made. Write us with full description of rank, color of background and color of stripes and we will quote prices promptly.

**Military Officers' White Uniform.** Bell top white cap with black leather visor; new; in assorted sizes. Price $1.50.

Fine White Cotton Duck Blouse, trimmed with white braid, with standing collar, with sword slit—without shoulder tabs or collar ornaments—new blouse in assorted sizes, $5.00. Fine quality Duck Trousers, with side and hip pockets, made in the best manner. Price, $1.50 pair. The whole uniform, Cap, Blouse and Trousers, all new, fine quality goods, for $8.00. Splendid summer uniform for bands.

### U. S. NAVAL GREELEY RELIEF EXPEDITION ARCTIC GOODS

Blanket Insoles (pair), 25c.
Woolen Socks, $1.00.
Buckskin-covered Socks, $1.50.
Leather Boots, cork-filled soles (pair), $6.00.
Heavy Wool Special Arctic Cloth, resembles Irish Frieze—Pants—new, moth-eaten, $5.00.

**Military Blue Cloth Dress Coat,** single breasted with white or light blue trimmings; $3.85.
Blue Cloth Trousers, good second-hand, $2.50.
Black cloth-covered Cork Helmets with brass front plate and spike, $1.10.

**Military Officers'** fine quality dark blue, fine wool cloth Blouse, trimmed with best quality black Mohair braid, in assorted sizes. Price, $7.25. In good, second-hand, serviceable order, cleaned and pressed. Lighter shade of fine blue wool cloth Trousers with 1 1-4-inch white stripe; good second-hand, cleaned and pressed, serviceable, $3.00.
Bell Top Officers' Cap with stamped gilt metal coat of arms; gilt lace chin strap; good quality blue cloth. Price $3.25.
U. S. Naval Officers' Complete Uniform, size 38, consisting of new chapeau, dress coat, service coat, society coat, trousers, epaulettes, dress belt and gilt buckle. Cost over $300. Price, $85.00 for the outfit.

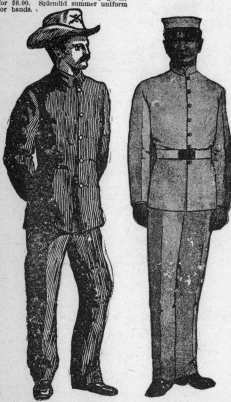

No. 8.

No. 4.

**NEW OLIVE DRAB SPIRAL PUTTEES.** Fine quality. Reduced to 90 cents per pair. Heavier quality, $3.50.
500 KHAKI ARMY COATS, with four outside pockets, buttoned flaps, new, dyed brown. Size 34 chest. Price, 50 cents.

**MARINE CORPS LINEN TROUSERS,** as used by the Marines when stationed in Panama, China or other warm countries. Offered NEW in SMALL sizes. Suitable for cadets, bell boys or messengers in the south. Price $1.00 each.

**ARMY LIGHT BLUE TROUSERS,** offered in good order, used, with white stripes. Price $2.75.
For those selected, little used the price is $3.50 pair.
**ARMY BLUE TROUSERS** without stripes, second hand. $2.50 up.
**GRAY TROUSERS,** West Point Cadet, with black stripes, used, in good condition. $2.50 pair.
**NOTE ALL TROUSERS OFFERED DO NOT RUN OVER WAIST 34 INCH.**

3. U. S. A. Soldier's Outfit. Fine Dark Blue cloth Cap, new, 75c; good second-hand, 50c.
Blanket, new, $5.00. Canvas Knapsack, with shoulder straps and coat straps, good second-hand, $1.75. Caliber 45 Blue Woven Web Cartridge Belt, almost new, 80c. Canteen, with leather sling strap; good, serviceable order; used only a few times, 60c. Mess Kit Outfit, price 60c set. Fine Cloth Blouse Coat, good second-hand serviceable order, cleaned and pressed, fine appearance, $2.50.
4. U. S. Officers' Society Coat, with either the U. S. N. gilt or black cloth covered buttons; new coats made of the finest black broadcloth complete with vest; cutaway pattern. Price $8.00.

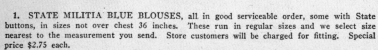

**1. STATE MILITIA BLUE BLOUSES,** all in good serviceable order, some with State buttons, in sizes not over chest 36 inches. These run in regular sizes and we select size nearest to the measurement you send. Store customers will be charged for fitting. Special price $2.75 each.

## 10180. GRAY UNIFORMS.

10180. GRAY UNIFORMS. To represent Civil War Confederate Soldiers. Gray wool cloth CAP, gray-colored cloth four-button COAT, brass buttons; gray cloth TROUSERS. Government contract goods altered to represent Confederate uniforms. In small to medium sizes. Price of the complete uniform, cap, coat and trousers, $4.35.

1563

West Point Cadet Pattern Fatigue Uniforms; fine gray cloth, black mohair trimmed, with blue cloth braided top cap. All in good serviceable order. Have been used; are now cleaned and pressed. Price, complete suit, blouse, trousers and cap, $6.25. Sizes, 32 to 36 in. chest measure. Cap separate, 58c; blouse separate, $3.00; trousers separate, $2.75.

1563. MARINE CORPS DRESS UNIFORM. White Helmet, 65 cents; Blue Cloth Coat, red trimmed, $3.75; Kersey Blue Cloth Trousers, $3.50; Red Stripes, cloth, pair, 75 cents; White Leather Belt with brass buckle, 90 cents; Chevrons, pair, 25 cents up.

West Point Cadet Dress Uniforms; fine gray cloth, cutaway-style dress coats, black mohair braid trimmed, with 44 gilt polished ball-shaped buttons; fine gray cloth trousers with 1½-inch black stripe, with black fur-covered shako with white pompon; in good second-hand serviceable order. Price for complete uniform, as specified, $7.00. Sizes, 32 to 36 inches chest measure. Coat separate, $3.50; trousers separate, $2.75; shako and pompon, 90c.

25 MILITARY AND SOCIETY SINGLE-BREASTED FROCK COATS. Made of the finest broadcloth in the best manner, with satin lining, in blue and in black colors. Maker's price, $25.00 to $30.00. Our price, $8.00. Assorted sizes.

U. S. A. OLIVE DRAB HEAVY WOOL CLOTH HOODS. Fine for automobile riding. NEW. Cost upwards of $5.00 to make. Our bargain price, 50 cents.

80. BLUE CLOTH BAND COATS. Standing collar, white cloth trimmings, 3 rows U. S. Eagle buttons, shoulder tabs, gilt braid, practically new coats. Pattern similar to West Point Cadet Dress Coats. Also 75 BAND COATS; similar trimmed with red cloth. Price, $3.85 each.

100 New Blue Fatigue Blouses with U. S. brass buttons, inside pockets, semi-lined, assorted sizes. Price, $3.25 each.

New Black Felt Helmets, small and large sizes only. Price, plain, without trimmings, 65 cents each. Trimmed with brass eagle plate and spike, 95 cents ea.

MILITARY OFFICER'S DRESS UNIFORM. Dress coat with epaulettes and belt; helmet and sword. Prices quoted on application.

100 Civil War Soldiers' Jackets and hats; part of lot made during Civil War time. Black Felt Hat with blue cord and tassel for infantry, with coat of arms ornament and feather. New goods, slightly aged. Price $1.50 each. New Sky Blue Cloth Jacket with standing collar, trimmed with braid; 12 brass Civil War Buttons. Price, $2.50 each.

OLIVE DRAB COTTON SHIRTS, all NEW, in assorted sizes from 14½ to 16, at reduced price of $1.50 each. Olive drab WOOL shirts, new at $3.00 each.

U. S. Army Double-seat Cavalry Trousers; slight difference in shade of cloth. Price $2.40 per pair.

U. S. Cavalry Trousers; stained and discolored. Price $1.90 per pair.

Fine Blue Cloth Riding Breeches, for use with leggins. In serviceable, secondhand order. Price $2.75 per pair.

Returning from a trip to Europe, a friend relates how he got acquainted with an old man who had a good farm in Ireland and who, against the advice of his friends determined to go to America. On the voyage the steamer encountered rough weather and while the old farmer was very sea sick, he was overheard saying, perhaps as he thought of the good advice he had refused to take, "I wush tae God some wan had tied me at hame with a rape."

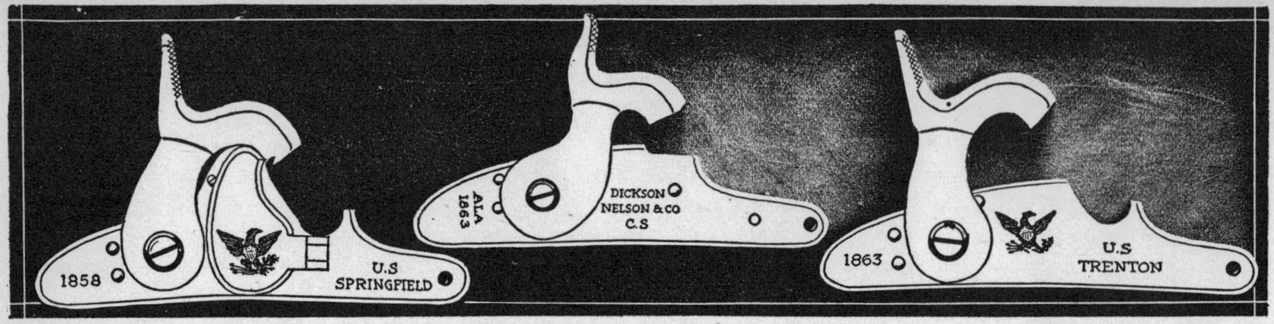


Collectors will find on this page a list of Civil War lock plates, many of which are exceedingly rare and hard to find nowadays. On page 90 will be found data concerning Civil War guns that tend to make these lock plates interesting to students and collectors. (See Model 1861, English Enfield and Model 1863 on page referred to above.) Here are some more facts concerning the guns for which these lock plates were made, all gleaned from Government sources. In 1861, 900,000 "Model 1855 Muskets" were contracted for; in 1862 but 20,806 of this vast number were delivered to the Government. But in 1863, 248,969 were completed. All these were called Model 1861, even up to the end of '63, except in three cases. Colt, Amoskeag and L. G. & Y. Windsor, Vt. The locks of the latter mentioned were not interchangeable with those of other contractors. A number of Confederate plates are included in the list. These were made to fit rifles patterned after the regulation Model of 1841, a number of which were made in the South, especially in Alabama and Georgia. Harper's Ferry Arsenal was abandoned by U. S. Troops on April 18, 1861. The Confederates promptly put out the fire started by the Federals, but not soon enough to save 16,000 finished rifles and muskets. A large portion of the machinery and unfinished parts were saved, boxed and sent by rail to Winchester, Va., by wagons to Strasburg and thence by rail to Richmond. Some eventually found their way to Fayetteville, N. C. Included in this lot of captured stuff was the die with which "U. S." and the eagle were stamped on the lock plates. This die was afterwards captured at Egypt, N. C. The "U. S." had been replaced with "C. S. A." with the well known inverted "S." Manton, the famous English gun maker, furnished Civil War muskets to our troops and the collection includes a lock plate bearing his name. The locks made in Germany were simply marked with an eagle, U. S. and the date 1861. Civil War Contract muskets cost Uncle Sam $18 to $20 each.

SPRINGFIELD LOCKS
1 U. S. Watertown—1863.
1 Harper's Ferry—1853.
1 Robbins & Lawrence—Windsor, Vt.—1849.
1 Robbins, Kendall & Lawrence, Windsor, Vt.—1847.

ASSORTED LOCKS
1 Parkers, Snow & Co., Meridan, Conn.—1863.
1 Whitneyville—undated.
1 U. S. Springfield Primer Lock—1858.
1 L. G. & Y., Windsor, Vt.—1862.
1 Amoskeag Manufacturing Co., Manchester, N. H.—1863.
1 Colts Pat. F. A. Mfg. Co., Hartford, Conn.—1862.
1 E. Whitney, N. Haven, Primer Lock—undated.
1 Manton—1862.
1 Remington, Ilion, N. Y.—1865.
1 U. S. Springfield—1861.
1 William Muir & Co., Windsor, Vt.—1863.
1 Bridesburg—1862.
1 S. N. & W. T. C., Fall, Mass.—1863.

EARLIER LOCKS
1 Remington, Herkimer, N. Y.—1852.
1 Tryon, Philadelphia, Pa.—1846.
1 Robbins & Lawrence, Windsor, Vt.—1849.

LOCK PLATES ONLY
3 U. S. Springfield, Maynard Lock Plates only. 1, 1858—1, 1859—1, 1860.
1 U. S. Harper's Ferry, Maynard Primer Lock only.

EARLIER LOCKS WITH HAMMERS MISSING
1 Remington, Herkimer, N. Y.—1852.
1 E. Whitney, N. Haven—1853.
1 Harper's Ferry, 1849.
1 Robbins & Lawrence, Windsor, Vt.—1851.
1 Tryon, Philadelphia, Pa.—1848.
1 Robbins, Kendall & Lawrence, Windsor, Vt.—1847.

ANY LOCK, $2.50 EACH.

CONFEDERATE LOCKS
3 Dickson, Nelson & Co.—C.S.—1863
4 Dickson, Nelson & Co.—C.S.—1864
1 Dickson, Nelson & Co.—C.S.—1865
} $5.00 EACH

1 Sharps Carbine Lock—hammer missing—marked S. C. Robinson Arms Manufactury, Richmond, Va.—1862.
1 stamped Georgia Armory—1862.
1 stamped C. S. A., Fayetteville—1863.
1 stamped P. Murray, Columbus, Ga.—undated.
1 stamped Cook & Brother, Athens, Ga.—1864. stamped with flag.

(YOUR SELECTION) $5.00 each.

BRITISH MADE LOCKS—FOUND WITH CONFEDERATE GUN PARTS
1 marked L. A. Co.—1862—stamped—Crown V. R.
1 stamped, small crown—1864—Enfield; also large crown V. R.
1 stamped 1861 Tower—large crown.
1 Tower 1861—large crown.
1 Potts & Hunt, London—undated.
1 stamped 1855—with hammer.
1 stamped E. P. Bond, London—undated.

(YOUR SELECTION) $2.50 each

## U. S. Revolvers—Continued

No. 7. LEFAUCHEUX PIN-FIRE ARMY REVOLVER. Caliber about .41. Made in France and also Belgium. This is a type of revolver in use in Europe in 1861. The government purchased 12,000 of these in that year at a cost of $13.00 each for Army use. Many were issued in the early days of the Civil War but they were soon discarded for American weapons. The metallic shell of the cartridge had a small pin attached at a right angle to the length. This meant that the shell could only be inserted but one way. These Lefaucheaux revolvers were made in many styles and sizes. The inventor, a Frenchman, was the first to use metallic ammunition in fire arms.

No. 8. LE MAT REVOLVER. This arm has two barrels, one of .44 caliber for the 10-shot percussion cylinder. The lower one is smooth bore of 12 ga. intended for a cartridge loaded with buckshot and fired by turning down the point of the hammer from the chamber in the center of the cylinder. Made in several styles and sizes both in France and England just prior to 1861. Used to a limited degree both by North and South, 1861-1865. The inventor, Col. Le Mat, was a French officer who located in New Orleans in the early 50's. The patent was taken out in 1856.

No. 9. FREEMAN REVOLVER. .44 caliber, 6 shots, percussion. Patented Dec., 1862, and made at Hoard's Armory at Watertown, N. Y. Barrel is seven and one-half inches long. The Rogers and Spencer revolver (No. 4) was a development of the Freeman. One of the rare weapons of the Civil War period. No record of any government purchase found.

No. 10. WESSON AND LEAVITT REVOLVER. Caliber .40, 6 shots. Patented in 1837. Made at Hartford, Conn. Cylinder turns by hand either way. Barrel is held by catch to the cylinder shaft which, when released, allows barrel to be raised. Cylinder slides off to load. Also made in .31 caliber and in several lengths of barrels. One of the earliest American revolvers.

No. 11. JOSLYN ARMY REVOLVER. Caliber .44, 5 shots, percussion. Patented by B. F. Joslyn in May, 1858. Made at Stonington, Conn. 1,100 purchased by U. S. for use in Army during Civil War. Barrel is 8 inches long and the arm weighs three pounds. The cylinder is removed by releasing screw in rear of frame. There were two models, the first one being made at Worcester, Mass., by W. C. Freeman, who received a contract for 500 in August, 1861.

No. 12. ADAMS ARMY REVOLVER. Caliber .44. Patented in England in 1853. This is one of the types purchased abroad by government agents. The weapon is noted for a remarkably fine grip and is double-action, a feature rare at this time. During the Civil War these revolvers were fabricated in this country at Chicopee Falls, Mass., by the Mass. Arms Co. Made in both .44 and .36 caliber and in several patterns. Many found their way to the South during the Civil War.

No. 13. RAPHAEL REVOLVER. Caliber .41, metallic cartridge. Made in France and purchased in 1861 (978 at $16.50 each). Cylinder is in two parts. Barrel is 5½ inches in length. No marks. The revolver takes a center-fire cartridge and is double action.

No. 14. PERRIN ARMY REVOLVER. Caliber .45. Civil war purchase from France. These weapons were originally made to use pin-fire cartridges and later changed to rim-fire. The hammer, which is made without a cocking piece, has no full-cock. The revolver is double action. 200 purchased in 1861 at $20 each. In spite of its peculiar construction this arm handled and functioned well.

No. 15. WARNER REVOLVER. Caliber .36. Percussion. Patented June, 1856. James Warner, the patentee, was manager of the Springfield Arms Co., the makers of these revolvers. Very similar in construction to the Wesson and Leavitt, No. 10, except the addition of the ramrod. Made in several calibers and patterns. Note the two triggers, the front one revolves the cylinder and as this is drawn to the rear it strikes the rear one to fire the piece. There is no record of government use during the Civil War.

No. 16. BUTTERFIELD REVOLVER. Patented December, 1855. Caliber .36, 7-inch barrel and 13½ inches total length. Also made in .44 caliber. This arm is provided with a disc-primer magazine situated directly in front of the trigger guard. Its action is automatic. Made in Philadelphia by J. S. Butterfield who also applied his primer idea to converted flintlock muskets. The pellets used in his magazine were like those used in Sharp's carbines.

No. 17. SMITH AND WESSON. Caliber .45, 6 shot Revolver. Model of 1917. This and the Colt .45 were the principal revolvers of the U. S. in the World War. 153,311 of these were made for our soldiers during the war. For military use this weapon and the .45 Colt, which it resembles very much in appearance, are considered the last word in revolver construction.

No. 18. SMITH AND WESSON. Caliber .38. Used by both Army and Navy Last patent date is 1898. These arms had 6½-inch barrels and a total length of 11½ inches. This model was soon replaced by the Model 1902, the first to have the catch under the barrel for the head of the ejector rod, a feature that has been retained ever since.

No. 19. ALLEN AND WHEELOCK. Caliber .44, 6 shots, percussion. Allen's patent January, 1857. This is the last model of Allen's, the first being No. 23. The peculiar shape of the frame is caused by the fact that the trigger-guard, upon being released, forms the ramrod. Made at Worcester, Mass. The patentee, Ethan Allen, became famous for his well known "pepperbox" revolvers of those days. About 500 of the Allen and Wheelocks were purchased by the government for Civil War use.

No. 20. BEAL'S PATENT REVOLVER. Caliber .44, percussion, 8-inch barrel. Patented September, 1858. Made at Ilion, by Remington. This is the first model of the famous Remingtons. 2,814 were purchased during the Civil War for Army use. All Remington revolvers are based on Beal's patents.

No. 21. SMITH AND WESSON REVOLVER. Caliber .45, 6 shots. This is the first of the .45 caliber revolvers made by this armory. Barrel is one inch longer than the Model 1917. The seat for the ejector rod was not a success for it was soon replaced by the catch. See No. 17.

No. 22. SCHOFIELD-SMITH AND WESSON REVOLVER. Caliber .45. This weapon, adopted in 1873 with the single action Colt .45, had a tip-up barrel held by a spring catch just in front of the hammer. The barrel is seven inches long and the gun weighed 2.5 pounds. This model was not, however, the first military Smith and Wesson of large caliber, for at least three years before a .44 caliber revolver was made and issued. These had an 8-inch barrel with a total length of 13½ inches. It is claimed that this model was the first made to use metallic cartridges, all those prior to this being altered from percussion. Both these Smith and Wessons were similar in appearance, the barrel catch, however, was of different design.

No. 23. ALLEN AND WHEELOCK. Caliber .36. Navy Revolver. The first model of the Allens. Made in several lengths of barrels. Like No. 19, the trigger-guard forms the ramrod when released.

No. 24. STARR REVOLVER. Caliber .44, 6 shots, percussion. Patented January, 1856, and made at Yonkers, N. Y. This arm is provided with a removable screw at the right side of the frame just back of the cylinder, enabling the barrel to drop down at the muzzle end and the cylinder removed. Barrel is 8 inches long, total length, 14 inches. Weight, 3 pounds. Also made with 6-inch barrel and double action, both in .44 and .36 caliber. 47,952 purchased by the government, 1861-1865, which makes the Starr one of the principal Civil War revolvers. In this connection some figures on Civil War purchases will be found interesting. From 1861 to 1865 there were purchased 373,971 revolvers of about 20 different makes, at a cost of six million dollars. Colt's Navy .36 tops the list at $27 each, while the Joslyn runs second at $22.50. Rogers and Spencer and Whitney revolvers cost but $12.00. About 15,000 of these arms were purchased abroad in 1861. Prices ranged from $20.00 to $13.00 each. From June, 1861, to Jan., 1862, contracts were entered into with nine contractors for 67,500 revolvers at a total cost of $1,756,000.

Our stock of military ready-made uniforms was originally made for soldiers whose average size would be medium; consequently we do not receive very many large sizes in the different lots, just about enough to fill company orders. Therefore orders for all large sizes we must either decline to fill or make extra charge. Cadet sizes are under 34-inch chest measure. Uniforms offered as motheaten will answer for property return.

The import duty on military uniforms of foreign soldiers is so great as to be almost prohibitive. For theatrical customers we can offer fine dark blue cloth uniforms used by American militia, trimmed in colors to represent very nearly the foreign soldier's uniform. We have books containing colored illustrations of British, French, Spanish, German, Italian, Russian, Austrian and Japanese soldiers' uniforms. State kind and quantity desired and we will name price.

25 Blue Cloth Blouses of fine cloth, elaborately trimmed with frogs across the breast. New goods. Assorted sizes. $6.50 each.

2 White Chaplain's Coats. Splendid. New goods. $7.50 each.

2 Fine Red Plush new Knickerbocker Trousers of "ye olden time." $3.50 pair.

8 Cadet Officers' fine dark blue cloth Blouses. Small sizes. New, handsome goods, $5.00 each, cheap at $15.00.

5 Grey Cloth Blouses. New goods handsomely trimmed in gold and black braid. $6.50 each.

2 Dark Blue Blouses, fine cloth. New goods, red trimmed, $6.00.

9 Dress Coats, dark blue, with red cloth trimmings. New goods. $7.00.

## GREY AND BLUE BANDMASTERS' UNIFORMS.

Coat — Cutaway style, made of fine cloth, elaborately trimmed, 3 rows of brass buttons. $4.75.

Trousers. Price, $2.95. Cap, with gilt cord or gilt lace. $1.25.

Epaulettes, black with white fringe. 95c.

## TRANSVAAL OFFICER'S DRESS COAT.
Used by Boer war officers in South Africa. In serviceable order. Price, $15.00.

1 Dark Blue Fine Cloth Blouse, with inlaid red trimming. Very showy. New goods. Price, $6.50.

Double-Breasted Gray Cloth Blouse, with black velvet collar. $6.50 New goods.

7 Dark Blue Fine Cloth Cutaway. Coats trimmed with white and gold. Handsome, showy. New uniforms. $6.50.

1 Green Cloth Cutaway, trimmed with white and gold. New goods. $6.50.

4 Dress Coats, dark blue, blue and gold trimmings. $7.00. New goods.

25 BAND UNIFORMS. Dark Blue Frock Coat of fine cloth, trimmed with white and light blue facings. Assorted sizes. Almost new. Price, $3.75.

We have carloads of Old Military Uniforms and Equipments, in fact everything required by Military Companies. To National Guard Officers or enlisted men, responsible for lost property, we can save money. Write us what you require, and we will quote bargain prices.

Complete West Point Cadet Uniforms, Gray Cloth Bell Top Cap, with black Mohair band and leather visor. Gray cloth Blouse Coat, trimmed with black Mohair braid. Cap and coat used, offered in cleaned and pressed serviceable order, with fine NEW white duck Military trousers, with side and hip pockets, in Cadet sizes, from 32 to 36 inches, complete uniform, $4.85.

1874.—200 Society or Band Uniform Dress Coats, dark Navy Blue Cloth, rows of gilt buttons, three rows of Mohair braid, with standing collar; lined and shoulder padded; full length skirts. Illustration is from photo. Used only a few times; offered cleaned and pressed, looking like new. Price, $4.85 each.

The London Court Journal says: "It is not generally known that Nelson's death was the origin of the black silk handkerchief which the sailor wears under his broad blue collar, tied in a loose knot in front. The scarf, or handkerchief, was first worn as mourning for the great admiral, and by some means or other it was retained and eventually became a part of the naval man's uniform. The white stripes around the broad blue collar also represent the victories at the Nile, Copenhagen and Trafalgar."

1814. Officers Fine Navy Blue Cloth Dress Coats, Full length skirts, 39 inches; with three rows of gilt buttons, 9 buttons in each row; with double row of mohair braid trimming on the breast, 2 inside pockets. Lined and padded at the shoulder. Two gilt buttons on each side of skirts. Standing collar with row of 1¼-inch mohair braid with gilt embroidered monogram, which we will remove if desired. White rubber collar attached, with loop for attaching epaulete or shoulder knot. Fine order. Practically as good as new, 37 in the lot. Price, $7.85.

U. S. Army Waterproof Blue Cloth Rain Coats, with large detachable capes, new, in assorted sizes; Army Blue Overcoat pattern; original cost upwards of $12. Our bargain price reduced to $5.00.

5512. NAVY BLUE HANDKERCHIEF. Standard indigo blue, full 28 inches, fast color. Price, 15 cents each; $1.50 dozen.

5504. TURKEY RED HANDKERCHIEF. Standard make, best quality, good full 28 inches. Price, 15 cents each; $1.50 dozen.

KHAKI SHOULDER TABS, colored, for different branches of the service. New. Price, 20 cents per pair.

U. S. ARMY FINE CLOTH. Green, intended for use as facing cloth and trouser stripes on fine military uniforms. Length from ¼ to 1½ yards, width 45 inches. Price at the rate of $1.50 per yard. The regulation goods cost upwards of $3.75 per yard. Sold as trouser stripes, our price is 70 cents per pair.

0-790. U. S. A. SANITARY WOOL SOCKS. Natural colored, double knitted, with EXTRA REINFORCED HEEL AND TOE. FREE FROM DYE. Soft wool and cotton. Durable sock for tender feet. All sizes. New. Bargain price, 30 cents per pair.

40 SOCIETY OR BAND BLOUSES. Finest quality blue, and in gray cloth. Blouse elaborately trimmed, assorted sizes, new goods. Regular $15.00 blouse. Our price, $6.50.

3 Dress Coats, dark blue, with white and gold trimmings. New goods, $7.00.

1,000 ABDOMINAL BANDAGES, kind worn round the stomach by U. S. Soldiers when in countries subject to hot days and cool nights to prevent sickness. All new, made of flannel; assorted sizes. Every camper should have one of these life-savers. Price, 35 cents each.

530 U. S. ARMY NEW FLANNEL CAPE LININGS. Yellow and Buff colored heavy flannel, cut for lining the large capes on soldiers' overcoats, as per illustration. Length around outside edge, 3½ yards. Average width, ¾ yard. Average weight, 10 ounces. Original cost would be upwards of $1.50. Our bargain price is 1½ yards flannel for 75 cents.

**PILL BOX CAP.** Not imported but fac-simile of the British service cap, with leather chin strap and braided band; for all practical purposes as good as new. 85 cents each.

Photograph of Fife and Drum Corps Uniforms and Equipments, equipped with our used, serviceable order gray bell top cap, West Point pattern blouse and trousers, drums, etc. Military organizations, cadet and drum corps can get outfits from us at a fraction of the original cost that will look as well as the highest priced, and far better looking than the ordinary cheap uniforms; in fact a drum corps outfitted by us at a cost of about $7.00 per uniform, received prize recognition in competition with a number of bands engaged in a large city on Memorial Day.

**BRITISH ARMY PILL BOX CAPS.** Blue cloth with leather chin strap, worn by British soldiers. (We have to pay a customs duty of 56 cents per pound and 50% of the cost. These *two rates added together* is the U. S. Government tariff duty on wool uniforms imported, either new or old.) We offer these caps in good serviceable order at $2.25.

**BLUE CLOTH TROUSERS.** Practically as good as new, $3.45. Those in used cleaned and repaired pressed order, $2.00.

**BRITISH ARMY SWAGGER STICKS.** Which the British soldier is required to carry when in uniform off duty. Offered with regimental crest, $2.25 each.

**U. S. A. OLIVE DRAB HEAVY WOOL CLOTH HOODS.** Fine for automobile riding. NEW. Cost upwards of $5.00 to make. Our bargain price, 50 cents.

**3095A. GILT EMBROIDERED SHOULDER STRAPS,** made up to order in any rank or color. In writing for prices state rank and exact color needed.

**3095B. OFFICER'S METAL SHOULDER STRAPS.** All ranks. New. 85 cents pair.

**BRONZE CAP ORNAMENT** as worn by army privates in all branches, screw back. Illustration is actual size. Price, 25 cents.

**NEW REGULATION BRASS finish,** 25 cents.

**VICTORY BUTTONS** in bronze or silver oxide. Sold by authorization from War Department, File No. A G 421-7. Either finish, 30 cents each.

**GOLD PLATED WATCH FOB** with Great Seal of the United States, with leather strap. Price, 20 cents.

**101083. INDIAN MOCCASIN BREECHES.** Tan colored leather with fringe on the sides, old, used, from artist's studio. Price, $6.85.

See other pages in this catalog for prices on drill books for Infantry, Cavalry and Artillery.

**CIVIL WAR WHITE BERLIN GLOVES.** From army contractor's stock left over at the close of the Civil War. Gloves are in small sizes. Are of fine quality and in good, serviceable order; the only thing about them which has deteriorated is the elastic tightening band in the nearly fifty years since they were made. Price, 10 cents

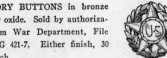

**0-813. U. S. NAVY EYE SHIELDS.** Fine wire gauze, with adjusting cord. All contained in neat box. From Brooklyn Navy Yard auction, 1912. Price, 15 cents each.

**218.—RUSSET LEATHER PUTTEE LEGGINS.** Fine quality, new, in assorted sizes, all one piece, molded to fit calf of the leg, 31½ inch small strap which passes round the outside of the puttee, small top strap with bronze buckles with adjusting clip, reinforced leather at the top, bottom and sides; good serviceable leggins that will wear and look well. Price, $4.50 per pair.

**208.—RUSSET LEATHER PUTTEE LEGGINS.** Made of one piece with long spiral strap, upper short strap, brass buckles and adjusters; finer quality than No 218. Price, $5.50 per pair.

**No. 214. NEW RUSSET LEATHER PUTTEE LEGGINS,** good quality suitable for use of cadet officers or others who do not wish heavy leggin. Size 14, 15 and 16 inch calf. Price, $3.50 pair.

**0-836. SCOTCH HIGHLAND CHIEFTAIN DRESS COSTUME.** Per 1825, illustrating our pair Murdock flint pistols, Scotch Claymore swords, powder horn and other Scottish goods listed for sale in our catalogue.

**0-984. ANCIENT BRITISH YEOMANRY OFFICER'S EPAULETS.** Gilt plate, scale pattern, richly ornamented with arms, cross, flags, drums, swords, etc. Marked "S. Nott, N. C." Price, $6.50.

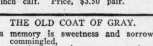

10193

**10193. U. S. ARMY OLIVE DRAB OVERCOATS, DYED BLACK.** Before being by Government it was ordered that these should be dyed, as the Army regulations forbid the use of Army clothing by civilians, unless changed. These fine heavy coats are suitable for drivers, private chauffeurs and others who wish a uniform coat. In sizes up to chest. Offered without hood. Only a small lot left. Price $4.50

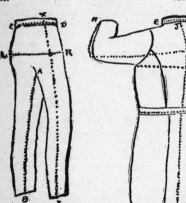

**Coat, Blouse and Trousers Measurements.**

For new uniforms made to order we require ALL the measurements shown in the above illustrations.

For uniforms that are offered all ready made up we require for the Trousers—the waist measure, C to D; the inside leg seam, A to B.

For the Dress Coat—the chest and collar measure; the sleeve measure from G to N.

For the Blouse—the chest measure from O to N; the sleeve measure, M to L.

**THE OLD COAT OF GRAY.**

Its memory is sweetness and sorrow commingled,
To me it is precious—more precious than gold;
In the rent, in the shot holes, a volume is written,
In the stains on the lining is agony told.
It was long years ago, when in life's sunny morning,
He rode with his comrades down into the fray,
And the old coat he wore and the good sword he wielded,
Were all that came back from the ranks of "the Gray." —*Blondine.*

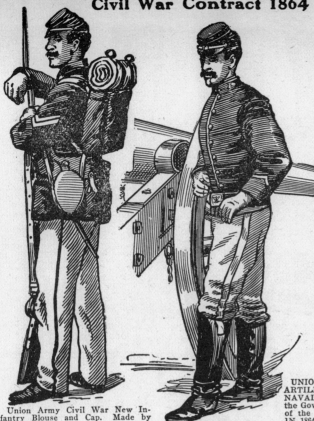

Union Army Civil War New Infantry Blouse and Cap. Made by contract, 1864.

Union Army Civil War New Artillery Jacket and Cap. Made by contract, 1864.

U. S. Navy Civil War Officer's Jacket. New. Contract, 1864.

Union Army Civil War New Cavalry Jacket and Cap. Made by contract, 1864.

FOREIGN ARMY UNIFORMS, used by the late Fred Remington for models, exchanged with us for other goods shortly before his death.

3178. One Cossack Soldier's Service Coat, orange-yellow color with long skirts, nickel trimmed ornaments carried in the two breast pockets; black cloth order; size 36. Price $10.00. From late Fred Remington.

3180. French Algier Soldier's Suit, with brown linen baggy - shaped trousers; black cloth coat; with red trimmings. Black cloth vest. Size 36. Serviceable second-hand. From the late Fred Remington. Price, $15.00.

3181. F r e n c h Algier Soldier's Blue Cloth Vest. Embroidered red fez cap. Price, $6.00.

French Soldier's Blue Cloth Overcoat, size 36. Used serviceable order. Price, $8.00.

Russian Cossack Soldier's Overcoat, with wide skirts. From the late Fred Remington. Price, $12.00.

Continental Coats for Society or Theatrical use. Cambric. Price, $4.50 each.

One French Algier Zouave Uniform, blue coat with yellow facings, with baggy blue cloth trousers, blue cloth vest, brown cloth leggings, red fez cap with tassel. Serviceable second hand order; size 36. Price, $22.50 Used by late Fred Remington on models.

Button Cleaners; made of hard wood; used by military men to clean buttons on uniforms; new. Price, 10c each; $1.00 a dozen.

**0-1204. UNIFORM BAND BLOUSE.** Fine blue cloth, ½-inch black mohair braid trimming around the collar, bottom and front, sword slits on the sides, 5 brass Excelsior buttons. Hook at the top band. Padded shoulder. Inside pocket. Assorted cadet sizes. In cleaned and pressed serviceable order. Price, $2.75 each.

**0-1205A. GRAY CLOTH CADET TROUSERS.** With 1½-inch black stripe. Used; serviceable order. Price, $2.50 per pair.

**UNION ARMY CIVIL WAR CAVALRY AND ARTILLERY JACKETS AND CAPS, AND NAVAL OFFICERS' JACKETS.** Left over in the Government Arsenals and Depots at the close of the great Civil War. Uniforms were MADE IN 1864 by army contractors. They are still in the ORIGINAL CASES, FREE FROM MOTHS and in PERFECT CONDITION. Some years after the war closed Gen. Benj. F. Butler introduced and passed a bill through Congress whereby the Government donated all the left-over uniforms then on hand to the FREEDMEN'S BUREAU. We remember in 1880 Gen. King trying to interest us in purchasing them from the bureau. We declined and some other fellow got them. Now, after nearly FIFTY YEARS this lot finds its way to Bannerman's Bargain Shop.

In other pages of uniforms in this catalogue are listed a small lot of the U. S. Civil War Cavalry Jackets at $3.85 each, and, as for Artillery Jackets, we know of none to be had and got; $6.50 each for some we made up new to fill an order. Recently we had a chance to purchase this fine lot and propose to offer Cavalry and Artillery Jackets at the bargain price of $2.50 each, and for a limited time we will accept orders from Grand Army Posts and Sons of Veteran Camps in lots of ONE DOZEN at price of $1.50 each, when order is received stamped with the seal of the post or camp.

As most of the volunteers were young men the sizes run from 32 to 36-inch chest measure. Do not waste time in ordering larger sizes, as we could only fill orders in larger than 36-chest sizes by having our tailors enlarge and for this work extra price would be charged. These uniforms are valuable as heirlooms of the time in which brave men fought the great battles of 1861-1865. They are valuable as a fine, showy service dress uniform. The jackets are made of blue kersey cloth, nine brass buttons, trimmed (with yellow braid for cavalry and red braid for artillery) around the sides and bottom, with bars of braid on the collar.

The Caps are of blue cloth, lined, leather peak and strap, and are roomy, comfortable kind worn by Gen. Sherman's soldiers when "marching through Georgia," wh'ch the Southerners named the soldier foragers, "Sherman's Bummers." Caps are CONTRACT OF 1864. Price, $1.00 each. In illustrating our artist has drawn the cavalry soldier as wearing the brass scale epaulette. These we can furnish at 50 cents a pair.

**GENUINE CIVIL WAR OVERCOATS,** with capes, in small and medium sizes, in serviceable order. They have been used, but would be suitable to theatrical, or movie production, or pageant. Complete with buttons. Offered without selection at $2.50 each. Special price in hundred lots.

Only a limited number of NAVAL OFFICER'S DARK BLUE JACKETS PURCHASED. They are made of fine quality dark-blue cloth, double-breasted, with two rows of 9 each gilt brass naval buttons on the breast, and with four smaller buttons on each cuff. Turndown collar. ALL NEW. In PERFECT CONDITION. Size 36. Price, $3.85 each, with special price to G. A. R. and Naval Posts for a limited time, on sealed order, $2.50 each.

**500 FINE DARK BLUE CLOTH SINGLE BREASTED MILITARY DRESS COATS,** trimmed with lighter shade of white cloth around the standing collar, cuffs and down the front of coat, all as shown in photograph. Price for coat, $3.25. Note that these fine coats have longer skirts than the ordinary.

**217 U. S. ARMY BANDOLIERS,** worn across the shoulder, holding 100 Cal., 30 or 45 Springfield Cartridges, blue or gray color. Price, $1.00 each; can also be used for Waist Belt, has inside Spring to keep Cartridges from falling out.

**2216A**

**2126A. FORTY U. S. MARINE BAND DRESS COATS.** New. Sold by reason of some slight changes in the regulation. The coats are all of bright red cloth, trimmed in yellow, with gilt buttons in assorted sizes. Handsome, showy uniform, which would cost upwards of $15.00 each to make. Our price, $5.85 each.

**TAN-COLORED CLOTH FIREMAN'S BLOUSE.** Fine cloth-lined, five-button blouse. Price, $6.50.

**30 BANDMASTERS' CUTAWAY DRESS COATS.** Elaborately trimmed, three rows polished brass buttons, fine cloth facings. Handsome, showy. New goods, assorted sizes, patterns and colors; finest cloth. Price, each, $7.50.

**NAVAL MILITIA WHITE UNIFORMS.** Used; require laundering. Blouse and trousers offered "as are," without regard to sizes. Price, $1.85 per suit.

**60. NAVAL MILITIA BLUE UNIFORMS, SHIRT AND TROUSERS.** Used; require laundering. Offered "as are," the suit, $4.50.

No. 1870.    No. 12.

U. S. Army Puttee Khaki Canvas Leggings.

No. 40C.    No. 40A.

**1890. SECOND HAND ARMY LEGGINGS**, heavy khaki canvas, in assorted sizes, with laces and under straps. Selected. Price, 45 cents per pair.

**3028. U. S. Army Brogan Shoes.** Made of calf leather, hand-sewed. Each pair has U. S. Officer's inspection mark. 110 pairs No. 12. Price, $1.95 a pair. New.

**Wooden Shoes**, for use as decoration; make good wall flower-pots, painted and decorated. Price, 50 cents each.

Puttee Legging.

**1853. Combs made of Wood.** Curious relic of the days of the American Revolutionary War period. Found in Nutmeg State collection. Size 3 inches long, 1 inch wide. Made of hardwood. Curious. Price, 25 cents.

**10,000 pairs new U. S. Navy Puttee Leggings.** From Navy Department auction. All new. In original boxes. Made of olive-drab shade of strong, heavy canvas, shaped to fit the leg; fastened with spiral strap and buckle. Some official blundered in ordering, forgetting that "Jack Tar" wore low shoes. Not suitable for attaching the puttee legging, consequently we secured for our customers a bargain. Our former price was $1.40; NOW REDUCED TO 95 CENTS PAIR. Sizes 1 and 2 only.

Note pages 367 and 372 where we show photographs of our place of business. These are included in the catalog for our new customers and for our mail order customers who do not have an opportunity to call and see us. We have been in this business since 1865, and we endeavor to give entire satisfaction to every customer, and to give a little more value than the prices indicate.

**1870.** 100 pairs White Canvas Leggings, made of heavy canvas, with brass eyelets and hook for quick fastening, with web strap bottoms. White metal buckle, assorted sizes. Length, 15 inches. Used a short time. Requires cleaning; complete with laces. In good serviceable order. Bargain price, 58 cents per pair.

**12.** Old pattern U. S. Navy Brown Canvas Leggings; light weight. Price, 60 cents pair.

**10977. Indian Bead Embroidered Moccasins.** Made by North American Indian squaws for British cowboy. Purchased at Arnold Museum sale. Indian tanned leather. Used. Serviceable. 2 pairs assorted. Price, $3.85 the pair.

**6. U. S. Army Leather Slippers.** From Government auction. Used a short time; are in serviceable order. Price, 85 cents pair.

**SCOTCH SOLDIERS KHAKI, SPATS, new.** Price, $1.25 pair.

U. S. Army Puttee Khaki Canvas Leggings. First pattern. Entirely new. Sold only by reason of strap fastening. These fine army puttees with laces. Suitable for anyone to wear. We have upwards of 1,400 pairs. Our former price, when obtained from the Government contractor, was 98 cents a pair. Our present BARGAIN PRICE 45 cents a pair. Large sizes.

**40C.** 5000 pairs full length heavy khaki colored cavalry leggings, used, but offered in good order with laces. Assorted sizes. No special selection. Price, 35 cents each.

**NEW LACES** for army khaki leggings, 5 cents per pair.

**BUCKLES** for under foot legging straps, used, 5 cents per pair.

**14. U. S. Navy Blanket Insoles**, from Greeley Relief North Pole Expedition, 3 thicknesses wool blanket stitched to canvas. Bargain. Price, 25 cents pair.

**40A.** 10,000 pairs Military Heavy Khaki Canvas Leggings; length, 12 inches. Used. OFFERED AS ARE, with laces and WITHOUT SELECTION OF SIZES. Price, 15 cents pair.

**LATE REGULATION U. S. A. OFFICERS' PUTTEE LEATHER LEGGINS**, with strap fastening. New. From $3.50 up.

**NEW SPIRAL PUTTEES OLIVE DRAB.** 90c pair. Heavier quality, $3.50 pair.

**Saddle Shoes**, German silver engraved. Length 10½ inches, weight 2 pounds. Fine order, like new. Price, $4.85.

3 Saddle Shoes, as illustrated, not engraved, same in size as above. Price, each, $4.00.

2 Saddle Shoes, same as above, in polished bronze. Price, each, $3.00.

2 Saddle Shoes, same as above, in polished bronze. Weight, 12 ounces. Price, $2.50.

No. 6.    No. 7.

**6.** 100 pairs Heavy Waterproof Canvas Knee Leggings, with inside spring on the side, with lace tops, made in the best manner of heavy colored canvas, same material as used in fine mackintoshes. Purchased at a great bargain, as slightly wet, at a fire underwriters' sale; the length is 20 inches; sell regularly for $1.00 pair. Our bargain price, 65 cents pair. Small sizes.

**7.** 1,000 pairs Heavy Waterproof Steel-gray Canvas Knee Leggings, side spring to the knee, with three patent quick-fastening buckles at the thigh. Purchased at fire insurance sale as slightly damaged by water. Price, 45 cents pair, $5.00 dozen pairs. Small sizes.

We wish to call your attention to pages 66, 67, 68, 69 and 366, where we show drawings and description of all the World War guns. This information is not to be found in any book on the World War, as we have obtained it from first hand sources having access to all the captured arms brought to this country by our government after the war. The drawings are all to scale and show every detail of gun, and the different styles of bayonets. This information would if in book form sell at one dollar per copy, whereas we include this in our catalog and charge only 50 cents for all.

On the last pages of the catalog we show interesting information of the various parts of the flint-lock, also various types of magazines used in army rifles, showing their development. Note also list of special bargains at one dollar each.

**50 U. S. BREAST CORDS.** For Engineer Corps. New. Red and white colors, with tabs and tassels. Very showy. Price, 65 cents each.

**50 U. S. BREAST CORDS.** For Hospital Corps, maroon and white colors, with tabs and tassels. New. Price, 65 cents each.

**DIVISIONAL CHEVRONS,** in colors. We have in stock most of the identification chevrons used by the various divisions of the U. S. Army during the War. These are the *best* grade. Send sketch of chevron desired, also division. Price 30 cents each.

**U. S. A. O. D. FLANNEL OVERSHIRT.** New, assorted sizes, with two outside pockets and turndown collar, $3.00.

### GENERAL LOGAN AND THE IRISHMAN.

Just before the capture of Savannah, General Logan with two or three of his staff entered the depot at Chicago one fine morning to take the car east on his way to join his command. The general, being a short distance in advance of the others, stepped upon the platform of a car and was about to enter it but was stopped by an Irishman with "You will not be goin' in there." "Why not, sir?" says the General. "Bekase this is a leddies' caer, and no gentleman'll be goin' in there without a leddy. There's wan sate in the caer over there, if yees want it." at the same time pointing to it. "Yes, I see there is one seat, but what shall I do with my staff?" "Oh, bother your staff!" was the petulant reply. "Go you and take the sate and stick your staff out of the windy."

**50 NEW GRAY BLOUSES,** in assorted styles, some with standing collars, some fold over or turned down. Some have four outside pockets, others only two. Styles as used by postmen, conductors, messenger boys and others. All in fine condition, in assorted sizes. Price, $4.85.

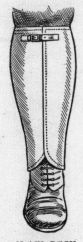 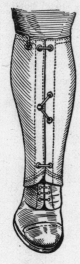

**NEW REGULATION OFFICERS' TAN LEATHER PUTTEE LEGGINS.** Inside clasp butting fastening, strap and buckle top fastening. Moulded to shape of leg. Length 12 inches. New. Made in imitation pig skin, $3.95 up.

**NEW U. S. A. REGULATION OLIVE DRAB HEAVY CANVAS PUTTEE,** laced in front, all sizes. New. 68 cents.

**1566 HOSPITAL CORPS STRETCHERS.** Second hand. Price, $2.50.

**VICTORY BUTTONS** in bronze or silver oxide. Sold by authorization from War Department. Either finish, 30c each.

**500 BLUE CLOTH BELL TOP ARMY CAPS.** Used a short time by State Militia; in serviceable order; bargain price, 90 cents each.

**500 NEW KHAKI BLOUSE COATS 50 CENTS EACH.** Late Regulation, dyed a seal brown (slightly darker color than that worn by the teamsters). All size No. 1 (33 inch chest); five brown color bone buttons, turn-down collar, four outside pockets, made of the *best khaki material.* Fine hunting coat—at the bargain price, 50 cents each.

**No. 17.**

**10 FINE CLOTH BLOUSES** in gray cloth; fancy trimmed with fine quality black braid; standing or rolling collar; fine linings. Handsome, showy uniform. New goods, assorted sizes. Price, $7.50 each.

**7. MILITARY CADET GRAY CANVAS LEGGINS.** The Regulation leggin, dyed a gray color to match Cadet gray uniforms. Leggins are soiled and stained, and need slight repairs. Used by mounted cadets. Offered "as are" at the bargain price of 18 cents per pair, with laces.

**Officers'**    **Army**

**100 ARMY WHISTLES,** of horn, in assorted patterns, in good condition, our selection. Price, 25 cents each.

**POLICE WHISTLES,** nickel-plated. 25 cents each.

**ARMY WHISTLES,** present style complete with chain from 50 cents up.

**BRONZE MEDAL BUST OF GENERAL GRANT,** made from set presented to Republican Club by Chester A. Arthur about the period of the Civil War.

Grant bust is in Lt. General U. S. A. uniform and measures 8½ inches, mounted on circular shield 11 inches, covered with blue cloth. **Price, $3.50.**

### THE "BROADWAY VAMP"

(Dedicated to the House of Bannerman, where such "Vamps" find inspiration)

When the "outfit" saw him coming—
  They named him "the Broadway Vamp";
Without a doubt, this kid was 'bout—
  The handsomest man in camp.

He didn't like to don the mitts—
  His ways were mild and mellow,—
On every side, he hurt their pride,
  They hinted he was "yellow."

And when the "outfit" crossed the pond—
  The bets were ten to one—
The "Broadway Vamp," would show his stamp
  And make a long home-run;

So when they hit the firing line—
  The C. O. called the "Top"—

"In the Chinese treaty ports certain parts of the city have been conceded to Europeans, over which part the consul of that country presides and in which the citizens of that country have their places of business, warehouses or godowns, as they are called. The consul acts as trial judge over all the territory conceded to his nation. This knowledge helped me to bluff a Chinese rowdy whom I met one evening while strolling along the Nankeen road. It seems that a poor old Chinese rickshaw man had done something to offend a stout young Chinese bully, who, when I met him, had hold of the rickshaw man's queue and was hauling him along, every little while slapping him in the face. A crowd of Chinamen had gathered around, but no one interfered. I got hot at seeing the poor man being beaten and wanted to stop it, but how? What would I say? Would I say "maskee"? No; it would mean "all right" as well as "let him alone"; but just then I happened to think that this was taking place in the British concession and knew that Chinese evildoers were afraid of the British consul's court, so, getting to where the rowdy could see me, I looked hard at him, as if I was an officer. The bluff worked well, for at once he stopped beating the old man and sneaked away."—Bannerman' New Yorker on the Yangtse-Kiang River.

**BRONZE BUST OF PRESIDENT LINCOLN.** Replica of the original one presented by Chester A. Arthur to Republican Club, mounted on 11-inch shield. Price, $4.85.

**"EXPERT RIFLEMAN BADGE."** Crossed guns on wreath suspended to a bar, with inscription title, with safety pin fastening; size 2x1½ inches; white metal silvered. Price, 65 cents each.

**"PISTOL EXPERT BADGE."** Crossed pistols on wreath suspended to bar, with title inscription, with safety pin fastening; size 1½x1⅛ inches; white metal silvered. Price, 78 cents each.

9

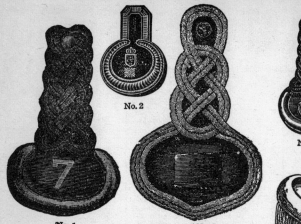

No. 2

No. 4    No. 5    No. 7    No. 6

No. 1    No. 3

No. 8

No. 1. Military Officer's Gilt Epaulettes, used a short time. Offered in good, serviceable order, $3.50 per pair.

No. 2. 10 Pair German Officer's Epaulettes with German Eagle and Crown ornamented rank designs. Used a few times, are in good, serviceable order; genuine (from Berlin.) Price per pair, $2.25.

No. 3. Officer's Shoulder Epaulettes, gilt cord, in good, second-hand order; various ranks in stock. Price, $3.00 per pair.

No. 4. 100 Pair New Band Epaulettes, red worsted shoulder knot and background, with gilt border, with or without anchor and world design, or with musician's lyre ornament. Pair of these handsome Epaulettes makes any Band Uniform complete; are complete with metal loops for attaching to coat. Worth $3.00 pair. Our bargain price, 95 cents per pair.

No. 5. General's Epaulettes, gilt lace with gilt fringe; used a short time, offered in good, serviceable order. Price, $8.50 per pair.

No. 6. Civil War Soldier's Shoulder Scales. New; slightly tarnished from 40 years storage. Have 2,000 pairs. Bargain price, 40 cents pair. Coat attachments, 20 cents per pair.

No. 7. Civil War Soldier's Epaulettes. All new; in green and yellow. Price. 50 cents per pair.

Buff Epaulettes, with blue border; polished brass frame. Price, $1.00 per pair.

No. 8. Gilt-lace Epaulettes; very slightly tarnished. Price, $4.75 per pair.

No. 1550    No. 1305    No. 10

No. 9

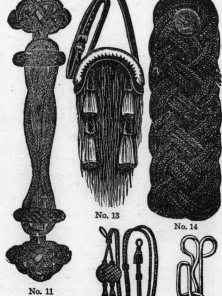

No. 11    No. 13    No. 14

No. 12

SPORRANS, No. 9, 13, 1305, 1550. We offer sporrans of no special design and without any special number of tassels. We get these from our British agent from time to time and must take whatever patterns we can obtain. Price is $3.50 each, in good second hand condition.

ST. ANDREWS CROSS ORNAMENT from Scotch sporrans, suitable also for use on cap or buzby. Price 50 cents each.

See other pages for articles of Scotch Highland Uniforms.

No. 10. White Hair Aigrette with wire for holding in hat. Price, 65c each.

No. 11. Coat or Cape Loop Fasteners with olive buttons, new. Price, 95c each.

No. 12. Late Regulation Army Aiguilettes colored worsted cord, with loops and tassels. Price, 65 cents each.

No. 14. Shoulder Knots of white mohair braid, with brass button. Price, $1.25 per pair.

No. 15.

No. 16    No. 18

No. 22

Marshall & Co. BEST QUALITY SHREWSBURY... 35

No. 19

No. 20

No. 17

No. 21    No. 23

No. 15. British Army Revolver Cord, braided, with tassels, with brass snap hook, worn around neck and attached to revolver, to prevent losing when dismounting; length 4½ feet. Price, 25c ea.

South African Set of Equipments: russet leather, with two shoulder slings, revolver holster and sword frog, with the revolver cord and snap hook. Serviceable order. Price, $8.85.

No. 16. 100 Pair U. S. Soldier's Suspenders, Price, 20c. per pair.

No. 17. German Army Officer's Silvered Shoulder Sash, with tassels, have been used, are in serviceable order. Price, $3.50.

No. 18. 200 Gross Peets Hooks and Eyes No. 4. Invisible eyes, 3 dozen package price, 10 cents.

No. 19. 138 Pounds of new U. S. Army Linen Thread. Unbleached Linen White-Brown in hanks. Good value for $1.00 pound, made by Marshall & Co. Our price, 50 cents per pound.

No. 21. Combination Waist Belt and Suspenders, from the U. S. Arsenal Auction invention of a soldier, made of fine russet leather, new bright metal fastenings. Price, $1.50 per pair.

No. 22. 500 Gross of DeLongs Hooks and Eyes No. 6, with hump, intended for use on army soldier's overcoat capes, all new, 3 dozen Hooks and Eyes in package. Price, 20 cents.

No. 23. British Army Officer's Silk Shoulder Sash with tassels; good, second-hand order. Price, $2.25.

U. S. ORDNANCE INSIGNIA. In heavy gilt metal, safety pin fastening. Size 1 inch. Price, 25 cents.

GILT MEDAL GEORGE V. REX, GEORGE FIFTH REIGNING KING OF ENGLAND. Soldier's insignia ornaments. Price, 35 cents each.

BRITISH ARMY ORDNANCE INSIGNIA. In heavy gilt metal, screw nut fastening. Size 1½ inches. Price, 35 cents.

State of New Jersey Militia Brass Belt Plate, with catch, 50c. N. Y. BRASS PLATES, 50 cents.

Old Brass Belt Plate, used by New York Military Company. Price, $3.75.

No. 50. Polished Brass Cross Belt Plate, with pin fastening for use on web belts, new, 30 cents

No. 49. N. Y. State Militia Brass Plate for web loop cartridge belt; by agreement with Adgt. General these plates will only be sold to members of the National Guard. Price, 40c each. Altered with plate over letters N. Y. 58c each, in doz. lots

U. S. Brass Belt Plate for use on web loop cartridge belt. Medium size, 40c.

No. 470. U. S. Navy Officer's Gilt Belt Buckle, circular centre, with U. S. coat of arms in blue enamel. Length, 3 inches; width, 1¾ inches. Price, $1.45.

No. 150. Nickel Plated Cartridge Plates, for web belts, with boar's head, with patent catches. Price, 35c, each.

No. 470. Colombia Guards Brass Belt Plate, for use web loop cartridge belts. Plates, 50c.; with belts, 95c.

Confederate Civil War Belt Buckle used by Texas Regiments, in good serviceable order. Valuable relic. Price, $2.00.

200 EXTRA LIGHT STAMPED BRASS EAGLE BELT PLATES, for use of cadets, on webbing belts. Price of plate with catches, 15 cents each. Price of plate on used white webbing belt, 30 cents per set.

SCOTCH ORNAMENT, 1⅝ inches long, showing St. Andrew holding cross and standing on two thistles. Bright finish. Can be used as ornament on sporrans or caps. Price 50 cents.

No. 1794. Sword Belt Studs, brass, 8 cents each; $5.00 per gross.
No. 1810. Sword belt loop and hook, brass, 35c each

Cast Brass Gilt Finished Belt Buckle for russet leather army belt, 1¾ ins. wide, new. Price, 25c, each.

PLEASE NOTE THAT BELT PLATES NUMBERS 470, 120, 25, 200, 72, 500, 210 and 520 are not always in stock. Allow above one week to have these made up. Price includes postage.

No. 1714. U. S. Naval Academy Belt Plate, cast metal, nickel plated, rope border and polished oval shaped letters; length. 3 x 2¼ ins. No catches. Price, 35c. each.

No. 1810.

No. 25. N. Y. State Coat-of-Arms Gilt Belt Plates for use on ladies' belts. 80c.

No. 120. Handsome U. S. Navy Gilt Buckle, with coat-of-arms in centre in relief, gilt polished; width, 1¼ ins.; length, 3 ins.; loops for 1½-in. belt. Price $1.00.

No. 48. Old Pattern U. S. A. Officer's Belt Buckle fine order, $1.00.

No. 47. Brass Belt Buckles for use on web loop cartridge belts, with coat-of-arms of Colombia, State of Panama, medium size, 90c. Brass Belt Buckles, with coat-of-arms of Colombia, State of Panama, in small size. Price, with belts, 90c. each; price of plates, either size, 35c. each.

No. 200. U. S. Coat-of-Arms Buckle for ladies' belt. Fine dull gilt buckle, size 1⅞ inches wide, 2⅝ inches long, with neat loops for fastening to the belt, with coat of arms design in bright gilt, with stars and field in hard blue enamel. Price, $.145. Can be sent by registered mail for 10c. extra.

Nos. 1771 and 1683. Brass Loops for Web Belts, 10c. each; $6.50 per gross.

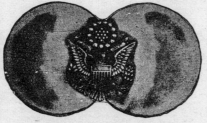

No. 72. Gilt Buckle for ladies' belt. U. S. Coat-of-Arms in centre. Price, $1.00.

No. 210. U. S. Coat-of-Arms Ornament made into neat belt buckles, with loop and catch for ladies' belts. Width, 1¾ ins.; length, 3 ins.; loops for 1½-inch belt. Price, $1.00.

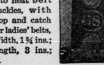

No. 520. Gilt Belt Buckle, for ladies' belt, with red, white and blue shield in U. S. Coat-of-Arms centre. Length, 2 inches; width, 1⅜ inches. Loops take 1¾-inch belt. Price, $1.45.

U. S. Army Brass Belt Buckle for web loop cartridge belts. New. Complete with two loop fasteners. Price, 35 cents.

No. 1771.

No. 1793. Brass Sword Belt Attachment, 25c each $30.00 per gross.

**United States Army Soldiers' Belt Buckle;** cast brass, serviceable; made at Government Arsenal. Price, 30 cents each; $3.00 per dozen.

**Sons of Veterans' Regulation Belt Buckles;** brass polished ormolu, gilt finished, with loops. Price, 40 cents each; $4.50 per dozen.

**United States Naval Officers' Service Belt Buckles;** brass polished, gilt finished. Price, 95 cents each; $11.00 per dozen.

**United States Army Officers' Belt Buckles;** brass polished ormolu, gilt finished. Price, 45 cents each; $5.00 per dozen.

**Confederate Relics—C. S. A.** Belt Plates, not original, but made in the same mold as those furnished to the Southern Army during Civil War. The original molds were found in ruins of Atlanta, Ga., after General Sherman burned the arsenals. Price, 65 cents each.

**Military Belt Plate** worn on cross-belts with dress uniforms; polished brass, pin fastening, with letters (assorted), nickel-plated; in good second-hand, serviceable order. Large stock. Price, 40 cents each; $4.50 per dozen.

**Massachusetts Coat-of-Arms Belt Buckle,** worn by soldiers of the Commonwealth many years ago; all in fine order; refinished in gilt like new; handsome relics. Price, $4.50 each.

**British Army Soldiers' Belt Buckle;** polished; in fine order; has crown, lion and motto; relics. Price, 75 cents each; $8.00 per dozen.

**Cross-Belt Plates,** as used by 71st New York Volunteers; also many other regimental numbers. Price, 40 cents each, with safety-pin fastening.

**"American Guard"** Public School Cadets' Regulation Belt Buckle; brass polished, with loops. Price, 35 cents each; $4.00 per dozen.

**United States Naval Officers' Dress Belt Buckle;** brass, silvered finish. Price, 95 cents each. Handsome.

**Cuban Guards' Belt Buckles;** polished brass, with coat-of-arms of Cuba in centre in white metal. Price, 75 cents each; $8.00 per dozen.

**O-717. SHIELD MADE OF 14 BRITISH ARMY OFFICERS' BELT BUCKLES.** Assorted buckles complete, with clasp mounts. Worn by British Army officers. Handsome designs, silvered and gilt. The base of the shield is red velvet covered. Size of shield 20x17 inches. Price, $35.00.

**United States Helmet Plate;** polished brass eagle. Size, 4⅛x5 inches. Price, 35 cents each; $3.75 per dozen. Handsome ornaments for decoration. Relics.

**State of New York Soldiers' Belt Buckles;** brass polished, with raised letters, S. N. Y., with loops. Worn many years ago; not now regulation; relics. Price, 30 cents each; $3.00 per dozen.

**Musicians' Belt Buckles;** polished brass, with harp surrounded by wreath. Price, 25 cents each; $2.50 per dozen.

**New York State Helmet Plate Ornament,** with eagle, Excelsior and State coat-of-arms; now obsolete; gilt finish, brass. Handsome relics. Size, 3x4 inches. Price, 40 cents each; $4.00 per dozen.

**Military Belt Buckles,** with either letters or figures in nickle or enamel; relics; brass polished; second-hand. Price, 40 cents each; $4.50 per dozen.

**United States Civil War Plates;** polished brass, lead backs, with loop for fastening on bridle. Handsome relic ornaments. Price, 20 cents pair; $1.50 per dozen.

**Civil War Carbine Sling Buckle;** brass; 3 inches. Price, 25 cents each; $2.50 per dozen.

**Spanish Seal;** size, ½x2 in.; "De la Ville," with space for inserting date, etc. Price, $4.50

**United States Soldiers' Shoulder Sling Buckles (1845-1865).** Polished brass, lead backs, with loops for thong fastening; handsome relics. Price, 20 cents each; $2.00 per dozen.

**NEW YORK STATE OFFICERS, LATE REGULATION BELT BUCKLE,** 2½ by 1⅞ inches, with silver wreath, and old English letters N. Y. in center. Complete with catch, in good order. Price 85 cents each. Price with second hand waist belt, $1.35.

**WEST POINT ARMY CADET BRASS CAP BADGE.** This is shield with helmet and dagger, surmounted by Eagle and Wreath. Size 1⅞ by 2 inches. Screw fastening. Price 50 cents each.

**U. S. Army Officers Extra Heavy Gold Finished Belt Plates** with silver plated wreath, complete with catch. All new. $1.00 each.

**United States Civil War Soldiers' Belt Buckles;** brass, lead backs; serviceable order; fine relic. Price, 25 cents each; $2.50 per dozen.

**Nickeled Anchor Ornament** with fastening wires. Size, 1 inch. Price, 20 cents each.

**U. S. Civil War Oval Plate** with letters U. S. as used on the Infantry Cartridge Boxes. These have the wire loops to attach to cover of box. Price 30 cents each.

**Polished Brass Cross-belt Buckles** with pin fastening; new. Price, 35 cents.

On Page 358 we show a large assortment of Navy buckles, also various styles of buckles with American and other flags.

**Brass Letters and Figures,** with fastening wires. Size, ½ in. .03 cts. ¾ " .05 " 1¼ " .10 " Some nickel-plated figures for coat collars, 12 cents each.

**Spanish Officers' Belt Buckles.** Came to New York in lot of old brass from Santiago, Cuba, in 1899; rare relics, cleaned and polished, gilt finished, with Spanish crown, coat-of-arms in centre in white metal. Price, $3.50 each. Some with castle in centre, $2.75.

Lot Spanish Soldiers' Brass Buckles with regimental numbers; assorted. Price, $1.50 each.

Lot Spanish Sappers' and Miners' Belt Buckles, with crossed axes, picks and spades. Price, $2.50.

Spanish Naval Officer's Belt Buckle, with Spanish crown and crossed anchors, with coral attached. Recovered from wrecked ship. Price, $5.00.

**Massachusetts Soldiers' Belt Buckles;** brass, with MASS. in raised letters. Relics. Price, 50 cents each.

**West Point Civil War Brass Belt Buckles.** Oval shaped, with U. S.; lead backs. Relics. Price, $1.00 each.

**Spanish Soldiers' Brass Hat Ornament,** in two sizes, 2x3 and 3x4 inches; brass metal, with cross cannon, crown and sunburst. 75c.

**British Officers' Belt Buckles,** with links; with lion head and crown on each part. Handsome relics. Price, $2.50.

**Brass Medal** from Guanabaco, Cuba. Price. 50 cents.

**Grand Army of the Republic Belt Plate.** Price, 25 cents each. New goods.

**Polished Brass Belt Buckle,** with loops; new. Price, 35 cents.

**Brass Buckle,** with tongue, for shoulder belts, 2½ inches wide. New. Price, 25 cents each.

British Officer's Buckle, from Cuba with lot of Santiago brass; relics. Price, $2.50.

"Jamaica, 1803," Brass Belt Buckle, oval shaped, from Cuba 1899. Rare relic. Price, $3.00.

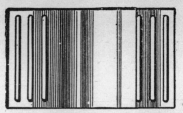

**1.—West Point Cadet Bras Belt Buckle,** for use with white web belt. The loops hold the belt without sewing; readily detached for laundering. Price, 35 cents each.

**No. 12. 17th British Lancers Helmet Plate,** "Death or Glory," with names of famous battles in which this regiment has taken part, in relief; with British arms, etc. Handsome relic; size, 8½ by 4½ in. $1.00.

**No. 3. Royal British Naval Officer's Gilt Belt Buckle** with Crown and Anchor, surrounded by Wreath. Size, 2¾ by 1¾ inches. For use on waist belt. Second-hand. Price $1.50 each.

**4.—Masachusetts Volunteer Soldier's Service Belt Buckle,** second-hand. Price, 40 cents.

**5.—U. S. Navy Sailor's Belt Buckle,** used on buff leather waist belt, Civil War pattern; length of buckle, 2⅛ inches; width, 2⅜ inches for belts 1⅝ inches wide; serviceable relic. Price, 15 cents each.

**6.—Palmetto Tree, South Carolina Buckle,** the State emblem, antique pattern buckle, pattern used in olden times. Price, $2.85.

**7.—Spanish Regulars Belt Buckle,** brass gilt finish, size 2¾ inches by 2¼ inches. This lot was used in Cuba by the Spanish Regular Soldiers. Price, $1.35.

**8.—Spanish Cuban Volunteer Soldier's Belt Buckle,** gilt finish. relic of Spanish War. Price, $1.35.

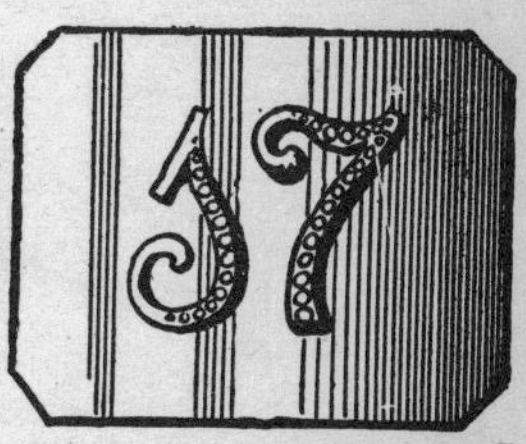

**9.—Spanish Regular Soldier's Cuban Campaign Belt Buckle,** came from Santiago, Cuba; rusty, no doubt gathered up from battlefield, sent to the U. S. in cargo of old brass. Price, $1.35 each.

**No. 648. CONFEDERATE OFFICERS BELT BUCKLES, RELICS.** In fair order. We obtained these a short time ago from a CONFEDERATE VETERAN who had picked them up on the BATTLEFIELD. Price $5.00 each.

**2205. BOER WAR SOLDIER'S BELT,** with fastener. Made for the Boers during the war in South Africa; can be used on any belt; polished brass plate, with South African insignia; length 2⅜ inches, height 1⅞ inches; in fine order. Price, 50 cents.

**649. SPANISH OFFICER'S BELT BUCKLE PRODUCED FROM THE ORIGINAL** after the Spanish-American War. The centre has the Spanish Coat of Arms. Price, $1.50.

**650. REVOLUTIONARY WAR PERIOD OFFICER'S BELT BUCKLE.** Produced from the original. Clasp pattern buckle, with eagle and 13 stars. Serviceable order. Price, $1.50.

**10577. BRITISH ROSE INSIGNIA.** Silvered metal, 1 1/16 inches in diameter. Price, 18 cents.

**0-837. NAVAL OFFICER'S MINIATURE BADGE BROOCH.** Silvered eagle and stars. gilt plated anchors, size 1¼x1½ inches, safety pin fastening, polished gilt back. Price, 75 cents.

**1568. ROYAL IRISH REGIMENT GILT ORNAMENT,** with harp and crown. Loop and pin fastening on back. Supposed to have been worn by Irish regiment in Boer war. Length, 1⅝ inches. Price, mailed, 50 cents.

**10576. COAST GUARD LIFE BOAT BADGE.** Silvered metal, 1¼ inches in diameter. Shield with life boat, with motto, "Always Ready, Courage, Humanity, Commerce, 1850." Two fastening loops on the back. Price, 25 cents, mailed.

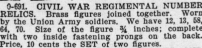

**British Naval Sailors** Silvered Ornament, as illustrated, full size loop fastener on back. Price 20 cents each.

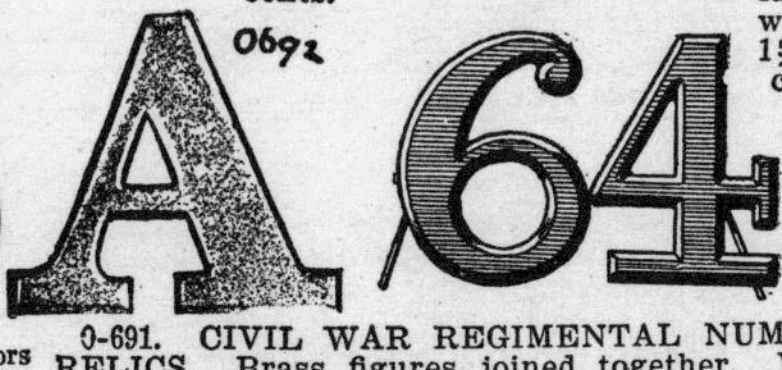

**0-691. CIVIL WAR REGIMENTAL NUMBER RELICS.** Brass figures joined together. Worn by the Union Army soldiers. We have 12, 13, 58, 64, 70. Size of the figure ¾ inches; complete with two inside fastening prongs on the back. Price, 10 cents the SET of two figures.

**0-692. ONE-INCH BRASS FIGURES AND LETTERS,** as worn on soldier's uniform 1858 to 1863. We can furnish the following figures, 1, 2, 4, 5, 6, 8, 9; in letters, B, C, D, G, H, I, K. These are all new, left over from the Civil War. In serviceable order as well as relics. Complete with fastening prongs. Price, 6 cents each; or 50 cents per dozen.

**2645. REVOLUTIONARY WAR HAT PLATE.** Shield, with eagle, wreath, 1776 and motto, "E Pluribus Unum." From Revolutionary War militia soldier's hat. Size 4½x3½ inches. Price, $7.50.

**0-809. SOUVENIR I. O. O. F. BADGE.** Oxidized metal, with silk ribbon, stamped "Souvenir Badge, Binghamton, 1889, I. O. O. F. P. M. Division of the Atlantic." From society goods' assignee sale. Price, 15 cents each.

**0-8010. CRUSADER KNIGHT IN ARMOR BUTTON BADGE.** Oxidized colored metal gilt, purple and green, with 12 silvered stars, battlement border, 1⅜-inch diameter. Price, 10 cents.

**0-677. U. S. COAT OF ARMS COPPER MOULD,** EAGLE WITH SPREAD WINGS, WITH STARS AND STRIPED SHIELD. Motto, "E Pluribus Unum." Length 12¾x6¼ inches, deepest recess ½ inch. Price, $4.85.

**U. S. N. BATTLE SHIP KEARSARGE HAT RIBBON,** as worn on sailors' hats. Gilt embroidered letters, kind that Jack gives as souvenir to his girl friends; new, black silk, 39 inches long, 1½ inches wide. Price, 60 cents each.

WE CAN FURNISH RIBBONS for the following named Navy War Ships, Torpedo Boats and Transports: Olympia, Constellation, Maine, Farragut, Sherman, Sheridan, Logan, Burnside, Meade, Crook, Dix and others. Your choice, 60 cents each.

**10814. BRITISH CYCLIST BADGE.** "T. Highland, Cyclist," in ½-inch gilt letters fastened neatly together. Size 1⅝x2⅛ inches. Brass back plate and fastening hooks. Price, 20 cents.

**0-693. SCOTCH HIGHLAND SOLDIER'S BOER WAR RELIC CAP BADGE.** Bronze color to match the khaki uniform; St. Andrew's Cross, with Scotch motto, "Nemo Me Impune Nacessit," ("No one attacks me with impunity") with thistle leaves and flowers. Size 1⅝x1¼ inches; fastening loop on the back. Price, 45 cents.

**British Navy Sailors** Silvered Ornament, foul anchor, crown in rope circle, length 1 7-8 inch, width 1 3-8, loop on back for fastening. Price, mailed, 50 cents.

**No. 16. BRITISH ROYAL COAT-OF-ARMS;** in bronze, gold finished; size, 1¼ by 1½ inches. Price, 50 cents mailed.

# Illustrated History of U. S. Military Small Arms

We are presenting to our readers on the following pages a concise illustrated history of U. S. Military Small Arms from the Revolutionary War to the present time. The arms are grouped under eight classes. These include all the principal weapons. Where only a slight difference occurs in the appearance of the guns they are covered in the text. The table shown on pages 54-55 shows at a glance the great study the subject has been given by ordnance experts since the early days, in fact no other country has spent the time and money endeavoring to obtain the best arms available for their armed forces. Other countries may have led us in the adoption of new types but we have profited by their mistakes. The data given is all taken from government documents after a search covering a number of years by James E. Coombes of Montclair, N. J., who also executed the drawings from which the illustrations were made.

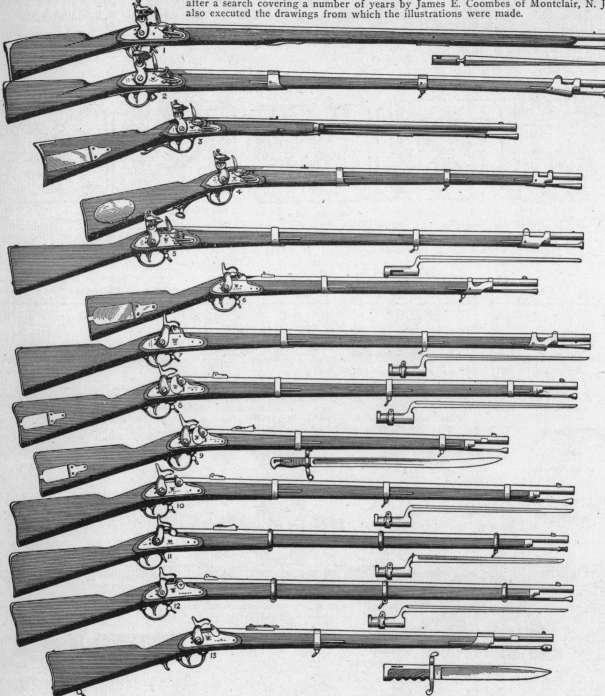

## Muzzle-loading Rifles and Muskets

The first U. S. military muskets were known as the "Committee of Safety" arms. In the spring of 1775 the 13 colonies through the various "Committees" provided muskets to arm the patriots for the coming year. About 200 gunsmiths produced these guns. Some were stamped with maker's names, some with simply an initial and some without any marks. After September 9, 1776, U. S. was used. The letters C. P., Continental Property, (or Commonwealth of Pennsylvania) were used, 1774 and 1775.

No. 1. REVOLUTIONARY FLINTLOCK MUSKET. This represents the type of musket made in the states prior to and during the Revolutionary War, the calibers varying from .72 to .80. They were generally without bands. Made principally in Massachusetts, Rhode Island, Maryland and Pennsylvania. They were all smooth bores and weighed 10 pounds and over. Very few bayonets are found with these pieces as less than half of the American soldiers were equipped with bayonets.

No. 2. U. S. SPRINGFIELD FLINTLOCK MUSKET. Model of 1795, Springfield Armory being established that year. These arms were faithful copies of the famous "Charleville" musket of France. Caliber .70, with a barrel 45 inches long. The arm weighed 9½ pounds. This model was made until 1808 when slight changes in the musket brought out the Model of 1808. These variations are so slight that they would not be apparent in an illustration. Caliber .69. Smooth bore, barrel same length as the model 1795. Made by contract as well as at government armories.

No. 3. HARPER'S FERRY FLINTLOCK RIFLE. Known as the Model of 1814, although made as early as 1804 in limited quantities. Caliber .53 with a 33-inch barrel. On account of the heavy barrel the gun weighed 9¾ pounds. Rifling had seven grooves. The butt-stock is provided with a patch box. Also made smooth bore with longer barrel. This arm was the official U. S. rifle until the adoption of the Model of 1819, No. 4. No bayonets provided for this gun.

Continued on Page 272

No. 4. Bandman's Cap Ornament (lyre) Gilt finish, 20 cts, Letters or figures 4 cents each extra, and will be brazed on when ordered in lots of a dozen or more.

**No. 1.** Cavalry Soldier's Hat Ornament. Crossed sabres, with screw fastening. Price, 14 cents each. When ordered in lots of a dozen or more, letters or figures will be brazed to the pin at a cost of 4 cents each.

**No. 2.** Infantry Soldier's Cap Ornament, with screw nut fastening, 14 cents each. Letters and figures brazed on when ordered in lots of a dozen or more, at a cost of 4 cents for each letter or figure.

Artillery Cap Ornament. Crossed cannon, gilt finish, screw nut fastening. Price, 25 cents each.

WE MAKE TO ORDER MOST EVERY KIND OF MILITARY ORNAMENT, AND SUGGEST THAT YOU SEND US SKETCHES OF WHAT YOU WANT, SO THAT WE MAY SUBMIT ESTIMATE. SOME OF THE ITEMS ON THIS PAGE ARE MADE TO ORDER, SO ALLOW TIME FOR THEM TO BE MADE UP.

No. 8. Bugler's Cap Ornament. New pattern. Price, 20 cents each. Letters and figures 4 cents each, brazed on when ordered in dozen lots.

**No. 5.** Boys' Brigade Cap Ornament. Screw back fastening, with ornament, with B B. Price 20 cents. Letters and figures 4 cents each extra, and will be brazed on when ordered in dozen lots.

No. 7. Signal Corps Cap Ornament. Price, 70 cents pair.

87,000 U. S. Army Gilt Collar Numbers. with 2 wires for fastening on back of number. The illustration is full size. Gilt plated All figures in stock. Price, 4 cents each. 40 cents a dozen, $4.00 per gross.

80,000 Brass Letters and Figures, half-inch size, with two wires in the back for fastening. *New* complete sets of figures, letters from "A" to "O" inclusive. Price, 3 cents each, or 30 cents per dozen, when ordered all of same number. $2.50 per gross when ordered all of same number.

**General's Stars** for shoulder straps, 10 cents each.

**No. 10.** Captain's Bars for shoulder straps, 10 cents each.

**No. 11**

No. 12. Majors Leaves, for shoulder straps 10c. each.

Chaplain's Cross Collar Ornament, silver plated, 50 cts. a pair.

No. 12. Lieutenant Colonel's Leaves. for shoulder straps, 10 cents each.

No. 13

**No. 13. BARS FOR BLOUSE OR COLLAR,** for SECOND LIEUTENANT, GILT FINISH. 50 cents per pair.

FIRST LIEUTENANT, SILVER FINISH. 50 cents per pair.

CAPTAIN, SILVER FINISH, smooth. 75 cents per pair.

CAPTAIN, CORRUGATED, imitation of embroidery. 50 cents per pair.

**No. 17.** Colonel's Eagle for shoulder straps. 10 cents each. Silver plated for collar ornaments, 90 cents a pair.

Nickle or Brass Wreaths for Cap ornaments, 10 cents each Letters or figures 4 cents each brazed on when ordered. in dozen lots.

**IDAHO KY. OR. U.S. ILL. N.J. N.Y.**

No. 19. Medical Officer's Gilt Collar Ornament (caduces) 40 cents a pair.

Collar Letter Ornaments for any State. with wire fasteners. Price, 12 cents each letter. Connected without extra charge when ordered in lots of a dozen or more. Periods 6 cents each.

**No. 20. U.S. Coat of Arms** Lapel Button, gilt metal, ⅝ inch, beautiful ornament. Price, 25 cents.

**No. 21.** Chaplain's Cross. gilt metal.

**No. 22.** Adjutant Collar Lapel Ornament, nickel metal, plated, 25 cents a pair. each.

**No. 23.** Metal Miniature Shoulder Strap Ornament, in any rank, in hard enamel colors. Price, 45 cents each.

**No.1 389.** Bronze Collar Ornament, infantry guns used short time by New York soldiers, Illustration is full size. Four loops on under side for attaching to collar of coat. Letters and figures are attached by brazing and can be taken off by heat. We offer *as are,* 12 cents each. We have for sale as illustrated, also with letters and figures, N. Y. 1 D., etc. 12 cents each set.

94  25  26

U. S. Army Spanish War Cap Ornaments, made of stamped brass, with wires for fastening. All new, in fine order. 60,000 crossed sabres. 8,000 crossed cannons. 20,000 crossed rifles. Price, 10 cents each, $1.00 per dozen, $9.00 per gross.

Nos. 31 and 32. Military Cross Gun Cap Ornaments. Polished brass with safety pin fastenings, lead filled. Job lot with figures and letters assorted. 12 cents each, $1.50 dozen. As are.

**No. 27.** U. S. Civil War Pattern Coat of Arms Hat Ornament in gilt metal, small size: 20 cts. Same in gilt embroidery, full size on dark blue cap cloth. Price. 95c.

**No.28.** United States Coat of Arms, gilt embroidered on dark blue cloth, for officers' caps. Price. $1.60 each. In gilt or bronze finish stamped metal.

**No. 29.** U. S. Gilt Bronze Cap Ornament, with letters in place of regulation sunburst. These fine cap ornaments can be furnished plain with sunburst or with small letters or figures as shown above at 5 cts. per letter extra when ordered in lots of ½ doz. All new; fine light, gilt metal.

**No. 30. Late Regulation** U. S. Army Gilt Brass Coat of Arms with loop or pin on back for attaching; size, 1 inch. Price, 25 cts.

No. 34. Veterinary Surgeon's Gilt Collar Ornament. Price, 45 cents per pair.

**No. 33.** Bugler Cap Ornament, old pattern, 15c. Civil War Cap Ornaments, in embroidered gilt, guns, sabres, etc. 50c. each.

British 'Army Gilt Ornaments. Relics; like new; with pin fastening; handsome souvenir for lady. Size, 1½ inches. Price, 40 cents.

**24 German Army Soldier Hat Ornaments,** brass, double-headed eagle design. Price, 50 cents each.

**40 Black and White Pompon Shako Ornaments.** Price, 20 cents each.

**80 Fluted Cross Ornament Design** Landwehr Kappes. Price, 30 cents each.

**100 Metal Maltese Cross Designs,** with German motto, "Fur Konig und Vaterland." 35c. each.

**1570. ROYAL MALTA MILITIA GILT BRONZE ORNAMENT MDCCC.,** gilt circle, with Maltese cross, wreath and crown; pin fastening on back; 2¼x1⅞ inches. Price, 50 cents.

**British Army Royal Fusiliers Cap Badge** ornament, with British crown motto inscription in white metal in centre, gilt polished brass; in fine order; size, ⅞x1⅝ in. 50c. Mailed.

**Royal Scots Grays,** centre design in exploding shell. Brass Helmet Badge; fine, serviceable order; gilt polished; 1⅝x3 ins. 50c. mailed.

**British Army Helmet Badge.** The Border Regiment. Design as shown in illustration taken from photograph. Size, 2¼x2½, white metal. Price, mailed, 50 cents each.

**6 British Belt Plates,** Dumbartonshire Volunteers, with design of elephant, castle and scroll work; same shape as the antique U. S. belt plate. Price, $1.00 each.

**King Edward VII. of Great Britain Defenders' Collar Badge,** gilt brass, with attaching loops; ⅞x1¼ ins. Price mailed, 35 cents.

**British Majesties Defenders' Collar Badge,** tiger rampant; on back for attaching; gilt brass, with hooks size, ⅞x1¼ inches. Price, mailed, 45 cts. French Flag, 17x27 inches, 60 cents.

**King Edward Design and Motto while Prince of Wales — Ich Dien (I serve) — in centre of brass helmet badge;** exploding shell; fine polished gilt brass with attaching loops; makes handsome ornament; size, 1⅝ x3 inches. Price, 50c. mailed.

**4 British Officers' Belt Buckles,** with crown and coat of arms design in centre; gilt background; silvered design in relief; size, 1¾x2 inches; have been in use; purchased in London in 1903; handsome buckle for lady. Price, $3.00.

**23 British Naval Belt Buckles,** nickel-plated Neptunes, with motto. Size, 2x3 inches; in good, second-hand, serviceable order. Price, $1.00 each.

**8 ditto,** size, 2½x3 inches. Price, $1.75 each.

British Crown Ornaments, in silvered metal with pin fastening, worn by soldiers of the King. Size, 1 in. Price, 20c. ea.

South African War Relic Buttons from London City Imperial Volunteer Regiment. Bronze, with crown in relief. Price, 10c. each.

British Army Ornament, bronze, imitation embroidery; bursting shell in flame with shamrock design. Price, 50 cents.

**British Army Helmet Plate.** The Prince Consort's Own Rifle Brigade, with names of battles: "Waterloo, Inkerman, Lucknow, etc." Bronze, dark colored. Size, 3 inches. Price, 60c. each.

Metal Ornament of the famous British "DEATH OR GLORY" Regiment. Skull and cross bones, with letters or glory. Price, $1.00.

**British Coat of Arms Brass Ornament. Price, $1.00.**

Metal Ornament, with King George's monogram; kind worn by British soldiers during American Revolutionary War period. Unique decoration. Price, $15.00.

**1567. BRITISH CROWN GERMAN SILVER ORNAMENT.** Full size illustration; 2 fastening loops on back. Supposed to have been worn on officers' shoulder straps during the Boer War. Price, mailed, 35 cts.

British Crown Ornaments, in white metal. Size, 1 inch. Price, 15 cents each.

**British Army Irish Reg't Ornament of Harp, in bronze; dark colored, with pin fastening; handsome souvenir.** Price, 50c. each.

**Musical Lyre Ornaments** for use on cap or collar of coat; bright metal, new, with wire fastenings. Price, 10c. ea.

**Scotch Regiment Thistle and leaf emblem.** Supposed to be relic from South Africa. Size, 2 inches. Price, 50 cents, with pin fastening.

**B391. LONDON POLICE HELMET BADGES;** size, 4½ in.; bordered with nickel letters and figures; "Metropolitan Police." Price, $1.50 each.

**British Army Officer's Shoulder Strap** rank badge. These were found attached to officers' uniforms purchased after the South African War. Size, 1 inch. Brass metal, ornamented and lacquered. Price, mailed. 60 cents.

**1571. CHESHIRE CONSTABULARY BADGE WITH PRINCE OF WALES MOTTO** in gilt coat of arms, "Ich Dien," with three plumes, silvered metal; 2 loop fasteners on back; size, 2x1⅝ inches. Price, 50c.

**British Army Royal Enniskillen Fusilier's Cap Badge,** gilt brass exploding shell with castle of Enniskillen in centre in white metal; handsome little ornament; with fastening loops; size, ⅞x1⅝. 50c., mailed.

**BRITISH ARMY COAT OF ARMS,** BRASS, size 3½ by 3½ inches. Price 50 cents each.

**BRITISH ARMY HELMET PLATES.** In this lot we have some for Derby, Dorset, Devon, Essex, Gibraltar, Gloucester, Hampshire, Kings Royal Rifles, Lancashire, Lancers 17th, Lancers Royal, Manchester, Middlesex, Royal Dragoons, East Surrey, Shropshire, Wiltshire, Warnich, York West and several other styles. All about 3 inches wide. Price 50 cents each.

**1572. BRONZE CONSTABULARY BADGE,** with King Edward's monogram E. R. VII.; size, 2½-inch diameter; loop fastening on back. Price, 50 cents.

**1573. British Army Pay Corps Silvered Ornament;** full size illustration. Price, 35 cts.

**1317. Rule Brittannia** Bronze Ornament, with fastening loop on back. Rare relic of Boer War. 80 cents each.

No. 6. 1st U. S. Army Corps Symbol.

No. 8. 3d U. S. Army Corps Symbol.

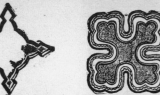

No. 9. 4th U. S. Army Corps Symbol.

No. 18    No. 20. Army Corps Badge.

NOS. 6, 8 AND 9. SPANISH WAR CORPS BADGES. IN HARD ENAMEL FINISH, WITH PIN BACK, BRASS EDGES. THESE BADGES ARE NOW SCARCE. WE OFFER THESE AT SPECIAL PRICE OF 65 CENTS EACH.

NOS. 18 AND 19. CIVIL WAR CORPS BADGES, BRASS EDGES, PIN BACK. THESE TWO STYLES ARE ALL WE HAVE LEFT OF A LARGE LOT. PRICE 65 CENTS EACH.

No. 9. British helmet badge in brass. Size 4 by 2 inches. Used by ROYAL DRAGOONS. Complete with fastenings. Price 50 cents.

No. 10. British King's Royal Rifles Regiment Helmet Ornament, lettered with names of battles; size, 1⅞ by 2½ in. Price, 60 cents each.

No. 20. German Helmet Plate Ornament; polished brass; size, 3¼ by 3½ inches. Price, 60 cents.

No. 21. German Eagle Ornament; brass; size, 3 inches in diameter. Price, 60 cents.

No. 22. European Soldier's Helmet Plate Ornament; brass finished; size, 3¼ by 3¼ inches. Price, 60 cents.

No. 25. French Military Uniform Button, with wreath encircling eagle in raised relief work. Price, 60 cents.

No. 1. German Military Belt Buckles; polished brass, with white metal centers; size, 2¾ by 1⅞ in.; complete with catches for attaching to waist belt. We paid a heavy import duty on these fine plates, which may make the price seem high to our German customers. Complete with leather waist belt, length up to 40 inches, $1.00. Price for plate without the belt, 68 cents.

No. 1.

No. 14. Liverpool Police Helmet Plate; brass finished; size, 3 by 2½ in. Price, 50 cents each.

British Army Helmet Badge, exploding shell, with three crowns in shield surrounded by laurel wreath; size 1⅝ by 3 inches; gilt brass, with fastening loops on the back. Price, mailed, 50 cents.

No. 23. Silver plated, $1.00    No. 24. Silver plated, $1.00

No. 25. Silver plated, $1.00

No. 26. Silver Plated. $1.00.

No. 27. Silver plated, 75c.

No. 28. Silver plated, 85c.

No. 29. Silver plated, $1.00.

No. 30. Silver plated, $1.00

No. 32. Silver plated, $1.00

No. 33. Silver plated, $1.00.

No. 34. Silver plated, 75c.

No. 35. Silver plated, 85c.

No. 36. Silver plated, 90c.

No. 37. Silver plated, 80c.

No. 38. Silver plated, 90c.

No. 39. Gilt and Enameled, $1.50.

ITEMS FROM No. 23 TO No. 39 ON THIS PAGE ARE MADE TO ORDER, AND ABOUT ONE WEEK'S TIME WILL BE NECESSARY TO GET THESE FROM THE FACTORY. MANY OTHER STYLES OF ORNAMENTS AND MILITARY MADE TO ORDER.

**No. 6**

**No. 6. Spanish Navy Sailor's Medal,** with ribbon, bar and pin fastening, crown, cross and anchor. Light white metal. Price, $3.95.

**No. 2**

**No. 2. Spanish War Medal** for presentation to soldiers for bravery in the Cuban campaign. Complete with colored ribbon and safety bar pin fastening. Purchased in Cuba in 1898. Price, $6.00.

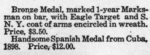

**No. 4**

**No. 4. Spanish Artillery Soldiers' Rosette.** Crimped silk, with artillery button. Worn on side of soldier's hat. From Cuba, 1898. Price, 50c.

Bronze Medal, marked 1-year Marksman on bar, with Eagle Target and S. N. Y. coat of arms encircled in wreath. Price, $3.50.

Handsome Spanish Medal from Cuba, 1898. Price, $12.00.

**No. 3**

**No. 3. Spanish War Medal** made of heavy white metal. Illustration is from photograph. Complete, with silk ribbon with bar and safety pin. From Cuba, 1898. Price, $6.50.

**No. 5**

**No. 5. Spanish Medal, from Cuba, 1898,** marked for presentation to soldiers who served in war against Carlists, 1873-1874. Silk ribbon with bar and safety pin fastening. $6.50.

**No. 17**

Miniature British Army Medals. Many soldiers wear these small light weight German silver medals in preference to the larger, heavier silver medals given by the British War Department.

No. 17 is for service 1901-1902 in South Africa. Complete with ribbon and bars. Price, $3.85.

**No. 18**

**No. 18. Long service and good conduct medal** with ribbon. Pric, $3.25.

**No. 8. Polished Brass Belt Buckle;** with British coat-of-arms; complete, with loops for attaching to belt. Handsome buckle for lady's belt. New; complete. Price, $1.00.

**No. 11. British Soldier's Helmet Plate;** brass, with British motto; size 4 by 4¾ inches. Price, 50 cents each.

**POLISH SOCIETY WAIST BELT BUCKLE.** Red background, with polished brass border, with Polish Eagle in center; complete with fastening loop. Price, 50 cents.

**No. 12. London Policeman's Metal Helmet Plate,** as worn by the Bobbies in the great metropolitan city; brass; dark-colored finish; lettered as per illustration; size 3½ by 4½ in.; 65 cents. Price, without the letters, 50 cents each.

**MEDICAL OFFICER'S INSIGNIA.** Nickel plated Maltese cross, with screw nut fastening. Price, 35 cts.

**10708. ARMY SOLDIER'S BELT BUCKLE.** Found in Germany, 1910, sold after the close of the Civil War with captured stores or left over from Blockade Runner Steamer cargo. Brass buckles with single star was adopted by the Confederate soldiers in Texas regiments. Size 2½ by 2⅜ inches. Price, 55 cents each.

U. S. Marine's Brass Cartridge Belt Buckles, with World Eagle and anchor ornament. Relics from cartridge belts that have been worn in Spanish and Chinese wars. Complete with fastenings. Price $1.00.

**No. 15. Lapel Shield** made for U. S. Volunteer War Veterans, in hard finished colored enamel, red, white and blue. Beautiful emblems. Price 15 cents each, mailed.

**No. 15**

**No. 12**

**No. 12. Confederate Veteran's Lapel Button** Colored enamel finish. Fac-simile Gen. Lee's Battle Flag. Price, 45c, mailed.

**No. 10. Sharpshooter's Lapel Badge,** 35 cents.

**No. 11. Sharpshooter's Lapel Target Badge.** Price, 35 cents.

**Sharpshooter's Bar and Badge,** 45 cents.

**No. 13. Sharpshooter's Lapel Target Emblem.** Price, 35 cents.

We can furnish British War Department Medal, Silk ribbons, one inch long for 50 cents for the following medals: Crimea, Canada 1866, Zulu, South Africa, 1878-1880; ribbon for medal given by Turkey to British in Crimea; Afghanistan, 1878-1880; Indian Mutiny, India, 1895; Burmah and Persia, 1885; (Queens), Egypt, 1884-1886; Khedieves, Egypt, 1898; Kings, South African, 1901-1902; Khedieves Bronze Star, 1882-1886; Queens, South Africa, 1899-1902; Coomasie Star, Chinese Medal of 1900, Queens, Egypt, 1898.

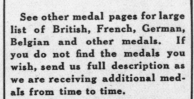

**No. 8**          **No. 9**

See other medal pages for large list of British, French, German, Belgian and other medals. If you do not find the medals you wish, send us full description as we are receiving additional medals from time to time.

**No. 19. German Soldier's Breast Plate Ornament;** polished brass, gilt finished; size 2¾x1⅞ in. 65c.

**Marksman's Bar. Price, 25 cents.**

**0-1052. SHIELDS IN RED, YELLOW AND BLUE CENTRE**, and rimmed with letters "B. F. C. E₁." Size 11x9½ inches. Reinforced hole for hanging. Price, 75 cents each.

**1090A. U. S. CROSS-GUN CAP ORNAMENTS.** Gilt finished, with screw nut fastening. Used on State militia caps. Some have figures and letters attached. We offer "as are"; no selection. second-hand order. Price, 10 cents each.

**1090B COMMISSARY CAP WREATH.** Gilt finished wreath, 2⅝ inches wide, with nickle-plated crescent moon centre, screw nut fastening. Have been used. second-hand, serviceable order. Price, 22 cents each.

**1090C. SIGNAL CORPS CAP WREATHS.** In used, serviceable order, with screw nut fastening. Price, 22 cents each.

**1090D. ELECTICIAN'S CAP WREATH.** Gilt finished, with 2⅝ inches, with nickle-finished electric rays centre, screw nut fastening. Used. Price, 22 cents each.

**10,000 OVAL-SHAPED CARTRIDGE BOXES**, holding 20 rounds of 43 calibre German Mauser or Spanish Remington or Springfield Ball Cartridges. Large, detachable loops for carrying on broad web or leather waist belts; also with brass buckle for use when worn on the dress cross belt. Boxes were made for German army. Used a short time; are in fine, serviceable order. Price, 40 cents each; 500 in russet leather, 50 cents each.

**7115. CADET OVAL-SHAPED CARTRIDGE BOXES**, holding 15 German Mauser cartridges 11 M/M. Black leather; practically new. Shaped to fit against body, with loops for attaching to the waist belt, also with brass buckle for attaching to cross belts for dress equipment. Neat boxes for the use of cadets. Size 6½x3½x 1½ inches. Leather is hand-sewed, weight 6½ ounces. Price, 40 cents each.

**10202A. U. S. MARINE CORPS SCARF PIN.** World, eagle, and anchor emblem in relief, gilt finish. Price, 50 cents.

**STEEL DOG COLLARS.** New. Finely nickeled, with name plate in adjustable medium sizes. Price, 95 cents each.

**0-1087. NAPOLEON BONAPARTE OFFICER'S BRASS GILT BUCKLE.** The first model, ROOSTER with outstretched wings standing on battle axe fasces, marked "Republique Française" in relief with raised border. Size 2¼ inches, as illustrated. Rare buckle even in France. Price, $10.00.

**0-1090. EMPEROR NAPOLEON WAR EAGLE BRASS BELT BUCKLE.** The eagle (with head facing the arrows) resting on fasces. Size 2½ inches. Relic. Price, $5.00.

**0-1088. FRENCH CADET OFFICER'S BRASS BELT BUCKLE.** Eagle with outstretched wings, the word "College" on top and in scroll, "D Estaires" in scroll at the bottom. Size 2¼ inches. Price, $5.00.

**0-1090E. LAPEL RANK BADGES.** Shoulder straps in miniature for use on outer garments or on lapel, fac-simile in gilt metal with Blue colored background. Large assortment job lot from assignee's sale. Bargain price, 30 cents each.

**6920. BRITISH OFFICER'S ANCIENT DISPATCH BOX.** With shoulder belt ornamented with gilt bronze plates, showing battle engagements (Java, Mahipoer, Nagpore), with socket plate for the metal ends of the breast cord, star with three cannon on the cover of the leather box, wood block with six holes. From the Caton Woodville collection. Price, $7.95.

**6920A. RUSSIAN OFFICER'S DISPATCH BOX.** With leather shoulder belt, ornamented with gilt bronze, with hand holding shield, with letters "F. I.," double headed Russian eagle on the cover, with sword, mace, flag and cannon balls on the ornamented gilt plate. From the Caton Woodville sale. Price, $7.85.

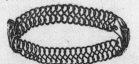

**0-1089. EMPEROR NAPOLEON SOLDIER'S WAR EAGLE HELMET PLATE.** With arrows bomb, crown and cross.

**10291. U. S. RUSSET LEATHER SABRE KNOT.** With leather tassel and brass stud for attaching to sabre or sword; in used serviceable order, full length 18 inches, weight two ounces. Price 25 cents.

**0-1183. U. S. COAT OF ARMS CAP BADGE.** Bent for to conform to the shape of the new regulation cap, with screw nut fastening. Price, 40 cents.

**0-1084A. U. S. COAT OF ARMS.** With screw nut fastening. Fine gilt finished. Made of heavy metal, extra fine quality, well finished. Price, 50 cents each.

**0-749 REAR ADMIRAL'S CIVIL WAR FLAGSHIP CANDLE-STICK.** Engraved with Rear Admiral's MONOGRAM U. S. N., 5¾ inch base, removable ornamental drip, quad-ruple pattern candle-stick used Civil War to Rear Admirals. May have been used by of the famous Admirals of the

**5920B. ANCIENT OFFICER'S DISPATCH BOX.** With shoulder sling, brass ornamented, with crown, shield, flags, cannon, etc. From the Caton Woodville sale. Price, $7.85.

**7121. U. S. MARINE CORPS WHITE BUFF LEATHER COLOR SLING AND FLAG CARRIER.** These have the single shoulder sling with 1⅞ inch wide sling with heavy brass buckle. Price $1.85 each.

**7121A. U. S. ARMY SLING FLAG CARRIER**, with wide black leather belt with brass buckle, with brass socket for end of flag pole. Price $1.25 each.

**U. S. A. INTRENCHING STEEL SPADE**, carried as part of soldier's equipment. Width, 7 in., length, 8¾ in., without handle. Price, 25 cents.

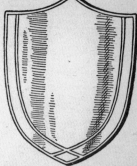

**0-1218. LODGE SHIELD.** Made of bright tin. Length 18x12½ inches, with moulded edges, as illustrated. Suitable for panoply decoration. Price, 68 cents.

**0-1058. WHITE METAL SHIELD BADGE.** Ornamented frame with diagonal cross bars. Size ¾ inch with fastening wire and loop on the back. Price, 12 cents.

**0-1046. METAL FLUTE.** Nickle-plated, length 15 inches, five holes. Price, $1.50.

**0-1047. METAL FLUTE.** Nickle-plated, inlaid with ebony wood mouthpiece, screw end piece, 14½ inches long. New. Price, $1.50.

TWO STARS and 10¼ inches high, with ruple silver plated. This furnished prior to and during the commanding flagships. Weight 2¾ pounds. Farragut, Porter, Dupont, or some Civil War. Price, $30.00.

**10033.** Sold. See other pages in this catalog for dunnage bags, haversacks and knapsacks. We have also various wide black leather slings for pack carrying.

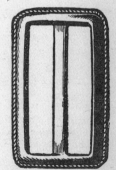

**0-1206C. WHITE WEB CADET WAIST BELTS.** With brass eagle or plain polished belt plate. Price, 50 cents.

**0-1140. EUROPEAN SIGNAL HORN.** Fine colored ox horn, 2¾ inches wide at the base, 12½ inches in length, German silver mouthpiece, which unscrews for cleaning the mechanism. Price, $3.75.

**0-1059. WHITE METAL BADGE FIVE-POINTED STAR, WITH OPEN HAND WITH HEART IN THE CENTRE.** With loop for ribbon. Size ¾ inch. Price, 15 cents.

**10141. U. S. A. JAPANNED METAL BELT SLIDE.** New, for 3-inch belts, imitation leather finish, weight 2 oz., 900 in stock. Price, 10 cents each, $1.00 per doz.

**10109. "IMPERIAL GENDARMERIE SURETE PUBLIQUE" BRASS BELT BUCKLE.** With French eagle stamped on the belt plate. Price $3.50.

INFANTRY.

ORDNANCE DEPT.

CAVALRY.

2D LIEUT. SHOULDER STRAP.

CAPTAIN SHOULDER STRAP

ARTILLERY.

(SUBSISTENCE) DEPT.

INSPECTOR-GENERAL'S DEPT.

MAJOR SHOULDER STRAP.

GENERAL SHOULDER STRAP.

JUDGE ADVOCATE-GENERAL'S DEPARTMENT.

ENGINEER'S DEPT.

SIGNAL CORPS.

OFFICER'S AIGUILLETTE.

U. S. NAVY OFFICER'S CAP ORNAMENT.

QUARTERMASTER-GENERAL'S DEPT.

PAY DEPT.

ADJT.-GENERAL'S DEPT.

MEDICAL DEPT.

POMPONS.

NAVAL WARRANT OFFICER.

U.S.N. SAILOR CORD KNOT EMBLEM.

HELMET CORD.

U.S.

FINE GILT OFFICER'S HAT CORD.

GILT OFFICER'S HAT CORD.

CORPS BADGE.

PRIVATE'S AIGUILLETTE.

German Soldiers' Helmet Plate. 75c. each.

European Army Helmet Plate.

CORPS BADGE.

We show on this page various ornaments and insignia, which are found with prices in other pages. A few of the articles are priced here, but these prices are for PLAIN ornaments, NOT embroidered or in embroidered finish.

We can make up to order the embroidered insignia, also cap and collar ornaments with different letters and figures, as used by private military companies, and by cadet academies and companies. Submit your sketch with the number of ornaments desired and we will quote prices and time of delivery.

On other pages in the catalog we list various foreign cap and helmet ornaments also medals. We have books showing uniforms of foreign countries before the World War, and if interested we shall be pleased to give you particulars and prices.

ARMY SOLDIERS' AIGUILLETTES, with tassels in red colored braid, finest quality, 40c each; new.

POMPONS, good, second-hand, 15c. each.

U. S. N. SAILORS' WHITE CORD KNOTS, 40c each; on blue cloth.

ARTILLERY HELMET CORDS, 20c each.

NAVAL WARRANT OFFICERS' ANCHOR and U S. N. CAP ORNAMENT, 75c.

CHEVRONS—Farriers; Apothecary's; Hospital; Artillery; Cavalry; Infantry. First Sergeant, 60c; Sergeant, 50c; Corporal, 35c.

SPANISH BRASS SEAL, half-inch thick, 3x5 inches, with letters "El Cejesta Imperia a Espanol Cuba," $5.00.

OFFICERS' SASH, crimson color, worsted; 6 feet long with tassels; new goods; $7.00.

CIVIL WAR EPAULETTE, new goods, left over since 1865. Assorted colors for different branches of service; 50c per pair.

GERMAN CUIRASSIERS' METAL HELMET PLATE with letters: "For God, King and Fatherland," 75c; size, 4½x 5 inches.

EUROPEAN ARMY BRASS HELMET PLATE with crown and wreath, star shaped, 75c each.

U. S. NAVY SMALL ARMS INSTRUCTIONS, 1907. Pocket size, 6x4 inches. 513 pages, fully illustrated. Flexible leather covers, with envelope flap. Contains everything that man should know about warships and guns to become a first-class man-o'-warsman. Military Drill, Target Practice, Landing-Force, Artillery Drill, First Aid to Wounded, Scouting, Camping, Etc., Etc. Valuable book to every outdoors man. Published at Naval Institute, Annapolis, Md., under direction of Navy Department. Price, 50 cents.

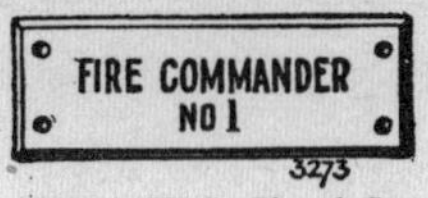

3273

**3273.** U. S. Signal Service, metal plate, nickeled, size 1 by 3 inches. Fire Commander No. 1, price 20c; similar plates marked "Headquarters," 25c; "S. W., B. D. Room" plates, 12c; "B. Intel" plates, 12c.

**3321.** Ohio Militia Brass Belt Plates used by Ohio Volunteers, sold after the Spanish War. Size 3⅛, 2¾. Weight 4 ounces. Price 30c.

U. S. Coat of Arms, collar size, gilt finished with pin fastenings. Size 1¼ by 1 inch. Price 25c.

King Edward VII Embroidered Crown, cloth background for use on military uniform. Size 1¾ inches. Price 35c.

Queen Victoria's Embroidered Crown, 1½ inches. Price 35c.

Embroidered Stars, 15c each.

3191. U. S. A. Cap Ornaments. Artillery Cross Cannons, with letters U. S. gilt finished, with safety pin fastenings. Length 1¾ inch. Price 15c.

3192. U. S. A. Cavalry Ornaments, Crossed Sabers with letters U. S., safety pin fastening, gilt finished. Price 15c.

3193. U. S. A. Infantry Crossed Rifle Cap Ornaments with letters U. S., safety pin fastenings, gilt finished. Price 15c.

3083

**3083.** Bank of England copper half penny button used on uniform coats of Bank Employeees, ⅞ inch diameter. Price 50c. Vest size ⅝ of an inch diameter, 30c.

3016

3016. Southern Soldier's Army Button, made in England during the Civil War, sent to South by Blockade Running Steamer in exchange for cotton. C. S. A. stamped on face, and on the back "superior quality." Illustration is fu.. size. Found in Bermuda, West Indies, (Blockade Running Headquarters). Price 20c each, $2.00 per dozen.

3194. Gilt Wreath with letters Q. M. D. (Quarter Master's Department), with safety pin fastening. Gilt finished. Price 15c.

3194a. Gilt Wreath Cap Ornaments, with nickeled cross flags with torch (emblem of U. S. Signal Corps with safety pin fastenings. Price 15c.

3002a. West Point Military Academy Cadet Uniform. coat Button worn by the graduating class; coat. Price 15c.

3043. Queen Victoria's medal star, with ribbon. Presented by the Queen to British Soldiers for service in the Ashantee War, 1896. On the reverse side, "From the Queen." The Queen was much affected by this small war for in it her son-in-law the Prince of Battenburg lost his life, $6.58.

5044

**3044. Bronze Star War Medal,** Crown, with ring and ribbon engraved (Kabul to Kandahar 1880), Commemorating one of the hardest marches in the British Service. An Irish Soldier gave vent to the feelings of the exhausted men by starting to sing, "Wait for the wagon and we will all have a ride." The commanding officer deemed the song at such a time as tending to mutiny, and at the end of the march poor Pat enjoyed bread and water in close confinement for a week. Price, $7.50.

3196

3196. New York City Coat of Arms Ornament, brass face, lead back, used on N. Y. Mounted Police Horse Equipments. Shield with 4 windmill sails, between the ends two beavers. Emblem of the Fur Trade, with two flour barrels each side sails and barrels. Emblem of the milling industry. Monopoly of 1678.

Crest, a Bald Eagle rising from a half globe.

Supporters, on the right Sailor in the dress of 1700 holding a sounding line. On the left side an Indian Chief with stringed bow. Size 3½ by 4 inches. Price 50c. Smaller size, 1¼ by 4 inches. Price 25c.

3358. Polished bronze relief figure of St. George and the Dragon. "England's Patron Saint." Size 7 inches, weight 1½ pounds. Price $2.50.

5037

5036. British Army Officer's gold plated Belt Buckle, ornamented with Lion Head with snake loop fastening. Sold.

3365. French Silver Medal, Emperor Napoleon III, Expeditione de Chine, 1860, engraved Takou, Chang Kia Wan Pali, Kiao Peking. Size 1¼ inches, weighs ⅜ of an ounce, no ring or ribbon. Price $8.50.

5037. British Army Officer's Dress Buckle, gold plated, with Lion and Crown in silvered metal. Loops for 1⅜ inch waist belt. Handsome buckle. Price $2.25.

5036b. British Army Officer's gilt and silvered buckle, clasp fastenings. Lion surmounting Queen Victoria's Crown. Price $2.00.

Sctoch Thistle, flower and leaf ornament, size 1¼ inches, nickeled metal, with fastenings. Price 45c.

British Lancers Emblem, embroidered cross lances with flags. Price 25c.

British Cavalry Emblem embroidered Bit. Size 1½ inch. Price 35c.

Embroidered Spur with cross whips. British Army Insignia. Price 30c.

Embroidered Crossed Sabres British Army Service. Size 2¾ inches. Price 35c.

Cross Cannon Artillery Emblem, embroidered, 2¼ inch. Price 35c.

Infantry Insignia, Crossed Rifles, British Army Service. Price 25c.

Embroidered Cannon. Price 50c.

Embroidered Drum. Price 40c.

Embroidered Wreath British Army, 2¼ inches. Price 18c.

BOOK ON RIBBONS AND MEDALS. Compiled by Commander H. Taprell Dorling, R. N. (British Royal Navy). Contains 177 pages showing 133 ribbons in COLORS of the BRITISH EMPIRE, with the different medals and foreign orders. Also 84 ribbons in COLORS for both British and foreign countries before the World War, with description of the medals and decorations with which they were used.

Part 3 shown 14 WORLD WAR RIBBONS IN COLOR, of various branches of the British service, also France and Greece. The British and foreign medals as issued to participants in the World War are illustrated and described. This book will be of great value to any veteran or collectors of medals. Price, $2.50 each.

Ordnance Corp Insignia Bursting Shell in flames in brass metal, 1½ inch. Price 30c.

5036a. British Artillery Officer's gold plated Belt Buckle, with snake link fastening with Artillery Motto, "Ubique," "Having served in all lands." British Lion surmounting Crown.

Embroidered Lozenge shaped Insignia, British Service. Price 12c.

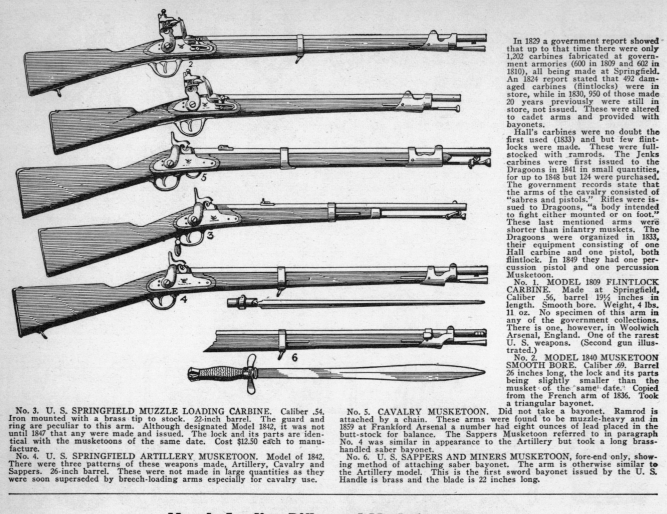

In 1829 a government report showed that up to that time there were only 1,202 carbines fabricated at government armories (600 in 1809 and 602 in 1810), all being made at Springfield. An 1824 report stated that 492 damaged carbines (flintlocks) were in store, while in 1830, 950 of those made 20 years previously were still in store, not issued. These were altered to cadet arms and provided with bayonets.

Hall's carbines were no doubt the first used (1833) and but few flintlocks were made. These were full-stocked with ramrods. The Jenks carbines were first issued to the Dragoons in 1841 in small quantities, for up to 1848 but 124 were purchased. The government records state that the arms of the cavalry consisted of "sabres and pistols." Rifles were issued to Dragoons, "a body intended to fight either mounted or on foot." These last mentioned arms were shorter than infantry muskets. The Dragoons were organized in 1833, their equipment consisting of one Hall carbine and one pistol, both flintlock. In 1849 they had one percussion pistol and one percussion Musketoon.

No. 1. MODEL 1809 FLINTLOCK CARBINE. Made at Springfield, Caliber .56, barrel 19½ inches in length. Smooth bore. Weight, 4 lbs. 11 oz. No specimen of this arm in any of the government collections. There is one, however, in Woolwich Arsenal, England. One of the rarest U. S. weapons. (Second gun illustrated.)

No. 2. MODEL 1840 MUSKETOON SMOOTH BORE. Caliber .69. Barrel 26 inches long, the lock and its parts being slightly smaller than the musket of the same date. Copied from the French arm of 1836. Took a triangular bayonet.

No. 3. U. S. SPRINGFIELD MUZZLE LOADING CARBINE. Caliber .54. Iron mounted with a brass tip to stock. 22-inch barrel. The guard and ring are peculiar to this arm. Although designated Model 1842, it was not until 1847 that any were made and issued. The lock and its parts are identical with the musketoons of the same date. Cost $12.50 each to manufacture.

No. 4. U. S. SPRINGFIELD ARTILLERY MUSKETOON. Model of 1842. There were three patterns of these weapons made, Artillery, Cavalry and Sappers. 26-inch barrel. These were not made in large quantities as they were soon superseded by breech-loading arms especially for cavalry use.

No. 5. CAVALRY MUSKETOON. Did not take a bayonet. Ramrod is attached by a chain. These arms were found to be muzzle-heavy and in 1859 at Frankford Arsenal a number had eight ounces of lead placed in the butt-stock for balance. The Sappers Musketoon referred to in paragraph No. 4 was similar in appearance to the Artillery but took a long brass-handled saber bayonet.

No. 6. U. S. SAPPERS AND MINERS MUSKETOON, fore-end only, showing method of attaching saber bayonet. The arm is otherwise similar to the Artillery model. This is the first sword bayonet issued by the U. S. Handle is brass and the blade is 22 inches long.

## Muzzle Loading Rifles and Muskets—Continued

No. 4. U. S. FLINTLOCK RIFLE. Model of 1819. Caliber .54. Barrel is 36 inches in length and the arm weighed 10¼ pounds. Made by contract principally at Middletown, Conn., and a few at Philadelphia by Deringer. Officially known as the "Common Rifle." The pattern rifles were made at Springfield. The guard and rear swivel are peculiar to this model. No bayonets provided. Reuben Ellis of New York obtained a contract to convert a number of these rifles to magazine (?) arms, by having the lock and its parts slide along a groove upon which were fastened four touch holes. The idea was to load the gun with four charges and by moving the lock rearward, fire each separately.

No. 5. U. S. FLINTLOCK MUSKET. Model 1822. Caliber .69. This is the most familiar of all flintlocks. Made in great quantities until 1840 with slight changes. Made by contract and at Springfield and Harper's Ferry. The shape of the butt-stock is peculiar to this arm. Complete weight 10 pounds with bayonet 16 inches long. In the 50's many of these were altered to percussion locks. At the outbreak of the Civil War, there not being enough of Model '55 to go around, some militia regiments were equipped with these .69 caliber altered weapons, and in several cases mutinies occurred as the soldiers refused to accept them. The last model flintlock is dated 1840, these being very similar to the 1822 type. The changes were of minor character, one being the butt-stock being given a comb at the top. This change and several others, however, took place prior to 1840. The manufacture of flintlocks was stopped in the spring of 1844.

No. 6. U. S. RIFLE. Model of 1841. Known as the Mississippi or Yager rifle. Caliber .54. Made at Harper's Ferry and Springfield Armories and by contract until 1855. When first made no provision was made for bayonets but later (1855) a long saber bayonet that carried its own attachment was provided. Many of these weapons were converted to breech-loaders in Civil War days, some of the Merrill system and still others by the Lindner. As the troops from Mississippi were the first to be equipped with the Model of 1841 they were given that name. The patch box cover and bands are brass.

No. 7. U. S. PERCUSSION MUSKET. Model of 1841. First issued at the front during the Mexican War and, it is claimed, the soldiers preferred the old flintlocks. Made at government armories and by contract. Caliber .69. About 1852 many of these muskets were rifled after a plan by Col. Minie of France, thus becoming the U. S. Minie rifle, caliber .69. A long range rear sight was added. The bayonets for these muskets were the first to have a clasp for better attachment to the barrel. Many used in the early days of the Civil War.

No. 8. U. S. MODEL 1855, MAYNARD PRIMER, MUSKET. Caliber .58. The priming magazine on this rifle was the invention of Dr. Edward Maynard of Washington. It was first experimented with on converted flintlocks as early as 1845 and finally adopted by order of Secretary of War Jefferson Davis in 1855, and condemned in 1860. The Maynard primer was a waterproof tape enveloping patches of fulminate placed at intervals throughout its length. This tape was coiled and placed in a round cavity in the lock plate, a hinged gate covering it. An arm from the hammer pushed the tape along, step by step, causing a patch of fulminate to project over the nipple. The end of the hammer had a sharp edge which came down close to the mouth of the primer cavity and cut off the tape beyond. Ordinary caps could also be used on the gun. Great difficulty was experienced in keeping the tapes dry, they becoming useless if allowed to become damp. Many used from 1861-1865.

No. 9. U. S. MODEL 1855 RIFLE. Same lock as the musket but shorter barrel and fitted for a long saber bayonet. Weight, with bayonet, 13 pounds. Principally made at Harper's Ferry Armory.

No. 10. U. S. MODEL 1861 MUSKET. The principal weapon of the Civil War. Caliber .58. The lock plate and hammer are identical with the Model '55 with the Maynard magazine eliminated. The U. S. fabricated 801,997 and purchased 670,617 of these during the years '61, '62, '63 and '64. Many firms accepted contracts for these and had to build a factory to make them in. It was late in 1862 before deliveries from contractors began in satisfactory quantities. It is of interest at this time to know that some were made in Germany. After the battle of Gettysburg 27,574 muskets were sent to Washington Arsenal. Of these 24,000 were loaded, 6,000 one load each, 12,000 two loads each, 6,000 had three to ten loads, and one had 23 loads.

No. 11. ENGLISH ENFIELD MUSKET. Caliber .577. Model of 1853. Used by both sides during the Civil War. The federal government purchased 428,000 in the early days of the struggle and the South received 400,000 during 1861-1862. An interesting detail of this transaction was that they were purchased by cotton certificates, no cash being available. These certificates represented cotton in the South. English contractors had to remove it at their own risk. In this connection some figures on Civil War arms may be of interest.

The U. S. Government purchased (1861-65), exclusive of those made at Springfield, 1,912,360 muskets and rifles, 407,923 carbines and 373,971 pistols and revolvers. This represents 69 different makes of weapons, the majority of which required special cartridges. Up to June 30, 1862, there were purchased abroad 726,705 muskets and 28,364 carbines and pistols. These varied in caliber from .54 to .72.

No. 12. U. S. SPRINGFIELD RIFLED MUSKET. Model of 1863. This rifle shows some changes from the Model 1861. The hammer, nipple-lugbands, ramrod were improved in design. The caliber remained the same, .58. In 1864 another model was brought out very much like the 1863. About the only change was the revival of the band springs and a slight change in the design of the bands. During 1864 Springfield Armory produced 276,200 arms. This was the greatest year's work there. The muskets averaged $10.69 each in cost. This is the last muzzle loader made by the government.

No. 13. U. S. "WHITNEYVILLE" NAVY RIFLE. Caliber .69. Known as the "Plymouth" rifle. Made by the Whitney Armory near New Haven, Conn. 10,000 of these were delivered to the Navy late in '63. They were intended to use the famous Dahlgren knife bayonet. This weapon had a 12-inch blade and weighed 2½ pounds. It is worthy of note that this arm was .69 caliber instead of the regulation (since 1855) .58 caliber. Remington also made a muzzle-loading rifle this year which was practically a copy of the Model 1855 Harper's Ferry (No. 9).

Our stock of Navy Rating Badges contains an assortment of blue and white badges, mostly old regulation. We offer these without regard to rank, for use in making pillow tops or for arm decoration. Price is 50 cents each, our selection. Prices on new badges for service quoted on application.

GILT EMBROIDERED SHOULDER STRAPS; new; made to order, of good quality gilt wire, by professional expert.

In ordering, state the color background desired.

200 GROSS U. S. ARMY BRASS BUTTONS, with brass backs, late regulation, in coat and sleeve sizes, loose, at special price of 25 cents per dozen; $1.50 per gross.

Major-General.

Brigadier-General.

Colonel.

Lieutenant-Colonel and Major.

Captain.

First Lieutenant.

OFFICERS SHOULDER STRAPS, stamped gilt metal border with any colored cloth center as may be desired. Second lieutenant, price, 50 cents a pair. All other ranks, 60 cents a pair. These shoulder straps are fac-simile of the gilt embroidered and will give good wear, retaiuing their gilt color longer than the expensive hand embroidered.

Second Lieutenant.

Collection of Relic Belt Buckles, Helmet and Shako Ornaments, worn by Soldiers in American, British and German service. Some very rare pieces, as will be seen by illustration, which is from photograph. **Price for the lot mounted on board, $45.00.**

No. 1769 Brass Belt Hooks. 7c. each, 75c. dozen.

No. 1786 Brass Belt Loop. 6c. each, 60c. dozen.

No. 1828 Belt Slide, 2½ inch. 15c. each, $1.50 doz.

No. 1795 Brass Hook for Canteens or Haversack Straps. 7c. ach, 75c. dozen.

No. 1800 10c. each, $1.00 dozen.

No. 359 Ring Plate, brass. 7c. each, 75c. dozen.

Collection of 81 Relic Belt Buckles used by soldiers in many wars. Mounted on board. Bargain price, $60.00.

Spanish Relics. Bugle ornaments. Price, 15c each.

Brass cross guns with loop fastenings, 10 cts. each. $1.00 dozen.

1 Buckle, West Yorkshire Regiment, with tiger. Price, $1.50.

Eagle Button made of dark hard for Army soldiers. Saving labor cleaning, dark color, avoiding target to enemy. Price, 5 cents each.

GILT BRASS BUTTONS with lyre, for musicians' uniforms, in coat size, 8 cts. each, 60 cts. per doz.; vest size, 35 cts. per doz., 5 cts. each.

Cross Cannon, Bugles and Sabres, Cap ornaments, late regulation. Brass, with loop, 10 cents each. $1.00 dozen.

Spanish Soldier's Belt Plate, First Regiment, $1.50.

12 British Army Bugle ornaments for helmet; size, 2x2½ inches. Price, 20c.

U. S. Marine Corps Belt Buckle; brass, with world, eagle, anchor emblem in center; kind worn on belts of Dewey's marines at Manila Bay. Price, 45c. each.

U. S. ARMY BRONZE BUTTONS, with coat of arms, overcoat size, price, 10 cts. each, 75 cts. per doz. Dress coat or blouse size, 8 cts. each, 60 cts. per doz. Vest size, 35 cts. per doz.

BUTTON BARS AND RINGS for attaching button to summer uniform. Easily detached for laundrying. Price, 3 cents each, 25 cents dozen.

No. 12. Gilt saber scarf pins, cross rifles and cannon. All new, gilt finished. These are made to order, and can be obtained when ordered with other goods. Price, 30 cents each.

Polished Brass Cap Ornaments, with the screw-nut fastening, for any branch of the service, 15c each; $1.75 per dozen.

1875. OFFICER'S GILT SHOULDER KNOTS, white background with brass fastener with embroidered rank bars. Rank of Captain and Lieutenant. Used only a short time. Offered in good serviceable order. Price, $2.85 pair.

Firemen's Belt Buckles, white metal, with letters F. D. in centre, 85 cents each.

It seems to be conceded that Scotland raises more and better engineers than any other land. There is a story of an American sea captain who made a wager that he would go on board any steamer, English, Chinese or Japanese, in the harbor of Hongkong, call down to the engine room, "Are you there, Mac?" and get an affirmative answer. He won his bet.

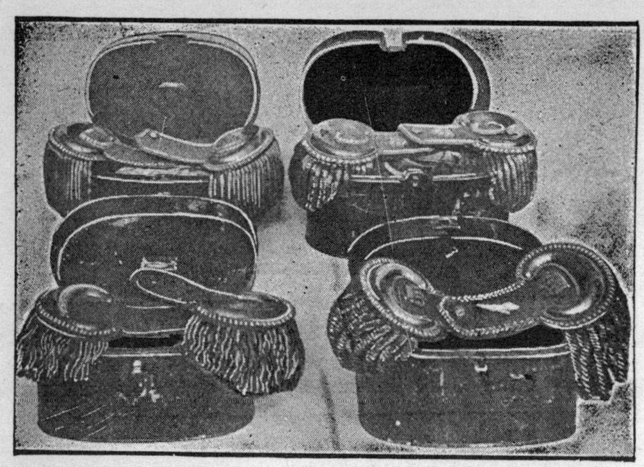

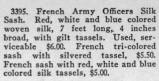

3395. French Army Officers Silk Sash. Red, white and blue colored woven silk, 7 feet long, 4 inches broad, with gilt tassels. Used, serviceable $6.00. French tri-colored sash with silvered tassel, $5.50. French sash with red, white and blue colored silk tassels, $5.00.

4. Civil War Sabre Knot. New leather strap which is attached to the sabre, with loop to go over the soldier's wrist to prevent losing in action; has leather tassel which adds to the beauty of the sabre when used for decorating. Price 20 cents each; $2.00 dozen. Have 10,000.

U. S. Cavalry Late Regulation Saber Knot, ¾-inch black bridle leather, with brass stud for attaching to saber, with two leather keepers with tassel; good, second-hand, serviceable order. Price, 25 cents.

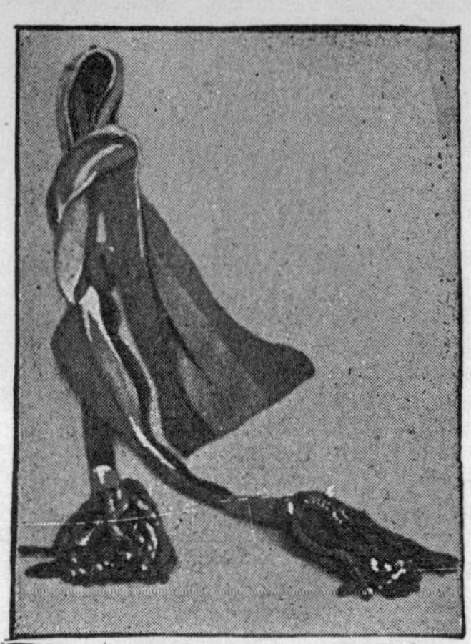

Military Officers Gilt Epaulette, with tin case, assorted patterns, in good second hand serviceable order. Price from $7.00 to $12.00 a pair.
Officers Gilt Epaulette in second hand serviceable order, much used. From $3.50 to $5.00 per pair.

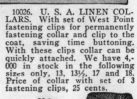

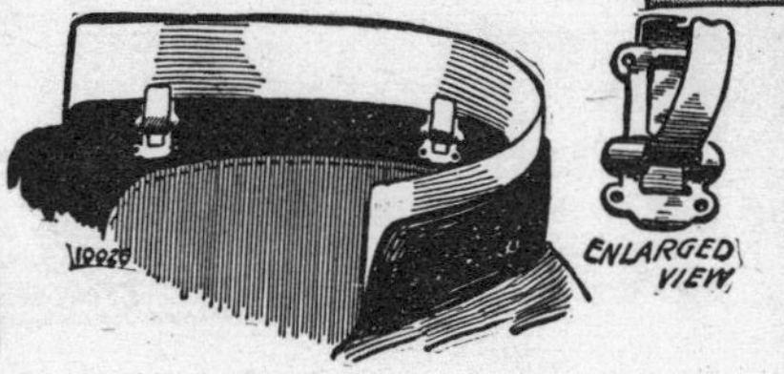
ENLARGED VIEW

10026. U. S. A. LINEN COLLARS. With set of West Point fastening clips for permanently fastening collar and clip to the coat, saving time buttoning. With these clips collar can be quickly attached. We have 4,000 in stock in the following sizes only, 13, 13½, 17 and 18. Price of collar with set of 3 fastening clips, 25 cents.

EXCELSIOR
NEW HAMPSHIRE
MASSACHUSETTS
INDIANA

New York. Massachusetts. New Hampshire. Ohio. Indiana.

MILITARY BUTTONS, 10 Cents Each.

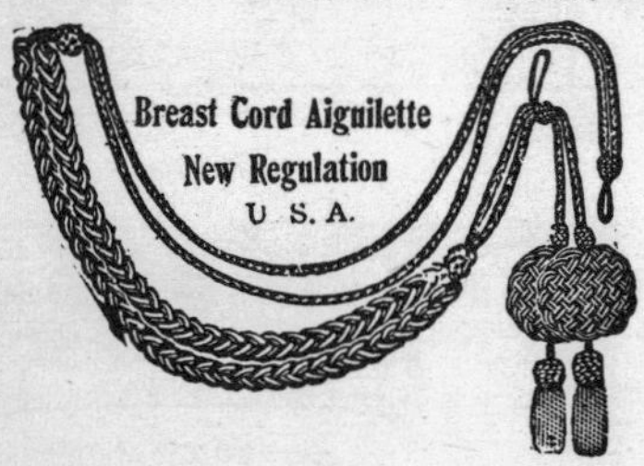
Breast Cord Aiguilette
New Regulation
U. S. A.

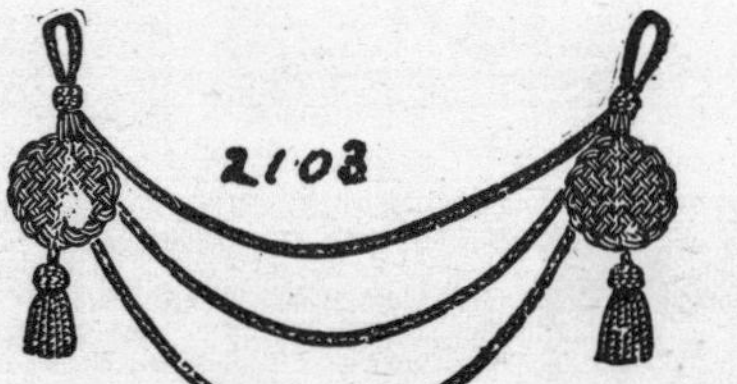
2103

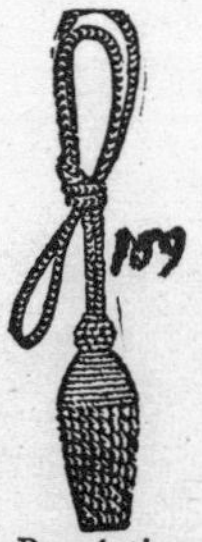
189

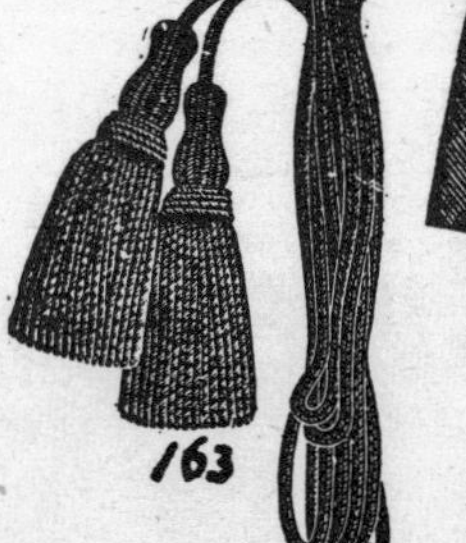
163

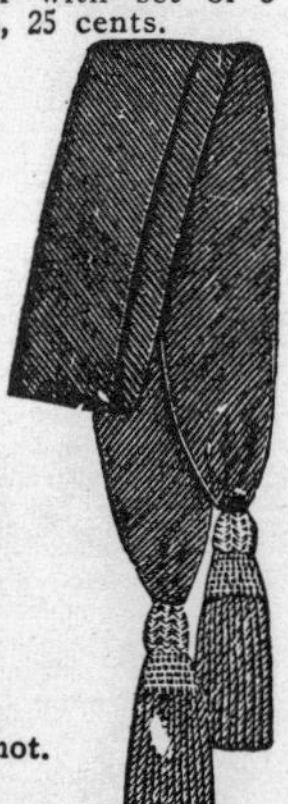

Army Officers Silk Waist Sash, with broad silk tassels, crimson color, 6 inches wide, 6 feet long, tassels 3¾ inches. Fine serviceable order. Price $7.50.

MILITARY BOOKS

3315. Description of Small Pox by Fisher, 13 illustrated colored plates. Published Boston, 1829, covers loose (complete), 73 pages. Size 13½-10½-⅝ inches. Price $1.45.

2103. Military Breast Cord (old regulation) with double tassels. Any desired color. Gives a neat dressy effect to any uniform. Price $1.15.

3319. Official Table of Distinces by Authority, Secretary of War for the guidance of U. S. Disbursing officers, 1881. 250 pages, size 9-6-1 inch. Price $1.25.

3302. Three volumes (Electrical Commission) Congressional Records, 44th Congress, 1887, size 11½ by 9½. 1⅜ inch thick. Price the set 3 volumes $3.00.

Regulation Russet leather sword knot. Price, 95 cents.

5042. Shoulder Sash Regulation Red colored, worn by British Army Non-Com. Officers, 3 inches wide, length 66 inches, 8 inch tassels. The material resembles silk and wool. Worn from the shoulder across breast. Gives a neat dressy appearance to any uniform. Price $1.85.

163. Military Worsted Hat Cords and tassels. Any desired color. Price 10c each.

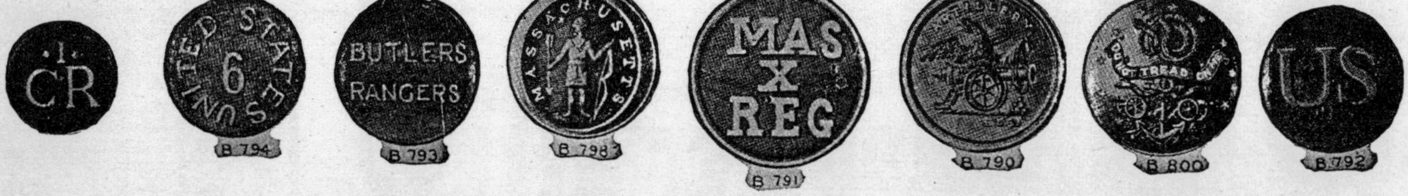
1
CR
B 794
UNITED STATES
6
B 793
BUTLERS
RANGERS
B 798
MASSACHUSETTS
MAS
X
REG
B 791
B 790
DONT TREAD
B 800
US
B 792

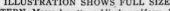

1776 to 1812 PERIOD RARE AND CURIOUS MILITARY BUTTONS ILLUSTRATION SHOWS FULL SIZE.

B 796. 1st Connecticut Regiment ancient pattern brass button. The oldest military organization in America. Price, $1.00.

B 794. BRASS BUTTON, kind worn on uniform of 6th U. S. Regiment. Price, $1.00.

B 793. BRASS BUTTON, kind worn on uniform of Butler's Rangers. Price, $1.00.

B791. Ancient Pattern 10th Mass. Regiment uniform button, Price $1.00.

B 798. OLD PATTERN Massachusetts soldier's uniform button. Price $1.00.

B 790. ANCIENT PATTERN U. S. ARTILLERY UNIFORM BUTTON. Price, $1.00.

B 800. One of the earliest pattern U. S. Artillery buttons, with rattlesnake and motto, "Don't tread on me." Price, $1.50.

B 792. Old pattern U. S. uniform button. Price, $1.00.

MILITARY BOOKS.

3045. U. S. Army Regulations, 1904, contains over 300 pages. Size 9 by 6, ¾ inch thick. Printed on fine quality paper. Cloth bound. Approved by Secretary of War, Wm. H. Taft, 1904. Price 75c.

3196. Manual Guard Duty, U. S. Army, Approved by War Department, 1898, pocket size, 78 pages, 450 in stock. Used serviceable. Spanish War Relics. Price 10c mailed.

3266. U. S. A. Judge Advocate's Digest of Opinions, revised 1901, leather bound, 876 pages, size 9½ by 7 inch. Valuable book for contractors and others doing Government business. Price $2.50.

3267. U. S. Army Field Regulations 1905, with amendments to 1907. 217 pages. Price 85c.

3268. Organization and Tactics, 4th edition. Wagner, U. S. A. 550 pages, cloth bound, 8¾ by 6¼ inches. Price $1.50.

3310. Decisions made by the Second Comptroller of the U. S. Treasury, 1865, relates to Civil War Contracts, Claims, Rates, Etc. Size 8½ by 5¾ by 1 inch. 279 Pages. Price $1.50.

3443. Electrical Engineers book (pocket) size Rules, Formulas, Tables, Data, Etc., by H. R. Kempe, London, with numerous illustrations, 1902. 300 pages. Size 5 by 3. Price 85c.

3325. Mercantile Navy List, 1871, Mayo, Cloth bound, 380 pages. 9½ by 6¾ by 1⅛ inches. Price 75c.

3444. The Storage Battery, Treadwell, 1902, illustrated, 257 pages, cloth covers, 7⅝ by 5¼. Price $1.00.

3445. Voltaic Cell, Park Benjamin. Its construction and capacity, 1893, illustrated, 562 pages. Price 85c.

3305. Velpeaus Operative Surgery, 3 volumes, size 9¼ by 6⅜ by 3 inches. Sheep bound, illustrated, from 850 to 1150 pages. Price for the 3 volumes $6.85.

3447. American Telegraph System Apparatus Operation. 563 pages, 450 illustrations. Wm. Maver, Jr., N. Y., 1898. Price $1.25.

3304. Six volumes of the American Chemist Journal of Theoretical Analytical Chemistry, 1870 to 1875. 478 pages each volume. Size 9¾ by 7¼ by 1⅜. The six volumes $5.00.

3448. Hand book of Practical Telegraphy, 8th edition, R. S. Culley, London, 1896, 442 pages, size 9 by 6, cloth bound, illustrated. Price $1.25.

3449. Hand Book of Electrical Testing, 6th edition, 1900, H. R. Kempe, London, 646 pages, illustrated. Size 8⅝ by 6. Price $1.50.

BOOK ON GERMAN MAUSER ARMY RIFLE

A twenty page booklet, profusely illustrated, on the most interesting and best known rifle of the war, "The German Mauser." A detailed description of the gun, showing its many attachments and thirty-eight bayonets. Price 45 cents.

3362. U. S. Navy Allowance Tables, 1880, showing the amount of Ordnance equipments and stores allowed for Navy War ships. Red cloth bound with Navy emblem, anchor and cross cannons. In gilt on cover, 33 pages, 9 by 6. Price 50c.

3320. N. Y. City Board of Health 5th and 6th Annual Reports 1874-75. Cloth bound, size 9⅝ by 7 by 2¼. 806 pages. Price $1.25.

Alabama. Arkansas. Arizona. California. Colorado. Connecticut. Delaware. Florida. Georgia.

Illinois. Indiana. Iowa. Kansas. Kentucky. Louisiana. Maine. Maryland. Massachussetts.

Michigan. Minnesota—N. G. Minnesota—Staff. Mississippi. Missouri. Montana. Nebraska. Nevada. New Hampshire.

New Jersey—N. G. New Jersey—State. New Mexico. New York. North Carolina. North Dakota. Ohio. Ohio—Staff. Oregon.

Pennsylvania. Rhode Island. South Carolina. South Dakota. Tennessee. Texas. Utah. Vermont. Virginia.

Set of Buttons, one from every State in the Union, arranged on **heavy cardboard**, with name of State printed underneath each button; all neatly arranged in cardboard box. Bright, new gilt polished buttons. **$2.50**

### SOUVENIR CARTRIDGE RELICS.

**West Point Cadet Uniform Bell Buttons**, Souvenirs, from Cadet Uniforms. Price 10c. each.

Staff

U. S. Army Present and Late Regulation Buttons. New. Price, 6 cents each; 60 cents dozen—

Spanish War Rifle Cartridges from U. S. Navy and captured Spanish Mauser Rifles, with powder removed and useful tool inserted in the bullet; can be carried in the pocket and looks like a loaded cartridge; by pulling out the bullet, reversing and inserting it in the shell you have either a buttonhook or a neat little manicure set, according to kind. The dotted lines in first illustration show the buttonhook as it appears inside the shell and the bullet sticking out, to all appearances like a regular loaded cartridge.

No. 8. No. 7. No. 12. No. 11. No. 15. No. 16.

No. 1, 21, 22 sold.

No. 2

No. 4

No. 17. No. 18. No. 19.

No. 5

No. 20. SCOTCH THISTLE, flower and leaves, BRASS, size 3¼x3⅛, used on helmet. Can be used on auto radiator, doors, or other places. Price, 50 cents each.

of cannon balls underneath and Spanish crown on top in raised design. Cuff buttons, 50 cents per pair; hatpin, 25 cents.

No. 20A. SCOTCH THISTLE, flower and leaves, BRIGHT metal, size 1½x 1¾ inch with loops to fasten to cap. NEW. Price, 45 cents each.

20A

The bottom illustration shows the Manicure Set ready for use. The shells are all highly polished, the bullets nickel-plated; the tools are made of steel. We have sold a great many, and to all they have given satisfaction; a useful article made from a death-dealing missile; valuable relics; the Mauser cartridges are stamped on the head with the year, initial and date and place of manufacture, mainly Karlsruhe, Germany. The U. S. Navy cartridge has stamped on the head, "U. S. N." Any of the above kind, price, 20 cents each; $2.00 per dozen.

No. 3

No. 25

No. 13 No. 14

No. 13 No. 14

No. 8.—Spanish Engineers Soldiers' Button, nickel finish, with Morro Castle, with Spanish crown surrounded with wreath. 50 cents per pair.

No. 15.—Spanish-Cuban Administration Soldiers' Button. Sunrays, surmounted with crown, surrounded by wreath. Cuff buttons, 50 cents a pair.

No. 16.—Spanish Guard Soldiers' Button, coat-of-arms with crown surrounded with wreath; letters G. M. or O. P. on each side of coat-of-arms; very showy button. Cuff button, 50 cents per pair; hatpin, 25 cents.

Nos. 2 and 3.—Spanish Regular Soldiers' Buttons. Spanish coat-of-arms in relief with crown and motto; worn by Spanish Regulars who returned to Spain. We have these buttons in both coat and vest size. Prices in cuff buttons, 50 cents per pair; hatpin, 25 cents.

No. 6.—Spanish Navy Sailors' Button. Anchor in oval with Spanish crown; rare, handsome button; in cuff buttons, 75 cents per pair; hatpin, 25 cents.

No. 14.—Spanish Artillery Soldiers' Button. Two crossed cannons with pile

Nos. 4 and 5.—Spanish Button Scarf Pins; vest size Spanish button, gold plated, with steel pin, making handsome scarf pin. Price, 25 cents.

Nos. 17, 18 and 19.—Cuff Buttons made from strand of the cable and Spanish soldiers' vest buttons. The bar is made from one of the strands, polished and plated, lettered "U. S. S. Maine," with loop for joining the spring link to the button; making a handsome, strong, serviceable pair of cuff buttons with link fastening; rare and valuable relic; made up for us by jeweler, who ordered cards on which to mount these relics, printed "Souvenir U. S. S. Maine." Admiral Philip gave us a more appropriate name by calling them "Memorials; the cable is a memorial of the Maine to all Americans." The Spanish-Cuban buttons a memorial of lost Cuba to the Spanish, both now

linked together. All of these cable relics are mounted on cards, on which is printed the history of the cable and the statement of the Naval officers, who vouch for its authenticity. Our price is 50 cents per pair. We will sell links and bars joined to any other button we have in stock at same price—U. S. Navy, U. S. Army, West Point Cadet, State, etc., etc.

No. 7 to No. 16.—Beautiful Pair of Gold-Plated Cuff Buttons, made from Spanish soldiers' buttons, which we purchased from the Spanish in Cuba, December, 1898. American soldiers returning from Cuba in fall of 1898 obtained $1.00 each for similar buttons. We have them in both lever and dumbbell fastenings. Price, 50 cents per pair, mailed. Buttons made up with hatpins, fine gold-plated. 25 cents.

The designs on the face of the buttons represent the different branches of the service in Spanish Army. No. 7 is No. 6 the button worn by Volunteer natives of Cuba, similar to American Militia—called by American soldiers Guerrillas—in whose ranks were found many who, hidden in the trees, armed with Remington rifles, fired upon surgeons and wounded, although under the protection of the Red Cross. This button has on the face a bugle with number of regiment, surmounted by Spanish crown.

No. 25.—U. S. coat-of-arms Scarf Pin, handsome gilt ornament with pin, kind worn by many Americans in foreign countries. Price 25 cents each, mailed.

**No. 1-2**

1. QUEEN'S MINIATURE MEDAL FOR THE BALTIC CAMPAIGN of 1854-1855. Reverse show Britannia seated with Naval Cannon and shells. Size 11-16th inch. With ribbon. Price, $3.85.

2. QUEEN'S MINIATURE MEDAL with yellow and black ribbon. Obverse show Queen Victoria in coronation robe with crown and sceptre; reverse Victory seated with battle flags and wreath, under which is word SUDAN. Size 11-16th inch. Price, $3.85.

SEE OTHER PAGES IN THIS CATALOG FOR FULL SIZE MEDALS OF GREAT BRITAIN, FRANCE, GERMANY AND OTHER COUNTRIES. Many special medals also shown. If you do not find listed the medals you wish, write us for prices.

10053. U. S. NAVY HAT RIBBON. Black silk, 3 feet long, 1⅝ inches wide, with name of the famous old warship Monongahela embroidered in gilt letters, worn on sailors' hats; the gilt is slightly tarnished. Bargain price, 10 cents each.

10054. SILK EMBROIDERED U. S. N. GILT HAT RIBBONS. From the U. S. S. Amphitrite. 10 cents each.

**No. 7**

7. MINIATURE QUEEN'S MEDAL for campaign of 1892 in East and West Africa. Complete with light yellow ribbon with black stripes. Size 11-16th inch. Price, $3.85.

No. 10. Confederate Belt and Buckle, sent to the South from England and captured on blockade running steamer, sold to us by U.S. Government after the close of Civil War as rebel, enameled leather, slightly sticky from long storage. Lion head, brass buckle. Price $1.50.

Sergeants' Gilt Lace Chevrons, old pattern; no longer regulation, practically new; slightly tarnished. Price, $1.00 pair.

No. 4 Civil War N. C. officers sword with shoulder belt, with U. S. buckle fine leather 2¼ inches wide worn over the shoulder, for Belt Sword, Scabbard and Buckle: theoutfit, price $4.25

**No. 8.** Civil War Soldier's Shoulder Belt and Cartridge Box, worn over the shoulders. Belt is 2¼ inches wide, complete with buckle, with brass U. S. cartridge box plate. This outfit formed part of the Civil soldiers' equipment, in connection with the Springfield rifle. The cartridge box has the inside tin box for holding 40 rounds of cartridges, the kind the soldier had to bite off the end before loading in the gun. Every G. A. R. veteran should have one of these old time serviceable relics to leave as an heirloom to his children. Price, $2.00.

**No. 19**

1782. Emergency Bandolier, drab color woven web, with six double pockets, for clips of 5 cartridges each, carried over the shoulder, can be furnished in khaki or white web as desired, used without belt plates. Price 40c. each.

No. 19. U. S. Navy German Silver Table Spoons. New. Slightly tarnished. Length 8¼ inches, bowl 1¾. Price 15 cents.

No. 14. 10,000 German Army Leather Bayonet Scabbard with inside steel spring, keeping leather from breaking. Complete with loop strap for attaching to belt, good as new. Price 20 cents each.

U. S. Army Officer's Gilt Belt plate, with silvered wreath and stars, gilt finish. $1.00 each.

New Army Chevron Pillow Tops, handsome and appropriate military souvenir. Colored cloth designs, silk stitched on heavy fine quality blue cloth (*not sewn together*, as in illustration), ladies, no doubt, preferring the work of arranging the different designs. The above assortment would cost to make, over $5.00. We have so many of these designs that we offer at the bargain price of 58 cents per set, $6.00 per dozen sets. Size of the pillow tops, illustrated, when sewn together measures 15½ inches square.

**G. A. R. HAT ORNAMENTS.** Stamped brass 2½ inch wreath, nickeled letters, safety pin fastening. Price, 15 cents each.

Fairbanks Army & Navy Folding Platform Scale for weighing up to 1200 pounds measures folded 1 ft. 10 wide 3 ft. 2 long, 61 inches high, needs adjusting offered as is Price $18.00.

Navy Capstan from Naval Auction. Cast Metal 2 ft. 3 high, 12 inches diameter in poor order for service, handsome outdoor ornament for lawn. Price $15.00.

Naval Steering Wheel. Hard wood brass hub 3 ft, 4 diameter, 6 spokes, serviceable relic. Price $18.00.

Shot Tower, Beekman St., New York, 150 ft. high, erected in 1856 by Richard McCullagh, torn down 1907, used in making shot by dropping melted lead at the top of the tower through seives or cullenders falling into tanks of water at the bottom, the molten metal assuming globular forms which cool and hardened in the descent. Previous to the high tower method it was a slow process as well as impossible to cast shot perfectly round. Greener tells that the use of high tower in making shot was the result of a dream that came to the wife of an English brass founder who dreamt that her husband stood at the top of the stairs and poured lead through a sieve that fell into the water in her wash tub at the bottom. The dream so impressed the good woman that she wakened and told her sprouse, who told her to go to sleep and not bother him with her dreams. On the dream being repeated the third time, they got up and acting it out, soon had a lot of beautiful round shot which was taken to London, patent obtained and sold to Maltby, Walker & Co., who for many years controlled the British market in lead shot.—From Bannerman's book in course of preparation, "Weapons of War."

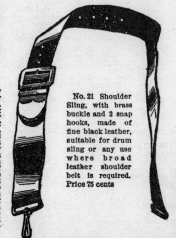

No. 21 Shoulder Sling, with brass buckle and 2 snap hooks, made of fine black leather, suitable for drum sling or any use where broad leather shoulder belt is required. Price 75 cents

No. 18 Revolutionary War Bayonet Scabbard, real old antique, in good serviceable order with brass mouth piece with stud for attaching to shoulder belt; kind used 1776 period. Price, 45 cents; with bayonet $1.40.

# Spanish War Buttons, Naval Hat Ribbons, Etc.

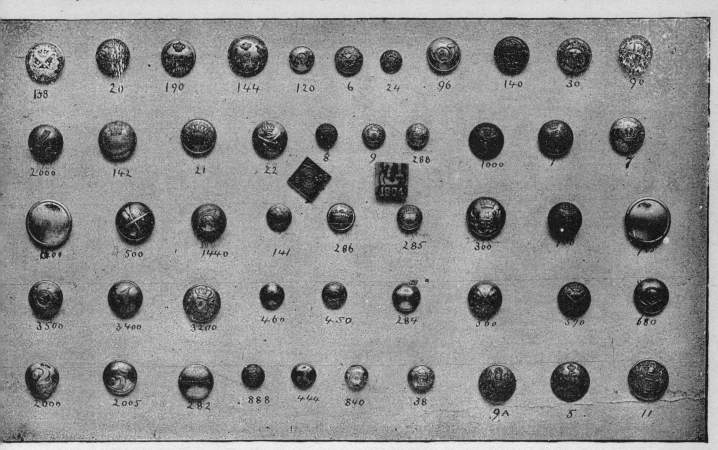

SPANISH WAR MILITARY BUTTONS from Cuba, 1898.  The number under illustration of button represents the quantity in stock.

Society Buttons, assorted patterns and designs, as illustrated.  Price, 10 cents each and 60 cents dozen.

Spanish Medal from Porto Rico . . . . . . . . . . . . Price, $3.50
Philippine Spanish Medal . . . . . . . . . . . . . . . Price, $5.50
Brass Plate, taken from the oldest house in San Juan, Porto Rico, Casa Blanca, once occupied by Ponce de Leon; size, 3½x5 inches; Indian figure holding wreath over head of Columbus, etc.  Price, $5.00

U. S. Navy Sailors Black Silk Hat Ribbons, with names of ship neatly embroidered in gold letters.  Your choice 75 cents each.

No. 61, U. S. S. Maine ; No. 12, Celtic; No. 48, Footer; No. 12, Hassler; No. 24, Junitata; No. 60, Montauk; No. 87, Minnesota; No. 71, Ossippe; No. 70, Passaic, No. 140, Rogers; No. 23, Trenton; No. 76, Wyandotte; No. 35, Wyoming; No. 47, Yorktown; No. 200, Amphitrite; No. 10, Lockport.

The following hat ribbons are very rare, from old ships:

Constellation, Marion, Nipsic, Nahant, Tennessee, Endeavor, Lancaster, Swatara.  Price, $5.00 each.

No. 36 and 144 (Alarm, Cugola), are in gold stamped letters.  Price, 30 cents each.

Spanish Navy Sailors, Silk Hat Ribbons.  Same as supplied by Spanish Naval Contractor in Havana, Cuba.

Infanta Maria Teresa, Cortes, Alfonso XII, Christobal Colon, Viscaya, Guardian, Almirante Oquendo, Furor, Alemanderes, Vazen N. de Ballon, Pizarro, Ponce de Leon, Reine Mercedes, Estrella, Descubridor.

The seven Santiago ships are emergency ribbons, painted letters; balance of list embroidered.  Price, $1.00 each.

Spanish Volunteer Soldier's Coat Ornament, worn on lapel of coat.  Brass, gold-plated.  Price, 20 cents each, mailed.

British Navy Warship Sailor Silk Hat Ribbons, embroidered in gilt letters, 85 cents each.

His Majesty's ships Nelson, Meteor, Defense, Victory, Howe, Thunderer, Hecla, H. M. S. Rapid.

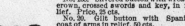

Wood button sticks to use in cleaning buttons without removing from coat.  10 cents each.

Spanish Metal 6-point Star, used on officers' uniforms to designate rank; imitation embroidery.  Price, 15 cts. each.

No. 138.  Silvered button with wreath, crown, crossed swords and key, in relief.  Price, 25 cts.
No. 20.  Gilt button with Spanish coat of arms in relief, 50 cts.
No. 190.  Gilt button with crown and letters A M in relief.  Price, 15 cts.
No. 144.  Silvered button with crown and castle in wreath.  Price, 35 cts.
No. 120.  Spanish - Cuban Volunteer vest-size Second Regiment button.  Price, 15 cts.
No. 6.  Guerro de E. M. Del Ejuercito in gilt letters, with crown, wreath and star, 50 cts.
No. 24.  Small gilt button, with crown, star and wreath in relief, 25 cts.
No. 96.  Spanish - Cuban Volunteer Second Regiment button with figure 2 and bugle in relief.  Price, 20 cts.
No. 140.  Spanish Naval Officers gilt button with crown and foul anchor.  Price, 40 cts.
No. 30.  Guerro de E. M. Del Ejuercito Spanish officers button with star, crown, wreath and motto in relief.  Price, 50 cts.
No. 90.  Spanish Engineer Soldiers gilt button.  Price, 50 cts.
No. 2,000.  Fourth Spanish Regulars Uniform button.  Price, 10 cents each; $1.00 per doz.
No. 142.  Spanish Administration Officers silvered button with crown and sun rays.  Price, 30 cts.
No. 21.  Spanish Cavalry Soldiers brass button with crown and carabineros.  Price, 50 cts.
No. 22.  Spanish Naval Gunners brass button with crown and crossed cannon with anchor.  Very rare.  Price, $1.00.
No. 8.  Spanish Regulars vest-size brass button with crown and coat of arms in relief.  Price, 40 cts.
No. 285.  Spanish Administration Officers silvered button.  Price, 20 cts.
No. 288.  Spanish Regulars Infantry button with crown and coat of arms.  Price, 15 cts.
No. 1,000.  Spanish Artillery Soldiers uniform brass button with crown, crossed cannon and shot.  Price, 15 cts.
B 1.  Spanish Military button, rare pattern, 50 cts.
No. 7.  Spanish Customs Officers in Cuba silvered button.  Pr.ce, 15 cts.
Squadron A Sharpshooters badge.  Price, 75 cts.
Seventy-first Regiment Sharpshooters badge.  Price, 75 cts.
No. 800.  Plain silvered button from Cuba.  Price, 5 cts. each; 50 cts. per doz.
No. 1,440.  Ancient Spanish Soldiers Cuban button with star and carbine.  Price, 20 cts.
No. 1,440.  Spanish Police Officers button with crown, coat of arms and O. P.  Price, 10 cts. each; $1.00 per doz.
No. 141.  Spanish-Cuban Cavalry Soldiers vest-size button with crown and carabineros, 10 cts. each; $1.00 a doz.

No. 286.  Silvered vest-size Spanish button with crown, 10 cts. each, $1.00 per doz.
No. 800.  Spanish Officers button with crown, key and three castles, with letters G. M.  Price, 15 cts. each.
No. 700.  Spanish Regulars Infantry Soldiers button with crown and coat of arms "Infanteria"  10 cts. each, $1.00 per doz.
No. 705.  Gilt finished plain buttons from Cuba, 10 cts. each, $1.00 per doz.
No. 3,500.  Fourth Regiment Spanish Volunteer Soldiers button, 10 cts. each, 60 cts. per doz.
No. 3,400.  First Regiment Spanish Soldiers Regulars Cuban button, 10 cts. each, 60 cts. per doz.
No. 3,200.  Spanish Regular Soldiers silvered button with figure 2.  Price, 10 cts. each; 75 cts. per doz.
No. 460.  Spanish button with crossed flags, 10 cts. each, 60 cts. per doz.
No. 450.  Spanish Volunteer Soldiers Third Regiment button, 10 cts. each, 60 cts. per doz.
No. 294.  Silvered plain button from Cuba, 10 cts. each, 60 cts. per doz.
No. 560.  Spanish button with crossed flags, medium size, 10 cts. each, 75 cts. per doz.
No. 570.  Medium size brass button used by Spanish Engineer Corps.  Price, 10 cts. each; $1.00 per doz.
No. 680.  First Regiment Spanish Volunteer Soldiers button, 10 cts. each, 60 cts. per doz.
No. 2,000.  Spanish Volunteers Fourth Regiment uniform button, partly bell shaped, 10 cts. each, 60 cts. per doz.
No. 2,005.  Spanish Regular Fifth Regular Silvered button, 10 cts. each, 60 cts. per doz.
No. 282.  Spanish gilt button Retirado, 10 cts. each, 60 cts. per doz.
No. 888.  Spanish Infantry Regulars small size button with coat of arms, 10 cts. each, 60 cts. per doz.
No. 444.  Spanish Regulars First Regiment vest button.  Price, 10 cts. each; 60 cts. per doz.
No. 840.  Spanish Volunteers silvered vest button, 10 cts. each, 60 cts. per doz.
No. 38.  Spanish Officials vest-size silvered button with crown, three castles and letters G. M.  Price, 20 cts. each.
No. 9.  A Napoleon First French Soldiers uniform button.  Price, 75 cts.
No. 5.  Brass button worn by Napoleon's Imperial Garde.  Price, $1.00.

No. 11.  A Napoleon Soldiers brass button, 75 cts.

Scotch Thistle button, 10 cts. each; $1.00 doz.

**No. 1.**

**No. 1.** War Medal given by Queen Victoria in 1854 to British soldier who fought in the famous battles of Alma, Inkermann and Sebastopol. Medal is complete with three bars, silk ribbon and safety clasp. Shows considerable wear. Illustration is from photo. Medals were not granted 50 years ago very freely. This is a prize. Price **$18.00.**

**No. 2.**

**No. 2.** War Medal given by Queen Victoria to British soldier for engagement at Alexandria, July 11th, 1882. Price **$8.75.**

**No. 3.** Bronze Star Medal given to British Army soldier for engagement at Alexandria, by Khedive of Egypt, 1882. Price **$8.75.**

These two medals are for the same engagement.

**No. 4.** War Medal given to

**No. 3.**

**No. 4.**

British soldier for Tirah Campaign in N. W. India Frontier. Complete with two bars Tirah and Punjab, 1897-1898. It was during this campaign that after the English soldiers were repulsed that the Scotch Gordon Highlanders were successful. The bugler, Findlater, who fell wounded, still played on the Highlander's stirring war tune, "The

**No. 5.**

Cock of the North." Price of this medal is **$10.00.**

**No. 5.** Queen Victoria Boer War Medal with two bars: WITTEBERGEN CAPE COLONY. With ribbon. Price **$7.00.**

**No. 4A.** War Medal for Tirah Campaign, with one bar; 1897-1898. Price **$8.50.**

**27-3.** QUEEN'S SOUTH AFRICAN MEDAL, with six bars.: SOUTH AFRICA 1901, LAING'S NEK, TRANSVAAL, RELIEF OF LADYSMITH, ORANGE FREE STATE, TUGELA HEIGHTS. Price $12.50.

**27-4.** QUEEN'S SOUTH AFRICAN MEDAL, with five bars: TRANSVAAL, RELIEF OF LADYSMITH, ORANGE FREE STATE, TUGELA HEIGHTS, CAPE COLONY. Price $11.50.

**27-5.** QUEEN'S SOUTH AFRICAN MEDAL, with four bars: BELFAST, RELIEF OF LADYSMITH, TUGELA HEIGHTS, CAPE COLONY. Price $8.50.

**27-6.** QUEEN'S SOUTH AFRICAN MEDAL, with three bars: TRANSVAAL, ORANGE FREE STATE, CAPE COLONY. Price $7.85.

**27-7.** QUEEN'S SOUTH AFRICAN MEDAL, with two bars: RELIEF OF LADYSMITH, TUGELA HEIGHTS. Price $6.75.

**27-8.** KING'S SOUTH AFRICAN MEDAL, with two bars: SOUTH AFRICA 1902, SOUTH AFRICA 1901. Price $6.25.

GOLD PLATED WATCH FOB with Great Seal of the United States, with leather strap. Price 20 cents.

QUEEN'S SUDAN MEDAL, with ribbon. Price $7.50.

QUEEN'S SOUTH AFRICAN MEDAL, with three bars, BELFAST, LAING'S NEK, DEFENSE OF LADYSMITH, with ribbon. Price $6.95.

QUEEN'S SOUTH AFRICAN MEDAL, with three bars, SOUTH AFRICA 1902, ORANGE FREE STATE, CAPE COLONY, no ribbon. Price $6.85.

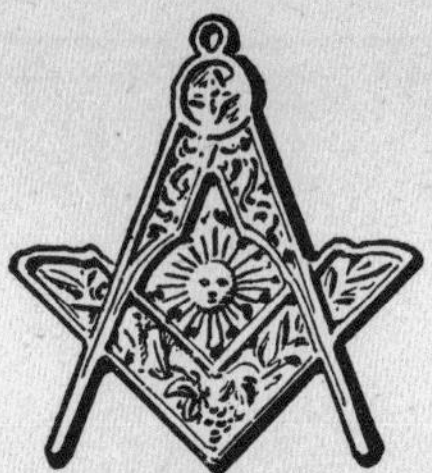

01226.

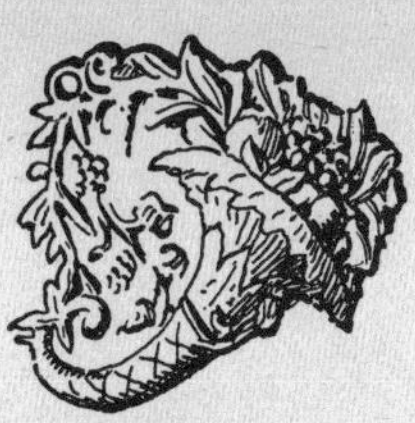

01227.

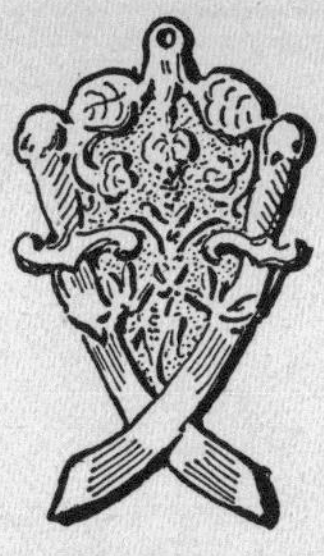

01225.

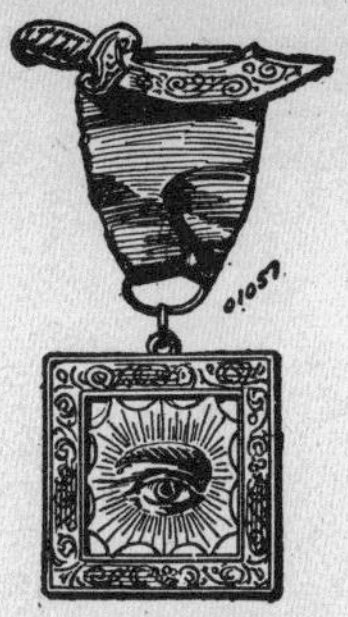

01057.

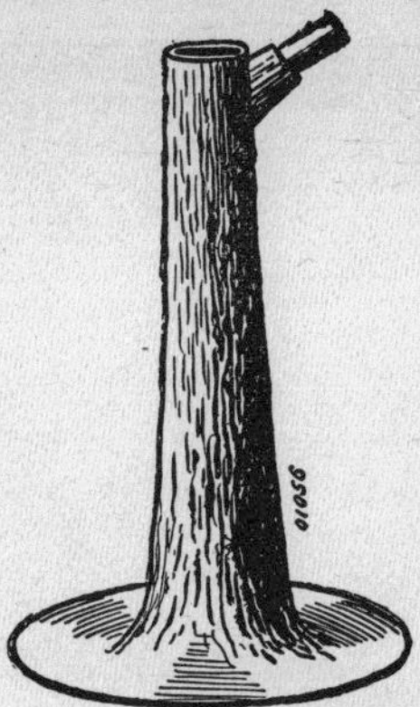

01056.

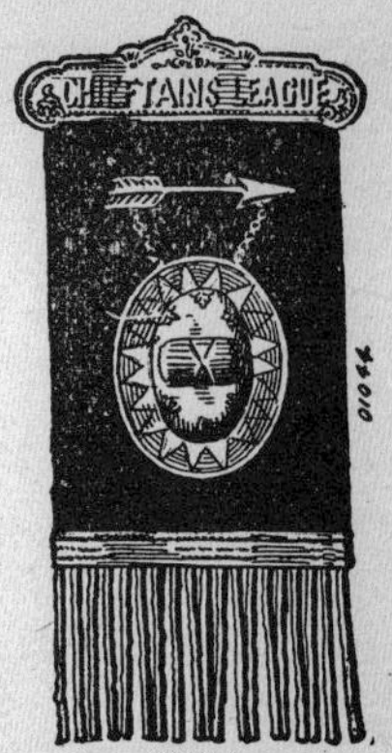


01044.

0-1226. LODGE JEWEL. with the ALL-SEEING EYE, polished silvered metal, 2½x2¼ inches. Price, 75 cents.

0-1227. CORNUCOPIA LODGE JEWEL. Silvered metal, relief ornamented, with hole for suspension ribbon. Length 1¾x2⅜ inches. Price, 50 cents.

0-1228. LODGE JEWEL OPEN BOOK, HOLY BIBLE. In relief ornamentation, with hole for ribbon, silvered metal 2x2¼ inches. Price, 75 cents.

0-1231. LODGE JEWEL SILVERED METAL. "SQUARE." With hole for ribbon, size 1¾x2⅜ inches. Price, 60 cents.

0-1232. LODGE JEWEL, COMPASS WITH SQUARE WITH CRESCENT MOON, MASKED FACE in centre. Size 2½x2¼ inches. Silvered metal. Price, 75 cents.

0-1233. LODGE JEWEL, "LEVEL." In silvered metal, with hole for ribbon, size 2 inches square. Price, 70 cents.

0-1234. LODGE JEWEL "LEVEL." Silvered metal ⅝ inch wide, 2¼ inches long, with suspension ribbon hole. Price, 45 cents.

0-1235. LODGE JEWEL CROSSED QUILL PENS. In silvered metal, relief ornamented, with ribbon hole, 2¾x1½ inches. Price, 60 cents.

0-1236. ANCIENT PATTERN SCIMITER. Worn suspended by ribbon, silvered metal, fruit and flower relief ornamented, 2½x1½ inches. Price, 75 cents.

0-1229. CROSSED KEYS LODGE JEWEL. In silvered metal, with hole for suspension ribbon, size 2⅝x1½ inches. Price, 65 cents.

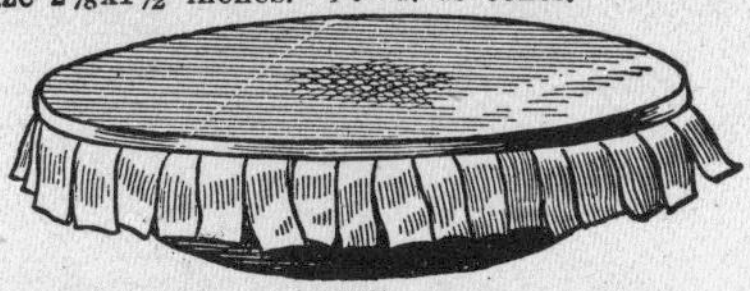

1208.

0-1208. LODGE DRUM OR TOM TOM. Regular 12½-inch drum head, stretched across wood bowl-shaped frame. Ornamented around the edges with colored cloth fringe. Height is 3¼ inches, width 12¼ inches. Good serviceable order. Offered with pair of drumsticks at the bargain price of $2.85.

0-1252A. LODGE DRUM. With 14-inch calfskin head, usually called TOM TOM. Broad bowl-shaped wood frame, with drum head attached to grommet and fitted over the edge of bowl, requires no tightening straps. Gives fairly good sound. Offered complete with pair of drumsticks. Price, $3.85.

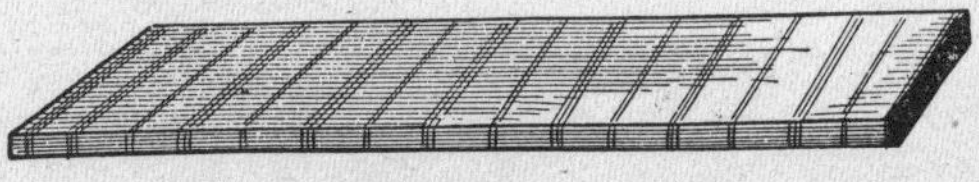

01220.

0-1220. RAIN SOUNDER. Wood frame 20½ inches long, 8 inches wide, 1 inch thick. Covered with ornamental striped cloth, containing small buckshot, which, when the frame is moved, gives forth the sound produced by rain. Price, 65 cents.

0-1251. LODGE HAND LAMP. Triangular-shaped, with wick, with handle, height 2 inches. Price, 25 cents.

0-1052. KNEELING CUSHION. Wood, frame black cotton drill covered and padded; length 24x15 inches, 1⅜ inches high. Price, $1.00.

0-1225. LODGE JEWEL CROSSED SCIMITER SWORDS. Silvered metal, polished backs, flowers and fruit ornamentation in relief scimiter suspended with hook and ribbon. Length 2¾ inches, width 1⅝ inches. New. Price, 60 cents.

0-1057. LODGE JEWEL BADGES. Ancient pattern scimiter sword, with safety pin fastening, with the all-seeing eye centre, ornamented border, attached to blue silk ribbon. Solid white silvered metal 2 inches square. Full length, with ribbon, 4¼ inches. Price, $1.50.

0-1057A. LODGE JEWEL BADGE. As above, with 3 keys in the centre of panel. Price, $1.50.

0-1057AA. SIMILAR CROSSED KEY BADGE, WITHOUT SCIMITER AND RIBBON BAR. Price, 75 cents.

0-1057C. LODGE JEWEL BADGE, WITH CROSSED BATTLE AXES AND TRUMPET. Price, $1.50.

0-1057D. LODGE JEWEL BADGE, WITH CROSSED KEYS. Price, $1.50.

0-1057B. LODGE JEWEL BADGE, WITH CROSSED QUILL PENS. Price, $1.50.

0-1060. ASSORTED LOT OF LODGE JEWELS. Triangular-shaped, average length 2 inches, with loops or rings for ribbons. Solid metal gilt-finished and polished.

Triangle, with raised border open work. Price, 50 cents.

With arrow in the centre. Price, 70 cents.

Cross swords centre; battle axe centre; knight with Oriental figure; crossed keys. Choice. Price, 75 cents each.

Triangular Lodge Level Badge, crossed keys and trowel; sword, battle axe and trowel. Price, $1.00.

Triangular lodge jewel badges, silver surface, polished, gilt finish, with arrow and battle axe. Price, 75 cents.

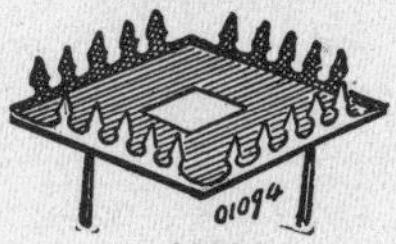

01094

0-1094. LODGE JEWEL HOLDER. Brass frame 1⅛ inch square, with two fastening wires on the back, ⅜-inch centre hole, 5 fastening clips on each side. Price, 10 cents each.

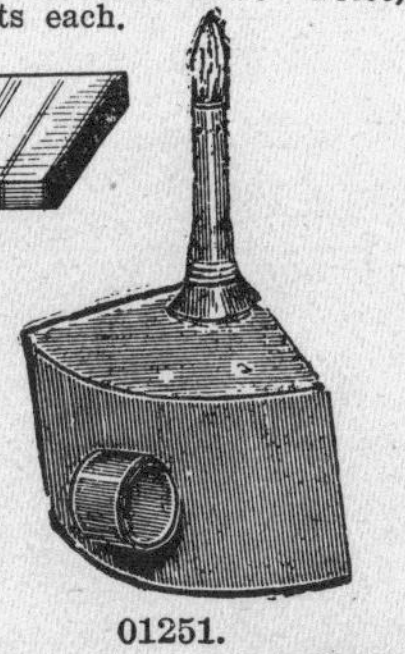

01251.

0-1056. METAL STAND FOR LODGE ROOM Cast metal 9 inches high, 3¼-inch base, ⅞-inch socket hole painted in red, yellow and blue colors buyer's choice of color. Weight 2 pounds 6 ounces. Price, 50 cents each.

0-1044. SOCIETY BADGE. Mounted on blue silk, with silvered fringe and bar with safety-pin fastening, lettered Chieftains' League, arrow with shield, suspended by small chains. Full length 6 inches, width 3 inches. Price, 65 cents.

0-1057J. BADGES. Without ribbons and scimiter bar, with finger pointing to a star. Price, 75 cents.

0-1057H. BADGES. Without ribbons and scimiter bar, with finger pointing to open Bible. Price, $1.50.

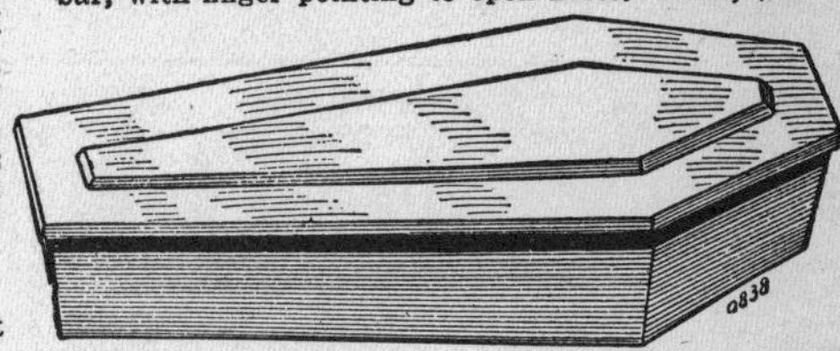

0838

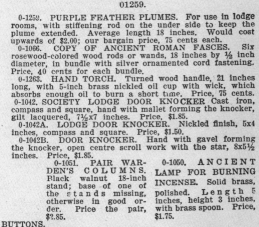

0-838. SECRET SOCIETY LODGE MINIATURE COFFIN. Polished walnut, length 19 inches, depth 3¾ inches, width 5½ inches. New. From assignee's sale society dealer's stock. Price, $4.85.

0-1061. WHITE METAL COFFIN BADGES. 2 inches long, silvered finish, with pin fastenings on the back Price, 50 cents.

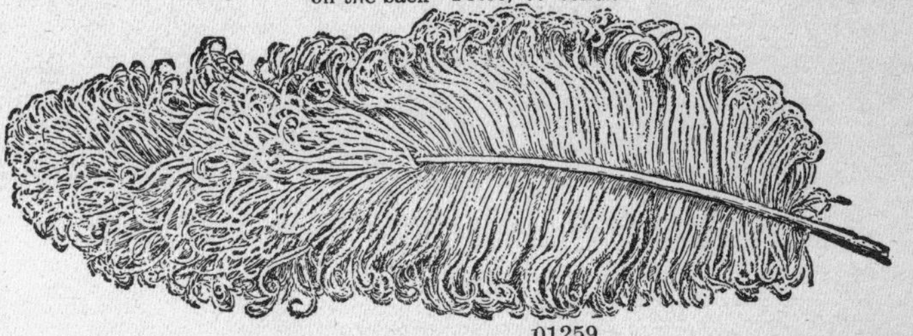

01259.

0-1259. PURPLE FEATHER PLUMES. For use in lodge rooms, with stiffening rod on the under side to keep the plume extended. Average length 18 inches. Would cost upwards of $2.00; our bargain price, 75 cents each.

0-1066. COPY OF ANCIENT ROMAN FASCES. Six rosewood-colored wood rods or wands, 18 inches by ½ inch diameter, in bundle with silver ornamented cord fastening. Price, 40 cents for each bundle.

0-1263. HAND TORCH. Turned wood handle, 21 inches long, with 5-inch brass nickled oil cup with wick, which absorbs enough oil to burn a short time. Price, 75 cents.

0-1042. SOCIETY LODGE DOOR KNOCKER Cast iron, compass and square, hand with mallet forming the knocker, gilt lacquered, 7½x7 inches. Price, $1.85.

0-1042A. LODGE DOOR KNOCKER. Nickled finish, 5x4 inches, compass and square. Price, $1.50.

0-1042B. DOOR KNOCKER. Hand with gavel forming the knocker, open centre scroll work with the star, 8x5½ inches. Price, $1.85.

0-1051. PAIR WARDEN'S COLUMNS. Black walnut 18-inch stand; base of one of the stands missing, otherwise in good order. Price the pair, $2.85.

0-1050. ANCIENT LAMP FOR BURNING INCENSE. Solid brass, polished. Length 5 inches, height 3 inches, with brass spoon. Price, $1.75.

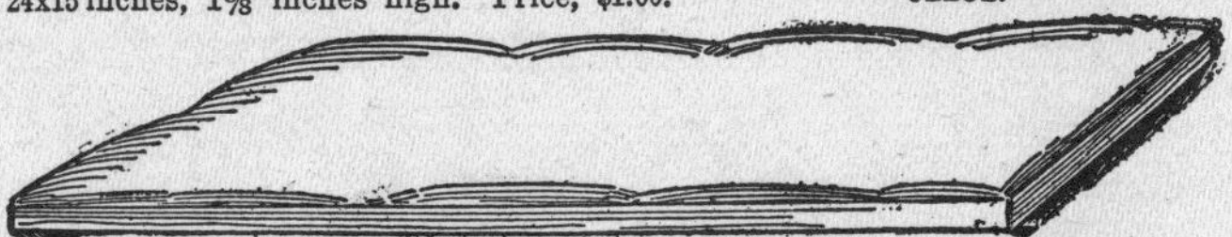

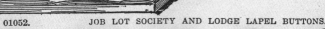

01052.

JOB LOT SOCIETY AND LODGE LAPEL BUTTONS.

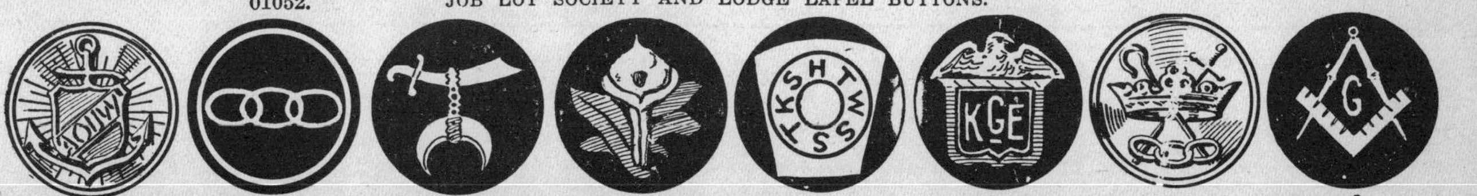


1 2 3 4 5 6 7 8

No. 1 is nickled; No. 7 gilt metal; the balance have woven covers with the insignia or design woven in silk metal backs. Illustration is 3/16 of an inch too large. Bargain price, 6 cents each, mailed. Buyer's choice.

**71-B. GERMAN MEDAL,** silver, with red, white and black ribbon. Obverse shows cross and wreath with 1870-1871. Reverse: German motto, with Crown, letter W and: FUR PELICHTTREUE IM KRIEGE. Price, $4.75.

**29-B. FRENCH GILT MEDAL** with red and white ribbon. Obverse shows head of woman marked: REPUBLIQUE FRANCAISE. Reverse: Swiss cross in center. SOCIETE DES SAUVETEURS BRANCHARDIERS, HONNEUR ET COURAGE, CHATILLON FONTENAY AUX ROSES. Price, $4.90.

**21-B. FRENCH SILVER LIFE SAVING MEDAL,** with crown, and blue, white and red ribbon. Obverse shows ANCHOR with letters C S on it. Reverse marked: LE COURAGE ET LA PROBITE SONT DEUX VERTUS QU ON NE PEUT CONTREFAIRE. MEDAILLE DES BELLES ACTIONS. Price, $5.50.

**186. BELGRAVIA CROSS FOR NAPOLEONIC CAMPAIGN,** including Waterloo. Obverse, center stamped 1815. Reverse, 1815. Yellow silk ribbon, blue border. Price, $12.50.

**25-B. FRENCH MEDAL FOR CAMPAIGN IN ITALY.** Similar to 25-B page 294. Price, $6.50.

**24-B. FRENCH ENAMELED DECORATION,** with fleur de lis silver clasp, with silver crown marked: TOUT POUR LA FRANCE, PAR LA FRANCE, ET AVEC LA FRANCE. Letters H E N I R intertwined. A very handsome piece. Price, $6.50.

**255. SPANISH MEDAL GIVEN FOR DEFENSE OF BALLAS,** 1874. Oval-shaped bronze medal, 1¼ inches wide, 1⅝ inches long. Good condition. Price, $8.50.

**62-B. PRUSSIAN MEDAL** with bust of Kaiser Wilhelm II. Reverse: Crown and wreath marked: DEN TAPFEREN STREITERN FUR DEUTCHLANDS EHRE. Gilt finish with ribbon. Price, $5.00.

**60-B. PRUSSIAN GILT FINISH MEDAL** with ribbon. Obverse shows crown over W II with short crossed swords, marked: DEN SIEGREICHEN STREITERN. Reverse shows German eagle over dragon. Price, $4.00.

**53-B. GERMAN GILT MEDAL** with ribbon. Obverse shows two crowns with letters W and F J. Reverse: Wreath and UNSERN TAPFERN KRIEGERN 1864. Price, $4.50.

**59-B. WILLIAM THE GREAT MEDAL,** silver finish, dull with bright yellow ribbon. Obverse show bust, marked: WILHELM DER GROSSE DEUTSCHER KAISER, KOENIG VON PREUSSER. Reverse: ZUM ANDENKEN AN DEN HUNDERSTEIN GEBURSTSTAG DES GROSSEN KAISERS WILHELM I 1797—22 Maerz—1897. Price, $4.50.

**43-B. HESSIAN SILVER MEDAL,** with light blue ribbon with two red stripes. Obverse shows bust marked: ERNST LUDWIG GROSSHERZOG VON HESSEN. Reverse shows wreath FU TAPFERKEIT. Price, $4.50.

**44-B. HESSIAN SILVER MEDAL,** similar to 43-B, but reverse marked: FUR KRIEGS VERDIENSTE. Price, $4.50.

**45-B. HESSE DARMSTADT MEDAL,** gilt finish with ribbon. Obverse shows crown over letter L. Marked: GESTIFTET AM 14 JUNI 1840. Reverse marked: FUR TREUEN IN FRIEGE with wreath. Price, $4.00.

**42-B. BAVARIAN OVAL GILT MEDAL** with red ribbon. Obverse shows bust marked LVITPOLD PRINZ REGENT VON BAYERN. Reverse: Crown over shield with IN TREVE FEST 1905. Price, $4.25.

**52-B. GERMAN GILT MEDAL** with red, white and black ribbon. Obverse marked with Crown over letter W, with German motto, and also DEM SIEGREICHEN HEERE. Reverse Cross with Wreath and 1870-1871. Price, $4.00.

**51-B,** same as 52-B. Price, $4.00.

**50-B. GERMAN CORONATION MEDAL** with bust of Kaiser and Kaiserin, marked: WILHELM KOENIG AUGUSTA KOENIGIN V. PREUSSEN. ZUR KROENUNG, AM 15 OCT 1861. Reverse shows coats of arms in miniature of the different provinces, around the edge, with royal shield in center. Gilt finish with yellow ribbon. Price, $5.50.

## MUSÉE ROYAL
### DE
### L'ARMÉE

No. 792/IV

Bruxelles, Le 10 Décembre, 1925.
Palais du Cinquantenaire.

Messieurs Francis Bannerman Sons,
501 Broadway, New York, U. S. A.

Messieurs: J'ai l'honneur de vous accuser réception et de vous remercier du magnifique catalogue d'armes et d'équipments que vous avez eu l'amabilité d'envoyer au Musée Royal de l'Armée.

Cet important ouvrage est dès à présent, mis à la disposition des collectionneurs qui fréquentent notre établissement, il leur sera même tout spécialement signalé.

Agréez, je vous prie, Messieurs, l'expression de mes sentiments distingués.

Le Conservateur en Chef.

Leconte.

**0-1244. RED, WHITE AND BLUE COLLAR AND BREAST SASH.** With rosette, silver tinseled star, with yellow fringe; length 2 feet. New. Price, $2.85.

**0-1244B. RED, WHITE AND BLUE VELVET COLLAR AND BREAST SASH.** With rosette, silver tinseled star; bottom of sash ends cross each other. Full length 3 feet; red, white and blue fringe. Price, $3.50.

**0-1245. BLUE VELVET SILK EMBROIDERED COLLAR SASH.** Silk lined, ½-inch silk lace binding, 2½-inch wide silver tassel. Full length 22 inches. Price, $3.85.

**0-1246C. BLUE VELVET SILVER LACE EMBROIDERED SASH.** ½-inch silver lace binding, 2½-inch silver fringe; lined and interlined. Bargain price, $5.85.

**0-1246. BLUE SILK COTTON SASH.** Watered silk lining, bound edges. New. Width 3 inches, full length 18 inches, with hook for jewel. Price, $1.25.

**0-1246A. BLUE COLLAR SASH.** 18 inches long, 3 inches wide, with snap hook. Price, 65 cents.

**0-1246B. BLUE CASHMERE CLOTH COLLAR SASH.** Silvered lace binding, with snap hook for jewel. Price, $1.25.

0-1246C.

**0-1247. REGALIA SASH.** Red velvet 3½ inches wide, with ½-inch silver lace binding on each side, 1¾-inch silver fringe, silvered lace embroidered crossed axes and flowers. Full length 22 inches. Maker's price, $9.00; our bargain price, $3.85.

We have a number in slightly different patterns from the illustration, all at bargain prices.

**0-1247A. REGALIA SASH.** Same pattern as No. 0-1247, handsomely ornamented with silvered lace embroidery and COLORED STONES, lined and interlined. Maker's price, $15.00; our bargain price, $6.85.

**0-1247B. REGALIA SASH.** Red plush with gilt lace binding and fringe, lined and interlined. Price, $2.85.

**0-1247C. REGALIA SASH.** Red plush, 2 rows of silvered lace binding, silvered fringe with silk embroidered BOW AND ARROWS. Price, $2.65.

**0-1247D. REGALIA SASH.** Red silk plush, silver fringe, 2 rows silvered lace binding, EMBROIDERED WITH CROSSED TOMAHAWK AXES. Price, $3.50.

**0-1247E. REGALIA SASH.** Red velvet 3½ inches wide with 2 rows of silvered lace binding, ½ inch wide on each side, lined and interlined, with SILVER EMBROIDERED CROSSED ARROWS, white beaded ornamental work. Price, $3.50.

**0-1248. REGALIA SASH.** Full width 4½ inches, full length 34 inches, red cashmere cloth with row of white binding on each side. Price, $1.65.

**0-1248A. REGALIA SASH.** Blue silk sash, with silvered lace binding, EMBROIDERED CLUBS. Price, $2.65.

**0-1249. POCAHONTAS REGALIA COLLAR SASH.** White plush velvet, with silverd lace and red velvet binding, silvered fringe, chain and leaf, 3 long chain lace tassels. Full length of sash 20 inches. Dealer's price, $45.00 per dozen; our bargain price, $2.85 each.

**0-1249A. POCAHONTAS REGALIA SASH.** In white cashmere with red silver fringe. Price, $1.60.

**0-1250. RED SILK COTTON PLUSH SASH.** With fine beaded embroidery, length 16 inches. Price, $1.50.

**0-1243. INDIAN CHIEF'S BEADED EMBROIDERED FEATHER HEAD DRESS.** Cloth cap with 3-inch blue flannel band, embroidered with white beads, with 7-inch blue feathers, with 6 yellow streamers ⅝ inch wide falling down over the back. An assorted job lot of feather head dresses in blue, yellow, white and green feathers and embroidered bands. Buyers' choice. Price, $3.50 each.

**0-1254. MASONIC APRONS,** cotton, blue trimmed like illustration, with various society emblems. All new. Price, 35 cents.

**0-1255. MASONIC APRONS,** lambskin, untrimmed with various society emblems. All new, no trimming or binding. Price, 95 cents.

**0-1048. FACE MASK.** Muslin stamped to shape of the face, with eye holes, in white, blue or yellow, at 10 cents each.

Masks with curtain covering mouth and chin, 15 cents each.

Some odd lots of wire face masks, 30 cents each. Masks with hair and mustache, $1.00 each.

Several officers of a British ship were dining with a mandarin at Canton. One of the officers wished a second helping of a savory stew, which he had the notion was composed of duck. Not knowing a word of Chinese the guest held up his plate to his host, remarking with smiling approval:

"Quack! quack! quack!"

But the countenance of the officer fell when the host, pointing at the dish, responded:

"Bow! wow! wow!"—Canadian Military Gazette.

# Job Lot Banners and Insignia.

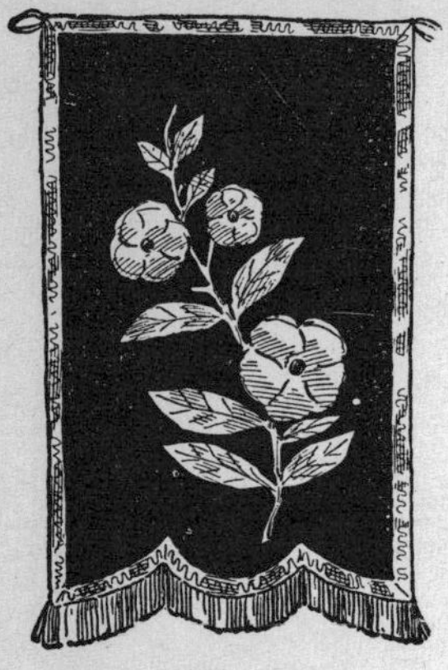

01267.

0-1267. RED SATIN BANNER. With gilt open work, 2-inch fringe, hand-painted LILY FLOWER and LEAF in centre. Size 21x30 inches. The flower is 15x9 inches. Price, $5.75.

0-1267A. PINK SATIN BANNER. Size 21x30 inches. Artistically painted in gold and oil colors, LILY and FLOWER. Offered at $6.75.

0-1267B. GREEN SATIN BANNER. Size 21x30 inches. BEE HIVE artistically painted in gold-leaf and oil colors. Make fine decoration for screen, or panel, offered unmounted at about half the cost of artist's work. Bargain price, $5.25.

0-1267C. WHITE SATIN BANNER. Size 21x30 inches. Artistically painted in gold-leaf and oil colors, CRESCENT MOON WITH MASKED FACE and 7 STARS. Fine work. Price, $5.25.

0-1267CC. SIMILAR ONE. With gold lace fringe. Price, $6.50.

0-1267D. SATIN BANNER. Size 21x30 inches. Hand-painted in oil and gold-leaf, NOAH'S DOVE BEARING OLIVE BRANCH. Price, $5.75.

0-1267E. PINK SATIN BANNER. Size 24x30 inches. NOAH'S DOVE WITH OLIVE BRANCH. Hand-painted, with gold-colored silk embroided wreath. Beautiful work. Price, $6.75.

0-1267F. BLUE SATIN BANNER. 18x24 inches, with monogram "F. H." in gold-leaf. Price, $2.75.

0-1267G. PURPLE SATIN BANNER. Size 21x24 inches. Artistically hand-painted in oil colors, with figure of MAN WITH ARM EXTENDED, with the name REUBEN in gold letters; scolloped bottom. Ready for mounting. New. Price, $4.75.

0-1267H. 2 RED SATIN BANNERS. Size 21x24 inches. Scolloped bottoms. Ready for mounting. Hand painted in oil with BULL and LETTERS EPHRAIM. Price, $4.75 each.

0-1268. ARTIST'S CREAM-COLORED CLOTH BANNER. Size 3 feet wide by 7 feet long. Artistic painting of THREE ANGELS WITH CROSS, CROWN AND OPEN BOOK. Price, $3.75.

0-1268A. CLOTH BANNER, WITH FIGURE OF ANGEL RISING OUT OF RED-SHAPED LILY, WITH HAND POINTING UPWARDS TO CROSS. 3 feet wide, 6 feet long. Price, $2.50.

0-1268B. SKELETON BANNER. Life-size figure of SKELETON painted on black background, with HAND HOLDING DEATH ARROW. Price, $2.50.

0-1266. SET OF FIVE LODGE BANNERS UNMOUNTED. Size 18 inches wide, 28 inches long. Artistically hand-painted on satin.

One in red, with BIBLE, SCALE, SAND GLASS and COFFIN.

One in white, with DEATH HEAD, SCYTHE and THREE-LINKED CHAIN.

One in blue, with the ARK and CHERUBIMS, BATLE AXE, SERPENT and ROD, GLOBE and HAND.

One in pink, with ARROW and BOW, QUIVER and ARROW and FASCES.

These banners would make a FINE DECORATION. They are painted in oil and we offer the set of 5 at half the cost of the artist's work. Price, $5.50.

0-1266A. FOUR SILK SATIN LODGE BANNERS. Similar in design to No. 0-1266. Design painted with gold-leaf. Width 21 inches, length 28 inches. Artistic work. New. Price the set of four banners, $10.50.

0-1266B. SET OF TWO SATIN LODGE BANNERS. Hand-painted, similar to the blue and red in No. 0-1266. For the set of two, $4.50.

0-1266C. BLUE SATIN LODGE BANNER. 18x28 inches. Hand-painted, with the [illegible] ARK, BATTLE AXE, SERPENT and [illegible] SPHERE and HAND. Price, $1.75.

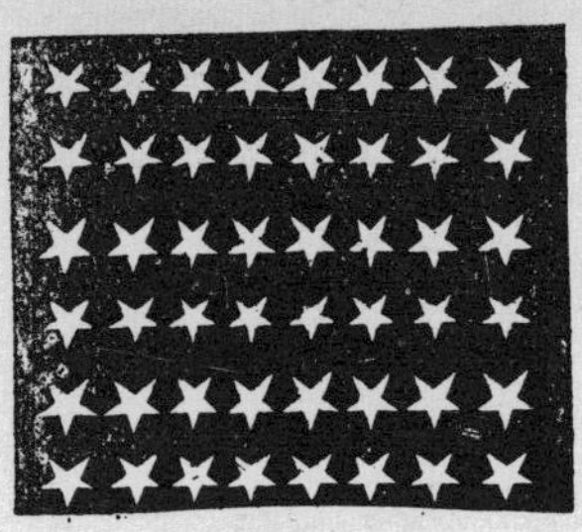

01260.

0-1260. BLUE SILK UNION JACK, WITH 38 COLORED STARS. Size 36x32 inches. Like new condition. Special banner silk, all in one piece, no sewing, hemmed borders; 4-inch gold stamped stars, with shaded edges, artistically hand-painted. Dealer's price upwards of $20.00; our bargain price, $9.85.

0-1260A. BLUE SILK UNION JACK. Size 45x34x38 inches. Gold stamped stars. New. Special banner silk all in one piece, 3½-inch gold stars, hand-painted edges. Dealer's price upwards $25.00; our bargain price, $10.85.

0-1047. SOCIETY FLAG POLE SPEAR HEADS, NICKLE-MOUNTED.

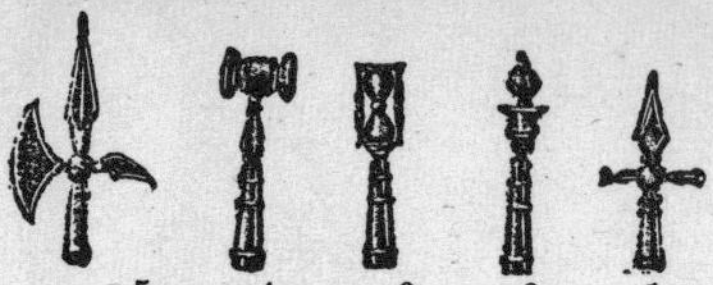

5 4 3 2 1

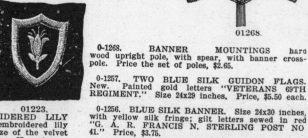

No. 1. Spear Head. With cross guard, 5¼ inches, 9/16-inch socket. Price, 85 cents.

No. 2. Flaming Torch. 4¼ inches long, 9/16-inch socket. Price, 75 cents.

No. 3. Sand Glass. 4 inches long, 9/16-inch socket. Price, 75 cents.

No. 4. Gavel or Mallet, 3¾ inches long, 9/16-inch socket. Price, 75 cents.

No. 5. Battle Axe. 5¾ inches long by 4 inches wide, 9/16-inch socket. Price, $1.00.

No. 6. Crescent Moon, with Face of Man, with 7 Stars. 4½x2¾ inches, 9/16-inch socket. Price, 85 cents.

No. 7. Bee Hive Flag Pole Top. 3⅝ inches by 1⅜ inches wide, 9/16-inch socket. 75 cents.

No. 7A. Bee Hive Flag Pole. 3⅛ inches long, 2¼ inches wide, ½-inch socket. Price, 65 cents.

No. 8. Lily Flower Flag Pole. 4½x2¼ inches, 9/16-inch socket. Price, 85 cents.

No. 9. Dove Bearing Olive Branch Flag Pole Top. 4¼x4½ inches, 9/16-inch socket hole. Price, $1.50.

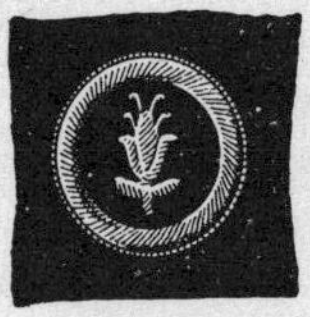

01222.

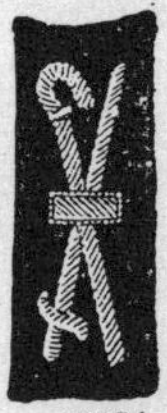

01221.

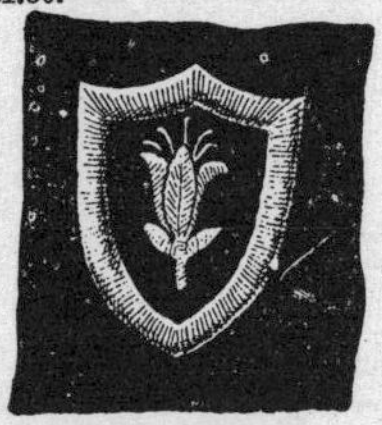

01223.

0-1222. SILVER EMBROIDERED LILY ON RED VELVET. Gilt embroidered lily flower in 2⅛-inch circle. Size of the velvet cloth 7¼ inches square. Price, 25 cents.

0-1221. SHEPHERD'S CROOK AND CROSS SWORD. Gold embroidered on blue cloth, with silver embroidered bar as illustrated. From dealer's society goods stock. Sold to us by assignee. In lengths 3¼ inches, also 2½ inches. Buyer's choice of size. Price, 20 cents each.

0-1223. SILVER EMBROIDERED SHIELD AND LILY FLOWER ON RED VELVET. Size of the shield 3¼x2¾ inches. Size of the red velvet cloth 4 inches square. New.

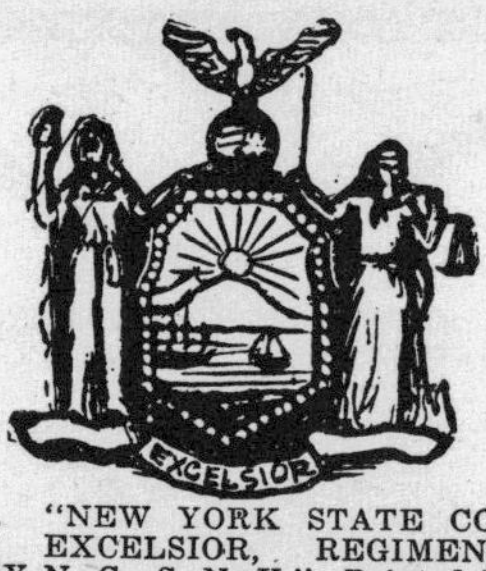


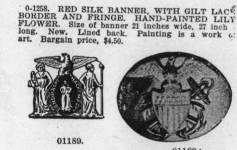

0-1261. "NEW YORK STATE COAT OF ARMS, EXCELSIOR, REGIMENT INFANTRY N. G., S. N. Y." Painted by artist on silk regimental flag in oil and gold. All ready for use, the number of the regiment only to be filled in, in the blank space. The flag is new, but is slightly shopworn, the oil painting slightly cracking, needs going over again by an artist. Size of flag is 6 feet long, 6½ feet wide. Blue banner silk, 3-inch silk fringe. Dealer's price is $80.00; our bargain price, $25.00.

Often we have been asked to sell from our museum exhibit some of our regimental flags, but have always declined to do so, which caused Tip of the New York Press to say about us in one of his articles: "What kind of a man is Bannerman that money won't buy some of his goods." This is a fine opportunity for anyone desiring to obtain regulation silk regimental flag.

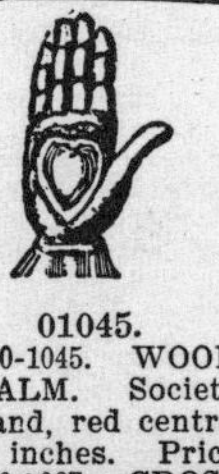

01045.

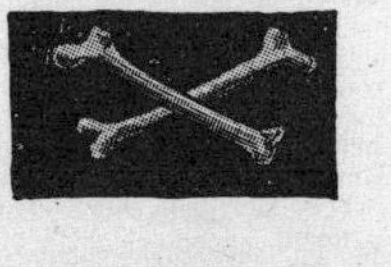

01067.

0-1045. WOOD HAND WITH HEART IN PALM. Society emblem. Gold lacquered hand, red centre heart, blue cuffs. Size 9¾x4 inches. Price, $1.50.

0-1067. CROSS BONES. For use in lodge rooms. White color, made of papier mache, [illegible] inches long. Life size. Price the pair, [illegible]

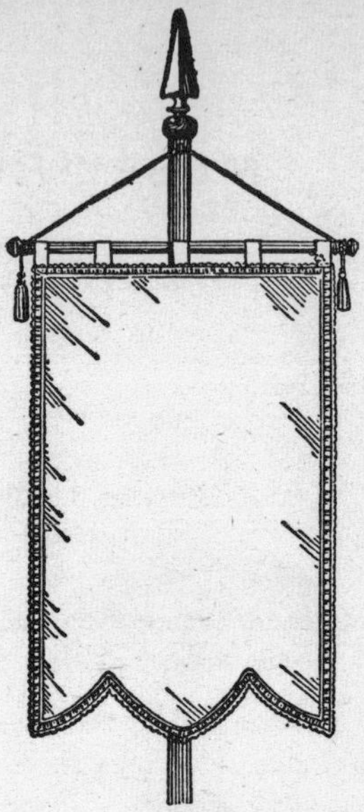

01268.

0-1268. BANNER MOUNTINGS hard wood upright pole, with spear, with banner cross-pole. Price the set of poles, $2.65.

0-1257. TWO BLUE SILK GUIDON FLAGS. New. Painted gold letters "VETERANS 69TH REGIMENT." Size 24x29 inches. Price, $5.50 each.

0-1256. BLUE SILK BANNER. Size 24x30 inches, with yellow silk fringe; gilt letters sewed in red "G. A. R. FRANCIS N. STERLING POST NO 41." Price, $3.75.

0-1258. RED SILK BANNER, WITH GILT LACE BORDER AND FRINGE. HAND-PAINTED LILY FLOWER. Size of banner 21 inches wide, 27 inch long. New. Lined back. Painting is a work of art. Bargain price, $4.50.

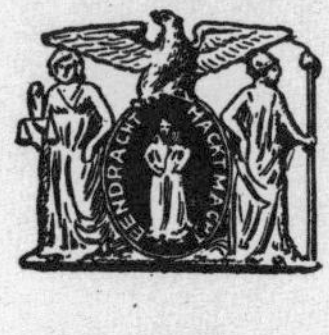


01189.

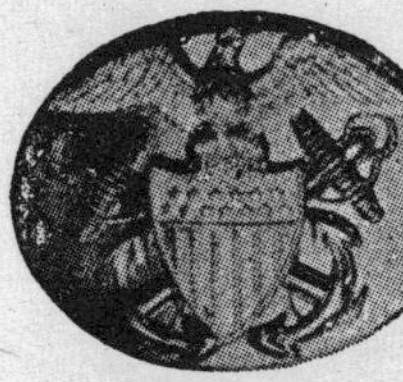

01189AA

0-1189. CITY OF BROOKLYN COAT OF ARMS AND MOTTO, COLLAR, OR COAT BADGE. Two female figure supporters, with centre figure and motto, "Een Dracht Macht." Size ¾ inch, with wire fastening. This motto is also that of President Kruger of South Africa. Price, 25 cents each.

0-1189AA. LADIES' BELT BUCKLE. With non-commissioned officer's insignia in relief. Gilt finish. Handsome souvenir buckle. Price, $3.45.

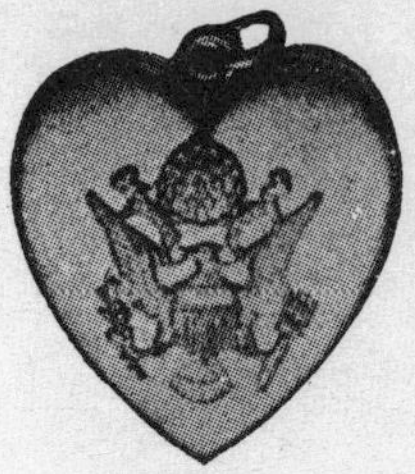

1190AA.

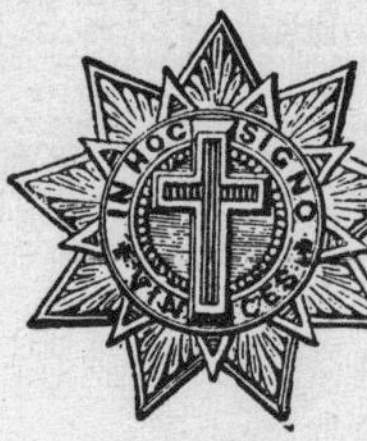


01043.

0-1190AA. HEART-SHAPED LOCKET. With U. S. Coat of Arms in hard enamel. Complete, with suspension loop. Gilt finish. Price, $2.40.

0-1043. BALDRIC STAR. 9-pointed star with SILVERED SUN RAYS. Raised border with motto. "In Hoc Signo Vinces." Gilt cross, with entwined serpent in silvered metal, red enameled background. Size 4 inches. Fastening loop on the back. In fine order. Price, $1.50 each.

0-1076. COLLECTION OF ANTIQUE BRASS BELT BUCKLES. Helmet plates, chin scales and military insignia, mounted on a wood board painted red, 29½ inches in diameter. 106 pieces, which include one Napoleon First Empire Eagle belt buckle, 11 antique brass helmet plates, with castle, Fleur-de-Lys, buckles with lion head cross, etc. Price for the collection, $25.00.

# UNITED STATES
# Presidential Bronze Medals

TWENTY-SIX BRONZE MEDALS, BEGINNING WITH PRESIDENT GEORGE WASHINGTON, DOWN TO EX-PRESIDENT WILLIAM H. TAFT. All are 76 millimetres in size (about 3 inches), 5mm. thick, are made of bronze, and are in perfect condition. Each medal weighs 8 ounces. The illustration shows the obverse, or face side, of each medal, the bust stamped in relief, the work of the best artists. In the early settlement of the United States a die was made for these medals, for presentation to Indian Chiefs as a peace medal.

*(Millimetres)*

Millimetre scale measurement showing size of medals.

291. George Washington, President U. S., 1789.
292. John Adams, President U. S., 1797.
293. Thomas Jefferson, President U. S., 1801.
294. James Madison, President U. S., 1809.
295. James Monroe, President U. S., 1817.
296. John Quincy Adams, President U. S., 1825.
297. Andrew Jackson, President U. S., 1829.

298. Martin Van Buren, President U. S., 1837.
299. Wm. Henry Harrison, President U. S., 1841.
300. John Tyler, President U. S., 1841.
301. James K. Polk, President U. S., 1845.
302. Zachary Taylor, President U. S., 1849.
303. Millard Fillmore, President U. S. 1850.
304. Franklin Pierce, President U. S., 1853.
305. James Buchanan, President U. S., 1857.
306. Abraham Lincoln, President U. S., 1861.
307. Andrew Johnson, President U. S., 1865.
308. Ulysses S. Grant, President U. S., 1869.
309. Rutherford B. Hayes, President U. S., 1877.
310. James A. Garfield, President U. S., 1881.
311. Chester A. Arthur, President U. S., 1881.
312. Grover Cleveland, President U. S., 1885-'93.
313. Benjamin Harrison, President U. S., 1889.
314. William McKinley, President U. S., 1897.
315. Theodore Roosevelt, President U. S., 1901.
316. William H. Taft, President U. S., 1909.

On the reverse side of the medals is TOMAHAWK and PIPE OF PEACE, with CLASPED HANDS. The reverse on all medals from No. 291 to No. 298, and from No. 300 to No. 302, are alike. Reverse of medal No. 299 has inscribed "INAUGURATED PRESIDENT OF UNITED STATES, March 4, 1841, died April 4, 1841"; No. 306 has inauguration and death dates on the reverse. The balance, from No. 308 down, have inscribed on the reverse, "PRESIDENT OF THE UNITED STATES," with date of INAUGURATION. Buyer can have his choice of any one of these medals at $2.00 each, the collection of 26 for $48.00, registered postage 20 cents each extra.

# BRONZE MEDALS
### Authorized by U. S. Congress to Naval Officers for distinguished Services in the Wars for Indpendance and 1812. Dies made in France.

**268. CAPT. EDWARD PREBLE,** Reverse shows STORMING FORTS, ATTACK ON TRIPOLI, 1804; obverse, Bust of Capt. Preble. Size, 65mm. Price, $3.85.

**269. CAPT. JOHNSTON BLAKELEY.** Reverse shows CAPTURE OF THE BRITISH SHIP REINDEER by Capt. Blakeley, Comdg. U. S. Ship Washington; obverse, Bust of Capt. Blakeley. Size, 65mm. Price, $3.85.

**270. CAPT. WILLIAM BAINBRIDGE.** Reverse shows CAPTURE OF THE BRITISH FRIGATE JAVA, 1812; obverse, Bust of Capt. Bainbridge. Size, 65mm. Price, $3.85.

**271. CAPT. CHARLES STEWART.** Reverse shows CAPTURE OF THE BRITISH SHIPS CYANE AND LEVANT, 1815; obverse, Bust of Capt. Stewart. Size, 65mm. Price, $3.85.

**264. CAPT. STEPHEN DECATUR.** Reverse shows CAPTURE OF THE BRITISH FRIGATE MACEDONIAN, 1812; obverse, Bust of Capt. Decatur. Price, $3.85.

**265. LIEUT. W. BURROWS.** Reverse shows CAPTURE OF THE BRITISH SHIP BOXER, 1813, as shown on page 302, No. 282; obverse side, as illustrated, arms trophy, arm, etc. Size, 65mm. Price, $3.85.

**266. CAPT. ISAAC HULL.** Reverse shows CAPTURE OF THE BRITISH FRIGATE GUERRIERE, 1812; obverse, Bust of Capt. Hull. (This medal is repaired at rim.) Size, 65mm. Price, $3.85.

**267. CAPT. THOMAS MACDONOUGH.** Reverse shows BATTLE OF LAKE CHAMPLAIN, 1814; obverse, Bust of Capt. Macdonough. (Medal dealer in Europe wanted upward of six dollars for this medal.) Size, 65mm. Price, $3.85.

**276. CAPT. JACOB JONES.** Reverse shows CAPTURE OF THE BRITISH SHIP FROLIC, 1812; obverse, Bust of Capt. Jones. Size, 65mm. Price, $3.85.

**277. COMMODORE OLIVER H. PERRY.** Reverse shows THE CAPTURE OF THE BRITISH FLEET ON LAKE ERIE, SEPTEMBER 10, 1812, with inscription, "WE HAVE MET THE ENEMY AND THEY ARE OURS"; obverse, Bust of Commodore Perry. Size, 60mm. Price, $4.50.

**278. CAPT. LOUIS WARRINGTON.** Reverse shows CAPTURE OF THE BRITISH SHIP EPERVIER, 1814; obverse, Bust of Capt. Warrington. Size, 65mm. Price, $3.85.

**279. COMMODORE OLIVER H. PERRY MEDAL, PRESENTED BY STATE OF PENNSYLVANIA.** Reverse shows THE CAPTURE OF THE BRITISH FLEET AT THE BATTLE OF LAKE ERIE, 1813; obverse, Bust of Com. Perry. Size, 65mm. Price, $3.85.

**272. CAPT. THOMAS TRUXTON** Reverse shows SEA BATTLE BETWEEN THE CONSTELLATION AND LA VENGEANCE, March 24, 1800; obverse, Bust of Capt. Truxton. Size, 58mm. Price, $3.85.

**273. CAPT. JOHN PAUL JONES.** Reverse shows CAPTURE OF THE BRITISH FRIGATE SERAPHIS, SEPTEMBER 23, 1779; obverse, Bust of Capt. Jones. Price, $4.50.

**274. CAPT. JAMES BIDDLE.** Reverse shows CAPTURE OF THE BRITISH SHIP PENGUIN, 1815, as shown on page 302, No. 283; obverse, Bust of Capt. Biddle. Size, 65mm. Price, $3.85.

**275. CAPT. JAMES LAWRENCE.** Reverse shows CAPTURE OF THE BRITISH SHIP PEACOCK, FEBRUARY 24, 1813; obverse, Bust of Capt. Lawrence. A few months later Lawrence was killed in the battle between the Chesapeake and the Shannon. Lawrence's dying words, "DON'T GIVE UP THE SHIP," is a motto in the United States Navy. Size, 65mm. Price, $3.85.

All the above medals were struck by act of Congress. The obverse side is shown in the illustration. The reverse contains inscription, battle scenes, etc.; the work of French artist. We can also furnish the following similar medals at $3.85 each, not illustrated:

LIEUT. McCALL AT THE CAPTURE OF THE BOXER.
CAPT. ELLIOT AT THE BATTLE OF LAKE ERIE.
CAPT. HENLEY AT THE BATTLE OF LAKE CHAMPLAIN.
LIEUT. CASSIN, BATTLE OF LAKE CHAMPLAIN.

All are size 65mm. bronze medals, in fine condition. Price, $3.85 each.

For millimeter measurement scale, see page 300. Any of the above medals can be sent by registered mail, 18 cents extra.

# Bronze Medals

**280.** BRONZE MEDAL AUTHORIZED BY CONGRESS TO OFFICERS AND MEN OF THE FRENCH, BRITISH AND SPANISH WARSHIPS FOR RESCUING MANY OF THE AMERICAN OFFICERS AND MEN OF THE "SOMERS," WRECKED OFF VERA CRUZ, 1846. Die made by American artist. Reverse shows the wreck, obverse the rescue. Size, 57mm. Price, $3.50.

**281.** HONORARY DIPLOMATIC MEDAL, PRESENTED TO RETIRING DIPLOMATS BY ORDER OF PRESIDENT JEFFERSON. Reverse illustration shown, inscribed "TO PEACE AND COMMERCE; obverse has the GREAT SEAL OF THE UNITED STATES. Size, 68mm. Price, $4.50.

**282.** Reverse illustration of bronze medal, No. 265, on page 301, authorized by Congress to LIEUT. W. BURROWS FOR CAPTURE OF THE BRITISH SHIP BOXER, 1813. Size, 65mm. Price, $3.85.

**283.** Reverse illustration of medal No. 274, page 301, authorized by Congress to CAPT. JAMES BIDDLE FOR THE CAPTURE OF THE BRITISH SHIP PENGUIN, March 23, 1814. Size, 65mm. Price, $3.85.

**84.** MAJOR-GENERAL ZACHARY TAYLOR. Reverse shows THE BATTLE OF PALO ALTO, 1846; RESACA DE LA PALMA, May 9, 1846. Obverse, Bust of General Taylor. Size, 65mm. Price, $3.85.

**85.** MAJOR-GENERAL EDMUND P. GAINES. Reverse shows BATTLE OF FORT ERIE, November 3, 1814; obverse, Bust of Gen'l Gaines. Size, 65mm. Price, $3.85.

**86.** GENERAL WINFIELD SCOTT. Reverse shows BATTLES OF CHIPPEWA AND NIAGARA, 1814; obverse, Bust of Gen'l Scott. Size, 65mm. Price, $3.85.

**87.** MAJOR-GENERAL WM. H. HARRISON. Reverse shows BATTLE OF THE THAMES, October 5, 1813; obverse, Bust of Gen'l Harrison. Size, 65mm. Price, $3.85.

**284.** BRIG.-GENERAL ELEAZER W. RIPLEY. Reverse shows BATTLE SCENES. MEDAL AWARDED FOR BATTLES OF CHIPPEWA, NIAGARA AND ERIE, November, 1814. Size, 65mm. Price, $3.85.

**285.** GENERAL GEORGE WASHINGTON RETAKING BOSTON, March 17, 1776. Reverse shows WASHINGTON AND STAFF BEFORE BOSTON; obverse, nude Bust of Washington. Size, 68mm. Price, $3.85.

**286.** REVERSE ILLUSTRATION OF THE GREAT MEDAL SEAL OF THE UNITED STATES, AN UNFINISHED PYRAMID, WITH THE DATE 1776 ON THE BOTTOM STONE; obverse shows the great seal of the United States. Size, 62mm. Price, $3.85.

The registered postage for any medal on this page is 18 cents extra, with the exception of No. 281. This is a larger medal, and the postage is 20 cents. We can furnish the following medals to U. S. Army Officers, not illustrated on this page, at the price of $3.85 each, all in perfect condition:

FOR THE BATTLES OF CHIPPEWA, NIAGARA AND FORT ERIE, MAJOR-GENERAL BROWN AND BRIG. GENERAL MILLER. Also medal to GOVERNOR SHELBY FOR THE BATTLE OF THE THAMES, AND TO MAJOR TAYLOR FOR THE BATTLE OF MONTEREY.

Millimeter measurement scale shown on page 300.

**93.** GENERAL ANTHONY WAYNE. Reverse shows THE CAPTURE OF THE BRITISH FORTIFICATIONS AT STONY POINT, HUDSON RIVER, 1779; obverse shown in illustration. Size, 55mm. Price, $3.85.

**94.** GEN'L HORATIO GATES. Reverse shows the SURRENDER AT SARATOGA, 1777. GATES RECEIVING BURGOYNE'S SWORD IN THE PRESENCE OF THE TWO OPPOSING ARMIES. Size, 56mm. Price, $3.85.

**95.** GENERAL NATHANIEL GREEN. Reverse shows THE BATTLE OF EUTAW SPRINGS, 1781; obverse, Bust of Gen'l Green. Size, 57mm. Price, $3.85.

**96.** GENERAL DANIEL MORGAN. Reverse shows BATTLE OF COWPENS, 1781; obverse illustration shows AMERICAN INDIAN PLACING WREATH ON HEAD OF MORGAN. Size, 56mm. Price, $3.95.

# Bronze Medals

Authorized by United States Congress to army officers and others for distinguished services in war. The dies for these early medals, were made by French artists. Illustrations show the obverse or face side; description gives size and price. Millimetre measurement scale on page 300.

88. COL. GEORGE CROGHAN. BATTLE OF SANDUSKY, 1813. Size, 65mm. Price, $3.85.

89. MAJOR-GENERAL ANDREW JACKSON. BATTLE OF NEW ORLEANS, 1815. Size, 65mm. Price, $3.85.

90. MAJOR-GENERAL ALEXANDER MACOMB. BATTLE OF PLATTSBURG, 1814. Size, 65mm. Price, $3.85.

91. OATH OF ALLEGIANCE TO CONSTITUTION, BUST OF WASHINGTON. Size, 30mm. Price, $3.00.

92. VALLEY FORGE CENTENNIAL, 1778-1878. BUST OF WASHINGTON. Size, 40mm. Price, $2.50.

97. MAJOR HENRY LEE, BATTLE OF PAULUS HOOK, August 19, 1779. Price, $3.85.

98. COLONEL JOHN E. HOWARD, BATTLE OF COWPENS, 1781. Size, 47mm. Price, $3.85.

99. WASHINGTON RESIGNING COMMISSION AND PRESIDENCY, 1797. Size, 54mm. Price, $3.00.

100. CAPTURE OF STONY POINT ON HUDSON RIVER. Reproduced copper medal, 1880. Size, 47mm. Price, $2.50.

101. COLONEL WILLIAM WASHINGTON, BATTLE OF COWPENS, 1781. Reverse shown. Obverse, Bust of Colonel Washington. Size, 47mm. Price, $3.85.

288. CITY OF PHILADELPHIA MEDAL TO CAPTS. CREIGHTON, LOW AND STOUFFER FOR RESCUE OF PASSENGERS FROM S. S. SAN FRANCISCO, 1854. Obverse shown. Reverse, wreck scene. Size, 75mm. Price, $6.00.

289. GENERAL U. S. GRANT, 1863, CAMPAIGN OPENING UP THE MISSISSIPPI RIVER. Reverse shown. Obverse, Bust of Gen'l Grant. Size, 103mm., rim 12mm. Price, $10.00.

290. MAJOR-GENERAL WINFIELD SCOTT, MEXICAN CAMPAIGN, March 9, 1848. Reverse shown. Obverse, Bust of Gen'l Scott. Size, 90mm. 3½ inches diameter, rim 8mm. Price, $7.50.

79. GILT MEDAL. LOUIS XVIII ENTERING INTO PARIS, May 3, 1824. Size, 42mm. Price, $5.00.

80. BRONZE MEDAL. GEORGE II TO AMERICAN COLONY INDIANS, 1757, ON CONCLUSION OF TREATY OF PEACE. Obverse shows Bust of King George II. Reverse, Indian and white man around campfire, with pipe of peace and inscription. Size, 44mm. Price, $6.50.

81. PRESIDENT LINCOLN EMANCIPATION BRONZE MEDAL, 1863. Size, 50mm. Price, $3.85.

82. BRONZE MEDAL. Obverse shown. In hoc signo vinces. Size, 40mm. Price, $6.50.

83. BRONZE MEDAL. Obverse shown (illustration is wrong end up), "Pont. M. A. Vn., Innocence XI," with crown, double-headed eagle. Reverse, lion on shield, with motto, "Revus Avaros Non Impleritor." Size, 38mm. Price, $6.50.

Any of the above medals can be sent by registered mail for 18 cents extra, with the exception of Nos. 288 and 290. These are larger and heavier; postage, 30 cents. Medal 288, postage 40 cents.

210. HENRY VI, 1422.    211. RICHARD I, 1189.    212. HENRY III, 1216.    213. WILLIAM III, 1689.    214. GEORGE III, 1760.

195. HENRY IV, 1399.    196. EDWARD VI, 1547.    197. QUEEN CAROLINE.    198. HENRY VII, 1485.    199. GEORGE IV, 1820.

15. KING STEPHEN, 1135.    216. GEORGE I, 1714.    217. QUEEN MARIA I.    218. HENRY V, 1413.    219. WILLIAM I, THE CONQUEROR, 1066.

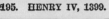

200. QUEEN MARIA I.    201. QUEEN ANNA, 1702.    202. QUEEN VICTORIA, 1837.    203. RICHARD II, 1377.    204. GEORGE II, 1727.

56        57        58        59        60

ORNAMENTAL BUTTONS, HANDSOME ENOUGH FOR BREASTPINS.

56 is 15-16 inch square.
57 to 60 is 1-16 inch in diameter.
56 is crimson center, with inlaid rows of white glass; border consists of small pieces of cut glass, in imitation f diamonds, set in metal frame.  Very handsome.
51 has black glass inlaid with small imitation glass diamonds border.
58. Golden-colored, fluted glass background, with border of similar pieces of glass, set in metal frames.
59. Pearl-colored glass, with metal flower center, with three imitation pearls.  (We use the word IMITATION PEARLS.  We are not experts.  They may be real.  We offer as are.)  With imitation glass diamond border.
60 is green glass center, with glass imitation diamond border.    THESE BEAUTIFUL BUTTONS  came from an ssignee's sale of high-class military and society goods.  Our price for BUYER'S  CHOICE of any of the buttons is EN CENTS EACH, with the exception of No. 59, 20 cents.

Buyer's choice of the above medals, $4.85 each. White metal, size 40mm. EXCEPTIONALLY FINE WORKMANSHIP. Good condition. The obverse, or face side, is shown in the illustration, and gives the name and title, with fine relief figure of head or bust. The reverse side gives the date of birth, date of crowning, and of death, together with the MOST IMPORTANT EVENTS that happened DURING THEIR REIGNS.

220. EDWARD III, 1327.    221. CHARLES II, 1660.    222. HENRY I, 1100.    223. EDWARD IV, 1461.    224. EDWARD V, 1483.

205. CHARLES I, 1625.    206. WILLIAM II, 1087.    207. OLIVER CROM-    208. EDWARD I, 1272.
WELL, 1653.
75. EDWARD II, 1307.

The above medals are 40mm. in size, are made of white metal. Obverse illustration shows the bust and title. The reverse has inscribed the dates of BIRTH, CROWNING AND DEATH of the KING, together with the most important events that happened during the King's reign. The excellent workmanship of the dies, in making these medals, is shown in the illustration. They are works of art. Are offered, buyer's choice, at $4.85 each.

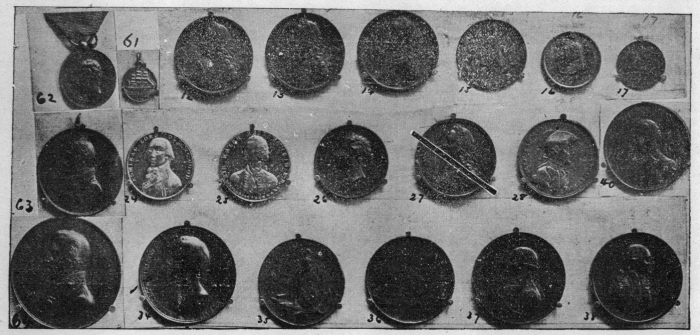

62. BULGARIAN BRONZE SERVICE MEDALS, with ribbon. Illustration is the obverse side. Reverse has Greek inscription within the ring. In good condition. Size, 25mm. Price, $6.85.

61. SMALL MEDAL, STRUCK FROM COPPER METAL; H.M.S. VICTORY, THE CENTENNIAL YEAR OF THE BATTLE OF TRAFALGAR. Illustration is the obverse side. Good condition. Size, 17mm. Price, $2.50.

12. GILT-BRONZE MEDAL, GEORGE II, 1758. Obverse shows the BUST OF GEORGE II. Reverse, two rows containing names of battles, around the border, with the date 1758. Good condition. Size, 42mm. Price, $6.50.

13. Same as No. 12, in better condition. Price, $7.50.

14. Same description as No. 12; fine condition. Price, $8.50.

16. QUEEN VICTORIA MEDAL, dated 1837-97. Pewter-gilt, poor condition. Size, 30mm. Price, $1.85.

17. QUEEN ANNE GILT-BRONZE MEDAL, 1703. Obverse shows BUST OF QUEEN. Reverse, a SEA BATTLE. Good condition. Size, 25mm. Price, $8.50.

63. SIR ROBERT WILSON, COPPER MEDAL, 1821. Obverse shown. Reverse, inscription, "CURIBUS SERATUS," within an OAK WREATH. Size, 40mm. Price, $7.50.

24. ADMIRAL LORD COLLINGWOOD, PEWTER MEDAL, 1805. Obverse shown in illustration. Reverse, the FAMOUS FLEET IN BATTLE FORMATION, October 21, 1805. Size, 38mm. Price, $5.50.

26. SIR JOHN MOORE, COPPER MEDAL, 1809. Price, $6.50.

28. GENERAL ELLIOTT ATTACKING GIBRALTAR, 1783. Reverse shows the FLEET ATTACKING ROCK OF GIBRALTAR. Pewter. Size, 40mm. Price, $5.50.

40. SIR RICHARD ONSLOW, ADMIRAL OF THE BLUE, 1798. Reverse shows SEA BATTLE. Good condition. Size, 50mm. Price, $7.85.

64. DUKE OF WELLINGTON, BRONZE. Born May 1, 1769; died September 14, 1852. Size, 52mm. Price, $7.85.

34. ADMIRAL NELSON BRONZE MEDAL, 1805. Size, 54mm. Price, $7.85.

35 and 36. ADMIRAL NELSON VICTORY OF THE NILE, 1798, as shown on obverse. Reverse, inscription, ALMIGHTY GOD HAS BLESSED HER MAJESTY. Sea Battle. Size 48mm. Price, $7.50.

37. MEDAL, INSCRIBED "EARL OF ST. VINCENT, ADMIRAL OF THE WHITE, 1797." The reverse shows FEMALE FIGURE, WEEPING, LEANING ON SPANISH SHIELD, WITH SEA BATTLE IN THE DISTANCE. Fine condition. Size, 48mm. Price, $8.50.

38. EARL HOWE, 1794. Reverse shows SEA BATTLE, June 11, 1794. Good condition. Size, 48mm. Price, $10.00.

45. BRONZE REGIMENTAL FIFTH FOOT FUSILIER MERIT MEDAL, March 10, 1767. Obverse, ST. GEORGE AND THE DRAGON, SCROLL INSCRIBED "QUO FATA OCANT." REISSUED April 25, 1805. Good condition. Size, 34mm. A rare medal. Price, $20.00.

18. CAPT. H. C. KANE, H. M. S. CALLIOPE, FROM FRIEND AND ADMIRER, THE MARQUIS DE LEUVILLE, FOR BRITISH SEAMANSHIP. Good condition. Size, 30mm. Price, $6.50.

19, 20 and 21. Obverse and reverse illustration of medals given for the Victory of the Nile, August 1, 1798. Size, 38mm. Pewter. Price, $3.85 each.

29 and 30 Nelson Medals obverse and reverse shown, Price, $8.50.

22. COPPER-BRONZE MEDAL, BELLE ISLE, 1759. Obverse inscription, "BRITAIN TRIUMPHED HAWK COMMANDED OFF BELLE ISLE, November 20, 1759." Reverse inscription, "FRANCE RELINQUISHES THE SEA," AMAZON AND WARRIOR IN COMBAT. Good condition. Size, 40mm. Price, $16.50.

23. MEDAL WITH BUST OF NELSON, GIVEN FOR THE VICTORY ON THE NILE, 1798. White metal. Size, 38mm. Good condition. Price, $5.85.

32. BOULTON'S BATTLE OF TRAFALGAR, NELSON MEDAL. Given to Heroes of Trafalgar. Bust of NELSON, with battle scene. October 21, 1805. In fine condition. Price, $14.85.

33. BOULTON, NELSON MEDAL, GILT-BRONZE. Same description as No. 31. Price, $14.50.

65. WATERLOO SILVER MEDAL. Obverse, HEAD OF KING GEORGE. Reverse, Emblematic flag, WELLINGTON-WATERLOO. Died June 18, 1815. Size, 1 1/10 inches. Price, $16.50.

66. FIELD MARSHAL WELLINGTON BRONZE MEDAL. Obverse, head of Wellington, with inscription. Reverse, "The Deliverer of Portugal and Spain, 1814. Size, 1 1/10 inches. Fair condition. Price, $6.50.

39. DUKE OF WELLINGTON LARGE BRONZE MEDAL. Fine condition. Obverse, BUST, INSCRIBED "ART COM D WELLINGTON." On the reverse, "VOTA REPUBLICA" within WREATH. Size, 55mm. Price, $9.75.

1. ADMIRAL DUNCAN'S DEFEAT OF THE DUTCH FLEET, GILT MEDAL. Size, 20mm. Good condition. Price, $4.50.

2. ADMIRAL SIR S. SMITH, 1799. Reverse inscription, "ACRE DEFEATED, BONAPARTE REPULSED, SYRIA SAVED, May 20, 1799." Size, 24mm. Good condition. Price, $4.50.

3. EARL HOWE, ADMIRAL OF THE WHITE K.G. THE FRENCH FLEET DEFEATED OFF USHANTE, June 1, 1794. Gilt. Size, 24mm. Price, $6.85.

4. ADMIRAL EARL ST. VINCENT, SPANISH FLEET DEFEATED, February 14, 1797. Gilt. Size, 24mm. Price, $4.85.

5, 6 and 7. LORD NELSON SILVER MEDALS, ST. VINCENT, ABOUKIR, TRAFALGAR. Size, 20mm. BUST OF NELSON, WITH FAMOUS SIGNAL MOTTO, "ENGLAND EXPECTS EVERY MAN TO DO HIS DUTY." Good condition. Size, 20mm. Price, $6.50 each.

8, 9 and 10. LORD NELSON GILT MEDALS, INSCRIBED, "ABOUKIR, 14 ENGLISH DEFEATED 15 FRENCH SHIPS, 10 TAKEN, 2 BURNT, August 1, 1798." Size, 20mm. Price, $4.80 each.

11. MEDAL WITH BUST OF GEORGE III, INSCRIBED "KING OF GREAT BRITAIN, FRANCE AND IRELAND." Reverse inscribed, "RESOLUTION, ADVENTURE SAILED FROM ENGLAND May 1, 1772." This medal was for CAPT. COOK'S DISCOVERY OF THE SANDWICH ISLANDS. Copper medal. Size, 42mm. Fine order. Price, $25.00.

41. BELGIUM COPPER-BRONZE MEDAL. Fine workmanship. BELGIUM COAT OF ARMS, "MALINES, 1886." Size, 50mm. Price, $7.50.

25 U. S. GOVERNMENT MEDAL CASES, for holding medals. Assorted sizes. Clasp fastening, velvet lined, leather covered. In good order. Price, 20 cents each.

42. BELGIUM COPPER-BRONZE MEDAL. Size, 50mm. COAT OF ARMS AND MOTTO ENGRAVED WITHIN OAK AND LAUREL LEAF WREATH, "MALINES, 1887." Price, $7.50.

73. POPE PIUS IX MEDAL. 1720. Size, 2 inches. Weight, 1½ oz. White, silvered metal. Reverse side has PONTIFICAL COAT OF ARMS. Price, $16.85.

### Write for prices on medals not shown in catalog.

74. LARGE MEDAL, INSCRIBED "PRESENTED TO THE MEN OF H.M.S. VICTORY WHO WERE PRESENT AT THE OPENING OF THE NELSON MONUMENT IN TRAFALGAR SQUARE, 1844." Obverse has BUST OF NELSON, WITH FAMOUS SIGNAL MOTTO. Reverse shows TRAFALGAR SQUARE. NELSON MONUMENT. DATED October 11, 1844. With suspension ring. Size, 62mm. White, silvered metal. Price, $15.00.

209. HENRY VIII MEDAL. Reverse. BORN 1491. CROWNED 1509. DIED 1547. In his reign, King Henry was excommunicated by the Pope, Bible was translated, dies first used in England. Size, 40mm.: pewter. Price, $4.85.

78. CQD S. S. REPUBLIC MEDAL. Obverse shown in illustration. Reverse inscription, "FROM THE SALOON PASSENGERS OF THE R.M.S. BALTIC AND R.M.S. REPUBLIC TO THE OFFICERS AND CREW OF THE S. S. REPUBLIC, BALTIC AND FLORIDA FOR GALLANTRY CONNECTED WITH THE RESCUE OF OVER 1700 SOULS, January 24, 1909. White, silvered metal, 1¾ inches in diameter, with ring and ribbon. In good condition. Price, $12.85.

233. LARGE SILVER PEACE MEDAL. Eagle with outstretched wings. "Paris. 3d of August. 1816," with inscription around the border. Diameter, 1½ inches. Good condition. Price, $10.00.

234. FREIDRICH WILHELM III SILVER MEDAL. "FOR SERVICES TO THE STATE." Size, 1 9/16 inches. Good condition. Price, $9.85.

239. GERMAN BRONZE CROSS MEDAL FOR 1866 CAMPAIGN. Size, 1⅜ inches. Good condition, with silk ribbon. Price, $6.50.

240. WATERLOO BRONZE MEDAL, given to German Soldier. Size, 1 1/16 inches. Good condition. Price, $8.75.

## BRITISH WORLD WAR MEDALS

**No. 81B. GILT METAL MEDAL**, marked on reverse THE GREAT WAR FOR CIVILIZATION 1914-1919, with ribbon. Price, $2.95.

**No. 82B. BRITISH WAR MEDAL**, showing man on horse back. Marked 1914-1918, with ribbon. Price $4.85.

**No. 84B. MONS STAR** with dates 1914-15, with ribbon. Price, $3.85.

**YSER BRONZE MEDAL, BELGIUM**, with red and black ribbon. Obverse has crown over letter A with wounded lion and word YSER. Reverse: Word YSER at top and figure of naked youth with staff and wreath, dated 17-31 OCT. 1914. Given for defense. Price, $7.50.

**OFFICIAL MEDAL**, made of STERLING SILVER, size 2¼ inches. Obverse shows head of CHRISTOPHER COLUMBUS in center with name above, with his three ships in circle sailing around him. On reverse the words: TO COMMEMORATE THE FOUR HUNDREDTH ANNIVERSARY OF THE DISCOVERY OF AMERICA BY CHRISTOPHER COLUMBUS. By authority of the committee of one hundred citizens of New York. With American and Spanish shields. Made by Gorham Mfg. Co. of New York. Price, $5.50.

**No. 108A. BRITISH MEDAL**, for Egyptian campaign, issued to E. MAY, on Her Majesty's Ship "ALEXANDRA" with one bar marked: ALEXANDRIA, 11th JULY. Medal is marked: EGYPT 1882. Navy medals from this campaign are scarce. Price $7.85.

**No. 108B. BRITISH MEDAL**, for Egyptian campaign. Medal marked: EGYPT 1882, no bars. Price, $6.50.

**B.D.-1. BRITISH DISCHARGE BADGE**, silver circle with words: FOR KING AND EMPIRE. SERVICES RENDERED. With the CROWN over monogram: GRI. This badge was given to soldiers upon honorable discharge. These are scarce here. Price, $1.50 each.

**No. D25. SET TWO CRIMEA MEDALS** with ribbons on silver breast bar. One silver British Medal like illustration No. 1 on page 278 and No. 123 on page 291, with FOUR bars: SEBASTOPOL, INKERMANN, BALAKLAVA, ALMA. Marked on edge: SOLVAN, R1 HORSE. Second medal is the French Crimea medal marked La Crimea 1855 as per illustration No. 175 on page 295. We offer the set of two with ribbons and two medal bar clasp at $32.00.

**No. 25-1. QUEEN'S SOUTH AFRICA SILVER MEDAL** with ribbon and FIVE bars; BELFAST, JOHANNESBURG, DRIEFONTEIN, PAARDEBERG, CAPE COLONY. Medal with so many bars are rare. Issued to D. McDONALD of the GORDON HIGHLANDERS. Price, $11.50.

**No. 25-2. QUEEN'S SOUTH AFRICA SILVER MEDAL** with FOUR bars: SOUTH AFRICA 1902, SOUTH AFRICA 1901, TRANSVAAL, NAVAL. Complete with ribbon. Price, $8.50.

**No. 151D. QUEEN'S SOUTH AFRICA SILVER MEDAL** with ribbon and three bars: TRANSVAAL, ORANGE FREE STATE, CAPE COLONY. Price, $7.85.

**No. 149D. QUEEN'S SILVER MEDAL** issued for service on PUNJAB FRONTIER 1897-98. Complete with ribbon. Price, $6.50.

**No. 164. FRENCH REPUBLIC COLONIAL MEDAL, WITHOUT BAR.** Obverse is shown with head wearing military helmet, and with the words: REPUBLIQUE FRANCAISE. On the reverse at edge: TONKIN, CHINE ANNAM, and the dates 1883-1885. In the center the words: SONTAY, BAC-NINH, FOUTCHEOU, FORMOSE, TUYEN-QUAN, PESCADORES. This is white silver medal complete with yellow ribbon with four green stripes. Price, $6.85.

**No. 190. POPE'S CROSS**, given to Volunteers who served in the Papal Brigade, under Major O'Reilley, in the Garibaldi Campaign. Reverse side shows the cross reversed or up side down, as tradition states that St. Peter was thus crucified. Price, $12.50.

**No. 27-1. CORONATION MEDAL**, in silver with ribbon, of King George the VI with his Queen, June 26th, 1902. Price, $8.00.

**No. 122. WATERLOO MEDAL**, Marked WELLINGTON, WATERLOO, June 18, 1815. Obverse shows head of King George. With ribbon. Price, $38.00.

**No. 27-2. GALLIPOLIS STAR** issued to officers who went through that campaign. Center of medal is red enamel, with silver crescent and Turkish inscription. A rare medal. Price, $8.50.

**No. 119. QUEEN VICTORIA JUBILEE MEDAL**, in bronze. OBVERSE MARKED: In commemoration of the 50th year of the reign of Queen Victoria, 20 June, 1887, with crown, and roses, thistles and shamrocks intertwined. Price, $16.00.

**No. 108. BRITISH MEDAL**, for Egyptian campaign. Medal marked: EGYPT, and obverse shows head of Queen Victoria. Bar marked: SUAKIN, 1885. Price, $7.00.

From time to time we are receiving other medals from Europe, given to soldiers of different countries. If you do not find listed the medals you want, send us description, and we will quote.

143. QUEEN'S SOUTH AFRICA MEDAL, with ribbon, with two bars marked: DEFENSE OF LADYSMITH, TALANA. Price $6.85.

132. EGYPTIAN THREE BAR MEDAL, inscribed: ABU-KLEA, THE NILE, TEL ELKEBIR. Medal similar to No. 108 on page 290. Rare with three bars. Price $13.50.

133. BRONZE STAR MEDAL presented to British Army soldiers for engagement at Alexandria by KHEDIVE OF EGYPT, 1882. This is one of the oldest styles of British Army Medals. Price $8.75.

134. TURKISH SILVER MEDAL FOR CAMPAIGN IN CRETE, dated 1285 Mohammedan, 1868 A. D. Price $12.50.

142. QUEEN'S SOUTH AFRICAN MEDAL with ribbon, with three bars marked: DRIEFONTEIN, PAARDEBERG, RELIEF OF KIMBERLEY. Price $6.85.

136. SOUTH AFRICAN, THREE BARS, INSCRIBED "BELFAST, DEFENSE OF LADYSMITH, ELANDSLAGTE." Reverse side shows Bust of QUEEN VICTORIA. Price $7.00.

122. WATERLOO, June 18, 1815. Reverse, WELLINGTON, WITH WINGED ANGEL STYLUS. Obverse as shown in illustration, GEORGE P. REGENT. Price. $37.50.

123. CRIMEAN WAR MEDAL, THREE BARS, INSCRIBED "ALMA, BALAKLAVA, SEBASTOPOL." Obverse shows Bust of QUEEN VICTORIA. Good condition. Price, $18.85. One in stock January, 1925.

124. CRIMEAN MEDAL, WITH ONE BAR, INSCRIBED "SEBASTOPOL." Price, $12.50.

126. CRIMEAN SILVER MEDAL, same as No. 123, but without any inscribed bar. Medal is marked CRIMEA, BUST OF QUEEN VICTORIA. Price, $10.00.

249. BRONZE MEDAL, "FREUEN KRIEGERN," FAITHFUL WARRIOR, MONOGRAM "C. U." Size, 1 1/16 inches. Price $6.75.

250. BRONZE MEDAL WITH GREEK INSCRIPTION. Obverse, TWO CROWNS, MONOGRAM, "F. E. A., 1853-1854-1855-1856." Size 1 1/16 inches, with purple ribbon, 3 yellow stripes. Price $6.85.

251. EMPEROR MAXIMILIAN SILVER MEDAL, WITH HEAD OF EMPEROR on the obverse. "AL MORITO MILITAIRE." On the reverse, with wreath. Size 1¼ inches. Price $14.50.

103. THREE-BAR CRIMEA MEDAL, INSCRIBED "BALAKLAVA, INKERMANN, SEBASTOPOL." Reverse shown in illustration. Obverse, QUEEN VICTORIA, 1854. Good condition. Awarded to James Price of DRAGOON GUARDS. Price, $18.50.

104. TURKISH CRIMEA SILVER MEDAL, AWARDED TO A FRENCH OFFICER. Obverse shown in illustration, inscribed "LA CRIMEA, 1855." Reverse, TURKISH INSCRIPTION WITHIN WREATH. Rare medal. Price, $20.00.

105. LONG SERVICE AND GOOD CONDUCT MEDAL TO CORP. JAMES PRICE, FIFTH DRAGOON GUARDS. Mate of No. 103. Price, $9.85.

102. GILT MEDAL, FIELD MARSHAL DUKE OF YORK, PRESENTATION OF COLORS BY HIS MAJESTY, August, 1813. Size, 1 9/16 inches; pewter. Price, $7.50.

Bronze medal with yellow and dark red ribbon. Obverse shows Roman Wolf over crossed axes and shield marked: S P Q R. Reverse with wreath and star marked: Roma Rivendicata Ai Suoi Liberatori. Price, $6.50.

156. QUEEN'S SOUTH AFRICAN MEDAL, with ribbon, with three bars marked: SOUTH AFRICA 1902, TRANSVAAL, ORANGE FREE STATE. Price $6.85.

157. QUEEN'S SOUTH AFRICAN MEDAL, with ribbon, with two bars marked: ORANGE FREE STATE, CAPE COLONY. Price $6.50.

118. QUEEN'S SOUTH AFRICAN MEDAL, with ribbon, with one bar marked: NATAL. Price $6.50.

SA-2. QUEEN'S SOUTH AFRICAN MEDAL, with ribbon, with one bar marked: CAPE COLONY. Price $6.50.

10

2B. **AUSTRIAN WAR MEDAL** with yellow and black ribbon. WAR CROSS in gold finish with AUSTRIAN coat of arms in SILVER set on. A very fine medal. Price, $6.50.

7B. **BRUSSELS BRONZE MEDAL** with ribbon, issued 1815. Obverse shows armed angel in combat with the devil. Reverse: BELGICI REGNI HABENAS CAPESSENTE WILHELMO NASSOVOEO, MDCCCXV. Price, $3.90.

12B. **BELGIAN LIFE SAVING MEDAL OF LEOPOLD II,** in silver with Crown. ISSUED TO J. C. LA FORGE. Price, $5.50.

70B. **SAXONY GILT FINISH MEDAL,** with red, white and black ribbon. Marked: 1870-1871. Price, $6.50.

18B. **BULGARIAN SILVER MEDAL** for campaign in CHILE. Red, white and blue ribbon with silver clasp. Obverse shows shield with word: MAPOCHO. Reverse: LA MUNICIPALIDAD DE SANTIAGO AL CUERPO DE BOMBEROS. Price, $4.50.

26B. **FRENCH MEDAL FOR CAMPAIGN IN MEXICO.** White ribbon with Mexican eagle and serpent. Obverse shows bust and NAPOLEON III EMPEREUR. Reverse: EXPEDITION DU MEXIQUE, with list of battles: CUMBRIES, CERRO-BORREGO, SAN LORENZO, PUEBLA, MEXICO, 1862-1865. Price, $10.00.

184. Obverse illustration of white medal, inscribed "VOORKRIGGS VER-RIGTINGEN," with KING'S HEAD. Reverse is plain. Size 1½ inches, with ribbon. Price, $6.50.

188. **AUSTRIAN WHITE, SILVERED, MEDAL. BUST OF KING.** INSCRIBED. Obverse. "FRANZ JOSEPH I, KAISER VON OESTRICH." Reverse. "MY FAITHFUL FOLK OF TYROL." 1866. Size, 1¼ inches. Price, $7.85.

189. **ITALIAN MEDAL. BY THE HUMANE RED CROSS SOCIETY FOR THE SIEGE OF PARIS,** 1870 to 1871. Copper. Size, 1⅜ inches. Price, $7.50.

262. **SILVER MEDAL, UNITED ITALY.** Obverse, illustrated. Reverse, inscribed "REDUCI DALLE PATRIE BATTAGLIE." Size, 1 1/16 inches. Blue silk ribbon, yellow center stripe. Price, $8.75.

191. **BRAZILIAN MEDAL FOR THE NAVAL BATTLE OFF REI-CHUELO,** June 14, 1865. Size, 1 inch. Price, $5.75.

110. **FOUR-BAR SOUTH AFRICAN SILVER MEDAL. BARS IN-SCRIBED** "RELIEF OF LADYSMITH, ORANGE-FREE STATE, TUGELA HEIGHTS, CAPE COLONY." Price, $8.50.

114. **TWO-BAR SILVER MEDAL,** INSCRIBED "SOUTH AFRICA, 1902, TRANSVAAL." Price, $7.50.

194. **KING LOUIS I PORTUGAL MEDAL FOR MILITARY VALOR,** 1868. WHITE, SILVERED MEDAL. Size, 1¼ inches. Price, $9.50.

111. **FIVE-BAR SOUTH AFRICAN SILVER MEDAL. BARS INSCRIBED** "BELFAST, DIAMOND HILL, JOHANNESBURG, ORANGE FREE STATE, CAPE COLONY." Price, $9.75.

173. 1 MINIATURE ST. HELENA FRENCH MEDAL. Gold finish with red and green ribbon. Price, $4.85.

173A. 1 MINIATURE MEDAL as above in bronze. Price, $4.50.

THE CROSS. Obverse shows figure of the POPE, as illustrated. Price, $20.00.

16. **EMPEROR NAPOLEON III. SILVERED WAR MEDAL,** given to French soldier for battles in Italy. Illustration shows the face side. On the reverse face is lettered "Campagne D Italie, 1850, Montebello, Palestro, Turligo, Magenta, Marignan Solferino." Measures 1¼ across faces. Complete, with silk ribbon. Price, $10.00.

71. **GRECIAN MILITARY BRONZE CROSS,** memento to the "BAVARIAN AUXILIARY CORPS." Blue silk ribbon. Size, 1¼ inches. Price, $5.75.

72. **GRECIAN MILITARY BRONZE CROSS,** same as No. 71. ⅟₁₆ inch (slightly smaller in size than No. 71). Price, $5.80.

52. **WHITE ENAMELED PAPAL CROSS WITH GILT METAL FLEUR DE LIS BETWEEN THE ARMS OF THE CROSS.** Obverse shows figure of the POPE, as illustrated. Polished gilt, width 3 inches; over 100 years old. Price, $20.00.

When Napoleon proposed the institution of the Legion of Honor he was told that "crosses and ribbons were the pillars of an hereditary throne, and that they were unknown to the Romans who conquered the world." His reply was that Rome rewarded the achievements of her citizens by many kinds of distinctions and that for the soldier as for all men in active life you must have *glory* and *distinction.* Recompenses are the food that nourish military virtue. —*Thomas Carter Book of War Medals.*

**25. FRENCH MILITARY UNIFORM BUTTON,** with wreath encircling eagle in raised relief work. Price, 60 cents.

**19. WATERLOO BUTTONS.** Brass, coat size, with raised eagle with spread wings. Marked: WATERLOO, R. S. G. These initials are ROYAL SCOTTISH GRAYS. Rare button. Price, $1.00.

**18. FRENCH REPUBLIQUE SILVERED MEDAL.** Illustration shows the face; on the reverse is shown rescue of French soldier. Size is 1⅝ inch. Price, $12.

**15. FRENCH REPUBLIQUE MEDALS** awarded in 1870 for Valeur et Discipline; size 1 1/16 inch. Illustration shows the obverse face. Reverse is lettered Republique Francaise, 1870; encircling medalion Valeur et Discipline, with silk ribbon. Price, $8.50 each. Not illustrated.

**168. FRENCH MEDAL.** Obverse shows BUST OF EMPEROR NAPOLEON III within a WREATH. Reverse, "CAMPAIGN D' ITALIA," and the names of six battles, dated 1859. White silver metal. Good condition. Size, 1¼ inches. Price, $10.00.

**169. FRENCH MEDAL,** same as No. 168, illustration showing the reverse side. Price, $7.85.

**170. FRENCH EXPEDITION TO MEXICO MEDAL.** Obverse shows BUST OF EMPEROR NAPOLEON III within a WREATH BORDER. Reverse, "EXPEDITION TO MEXICO, 1862 to 1863," with the names of five captured cities. With MEXICAN EAGLE and SNAKE MOTTO: ribbon. Size, 1¼ inches. Price, $10.00.

**171. FRENCH EXPEDITION TO MEXICO MEDAL,** same as No. 170. Price, $10.00.

**172. BEAUTIFUL BRONZE MEDAL.** Inscribed on the obverse, "NAPOLEON I. EMPEROR," with BUST, with WREATH BORDER SURMOUNTED BY CROWN. The reverse, "CAMPAIGN 1792 to 1815. A SES COMPANIONG DE GLORIA SA DERNIESE PENSER ST. HELENE, 5 MAI 1821," with WREATH BORDER. Size, 1 3/16 inches in width. Price, $9.50.

**21. FRENCH MILITARY BUTTON.** Eagle encircled by wreath in relief ornamental work. Price, 50 cents.

**257. ITALIAN THREE-BAR SILVER MEDAL FOR SERVICES IN THE WAR OF INDEPENDENCE,** 1848-1859-1870. Reverse shown in illustration. Obverse, head of EMPEROR VICTOR EMANUEL. Good condition. Size, 1 3/16 inches. Worn by a veteran of three wars. Price, $15.00.

**159. NAPOLEON III, EMPEROR FRENCH, MEDAL,** similar to No. 158, illustration showing the reverse, with names of four captured cities, dated 1860. In good condition. Size, 1¼ inches. Price, $9.50.

**20. FRENCH IMPERIAL GUARDS** brass buttons, coat size with eagle and crown. Marked on edge GARDE IMPERIALE. Price, $1.00 each.

**161. FRENCH REPUBLIC MEDAL,** same as No. 160. Illustration shows the reverse, SUNBURST AND STAR, DAHOMEY, ANCHOR and FLAGS within WREATH FOR BORDER. Price, $9.50.

**162. FRENCH MADAGASCAR MEDAL,** 1862. Obverse, "RADANA, M' PANIRA." Silvered white metal, with ribbon. Size, 1⅜ inches. Price, $9.50.

**163. FRENCH REPUBLIC MEDAL FOR THE EXPEDITION TO MADAGASCAR.** Good condition. Size, 1¼ inches, with silk ribbon. Price, $9.50.

**237. OVAL-SHAPED IRON SURGEON MEDALS,** 1815 Campaign, culminating at Waterloo. 1 inch wide, 1¼ inches long. Complete, with silk ribbon. Price, each, $7.50.

**165. FRENCH REPUBLIC COLONIAL MEDAL,** white silvered metal, with ribbon. Price, $9.00.

**67. PERSIAN SILVER MEDAL, ORDER OF THE LION AND SUN.** Reverse is covered with Persian inscription. In good condition. Size, 1 5/16 inches, with ribbon. Price, $18.00.

**46. ANCIENT SARDINIA ORDER OF ST. MAURICE and ST. LAZARUS, WHITE ENAMELED CROSS;** green enameled points. Rare medal, over 100 years old. Price, $17.50.

**76. IRON CROSS WITH WREATH BORDER, GREEK INSCRIPTION,** 1845. Black silk ribbon, white stripes. Bavarian services in Greece. Size, 11/16 inch. Price, $6.00.

**Nos. 49-50. 6 FRENCH LEGION OF HONOR MEDALS.** All in good order, showing signs of wear. With crown and red ribbon, with bust and words NAPOLEON, EMPERUER DES FRANCAIS. On reverse FRENCH EAGLE with words HONNEUR ET PATRIE. These medals full size. Price $14.50 each.

**No. 48. 2 MINIATURE MEDALS,** as above with red ribbon. Size one-half inch. Price $7.85 each.

**No. 47. 1 MINIATURE MEDAL,** as above with gold finish, red ribbon. Price $9.85 each.

**68. FRENCH & GERMAN CAMPAIGN** 1870-1871. Bronze Cross, inscribed as illustrated. White ribbon with Red Cross. Price, $10.00.

**54. MALTESE COPPER CROSS, ROPE BORDER, INSCRIBED, "LONDON, A.D. 1868, L.R.N.,"** with LATIN INSCRIPTION. Red silk ribbon, with safety-pin bar. Size, 1⅜ inches. Price, $5.75.

66B. PRUSSIAN MEDAL OR BADGE issued to wounded soldiers. Bright finish with pin clasp fastening. Price, $2.50.

65B. PRUSSIAN WAR ORNAMENT worn by the Motor Cycle Corps. This one used by CORPS 40. Crown and numerals in gilt finish, wreath wings and wheel in bright finish. Pin clasp. Price, $2.25.

259. SICILIAN SILVER MEDAL FOR "AL VALORE MILITAIRE SPEDIZIONE D ORIENT, 1855-1856." Size, 1¼ inches. Rare. Price, $12.50.

260. SICILIAN MEDAL GIVEN FOR 25 YEARS' MILITARY SERVICE. BUST FERDINAND II. Reverse, 25 Annin, etc. Size, 1½ inches. Price, $8.85.

39B. MAXIMILIAN JOSEPH WAR MEDAL, with ribbon. Obverse shows bust of Joseph, marked: MAXIMILIAN JOSEPH KOENIG VONBAIERN. Reverse Lion with crown, short sword and shield. Price, $3.75.

25B. FRENCH WAR MEDAL with ribbon. Obverse shows head with words: NAPOLEON III EMPEREUR. Reverse marked: CAMPAIGNE D' ITALIE, 1859, with list of battles as follows: MONTEBELLO, PALESTRO, TURBIGO, MAGENTA, MARIGNAN, SOLFERINO. Price, $10.00.

17B. BULGARIA BRONZE MEDAL with ribbon, issued 1885. Obverse shows bust of ALEXANDER I. Reverse: FIGURE OF VICTORY ON EAGLE. Price, $3.50.

128. BRITISH MEDAL for campaign in AFGHANISTAN, during 1878-79 and 80. Reverse shows crowned head of Queen Victoria. Price $7.85.

27-9. FRENCH CROIX DE GUERRE with bronze star, with ribbon. Price $9.75. We have also medals with gold stars, also palms.

27-10. BRITISH MEDAL for campaign in CHINA in 1900. Reverse shows head of Queen Victoria at time of Jubilee. Price $8.50.

27-11. GERMAN IRON CROSS. Obverse has oak leaves with crown over F W and date 1813. Reverse has crown with letter W and date 1914. Price $3.50.

27-12. BELGIAN MEDAL, with enamel cross with letters L L entwined. With ribbon. Price $7.85.

SH-8. BELGIAN CROIX DE GUERRE with crown and ribbon. Price $7.95.

NATIONAL DEFENSE BADGES, or Badges for Service. A badge for service adopted by the War Department as evidence of military service rendered. Persons entitled to wear the badges are:

a. (1) Those who have served honorably as enlisted men, field clerks, warrant officers, nurses or commissioned members of the military forces in time of war.

(2) Those who have served honorably in the Army of the United States and have been trained and qualified in the grade of private or in a higher grade, including warrant officers, contract surgeons and veterinarians, nurses and commissioned officers.

(3) Those who have served honorably in a military unit conducted under the War Department or have been trained and qualified as a private or in a higher grade.

(b) Next of kin are NOT authorized to wear the badge for service.

(c) Except where other regulations govern, the length of service and training required for qualification for the badge for service will be as follows, such service and training to have been considered honorable and satisfactory by the commanding officer:

(1) Two months service in the Regular Army.

(2) One year's service in the National Guard.

Description of Badge: A dexter eagle with wings displayed perched within a ring which displays seven white and six red vertical stripes with a blue chief bearing the words NATIONAL DEFENSE, the dexter wing of the eagle behind the ring, the sinister wing in front of the ring. We are authorized to sell these to persons qualified to wear them, Authorization No. A G 095. Price 25 cents each.

When Napoleon I surrendered on board H.M.S. Bellerophan, he was received by a captain's detachment of Royal Marines. After acknowledging the salute, he minutely inspected the men, and having remarked that they were very fine and well appointed, the Emperor added: "Are there none amongst them who have seen service?" Upon being told that nearly all of them had seen much service, he exclaimed: "What! And no marks of merit?" The officer in command explained that it was not customary to confer medals, except upon officers of the highest rank; to which the ex-Emperor replied: "Such is not the way to excite or cherish military virtues."—Quotation from D. Hastings Irwin's Book on Medals.

# MEDALS

**25-4. SPANISH WAR BRONZE MEDAL.** Obverse shows Battleship BROOKLYN with U. S. S. BROOKLYN, SANTIAGO DE CUBA, JULY 3, 1898. Reverse: IN COMMEMORATION OF THEIR HEROISM AT THE DESTRUCTION OF THE SPANISH FLEET. FROM THE CITIZENS OF BROOKLYN TO THE MEN BEHIND THE GUNS. Price, $12.00.

**25-5. GEORGE THE THIRD BRONZE NAVAL MEDAL.** Obverse shows bust of King George, marked: GEORGE III., KING OF GR. BRITAIN, FRANCE, IRELAND, ETC. Reverse shows two ships in battle. Marked: RESOLUTION. ADVENTURE. SAILED FROM ENGLAND MAY 11, MDCCLXXII. NO RIBBON. Price, $10.00.

**25-6. CULLODEN MEDAL,** made of bronze. Reverse shows officer on horseback with sword and pistols. Marked: WILL. DUKE CUMBERLAND. BORN JS AP J72J. Reverse: CAVALRY and INFANTRY IN THE CHARGE. Marked: REBELLION JUSTLY REWARDED. CULLODEN J6, AP, J746. Price, $12.50.

**25-7. SPANISH WAR RELIC.** Four Spanish silver coins melted together. Piece brought back from Cuba by American soldier who served in Spanish American War. Price, $4.50.

**190. POPE'S CROSS, GIVEN TO VOLUNTEERS WHO SERVED IN THE PAPAL BRIGADE,** UNDER MAJOR O'REILLY, IN THE GARIBALDI CAMPAIGN. Reverse side shows the cross reversed, as tradition states that ST. PETER WAS CRUCIFIED WITH HIS HEAD DOWNWARD. Obverse is shown. Inside wreath border. A rare medal, given by the Pope. Size of medal, 1½ inches. Price, $12.50.

**170. FRENCH EXIDITION TO MEXICO MEDAL.** Obverse shows BUST OF EMPEROR NAPOLEON III. within a WREATH BORDER. Reverse, "EXPEDITION TO MEXICO, 1862 to 1863," with the names of five captured cities. With MEXICAN EAGLE and SNAKE MOTTO. Size, 1¼ inches. No ribbon. Edge chipped. Price, $7.00.

## THE IRON CROSS

The Germans who perform heroic deeds in the present war are being rewarded with The Iron Cross. The cross is a Maltese cross of cast iron edged with silver.

The Iron Cross has been used on but two previous occasions in Germany's history. Frederick William III, King of Prussia, established the Iron Cross as a reward for his soldiers who displayed remarkable bravery in the wars against Napoleon. William I re-established the decoration during the Franco-Prussian War. Emperor William II has now revived the order for the present conflict, and a considerable number of Iron Crosses have already been awarded.

The cross is suspended by a black ribbon with two white stripes. In the center of the cross is a spray of three oak leaves. In the upper limb are the initials of the monarch who presented it, and in the lower part the date. There are three classes of crosses, indicated by the position in which they are worn. The Grand Cross is worn at the throat, the First Class Cross as an order on a ribbon, and the Second Class is fastened on the breast.—The American Boy.

No. 22.

**241, 242. PRUSSIAN BRONZE MEDALS, given for 1813-1814 CAMPAIGN.** Size, 1 1/16 inches, with ribbon. Good condition. Price, each, $5.50.

**243. FREDERICK WILHELM IV BRONZE MEDAL FOR CAMPAIGN 1848-1849.** Size, 1 1/16 inches, with silk ribbon. Price, $5.50 each.

**244, 245.** Illustrations shows obverse and reverse of medals given by EMPEROR WILLIAM FOR FRENCH-GERMAN WAR CAMPAIGN, 1870-1871. White metal. Size, 1 1/16 inches, with silk ribbon. Price, $6.50 each.

**22. FRENCH MILITARY BUTTON,** with eagle and crown in raised ornamental work. Price, 50 cents.

**247. SERVIAN IRON CROSS FOR SERVICES** in CAMPAIGN 1885-1886 AGAINST TURKEY. Price, $7.85.

**248. "FREDERICK AUGUSTUS HERZOG ZU NASSAU" SILVER MEDAL FOR DISTINGUISHED SERVICES AT WATERLOO.** Size, 1 1/16 inches. Silk ribbon. Price, $14.50.

**235 and 236. BRONZE MEDALS FOR THE "CAMPAIGN OF 1813-1814,"** that preceded Waterloo. Size, 1 1/10 inches, with silk ribbon. Price, $6.75 each.

**175. SILVER MEDAL, PRESENTED TO FRENCH OFFICER, "LA CRIMEA, 1855."** ARMS, TROPHY AND FLAGS. Reverse: TURKISH inscription. Size, 1⅞ inches; silk ribbon and two buckle loops. Price, $15.00.

**225. "QUATRE BRAS" DUKE OF BRUNSWICK BRONZE MEDAL,** (WATERLOO, 1815). Size, 1 7/16 inches. Good condition. Price, $9.85.

**228. "FUR TRUEN DIENST IN EINEM FELD JUGE" MEDAL.** Obverse, Crown within Wreath. Size, 1⅛ inches. Good condition. Price, $5.75.

**229, 231, 232. PRUSSIAN BRONZE MEDALS FOR MILITARY SERVICES IN CAMPAIGN 1813-1814,** that led up to the defeat of Napoleon at Waterloo in 1815. Size, 1⅛ inches, with ribbon. Good condition. Price, each, $5.75.

**230. PRUSSIAN WATERLOO BRONZE MEDAL, 1815.** Size, 1⅛ inches. Fine condition. Complete with ribbon. Price, $8.75.

Illustration of stock of Bronze and Gilt Military, Naval and Yacht Organization Buttons, sold to us by the assignee of Raynold & Co., 99 Fourth Avenue, N. Y. City. The three top rows of buttons (with the exception of item No. 141) are in BRONZE FINISH, the balance in GILT. ALL ARE NEW. The NUMBERS represent the quantity on hand, as well as for identification in ordering. Organizations who have heretofore purchased their buttons from Raynold can now obtain them from us, at the price of 5 cents singly, 50 cents per dozen, $5.00 per gross.

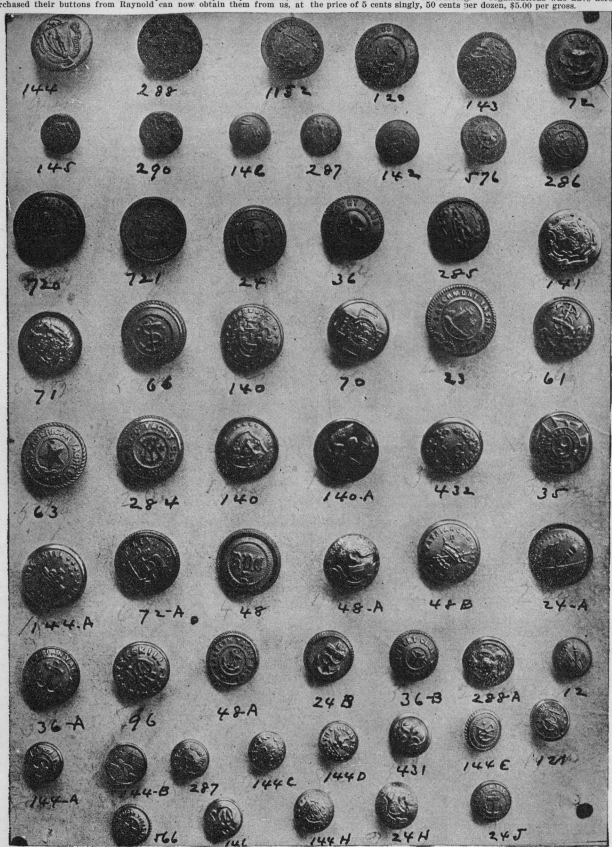

0-709. COLLECTION OF 100 BRITISH SOLDIERS' ARMY UNIFORM BUTTONS, all different. Upward of half of the lot were used in old-time NUMBERED REGIMENTS. Some worn by British Red Coat Regiments in the War of the American Revolution. All were in service. Price for the collection of 100 buttons, $50.00.

0-710. COLLECTION OF 71 BRITISH ARMY SOLDIERS' UNIFORM BUTTONS, all different. Some have silver fronts, copper backs: some in pewter. Price for the collection of 71 BUTTONS, $35.00.

0-711. BRITISH ARMY NUMBERED REGIMENTAL BUTTONS, Nos. 93, 94, 12, 17, 22, 83, 7, 3, 31, 65, 25, 14. Price, 50 cents each.

'Why should we wear medals and decorations on the left breast and not on the right? The gallant Knights of the Crusades placed their medals and insignias on the left breast because it was the shield side and also because the heart that beat in honor and fealty to its King was on that side under the badge of honor.— *National Guard Magazine.*

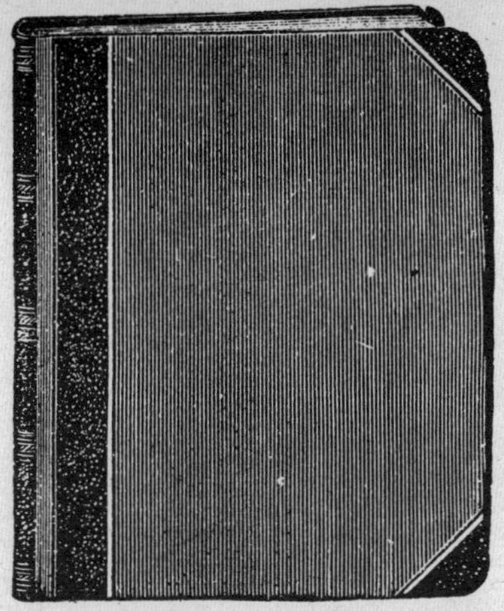

0-1068. EXTRA LARGE SIZE NEW COPYING BOOK. For plans, etc. From the U. S. Navy Department. Size of the pages 20x16 inches. First quality light-weight paper, 500 numbered pages, heavy black cover. Have 16 in stock. Would cost upwards of $5.00 each. Our bargain price, $1.85 each.

0-1069. EXTRA LARGE SIZE NEW COPY BOOK. Page is 22x20 inches. 400 pages. From U. S. Navy auction. 15 in stock. Good value for $5.00 each. Our bargain price, $1.85 each.

0-1070. SUPERFINE QUALITY 1,000-PAGE HEAVY WRITING PAPER U. S. NAVY BLANK BOOK. Size of the page 15x11¾ inches. Pages numbered from 1 to 1,000. Heavy canvas covered backs, with inside pocket flap in the cover. Book is 4 inches thick and would cost upwards of $10.00. Our bargain price, $4.85.

0-1071. BOOK OF SUPERFINE QUALITY HEAVY PAPER. Ruled and printed with the days of the month on each double page for copying the "daily analysis of cost of labor." Useful for the purpose intended, or for a good account book. 300 DOUBLE pages, size 15x11 inches, heavy canvas cover. Price, $1.50 each.

0-1072. JOB ORDER BOOK. Fine quality writing paper. Size 16x10¾ inches. Book is 2½ inches thick. Printed for two orders on each page. Size of each order 6¼x8 inches, with stub 4½x8 inches. Price, $1.40.

## MILITARY BOOKS, ETC.

MILITARY INSTRUCTOR'S MANUAL. By Captain James P. Cole, 59th Infantry, Instructor 3rd Battalion, 17th Provisional Training Regiment, Plattsburg, N. Y., and Major Oliver Schoonmaker, 76th Division, Assistant Instructor 3rd Battalion, 17th Provisoinal Training Regiment, Plattsburg, N. Y., 506 pages, 4¾ inches, by 7½ inches, cloth bound contains Infantry Drill Regulations, Physical Training, Use of Modern Arms, including the army rifles, the army pistol and machine guns. Map Sketching, notes on army regulations, feeding men, personal hygiene and first aid, signalling, and other valuable chapters for those interested in work done at Plattsburg training camp. Price, postage paid in U. S. 75 cents.

U4-13. THE NAVAL HOWITZER ASHORE, by Foxhall A. Parker, Commander U. S. Navy, 1865. Contains many charts and full page illustrations. 64 pages. Price, $1.00.

U4-14. ELECTRICAL INSTRUMENTS AND TELEPHONES OF U. S. SIGNAL CORPS, 1905. 316 pages, fully illustrated, showing instruments and other equipment. Price, $2.00.

3312. SPANISH WAR, 1898, REPORT OF ORIGIN AND SPREAD OF TYPHOID FEVER IN U. S. MILITARY CAMPS, 1898. Published in 1904. Cloth bound, 721 pages, sixe 12x10x1¾. Price, $1.85.

3313. MEDICAL REGISTRY N. Y., N. J. AND CONN., 1878. Cloth bound, size 7¼x5¼x1 inch. Price, 90c.

3271. U. S. ARMY MEDICAL DEPT. TRANSFER BLANK BOOK. Printed headings, ruled, size 11x4⅜x1 inch. Price, 45c.

3316. GEOLOGY OF THE UNITA MOUNTAINS. With atlas. By J. W. Powell, 1876. For Department of Interior, Washington. Illustrated, cloth bound, size 12x9⅜x1¾ inches, 218 pages. Price, $1.45.

3270. HOSPITAL CORPS U. S. ARMY MORNING REPORT BLANK BOOK. 11x7¾x1½ inches. Printed on fine quality paper, with printed and ruled headings. New. Slightly stained. Price, $1.00.

3309. DIGEST SECOND COMPTROLLER TREASURY, 1865. Giving Government decisions as to payments. Civil War Contracts. Price, $1.50.

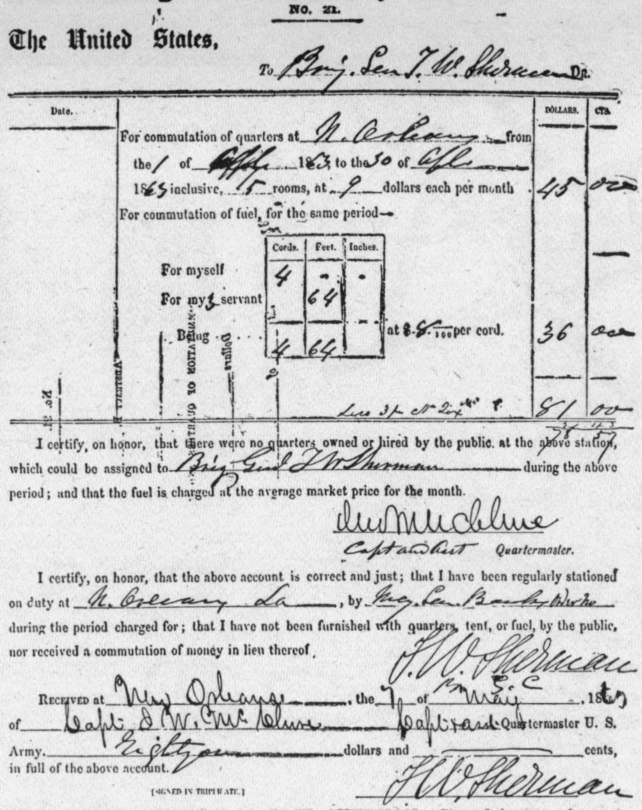

NO. 21.

The United States,

To Brig. Gen. T. W. Sherman Dr.

| Date. | | DOLLARS. | CTS. |
|---|---|---|---|
| | For commutation of quarters at N. Orleans from the 1 of April 1863 to the 30 of April 1863 inclusive, 5 rooms, at 9 dollars each per month | 45 | 00 |
| | For commutation of fuel, for the same period — For myself: Cords 4; For my servant: Feet 64; Being 4 cords 64 feet, at $8.00 per cord. | 36 | 00 |
| | | 81 | 00 |

I certify, on honor, that there were no quarters owned or hired by the public, at the above station, which could be assigned to Brig. Genl. T. W. Sherman during the above period; and that the fuel is charged at the average market price for the month.

J. W. McClure
Capt. and Asst. Quartermaster.

I certify, on honor, that the above account is correct and just; that I have been regularly stationed on duty at N. Orleans La., by Maj. Gen. Banks' Orders during the period charged for; that I have not been furnished with quarters, tent, or fuel, by the public, nor received a commutation of money in lieu thereof.

T. W. Sherman

Received at New Orleans, the 7 of May, 1863, of Capt. J. W. McClure Capt. and Asst. Quartermaster U. S. Army, Eighty-one dollars and — cents, in full of the above account.

[SIGNED IN TRIPLICATE.]

T. W. Sherman

AUTOGRAPH OF GENERAL T. W. SHERMAN. Signed in two places to pay receipt in April, 1863, at New Orleans, La., when serving as brigadier-general under Major-General Banks. Upper signature certification regarding commutation of quarters; the lower signature on receipt of the money, $81.00, rent and firewood for the month. Price, $20.00.

0-672. BOOK OF WATER-COLOR DRAWINGS OF HISTORICAL BRITISH NAVAL AND MILITARY TROPHIES. From the days of Queen Bess to Queen Victoria. By J. Wm. Gibbs, with descriptive notes by Richard R. Holmes, F. S. A. Dedicated by permission to Her Majesty Queen Victoria. Book is 12x16, 1¾ inches thick, and contains 36 plates, with descriptive notes. We purchased this handsome book in order to obtain description and illustration for our book on Weapons of War, expecting to sell the book at a reduced price after serving our purpose. Among the plates are the swords of Oliver Cromwell, Duke of Marlborough, Duke of Wellington, Lord Nelson, General Wolfe, Captain Cook and Bonaparte, with illustration of American flags captured in war of 1812, pistols, guns, powder horns, etc. Book is in fine order in case, showing colored drawings of Lord Nelson's famous Battle of Trafalgar signals. Publisher's price, 7 pounds 7 shillings, equal to $36.75. We offer the book at the bargain price of $18.50.

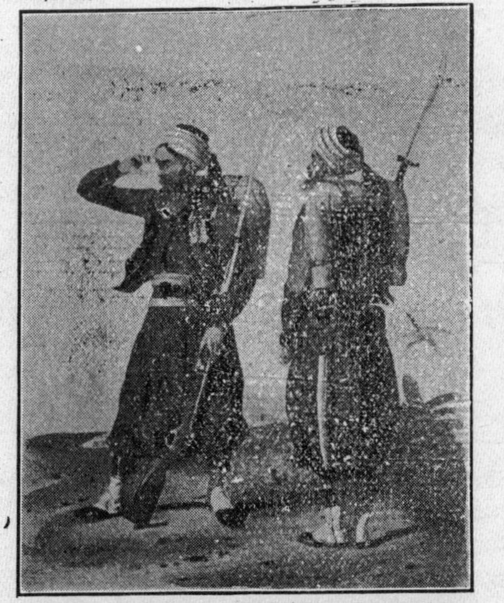

0-1166. SIXTEEN COLORED ILLUSTRATIONS OF FRENCH ARMY SOLDIERS. Size of each page is 9x12 inches. The collection includes Zouaves, Chasseurs, Generals, Grenadiers, Dragoons, Garde de Paris, Sapeurs, Pompiers, Cantoniers, Infanterie, Gendarmerie, Hussars. A WORK OF ART. Printed in Paris. Gives correct details of antique French military uniforms and weapons, period about 1840. Suitable for framing. Price for the collection of 16 plates, $15.00.

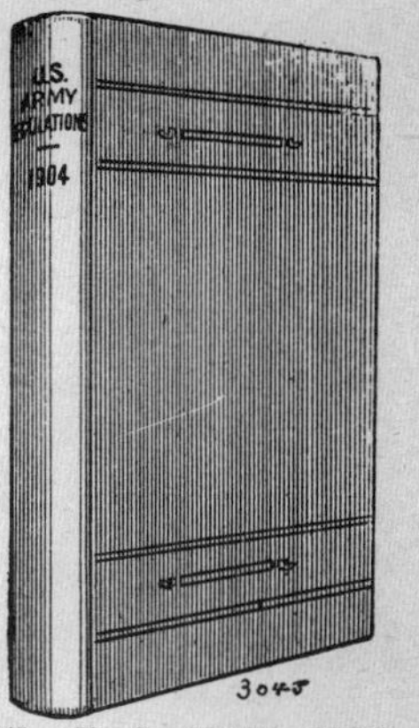

3045. U. S. ARMY REGULATIONS. Full of valuable information, which every one connected or doing business with the army should know. Size 6x9 inches. Price, 90 cents.

0-787. BOOK CONFEDERATE JOURNAL, HOUSE OF REPRESENTATIVES, STATE OF GEORGIA, MILLEDGEVILLE. From November 6 to December 14, 1861. 462 pages, 9x6 inches. Full account of the early days of the Confederacy in Georgia. Captured by soldiers in General Sherman's army when he went marching through Georgia. Price, $10.00.

Delta, O.
Aug. 2, 1925.

Sirs:—I received the camping equipment, also the catalog. The things were in very much better condition than I expected. I am well satisfied with your dealing and will send another order soon.

Yours truly,

OATES VAN DOREN.

U4-11½. FRENCH-ENGLISH MILITARY TECHNICAL DICTIONARY, by Cornelis De Witt Willcox, Major U. S. A. Coast Artillery. 1910. 492 pages. Price, $3.50.

0-668. ORIGINAL MAP "A PLAN OF THE OPERATIONS OF THE KING'S ARMY, under the command of General Sir Wm. Howe, K. B., New York and East New Jersey, against the American forces commanded by General Washington, from the 12th of October to 28th of November, 1776, whereon is particularly distinguished the engagement on the White Plains, the 28th of October. By Claude Joseph Sauthier. Engraved by Wm. Faden, 1777. Published as the act directs, February 5, 1777, by Wm. Faden, corner St. Martens Lane, Charing Cross, London." Sixe 22½x30 inches. This rare map came from the Donderin sale of Revolutionary War relics at Matteawan, New York. Well preserved order. Price, $50.00.

## U. S. ARMY BOOKS

| | |
|---|---|
| 10 Manual of Guard Duty, 1902 | $0.25 |
| 5 Field Service Regulations, 1905 | .75 |
| 9 Manuals for Army Cooks, 1896 | .75 |
| 3 Army Issue Ration Tables | .50 |
| 4 Manuals Subsistence Dept | .75 |
| 30 U. S. A. Krag Rifle, 1899 Regulations | .75 |
| 60 U. S. A. Springfield .45 Rifle and Revolver | .25 |
| 9 War Dept. Regulations for Militia | .75 |
| 28 U. S. A. Regulations, 1908 | .75 |
| 5 Kentucky State Guard Regulations | .50 |
| 2 Infantry Drill Books, 1904 | .25 |
| 3 Manuals for Court Martial | .75 |
| 40 Blank Company Property and Clothing Books, Size, 10½x16½ inches, 1 inch thick, weighs 7 pounds, ruled headings. Price, each | 1.00 |

No. 499. FRENCH-ENGLISH MILITARY TECHNICAL DICTIONARY, by Col. C. DeWitt Willcox, U. S. A., Professor of Modern Languages at West Point. Published by Harper & Brothers, New York. It contains all the latest terms of aviation, trench warfare, artillery and camouflage, military slang, etc. 584 pages on glazed paper, size 6x9 inches. 1917 edition. Regular price was four dollars. Our bargain price $1.00 each. Allow postage on three pounds.

**θ-797. FOLDING HAMMOCK OR YACHT CHAIRS.** Appreciated by all travelers on the sea and by convalescents. Can be adjusted to any desired position. Folds up flat. Hard wood, varnished frame, heavy brown canvas seat and foot rest, flat arms, weight 14 pounds. New, $2.50.

**NEW YORK CITY FIRE DEPT. BATTERING RAM.** Used in time of fire to batter in doors of warehouses. Heavy hard-wood log about 7 inches in diameter, shod on end with iron, with carrying straps on side, with guiding pole. Price, $15.00.

**U. S. NAVY BOAT AWNINGS** in best quality navy canvas; flat view shows form with stretchers and tie ropes. Offered in fine condition:

For 14 ft. boat............Price, $5.00    For 20 ft. boat............Price, $10.00
For 16 ft. boat............Price, 7.00     For 28 ft. boat............Price, 14.00
For 18 ft. boat............Price, 7.50     For 30 ft. boat............Price, 16.00

**SEA ANCHOR,** for vessels up to 1,000 tons. Made of very heavy canvas, cone shaped, 3 inch rope, 5 ft. mouth, 7 ft. long, weighs 100 lbs. Price, $35.00.

**SEA ANCHOR,** 3 ft. mouth, 4 ft 7 in. long. Price, $20.00.

**3419. ABDOMINAL BANDAGES.** Kind worn around the stomach by U. S. soldiers when in countries subject to hot days and cool nights to prevent sickness. All new. Made of flannel. Assorted sizes. Every camper should have one of these life-savers. Price, 25 cents each.

**COTTON DUCK.** Such as is used in the manufacture of tents, etc., can be divided into three general divisions, based on quality:

**U. S. ARMY STANDARD DUCK.** 28½ inches wide. Made in the following weights per lineal yard: 8 ounces, 10 ounces, 12 ounces and 15 ounces. Used for all Government purposes, and the CLEANEST, CLOSEST, STRONGEST and MOST DURABLE duck POSSIBLE TO CONSTRUCT.

**DOUBLE FILLING DUCK.** 29 inches wide. Made in same weights as Army Duck, but NOT OF SUCH GOOD COTTON, NOR SO FINELY WOVEN. This duck is well suited for tents and covers where a first-class article at a moderate price is required.

**SINGLE FILLING DUCK.** 29 inches wide. Made in 7 ounces, 8 ounces, 10 ounces, 12 ounces, per lineal yard. These goods are made of coarser yarns and of poorer cotton than the above grades. They are low-priced, and make fairly satisfactory tents and covers, where great durability to withstand hard usage is not the first essential. THIS IS THE GRADE ON WHICH MANY DEPARTMENT STORES QUOTE SUCH ATTRACTIVE PRICES, CLAIMING THAT THEY ARE "STANDARD ARMY GOODS." When we quote U. S. Army we mean Army standard such as made up to Army specification.

**See page 361 for ARMY TENTS.**

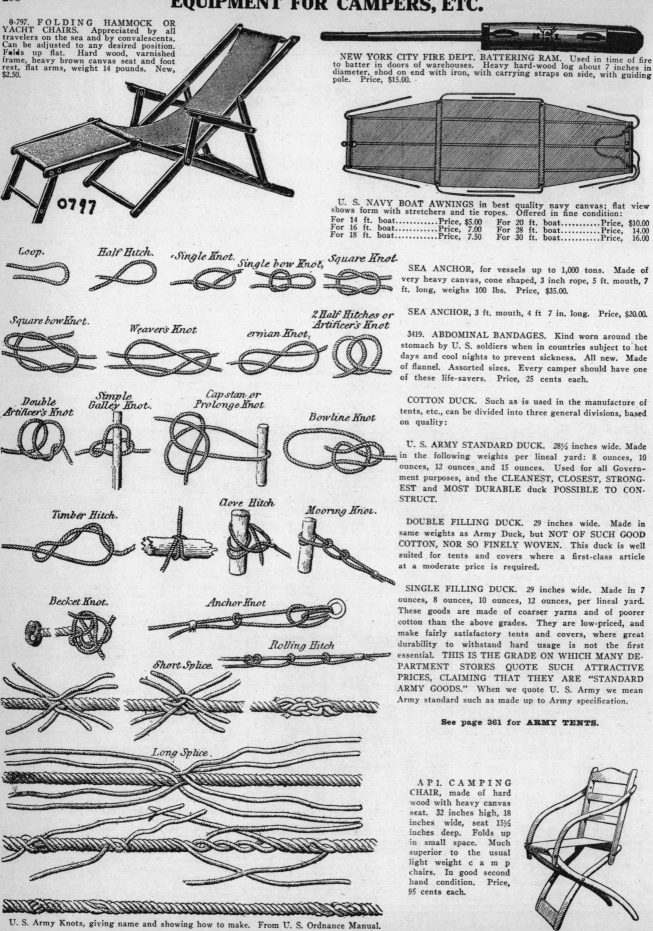

Loop.   Half Hitch.   Single Knot.   Single bow Knot.   Square Knot.

Square bow Knot.   Weaver's Knot.   erman Knot.   2 Half Hitches or Artificer's Knot

Double Artificer's Knot.   Simple Galley Knot.   Capstan or Prolonge Knot.   Bowline Knot.

Timber Hitch.   Clove Hitch.   Mooring Knot.

Becket Knot.   Anchor Knot.   Rolling Hitch.   Short Splice.

Long Splice.

U. S. Army Knots, giving name and showing how to make. From U. S. Ordnance Manual.

**AP1. CAMPING CHAIR,** made of hard wood with heavy canvas seat. 32 inches high, 18 inches wide, seat 15½ inches deep. Folds up in small space. Much superior to the usual light weight camp chairs. In good second hand condition. Price, 95 cents each.

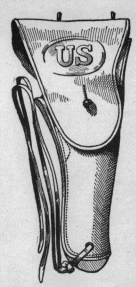

**U. S. NAVY PISTOL CARTRIDGE POUCH.** Civil War Relic used also for holding percussion caps for Navy rifles. U. S. N. stamped on cover made of black leather with two loops on the back for the 1¾ inch waist belt; serviceable relic. Price, 25 cents.

**RUSSET LEATHER HOLSTER** for Colt's automatic pistol, calibre 45; second-hand, 95 cents each.

**3007. U. S. M. C. LEATHER SIDE ARM SWORD FROG,** will fit any scabbard. New. Price, 25 cents each.

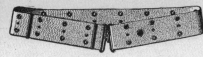

**WEB WAIST BELT,** 2½ inches wide, with eyelets for attaching holster. Offered in good serviceable order with plain catch at 78 cents each. New ones, $1.80 each.

**ARMY OLIVE DRAB WEB TROUSER BELT,** new. 1 inch wide with bronze buckle. Price, 20 cents.

**ARMY CLEANING BRUSH** with stiff hair bristles on brass wire with leather thong. Suitable for cleaning revolvers from calibre 44 up. Price, 25 cents each. $2.00 per dozen.

**SECOND HAND WEB CLIP HOLDER** for two automatic pistol clips, 45 cents each.

**NEW WEB POCKETS** for two clips rifle cartridges, 75 cents each.

**WEB HOLDERS** with three pockets of two compartments each for half moon revolver clips, second hand, 40 cents each.

**500 CIVIL WAR REVOLVER HOLSTERS,** serviceable relics. Price, 50 cents each.

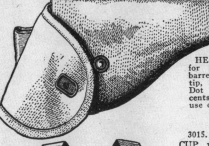

**HEAVY WEB HOLSTERS,** for any revolver with 5-in. barrel or shorter. Have metal tip, large flap with Lift the Dot quick fastener. Price, 60 cents each. Has belt loop for use on any belt.

**3015. ANCIENT METAL OIL CUP** with screw top and oil dropper. Made of iron with broad base. Cannot easily tip over. One drop of oil at a time directly on the spot where needed. Old time serviceable relic. Useful household article. Price, 25 cents each, $2.50 per dozen.

**200 U. S. STEEL CLEANING RODS.** For pistols and revolvers. Length 11 inches, with hole in end for cleaning rag; will fit any pistol from calibre 22 up. Price, 10 cents each.

**WALNUT REVOLVER STOCK** for Colt's Army Revolver. Double stock, with inletting cuts for the metal parts. Price, 45 cents.

**10707D. BRASS TOMPION,** used in the muzzle of antique guns. Length, 1¾ inches. Fit any gun 45 calibre or over. Tompions help keep gun from rusting. Price, 15 cents.

**1919. BRITISH ARMY SAM BROWNE TAN HOLSTERS,** almost new with top flap. Length of top is 9 inch. These will fit most any revolver, also Luger pistol. Price, 85 cents each.

**1919A. BRITISH ARMY TAN OPEN HOLSTER.** This is without flap but has top strap to keep pistol from coming out. There is holder on back for cleaning rod. Small end is open, so that any revolver may be carried in it. Almost new. Price, 55 cents each.

**U. S. NAVY CIVIL WAR HOLSTERS** for Colts, Remington or Whitney revolvers. Black leather, serviceable. Price 50 cents each.

**150,000 U. S. ARMY LEATHER GUN SLINGS** for Springfield Army Rifle, made at Government Arsenal of finest quality leather, fitted with brass studs and the double claw brass adjusting hooks, in used, serviceable order. Price, 30 cents each.

**3356. BRITISH ARMY REVOLVER HOLSTER.** Heavy Tan Leather, riveted, loop for attaching to waist belt, strap for tightening the cover flap. Length at the top 8 inches, at the bottom 11 inches, weight 6 ounces. Will take any large size cylinder revolver Price, 35 cents.

**ARMY OLIVE DRAB BELTS** with *small* clip pockets without suspender, in second hand condition. 60 cents each.

**ARMY OLIVE DRAB BELTS** with pockets for rifle clips, 50 cents each.

**SUSPENDERS** for rifle belts are 40 cents per set extra.

**No. 1817A. NEW U. S. NAVY OFFICER'S WOVEN WEB HOLSTERS,** made of heavy drab web, with bronze cap and rivets. Bronze U. S. N. button snap fastener, made for U. S. Navy Academy, with loop for attaching to waist, belt length on top 9 in. Price 70 cents each; will hold Colts Navy 38-cal. service revolver.

**FROM ADVENTURE MAGAZINE**

If you have it not, I would suggest that you send fifty cents to Francis Bannerman's Sons, 501 Broadway, N. Y., for their illustrated catalog. They are the largest arms dealers in the world—old arms. The catalog is an education in this line and has illustrations of nearly all kinds of arms, ancient and modern.

**U. S. TAN LEATHER REVOLVER HOLSTERS,** for Cal. 38 Smith & Wesson or other army revolvers. Made of the best bridle leather with the large loop for use on the calibre 30 web cartridge belt. Stamped Rock Island Arsenal, 1907. We secured upwards of 5,000 of these fine serviceable holsters, sold to us only because they were obsolete by reason of the adoption of the automatic. Our bargain price, 85 cents each.

**BLACK LEATHER HOLSTERS,** for calibre 45 revolvers, in fine order. Price, 45 cents.

# BELTS.

No. 11. U. S. Navy Marine Belt and Buckle. Same as was worn by marines in Spanish-American War. Belt of white buff leather. Brass buckle. Plain. Price, $1.00.

For use of military companies and school, we offer black or russet waist belts, in good order, fitted with the heavy brass belt plates, marked U. S. or N. Y., or N. J. Prices will be quoted on application. If full sets of equipment as shown on pages 304 and 315 are not desired, we can supply any part, and will quote prices on parts needed.

No. 12. U. S. Late Regulation Waist Belt and Plate. As used by the U. S. Army. Made of grain leather, with adjusting hooks for length. Good, second-hand, serviceable order, with loop for attaching shoulder slings to the buckle in use at the time when the soldier carried his cartridge boxes on the waist belt. Price, 65 cents each.

No. 13. Soldiers' Souvenir Button Belt. Military belt and buckle with 12 assorted military coat buttons. Handsome souvenir for the ladies. Each set has one U. S. Naval Officer, includes one West Point Cadet and one U. S. Army Officer button. Price, 95 cents.

No. 15. British Army Officer White Enameled Leather Sword Belt, with sling, straps and either silvered or gilt buckle, with British Coat of Arms and Motto:

Honi suit qui mal y pence.

Purchased in London after South African War. No doubt relics. Are offered in good second-hand, serviceable order. Price, $4.50 each.

No. 1715. Cadet Khaki Web Waist Belt, with our regular brass eagle coat of arms belt plate; double thick woven ribbed web, 2½ inches wide; longest length, 29 inches; can be furnished up to 36 inches by joining. Price, 45 cents each.

No 18. 1,200 U. S. Cavalry Web Loop Cartridge Belts with sabre hook; loops for 50-calibre 45 ball cartridges, bar-buckle fastening. Good, second-hand, serviceable order. Price, 75c. each; $7.00 doz.

1,713A. Revolver cartridge belt in gray or khaki colored woven web; cartridge loops are woven into body of the belt; for holding 55 cartridges, in size from 38 to 45 calibre; with plain polished brass belt plate. Price, 65 cents each.

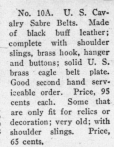

No. 10A. U. S. Cavalry Sabre Belts. Made of black buff leather; complete with shoulder slings, brass hook, hanger and buttons; solid U. S. brass eagle belt plate. Good second hand serviceable order. Price, 95 cents each. Some that are only fit for relics or decoration; very old; with shoulder slings. Price, 65 cents.

No. 1723. Cartridge Sword Belt; woven web belt, with loops woven in body of the belt, for holding 50 cartridges from 32 sporting model up to calibre 44, including United States Navy calibre 30 and the 7 m/m. cartridge; adjustable sword slings, with brass snap hook; with polished brass plate; practically new. Price, $1.20 the outfit.

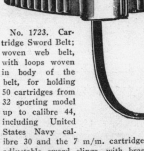

No. 1,712. U. S. Signal Corps Cartridge Belt. new double thick gray color, woven web, with loops for holding 32-10 guage cartridges; made for use U. S. Signal Corps; will hold ordinary paper or brass 10-gauge cartridge; offered with metal loop fastenings; made for U. S. Government and not to be compared with the cheap, ordinary kind sold by sporting goods dealers. Price, 65 cents.

No. 1,720. U. S. Navy Cadet Cartridge Belt with nickel plate, new gray woven web with loop for holding 45-calibre .30 cartridges; belts have patent nickel adjustable fasteners in lengths up to 40 inches; have eyelets for attaching either holster or bayonet scabbard; will also hold 30 40 sporting cartridges or any of the high power small bore rifle cartridges. Price, $1.00.

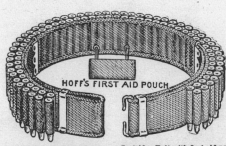

HOFF'S FIRST AID POUCH

No. 22. U. S. Army Krag-Jorgensen Cartridge Belt with first aid pouch; double row belt, holding 100 calibre 30 Krag-Jorgensen or Mauser cartridges; with brass loops, adjustable fasteners; in fine order; used a short time; for all practical purposes as good as new. Price, 60 cents each. With first aid pouch, 25 cents extra.

No. 21. 50 U. S. Army Sword Belts, russet leather with sling straps and snap attachment. offered in good, second hand, serviceable order. Price, $1.85 each.

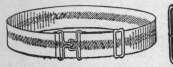

No. 19. Cadet Belt, white web, with loop fastening design, size 28 to 34 inches. Price, 30 cents.
No. 24. Small Gilt Buckle for adjusting length on U. S. Army officers' sword belts. Price, 12 cents each.
No. 25. U. S. Arsenal Made Heavy Gilt Sling Hooks, for snapping the sling straps into the scabbard rings. Price, 50 cents per pair.

OFFICER'S BLACK LEATHER BELTS, complete with eagle or U. S. brass belt plate, with two sword slings, with snaps. This style now used by officers of societies, and private military and cadet companies. Special price, $1.75 each.

No. 1718. 5,000 Pieces new woven double thick khaki colored Ribbed Belts, width 2¼ inches, 28 inches long; similar to fine heavy web used in the U. S. regulation cartridge belt suspenders. For sale at bargain prices.

No. 27.        No. 28.
No. 27. U. S. Navy Buff Leather Sword Frogs for holding non-com. swords, antique side arm swords and sword bayonets and cutlasses, 20 cents each.

No. 28. Hagner's Patent Sling Straps, made for use on army belts period of 1870-1880. Can be attached to any waist belt for purposes of altering to sword belt. Equal to new. Price 25 cents. With two brass snap hooks, 25 cents additional.

No. 29

No. 29. Illustration showing soldier equipped with bandolier cartridge belt, carried on shoulder; holding 100 .45 cartridges. With cartridge waist belt holding 50 cartridges calibre .45. With this outfit the soldier can load and fire the old regulation Springfield breech-loading calibre .45 rifle almost as quickly as the magazine rifle. We can supply bandoliers with combination shoulder or waist fastening, at 85 cents each. Web loop cartridge waist belt, 50 cents each. $5.00 per doz., upwards,

No. 30

No. 30. Illustration showing safe position of Krag Cartridges, carried in double-row, web-loop belts.

No. 30A. 70 Bright Colored Worsted Web Loop and Cartridge Belts. Red, yellow or blue colored belts, with loops for holding .45 calibre cartridges. Very showy. Practically new; with plain, polished, brass belt plates. $1.00 each.

No. 31

100,000 Web Loop Cartridge Belts. Worn only a few times; all in serviceable order, made originally for the U. S. Volunteers in Spanish-American War, for holding 50 rounds of 45-calibre cartridges. We find that they can be used for holding the Spanish Mauser, 30-calibre, Spanish Remington 48-calibre, 45-calibre Springfield and the 50-calibre Springfield. Note that our engraving shows these four different kinds of cartridges inserted in the loops. Complete with brass loops, adjustable fastenings. Price, 30 cents each;

No. 32

5,009 U. S. Volunteer Blue Woven Web Cartridge Belts with loops for 45-70 Springfield cartridge; U.S. brass adjustable belt plate; practically new, 60 each;

No. 33

500 Relics Spanish War. N. Y. State blue woven web 45-caleartridge belts, kind used by 71st Regt. in Cuba, 1898. At close of war we obtained from veteran one of these belts, which we value at $5.00. At late Army auction we obtained all that was turned in—several hundred—so price is now 75 cents each. All in good serviceable order.

No. 39

Illustration showing the proper way to remove cartridges from web loop cartridge belt.

No. 34

No. 34. 100 U. S. Army Revolver Cartridge Belts, holding .38 Brass book fastenings, second-hand serviceable order, 45 cents each.

No. 37. Illustration showing U. S. A. KRAG RIFLE EQUIPMENT, holding over 200 Krag cartridges, consisting of bandolier worn over the shoulder, double row woven web cartridge belt, with cartridge wristlet.

Woven Web Cartridge Wristlet, with loops, holding 20-calibre 30 or 7 mm Mauser cartridges. Note illustration No. 37 for method of using. Price, 38 cents each.

No. 38

LEATHER BELT, with web loops for 20 caliber 30 Army or sporting cartridges, in second hand order. Price of outfit, 60 cents. Price of web loops only, to be used on any waist belt, 20 cents each.

U. S. ARMY MUSICIANS' DRESS WAIST BELTS. New enameled colored leather, with bronze buckle. 77 in pale blue, infantry; 32 red, artillery; 46 yellow, cavalry. Choice. Price, 75 cents each.

No. 10. NON-COMMISSIONED OFFICER'S BLACK ENAMELED LEATHER SIDE ARM SWORD BELT, with eagle or plain brass buckle, with sword frog. Good serviceable, refinished order. Used a short time. Price, 95 cents the outfit.

No. 40. 10,000 New U. S. Army Service Equipment Web Loop Cartridge Belts, holding 50 cartridges, Cal. .45; will also with a little pressure fit Cal. .50 cartridges; complete with steel scabbard, with U. S. swivel frog with hook attachment for attaching to any part of the belt as desired. Complete with polished cast-brass U. S. belt buckle; with adjustable loops, practically new. Price, $1.50 the set, in blue, or gray color. For those in good second-hand serviceable order, in gray color, with brass loop belt fasteners, the price is 75 cents a set.

U. S. Web Loop Cartridge Belts, for holding 100 Cal. .30 cartridges; new; with steel scabbard. Price, $1.50 the set.

100,000 Service Equipments can be furnished in good second-hand serviceable order same as this illustration, with U. S. A. brass loop fasteners instead of the brass buckle, and the price will be in gray, 75 cents set; in blue, 90 cents set.

No. 8. 10 GERMAN ARMY OFFICER SILVERED BELTS (FELDBINDEN), with fine buckle, with ornamented wreath, with Wm. II. monogram; used a few times by German officer (purchased in Berlin), in good serviceable order. Price, $2.50 each.

2 GERMAN SABERTASCH "FRESSHUT," with German eagle and crown ornaments; embroidered. Fine second hand serviceable order. Price, $5.00.

No. 36. Illustration showing late regulation U. S. Service Uniform and Equipment. Note the web loop gun sling, attached to Springfield B. L. Rifle, which we sell at 35 cents each. Woven web loop cartridge waist belt, at 30 cents each upwards.

**MP1.—500 U. S. ARMY AXE OR HATCHET HOLDERS.** Made of extra heavy olive drab webbing bound with tape and riveted at several points. Width 6 inches with large flap.

Fitted with swivel attachment to be used on any belt. Non-corrosive buckle and russet strap. Made at Rock Island Arsenal. ALL NEW. Price, 35 cents each.

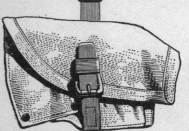

90 Military Cadet Woven-web Cartridge Belts, with cadet-size loops for holding the 45 or 50 calibre cartridge. New. Blue color. Price, 75c. each.

**21A. OFFICER'S RUSSET LEATHER SWORD BELT,** with non-corrosive metal buckle. Gov't bronze regulation finish, with 10203A belt loop attachment, bronze finish, Government made fine quality tan leather sling straps and snap hooks. Far superior to any trade made belt, complete at the bargain price, $2.25.

**10030. U. S. A. Russet Leather Belt Hanger.** For attaching to the ordinary waist belt for carrying side arm sword; made at the Government Rock Island Arsenal, practically as good as new. Price, 35 cents each.
**10030A. U. S. A. Black Leather Belt Hangers.** Gov't arsenal make, practically as good as new. Price, 30 cents each.

Ohio Officer's Belt Buckle, with State coat-of-arms, $1.00.

United States Navy Regulation Blue Web Belt. For holding clips of navy magazine or Mauser rifle cartridges. Second-hand, serviceable. 75 cents.

90 Mauser Cartridge Belts, blue web, with loops for holding single cartridges. Also with pockets for holding clips. All new, with the U. S. brass loop adjustable fastenings. Price, 95 cents each.

Hibernian Rifle Web Loop Cartridge Belt, holding 50 ball cartridges, either calibre 45 or 50, with brass plate and letters H.R.; either in blue or gray colored web; used only a short time; are in good, serviceable order. Price, 90 cents each.

British Soldier's Braided Hat Cord, with acorn tassels. Price, 35 cents each.

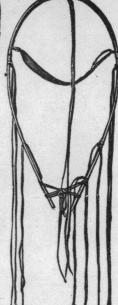

U. S. Army Dodge Yoke, for carrying the soldier's blanket, overcoat, etc., wrapped around the yoke and carried over the shoulder. Fitted with white leather tie straps. Yoke is light hardwood, weighing only a few ounces. 30 in stock. Price, $1.00 each.

**10011. STEEL CHAIN BURNISHER.** With leather handles, used for polishing round steel surfaces. Price, 65 cents.
See page 74 for British Army steel burnishing pads, size 5x5 inches, at 95 cents.
**CAVALRY SABRE BELTS.** Black leather with stamped eagle buckle with Hagner pattern sling attachment, with sling straps, with fastening studs, in used serviceable order. Price, 75c.

U. S. Navy Woven-web Cartridge Belt, with loops for holding 30 calibre 45 ball cartridges and 4 pockets for cartridges in clips; will answer for the Mausers. Illustration shows the small Mauser cartridges in the loops and two clips in each pocket, making a total of 70 Mauser cartridges carried in each belt. Have been much used; are in fair order only. Price, 85 cents each.

U. S. Army Buff Leather Waist Belt, with cast brass spread eagle buckle. New. Fine, heavy buff leather, alum or Indian tanned; blacked on outside, buff on inside. Price, 75c. each.

Black Leather Waist Belt, with heavy stamped brass belt buckle, with the spread eagle design. Hook for adjusting the length. Good, second-hand, serviceable order. 65c. each.

U. S. Army Officer's Gilt Lace Sword Knot. New. Price, $1.65 ea.

New Bandoliers; made of woven web canvas, with loops for holding cartridges. Similar to the Cartridge Waist Belt, only much longer, for carrying over the shoulder. For either the 45 calibre or Mauser rifle cartridges. 150 in blue, price, 95c. each; 170 in gray, 85c. ea.

50-Calibre U. S. Army Cartridge Belt, with loops for holding the regulation 50-70 Springfield ball cartridges. In good, second-hand, serviceable order. Price, 75c each. Price with steel scabbard, 50c. extra.

Russet Leather Sword Knots. New. 75c. each.

Antique Port Fire Case. Used in U. S. Army to carry port fire for signaling purposes; long since obsolete. Made of russet leather with sling strap for carrying over the shoulder. Diameter, 3¼ in.; length, 15 in. Price, 75c. each.

**10203A. BELT AND SWORD SLING ATTACHMENT.** Gov't cast brass, bronze finish slides, that will fit over any waist belt 1⅞ inches wide; Government made russet leather sling straps attached to the slide loops, with Government bronze finish, sword hook, belt studs for attaching to scabbard rings. These new russet leather sword slings with detachable belt slide will convert any waist belt into an officer's sword belt. Price, 75 cents.

U. S. Soldier's Russet Leather Waist Belt, with cast brass U. S. belt buckle. New. Price, 90 cents each.

**10732. U. S. A. SOLDIER'S BLACK LEATHER WAIST BELT;** made at Government Rock Island Arsenal; complete with cast brass U. S. belt plate; hook for adjusting length; used; offered in good serviceable order. Price 60 cents.

U. S. Marine Band White Buff Leather Drum Slings, with brass buckle. Good, second-hand, serviceable order. Price, $1.85.

British Army Officer's Gold Lace Belt, with handsome buckle. Complete, with sling strap. Fine, neat dress belt. Price, $7.50.

2,000 30-Calibre Double Row Tan Color Belts. Made by Spaulding under contract for U. S. Army in 1898. With loops for 100 calibre 30 U. S. rifle or Mauser cartridges. Almost new. 75c. each; $8.00 per dozen.

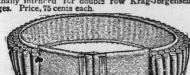

150 Shot Gun Cartridge Belts. 12 gauge new; woven web in blue or gray; loops for 28 cartridges; worn around the waist; originally intended for double row Krag-Jorgensen cartridges. Price, 75 cents each.

100 new Russet Leather Waist Belts, with loops for holding 45 cartridges. Made for U. S. Army during Spanish war. Handsome belt. Price, $1.50.
New York State Officer's Belt Buckle, with N. Y. in center. Not regulation. Price, 75 cents.

1,000 BLUE WEB 30-CALIBER DOUBLE ROW CARTRIDGE BELTS, with loops for holding 100 caliber .30 U. S. rifle or Mauser cartridges. Complete, with adjustable fastenings. Price, 60 cents each.

2 Napoleonic Cartridge Boxes, made of leather, with the French eagle in brass in the center of the cover, with brass flaring shell on the corner of the box. This kind of box is shown on the great battle pictures of Napoleon. Rare pieces. Price, $5.00 each.

U. S. S. Olympia Sailor's Cartridge Belts, with loops for holding 50 rounds of 45-calibre cartridges. All in serviceable order. Sailor's number stenciled on the back of each belt. Serviceable. Relics. Price, 85 cents each.

# EQUIPMENTS.

**550 Sets Cadet Naval Equipments,** consisting of leather waist belt with polished brass belt buckle, with small leather U. S. Navy Cartridge box, with steel bayonet scabbard, with U. S. N. on brass swivel frog. Scabbard will fit any U. S. Springfield bayonet. Equipments have been in use, and are offered in good serviceable order at 85 cents the complete set.

**U. S. Krag, McKeever Cartridge Box;** russet leather, with 20 inside loops for holding Calibre 30 smokelesspowder ball cartridges; oxidized; bronze trimmings; used only a short time offered in good, serviceable order; price 75 cents each.

TOP VIEW, OPEN.

FRONT VIEW

**10206A. 20,000 SPANISH REMINGTON OR MAUSER .43 CALIBER LEATHER CARTRIDGE BOX,** fine serviceable order; will also hold 20 rounds of any of the Springfield or any high power rifle cartridges; loops on the back for waist belt, side strap fastening, small, neat cover. Presents dressy appearing front, edges are bound with soft leather, hand sewed, size of box is 7 inches long, 4 inches high, 2 inches wide, weight 14 ounces. Price, 35 cents. Bargain price for the lot.

**2201. Boer War Soldier's Belt,** with frog, for the Mauser rifle side arm sword bayonet; will most any of the side arm swords, made of best quality new white buff leather, 1 7-8 inches wide, in assorted lengths up to 40 inches, with polished brass buckle, with South African Republic monogram; new, and sold to us by reason of failure to deliver to the Boers during the war with Great Britain; 500 in stock; bargain; price $1.00 each.

**U. S. Army Buff Leather Sword Belt,** with sword frog, practically new and fitted with stamped brass eagle belt buckle, black color on the outside, buff color on the inside, price $1.00.

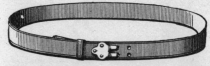

**1,000 Olive Drab Woven Web Cartridge Belts,** with pockets for holding cartridges in clips; 9 pockets in each belt, holding two clips of 5 cartridges each; practically new belts, with loop fastenings; width 3½ inches; good sized lengths; illustration shows clips of cartridges in pockets for the Krag, Lee Navy, Mauser 7 m/m and 7.65 m/m; bargain; price of belts. 75c each.

**2436. Russet Leather Waist Belt,** with polished brass, double claw hook fastening (hook more readily adjusted than buckle); can be furnished in all sizes up to 60 inch, making these belts especially desirable for large men, who are unable to obtain large size belts; 1 1-4 inches wide; best quality Government leather; offered in used, serviceable order; price 30 cents each.

**2,000 Clip Cartridge Belts;** olive drab color; heavy woven web; 3½ inches wide; all lengths up to forty inches; russet leather strap, with glove snap fastening over each pocket; metal loop fastenings; practically new belts; price 95 cents each.

**10492. BRITISH HIGHLAND OFFICER'S BLACK WATCH SWORD BELT.** With sling straps, snap hooks, silvered buckle. Complete. Price, $4.50.

**SCOTCH ARMY OFFICER'S SWORD BELT.** Plate engraved "Perth Highland Volunteers." Complete with sling straps, snap hooks. Price, $3.85.

**2673. REVOLUTIONARY WAR SOLDIER'S HAVERSACK.** From 1777 to 1778. From the Brooks collection. Carried by Private Martin Kirtland, with the Sixth Regiment Connecticut Line. Size 15x14 inches. Made of coarse homespun flax, The front flap is waterproofed and painted red, with oval space with letters "M. K." in white. Serviceable. Price, $15.00.

**German Army Fife Holder,** with frog for attaching to Waist belt; made of black leather, with brass hinged top; will hold 15½ inch fife; diameter 1¼ inches; price $1.40.

**German Army Soldiers' Sword Belt,** with chain hook for sword; with detachable leather sling, with snap fastening for revolver; used, serviceable order; price $1.50.

**German Army Equipments;** black leather; 2 inch shoulder belt, with buckle; cartridge box, with Emperor's monogram on cover; used, serviceable order; price $3.50.

**European Army Side Arm Sword Frog,** black leather, practically new. Price 25 cents each.

**U. S. Navy Revolver Cartridge Box,** small leather box for holding revolver cartridges; with loop for attaching the box to the waist belt, as per illustration on page 167 of the catalogue; price 45 cents each.

**German Army Sanitary Glass Water Bottle Canteen,** the upper part is covered with leather; the lower part with heavy block tin, which answers for drinking; cup; black leather shoulder sling strap, with buckle, second-hand, serviceable. 98 cts each.

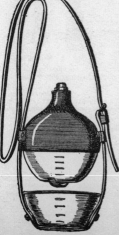

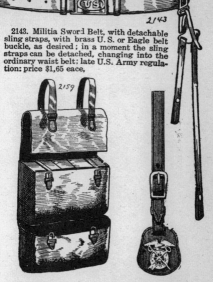

**2143. Militia Sword Belt,** with detachable sling straps, with brass U. S. or Eagle belt buckle, as desired; in a moment the sling straps can be detached, changing into the ordinary waist belt; late U. S. Army regulation; price $1.65 each.

**Civil War Combination Cartridge Box and Haversack,** wood frame, covered with waterproof canvas, with inside box for holding upwards of 100 cartridges, with small tin for musket caps. The bag part is at the bottom. The cover serves to cover both box and haversack; complete with shoulder sling, practically new; sticky from long storage; valuable only to collectors; price $1.00 each.

**2437. Military Watch Fob.** made of fine black leather, with buckle; with Army device in gilt or bronze; illustration shows insignia of Quarter Master's Department; we can furnish insignia for Infantry-Cross Rifles; Cavalry-Cross Sabres; Artillery-Cross Cannons; Hospital Corps Cross; price 50 cents each.

**U. S. A. Later Regulation Mess Pan,** with deeper pan than in the older pattern; made of heavy block tin; with folding handle; with cover, which can be used as a plate. with ring for carrying on the belt; used; serviceable order; price 15 cents each.

**British Army Infantry Soldiers' Swagger Stick,** required to be carried by Army Regulations in the Soldier's hand when in uniform off duty. Serves to keep hands out of pockets and gives the soldier a smart, natty appearance. White metal top and tip. Price $1.25. A few with British Army Regimental Crests, $2.25.

**U.S. Navy Primer Box;** black leather with loop on the back for attaching to any waist belt; 2 inches in width; inside measurement of the box 3 1-8 inches long, 3 1-8 inches high, 2 inches wide; in used, serviceable order; price 40 cents each.

**2230. German Army Mess Kit,** made of heavy block tin; oval shape; coffee tin, with inside attachment, with handle for use as fry pan; in used, serviceable order; price $1.00 each.

**1,000 U. S. A. Clothing Bags;** size of the bag 14 inches wide 14 inches long, with inside compartments; made of heavy water repelling drab colored canvas; offered in used, serviceable order, with leather sling strap; price 75 cents.

**50 U. S. Army Leather Haversacks,** with leather shoulder sling strap; bag measures 13 in. x 13 in.; bellows shape at the bottom and sides; fine soft black leather; used, serviceable order; price $1.50.

**0-960. ANCIENT PERSIAN GUN EQUIPMENT WAIST BELT.** Buff leather with two hand-made buckles with leather pouches, with home-made brass plate. Price, $3.85.

**CONFEDERATE'S ARTILLERY SWORD BELT.** English tan wax finished leather, with frog for short scabbard with brass loops and buckle, new, requiring cleaning. Width of the waist belt, 2¾ inches. Assorted sizes. Price, $1.00.

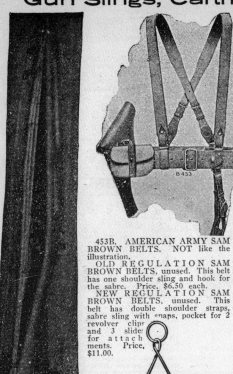

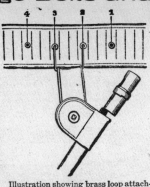

Illustration showing brass loop attaching the bayonet scabbard to eyelets in the web locp cartridge belt.    Price of brass hooks, 15 cents each.

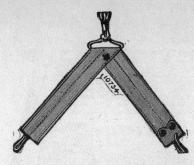

**10734. U. S. CAVALRY CANTEEN SLING STRAP.** Khaki web with bronze hooks for attaching to the canteen with bronze snap hook fastening to the waist belt. Price, 25 cents.

**453B. AMERICAN ARMY SAM BROWN BELTS.** NOT like the illustration.
**OLD REGULATION SAM BROWN BELTS,** unused. This belt has one shoulder sling and hook for the sabre. Price, $6.50 each.
**NEW REGULATION SAM BROWN BELTS,** unused. This belt has double shoulder straps, sabre sling with snaps, pocket for 2 revolver clips and 3 slides for attachments. Price, $11.00.

**U. S. McKeever Dress Equipment.**
Cartridge box with 20 loops for holding cal. .45 cartridges. Black leather waist belt, with brass eagle or U. S. buckle. With steel scabbard, with swivel frog. All in good refinished serviceable order. 95 cents the set.

**U. S. Army Late Regulation Service Equipment,** blue or grey colored, woven web cartridge belts, with loops for holding cal. .45, or with a little pressure at the start, the .50 caliber cartridges; with U. S. brass buckle, with steel bayonet scabbard attached, with swivel frog. All in good serviceable order, used only a short time. $1.25 the outfit.
With new khaki colored web cartridge belt for single row .30 calibre cartridge, with new steel scabbard. Price, $1.50 the outfit.

Illustration showing woven web drab colored gun sling, attached to U. S. rifle. We have 2,000 of these fine gun slings; will fit any gun. Good serviceable order. Used only a short time. Price, 35c. each.

**MINIATURE CANTEEN.** Fac-simile of the soldier's canteen. For use as personal ornament. Made of gilt metal, with ring and chain links, as illustrated. Trifle larger in size than 25-cent piece. Neat-looking charm. Price, 50 cents.

**No. 4. Civil War Sabre Knot.** New leather strap which is attached to the sabre, with loop to go over the soldier's wrist to prevent losing in action; has leather tassel which adds to the beauty of the sabre when used for decorating. Price 20 cents each; $2.00 dozen. Have 10,000.

**10737. NEW REGULATION GUN SLING.** Made at the Government Rock Island Arsenal, 1903-1907. Russet leather, with bronze loop in the center, with double hook claw adjusting hooks at each end. Full length of the sling, 4 feet. Offered in good, serviceable order. Price, 75 cents each. New, $1.25.

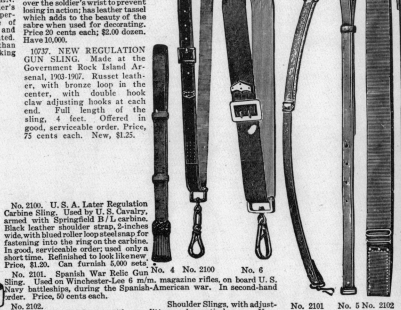

**U.S. Late Regulation Sword Belt Sling Outfit.** Finest quality ¾-inch bridle leather sling straps, with polished brass studs for attaching to sword or sabre rings. Fitted to patent light weight brass plate, with hook, for quick attaching to waist belt, thus converting in a moment, the ordinary waist belt into a sword belt. The short sling is 9½-inches long. The long sling is 23-inches. NEW Price of the outfit, 35c.

**No. 2100. U. S. A. Later Regulation Carbine Sling.** Used by U. S. Cavalry, armed with Springfield B/L carbine. Black leather shoulder strap, 2-inches wide, with blued roller loop steel snap for fastening into the ring on the carbine. In good, serviceable order; used only a short time. Refinished to look like new. Price, $1.20. Can furnish 5,000 sets.

**No. 2101. Spanish War Relic Gun Sling.** Used on Winchester-Lee 6 m/m. magazine rifles, on board U. S. Navy battleships, during the Spanish-American war. In second-hand order. Price, 50 cents each.

**No. 2102.** Shoulder Slings, with adjusting buckle, intended for use with navy litters. Are entirely new. Very suitable for use as shoulder straps, supporting any weight, in connection with handles. Price, 20c. each.

No. 4    No. 2100    No. 6

No. 2101    No. 5  No. 2102

**No. 2103.** 150,000 U. S. Government Russet Leather Gun Slings, made at Rock Island Arsenal, of the best quality russet leather, with double hook, brass claw fasteners. With brass adjusters. Used only a short time. Are offered in serviceable, complete order, at bargain price of 30 cents each.

**11044. U. S. A. REGULATION DRESS EQUIPMENT;** russet leather McKeever cartridge box, with inside web loops for holding 20 caliber .30 Krag or Springfield ball cartridges; with russet leather waist belt with bronze buckle; equipment has been used; is offered in good refinished serviceable order at $1.38 per set. Krag steel scabbards can be furnished at 60c each if desired.

**Captured Spanish Gun Slings.** They came to us attached to Mauser repeating rifles; also on captured Spanish Remington B. L. rifles, purchased from the U. S. Government and sold to us as captured in Cuba and Porto Rico. Leather slings in poor order. Valuable only for relics. Price, 30 cents each.

No. 2103

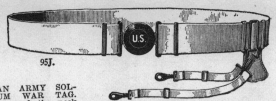

95J.

No. 45

**10495. EUROPEAN ARMY SOLDIER'S ALUMINUM WAR TAG.** With string worn around the neck when on war service, for battlefield indentification. Price, 50 cents.

**10445. U. S. ARMY DOUBLE SNAP STEEL HOOK.** Bronze finished. Length 3½ inches. New. Price, 8 cents each; 68 cents per dozen.

**2675. REVOLUTIONARY WAR CARTRIDGE BOX, 1777 to 1780.** Carried by Roger Walch, Coventry, Conn., while serving in Col. Sherburn's Regiment. Black leather, length 9½ inches, 2½ inches wide, 6½ inches high. Wood block for holding two rows 10 cartridges each; block in front for holding 4 cartridges, making total capacity 24 rounds. A few calibre 69 cartridges of period 1824, as used in the old mustering days, now in the box. White buff shoulder sling strap 2 inches wide. A rare old relic from the Brooks collection. Price, $25.00.

**No. 95J. 500 U. S. ARMY OFFICER'S WEB BELTS,** made by Mills. Two inches wide, adjustable for length. Heavy bronze buckles with letters U. S. raised. Detachable web saber slings, adjustable, with swivel bronze snaps. Web chafing piece under sling attachment. All in fine order. Received after the war. Price $1.00 each.

**No. 45. 1000 Shot Gun 16 Gauge Cartridge Belts** woven web belts with cartridge loops woven in the body of the belt, under Genl. Mills' patent. New belts with adjustable brass loop fastening. Superior to the ordinary sporting trade—cheap belts with loops sewed on light weight webbing. Manufacturers price, $1.25. Our bargain price, 60 cents.

No. 46

**No. 46. 1000 Khaki Web Belts,** for either .30 Calibre or .45 Calibre Cartridges, made by contract for the U. S. Government in 1898. Are complete with Brass loop, adjustable. New quality, 65 cents each. Good serviceable used belts, 40 cents each.

**No. 49. Illustration of U. S. Infantry Soldier in Khaki Uniform, with regulation calibre .30 rifle and equipment.** We can furnish NEW woven web gun slings at 25c. NEW Emergency bandoliers at 40c. NEW woven web clip cartridge belt at $1.00. NEW suspenders, 65 cents per pair. NEW late regulation hats, $12.50.

NEW late regulation khaki coat and trousers, $4.50 suit.

No. 48

**No. 48. Emergency Clip Cartridge Bandolier,** double pocket each holding clip of 5 cartridges. Worn over the shoulder. Can furnish in khaki. Price, 45 cents each, in white, each 35 cents.

**No. 50. U. S. A. CLIP CARTRIDGE BELTS,** without suspenders, in serviceable order at 50 cents each.

Calibre 30, gray and blue web belts with double row of loops at 60 cents each. Calibre 45, single row gray or blue web belts, 45 cents each.

No. 50

No. 52

**No. 52. Illustration showing back view of U. S. soldier equipment and uniform.** We can furnish leggins from 25 cents a pair upwards. New leggins, 75 cents a pair.

No. 49

No. 1726

10485.

**0-658. CADET WHITE WEB WAIST BELTS.** 2 inches wide, cadet length, 24-32 inches, requiring laundering. Offered as are, at 8 cents each.

**10485. BRITISH ARMY ALUMINUM CANTEEN.** With felt thermos cover, with snap button fastening. Used, but offered in good serviceable order. Contractor's price, $2.50; our bargain price, $1.25.

**3,000 BOY SCOUT CANTEENS, NEW.** Khaki cloth covered with shoulder strap. Holds one pint (half the regulation army size). Metal cap covering cork with chain attached. Weighs 7 oz.; width 6 inches in diameter. We purchased the entire stock from a manufacturer retiring from business whose price was 75c each. Our bargain price, 40 cents each.

U. S. ARMY ENGINEERING DEPARTMENT SHOVEL, 30 inches long, T handle, blade 7 inches wide by 10 inches long, pointed, unused. Weight, 2¾ pounds. Price, $1.00.

DRIVERS' GOGGLES with amber colored glass, in pocket case. Price, $0.50.

U. S. ARMY MARCHING COMPASS, 2⅜ inches in russet leather case with belt hook. Unused. Price, $1.50.

USED REGULATION ARMY SPURS of non-corrosive metal with new russet leather straps. This model has no rowels. Per pair, $0.85 including straps.

0-1329. HOSPITAL CORPS ORDERLY'S TONGUE DEPRESSOR. Nickel plated metal measures 8 inches around outer edge. Three-grooved handle; hole in blade 1 by ⅝ inch; weighs 3¼ ounces. Good condition. Price, 35 cents.

0-1330. MEDICAL GAUGE GLASS, with leather holder, from Militia Medical Auction, Length, 4 inches; diameter of stand and mouth, 2 inches. Black leather hand-sewed holder. Condition equal to new. Price the outfit, 45 cents.

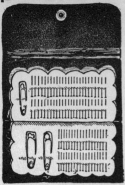

HOSPITAL CORPS OR-DERLY'S LEATHER POCKET CASE, with pocket and flap (snap fastening), with four folds flannel. No contents. Size of case, 5¼ by 3 in. Price 35 cents.

**10737. NEW REGULATION GUN SLING.** Made at the Government Rock Island Arsenal, 1903-1907. Russet leather, with bronze loop in the centre, with double hook claw adjusting hooks at each end. Full length of the sling, 4 feet. Used a short time. Offered in good, serviceable order. Price, 50 cents each.

MILITIA CANTEENS, with canvas covers and webbing sling without adjusting buckles. All second hand, much used but serviceable. Price, 30 cents each.

10481. BRITISH BOY SCOUT EQUIPMENT. Tin box, oval-shaped, size 4x3x1½ inches. Two compartments enclosed in a khaki covered pouch, with loop for fastening to the waist belt, with button on the flap cover. New. Intended for use of Boer War artillery gunners for holding gun oil. Never used; could be used as small canteen. Very neat looking. Price, 25 cents each.

0-676. U. S. A. LEATHER PICK AXE HOLDER WITH SHOULDER SLING STRAP. Made of fine, heavy black leather to cover the blade of the steel pick, tightening straps, shoulder sling, with loop for handle. Cost over $1.00 each to make. We have 1,980 in stock. Weight 1¾ pounds. Price, 35 cents each.

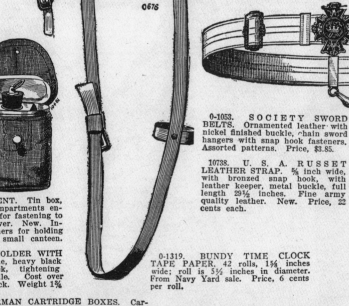

7114. GERMAN CARTRIDGE BOXES. Carried by German army soldiers in the war with France. Leather box size 7x4x2½ inches, with loops in the back for waist belt. Different inspection dates stamped on the leather, some in the lot as early as 1860, I. R., '63, etc. Serviceable relics offered as is, no selection of dates. Price, 50 cents each.

6919. POLISHED STEEL BOX having two compartments for holding small charge of powder and shot. Carried in pocket by sportsmen about the period of 1840. Spring cover at each end, length 3½ inches, 1½ inches diameter. Price, $1.75.

25 WOVEN WEB CARTRIDGE BELTS. With Massachusetts brass belt plate. Used, serviceable order. Price, 60 cents each.

0-1053. SOCIETY SWORD BELTS. Ornamented leather with nickel finished buckle, chain sword hangers with snap hook fasteners. Assorted patterns. Price, $3.85.

10738. U. S. A. RUSSET LEATHER STRAP. ⅝ inch wide, with bronzed snap hook, with leather keeper, metal buckle, full length 29½ inches. Fine army quality leather. New. Price, 22 cents each.

0-1319. BUNDY TIME CLOCK TAPE PAPER. 42 rolls, 1⅝ inches wide; roll is 5½ inches in diameter. From Navy Yard sale. Price, 6 cents per roll.

ENGINEER'S SKETCHING BOARD, as made for U. S. ARMY. Board 12½x15 inch, white pine, reinforced strips on end to prevent warping and splitting. Trough compass 3 inch needle, set in flush with one edge. Four clap screws for holding paper. Stamped on board: inch scale, plotting scope scales and tangent scale, inch scale, 1, 3 and 6 inches to the mile, in hundreds of yards. Threaded brass plate on reverse side of board to take tripod bolt. Complete with standard camera tripod. Price for this fine outfit, only $5.00.

10538. ARMY SERVICE COLLAR BUTTON. With cross rifles for artillery or cross swords for cavalry, with company letters. Job lot. Bronze finish. 1-inch diameter, screw nut fastening. Cannot furnish in special design. Offered only our selection. Price, 10 cents.

10202B. U. S. N. CHIEF PETTY OFFICERS' SCARF PIN. Letters U. S. N. with anchor and rope emblem, gilt finish. Price 50 cents.

10041. U. S. S. BRONZE COLLAR ORNAMENTS. With safety pin fastening; from the U. S. Quartermaster's auction sale; ⅝ inch letters, solid brass, bronze lacquered, 1,500 in stock. Price 10 cents each, 80c per dozen.

Walnut Steering Wheel from yacht Three Friends, not Cuban filibuster steamer, but New York Tammany Men's yacht, complete with frame; size, 32 inches ....Price, $15.00

Mauser Rifle, with Santiago Arsenal Spanish Record label pasted on gun, one of lot captured July, 1898; relic only....Price, $20.00

Spanish Seal, oval, 2½x1½ inches, brass, used Havana military arsenal; fine order; Gua Civil De Isle De Cuba, with blank space....Price, $6.00

Clearance Paper, issued by President John Adams, with seal of U. S., 1797, printed in four languages....Price, $20.00

Suit of Nickeled Armor for Horse and Man, made by noted English maker; fine order. Can be seen at our salesrooms, mounted on stuffed war horse of General Roberts of Civil War fame....Price, $250.00

Spanish Band Cymbals, from Santiago. Two odd ones, 12 inches; poor order; relics....$2.00 each

Coir Mat, with name "Corsair" worked in it. Size, 7 ft. long, 3½ ft. wide; in fine order; relic. Corsair now Gloucester....Price, $20.00

Part of Spanish Torpedo, Rudder and Propeller, found on deck of Viscaya after the explosion; relic....Price, $30.00

CAPTURED SPANISH OFFICER'S SABRE. Blade is 28 inches long and has been sharpened. Came to United States Arsenal along with lot of private captured sabres. Price, $12.00.

Spanish Powder Tanks from one of the wrecked warships at Santiago, Cuba; hold 300 pounds; price, $60.00. Spanish Powder Charger for 11-inch breech-loading rifle, copper, 3 ft. long; price, $65.00. Spanish Cartridge Shells found on deck of wrecked warship, 1-pounder 75 cents, 3-pounder $1.25, 6-pounder $1.50. Spanish Torpedo War Head that contains the explosive, when attached to torpedo; now free from powder; measures 14 in. long; made of copper; price, $20.00.

Seal of Philippine Islanders, captured at Congress Hall, Malabon, by member of Utah Battery. Carved on hard wood; beautiful work; rare relic. Price, $150.00

Civil War McClelland Saddle, used through the war by Major A. F. Greene. Rawhide covered; in serviceable order; vouched for....Price, $20.00

General's Saddle, Civil War period, facsimile of one used by General Grant. We will loan this saddle to sculptors for modeling. Terms on application.

Headless Shell Extractors and Drifts for the Springfield 45-70 breech-loading rifle ....50 cents per set

Zulu Battle Shields, made of bull hide, with spear, $10.00, $12.00, $14.00 and $16.00 each, according to size.

British Life Guard Steel Cuirass. Front and back piece, with polished brass shoulder scales....Price, $12.00 per set

Brass Stair Plate from the Spanish warships sunk off Santiago, Cuba, 19x6 inches, about 20 pounds, $6.00; larger one from the Viscaya, warped by fire; has anchor monogram, $8.50.

Megaphone from Corsair, $3.75; exploded brass shells from Corsair, 6 inches long, 2½ inches in diameter; fine relics, 75 cents.

N. Y. State Artillery Belt, used in War 1812; red leather, with plate. Price, $2.50.

Coat of Mail, made of caribou horn, with brass chain interwoven; supposed to have been captured by the Moros from the Spaniards in the seventeenth century; found on the Island of Jolo (New York import house had one similar to this for which they wanted $450.00). Price, $275.00.

Complete Suite of Japanese Armor, including metal helmet; purchased at Singapore. Price, $35.00.

Japanese Triangular Point Spear; peculiarly polished black handle. Price, $7.00.

Shield from Celebu Islands; long and angular, with hair and bone ornamentation; blood stains on back from service the day previous to Captain Moss' purchase of same from native, about August, 1901. Price, $22.00.

1812 Artillery Saber; in old Long Island family since 1812 (name given to purchaser); good order. $15.00.

Russian Collection of 5 Swords; Naval Officers'; Tassock, used period of Peter the Great; 1833 Dragoon Saber; Circassian Dagger; Dress Sword; all in good, second-hand, serviceable order. Price for the lot, $68.00.

No. U 1-40. THE ARTILLERIST'S MANUAL AND BRITISH SOLDIER'S COMPENDIUM, by Major F. A. Griffiths, R. F. P. Royal Artillery. Published in London, in 1856. Illustrated with many full page plates. Has chapters on Carbine Exercises, Ordnance, Ranges, Gunnery, etc. Size 4x6½ inches, 345 pages. Price $1.50.

Admiral Dewey's Bamboo Chair, one worn out on the Olympia while at Manila; given to the ship's carpenter, who presented it to us for our museum.

Percussion Cap Blunderbus, with swivel for mounting on wall or boat; weighs about 20 pounds; fine order....Price, $15.00

Spanish Bronze Bell, mounted on metal stand, which came to New York in cargo of old brass from Santiago wrecked Spanish warships; supposed to have been on board some of the Spanish torpedo boats; 6½-in. mouth; perfect order. Price, $50.00

Gatling Gun Circular Feed Case; bronze mountings....Price, $7.50

Brass Figures from the wrecked Spanish warships; used to show the depth of water, 8, 0; 6 and 8 inches long....$2.50 each

Brass Name Plates from the cabin doors on Admiral Cervera's warship, 2 inches wide, 6 to 8 inches long. Some are partly burned....Price, $5.75 each

African Spears, set 4, sold by New York Customs Officers. Spear and socket are native work, decorated with colored fibre at centre; rare specimens. Price, $40.00 the set; will sell singly if desired, $12.00 each.

Powder Measure.—Large bronze powder measure used at Morro Castle to measure charge for antique mortars; is marked "Decalitro de Malabouche Valencia;" shot went through one side and made deep indentation on the opposite side. This rare relic came from Santiago in cargo of old brass; weight, 20 lbs.; 10 in. across top, 10 in. deep....Price, $

Spanish Engineer Officer's Brass Belt Buckle with Morro Castle Spanish crown in white metal on the centre; handsome and rare buckle; relic. Price, $2.75

Insurgent Filipino Sergeant of Infantry Uniform; blouse and trousers from Van Camp collection. Price, $6.85.

South Sea Islander Brass Pipe; native work. Price, $3.50. Pipe in carved wood. Price, $1.85.

Old-time Dagger, fine steel blade, with leather scabbard; brass tipped. Price, $4.50.

U. S. A. Officer's Sword, found in hospital, San Juan, Cuba; we are unable to find owner and now offer it for sale; rare relic, vouched for...Price, $20.00

Spanish Bronze Indicator from the bridge of one of the wrecked warships; marked Barbord-Tribord; stands 40 inches high on base-plate; 13 inches wide; is incomplete; weighs under 100 pounds....Price, $75.00

Spanish Torpedo Propellers and Rudders, 22x14 inches; weigh about 60 pounds; relic from Santiago....Price, $50.00

Spanish Torpedo War Head, free from powder; 28x14 inches; conical shaped; copper ....Price, $30.00

Sword Handles; Spanish officers' sword handles, with coat-of-arms of Spain ....Price, $3.00

Brass Sun Dial, from Cuba, for use in latitude 25½; 10-inch face; engraved ....Price, $9.50

Stirrups.—Spanish old-time copper stirrups; rare pattern, $6.00. Others in bronze, $1.75 each.

Spanish Torpedo Engine, copper, valuable as relic only; recovered from wreck of Spanish warship; weighs over 100 pounds....Price, $20.00

Bronze Port-Hole Cover, circular, 16 inches in diameter, with over 20 shot holes; fine specimen, showing effect of U. S. Navy shooting; recovered from wreck; weighs about 30 pounds....Price, $50.00

Bronze Relics, large assortment, recovered from Spanish wrecks; door-plates on cabins, port-hole frames, railing, gongs, cartridge shells from 6-pdr. to 6 inches, etc. Prices on application.

Antique Quill Cannon Primers, valuable as relics only (cannot be mailed) Price, 10c. each

Bayonet Scabbards; nickel-plated steel....Price, 75c.

Ebony Walking Cane; silver mounted. Price, $2.50.

Spanish Dead-light, with glass; 8 inches in diameter; circular; from wreck. Price, $15.00

Clark Russel's Patent Log for U. S. N. Warship; circular; brass. Price, $4.50

U. S. N. Gunner's Rapid-fire Cannon Cartridge Box for 1½-inch diameter cartridge, with shoulder belt; holds 20 cartridges; size, 6x13 inches; relic. Price, $6.00

U. S. Gunner's Level, with spirit gauge; in walnut case....Price, $4.50

Set of Polished Steel Gauges from U. S. Arsenal at Harper's Ferry, for gauging the parts of the model 54, muzzle-loading rifle while being manufactured; gauges for 200 operations; packed in compartment case....Price, $35.00

Brass Lantern used by Gen. Shafter in his tent in Cuba at Siboney; it began to leak, so he threw it away. Sergeant Ralston, now lieutenant of Tenth Infantry, saved it and sold it to us as a relic; our price for this old $1.00 lantern is $20.00; vouched for.

Weather Vane from the old Frigate Roanoke; 6-ft. guide, with compass letters; fair order....Price, $20.00

U. S. N. Surveyor's Compass, from the Raleigh after the battle of Manila Bay; is incomplete; relic....Price, $15.00

U. S. S. Trenton Bronze Gong, recovered by divers from the wreck at Samoa; 10-inch diameter; rare relic....Price, $35.00

Seven-and-one-half-inch Bronze Gong from Spanish wrecked warship, Santiago; relic only....Price, $6.00

U. S. Navy Fire Hook, used in fighting fire....Price, $2.50

Double Pulley Block, with two brass wheels, recovered from the wreck of the Spanish warship, Reina Mercedes; 6 in.; in serviceable order....Price, $5.00

U. S. Navy Iron Shot and Shell Hooks, used on warships to hoist shells from the deck to the gun....Price, $1.85 each

U. S. Navy Divers' Electric Lamp, with reflector and large guard; about 100 candle power; relic....Price, $7.50

Piece U. S. Navy 8-in. Shell, fired into Santiago, Cuba, from U. S. N. warship; size, 4x5 inches....Price, $3.00

U. S. N. Battleship Electric Signaling Outfit, Siemens & Holske, Vienna, with 4 lamps, red and white, double electric switchboard, and about 100 pounds cable; seems to be in working order....Price, $30.00

Revolutionary War Captain's Commission, signed by John Hancock, with Seal of Commonwealth of Massachusetts, 1781, to Capt. Thomas Eaton, as captain of militia; also his resignation in 1787, framed in glass case....Price, $25.00

Philippine Walking Cane, made with alternate black and white polished horn from caribou and water buffalo; cartridge tipped; silvered head. Price, $6.85.

Collection of 22 different kinds of Antique Lamps and Lanterns; some are very rare....Price for the lot, $150.00

Plaques of distinguished British Generals of South African War; size, 10 inches, colored....Price, $1.00 each

Button Pictures; ornaments of British War Generals....Price, 10 cents each

Old Norman Battle Ax from Edinburgh, Scotland, collection, no shaft. Price, $15.00

Stone Cannon Ball from Flodden Battlefield, 7 inches....Price, $20.00

Confederate Cedar Wood Canteen, carried by Virginia Volunteers, Price, $5.00

No. U3-10. A CONCISE SYSTEM OF INSTRUCTION and Regulations for THE MILITIA and VOLUNTEERS of the United States, with exercises and movements for the INFANTRY, LIGHT INFANTRY, AND RIFLEMEN, CAVALRY AND ARTILLERY. Prepared by Brevet Capt. S. Cooper. Published in Philadelphia in 1836. Many illustrations. Give drum music. Size 4½x7 inches....Price, $2.00

U. S. Navy Sailor's Palm for sewing sails, etc. Relic....Price, 75 cents

President Kruger South African Army Brass Buttons....Price, $2.00 each

South African Volunteer Soldiers' Buttons. Relics....Price, 50 cents each

Spanish Cartridge Box, with shoulder belt equipment....Price, $2.85

British War Office Manual of Military Law, 1024 pages, 1899..Price, $3.00

British Soldiers' Enlistment Papers for Boer War....Price, $2.00

South Africa Basuto Native's Bangle Charm, a cure for rheumatism, given to British soldier....Price, $2.50 per pair

South African Mounted Rifle Belt Plate, with British coat-of-arms, Price, $1.50

British Jack Spurs; pair used by trooper in Brabant's Horse; good order; relic ....Price, $2.00

S.S. Niagara Circular Life Preserver, 2½ ft. diameter, with name of ship painted on it; sold at Navy Yard auction after close of Spanish War. Price, $5.00

Buttons from Bank of England employee's uniform; facsimile of British penny; relic....Price, 40 cents each

British Military Buttons; large assortment; over 30 varieties, Price, 25 cents each

British Button, with "92"; from uniform famous 92d Regiment, Price, 50 cents

British Button, with Prince of Wales coat-of-arms and 3 plumes, Price, 50 cents

U. S. Navy Officer's Gilt-finish Button, ⅝-in.; also 1-inch size, with eagle, anchor and 13 stars....Price, 10 cents

Button from every State in the Union, mounted on cardboard, boxed, with name printed underneath; also army and navy buttons; all fine, new buttons; regular collection....Price for set of 48 buttons, mailed, $2.50.

British Soldier's Emergency Package of Bandages for the wounded; carried through South African campaign....Price, $1.00

Boer Handcuffs for British prisoners, from South Africa....Price, $2.50

Spanish Soldier's Leather Leggin, recovered from wounded soldier at El Caney....Price, $2.85

Civil War Tent Stove; sheet iron....Price, $6.00

Collection of 5 Old Brass U. S. Navy Battle Gongs; relics of old wooden ship....Price, $100.00

Russet Leather Pouch with name of D. J. Botha written on inside of flap; found near Pretoria, South Africa....Price, $3.00

Small Brass Anchor Ornament, from Spanish; size, 4½x2½ inches, Price, 75 cents

**5011.** British Army Water Bottle. Glass bottle covered with black leather, with straps for tightening the leather cover around the neck part, and strap loop on the back for attaching to waist or cartridge belt. Fitted with new corks (glass easily cleaned). Weight 1¼ pounds. Price, $1.00.

**5012.** European Army Canteen. Enameled mouthpiece, shoulder sling straps, with brass buckles for adjusting 5½x2½ inches, weight 17 ounces. Price $1.00.

**5013.** Aluminum Water Bottle, with detachable felt cover, used. Offered in serviceable order. Partly oval shaped, size 8 inches, with tan leather shoulder sling strap, length 7½ inches. Price $1.25.

**U. S. Cavalry Canteen,** with short sling strap, either in black leather or woven web khaki, with snap hook for attaching to the saddle; new at $1.00 each; in good, second-hand, serviceable order, price, 65 cents each.

**35,000 U. S. Army Canteens.** Drab colored heavy canvas covers, with inside wool covers to keep contents cool, with bridle leather carrying strap, with brass hooks for adjusting the length. Used. Our price is 50 cents each. We show photographic view.

**5000 Canteens** same as above, but which have been a long time in use, and which we offer as are for relics or decoration. No doubt some can still be used, and are as good as some that are offered for sale in the market at high prices. Our price is 35 cents each.

**10108. BRITISH ARMY SOLDIER'S EQUIPMENT.** Consisting of waterproof canvas knapsack, white buff leather cartridge pouches, with white buff leather, shoulder sling strap with brass belt plate, etc. Serviceable order. Price, $3.85.

**500 German Army Canteens,** "Feldflaschen," as shown in photograph. Special glass bottle covered with leather, with shoulder sling, cork, with ring and strap. Useful for campers; holds about 3 pints; 7 inches long, 5 inches wide, 3 inches deep. Price, 75 cents each. Have been in use, but are in good, serviceable order.

British Army Enameled Tin Canteen, covered with felt (slightly moth eaten). Complete, with shoulder sling; second-hand; serviceable; metal bound cork. Price, 80 cents.

**United States Army Mess Kit,** consisting of knife, fork, spoon, mess pan (which can be used for frying) with cover, and tin cup, as per illustration. Second-hand, serviceable order. Price, 48 cents the set.

**28,000 U. S. Army Soldiers' Heavy Block Tin Cups;** furnished to Spanish War soldiers encamped in the South. Many of these cups are practically new; for such the price is 15 cents, and for those in good, second-hand serviceable order price 8 cents each, or 80 cents dozen; $60.00 per 1,000.

**BRITISH ARMY SOLDIER'S OLD TIME BODY BELT.** White buff leather, with brass clasp engraved "Nottinghamshire Regiment." Price $2.00.

**BLACK LEATHER SWORD BELT,** officer's, with brass belt plate engraved "Bombay Medical Society." Price $3.00.

**WHITE BUFF LEATHER BELT** with Lion, Crown and British monogram "Dieu et Mon Droit." Price $2.00.

**1313.** British Army Water Bottle, Boer War relic, with buff leather straps and large frog for attaching over the web loop cartridge belt; with open stud fasteners; second-hand, serviceable order. Price, $1.00 each.

**1878.** Congo Canteen, made of carved and ornamented gourd; unserviceable; only fit for decoration. Price, $5.00.

**3440.** U. S. A. Soldier's Telescope Suit Case, closed measures 18¾ by 9½ by 16 inches, with 3 heavy leather straps with loops, which pass around the middle and ends of the case; with adjustable carrying handle. Cases are made of heavy fiber superior quality. For government use. Used a few times, offered in serviceable order. Price 95 cents each.

British Army Mess Tins, showing opened and closed; made of heavy tin. Set, $1.

British Army Wood Canteen, with white buff leather straps. In serviceable order. **Price, 85 cents each.**

Austrian Army Canteen, heavy glass flask covered with block tin; in two sections, joined together with canteen cord, with flask inclosed in center. Canteen cork in center of cup-shaped cover, which serves as drinking cup. Convenient for tourists and campers. Price, $1.00 each.

**Buzzacot Packed**

Old C. S. A. Civil War Battle Canteen. Relic, $1.00.

Old Civil War Canteen. Relic, 50 cents.

Old fashioned long Sickle, from Southerner's collection of relic weapons, $1.00.

Old Civil War Cartridge Box from Southerner's collection, $1.00.

Revolutionary War Wood Canteen; good condition; barrel shape. Price, $10.00.

Old Relic Civil War Battlefield Cap Box, 25 cents.

Buzzacott 100 Men Cooking Outfit, made of heavy steel and bar iron skeleton grate stove with two steel ovens, and covers, two iron kettles, 7 inches deep, 14 inches diameter, 2 12-inch steel fry pans, 100 tin coffee cups, 100 each knives, forks and spoons. All in good, second-hand serviceable order. Price, as specified without boilers, $20.00 each outfit.

Buzzacott 25 Men Cooking Outfit, same as above, but smaller in size, with one iron kettle and one fry pan, and 25 each cups, knives, forks and spoons. $15.00 the outfit.

3B. AUSTRIAN OFFICER'S GILT SERVICE CROSS for eight years' service. Yellow and black ribbon. Price, $4.50.

46B. MECKLEBURG SCHWERIN GILT CROSS, marked with crown F F 1914. FUR AUSZEICHNUNG IM KRIEGE. With ribbon. Price, $20.00.

55B. OFFICER'S GILT CROSS FOR 15 YEARS SERVICE. With blue ribbon. Price, $4.50.

57B. TWENTY-FIVE YEARS' SERVICE CROSS with blue ribbon. Obverse marked with crown over F W III. Reverse X X V in circle in center. Medals for such long service are rare. Price, $7.00.

38B. KING LUDWIG'S WAR CROSS, bronze with black enamel. Shows bust of king. Reverse marked 7 I 1916. With blue and white ribbon. Price, $4.00.

54B. PRUSSIAN DUPPEL SILVER CROSS, with blue, white and black ribbon. Obverse shows Prussian eagle mount on cannon, DUPPEL 18 APR. 1864. Price, $4.00.

68B. SAXONY WAR CROSS with ribbon. Made of bronze, dull finish. Note that this cross is of different shape from the regular German cross. Marked: WELT-KRIEG, 1915. Price, $5.00.

4B. FRANCIS JOSEPH OF AUSTRIA GILT MEDAL with yellow and black striped ribbon. Shows bust of Francis Joseph, with 2 DECEMBER 1873. Price, $4.00.

5B. FRANCIS JOSEPH OF AUSTRIA silver medal with white and red striped ribbon. Marked: DER TAPFERKEIT over draped flags and wreath. Price, $4.00.

6B. FRANCIS JOSEPH BRONZE MEDAL with ribbon, similar to 5B. Price, $3.75.

32B. BADEN LARGE SILVER FINISH MEDAL, with bust marked: FRIEDRICH II GROSSHERZOG VON BADEN. Reverse: FUR VERDIENST. With yellow and red ribbon. Price, $5.50.

33B. BAVARIAN BRONZE MEDAL with red ribbon. Marked with bust and MAXIMILIAN II GOENIG V. BAYERN. Reverse: IN TREUE FEST 1849. Price, $4.00.

58B. PRUSSIAN SILVER MEDAL with orange and white ribbon. Marked with bust and FRIEDRICH WILHELM III KOENIG VONPREUSSEN. Reverse: FUR RETTUNG AUS GEFAHR, with wreath. Price, $6.50.

30B. GUATEMALA SILVER MEDAL, marked 1902. Reverse shows capitol building, MANUEL ESTRADA CABRERA FUNDADORA DELA FIESTA DE MINERVA. With blue and white ribbon. Price, $5.50.

34B. BAVARIAN CROSS, silver with blue ribbon. Obverse has raised gold crown over letter L in center with 1870-1871 at edge on wreath. Reverse has RED CROSS on white enamel back with black border. Price, $20.00.

40B. BAVARIAN BRONZE WAR CROSS for 14 years' service. With light blue ribbon with white edges. Price, $5.50.

41B. BRUNSWICK WAR CROSS, bronze, with purple ribbon. Marked: FUR VERDIENST IN KRIEGE. Reverse with Crown, E A 1914. Price, $5.00.

61B. PRUSSIAN CHINA MEDAL 1900, 1901, for non-combatants. With yellow, red, white and black ribbon. With crown over letter W. Reverse: German eagle over dragon. Price, $3.50.

64B. PRUSSIAN GILT MEDAL with red, white and black ribbon. Obverse has cross with crown at each end with letters W R A V. Reverse: FUER VERDIENSTE VM DAS ROTHEKREVZ, with wreath. Price, $5.00.

69B. SAXONY WAR MEDAL, SILVER, with green and white ribbon. Obverse shows bust of WILLIAM ERNST OF SACHSEN. Reverse: DEM VERDIENSTE 1914. Price, $5.00.

Dodge Blanket Roll Support.

**10483. BRITISH ARTILLERY SOLDIER'S CARTRIDGE BOX.** Patent leather, with loops for belt, with metal cannon ornaments on the cover. Size of the box 6¼x4x1½ inches. Price, 60 cents each.

**10593. CANTERBURY CATHEDRAL MARBLE DEATH HEAD.** Part of the architectural ornamentation removed by contractor on restoration work. The length is 8 inches, width 6 inches, 4¾ inches. Beautiful piece of ancient sculptural work from famous cathedral. Price, $25.00.

**NEW U. S. GOVT. CANTEENS,** with web sling, with open brass loops, double covered, outside covering drab colored canvass, inside cover wool, with U. S. Stamp, the hall mark of perfection; with brass chain attached to cork. Price, $1.65.

**500 Dodge Patent Blanket Roll Supports,** whereby the soldier or tourist can carry his outfit rolled up in blanket adjusted to the support, which consists of light bent hickory wood with leather lacing straps and studs, and is carried across the shoulder without compressing the chest or back. All in fine serviceable order. Price, $1.00 each.

Spanish Officer's Russet Leather Revolver Holster, stamped "Catalina, Havana." From Cuba, 1898. Holds 44-caliber S. & W. revolver. Relics. $1.50 ea. British Army South African War Canteen; made of enameled tin with metal screw-top; heavy wool cloth covered; in good, second-hand, serviceable order. Price, $1.00 each. Leather Canteen; rare pattern from London collection; good, serviceable order. Price, $2.75.

U. S. Army Vegetable Basket which goes with Buzzacott cooking outfit. New; fine potato basket; made of wire. Price, separate, 20c.

**No. 1807. BOER WAR BRITISH ARMY REVOLVER HOLSTER** made of fine russet leather, bridle quality, riveted with brass cover, opening at muzzle end, with 3-inch loop on back for cartridge belt with fastening flap strap, that goes completely around the butt of the revolver fastening to brass stud, adapted for any army revolver with barrel not longer than 6 inches. Price, 75 cents.

**3298. U. S. A. LEATHER SHOULDER SLING STRAP,** with brass hooks for adjusting the length. Brass hooks for attaching to the Haversack or the article to be carried. Made at the Government Arsenal, of the best bridle leather, 2 inches wide across the shoulder, tapering to 1¼ inches at the end. Weighs 7 ounces, cost upwards of $1.00 each to make. We have about 50,000 in stock. For sale at the bargain price of 35 cents each.

**3104. NEW BLUE WEB CARBINE SHOULDER SLING,** 1⅝ inches wide. Heavy web with strong snap buckle attached by leather, made for a prominent Arms Co. Suitable for any purpose requiring weight carried from the shoulder. Suitable for Post Man, Drummer, suit cases, etc. Must have cost $1.00 each to make, we have 700 in stock. Our bargain price is 35 cents each.
**3104A. NEW LEATHER CARBINE SHOULDER SLING STRAPS,** with strong steel snaps. Same appearance as 3104, only in leather. Price, 75 cents each.

**1558. BRITISH ARMY OFFICER'S SABRETASH,** new fine white buff leather. Entire upper side with fine enamel facing, with brass buckle, loop and extension. With silvered buckle SOUTH WALES BORDERERS around the rim. With centre ornament, surrounded by wreath. All in relief, short and long sword slings. With white enameled buff sling strap from belt to pouch, black enamel leather pocket, size 6x9 bellows shaped, practically new, with British gilt coat of arms ornament on cover. Buckle is worth half the money asked for the outfit. Price, $8.75.

**1558C. 5 BRITISH ARMY OFFICER'S SABRETASHES,** similar to No. 1553, but without enamel facing on white buff leather, and with British gilt coat of arms. Buckle in second hand serviceable order. Price, $6.85.

**1558D.** Similar to illustration, but with silvered British coat of arms and officer's buckle. Price, $7.85.

**1558A. SABRETASH,** similar to illustration. Not quite so new, but good serviceable order, with gilt buckle, V. R. With cannon surrounded by wreath with British motto. "Mon Dieu Mon Droit," with V. R. gilt ornament on pouch. Price, $7.85.

**1558B. SABRETASH,** similar to No. 1558, but without enamel facing on white buff leather. Price, $7.25.

**PLAIN ENAMELED LEATHER WAIST BELT,** with light stamped brass belt plate, without sling straps; in second hand, serviceable order. Price, 45 cents each.

**No. 1807B. ADMIRAL DEWEY'S FLAG SHIP OLYMPIA REVOLVER HOLSTER,** black leather Colts Cal. .38 with U. S. N. stamped on cover, puchased at Boston Navy Yard auction shortly after the return of the Olympia; vouched for by the officers who received and had charge of the stores from the Olympia. Price, 75 cents each.

**9. U. S. EAGLE BELT AND PLATE.** With hook for adjusting length. Made of bridle leather; in good, serviceable, second hand order; superior to any cheap, made-up leather belts; plate is of brass. Price, 90 cents each.

**No. 1312. KING OF PORTUGAL SADDLE HOLSTERS** with gilt Coat of Arms on each cover. Holsters are made of russet leather, hand sewed, with gilt ornamented end caps, patent leather cover; in good second hand serviceable order; vouched for. Price, $28.00 pair.

**50 REVOLVER HOLSTERS** stamped N. Y., used by N. Y. Cavalry Squadrons A and C at Porto Rico. In fine order; 38 cal. Relics Spanish War. $1.50 each.

**500 Old Style Saddle Holsters** for pistols; fine, serviceable order. Price, $5.00 pair.

56B. GERMAN OFFICER'S SILVER MEDAL FOR TWENTY YEARS' SERVICE. Obverse has gold center with CROWN and monogram W R REVERSE MARKED in gold center X X. With blue ribbon. Price, $6.00.

37B. BAVARIAN SILVER CROSS surmounted by Crown and crossed short swords. Center black enamel with white edge marked MERENTI with crown over letter L in silver. Reverse has raised silver lion in center with 1866. White and blue ribbon. Price, $15.00

48B. PRUSSIAN OVAL IRON MEDAL for WATERLOO CAMPAIGN. With white ribbon with black and orange edges. Obverse has German motto with crown over monogram. FURPFLICHTREUE IM KRIEGE. Reverse shows cross with 1815. This is a rare medal. Price, $8.50.

67B. PRUSSIAN MUNITION WORKERS' CROSS with ribbon with white and black stripes with red edges. Dull finish. Crown and W R in center. Reverse FUR KRIEGS HILESDIENST. Price, $5.00.

36B. BAVARIAN BRONZE CROSS with ribbon. Similar to 37B. Price, $8.50.

71B. SCHAUMBERG LIPPE GILT WAR CROSS with blue and white ribbon. Marked with crown over letter A. FUR TREUE DIENSTE 1914. Price, $5.00.

74B. FRANCO-PIEDMONT SILVER MEDAL with green, white and red striped ribbon. Obverse marked: HOPITAUX DE MILAN. AUX BLESSES ET MALADES DE L'ARMEE ALLIEE FRANCO-PIEDMONT-AISE LES COMMERCANTS DE MILAN. Reverse: 5 JUIN 1859. Price, $5.00.

72B. WURTEMBURG SILVER MEDALS with yellow and black ribbons. Obverse shows bust and WILHELM II KOENIG VON WUERTTEM-BERG. Reverse: FUR TAPFERKEIT UND TREUE, in wreath. Price, $5.00.

76B. ROUMANIAN SILVER MEDAL with red ribbon. Shows bust marked: CAROLUS I PRINCEPS ROMANIAE. Reverse: BENE MERENTI in wreath. Price, $6.00.

13B. LEOPOLD II GILT MEDAL FOR MERIT AND LONG SERVICE, with red, yellow, and black striped ribbon. Medal in shape of cross with wreath, surmounted by crown. Center marked L II. ARMEE MERITEAN-CIENNETE. Reverse has Belgian Lion in center, marked: L'UNION FAIT LA FORGE. Price, $8.00.

19B. GERMAN BRONZE MEDAL, with red and yellow ribbon. Crowned lion in center with short sword. Marked at edge: URHEUDESTA FUR TAPPERHET. Reverse: SUOMEN KANSALTA 1918, in wreath. Price, $4.00.

1B. AUSTRIAN SILVER MEDAL of 1797, with yellow and black ribbon. Obverse shows bust, marked: FRANZ IIR. K. ERZII ZU OEST GEF GRAF VON TYROL. Reverse: DEN TAPFEREN VERTHEIDIGERN DES VATERLANDES MDCCXCVII, in wreath. This is a rare old medal. In good order. Price, $6.50.

SH1. BRITISH MILITARY MEDAL, silver, with blue ribbon with red and white striped center. Obverse shows bust of King George V. Reverse: Wreath with crown over G R v. FOR BRAVERY IN THE FIELD. Price, $18.00.

SH2. TURKISH STAR DECORATION, with pin clasp. Taken from GER-man prisoner by Canadian soldier. Red enamel center with silver edge, and silver crescent with Turkish inscription in center. Price, $6.50.

SH3. GERMAN SOLDIERS WOUNDED BADGE. Made of block tin, black enameled showing wreath with trench helmet and two crossed short swords in center. Price, $1.00.

SH4. BRONZE WURTEMBURG CROSS. Has crossed swords at center, with crown and 1915. KRIEGSVERDIENST. Long blue and red ribbon. Price, $4.50.

SH5. GERMAN HANOVERIAN OFFICER'S CROSS. Made of black en-amel with silver edges and green enameled wreath. 1914 in raised silver letters. In center silver circle is shown crown with monogram and X X V II. With clasp. Price, $6.50.

SH6. ITALIAN WAR CROSS, bronze with blue and white ribbon. Cross marked with crown monogram V E III MERITO DI GUERRA. Price, $5.50.

SH7. GREEK SILVER WAR CROSS, 1916 1917 with black ribbon with blue edge. Medal in shape of wreath with short sword and bar across center. Price, $5.85.

SH8. BELGIAN BRONZE CROIX DE GUERRE, with red ribbon with narrow green stripes. Bronze cross is surmounted by bronze crown. Price $7.95.

27C. FRENCH BRONZE CROIX DE GUERRE with silver star and ribbon. Price $9.00.

27E. FRENCH BRONZE CROIX DE GUERRE, with bronze and ribbon. Price $9.50.

BM. BAVARIAN WHITE ENAMELED CROSS, silver trimmed with monogram L L in center circle, with two pointed crown with red and black striped ribbon. Price $7.50.

MM. BAVARIAN SILVER MEDAL, MINIATURE, with monogram L L on enamel center, with silver crown, and blue ribbon with black center stripe. Medals in this size are rare in Europe. Price $5.00.

AV. AMERICAN VICTORY MEDAL, without bars, as issued by the United States after the World War. Complete with ribbon. Price $3.50.

RARE COLLECTION OF CONFEDERATE BILLS AND STAMPS. Made up into scrap book at time of Civil War by a Confederate soldier. Contains bank notes of every denomination as issued by the Confederacy, and by the various banks of the South. Has about one dozen original envelopes with address and the Confederate postage stamps. This is a very rare collection and should be in some Southern museum. Price $150.00.

**3,000 U. S. ARMY HORSE HOBBLES** for attaching to horses while in camp, allowing them to graze without wandering off. These were made at the U. S. Government Rock Island Arsenal. Anyone having care of horses or other animals can use these fine hobbles to advantage. Keep you from wearing the hide off your heels looking up lost animals. Soft leather inside, swivel center link. Must have cost upwards of $3 to make. Our bargain price is 50c each.

**WHITE MILITIA BED SACK.** Length 6 feet 3 inches, width 2 feet 6 inches, 4 inches deep, weight 28 ounces, opening slit in center. Good second hand order. Price, $1.50.

**500 KHAKI BED-SACKS,** used, with full length opening, only $1.40 each.

**LATE PATTERN ARMY ROUND MESS-PANS,** 8½ inches, of heavy block tin, in used, serviceable order. Weight 18 ounces. Price 25 cents each. $2.50 per dozen.

**40,000 ARMY CAN-VAS HAVERSACKS** with rings; in used, serviceable condition. 13 inches long, 9½ inches wide, weight 20 ounces. Have pocket on inside of cover. Offered without slings at 55 cents each. Leather shoulder sling 35 cents extra. Web sling, No. 10734, for attaching to belt, 25 cents extra.

**1,000 NEW WATER-PROOF HAVER-SACKS.** With inside detachable bag, which can be removed for washing. Made for use of U. S. Army during Civil War. Never used; still in the original cases. Black water-proofed canvas, with shoulder sling, with leather strap and buckle. Useful bag for soldier, camper, scholar or anyone requiring bag with shoulder strap. Bargain price, 15c each.

**50,000 ARMY CANVAS HAVER-SACKS** in second-hand, serviceable condition, 11 inches long, 7½ inches wide, weight 16 ounces. Two rings on back for use with sling. Offered without slings at 35 cents each. Leather shoulder sling 35 cents extra. Web sling, No. 10734, for attaching to belt, 25 cents extra.

**ARMY KNAPSACK.** Made of heavy drab colored water repellent canvas. Light steel frame, forming two box like compartments, full size 15x12 inches, with bellows shaped canvas sides (which expand in filling). The frame always keeps the knapsack in shape. Side flaps with tightening straps with 2-inch wide shoulder carrying straps; with snap buckles; with two extra straps that can be used for supporting the waist belt. Side straps have thongs for fastening the blanket. These bags are in fine serviceable order. We have 12,000 in stock. Weight is 3½ lbs. Made to army specifications at a cost of $3.85 each. Our BARGAIN PRICE, 75 CENTS EACH, $7.00 DOZEN.

**U. S. ARMY KNAPSACKS** from U. S. Government Arsenal. Obsolete on the adoption of the Blanket Roll (some branches of the U. S. Military still retain this pattern knapsack, PREFERRING it to the blanket roll). Made of heavy drab canvas to repel water; with large body bag with cover; with bridle leather shoulder straps with brass hooks for quick adjusting. We offer them for sale as the BEST KNAPSACK EVER MADE, suitable for soldiers. Farmers, Campers, Tourists—anyone requiring a good knapsack—this is your opportunity. We have sold over 80,000 of these the past five years. Our bargain price for repaired order, $1.75 each.

View of the U. S. Light Artillery Knapsack, empty, folded up. Measures 4x17 inches. Weighs 2½ pounds.

U. S. Artillery Knapsack.

**600 U. S. ARTILLERY VALISE KNAPSACKS.** Made of heavy flax canvas. Consists of the body bag with cover and flaps, with two long tan leather wrapping straps (5½ feet), with handle carrying strap, offered in used, serviceable order for a short time at 70 cents each. $6.00 dozen.

**U. S. Cavalry Late Regulation Saber Knot,** ¾-inch black bridle leather, with brass stud for attaching to sabre, with two leather keepers with tassel; good, second-hand, serviceable order. Price, 25 cents.

**Confederate Box Knapsack,** made in England and sent South by blockade-running steamers in exchange for cotton; made of linen canvas, lined, waterproofed, black color, with English tanned leather straps, inside measurement of box 13 inches long, 11½ inches wide, 4 inches deep; inside folding cover with side straps, with shoulder sling straps, with blanket coat straps; inside compartment in flap cover; new and good serviceable order, light weight box pattern knapsack. Price, $1.00 each.

**Blanco for Whitening Buff Leather Equipments, Gloves,** Helmets, etc.; gives an evenness of color, glossy, satin like, white appearance, which will not readily rub off. Packed in zinc box with sponge; very simple to apply; full directions in each box. Regular price, 25 cents a box; our price, 20 cents a box.

**Antique European Army Fur-covered** Knapsacks, complete with straps. Genuine relics. For use of theatrical companies or decoration. Price, $1.50.

**7123. U. S. ARMY MOSQUITO HEAD GUARDS,** for protection against insects. Made of the best quality netting, with light collapsible frame, tape bound, with small shot at bottom to hold in position. Weight 6 ounces. Made to wear over any hat. Price 20 cents each.

**F. M. 1. ARMY BOMB BAGS,** made of heavy drab canvas, inside bottom reinforced with soft russet leather. Large flap cover has bronze buckle. Shoulder strap adjustable. 1½ inch wide with buckle. Bag is 10 inches long, 5 inches wide, 6 inches thick. Will hold thermos bottles, cameras, etc. Fine for hikers and campers. Price, 85 cents; $9.00 a dozen.

**C23. CANVAS KNAP-SACKS,** medium size for boy or woman hikers. Size is 13x9½ inches, weight only 20 ounces. Fitted with two shoulder slings. In serviceable order, only $1.00 each.

**ARMY FIELD RANGES,** in good second hand condition, without pots or pans. Prices and sizes quoted on application.

**1386B. NON-COM. OFFICER'S BLACK LEATHER SWORD BELT** with U. S. brass buckle, with brass hook for adjusting with side arm sword frog; in good serviceable order, used a short time, refinished. Price, 95 cents.

**1,000 U. S. Army Civil War Knapsacks,** new, made of canvas, blacked, waterproofed, slightly sticky from long storage, complete with leather shoulder straps; large, roomy knapsack; genuine Civil War relics. Price 55 cents each.

**U. S. Army Knapsack,** late regulation carrying braces, worn over the shoulders, with straps for attaching haversack, knapsack or other load to be carried; new; complete with brass buckles. Price, 35 cents set, as per illustration.

**6,000 Merriam Patent U. S. Army** Knapsacks. Made with side braces and straps to cross the hips and supporting braces to take weight of load from the shoulders, leaving the chest free from all constriction, so that coat can be opened without deranging the equipment. The pack is divided into two compartments for clothing and rations. Good, serviceable order. Price, 70 cents.

**7,000 State Militia Knapsacks.** Made on frame covered with canvas and leather, with shoulder sling; size, 14x15x4 inches. Cost New York State $3.50 each. In fine, serviceable order, complete with blanket straps. Price for ones refinished like new, without the regimental number, $1.00 each. For those in good, serviceable order, with regimental number, 65 cents. Old ones for decorating, 45 cents.

**500 U. S. Army Gunners' Leather Haversacks.** Made of russet leather, with shoulder sling; size, 12½x13 inches. Good, serviceable, second-hand, $2.25 each.

**6,000 Merriam Knapsack Packs,** with blanket roll straps. Used only a short time. Highly recommended by U. S. Army officers and surgeons for its even distribution of the weight of the pack. Made of strong brown canvas, with leather straps. N. Y. State Militia marking on cover. Illustration shows how the hip straps support the weight, the blanket and canteen carried on the pack. If any box knapsack is desired, then we can recommend this pattern as the best. Offer wanted for the lot of 6,000. All in good, serviceable order. Price of single knapsack, 70 cents.    A very low price will buy the lot.

**Full Dress Equipments.** Leather Waist Belt, with polished brass belt plate; Leather Cartridge Box, with buckles for cross-belt loops to fasten to; Leather Bayonet Scabbard, brass tips; White Web Cross Belt, with polished brass plate, pin fastening. All new goods. Per set, $1.65.

**United States Army Revolver Equipment.** Leather belt, with brass buckle and loop; woven web 12-loop revolver cartridge holder; United States Army heavy leather holster, for either 38 or 45 calibre revolver. All in serviceable order. $1.00 the set.

**United States Navy Late Regulation Double Cartridge Belt,** holding 100 rounds 45-calibre cartridges. Complete, with shoulder sling. Price, $1.20.

**Spanish War Soldiers' Tan Web Cartridge Belt.** For holding either 30-calibre or 45-calibre ball cartridges. With sword hook for cavalrymen, with polished brass belt buckle or hooks if desired. Good, second-hand, serviceable order. Used only a few times. Price, 75 cents.

**Enameled Leather Waist Belt,** with plain brass belt plate, with leather frog for holding sword, bayonet or non-com. officer's sword. 50c. set, as per illustration.

**Spanish Mauser Cartridge Box.** Used by Spanish soldiers in war with United States, 1898. Holds the Mauser cartridge in clip. Real, genuine relic. $1.50 each. We have the Spanish shoulder belt attachment. Price, $2.50 each.

**United States 45-70 Springfield Breech-Loading Rifle Equipments.** Woven web loop belt, with burnished brass plate, with loops for adjusting length, with swivel steel scabbard. All in serviceable order. Makes full set fatigue equipments. $1.00 per set, as per illustration.

Collection of 50 assorted kinds of Cartridge Boxes as used during Civil War. Price for lot, $50.00. Some are very rare.

**Austrian Leather Cartridge Box.** Same pattern as used formerly in German Army. Price, 60c. each.

**United States Navy Battle Axe Belt and Holder.** Made of heavy leather. Large enough to fully protect the blade of an ordinary axe. Price for the set, 65 cents. (This price does not include the axe.) Price of axe holder, without belt, 25 cents.

**200 Mann's Patent Cartridge Boxes,** with shoulder slings, 60 cents each.

**10465. WATERLOO PERIOD CARTRIDGE BOX,** leather, with 2 tin compartments for cartridges and flints; with white buff leather shoulder sling; box is 3 inches wide, 4 inches deep, 8 inches long. Price $8.00.
**10464. ANCIENT LEATHER POWDER BAG;** double pockets for powder and shot, with detachable brass loading charger; with shoulder sling. Price, $6.85.

**6,000 Leather Cartridge Boxes with Wood blocks.** With holes bored to hold 20 50-calibre metallic cartridges. Has brass plate on the cover. Not for use with plate in New York State, as these boxes are still used for dress equipment. We can substitute plain nickel plate if desired. Price of box, as per illustration, 35 cents each; nickel plate, if desired, 8 cents extra.

**Spencer Cartridge Box.** Wood, covered with leather. Contains 10 tin tubes. Each tube holds 1 complete round of 7 cartridges for the Spencer carbine or rifle, all of which can be emptied at one operation into the magazine of the gun, making quick loader. New, with shoulder sling with hooks for adjusting length. Price, 70 cents each.

**0-992A. CONFEDERATE OFFICER'S TELESCOPE.** Captured at Smudden's Plantation, Pee Dee, Georgetown, S. C., 1864, by Halstead Reed. From the A. E. Brooks collection. Length closed, 20 inches, diameter 2½ inches, brass case leather covered. Powerful glass. Full length 3 feet (when opened out). Leather on case requires stitching, otherwise in serviceable order. Price, $15.00.

**CADET WHITE WEBBING,** roll of 12 yards, 2 inches wide, $1.50.

**United States Navy Cartridge Box** for holding 20 metallic ball cartridges. Opens endwise. Small, neat box, with loops on the back for attaching to the waist belt. In good, second-hand, serviceable order. Price, 35 cents each.

We have an assorted lot of **MUSIC POUCHES,** and will quote prices on application. Write us how many are needed.

**36,000 Civil War 58-Cal. Springfield Leather Cartridge Boxes.** Heavy leather. With two compartments for holding the old-style paper cartridge. All new. In fine, serviceable order. 30 cents each.

**500 Patent Leather Cartridge Boxes.** Used by National Guard as dress equipment. Good, serviceable order. Price, 35 cents each.

**Captured Spanish Mauser Cartridge Belts,** for holding clips of cartridges. Old relics. Price, $1.50 each.

**United States Navy Small Size Cartridge Box.** Made of leather, with tin compartments for holding the old-style cartridges. obsolete. Fine **Cadet Cartridge Box,** 40

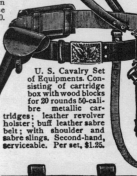

**U. S. Cavalry Set of Equipments.** Consisting of cartridge box with wood blocks for 20 rounds 50-calibre metallic cartridges; leather revolver holster; buff leather sabre belt; with shoulder and sabre slings. Second-hand, serviceable. Per set, $1.25.

**6,000 Cartridge Boxes,** with wood blocks to hold 20 rounds of 50-calib. metallic cartridges. Made of leather. All new and in fine, serviceable order. Price, 35 cents each.

**Antique United States Army Leather Cartridge Box.** Cover is as per illustration. Box is large size. Made to hold the old-style flint-lock ball cartridges. Upward of 100 years old. Limited number for sale. Handsome ornament; valuable relic. Price, $3.00 each.

**800 U. S. Army Gunners' Russet Leather Pouches,** with waist belt. Complete. Good as new. Size of box is 6x7 inches, 2 inches wide at the top. Price of box and belt, 60c.

**United States Army Latest Regulation Steel Scabbard,** with swivel frog with brass hook for adjusting to the present regulation web-loop cartridge belt. All in serviceable order. Price, 40 cents each.

**Despatch Shoulder Belt,** with 8-inch brass buckle, with swivel snap hooks for attaching to despatch boxes. Can also be used for drum slings. Almost new. $1.25.

**10451.** Oriental Chieftain's Belt Buckle; silvered metal ornamented with flower designs in red and green; fancy buckle; width 2½ in., length 8½ in. Price, $6.50.

**10460.** British Officer's Sabertash; size of the pocket, 12x13½ in.; ornamented with gold letters and embroidered coat of arms, with motto, "Ubique Quopas et Gloria Sucumb;" originally cost upwards of $50.00; complete with gilt strap. Price, $12.50.

**United States Non-Commissioned Officer's Sword Belt,** with frog attached. Made of new black buff leather. Complete, with solid brass eagle belt plate, with spread eagle and German silver wreath. Price, $1.00 each.

**United States Army Carbine Slings,** with brass buckle. Narrow width. Used in 1898. Good as new. Price, $1.00.

**10000 Sets Cadet Equipments, suitable for small boys.**

Small wool-lined Cartridge Box, with nickel plate on box. Plain Brass or Eagle Belt Plate. White Web or Leather Waist Belt, Bayonet Scabbard. Price, per set, 75 cents.

Enlarged View of Leather Cartridge Box in Sets of Cadet Equipments. Price for this Cartridge Box,

**1000 Sets Boys' Brigade Equipments.**

Leather Cartridge Box (with nickel plate), large enough to hold Bible. Black Leather Waist Belt. Belt Plate with fastener for adjusting length. Bayonet Scabbard. Cadet size, made to fit any length scabbard. Price, 85 cents per set. All in good, serviceable order.

**1500 Sets Cadet Equipments.**

Large sized Cartridge Box for holding Bible. Polished brass belt plate, swivel scabbard. Price, per set, 95 cts. All in good serviceable order. Any belt plate as desired.

Front view of Cartridge box in N. Y. State Equipments, showing appearance of box when cover is closed. Price for this box, 35 cts. N. G. Brass Plate, 15 cents extra.

**1200 Sets N. Y. State Regulation Equipments.**

All in good order. Frazier's Patent Cartridge Box holding cal. 50 cartridges. Bayonet Scabbard and either Enameled or Grain Leather Waist Belt, as desired. S. N. Y. Plain Brass, Matted Brass or Eagle Belt Plate furnished. Price, per set, $1.00.

100 National Guard Dress Cartridge Boxes. Patent leather covers with polished brass band around edges, 60 cents each.

**1000 Sets Cadet Equipments.**

Small Navy Cartridge Box. Black Leather Waist Belt. Brass lead filled, U. S. Belt Plate (Civil War pattern). Full length Leather Bayonet Scabbard, 18 inches. Price, per set, 75 cents. With plain polished brass plate, 78 cents set. Good second-hand equipments.

**1000 Sets Baptist Boys' Brigade Regulation Equipments.**

Leather Box (with nickel plate), large enough to hold Bible. Black Leather Belt. Any desired Belt Plate, Eagle, Plain Brass, Matted Brass, with fastener for adjusting length. Bayonet Scabbard to fit bayonet, with swivel frog. Price, 90 cents per set. All in good, serviceable order.

**6000 Sets Breech Loading Rifle Equipments.**

Wood blocks in Cartridge Box for 20 rounds. Wood block can be taken out and room made to hold Bible. Plain polished brass plate, or other kind as desired. Price, $1.00 set.

Enlarged View of Breech Loading Rifle Cartridge Box. Price for this box, 35 cents. (Nickel Plate, 10 cents.)

**500 Sets U. S. Navy Muzzle-Loading Equipments.**

Same as used in Civil War. All in cleaned and repaired order. Price, per set, 65 cents.

Tin Magazines for 58 Cal. Cartridge Boxes, new, 10 cents each.

**1500 U. S. Government Cartridge Boxes,** furnished to the Militia for 45—70 cal. metallic cartridges, wood block, holds 20 cartridges, brass frame, neatest box made. In serviceable order, 50 cents each.

2nd-hand Sets of Equipments for Stage, Artists or Sculptors, as low as 50 cents set, according to pattern selected.

**5000 Sets U. S. Army Civil War Equipments.**

For Caliber .58 and .69 Muskets. All in good refinished order. Price, $1.50 set.

Good second-hand equipments.

**U. S. Army Regulation Sets, McKeever Equipments,**

Black Leather Waist Belt. U. S. or Eagle Belt Plate. McKeever Cartridge Box for 45—70 Cartridge. Steel Bayonet Scabbard, with swivel frog. Price, $1.00 per set.

View of the U. S. Regulation Cartridge box when opened up, ready for withdrawal of the Cartridges. Price for this box, 35 cents.

**600 Sets Cadet Equipments.**

Cartridge Pouch is large enough to hold medium sized book. All in serviceable order. Price per set, 80 cts.

Enlarged View of Cartridge Pouch, Army Regulation time of General Custer's Indian Campaign. Price for this Pouch, 35 cents.

This Pouch can be used by Sportsmen in carrying Cartridges. Price complete with Waist Belt and Buckle 75 cents.

English Army Life Guard Cartridge Box, with Polished brass plate. Royal Coat of Arms. Price, $1.25 each.

Old time very large Leather Cartridge Box. $1.00.

Confederate Army Cross Belt and Bayonet Scabbard. Genuine Relics. $1.00 for Belt and Scabbard.

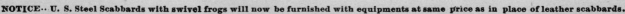

**NOTICE.·** U. S. Steel Scabbards with swivel frogs will now be furnished with equipments at same price as in place of leather scabbards.

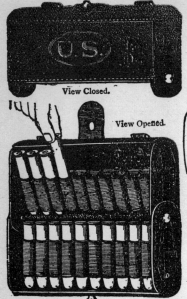

View Closed.

View Opened.

**U. S. Army Regulation Dress Cartridge Box;** now obsolete under new regulations; wherein the web loop cartridge belt is adopted. Made of fine bridle leather, with loops for attaching to the waist belt; swings open on swiveled brass rod; has web loops which hold 20 calibre Springfield .45 rifle ball cartridges; letters U. S. in oval are pressed in the leather cover; we can cover over the letters if desired by putting on a neat name plate; cost of this plate is 15c. These boxes are cleaned and polished and look like new; the size is about 3½x7½ inches, and it is one of the neatest and lightest cartridge boxes made. We have 10,000 in stock. Old price was 60c. each; now reduced to 40c. each, or complete, with leather waist belt, eagle buckle and steel bayonet scabbard, all like new, price, $1.00 the set.

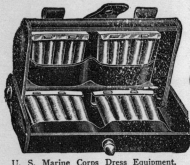

**U. S. Marine Corps Dress Equipment.** In fine order, practically new. Consisting of McKeever Cartridge Box, with loops for holding 4 clips (20) Lee Navy 6 mm. Cartridges, white web waist belt, with polished brass belt buckle, with scabbard for the Lee Knife Bayonet. Price, $1.65 set.

**U. S. ARMY AND NAVY BANDOLIERS,** 8 cents each. 9 pockets holding 2 clips of 5 cartridges each, for the KRAG, Cal. 30 SPRINGFIELD and ALL OF THE HIGH POWER MAUSER rifles. 20,000 in stock.

New Large-sized Wool-lined Leather Boxes; about 8x7x1½ inches, with white wool lining attached to the fleece. We have about 250. Price, 50 cents each.

**3,000 New Cadet Cartridge Boxes.** Made of black leather. Price, 30 cents each.

Napoleon's Old Guard Cartridge Box; large size; with the French eagle and four exploding shells; brass ornaments on the cover same as shown in the old battle pictures. Price, $5.00 each.

**25,000　　Leather Boxes,** made for use of U. S. Army during Civil War to hold soldier's 40 rounds of ball cartridges. Are now obsolete. Price, 30 cents each, or $25.00 per 100. Will name a very low price if the lot is taken.

**300 German Army Cartridge Boxes;** size 4½ inches long, 2 inches deep, ⅝ wide. Made of fine leather, hand sewed, with loop for 1⅞-in. waist belt; loops inside the box for holding cartridges; a number of these boxes can be carried on the waist belt; suitable for cadet companies; good order. Price, 25c. each.

**Army Musician's Pouch,** made of enameled leather; used for carrying music; has loop by which it is attached to the waist belt. All in good serviceable order. Used only a few times. 50c. each.

**Nos. 1, 2 and 3.** Illustrations showing UNION ARMY CAVALRY SOLDIER, CIVIL WAR PERIOD, equipped with Spencer quick loading carbine cartridge box. The box is made of light wood, covered over with leather, with 7 holes in the wood block, which contains tin tubes holding 7 cartridges. The soldier, by pushing aside the cover in the butt plate of the stock, and inserting the mouth of the tin tube into the opening, could at one operation load the 7 cartridges, the full charge, into the magazine of the gun. We offer the cartridge box, with adjustable sling straps and tin tubes, at 90 cents the outfit.

**100 U. S. Army and Navy Revolver Cartridge Boxes;** new; made of fine black leather; hand sewed; attaches to the waist belt. Price, 50c.

**BLACK LEATHER BODY BELT,** lettered in relief, "VOL. BATTL. GORDAN HIGHLANDERS," with "V" in the center. Price $3.85.

**BLACK LEATHER BODY BELT,** with brass plate marked "Queen's Own Regiment," with figure "50" in the center. Price $3.85.

**10487. BRITISH ARMY WAIST BELT,** with clasp plate inscribed "Border Rifle Volunteers," with Royal Crown with motto, "Doe or Die;" small buckle for adjusting length; russet leather. Price $1.25 each.

**500 U. S. M. C. New Dress Equipments,** consisting of McKeever cartridge box, black leather waist belt with cast polished brass U. S. Buckle, with hook for adjusting the length; with steel scabbard with brass swivel frog. Price, $1.70 the set. The same set in good, serviceable, second-hand order, 95 cents the set.

This set of U. S. Dress Equipments with McKeever cartridge box in *russet* leather with *russet* waist belt, with polished brass U. S. buckle, with steel scabbard, *russet* leather, covered with *plain russet* frog. All like new, with loops for holding the Springfield .45 cal. cartridges. Price, $2.40 set.

**1520. MAUSER RIFLE CLIP CARTRIDGE BOX.** Made of fine leather, hand sewed with fastening strap on cover; with inside strap for raising quickly the clip of cartridges; two inch belt loop. Box is 3½x¾x2¾ inches. Second hand order. Price, 35 cents each.

**61B. BLACK LEATHER WAIST BELTS** with brass bar buckles, in assorted sizes up to 60 inches. Width 1½ inches. Price, 75c.

**NEW RUSSET COAT STRAPS,** 42 inches long, with bronze buckle. Strong strap, very useful on camping or auto trips. Price, per pair, 50 cents.

**No. 1519A.** British Volunteer Soldiers' Cartridge Pouch, made of patent leather, with crown and bugle metal ornament on cover, with loop on back for inserting waist belt. Second-hand serviceable order. Neat decorative ornament. Price, 65 cents.

**No. 1255.** Ancient Bandolier, suspended from shoulder across the breast, with engraved brass tubes 4 inches long, ½-inch bore for carrying charge of powder for ancient guns, with cloth stoppers attached to belt by small chains; leather shows great age; 5 series; 2 tubes each; some of the tubes missing; small leather powder box, with flap; size, 4½ x 3½. Very rare genuine old piece. $50.00.

No. 1255.

# Flags
## FLAGS OF OUR COUNTRY.
### PRINTED IN EXACT COLORS

TEN 4 x 6 INCH PRINTED SILK FLAGS,
MOUNTED ON EBONIZED STAFFS WITH ORNAMENTS

## COLONIAL, REVOLUTIONARY, 1812 and "OLD GLORY"

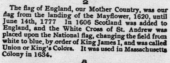

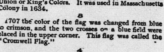

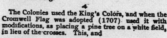

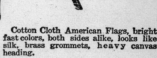

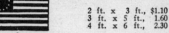

REVOLUTIONARY FLAG

FLAG OF 1812

OLD GLORY

**1**
Sebastian Cabot landed at Labrador 1497, and planted on North American soil the Red Cross flag of England, the Ensign of King Henry the Seventh.

**2**
The flag of England, our Mother Country, was our flag from the landing of the Mayflower, 1620, until June 14th, 1777 In 1606 Scotland was added to England, and the White Cross of St. Andrew was placed upon the National flag, changing the field from white to blue, by order of King James I, and was called Union or King's Colors. It was used in Massachusetts Colony in 1634.

**3**
1707 the color of the flag was changed from blue to crimson, and the two crosses on a blue field were placed in the upper corner. This flag was called the "Cromwell Flag."

**4**
The Colonies used the King's Colors, and when the Cromwell Flag was adopted (1707) used it with modifications, as placing a pine tree on a white field, in lieu of the crosses. This, and

**5**
The plain white flag with a pine tree, were regarded as the flags of Massachusetts Colony for some time. In 1775 the Pine Tree flag was decided on for our vessels.

**6**
The Southern States, or then Colonies, from 1776 to 1777, used the Snake flag.

**7**
The first striped flag was raised at Washington's Headquarters, Cambridge, Mass., January 2nd, 1776. It was called the "Cambridge Flag," and known in England as the "Rebellious Stripes." Lieut. John Paul Jones hoisted this flag on his vessel the "Alfred," and said "The flag of America floats for the first time over an American Man-of-War."

**8**
June 14th, 1777, Betsy Ross made the first flag of thirteen stars and thirteen stripes.

**9**
Vermont was added to the Union in 1791, and Kentucky in 1792. In consequence two additional stars and stripes were added to the flag, making a flag of fifteen stars and fifteen stripes. This was the flag of the War of 1812, and was known as "The Star-Spangled Banner."

**10**
April 4th, 1818, a bill was passed by Congress, reducing the number of stripes to thirteen, and increasing the number of stars to one for each State.

Price per set, $2.50.

Cotton Cloth American Flags, bright fast colors, both sides alike, looks like silk, brass grommets, heavy canvas heading.

2 ft. x 3 ft., $1.10
3 ft. x 5 ft., 1.60
4 ft. x 6 ft., 2.30

THE CHRISTIAN FLAG. These can be furnished in silk or wool bunting. Prices quoted on application.

---

U. S. A. WOOL BUNTING FLAGS at bargain prices.
Size 3 ft. x 5 ft., $2.95
Size 4 ft. x 6 ft., 3.90
Size 5 ft. x 8 ft., 5.85
Other sizes in proportion.
Heavy yellow worsted fringe sewed on any of these flags at 80 cents each EXTRA.

### HOLIDAYS
*When the flag should be displayed at full staff*

Lincoln's Birthday .... February 12th
Washington's Birthday . February 22nd
Battle of Lexington .... April 19th
*Memorial Day ........ May 30th
Flag Day .............. June 14th
Battle of Bunker Hill... June 17th
Independence Day ...... July 4th
Columbus Day ......... October 12th
Battle of Saratoga...... October 17th
Surrender at Yorktown.. October 19th
Evacuation Day ....... November 25th

*On Memorial Day, May 30th, the Flag should fly at half staff from sunrise to noon and full staff from noon to sunset.

*In order to show proper respect for the flag the following ceremony should be observed:*

It should not be hoisted before sunrise nor allowed to remain up after sunset.

At "Retreat" sunset, civilian spectators should stand at "attention" and uncover during the playing of the "Star-Spangled Banner." Military spectators are required by Regulation to stand at "attention" and give the military salute. During the playing of the National Hymn at "Retreat" the flag should be lowered but not then allowed to touch the ground.

When the National Colors are passing on parade or in review, the spectator should, if walking, halt, and if sitting arise and stand at "attention" and uncover.

When the National and State or other flags fly together the National Flag should be placed on the right.

When the flag is flown at half staff as a sign of mourning, it should be hoisted to full staff at the conclusion of the funeral.

In placing the flag at half staff, it should be first hoisted to the top of the staff and then lowered to position, and preliminary to lowering from half staff, it should be first raised to the top.

The National Salute is one gun for every State. The International Salute is, under the Law of Nations, 21 guns.

The Statutes of the United States have forbidden the use of the Flag in registration of trade-marks.

REGULATION DESIGN AMERICAN FLAG, stars in effect July 4th.

U. S. ARMY SILK FLAG CORD AND TASSELS, blue and white color; new; never used; slightly stained. Price, $1.85.

"We took the stars from Heaven: red from our Mother Country, separating it by white stripes, thus showing that we have separated from her, and white stripes shall go down to posterity representing Liberty." Sayings of George Washington, from the "Albany Argus."

---

No. 7.

FLAG POLE SHOULDER BELTS, in black leather with socket for flag pole. Almost new. Price, 95 cents each.

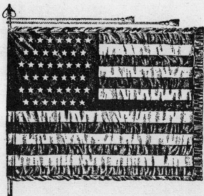

### U. S. NATIONAL REGULATION SILK FLAG.
Made of fine flag silk, sewed stripes, with embroidered stars. With yellow silk bullion 2-inch fringe, with silk cord and tassels. With rain cover and leather carrying sling. Prices quoted on application to Legion Posts, Schools and Military Companies.

And when we wanted an emblem
To carry in war and peace,
A flag to tell the nations
That the Union never should cease:
We looked to the heavens above us,
To the stars in the fair blue skies,
And we copied the red from the sunset clouds
In the West when the daylight dies.

Pelig D. Harrison, in his book, "The Stars and Stripes, and Other American Flags, published by Little & Brown, Boston, tells a story which has never been contradicted: That when Theodore Roosevelt, Sen., the father of President Roosevelt, flew the Stars and Stripes from his house in this city, after the capture of Fort Sumpter, by the Union Army, his wife, who was Martha Bullock, of Georgia, hung the Stars and Bars out of the bedroom window. A crowd gathered in the street and demanded a removal of the flag. Mr. Roosevelt besought his wife to have the Confederate emblem removed, but she refused to have it taken in. He therefore went out to the crowd and explained the situation, and dwelt so feelingly upon his wife's love for her native section, that the crowd permitted the Stars and Bars to remain."

---

No. 10.

HEAVY BUNTING FLAG, with four white star and foula anchor, size 10x12 feet. Price, $12.50.

AMERICAN FLAG, with 45 stars, size 12x20 feet, in fine order. Price, $20.00.

SPANISH ENSIGN, wool bunting, second hand, size, 8x16 feet. Price, $15.00.

No. 10. GUIDON FLAG POLE, polished ash, with acorn top; 4½ ft. long, 40 cents.

FRENCH FLAG, made of heavy bunting, like new. Size 20x38 feet. A bargain at $18.00.

BRITISH ENSIGN, of heavy bunting, like new. Size 10x18 feet. At reduced price of $12.00.

Used lot of 24 assorted muslin National Flags, size 20x30 inches, mounted on poles, each one different, $2.20 the set.

Set of 12 assorted National Flags, size 20x30 inches, on poles. Price, $1.00 set.

Facsimile Admiral Dewey's Flag, 20x30, with letters, "Welcome Dewey," 10c.

**FLAG SPEAR TIP**, found on the Warrentown Turnpike on the retreat of the Union forces from the first battle of Bull Run, by William Hamilton, Sutler with the Union Army. Spear is made of German silver; length 8½ inches; 6½-inch cross guard. Price, $8.75.

**Admiral Sampson's Pennant**, used on the Flagship New York during the Spanish war. In poor order from long service. Price, $100.00. U. S. N. Pennant from the U.S.S. Hornet. In fair order. Price, $50.00.

**U. S. New Bunting Flags,** made of best quality bunting, with 45 stars, machine sewed. Large flags have rope headings and reinforced ends. Compare these prices and see how cheap we can sell you a No. 1 Standard Bunting Flag. Warranted fast colors. All wool.

### Prices are coming down. Tell us size wanted and we will quote.

**FLAG POLE EAGLE ORNAMENTS IN DIFFERENT SIZES.** We do not carry all sizes in stock, and will quote on application. Note that we will quote prices complete for flag, pole, eagle and carrying sling.

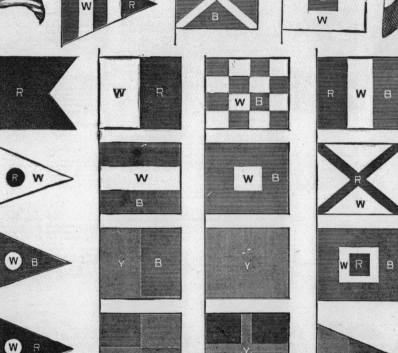

**ADMIRAL DEWEY'S BATTLE FLAGS.**

Captured Spanish Volunteer Battle Flag from XIII. Battalion in Puerto Rico. Fitted with pole, spear and cords. Rare relic. Size, 3 ft. wide by 4½ ft. long. Made of bunting. Price, $250.00.

Spanish Flag fitted to Lance. Blade of lance is marked in the steel "Toledo." Flag is 2x2 ft., of cotton bunting, and has Spanish Coat of Arms in centre. Price complete, $50.00.

Silk Guidon Flags with Poles, with regimental numbers. Relics. Sizes, 1½x2 ft. and 2x3 ft. Price, $10.00 each.

Assorted Naval Signal Flags, not in sets, 6x8, suitable for decorating, $2.50 each.

U.S. Navy Rear Admiral's Flag, 3x8. Relic. Price, $4.50.

Silk Regulation Flag, tattered and torn, rare relic. Originally 8 ft. long. Price, $60.00.

Flag Poles, 8 ft. long, 75c. each.

Pole and Spear, $1.75 each.

Polished Wood Balls, 4½ inches in diameter, gilded, for large poles, 85c. each.

Assorted Bunting Flags, 1½x2 ft , 20c. Small American Flags, 2x3 ft., same as furnished Lieut. R. E. Peary (on poles), 50c.

U. S. S. Maine Flag, used on the Maine in 1896. Vouched for by Navy Department record ; 3x5; fair order. Price, $75.00.

**U. S. Army Late Regulation Silk Flag Cord** with handsome heavy Tassels. Blue and white, 8 ft. long, new. Price, $1.00.

**U. S. Signal Flags from the Olympia.** These flags when turned in would under general orders have been condemned to be burned. We found this out and wrote the Honorable Secretary of the Navy, asking that they be given to us for our Museum collection. The Secretary gave us an order for them, but upon presenting the order to the storekeeper of the Boston Navy Yard we were told that we were "too fresh, the flags had not yet been surveyed and condemned." We said we would wait until they were surveyed and condemned. After waiting several months the Board of Officers reported that the flags should be sold at auction. At the auction sale, June 5, 1900, lot No. 17, we were the purchasers not only of the three sets of Signal Flags, but also a few Pennants and U. S. Flags, all from the famous ship. Had these flags been given to us gratis for our Museum we should have held them and offered none for sale, but now we feel free and will offer one set of Signals from the U. S. Flagship Olympia and the price is $800.00 for the 19 flags. The other two sets are not for sale; will be added to our Museum collection. Neither is the large blue flag with the four white stars which was on the ship as a Rear Admiral's flag. But when Commodore Dewey was made full Admiral the necessary two extra stars were sewed on this flag, thus making it an Admiral's flag, and as such flown from the masthead of the Olympia at Manila and on Dewey's triumphal voyage home until he arrived at New York, when Admiral Farragut's old flag was presented to Dewey and this flag was turned in, eventually finding its way to our Museum, where it is now and is not for sale.

These flags were used on the Olympia at the Battle of Manila Bay to signal to the fleet. Commodore Dewey's orders among the many signals were, as we understand it, "Remember the Maine," " Engage the enemy," "Haul off for breakfast," " Report casualties," "Renew battle," etc., etc. Also the orders at the taking of Manila in connection with the Army. We have had these flags preserved in moth-proof preparation. It is a rare chance to obtain one set of these 19 flags for $800.00. Flags are fully authenticated.

Also from Admiral Dewey's Flagship, the Olympia, we purchased 1 British flag, 2 German flags, 2 narrow pennants. Prices upon application.

**FLAG POLE SPEAR HEADS** in brass. Prices quoted on any length.

**SPENCER GUN CLUB.**

**BURGEES AND FLAGS IN SPECIAL SIZES AND DESIGNS MADE TO ORDER.** Send us your sketch with all measurements and we will quote price in cotton or bunting.

French Flag, made of heavy bunting like new. Size 20x38 feet. A bargain at $26.00.

British Ensign, of heavy bunting, like new. Size 10x18 feet. At reduced price of $18.00

Lot of U. S. Navy Signal Flags we sold to New York City and used at New York City Columbian Celebration, in 1 92, decorating Fifth Avenue from 23d to 34th Streets, also President's Grand Stand, and which we repurchased. In sets consisting of 15 assorted Square Flags, 6x8½ feet, 6 Streamer Flags, 4x16, warranted fast colors, all wool, in fair order, per set, $27.50. Cost the U. S. Navy $100.00 set.

Assorted Navy Streamer Flags, 4x16. Price, $2.50 each.

Lot of Spanish Flags left over from Columbian Celebration, good bunting; 4x6 ft., $1.50; 5x8 ft., $2.00; 6x10 ft., $2.50; 5x8 ft. Irish Flag, $5.00; 6x10 ft. German Flag, $4.00; 5x8 ft. French Flag, $3.50; 5x8 ft. Swedish Flag, $4.50.

Confederate Bunting Flags remade up from second-hand flags. Not relics. Theatrical use. 3x5, $6.00; 5x8, $7.50; 6x10, $9.00.

British Flags, 3x5 ft., $3.50; Canadian Flags, 3x5 ft., $3.75; British Flags, 3 feet long, $4.00.

Union Jacks, relics from warships, purchased from the U. S. Navy Department, 6 feet long. Price, $4.00.

New York State Silk Regimental Flag, tattered and torn. Relic. $50.00.

Colored plate showing 240 Merchant Signal Flags trading to Port of New York in 1854, in glass frame. Price, $15.00.

Confederate Flags for decorating. Colors stamped on cotton. Size, 2x3 feet. Price, $2.50 each.

Window Flag Pole Holders. Galvanized malleable iron; fit ordinary size pole, from 6 to 10 feet. Price, 40c. Large Adjustable Brackets for 1½-inch Poles, $1.50 each.

Union Jacks, 45 Stars :

| | | | | |
|---|---|---|---|---|
| 3x2 feet | $2.50 | 8x 6 feet | $7.00 |
| 4x3 " | 3.00 | 10x 8 " | 10.00 |
| 5x4 " | 3.50 | 12x 9 " | 12.50 |
| 6x4½" | 5.00 | 15x12 " | 20.00 |

British Jacks:

| | | | |
|---|---|---|---|
| 5x7 feet | $6.00 | 8x10 feet | $9.00 |

Set of 12 different British Flags, used for decorating in England in honor of British regiments returning from Boer War in South Africa. Flags are all different and in fine order; about 2 feet long; make handsome decorations. Price, $25.00 the set.

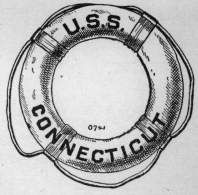

**0-740. RELIC U. S. S. MAINE, CORK LIFE BUOY.** From Brooklyn Navy Yard auction. It is the custom of the Navy Department to dispose of equipment bearing names of ships that have been stricken from the navy list upon the listing of new ship of the same name. Outside diameter of the ring buoy is 30 inches, inside 16 inches, thickness 4 inches, width 6½ inches. Made of blocks of cork covered with waterproof canvas and painted white, with bands and life ropes. We believe these relics of the historical ship were brought to New York with other stores and equipments directly after the explosion of the Maine in Havana and before the declaration of war with Spain was made. We have a few of these buoys left from our museum salesroom collection that we offer at the bargain price of $25.00 each.
4 LIFE RING BUOYS. From the U. S. S. Paducah.
2 RING LIFE BUOYS. From the Hannibal.
2 from the TORPEDO BOAT Winslow.
1 each from the Nebraska, Tennessee and Wheeling. Buyer has the choice. Price $7.50 each.

**1776. U. S. NAVY BATTLE RATTLE.** Kind that was fixed to the mast on board oldtime navy frigates. Used to call the crew to quarters before the advent of steam— "Spring the rattle and every man to his station." These old-time relics are one of the greatest bargains we have to offer. Made of handsome polished hard wood. An ornament for any library or den. Unique alarm call for dining-room. Price, $7.50 each.

**0-746. ADMIRAL DEWEY'S REAR ADMIRAL FLAG.** Used on the Olympia at Manila Bay. Not flown during the naval battle, as Dewey then had rank of COMMODORE and entitled to fly the commodore flag, which had ONE star. After the battle of Manila Bay and before the capture of Manila Congress promoted Dewey to Rear Admiral, when this flag was flown from the flagship. This is an historical relic vouched for by all the facts coming into our possession, of which we will give purchaser certificate under notary's seal. Size of the flag 34x64 inches. Blue flag with two 9-inch white stars. Price, $100.00.
**0-746A. ADMIRAL DEWEY'S REAR ADMIRAL FLAG.** Similar to the above, but size smaller, 32x48 inches. Price, $100.00. Evidently much used, as the outer end has new piece attached, evidently done on board ship to continue in service.

**0-741. LIFE RING BUOYS.** From the U. S. S. Connecticut. Outside diameter 19 inches, inside 9 inches, width 5½ inches, thickness 3½ inches, cork blocks covered with waterproof canvas, painted white, with bands holding life rope, with name of the ship, as per illustration. In serviceable order. Price, $6.50.
3 same size, marked Tennessee. Price, $6.50 each.
3 marked Lawson. Price, $3.50 each.

**0-742. U. S. FLAGSHIP OLYMPIA PENNANT.** Turned into the Boston Navy Yard on the arrival of the Olympia after the battle of Manila Bay and sold to us by the Navy Department. Catalogued as "Bunting flags from the Olympia." The identical flags used by Admiral Dewey on the battleship. This pennant is the regular navy pennant displayed from all navy ships when in commission. Is marked No. 3, width at the heading 4½ inches, is now 11 feet long (originally much longer, part worn off in service), blue field with 13 white stars, red and white stripes; soiled and partly smoke stained. Offered with signed certificate guaranteeing the above facts. Price, $50.00.
**0-742A. FLAGSHIP OLYMPIA PENNANT.** 12 feet long, 4 inches wide at heading. Same guarantee to facts as No. 742. This pennant is size smaller than No. 742 and has 7 stars in the field. Price, $40.00.
**0-742A. FLAGSHIP OLYMPIA PENNANT.** 7 feet long, heading worn off in service. Price, $30.00.
**0-745A. FLAGSHIP OLYMPIA SMALL SIGNAL FLAG.** White background, diagonal red cross. Size 18x26 inches. Slightly smoke stained. Price, $25.00.

**0-748. UNION JACK FROM THE U. S. FLAGSHIP OLYMPIA.** Size 6x7 feet, blue field, 45 six-inch white stars. Flag shows considerable service; it has a number of patches. Historical relic that will increase in value with age; guaranteed with notary's seal. Price, $150.00.

**2425. AMERICAN FLAG UNIONS.** From flags used by U. S. Army, which became obsolete after the number of stars were increased by the entrance of additional States in the Union, the law requiring a star for every State. Stamped wool bunting, 28 inches wide, 34 inches long, canvas heading, with two brass gromets, 35 stars. Will answer for decorating. Price, $1.40 each.

**218. GUIDON FLAG COVERS.** Price, 75 cents each.

**SECRETARY OF NAVY FLAG.** Blue bunting flag with white star in each corner, with foul anchor in the centre. Used on Navy flagships. Size 10½x12 feet. Fair order. Price, $10.00.

**U. S. ARMY GARRISON FLAGS.** National flags made of army quality bunting, 20-foot hoist, 36-foot fly. These fine, large flags are only issued to important posts having large garrisons, and are hoisted only on great occasions. Flags were made obsolete by the addition of new States, as the law requires a star for each State in the Union. Are in serviceable order; will answer for decoration. Regular price, $40.00; our bargain price, $22.50 each.

**0-694. U. S. CAVALRY GUIDON RELIC ENSIGN.** Silk (faded), gold stamped letter "A." Said to have been used by Custer's 7th Cavalry. Purchased at Government Schuylkill Arsenal auction in 1886. The stripes are sewn together. Rare old banner. Price, $100.00.

**0-695. OLD STATE OF NEW YORK 54TH REGIMENT BLUE SILK GUIDON.** With gold stamped letters 54. Size 17x19 inches. Price, $30.00. Also one of 32d Regiment. Price, $30.00.

**0-698. U. S. SILK ENSIGN.** With embroidered figure 32 in the centre of the blue field, hand-sewed silk stars. 32d Regiment State of New York marker's flag. Size 16x18 inches. Only in fair order. Price, $45.00.

A SIMILAR FLAG used by the 49th Regiment. Price, $45.00.

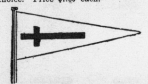

**0-743. CHURCH PENNANT FROM ADMIRAL DEWEY'S FLAGSHIP OLYMPIA—STORM OR BOAT PENNANT.** White pennant with the blue (Latin) cross. Rope heading. Width at the heading 20 inches, length of fly 28 inches. Hand sewed. Made at the Brooklyn Navy Yard Flag Department by widows of naval seamen. This flag is offered with guarantee as to facts. Price, $36.00 as above.

**0-744. FLAGSHIP OLYMPIA'S U. S. STORM ENSIGN OR CUTTER FLAG.** Looks as if made on board ship. 13 white stars on blue field, 7 red and 6 white stripes, 21 inches square. During storm warships display a small ensign called storm flag. Slightly smoke stained, otherwise in serviceable order. Price, $50.00.

**0-745. OLYMPIA'S SIGNAL FLAG.** No. 22. Size 18½x29 inches, with the flag figure 22 in blue; no doubt secret code. Turned in with other flags on the arrival of the Olympia at Boston Navy Yard. Price, $25.00.

**0-795. CONFEDERATE FLAG.** Made of cotton bunting. New. The pattern carried by soldiers in the Civil War from State of Texas.

**0-696. 17TH CENTURY FRENCH BANNER.** From French nobleman's collection. Size 4x7 feet, triangular-shaped, red background, green border with letters and symbols, soft cotton material. Rare old banner on pole with spear head. Price, $75.00.

> ### BATTLE FLAGS.
>
> Battle flags are sacred things,
> Death's great glistening angel wings,
> When he is most glorious
> As a love most valorous.
>
> Dying eyes have on them turned,
> Glowing hopes in hearts have burned
> Where they led in gallant strife
> Free will asking death or life.
>
> Standards of our manhood true,
> Symbols red and white and blue,
> Sing the story of our sires,
> Kindle for us, too, your fires.
> —JOHN M. DUNPHY.

**0-702. 17th CENTURY VENETIAN FLAG.** Blue with winged lion holding sword and open book, *Pax Evan Tibi Gelis Mav Cepenet.* Size two feet square, gilt lace fringed border. The Doge of St. Mark was the patron saint of Venice. This flag was sold to Metropolitan Museum of Art in New York City.

**0-699. SILK ARTILLERY FLAG.** With gold stamped figure "2" in the centre, "State of New York 2nd Battery." Size originally 26x30 inches, now measures 26x20 inches. Is all tattered and torn. A relic. Price, $20.00.

**0-700. SILK ARTILLERY BATTERY FLAG.** Embroidered with crossed cannon, figure "2" and letters "S. N. Y." Size 25x23 inches. Relic. Price, $20.00.

**0-705. ANCIENT FRENCH BANNER.** 6 feet square, red and white silk in form of cross with oval-shaped embroidered silvered letters. From French nobleman's collection. Price, $100.00.

**WHITE ENSIGN.**

3231. Royal White Ensign used on British warships, size 9 by 15½ feet; good order; finest quality bunting. Dealer's price about $40.00, our bargain price $40.00.

We have in stock the following National Flags, all best quality wool bunting, used a short time on U. S. Navy Warships for display while in Foreign Countries, 9 foot hoist, 15½ foot Flag. In good serviceable order at the bargain price of $6.85 each.

1 Venezuela. 1 Brazilian.
1 Austria. 1 Swedish.
2 British. 2 Bolivian.
2 Danish. 2 Nicaragua.
2 French. 1 Uruguay .
2 Russian. 1 San Domingo.
2 Italian. 1 Guatemalian.
2 Spanish. 1 Grecian.
1 Mexican.

And the following National Flags 13 foot hoist, 25½ foot flag:

1 Columbian.
1 Paraguay.
1 Costa Rico.

Serviceable historical flags used on board U. S. warships while in foreign ports. For sale at $10.85 each, which is only a fraction of their original cost.

**CONFEDERATE STAR AND BARS**

**CONFEDERATE NATIONAL**

3232. Confederate Star and Bars and Confederate National Flags sewed stars, fast color cotton bunting.

**Prices on these flags will be quoted on application. State size and style desired.**

**Prices on these flags will be quoted on application. State size and style desired.**

**UNION JACK**

**SCOTLAND.**

**Prices on these flags will be quoted on application. State size and style desired. Allow a few days for them to be made up.**

was termed a "COPPER HEAD." The public tore down the flag and broke up the meeting. The flag is about 12 feet square. Offered with a portrait of Valindingham; all fully vouched for. Price $25.00.

**U. S. Army Regulation Spear Head for Flag Poles.** Length 8 inches, in nickel or brass. Price $1.90.

3246

3246. U. S. Navy Bronze Flag Halliard Swivels, for quickly attaching signal flags with swivel to keep the halliard from twisting. Length 2¾ inches, used on warships. In serviceable order. Price 45 cents each.

3246a. U. S. Navy Flag, Halliard Swivels, galvanized iron, double snaps, length 4 inches. Price 25c each. Used on warships.

3294. American Flag, home made, displayed during Civil War Times over Main St., Dayton, Ohio, at public meeting addressed by C. L. Valindingham who

**S. N. ARMY REGULATION WIG WAG SIGNALING FLAGS** consisting of white flag, size 4 by 4 feet, with 15 inch red square in the centre and 4 by 4 feet red flag with 15 inch white centre for sale at $1.70 the pair.

WIG WAG FLAG POLES 9 feet 10 inches long, ash wood. Price 85 cents each. Also set of three sectional ash wood flag poles with brass joints, full length when assembled 11 feet. Price the set $2.45.

3452. U. S. ARMY WIG WAG CANVAS BAG FLAG OUTFIT for holding jointed wig wag flag poles and flags. Length 4 feet, with 2 small tightening straps; also, shoulder sling strap. Price 65 cents.

SIX THOUSAND POUNDS U. S. NAVY BUNTING SIGNAL FLAGS used on Board Navy Battleships made of the highest grade special quality all wool bunting as per Navy Specifications. Made up into flags at the N. Y. Navy Yard by Widows of Navy Sailors. Flags furnished as part of the navigation equipment to U. S. Warships. No doubt many of these flags are historical as they were sold to us after the close of the Spanish War. Navy Regulations forbid marking on the flags of the battle engagements. Those who have witnessed a ship in port on holidays dressed with the many colored Navy signal flags, know what a beautiful sight they present. To those who wish to decorate for any celebration, these flags are more desirable than any others and will give great satisfaction. We have for over 45 years supplied flags for decorating New York City, especially since 1889 when the late Stanford White as Chairman of a Committee, gave contract for flags to a theatrical decorator. The morning before the celebration a slight rain storm destroyed all the flags which were not of fast colors and as a party said they looked like a field of carnage "DESECRATION" instead of "DECORATION." We were called upon, and furnished flags within 6 hours time, which decorated 11 blocks of Fifth Avenue, from 23rd to 34th Streets, including the President's stand at Madison Square.

Our Flags are fast colors, no amount of rain can change them. They were only sold by reason of the change in the U. S. N. Signal Code. Some of the flags are entirely new. We have packed them into bales, consisting of 10 Steamer Flags from 3 to 5 feet wide and 10 to 20 feet long, with 15 square flags from 3 to 9 feet wide and from 5 to 15 feet long. Assorted colors and patterns complete, with ropes ready for hoisting. These bales of 25 flags weigh from 35 to 75 pounds per bale according to the sizes of the different flags. OUR BARGAIN PRICE PER BALE IS 90c PER POUND.

| THE FLAG GOES BY. | | |
|---|---|---|
| Hats off! | Hats off! | March of a strong land's swift increase; |
| Along the street there comes | The colors before us fly; | |
| A blare of bugles, a ruffle of drums | But more than the flag is passing by. | Equal justice, right and law, |
| A flash of color beneath the sky. | | Stately honor and reverend awe; |
| Hats off! | Sea-fights and land-fights, grim and great, | |
| The flag is passing by! | Fought to make and to save the State; | Sign of a nation, great and strong To ward her people from foreign wrong; |
| Blue and crimson and white it shines, | Weary marches and sinking ships; | Pride and glory and honor—all |
| | Cheers of victory on dying lips; | Live in the colors to stand or fall. |
| Over the steel-tipped, ordered lines. | Days of plenty and years of peace: | —HENRY HOLCOMB BENNETT. |

Illustration showing hotel building in New York City, decorated with our U. S. Navy Signal Flags made of Fast colored bunting that will stand wind or rain.

**"Veterans of the War."**—Our battle-scarred treasures. Collection of old flags, many of which are relics from the great Civil War, 1861-1865; the Spanish-American war; the Franco-German war; the Boer war in South Africa, etc., etc. National and regimental colors, in silk and bunting. We prize these too highly to offer any for sale, and mention them here in order to show our out-of-town customers one of the many attractions of a visit to our free War Museum.

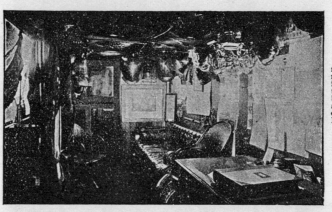

**Revolutionary War Relic.**—Bow stem of the British Powder Ship Morning Star. Blown up in New York Harbor during war of 1776; size, 8 feet long, 10x 12 inches; excavated in 1893. Price, $50.

**"Jeff Davis' Neck Tie."**—Bar of railroad iron which formed part of the track removed by General Sherman's soldiers in their march through Georgia during the Civil War, and in order to prevent being relaid was bent, while heated, around a tree or telegraph pole and called by the soldiers as per our heading. Rare relic. Price, $125.00.

**General Manager's Den.**—Our office, fitted up with cuirasses, helmets, flags, engravings, swords, shields, etc.; pronounced by experts one of the most handsomely decorated dens known. Note the sofa, which was used by Admiral Sampson on the flagship New York, off Santiago, 1898. The electric chandeliers, from the cruiser yacht Corsair. The navigator's globe, from the flagship Olympia. We will sell this valuable serviceable relic, fully authenticated, for $150.00. It is 14 inches in diameter. When in New York call and see us and rest yourself on our relic sofa. Note that we keep one book for cash sales.

**U. S. S. Cruiser's Binnacle.**—Veteran of the Civil War; made of solid black walnut with bronze-gilt trimmings, with glass sides set in bronze Complete with compass; stands about 5 feet high. Handsome ornament. Price, $100.00.

**"Spanish War Veterans."**—Name boards of fine yachts purchased by the U. S. Navy Department during the Spanish war for use as cruisers and dispatch boats. Gold letters on walnut, rosewood or mahogany decorated boards, as shown in the illustration; choice. Price, $20.00 each.

**Admiral Dewey's Anchor** from the U. S. S. Flagship Olympia. Used for anchoring the target during rifle practice. Size about 3 feet, weight about 100 lbs. Price, $60.00 each, or $100.00 pair. Make fine pair of relic andirons.

**Civil War Binnacle.**—Made of black walnut with bronze gilt mountings; stands about 4 feet high. Handsome ornament. Price, $60.00. Fitted with compass, $75.00.

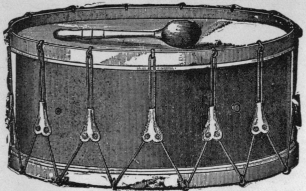

BASS DRUMS. We do not carry these in stock, but can quote on them in assorted sizes.

**THE SPIRIT OF 1776.**
Write us for prices on equipment for your band or drum corps. We can supply uniforms complete or any part, also drums, bugles and fifes.

Ancient Military Fifer. From Bannerman's book of "Weapons of War."

Trumpet Mutes to deaden the noise in practising; used, 30c.

**CIVIL WAR DRUM STICK HOLDER**, with attachment to fasten to the belt, polished brass; relics; 25 cents.

New Drum Major's Batons. Heavy Brass Bell shaped Top, with eagle coat of arms. Top is removable to add more weight if desired. Brass end tip is 8½ in. long. Stock is of hardwood. Total length of baton 49½ in. Each baton complete with heavy silk cord and tassels. Bargain price, $4.85.

**RED BREAST CORDS**, new for use on bugles. Price, 40 cents.
**GERMAN ARMY SNARE DRUM**; purchased in Hamburg in 1892, after the return of the troops from China; fair order, patched head; relic. Price, $12.50.
No. 1310. BELGIAN ARMY DRUM, 15½-inch head 11 inches high, with white buff leather tightening loops, polished brass shell, white and blue painted rims, with sticks, $15.00.

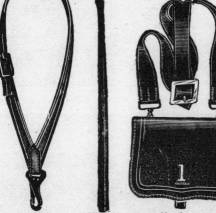

No. 1730       No. 13       No. 5
No. 1730. WOVEN KHAKI WEB DRUM SLINGS. Double thick web, with buckle for adjusting length; 1⅝ in. wide, with snap hook. Price, 48 cents.
No. 1731. BLUE WEB DRUM SLINGS, with snap hook with adjustable buckle. Practically new. Price, 35 cents.
No. 13. U. S. ARMY NEW POLISHED HARDWOOD DRUM STICKS. Price, 40 cents per pair.

No. 5. MILITIA BAND MUSIC POUCHES. Black leather, with shoulder sling, with brass adjusting buckle and end tip, with snap hook; used. Offered in good repair, serviceable order, with figure on cover. Price, 85 cents.

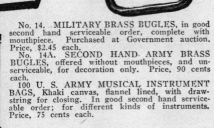

No. 14. MILITARY BRASS BUGLES, in good second hand serviceable order, complete with mouthpiece. Purchased at Government auction. Price, $2.45 each.
No. 14A. SECOND HAND ARMY BRASS BUGLES, offered without mouthpieces, and unserviceable, for decoration only. Price, 90 cents each.
100 U. S. ARMY MUSICAL INSTRUMENT BAGS, Khaki canvas, flannel lined, with drawstring for closing. In good second hand serviceable order; for different kinds of instruments. Price, 75 cents each.

No. 7       No. 8
No. 6. NEW HARDWOOD FIFES, army pattern, good quality. Price, 55 cents.
No. 7. NEW BRASS BUGLES, olive drab color, dull finish, length 9 inches. Price, $2.95 each.
No. 7A. NEW BRASS POLISHED BUGLE, length 9 inches. Price, $3.25 each.
No. 8. NEW BRASS POLISHED ARMY PATTERN BUGLE, length 16 inches. Price, $3.40.
*Note that these are reduced prices and are lower than quoted before the war. Bugles at prices shown are not fitted with chains.*

10450. BATTLE OF WATERLOO PERIOD ARTILLERY COPPER BUGLE; in serviceable order with the exception of a few dents; from British collection. Price $20.00.

UNITED STATES ARMY LEATHER CYMBAL BAGS, assorted sizes, used a short time by Spanish War Volunteers, in fine serviceable order, like new, $1.75.

UNITED STATES ARMY TAN DUCK CYMBAL BAGS, assorted sizes, good order, 65 cents.

OFFICER'S BRASS SIGNAL TRUMPET, relic, $5.00.

SPANISH MILITARY BUGLE from Santiago, Cuba, old and battered, relic only, $2.00.

COLLECTION UNITED STATES NAVY BAND INSTRUMENTS, 10 pieces for the lot. Price, $38.00. Relics from the Spanish War.

One day after the great sea battle off Santiago a sailor dressed in Uncle Sam's uniform came to our store and offered to sell us a Spanish flag, which he claimed was taken from one of Admiral Cervera's sunken war ships. We examined it and told him that he was mistaken, that we doubted if the flag had ever been on any of the Spanish ships. Jacky got angry and pulling out his discharge papers handed them to us to see that the name in the discharge was the same as was tattooed on his arm. Still we were not convinced, and finally showed him that marked on the heading of the flag was "Spanish Ensign" and asked him would the Spanish be likely to mark their flags in English? The flag was a National Spanish flag, such as is carried by U. S. Navy ships, who carry flags of all nations. Had it been of any of the Spanish war ships it would have likely been marked "Espanol Bandera" instead of "Spanish Ensign."

No. 4       No. 16
No. 15. 23 U. S. ARMY MUSICIAN STANDS; fold up, occupy little room, are all in second hand serviceable order. Full height about 5 feet. Price, 60 cents each.

No. 1309. GERMAN ARMY DRUM, brass shell, bands painted red and white, 15-inch head, 11-inch side. Complete with sticks. All in serviceable order; relic. Price, $15.00

No. 4. NEW BAND EPAULETTES, worsted cord, gilt brass rim, with lyre ornament. Bargain price, $1.25 per pair.
No. 16. MOUTHPIECE, for Fife or Piccolo, white metal. Price, 15 cents each.

No. 17. U. S. ARMY STEEL TRIANGLES, serviceable relics from U. S. Government sale after the close of the Spanish War. 6-inch size, 40 cents; 8-inch, 60 cents; 11-inch, 75 cents. One 10-inch triangle, which seems to have been made in camp. Rare relic. Price, $2.00.

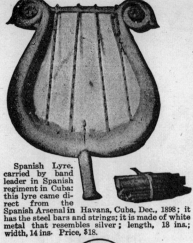

**Spanish Lyre,** carried by band leader in Spanish regiment in Cuba; this lyre came direct from the Spanish Arsenal in Havana, Cuba, Dec., 1898; it has the steel bars and strings; it is made of white metal that resembles silver; length, 18 ins.; width, 14 ins. Price, $18.

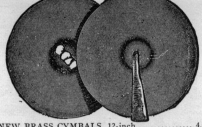

NEW BRASS CYMBALS 12-inch ............ 4.85
7-inch ............$1.30  13-inch .............$5.90

SPANISH WAR SNARE DRUM issued to 1st New York Volunteers, record cut on the hoop in "Camp Black, Camp Presidio, Camp Honolulu." Fully authenticated by Government Quartermaster. Price, $35.00.

TWO ARMY FIFES, with metal keys, needs repair, $1.00 each.

UNITED STATES ARMY DRUM COVERS for snare drums, assorted, 50 cents each.

AFRICAN SAVAGE DRUM OR TOM-TOM, crude affair; piece of skin stretched over circular shaped wood; decorated; from Prof. Simmons collection; $7.50.

**U. S. Navy Brass Bugle,** as used on board battleships; also used by marine band. Relics for decorating. Price, $1.75. 18 bugles on hand: serviceable; $2.75.

**War Club,** native work. Price, $3.50.

1005. African Native Tom Tom Drum, with stick and strap. Price, $15.

No. 61. Dinner Bell, made from part of the brass received from the U. S. S. Maine. Size, 2¾ ins. high, 2½ ins. diameter. with copy of affidavit, with red white and blue silk ribbon. Sold at Worlds Fair at $1. Price, $1.00.
Old Cast Iron Bell from New York Navy Yard Auction, May, 1907, 17 ins. diameter, 10 ins. high. Old relic; history unknown. Price, $15.

1746. Antique Castanets, concave disks of wood, held in the palm of the hand, and clapped together to produce musical sound; carved and decorated. Price, $6 pair.

Captured Filipino War Drum. from U. S. A. Captain Collectiou. Price, $20.

Civil War Military Drum in second-haud order relic: repaired; with new calfskin batter head C. W. sheepskin head.

1813. Congo Native Loom, with piece of fibre cloth in process of making, together with ½ doz. pieces of finished material : ingenious ornamented pattern: some with raised fibre: artistic work from native standpoint: size of loom, 2 ft. wide: brought from the Congo by Belgian Government official. Price of the outfit, $50

Whip with Bamboo Handle. Price, $1.60.

Music Bags for the Alto, 32 ins. long, 18 ins. at the top. 12 ins. at the rounded bottom. A good use ful bag for any desired service. Price, 65c. each.

U. S. A. Khaki Music Bags : a good, serviceable neat bag for any use : made of khaki canvas. cotton, flannel lined; average length, 34 ins., 16 ins. at the bottom, 14 ins. at top; round bottoms with rope drawing cord. Price, 75c. each.

Estey Organ from the U. S. S. Newark; good, second-hand order; has 10 stops, 2 knee swells;, brass letters "U. S. S. Newark": from Boston Navy Yard auction sale, on return of ship from the Philippines ; useful relic. Price, $50.

**U. S. NAVY BATTLE RATTLE.** From auction at Brooklyn Navy Yard at close of Civil War. Hand rattles were used on board navy battleships from the days of John Paul Jones up to and through the Civil War. Rare relics. Price, $3.75.

UNITED STATES ARMY DRUM VALISE, for carrying snare drum, tan covered canvas, with pocket for the sticks, folds up together, was made for use during the Spanish war, $1.00.

U. S. NAVY BOATSWAIN WHISTLE. Supposed to be silver. Relics Price, $2.00 each.

Bamboo Hammock, in serviceable order. Price, $10.

Filipino Hat, $1.

Illustration showing Old Battle Flags on exhibition in our salesroom, with reading notice taken from the N. Y. Herald, September, 1907: "It may surprise many readers to learn that on Broadway, in the heart of New York city, are flags on exhibition that waived triumphantly from the Olympia in the sunlight of that wonderful morning when Dewey sailed into Manila harbor with shells thundering and crashing and guns belching fire, as forts burst into flame and ships sank under Dewey's terrifying bombardment.

You can see those same flags at a Broadway war supply company establishment. All the signal flags from the Olympia were sold to the dealer by the U. S. Navy Department after the famous battle in Manila Bay, in which they were used by Admiral Dewey in giving orders to the fleet to 'Engage the enemy,' 'Haul off for breakfast,' 'Renew battle,' 'Remember the Maine,' etc. The collection includes Admiral Dewey's Bamboo chair, also his flag, originally a rear admiral's flag and altered on board the Olympia when Congress revived the rank of admiral, is the first admiral's flag since Farragut's and Porter's."

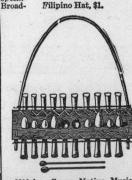

Illustration showing uniform and drum of 'Ye ancient drummer with hes drume.'

U. S. NAVY SPEAKING TRUMPETS. Relics.
Brass. Price, $5.00
Tin... " 1.00
Officer's " 6.50

ANTIQUE CARVED WOOD TANKARD. Barrel-shaped, with wood hoops, carved lid and handle, 5½ inches diameter, 10 inches high. Price, $4.85.

2219 A. Congo Native Musical Instrument Xylophone, 10 bars suspended from cross-piece. Over the last bar, fastened in the cross-piece, is a gourd to give tone ; length of bars 13¼ by 1½ by ¾ ins. ; cross-piece measures 24 by 4½ by ¾ ins. This Rare instrument, suitable for museum exhibit. Price, $15.

Organ used on board the U. S. S. Baltimore with silvered plate engraved "Presented to the U. S. S. Baltimore in Loving Memory of Mrs, C. R. P. Rodgers by the Army and Navy Auxilary, Washington, D. C., 1890." Keyboard is 2 ft. 9 ins. by 3 ft. 10 ins. long, 2 ft. 10 ins. wide, 3 ft. 6 ins. high; made of hardwood Price, $50.

11

Old Newgate Prison in London was torn down in 1903. Before turning over the prison to the firm of Holloway & Co., who had the contract for its removal, an auction sale was held in February and many historical relics connected with the old prison were auctioned off. One of the wooden doors from the cell in which, it is claimed, the great English highwayman, Dick Turpin, was confined, was purchased by the British Premier, A. J. Balfour, for $600.00. Our buyer was in London in August and made a visit to the prison, which had then been removed, in some places down below its original foundations. The workmen in excavating had uncovered an older prison, which history reports as having been in use in Mayor Dick Whittington's time. They had also dug up part of the "Old Roman Wall," and our buyer secured a piece of it, also one of the old "Roman Tiles." With the aid of Holloway & Co.'s superintendent, who was in charge of the work of tearing down and removal, who seemed to know every nook and corner, having read about everything connected with the history of the prison, we secured what he considered was one of the most historical pieces—the old dungeon door, as illustrated on this page, through which prisoners condemned to death had to pass to the place of execution. The frame of this door is 3 inches wide, and extends 8 inches beyond the door proper. The bars are hand-forged iron, 1¼ inches square. The door has two large iron bolts with places for padlocks. This door was on the lower tier, near where the condemned men were buried. We also secured a few of the heavy hand-forged grilles, which were set in the mason work for purposes of ventilating the dungeons. The rim bars in the grilles are 1½ inches square. Also see illustration of the iron frame which held the lantern; it is 3¾ feet long; place for lantern is 14 inches square.

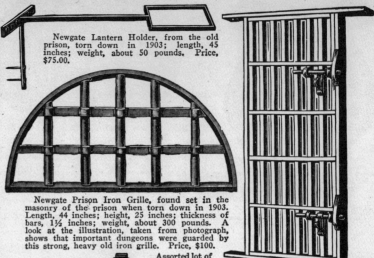

Newgate Lantern Holder, from the old prison, torn down in 1903; length, 45 inches; weight, about 50 pounds. Price, $75.00.

Newgate Prison Iron Grille, found set in the masonry of the prison when torn down in 1903. Length, 44 inches; height, 25 inches; thickness of bars, 1½ inches; weight, about 300 pounds. A look at the illustration, taken from photograph, shows that important dungeons were guarded by this strong, heavy old iron grille. Price, $100.

Assorted lot of U. S. N. Binoculars and Spy Glasses, sold at Mare Island Navy Yard, California, after the Spanish War. Relics in fair order. Price $7.50 each.

Old London Newgate Prison Door, size 5 feet 10 inches high, 2 feet 4½ inches thick; weight about 500 pounds; vouched for. Original bill of sale from contractors who tore down the Prison will be given to the purchaser. This old prison is connected with the American Revolutionary War history, for many of the captured American seamen were confined there, some of whom were sentenced to death and had to pass through this door. Price $450.00.

Map of Burial Plot, San Juan, Cuba, of American soldiers. Used by U. S. Government in locating for removal to United States the bodies of the American soldiers who died at the battle of San Juan. With United States War Department printed Burial Service in Spanish and other papers fully vouched for; at our Museum Salesroom Exhibition; will consider offer.

Chinese Cymbals, 14 inch diameter, new. Price, $4.85 the pair.

U. S. Army Cymbal Bags. Leather, army size. Price $1.75. U. S. Army Khaki Duck Cymbal Bags. Assorted sizes. Price 65 cents each.

Ancient Hand Rattle used on board old time navy war ships. Price, $3.75.

3455. Castanets, Spanish Model, Ebony, new, small to medium sizes, 90 cents a pair. Large sizes. Price $1.25 a pair.

3417. Patriotic Watch Fob, red, white and blue colored silk ribbon, with brass adjusting buckle, with gilt snap; attached to tin shield with American Stars and Stripes in colors. Width of the shield, 1⅛ inches; full length, 5 inches. Price, 15 cents.

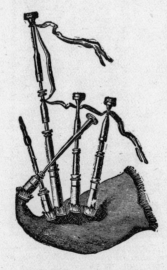

SCOTCH BAG PIPES. Imported to order.

U. S. Naval Officer's Cap Ornament, silvered and gilt metal finished foul anchors, shield and eagle, with pin fastening. New. Price $1.00 each. With buckle loops for attaching to belt for lady. Price $1.25.

### "THE RETURN."

I stood with the throng that waited
    The sound of the pipe and drum,
Till I heard a far-off murmur,
    Do you hear? They come! They come!
But I saw them not; I was dreaming
    Of the lads who come not home;
The brave true lads, who are sleeping
    In that land across the foam.
My heart was beating wildly
    At the sound of their martial tread;
And I tried to cheer but I faltered,
    For my thoughts would turn to the dead.
Their country called, and they followed,
    Forsaking their homes, their all;
And now when their friends turn homeward,
    They hear not the bugle call.
So I bowed my head and was silent,
    There were others. I knew, could cheer;
I grudged not the palm to the victors,
    Though I gave to the dead my tear.
My thoughts were too deep to utter,
    Too sad for the voice, or pen,
For I mourn o'er the dear Highland laddies,
    Who will never come back again.    A. R. F.

CRAFTSBURY, VERMONT, Oct. 29, 1923.
FRANCIS BANNERMAN SONS,
New York, N. Y.
  *Gentlemen:*
  Let me thank you for the promptness in forwarding the goods I ordered last Wednesday. They came to-day; some service.
      Very truly yours,
          F. C. KEIR

**10068.—U. S. BRASS DRAWER PULL HANDLES.** With inside glass cover for insertion of label describing contents; new. Price, 35 cents each.

**10072.—U. S. MEDICAL DEPARTMENT PILL FORMING MACHINE.** Brass forms, guides and rollers, hard wood frame and handles. Length of frame 11½ inches, width 3¼ inches; new, never used, slightly water stained. Price, $1.00 each.

**ARMY HOUSEWIFES.** New. Every camper or traveler should have one in his kit. Price, 75 cents each.

**C22. WORLD WAR RELICS.** Collected by officer in French Aviation Corps, M. Henri Julliot, mostly from battle of the Marne. Lot includes about 46 pieces, consisting of trench helmet, gas mask, shells, shrapnel and fragments. Collector's photograph on glass in colors included also. Price for collection, $60.00.

**U. S. EMERGENCY RATIONS.** Contain bread and meat component; also chocolate component; calculated to subsist one man one day. Prepared by Armour Packing Company in sealed metal container. Weight, 1½ pounds. Price, 35 cents each.

**10134.—U. S. VETERINARY SURGEON'S FILE BLADES.** For use on horses teeth. Regulation size, new, very slightly tarnished. Price, 18 cents each.

**10070.—U. S. MEDICAL DEPARTMENT CALL BELLS.** Silvered bell, Japanned base; new, serviceable order, from the fire sale. Price, 45 cents each.

**10074.—U. S. A. MEDICAL DEPARTMENT ODORLESS COMMODE.** New, never used, from recent army building fire sale; height 17 inches, diameter 12 inches. Made of zinc with heavy galvanized steel bottom, double at the top forming a flat seat; sloping sides near the top which allows the heavy rubber ring inserted between the edges of the double covers to fit tight, preventing any odor from escaping; side hook on the cover for hanging to the pail when not in use. Outside slightly paint scorched, otherwise in serviceable order like new. We purchased this lot believing our customers would appreciate for *family camping tents.* They are worth $5.00 each, our bargain price, $1.85.

**10069.—U. S. MEDICAL DEPARTMENT SPATULA.** Hard wood handles, flexible steel blades very slightly rusted; 3 inch blade, price 15 cents, 5 inch blade, price 25 cents.

**6071. NEW U. S. NAVY SAILOR CLOTHES OR DUNNAGE BAG.** Made at the Navy Yard of heavy cotton canvas, waterproofed, black color, for U. S. Navy sailors' use, with eyelet holes for draw rope fastening, round bottom, length 40 inches, diameter 13 inches. Superior to any bag in the market. Price, $1.25 each.

**10137. MULFORD'S GLASS ASEPTIC SYRINGES.** Containing veterinary tetanus antitoxin. Marked to be exchanged after October, 1909. Price, 25 cents per box.

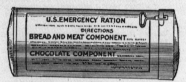

**10061.—U. S. ARMY STAMPED STEEL ENAMELED STEW PANS.** With steel handle, 8½ inch diameter, 4¾ inches deep. New, never used, enamel very slightly chipped, weight 3 lbs., 5 oz. Bargain price, 50 cents.

**10062.—U. S. ARMY STAMPED STEEL AGATE ENAMELED DIPPER.** 5½ inch diameter, 3 inches deep, handle 10 inches; new, never used, enamel very slightly chipped. Price, 15 cents each.

**10163.—U. S. A. MEDICAL DEPARTMENT STOMACH PUMP.** New, in rosewood case, size 13 by 6¾ by 2¾ inches with lock and name plate engraved "Med. Dept. U. S. A."; velvet lined, nickel-plated instruments. Made by S. Tieman & Co. We have forty in stock, all new (rubber tubing deteriorated). Bargain price, $6.85 each.

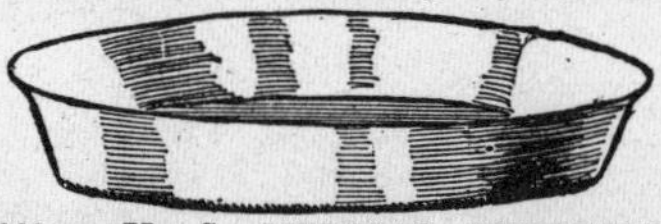

**10060.—U. S. MEDICAL DEPARTMENT MILK PAN.** From the late fire sale, new, never been used, very slightly tarnished, made of heavy stamped tin, 14 inch diameter, 3¼ inches deep, flared edge, weight 1 lb. Bargain price, 15c. each.

**10135.—U. S. A. HYPODERMIC SYRINGE OUTFIT.** In leather lined case with about 12 vials (empty); used, requires overhauling; offered as are at $1.00 per case outfit.

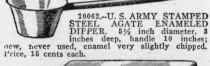

**10073.—U. S. MEDICAL DEPARTMENT SANITARY ENAMELED METAL TABLE TOP.** Size 16 by 20 inches, weight 27 lbs. Rolled edges, white porcelain; new, never used, enamel slightly stained, useful for any purpose requiring flat enameled service. Price, 75 cents.

## MILITARY BOOKS.

**3317. TREATIES ON FEVERS.** Published by Blanchard & Lea, 1861. Cloth bound, 362 pages, size 9½x6¼x1 inch. Price, 85 cents.

**10063. U. S. ARMY MEDICAL PRESCRIPTION BLANK BOOK.** Brown canvas cover, size 15x11½ inches, width of the back 3¾ inches, 150 pages strong, heavy brown paper. New, never used, slightly water stained. Bargain price, 75 cents.

**10163A. SET U. S. ARMY SURGICAL INSTRUMENTS.** In rosewood case, in leather pouch, with broad leather shoulder sling strap with adjustable brass buckle. The case measures 8¼x5¼x2 inches, nickel hinges and sliding catch, steel instruments nickel plated. The knives, lances, saw, etc., have detachable handle; 21 pieces, with sewing silk, needles, silver wire, etc. Looks complete (all receptacles in the box filled). Price for the instruments in rosewood case with pouch and sling, $9.85.

**10136. SCHIEFFELIN & CO.'S TETANUS ANTITOXIN.** Containing 1,500 Lederle antitoxin units, improved antiseptic syringe, in original packages, marked to be exchanged after September 15, 1909. Offered at 25 cents per box.

**3269. U. S. ARMY REGISTER AND PRESCRIPTION BLANK BOOK.** New, cover slightly stained, illustrated with printed example in fly leaf, leather covers, 8x5¼x⅜ inches. Price, 25 cents each.

**3318. DISEASES OF THE ALIMENTARY CANAL.** By Habershaw, 1859. 312 pages, size 9½x6⅜x1 inch. Price, 85 cents.

**3303. FIVE VOLUMES of the London Chemical News, Journal of Physical Science, Practical Chemistry as Applied to Pharmacy, Arts and Manufactures,** American Report. 300 pages. Size 9¾x7¼x⅞ inches, 1868 to 1870. Price, $4.00 the lot of 5 volumes.

**U3-2. THE MILITARY FORCES OF THE CROWN.** Their Organization and Equipment. By Colonel W. H. Daniel, P. S. C. Published in London in 1901. Large colored map of the world showing the British empire. Size 5x7½ inches, 256 pages. Price, $1.50.

**ILLUSTRATED BOOK SOUTH AFRICAN WAR.** By Capt. A. T. Mahan, U. S. Navy. 216 pages, 11½x17 inches. Many full page illustrations in color. Book is now out of print. Bargain price, $6.85.

**BOOK ON GERMAN MAUSER ARMY RIFLE.** A twenty page booklet, profusely illustrated, on the most interesting and best known rifle of the war, "The German Mauser." A detailed description of the gun, showing its many attachments and thirty-eight bayonets. EVERY VETERAN OF THE WORLD WAR WILL WANT A COPY OF THIS BOOK. Price 45 cents.

**MILITARY LITTERS.**

army model, well seasoned hard wood frame, malleable iron extension braces and legs (rounded for sliding into ambulance), strong, heavy canvas. Litter folds up for convenience in carrying when not in use. Extended full length of carrying poles is 7½ feet, width of canvas 22 inches, length 5 feet 11 inches. Suitable for military companies, factories, mines, etc. Price, $2.50.

**U. S. ARMY FIRST AID PACKAGE,** with brass loops for attaching to the waist belt, hermetically sealed, opened by a pull on the ring, brass metal box, size 2½x4½ inches. Weight, 5 ounces. Contains full First Aid Package outfit. Price, 20 cents.

**No. 3.—U. S. ARMY SURGEON'S NICKEL-PLATED METAL CROSS,** with screw-nut fastening. New; 5,000 in stock. Price, 10c each; $1.00 per dozen; $7.00 per 100.

No. 3

**8 U. S. Army Restraining Sets,** in small, wood trunk. Size, 7x13x16 inches. Looks like new, as never have been used; well made. Price, $8.50 per set.

**3021. MEDICAL BELT BUCKLE.** With Caduceus emblem of medical department. Buckle is gilt finished brass, with Caduceus in centre in raised or relief work. Fine buckle for lady's belt. Price, $1.50.

**U. S. Hospital Corps Handbook,** by Deputy Surgeon-General Smart, 1898. Size, 5x7½ ins.; 350 pages, cloth bound; illustrated. Regular price, $1.00. Our price, 45 cents.

**Wheel Table Bed.** New; in fine order. Price, $15.00.

**U. S. Navy Aspirator Brass Pump.** Price, $4.00.

**U. S. Navy Ambulance or Hospital Cot.** Canvas, with loops for strapping "Jack" while being lowered to "Sick Bay." Complete, as per cut. Price, $8.50 each.

**Fleming's Electrical Medical Battery.** In walnut case, 6x8x7 inches. Price, $3.50.

**60 Pairs Hospital Slippers,** used few times; assorted sizes. Price, 50 cents a pair.

**U. S. Army Rubber Blankets.** Size, 72x42 ins.; weight about 2½ pounds. Price, $1.00.

**Spanish Surgeon's Leather Haversack,** with field outfit. New. Price, $2.00.

**U1-32. ELEMENTS OF WAR, MASSACHUSETTS MILITIA.** Written by Isaac Maltby, Brigadier General in the Fourth Mass. Division. Published in Boston in 1813. For use of Militia officers. Sheepskin cover; 208 pages; size 4x7 inches. A Rare Book. Price, $4.50.

**U1-33. A MILITARY DICTIONARY** explaining and describing the Technical Terms, Works and Machines Used in the Science of War. Published in Dublin in 1780. Size 4½x7½ inches. A rare book in good condition. Price, $6.00.

**U1-34. NOTES ON MILITARY HYGIENE** for officers of the Line, by Brig. Gen. Alfred A. Woodhull, U. S. A. Size 4x6½ inches; 239 pages. Price, 50 cents.

**Head Nets,** for use as protection against mosquitoes. Like new; fine, serviceable order; from U. S. Army; made of light netting. Price, 45 cts.

**U. S. Medical Bed Pan.** Made of pewter-like metal; new, but knocked about in army transports. Price, 65 cents.

**Galvanic Medical Battery,** hand power, in working order. From U. S. Navy. Price, $3.75.

**400. ELEMENTARY NAVAL ORDNANCE AND GUNNERY.** Includes Close-order Infantry with 1918 Drill Regulations. By Lt. M. C. Ramsey, in charge of Naval Ordnance and Gunnery at U. S. N. Officer's Training School at Harvard University. 412 pages, size 5 by 7¼, on heavy glazed paper. Many drawings of cannon, machine guns, projectiles, etc. Large detail sketch of 12 inch 2 gun turret. Chapters on NAVAL GUNS, BREECH MECHANISMS, TURRETS, PROJECTILES, FIRE CONTROL, TORPEDOES, BATTLE DRILLS, ETC. A fine text book for individuals or schools. Price, postage paid in U. S., 65 cents.

**BOOK ON RIBBONS AND MEDALS.** Compiled by Commander H. Taprell Dorling, R. N. (British Royal Navy.) Contains 177 pages showing 133 ribbons in COLORS of the BRITISH EMPIRE, with the different medals and foreign orders. Also 84 ribbons in COLORS for both British and foreign countries before the World War, with description of the medals and decorations with which they were used. Part 3 shows 14 WORLD WAR RIBBONS IN COLOR, of various branches of the British service, also France and Greece. The British and foreign medals as issued to participants in the World War are illustrated and described. This book will be of great value to any veteran or collector of medals. Price $2.50 each.

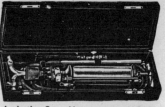

**Aspirating Set.** Almost new; rubber has deteriorated. Size of pump, 4¾ inches by 1 inch diameter; in wood case. Price, $5.85.

**WASHINGTON BRONZE PLAQUE,** size 11x 7½ inches, with bolts for fastening to shield. Weight, 3 pounds 7 ounces. Price, $3.85.

**Pocket Flasks,** hold about 4 ounces of liquid, about ¼ pint; are in fine, serviceable order; made of glass, with metal screw-top; top part covered with leather; the bottom part is of metal, which can be taken off and use as a cup. Price, 65 cents.

**U. S. Army Surgeon's Microscope,** with lens and slides. All contained in rosewood case, with strap. Size, 14x8x10 inches. Contract price, $75.00; will sell for $30.00.

**Stethoscope,** from U. S. Army Medical sale. Price, $5.75.

**U. S. Navy Greely Relief Expedition Medicine Chest,** filled with medicine, used in resuscitating General Greely and comrades. Price, $20.00.

**Sets of Metal Marking Figures,** with brass holder. Complete marking outfit; looks like new; in tin box, 8x4½x1¼ ins. Price, $2.85.

**D9. NINE VOLUMES. REFERENCE HANDBOOK OF THE MEDICAL SCIENCES,** embracing the entire range of Scientific and Practical Medicine and Allied Science. Edited by Dr. Albert H. Buck, New York City, 1887. Each volume contains about 800 pages; size 8x11 inches. Price for full set of nine volumes, $10.00.

**8,000 U. S. Army Soldiers' First Aid Packages.** Complete, with illustrations and directions showing how to apply the medicated bandages. The contents of each package consists of 2 antiseptic compresses of sublimated gauze in oiled paper; 1 antiseptic bandage of sublimated cambric with safety pin, 1 triangular bandage with safety pin, (tarnished), with mode of application illustrated on same. Useful article that may be the means of saving life, and should be on hand at all places where workmen are employed, as well as by militiamen in service. Size of package: 3 inches wide, 4 inches long, 1 inch thick. Cost 25 cents each by contract. Our price, 10 cents

**U. S. Navy Surgeon's Case of Autopsy Intruments,** Incomplete. Price, as is, $4.50.

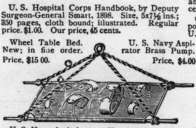

**U. S. ARMY HOSPITAL CORPS LITTER.** Cover made of heavy canvas iron legs, and stretchers, in second hand condition. Folds up when not in use. Price, $2.50 each.

**2242. U. S. ARMY TOURNEQUET.** Brass buckle, with roller, with web strap. New. Made for use during the Civil War period. Fine, serviceable order. Valuable in any manufacturing establishment in case of accident to stop flow of blood. Chamois leather pads. Price only 35 cents each.

**0-979. ANCIENT POCKET LANCE IN FOLDING BRASS CASE.** Engraved "G. W. Smith." 2 sharpened lance points encased in folding iron blades. Curious. Price, $1.85.

**U. S. ARMY BACON TINS,** length 7 inches; new, made of heavy block tin at special price of 15 cents each. Allow postage on 2 pounds.

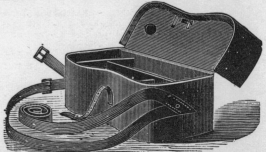

**400 Civil War U. S. Army Surgeon's Field Cases.** New; now obsolete. Wood frame, leather-covered, with waist belt and shoulder sling, compartments to hold bottles, etc. Handy medicine chest for boy's brigade companies or home use. Price, 75 cents each.

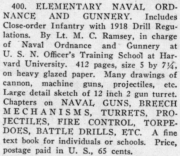

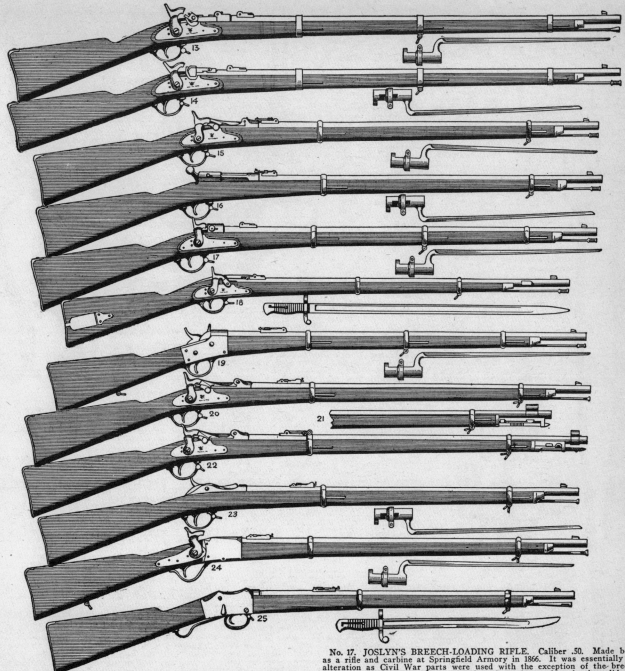

**No. 13. BERDAN'S ALTERATION OF A SPRINGFIELD MUSKET TO A BREECH-LOADER.** This was known as the "Slam Bang" system. The block was jointed in the center and if closed rapidly made two distinct sounds or clicks, hence the name. This system had a limited use but it was one of the important arms of the period. From 1865 to 1880 the government tested one hundred and four different breech-loading systems both in single loaders and magazine arms. Of these fourteen were actually used either by the Army, Navy or Militia during that time. In 1880 the .45 caliber Springfield was well established in the hands of the troops and the desire to experiment except with magazine arms was practically stopped.

**No. 14. MILLER'S ALTERATION TO BREECH-LOADER.** Another one of the systems which were based along the lines of the Allin, i.e., the block swinging up and forward. This arm had a very efficient extractor for which the government paid $18,000 to control. This system saw limited use in several states by the militia regiments prior to 1873.

**No. 15. U. S. SPRINGFIELD BREECH-LOADING RIFLE.** Model of 1870. Caliber .50. This arm shows some changes from the Model 1868, noticeably in the rear sight, breech-block and the fact that it had but two bands. This is the last of the .50 caliber arms and also the last U. S. rifle to be left bright. The model 1870 finished what was known as the "alterations," that is, using old parts to make new model guns. Made also as a carbine.

**No. 16. WARD-BURTON BREECH-LOADING RIFLE.** Model of 1871. Caliber .50. Made at Springfield Armory both in rifle and carbine models. This arm was the first bolt action to have the firing-pin in the bolt and the first to use a center fire cartridge. It was not a success, however, as reports from the army stated that "the system was dangerous and always out of order." The Ward-Burton did not see much use and was soon consigned to the junk pile.

**No. 17. JOSLYN'S BREECH-LOADING RIFLE.** Caliber .50. Made both as a rifle and carbine at Springfield Armory in 1866. It was essentially an alteration as Civil War parts were used with the exception of the breech block and hammer. As there were but three thousand made they did not see much use in the regular Army.

**No. 18. MERRILL'S PATENT BREECH-LOADING RIFLE.** Caliber .54. Navy model. This breech-loading system was first brought out in 1858 and was the outcome of the well known Jenks. Carbines and rifles alike were made at Baltimore and these saw extensive service from 1861 until after the Civil War. The breech action was later adapted to the use of a rim-fire metallic cartridge and used until the 70's.

**No. 19. REMINGTON PATENT BREECH-LOADER.** Caliber .50. Model of 1870 and made at Springfield Armory. This particular Remington was an alteration as Civil War parts were used to complete the gun. Made for Navy use. The Remington action first appeared just at the end of the Civil War. It was originally known as the "Rider," being based on Joseph Rider's patent of December, 1863. The first form was known as the "split-breech." This was the first use of the Remington system by the U. S. Various modifications were made on the breech mechanism until the 80's when it became standardized. The Remington was used with great success by the Army, Navy and Militia for many years. The calibers ranged from .56 to .45 in the U. S. service and for foreign governments it was easily chambered to use the standard ammunition. In the World War it saw extensive use in various calibers. The Remington system is perhaps the best known American arm abroad and today it cannot be surpassed as a single loader for strength and durability. The action is practically "fool-proof."

**No. 20. U. S. SPRINGFIELD RIFLE.** Model of 1873. Caliber .45. The first step in the reduction of caliber as applied to regular Army rifles and carbines. This arm was adopted after exhaustive tests of about fifty different systems, both domestic and foreign. This arm was in use with changes in sights and bayonets until 1894 by the regulars and was always preferred to any of the magazine guns issued during this time. The militia used it

*Continued on Page 363*

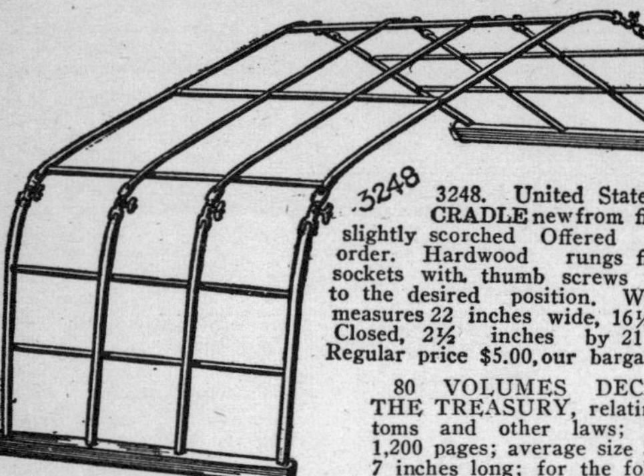

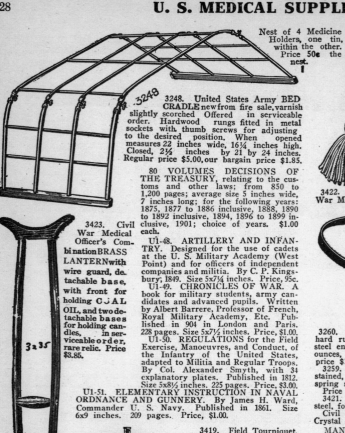

Nest of 4 Medicine Holders, one tin, within the other. Price 50c the nest.

3248. United States Army BED CRADLE new from fire sale, varnish slightly scorched Offered in serviceable order. Hardwood rungs fitted in metal sockets with thumb screws for adjusting to the desired position. When opened measures 22 inches wide, 16¼ inches high. Closed, 2½ inches by 21 by 24 inches. Regular price $5.00, our bargain price $1.85.

80 VOLUMES DECISIONS OF THE TREASURY, relating to the customs and other laws; from 850 to 1,200 pages; average size 5 inches wide, 7 inches long; for the following years: 1875, 1877 to 1886 inclusive, 1888, 1890 to 1892 inclusive, 1894, 1896 to 1899 inclusive, 1901; choice of years. $1.00 each.

U1-48. ARTILLERY AND INFANTRY. Designed for the use of cadets at the U. S. Military Academy (West Point) and for officers of independent companies and militia. By C. P. Kingsbury, 1849. Size 5x7¼ inches. Price, 95c.

U1-49. CHRONICLES OF WAR. A book for military students, army candidates and advanced pupils. Written by Albert Barrere, Professor of French, Royal Military Academy, Etc. Published in 904 in London and Paris. 228 pages. Size 5x7½ inches. Price, $1.00.

U1-50. REGULATIONS for the Field Exercise, Manoeuvres, and Conduct, of the Infantry of the United States, adapted to Militia and Regular Troops. By Col. Alexander Smyth, with 34 explanatory plates. Published in 1812. Size 5x8½ inches. 225 pages. Price, $3.00.

U1-51. ELEMENTARY INSTRUCTION IN NAVAL ORDNANCE AND GUNNERY. By James H. Ward, Commander U. S. Navy. Published in 1861. Size 6x9 inches. 209 pages. Price, $1.00.

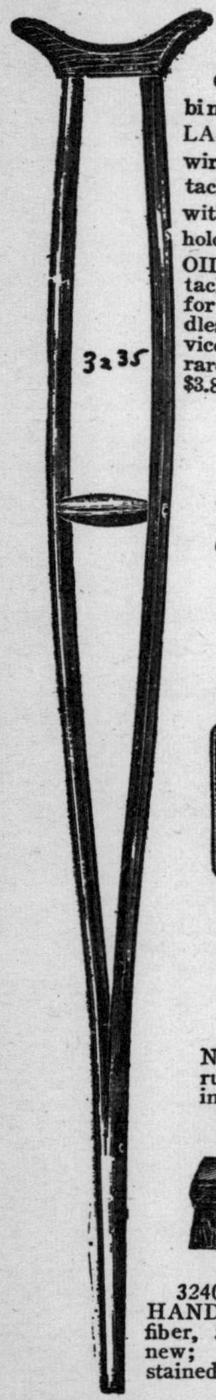

3423. Civil War Medical Officer's Combination BRASS LANTERN with wire guard, detachable base, with front for holding COAL OIL, and two detachable bases for holding candles, in serviceable order, rare relic. Price $3.85.

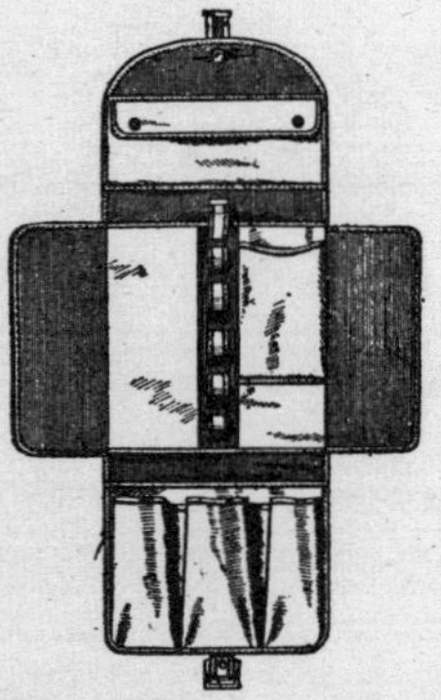

3419. Field Tourniquet, stamped U. S. A., brass, roller buckle, with chamois leather pad 1⅜ inches. Price 25c.

3455. Tieman's Improved PAD TOURNIQUET for use in Civil War, new, with printed directions. Price $1.00.

3436. BRASS SPIRAL TOURNIQUET with large brass thumb screws with chamois leather pads, new. Price $1.00.

NEW TOILET KIT of heavy olive drab cloth with rubberized lining, seven compartments. Size, open, 9 inches wide, 24 inches long. Price, 65 cents.

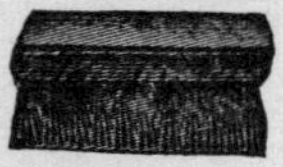

3240. U. S. Army HAND BRUSH, white fiber, 5 by 1½ inches; new; slightly fire stained. Price 5c.

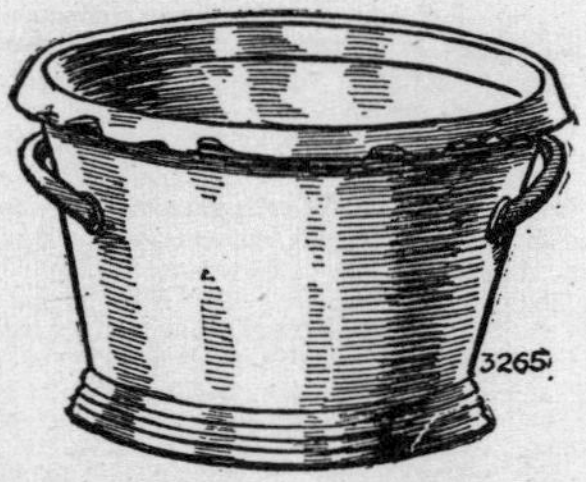

3235. U. S. Army Crutches, 900 pair in stock, new, purchased from U. S. Army Medical Department, very slightly damaged at the recent fire sale. Crutches are only varnish stained. All in serviceable order, length 4 feet 4 inches, made of hard wood, weighs 3 pounds the pair. Dealer's price, $2.00. Our bargain price 48c a pair.

United States Medical Army Department, FOOT BATH TUB, new, made of heavy steel, white enameled, slightly damaged at late fire sale. Weight about 5 pounds, measures 14x10½ inches. Our bargain price, $2.00.

3361. U. S. Army Officer's Post Mortem case of instruments, mahogany case, 12½x5x2¼ inches, brass, with plate engraved U. S. A. on the cover, brass corner braces, contains 15 instruments. Some with white and some with hard rubber handles. Made by Bernstein & Son, N. Y. Used, requires cleaning. Price "as is" $7.85.

Civil War Medical Supplies found in State Arsenal, Trenton, N. J., 40 years after the war was over. All in original packages overlooked and never sent to the seat of war. They were packed along with a lot of drugs.

3427. Civil War Urinal (hospital size), with handle, new, found stored in old State Arsenal, never sent to the seat of war. Length 10, base 4½, height 4½ inches, with hanble 4½ inches, crockeryware. Price 50c.

3428. Medicine Cup, with spout and handle, new, crockery length 6 inches, width 3½, height 2¼ inches. Price 25c.

3429. U. S. Civil War graduated MEDICINE GLASS. Width 4 inches, height 6 inches, diameter 3½. Price 45c.

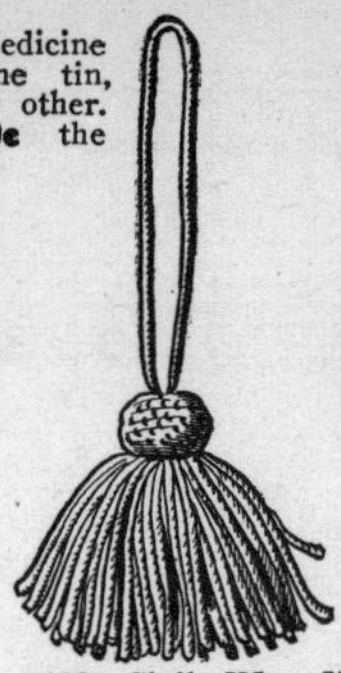

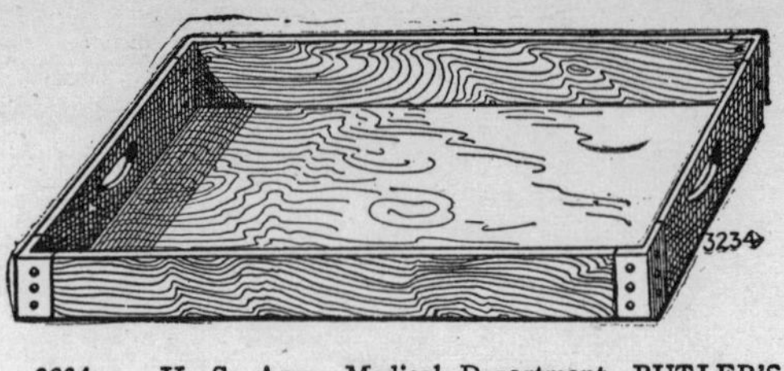

3234. U. S. Army Medical Department, BUTLER'S TRAY, new, slightly damaged at fire sale. Serviceable order, made of hardwood with brass corner braces. Locked corners, open handles. Size 30 inches long, 18 inches wide, 4¾ inches deep. Neat, strong, serviceable tray. Price 95c.

3422. Civil War Yellow Tassel, with loop, new, found packed away with Civil War Medical Stores, intended to be worn by army convalescents. Price 10c.

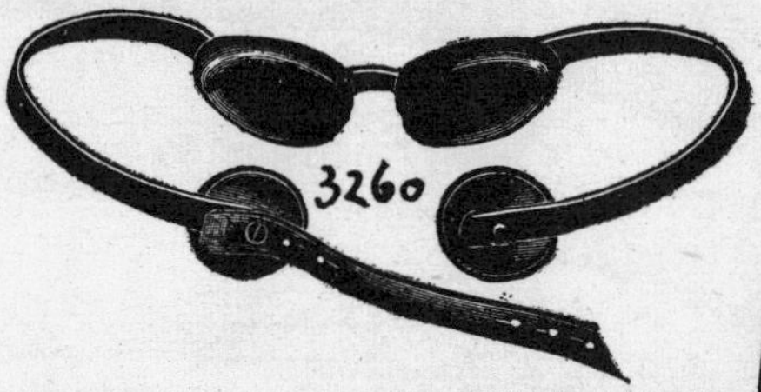

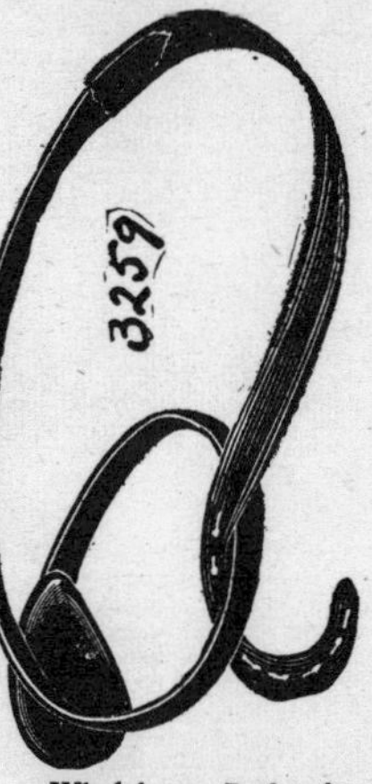

3260. U. S. Army DOUBLE TRUSS, adjustable hard rubber sanitary pads, nickel holders, spring steel enameled, with leather straps. Weight 12 ounces, *new*, slightly stained by fire. Our bargain price $1.45.

3259. U. S. Army SNGLE TRUSS, NEW, fire stained, hard rubber pads, nickel holder, enamel spring steel, leather straps. Weight 7 ounces. Price 95c.

3421. U. S. Army Tongue Depressor, nickel steel, folding, size opened 11 inches. Price $1.25.

Civil War Razor Strap, Saunder's, New York Crystal Palace, 1853. New. Price 50c.

MANUAL OF MILITARY FIELD ENGINEERING. Sixth Edition, by Major Wm. D. Beach, U. S. A. 288 pages. Fully illustrated. Use of Cordage and Spars, Bridges, Telegraph, Railroads, Camping, Etc. Size 7x5¼ inches. Price, 75 cents.

Whalebone Rod with Sponge, white ivory tipped handle, 12½ inches long, ¼ inch diameter. Price 25c.

U1-53. REPORT OF THE SECRETARY OF THE NAVY, with an Appendix containing Bureau Reports. Published in 1866 at Washington. Size 6x9 inches. 226 pages. Price $1.00.

U1-54. A MANUAL OF NAVAL TACTICS, with analysis of the principal Modern Naval Battles. By Commander James H. Ward, U. S. N. Many sketches. 208 pages. Size 6x9 inches. Price $1.50.

U1-55. DRILL REGULATIONS FOR COAST ARTILLERY U. S. ARMY, 1909. Many sketches and charts, with Index. 242 pages. Size 5½x8 inches. Price 60c.

U1-56. A SYSTEM OF CAMP DISCIPLINE, MILITARY HONOURS, GARRISON DUTY, and other regulations for the Land Forces, including Kane's Discipline for a Battalion, also General Kane's Campaigns of King William and the Duke of Marlborough. Printed in London in 1757. A rare military book. Sheepskin covers. Size 5x8 inches. 217 pages, with Colored Maps and Battle Order. Price $6.00.

U1-57. SYSTEM OF EXERCISE AND INSTRUCTION OF FIELD ARTILLERY, including manoeuvres for Light or Horse Artillery. Published by the War Department in 1829. Many full page illustrations. Size 4½x7½ inches. 78 pages. Price $2.25.

U1-58. MANUAL OF INSTRUCTION for the Volunteers and Militia of the Confederate States. By William Gilham, Colonel of Volunteers. Published in Richmond in 1862. This Is a Rare Confederate Book. Size 5x7½ inches. 502 pages. 82 full page plates showing formations, etc. Price $10.00.

3324. Civil War Medical Knapsack with Bottles, Stoppers and TIN CANISTERS, made of wicker work, with compartments water proofed, canvas covered, with top and side openings, new, never used, height 18½ inches, width 15 inches, with willow trays. Price $4.85.

3423a. U. S. A. Civil War Coffee Mill, new, with thumb screws for attaching, intended for hospital use. Height 9½ inches, width 6½ inches by 3½ inches deep with handle. Price 85c.

3425. Civil War hard rubber syringe, NEW, in original box, length closed 5 inches, opened 7 inches. Price 85c.

3426. Hard rubber ENEMA SYRINGE, NEW, in original box. Left over from Civil War Stock. Closed measures 15 inches, opened 22 inches; new. Price $2.50.

United States Civil War Medicine Glass, graduated. Length 3½ inches, diameter 2 inches. Price 30c.

Nest of four MEDICINE GLASSES, one within the other. Price the set, 50c the four.

3431. BOOK, THOMAS CONSPECTUS, new. Published by S. S. & W. Wood, 1861. Size 6¼x4¼x1¼ inches, 322 pages. Price $1.00.

3432. Pocket Set Surgical Instruments for Civil War Surgeon, new, in leather case, 14 pieces, few of the instruments very slightly rusted. Size of the case 5¾x8¾, silk-lined, folding flaps. Morocco, made by V. W. Brinkerhoff, N. Y. Price $10.00.

Dental Surgeon's Instruments, made by M. Bernstein & Son. Black leather case, chamois leather lined, size 7½ by 9 inches, 8 pieces Price $5.00.

3434. Civil War Suspensories, 36 inch cloth waist belt, cotton, new, Civil War stock. Slightly stained from long storage. Price 25c.

3435. Civil War Scarificator Brass, new, in leather covered box, felt lined, size of the box, 3x2¼x2⅜ inches. Price $3.00.

16. ANTIQUE EUROPEAN CANDLE SNUFFERS, in assorted sizes and patterns, average length 6 inches. All very old, but serviceable. Price $3.00 each.

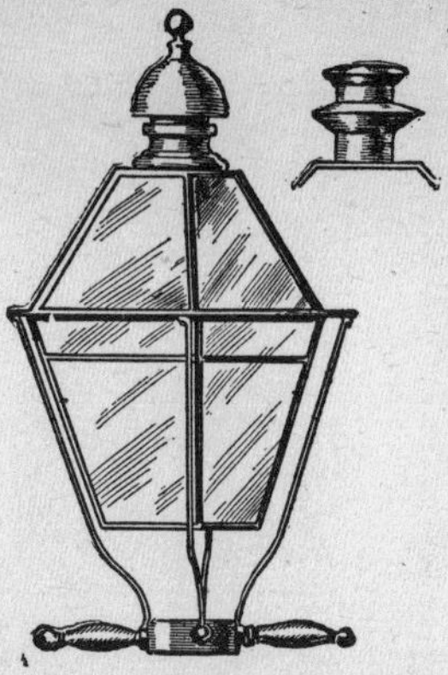

10178. NEW YORK CITY SQUARE LAMPS. Old pattern street lamps, with ½-inch round iron guards fitted to frame, wherein the lamp rests. The guard irons are bolted to cast iron cross guard, with 2⅝-inch square hole for post. The width of the lamp, where it rests in the frame, is 20 inches; height from cross guard to resting frame is 24 inches, total height 28 inches, widest width 16 inches; four upper and four lower glass lights; weight 27 pounds. Used. In second-hand, serviceable order, carefully packed, each lamp and frame in barrel. Useful ornament to any country place. Must have cost upwards of $20.00 to make. We have 100 in stock. Our bargain price, $3.85 each.

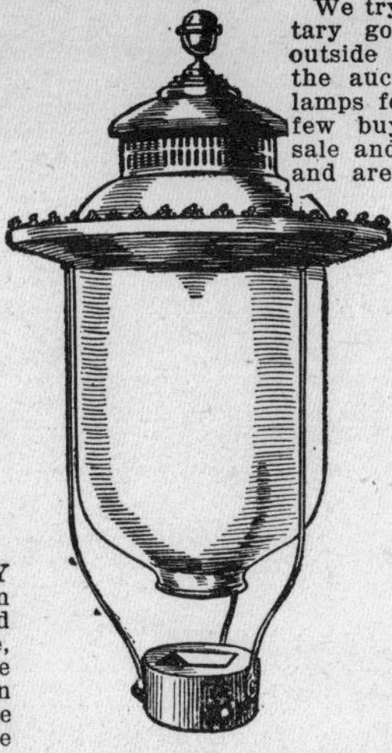

10262. NEW YORK CITY BOULEVARD LAMP. Stands 33 inches high, globe 11 inches in diameter, 14 inches high, four ⅜-inch guard irons bolted to iron base, with 2⅝-inch hole for post; COPPER TOP BRASS VENTILATOR. About 100 in stock. Used a short time on New York City boulevard. Offered in serviceable, second-hand order, packed in barrels for shipment. Price, $5.85.

We try to adhere strictly to military goods. Lamps are a trifle outside of our line. We attended the auction in order to purchase lamps for our Island grounds, but few buyers were present at the sale and we secured the entire lot and are giving our customers the benefit of our great bargain. The lamps are offered at a fraction of the cost. Are very suitable for lighting suburban home or village.

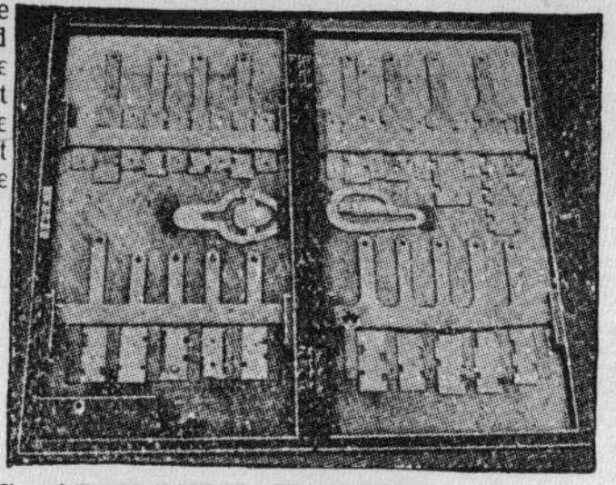

3992. U. S. ARTILLERY HARNESS GAUGES. Used during the Civil War in making harness parts interchangeable in the field. Each gauge named and numbered with crossed cannon and shell in flames (U. S. Ordnance insignia). In walnut case, size 25x14¾ inches Lined with heavy buff leather. Must have cost upwards of $1000.00 to make. Bargain price for the outfit, $19.85.

10179. NEW YORK CITY FIRE DEPARTMENT STREET LAMPS. Similar to No. 10178, only trifle smaller and more ornamental. Price, $4.25.

A sentry, while on duty, was bitten by a valuable retriever, and drove his bayonet into the dog. Its owner sued him in the County Court for its value, and the evidence given showed that the soldier had not been badly bitten after all. "Why did you not knock the dog with the butt end of your rifle?" asked the judge. The court rocked with laughter when the sentry replied: "Why didn't he bite me with his tail?"—London Daily News.

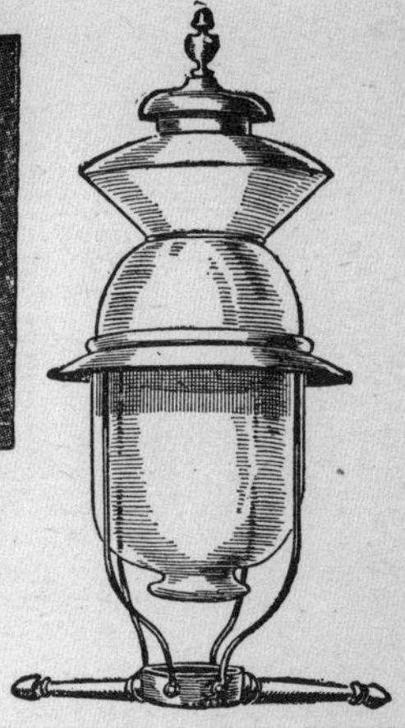

10177. NEW YORK CITY BOULEVARD LAMPS. With round globe, with iron frame, with folding top with reflector. Used on New York City street. Sold on account of change in regulation. The frame consists of four ⅜-inch round iron guards, attached to heavy cast iron cross bar, with 2¾-inch square hole opening for the pole. Top of the guard iron is joined to round iron ring forming the rest for the globe. The length of the cross guard is 22 inches, the height from the cross guard to the rim of the globe is 19½ inches, total height 42 inches, diameter of the globe 12 inches, weight 31 pounds. Must have cost over $25.00 to make. We have about 200. We offer them in second-hand, serviceable order, each packed in barrel. Fine, useful ornament for suburban home. At the bargain price of $4.85.

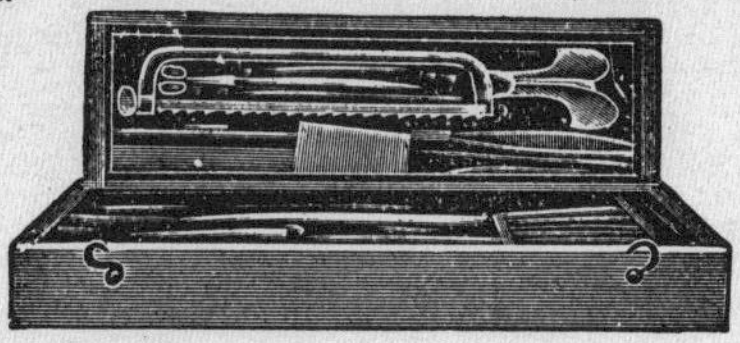

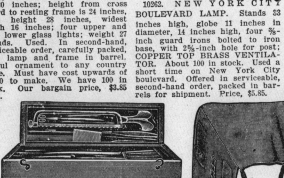

U. S. A. SURGEONS' FIELD MAJOR OPERATING SETS. The sets now in stock are incomplete and we prefer to sell to customers who can call and make own selection. All in fine hard wood cases. Prices from $8.00 up.

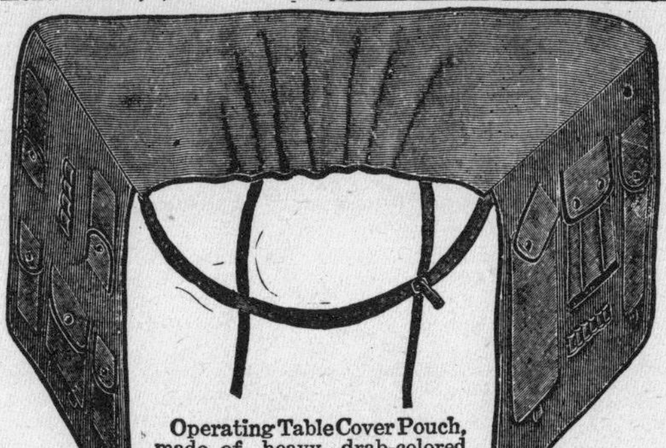

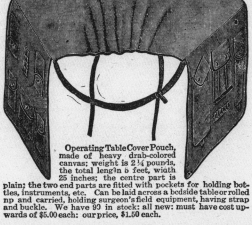

**Operating Table Cover Pouch,** made of heavy drab-colored canvas; weight is 2¼ pounds, the total length 5 feet, width 25 inches; the centre part is plain; the two end parts are fitted with pockets for holding bottles, instruments, etc. Can be laid across a bedside table or rolled up and carried, holding surgeon's field equipment, having strap and buckle. We have 90 in stock: all new: must have cost upwards of $5.00 each: our price, $1.50 each.

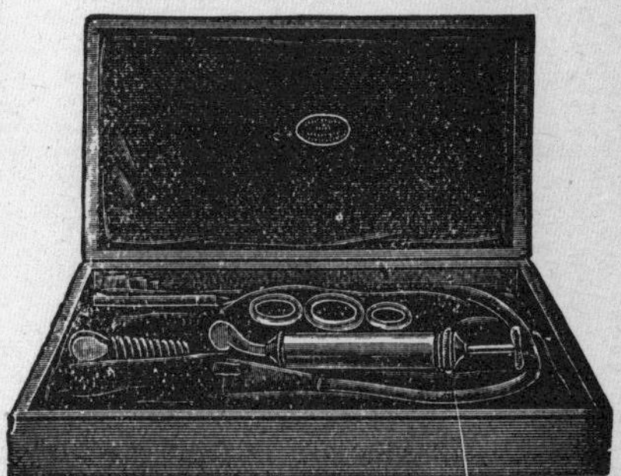

No. 7. United States Army Stomach-Pump Sets, Tieman make; are in good serviceable order, like new; rubber may require renewing. Price, $5.00 set; all contained in polished mahogany brass bound case. Size, 13x7x2½ inches.

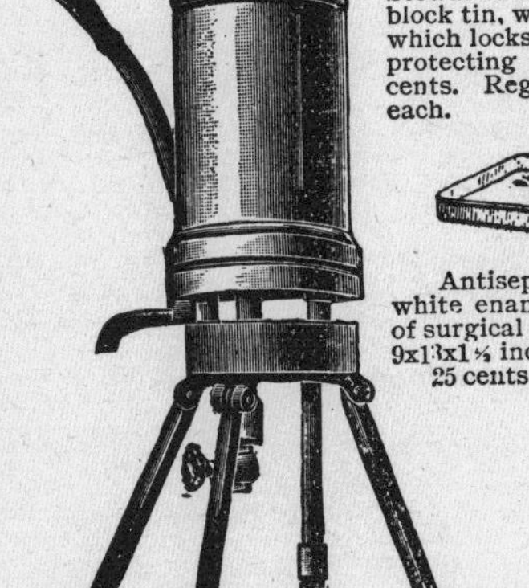

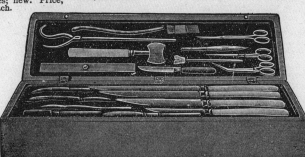

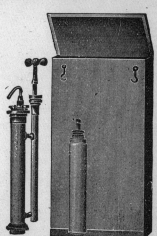

Two Pasteur Germ-Proof Filters, nickel-plated cylinder. Length, 12 inches; diameter, 5⅛ inches; stroke of pump, 4½ inches; has been used; requires new rubber hose: complete, with special box. Legs fold up; seems to be in order; offered as is. Price, $6.00.

19 United States Army Steward's Trays, new; heavy block tin, with folding handle which locks by a spring; has protecting rim. Price, 50 cents. Regular price, $1.00 each.

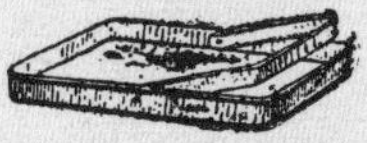

Antiseptic Lipped Tray, white enamel, for immersion of surgical instruments. Size, 9x13x1½ inches; new. Price, 25 cents each.

14 Bed Trays, purchased for use of United States Army Medical Department; new, never used, only wear was received in transportation. Made of ash. Tray stands on four small legs that can be folded underneath; size, 23 inches long, 16 inches wide, 10¼ inches high. Price, 75 cents.

600 Bed Ticket and Card Holders, bronze lacquered tin; length, 6 inches; 3⅛ inches wide, with hole at the top and turned edges for holding record of patient in hospital; new. Price, 5 cents each; 30 cents per dozen; $2.00 per hundred.

Hard-Rubber Trays, new, for sterilizing surgical instruments. Size, 11½ inches by 9⅛ inches, 1 inch deep. Price, 75 cents each.

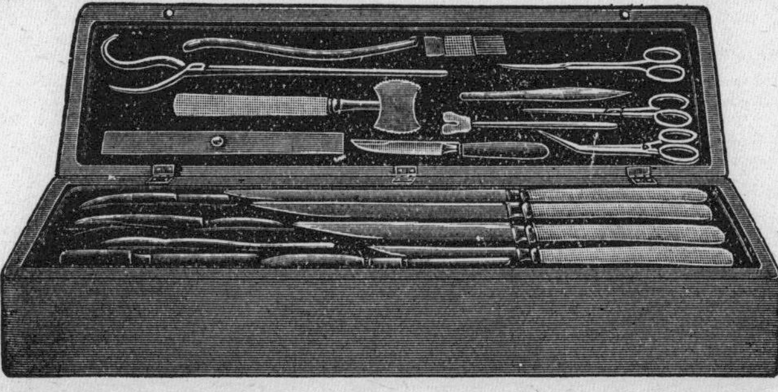

U. S. A. SURGEONS FIELD MAJOR OPERATING SETS. The sets now in stock are incomplete and we prefer to sell to customers who can call and make own selection. All in fine hard wood cases. Prices from $8.00 up.

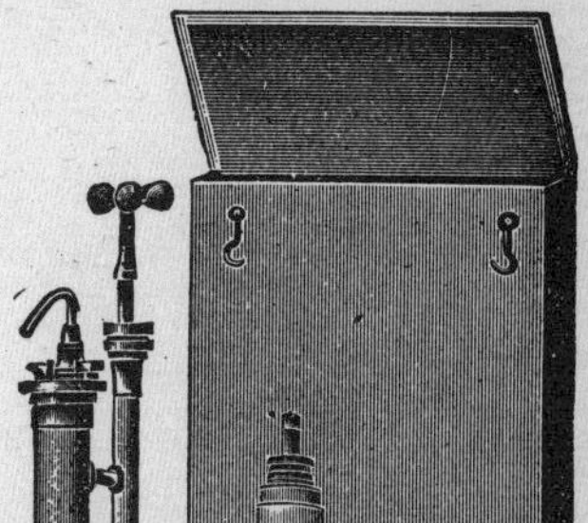

Five Berkefeld Germ-Proof Filters, new, with extra filter; nickel-plated cylinder. Full length, 15 inches; diameter, 2½ inches; stroke of pump, 10 inches. Complete, with special packing box, all as shown in illustration. Price, $4.50 each.

3154. TROPICAL DISEASES, Manson. 130 illustrations, 2 colored plates. Wood, publisher, 1903, New York. 756 pages, 7½x5½ inches. Price, 60 cents.

3155. WOUNDS IN WAR, by Surgeon A. W. F. Stephenson. Publisher, Wood, New York, 1898. Illustrated; 437 pages, 9½x6½ inches. Price, 60 cents.

3156. BRITISH MEDICAL JOURNAL, Volume I and II, 1879-1884. 1,000 pages, each size 10½x9. Illustrated. Price, $1.75 each volume.

3157. LONDON LANCET, 1,480 pages. Size 11¾x8½x3¼ inches. Partly leather bound, 1868-1867-1891. Illustrated. Price, $2.00 per volume.

3306. SYSTEM OF SURGERY, HOLMES. Published by Wood & Co., 1883. Illustrated, sheep bound, 10¼x6¾x2⅛ inches; 3,000 pages in the 3 volumes. Publisher's price, $16.00 the set; our price, $4.50.

3162. MANUAL FOR ARMY COOKS. Published by U. S. War Department, 1896; 306 pages, 7¼x4¾ inches; much used. Complete, 95 cents.

3167. ATLAS OF SKIN AND VENERAL DISEASES, Morrow. Illustrated; colors; size 17x13¼ inches; morocco bound. Price, $5.00.

3163. U. S. NAVY, COOK BOOK MANUAL. Published by order of Secretary of the Navy, 1902. Canvas covered; 8¼x5¼; 32 pages. Price, 50 cents.

MARINE CORPS BOOK, 1903. Manual of Practical Instruction to Officers in Field Work, Trenches, Range Finding, Countersigning, Landing, Submarines, Mines, etc. Illustrated; size 9x5½ inches; 78 pages. Price, 35 cents each.

14 ANATOMICAL MAPS used in West Point classes, mounted on rollers; serviceable order. The lot, $5.00.

12 ANATOMICAL CHARTS, by Prof. Theodore Eckhardt of Vienna. Used in classes at West Point Military Academy; serviceable order. Price, $3.85.

No. 5. NOTES ON MILITARY HYGIENE for officers of the line, by Woodhull. Used by West Point cadets as text books. Size 4x7 inches; 238 pages. 55 cents each.

No. 7. ANATOMY, PHYSIOLOGY AND HYGIENE, by Roger M. Tracy, M. D. Used at West Point as text book. 5x7 inches; 353 pages; illustrated. Series No. 3. 75 cents.

U2-1. NAVAL TACTICS, Fleet Evolutions Under Steam Alone. 83 pages; many full page drawings of fleet formations. Price, 75 cents.

U2-2. NAVAL LIGHT ARTILLERY, AFLOAT AND ASHORE, by Lt. S. B. Luce, 1862. 120 pages, with 21 plates, full page, showing cannon, formations, etc. Price, $1.00.

U2-3. THE VOLTAIC CELL (BATTERY), its construction and its capacity, by Park Benjamin, 1899. Fully illustrated. Price, $1.50.

U2-4. DESCRIPTION OF THE 2.95-INCH MOUNTAIN GUN, CARRIAGE, AND PACK OUTFIT, VICKERS-MAXIM. Illustrated with 27 plates. Price, $1.00.

D1. STATISTICS, MEDICAL AND ANTHROPOLOGICAL, of the Provost-Marshall-General's Bureau. Records of the examination for military service on the Armies of the United States during the late war of the Rebellion. Volume I, 1875, 568 pages. Size 9x11½ inches. Price, $3.00.

D2. MANUAL OF ARTILLERY EXERCISES FOR HORSE GUARDS, January 1860. Published in London; 303 pages, with many illustrations. Price, $1.00.

D3. LAWS RELATING TO THE NAVY AND MARINE CORPS, AND THE NAVY DEPARTMENT, July 1, 1865. 253 pages; size 6x8½ inches. Price, $1.00.

D4. MERCANTILE NAVY LIST AND MARITIME DIRECTORY FOR 1871. Published in London; 379 pages. Price, $1.00.

D5. DANGER, DISTRESS AND STORM SIGNAL CODES for the Signal Service Sea-Coast Stations and Mariners. 89 pages. Price, 70 cents.

D6. KRUPP AND DE BANGE, by E. Monthaye, Captain on the Belgian General Staff. Published in New York, 1888. Several full page charts showing guns and breech mechanisms. Price, $2.00.

Printed in 1814; 424 pages. Price, $2.00.

D11. MANUAL FOR THE MEDICAL DEPARTMENT U. S. ARMY, 1916. Corrected to April, 1917. 395 pages. Price, $1.20.

D12. HANDBOOK OF PRACTICAL TELEGRAPHY, by R. S. Culley, 1885. Fully illustrated with drawings of various instruments and connections. 442 pages. Price, $1.00.

D13. TABLES OF GUN PLOTTING PRACTICE, Navy Dept., 1891. 27 pages. Price, 40 cents.

U1-1. THE ATLANTIC COAST, the Navy in the Civil War, by Daniel Ammen, Rear Admiral, U. S. N., 1883. Size 5x7½ inches; 273 pages with index. Price, $2.00.

U1-2. BRITISH TEXT BOOK OF SMALL ARMS, 1904. Published in London. Size 6x8½ inches; 327 pages including appendices. Fully illustrated. Price, $3.50.

U1-3. NAVAL AND MILITARY TECHNICAL DICTIONARY OF THE FRENCH LANGUAGE, by Robert Burns, of Royal Arsenal, Woolwich, England, 1852. In two parts, French-English and English-French. Size 5x7½ inches; 320 pages. Price, $3.45.

U1-4. THE AMERICAN BATTLESHIP IN COMMISSION, as seen by an enlisted man. Includes many man-o'-war yarns. From library of U. S. S. Eagle. Size 5x7¼ inches; 248 pages. Many half tone illustrations. Published 1906. Price, 95 cents.

U1-5. THE BLOCKADE AND THE CRUISERS, by James R. Soley, Professor U. S. N.; dated 1883. Part one of The Navy in the Civil War. See U1-1. 257 pages with index; size 5x7½ inches. Price, $2.00.

U1-6. ALLOWANCES ESTABLISHED FOR VESSELS OF THE UNITED STATES NAVY, 1864. Issued by Navy Department. Shows outfits and equipment needed by the various departments of war vessels. Size 6x9 inches; 164 pages. Price, $1.50.

U1-7. THE SOLDIERS HANDBOOK, issued by the Secretary of War, 1905. Gives various information that a soldier should have, apart from drilling. Some headings are rank of officers, salutes, pay, army code, outlines of first aid, etc. Paper covered, size 4x6½ inches, 92 pages. Price 60 cents.

U1-8. WOMEN OF THE (CIVIL) WAR, Their Heroism and Self Sacrifice, by Frank Moore. Illustrated with steel engravings. Published in 1866. Size 6x9 inches; 596 pages. Price, $4.50.

U1-9. HISTORICAL SKETCH of the Organization, Administration, Material and Tactics of the Artillery, United States Army, by First Lieut. William E. Birkhimer, Third Regt. U. S. Artillery. Published 1884. Covers period from 1745 to 1884. Has appendix with list of all Artillery officers in different wars. Size 6x9 inches; 406 pages. Price, $5.50.

U1-10. ADJUTANT GENERAL'S REPORT OF STATE OF NEW YORK for Year 1861. Lists officers of the different regiments with rank, the equipment of the different regiments. Contains much valuable history of N. Y. State in the Civil War. Size 6x9 inches; 735 pages. Price, $4.50.

3264. A DIGEST OF OPINIONS OF THE JUDGE-ADVOCATES GENERAL OF THE ARMY, originally compiled by Col. W. Winthrop; revised by Major Charles McClure; published in 1901. Size 6¼x9¼ inches; 876 pages; sheepskin covers. Price, $2.50.

U1-11. ORDNANCE AND GUNNERY, prepared for the use of the cadets at the U. S. Military Academy, by Brevet-Col. J. G. Benton. Published 1875. Size 6x9 inches; 585 pages. Price, $4.80.

U1-12. ORGANIZATION AND TACTICS, by Major Arthur L. Wagner. Published 1901. Officially recommended from the headquarters of the Army to officers subject to examination for promotion. Size 6x8½ inches; 551 pages. Price, $2.00.

Edited by Charles K. Gardner of Major Gen. Brown's division. Published 1860. Size 5x8 inches; 640 pages. Price, $10.00.

U1-16. ORDNANCE INSTRUCTIONS FOR THE UNITED STATES NAVY, published in 1880. Fully illustrated. Size 6x9 inches; 511 pages. Price, $2.50.

U1-17. INSTRUCTIONS FOR NAVAL LIGHT ARTILLERY, Afloat and Ashore, prepared for the U. S. Naval Academy by Lt. Wm. H. Parker. Revised by Lt. S. B. Luce, U. S. N. Published 1862. Size 6x9 inches; 120 pages; many illustrations. Price, $1.50.

U1-18. TREATISE ON FORTIFICATIONS AND ARTILLERY, by Major Hector Straith, late major in Her Majesty's Army. Published in London, 1850. Chapters on Field Fortifications, Permanent Fortifications, Gunpowder, etc. Size 6x9 inches; 774 pages. Price, $4.50.

U1-19. A MANUAL OF NAVAL TACTICS, with Analysis of Modern Naval Battles, by Commander James H. Ward, U. S. N., with appendix from Sir Howard Douglas' "Naval Warfare with Steam." Published in 1859. Size 6x9 inches; 209 pages. Price, $2.00.

U1-20. THE MILITARY LAW OF THE STATE OF NEW YORK as Amended to Nov. 1, 1911. With Related Extracts from Other Statutes of the State. Size 5½x8 inches; 184 pages. Price, 75 cents.

U1-21. TEXT BOOK OF ORDNANCE AND GUNNERY, by Lt. Commander R. R. Ingersoll, U. S. N. Published 1894. Used by Naval Cadets. Many full page illustrations. Size 6x9½ inches; 265 pages. Price, $3.50.

U1-22. DER WELTKRIEG DEUTSCHE TRAUME, Roman von August Niemann. Written in German. Size 6x8½ inches; 386 pages. Price, $2.00.

D17. OBSERVATIONS ON MILITARY LAW AND THE CONSTITUTION AND PRACTICE OF COURTS MARTIAL, with summary of the Law of Evidence. By William C. De Hart, Captain U. S. Artillery. 1846. 433 pages. Price, $1.50.

U1-24. REPORT OF THE SECRETARY OF WAR, Volume III, being part of the Message and Documents communicated to the Two Houses of Congress at the beginning of the First Session of the 49th Congress. 689 pages; size 6x9 inches. Price, $2.50.

U1-25. A MILITARY, HISTORICAL AND EXPLANATORY DICTIONARY including the Warriors' Gazetteer of the places remarkable for Sieges or Battles. Written by Thomas Simes, Esq., and published in Philadelphia in 1766. Size, 5x8 inches. A Rare Military Book. Price, $7.00.

U1-26. REPORT OF THE CHIEF OF ORDNANCE to the Secretary of War for the year 1881. Many full page illustrations of equipment and war material. 560 pages; size 6x9 inches. Price, $3.50.

U1-27. REPORT OF CHIEF OF ORDNANCE FOR YEAR 1882. 541 pages. Price, $3.50.

U1-28. KAISER FRIEDRICH III, by Professor Dr. J. W. Otto Richter. Printed in German in Berlin. Many Illustrations of Royal Family and Battles. Size 8x11 inches; 338 pages. Price, $3.25.

U1-29. NOTES ON SEA-COAST DEFENSE, consisting of Sea-Coast Fortification, the Fifteen-Inch Gun, and Casemate Embrasures, by Major J. G. Barnard. Published 1861; size 6x9 inches; 110 pages. Price, 75 cents.

U1-30. REVERIES OR MEMOIRS CONCERNING WAR, by Maurice Count De Saxe, Marshal-General of the Armies of France. To which is annexed his Treatise Concerning Legions, or the Plan for New-Modelling of the French Armies. Illustrated with copper plates. Translated from the French. Published in Edinburgh, 1759. Price, $8.00.

U1-31. PROJECTILE WEAPONS OF WAR AND EXPLOSIVE COMPOUNDS, including some New Sources of Warfare, with special reference to Rifled Ordnance in their chief varieties. Shows Armstrong's Wrought Iron Breech-Loading Guns with shells and fuses. Published in London, 1859. Author, J. Scoffern, M. B. Size 5x7½ inches; 376 pages. Price, $3.00.

Section of the Great Steel Cable recovered from the wreck of the U. S. S. Maine, in Havana Harbor. "In April, 1898, there was landed at the ordnance dock, New York Navy Yard, from the Merritt Wrecking Compan's steamer Lone Star, a miscellaneous assortment of stores and material saved from the wreck of the U. S. S. Maine. All that was fit for further use, such as anchors, chains, guns, etc., was at once put in store for issue to other vessels. But there was one item in the cargo that puzzled the officials, viz., the steel wire cable which had been removed from the Maine, all snarled and twisted from the force of the explosion and the hurry of the wreckers. Even the man who has the privilege of gleaning anything of value from the refuse in the dump refused to take it. The officials of the yard, tired of seeing the old mass taking up valuable room, finally concluded to bury it in the old dump hole, and, with a force of men and horses, nearly a year after its arrival, it was thrown in, soon to be buried along with old refuse. Thereupon, one of our advertisers, F. Bannerman, wrote to Admiral Philip, suggesting that the old wire was worthy of better use; that in a dump hole it would cause trouble in future building operations: that the National Museum would be pleased to have some of it; that he would be glad to take it away at his own expense and present the Washington Museum with a suitable sample mounted for exhibition, and the balance made up into souvenirs, Admiral Philip sent the letter to the Navy Department at Washington, and they wisely agreed to accept this offer. To-day the National Museum has in the relic case of the U. S. S. Maine a piece of the cable. Museums have specimens, and our readers will see illustrations of the use the wire has been put to in our advertising columns; certainly a much better use than filling in low ground, affording as it does, something that every patriotic American will be proud to wear."---Army and Navy Journal, August 19, 1899.

Section is about 2 in. in diameter and about 5 in. in length, with polished brass band around the centre, engraved "Cable from the U. S. S. Maine." Price, $5.00.

U. S. Navy Cutter, in good order. Length, 21 feet; 6 foot beam. Suitable for naphtha engine. Price, $70.00. Can be seen by appointment at our Erie Basin storehouse.

**Battle Manila Bay Relics.**
U. S. Flagship Olympia.

10 Revolver Cartridge Boxes, stamped "U. S. N." Price, 50 cts. each.

41 Cutlass Frogs, leather, attached to the waist belt for holding cutlass scabbard. Price, 50 cents.

120 Revolver Holsters, for 38-calibre revolver, Price, 45 cents.

Ax Frogs, for holding axe attached to waist belt. Price, 35 cents.

1 Copper Adze, from magazine. Price, $5.00.

15 Fire Buckets, leather. Price, $2.50 each.

10 U. S. N. Battle Axes, showing wood handle worn very thin by constant scraping in cleaning. Price, $2.50 each.

Set Carpenter's Steel Boring Bits, fairly good order; 14 pieces, from ⅜ to 1⅝ in. Price, $2.50.

9 Miscellaneous Boring Bits, good, second-hand; relics. The lot, $1.25.

7½-inch Brass Elevating Wheel. Price, $1.00.

9-inch Brass Elevating Wheel. Price, $1.50.

Rubber Ponchos, with sailor's number stenciled on the back, second-hand, fair order only. Price, 50c. each.

1 Old Spanish Book, from Cavite, brought by sailor on the Olympia. Price, $5.00.

Piece of Olympia Log Line, 36 feet long, ⅜-in. diameter; cable laid rope, with fathom marks inserted; fine order. Price, $3.75.

Sheets of Band Music, no doubt used in celebrating the victory of May 1, 1898. Price, 50c. piece; $20.00 the full set; national airs.

7 Embroidered Curtains, from U. S. Flagship Olympia, removed from officers' staterooms at Boston Navy Yard on return of Admiral Dewey from Manila. Size, 22x26 in. Price, each, $5.00.

U. S. S. Olympia Knives and Forks, 6 silver-plated knives with U. S. N. in monogram on handle and 6 forks, assorted. Turned in to storekeeper at Boston Navy Yard from the Olympia on arrival after the battle of Manila Bay. These would have brought $25 each if they could have been obtained during the celebration over Admiral Dewey's return. We now offer the 12 pieces for $4.50. Rare relics.

Japanned Tray, 12x15, serviceable order, Price, $1.50.

Frying Pan, serviceable order. Price, 75c.

Relic of U. S. S. Maine, small bronze Tea Bell, which is composed of some of the bronze from the capstan of the U. S. S. Maine. See illustration of Capstan Certificate is given with each bell. Beautiful, useful souvenir relic. Price, $1 each; has silk red, white and blue ribbon, and on the handle is cast letters "Remember the Maine.

2 U. S. NAVY FOLDING BOATS, used a short time on Spanish War Torpedo boats, offered in good second-hand serviceable order, with oars, row-locks and rudder. Boat is made of hard wood frame covered with extra heavy canvas, with iron tightening braces. Illustration is taken from photograph. The size is 18 feet, 10 inches long; 6 foot beam, and shows the two parts joined together making the completed boat; size of each part when folded is 9 feet long by 12 inches wide by 3 feet 6 inches high. This style of boat was adopted for use on all the U. S. Navy Torpedo Boats, owing to limited deck space. Price, F.O.B. New York, $48.50 complete boat.

**Battle of Santiago Relics**

Propeller Wheel from Spanish launch; bronze metal, four blades; diameter 1¾ in., length from shaft to end of blade 14 in., useful relic, weighs about 50 pounds, in serviceable order. Price, $20.00.

Also 3 Blade Bronze Propeller Wheel, diameter of shaft ¾ inch, length of blade 15 inches, in fine order. Price, $20.00

Also Spanish Propeller Wheel, recovered from wrecked warship; 4 blade propeller wheel, bronze, one blade broken off, relic only, supposed to have been burnt with the ship and fallen into the hold; length from shaft to end of blade 16 inches, valuable for use to cast medals or souvenirs

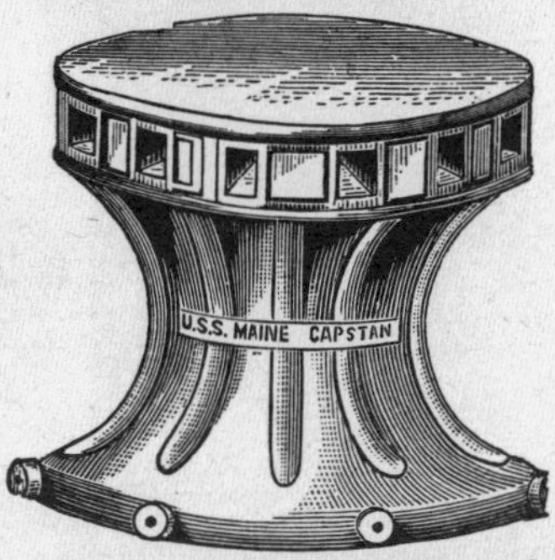


U. S. S. Maine Capstan; weighs 1,700 pounds brought to the New York Navy Yard, April 29, 1898; the top cover was reserved to be erected on the top of the monument for the Main dead at Arlington Cemetery; relic. Price, $2000.00.

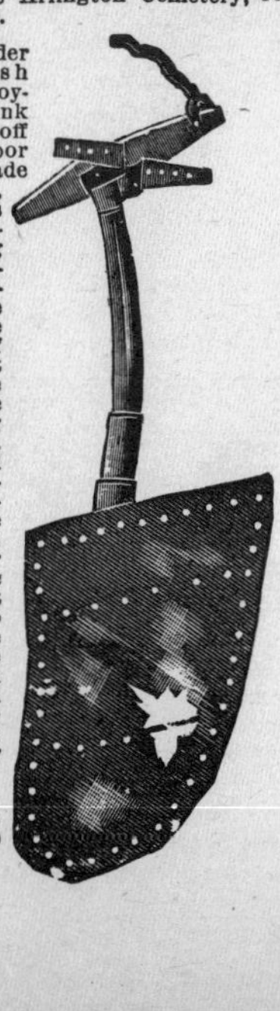

Brass Rudder From Spanish Torpedo Destroyer Furor, sunk fathoms deep off Santiago Harbor July 3, 1898. Blade shows shot hole, post is bent, thus disabling the vessel and confirming Commander Wainwright of the Gloucesters story of the battle: "We were within 600 yards of her and every shot appeared to strike * * * and now came the most exciting moment of the day. The Furor turned toward us. It appeared to be a crucial situation. She might succeed in torpedoing us, or she might escape up the harbor; but as she continued to circle it became evident that she was disabled, and her helm jammed hard over. Our fire had been too much for her." *Century Magazine.*

Length of rudder is 5½x2¼ feet wide weight, about 400 lbs. Price, $2000.00.

## THE UNITED STATES CORVETTE KEARSARGE.

Photographic Copy of the Log Book of the U. S. Sloop of War Kearsarge, on the 19th day of June 1864 when under the command of Captain John A. Winslow, off Cherbourg, France, engaged and defeated the famous Confederate Privateer Alabama, commanded by Captain Semmes. Size of the photo copy is 10½ x 6¼ inches. Gives the watches from 4 A. M. to 8 P. M. Tells how the Alabama began firing broadsides at 10:57 at 1,000 yards range; how the Kearsarge returned the fire at 11 A. M., and continued firing until 12, when the Alabama ceased firing and showed signs of distress, etc., etc. The story of a great naval battle very simply told. Price of copy, **$1.00.**

Steam Gauge, from wreck of U. S. Warship Kearsarge, serviceable order, **$18.00.**

Brass railing, 1½ inches in diameter, **$2.00** per foot.

Brass Stair Plate from wreck of U. S. Warship Kearsarge, **$7.00.**

10058. U. S. NAVY CANDLE-STICK. Entirely new, made of extra heavy blocked tin, brass adjuster, tin snuffer attached to the handle with brass chain, stamped bottom, diameter 6 inches, flared sides, 8½ inches across the top, 4 inches high, weight 1¼ pounds. Broad bottom to prevent tipping; 200 in stock. Worth $1.00 each, our bargain price, 30 cents each.

BRONZE BINNACLE, from Commodore Elbridge T. Gerry's Yacht Electra. Width of the bowl taken at the lamps is 18 inches; height 44 inches; in fine polished order, complete with glass. Price, $20.00.

BRONZE BELL U. S. NAVY GUNBOAT "MACHIAS," weighs 80 pounds, fine tone, complete with clapper. Engraved 1¼-inch letters, "U. S. S. MACHIAS, 1891." Price, $75.00.

U. S. S. KENTUCKY CAPSTAN, built with the ship, removed after few years' service for later improved model; heavy bronze top 35 inches in diameter; has the name "U. S. S. KENTUCKY" in 3-inch letters, while around the rim in 1-inch letters is the name of the builders, "Newport News Ship Building Co." Base, 44 inches; height, 35 inches. The hand spike holes are square shape, and are of heavy bronze. Weight of capstan, 3,500 lbs. We have two of these fine capstans, which are very suitable for out-door decoration in garden (or grounds) as tea table or ornament. All metal, nothing to wear out. Very appropriate for Kentucky home grounds. Our price is $375.00 each, one or both.

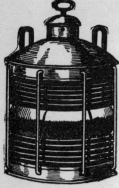

**27.**—Large White Light from U. S. S. Newark; polished brass, heavy ribbed glass, 26 inches high; 12 inches diameter; weight 40 pounds. Price, $25.00.

**27A.**—One Large White Light from U. S. S. Minneapolis. Price, $25.00.

**27B.**—Two Large Brass Lights, from U. S. S. Minneapolis, with heavy ribbed glass (broken); height 26 inches; weight, originally 40 pounds. Price, $15.00 each.

U 1-46. THE DEVELOPMENT OF ARMOR FOR NAVAL USE, as prepared by the U. S. Naval Institute, by Lieut. E. W. Very, U. S. N. We believe that he is the inventor of the famous Very Signal Pistol used for many years in the U. S. Navy. Size 6x9 inches, 591 pages. Price $1.50.

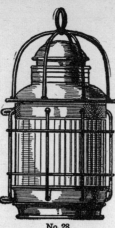

**No. 28**

**28.**—Large Mast Head Light; height 27 inches; diameter 13 inches; weight, 36 pounds; heavy ribbed glass, $25.00.

**28A.**—U. S. S. Mayflower Mast Head Light, from President's yacht; height, 23 inches; width 13 inches; weight 25 pounds. Price, $22.00.

**28B.**—Copper Mast Head Light from U. S. S. Buffalo; 20 inches high; 11 inches wide; weight 18 pounds. Price, $17.50.

**28C.**—Copper Light from U. S. S. Marcellus (Collier); height 21 inches; width 10 inches; weight 23 pounds. Price, $17.50.

**28D.**—Large Brass Mast Head Light from U. S. S. Iowa; 20 inches high; 12 inches diameter; weight, 24 pounds. Price, $25.00.

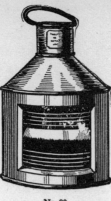

**No. 29. Pair of Side Lights,** white metal 21 inches high, 14 inches wide, weight 18 pounds each. Red and green color, heavy ribbed glass.

**29A. Pair of Copper Side Lights,** red and green, from U. S. S. Supply, height 24 inches, width 15 inches, weight 28 pounds each, price the pair $32.00.

**29B. Pair of Side Lights** from U. S. S. Columbia, white, length 18 inches, width 12 inches, weight 16 pounds each. Price, pair $30.00.

**29C. Pair of Red and Green Side Lights,** from Navy War ship, name not known, height 20 inches, width 13 inches, weight 18 pounds each. Price pair, $35.00.

P A R K E R ' S NAVAL HOWITZER ASHORE; illustrated; 25 folding plates; 64 pages; showing drill and maneuvers with Naval Howitzer; size 6 by 9 inches. Price $1.50; postage 9 cents.

"P A R K E R ' S NAVAL HOWITZER AFLOAT"; 75 pages; 6 by 9 inches; many illustrated pages; price $1.00; postage 7 cents.

"TABLE OF RANGES FOR ARMY AND NAVY CIVIL WAR CANNONS, with the method of finding the distance of an object at sea;" by Lt. W. P. Bucker, U. S. N.; 79 pages. Price $2.50.

10212. H A N D BOOK ON NAVAL GUNNERY; pocket size, by Radford; 260 pages; 5½x4x1 inches; numerous illustrations. Price, 85 cents.

**No. 30**

**30.**—Red Glass Lantern from U. S. S. Dixie; white composition metal; height 21 inches; diameter 10 inches; weight, 8 pounds. Price, $12.00.

**30A.**—Three Copper Lanterns, ruby red, from U. S. Navy warships, purchased at Navy Yard auction, on return of Navy battleships after the Spanish War; height 16 inches; diameter 12 inches; weight, 8 pounds. Price, $10.00 each.

Old time London Police Lantern with Horn Sides. Place for candle. The origin of the Lantern "Lamp Horn" afterward called Lantern.

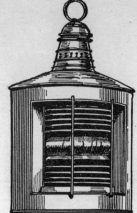

**No. 31**

**31.**—Pair of Side Lights, red and green, heavy ribbed colored glass; height 27 inches; diameter, 13 inches; weight, 24 pounds. Price pair, $35.00.

**31A.**—Pair of Side Lights, similar to No. 31, from U. S. S. Supply. Price, $30.00.

**31B.**—One Red Side Light from U. S. S. Dixie similar to No. 31. Price, $18.00.

**31C.**—Pair of Red and Green Side Lights, in size similar to No. 31; from U. S. Navy battleships; came to us unlabeled; name of ship not known; Price, $30.00 the pair.

U. S. A. Copper Air Compressor; diameter, 16 inches; length, 21 inches; with gauge; nickel plated. Price, $7.50.

ANTIQUE U. S. ARMY TIN LANTERN, from old U. S. Arsenal. Used with candle. Sold to western museum.

Old Time Lantern from Portsmouth Navy Yard, England. Fine relics.

**No. 26**

**26.**—Pair Old Brass Side Lights, red and green; from U. S. torpedo boat. Heavy colored ribbed glass; height, 16 inches; width, 11 inches; weight the pair, 20 pounds. Price, $22.00.

**26A.**—Pair of Side Lights, from U. S. S. Montgomery, white metal; height, 10 inches; width, 7 inches; weight the pair, 6 pounds. Price, $10.00.

**26B.**—One Copper Side Light, white from U. S. S. torpedo boat Cushing; height, 18 inches; width, 12 inches; weight, 15 pounds. Price, $12.00.

**26C.** — One Green Side Light, from U. S. S. Marcellus brass; weight, 15 pounds. Price, $10.00.

U. S. Navy Polished Copper Battle Lantern with Horn sides. Purchased from U. S. Navy Dept. as Battle Lantern; used on old-time Navy warships; has place for candle. Price, $12.00.

NAVY BRONZE SHIP BELLS, polished, weight 21 lbs., height over all 10½ in., diameter of mouth 9¾ in. All in fine order. Price, $12.50 each.

British Navy Antique Lantern; from the Portsmouth dockyard; relics. $2.50.

U. S. Navy Polished Copper Lantern, with Horn instead of Glass; very ancient; used with candle; from U. S. Navy Department Auction. Price, $4.50.

British Navy large size Bulls Eye Dark Lantern; relics. $4.50.

**1880.**—Old time U. S. Navy Copper Lamp, fitted inside for candle; size 11 by 8 inches; weight, 2¾ pounds.

**U. S. NAVY CARVED HEAD BOARD** removed from one of the Civil War Battleships at close of war. (Name unknown.) Artistic piece of wood carving, as well as valuable relic. At the same auction we purchased the head board of the historic old Hartford, which we sold to Mr. Harper, of Harper Bros., Publishers, for preservation in rooms of the Larchmont Yacht Club. Price for above head board, $250.00.

Steering Wheel from U. S. Navy ship "Supply." Used during Civil War carrying supplies to the ships on blockade duty. 6 feet high. Fine order. Walnut. Price, $20.

7-foot Walnut Wheel. Name of ship unknown. Price, $18.00.

**ADMIRALTY MANUAL** for the deviations of the compass; 218 pages; size 6x9 inches; red cloth binding. Price, 75 cents.

Weather Vane, made in China, before the war, for the old U. S. Frigate "Roanoke." $20.00.

Spanish War Steering Wheel. Walnut, bronze bushing. In fine order. From Navy auction after closing Spanish war. 3 ft .diameter. Fine order. Price, $12.50.

**SCOTCH HEAD BOARD** found on old wreck on island in Pacific Ocean. Small size indicates old time privateer, such as used by British Admirals Drake or Cook. Coat of Arms belongs to the Fleming family, ship merchants of Glasgow, Scotland, since 1643. *Let the deed show.* Rare old relic. Price, $100.00.

**U. S. NAVY GANGWAY HEAD BOARD.** Fine black walnut, artistically carved, as shown in the illustration, from one of the Civil War battleships. Name unknown. Nearly three inches thick, with polished brass band protecting the sides. Valuable relic. Price, $250.00.

Admiral Dewey's Navigator's Globe, from the U. S. Flagship Olympia; is in good, serviceable order. Now a famous relic, since it was used to navigate the ship in and to the Manila Bay battle; brass fittings. Price, $150.00.

U. S. Navy Boat Fenders, made of leather, cork filled, to hang over side for protection, all in serviceable order. 80 cents each.

Cross Tree from old Civil War ship, suitable for joining two parts of large flag pole. $10.00.

**U. S. NAVY CIVIL WAR SHOT PLUG.** Heavy iron plate covered with thick rubber to let down over the side of ship to plug up shot hole and prevent leaking. Valuable relic. 2 feet square. $10.00.

**CIVIL WAR BATTLE LOGS,** with cannon balls imbedded, cut from the battlefields of the South. Two balls in pine log. Price, $30.00.

One 8½ feet high with 6 12 Pounder spherical shot in it, fired at General Corse's Union Battery at Alatoona Pass when besieged by General French, C. S. A. It was at this battle that General Sherman sent the famous signal, "Hold the Fort for I am Coming." This is one of the best war logs that ever left the South. Price, $275.00.

**U. S. NAVY BATTLE GONG, for** calling men to quarters for battle; used on the old wooden warships. Obsolete with the introduction of steam. Rare old relic. Polished brass. $22.00.

Spanish Sword Decoration. Toledo Blade Swords, made up into shape of eight petal flower, same as can be seen in the Tower of London; 72 blade ends, 12 inches long, 8 in each leaf; fastened on board. Handsome relic. Price, $45.00.

United States Navy Yard, New-York. 1st March 1852

Received from SAMUEL P. TODD, Purser in the U. States Navy, One hundred ninety one Dollars fifty eight Cents, on account of my Pay, &c.

$191 58/100

receipts and are genuine. Disbursing officer obtained duplicate receipts, one for Navy Department, one for his own protection

John L. Worden, hero of the Monitor, Autograph.
Schooner Scorpion at Battle of Lake Erie, War of 1812, Frolic. Admiral Braine, first receipt as middy in 1840, jr. Commodore M. C. Perry, Theodore Dahlgren, War of 1812, T. A. M. Craven, who, in the Battle of Mobile Monitor Tecumseh, etc., etc. Confederate Army Officers' Pay Receipts, from

Autographs of Naval Officers Prominent in the Civil War. We have over 8,000 different autographs. Prices ranging from Commodore Hiram Paulding, as in above cut, signs for $191.58 on account of his pay, March 1, 1852. These signatures are attached to pay

Stephen Champlin, who commanded Commodore Jacob Jones, hero of Wasp— Admiral R. W. Meade, signed as Lawrence Kearney, hero of Bay, went down with his ship, the

$5.00

A

**THE YANKEE SOLDIER**

He's tough;
Enough to make his Mother sad—
Enough to make his Daddy mad,
And all the neighbors sure were glad,
When Johnny marched away.

He's rough;
Enough to get an awful "rep"
Enough to show a lot of "pep"
He didn't fail to fall in step—
When Johnny marched away.

His bluff;
Enough to bring him nicely through—
Enough to teach him what to do—
Enough to keep from getting blue,
When Johnny marched away.

"ENOUGH"
The word he wouldn't say
Until in his own Yankee way;
He put the German horde at bay;
John marched home to-day.

*F. Theodore Dexter.*

Civil War Paymaster's Safe, with duplicate records of property seized from the Confederates by Generals Banks and Butler at New Orleans during the Civil War. About 50 pounds of valuable papers, relics of the war. Packed in iron safe. Price, $500.00.

**U. S. Navy "Jacob's Ladder,"** made of heavy wire rope with iron rungs; make splendid fire escapes; coil up under window, ready to throw out. 25 to 30-foot lengths. Price, 35 cents foot.

**RUBBER LIFE PRESERVING SUITS.** Kind issued on board transports during the war. Will keep wearer dry and afloat for several days. Lined with fiber which has many times the sustaining power of cork. Have lead soles to keep wearer in upright position in water. We offer these suits almost new, packed for shipment at $12.00 each.

**U. S. Navy Sailor's Razor Combination Strop,** with screw tightening handle. Two sides for the different stages of honing. *The U. S. Navy always gets the best.* These fine new strops no doubt have cost upwards of $2.00 each. They were in with sale of lot of other goods. To sell off the lot we offer them at bargain price of 50 cents each. All new and perfect.

137v. **Pair of Antique leg Irons. In well preserved order, Unique fastening,** Price the pair, **$15.00.**

**U. S. NAVY LEG IRONS.** Kind used in Navy during the Civil War. Invented by Sergeant of Marines named Lillie, who died while in irons of his own invention during an attack of delirium tremens. Rare relics, only a few pairs left. No keys. $10.

**10971 PAIR BRITISH NAVY HAND-CUFFS,** with key (same pattern as our U. S. Civil War handcuffs, page 289); from Middlebrook Museum; history lost, probably famous relic; condition serviceable, but rusty. Price, $3.85.

**3210. CHICKAMAUGA BATTLE FIELD WAR LOG.** Pine log, with 12-pounder solid shot, two grape shot and a number of rifle bullets embedded. Log is 14 inches in diameter, 30 inches long. Part of a tree found in a creek near Col. Gordon's headquarters. Weight 68 pounds. Price, $25.00.

**IRON BODY GIRDLE,** once the property of Queen Victoria's father. Engraved H. R. H., Duke of Kent. Old fashioned Shackle used in olden times to confine prisoners. Rare Relic. From Edinburg collection. Price $25.00.

WE HAVE AN ASSORTED LOT OF UNSERVICEABLE NAVY IRONS FOR COLLECTORS, OFFERED AT OUR SELECTION AT $1.00 PER PAIR. (Allow postage on three pounds.)

**U. S. NAVY HAND AND LEG IRONS,** Tower patent, without key, with chains. Price $1.50 pair.

**Rare old London Handcuffs.** With Key, $6.00. Collection 12 different kinds of Shackles. As used at different periods in the U. S. Navy. Price. $50.00.

**THE MATTATUCK HAND AND LEG IRONS, NEW, WITH KEY. THIS STYLE HAS THREE LINK CHAIN.** These are a World War contract irons, and are not as well made as regular Navy irons. Price, $1.25 pair.

1322A. **40 Pairr Rankins Patent, U. S. Navy Leg Irons, with chains; no Keys.** Price $2.00 pair.    1322

PROCLAMATION
To The Inhabitants of Kentucky
Fellow Countrymen
I Have Kept my Promise

No Power on Earth Can Make Us Slaves

John H. Morgan

**1908. OLD U. S. NAVY LEG IRONS.** Palmer's patent. Price $2.50 per pair.

**BLAKESLEY'S PATENT POLICE NIPPERS.** With automatic spring opening and closing device. Great strength with little weight. Nickle plated like new. Bargain price, 90 cents.

**1703. 2 ANCIENT HANDCUFFS.** Look like hand-forged, with antique pattern key. Price for set of two pieces, with two keys, $15.00.

2202.

**2202. NAVAL ANCHOR DESK WEIGHTS.** Enameled iron stand with gilt anchor. Size 3¾x2 inches, ½ inch thick, length of the anchor 2½ inches. Handsome ornament for naval man's desk. Price, $4.75.

**3358A. CIVIL WAR U. S. MAGNETO ELECTRIC SIGNAL TELEGRAPH, No. 89.** Stamped 1859-1863. Contained in walnut case full brass bound, with handles and leather straps. Size 10½x12x14 inches, weighs upwards of 100 pounds. Upper part contains operating levers, bell, German silver face plate with alphabet and numerals up to 50. Side door opening to lower part, wherein are magnets, wire wound coils, bronze works, etc., all in order except directing handle needs brazing. No doubt used for telegraphing by the Union Army. Rare relic. Price, $50.00.

**3348. BRASS SEAL WITH WOOD HANDLE.** Used in making wax impressions U. S. A. Face size 1 inch, full length 4¼ inches. Present inscription can be removed and reinscribed as desired. Price, 45 cents.

**10129. U. S. N. HARNESS CASK.** Used on board ship for holding salt beef and pork for immediate use. Called harness cask, we presume, from the fact that the sailors call salt provisions "salt horse." Regulation ship equipment, polished oak staves with two inside compartments, with brass hinges, loops, etc. Height 31 inches, oblong base 27x34 inches, oblong top 22½x28 inches. Cost upwards of $25.00 to make. Our bargain price, $8.85.

10129

**3227. PROCLAMATION PASTER.** Pasted on panels of doors of houses and barns in Kentucky by order of Col. John H. Morgan, C. S. A., August, 1862. Panel is of Georgia pine, length 2 feet, width 14 inches. The price. $85.00.

PROCLAMATION.
**To the Inhabitants of Kentucky.**
Fellow Countrymen:—
**I HAVE KEPT MY PROMISE.**

At the head of my old companions in arms, I am once more amongst you, with God's blessing no more to leave you.

Deprived as you are by these Northern Despots of all true information respecting the War, you are probably unaware that our holy Southern Cause is everywhere in the ascendant.

The so-called "Young Napoleon," McClellan, has retreated from the Peninsula. Stonewall Jackson, the "invincible," is asserting the superiority of our Southern Banner against the armies of Pope, Banks, Fremont, Burnside and that of McClellan, who has joined them. His ultimate success is assured. NO POWER ON EARTH CAN MAKE US SLAVES.

Bragg in Tennessee is steadily advancing with an overwhelming force on Buel, who is retreating, whilst New Orleans is on the eve of being torn from the clutches of "Butler, the infamous," and restored to its legitimate and Confederate Government.

Kirby Smith, at the head of a powerful army, is already in your State, whilst Forrest, Woodward and myself have already proven to the Yankees our existence by taking Murfreesboro, Galatin and Clarksville, burning the railroad bridges and damaging seriously the enemy.

AROUSE KENTUCKIANS! shake off that listless feeling which was engendered by the presence of a powerful and relentless enemy. He is no longer to be feared! We have drawn his eye-teeth; there will soon be nothing left of him but his roar!

Let the old men of Kentucky, and our noble-hearted women, arm their sons and their lovers for the fight! Better death in our sacred cause, than a life of slavery!

Young men of Kentucky, flock to my standard. It will always wave in the path of honor, and history will relate how you responded to my appeal, and how, by so doing, you saved your country.                                    JOHN H. MORGAN,
August 22, 1862.    Col. Commanding Brigade, C. S. A.

**FAC-SIMILE COPY OF GENERAL ROBT. E. LEE'S FAREWELL ADDRESS TO HIS ARMY.** Dated Headquarters of Army, No. Va. 10th, April, 1865, with engraving of General Lee, printed on cardboard paper, suitable for framing. Size 10x16 inches. Price, 25 cents.

# Naval Bells, Binnacles, Compasses, Etc.

Bronze Bell from the Spanish Cruiser, "Christobal Colon." Valuable relic. Price, $1,000.

MILITARY INSTRUCTORS MANUAL. By Captain James P. Cole, 59th Infantry, Instructor 3rd Battalion, 17th Provisional Training Regiment, Plattsburg, N. Y., and Major Oliver Schoonmaker 76th Division, Assistant Instructor 3rd Battalion, 17th Provisional Training Regiment, Plattsburg, N. Y., 506 pages, 4¾ by 7½ inches, cloth bound, contains Infantry Drill Regulations, Physical Training, Use of Modern Arms, including army rifle, army pistol and machine guns. Map sketching, notes on army regulations, feeding men, personal hygiene, and first aid, signalling and other valuable chapters for those interested in work done at Plattsburg training camp. Price, postage paid in U. S., 75 cents.

of set of chimes.
8 inch face.....$7.50
8¼ "   " .....9.00
9¼ "   " .....13.00

Small Ship Bell, engraved "Pensiero Chiavari, 1868." Relic from wreck. $1.00.

Old Bronze Church Bell, made in Santa Roche, 1637. Relic only (cracked). Weighs about 40 pounds. Price, $150.

U. S. Navy Taffrail Log, for measuring speed of ship; polished brass; equal to new. $4.85 each. Assorted patterns.
U. S. Navy War Ship leather Fire Buckets. $1.50 each. Paper holder for military man's library.

Old Spanish Bronze Church Bell, stands 20 inches high, 20 inches across the mouth (cracked); relief ornamented with letters, "Fabrica de an Matanzas por Mrs. Caro de Menoz Maria Ano de 1834 Sito de Jesus;" fine old relic from Cuba after the Spanish War; handsome ornament; many of these old bells have been used as flower pots; weighs upward of 200 pounds. Price, $60.00.
U. S. Navy Iron Steering Wheel, 2⅓ feet diameter, Price, $4.50.

U. S. Navy Artificial Horizon, $5.00.

10-inch Dry Compass in fancy binnacle box; made by Fordsham & Keene, Liverpool, England. Requires glass and other minor repairs. From the Boston Navy Yard, June, 1900. Price, $15.00.

9-inch Azimuth Circle with Vernier Vanes. Prisms, in mahogany case. New, with brass hooks. Made by E. S. Ritchie, Boston, Mass. Price, $10.00.

Another one, same size, made by Blunt, used. Price, $8.00.

Steam Gauge, 10½-inch; made by American Steam Gauge Company; seems to be in order; from the Boston Navy Yard, June 8, 1900. Price, $7.50.

10-inch Compass from the United States Collier Alexander; made by Constantine, Pickering & Co., Middleboro; requires fresh alcohol to put in serviceable order. Price, $10.00.

U. S. Navy Life Saving Cork Ring, 29 inches outside diameter. Cork covered with canvas, with rope life line. From U. S. Navy Spanish War emergency ships. Canvas cover needs slight repairing. Price, $5.00.

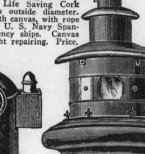

Pair Boat Compass Binnacles (from U. S. Navy auction). vouched for as having been used on the U. S. S. New Orleans. Brass, 11 in. high, 8 in. diameter (needs repairs), Relic of famous ship; fitted with electric light; will make handsome and appropriate ornament in "den" of some New Orleans man's home. Price, $20 pair.

Deep-sea Sounding Machine, with automatic registering machine. 225 fathoms. New. Price, $6.00.

Thompson Deep-sea Sounding Machine; in walnut case. Stands 2½ feet high by 15 inches wide; 2 feet long. Reel and wire; good, second-hand order. Price, $25.00.

7-inch Card Compass, made by Robert Merrill, New York. In box. Price, $5.00.

8½-inch Spirit Compass, made by Ritchie, Boston; seems to be in working order. Price, $10.00.

9½-inch Compass, made by Ritchie, Boston; turned in from United States Cruiser Raleigh, the ship that fired the first gun at the Battle Manila Bay. Glass is wrecked and needs repair. Price, $25.00.

11-inch Spirit Compass; made by Featherson, Dundee, Scotland; alcohol has leaked out and discolored the card; otherwise seems to be in good order. Price, $12.00.

U. S. Navy Brass Mounted Binnacle, used in old-time wooden warships; height, 5 feet.; made of polished rosewood. Bronze trimmed. Handsome ornament. Price, $90.00. Smaller size, $75.00.

Brass Gong from the engine room of the wrecked U. S. war ship "Trenton." Price, $35.00.
U. S. Navy Devils Claw, anchor hook. $3.00.
U. S. Navy Spectacle, iron hook used on sails. $2.00.
U. S. N. Sextant. Relic. $3.75.
U. S. N. Compass, made by Fordsham & Kerr, Liverpool, England; size, 10 inches; requires new glass and steps (slight repairs). Price, $20.00.
U. S. N. Boat Compass, 5-inch face; relic only; out of order. Price, $5.00.
U. S. N. Compass, made by Robt. Merrill, N. Y.; out of order. Price, $3.00.
Liquid Compass, made by Ritchie Bros. U. S. N., 10 inch; seems to be in order. Price, $5.00.
Tell-tale Compass; in order. $10.00.
Deep Sea Lead and Line, 74 lbs. of rope, $8.00.
Spanish war ship "Reine Mercedes" Double Sheaved Brass Pulley Block; removed after the Battle of Santiago. Price, $3.50.
U. S. Navy Ship Electric Signalling outfit; with lamps to hang in rigging; copper wire cable, switchboard, etc.; as is; needs repairs. Price, $50.00.

U. S. Navy polished bronze ship bells, weight 21 lbs., height overall 10½ inches, diameter of mouth 9¾ inches. Special price, $12.50 each.

Old U. S. Navy War Ship Constellation.s Binnacle and Compass, Polished walnut frame, brass bound: glass set in brass frame. We believe this is the original binnacle that was on board this famous old war ship during the historic battles. Sold to Valley Forge Museum.

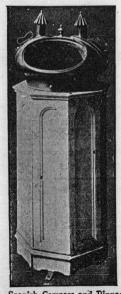

Spanish Compass and Binnacle from the Pedro, Philippine Islands, brought by the Olympia to the Boston Navy Yard. In fine, serviceable order, complete with binnacle and lamps. Price, $75.00.

# ARMY AND NAVY GOODS

Commander Peary on each and every trip obtained from us his outfit of guns, swords, etc., for rewarding and trading with the Native Esquimos, also the Pemmican, and other Arctic Stores we purchased at the U. S. Navy Department Auction, on the return of Greeley Relief Expedition.

**10078. U. S. N. BUOY SIGNAL TORCH.** Copper flask, 7 inches long, 2½ inch diameter, 3½ inch torch holder, spring clips at the base, wt., 1 pound. Price, $1.85.

**10067. U. S. NAVY BRASS DECK LANTERN.** Opening top, detachable lock clasp fastened bottom, six upright brass wire guards, two round guards; burns signal oil. Lantern is similar to the kind carried by train conductors; used on navy warships. Offered in serviceable order, weight, 3 pounds 6 ounces.

**D10.** SYSTEM OF THEORETICAL AND PRACTICAL CHEMISTRY, by Frederick Accum. Printed in 1814; 424 pages. Price, $2.00.

**D7.** ELDRIDGE'S COAST PILOT No. 2, Chatham, Mass., to the Rio Grande. Gives all sailing directions between these two points; 536 pages. Price, $1.50.

**D8.** PORT REGULATIONS IN FOREIGN COUNTRIES. Reports from the Consuls of the United States. Printed in Washington, D. C., 1891. 732 pages, paper cover. Price. 60 cents.

**10095. BASE BALL CATCHER'S MASK.** Used U. S. N. teams, spring steel guards, tan leather straps, hair filled pads, Spaulding's make; offered in serviceable second hand order. Price, 50 cents.

**10020. SIREN-TORPEDO WHISTLE.** Gives loud shrill sound like the signal of the torpedo boat. Price, 85 cents.

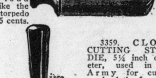

**3079. COMMANDER PEARY'S ARCTIC SLEIGH,** wood and iron, cross bars fastened with rawhide thongs. Used by Peary on Expedition previous to his discovery of the North Pole. Length is 11½ feet, width 3 feet, height 1 foot. In used, serviceable order. Sold to VALLEY FORGE MUSEUM.

**3359. CLOTH CUTTING STEEL DIE,** 5¼ inch diameter, used in the Army for cutting wool cloth for powder bags. Steel knife is in sectional parts, easily detachable, hammer head handle. Price, $5.00.
**3359A. SIMILAR DIE,** 3⅞ inch diameter. Price, $4.00.

**10012. CHAIN KEY RING WITH SNAP HOOK.** Nickel plated. Price, 18 cents.
**10150.** SET 49 STATE BUTTONS. In fine gilt and bronze, mounted on card with name of state under each button. This new up-to-date set supersedes the old set advertised on page 187. Price for the new set, 49 buttons including Oklahoma button, $2.50.

**3357. U. S. NAVY ELECTRIC BATTERY,** for raising and lowering Boats on Warships. Mahogany case, double folding covers with brass hinges and locking bolts. Stands on 4 small brass studs. Box contains 4 white rubber jars, metal lined with brass connecting screws, size of box 8 inches square. Price, $4.85.

**10092. NOSE MASKS.** Rubber, from U. S. N. Gymnasium, Morrills patent; used, offered in serviceable order. Price, 75 cents each.

**10093. RUGBY FOOT BALLS,** U. S. N. Used in U. S. N. gymnasium; offered in serviceable order, with new bladder finest quality heavy tan leather. Price, $2.50.

**10091. U. S. N. MASK FOR USE IN BROAD SWORD FENCING.** Strong steel guards with head, cheek and chin piece, hair filled pads; must have cost over $8.00 each to make; for all practical purposes, as good as new. Bargain price, $2.45 each.

**10071. U. S. NAVY STEEL SCRAPER.** New steel, sharpened ready for use. Can be used held in the hand, or attached to handle, fastened with screw nut; 4 inch diameter, ¼ inch thick. Price, 45 cents each.

**U. S. ARMY SIGNAL CORPS PORTABLE FIELD TELEPHONE.** Walnut box with leather shoulder sling strap, with magnet bells, one piece mouth and ear receiver and transmitter. Size of box, 11x7x7¼ inches. Brass round corners, hinges and catches. In repaired serviceable order. Made by Lambert & Schmidt, Weehawken, N. J. Handy outfit for connecting camp with town. Electrician says good for 25 miles. Price, $16.50.

**10058. U. S. NAVY CANDLE STICK.** Entirely new, made of extra heavy blocked tin, brass adjuster, tin snuffer attached to the handle with brass chain, stamped bottom, diameter 6 inches, flared sides, 8½ inches across the top, 4 inches high, weight 1¼ pounds. Broad bottom to prevent tipping; 200 in stock. Worth, $1.00 each, our bargain price, 30 cents each.

**3301. U. S. A. FIELD DESK.** Used by Military Officers to hold books and papers while on the march and in the field. Length 32 inches, 19 inches wide, 19 inches high. Three drawers with compartment for holding the folding iron stand. With corner irons, rope handles with brass padlock. Offered in used, serviceable order. Price, $9.85.
**3301A.** Similar desk without the folding iron stand. Offered with 2 folding camp stools which will serve as stand, also as seat. Price, $8.85.

**10066. U. S. NAVY BOAT SIGNAL BRASS LANTERNS.** With glass bull's eye reflector, ventilated top, carrying handle, with adjustment for fastening to the belt, burns signal oil, weight, 2 pounds; used on U. S. Navy warships; some are engraved (boat signal); offered in used serviceable order. Price, $3.85.

---

**POEM ON PEARY'S SLEIGH THAT REACHED THE POLE**

Rude thing of wood and iron with sinew lashed,
O'er arctic pressure ridges rudely dashed;
Most famous vehicle in all the world;
One triumph sledge of all those northward hurled
Through long processions of the centuries;
Type of the alert and supple energies
That won where force and mighty ships had failed;
Though light and yielding, firm as if stout-mailed;
Keen, lithe, and like the wind that sought the goal.
Sure as a thought projected at the pole.
*Walter F. Longacre.*

**3098. COMMANDER PEARY'S ARCTIC ICE SAW,** used sawing passage for ship through the ice on expedition previous to discovery of the North Pole. Length, 18 feet; width, 6 inches; teeth, 2¾ inches. A Museum exhibit. Price, $15.00.

**U. S. NAVY BATTLESHIP ELECTRIC DECK LAMP.** With 18 feet of flexible ⅝-inch cable, white metal lamp, safety bars and rings, 12 inches long, 6 inches in diameter, 16 candle power, with electric bulb, with large glass protector, with handle and rings. Appears to be in serviceable order. Price, $5.85.

**10728. GARDEN PARTY LAMPS.** In assorted colors, red, blue, white, opal and turquoise. Bucket-shaped with five-hour candles. Part of the lot made for use in London at the coronation of King George V. Lamps are 3½ inches in depth, 2¾ inches in diameter. Ribbed reflecting squares, brass wire for attaching to small chain or wire. Gives beautiful effect hung between trees. The candles are made of fine hard wax, with high melting point that will burn for about five hours. We offer the lamps in sets of one dozen assorted colors, with two candles for each lamp, at $3.00 per dozen lamps.

**SPANISH WAR BATTLE RELIC.** Electric signaling device. Used on board navy battleships for sending battle orders to the different stations. Size is 10 inches in diameter, 4 inches high. Purchased at Brooklyn Navy Yard auction on the return of the warships after the Spanish War. No doubt used on board the U. S. Navy ships at battle of Santiago and Manila Bay. Price, $5.85.

**10552. BRITISH ARMY BULL'S EYE LANTERN** with metal hook for attaching to the waist belt with carrying handle, with bulls eye reflector, with adjustable shutter with hole in the bottom for fastening on pole. Used, serviceable order. Price, $2.85.

**10190. BRITISH ARMY SOLDIERS IRON BREAST PLATE,** old rusty; period of 1760. Price $20.00.

**10467. YOUNG ZULU WARRIOR'S HIDE SHIELD,** with Assegai; length 17x10 inches. Price, $7.85.

**FLAG COVERS,** rubber, new. 50 cents.

**FLAG MARKER GUIDON COVERS,** rubber, new. 50 cents.

WE HAVE AN ASSORTED LOT OF UNSERVICEABLE NAVY IRONS FOR COLLECTORS, OFFERED AT OUR SELECTION AT 50 CENTS PER PAIR. (Allow postage on three pounds.)

**C16. GRAY METAL HELMET TOPS,** captured by American troops at Coblenz Arsenal from the Germans. These are new and were intended to ornament the helmets of the troops who expected to march through the Arc de Triomphe in Paris some day. An interesting souvenir of the war. Price, 25 cents each.

**1809. British Army Folding Ambulance Litter.** Heavy brown canvas, hard wood frame, side handles which fold underneath when not in use. Three-inch brass wheels for saving jar carrying incidental to shifting. Used serviceable order. Price, $4.85.

**10192. PAIR OF INDIA HEAVY IRON FIGHTING SHIELDS,** 11 inches in diameter complete, with arm straps, and pads. Copper disk center. Arm strap attached with ornamental copper rivets. SHIELD IS COVERED WITH SWORD CUTS. Price $15.00 each.

These Grape Shot were fired Sep 8, 1855 at the REDAN

**10967. PAIR CRIMEAN WAR GRAPE SHOT RELICS.** Miniature marble stands 5 inches, each mounted with three grape shot. Sculptured letters stating these grape shot were fired September 8th, 1855 at the MALIKOFF. The other marble stand is mounted with three grape shot is marked fired September 8th, 1855, at the REDAN. Price the PAIR $8.85.

**U4-2. TEXT BOOK OF ORDNANCE AND GUNNERY, 1884.** Prepared for the use of the Cadets at the Naval Academy. Illustrated with many full page drawings and large charts. Chapters on Explosives, Torpedoes, Machine Guns, etc. Size 6x9 inches, 218 pages. Price, $1.50.

**10944A. PIPE BERTHS FROM IRISH RACING YACHT** Shamrock, which Sir Thomas Lipton raced for the America Cup. Made of STRONG EXTRA LIGHT galvanized tubing, filed joints to reduce the weight. Price $2.00 each.

**BOOK ON GERMAN MAUSER ARMY RIFLE.** A twenty page booklet, profusely illustrated, on the most interesting and best known rifle of the war, "The German Mauser." A detailed description of the gun, showing its many attachments and thirty-eight bayonets. EVERY VETERAN OF THE WORLD WAR WILL WANT A COPY OF THIS BOOK. Price 45 cents.

Chiswick, London.
March 11, 1926.

Sirs:—

I have to thank you for your letter and the catalog. I take this opportunity of saying that I think the list a most remarkable production and of the greatest interest. The vast number of weapons so faithfully reproduced in the illustrations, reflect a most marvelous credit upon yourselves, for the patience, knowledge and experience in listing so many pieces besides collecting them.

Yours very truly,
S. FLADGATE.

**10944. U. S. NAVY WARSHIP SIGNAL LIGHT LENSES,** Fresnel ribbed glass; ruby red; length 5¾ inches, diameter 5½ inches, ½-inch thick; new, obsolete on the adoption of the electric lamps. 79 in red, price $1.50 each; 125 in green, price $1.25 each.

Sketch by Artist Luke Sullivan, at time of his death some years ago, the oldest member of London Society of Artists. Sketch is in ink, size about 6 inches square and represents King of Prussia's ancient soldier with spade bayonet. Price $10.00.

**MILITARY INSTRUCTORS MANUAL.** By Captain James P. Cole, 59th Infantry, Instructor 3rd Battalion, 17th Provisional Training Regiment, Plattsburg, N. Y., and Major Oliver Schoonmaker 76th Division, Assistant Instructor 3rd Battalion, 17th Provisional Training Regiment, Plattsburg, N. Y., 506 pages, 4¾ inches, by 7½ inches, cloth bound contains Infantry Drill Regulations, Physical Training, Use of Modern Arms, including the army rifles, the army pistol and machine guns. Map Sketching, notes on army regulations, feeding men, personal hygiene, and first aid, signalling, and other valuable chapters for those interested in work done at Plattsburg training camp. Price, postage paid in U. S., 75 cents.

**10191. ORIENTAL BODY ARMOR,** 12-inch circular breast plate with 3 inch bottom and side plates attached to the circular body plate with link chains. Has MAKER'S SEAL. Stamped circular plate has raised center with fluted rays. Old and rusty. Used by Dudley Hardy the British painter. Rare, price $30.00.

**D14. NEAR VISION TEST TYPES, MEDICAL DEPT. U. S. ARMY.** Three folded parts used in testing eye sight. Length open 16½ inches. Price, 25 cents.

**D15. TREATISE ON FIELD FORTIFICATION,** including Intrenchments, Attack, Defense and Permanent Fortifications. By. D. H. Mahan, Professor at West Point. Printed in 1864. 168 pages. Price, $1.00.

**D16. AMERICAN TELEGRAPHY:** Systems, Apparatus, Operation. By William Maver, Jr., 1898. 563 pages, fully illustrated. Price, $1.50.

**D17. OBSERVATIONS ON MILITARY LAW AND THE CONSTITUTION AND PRACTICE OF COURTS MARTIAL,** with summary of the Law of Evidence. By William C. De Hart, Captain U. S. Artillery. 1846. 433 pages. Price, $1.50.

**D18. REGULATIONS FOR THE ARMY OF THE UNITED STATES.** 1857. 457 pages, with appendix. Price, $1.00.

**D19. HUMAN PHYSIOLOGY, STATICAL AND DYNAMICAL,** or the Conditions and Course of the Life of Man. By John William Draper, M. D., LL. D. 1856. 649 pages. Price, $2.00.

**D20. MEDICAL LEXICON OF MEDICAL SCIENCE** with a vocabulary of Synonyms in Different Languages. By Robley Dunglison, M. D., M. A. P. S. 1839. 821 pages, size 6x9½ inches. Price, $2.00.

**D21. THE AMERICAN CHEMIST,** July 1870 to June 1871. 478 pages. Price, $1.25.

**D22. COMPANY SICK REPORT.** Book contains printed forms for daily reports of sickness in Company and Regiment. Price, 50 cents.

**D22. EXPERIMENTAL RESEARCHES IN STEAM ENGINEERING.** By Chief Engineer B. F. Isherwood, U. S. Navy. 1863. Many full page charts and drawings. 355 pages, size 9½x12 inches. Price, $1.50.

**D23. REPORTS OF EXPERIMENTS ON THE STRENGTH AND OTHER PROPERTIES OF METALS FOR CANNON.** By Officer of the Ordnance Dept., U. S. Army. 1856. 428 pages, size 9½x12½ inches. Many full page drawings. Price, $1.00.

**ADMIRALTY MANUAL** for the deviations of the compass; 218 pages; size 6x9 inches; red cloth binding. Price, 75 cents.

**GUNNERY DRILL BOOK,** for U. S. Navy, 1893; 98 pages; size 5x7½ inches. Price, $1.00.

**U. S. N. INSTRUCTIONS FOR INFANTRY AND ARTILLERY,** 1890; 750 pages; 6x9 inches; red leather binding. Price, $1.00.

**DISTANCE AND BEARING** tables for the assistance of the navigator; 33 pages; 6x9 inches. Price, 25 cents.

**80 VOLUMES DECISIONS OF THE TREASURY,** relating to the customs and other laws; from 850 to 1,200 pages; average size 5 inches wide, 7 inches long; for the following years: 1875, 1877 to 1886 inclusive, 1888, 1890 to 1892 inclusive, 1894, 1896 to 1899 inclusive, 1901; choice of years. $1.00 each.

**10212. HAND BOOK ON NAVAL GUNNERY,** pocket size, by Radford; 260 pages; 5½x4x1 inches; numerous illustrations. Price, 85 cents.

PLEASE NOTE THAT WE DO NOT PAY POSTAGE. MAKE ALLOWANCE FOR THIS IN YOUR REMITTANCE. WE DELIVER TO EXPRESS OFFICE FREE.

**MANUAL OF MILITARY FIELD ENGINEERING.** Sixth Edition, by Major Wm. D. Beach, U. S. A. 288 pages. Fully illustrated. Use of Cordage and Spars, Bridges, Telegraph, Railroads, Camping, Etc. Size 7x5¼ inches. Price, 75 cents.

**U. S. NAVY SMALL ARMS INSTRUCTIONS,** 1907. Pocket size, 6x4 inches. 513 pages, fully illustrated. Flexible leather covers, with envelope flap. Contains everything that man should know about warships and guns, to become a first-class man-o'-warsman. Military Drill, Target Practice, Landing-Force, Artillery Drill, First Aid to Wounded, Scouting, Camping, Etc., Etc. Valuable book to every out-doors man. Published at Nav l Institute, Annapolis, Md., under direction of Navy Department. Price, 50 cents.

**10214. SET TEN NAVAL MANUALS,** from 1900 to 1909; numerous illustrations; 450 pages each volume; size 10x7x1⅝ inches. Price, the ten books, $6.50.

**10214. 2 SETS, FROM 1901 TO 1909;** nine books, $5.50.

**10214A.**
1 volume, two sets, 1903 to 1904.
3 sets 1905.
2 sets 1906.
6 sets 1907.
2 sets 1908. Price, 50 cents each volume.

**10215. SIXTEEN VOLUMES OF GOSPEL HYMNS;** 1, 2, 3, 4, with music; size 8x5½ inches; used by crews of U. S. Navy battle ships; serviceable relics. Complete set of 16 books for $2.00.

**10216. GOSPEL HYMN BOOKS,** pocket size; 1, 2, 3, 4, words only; size 5x3½ inches; 304 pages; used on naval war ships. 30 volumes for $2.50.

**10217. BOOK OF COMMON PRAYER WITH PSALMS,** used divine service on board U. S. Navy warships; size 5½x4 inches. 12 volumes for $1.50.

**2207.** "Manual of Naval Tactics," by Commander H. J. Ward, U. S. N., 1859 to 1869; 208 pages, size 6 by 9 inches; illustrated; contains critical analysis and description of the famous battles of Trafalgar, Nile, Perry's Victory on Lake Erie, and others. Price $1.00.

**MILITIA MEDICAL EQUIPMENT.** Hard Rubber Bottles, one pint, 20 cents each.

20 Blue Webb Belts, for Hospital Corps privates, 45 cents each.

1 Civil War Pattern Medicine Case, leather covered case about 1 ft. x 6 ft. x 7 in., containing medicine bottles with compartments for drugs, etc. Price, $25.00.

2 Hospital Corps Knapsacks, old pattern, State Militia, with outfit. $10.00 each.

29 Hypodermic Syringes, pocket set (incomplete). Price 75 cents the set.

**SAILING DIRECTIONS** for the Gulf and River of St. Lawrence, with chart; 372 pages; 6x9 inches; cloth binding. Price, $1.00.

**SYSTEM OF ACCOUNTABILITY, U. S. MARINE CORPS,** 1911. Selection of Arms, Equipment, Purchases, Rations, Transportation, Recruiting, Selection of Horses, Pitching Tents, Care of Furniture, Etc., Etc. Useful book. Size 9½x6 inches; 146 pages. Price, $1.00.

**FORMS OF PROCEDURE FOR NAVAL COURTS AND BOARDS,** 1902. By Lauchheimer. 302 pages; 9x6 inches. Price, 75 cents.

**GOVERNMENT SALARY TABLES,** 1904. Prepared by the U. S. Treasury Dept. for use of U. S. Paymaster. Cloth bound; size 9x6 inches; 273 pages. Price, 75 cents.

**INTIMATE GLIMPSES OF AMERICAN GENERALS OF INDUSTRY.**
No. 48. Mr. Bannerman, the military outfitter, goes to camp with his regiment.

From "LIFE," Oct. 26, 1922.
Reproduced by permission Life Pub. Co., N. Y. City.

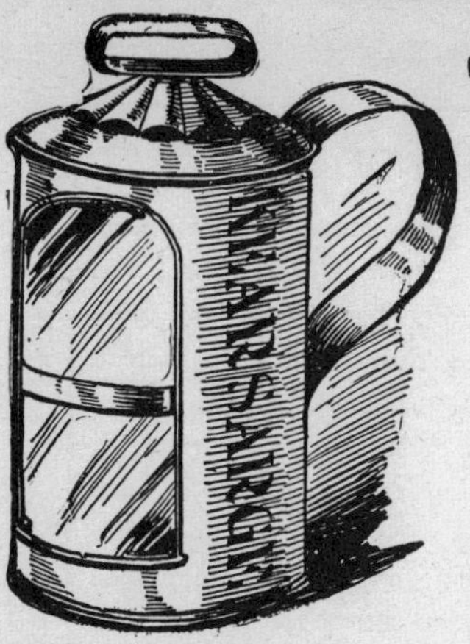


2240

No. 2240, U. S. N. Kearsarge Battle Lantern; from Portsmouth Navy Yard sale after the return of the Kearsage from the famous battle with the Confederate Cruiser "Alabama." The lantern is of copper, with Horn light; length 14 inches; diameter 6¼ inches; weight 6¾ pounds. We believe this lantern to have been used in the magazine of the Kearsarge in the battle with the Alabama. It came to us from the Navy Yard, with the name of the ship stenciled on the side, as per the above illustration;(such marking is prohibited by naval regulation) price $75.00.

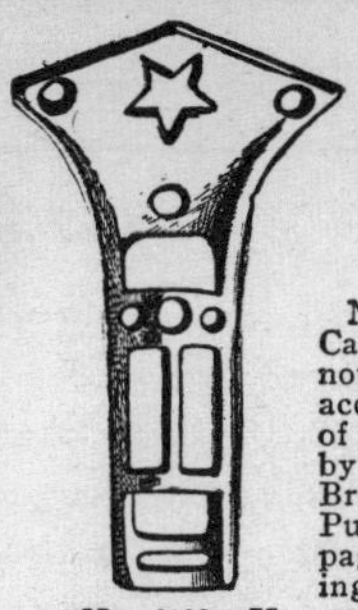

No. 2182. U. S. Army Cast Metal Flag Pole Holder; width of base 4¾ inches; length 10 inches; inch for 1¼ made flag pole; 3 holes for fastening; new offered as are; price 18 cents each.

No. 2406. Brass Sun Dial; 3 inches in diameter; marked 2¼ inches; with eighth hour marks from 4 a. m. to 8 p. m.; with motto "Early to rise"; price $5.00.

No. U 1-59. An Essay on Shooting. Containing the various methods of forging, boring, dressing gun barrels used in France, Spain and England. Recoil, powders, bore, range, shot, wads, etc. Printed in London in 1791. 313 pages, size 5x8½ inches. Price $5.00.

No. U 1-60. Siege Artillery in the Campaigns Against Richmond, with notes on the 15-inch gun, illustrated by accurate drawings of a large collection of the rifle projectiles and fuzes used by each army in Virginia, by Bvt. Brig. Gen. Henry L. Abbot, U. S. A. Published in 1868. Size 6x9 inches, 183 pages, also six large plates of drawings. Price $3.00.

No. U 1-61. Annual Reports of the War Department for Fiscal Year Ended June 1901. Report by Chief of Ordnance, U. S. A. Many full page photographs and drawings. Covers all work and experiments made and conducted by the U. S. Army. Size 6x9 inches, 804 pages. Price $6.00.

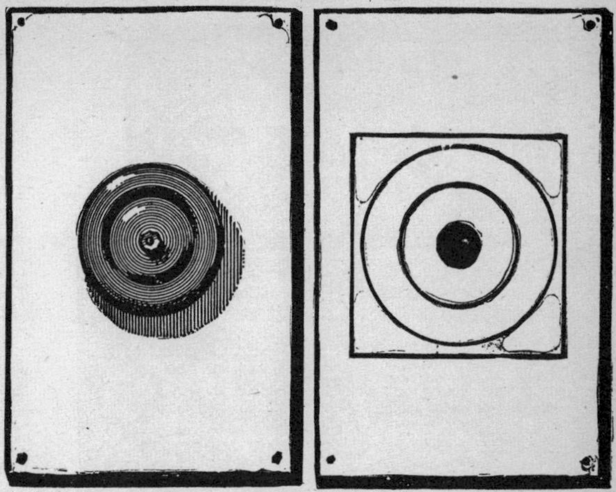

U. S. Army Iron Target Plates; complete with 8 inch bell, which rings when bullet strikes the center; illustration shows front and rear views; plates are ⅝ inch thick; 30 inches high; 20 inches wide; weight about 100 pounds; practically new; size of the bull's eye square is 6 in. by 7 in. Also some with the bull's eye square size 9x10, and 12x14; your choice of the three sizes; 75 in stock; $3.25 each.

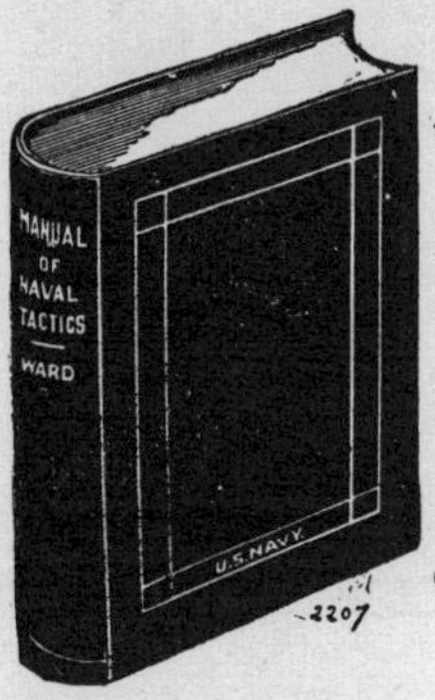


Now Infantry Drill Regulations with 150 interpretations, authority War Dept. 1904. 285 pages 5½ x4½ inches. Price, 75 cents.

No. 2207. "Manual of Naval Tactics," by Commander H. J. Ward, U. S. N., 1859 to 1869; 208 pages, size 6 by 9 inches; illustrated; contains critical analysis and description of the famous battles of Trafalgar, Nile, Perry's Victory on Lake Erie, and others; price $1.

No. 2208. "Scott's U. S. A. Infantry Tactics;" in three volumes; pocket size, 3½ by 5½ inches; 200 pages each volume; illustrated plates; weapons, drill regulation, evolution, Military music, etc.; price $5.00 the set; old volumes, No. 1, $1.50 each.

"Letters on Artillery," by Prince Kraft Zu Hohenlohe Ingelfingen, translated by N. L. Walford, R. A. A complete and interesting story of the use and results of the Field Artillery in the Wars of 1866 and 1870, with full accounts of the battles; 6 folding plates and plans of battle fields; 427 pages; size 5 by 7 inches; price $1.25; postage 12 cents extra.

"Captain Mordecai, Ordnance Department, U. S. A.," Experiments on Gun Powder at Washington Arsenal 1843 to 1844; 328 pages; size 6 by 9 inches; contains number of plates; price $1.00; postage 10 cents.

"Ballistics," by J. L. Meigs and R. R. Ingersol, U. S. N.; prepared for use of Cadets at the U. S. Navy Academy at Annapolis; 129 pages; size 6 by 9 inches; price 75 cents; postage 7 cents.

Parker's Naval Howitzer Ashore; illustrated; 25 folding plates; 64 pages; showing drill and manouevers with Naval Howitzer; size 6 by 9 inches; price $1.50; postage 9 cents.

"Parker's Naval Howitzer Afloat"; 75 pages; 6 by 9 inches; many illustrated pages; price $1.00; postage 7 cents.

"Table of Ranges for Army and Navy Civil War Cannons, with the method of finding the distance of an object at sea"; by Lt. W. P. Bucker, U. S. N.; 79 pages; price $2.50.

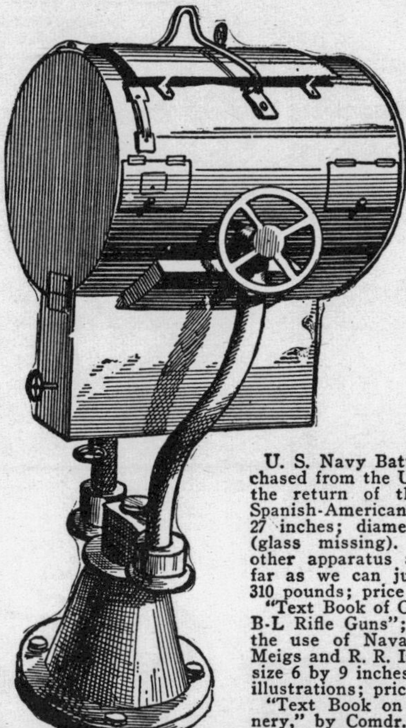

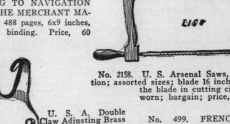

U. S. Navy Battle Ship Search Light; purchased from the U. S. Navy Department after the return of the Battle Ships after the Spanish-American War; height 5 feet; depth 27 inches; diameter of the light 21 inches (glass missing). The electrical wire and other apparatus appears to be complete as far as we can judge; offered as is; weight 310 pounds; price $50.00.

"Text Book of Ordnance and Gunnery Navy B-L Rifle Guns"; prepared and arranged for the use of Naval Cadets by Lieuts. J. L. Meigs and R. R. Ingersol, U. S. N.; 262 pages; size 6 by 9 inches, with numerous plates and illustrations; price $2.50; postage 17 cents.

"Text Book on Naval Ordnance and Gunnery," by Comdr. A. P. Cooke, U. S. N.; 687 pages, with 128 pages of appendix; total 815 pages; gives detail of the manufacture of cannon, explosives, ordnance, etc.; size 6 by 9 inches; price, $4.80; postage, 35 cents.

"Submarine Mines," by Major R. H. Stotherd, R. E.; 318 pages; 6 by 9 inches; with numerous illustrations; price $1.50; postage 12 cents.

"Manual of Artillery Exercises"; English Horse Guards, 1860; 303 pages; 5½x8½ inches; price $1.50; postage 9 cents.

"The Fleet Drill Book," containing also the Tactical signals for the manouevering of vessels; 116 pages; size 6x9 inches; price $1.50; postage 7 cents.

No. U 1-40. The Artillerist's Manual and British Soldier's Compendium, by Major F. A. Griffiths, R. F. P. Royal Artillery. Published in London, in 1856. Illustrated with many full page plates. Has chapters on Carbine Exercises, Ordnance, Ranges, Gunnery, etc. Size 4x6½ inches, 345 pages. Price $1.50.

U 1-41. Manual of Military Law, Official Copy as Issued by British War Office in 1899, in London. 1024 pages, size 5x7½ inches. Price $2.00.

No. U 1-43. The Political and Military History of the Campaign of Waterloo, translated from the French of General Baron De Jomini, by S. V. Benet, U. S. Ordnance. Published in New York in 1854. Size 5x7½ inches. 227 pages. Price $1.25.

No. 400. ELEMENTARY NAVAL ORDNANCE AND GUNNERY. Includes Close-order Infantry with 1918 Drill Regulations. By Lt. M. C. Ramsey, in charge of Naval Ordnance and Gunnery at U. S. N. Officer's Training School at Harvard University. 412 pages, size 5 by 7¼, on heavy glazed paper. Many drawings of cannon, machine guns, projectiles, etc. Large detail sketch of 12 inch 2 gun turret. Chapters on NAVAL GUNS, BREECH MECHANISMS, TURRETS, PROJECTILES, FIRE CONTROL, TORPEDOES, BATTLE DRILLS, ETC. A fine text book for individuals or schools. Price, postage paid in U. S., 65 cents.

No. U 1-38. Hand Book for Active Service containing practical instructions in campaign duties. By Egbert L. Viele, late U. S. A., Captain Engineers Seventh Regiment, N. G., N. Y. Dedicated to Seventh Regt. N. Y. National Guard. Published in 1861. Size 5x7½ inches, 252 pages. Price $1.50.

No. U 1-39. The American Militia Officer's Manual, containing a system of instruction for Infantry, Field and Horse Artillery, Cavalry and Riflemen; with an Appendix. By J. G. Dyckman, former major of light infantry in the service of the United States. Published in 1824. Size 4x7 inches, 216 pages. Price $2.00.

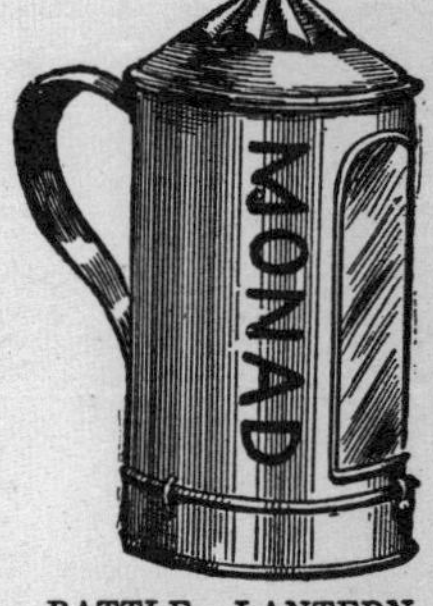


BATTLE LANTERN. From U. S. Navy Civil War double turret monitor Monadnock. Copper frame, horn light, diameter 5 inches, length 11 inches. Price, $20.00.

ANTIQUE TANKARD OR TOBACCO BOX. Made of ornamented hard wood, with carved cover and handle, 5 inches diameter, 5½ inches high. Price, $5.00.

No. U 1-36. Cavalry; Its History, Management and Uses in War. By J. Roemer, late an officer in the service of the Netherlands. With illustrations. Published in 1863. Size 6x9 inches, 515 pages. Has chapters on rifled fire arms, field service, horse, etc. Price, $3.50.

LAWS OF THE U. S. RELATING TO NAVIGATION AND THE MERCHANT MARINE. 488 pages, 6x9 inches, leather binding. Price, 60 cents.

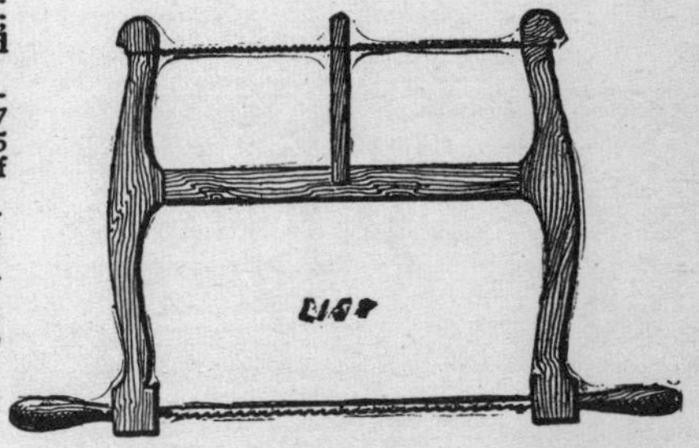

No. 2158. U. S. Arsenal Saws, as per illustration; assorted sizes; blade 16 inches; handle turns the blade in cutting circles; new, shop worn; bargain; price, 75 cents each.

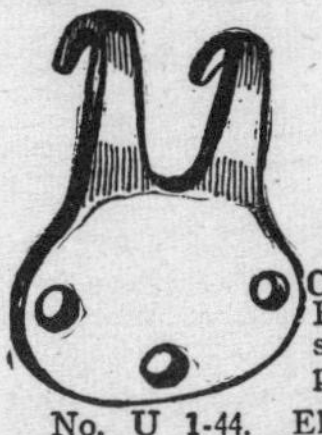

U. S. A. Double Claw Adjusting Brass Hook for gun sling; size 1¼x1½ inches; price 10 cents each.

No. U 1-44. Elements of Rhetoric and Literary Criticism by Rev. James Robert Boyd. Published in 1857 in New York. Size 4½x6½ inches. 333 pages. Price 75 cents.

No. U 1-46. The Development of Armor for Naval Use as prepared by the U. S. Naval Institute, by Lieut. E. W. Very, U. S. N. We believe that he is the inventor of the famous Very Signal Pistol used for many years in the U. S. Navy. Size 6x9 inches, 591 pages. Price $1.50.

No. 499. FRENCH-ENGLISH MILITARY TECHNICAL DICTIONARY, by Col. C. DeWitt Willcox, U. S. A., Professor of Modern Languages at West Point. Published by Harper & Brothers, New York. It contains all the latest terms of aviation, trench warfare, artillery and camouflage, military slang, etc. 584 pages on glazed paper, size 6x9 inches. 1917 edition. Regular price was $4.00. Our bargain price $1.00 each. Allow postage on three pounds.

Iron Money Box. The bank of some nobleman in bygone days. Massive intricate lock, inside compartment for the "yellow fellows." Length, 31 inches; width, 16 inches; depth, 15 inches; weight over 100 pounds.

NAVY SIGNAL LANTERN, oxydized finish, with heavy ribbed white glass. In fine order. Many customers have made these into electric lamps for both use and decoration. Price $4.50 each.

## WEAPONS OF WAR

In some of our recent catalogs we have mentioned that we were at work on a book to be called "Weapons of War," and in these catalogs we have shown illustrations which will appear in this new book. Much of the information necessary has been secured and tabulated, but owing to the death of Mr. Francis Bannerman and for various other causes since that time, it has been impossible to complete the work and have it published promptly as we had expected. We are still at work on this and progressing slowly. It may be several years before the book can be completed and published.

U. S. Navy Paymaster's Iron Safe, with combination lock. Size, 16 by 22 inches. Requires aid of locksmith, as the marked combination does not operate the lock. Offered as is. Price, $15.00.

Captured Spanish Safe. Size, 17x17x27 inches. Juan Menendez painted on door. In good order. From late navy yard auction. With working combination lock. Price, $45.00.

8 Sets State Militia Signalling Set, as shown in the two photographic illustrations. Leather carrying case, torch and fixtures, large copper lantern for oil, etc. Price per set as shown, $3.50

35 Singer Power Sewing Machines, No. 16-85, complete with fine tables, shafting and pulleys. Practically new machines. Purchased by U. S. Government to manufacture Web Loop Cartridge Belts. Bargain price for the entire lot. $450.

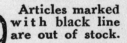

### Articles marked with black line are out of stock.

This poem was found written on Confederate note at the close of the Civil War. Kindly loaned to us for use in our catalogue by Gen. Jos. G. Story, N. Y. N. G. Price of Confederate bank note with poem printed on the back, $2.85. Please note that our catalogue, including this poem, is copyrighted.

### IN MEMORIAM.

Respectfully Dedicated to the Holders of Confederate Treasury Notes.

Representing nothing on God's earth now,
  And naught in the water below it—
As a pledge of the nation that's dead and gone,
  Keep it, dear friend, and show it—

Show it to those who will lend an ear
  To the tale that this paper can tell,
Of liberty born, of patriot's dream—
  Of the storm cradled nation that fell.

Too poor to possess the precious ores,
  And too much of a stranger to borrow,
We issued to-day our promises to pay,
  And hope to redeem on the morrow.

The days rolled on and weeks became years,
  But our coffers were empty still;
Coin was so rare that the Treasury quaked,
  If a dollar should drop in the till.

But the faith that was in us was strong indeed,
  And our poverty well discerned;
And these little checks represented the pay
  That our volunteers earned.

We know it had hardly a value in gold,
  Yet as gold her soldiers received it;
It gazed in our eyes with a promise to pay,
  And each patriot soldier believed it.

But our boys thought little of price or pay,
  Or of bills that were over due;
We knew if it brought us bread to-day,
  'Twas the best our poor country could do.

Keep it, for it tells our history o'er,
  From the birth of its dream to the last;
Modest and born of the angel Hope,
  Like the hope of success it passed.

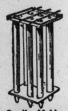

Candle Molds.
Ancient Candle Molds for making tallow candles, found in old marine store in Virginia. Price, $10.00.

Patrick Henry's Signature as Governor to land grant, with the seal of Commonwealth of Virginia in 1785, to 1,000 acres of land. "In Ohio County on the Point Pleasant Fork, 3 miles from the Ohio River." We value this signature at $75.00.

Signature of William H. Seward, Dec. 31, 1860, on letter, $10.00.

Signature of Mayor Albert Wharton, Philadelphia, 1815, on parchment deed of land, $25.00.

Small Wood Butt with brass hoops, filled with sand or sawdust, placed between decks for use as spit box; fine order, like new; 12 inches diameter, 7 inches high. Price, $3.00.

Parchment Deed dated 1787, with old seal and signatures of prominent Philadelphia men, viz.: Francis Gurney, William Semple, Alexander Addison, George Plumstreet, William Pollard. Price, $25.00.

Plaster Cast from the Dewey Arch; the pair of arms and hands holding up the scroll with the letters "McCullough"; fair order. This, we believe, is the largest piece saved. Price, $25.00.

Wood Shovels. Part of United States Navy Yeoman's Outfit. For use in handling potatoes. New. Value for $1.00 each. Price, 45 cents.

## MILITARY BOOKS.

**U. S. Army Ordnance Book   U. S. Army Regulations   U. S. Navy Ordnance Book**

U. S. Army Regulations, 475 pages; size 6x9 inches; full of information required by army officers; new books; 90 cents. Middle book in group of three books illustrated above.

U. S. Navy Ordnance Instructions, 1861. Issued by the Navy Department for use of naval officers. Part 1 relates to the preparation of war vessels for battle, officers' duties, etc.; Part 2, the equipment of boats, etc.; Part 3, ordnance and stores; size 6x9½ inches, 300 pages, with illustrations and valuable information for any one interested in military matters. First book on the right of illustrations. Price, 70c.

United States Army Ordnance Manual. Published by the War Department for the use of army officers. Gives full details for manufacture, care and use of cannons, bombshells, arms, and equipments, etc. 33 illustrated plates, containing valuable receipts, tables, etc. First book on the left of the three books illustrated above. Size 5x7 inches; 560 pages, with appendix containing over 200 illustrations, among which are 25 different kinds of knots. Valuable book that will help furnish a military education. Price, $1.50.

1818-1823 Army Records. Containing enlistment and discharge of soldiers in the vicinity of Boston. Also signatures of army officers attached to their pay receipts. About 60 pounds of valuable old papers. Packed in iron safe. Price, $500.00.

U. S. Army Magazine Rifle Book, with illustrations; used by U. S. Marine Corps. Price, 75 cents.

Book of Companions of the Loyal Legion by Hamersly Co., containing illustrations from photographs of officers. Size of books, 9x6½ inches; pages 395. **Price, $7.00.**

MANUAL OF GUARD DUTY. 30 cents.
HOSPITAL CORPS HANDBOOK. By Deputy Surgeon-General Charles Smart, U. S. A., 1898. Books are new and treat of hospital duties. Size 5x7½ inches, 350 pages, cloth covered. anatomy and physiology and the special duties of the Hospital Corps. Illustrated. Valuable book. Regular price, $1.00; our price, 45 cents.
MARINE INTERNATIONAL LAW. By Commander Henry Glass, U. S. N. 250 pages, 6x9 inches. leather binding. Price, $1.00.
HEYLES' STATUTES OF THE U. S. Relating to revenue, commerce, navigation and currency, to which are prefixed the Declaration of Independence and Constitution. 837 pages, size 2½x7x10 inches, leather binding. Price, $1.00.
REVISED STATUTES OF THE U. S. 1085 pages, leather binding, size 8x11½ inches. Price, $1.25.

ATLANTIC LOCAL COAST PILOT—CAPE HENRY TO WINYAH BAY. With charts, 800 pages, 8x11½ inches. Price, $1.00.
U. S. GOVERNMENT, its origin and practical workings, including the Declaration of Independence, Constitution and description of the three divisions of Government. By Geo. N. Lamphear. 235 pages, 6x9 inches, leather binding. Price, $1.50.
ANNUAL REPORT OF THE U. S. LIFE-SAVING SERVICE. Contains detailed account of rescues, wrecked ships, persons saved from drowning, etc. Average 400 pages, 6x9 inches, years 1893-1900. Choice of years, $1.00 per copy.
AZIMUTH TABLES. Giving the time bearing of the Sun at intervals between sunrise and sunset, for parallels and latitude between 61 degrees north and 61 degrees south, inclusive. Size 9x12 inches. Price, 60c.
U4-17. SKETCH OF ALL THE INVASIONS OR DESCENTS UPON THE BRITISH ISLES, from landing of William the Conqueror to the present time. To which are prefixed thoughts on the French Invasion of England. By General Dumourier. Translated from the French. Published in London in 1803. 46 pages, including large Maps. Price, $6.00.

Book on Springfield Breech Loading Rifle. Illustrating different parts with names. Care of rifle, trajectory, etc. Information given in this book will be of benefit to all who use the Springfield B-L Rifle. Price, 10c.

Farrow's Military Encyclopedia. This is the standard military encyclopedia of the world, and the only one of its kind in the English language. It has the indorsement of the War Department and the leading military commanders of America and Europe. It is issued in three large octavo volumes of about 1,000 pages each, printed on fine paper from new electrotype plates, profusely illustrated and handsomely bound. It is a complete library of military information, both for military and non-military people. Set, 3 volumes. Price, $40.00.

Infantry Drill Regulations, 50 cents.
Cavalry Drill Regulations, $1.00.
Artillery Drill Regulations, $1.00.
Manual of Arms for the Springfield caliber 45 and Krag-Jorgensen caliber 30. Price, 15 cents.
United States Army 1863 Manual. Illustrated. With rules for caring for guns. Price, 10 cents.
Book marked from library of old U. S. S. Kearsage. Price, $5.00.
Book of Photos. Illustrations of officers who served in Spanish War. Size of book, 10½x7¼; pages 262. Price, $7.50.
Book Containing Records of Living officers of the U. S. Navy and Marine Corps. Published by Hamersly, 1902. Size of book, 10½x7¼ inches; 511 pages. Price, $10.00.

### GUNNERY AND NAVIGATION BOOKS USED BY U. S. REVENUE OFFICERS.

U. S. NAVY ORDNANCE POCKET MANUAL. Pocket size. Manual of exercise for great guns and small arms, equipment of boats, progressive instruction for gun and powder divisions, and directions for target practice with machine guns, small arms, etc. 484 pages, size 4x5½ inches. Red binding. Price, $1.00.
GUNNERY CATECHISM. As applied to the service of Naval Ordnance. 197 pages, 4x6 inches, cloth binding. Price, 60 cents.
U4-18. DEUTSCHE HELDEN aus der Zeit Kaiser Wilhelms des Grossen von Hans Kraemer. Many Double Page illustrations in Colors, with drawings and photographs. 348 pages. Printed in German. Price, $4.00.
U4-19. ZUR GESCHICHTE DER COSTUME. Costumes and dress of various peoples. Fine book for costumer or those interested in correct costumes for private theatricals. Size 9x13 inches. Printed in German. Price, $5.00.
U4-20. THE BRITISH NAVY, with illustrations, maps and diagrams. Frontispiece is portrait of Queen Victoria. Published in 1898. Shows various British Naval Uniforms, ratemarks, flags. History of British Navy for early times. 327 pages, size 7x9½ inches. Price, $6.00.

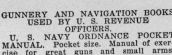

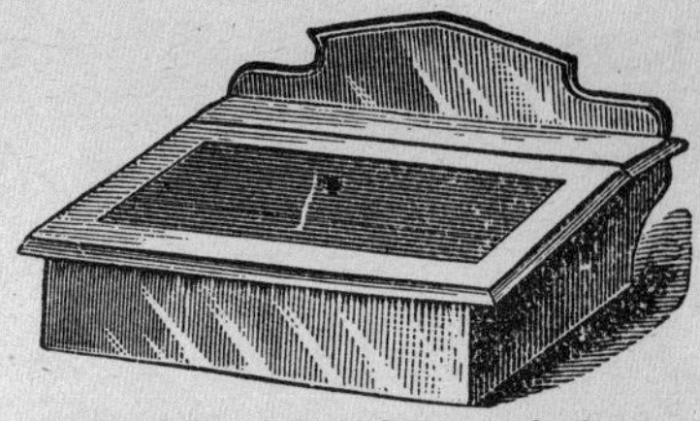

Army Officers' Field Desk, made for use during the Spanish War; new, as per illustration; size, 12x14 inches, with hinged cover; made of hard wood; oil finished; light and handy for use of army office while on the march. Handy Desk, with place for letters and writing materials. Price, 75 cents.
Civil War Officers' Field Desk. Used by Major A. F. Green, N. Y. Volunteers. Was once captured by Gen. Mosby, C. S. A. Price, $20.00.
We call special attention to the collection from the BRITISH NATIONAL EXPOSITION, at Wembley. These pieces were held as one collection, and we purchased them as such. We are now offering them in pairs and single pieces to collectors and museums. We suggest that you make early selection if you are interested.

**Gew 98**

The German Mauser Rifle Model of 1898 Its Use and Development In the World War.

**BOOK ON GERMAN MAUSER ARMY RIFLE**

A twenty page booklet, profusely illustrated, on the most interesting and best known rifle of the war, "The German Mauser." A detailed description of the gun, showing its many attachments and thirty-eight bayonets. EVERY VETERAN OF THE WORLD WAR WILL WANT A COPY OF THIS BOOK. Price, 45 cents.

**U. S. Light House Time Markers;** marks time in parts of seconds. Used to time flash lights. Serviceable order. Some with watch cases. $4.00.

THE AMERICAN WATCHMAN TIME DETECTOR. In box with glass cover, 15 inches square, 10 inches high. Said to be in serviceable working order. Offer wanted.

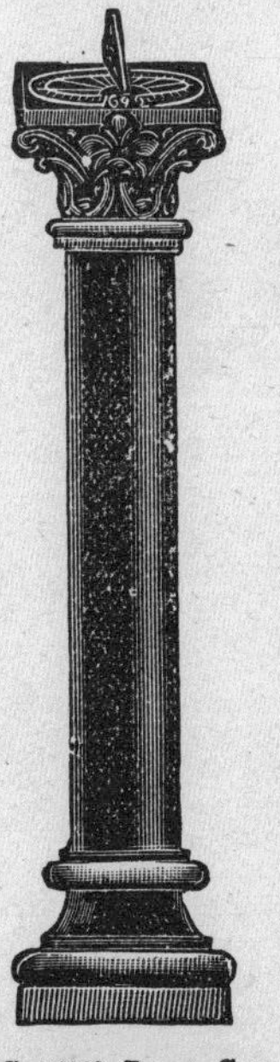

**Cut 1392. Bronze Sun Dial;** date 1619, with figures from 8 to 12 and 1 to 7; mounted on 22 inch pedestal; pedestal is made of baked clay; size of sun dial, 4¼x4¼. Price, $25.00.

Admiral Dewey's Printing Press, from the U. S. Flagship Olympia; used in printing orders, etc.; also used in printing the newspaper, *The Bounding Billow*, celebrating Fall of Manila and the Battle of Manila Bay. We purchased this historic press at the Boston Navy Yard on the return of the Olympia. The size is: height, 41 inches; width, 30 inches; 13½x9-inch plate; is worked with foot treadle; needs rollers and inking plate. Will sell the whole outfit, as illustrated, for $175.00. We purchased this outfit expecting to print copies of the little paper, *The Fall of the City of Manila and the Battle of Manila Bay*. About 1,000 copies of these papers were printed and have now become valuable relics. But New York printers estimated such high cost that we did not care to venture, and now offer this historical press for sale.

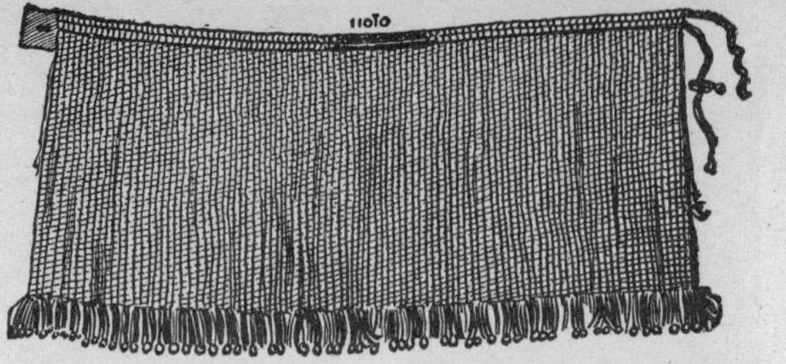

**10471.** AFRICAN NATIVE-MADE DRESS. Length 26 inches. Beads and sea shell ornamentation. Price, $10.00.

**10468.** AFRICAN NATIVE'S COPPER BANGLE CHAIN. Price, $2.85.

AFRICAN NATIVE'S BEAD NECKLACE. Ornamented with sea shells, black and white beads. Price, $1.75.

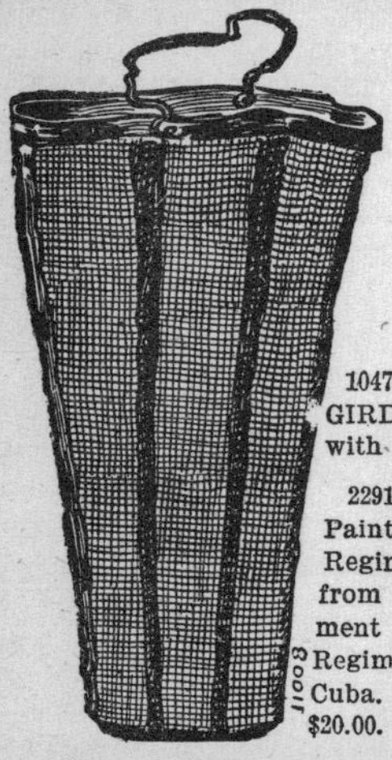

**10469.** AFRICAN NATIVE'S BEAD GIRDLE. Leather ornamented, with colored beads and fringe. Length 26 inches. Price, $2.50.

**10472.** AFRICAN NATIVE'S LEATHER FRINGED DRESS. Length 27 inches, depth 13½ inches. Similar to No. 10471. Price, $7.50.

**10470.** AFRICAN NATIVE'S BEAD GIRDLE. Woven fibre, ornamented with sea shells. Price, $3.50.

**2291.** SPANISH WAR DRUM. Painted eagle, shield and scroll; 71st Regiment N. G. N. Y. Purchased from N. Y. State Ordnance Department after the return of the 71st Regiment from the Spanish War in Cuba. Serviceable relic. Price, $20.00.

**11008.** ANCIENT KAFIR NATIVE'S BEAD EMBROIDERED BAG. Used by the NATIVE WOMEN FOR CARRYING BABY. Width at the mouth 11 inches, at the bottom 6½ inches, length 24 inches. Made of leather, the front covered with white and black beads. Rare relic from Lady Stewart's collection. Price, $20.00.

**11009.** ANCIENT SOUTH SEA ISLAND NATIVE'S NECKLACE. About 1 foot long. Made of cowrie shells. From Arnold Museum. Price, $3.85.

**0-1265AA.** DESK WEIGHT. Made from iron plates from the Confederate RAM Virginia (Merrimac). Relic of the most famous naval battle of the Civil War—the first encounter between ironclads. We recently secured two of the end plates from a party in Virginia, whose father served on board during the fight. One plate we reserve for our museum, the other we will cut up into 1½-inch desk weights, stamp on each of the four polished sides, name of ship and date of battle, thickness of plate 1¾ inches, weight 1 pound. A rare souvenir. Price, $3.85.

**1010.** AFRICAN NATIVE WOMAN'S BEADED WAIST GIRDLE (full dress). String of beads 5 inches long attached to the leather strap, with fibre tassels, beaded ends. From Lady Stewart's collection. Bead portion 11 inches. Price, $12.50. Somewhat similar to No. 10471.

**11011.** AFRICAN NATIVE DANCING GIRL'S FULL DRESS. Consisting of leather strips 11 inches long, fastened to the body girdle, ornamented with beads and cowrie shells. Length 20 inches. Price, $14.50.

AFRICAN NATIVE'S COLORED FIBRE CROWN CAP. With tassel and fringe. Curious relic. Price, $2.50.

AFRICAN NATIVE'S LACE COAT. Made of pieces of wood laced together like beads. Price, $5.00.

**11012.** AFRICAN NATIVE WOMAN'S BEADED FULL DRESS. Worn suspended from the neck by a leather thong, covered with brass rings. Very curious. Quite out of the ordinary even in Africa. Strings of beads are attached to the beaded centre. Length of beaded work 14 inches. From Lady Stewart's collection. Price, $15.00.

**0-978AA.** MILITARY DICTIONARY. By Col. H. L. Scott, U. S. A. 1861. Cloth bound, illustrated; 674 pages, 9x4¾ inches. Price, $5.00.

**0-978.** JOAN OF ARC MEDAL SEAL. Silvered medal, engraved "Domreny, 1412; Rouen, 1431." Ornamented gilt medal seal, ready for cutting. Price, $5.00.

**0-1264.** AUTOGRAPH REGISTER. For duplicating sale slips. Length 8 inches, widest width 7 inches, stands 8 inches high, 3 rollers for paper and carbon, writing part measures 5x3½ inches. Bargain price, $2.75.

**0-1265.** AUTOGRAPH REGISTER. For copying bill heads. Size of the desk copy plate 8x10 inches, wood frame, nickeled metal stand 6¼ inches high. Full length 15 inches; 10½ inches wide. Bargain price, $2.75.

MILITARY OVERCOATS, WITH CAPES. Heavy blue cloth, green flannel lined (ambulance corps). Assorted sizes 33 to 36-inch chest measure. Used; serviceable; cleaned and pressed. Price, $5.50 each.

ARTILLERY OVERCOATS, WITH CAPES. Heavy blue Kersey cloth, with red flannel lined capes. Used; serviceable order. Military sizes 33 to 36-inch chest measure. Price, $5.50. (We have a few in larger sizes for company orders only, not for sale singly.)

**10884.** VERY OLD KEY, found in the grounds of Rochester Cathedral; hand forged, with post and numerous wards; length 5¼ inches; from London collector. Price, $5.00.

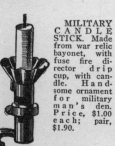

MILITARY CANDLE STICK. Made from war relic bayonet, with fuse fire director drip cup, with candle. Handsome ornament for military man's den. Price, $1.00 each; pair, $1.90.

**1290.** ANTIQUE KEY. Found in Chester, England. Perhaps some old castle; rusty; unserviceable. Relic. 5¼ inches long. Price, $1.50.

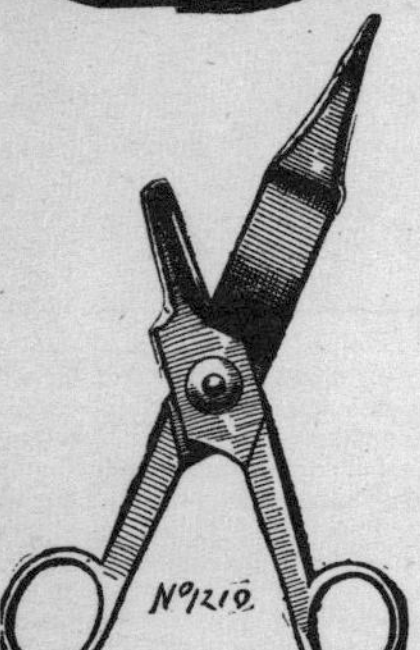

**1210.** BRITISH ARMY ANTIQUE CANDLE SNUFFERS. Stamped with the British Government broad arrow mark, showing Government ownership. Part of old-time equipment From London collection. Price, $3.50.

**1296.** ANTIQUE BRASS DOOR KNOCKER. Egyptian model. From London collection. Complete order with screws and washer, length 4⅝ inches, width 3 inches. Price, $10.00.

**1297.** ANTIQUE BRITISH LION HEAD DOOR KNOCKER. Has had innumerable coats of paint. Is complete, length 7 inches, width 4½ inches. Price, $10.00.

**1298.** HANDSOME OLD ORNAMENTED DOOR KNOCKER. Centaur, with wings, supporting circle, etc., length 8½ inches, 5 inches wide; serviceable order. Price, $10.00.

**1292.** ANTIQUE KEY. History unknown. Rare old ornamental pattern. 6 inches in length. Price, $1.50.

**6903.** WOOD CHAIN. Made of hard wood by African natives with primitive cutting tools, links measure 3½ inches in length, 2½ inches in width, full length 3 feet. Price, $4.85.

**1291.** ANTIQUE KEY. History unknown. Shows unique work. Broken and brazed. Found in London collection. Price, $1.50.

**1293.** ANTIQUE OLD KEY. Badly rusted, length 5¼ inches. Price, $1.50.

**3279.** LIBBY PRISON LOCK. Taken from the old tobacco warehouse in Richmond, Va., used as prison during the Civil War. Vouched for by affidavit of party who sold it to us. Price, $20.00.

**1300.** Sold.

**1301.** AMERICAN BRASS EAGLE DOOR KNOCKER, copy of one found in a London collection. Size 5x9 inches. In good order. Price, $8.50 each.

**1295.** ANTIQUE DOOR KNOCKER. With Liberty face. In good serviceable order, with screws ready for attaching to door. Found in London collection. Length 8 inches, width 5¾ inches. Very suitable for secret society lodge room. Price, $10.00.

Reproduction of this door knocker in brass. Price, $7.00.

**0-851.** ANCIENT DOOR LOCK AND KEY FROM THE CHALK CHURCH, GRAVESEND, ENGLAND. Lock is hand forged iron, complete on heavy part of the oak door, 4 inches thick, 19 inches long, 8 inches wide, 9½-inch key, 3 inches wide at the handle. Came from the sale of George Arnold Museum. Fairly well preserved. A museum exhibit offered with the Chalk Church OFFERTORY BOX. Made of old English quartered oak. Hand forged iron band straps, with rose ornamentation, with hasp for the lock. Well preserved. Size of the frame 21x10 inches, box is 10x5¼x7¾ inches. Price for the lock, key and offerty box, $25.00.

(Near Wheel Horse)

GATLING GUN HARNESS, with leather snap collars, hames and tugs attached; bridle, halter and nose bag; traces, breeching, whip and McClellan riding saddle. All in good, serviceable order. Price, $35.00 per horse.

Francis Bannerman

**MILITARY GOODS**

**501 Broadway,**
Near Broome St.,
New York

U. S. ARMY ARTILLERY HARNESS, Civil War pattern, wheel horse; bridle complete, collar, hames and tugs, pole strap, halter, feed bag, riding and valise saddles, valise, breeching, breast strap, traces, driver's whip, pole pad, leg guard, breeching girth, all in fine, serviceable order, almost new. Price, per horse, for lead and wheel, $22.50. Wheel horse separate; price, $25.00 per horse.

U. S. ARMY ARTILLERY HARNESS, lead horse, Civil War pattern; bridle, halter, collar, hames with tugs, traces, crupper, back strap, girth, saddle, valise, driver's leg guard, nose bag, whip, all in fine, serviceable order, almost new. Price, per horse, wheel and lead, $22.50; lead horse separate, $20.00 per horse.

TOP VIEW OF THE McCLELLAN SADDLE TREE, showing the way the side bars are ironed and fitted (like the knees and ribs of a ship) to the pommel and cantle. The natural and cradle-like seat for the rider.

SIDE VIEW OF THE U. S. ARMY McCLELLAN SADDLE and the correct way to take the measurement of the seat. These saddles are made at the Govt. Rock Island Arsenal, on the most scientific principles for the safety and comfort of both man and horse. This pattern saddle, with some few minor changes, has been the regulation saddle for almost 50 years.

VIEW OF THE McCLELLAN ARMY SADDLE with the rawhide calfskin cover —ready for the black or russet leather outer covering. This rawhide is sewed on while wet, that when it dries it shrinks and binds the wood parts together so as to be nearly indestructible.

U. S. ARMY POLE STRAPS, 56 inches long, 1¾ inches wide, 4-ply leather, over ½ inch thick, 4 rows of hand stitching, iron buckles with loop, used; are in good second-hand serviceable order. Some of our customers use these for traces by putting on trace chains. Our bargain price is 75 cents each.

U. S. ARMY HOOD STIRRUP. 4-inch foot rest; in good, second-hand serviceable order. Manufactured at Government Arsenal. These are the stirrups we furnish with the McClellan saddles. For sale separate, $1.75 pair.

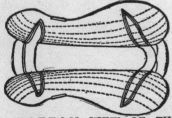

BOTTOM VIEW OF THE McCLELLAN ARMY SADDLE TREE, showing the easy, graceful curves which conforms to the horse's back and prevents injury.

NEW U. S. ARMY TOOL BAG for armorers; with shoulder straps; with brass padlock and key. Has inside straps for holding tools in place. Width, 8 inches; depth, 8 inches; length, 13½ inches. Price, $5.00.

A correspondent of the London Mail says that women always rode astride till Queen Elizabeth, in order to show a magnificent dress upon a certain State occasion, rode sideways, and so set the fashion.

The U. S. A. McClellan Saddle, with its open seat, is the safest and best saddle for ladies to use in riding astride.

A short time ago we submitted a bid to a State organization to supply U. S. McClellan Army Saddles. The order went to a prominent saddle maker, who supplied new saddles, imitations of the McClellan. The first week the saddles were used, a number of the horses developed sore backs on account of the side bars of the saddle being rounded instead of dished to lie flat on and conform to the shape of the horse's back. The parties offered to trade us their new saddles for our old ones, but we would not put them in stock.

**No. 9.**
U.S. Army Officers' Whitman Saddle, Russet, Leather covered, with hooded stirrups, hair cinch and coat straps; saddles made on Whitman trees from Government Arsenal Sale; cinch is made of long horsehair at U. S. Rock Island Arsenal. Second hand, $17.50.

Whitman Saddle Trees, covered with rawhide, $4.50 each.

For saddle bags for Whitman and McClellan saddles, see this and other pages. We recommend a hair pad for use under saddle.

**10,000 U. S. ARMY HORSE HOBBLES** for attaching to horses while in camp, allowing them to graze without wandering off. These were made at the U. S. Government Rock Island Arsenal, and are only sold off by reason of change from black to russet color leather. Anyone having care of horses or other animals can use these fine new hobbles to advantage. Keep you from wearing the hide off your heels looking up lost animals. Soft leather inside, swivel center link. Must have cost upwards of $3.00 to make. Our bargain price is 50 cents each, or $5.00 per dozen.

**100 U. S. A. RUSSET LEATHER WATERING BRIDLES.** Made at Rock Island Arsenal, with forged steel bridle and bit with spring snaps for quickly attaching to headstall of bridle. Used. Serviceable order. Price, $1.35 each.

**No. 12**
**50 U. S. Artillery Valise Saddles.**
padded stitched seats, heavy leather skirts, wood stirrups, complete with leather girths. Excellent saddle for boys. Superior to any cheap saddle. Tree is strong, hard wood, then covered with heavy rawhide calfskin then covered with leather, with brass rims. Price, $6.50 each. We offer the Valise saddle trees only, with rawhide cover, new at 50 cents each.

**U. S. ARMY LEATHER SADDLE BAGS,** later regulation; made of fine leather, at the Government Arsenal. We have sold a great many to wholesale saddlery houses; they could not make them for less than $10.00. We offer this pair of fine bags, in good, serviceable order, almost new, $3.50; second hand bags, $2.25.

See No. 14D page 351.

**2199. BRITISH ARMY OFFICER'S MARTINGALE AND CRUPPER.** With relief ornamentation of lion, crown, etc. Used, serviceable order. Price the set, $5.00.

**FROM KATE FIELD, IN "THE CHICAGO TIMES-HERALD"**

"Man naturally rides astride of a horse because in no other way can a perfect balance and complete control be attained without artificial aid. Primitive woman copied her lord and master even when the era of barebacks succumbed to saddles. It remained for 'civilized' convention to devise the side saddle and skirt of dangerous length with death in every inch. Why this departure from common sense? Because in the days of Queen Elizabeth a noble dame was too deformed to ride astride as women had always ridden up to that time. To cover the physical defects of one woman a whole sex has been punished for centuries!"

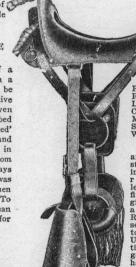

**200 U. S. ARMY REGULATION RUSSET LEATHER COVERED McCLELLAN SADDLES.** With coat and stirrup straps, with 4-inch wood stirrups, russet leather covered, fine hair cincha girth. All made at Government Rock Island Arsenal and issued to U. S. Cavalry. Used a short time. Offered in good second-hand, repaired order. Price, $11.95 each.

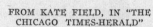

**10205A. LARIAT HONDAS.** Brass, with outside groove for lariat rope, inside smooth polished. Price, 25 cents.

**20 PAIRS RUSSET SWEAT LEATHERS.** For McClellan Saddles. Used. Serviceable. Price, $1.85 per pair.

**40 U. S. WOVEN WEB SURCINGLES.** With heavy russet leather billet straps. Used. Serviceable. Price, 95 cents each.

United States Artillery Officer's Outfit; black leather covered saddle with stitched leather seat, with polished brass bound edges, with large leather skirts, with stirrup straps and hooded wood stirrups, with martingale, crupper and new double rein bridle, all for $16.59.

We fit out many Central and South American mining companies with their full equipment of saddles, bridles, saddle bags and pack saddles. This equipment can be purchased from us at wholesale prices and is far superior to the native made saddlery. We also equip cavalry companies with saddles, pads, and complete uniforms. Send us a list of your requirements and we shall quote bargain prices.

RUSSET U. S. ARMY McCLELLAN SADDLES, not saddles the Government purchased during the emergency caused by the war and recently sold off at any old price, but genuine Rock Island Arsenal made Trees, with the heavy rawhide calfskin covers, with outer covering of fine leather, fitted with brass rings and mountings, with coat straps, with strong, heavy leather stirrup straps, with large tread wood stirrups, with leather covered hoods, with hair cinch, with long rawhide cinch straps; all in fine second-hand serviceable order. The strongest, best and easiest riding saddle ever made. We purchased this lot expecting to sell them to the Japs, but on arriving at Tokyo found that the saddles were too large for Japanese men and horses. Our price is $9.85 for a second hand saddle. SELECTED SADDLES, $13.50 each.

No. 2

**MILITARY OFFICERS' HORSE EQUIPMENT OUTFIT.** Double rein bridle with shoemaker steel forged bit, with with curb chain, with bands; polished brass buckles; martingale with breast straps in colored leather to match the bridle; with brass shield; with either nickeled figure or eagle; with genuine McClellan Saddle; with hood stirrups; with sweat leathers; with coat straps; with under housing of fine blue cloth, canvas lined with 1 inch gilt lace border; all in fine serviceable order; Price, $34.00.

No. 3.

No. 3. 2,700 new U. S. Army Rock Island Arsenal-made hair Cinchs; 24 strand, dark colored horse hair: 3 twist, bronze cinch rings, with dark colored russet leather covered safes, stamped in each cinch "*Rock Island Arsenal, 1893*," with the initials of the Government inspecting officer. Hand stitched 4½ inch bronze ring: new, perfect goods; superior to any cinch usually made by saddle manufacturers. Width, 8 inches. We have these fine cinches: 14 inches in size, measured from ring to ring, price; $2.00;

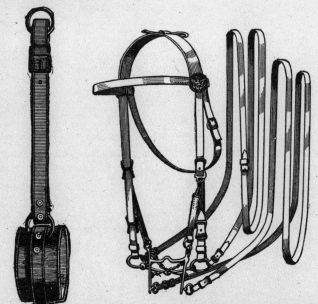

No. PQM. MARINE CORPS PONCHOS, pliable rubberized fabric, light olive drab color, weight 3½ pounds. Opening in center to use as cape, and fitted with snaps to use as a blanket. All in good order, size 68 inches wide by 84 inches. Snaps along each long edge so that two may be fastened together to form a shelter tent. In remitting allow postage on 3 pounds. Price $2.00 each. This is the size and style used on horseback, as it covers the knees and back of saddle.

No. U 1-36. Cavalry; Its History, Management and Uses in War. By J. Roemer, late an officer in the service of the Netherlands. With illustrations. Published in 1863. Size 6x9 inches, 515 pages. Has chapters on rifled fire arms, field service, horse, etc. Price $3.50.

1741E. U. S. ARMY VALISE TREE which we have fitted up with second hand straps; girth and wood stirrups; will answer for strong, cheap saddle for boys. Price, $3.85. Cheapest saddle on the market.

**No. 22. NEW PONY HOBBLES,** double leather, 2½ inches wide, about 1 foot long, with buckle and strap to go around the animal's leg with ring attached to strap 15 inches long, whereby the animal can be picketed to lariat; all made of heavy leather, double handstitched and riveted. Price, 65 cents.

**No. B1. 500 U. S. ARMY RUSSET LEATHER BRIDLES,** as per cut, with double reins and two bits. Probably made for use of officers. Bronze rosettes with eagle, adjustable cheek pieces. One bit is curb with chain, and is attached to cheek pieces with small snaps on special buckles, so that the extra bit and reins may be removed entirely. The other is bar bit with long side bars and rings. The curb bit, reins and snaps could be used on halter, thereby making two bridles from this one. ALL NEW. Price, $4.50 each.

No. B2. 300 U. S. ARMY HEAVY RUSSET LEATHER BRIDLE, as made for use in World War. ALL NEW. Single rein with extra long single end for use as lash. Bronze rosettes with U. S. Eagle Cheek pieces adjustable by special patent buckles. Fine steel bit made at Rock Island Arsenal, with long side bars and rings. Price, $3.00 each.

No. B3. 100 SINGLE REIN RUSSET LEATHER BRIDLES like No. B2, fitted with martingale, WITHOUT breast straps. This special style of martingale used to keep horse from rearing. Price, $3.50 each.

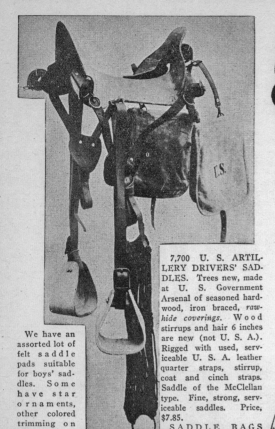

102

**48. UNITED STATES ARMY HEAVY KHAKI COLORED CANVAS HORSE COVERS,** with straps and surcingle; used. Offered in repaired serviceable order. Price, $1.50 each.

**10024. U. S. ARMY MODEL 92 BIT.** Guaranteed forged steel; not to be compared with the cheap, malleable cast iron style usually for sale. These bits are offered in cleaned, serviceable order. Used only a short time. 9,000 in stock. Regular price for this quality is $3.00; our bargain price, 90 cents each.

**7,700 U. S. ARTILLERY DRIVERS' SADDLES.** Trees new, made at U. S. Government Arsenal of seasoned hardwood, iron braced, *rawhide coverings.* Wood stirrups and hair 6 inches are new (not U. S. A.). Rigged with used, serviceable U. S. A. leather quarter straps, stirrup, coat and cinch straps. Saddle of the McClellan type. Fine, strong, serviceable saddles. Price, $7.85.

SADDLE BAGS FROM $1.75 pair up.

We have an assorted lot of felt saddle pads suitable for boys' saddles. Some have star ornaments, other colored trimming on edge. Price, $1.00 each.

**190.—U. S. ARMY NON-CORROSIVE SILVERED BITS, OFFICER'S.** Pelham's pattern; new; "never rust"; loose check; similar to Model 92 Regulation port bit, but with rings for double reins (officers); from Rock Island Arsenal; cost upwards of $40.00 a dozen. Our bargain price, all new, perfect order, $1.45 each.

**BRITISH ARMY MOUNTED SOLDIER'S SWAGGER WHIP.** Required by Army regulations to be carried by soldier when in uniform off duty. Rawhide covered, russet leather - covered handle, 40 inches long. Price, plain, at $1.55 each. A few with the regimental crests, $2.55.

**102.—U. S. ARMY McCLELLAN SADDLES.** Sold by reason of change in army regulations, which now require that all equipments be of russet leather to correspond to the olive-drab uniform. It is almost unnecessary to say anything about the splendid merits of the U. S. Army McClellan saddle. It is acknowledged to be the *best in the world.* For *over fifty years* the *U. S. Army regulation,* the pride of both the Union and Confederate officers in the four years of campaign and battles during the Civil War, the envy of foreign officers attached to the allied armies at Pekin, China, relief engagements.

Saddle is made of seasoned hard wood, strongly bound together with steel braces. The tree covered first with rawhide calfskin, then finish covered with fine bridle quality leather seat. The only men's saddle suitable for women to ride. Knowing the merits of the McClellan army saddle, we far outbid all bidders at the auction. After the sale we heard of an officer who remarked to another that "Bannerman has paid a good price for the large lot of saddles." He received answer, "If I had my way Bannerman would not have the saddles. I would have stripped off the black leather and recovered the trees with russet and issued them as regulation saddles."

It is doubtful if any more McClellan saddles will be offered at the Government sales. *If you have use for a good McClellan saddle do not put off buying or you may lose your chance.* We offer without option *for a limited time black leather covered Government McClellan army saddles,* late regulation, with 4 inch tread wood stirrups, covered with leather hoods, with hair cinches, coat and stirrup straps, *complete,* used only a short time. Saddles required repairing; are in serviceable order. Price, $6.95. ea.

## Selected Saddles Which Required Only a Few Repairs, $11.50 Each.

**10037.—U. S. A. BRIDLE CURB CHAIN AND RUSSET STRAP.** Made of non-corrosive white metal with army circle curb locking hooks, which lie flat against the horse's lower jaws. Price 48c. Price of chain and hooks, without the leather strap, 25 cents.

Vickers-Maxim ammunition carriers for use on light steel frames attached to pack saddles; carrier made of light steel with handle, one end opening for insertion of projectiles in the three brass shell holders. We have 200 in stock. Our bargain price $4.85 each.

Light steel frames for carrying ammunition boxes, etc., on pack saddles; complete with leather straps and attaching loops; good, serviceable order. Length, 17½, width 8½, height 10½ inches; weight 8½ lbs. Price, $4.85.

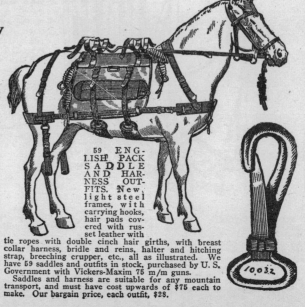

**59 ENGLISH PACK SADDLE AND HARNESS OUTFITS.** New, light steel frames, with carrying hooks, hair pads covered with russet leather with tie ropes with double cinch hair girths, with breast collar harness, bridle and reins, halter and hitching strap, breeching crupper, etc., all as illustrated. We have 59 saddles and outfits in stock, purchased by U. S. Government with Vickers-Maxim 75 m/m guns.

Saddles and harness are suitable for any mountain transport, and must have cost upwards of $75 each to make. Our bargain price, each outfit, $28.

**U. S. ARTILLERY FOLDING CANVAS WATER BUCKET,** made at the Government Rock Island Arsenal; of heavy drab color water repelling canvas; 12 inches high; 11 inches in diameter; weighs 26 ounces; used, good serviceable order. Price, 85 cents.

**CANVAS SADDLE BAGS** for use on McClellan Army Saddles, fitted with new leather for attaching to cantle of the saddle. Made up in excess of order from the French government. Bargain, $1.75 pair.

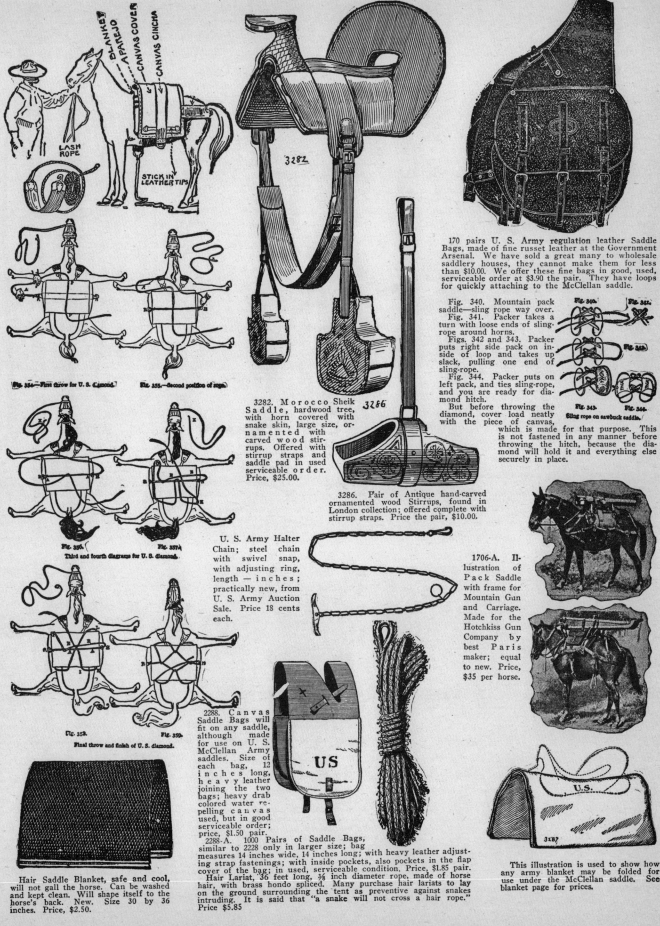

BLANKET

APAREJO

CANVAS COVER

CANVAS CINCHA

LASH ROPE

STICK IN LEATHER TIPS

3282.

Fig. 354.—First throw for U. S. diamond.

Fig. 355.—Second position of rope.

Fig. 356.

Fig. 357.

Third and fourth diagrams for U. S. diamond.

Fig. 358.

Fig. 359.

Final throw and finish of U. S. diamond.

3282. Morocco Sheik Saddle, hardwood tree, with horn covered with snake skin, large size, ornamented with carved wood stirrups. Offered with stirrup straps and saddle pad in used serviceable order. Price, $25.00.

3286.

3286. Pair of Antique hand-carved ornamented wood Stirrups, found in London collection; offered complete with stirrup straps. Price the pair, $10.00.

U. S. Army Halter Chain; steel chain with swivel snap, with adjusting ring, length — inches; practically new, from U. S. Army Auction Sale. Price 18 cents each.

170 pairs U. S. Army regulation leather Saddle Bags, made of fine russet leather at the Government Arsenal. We have sold a great many to wholesale saddlery houses, they cannot make them for less than $10.00. We offer these fine bags in good, used, serviceable order at $3.90 the pair. They have loops for quickly attaching to the McClellan saddle.

Fig. 340. Mountain pack saddle—sling rope way over.

Fig. 341. Packer takes a turn with loose ends of sling-rope around horns.

Figs. 342 and 343. Packer puts right side pack on inside of loop and takes up slack, pulling one end of sling-rope.

Fig. 344. Packer puts on left pack, and ties sling-rope, and you are ready for diamond hitch.

But before throwing the diamond, cover load neatly with the piece of canvas, which is made for that purpose. This is not fastened in any manner before throwing the hitch, because the diamond will hold it and everything else securely in place.

Fig. 340. Fig. 341.

Fig. 342.

Fig. 343. Fig. 344.

Sling rope on sawbuck saddle.

1706-A. Illustration of Pack Saddle with frame for Mountain Gun and Carriage. Made for the Hotchkiss Gun Company by best Paris maker; equal to new. Price, $35 per horse.

2288. Canvas Saddle Bags will fit on any saddle, although made for use on U. S. McClellan Army saddles. Size of each bag, 12 inches long, heavy leather joining the two bags; heavy drab colored water repelling canvas used, but in good serviceable order; price, $1.50 pair.

2288-A. 1000 Pairs of Saddle Bags, similar to 2228 only in larger size; bag measures 14 inches wide, 14 inches long; with heavy leather adjusting strap fastenings; with inside pockets, also pockets in the flap cover of the bag; in used, serviceable condition. Price, $1.85 pair.

Hair Lariat, 36 feet long, ⅜ inch diameter rope, made of horse hair, with brass hondo spliced. Many purchase hair lariats to lay on the ground surrounding the tent as preventive against snakes intruding. It is said that "a snake will not cross a hair rope." Price $5.85

US

Hair Saddle Blanket, safe and cool, will not gall the horse. Can be washed and kept clean. Will shape itself to the horse's back. New. Size 30 by 36 inches. Price, $2.50.

U.S.

3137.

This illustration is used to show how any army blanket may be folded for use under the McClellan saddle. See blanket page for prices.

**CW2. U. S. ARMY LARGE SIZE LEATHER SADDLE BAGS**, 15x14 inches, used on McClellan Army Saddles, offered in repaired serviceable order. $3.50 per pair.

**3288. U. S. A. RUSSET LEATHER HOLSTER**, for holding the combination Springfield Service Rifle and Carbine. Complete with saddle straps made at U. S. Rock Island Arsenal. Hand sewed with brass buckles. Made of the best leather stiff sides. Is longer and wider than the old regulation in order to hold the new combination Infantry and Cavalry rifle. Length is 31¾ inches and the width is 7 inches. Weight, 2 pounds 2 ounces. Offered in cleaned, repaired, serviceable order. Price, $2.50.

**CW3. UNITED STATES ARMY SADDLE BAG.** Late regulation. Made of fine black bridle leather. Will fit any saddle. Cost to make upward of $6.00 per pair; our price $4.25 per pair. Size, 14x12 inches.

**CW3**

**CW1. UNITED STATES ARMY CANVAS SADDLE BAGS.** Good, 2d-hand, serviceable order. Leather lined, with strap, etc. These bags fit on all McClelland saddles. Size, 15x14 inches. Price, $1.75 pair.

**German Army Gunner's Leather Tool Bags**, with shoulder sling strap: also hand carrying strap, made of sole leather, hand sewed, reinforced ends, size 10, 6, 7½ inches with hook fastenings, fine serviceable order. Price $5.85.

**7109. Iron Hames**, length 27½ inches, new, originally nickled, now slightly rusted, assorted patterns. Price 70 cents per pair.

**7110. Iron Hames**, 21½ inches, new, originally nickled, slightly rusted, assorted patterns. Price 45 cents per pair.

**New Padded Leather Seats** for 10 and 12 inch army saddles, army reserve stock. Price $1.50 each.

**NEW COMMERCIAL BRIDLES**, russet leather with army bit. Price, $2.95.

**1711. U. S. Army Breast Chains**, used on Artillery harness, 32 inches long, 5½ inch toggle ends, weight 2½ pounds, 1,200 in stock, in serviceable order. Price 25 cents each.

**3367. U. S. Army Artillery Lead Wire Rope Traces**, leather covered, same as 3366, length 8 feet 10 inches, weight 3 pounds. Price $3.58.

**100 McCLELLAND CIVIL WAR CAVALRY SOLDIERS' SADDLE BAGS**, with loops for attaching to McClellan saddle. Made at United States Arsenal. Price, $1.40 per pair.

**3366. U. S. Army New Pattern Steel Wire** leather covered **TRACE**, used with Artillery wheel harness, chain loops for fastening to hames, hook and toggle for attaching to the limber bar. The wire rope is ⅜ inch thick, covered with leather, hand sewed, full length 5 feet, 4 inches, weight 2½ pounds. Used, serviceable order, $2.85 each.

"Moderator"

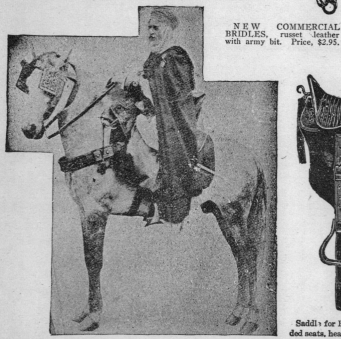

3366

**Ancient Army Ball Remover and Cleaner** for calibre 69 gun (¾-inch bore). Worm end, drill on the other; with open slot for the cleaning rag, at one Price 25c.

**Saddle for Boys**, 10 inch padded seats, heavy leather skirts, open wood stirrups, adjustable straps, used as part of the U. S. Army Artillery harness for carrying the gunners outfit, also used as a riding saddle in emergency. Offered in cleaned, repaired serviceable order. Strongest saddle made. Price, $6.50.

**3282. Algerian Sheiks, Bridle**, gilt embossed cloth and leather, hand forged native made bit, with large mouth ring, used by the late Frederick Remington in illustrating. The bridle is complete with saddle bags, with gilt embroidered cinch, native made. The outfit, bridle, cinch and saddle bags, $22.85.

**3385. French Cavalry Officer's Bridle and Saddle Bags**, used by the late Frederick Remington in illustrating. Bridle has double reins, forged steel French army bit, with curb chain, tan leather saddle with double pigskin skirts, complete outfit in good serviceable order. Price $25.00.

**F. M. 2. ARMY RECRUIT BAG**, or rucksack, made of canvas with draw rope at top to close. Flap to cover opening. Shoulder straps attached in center at top, and fastened at bottom corners. Both straps adjustable, with snap on one for ease in putting on. Price, $1.00 each.

### THE McCLELLAN ARMY SADDLE.

The national financial deficit for the year just closed is in part caused by the great waste made necessary by the rapid advance in improvements in military armament.

Battleships which were the flower of the navy in 1898 are now superseded by the new and more powerful Dreadnaughts. The Krag military rifles, with which troops were armed during the Spanish War, are now laid aside in the Government arsenals held as the army reserve gun, superseded by the new Springfield high power magazine rifle.

We can recall only one article of the military soldier's outfit that has stood the test of time, practically unchanged, namely, the saddle planned by Captain McClellan, who, while military attache in Europe in 1857, conceived the idea from the Hungarian saddle, on which he improved. His saddle was adopted as the U. S. regulation saddle in 1858. During the allied armies' march to Pekin, China, during the Boxers' War, the British army officers who had a chance to examine the United States Army McClellan saddle became very much interested in it, and declared it the best saddle of all the nations. Captain McClellan, during the Civil War, was the commanding officer of the Union army of the Potomac, familiar to the soldier as "Little Mac," father of former Mayor McClellan of New York City. During the Civil War the McClellan saddle was in use, with the tree covered with rawhide calfskin, with large leather skirts. After the Civil War the saddle had the skirts removed, and was covered with fine black leather over the rawhide. In this shape it was used until the recent change of uniforms from blue to olive-drab (dust color), when in order to match the uniforms, the saddle and equipments were changed from black to russet leather. Some 20,000 of these black leather covered saddles were sold from Rock Island Arsenal to Francis Bannerman, of New York City. One of the army officers, it is stated, expressed his opinion of the sale "that if he had his way the saddles would not have been sold, but would have been recovered with russet leather, and reissued for service."—Harness Herald, of St. Louis, Mo.

### EQUIPMENT OF A PRIVATE—1792—U. S. ARMY-PENNSYLVANIA MILITIA

| | |
|---|---|
| A Fire Lock | $15.00 |
| A bayonet | 2.00 |
| A ramrod | 1.00 |
| A cartridge box | 4.00 |
| A bayonet | 1.00 |
| Scabbard ($2/3) | .66 |
| A cartridge ($1/5) | .20 |
| A flint ($1/20) | .05 |
| A gun worm ($¼) | .25 |
| A screw driver ($1/20) | .05 |

(Extract from an act of the regulations of the Militia of the Commonwealth of Pennsylvania, Lancaster, Printed by Charles Bailey, in 1802.)

(From the rules ordered by Congress in March 29, 1779, signed by John Jay, President, Attested by Charles Thomason, Secy.)

**No. 40 KE. COMBINATION KNIFE** with fork, cap lifter and spoon with can opener. Has patent stag handle, brass lined, with nickel silver bolster and shield. The knife, fork and spoon close into the handle just as the blades of a pocket knife, as shown in illustration. Fork can be separated according to need. Price, new, $1.80, complete.

**No. 40N. NEW MODEL U. S. NAVY JACK KNIFE**, length open 5¾ inches. Has large blade, also small manicure blade. Loop for lanyard. Price, 60 cents.

**No. 40K. CAMPERS' COMBINATION KNIFE.** Length, 3½ inches with stag handle, large blade, screw driver, can opener, leather punch. High grade knife, NEW. Price, $1.50.

**F. M. 1. ARMY BOMB BAGS**, made of heavy drab canvas, inside bottom re-inforced with soft russet leather. Large flap cover has bronze buckle. Shoulder strap is adjustable, 1½ inches wide with buckle. Bag is 10 inches long, 5 inches wide, 6 inches thick. Will hold thermos bottles, cameras, etc. Fine bag for hikers and campers. Price, 85 cents; $9.00 a dozen.

## "Old Glory's" Baptism Traced to Fort Stanwix

### Historians Find Evidence Improvised Colors in 1777 Were Original Stars and Stripes

WASHINGTON, July 18 (A-P).—Army historians have unearthed evidence that the Stars and Stripes got its baptism of fire in land battle in the defense of Fort Stanwix, New York, August 2, 1777. The colors improvised by the garrison appear to have shown both the alternative stripes of red and white and the "stars of glory" set upon a field of blue cut from a "camulet cloak taken from the enemy at Peekskill."

At the request of historical societies, the War Department began a search which has brought to light a work entitled "A Narrative of the Military Actions of Colonel Marinus Willett," who was a member of the garrison. It describes the necessity for making a flag when the enemy invested the fort, and adds that "a decent one was soon contrived."

"The white stripes were cut out of ammunition shirts; the blue out of the camulet cloak taken from the enemy at Peekskill, while the red stripes were made of different pieces of stuff procured from one and another of the garrison," the narrative says. Quoting a letter written by Lieutenant Colonel Willett, at Hartford, Conn., August 21, 1777, it adds, speaking of the final action at Fort Stanwix on August 6:

"We totally routed two of the enemy's encampments, brought off upwards of . . . five colours, the whole of which on our return to the fort were displayed on our flagstaff under the Continental flag."—From *N. Y. Herald-Tribune* July 19, 1926.

While we're at Christmas, the H. T. carried an advertisement of Flint Lock Pistols in Working Order under the classification of Unusual Christmas Gifts last week. . . . We look for an outburst of period firearms among the local banditti toward the first of the year.—From *N. Y. Herald-Tribune*, Dec. 16, 1925.

Blue Web Saddle Girth. Price 25 cents.

Larger view of the U. S. Army Snap Hook in the link strap. Price for hooks separate from the strap 5 cents each, 40 cents per dozen.

No. 21    No. 22

21. Black Leather Spur Strap with buckle, second-hand, 10c each.

22. U. S. Cavalry Link Strap, with buckle and snap link; strap is 15 inches long, ¾ inch wide, heavy bridle leather, used to link the horse to the halter ring of the next horse, new. Price, 20 cents each.

No. 14

14. Polished Brass Bridle Rosette, as used on U. S. cavalry bridles. Price, 25 cents per pair. No extra charge for these on bridles costing $2.00 each or over.

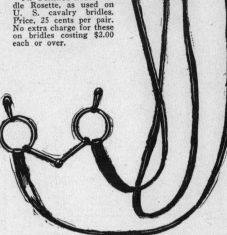

No. 5

No. 3

3. Illustration showing the No. 4 woven web halter on the horse with the No. 5 watering bridle lines and bit snapped into the halter, ready for use as COMBINATION HALTER AND BRIDLE.

U. S. Cavalry Curb Bridles, with forged steel bits. Bridles have been in use, are in second-hand order. Price, $1.20 each.

100 Civil War Army Bridles, with Government steel bits. Valuable only as relics or for decoration; not serviceable. Price, 75 cents each.

5. 10,000 New U. S. A. Combination Halter Bridles, with reins, bit and snap hooks, for quickly attaching to any 5 ring halter, in a moment making the combination of halter and bridle; reins are of the best bridle leather, 5 feet long, with steel bit and snaps, just purchased at recent Government Auction; in order to start the sale will offer a limited number of these fine new Watering Bridles for 90 cents for bridle, with bit and snap hook, or $9.00 per dozen. $1.80 for Bridle and Halter complete.

No. 19. U. S. A. Artillery Halter, strong heavy leather. Price with tie strap 90c. each, with combination bridle, reins and bit. Price $1.80

56 inches long    No. 26 Price 75 cents.

90 inches long

27. U. S. Artillery Wheel Traces. Length of leather 4 feet 2 inches, in serviceable order.

28. U. S. Artillery Lead Trace, leather is 6 feet long, second-hand serviceable order.

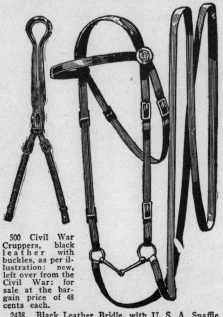

2160. U. S. Civil War Bridle, black leather head stall; left over from Civil War stock, with brass rosette U. S. Monogram; with new Spanish War stitched bridle reins, 5 feet long; with forged steel curved bit; price $2.45 each.

80 U. S. A. Russet Leather Link Straps, for quickly attaching to Cavalry horses bridles to link them together, used only a short time, in good, serviceable order: price 75 cents each.

No. 1311

No. 1311. Kings Bridle with gilt crown attached to chin strap, handsomely ornamented, gilt buckles and keepers, gilt metal head bands over the leather, silvered ornamented crown on the gilt rosettes, ornamented gilt nose and head bands, royal coat of arms in gilt. This fine bridle was used by the King of Portugal. It has the royal coat of arms, is in good serviceable order. We have supplied handsome silvered bit and patent leather rings to complete; rare relic. Price, $50.00.

500 Civil War Cruppers, black leather with buckles, as per illustration: new, left over from the Civil War: for sale at the bargain price of 48 cents each.

2438. Black Leather Bridle, with U. S. A. Snaffle Steel Bit, with brass U. S. A. monogram rosette, the head stall is Civil War pattern, fitted with new Spanish War steel snaffle bit and stitched reins, 5 feet long. Price, $1.95.

**1766. UNITED STATES CAVALRY CRUPPERS.** Sold on a slight change in the regulations. Price $1.00.

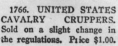

**1389. ARMY SADDLER'S FILES,** 3 cuts, 8⅞ inches long, ⅞ inch wide, new. Price, 20 cents.

**U. S. CIVIL WAR CARBINE SOCKET,** attached to the saddle strap to hold the cavalrymen's carbine; new. Relics of 1861 to 1865. Price 15 cents each.

**1388. SADDLER'S GLASS SLICKERS,** 5 by 4½ by ⅝ inches thick, with hard wood handle; new; from Government Arsenal. Price, 35 cents each.

**ARMY OLIVE DRAB SLICKERS,** offered in serviceable order, in assorted sizes at $1.85 each.

**U. S. CARBINE SOCKET.** Hartman's patent, used about General Custer's time, has opening for quickly raising the carbine without having to withdraw, as in Civil War kind; almost new. Price, 20 cents.

**U. S. ARMY CARBINE BOOT,** late reguation, almost new. Made of heavy bridle leather, complete with straps, hold any carbine, cost to make upwards of $6.00. Our price, 40 cents each.

**10972. PETER THE GREAT, EMPEROR OF RUSSIA STIRRUPS,** from the Arnold Museum Sale, Milton Hall, Gravesend, England. The stirrups are of light hand forged iron, reinforced at the edges; swivel bar; the front with iron design, double headed eagle and crown "Russian Emblem;" length at the foot-rest 9½ inches; width 4½ inches; height of arch 4½ inches; each stirrup weighs 2 pounds; rare relics. Price $50.00 the pair.

**10906. GERMAN ARMY BRADOON BIT,** relic of the French-German War, 2¼ inch rings. Price 15 cents each, $1.50 per dozen.

**11043. MILITIA OFFICER'S HALTER BRIDLE;** double reins, with halter tie strap; black leather used, offered in good serviceable refinished order. Price $3.65.

**COWBOY REVOLVER HOLSTER,** made of fine heavy russet leather. Will hold most any revolver, plain finish. Price, $1.25 each.

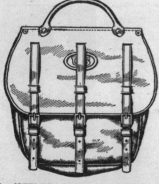

**14D. NEW BLACK LEATHER BAG,** suitable for carrying papers, books or tools. Size 11x12x3 inches. With handle or long shoulder sling. Special price, $3.25 each.
Second hand Bags as above, in serviceable order, $1.95 each.

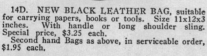

**10973. ANTIQUE WOOD STIRRUPS,** 18th century period, from Moscow, Russia; dark colored hardwood, bound with hand torged irons; embossed metal fronts, crescent shaped; length 7½ inches, width 4½ inches, height 4 inches. From Arnold Museum Sale. In serviceable order. Price $12.00 the pair.

**KHAKI RUBBERIZED FABRIC PONCHO,** size 45x72 inches, in fine condition, little used. This is a recently adopted poncho with buttons along edge. Good protection when riding. Price, $1.00.

**3231.** 2½ INCH U. S. BRONZE LACQUERED ROLLER BUCKLE. 6 cents each, 50 cents per dozen, $3.00 per gross.

**FM4. CAVALRY CANTEEN COVERS,** made of drab canvas lined with heavy felt to keep contents cool. Two top snaps, thong at bottom to attach to saddle spider, adjustable leather strap around entire cover, with snap at top to attach to saddle ring. Price with new aluminum canteen and cup, $1.50. Cover only 75 cents.

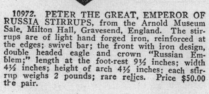

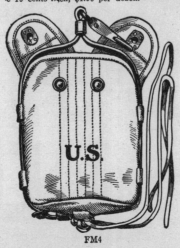

FM4

**5076. NEW U. S. BRONZE LACQUERED BAR BUCKLE;** takes ⅞ inch strap; obsolete pattern. 3 for 10 cents, 25 cents per dozen, $2.00 per gross.

**U. S. CURRY COMB,** with flexible leather back—the Ideal Curry Comb. Bargain price, 50 cents each.

**10466. OLD TIME BRITISH ARMY HORSE BIT,** with brass rosette, ornamented with "Crown and Lion, Peninsula, Waterloo. Price $4.85.

**10440. SOUTH AFRICAN BOER WAR RHINOCEROS HIDE WHIP.** German silver wire mountings; 5 feet. Price $6.85.

**1128. NEW U. S. A. SNAP HOOKS FOR ⅝ INCH SLING STRAP;** black lacquered finish; obsolete; from U. S. Government arsenal; makes fine snap for sword; full length 2¼ inches. Price 5 cents each, 50 cents per dozen.

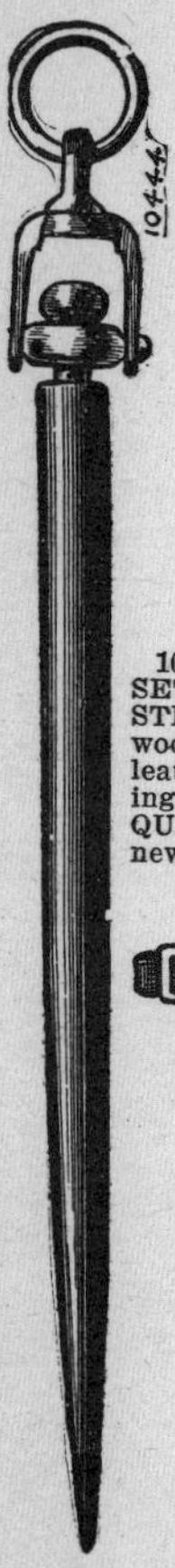

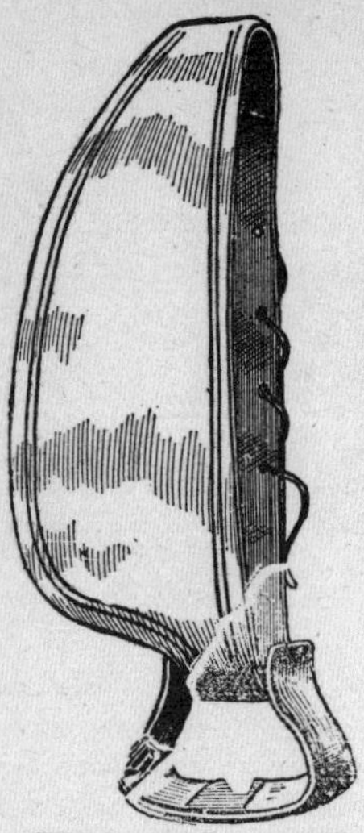

10296B. TEXAS SADDLE RUSSET LEATHER STIRRUP STRAPS, WITH FENDERS. Large wood stirrups, covered with russet leather. Complete with lariat lacing. Made of the FINEST QUALITY LEATHER. Entirely new. Price, $10.00 per pair.

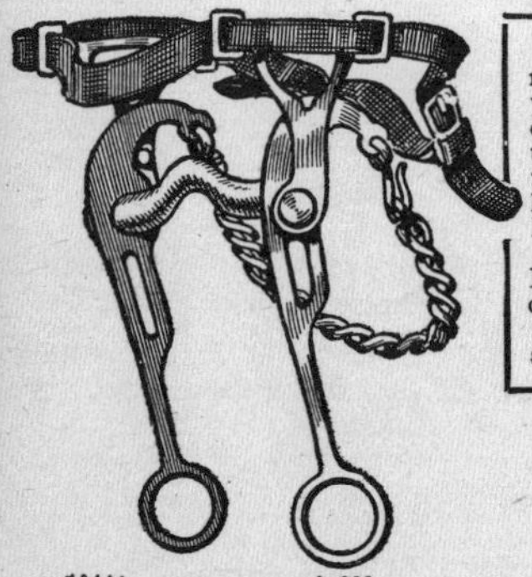

10444. 0-829

10444. U. S. ARMY PICKET PIN. With double swivels and adjustable shackle, steel forged, with solid hammer head. Full length 18 inches, diameter ⅞ inch, weight 21 ounces. Made at the Government Rock Island Arsenal, 1903. A necessity on every farm. Price, 45 cents.

0-829. U. S. A. HORSE TRAINER'S BIT. Johnson's patent. Offered complete, with russet leather nose strap, polished steel curb chain and hooks, as illustrated. Trainer has powerful lever on the horse. Equipped for single or double lines. Nickeled steel. From the Rock Island Arsenal. In good order; equal to new. Price, $1.50.

10032. U. S. A. SNAP HOOKS. 14,000 IN STOCK. Loop takes ¾-inch strap. Steel springs. From the Rock Island Arsenal auction. Price, 5 cents each; 30 cents per dozen; $2.85 per gross.

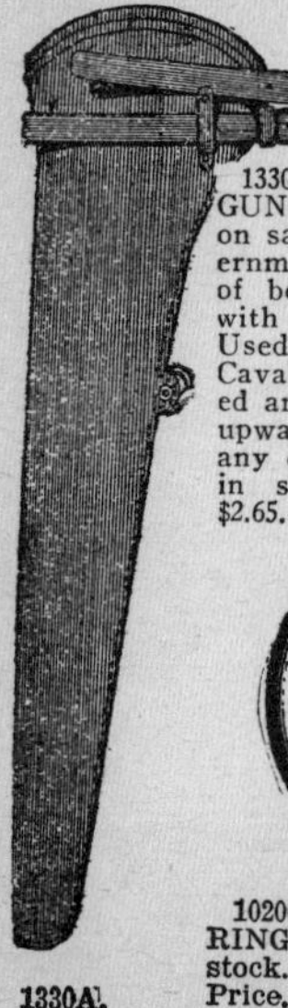

1330A. RUSSET LEATHER GUN CASES. For carrying gun on saddle. Made at U. S. Government Rock Island Arsenal of best quality leather, fitted with loops and fastening straps. Used a short time by U. S. Cavalry. Are offered in cleaned and serviceable order. Cost upwards of $4.00 each. Will fit any ordinary sporting rifle. 500 in stock. Our bargain price $2.65.

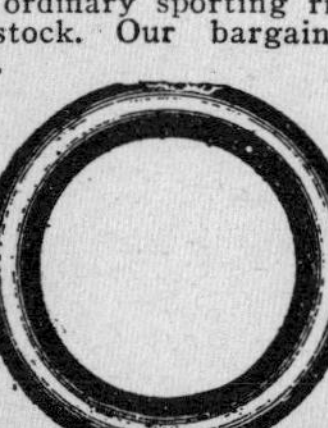

10200.

10200. U. S. A. HARNESS RINGS. Size 1¼-inch. 9,000 in stock. New blue steel color. Price, 25 cents per dozen.

1330A.

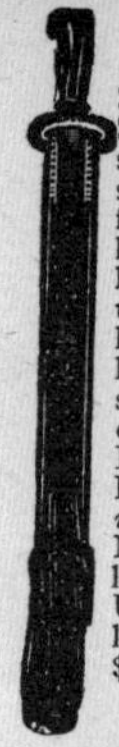

No. 301. U. S. A. LINK STRAPS. Russet leather with snap hook for fastening to horse's bit to keep in line; useful in team harness to keep horses from snapping at each other; *new*. Price, 35 cents. Russet leather, *used*, 25 cents. New, black leather, 20 cents. Used, black leather, 14 cents. $1.25.

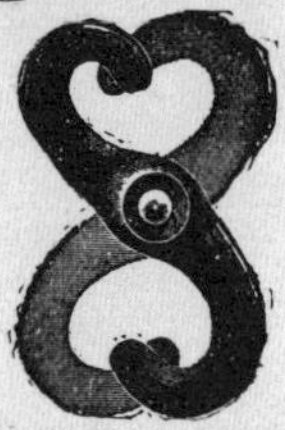

7,000 U. S. ARMY CONNECTING SHACKLES, forged steel. Size, $2\frac{1}{4}$x$1\frac{1}{16}$ inches. Price, 10 cents each; $1.00 per dozen; $10.00 per gross.

A Kentucky man writes regarding the short delay while waiting for a new edition of our catalogue to be printed, "Just send it when you can, I am like the Ohio man's wife, I want one for a bible."
California Railroad Manager writes: "Your catalogue is indispensable, send it as soon as possible."

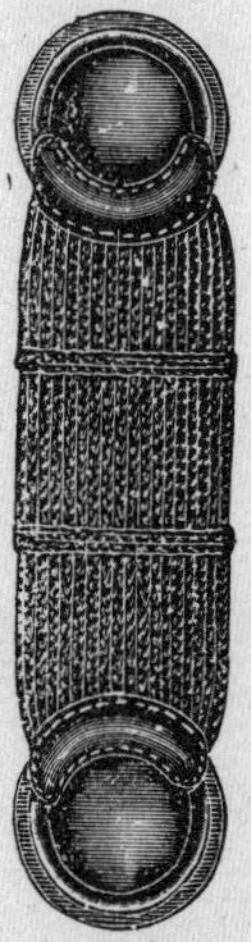

3506.—U. S. HAIR CINCH SADDLE GIRTH. Made at Government Arsenal, all hair, 23 rope strands attached to 4 inch rings, black leather safe under the rings, hand sewed; in assorted sizes, used, serviceable order. Price, $1.45. Russet leather safes $1.65.

10287. U. S. A. BRIDLE AND REINS WITH BRIDOON BIT. Heavy fine quality stuffed black leather; noncorrosive silvered steel bit, with swivel cheeks, hand sewed, like new, bronze regulation buckles; finest quality leather watering bridle. Price, $1.85.

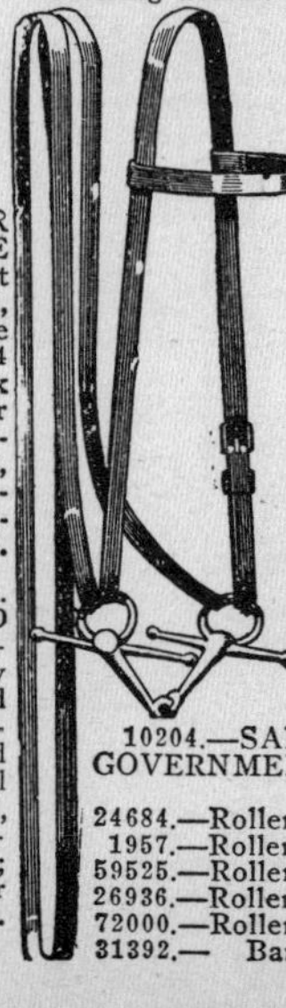

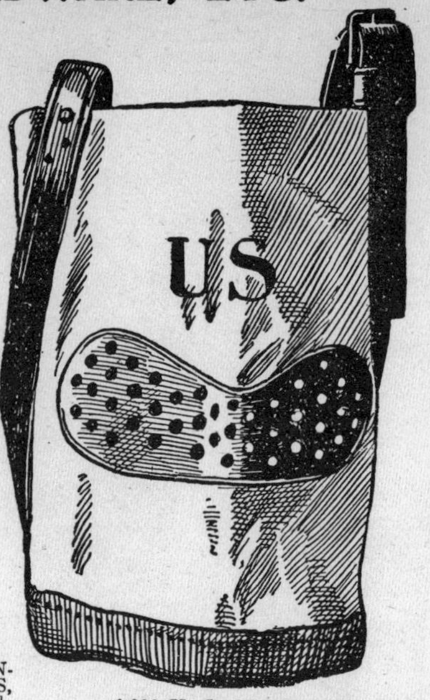



1,000 U. S. ARMY FEED BAGS. Made of strong, heavy white canvas duck, with leather bottom, and strap with leather ventilator. Best and strongest feed bag made. Price, 50 cents each.

CIVIL WAR PICKET PIN. Round iron about 1¼ inches in diameter, 3 feet long, used to drive into the ground for picket stations. Price, $3.50.

1800. — U. S. CAVALRY PICKET PINS. Forged steel pointed pin, 15 inches long, ⅝ inch shanks for driving into the ground, for tying horses to while grazing; swivel shackle attached to head of the pin which keeps the lariat rope from twisting. Far superior to the old model picket pin illustrated on page 256; useful on every farm; condition practically as good as new. Price, 45 cents.

HORSEMAN'S WATCH FOB. Russet strap attached to short nickled stirrup. Price, 25 cents.

WHITMAN WATERING BRIDLES. Used by U. S. Army Experimental Board; offered in serviceable order. Price, $1.85.

10262A. — POLICE BOULEVARD GREEN GLASS LAMP GLOBES. For use in boulevard lamps, 12 inches in diameter, globes lettered "Police"; new and in perfect order; 50 in stock. Price, $1.00 each.

10262B.—PLAIN GLASS GLOBES. For Boulevard lamps, 12 inches in diameter, 35 in stock. Price, $1.00 each.

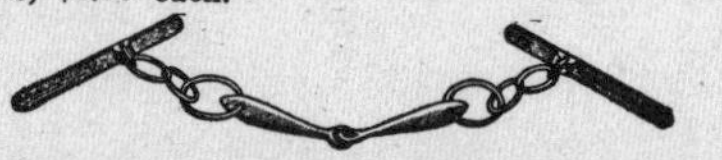

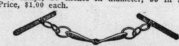

10294.—CIVIL WAR BRIDOON BIT. Kind used by Union Cavalry on watering bridle, made of forged steel with rings for reins and three link chain toggles for hooking into the ring of the halter, connecting the halter with bridle. Called watering bridle from the fact that it was quickly attached to the halter, the soldiers using it when watering horses.

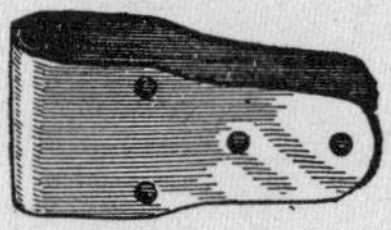

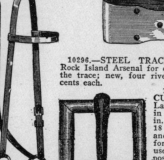

10296.—STEEL TRACE CLIPS. From Rock Island Arsenal for connecting chain to the trace; new, four rivet holes. Price, 15 cents each.

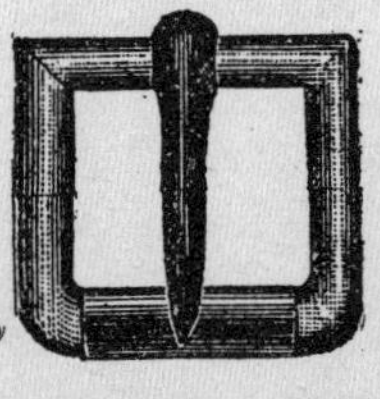

1678. — U. S. A. CURB STRAPS. Late regulation, new, in black leather, ⅝ in. wide, full length 18 in., with buckles and keepers; doubled for use as curb strap, useful for any purpose requiring good leather strap. Price, 8 cents each.

10204.—SADDLERY HARDWARE FROM U. S. GOVERNMENT ROCK ISLAND AUCTION—

| | | | | Price per | Price per |
|---|---|---|---|---|---|
| 24684.— | Roller buckles | 1½ | in., new, | doz. $0.35, | gross $3.00 |
| 1957.— | Roller buckles | 1¼ | in., new, | doz. .30, | gross 2.40 |
| 59525.— | Roller buckles | 1 | in., new, | doz. .25, | gross 2.00 |
| 26936.— | Roller buckles | ¾ | in., new, | doz. .20, | gross 1.50 |
| 72000.— | Roller buckles | ⅝ | in., new, | doz. .15, | gross 1.20 |
| 31392.— | Bar buckles | ¾ | in., new, | doz. .20, | gross 1.50 |

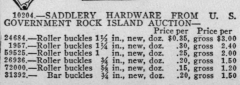

U. S. ARMY BLUE WEB SURCINGLE, with heavy harness leather strap, with hand sewed buckle straps and keeper loops. Full length is 60 inches; wool web 3½ inches wide; leather strap measures 30 inches. Price, 55 cents each.

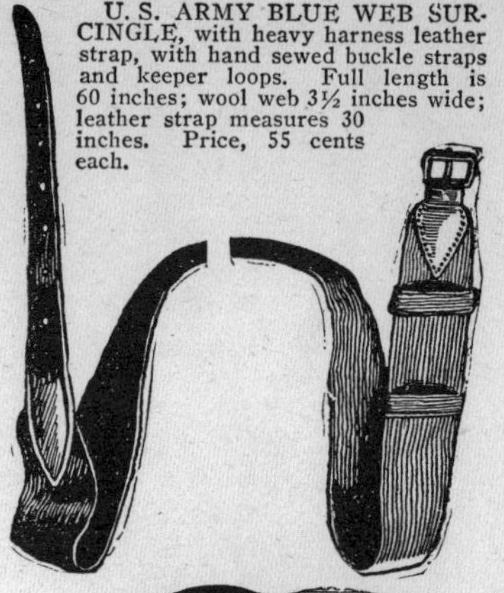

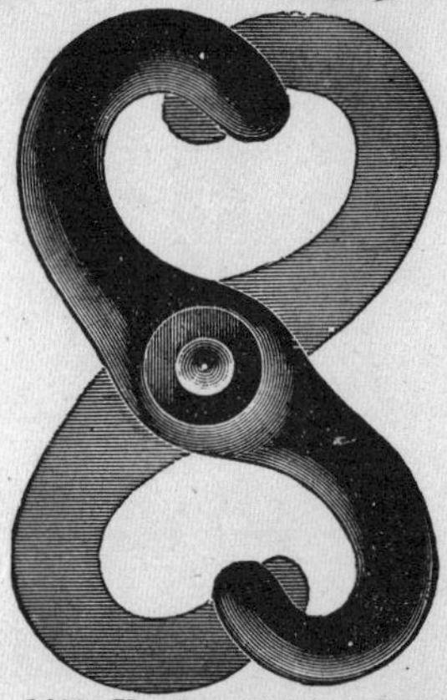

6,000 U. S. ARMY FORGED STEEL SHACKLES, for quickly connecting two parts of chain. Size, 2½ inches long, 1½ inches wide. Price, 12 cents each; $1.25 per dozen; $12.00 per gross.

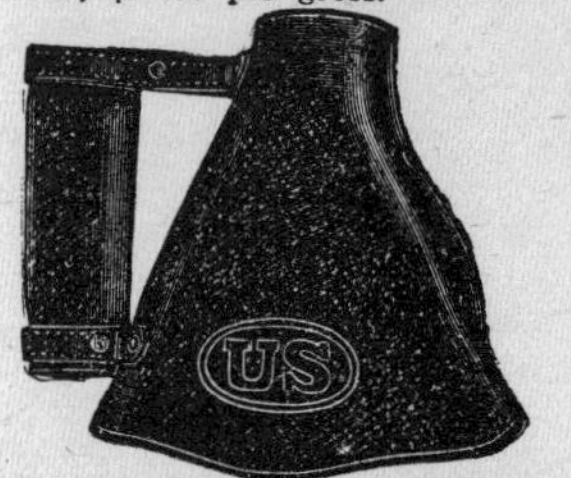



28 U. S. GUIDON STIRRUPS. Hard wood stirrup with 4 inch tread, covered with russet leather hoods, with russet leather socket attached for holding the guidon flag pole; practically new. Price, $2.00 each.

25 U. S. GUIDON STIRRUPS. Black leather, old pattern, small size, serviceable order. $1.50 each.

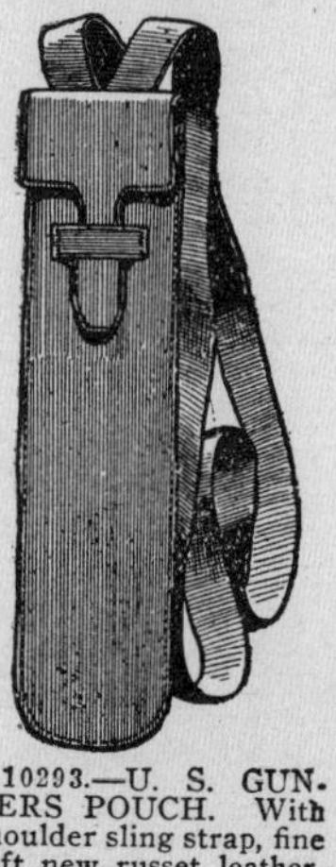

10293.—U. S. GUNNERS POUCH. With shoulder sling strap, fine soft new russet leather, hand sewed. Length of the pouch 10 in., width 2½ in. Shoulder sling 40 in., ⅝ in. wide. Price, 35 cents.

No. 600. Pair of Brass Barrel Flint Lock Pistols, used by General George Washington, purchased at Auction Sale held by the receiver, J. P. Leachman, of the estate of S. A. Marsteller. Sale was ordered and held at the County Court House, Manassas, Va.

Description.—Brass barrels, 8 inches long, ⅝-inch smooth bore; slightly bell-shaped at the muzzle. Lock plate is marked Hawkins (famous English gunsmith of Revolutionary War period). On the barrel is marked "London," with proofmarks, crown and G. P., which means "Gunmaker's Proof," as authorized by charter given to the Gunmakers' Guild in 1634, R. V., with second proofmark crown V. The stock is old English walnut with carving around the breech pin, with knob butts (both stocks were broken and show repairing). The pistols are heavily mounted in silver. There is a silver band on the stock, engraved "Gen'l G. Washington." There is a silver name plate, showing man's head with ornamented relief work of draped flags, Rose and Thistle. On the side opposite the lock there is a heavy silver plate with lion, unicorn, cannon balls, draped flags, etc.; silver thimble ramrod-holders, engraved silver guard lever, silver butt with head surrounded with ornamental relief work. Full length of each pistol is 15 inches. They show considerable wear; part of one of the stocks at the muzzle end is broken off.

History.—These pistols were given by General Washington to his private secretary, Bartholomew Dandridge. (See Lossings "Life of Washington" for letter from Washington to Dandridge, thanking him for his six years' service as his private secretary.) The inscription on the name plate shows that these pistols were presented to Washington. At the Administrator's sale of personal effects of Bartholomew Dandridge, held in Alexandria, Va., April 20, 1804, these pistols were bought by Col. Philip G. Marsteller, who was an intimate

In March, 1903, sealed bids were received by the sheriff for the purchase of these rare relics (Confederate General Mosley's daughters bid for these pistols; were within small sum of our bid), but the court refused to confirm the sale, as there had been an offer made in 1892 of $5,000.00 for these pistols for exhibition at Chicago's World's Fair. So sale was ordered at Public Auction, when we became the purchasers. With the pistols we obtained the bill of sale given to Col. Philip G. Marsteller in 1804. Mr. Marsteller certified on the bill of sale given to us by Sheriff Leachman that these pistols are the identical ones in his family known as Washington's pistols. We have the copy of the records of the Alexandria Will Court; We have the certificate and seal of the Prince William County Court, certifying to the order of court placing these pistols and other property in Sheriff Leachman's possession, with order to sell the same; also sheriff's circulars and advertisement of sale.

George Washington Bassett Pair Flint Lock Duelling Pistols; all vouched for by original letters (which went to the purchaser of these pistols) from Mr. Basset and Ex-Governor Wise of Virginia. Pistols are in serviceable order; contained in walnut case as shown by photograph. Presented by French Officer, Battle of Yorktown period to Col. Brownell Bassett of Eltham, New Kent, Virginia, Member of Congress from Williamsburg, Va.; the pistols descended to Col. Bassett's son, George Washington Bassett.

George Washington Basset's wife was granddaughter of General George Washington's only sister. Governor of Virginia Henry A. Wise, in 1875, gave letter vouching for G. W. Bassett, then a man over 80 years old. Pistols have brass barrels showing much wear on the muzzle. Ornamented silver lock, plate, guard lever and mountings, name plate engraved, "Mr. G. Washington Bassett." Engraved on the barrel of the pistol is "Buckmaster, London," with old time British proofmarks; full length, 13½ inches; fine order.

Both pairs sold to Mr. Litchfield of Brooklyn, N. Y., for presentation to a Museum. We show them with description, as we believe some of our customers will be interested in this bit of American history.

friend and acted as one of Washington's pallbearers. The price paid at the sale was £6 3s. The original bill of sale belongs with the pistols. The sale report is recorded in Will Book B, page 67, Alexandria City Orphan's Court. When Col. Philip G. Marsteller died, these passed to his son, S. A. Marsteller, who died in Prince William County, Va., about 30 years ago. They remained in his family until last year, when suit was brought to settle up his estate, and these pistols, together with other personal property (see page — for Col. Marsteller's sword), were placed with Sheriff Leachman as Receiver.

## The Iron for Parrot's Guns

In the Palisades Interstate Park, a great playground of New York city and State, lies a tract of 10,000 acres, once called Greenwood and owned by Robert P. Parrott, the inventor of the Parrott gun, and his brother, which had a not unimportant role in the Civil War. On this tract was produced the iron, dug from mines and smelted in a cold blast charcoal furnace, which, transported over the hills to the West Point foundry at Cold Springs, was made into cannon. The most important product of this foundry was the Parrott gun, an effective weapon of longer range than any the South could make or buy, and which an officer of the Confederacy who suffered from the deadly precision of its first fire described as "excelling any artillery ever before brought on the field in siege operations."

The early iron industry of Orange county is almost forgotten to-day. Few traces of it remain except the stacks of the old Greenwood furnace and of the Queensboro furnace built in the latter part of the eighteenth century and still to be seen near the road from Bear Mountain Inn to Tuxedo. We are indebted to R. D. A. Parrott, a nephew of Robert P. Parrott, for the little known history of his uncle's part in developing the mineral resources of this region.

Robert P. Parrott was graduated from the United States Military Academy in 1824; he was assigned to the Ordnance Department, and after some service in the Creek Indian wars was stationed at West Point. He resigned from the army to take over the cannon factory, and he finally succeeded in acquiring 7,000 acres of land in Orange county with the mineral rights and the Greenwood furnace.

The furnace was on the edge of a small lake

in the midst of a vast wooded tract. The houses of the furnace men, miners and wood choppers were scattered through the mountains. The labor of these men was irregular; the free use of the land for grazing, the opportunity for securing free wood for domestic use, as well as for making baskets, spoons and ladles, and the use of the woods for hunting and fishing "all tended," writes Mr. Parrott, "to make the mountaineers indifferent to discipline." Nevertheless, many of them enlisted and went to the front in the Civil War, and those who remained did yeoman service at the iron mines and furnace. An important branch of the work was the cutting of 10,000 cords of wood and turning it into charcoal.

The Greenwood charcoal iron was selected for making guns on account of its remarkable tensile strength. This quality was the achievement of years of experiment and investigation by Robert P. Parrott. To him the production of strong iron was a task and at the same time a means to a patriotic end. Because he used this superior metal he was able to have guns of high effectiveness at the front when the Civil War began. And he kept on furnishing them as fast as the West Point foundry could make them until the end of the war. Writing of the Parrott gun R. D. A. Parrott quotes his uncle's words describing it:

"I was led to the construction of my gun wholly by my own experiments and conclusions. It is a hooped gun of the simplest kind, composed of one piece of cast iron and one of wrought iron. It has no taper, no screws, no successive layers of hoops. It is, however, no hasty expedient; but devised upon the result of years of experience and practical trials, and has a definite and consistent plan."

He made no claim for originality in inventing a hooped gun; neither did he claim that the rifling of the gun was original. His system, however, was new, he had the strong iron he needed and he conceived improvements on all other big guns.

Mr. Parrott cites as an evidence of his uncle's stanch patriotism the fact that when he was importuned to raise the price of his guns because the Government could not do without them he refused, and that when the end of the war came he proposed of his own accord to cancel contracts for work unfinished. "The Government accepted this loyal offer and the manufacture of Parrott guns ceased."

The Greenwood furnace was thus clearly linked with the operations of the Civil War from the first to the last shot fired; and these early iron workers, by availing themselves of their resources of ore and wood and carrying their industry to its high point of excellence, became national benefactors and achieved a position of historic importance. The Greenwood tract, increased until it included more than 10,000 acres and representing thirty-three separate purchases, remained after the war in the possession of Robert P. Parrott's brother. The fact that the owner of so large a tract cooperated with the late E. H. Harriman made possible the expeditious working out of the plan for the extension of the Palisades Interstate Park across the divide to the western boundary of the Hudson Highlands. The old furnace, near what is now the town of Arden, made its last blast in 1871, but its stack, already properly marked with tablets, will be preserved.

*—From N. Y. Herald, March 6, 1921.*

# SADDLERY:

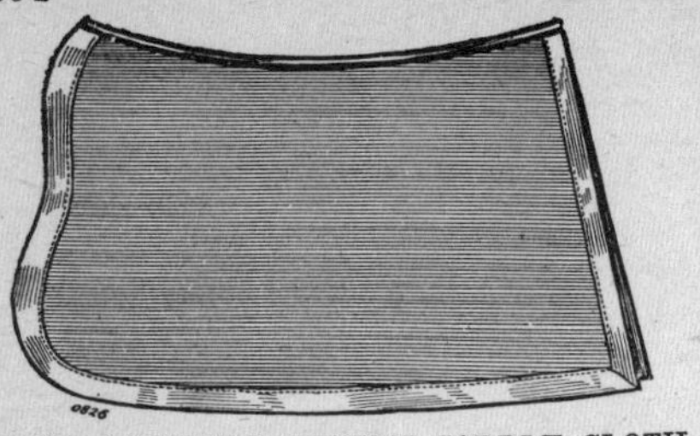

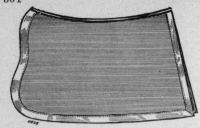

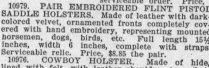

0-826. OFFICER'S SERVICE SADDLE CLOTH OR CHEVRAC.
HEAVY DARK-BLUE CLOTH, with regulation 1-inch colored leather binding around the edges, 1¼-inch black leather binding in the centre. Heavy waterproof canvas lined. New and of fine quality. Made at the U. S. Rock Island Armory. We have 11 with artillery red border, 7 in robin's-egg blue border for infantry officers and 4 with yellow binding for cavalry. Bargain price, buyer's choice, $3.85 each.

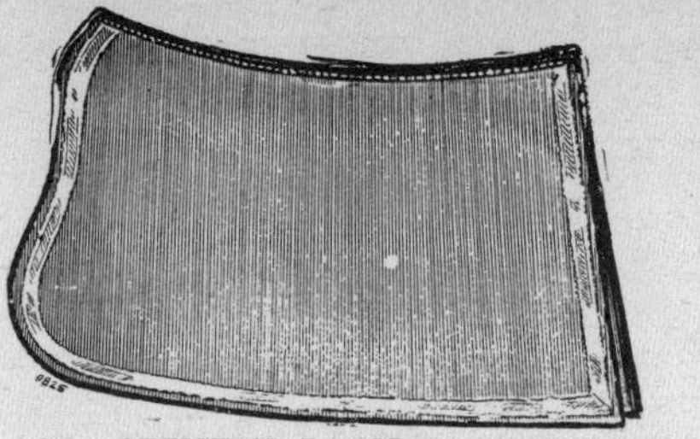

0-825. OFFICER'S DRESS PARADE SADDLE CLOTH OR CHEVRAC. Heavy dark blue cloth, with row of 1-inch gilt lace ⅜ inch from the edge, 1¼-inch leather binding over the centre, heavy waterproof enameled cloth lining, widest width 31 inches, at the centre 26 inches, depth of skirt 19 inches. 36 in stock. ALL NEW and of the finest quality. Made at the U. S. Rock Island Arsenal, and far superior to the ordinary cheap trade made saddle cloths. Bargain price, $5.85.

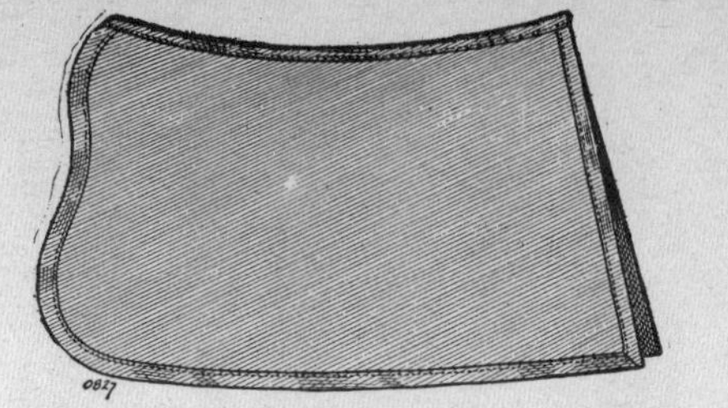

0-827. OFFICER'S OLIVE DRAB SERVICE SADDLE CLOTH. Extra fine colored olive-drab canvas facing cloth,
Bound around the edges and in centre with slightly darker shade of olive-drab binding cloth. Heavy olive-drab waterproof canvas lined. 25 in stock. Made at the U. S. Rock Island Arsenal. Practically new. Bargain price, $3.25 each
0-824. U. S. A. KHAKI CANVAS SADDLE CLOTH. Size 30 inches on the seat, 19-inch skirts. Heavy khaki-colored cloth canvas. Made at the U. S. Rock Island Arsenal. Double sewed at the seat, reinforced edges. Have been used. Flanks pierced for fastening the insignia. 60 in stock in serviceable order. Price, 75 cents each.

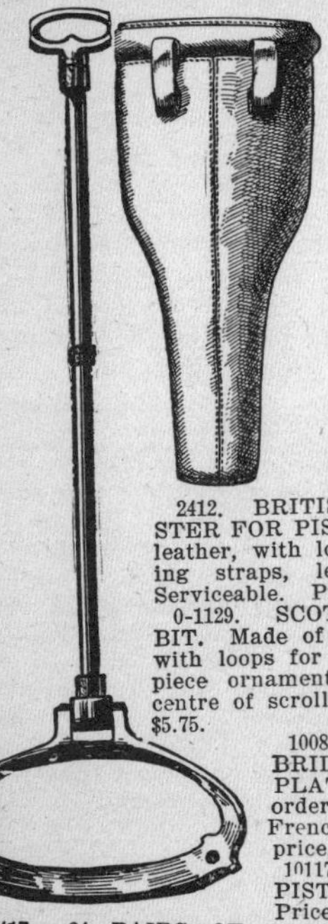

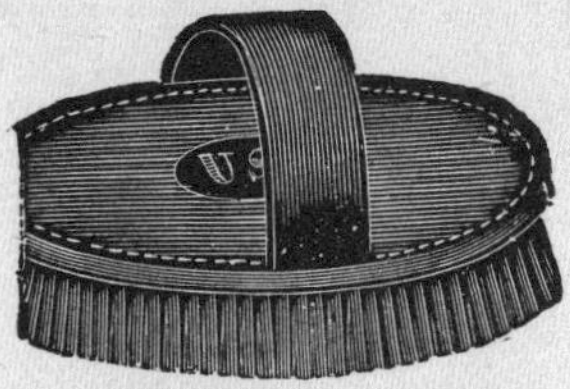

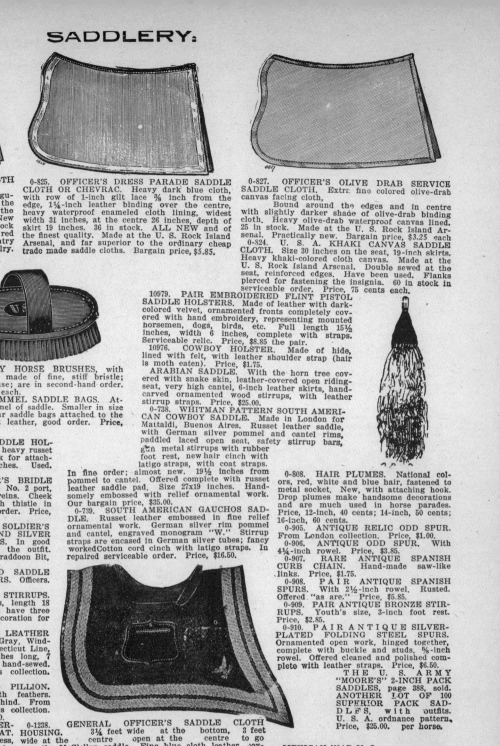

U. S. ARMY HORSE BRUSHES, with leather backs; made of fine, stiff bristle; have been in use; are in second-hand order. Price, 60 cents each.
U. S. A. POMMEL SADDLE BAGS. Attached to pommel of saddle. Smaller in size than the regular saddle bags attached to the cantle. Russet leather, good order. Price, $2.65 pair.

2412. BRITISH ARMY SADDLE HOLSTER FOR PISTOL. Made of heavy russet leather, with loop on the back for attaching straps, length 13½ inches. Used. Serviceable. Price, $1.75.
0-1129. SCOTCH OFFICER'S BRIDLE BIT. Made of German silver, No. 2 port, with loops for three sets of reins. Cheek piece ornamented with Scotch thistle in centre of scroll. Serviceable order. Price, $5.75.
10081. FRENCH SOLDIER'S BRIDLE BIT AND SILVER PLATED STIRRUPS. In good order. Price, $5.85 the outfit. French Soldier's Braddoon Bit, price, $1.00.
10117. PAIR OLD SADDLE PISTOL HOLSTERS. Officers. Price, $4.50.
2417. 24 PAIRS OF ANTIQUE METAL STIRRUPS. With stirrup irons, ornamented swivel loops, length 18 inches, stirrups 3¾ inches. The stirrup rods have three ornamented brass bands. Will make fine decoration for den. Price, $1.75 each stirrup.
2674. REVOLUTIONARY WAR OFFICER'S LEATHER SADDLE BAG. Belonged to Col. Ebenezer Gray, Windham, Conn., officer in the 6th Regiment Connecticut Line, 1777 to 1778. Russet-colored leather, 20 inches long, 7 inches diameter, embossed leather ends, hand-sewed. Valuable only as relic. From the Brooks collection. Price, $15.00.
2117. REVOLUTIONARY WAR PERIOD PILLION. Leather-covered saddle cushion filled with feathers. Usually used as saddle for woman to ride behind. From the Coles family, Glastonbury, Conn., Brooks collection. Pillions are now rarely met with. Price, $15.00.
0-718. SOUTH AMERICAN COWBOY SILVER-MOUNTED RAWHIDE BRIDLE AND LARIAT. Bridle is combined with halter, double thickness, of Indian-tanned hide, hand-sewed and bound together with silver rings, Turk's head knot for throat fastening. RAWHIDE LEATHER BIT clamped together with silver rings, with Turk's head knot instead of fastening buckle. Rawhide halter strap, partly double thick, hand-sewed, clamped with silver rings and ornamented, 8½-foot halter strap. Lariat is made of Indian-tanned rawhide 18 feet long, all in one piece, with 1¾-inch heavy silver lariat ring. Handsome, serviceable outfit. Price for bridle and lariat, $38.50.

10979. PAIR EMBROIDERED FLINT PISTOL SADDLE HOLSTERS. Made of leather with dark-colored velvet, ornamented fronts completely covered with hand embroidery, representing mounted horsemen, dogs, birds, etc. Full length 15½ inches, width 6 inches, complete with straps. Serviceable relic. Price, $8.85 the pair.
10976. COWBOY HOLSTER. Made of hide, lined with felt, with leather shoulder strap (hair is moth eaten). Price, $1.75.
ARABIAN SADDLE. With the horn tree covered with snake skin, leather-covered open riding-seat, very high cantel, 6-inch leather skirts, hand-carved ornamented wood stirrups, with leather stirrup straps. Price, $25.00.
0-738. WHITMAN PATTERN SOUTH AMERICAN COWBOY SADDLE. Made in London for Mattaldi, Buenos Aires. Russet leather saddle, with German silver pommel and cantel rims, paddled laced open seat, safety stirrup bars, gun metal stirrups with rubber foot rest, new hair cinch with latigo straps, with coat straps. In fine order; almost new. 19½ inches from pommel to cantel. Offered complete with russet leather saddle pad. Size 27x19 inches. Handsomely embossed with relief ornamental work. Our bargain price, $35.00.
0-739. SOUTH AMERICAN GAUCHOS SADDLE. Russet leather embossed in fine relief ornamental work. German silver rim pommel and cantel, engraved monogram "W." Stirrup straps are encased in German silver tubes; fancy workedCotton cord cinch with latigo straps. In repaired serviceable order. Price, $16.50.

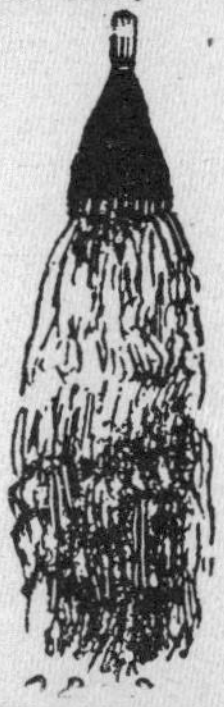

0-808. HAIR PLUMES. National colors, red, white and blue hair, fastened to metal socket. New, with attaching hook. Drop plumes make handsome decorations and are much used in horse parades. Price, 12-inch, 40 cents; 14-inch, 50 cents; 16-inch, 60 cents.
0-905. ANTIQUE RELIC ODD SPUR. From London collection. Price, $1.00.
0-906. ANTIQUE ODD SPUR. With 4¼-inch rowel. Price, $3.85.
0-907. RARE ANTIQUE SPANISH CURB CHAIN. Hand-made saw-like links. Price, $1.75.
0-908. PAIR ANTIQUE SPANISH SPURS. With 2½-inch rowel. Rusted. Offered "as are." Price, $5.85.
0-909. PAIR ANTIQUE BRONZE STIRRUPS. Youth's size, 3-inch foot rest. Price, $2.85.
0-910. PAIR ANTIQUE SILVER-PLATED FOLDING STEEL SPURS. Ornamented open work, hinged together, complete with buckle and studs, ⅝-inch rowel. Offered cleaned and polished complete with leather straps. Price, $6.50.
THE U. S. ARMY "MOORE'S" 2-INCH PACK SADDLES, page 388, sold. ANOTHER LOT OF 100 SUPERIOR PACK SADDLES, with outfits. U. S. A. ordnance pattern. Price, $25.00. per horse.

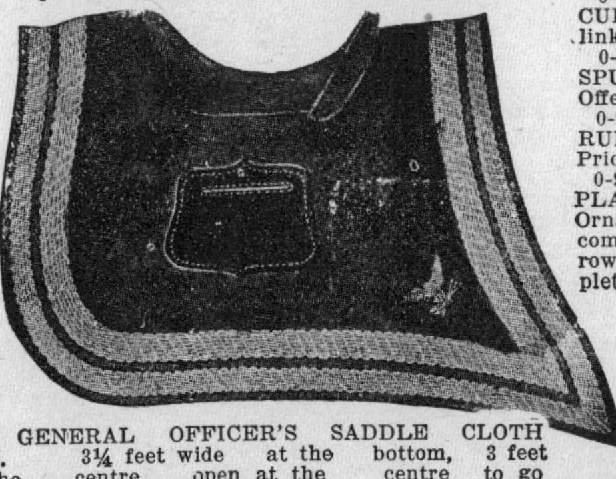

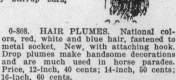

0-1238. GENERAL OFFICER'S SADDLE CLOTH HOUSING. 3¼ feet wide at the bottom, 3 feet wide at the centre open at the centre to go over the McClellan saddle. Fine blue cloth leather covered with two rows of gilt braid 2½ inches in width around the front, back and bottom, with 3-inch embroidered gilt eagle on the corners. Have been used. Offered in good, second-hand serviceable order. Price, $15.00.

MEXICAN WAR U. S. BRIDLE ROSETTE. Polished brass fronts with letters U. S. Lead filled back with strap loops. Kind used in Mexican and early part of Civil War. Good condition. Price, 15 cents each; 25 cents pair.

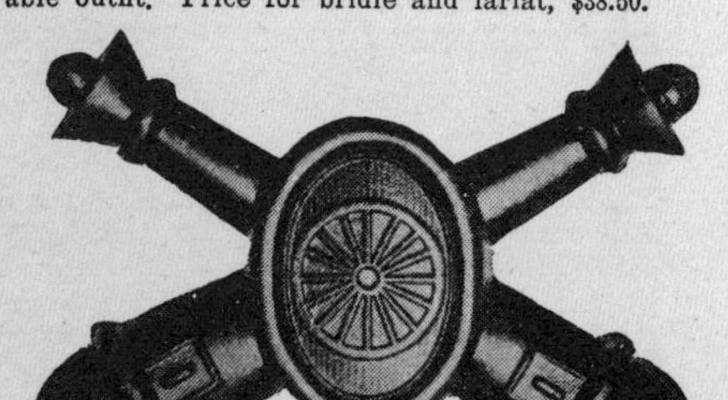

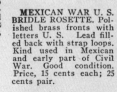

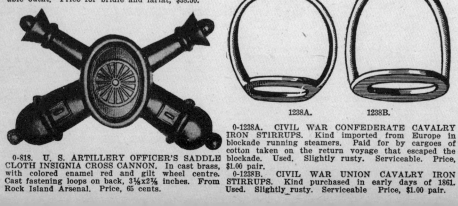

0-818. U. S. ARTILLERY OFFICER'S SADDLE CLOTH INSIGNIA CROSS CANNON. In cast brass, with colored enamel red and gilt wheel centre. Cast fastening loops on back, 3⅛x2⅞ inches. From Rock Island Arsenal. Price, 65 cents.

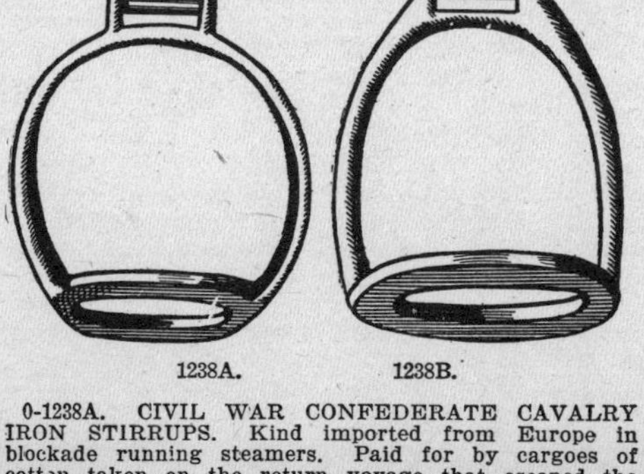

1238A. 1238B.

0-1238A. CIVIL WAR CONFEDERATE CAVALRY IRON STIRRUPS. Kind imported from Europe in blockade running steamers. Paid for by cargoes of cotton taken on the return voyage that escaped the blockade. Used. Slightly rusty. Serviceable. Price, $1.00 pair.
0-1238B. CIVIL WAR UNION CAVALRY IRON STIRRUPS. Kind purchased in early days of 1861. Used. Slightly rusty. Serviceable Price, $1.00 pair.

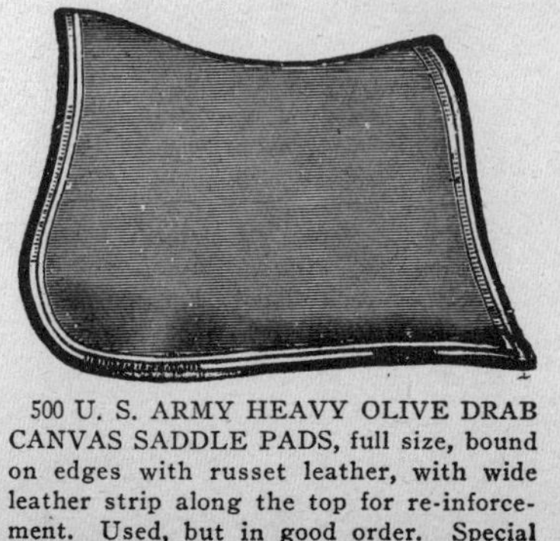

500 U. S. ARMY HEAVY OLIVE DRAB CANVAS SADDLE PADS, full size, bound on edges with russet leather, with wide leather strip along the top for re-inforcement. Used, but in good order. Special price 65 cents each; $6.50 per dozen.

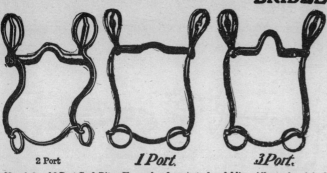

2 Port    1 Port.    3 Port.

**Nos. 1, 2 and 3 Port Curb Bits.** Shoemaker forged steel curb bits. All new, in original cases. From stock left over after the Spanish war. Made of the best hand-forged steel, finely finished; each bit wrapped in paper. Suitable for single or double reins. In three sizes. For over 20 years the Shoemaker was the U.S.A. regulation bit. President Roosevelt used this pattern bit while Colonel of the Rough Riders in the Spanish-American war. Dealers' price, $4.00 each. Our bargain price, your choice of the three sizes, 60c each; $5.00 per dozen.

Illustration of cowboy throwing the lariat.

**U. S. Civil War Cavalry Bits,** without brass U. S. side pieces, old bits regalvanized like new. 30c. each, $3.00 per dozen.

**Set of U. S. Army Gauges for Officers' Bits,** made of fine polished steel; complete set gauges with sample bit in mahogany case, lined with velvet; size, 20 inches long, 11 inches wide, 3 inches deep. Price, $5.00.

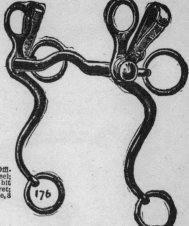

**No. 176. Military Curb Bit,** with swivel snap hooks, for use with halter bridles, cast steel nickel plated, with rings for single or double reins. **Not** U.S.A. Practically new. Price, $2.25.

**No. 176A. U. S. Army Model 1892** Forged Steel Curb Bit, made at Rock Island Government Arsenal. Has been used. Are in second-hand serviceable order. Price, $1.25 each.

**No. 176B. U. S. Army** Officer's Model 1892 Curb Bit, made of magnolia metal (resembles German silver), prevents rust. With rings for double reins. Practically as good as new. 600 in stock. Good value for $4.00. Our bargain price, $1.50 each.

**No. 1383A. Prussian Army Bit,** with German regimental letters and figures; assorted sizes, with curb chain and hooks. We had an order recently for equipping a company with McClellan saddles and bridles. The order included Prussian bits, and in order that we might fill the order correctly, the party sent us a sample bit for which they paid $3.00. On examination we found it was almost the same bit that we purchased in Berlin and that we are now offering at $1.00 each.

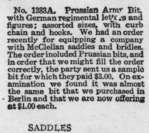

**No. 177. 10,000 Forged Steel U. S. Army Snaffle** or Bridoon Bits, with snaps for attaching to halter, as used on halter bridles. These bits are all new, left over surplus, after the Spanish war in 1898. Manufacturer's price, $1.00 each. Our bargain price, 35c. each. We can offer these fine new bits, with new black leather full length U. S. A. bridles lines at 90c. for the bit and lines.

## SADDLES

In the "London Illustrated News" are pictures of several European princesses riding astride on horseback. There is nothing immodest in the situation at the present day; but twenty years ago a girl or woman astride was looked upon with grave apprehension by all who had her welfare at heart. She was classed among the "wicked tomboys" who climbed trees and waded in small streams for diversion. Now, we look upon this riding astride as something novel. Some parents regard it with holy horror. Possibly they have overlooked the historical fact that before side saddles were invented, in 1380, all women rode astride. Sallie Elliot could sit a barebacked horse in womanly fashion, and I have seen men of the farm, riding to and from the fields in the same style, carrying plows on their shoulders.

**No. 22.—30,000 Model of** 1863, New, U. S. Army Forged Steel Curb Bits. This pattern bit was used by the many thousands of Cavalry and Artillery men during the Civil War, who can testify to its merits. Price, 50 cts. each; with curb chain, 65 cts. each.

**No. 955. Spanish Bit,** cast steel, smooth filed, blued finish. Price, 60c. Nickel plated, 90c.

**Mexican Spurs** with 4-inch Rowels, with jangle and chains, complete with plain straps. New. Offered in dozen lots only. Prices on application.

Illustration showing Port Bit in horse's mouth, with room for the tongue under the port, resting on the bars, the proper place for controlling the horse. A properly fitted Port bit is not a harsh bit, and is necessary to the mounted soldier, allowing him to guide his horse in the lightest possible manner, with ample leverage provided by the port and curb chains to bring his horse to an instant halt.

**500 Civil War U. S.** Cavalry Bits, steel bits with U. S. in brass letters, different sized curbs, good serviceable second-hand order, used in Civil War. 40c. each.

**British Army Bits,** brass monogram with crown and letters. Price, $1.50.

**U. S. Cavalry Bit,** with large ring curb as per illustration, used to break in wild horses; new bits. Price, $1.50 each.

**Confederate Army Bit** made at Augusta Arsenal during the Civil War; crude relic. $4.00.

**No. 2. — Shoemaker** Forged Steel Bit, used, rusty, without bottom bars. Price 30 cts. each.

**South American Broncho Buster, Fancy Bits,** $2.50 each. One pair in German silver, odd shape, $3.75.

**Mexican Bits** with high roller curbs, rusty, recovered from wreck of vessel bound for Mexico. Various patterns, 45 cents each.

**Mexican War Officers'** Bit, brass covered, with U. S. and 21 stars; rare relics. $6.75.

**U. S. Civil War Officers' Bits,** steel, covered with brass; takes fine polish. U. S. A. in brass letters on each bit; takes double reins. Price, $1.25.

Assortment of four kinds of Mexican Bits, $1.00 each.

**German Army Watering Bit,** with chain for fastening to halter. Price, 50 cents.

**No. 1**

**U. S. ARMY CAVALRY SPURS.** Brass polished with straps. Price, $1.25 pair.

**No. 2**

**U. S. ARMY POLISHED BRASS SPURS** with blued steel rowels; new goods; never out of the original cases until we sent them to be polished. Price, with straps, 75 cents per pair; unpolished, without straps, 45 cents per pair; serviceable second-hand straps, 15 cents per pair.

**MILLS PATENT U. S. ARMY SPURS,** metal rowel and holder, strongly riveted to leather heel band, adapting itself to ball of the boot, and held there firmly by friction, without pain, discomfort or chafing. Retail price, $1.75; our price, 90 cents.

**1716**

**BRITISH ARMY SOLDIERS JACK SPURS,** complete with leather straps. In good second-hand serviceable order. Price, 95 cents pair.

**1717**

**No. 25. LIGHT, NICKELED STEEL SPURS,** with straps. Price, $1.00 pair.

**No. 17.**

**CENTRAL AMERICA COW BOYS' GERMAN SILVER SPURS,** with plain leather straps, $3.85 pair.

**No. 4**

**GERMAN SPURS** (SPOREN), from Berlin, serviceable, light, polished steel, fine order. Price, 65 cents pair.

**No. 5**

**U. S. A. REGULATION OFFICER'S BOX SPURS,** nickel; best quality; new Price, $1.80 pair. **OLD BRASS SPUR,** with letters, C. S. (Confederate States) on it, found near Corinth, Miss. Broken, relic only. Price, $2.50.

**19. CENTRAL AM. COW BOYS' FANCY GERMAN SILVER SPURS,** with handsome hand-carved russet leather straps, with German silver conchs. Price, $5.85 pair.

**No. 19.**

**No. 6.**

**800 PAIRS NICKEL-PLATED STEEL SPURS,** neat, handsome, light and strong spurs, complete with strap. Price, 85 cents pair; $9.00 dozen pair. New goods.

**No. 7.**

**7. NEW U. S. ARMY REGULATION OFFICER'S NICKEL SPURS,** complete, with russet leather straps; all new, best quality. Price, $2.25 pair.

**COW BOYS' FANCY GERMAN SILVER SPURS,** with buckle loops, and hand-carved leather straps and conchs, practically new. Price, $4.85 pair.

**No. 16.**

**No. 15.**

**15. SOUTH AMERICA COW BOYS', FANCY GERMAN SILVER SPURS,** with buckle and loops, with hand carved russet leather straps and German silver conchs, practically new. Price, $6.85 pair.

**60 U. S. ARMY CANVAS HARNESS SACKS,** strong, heavy canvas, with leather handles, well bound; used for packing harness not required on the march. Measures 38 by 61 inches. Price, $3.50 each.

**GERMAN ARMY OFFICER'S SADDLE CLOTH "SCHABRAKEN,"** Blue Cloth embroidered with Imperial Eagle and red trimmed stars, as shown in photograph. This cloth used a few times, is in good serviceable order. Price, $12.00.
One similar, except ornamental design is slightly different. Very showy, fine order. Red border on blue cloth, gilt lace. Price, $10.00.

Correct position of Rider, Horse and Saddlery. Dotted lines show level and centre of balance.

**NEW MONEY BELT** of heavy olive drab cloth, with rubberized lining, four compartments. Width, 3¼ inches. Price, 35 cents.

**HAIR LARIAT,** 36 feet long, ⅜ inch diameter rope, made of horse hair, with brass hondo spliced. Many purchase hair lariats to lay on the ground surrounding the tent as preventive against snakes intruding. It is said that "a snake will not cross a hair rope." Price, $5.85.
**ROPE LARIAT,** 40 feet, with polished brass honda, and finished with Turks head. Reduced to 95 cents each.

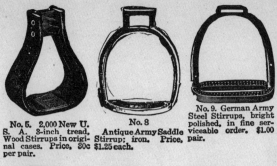

**No. 5.** 2,000 New U. S. A. 3-inch tread. Wood Stirrups in original cases. Price, 30c per pair.

**No. 8** Antique Army Saddle Stirrup; iron. Price, $1.25 each.

**No. 9.** German Army Steel Stirrups, bright polished, in fine serviceable order. $1.00 pair.

**No. 10.** 50 Color Bearer Stirrups, with socket attached to carry the guidon flag pole. Good as new. Price, $1.50 each.

**No. 11** Texas Stock Stirrups. Price, $2.00 a pair.

**No. 12.** U. S. Army Officer's New Regulation Stirrups, star steel silver quality. Price, $3.00 per pair.

**No. 13.** U. S. Artillery brass stirrups. $1.50 per pair.

**No. 14** European Army Iron Stirrup; ancient. $1.50.

**No. 163.** Metal Stirrups; new, 3¼ inch tread. Per pair, 65c.

**No. 15.** Ancient Hand Forged Saddle Stirrups, rare serviceable relics, handsome ornaments. Very cheap at $1.50 per pair.

**No. 1186.** Antique German Hand Forged Iron Stirrups. Price, $1.50 a pair. One odd stirrup, 75 cts. These odd stirrups make unique fastenings for drapery in cosey corners.

Military Port Bit for double reins, cast steel, bent cheek. $1.25.

**No. 22.** New Rock Island Arsenal Hair Cinth with Russet Leather Safes and Bronze Rings. Perfect. Price, $2.50.

**No. 19.** 3,000 United States Army Curb Chains, Artilery, blued steel, with chain hooks, new, in original boxes. Price, 20 cents each; $1.80 per dozen; with leather safes, $1.00 per dozen extra.

**No. 7.** Wind Jammer for breaking wild horses. Price, $1.50.

**No. 16.** South American Cowboys Wind Break, used in breaking horses. Price. $2.50.

**No. 6.** Broncho Busters Nose Break. Price, $1.00.

**No. 24.** 500 U. S. Halters; genuine Government Halter, not imitation, made up from old government leather, but every halter is both sewed and rivited. All in good second hand serviceable order. Price, 35 cents each.

Cowboy Pattern Hand Forged Steel Spade Bit, with silver inlaid decorative relief work. Prices on application.

**No. 23.** U. S. Army Mane Combs as issued to cavalrymen for use in grooming their horses; made of malleable metal; new, 10c. each.

**No 21.** Large size Wood Stirrups, 3½ inch tread; 7 inches high; strongly rivited and bolted; ¾-inch thick; new fine quality. 40c. pair; $4.00 dozen.

Mexican Wood Stirrups, large size, 80 cents per pair.

Mexican Hooded Stirrup, with sweat leather, hand carved, handsome decoration. Price, $6.50 per pair; one extra large pair, carved and decorated. Price, $8.00

800 New U. S. Army Hames Straps, 23 inches long, 2¼ inches wide; best quality bridle leather. Price, 25 cents each.

A. 3,000 New U. S. Cavalry Tie Straps; best bridle leather, hand sewed; full length, 25 inches; with snap hook, with brass link for adjusting length. All horsemen should have this handy strap. Price, 18 cents.

**No. 17.** 12,000 New Carbine Swing Swivel shap hooks, 20 cents each. Best forged steel, U. S. Government quality. $2.00 dozen; $20.00 gross.

**No. 18**

9,000 new United States Artillery Bits, with No. 2 small port. Double XX tinned, looks like nickel-plating. Made of forged steel. Price, 65 cents each; $6.75 dozen; $60.00 gross.

**No. 20.** U. S. Army Neck Halter, heavy leather 2½ inch wide, 38 inch long, with 4 foot steel chains, with swivel and rings. Good as new. Price, $1.00 each.

U. S. Army Curry Combs in good serviceable order, for all practical purposes, as good as new. Price, 35 cents each.

99 U. S. Cavalry Soldier's Hoof Hooks, for removing obstructions from horses' feet. Blued steel sharpened hook with ring. Full length, 5 inches. New. Price, 15 cents each.

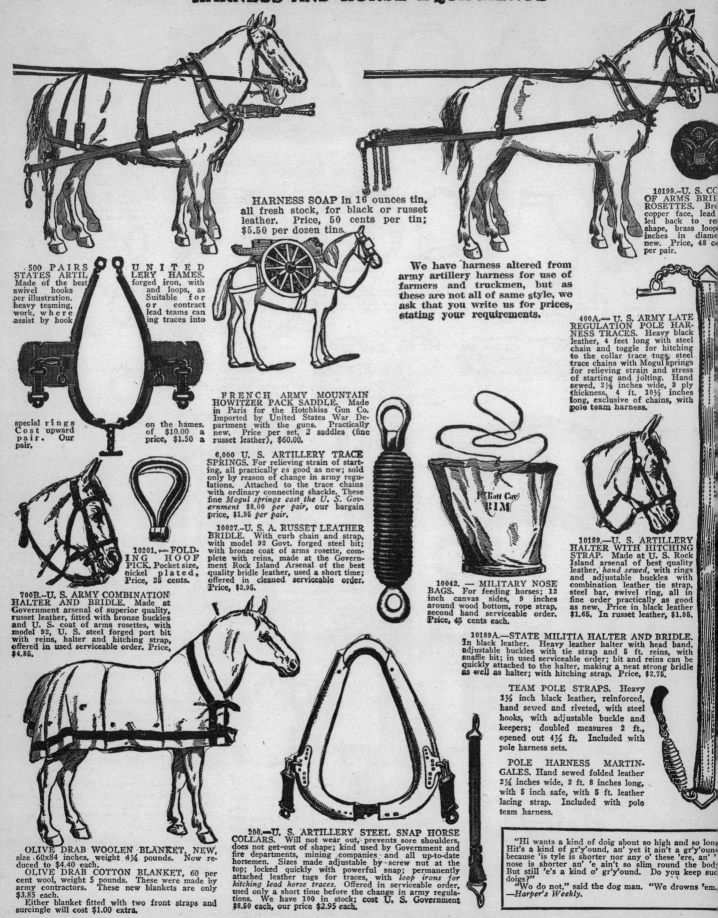

**HARNESS SOAP in 16 ounces tin,** all fresh stock, for black or russet leather. Price, 50 cents per tin; $5.50 per dozen tins.

We have harness altered from army artillery harness for use of farmers and truckmen, but as these are not all of same style, we ask that you write us for prices, stating your requirements.

**10199.—U. S. CO OF ARMS BRI ROSETTES.** Br copper face, lead led back to re shape, brass loop inches in diame new. Price, 48 c per pair.

**500 PAIRS UNITED STATES ARTIL LERY HAMES.** Made of the best forged iron, with swivel hooks and loops, as per illustration. Suitable for heavy teaming, or contract work, where ing traces into assist by hook special rings Cost upward on the hames. pair. Our of $10.00 a pair. price, $1.50 a pair.

**400A.— U. S. ARMY LATE REGULATION POLE HAR NESS TRACES.** Heavy black leather, 4 feet long with steel chain and toggle for hitching to the collar trace tugs, steel trace chains with Mogul springs for relieving strain and stress of starting and jolting. Hand sewed, 2⅜ inches wide, 3 ply thickness, 4 ft. 10½ inches long, exclusive of chains, with pole team harness.

**FRENCH ARMY MOUNTAIN HOWITZER PACK SADDLE.** Made in Paris for the Hotchkiss Gun Co. Imported by United States War Department with the guns. Practically new. Price per set, 2 saddles (fine russet leather), $60.00.

**6,000 U. S. ARTILLERY TRACE SPRINGS.** For relieving strain of starting, all practically as good as new; sold only by reason of change in army regulations. Attached to the trace chains with ordinary connecting shackle. These fine *Mogul springs cost the U. S. Government* $8.00 *per pair,* our bargain price, $1.95 *per pair.*

**10201.— FOLD ING HOOF PICK.** Pocket size, nickel plated. Price, 25 cents.

**10027.—U. S. A. RUSSET LEATHER BRIDLE.** With curb chain and strap, with model 92 Govt. forged steel bit; with bronze coat of arms rosette, complete with reins, made at the Government Rock Island Arsenal of the best quality bridle leather, used a short time; offered in cleaned serviceable order. Price, $2.95.

**10042. — MILITARY NOSE BAGS.** For feeding horses; 12 inch canvas sides, 9 inches around wood bottom, rope strap, second hand serviceable order. Price, 45 cents each.

**10189.— U. S. ARTILLERY HALTER WITH HITCHING STRAP.** Made at U. S. Rock Island arsenal of best quality leather, *hand sewed,* with rings and adjustable buckles with combination leather tie strap, steel bar, swivel ring, all in fine order practically as good as new. Price in black leather $1.65. In russet leather, $1.85.

**700B.—U. S. ARMY COMBINATION HALTER AND BRIDLE.** Made at Government arsenal of superior quality, russet leather, fitted with bronze buckles and U. S. coat of arms rosettes, with model 92, U. S. steel forged port bit with reins, halter and hitching strap, offered in used serviceable order. Price, $4.85.

**10189A.—STATE MILITIA HALTER AND BRIDLE.** In black leather. Heavy leather halter with head band, adjustable buckles with tie strap and 5 ft. reins, with snaffle bit; in used serviceable order; bit and reins can be quickly attached to the halter, making a neat strong bridle as well as halter; with hitching strap. Price, $2.75.

**TEAM POLE STRAPS.** Heavy 1½ inch black leather, reinforced, hand sewed and riveted, with steel hooks, with adjustable buckle and keepers; doubled measures 2 ft., opened out 4½ ft. Included with pole harness sets.

**POLE HARNESS MARTIN GALES.** Hand sewed folded leather 2¼ inches wide, 2 ft. 8 inches long, with 5 inch safe, with 5 ft. leather lacing strap. Included with pole team harness.

**OLIVE DRAB WOOLEN BLANKET, NEW,** size .60x84 inches, weight 4¼ pounds. Now reduced to $4.40 each.

**OLIVE DRAB COTTON BLANKET,** 60 per cent wool, weight 5 pounds. These were made by army contractors. These new blankets are only $3.85 each.

Either blanket fitted with two front straps and surcingle will cost $1.00 extra.

**200.—U. S. ARTILLERY STEEL SNAP HORSE COLLARS.** Will not wear out, prevents sore shoulders, does not get out of shape; kind used by Government and fire departments, mining companies and all up-to-date horsemen. Sizes made adjustable by screw nut at the top; locked quickly with powerful snap; permanently attached leather tugs for traces, with *loop irons for hitching lead horse traces.* Offered in serviceable order, used only a short time before the change in army regulations. We have 100 in stock; cost U. S. Government $8.50 each, our price $2.95 each.

**0-1307 NAVAL OFFICER'S PATTERN BRONZE BUCKLE,** end fastening. Loops take 1½-inch belt, size of the plate 2¾ inches long, 2 inches wide. Offered in blued or in gilt finish. Center has the naval monogram, eagle and anchor, and 13 stars surrounded by wreath. Handsome, showy buckle. Price, 35 cents.

**0-1310. AMERICAN CROSSED FLAGS BELT BUCKLE,** in either gilt or silvered finish. Flag is in relief, with stars and stripes in colored enamel. Size, 2¾ inches by 1¾ inches. Loops take 1⅝-inch belt. Price, 45 cents.

| NOTE WHOLESALE PRICES ON THESE FINE BUCKLES. | |
|---|---|
| O-1307. Per dozen | $3.50 |
| O-1310. Per dozen | 4.50 |
| O-1305. Per dozen | 2.50 |
| O-1308A. Per dozen | 1.50 |
| O-1309. Per dozen | 4.60 |
| O-1309A. Per dozen | 2.00 |

**0-1305. GOLF BELT BUCKLE,** gilt-bronze, patterned after the U. S. Naval Officer's buckle, with wreath border and pair of crossed golfing sticks and balls in center. Loops take ½-inch belt. We offer the buckles, all new, at bargain price of 30 cents each, or with russet or black leather waist belt, 65 cents each.

**0-1308. PEACE EAGLE BELT BUCKLE** (with the eagle head facing olive branch), stamped brass. Loops take 1⅝-inch belt. Size, 2⅞ inches by 1¾ inches. Price of the buckle, 20 cents; fitted with used, serviceable russet leather gun sling as waist belt. Price, 50 cents.

**0-1316. BUCKLE WITH HAND HOLDING FLAG,** fine gilt, with beveled edges. Size, 2⅝ inches by 1¾ inches; 1½-inch loops. Price of buckle, 40 cents; with belt, 60 cents.

**0-1313. OFFICER'S AMERICAN FLAG BELT BUCKLE.** Small flag in colored enamel, eagle, two crossed swords, officer's pattern. Size, 2¼ inches by 2¾ inches; 1½-inch loops, in gilt or silvered finish. Price, 40 cents; with silk ribbon belt. 65 cents.

**0-1312A. ENAMELED COLORED AMERICAN FLAG BELT BUCKLE,** with pole tassels within wreath. Flag is small size, has nine stripes; ormolu gilt finish. Size, 2¾ inches by 2⅛ inches; 1½-inch loops. Price of buckle 40 cents; with silk belt, 65 cents.

**0-1309. AMERICAN FLAG FINE GILT BELT BUCKLE.** Brass, with raised flag in red, white and blue enamel finish. Size of the buckle, 2½ inches by 2 inches, complete with loop fastening. Handsome buckle. Price, 50 cents. A job lot offered with cadet blue watered silk waist belt, lady's size, 75 cents.

**0-1309A. AMERICAN FLAG BELT BUCKLE,** size 2½ by 2 inches, with raised stars and stripes. Flag finished in colored enamel. The manufacturer made an error in putting only eleven stripes, in consequence we offer these fine buckles at 25 cents, in either gilt or silvered finish.

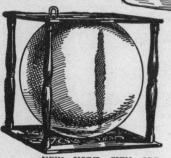

**0-1306. U. S. S. MAINE SOUVENIR BELT BUCKLE.** Square buckle; is 3 inches long, 2 inches wide; loops take 1⅝-inch belt. Battleship is stamped in the center, with the inscription, "U. S. S. Maine, destroyed Feb. 15, 1898," with American flag in colored enamel. This handsome belt buckle is offered in either silvered or gilt finish at 25 cents, or fitted with cadet blue watered silk, lady's size waist belt, at the bargain price of 50 cents.

**0-1314. NAVAL ANCHOR FLAG BUCKLE,** two anchors with American flag center, eleven stripes in colored enamel. Size, 2¾ inches by 1¾ inches; 1½-inch belt loops. Price, 75 cents.

**0-1313A. AMERICAN OFFICER'S SWORD-FLAG BELT BUCKLE,** scalloped edges, two officer's pattern swords, with small colored enamel flag in gilt finish. Size, 2⅝ inches by 2⅛ inches. Loops take 1⅝-inch belt. Price, 40 cents; with belt, 65 cents.

**0-1315. BUCKLE,** with two American Eagles in colored enamel, with flag in the center; gilt finished. Size, 2⅝ by 1¾; 1½-inch loops. Price, 40 cents; with silk belt, 65 cents.

**0-1308A. CROSSED RIFLE BELT BUCKLE,** size 3¼ inches by 1¾ inches. Loops take 1½-inch belt. Price of the buckle, 20 cents; with gun sling waist belt, 50 cents, offered in either gilt or silvered finish.

**0-1335D. NEW SEAMLESS ALUMINUM CANTEEN;** holds one quart; weight, with leather sling strap, 10 ounces. Made to lie against the body. Screw top, cork lined; length, 7 inches; diameter, 5 inches. Price, $1.95.

**0-1335. FOLDING CAMP COT WITH MOSQUITO CANOPY.** Rope-bound canvas cot, rope ends projecting for holding cot in position by iron anchor driven in ground. Two-piece mosquito netting over arched iron rods. Inventor's models; 15 in stock. We cannot recommend. They are not as strong or as easily put up and kept in place as other cots. We offer for sale only to city customers who can call, examine and accept. Price, $1.50 each.

**0-1335B. USED BLUE CLOTH BELL-TOP CAPS,** cleaned, serviceable order, at 55 cents each.

**0-1312. AMERICAN FLAG ROUND BELT BUCKLE,** stars and stripes in relief, in colored enamel, within wreath. Size, 2¼ inches in diameter, gilt finish; 1½-inch loops. Price of the buckle, 40 cents; with silk belt, 65 cents. Good value for $1.00 each; job lot. Our bargain price, 40 cents each.

**0-13311A. AMERICAN AND CUBAN FLAG BELT BUCKLE,** gilt finish, size 2⅝ by 1¾ inches. Loops take 1½-inch waist belt. Price of the buckle, 40 cents; with blue silk belt, lady's size, 65 cents.

**0-1334. CONFEDERATE OFFICER'S SWORD,** with letters C. S. cast between the handle guards; straight cut-and-thrust 31¼-inch blade, No. 344; two brass guards; brass scabbard, lower part missing. Price, $30.00.

**0-1334A. CONFEDERATE OFFICER'S PISTOL.** Made up from parts captured in battle. Derringer pattern, chased lock, "Lewis & Tomes"; 36 calibre; 7-inch barrel, marked Allen. Price, $25.00.

**NEW YORK STATE OFFICERS MILITIA BELT PLATES.** With old English letters N Y in wreath, on pebbled back-ground. Size 2½x 2 inches, take belt 1¾ inches wide. These are the same style as used by the officers of all the famous N. Y. State regiments. Price 50 cents each. Complete with used black waist belt $1.00.

**U. S. A. GENERALS' NEW GOLD PLATED CLASP BELT BUCKLE** with wreath and Coat of Arms in relief, made at Government Arsenal. Price, $4.50.

**NEW NAVY CHEVRONS.** Embroidered blue silk eagle, crossed flags with two cloth red-edged bars. 50 cents. Navy Chevron with eagle, anchor, arrow and bars. 45 cents.

**U. S. N. SAILORS' SHAVING AND TRINKET BOX.** Hard rubber, beautifully ornamented with naval motto, *"Don't Give up the Ship,"* U. S. N. and foul anchor, mirror set in cover. Size, 3x1½ inches. Price, 45 cents.

**U. S. MARINE CORPS BUTTON.** New, gilt and in bronze, Eagle-world-anchor emblem. Cost price, 5 cents each.

**2017. REVOLUTIONARY WAR SOLDIER'S BUCKSKIN BREECHES.** Worn by Daniel Miles, Glastonbury, Conn., while serving as a soldier of Third Regiment of Connecticut Line, 1777 to 1778. Front pocket, knee buttons. Serviceable order. From the Brooks collection. Price. $20.00.

**NEW YORK CITY OLD-TIME BALLOT-BOX,** relic of the days when Boss Tweed ruled the city. Can be used as an aquarium. Size, 12 inches wide, 12 inches long, 30 inches high. Heavy glass globe 10 inches wide, 10 inches deep; weighs 39 pounds. Top, bottom and frame artistic iron casting, good glass; will make a splendid fish globe. Must have cost the city $50.00 each. Our bargain price, $2.85.

**5,000 ABDOMINAL BANDAGES.** Kind worn around the stomach by U. S. soldiers when in countries subject to hot days and cool nights to prevent sickness. All new assorted sizes. Every camper should have one of these life-savers. Price, 35 cents each.

**0-1335C. U. S. ARMY STANDARD FIELD RANGE No. 1,** all parts made of steel and malleable iron, to stand the hard knocks in service and transportation. Will cook for 150 persons; burns wood or coal. Two folding metal handles at each end; 15,000 in use by U. S. Gov't since their adoption in 1898; used by State Militia; are in good, serviceable order, without cooking utensils (which can be purchased at any good hardware store, kind and quantity as desired.) Price on request.

**3 MEDICAL AND SURGEONS' METAL FIELD CHESTS.** Size, 22x16x17 inches. Metal reinforced frames with 6 drawers and 8 compartments with hard rubber bottles, screw tops. Chest is covered with heavy leather, has hasp and lock, carrying handles. Bargain price, $12.00 each.

**1 ARDOIS ELECTRIC SIGNAL OUTFIT,** 4 double end red and white prism glass lamps, with wire coils, $15.00.

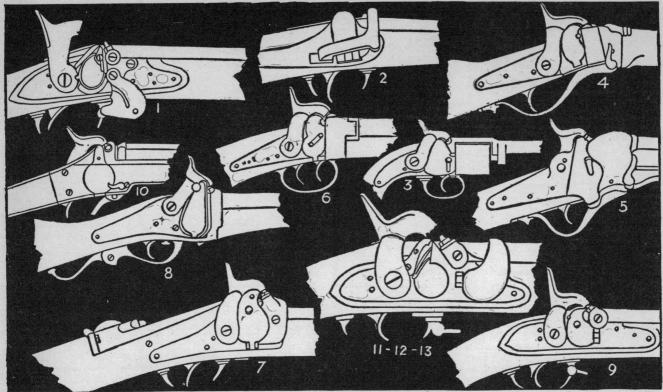

This improvement in firearms was the invention of Edward Maynard, who submitted his idea to a board of Ordnance officers at West Point in January, 1845. The original idea was the improvement of flint-locks to percussion and the first alterations had the primer magazine entirely outside of the lock plate and did not admit of the use of regular caps. In 1851 the Ordnance Department suggested the improved lock in which the primer magazine was imbedded in the lock plate and which later became the well-known model of 1855 used in both rifles and pistols. Up to 1857 Maynard had received $75,000 for the use of his idea. According to Government reports the first alterations were made at Springfield Armory in 1848, about 300 flint-locks being improved by the addition of the primer.

After a careful study of available records we find that there were different weapons that were equipped with the Maynard device, as follows: No. 1, The flint-lock alteration referred to above; No. 2, Jenks' Carbines about 1847; No. 3, Wesson and Leavitt's Revolvers, dated in the '50s; No. 4, First model Sharp's Carbines, late '50s; No. 5, Second model of Sharp's a year or so later than No. 4; No. 6, Green's Carbines, date 1857; No. 7, Merrill, Latrobe and Thomas' Carbines, date about 1856; No. 8, Symme's Carbines, 1858; No. 9, Remington's alteration of the model 1842 musket in 1857; No. 10, Maynard's own carbines 1859, and 11, 12 and 13, The familiar Model of 1855 Rifle, Musket and Pistol made at Springfield Armory and also at Harper's Ferry until 1860. The illustration shows the magazine with the "gate" open, disclosing the "fingers."

## Successful Types of Magazines

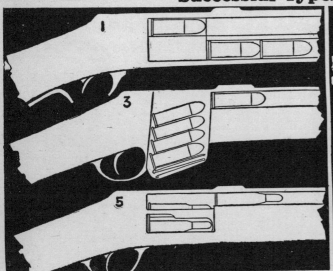

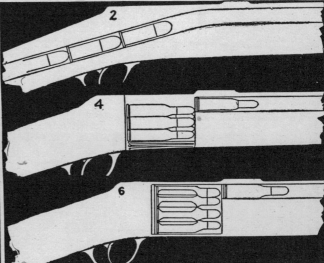

There have been six successful types of magazines as adapted to Military Rifles and Carbines. Another type, although tried both here and abroad, known as the gravity feed, was never adopted by any of the powers. The first system shown, No. 1, is the invention of Tyler Henry brought out in the United States in 1860. In this, the cartridge are inserted in a tube underneath the barrel and fed into the chamber by a coiled spring. In addition to the Henry rifles it has been used in the Ball, U. S. 1863; Lebel, France, 1886; Kropatschek, France, 1878; Mauser, Germany, 1884; Jarman, Sweden, 1887; Vetterli, Swiss, 1874; Murata, Japan, 1887; Turwirth, Austria, 1875; Remington Keene, U. S., 1880; Ward Burton, U. S. Experimental, 1875; Mannlicher, Austria, 1882; Sharp, 1878, Buffington, 1878, Gray, 1866, the last three all U. S. experimental, and the Pieri in Italy about 1872. Winchester rifles are still made today on this system.

The next to be brought out, No. 2, was the Spencer type, the tube however being in the butt stock. Christopher Spencer was the inventor in 1860. Other rifles to use this idea were the well-known Hotchkiss 1878 and 1883 models; the Chaffee-Reece, U. S. 1884; Triplett and Scott, U. S. 1865; Evans, 1885; Schulhof, China, 1884; Mannlicher, 1880 and Straw U. S. Experimental, 1866.

The third type (No. 3) was the invention of James P. Lee, dated 1879. This is the first of the centrally located magazines. It was at first loaded singly but later a clip was used. Some famous guns have used this system, notably the Lee-Enfield of England, 1892-1921; Schmidt-Rubin, Swiss, 1889-1921; Dadateau, France, 1895; also Berthier of France 1891; the Russian Mouzin, 1891-1921; the Ross, Mark III Canada, Mauser, 1889; Belgium, 1890; Turkey 1891, Argentine; Remington-Lee, U. S. N., 1880; Mannlicher, 1888; Vetterli-Vitali, Italy, 1887; Beaumont-Vitali, Holland, 1888; the Winchester Model 1895; the Lee Straight Pull, U. S. N., 1895.

No. 4 is the famous Mauser type, the most successful of all systems. Here we find the magazine entirely within the stock. First brought out in the Spanish model of 1893. It has since been used in our Springfield 1903, the Arisaka of Japan and the Ross of Canada. Other Mauser models using it are dated 1895, 1896, 1898, 1899, 1902, 1903, 1904 and 1917.

No. 5 is the Krag-Jorgensen, the invention of two Danish military officers. In this we find the cartridges, loaded singly and fed by a spring from the right side to the left and upward into the chamber. Introduced in Denmark in the model of 1889 and still in use in Norway in 1894 and in the United States in 1892.

The last shown (No. 6) is the Schulhof, an Austrian invention of 1888. Here we find the cartridges revolve on a ratchet wheel, the top shell being forced into the chamber by the bolt. Loaded both by clip and singly. Used today by Greece is the Mannlicher-Schonauer, in the Blake U. S. about 1895, Savage U. S. Mannlicher 1887. Also 1888 and 1900.

# ARMY TENTS

Most of the Army Tents can be used without a fly or extra cover. We have flies in stock and can quote on any that may be needed.

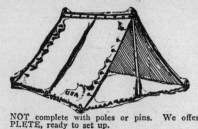

63A. 1,000 U. S. A. SHELTER TENTS. Khaki canvas, in 2 parts that button together. The size is 5 feet 2½ inches, with extension flaps 2½ feet; height, 3½ feet. Open at one end; allows a number of tents to be joined together. Weight, 5 pounds. Used. Offered in serviceable order with 2 new pattern 3 joint folding poles and round pins at $3.50 each. Please note that most of these tents offered by other firms are good second-hand tents COMPLETE, ready to set up.

NOT complete with poles or pins. We offer

500. U. S. ARMY PYRAMID TENTS; size 16x16 feet with 3-foot wall. Made for the Army of heavy khaki duck, contract make. These tents have been used, but have been overhauled and repaired. We offer them in good serviceable order, complete with upright pole and pegs at special price of $35.00 each, up.

7121. U. S. ARMY MOSQUITO BARS, best quality mosquito netting, tape bound, illustration shows use on army folding camp cot, attached to four light upright sticks stuck in the ground at each corner. Length 8 feet, height 5 feet 10 inches, width 2 feet 9 inches, weight 18 ounces. Price $1.50.

MOSQUITO BAR FRAMES to fit on end of cot. Hard wood with metal trimmings. 90 cents pair.

## HOW TO PITCH A TENT

Having unrolled the tent in the position you want it when up, place the ridge pole, rounded side up, inside the tent, on a line with the large eyelet holes, which are in the center of the roof; then insert the uprights in the holes bored in the ridge pole, and let the pikes in the upright pole come through the top of the tent. If a fly is used let the pikes also go through that, in the same way as the tent; then take hold of the uprights and raise tent and fly together; secure the corner guys first, then the others between them. Do not drive the pegs straight, but angling. The tent now being up and guys adjusted so that they bear equal strain, proceed to dig a V-shaped trench around the tent, about three inches deep; this will insure a dry floor. Do not take the tent down when wet or damp. Heat and dampness are the cause of mildew.

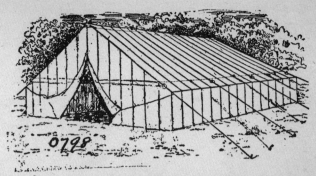

0798. U. S. ARMY HOSPITAL WARD TENTS. Made of heavy khaki duck. Size is 16 feet wide, 50 feet long, 11 feet high, with 4½ foot wall. In size this equals 4 pyramid tents and is suitable for camp for a large number of people. Have sold a number to contractors on highways, railroads and other construction. These tents have never been used but are slightly soiled OUTSIDE from storage. We offer these fine tents WITH POLES. Price $150.00.

ARMY STORAGE TENTS, KHAKI COLOR, size 20x20 feet, with 5 foot wall, 11 feet high. Uses three uprights and one ridge pole. We offer these tents in fine order with three uprights, NO ridge pole at $88.00 each.

$2⁵⁰

U. S. NAVY SAILOR'S HAMMOCK. New, but slightly stained. Made at the Government Navy Yard. Of one piece of extra-heavy canvas. Measures 40½ inches wide, 68½ inches long, 2-inch turned border at each end, with 12 hand-worked grommet holes, ¾-inch hem on sides. Hammock weighs over 5 pounds with clews, $2.50.

ARMY HAMMOCKS. These are slightly smaller than the Navy hammocks, and much lighter in weight. They are second hand, somewhat soiled, but offered at low price of 95 cents each.

COOKING GRATES, used by N. Y. State troops. General Storey recommended these grates as the best and simplest cooking grate made. Made of wrought iron piping joined together. Size, 25x37 inches. Weight, about 22 lbs. Price, $1.95 each.

PRICES QUOTED ON NEW TENTS IN ANY SIZE OR SHAPE. EYE SHIELDS, made of celluloid, with elastic head band. Useful to keep out dust in working or driving. Price, 35 cents each.

FIFTY U. S. ARMY WALL TENTS. 14 feet 4 inches long, 14½ feet wide, 10 feet high, 4½ foot wall, height of door flap 8 feet 9 inches, weighs 96 pounds. Made of heavy army standard cotton canvas. Open flaps at each end allow a number of tents to be joined together. Ventilator or stove pipe openings. Twelve-inch canvas sod cloth. Offered in serviceable order, with poles, pegs and ropes. Price, $50.00, up.

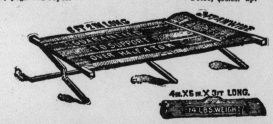

0-792. ARMY FOLDING COTS, fitted with NEW tan covers. The wood frames have been used but are in good order. New covers have been put on. These cots are better than the cheap imitations. Price, $2.75 each.

**U. S. NAVY SAILOR'S HAMMOCK.** New, but slightly stained. Made at the Government Navy Yard. Of one piece of extra-heavy canvas. Measures 40½ inches wide, 68½ inches long, 2-inch turned border at each end, with 12 hand-worked grommet holes. ¾-inch hem on sides. Hammock weighs over 5 pounds with clews, $2.50.

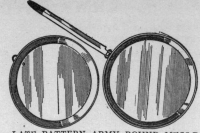

**LATE PATTERN ARMY ROUND MESS-PANS,** 8½ inches, of heavy block tin, in used, serviceable order. Weight 18 ounces. Price, 25 cents each. $2.50 per dozen.

**3298. U. S. A. LEATHER SHOULDER SLING STRAP,** with brass hooks for adjusting the length. Brass hooks for attaching to the Haversack or the article to be carried. Made at the Government Arsenal, of the best bridle leather. 2 inches wide across the shoulder, tapering to 1¼ inches at the end. Weighs 7 ounces, cost upwards of $1.00 each to make. We have about 50,000 in stock. For sale at the bargain price of 35 cents each.

**OLIVE DRAB WOOLEN BLANKET, NEW,** size 60x84 inches, weight 4¼ pounds. Now reduced to $4.40 each.

**OLIVE DRAB COTTON BLANKET,** 60 per cent wool, weight 5 pounds. These were made by army contractors. These new blankets are only $3.85 each.

**NEW FINE QUALITY OLIVE DRAB WOOL BLANKETS,** direct from factory, never used; size 66x84 inches; weight 4 pounds. Now offered at reduced price of $5.00 each.

**No. 244. ARMY ENGINEER SOLDIERS' STEEL SHOVEL AND PICK;** 5¾ inches wide, 7½ inches long; total length, 20 inches; with pick shaped handle. Very strongly made; valuable to miners on prospecting trip or for gardening; fine steel. Adopted by Military Schools. 500 in stock. Price, $1.25 each.

**No. 2. U. S. ARMY HUNTING KNIFE.** With leather scabbard and brass hanger for attaching to cartridge belt; fine tempered steel blades. Made at Government arsenal; brass guard, harness-leather scabbard. Length of blade, 8 inches; width, 2 inches. Price, with scabbard, $1.25 each.

**U. S. ARMY FIRST AID PACKAGE,** with brass loops for attaching to the waist belt, hermetically sealed, opened by a pull on the ring, brass metal box, size 2½x4½ inches. Weight, 5 ounces. Contains full First Aid Package outfit. Price, 30 cents.

**PQM. MARINE CORPS PONCHOS,** pliable rubberized fabric, light olive drab color, weight 3½ pounds. Opening in center to use as cape, and fitted with snaps to use as a blanket. All in good order, size 68 inches wide by 84 inches. Snaps along each long edge so that two may be fastened together to form a shelter tent. In remitting allow postage on 3 pounds. Price $2.00 each.

**U. S. A. BUZZACOT COOKING OUTFIT.** Made of steel. Illustration shows view packed. Contains stove grate, oven or boiler and cover. Size, 24x34x12 inches. Price, $7.00.

6071

**DUFFLE BAGS,** made of heavy khaki tent duck. Size 36 inches long with cope drawstring. Second hand. Price, $1.30.

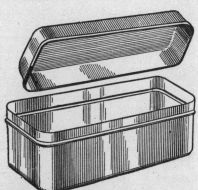

**40,000 U. S. ARMY CANTEENS,** with leather sling brass hooks and snaps for infantry, or with short slings and snap for cavalry. Made of heavy tin, with chained cork, with double covers, one of heavy wool cloth, outside cover of heavy canvas, used, 50 cents each.

**No. 14D. NEW BLACK LEATHER BAG,** suitable for carrying papers, books or tools. Size 11x12x3 inches. With handle or long shoulder sling. Special price, $4.50 each.

Second Hand Bags as above, in serviceable order, $3.00 each.

**No. 1270D. NEW MACHETES,** from salvaged ship. Water stained with paper wrapping stuck to blade. These are made by famous American makers. Offered without scabbards at $1.25 each.

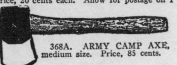

**NEW BACON CANS** made of heavy block tin, entirely new. Handy for small lunch box or for keeping fishing tackle or small tools. Price, 20 cents each. Allow for postage on 1 lb.

**368A. ARMY CAMP AXE,** medium size. Price, 85 cents.

**NEW ALUMINUM MESS PANS, WITH COVER.** Lower part has long handle and can be used as fry pan while top may be used as plate. Price, 45 cents each. Allow for postage on 1 lb.

**MESS PANS,** second hand made of heavy block tin, complete with top. Now reduced to 15 cents each. Allow for postage on 2 lbs.

**NEW ALUMINUM CANTEEN,** complete with new cup and second hand army made cover. Cup fits over bottom of canteen and both go into cover. There are belt hooks on cover, also snaps for quickly detaching. Price of ONE DOLLAR, includes canteen, cup and cover. Allow for postage on two pounds.

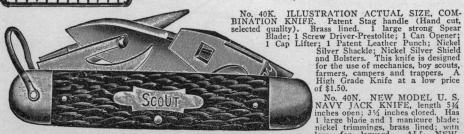

**COOKING GRATES,** used by N. Y. State troops. General Storey recommended these grates as the best and simplest cooking grate made. Made of wrought iron piping joined together. Size, 25x37 inches. Weight about 30 lbs. Price, $1.95 each.

**ARMY HOUSEWIVES.** New. Every camper or traveler should have one in his kit. Price, 75 cents each.

**U. S. A. INTRENCHING STEEL SPADE,** carried as part of soldier's equipment. Width, 7 inches; length, 8¼ inches; without handle. Price, 25 cents.

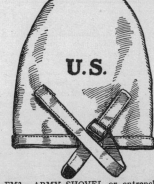

**No. 40K. ILLUSTRATION ACTUAL SIZE, COMBINATION KNIFE.** Patent Stag handle (Hand cut, selected quality). Brass lined. 1 large strong Spear Blade; 1 Screw Driver-Prestolite; 1 Can Opener; 1 Cap Lifter; 1 Patent Leather Punch; Nickel Silver Shackle; Nickel Silver Shield and Bolsters. This knife is designed for the use of mechanics, boy scouts, farmers, campers and trappers. A High Grade Knife at a low price of $1.50.

**No. 40N. NEW MODEL U. S. NAVY JACK KNIFE,** length 5¾ inches open; 3¼ inches closed. Has 1 large blade and 1 manicure blade; nickel trimmings, brass lined; with loop for lanyard. ALL NEW.

**FM3. ARMY SHOVEL** or entrenching tool holder. Made of heavy drab canvas, with web strap and buckle to attach on handle. Wire fastening to attach to any belt. Will also carry hatchet or axe. Width at opening 7 inches, length 8 inches. Price 30 cents each; $3.00 dozen.

Price, 60 cents each.

**U. S. NAVY WHITE LANYARDS,** second hand, serviceable, for use with knife. Price, 12 cents each.

No. 8. BROWN-MERRILL BREECH-LOADING RIFLE. Patented in October, 1871. Caliber .58. Altered from a muzzle-loading English Enfield Model of 1857. It will be noticed that the bed of the side lock-plate is filled in. Hammer is in rear of the bolt, which had the usual one-quarter turn to the left and back. A few states in the east purchased these rifles to arm the militia. This is the same Merrill who invented the rifle and carbine shown elsewhere. These rifles were made by the Brown Mfg. Company of Newburyport, Mass.

No. 9. U. S. SPRINGFIELD RIFLE. Model of 1866. This is a Civil War muzzle-loader altered. The caliber has been reduced from .58 to .50 by inserting a tube in the original barrel. The hammer is new, but the old lock-plate and its parts are retained. Up to 1873 all breech-loaders made at Springfield were alterations of Civil War guns and with the exception of the breech mechanisms, the original arms were used. In 1868 a new rear sight was used and in 1870 when another model rifle and carbine was introduced an improved rear sight was employed. All these arms were of caliber .50. The breech mechanism is practically the same as was afterwards used on the Models 1873-1884-1888, the familiar block operation up and forward upon the axis of the barrel. This system was the invention of E. S. Allen of the Springfield Armory. See No. 12.

No. 10. SHARP'S BREECH-LOADING ALTERATION OF A SPRINGFIELD RIFLE. Model of 1870 and made at Springfield Armory. Caliber .50. This system was the invention of Christian Sharp and brought to the attention of the government in 1848. The first arms were percussion, some using the famous Maynard primer and many using a priming feature introduced by Sharp in 1852. This system was used as a military arm for forty-five years and saw excellent service in the Civil War. Made in many styles, both in carbines and long rifles. The illustration shows what was practically the last Sharp's used. The system was very easily changed from percussion to metallic cartridge. The Confederates made Sharp's carbines in Richmond during the war in large numbers. The Sharp's Company started business at Hartford in 1851, moved to Bridgeport in 1875, and went out of business in 1881. The system was so well liked by the government that immediately after Lee's surrender 30,000 percussion rifles and carbines were sent to Hartford to be converted to metallic cartridge arms. The Sharp's was pronounced the best of all breech-loading systems used in the Civil War.

No. 11. MILBANK'S BREECHLOADING ALTERATION OF CIVIL WAR SPRINGFIELD RIFLES. Caliber .58. The breech block swings to the right and forward, being locked in place by the spur on the end of the hammer. Patented by J. M. Milbank in 1867. In 1870 the Fenians staged a raid on the Canadian border, obtaining a number of these rifles to arm themselves, and hence Milbank's alteration was always called the "Fenian" gun. Used by militia regiments about 1868-1870.

No. 12. E. S. ALLIN'S BREECH-LOADING ALTERATION OF CIVIL WAR SPRINGFIELD RIFLES. Made at Springfield Armory as Allin was employed there. This arm is the beginning of the famous Springfield breech-loader as used until the adoption of the Krag-Jorgensen. In 1865 5,000 of the Allins were made and issued for trial in the Army. They had a coiled spring enclosed in a tube to work the ejector. Several inventors claimed that Allin infringed on their systems and several suits against the government came out of these claims. An interesting item concerning U. S. arms at this time is the following: On June 30, 1871, the War Department report stated that ten million dollars had been turned into the public treasury from the sales of small arms and ordnance stores to European countries. This was the Franco-Prussian war period.

No. 20——

until 1902 (in some states until 1906), although it was late in the 80's that these troops received them. Made as a carbine and also a cadet arm. Some interesting experiments were made at Springfield about 1874 to make this model a repeater. Holes were bored in the butt-stock to hold extra shells. These were held in place by a sliding cover; also a block, holding 10 cartridges was strapped to the right side of the arm just in front of the lock plate. None of the several experiments were adopted, however, as they would have been a hindrance rather than an improvement in actual service.

No. 21. MODEL OF 1884 SPRINGFIELD RIFLE. The first of the rod bayonet rifles. This bayonet was triangular in form. Although called Model 1884, they were made in 1880. As the catch was not satisfactory few were issued for actual use. At this time a front sight cover was also brought out both on rifles and carbines. Up to 1889 all triangular bayonets used on standard arms were those fabricated during the Civil War. The sleeve fitted the altered .50 caliber barrels and for the .45 caliber the sleeve was altered to fit.

No. 22. MODEL OF 1888, SPRINGFIELD RIFLE. The last of the .45 caliber arms. The ramrod bayonet is round in form and extends 15½ inches beyond the muzzle when extended for use. This model was equipped with the famous Buffington rear sight, a popular one in the service. The rod bayonet is distinctly an American idea. Hall used it in the 30's, we find it revived in 1880 and in use 1884 and 1888, and until the adoption of the Krag in 1892. In 1903 it was again revived but soon discarded. Although it was hardly a bayonet in the real sense it certainly would have proved as efficient as the Lebel bayonet of France did in the World War.

No. 23. LEE "SINGLE-ACTION" RIFLE. Caliber .45. Model of 1875. 140 of this system were made in 1875 at Springfield Armory under the personal supervision of the inventor, James P. Lee, well known for his magazine invention used both by the U. S. and England for many years. The breech-block drops down in front, similar to the Peabody. Cartridge is ejected by striking hammer sharply with the palm of the hand. The stock and fittings of the rifle are similar to the regular model 1873. Experimental only and no record of its use has been found.

No. 24. PEABODY'S PATENT BREECH-LOADING RIFLE. Caliber .45. A militia gun only, as no record has been discovered showing its use by the regular Army, although tested by various ordnance boards from 1865 until 1872. Made both as a rifle and carbine. Connecticut adopted the Peabody for its militia in 1871. It is interesting to note that in this year (1871) some of the New York militia regiments were still armed with muzzle-loading rifles. In view of the fact that the breech-loader was an established success for over ten years, this seems hard to believe. It also seems strange that militiamen were using .45 caliber single loading rifles in 1906 or twelve years after the Krag-Jorgensen was first issued.

No. 25. PEABODY-MARTINI RIFLE. Caliber .45. Used experimentally by the Navy only about 1880. This system is practically the same as the regular Peabody with the exception that the hammer is concealed in the block. England used this system for some years with the Henry rifled barrel. Some of these Navy rifles were equipped with cutlass bayonets having blades 27 inches long. This is about twice the length of the average bayonet blade of today. Made by the Providence Tool Co. of Providence, R. I., who also made the regular Peabody.

## Colt Revolvers—Continued

No. 6. COLT'S ARMY REVOLVER. Caliber .44, 6 shots. Length 14 inches, barrel 7½ inches long and weight 4 lbs. Known as the "Dragoon" model. Stamped U. S. M. I., U. S. M. R., or U. S. Dragoons. Made from 1848 to 1850. Some were fitted for shoulder stocks and some were not. They were also made with fluted cylinders but this particular type is rare. They were designed at first to be carried in holsters and called "holster" revolvers, but later the Dragoons, a military unit intended to fight either mounted or on foot, were armed with them. Colt took out a patent on shoulder stocks in 1859, a separate one being applied for on the canteen idea. In December, 1858, Secretary of War Floyd approved of the following regulation for the issue of Colt revolvers with shoulder stocks:

"Two pistols and one stock for each man, one pistol in holster on belt, one pistol in holster on saddle and stock at left rear side."

No. 7. COLT'S FIRST MODEL BELT REVOLVER. Model of 1848, known as the "Wells-Fargo," as that company used this arm for its messengers. No loading-lever is provided on this model. It was made in six, five, four and three-inch barrels. These were the first revolvers to be made by Colt in Hartford. Caliber .31, five shots. They were improved in several details in 1851.

No. 8. COLT'S "OLD MODEL" BELT. Pattern of 1849, caliber .31, 6 shots. Made in six, five, four and three-inch barrels. In the smaller sizes they were known as "Pocket" revolvers. A number of variations of this model exist, some were .34 caliber, some were five shots only. Another "Belt" model was made soon after this of .36 caliber with a 5½-inch barrel and a notched cylinder. These revolvers were made until 1873.

No. 9. This is the NAVY, CALIBER .36 REVOLVER, without a shoulder-stock.

No. 10. COLT'S "NEW MODEL" BELT. Caliber .36. First brought out in 1862, and made in 6½, 5½, 4½ and 3½ inch barrels. This model is a reduced facsimile of the Army .44 Model of 1860, with the exception of the fluted cylinder. Many of the 6½-inch barrel model used in the Civil War by officers.

No. 11. COLT'S .44 ARMY. Model of 1860. Altered to use metallic cartridges. Caliber .45. The old ramrod and lever has been removed and an ejector added to the right side of the barrel. Also the rear end of the cylinder is altered and a gate provided to facilitate loading and ejecting. The barrel length is the same as in the original form. These altered weapons were much used in the 70's before the introduction of the Models of 1873.

No. 12. Another .44 ARMY altered by a different method. It is hard to say just how many methods were adopted to alter percussion arms to use metallic cartridges, the writer has seen ten or twelve different patterns. Army, Navy, Holster, Belt and Pocket models were all altered and as private individuals took up the work in addition to the armories it is easy to see that the types are numerous. As an Army weapon the altered revolver was soon displaced by the Model 1873 (see No. 13).

No. 13. COLT'S SINGLE-ACTION MODEL 1873, CALIBER .45 ARMY REVOLVER. Made in two patterns. The one shown, the "Cavalry," had a barrel 7½ inches long. The "Artillery" model had a barrel 5½ inches in length. These were the first straight metallic cartridge revolvers to be made by Colt. They were first issued to the Army in 1875 and were still being issued during the Spanish war. The "Cavalry" model was a great favorite in the west for many years and preferred to the more modern double-action types. Issued at the same time as the "Schofield" Smith and Wesson, caliber .45, but considered superior in every way and were used many years after the "Schofield" was discarded.

No. 14. COLT'S DOUBLE-ACTION ARMY REVOLVER. Caliber .45, 6 shots, weight 2 pounds 7 oz. Barrel is 7½ inches long. The last patent date on this revolver is 1880, and they appeared soon after. This is the first double-action Army revolver made by Colt. It was also made as a "Frontier" model and so-called, but it did not have the popularity of the Model 1873 single action.

No. 15. COLT'S AUTOMATIC PISTOL. Browning's Patent. Caliber .38. First tried in an Army test January, 1902, 200 being purchased. The magazine held 8 cartridges. The Navy also purchased some for trial. These can be distinguished by the "U.S.N." on the slide and the plain wooden handles. As there was a growing demand for a larger caliber in revolvers (the official caliber was .38 at this time), so it was also with the automatic pistol; so in 1907 a board, after exhaustive tests, recommended the adoption of the .45 caliber Colt Automatic that had been presented for its study and approval. This model held 7 cartridges, had wooden handles and weighed 2 pounds 2 oz. The barrel was one inch shorter than the .38 caliber but the handle was set at the same angle to the barrel as the .38. Very few of these were purchased as it was soon superseded by the model shown in our illustration No. 19.

No. 16. COLT'S DOUBLE ACTION REVOLVER. Caliber .38, solid frame with swing-out cylinder, the first of this type. The Navy was the first arm of the service to adopt this famous weapon. This was in 1888. The Army soon followed in 1892. There were five models of this revolver brought out, the last dated 1903. It was owing to the "lack of stopping power" of this gun as proved in the Philippines that the agitation for the old .45 caliber was started in 1900. The Navy model of No. 16 had black rubber handles, while the Army and Marines used plain wooden handles.

No. 17. COLT'S DOUBLE ACTION. Caliber .45 Revolver. In our last paragraph mention is made of the agitation for the .45 caliber revolver. This gun is the first answer to it, for in 1902 a number of these were sent to the Philippines. The barrel is 6 inches long and the total length is 11 inches. Black rubber handles. This arm is distinguished by an abnormally large trigger and trigger-guard. Compare it with No. 14, which is clearly the weapon it was designed after. This model met all requirements for in spite of its clumsy appearance it handled well and was popular with the Army. It was discarded, however, in 1907, when the new model Colt .45 caliber revolver made its appearance. This arm resembled the present regulation revolver with some slight exceptions. In this connection is another interesting item regarding U. S. military pistols. On April 6, 1901, $15,000 was appropriated for the purchase of 1,000 caliber .31 Luger Automatic pistols. They were made in Germany and were stamped with a large American Eagle on the barrel. They were not popular with the troops and in 1907 they were called in and sold.

No. 18. COLT'S DOUBLE ACTION CALIBER .45 REVOLVER. Model of 1917. From April, 1917, to December, 1918, over 150,000 of this model were made and issued to the American fighting forces. This arm together with the Smith and Wesson, Model 1917, represents the last word in military revolver construction. They are loaded by clips and hold six rimless cartridges.

No. 19. COLT'S AUTOMATIC CALIBER .45 PISTOL. Model of 1911. This is the principal small arm of the war. From April, 1917, until December, 1918, the Colt people turned out 425,500 of them and Remington 13,152, the latter named, however, had only started production in September, 1918. In addition to being used by the U. S. troops it was also supplied to all of the Allied governments in spite of the fact that they had official weapons of their own.

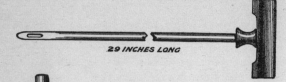

**29 INCHES LONG**

**C21. MAUSER RIFLE RAMROD** for any rifle from calibre 30 up. The end is made with eyelet for wiping rag, and flattened to avoid jamming. Leather washer protects end of gunbarrel. The handle is swiveled so that the rod may turn with the rifling. Price, 85 cents each.

**AERIAL FLARE.** Made for U. S. Air Service to be used in proposed bombing expeditions over enemy territory. This Flare has four vanes to retain the vertical position when falling toward the earth. Revolving air screw on nose explodes the charge at desired elevation, giving forth a blinding white light, concealing the plane and enabling the bomber to discern the object of attack. Length, 47 inches; diameter, 7 inches; weight, 4¾ pounds. Price, $45.00.

**WORLD WAR MEDALS**

**C17. HEADLESS SHELL EXTRACTOR** for German Mauser, model 1888 or 1898. Fits on end of bolt like cartridge. New. Our bargain price, 50 cents each.

**81B. BRITISH VICTORY MEDAL,** showing angel with chain armor and robes, holding olive branch. On reverse THE GREAT WAR FOR CIVILIZATION 1914-1919. With ribbon, $2.95.
**82B. BRITISH WAR MEDAL,** silver, showing head of KING GEORGE. On reverse NAKED MAN ON HORSE, BARE BACK, WITH ROMAN SHORT SWORD. Complete with ribbon. Price, $4.85.
**84B. MONS STAR WITH CROSSED SHORT ROMAN SWORDS WITH WREATH AND CROWN,** 1914, and letters G. V. With ribbon. Price, $3.85

**C15. GERMAN MAUSER, MODEL OF 1898, BREECH-COVER.** Battlefield relics, used by the Kaiser's troops to keep mud and dirt out of the breech of the rifle while in the trenches. Can be attached in a minute. Rare, as very few reached this country. 85 cents each.

**C16. GRAY METAL HELMET TOPS,** captured by American troops at Coblenz Arsenal from the Germans. These are new and were intended to ornament the helmets of the troops who expected to march through the Arc de Triomphe in Paris some day. An interesting souvenir of the war. 25 cents each.

To some we have added to weight so that tip may be used as paper weight. Price, 45 cents.

**C19. ANTI-DIMMING STICK FOR GAS MASKS.** Full instructions for use. When to use the Anti-Dimming Stick. The composition is to be applied to the eyepieces of the Gas Mask, weekly or after each time that the Mask has been worn. This may be also applied to wind-shields, lamps, telescopes, eye glasses, etc. Price, 15 cents each.

**C18. GERMAN MAUSER MUZZLE COVER.** Battlefield relics of the World War. Very valuable to keep the barrel clean. Can be attached in a second. Very strongly made, will last for years. 50 cents each.

**BARRELS FROM CAPTURED GERMAN MAUSER RIFLES.** These are 30 inch, in much used condition, offered as are without selection at $1.30 each. Weight about 3 lbs.

**U. S. ARMOR PIERCING CARTRIDGES,** Model of 1917, cal. 30, same size shell as service cartridge Model 1906. Bullet has lead tip to prevent slipping on armor plate and has a hard steel bullet under the nickel jacket. Made at Frankfort Arsenal for aircraft use only. Loaded with 45.5 grains I. M. R. powder. Price, $6.00 per 100.

**AUSTRIAN WORLD WAR BAYONET.** Devised by the Austrian ordnance experts toward the end of the War when materials were scarce. Consists of a single piece of steel forming the blade and twisted half way around to form a bar or strip to attach to bayonet lug. Barrel aperture is a simple piece of angle-iron with a hole for the barrel. On the right is a spring to hold it secure when attached. The entire bayonet is held together with two rivets. Fits the model 1895 Mannlicher. Price, $5.00.

**GERMAN STEEL CARTRIDGES.** These are the 8 m/m. cartridges with drawn steel copper washed bullet. Made by the Germans during last part of war when copper was hard to obtain. Very rare cartridge for collectors. Offered with powder at 25 cents each. Please note that percussion caps, primers and loaded cartridges cannot be sent by mail.

**RUBBER LIFE PRESERVING SUITS.** Kind issued on board transports during the war. Will keep wearer dry and afloat for several days. Lined with fiber which has many times the sustaining power of cork. Have lead soles to keep wearer in upright position in water. We offer these suits almost new, packed for shipment at $12.00 each.

**WORLD WAR RELICS**

1 GERMAN CARTRIDGE BOX, $1.00.
14 GERMAN BAYONETS, $5.00 each.
1 AUSTRIAN HOMEMADE BAYONET, $5.00.
1 GERMAN MACHINE GUN, $150.00.
2 FRENCH BAYONETS, $10.00 each.
1 FRENCH BAYONET with Frog, $15.00.
1 FRENCH BAYONET, without Scabbard, $8.00.
1 GERMAN OFFICERS' TUNIC, $10.50.
2 FRENCH CAPS of 1870, $2.00 each.
1 FRENCH NAPOLEON 2nd LEATHER SHAKO, with Eagle, $10.00.
1 GERMAN HUSSAR'S RED AND GOLD SABRETASCHE, $2.50.

**BK-1. ARMY BRASS CARTRIDGE CASES,** empty, size 2½ inches by 9¼ inches, weight 1½ pounds. Price, $1.95 each.

**BK-2. ARMY BRASS CARTRIDGE CASES,** empty, size 5 inches by 16¾ inches, weight 7 pounds. Price, $5.00 each.

**FM5. U. S. ARMY WAR ARMOR,** designed for and used by the MACHINE GUNNERS. Jointed throughout and padded on chest with heavy crude rubber. Sections fastened together with soft russet leather straps. Full length 30 inches, widest part 16¾ inches, weight 5¼ lbs. This can be worn under the clothing. A rare relic of the War. Price, $4.50.

**BK-3. ARMY BRASS CARTRIDGE CASE,** empty, WITHOUT BASE. LENGTH 19¼ inches, diameter at bottom 4 inches, weight 4½ pounds. Price, $3.00 each.

**GERMAN PERISCOPE.** Complete specimen of type used in the German Trenches during the "World War." Length, expanded, 105 inches. Appears to be in original condition. An interesting and useful instrument. Price, $75.00.

**FRENCH OFFICER'S "LEBEL" REVOLVER. MODEL OF 1892.** This is the regulation weapon of the French during the World War. The calibre is 8 m/m. or .31 and the cylinder is adapted for 6 cartridges. A peculiar feature of this arm is that the cylinder swings out to the right instead of the left as in U. S. weapons.
Revolver without holster or cartridges. Price, $23.00.

**FRENCH ARMY CARBINE.** Battlefield relic of the world war. This interesting weapon is shown in the French section of our illustrations of world war guns. Price for this specimen just as it was picked up on the field by an American soldier is $35.00. We can supply the bayonet for an additional $10.00.
REVOLVER without holster or cartridges. Price $23.00.

1 **MAUSER BAYONET** with steel scabbard attached by frog to leather belt which is fastened by the well known "Gott Mit UNS" buckle, in original condition as taken from the Battle Field. This bayonet is shown on page 6. (See cut No. 1 in Book on the German Mauser Rifle, by Coombes & Aney). We offer this set of German equipment with copy of book on Mauser Rifle for $12.50.

6 **METAL COFFINS.** Taken from German ships, seized by the United States when war was declared against Germany. Sold at U. S. Navy Sale. Price, $15.00 each.

**RED, WHITE and BLUE HAT CORDS,** as used by the preparedness camps, such as Plattsburg, etc. All new; fine for cadets or other patriotic companies. Price, 10 cents each.

## LOT OF CAPTURED WAR RELICS

**VC-1. GERMAN DUGOUT HANGING LAMP,** acetylene gas, with two parts, 9½ inches high, with 5 inch reflector, with 5½ inch wide iron hook for hanging. Made by ARNOLD NACHF, DRESDEN. Taken from captured dugout by U. S. A. surgeon. Price, $30.00.

**VC-3. GERMAN TRENCH PERISCOPE, GRAY COLOR.;** length closed 11½ inches, open 19 inches. Has hook for attaching to belt. Marked: D.R.G.M. A battle field relic. Price, $5.00.

**VC-4. ARTILLERY SHOULDER TAB,** cut from uniform of dead soldier, by American surgeon. 4½ inches long, all red with olive drab back. Marked with flaming shell (Ordnance) and number 41 embroidered in yellow. Price, $2.50.

**VC-5. U. S. ARMY TRENCH HELMET,** picked up after a charge. Painted a very dark green with the emblem of the 27th Division, New York Troops. Marked with owners name on inside: WILKINSON, size 6⅞. Price, $12.00.

**VC-6. SECTION OF GERMAN MACHINE GUN BELT,** with cartridges. Taken from German gunner on capture. 19 inches long, with 18 high power cartridges. Price, $4.50.

**C24. U. S. ARMY TRENCH HELMETS,** as issued for use in France. Fine souvenir of the war. Allow postage on five pounds packed. Price only 85 cents each.

**WAR RELICS,** sold by U. S. Government, showing actual use in service, some dented and battered. Price, $10.00 each.

---

**C22. WORLD WAR RELICS, Collected by officer in French Aviation Corps, M. Henri Julliot, mostly from battle of the Marne. Lot includes about 46 pieces, consisting of trench helmet; gas mask, shells, shrapnel and fragments. Collector's photograph on glass in colors included also. Price for collection, $45.**

---

**ARMY RELIC GAS MASKS** with bag, like illustration, sold by U. S. Government at auction as WAR RELICS. These are not serviceable, but are offered as genuine relics of the World War. Price, $5.00 each.

**U. S. NAVY GAS MASKS,** new, never used. These are of a model entirely different from that used by the Army, as the Navy mask has the container on TOP of Head piece and no bag is used. These are ready for the chemicals, and are recommended for the use of Firemen, Miners and Gas Workers. Price, $1.00 each.

**THESE TWO FLAGS** were sold at auction with other goods as War Relics.

**FRENCH FLAG,** made of heavy bunting, like new. Size, 20x38 feet. A bargain at $18.00.

**BRITISH ENSIGN,** of heavy bunting, like new. Size, 10x18 feet. At reduced price of $12.00.

**FRENCH POIGNARD BAYONETS,** four sided; ⅝ inch diameter at socket; 20½ inch blade, tapered to sharp needle point; German silver mountings; knurled head spring. Diameter of socket for rifle barrel 9/16 inch. Rare pattern, fine order, like new. With blued steel round scabbard, ¾ inch diameter at mouth-piece. Neat knob tapered tip with loop and black frog with adjusting buckle. This bayonet was sold to us by American soldier on his return with Army from overseas. A fine relic of the War. Price, $15.00.

**CJX. U. S. ARMY WORLD WAR TRENCH KNIVES.** Model 1917 without scabbards. Knobbed handle with triangular shaped blade. Price, $4.50 each.

**R1. U. S. ARMY RIFLE TRENCH MIRRORS,** Model 1917-18, to attach to end of bayonet. By removing this gun attachment, the mirror may be carried in pocket or handbag. Mirror is set in metal with metal hinged cover, all painted olive drab color. Size 3½x1¾ inches. This is a rare relic of the World War. Price, 25 cents each; $2.00 dozen.

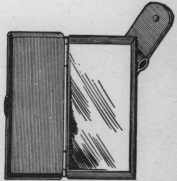

**CAPTURED GERMAN MACHINE GUN, SPANDAU MODEL,** caliber 7.9 m/m. This came to us with other World War equipment. Length over all including silencer, 55 inches. Barrel 28½ inches. Weight, 33 lbs. Has stiff leg tripod. Marked No. 6708 MG. 08/15 S. & H. BERLIN 1918. Price, $100.

**84-BA. MONS STAR,** with one bar marked, 5th AUG. 22nd. NOV. 1914. With ribbon. Price, $4.85.

**U S 1. AMERICAN VICTORY MEDALS** with ribbon, in good order. Price, $3.50 each.

**AMERICAN VICTORY MEDAL** with ribbon. Shows angel with shield and short sword. On reverse: AXE and SHIELD, with names of countries allied: FRANCE, ITALY, SERBIA, JAPAN, MONTENEGRO, RUSSIA, GREECE, GREAT BRITAIN, BELGIUM, BRAZIL, PORTUGAL, RUMANIA, CHINA. Price, $3.50 each.

**CJZ. U. S. ARMY WORLD WAR TRENCH KNIVES WITH STEEL SCABBARDS,** Model 1918. Scabbard has two heavy wire attachments on back to hold on belt. Large brass handle, dull finish, as shown in cut. 7-inch blade, one inch wide, with two ridges in center. Price, $5.00 each.
PLEASE NOTE THAT THE RESTRICTIONS REGARDING DANGEROUS WEAPONS APPLIES TO SALE OF THESE TRENCH KNIVES. WE MUST HAVE PERMIT FROM YOUR CHIEF OF POLICE WITH YOUR ORDER.

SEE OTHER PAGES IN THIS CATALOG FOR LIST OF MEDALS FROM DIFFERENT WARS.

## Continued from Page 66

FIG. G. IS THE CARBINE OF 1888, with the same sling arrangement and stacking hook of the Model of 1898. Attention is called to the front sight protector. This is peculiarly German as they used this device on the old "Needle"—Carbines of the early '70's.

FIG. H. THIS IS THE MAUSER AUTOMATIC PISTOL, with detachable shoulder. Stock which forms a holster for the piece when not in use, the rear end being hinged forming an opening for the insertion of the arm. This pistol holds ten shots, clip-loaded, the magazine being in front of the trigger guard. It is equipped with an elevating rear sight, graduated to 1000 metres. Many thousands of these weapons were used in the War, it being a great favorite with the officers. Other German small arms were the Luger, well known in this country and the Mauser .25 calibre or "Kamerad" pistols; both these are shown elsewhere in this volume.

FIG. I. During the war, the Germans captured so many French, Russian and Belgian rifles, that they made ammunition for them and used them; they were not very fond of the French needle bayonets, so they devised a scheme of using their own bayonets in the captured arms. In Fig. I, we show how a sleeve just the length of a bayonet handle slipped over the muzzle-end of the gun, with a lug on the right side, enabled the Germans to use their knife bayonets. The lower illustration shows the top view with the bayonet on the sleeve, the upper one shows the sleeve on the French Lebel Rifle. This was also done to the Russian Rifles. That Germany was in sore straits at times for weapons is shown by the fact that rifles of by-gone days were found to have been used, for example, thousands of the first (single-loading) Mauser, Model of 1871, were included in the allotted share of captured arms to the U. S. These were .43 calibre, taking the old fashioned lead bullets. We also find the same rifle converted to the magazine gun (Model 1884) included, also calibre .43. Both these rifles are shown elsewhere in our catalogue.

## Continued from Page 67

FIG. E. REMINGTON, SINGLE SHOT RIFLE. Made at Ilion, N. Y., for the French in the early part of the War, and chambered to take the 8 m/m. Lebel cartridge. It will be noticed that the rifle is equipped with a hand guard and a very long bayonet (16-inch blade), making it a more up-to-date weapon than our familiar Remington of thirty or forty years ago.
There were several other types of rifles found to have been captured by the Germans from the French. For example, the Gras, an alteration of the Chassepôt of 1870, designed to take an 11 m/m. cartridge, even the Chassepôt itself was found in large quantities. The principal revolver of the French Army was the Lebel, Model of 1892. This is shown elsewhere in our catalogue.

FIG. F. BELGIAN MAUSER MAGAZINE RIFLE. Model of 1889. Calibre, 7.65 m/m. Five shots. This is the first of the Mausers to use the Lee type of magazine, familar to us as it was used in this country in the '80s. Soon discarded, however, for the '93 model, which had the magazine all within the stock. The rifle has a mantle or tube protection for the barrel instead of the usual hand guard. No improvements have been made on the piece since its introduction, 30 years ago. During the war the bayonet blade was made longer, 6 inches being added making it 16 inches long, both types are shown in the illustration.

FIG. G. BELGIAN MAUSER MAGAZINE CARBINE, same calibre and number of shots as the long rifle and taking the same bayonets. The barrel of this weapon is 18 inches long against 30 for the rifle. There was also used 2 types of "short" rifles, the barrels being about 20 and 23 inches in length, all being designed to take bayonets.

FIG. H. BELGIAN COMBLAIN RIFLE. Single shot and 11 m/m. or .43 calibre. This weapon was used in large numbers and dates back from 1870. It has the falling breech-block of the Peabody type, and was the official weapon of Belgium in the '70s. The bayonet is patterned after the famous Chassepôt of France, having a blade over 20 inches long and a bras handle. Like the other countries Belgium was forced to bring into use old time weapons even the ancient Alóini-Braendlin being found among the captured arms.

FIG. I. TURKISH MAUSER MAGAZINE RIFLE. Model of 1895. Five shots, calibre 7.65 or 3.01 inches. This arm is a variation of the Spanish model of 1893, with the addition of a cut-off. The rifle is unique in this respect as it is the only Mauser that ever used a cut-off. The mechanism of this feature shows just forward of the bolt handle. The bayonet blade is 10 inches long; some however were found 16 inches in length. A few Model 1891 Mausers were found. This arm is similar to the Belgian rifle, except that it had a short hand guard between the rear sight and the middle band and as mantle to the barrel. Same calibre and number of shots.

FIG. J. TURKISH MAUSER MAGAZINE RIFLE. Model of 1903. Calibre, 7.65 m/m. or .301, and holding 5 cartridges in the magazine. This is the principal weapon of the Turkish Army, modeled after the '98 model of Germany, the principal difference being in the rear-sight and hand guard. The Mauser of 1910 used by Mexico is very much like this arm in general appearance.
The bayonet of the Turkish rifle is designed principally from the original pattern, used on the '98 German model, with the exceptions of the handle and curved guard. Blade is 21 inches long.

## Continued from Page 68

FIG. D. CANADIAN ROSS MAGAZINE RIFLE, MARK III. Model of 1916. Calibre, .303; five shots. This rifle is an outcome of the War, as it is the first Ross to load with a clip, also the magazine of former models is discarded for the Lee type. The rear sight, while different in principle

from the Enfield pattern, 1914, is of the same type and position. The straight pull bolt is new and much stronger than previous models. It is said that but few of these guns actually found their way to the front, but photos of the Royal Navy and its activities show sailors and marines armed with them. The bayonet blade is 10 inches in length and quite broad. In the illustration the bolt is drawn back showing the receiver open ready to receive the cartridges. The Mark III is equipped with a cut-off and a safety lock. These weapons were made in Quebec where the Ross Rifle works were located.

FIG. E. SERBIAN MAUSER MAGAZINE RIFLE. Model of 1910. Calibre, 7 m/m., five shots. This rifle is very similar to the Spanish model of 1893 in appearance. It however has a bolt like the '98 German Mauser, with the receiver cut away at the left for the better manipulation of the cartridges in loading. The usual safety is provided but no cut-off. There were several patterns of bayonets used on this rifle, with blades varying from 10 to 16 inches. The specimen shown was made in this country during the War under contract, it has a 10-inch blade.

FIG. F. ROUMANIAN MANNLICHER MAGAZINE RIFLE. Model of 1893. Calibre, .256; five shots. The rifle, which is shown with the bolt drawn and the breech open, is of the usual Mannlicher pattern wherein the clip forms a part of the magazine mechanism. This rifle was a great favorite in England before the war on the shooting ranges, on account of its handiness and accuracy. The Dutch Mannlicher is identical with the exception of the rear sight and upper band. Bayonet blade is 10 inches in length.

FIG. G. ROUMANIAN MANNLICHER MAGAZINE CARBINE. Same calibre and number of shots as the long rifle. The rear sight is shorter and sighted only to 1800 metres. There is no hand guard and the arm does not take a bayonet. The sling is attached to two swivels, one on the lower band and the other on a plate on the butt stock. Both these rifles carry short cleaning rods.

FIG. H. PORTUGAL, MAUSER-VERGUIERO MAGAZINE RIFLE. Calibre, .256 or 6.5 m/m., five shots. Model of 1904. This Mauser differs from the others at the breech as the bolt handle is placed farther forward so that it sets in front of the rear end of the body and directly over the magazine. (See cut.) The safety is also of a different pattern. The fore end is the same as the model 1907, the standard arm of China. The bayonet blade is 10 inches in length and has a handle of a new design. The magazine is the same as the model '98. This is the smallest calibre yet used in a Mauser rifle.

FIG. J. GREEK MANNLICHER SCHOENAUER MAGAZINE RIFLE. Model of 1903. Calibre, .256; five shots. This rifle differs from all the other Mannlicher models as it has a rotating platform which is provided with 5 grooves to hold the cartridges. This platform is worked by a coiled spring which is compressed by the insertion of the shells. Like the Mauser the entire mechanism is within the stock. The bayonet has the usual 10-inch blade and is like the Austrian pattern of 1895, having the cutting edge on top when fixed on the rifle.

FIG. I. GREEK MANNLICHER MAGAZINE CARBINE. Same pattern and calibre as the long rifle. Also same mechanism and number of shots. Barrel is 20½ inches long and is equipped with a cleaning-rod. The bolt handle is turned down so as to be easily inserted in the saddle boot. The carbine takes the same bayonet as the rifle. The knob on the bolt handle is quite large and bored out for lightness.

## Continued from Page 69

FIG. F. RUSSIAN MOUZIN MAGAZINE RIFLE. Model of 1901, officially known as the "3 line rifle," also "Nagant." Calibre .31, five shots, magazine is of the Lee type. The bayonet is the old fashioned sleeve and lock pattern, with a four fluted blade, which is intended to be always carried fixed, no scabbards being provided. The U. S. purchased over 280,000 of these from manufacturers in this country for training purposes. No changes have been made in the weapon since its introduction twenty years ago. Also made without sling swivels, holes being bored in the stock for the purpose of carrying.

FIG. G. MOUZIN CARBINE, action is the same as the rifle, barrel being 11 inches shorter or 20 inches against the 31 inches of the rifle. The Russian rifle was also made with 28-inch barrel. The Germans made ammunition and adapted their own bayonets to these guns.

FIG. H. WINCHESTER, MODEL OF 1895 MAGAZINE RIFLE, chambered to take the Russian cartridge. Supplied by the Winchester Arms Co., to the Russians in the early part of the war. This rifle has a barrel, 28 inches long and a bayonet with a 16-inch blade. It is also equipped with a cartridge clip guide at the top of the receiver. Otherwise the rifle is familar in this country. Other rifles used by the Russians, were the old single shot Berdan of 1886, Mark II and some single shot Remington of large calibre.

FIG. I. JAPAN ARISAKA MAGAZINE RIFLE. Model of 1907, officially known as "38th year model." Calibre is 6.5 m/m. or .256 inches. The magazine is a copy of the Mauser with a few changes. A dust-cover easily attached is part of the equipment. The bayonet resembles the English bayonet of 1903. Thousands of these rifles were sold by Japan to Russia during the war and many found their way into German hands by capture. Magazine holds 5 cartridges.

FIG. J. JAPANESE ARISAKA CARBINE. Same mechanism as the "38th year" rifle. Barrel is 19 inches long. The dust cover is shown on the carbine in the illustration. Takes same bayonet as long rifle. An earlier model of this gun was without a hand guard. Many of these found in the hands of the Bolsheviki, in Eastern Russia.

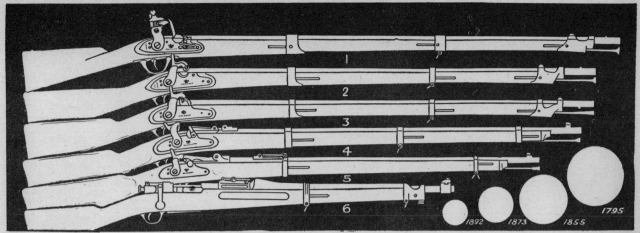

No. 1. Model 1795. Springfield Flint-lock Musket, Calibre .70.
No. 2. Model 1822. Springfield Flint-lock Musket, Calibre .69. Altered to percussion in the '50s.
No. 3. Model 1842. Springfield Percussion Musket. Calibre .69. (All of the above are muzzle-loading and smooth bore.)

No. 4. Model 1861. Springfield Percussion Rifle. Calibre .58. Altered to breech-loader in 1865.
No. 5. Model 1873. Springfield, Breech-loading, single shot rifle. Calibre .45.
No. 6. Model 1903. Springfield Magazine Rifle. Calibre .30, 5 shots.

NOTE: The six guns shown above are drawn to the same scale showing at a glance the correct lengths. The circles showing calibres are exact size.

## THE PARTS OF A FLINTLOCK

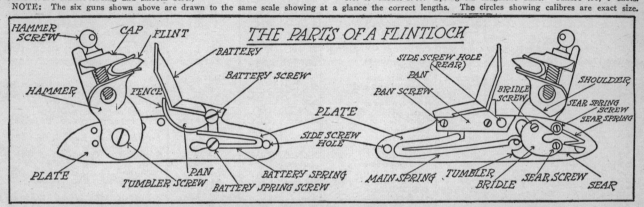

## VARIOUS METHODS USED TO ALTER FLINTLOCKS TO PERCUSSION

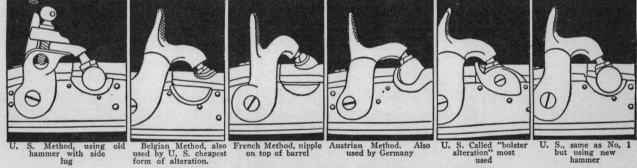

U. S. Method, using old hammer with side lug

Belgian Method, also used by U. S. cheapest form of alteration.

French Method, nipple on top of barrel

Austrian Method. Also used by Germany

U. S. Called "bolster alteration" most used

U. S., same as No. 1 but using new hammer

## MAGAZINE RIFLES OF THE POWERS—1914-1918

| Country | Austria | Belgium | Denmark | England | Canada | France | Germany | Greece | Holland | Italy | Japan | Portugal | Roumania | Russia | Spain | Switzerland | Turkey | U. S |
|---|---|---|---|---|---|---|---|---|---|---|---|---|---|---|---|---|---|---|
| Model of Year... | 1895 | 1889 | 1889 | 1903 | 1907 | 1886 | 1898 | 1903 | 1895 | 1891 | 1907 | 1904 | 1893 | 1901 | 1893 | 1900 | 1895 | 1903 |
| Name ......... | Mannlicher | Mauser | Krag-Jorgensen | Lee-Enfield | Ross | Lebel | Mauser | Mann-Schoenauer | Mannlicher | Carcano | Arisaka | Mauser | Mannlicher | 3 line Mouzin | Mauser | Schmidt Rubin | Mauser | Springfield |
| No. of Cartridges. | 5 | 5 | 5 | 10 | 5 | 8 | 5 | 5 | 5 | 6 | 5 | 5 | 5 | 5 | 5 | 6 | 5 | 5 |
| Magazine Type... | Box | Box | Box | Box | Box | Tube | Box | Box | Box | Box | Box | Box | Box | Box | Box | Box | Box | Box |
| Weight (with bayonet) ...... | 8 lb. 6 oz. | 9 lb. 9 oz. | 10 lb. 4 oz. | 9 lb. 10 oz. | 9 lb. 1 oz. | 10 lb. 1 oz. | 9 lb. 14 oz. | 8 lb. 5 oz. | 10 lb. 6 oz. | 9 lb. 3 oz. | 9 lb. 9 oz. | 9 lb. 9 oz. | 9 lb. 9 oz. | 9 lb. 11 oz. | 10 lb. 5 oz. | 8 lb. 10 oz. | 10 lb. 8 oz. | 9 lb. 8 oz. |
| Length (without bayonet) ...... | 4 ft. 2 in. | 4 ft. 2 in. | 4 ft. 5 in. | 3 ft. 9 in. | 4 ft. 4 in. | 4 ft. 4 in. | 4 ft. 1 in. | 4 ft. | 4 ft. 3 in. | 4 ft. 3 in. | 4 ft. 3 in. | 4 ft. | 4 ft. 1 in. | 4 ft. 4 in. | 4 ft. 1 in. | 3 ft. 8 in. | 4 ft. 1 in. | 3 ft. 8 in. |
| Length of Barrel. | 30.12 | 30.67 | 32.9 | 25.19 | 28 | 31.5 | 29.05 | 28.5 | 31.1 | 30.7 | 31.3 | 29.08 | 28.56 | 31.5 | 29.03 | 23.3 | 29.1 | 23.7 |
| Calibre, mm...... | 8 | 7.65 | 8 | 7.7 | 7.62 | 8 | 7.9 | 6.5 | 6.5 | 6.5 | 6.5 | 6.5 | 6.5 | 7.62 | 7 | 7.5 | 7.65 | 7.62 |
| Calibre, inches.... | .315 | .301 | .315 | .303 | .3 | .315 | .311 | .256 | .256 | .256 | .256 | .256 | .256 | .30 | .276 | .295 | .301 | .30 |
| Rifling (number grooves) ...... | 4 | 4 | 4 | 5 | 4 | 4 | 4 | 4 | 4 | 4 | 4 | | 4 | 4 | 4 | 3 | 4 | 4 |
| Twist (1 turn in inches)...... | 9.84 | 9.84 | 11.8 | 10 | 10 | 9.45 | 9.39 | .... | 7.87 | .... | 7.87 | 7.78 | 7.87 | 9.5 | 8.68 | 10.6 | 10 | 10 |
| Sighted for yards. | 2132 | 2187 | 2078 | 2800 | 2200 | 2187 | 2187 | 2187 | 2187 | 2187 | 2187 | .... | 2187 | 2096 | 2187 | 1312 | 2187 | 2850 |
| Cartridge weight, grains ........ | 455 | 441 | 460 | 415 | 415 | 415 | 431 | 348 | 338 | 331 | 348 | .... | 350 | 363 | 373 | 424 | 416 | 392 |
| Muzzle velocity, f. s. ........ | 2034 | 2034 | 1968 | 2060 | 2068 | 2380 | 2960 | 2223 | 2433 | 2395 | 2396 | 2347 | 2400 | 1985 | 2296 | 1920 | 2066 | 2700 |

# 1826—THE BREECHLOADER IN THE SERVICE—1917

A COMPLETE LIST OF THE BREECHLOADING ARMS USED OR EXPERIMENTED WITH BY THE U.S. ORDNANCE DEPARTMENT FROM THE INTRODUCTION OF THE "HALL" IN 1826 TO THE "ENFIELD IN 1917. THE NAMES IN CAPITALS (SEE SECOND COLUMN) ARE THE SYSTEMS ACTUALLY USED IN SERVICE. THE FOLLOWING ABBREVIATIONS ARE USED: F.L. FLINTLOCK, PERC., PERCUSSION CAP, R., RIFLE, C., CARBINE, P., PISTOL, REV., REVOLVING, ROT., ROTATING, SI.Bbl., SLIDING BARREL, S.W., SWINGING, FAL'G, FALLING M.C., METALLIC CARTRIDGE, MAG., MAGAZINE, H.F., HARPERS FERRY, S.P., SPRINGFIELD, EXP., EXPERIMENTAL. ALL WEAPONS NOT SPECIFIED "MAG" IN SEVENTH COLUMN ARE SINGLE LOADING ONLY.

| No. | NAME | Date of Pat. | INVENTOR | Operation | ARM | SYSTEM | WHERE MADE, REMARKS |
|---|---|---|---|---|---|---|---|
| 1 | HALL | May 1811 | J. H. Hall | Rising Block | R.C.P. | F.L. Perc. | H.F. & Middletown. Used 1826-'61 |
| 2 | COLT | Feb. 1836 | Samuel Colt | Rev. | " | Perc. M.C. | Paterson, N.J., & Hartford. |
| 3 | JENKS | May 1838 | Wm. Jenks | Lever | R.C. | F.L. Perc. | Herkimer, N.Y. 1840-'55 |
| 4 | SHARPS | Sept. 1848 | C. Sharps | " | R.C.P | Perc. M.C. | Hartford. Used 45 Years |
| 5 | GREENE | Jun. 1854 | J.D. Greene | Rot. Bbl. | C. | Perc | Chicopee Falls. Trial 1856-57 |
| 6 | Howe | Oct. " | J. C. Howe | Lever | " | " | Model only. " 1857 |
| 7 | PERRY | Nov. " | A. D. Perry | " | " | " | Newark, N.J. " '55 Navy |
| 8 | JOSLYN | Aug. 1855 | B. F. Joslyn | Top Lever | " | " | Stonington, Conn. Used 1860-65 |
| 9 | MERRILL | Jan 1856 | J.H. Merrill | " | " | " | Herkimer, N.Y. (Remington) |
| 10 | GIBBS | " " | L. H. Gibbs | Sl. Bbl. | " | " | New York. Used 1860-65 |
| 11 | BURNSIDE | Mar. " | A. E. Burnside | Lever | " | " | Bristol, R.I. " |
| 12 | Schroeder | Jun. " | H. Schroeder | Sl. Bbl. | " | " | Models only. Trial 1858 |
| 13 | Mont Storm | Jul. " | Wm. Mont Storm | Rising Block | R. C. | " | Partly by Gov't. 1859-'60 |
| 14 | SMITH | Jun. 1857 | G. Smith | Bbl. Tips | C. | " | Chicopee Falls. Used 1861-'65 |
| 15 | GREENE | Nov. " | J. D. Greene | Bolt | R. | " | Milbury, Mass. " |
| 16 | Morse | Jun. 1858 | G.W. Morse | Rising Block | R. | M. C. | Sp. Armory. Trial 1859-'60 |
| 17 | MERRILL | Jul. " | J.H. Merrill | Top Lever | R.C. | Perc. | Baltimore. Used 1861-'65 |
| 18 | STARR | Sep. " | E. S. Starr | Lever | C. | " | Yonkers, N.Y. " " |
| 19 | SYMMES | Nov. " | J.C. Symmes | " | " | " | Exp. 1858 |
| 20 | SHARP & HANKINS | Jan. 1859 | C. Sharps.—Hankins | Sl. Bbl. | R. C. | M. C. | Phila., Pa. Used 1862-1871 |
| 21 | LINDNER | Mar. " | Edw. Lindner | Rising Block | C. | Perc. | Used 1861-1865 |
| 22 | WESSON | Oct. " | F. Wesson | Fal'g Bbl. | " | M.C. | " 1870 |
| 23 | Arnold | Nov. " | W. H. Arnold | Top lever | R. | Perc. | Exp. 1859 |
| 24 | MAYNARD | Dec. " | Edw. Maynard | Fal'g Bbl. | C. | M. C. | Chicopee Falls. Used 1861-'65 |
| 25 | SPENCER | Mar. 1860 | C. Spencer | " Block | R.E.C. | M. C. | Bristol, Conn. Boston & Prov. R.I. |
| 26 | GALLAGER | July " | M.J.Gallager | Fal'g Bbl. | C. | Perc. | Phila. Used 1861-'65 |
| 27 | Maynard | Oct. " | Edw. Maynard | Rot. Block | R. | " | Model only. Exp 1860 |
| 28 | HENRY | " " | Tyler Henry | Lever | R.&C. | M. C. Mag. | New Haven. Used 1861-'65 |
| 29 | BALLARD | Nov. 1861 | C.H. Ballard | " | " | Perc. & M.C. | New York. " |
| 30 | National | Dec. " | D. Moore | " | C. | M. C. | Model only. Exp. 1866-68 |
| 31 | Johnston | May 1862 | W. Johnston | " | " | " | " |
| 32 | JOSLYN | Jun. " | B.F. Joslyn | Sw. Block | R.&C. | " " | Stonington, Conn. Used '64-71 |
| 33 | PEABODY | Jul. " | H.O. Peabody | Lever | " | " " | Prov. R.I. Exp. 1865-'70 |
| 34 | COSMOPOLITAN | Oct. " | Gwin & Campbell | " | C. | Perc. | Hamilton, O. Used 1862-65 |
| 35 | Armstrong & Taylor | Nov. " | Armstrong—Taylor | Rot. Bbl. | R. | M. C. | Model only. Exp. 1866 |
| 36 | White | Jan 1863 | L.S. White | Lever | C. | " " | " |
| 37 | BALL | " " | A. Ball | " | " | M.C. Mag. | Windsor, Vt., Used 1864-'67 |
| 38 | Underwood | " " | H. Underwood | Sw. Block | " | M.C. | Model only. Exp. 1865 |
| 39 | Cochran | July " | J.W. Cochran | Lever | R.E.C. | " " | " |
| 40 | Percy | Aug. " | J. Percy | Fal'g Bbl. | C. | " " | " |
| 41 | PALMER | Dec. " | Wm. Palmer | Bolt | " | " " | Windsor, Vt. Used 1864 |
| 42 | REMINGTON | " " | J. Rider | Fal'g Block | R.&C. | " " | Remington & U.S. Used '65-90 |
| 43 | Stevens | Jan. 1864 | W.X.Stevens | " | C. | " " | Model only. Exp. 1866 |
| 44 | Mix & Horton | " " | L. Mix | Lever | R. | " " | " |
| 45 | WARNER | Feb. " | James Warner | Sw. Block | C. | " " | Worcester, Mass. Used '64-67 |
| 46 | Rowe | Apr. " | A. H. Rowe | Rot. Bbl. | C. | " " | Model only. Exp. 1867. |
| 47 | Smith | " " | J. Smith | Sw.Block | C. | " " | " |
| 48 | Richardson | " " | G.J. Richardson | Lever | C. | " " | " |
| 49 | Goulding | May " | J. Goulding | Sw. Block | C. | " " | " |
| 50 | Hammond | Oct. " | H. Hammond | Rot. Block | C. | " " | " |
| 51 | Wright | Nov. " | E.S. Wright | Sw. | C. | " " | " |
| 52 | TRIPLETT & SCOTT | Dec. " | L. Triplett | Rot. Bbl. | " | M. C. Mag. | Meriden, Conn. Used 1865-70 |
| 53 | Fitzgerald | Jan. 1865 | | Lever | " | M. C. | Model only. Exp. 1867 |
| 54 | MILLER | May " | W.H. Miller | Sw. Block | R.&C. | " " | Meriden, Conn. " |
| 55 | STARR | — | E. S. Starr | Lever | C. | " " | Yonkers, N.Y. " " |
| 56 | Maynard | — | Edw. Maynard | Fal'g Bbl. | C. | " " | Chicopee Falls. " " |
| 57 | Riche | — | J. Riche | Sw. Block | C. | " " | Model only. " " |
| 58 | ALLIN | Sept. '65 | E.S. Allin | " | R. | " " | Sp. Armory. In use 1866 — |
| 59 | Howard | — | H. Howard | Sl'dg Bbl | " | " " | Model only. Exp. 1867 |
| 60 | Merrill | — | J. H. Merrill | Top Lever | " | " " | Baltimore. " '68 |
| 61 | SPRINGFIELD | 1866 | Ordnance Dep't | Sw. Block | R.&C. | " " | Sp. Armory. Used 1866-'94 |
| 62 | Beal | Jan. 1866 | F. Beal | Sl'dg Bbl. | R. | " " | Model only. Exp. 1868 |
| 63 | Berdan | Feb. " | H. Berdan | Sw. Block | R. | " " | " " |
| 64 | Grey | Apr. " | J. Grey | Lever | C. | M. C. Mag. | " " |
| 65 | Robertson-Simpson | Mar. " | J. Robertson | " | C. | M. C. | Made by Sharps. |
| 66 | Meigs | May " | J.V. Meigs | " | C. | M.C. Mag. | Lowell, Mass. |
| 67 | Laidley & Emery | " | S. Laidley | Fal'g Block | C. | M.C. | Model only. |
| 68 | Burke | June " | J. Burke | " Bbl. | R. | " " | " |
| 69 | Hayden | Aug. " | H.W. Hayden | Lever | R. | " " | " |
| 70 | Norny | " | | " | R. | " " | " |
| 71 | Winchester | Sep. " | O.F. Winchester | " | R. | M.C. Mag. | New Haven " 1872-4 |
| 72 | Coleman | Nov. " | C.C. Coleman | " | R. | M. C. | Model only " 1867-8 |
| 73 | Wolcott | " " | H.H. Wolcott | " | R. | " " | " " |
| 74 | Yates | Dec. " | Theo. Yates | Fal'g Block | C. | " " | " " |
| 75 | Straw | " | | Lever | C. | M.C. Mag. | " " |
| 76 | Fields | " | | " | C. | " " | " " |
| 77 | Chassepot | Jan. 1867 | A.A. Chassepot | Bolt | R. | Needle gun | French Army Rifle 1872 |
| 78 | Smith | " | S. Crispin | Fal'g Bbl. | C. | M. C. | Chicopee Falls. " 1867 |
| 79 | Milbank | Feb. " | J.M. Milbank | Sw. Block | C. | " " | Phila. Pa. " 1872 |
| 80 | SHARPS | " | C. Sharps | Lever | R.E.C. | " " | Hartford. Used 1868-'80 |
| 81 | Root | Jun. " | E.K. Root | Top " | C. | " " | Model only. Exp 1867 |
| 82 | Hubbell | " " | W.W. Hubbell | Sw.Block | C. | " " | " " |
| 83 | Roberts | " " | B. S. Roberts | Lever | R. | " " | " '67-'72 |
| 84 | Werndl | " " | J. Werndl | Sw. Block | R.C. | " " | Austrian Army Rifle " |
| 85 | Gwyn | — | | Fal'g | C. | " " | Hamilton, O. Exp. 1868 |
| 86 | Jenks | Feb 1868 | B.H. Jenks | | C. | " " | Model only. |

| NO. | NAME | Date of Pat. | INVENTOR | Operation | ARM | SYSTEM | WHERE MADE – REMARKS |
|---|---|---|---|---|---|---|---|
| 87 | Mauser | June 1868 | Paul Mauser | Bolt | R. | M C. | Germany. Exp. test 1872 |
| 88 | Wilson & Flathers | July 1868 | —Wilson—Flathers | Sw. Block | " | " " | Model only. " " 1868 |
| 89 | Allen | Dec. " | E.Allen | Sw. Block | C. | " " | |
| 90 | Vetterlin | Dec. " | F.Vetterlin | Bolt | R. | M.C. Mag. | Switzerland, 1872 |
| 91 | WARD-BURTON | Aug.1869 | W.G.Ward- B.Burton | | R.&C. | M.C. | Sp. Armory. Used 1871-76 |
| 92 | Morgenstern | | Wm. Morgenstern | Sw. Block | R | " " | Model only. Exp. test 1872 |
| 93 | Joslyn-Tomes | Nov. 1870 | B.F.Joslyn | Bolt | R.&C. | " " | New York, " " |
| 94 | Berdan | | H. Berdan | | R | " " | Hartford, " " |
| 95 | Elliott | Dec " | W.H.Elliott | Fal'g Block | " | " " | Model only. " " |
| 96 | Lee | May 1871 | James P. Lee | Lever | " | " " | |
| 97 | Whitney | June " | E. Whitney | Fal'g Block | " | " " | New Haven, |
| 98 | Stetson | July " | G.R.Stetson | Lever | " | " " | Model only. " |
| 99 | Evans | Sep. " | W.R.Evans | | R.&C. | M.C. Mag. | Mechanic Falls, Me., |
| 100 | Merrill | Oct. " | G. Merrill | Bolt | R | M.C.. | Newburyport, Mass., |
| 101 | Martini | Nov. " | F.V.Martini | Lever | " | " | English Army Rifle, |
| 102 | Freeman | Jan 1872 | A.T.Freeman | Fal'g Block | " | " | Model only Exp. |
| 103 | Thomas | May " | J.F.Thomas | " " | " | " | " " " |
| 104 | Earnest | July " | G.H.Earnest | Sw. Block | " | " | " " " |
| 105 | Updegraff | Aug. " | H.Updegraff | Fal'g | " | " | " " " |
| 106 | Whittemore | Sep. " | J.M.Whittemore | Bolt | " | " | " " " |
| 107 | Van Choate | Oct. " | S.F.Van Choate | " | " | " | " " " |
| 108 | Westley-Richards | Dec. " | Westley-Richards | Top lever | " | " | English Military Rifle |
| 109 | Ward-Burton | | W.G.Ward-B.Burton | Bolt | R.&C. | M C. Mag. | Model only. Exp. " |
| 110 | Werder | — | F.Werder | Fal'g block | R | M.C. | Bavarian Army Rifle " |
| 111 | Helm | — | | Rev. | " | " | Model only. Exp. " |
| 112 | Wohlgemuth | | F.W.Wohlgemuth | Bbl. Tips | " | " | " " " " |
| 113 | Snell | | O.Snell | Sw. Block | " | " | " " " " |
| 114 | Muir-Mont Storm | | Muir & Mont Storm | Fal'g | " | " | " " " " |
| 115 | Beals | | A.C.Beals | Lever | " | " | " " " " |
| 116 | Broughton | | J. Broughton | " | " | " | " " " " |
| 117 | Broughton | | " | Sw. Block | " | " | " " " " |
| 118 | Broughton | | " | " | " | " | " " " " |
| 119 | Dexter | | W.G.Dexter | Fal'g | " | " | " " " " |
| 120 | Gardner | | W.Gardner | Sl. BBL. | R | " | " " " " |
| 121 | Greene | | J.D.Greene | Bolt | | M.C. Mag. | " " " " |
| 122 | Milbank | Mar. 1873 | J.M.Milbank | | | M.C. | " " " " |
| 123 | Robertson | | | Lever | " | " | " " " " |
| 124 | Spencer | Feb. 1873 | C.Spencer | " | " | " | " " " " |
| 125 | Stillman | | J.Stillman | Sw. block | " | " | " " " " |
| 126 | Rumsey | | | Lever | " | M.C. Mag. | " " " " |
| 127 | Conroy | Dec. 1873 | L.Conroy | Fal'g block | " | M.C. | " " " " |
| 128 | LEE | Mar. 1875 | James P. Lee | | " | " | Sp.Armory. Used 1876-9 |
| 129 | Lee | — | | Sl. BBL. | " | " | Model only, Exp-test 1872 |
| 130 | Sharps-Borcherdt | — | C. Sharps | Lever | " | " | Hartford, |
| 131 | Smoot | | W.S.Smoot | Sl. BBL | " | " | Model only, |
| 132 | HOTCHKISS | Aug.1869 | B.B.Hotchkiss | Bolt | R.E.C. | M.C. Mag. | New Haven. Used 1878-1885 |
| 133 | LEE | | J.P.Lee | " | " | " | Bridgeport Ellion Used 1880-'98 |
| 134 | KEENE | Feb.1874 | —Keene | " | R. | " | Ilion, N.Y. (Remington) " '85 |
| 135 | Franklin | — | W.B.Franklin | " | R. | " | Hartford. Exp. test 1877 |
| 136 | Hunt | — | C.B.Hunt | " | R. | " | Model only " " |
| 137 | Sharps | — | C.Sharps | " | R. | " | Hartford, " " |
| 138 | Lewis-Rice | | —Lewis—Rice | Lever | R. | " | Model only. " " |
| 139 | Buffington | | A.R.Buffington | Lever | R. | M.C.Mag. | Model only. Exp. test 1877 |
| 140 | Miller | | W.H.Miller | Sw. Block | R. | " | |
| 141 | Tiesing | | —Tiesing | Lever | " | " | New Haven " " |
| 142 | Clemmons | | G.F.Clemmons | Sw. Block | " | " | Model only " " |
| 143 | Burgess | | A.Burgess | Lever | " | " | New Haven " " |
| 144 | Chaffee | | R.S.Chaffee | " | " | " | Model |
| 145 | CHAFFEE-REECE | | " - J.N.Reece | Bolt | " | " | Sp. Armory In use 1884-1889 |
| 146 | Boch | | P. Boch | Bolt | " | " | New York Exp. test 1882 |
| 147 | Russell | | A.H.Russell | Bolt | " | " | Model " " |
| 148 | Traube | | Wm. Traube | Bolt | " | " | Louisville " " |
| 149 | Dean | | C.J.Dean | Lever | " | " | Wash. D.C. " " |
| 150 | Marlin | | J.M.Marlin | " | " | " | New Haven " " |
| 151 | Spencer-Lee | | C.Spencer & J.P.Lee | Pump Ac. | " | " | N.Y. Francis Bannerman. " |
| 152 | Jones | | A.S.Jones | Sw. Block | " | " | Dakota Exp. test |
| 153 | Elliott | | H.Elliott | Bolt | " | " | Model |
| 154 | Rubin | Mod. 1881 | J.Rubin | " | " | " | Switzerland " " |
| 155 | Schulhof | " 1882 | —Schulhof | " | " | " | Austria " " |
| 156 | KRAG-JORGENSEN | | O.Krag- E.Jorgensen | " | R.&C. | " | Sp. Armory, In use 1894-1903 |
| 157 | Lee-Speed | Mod. 1890 | J.P.Lee | " | R.&C. | " | England Exp. test 1892 |
| 158 | Mannlicher | " 1888 | F.Von Mannlicher | " | R.&C. | " | Austria " " |
| 159 | Kropatschek | " 1878 | V.Kropatschek | " | R. | " | France (Navy) " " |
| 160 | Murata | " 1887 | | " | " | " | Japan (Army) " " |
| 161 | Ford | | J.Ford | " | " | " | Quebec " " |
| 162 | Schmidt | | R.Schmidt | " | " | " | Switzerland " " |
| 163 | Berthier | Mod.1891 | —Berthier | " | Carb. | " | France (Navy) " " |
| 164 | Kelton | — | J.C.Kelton | " | R. | " | Washington " " |
| 165 | Sporer | — | M.Sporer | " | " | " | Hartford " " |
| 166 | Pitcher | — | —Pitcher | " | " | " | Neilsville, Wis " " |
| 167 | Bruce | | L.F.Bruce | " | " | " | Springfield, Mass. " |
| 168 | Fogerty | | G. Fogerty | " | " | " | Cambridgeport, " |
| 169 | Hampden | | T.B.Wilson | " | " | " | Springfield, " |
| 170 | Durst | | M.H.Durst | " | " | " | California. Exp. " |
| 171 | Miles | | D.D.Miles | " | " | " | Aurora, Ill. " |
| 172 | Larsen | | I. Larsen | Lever | " | " | Chicago " |
| 173 | Savage | | A. Savage | " | " | " | Utica, N.Y. " |
| 174 | Mullins | | J.M.Mullins | Sw. Block | " | " | Kentucky. " " |
| 175 | Blake | | J. Blake | Bolt | " | " | New York " 1893 |
| 176 | Russell-Livermore | | A.H.Russell | " | " | " | Boston " |
| 177 | White | | H.R.White | " | " | " | Model only " |
| 178 | Van Patten | | H.G.Van Patten | Pump Act. | " | " | " 1895 |
| 179 | Briggs-Kneeland | | Briggs-Kneeland | Bolt | " | " | " " |
| 180 | Daudeteau | Mod. 1895 | J.Daudeteau | " | " | " | French Navy. |
| 181 | LEE | | James P.Lee | " | " | " | U.S. NAVY. Used 1896-1901 |
| 182 | WINCHESTER | | | Lever | " | " | New Haven, 1899 |
| 183 | SPRINGFIELD | " 1903 | Modified Mauser | Bolt | " | " | Sp. Armory, IN USE |
| 184 | ENFIELD | " 1914 | British Government | " | " | " | Modified English, " 1917-18 |

ON the back cover we show one view of Bannerman Island used for storage. In the view of first floor of store or salesroom, we show on the right U. S. Navy cutlasses with large brass guards, gong from Battleship Kearsarge, marine corps drum and American pistols, both Army and Navy patterns. To the right of post may be seen the long barrel and muzzle of the famous dynamite gun used by Colonel Roosevelt and his ROUGH RIDERS in Cuba. This is one of the most valuable Army relics of the Spanish War. In front of this appears the edge of the capstan of the U. S. S. MAINE blown up in Havana Harbor. We believe this to be the largest genuine relic of the Navy in the Spanish War. Behind the dynamite guns are various models of the rapid fire machine guns, including some used in the World War. On the stairway leading to Uniform and Insignia Department, are pictures of European Soldiers in full uniforms, also Union and Confederate soldiers of the Civil War, and full set of pictures of all the uniforms used in the Army of the United States from the beginning.

In the photograph showing display of guns, we have the bows of early times, with cross-bows, flint lock muskets, percussion lock guns of many countries. Swords and sabers of various European countries are also shown.

---

We are showing these different photographs of our salesrooms for the reason that some new customers seem to think that we are like all the other so-called Army and Navy Stores, and are an outgrowth of the last war, when the Government began selling its surplus and obsolete equipment. WE HAVE BEEN IN THIS BUSINESS SINCE 1865, and we are the only dealers in army auction goods that have been in business for so long a time. Many small merchants have added army goods to their stocks and cannot fill orders except for a few items. Look through the pages of our catalog and you will see what an enormous stock we carry. In most cases, we make shipment the same day that order is received, either by express or by mail (when postage is sent.) Freight shipments are made one or two days after receiving order. To avoid delay in receiving your order, please send us Postal or Express Money Order, Bank Draft or certified check. We give faithful description of goods and want EVERY customer entirely satisfied.

We ask you to read history and other interesting facts about our business on pages 2, 3, and 4. We are always glad to have our mail order customers call and look over our collection of weapons and other curios.

IN THE MARCH 1, 1917, ISSUE NATIONAL SPORTSMAN, APPEARS:

Do you know anything about Francis Bannerman, 501 Broadway, New York, N. Y.? He seems to be an extensive dealer in second-hand military firearms.

Answer. Francis Bannerman is a reliable dealer in Military arms of all kinds, both second-hand and new. If he tells you that the rifles you wish to purchase are serviceable, you can depend upon what he says.

## MR. FRANCIS BANNERMAN, 1851 — 1918

MANY OF OUR CUSTOMERS KNOWING OF OUR LONG ESTABLISHED BUSINESS IN GOVERNMENT AUCTION GOODS, have lately received price lists issued by TRADERS WHO START UP SMALL STORES and publish a price list in which are FAC-SIMILE ILLUSTRATIONS taken from OUR COPYRIGHTED CATALOGUE, which gives our friends an impression (which is what these unscrupulous traders intend) that they are in some way ASSOCIATED WITH US.

PLEASE REMEMBER THAT WE HAVE NO BRANCH SALES STORES EITHER IN THE UNITED STATES OR IN EUROPE. ALL OUR BUSINESS IS TRANSACTED FROM OUR OFFICE, 501 BROADWAY, NEW YORK CITY.

We have been asked to join in forming a syndicate to control the PURCHASING AND SELLING OF GOVERNMENT AUCTION GOODS under the title of THE FRANCIS BANNERMAN MILITARY AUCTION GOODS COMPANY. Our reply to these "would-be competitors"—That such a syndicate was against the Sherman Law; that we were not law-breakers, neither would we have anything whatever to do with THEM, or to allow any such use of our name. That for nearly half a century we had fought (out-bid) these WINDY BIDDERS and SPECULATORS at all the Government auction sales from Maine to California and would go down to the "Valley of the Shadow" with OUR BANNER FLYING IN DEFIANCE OF THEM AND THEIR METHODS. That we would not associate or compromise.

Nearly the last words of advice given me by my old Scotch grandmother was, "Laddy, never let your banner trail in the dust."

A business friend once told us that he could make more money out of our business than we were doing. Our reply was, "No doubt of it, but that MAKING MONEY WAS NOT OUR CHIEF AIM IN LIFE." We said, "Supposing you did make more money and became a millionaire, you would then stand among the fast increasing long line of millionaires, but so far from the head that YOU WOULD BE A TAIL-ENDER, whereas I stand as THE FOUNDER of a line IN UTILIZING OLD GOVERNMENT WASTE, in which I am not only the head but the whole show, carrying on a LARGE BUSINESS DIFFERENT from that of any other private individual. ABLE TO SAY TO GOVERNMENT OFFICIALS when they wish to buy my goods, 'Gentlemen, the same Government auction terms you ask of me when I buy your goods, "FIRST YOUR MONEY, THEN YOU GET MY GOODS,"' the same terms with which we began this business forty-eight years ago."

When the corporation which stands for the greatest wealth in the world, THE STANDARD OIL COMPANY, wished to purchase our goods they cheerfully complied with our terms and SENT US THE MONEY IN ADVANCE.

The gladdest, happiest day is NOT when we fill a large Government order, but when we join a group of poor boys from the city with whom it is our privilege during the week to study the Bible lessons, and we make an excursion up the Hudson to our Island where they shoot off the cannons on the fortifications, EAT AND PLAY, BOAT AND SWIM, having THE DAY OF THEIR LIVES—AND OURS.

Francis Bannerman in 1917 Catalog.

## GENERAL INDEX

# BANNERMAN ISLAND

THIS view is taken from the south-east and shows the extensive breakwaters, by which are formed inside canals or waterways, so that we can ship through either the west or east channel. Large boats can take on cargo at the dock. Behind the towered warehouse shown are other large ones, necessary for storing our great stock of Military Goods.

The building in center is the residence of Mr. Francis Bannerman and used by him until his death. It is still used by other members of the family.

VISITORS ARE NOT PERMITTED TO LAND, ON ACCOUNT OF THE MANY EXPLOSIVES STORED HERE.

## BANNERMAN ISLAND
### At the foot of Storm King Mountain, about Four Miles North of West Point

What an important part Polopel's Island had in the war of the Revolution, lending its name to the obstructions placed across the channel in 1776 to prevent the passage of the British fleet;—graced by the presence of General Washington and his staff on his inspection tours of the fortification and crib construction while his army lay encamped at New Windsor on the opposite shore;—housing the workmen engaged in building the Cheveau de Frieze obstruction, no doubt with part of the lot of 500 axes requisitioned by General Clinton from the neighboring farmers. N. P. Willis often rowed over from Cornwall, and here perhaps received inspiration for his greatest poems, but that was before the time of "The Iron horse that never tires,
Dashing along at lightning speed, On either bank with noisy roar."
Many of the people of Newburgh, West Point and vicinity believed it to be a public misfortune when the island was sold to Francis Bannerman Sons of 501 Broadway, N. Y. City, for the storage of war weapons and explosives, as it necessarily prevented the landing on the island of picnic parties. Its purchase was a God-send to the Bannermans, as at the close of the Spanish war they had bought up practically all of the arms and ammunition captured from the Spanish, and had to find some place outside of New York City for the storage of over 20 millions of cartridges. In the castellated buildings are stored vast quantity of war material, guns, swords, cannon, ammunition, etc., in fact, everything to equip an army.

See Page 370